T0180509

Lecture Notes in Electrical Engineering

Volume 946

The book series *Lecture Notes in Electrical Engineering* (LNEE) publishes the latest developments in Electrical Engineering—quickly, informally and in high quality. While original research reported in proceedings and monographs has traditionally formed the core of LNEE, we also encourage authors to submit books devoted to supporting student education and professional training in the various fields and applications areas of electrical engineering. The series cover classical and emerging topics concerning:

- Communication Engineering, Information Theory and Networks
- Electronics Engineering and Microelectronics
- Signal, Image and Speech Processing
- Wireless and Mobile Communication
- Circuits and Systems
- Energy Systems, Power Electronics and Electrical Machines
- Electro-optical Engineering
- Instrumentation Engineering
- Avionics Engineering
- Control Systems
- Internet-of-Things and Cybersecurity
- Biomedical Devices, MEMS and NEMS

For general information about this book series, comments or suggestions, please contact leontina.dicecco@springer.com.

To submit a proposal or request further information, please contact the Publishing Editor in your country:

China

Jasmine Dou, Editor (jasmine.dou@springer.com)

India, Japan, Rest of Asia

Swati Meherishi, Editorial Director (Swati.Meherishi@springer.com)

Southeast Asia, Australia, New Zealand

Ramesh Nath Premnath, Editor (ramesh.premnath@springernature.com)

USA, Canada

Michael Luby, Senior Editor (michael.luby@springer.com)

All other Countries

Leontina Di Cecco, Senior Editor (leontina.dicecco@springer.com)

** This series is indexed by EI Compendex and Scopus databases. **

Rajesh Doriya · Badal Soni · Anupam Shukla ·
Xiao-Zhi Gao

Editors

Machine Learning, Image Processing, Network Security and Data Sciences

Select Proceedings of 3rd International
Conference on MIND 2021

 Springer

Editors
Rajesh Doriya
Department of Information Technology
National Institute of Technology Raipur
Raipur, Chhattisgarh, India

Anupam Shukla
Indian Institute of Information Technology
Pune, India

Badal Soni
Department of Computer Science
and Engineering
National Institute of Technology Silchar
Silchar, India

Xiao-Zhi Gao
Faculty of Science and Forestry, School
of Computing
University of Eastern Finland
Kuopio, Finland

ISSN 1876-1100   ISSN 1876-1119 (electronic)
Lecture Notes in Electrical Engineering
ISBN 978-981-19-5870-0   ISBN 978-981-19-5868-7 (eBook)
https://doi.org/10.1007/978-981-19-5868-7

Preface

Welcome to the proceedings of the Third International Conference on Machine Learning, Image Processing, Network Security, and Data Sciences (MIND 2021), which was held in National Institute of Technology Raipur, from December 11 to 12, 2021. Since its inception in 2019, the MIND conference series has featured some of the most innovative and fascinating basic and applied research in the flourishing research area centered on machine learning and computational intelligence, image processing and computer vision, network and cybersecurity and data sciences and big data. This tradition of exemplary interdisciplinary research has been kept alive in 2021 as evident through the imaginative, exciting and diverse set of papers spanning the fields of artificial intelligence, data science, computer science, engineering, computer vision and linguistics. The MIND 2021 conference program featured a rich portiere of original research embodied through oral presentations, posters, invited talks and workshops. In all, we received 273 submissions, and each paper was reviewed by at least two expert reviewers (most papers received three reviews). Seventy-one out of the 273 regular papers were accepted as oral presentations (26 percent which is the lowest from all the previous MIND conferences). The conference also featured invited talks by two outstanding professors, one Associate professor and one industrial expert: Prof. R. K. Shyamasundar (IIT Bombay, India), Prof. Ugo Fiore (Parthenope University, Italy), Dr. Shirin Dora (Loughborough University, UK), and Ms. Kamiya Khatter (Springer, Nature, New Delhi, India). The conference was kick-started by a full day of different activities with a keynote talk, workshops, and oral presentation on cutting-edge topics including machine learning, deep learning, natural language processing, image processing for a robotic vision for path planning, cloud computing, and algorithm for its security for fog and edge vehicular network, different challenges, and problems in the Internet of Things, network and cybersecurity for the new era of a cyber-physical system. The conference also included an interactive events session where a number of researchers discuss their affective interfaces and technologies virtually due to the pandemic situation. In keeping with MINDs tradition of promising and arena the next generation of researchers, the conference featured a consortium where 27 students presented their presentation on machine learning, 12 students on deep learning, 6 students on image processing and computer vision, 7 students on cloud computing and algorithm, 6 students on the Internet of Things, 6 students on the network and cybersecurity, and 6 students on natural language processing.

The MIND 2021 conference would not have been possible without the vision and dedicated effort of a number of people. We are indebted to the Program Committee and the Senior Program Committee for their exceptional work in reviewing the submissions and helping us select the best papers for the conference. We would like to acknowledge Prof. Rakumar Buyya (University of Melbourne, Australia), Prof. Salah Bourennane (Ecole Centrale De Marseille, France), Prof. Xiao-Zhi Gao (University of Eastern Finland, Finland), and Prof. Ching-Hsien Hsu (Asia University, Taiwan) who organized the MIND group. We are grateful to Prof. R. K. Shyamasundar who enlightened us on the latest trend in the areas of real-time distributed systems, programming languages, logic programming, reactive systems, and formal methods. Thanks to Prof. Ugo Fiore who enlightened us with the latest tool on data science and security with advanced optimization techniques. Thanks to Dr. Shirin Dora to share a wonderful talk on computational neuroscience with predictive deep learning techniques and spiking neural networks that close with mimic natural neural networks, and also thanks to Ms. Kamiya Khatter to give the expert talk on plagiarism tools, techniques, research tools, and journals scope for publishing the papers.

In conclusion, 2021 appears to be a fantastic year for Machine Learning, Image Processing, Network Security and Data Sciences. The keynotes, virtual oral and poster presentations, workshops did online model only and the attendees are from all over the world. The program was conducted in virtual mode due to the COVID-19 pandemic situation at NIT Raipur, and all contributed to the third MIND conference being held in Raipur being intellectually stimulating, enjoyable, and memorable.

Raipur, India   Rajesh Doriya
Silchar, India   Badal Soni
Pune, India   Anupam Shukla
Kuopio, Finland   Xiao-Zhi Gao

Acknowledgements

We are grateful to Prof. A. M. Rawani, Director, NIT Raipur, Prof. Prabhat Diwan, Dean (R&C), NIT Raipur, Dr. Rakesh Tripahi, HOD (IT), NIT Raipur, Dr. Rajesh Doriya, NIT Raipur, Dr. Sanjay Kumar, NIT Raipur, Dr. Gyanendra Kumar Verma, NIT Raipur, Dr. Rekh Ram Janghel, NIT Raipur, India, Dr. Badal Soni, NIT Silchar, and Dr. Tirath Prasad Sahu, NIT Raipur, India to organizing the MIND 2021 conference. We would like to thank members of the MIND 2021 Advisory Committee, Publicity Committee, Technical Program Committee, and Steering Committee for their advice and support. Finally, thanks to the authors for sending us their best work and to all the attendees who bring MIND to a successful program. Dr. Rajesh Doriya and Dr. Gyanendra Kumar Verma would also like to thank Prof. A. M. Rawani for encouraging the MIND team to host the 2021 conference and Prof. Prabhat Diwan, Gratch for his invaluable support and assistance throughout the year leading up to the conference. We are obliged to the student volunteers from the National Institute of Technology Raipur, who were invaluable in numerous respects. Thanks to the student, research fellow, and staff of Conference Planning and Operations at the National Institute of Technology, Raipur. Finally, we would like to thank Dr. S. P. Sahu, NIT Raipur, Dr. Mridu Sahu, NIT Raipur, Dr. Manu Vardhan, NIT Raipur, Dr. Baidyanath Bag, NIT Raipur, Dr. Mahendra Kumar Murmu, NIT Kurukshetra, Dr. Naresh Babu M., NIT Silchar, Dr. Sudhakar Pandey, NIT Raipur, Dr. Naresh Kumar Nagwani, NIT Raipur, Dr. R. N. Patel, NIT Raipur, Dr. Arup Bhattacharjee, NIT Silchar, Dr. Chandrashekhar Jatoth, NIT Raipur, Prof. Awadesh Kumar Singh, NIT Kurukshetra who generously provided invaluable support and advice time to time.

Contents

Machine and Deep Learning

Beta Artificial Bee Colony Algorithm for EMG Feature Selection 3
Padmini Sahu, Bikesh Kumar Singh, and Neelamshobha Nirala

Distributed Deep Learning for Content-Based Image Retrieval 19
U. S. N. Raju, Debanjan Pathak, Harika Ala, Netalkar Rohan Kishor,
and Hillol Barman

Automated Detection of Type 2 Diabetes with Imbalanced
and Machine Learning Methods 29
G. Anirudh and Upasana Talukdar

Deep Transfer Learning and Intelligent Item Packing in Retail
Management 41
Mohammad Alodat

Prediction of Polycystic Ovarian Syndrome Using Machine
Learning Techniques 53
Asis Kaur Baweja and M. Kanchana

Medical Image Fusion for Diagnosis of Alzheimer Using Rolling
Guidance Filter and Parameter Adaptive PCNN 65
K. Vanitha, D. Satyanarayana, and M. N. Giri Prasad

Effectiveness of Ensemble Classifier Over State-Of-Art Machine
Learning Classifiers for Predicting Software Faults in Software
Modules 77
Mansi Gupta, Kumar Rajnish, and Vandana Bhattacharya

A Machine Learning Approach for Detection of Breast Cancer
in Women Using Advanced GLCM 89
L. Kanya Kumari and B. Naga Jagadesh

Sales Prediction Using ARIMA, Facebook's Prophet and XGBoost Model of Machine Learning 101
Sushila Ratre and Jyotsna Jayaraj

Modeling Concept Drift Detection as Machine Learning Model Using Overlapping Window and Kolmogorov–Smirnov Test 113
K. T. Jafseer, S. Shailesh, and A. Sreekumar

Wearable Sensor-Based Framework for the Detection of Daily Living Activities Utilizing In-Depth Features 131
Updesh Verma, Pratibha Tyagi, and Manpreet Kaur

Implementing Robotic Path Planning After Object Detection in Deterministic Environments Using Deep Learning Techniques 157
R. Gayathri, V. Uma, and Bettina O'Brien

SDDSCNet: Siamese-Based Dilated Depthwise Separable Convolution Neural Network with Wavelet Fusion for Change Detection 171
Parmeshwar S. Patil, Prathmesh R. Bhosale, Raghunath S. Holambe, and Laxman M. Waghmare

Evaluation of Customer Care Executives Using Speech Emotion Recognition 187
Battula Pragati, Chandana Kolli, Diksha Jain, A. V. Sunethra, and N. Nagarathna

Deep Convolutional Neural Network Approach for Tomato Leaf Disease Classification 199
Surabhi Lingwal, Komal Kumar Bhatia, and Manjeet Singh

Cognitive Load Classification During Arithmetic Task Using Single Convolution Layer-Based 2D-CNN Model 209
Aman Anand Rai and Mitul Kumar Ahirwal

Plant Leaf Diseases Detection Using Deep Learning Algorithms 217
Vikki Binnar and Sanjeev Sharma

Performance Comparison of the Classifiers for Betel Vine Disease Prediction 229
S. Aneesh Fathima and M. Nandhini

Enhanced Object Detection in Floor Plan Through Super-Resolution 247
Dev Khare, N. S. Kamal, H. B. Barathi Ganesh, V. Sowmya, and V. V. Sajith Variyar

Attention-Based Bitemporal Image Deep Feature-Level Change Detection for High Resolution Imagery 259
Nitesh Naik, K. Chandrasekaran, M. Venkatesan, and P. Prabhavathy

Prostate Cancer Grading Using Multistage Deep Neural Networks 271
Ramya Bygari, K. Rithesh, Sateesh Ambesange,
and Shashidhar G. Koolagudi

**Analyzing Wearable Data for Diagnosing COVID-19 Using
Machine Learning Model** 285
Manpreet Kaur Dhaliwal, Rohini Sharma, and Naveen Bindra

**Comparative Analysis of Classification Methods to Predict
Diabetes Mellitus on Noisy Data** 301
Uppalapati Padma Jyothi, Madhavi Dabbiru, Sridevi Bonthu,
Abhinav Dayal, and Narasimha Rao Kandula

**A Robust Secure Access Entrance Method Based on Multi Model
Biometric Credentials Iris and Finger Print** 315
Pranay Yadav, Nishant Chaurasia, Kamal Kumar Gola,
Vijay Bhasker Semwan, Rakesh Gomasta, and Shivendra Dubey

**Region Classification for Air Quality Estimation Using Deep
Learning and Machine Learning Approach** 333
Sumneet Kaur Bamrah, Shruti Srivatsan, and K. S. Gayathri

**Neuroevolution-Based Earthquake Intensity Classification
for Onsite Earthquake Early Warning** 345
Siddhartha Sarkar, Anubrata Roy, Bhargab Das, and Satish Kumar

**Detection of Credit Card Fraud by Applying Genetic Algorithm
and Particle Swarm Optimization** 357
Debachudamani Prusti, Jitendra Kumar Rout, and Santanu Kumar rath

**Traditional Indian Textile Designs Classification Using Transfer
Learning** 371
Seema Varshney, C. Vasantha Lakshmi, and C. Patvardhan

**Classification of Electrocardiogram Signal Using Hybrid Deep
Learning Techniques** 387
Ishu Garg, Saroj Kumar Pandey, Rekh Ram Janghel, and Anupam Shukla

**Fault Diagnosis in Wind Turbine Blades Using Machine Learning
Techniques** 401
Hema Sudheer Banala, Sudarsan Sahoo, Manas Ranjan Sethi,
and Anup K. Sharma

Real-Time Detection of Vehicles on South Asian Roads 413
Rutuparn Pawar, Shubham Gujar, Suyash Chougule, Rutuja Pote,
Dipti Pandit, and Yogesh Dandawate

**Stock Market Prediction Using Ensemble Learning
and Sentimental Analysis** 429
Tinku Singh, Siddhant Bhisikar, Satakshi, and Manish Kumar

Multiple Feature-Based Tomato Plant Leaf Disease Classification
Using SVM Classifier 443
Venkata Lalitha Narla and Gulivindala Suresh

A Methodological Review of Time Series Forecasting with Deep
Learning Model: A Case Study on Electricity Load and Price
Prediction 457
Ayush Sinha, Tinku Singh, Ranjana Vyas, Manish Kumar, and O. P. Vyas

Unexpected Alliance of Cardiovascular Diseases and Artificial
Intelligence in Health Care 481
Rishika Anand, S. R. N. Reddy, and Dinesh Kumar

A Novel Smartphone-Based Human Activity Recognition Using
Deep Learning in Health care 493
Vaibhav Soni, Himanshu Yadav, Vijay Bhaskar Semwal,
Bholanath Roy, Dilip Kumar Choubey, and Dheeresh K. Mallick

An Enhanced Deep Learning Approach for Smartphone-Based
Human Activity Recognition in IoHT 505
Vaibhav Soni, Shashank Jaiswal, Vijay Bhaskar Semwal,
Bholanath Roy, Dilip Kumar Choubey, and Dheeresh K. Mallick

Classification of Indoor–Outdoor Scene Using Deep Learning
Techniques 517
Bagesh Kumar, Harshit Gupta, Shriyash Pravin Ingale, and O. P. Vyas

Prediction of the Reference Evapotranspiration Data from Raipur
Weather Station in Chhattisgarh using Decision Tree-Based
Machine Learning Techniques 537
Abhishek Patel and Syed Taqi Ali

Application of 1-D Convolutional Neural Network for Cutting Tool
Condition Monitoring: A Classification Approach 547
Sonali S. Patil, S. S. Pardeshi, Nikhil Pradhan, Abhishek D. Patange,
and Jay Shah

Image Processing and Computer Vision

Wireless Surveillance Robot for Industrial Application 561
Rishabh Singh, Anjali Kushwah, Preeti Warrier, and Shraddha Oza

An Iterative Posterior Regularized NMF-Based Adaptive Wiener
Filter for Speech Enhancement 575
Sivaramakrishna Yechuri and Sunny Dayal Vanambathina

ADASemSeg: An Active Learning Based Data Adaptation Strategy
for Improving Cross Dataset Breast Tumor Segmentation 587
Arnab Kumar Mishra, Pinki Roy, Sivaji Bandyopadhyay,
and Sujit Kumar Das

Dense Disparity Map Generation for Images Captured by Lunar Rover Navigation Camera 603
Yukti Khosla, U. Rachna, Y. Narendra Reddy, Shikha Tripathi, Amit Maji, and Jayanta Laha

Threat Detection in Self-Driving Vehicles Using Computer Vision 617
Umang Goenka, Aaryan Jagetia, Param Patil, Akshay Singh, Taresh Sharma, and Poonam Saini

Natural Language Processing

KDC: New Dataset for Kannada Document Categorization 633
R. Kasturi Rangan and B. S. Harish

The Ties that Matter: From the Perspective of Similarity Measure in Online Social Networks 647
Soumita Das and Anupam Biswas

Comparative Study of Abstractive Summarizers (Sequence2Sequence Models) 659
Vijay Karunakaran and Manoj Das

Comparative Analysis of Lexicon-Based Emotion Recognition of Text 671
Anima Pradhan, Manas Ranjan Senapati, and Pradip Kumar Sahu

A Comprehensive Understanding of Text Region Identification and Localization in Scene Imagery Using DL Practices 679
Ritu Devi and Bijendra Kumar

TCRKDS: Towards Integration of Semantic Intelligence for Course Recommendation in Support of a Knowledge Driven Strategy 693
Harsh Shaw, Gerard Deepak, and A. Santhanavijayan

Network Security and IoT

Developing MCDM-Based Technique to Calculate Trustworthiness of Advertised QoE Parameters in Fog Computing Environment 705
Shefali Varshney, Rajinder Sandhu, and P. K. Gupta

Data Clustering Approach on the Basis of Data Sensitivity for Implementation of Secure Cloud Computing Environment 715
Rajdeep Singh and R. K. Pateriya

An Approach for Energy-Efficient Resource Allocation Through Early Planning of Virtual Machines to Servers in Cloud Server Farms 725
P. Kumar, S. Vinodh Kumar, and L. Priya

**negSPUC: Trees-Based Single-Phase High-Utility Itemset Mining
Algorithm with Negative Profit Values** 739
B. Anup Bhat, S. V. Harish, and M. Geetha

**LoRa-Based IoT Architecture Using Ant Colony Optimization
for Intelligent Traffic System** 751
Sarita Simaiya, Umesh Kumar Lilhore, Jasminder Kaur Sandhu,
Jyoti Snehi, Atul Garg, and Advin Manhar

**Energy Saving Techniques for Cloud Data Centres: An Empirical
Research Analysis** 763
Arif Ahmad Shehloo, Muheet Ahmed Butt, and Majid Zaman

Preliminary Conceptions of a Remote Incoercible E-Voting Scheme 781
Nazia Jahan Khan Chowdhury, Shinsuke Tamura,
and Kazi Md. Rokibul Alam

**Evaluating Data Migrations with Respect to Interoperability
in Hybrid Cloud** 795
S. M. Barhate and M. P. Dhore

**Secure Management of Digital Academic Certificates Using
Blockchain Technology** 805
Anindya Kumar Biswas, Mou Dasgupta, and Sangram Ray

Tracking of Fall Detection Using IMU Sensor: An IoHT Application ... 815
Vijay Bhaskar Semwal, Abhishek Kumar, Pankaj Nargesh,
and Vaibhav Soni

**Avenues of Graph Theoretic Approach of Analysing the LIDAR
Data for Point-To-Point Floor Exploration by Indoor AGV** 827
Rapti Chaudhuri, Jashaswimalya Acharjee, and Suman Deb

**Combined Cryptography and Text Steganography for Enhanced
Security Based on Number System** 839
Bubai Das, Santanu Mondal, and Kunal Kumar Mandal

Analysis of Mirai Malware and Its Components 851
Shubham Kumar and B. R. Chandavarkar

**Realization of 5G NR Primary Synchronization Signal Detector
Using Systolic FIR Filter** 863
Aytha Ramesh Kumar, K. Lal Kishore, and Parepalli Sravanthi

**Composition of Static and Dynamic Analysis for Algorithmic-Level
Code Semantic Optimization** 877
Mehul Thakral, V. C. Skanda, Bhavna Arora, G. R. Dheemanth,
and N. S. Kumar

A Framework for DDoS Attack Detection in SDN-Based IoT Using Hybrid Classifier 889
Pinkey Chauhan and Mithilesh Atulkar

Modeling Solar Photo-Voltaic Power Generation System with MPPT Controller 901
Babita Panda, Aman Sharma, Sudip Nandi, Arjyadhara Pradhan, Lipika Nanda, and Sarita Samal

About the Editors

Rajesh Doriya received his B.E. from MITS Gwalior, M.Tech. from IIIT Allahabad, and Ph.D. from IIIT Allahabad, India. He has got teaching experience of over 10 years, and presently, he is working as an Assistant Professor in the Department of Information Technology, NIT Raipur. He is associated with research projects at the Institute for System Studies and Analyses (ISSA) lab of DRDO, New Delhi, India, and the Division of Remote Handling and Robotics (DRHR) lab of BARC Mumbai, India. He has authored over 50 research papers published in international Journals and Conferences. His research interests include distributed computing, cloud computing, artificial intelligence, robotics, soft computing techniques, network security, etc.

Badal Soni is an Assistant Professor in the Department of Computer Engineering, National Institute of Technology (NIT) Silchar, India. He completed his B.Tech. from Rajiv Gandhi Technical University (formerly RGPV) Bhopal, India, and M.Tech. from Indian Institute of Information Technology (IIITDM) Jabalpur, India. He received his Ph.D. from NIT Silchar, India. He has teaching and research experience of over seven years in computer science and information technology with a particular interest in computer graphics, image processing, speech, and language processing. He has published over 50 papers in international journals and conference proceedings. He is a Senior Member of IEEE and a professional member of various bodies like IEEE, ACM, IAENG, and IACSIT.

Anupam Shukla is working as Director at the Indian Institute of Information Technology, Pune. Before this, he was a founding Dean of Sponsored Research and Consultancy, Professor in the Department of Information and Communication Technology (ICT) at ABV-Indian Institute of Information Technology and Management (ABV-IIITM), Gwalior, and a visiting professor at Florida International University, USA, and Indian Institute of Management (IIM), Rohtak. He has 32 years of teaching and research experience. He is globally renowned for his research on artificial intelligence, which has won him several academic accolades and resulted in collaborations with academicians worldwide. To his credit, he has five patents, five books, and 190 peer-reviewed publications. He is the mentor of 17 doctorates and 146 postgraduate theses.

Xiao-Zhi Gao received his B.Sc. and M.Sc. degrees from the Harbin Institute of Technology, China, in 1993 and 1996, respectively. He obtained his D.Sc. (Tech.) degree from the Helsinki University of Technology (now Aalto University), Finland, in 1999. He has been working as a professor at the University of Eastern, Finland, since 2018. He has published over 450 technical papers in refereed journals and international conferences. His research interests are nature-inspired computing methods with their applications in optimization, data mining, machine learning, control, signal processing, and industrial electronics.

Machine and Deep Learning

Beta Artificial Bee Colony Algorithm for EMG Feature Selection

Padmini Sahu, Bikesh Kumar Singh, and Neelamshobha Nirala

1 Introduction

EMG signal is a bioelectrical signal expressed by the activity of muscle during contraction. EMG is a non-invasive technique, and it is related to the upper limb information of the body [1]. EMG data is collected by surface EMG (sEMG) sensors placed on the surface of the skin. sEMG sensors are mainly used in different types of experiments such as lab experiments, field experiments, etc. Muscular activity of the body can be recorded, measured, and analyzed to explore and identify various research areas such as biomechanics, rehabilitation, sports science, clinical diagnosis, man–machine interface, and so on. EMG signal can be applied into the development of an interface model for people with disabilities such as electric wheelchairs, prosthesis control, robotics (robot control), virtual word, and so on. In this work, prosthesis control based on non-invasive adaptive prosthetics is considered for classifying hand movements [2]. Recent scientific research has proposed various methods in the field of the hand prosthetics such as hybrid prosthetics, passive prosthetics, robotic hand prosthetics, and so on [3, 4]. The present work is based on the investigation of the robotic hand prosthetic followed by 67 intact subjects and 11 transradial amputated subjects. Generally, the upper link of hand prostheses is controlled using more than one EMG signal. There are many movements in the muscular activity of the amputees leading to various problems that need to be identified and isolated. To

P. Sahu (✉) · B. K. Singh · N. Nirala
Department of Biomedical Engineering, National Institute of Technology Raipur, Raipur, India
e-mail: psahu.phd2019.bme@nitrr.ac.in

B. K. Singh
e-mail: bsingh.bme@nitrr.ac.in

N. Nirala
e-mail: neelanir.bme@nitrr.ac.in

© The Author(s), under exclusive license to Springer Nature Singapore Pte Ltd. 2023   3
R. Doriya et al. (eds.), *Machine Learning, Image Processing, Network Security and Data Sciences*, Lecture Notes in Electrical Engineering 946,
https://doi.org/10.1007/978-981-19-5868-7_1

eliminate these problems, enhance classification performance by choosing the right feature selection techniques [2, 3, 5].

FS is a preprocessing and essential step to remove redundant and irrelevant information of the problem as well as reduce the number of feature and classifier complexity. There are three types of FS techniques: (i) filter techniques, (ii) wrapper techniques, and (iii) hybrid techniques. The filter technique is used for statistical techniques such as mutual information, distance information, and correlation information. Examples of filter techniques are correlation-based feature selection, information gain, ANOVA, principal component analysis (PCA), and so on [6]. Whereas the wrapper technique is based on finding the optimal feature subset from the actual feature set. It includes feature selection-based meta-heuristic algorithms such as binary artificial bee colony algorithm (BABC), binary particle swarm optimization (BPSO), binary ant colony optimization (BACO), binary crow search algorithm (BCSA) [7–10]. The third type of hybrid feature selection technique is a combination of filter and wrapper technique that improves the classification accuracy. Examples of hybrid techniques are hybrid serial GWO-WOA [11], TOPSIS-Jaya [12], and so on. Compared to all three techniques, the hybrid technique is faster than the wrapper technique, and the filter technique is a simple structure with a fast processing process. However, all feature selection techniques provide better classification accuracy with different domains and regions, therefore the major interest of researchers in the feature selection area.

In recent years, real-world problems are getting more and more challenging, thus requiring more flexible, robust, and efficient algorithms in feature selection. One of the most promising swarm algorithms of feature selection for optimization is artificial bee colony (ABC) and has great potential with proper modifications. It is a new approach proposed by Karaboga [13], and since then, there has been a rapid increase in the interest of ABC. ABC has been successfully applied to many fields like machine batch processing of a machine [14], designing two-channel quadrature mirror filter banks [15], loudspeaker design problems [16], etc. In [17], a two-archive multi-objective ABC algorithm (TMABC-FS) is developed for the cost-sensitive FS problem of machine learning [16, 17]. ABC has the potential of solving local and global optimization problems. Several benchmark functions [18] have been tested to validate the performance of ABC. As per no free lunch theorem, no specific meta-heuristic algorithm is regarded as best that gives best solution for all optimization problems. The standard ABC algorithm however demands alteration for many practical applications due to its inefficiency in balancing both exploration and exploitation phases during searching. The solution generated after each run by the solution search equation of the algorithm has an equal probability of being a positive or negative result. For ensuring better and effective results from the algorithm, the two phases need to be well balanced as excessive exploitations lead to premature convergence to local minima and excessive explorations result in slow convergence. Thus, Gaussian artificial bee colony (GABC) [19] was proposed to counterbalance between exploration and exploitation. It outperforms standard ABC by taking random values from Gaussian distribution over a uniform distribution.

Although GABC is better than the standard ABC, it still needs improvements in terms of convergence and better exploration capability. We propose a beta artificial bee colony (BetaABC) algorithm to further increase its performance by introducing beta distribution in search space. This algorithm avoids premature or slow convergence, and after comparison with ABC and GABC with different parameters, it proves to be better, in terms of global optimization. Hence, the key contributions of the proposed method are listed below:

1. A novel variant of ABC, i.e., beta artificial bee colony (BetaABC) is proposed and validated on 10 benchmark functions.
2. Binary beta artificial bee colony (BBABC)-based FS is proposed for EMG signal classification.
3. DWT is employed to extract various features from EMG signal.
4. The proposed BBABC is applied for FS and classification of prosthetic hand movements using EMG signal.
5. The extensive experiment is performed to validate proposed BBABC with BABC, and BGABC.

2   Methods and Implementation

2.1   EMG Data

The raw EMG data is taken from the public domain non-invasive adaptive prosthetics (NinaPro) dataset for prosthetic hands [3]. In this study, the third version of the NinaPro dataset (DB3) that comprises EMG signals acquired from 11 amputee people for 17 hand movements (Exercise A) is used. There are 12 EMG electrodes with a 2000 Hz sampling frequency which are used in the experiment. Each subject was asked to perform 6 movement repetitions with 5 s of action and 3 s of rest.

2.2   Feature Extraction Using DWT Method

Discrete wavelet transform (DWT) is a widely used feature extraction method in signal processing that decomposes signals in a time–frequency domain. The signals are decomposed into multi-resolution coefficients, i.e., low-pass filter and high-pass filter. Low-pass filters are represented in approximation levels (A) and high-pass filters are represented in detail levels (D) [20]. The popular mother wavelet-like sym4, sym6, coif4, coif5, db4, db6, bior2.2, bior2.4, and bior4.4 of the DWT method were selected to extract the features from raw EMG signals. Recent research shows that the decomposition at the fourth level with db6 gives promising results in EMG signal classification. Therefore, the DWT method at the fourth decomposition level with db6 is used in the current work [21, 22]. In literature, twenty-four popular statistical

Table 1 Twenty-four statistical EMG features

S. No	Feature	Feature name	S. No	Feature	Feature name
1	RMS	Root mean square	13	EWL	Enhanced wavelength
2	MAV	Mean absolute value	14	SI	Simple square integral
3	WL	Wavelength	15	MMAV	Modified mean absolute value
4	VAR	Variance of EMG	16	MMAV2	Modified mean absolute value 2
5	ZC	Zero crossing	17	DASDV	Difference absolute standard deviation value
6	AE	Average energy	18	VO	V-order
7	LD	Log detector	19	MYOP	Myopulse percentage rate
8	WA	Willison amplitude	20	IEMG	Integrated EMG
9	SKEW	Skewness	21	SD	Standard deviation
10	KURT	Kurtosis	22	DVARV	Difference variance value
11	MFL	Maximum fractal length	23	TM	Temporal moment
12	AAC	Average amplitude change	24	MAD	Mean absolute deviation

features have been used to extract valuable information from each wavelet coefficient as given in Table 1 [22–27].

2.3 Background

2.3.1 Artificial Bee Colony

ABC consists of two components: bees (the process of decision making for selection of the position of food) and food source (position in space). It defines two types of behavior: nectar source identification and food source abandonment. Also, the bees are categorized into three class namely—employed, onlooker, and scout bees [13]. The job of the employed bees is to visit identified food sources while the job of the scout bees are to search new food sources around the hive. The job of the onlooker bees is to stay and watch the employed bees at the hive in order to identify the food sources. In the whole process, some bees are employed to search the food randomly around the hive. These bees are responsible for collecting, bringing, and depositing some nectar from identified food sources to the hive. After depositing, their job is to share the information through various dance about quantity and quality of the nectar of food sources with the bees (onlookers) waiting in a hive [28]. The bee colony now enters a cycle of iterations and the following steps are followed: (1) after the information is shared, the employed bee either becomes onlooker after the food source is abandoned or continue to forage the site visited earlier; (2) onlookers in the hive will follow employed bees simultaneously based on the information received to forage further on some memorized sources of food; and (3) some of the scouts will start random search spontaneously [13, 28, 29]. The food sources are randomly initialized using the below expression:

$$a_i = l_k + \text{rand}(0, 1)^*(u_k - l_k) \tag{1}$$

where a_i is the ith solution in the population, k is a randomly selected parameter index, u_k and l_k are upper and lower bound constraints for the solution search space of objective function to be optimized. Onlooker bee selects the food sources influenced by employed bees based on the probability:

$$Pb_i = \text{fitness}_i / \sum_{n=1}^{SN} \text{fitness}_i \tag{2}$$

to calculate the fitness values, we use the following equation:

$$\text{fitness}_i = \begin{cases} \frac{1}{1+f} & \text{if } f \geq 0 \\ 1 + abs(f) & \text{if } f < 0 \end{cases} \tag{3}$$

The following equation is used for greedy selection to update the solution:

$$\left.\begin{array}{l} a = a_{new} \\ f = f_{new} \end{array}\right\} \text{if fitness}_{new} > \text{fitness}_i(a_i)$$

a and f remains the same if $\text{fitness}_{new} < \text{fitness}_i(a_i)$ (4)

where f represents the food source. Onlookers will explore all the locations that seem promising and might have a higher probability than other locations. The following equation is used to generate candidate food sources from the previously memorized ones as:

$$b_{i,j} = a_{i,j} + 2(r - 0.5)\big(a_{i,j} - a_{k,j}\big) \tag{5}$$

2.3.2 Gaussian Artificial Bee Colony (GABC)

A common problem with meta-heuristic methods is that poor balance between the exploitation and exploration capability and thus suffers from either very slow convergence due to excessive exploration or premature convergence due to excessive exploitation [19]. In GABC, the improvement has been made to generate candidate food sources as per the following alternative:

$$b_{i.j} = \begin{cases} a_{i,j} + \emptyset_{i,j}(a_{i,j} - a_{k,j}).\theta.\rho \text{ if } r_2 > z \\ a_{i,j} + \emptyset_{i,j}(a_{i,j} - a_{k,j}).2.\rho \text{ if } r_2 <= z \end{cases} \tag{6}$$

where $\emptyset_{i,j} = 2.(r_1 - 0.5)$, $\emptyset$ is a random number in the range $[-1,1]$, and i, j, k are indexes of dimension of a solution, and $r1, r2 \in [0,1]$ are random numbers generated from uniform distribution and

$$\rho = 0.5 - 0.25\frac{\text{iter}}{\text{maxiter}} \tag{7}$$

and θ is a number generated from Gaussian distribution; iter and maxiter represent current and total iterations, respectively. The parameter z is used to balance the tradeoff between Gaussian and uniform distribution.

3   Proposed Methodology

3.1   Beta Artificial Bee Colony (BetaABC)

Although GABC is better than the standard ABC, it still needs improvements in terms of convergence. Therefore, we propose BetaABC to further avoid slow or premature convergence. The proposed method uses beta distribution over uniform or Gaussian distribution that increases the search space which in turn gives a better balance between exploration and exploitation capability. In GABC, a list of random samples is drawn from a normal distribution and Gaussian distribution. The distribution is dependent on many parameters like loc, scale, and size. The number of samples is equal to the value of the size of the argument. Furthermore, in each iteration, the results will be slightly different due to their randomness nature but will follow the same distribution and general shape. Unlike GABC, the proposed method uses beta distribution to draw samples. It has the probability distribution function

$$f(x; a, b) = \frac{1}{B(\alpha, \beta)}x^{\alpha-1}(1 - x)^{\beta-1} \tag{8}$$

where B is the beta function

$$B(\alpha, \beta) = \int t^{\alpha-1}(1 - t)^{\beta-1}\text{dt} \tag{9}$$

where a and b are oats or an array of oats, size is int or tuple of int and α & β are positive values.

4 Proposed Binary BetaABC for EMG Feature Selection

The presence of redundant and irrelevant information in a problem makes the classification of EMG signals excessively difficult, which also reduces the performance of their classification models. Therefore, the proposed BetaABC is converted into its binary version called binary BetaABC (BBABC) to solve the feature selection problem in EMG signal classification. The dimension of the search space is equal to the number of features in EMG dataset. The following matrix G $(E \times F)$ shows the possible solution to be selected as optimal feature subset. Here, E represents the population size, and F represents the number of features. Our main objective is to select S optimal features from the original EMG dataset, where $S \ll F$. The example of possible solution is given below:

$$G = \begin{bmatrix} 1 & 0 & 1 & 0 & 0 & 0 & 1 & 1 \\ 1 & 0 & 1 & 0 & 1 & 0 & 1 & 0 \\ 0 & 1 & 1 & 1 & 0 & 0 & 0 & 1 \\ 0 & 1 & 1 & 0 & 0 & 1 & 0 & 0 \\ 1 & 0 & 0 & 0 & 0 & 0 & 1 & 1 \end{bmatrix}$$

where G has a population size of 5 with 8 dimensions. Bit 1 shows the feature is selected, whereas bit 0 shows the feature is not selected. So the first solution represents the 1st, 3rd, 7th, and 8th features that were selected. The second solution represents the 1st, 3rd, 5th, and 7th features were selected, and so on.

Algorithm: Beta Artificial Bee Colony (BetaABC)

---

1. Initialize population of solutions $a_{i,j}$ using Eq. (1)
2. Evaluate the population
3. Run = 1
4. Produce new food sources $b_{i,j}$ in the neighborhood of $a_{i,j}$ for employed bees using Eq. (6) with θ generated from Eqs. (8) and (9)
5. Calculate probability values P_{bi} for $a_{i,j}$ with the help of their fitness values using the Eq. (2)
6. Calculate the value of fitness$_i$ using Eq. (3)
7. Apply greedy selection process between $a_{i,j}$ and $b_{i,j}$ by using Eq. (4)
8. Produce new food sources $b_{i,j}$ in the neighborhood of $a_{i,j}$ for onlooker using Eq. (6) with θ generated from Eqs. (8) and (9)
9. Produce new positions bi for onlooker from the a_i selected depending on P_{bi} and evaluate by using Eq. (2)
10. Calculate the value of fitness$_i$ using Eq. (3)
11. Apply greedy selection process for the onlookers between $a_{i,j}$ and $b_{i,j}$ by using Eq. (4)
12. Find the abandoned sources, if exists, and replace them with new random solution a_i for scout using equation
$a_{i,j} = \min_j + \text{rand}(0, 1)^* (\max_j - \min_j)$
13. Memorize the position of best food source achieved so far
14. Run = Run + 1
15. Repeat step 4 to 14 until Run = Maximum runs

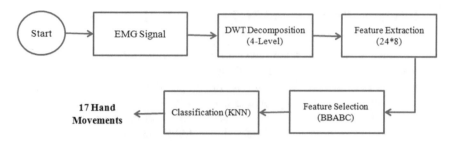

Fig. 1 Flow diagram of proposed BBABC for EMG signal classification

Figure 1 shows the flow diagram of the proposed BBABC for EMG feature selection and classification. Initially, raw EMG signals are preprocessed, and features are extracted from preprocessed EMG signal using DWT to form an original feature set. The extracted feature set contains 24 statistical features on 8 coefficients obtained at 4th level of DWT decomposition using db6 mother wavelet. The proposed BBABC is used to find the optimal feature subset from the extracted feature set. In the feature selection process, the fitness function is used to evaluate the performance of the classification. If the solutions give the same fitness value, then solution with fewer features is selected. Finally, the optimal feature subset obtained by the proposed BBABC is fed into the KNN classifier for EMG signal classification.

5   Experimental Analysis

Experimental analysis is divided into two sections: Section-I investigates the proposed BetaABC with ABC and GABC on 10 benchmark test functions that have been tested to validate its effectiveness and Section-II investigates the proposed BBABC for EMG feature selection on 11 amputee subjects.

Section-I: Experimental results of proposed BetaABC on benchmark functions

This section presents the comparative results of proposed BetaABC with ABC and GABC on different parameters. A set of 10 benchmark test functions have been used to validate the performance of BetaABC. These benchmark functions are used for the verification of many stochastic optimization algorithms. The necessary information about the functions, their mathematical representations, search range, and desired optimal solution is showcased in Table 2. All the test functions used for experimental verification are minimization functions.

The results of BetaABC are compared with the results of ABC and GABC for each benchmark function with different values of the parameter. The efficiency of the BetaABC algorithm depends on the parameter z that ranges from 0.1 to 0.9. The benchmark functions were run for several evaluations as the population size used for the experiment is 35, number of iteration is 100, and the value of z is

Table 2 Benchmark functions used in experiment

S. No	Function name	Mathematical representation	Search range	Optimal solution
1	**Alpine**	$f_1(x) : \sum_{i=1}^{D} \lvert x_i \sin(x_i) + 0.1x_i \rvert$	$[-10,10]$	0
2	**Booth**	$f_2(x) : (x + 2y + 7)^2 + (2x + y - z)^2$	$[-10, 10]$	0
3	**Beale**	$f_3(x) : (1.5 - x + xy)^2 +$ $(2.25 - x + xy^2)^2 + (2.625 - x + xy^3)^2$	$[-4.5, 4.5]$	0
4	**Chung**	$f_4(x) : (\sum_{i=1}^{D} x_i^2)^2$	$[-100, 100]$	0
5	**Branin**	$f_5(x) : (x_2 - 5.1x_1^2/4\pi^2 + 5x_1/\pi - 6)^2 +$ $10(1 - 1/8\pi)cos(x_1) + 10$	$[-15, 15]$	0
6	**Sphere**	$f_6(x) : \sum_{i=1}^{D} x_i^2$	$[-100, 100]$	0
7	**Griewank**	$f_7(x) : \sum_{i=1}^{D} \frac{x_i^2}{4000} - \Pi \cos\left(\frac{x_i}{\sqrt{i}}\right) + 1$	$[-600, 600]$	0
8	**Rastrigin**	$f_8(x) : \sum_{i=1}^{D} [x_i^2 - 10 \cos 2\pi x_i + 10n]$	$[-5.12, 5.12]$	0
9	**Schaffer**	$f_9(x) : 0.5 + \frac{\sin^2(x_1^2 + x_2^2)^2 - 0.5}{1 + 0.001(x_1^2 + x_2^2)^2}$	$[-100, 100]$	0
10	**Schwefel**	$f_{10}(x) = 418.9829n - \sum x_i \sin(\sqrt{\lvert x_i \rvert})$	$[-500, 500]$	0

0.5. The experiment was run 20 times independently for dimensions $D = 2$, and three statistical values, i.e., best, worst, and the average values, are noted from these experiments which are given in Table 3. It shows that the proposed BetaABC achieves higher or competitive results than ABC and GABC in all three statistical parameters. Convergence graphs based on fitness values are also plotted for comparison between ABC, GABC, and BetaABC on all benchmark functions as shown in Fig. 2. BetaABC is outperforming than ABC and GABC with suitable parameters.

Section-II: Experimental results of proposed BBABC on EMG signal classification

This section presents the performance of the proposed BBABC with BABC and BGABC for EMG feature selection. The EMG signals from 11 amputee subjects were collected from exercise A of the NinaPro DB3. Thereafter, the mother wavelet db6 of the DWT method was applied to decompose the EMG signal into the fourth decomposition level. Twenty-four statistical features were extracted from each DWT coefficient (four details and four approximations). In total, 2304 features (12 EMG channels × 8 DWT coefficients × 24 statistical features) were extracted from each EMG segment of each subject. The feature selection based on proposed BBABC is applied to select the optimal feature subset. The KNN classifier is used in the

Table 3 Fitness values of proposed BetaABC with ABC and GABC on 10 benchmark functions

		ABC	GABC	BetaABC
Alpine	Best	1.76E−12	4.54E−06	**1.16E−12**
	Worst	257.4853375	265.145999	**216.5156087**
	Avg	43.03078019	58.84823994	**36.77360991**
Booth	Best	0.24078979	0.11078979	**0.003078979**
	Worst	3.385294	14.20313	**3.185294**
	Avg	0.018105	0.138345	**0.0018105**
Beale	Best	0.34078979	0.18078979	**0.06078979**
	Worst	0.103797	**0.092382**	31.55422
	Avg	0.005416	0.001215	**2.08101E−06**
Chung	Best	**1.26E−12**	3.5421E−06	1.26E-12
	Worst	8,044,898.158	**7,362,745.454**	54,221,365,634
	Avg	87,181.57425	123,664.834	**85,181.57425**
Bramin	Best	20.05231234	20.08231234	**19.67231234**
	Worst	264.688204	371.9663214	**121.6889116**
	Avg	97.24972072	176.9312544	**26.80310608**
Sphere	Best	295.6037754	486.0067942	**135.6037754**
	Worst	292,744.4611	281,216.3629	**2913.386937**
	Avg	40,083.58003	68,324.75694	**904.6985949**
Griewank	Best	0.089460346	0.056780414	**0.029460346**
	Worst	0.059923658	0.071359047	**0.029923658**
	Avg	2.935520787	3.978498861	**2.635520787**
Rastrigin	Best	0.24972072	0.9312544	**0.103106079**
	Worst	1540.874042	1657.699314	**1530.874042**
	Avg	394.7383831	529.3521708	**392.7383831**
Schaffer	Best	0.21972072	0.7312544	**0.103106079**
	Worst	292,744.4611	281,216.3629	**2913.386937**
	Avg	40,083.58003	68,324.75694	**904.6985949**
Schwefel	Best	10.32063	13.14079	**8.13034**
	Worst	**839.924873**	2109.400154	2018.472328
	Avg	264.688204	371.9663214	**121.6889116**
Ranking (W|T|L)	Best	0|1|9	0|0|10	**9|1|0**
	Worst	1|0|9	2|0|8	**7|0|3**
	Avg	0|0|10	0|0|10	**10|0|0**

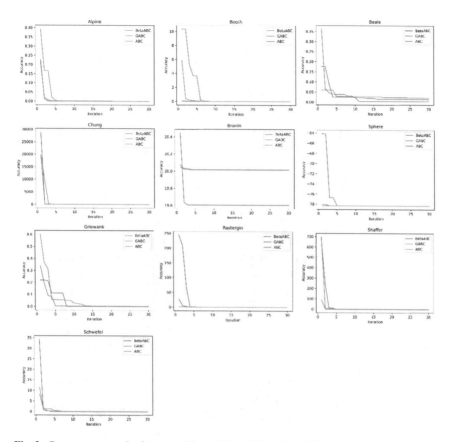

Fig. 2 Convergence graph of proposed BetaABC on 10 benchmark functions

experiment for the classification of 17 different hand movements from 11 amputee subjects. The two metrics, namely maximum accuracy and feature selection ratio, are used to evaluate the performance of the algorithms.

Table 4 shows the maximum accuracy and standard deviation of proposed BBABC with BABC and BGABC in which the best results are highlighted by bold text. It is observed that the proposed BBABC achieves the highest accuracy than the other two methods. The ranking of three methods is also given based on win/tie/loss (W/T/L) statistical measure. The W/T/L measure is also suggesting that the proposed BBABC-based feature selection method is outperforming than other methods. In Fig. 3, the comparison between BABC, BGABC, and BBABC is demonstrated by the convergence graph based on classification accuracy. The convergence graph is also showing that BBABC-based feature selection gives better classification accuracy than BABC and BGABC on 11 amputee people.

Table 5 shows the comparison of three feature selection methods BABC, BGABC, ad BBABC based on feature selection ratio, i.e., the number of selected features

Table 4 Maximum classification accuracy with different ABC variants on 11 amputee subjects

Dataset		BABC	BGABC	BBABC
Subject 1	Avg	94.0983363	93.97058824	**94.09902555**
	Std	0.06302035	0.141347924	0.148025472
Subject 2	Avg	94.1176471	94.11764706	**94.58057041**
	Std	1.4283E-13	1.42832E−13	0.181260089
Subject 3	Avg	70.4426619	70.48128342	**70.57070707**
	Std	0.30304797	0.402824981	0.411057384
Subject 4	Avg	79.3850267	79.33155081	**80.21717172**
	Std	0.15265282	0.215227447	0.225440775
Subject 5	Avg	51.9266191	49.77421272	**52.11194949**
	Std	0.59257832	0.456221937	0.599318693
Subject 6	Avg	92.1078431	91.15418895	**92.17498515**
	Std	0.16090162	0.221699518	0.234779968
Subject 7	Avg	42.6619133	43.73291741	**44.17142008**
	Std	0.43284192	0.504772212	0.515929897
Subject 8	Avg	91.1764706	91.17647059	**91.19647059**
	Std	1.5711E−13	1.57115E−13	1.57115E−13
Subject 9	Avg	94.1161616	94.11764706	**94.12764706**
	Std	0.01477997	1.42832E−13	5.71327E−14
Subject 10	Avg	58.9913844	56.56565656	**62.88264409**
	Std	0.47960023	0.398101122	1.14265E−13
Subject 11	Avg	91.1586453	91.7409388	**92.62147059**
	Std	0.17735961	0.236479486	0.437655323
Ranking	**W|T|L**	0|0|11	0|0|11	**11|0|0**

divides by the total number of features. It is observed that the proposed BBABC method wins 7 times in selecting the minimum number of features.

6 Conclusion

This paper proposes a new variant of ABC algorithm called as BetaABC algorithm inspired from GABC algorithm aiming to improve its performance by maintaining a proper balance between the exploitation and exploration of the search space. The Uniform distribution used in the estimation of new search space solution is replaced with beta distribution which gives the better results than the existing algorithm. The performance of proposed BetaABC is evaluated on 10 benchmark functions and an obtained result suggests that it is outperforming the standard ABC and GABC. Further, a binary version of BetaABC called BBABC is proposed to solve the FS

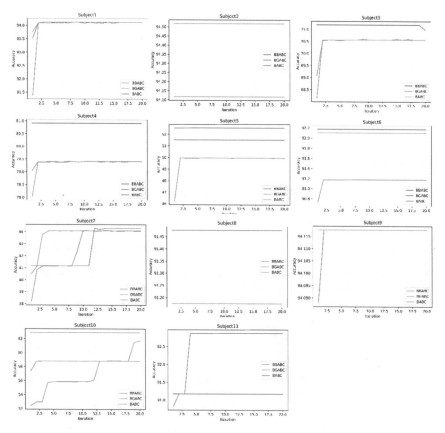

Fig. 3 Convergence graph of proposed BBABC with BABC and BGABC on 11 amputees

Table 5 Average feature selection ratio of BBABC with BABC and BGABC on 11 amputees

Dataset	BABC	BGABC	BBABC
Subject 1	0.51	0.45	*0.33*
Subject 2	0.47	0.42	*0.31*
Subject 3	0.5	0.47	*0.37*
Subject 4	0.5	0.5	*0.49*
Subject 5	0.49	0.54	*0.3*
Subject 6	*0.4*	0.41	0.54
Subject 7	0.41	0.41	*0.27*
Subject 8	0.48	*0.44*	0.51
Subject 9	0.71	*0.53*	0.75
Subject 10	0.5	0.49	*0.27*
Subject 11	*0.48*	0.63	0.6
Ranking	2|0|9	2|0|9	*7|0|4*

problem of EMG signal classification. The accuracy and feature selection ratio is taken into consideration to validate the performance of the proposed BBABC with BABC and BGABC on 11 amputee subjects. It can be inferred from the experimental results and statistics that BBABC with appropriate parameters is giving either better results or competitive to other variants of ABC. Further improvements are to be expected keeping in view to the increasing popularity of the other variants of ABC.

References

1. Azhiri RB et al (2021) EMG signal classification using reflection coefficients and extreme value machine. arXiv preprint arXiv:2106.10561
2. Phinyomark A et al (2009) A novel feature extraction for robust EMG pattern recognition. arXiv preprint arXiv:0912.3973
3. Atzori M et al (2014) Electromyography data for non-invasive naturally-controlled robotic hand prostheses. Sci Data 1:1–13
4. Shi W-T et al (2018) A bionic hand controlled by hand gesture recognition based on surface EMG signals: A preliminary study. Biocybernetics Biomed Eng 38:126–135
5. Sharma T et al (2021) Decomposition and evaluation of SEMG for hand prostheses control. Measurement 186:110102
6. Bommert A et al (2020) Benchmark for filter methods for feature selection in high-dimensional classification data. Comput Stat Data Anal 143:106839
7. Chuang L-Y et al (2008) Improved binary PSO for feature selection using gene expression data. Comput Biol Chem 32:29–38
8. Karaboga D, Basturk B (2008) On the performance of artificial bee colony (ABC) algorithm. Appl Soft Comput 8:687–697
9. Aghdam MH et al (2009) Text feature selection using ant colony optimization. Expert Syst Appl 36:6843–6853
10. Chaudhuri A, Sahu TP (2021) Feature selection using Binary crow search algorithm with time varying flight length. Expert Syst Appl 168:114288
11. Mafarja M et al (2020) Efficient hybrid nature-inspired binary optimizers for feature selection. Cogn Comput 12:150–175
12. Chaudhuri A, Sahu TP (2021) A hybrid feature selection method based on Binary Jaya algorithm for micro-array data classification. Comput Electr Eng 90:106963
13. Karaboga D, Basturk B (2007) A powerful and efficient algorithm for numerical function optimization: artificial bee colony (ABC) algorithm. J Global Optim 39:459–471
14. Melouk S et al (2004) Minimizing makespan for single machine batch processing with non-identical job sizes using simulated annealing. Int J Prod Econ 87:141–147
15. Upendar J et al (2010) Design of two-channel quadrature mirror filter bank using particle swarm optimization. Digital Signal Process 20:304–313
16. Coelho LDS et al (2012) A chaotic approach of differential evolution optimization applied to loudspeaker design problem. IEEE Trans Magn 48:751–754
17. Zhang Y et al (2019) Cost-sensitive feature selection using two-archive multi-objective artificial bee colony algorithm. Expert Syst Appl 137:46–58
18. Tang K et al (2007) Benchmark functions for the CEC'2008 special session and competition on large scale global optimization. Nat Inspired Comput Appl Lab USTC, China 24:1–18
19. dos Santos Coelho L, Alotto P (2011) Gaussian artificial bee colony algorithm approach applied to Loney's solenoid benchmark problem. IEEE Trans Magn 47:1326–1329
20. Ahlawat V et al (2021) DWT-based hand movement identification of EMG signals using SVM. In: Proceedings of international conference on communication and artificial intelligence, 2021, pp 495–505

21. Chowdhury RH et al (2013) Surface electromyography signal processing and classification techniques. Sensors 13:12431–12466
22. Too J et al (2019) EMG feature selection and classification using a Pbest-guide binary particle swarm optimization. Computation 7:12
23. Too J et al (2019) Hybrid binary particle swarm optimization differential evolution-based feature selection for EMG signals classification. Axioms 8:79
24. Subasi A (2012) Classification of EMG signals using combined features and soft computing techniques. Appl Soft Comput 12:2188–2198
25. Too J et al (2019) Classification of hand movements based on discrete wavelet transform and enhanced feature extraction. Int J Adv Comput Sci Appl 10:83–89
26. Too J, Abdullah AR (2021) Opposition based competitive grey wolf optimizer for EMG feature selection. Evol Intel 14:1691–1705
27. Junior JJAM et al (2020) Feature selection and dimensionality reduction: an extensive comparison in hand gesture classification by sEMG in eight channels armband approach. Biomed Signal Process Control 59:101920
28. Karaboga D, Akay B (2009) A comparative study of artificial bee colony algorithm. Appl Math Comput 214:108–132
29. Cao Y et al (2019) An improved global best guided artificial bee colony algorithm for continuous optimization problems. Clust Comput 22:3011–3019

Distributed Deep Learning for Content-Based Image Retrieval

U. S. N. Raju⑩, Debanjan Pathak⑩, Harika Ala⑩, Netalkar Rohan Kishor, and Hillol Barman

1 Introduction

The term content-based image retrieval suggests the image retrieval procedure is focused on the image's information. As a result, color, shape and texture are chosen as image features. Feature extraction approaches such as color histogram [1], color correlogram [1], color autocorrelogram [2, 3] and inter-channel voting between hue and saturation [4] can be used on an image to obtain color features. ULBP [5], LBP [5], LDP [6], LEP [7], LTrP [8], CS LBP [9] can all be utilized to extract texture features. GLCM is another texture feature descriptor that gives information about the image's pixel pair co-occurrence [10, 11]. Fourier descriptor [12], HOG [13], wavelet Fourier descriptor [13], convex hull [14], angular pattern and binary angular pattern [15] and others are utilized to extract shape information. Various image retrieval algorithms are reviewed and explained in [16–18].

Zheng et al. [19] have given the survey on image retrieval, which mentioned scale invariant feature transform (SIFT) and DCNN as two prime methods for image retrieval problem. One new CBIR model was proposed by Peizhong et al. [20] which combines both high-level and low-level features of an input image. To extract low-level features dot-diffused block truncation coding (DDBTC) is used. CNN is frequently used for extracting high-level features. Among various DCNN (AlexNet, VGG, ResNet,), Ye et al. [21] proposed a new CBIR method that used DCNN feature with weighted distance. The method is divided into two phases. In the 1st phase, known as the offline phase, feature extraction and class leveling of an input image

U. S. N. Raju (✉) · D. Pathak · H. Ala · N. R. Kishor · H. Barman
Department of Computer Science and Engineering, National Institute of Technology Warangal, Warangal, Telangana State 506004, India
e-mail: usnraju@nitw.ac.in

© The Author(s), under exclusive license to Springer Nature Singapore Pte Ltd. 2023   19
R. Doriya et al. (eds.), *Machine Learning, Image Processing, Network Security and Data Sciences*, Lecture Notes in Electrical Engineering 946,
https://doi.org/10.1007/978-981-19-5868-7_2

are done based on fine-tuned DCNN. In the 2nd phase, known as the online phase, the weightage factor of each class is calculated based on the probability of a query image belonging to that particular class. Distance between the retrieved images and the query image is determined based on the calculated weighted factor. Zar Nawab Khan Swati et al. [22] proposed a new CBIR method based on DCNN. VGG16 architecture is used as DCNN. A novel CBIR framework is proposed by Adnan Qayyum et al. [23] which is divided into two stages. First stage is the classification stage, where the training of a DCNN is performed on a medical image dataset based on supervised learning. In the 2nd stage, the last three fully connected layers of trained DCNN are used to extract feature from the input image.

Hadoop Distributed File System. Hadoop is an open-source distributed file system. It is a file system that is commonly utilized in distributed contexts. When a cluster of nodes is built, each node contributes a certain volume of memory to HDFS. HDFS is Hadoop system's pillar, storing data through replication and storing separate different racks data copies for the purpose of fault tolerance. Also, the replication factor could be any number; however, three is the most common. It keeps three Java virtual machine process status tool (jps) files for storage: data node, secondary name node and name node. There will be a single name node and a single secondary name node in the entire cluster, although there can be n data nodes. It has two JPS for processing: resource manager and node manager, with n node managers and one resource manager in the cluster. HDFS is utilized for accumulation of a huge figure of images in this study because it is unfeasible to hold all of them in a solo system. The map-reduce programming model is utilized to decrease the time of processing for the vast numbers of images.

Spark. Spark uses resilient distributed database (RDD) as a general data representation. RDDs are immutable distributed collection of objects. An original RDD cannot be changed, but new RDDs can be created by performing coarse-grain operations, like transformations, on an existing RDD. The features of RDD in Spark are resilience, fault tolerance, distributed, immutability, lazy evaluation, cacheable, in-memory computation and partitioning. RDDs are divided into small chunks called partitions, and when an action is performed, a task is launched per partition. This means that for higher number of partitions, there would be more parallelism. Spark decides on the number of partitions to be created by dividing the RDD, but the number of partitions can also be specified when creating RDD. These partitions are then divided across all the nodes in the cluster. Driver creates an execution graph based on the transformation operations and starts the execution on the execution graph based on the action operation encountered on the RDD. Spark transformation is a function that creates a new RDD from the existing RDD on performing an action. It takes RDD as input and creates one or more RDDs. An action is a process which activates the execution of RDD conversions and yields a value. By using the distributed technologies (Hadoop and Spark), which supports DDL, CBIR is explored and detailed description is given in methodology section. By using these technologies, CBIR is explored and detailed description is given in methodology section.

2 Methodology

In this paper, we have used two different in-house and self-made clusters of computers using Hadoop 3.3.0 and Spark 3.1.1. The two different clusters and the configurations are shown in Tables 1 and 2.

In DDL model for CBIR, initially part of the image dataset is used for distributed learning on cluster of computers. This distributed learning can be done in any of three modes: synchronous, asynchronous and Hogwild. Once it is done, we obtain the trained model. For this trained model, all the images from the image dataset are given and features are extracted and these features are stored as feature vectors of these images. Whenever any image is given as a query, the same trained model is utilized for the purpose of feature extraction and these feature values are compared against features in the 'feature database.' Based on this comparison, we obtain the distance and from this distance, a rank matrix is obtained. By using this rank matrix, different performance measures can be obtained. The complete procedure can be seen in Fig. 1. Three different modes of DDL are explained here.

Synchronous. All the slave nodes return the weight updates at the same time to the master node which calculates the updates and transfers the updates to all the slave nodes at the same time. If any of the nodes are slow, then all the other nodes have to wait for them. This results in the wastage of their computational time.

Asynchronous. When the master node receives an update from a slave node(s), it applies a MUTEX lock on the shared variable to perform operations based on the updates received from the node(s). After the operations are finished, the corresponding updated model is sent to the respective slave node(s). Even though this is better than synchronous, it still has a computational overhead due to MUTEX locks.

Table 1 Configuration of cluster-1 which is made at our NIT Warangal, big image data processing lab

Node type	Ram size (GB)	Processor	CPU cores
Master	16	Intel i7-4770	8
Slave1-Slave4	16	Intel i7-4770	8

NIT Warangal-In-house Cluster: 1 + 4

Table 2 Configuration of cluster-2 which is made at our NIT Warangal, big image data processing lab

Node type	Ram size (GB)	Processor	CPU cores
Master	16	Intel i7-4770	8
Slave1-Slave10	16	Intel i7-4770	8
Slave11-Slave15	8	Intel i7-4770	8

NIT Warangal-In-house Cluster: 1 + 15

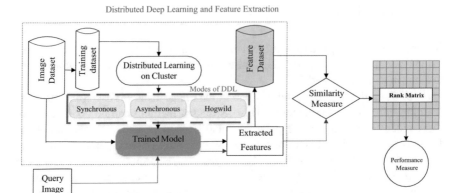

Fig. 1 Block diagram of CBIR using DDL

Hogwild. In Hogwild, all the processors have an equal access to shared memory and hence are able to modify any individual component in the memory at will. At first, it might seem that such a lock-free scheme would fail as the processors could overwrite each other's progress. But when the data access is sparse the individual modifications are only a small part of the decision variables. Due to this, it has been shown that memory overwrites are rare and thereby introducing barely any error into the computation even when they occur [24]. The mechanism of updating the parameters for all these three modes is shown in Fig. 2.

In this paper, the CBIR is implemented in Python with the help of various libraries which supports DDL. One such library used is Elephas [25] which introduces deep learning model into the distributed environment. Elephas brings any deep learning model implemented in Keras to spark. HDFS is used for the purpose of storage. Elephas uses Spark's RDDs and data frames to create a data-parallel algorithms class above Keras. The Keras models are first set on the driver and then divided and distributed to all workers with the parameters of the data and model. The Spark workers deserialize the model that they have been given and train it on the data chunk they have. The workers submit their gradients to the drivers for updating while training the model. With the help of an optimizer, the driver's 'master' model is updated. Gradients are taken concurrently or asynchronously by the optimizer. We have used AlexNet which was available in Keras and given it to Elephas, which has converted into distributed model. As it is not supporting the transfer learning, in this paper, the AlexNet is trained from start with all the three modes to get the trained model for CBIR which we use to extract the features.

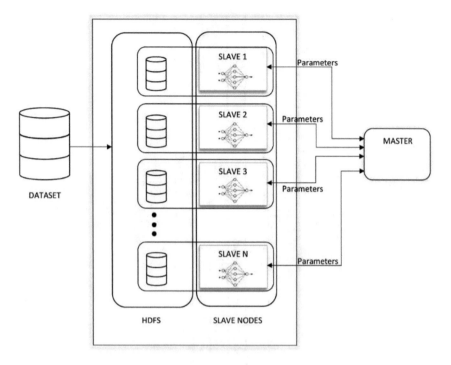

Fig. 2 Mechanism for updating the parameter in DDL

3 Results and Discussion

To test the performance with the three modes in the DDL, we performed some test results on the digit recognition on Modified National Institute of Standards and Technology (MNIST) dataset using the in-house clusters.

MNIST dataset is the handwritten digits image dataset. The dataset consists of 28 × 28 pixels images which are grayscale. There are of single handwritten digits from 0 to 9 and both included. It has a train set comprising 60,000 examples, and a set of test examples of count 10,000. The results for digit recognition using DDL for MNIST dataset are shown in Table 3.

We used the Corel-1000 image dataset to test the proposed model and determine CBIR's performance. This dataset [26] contains 1000 photographs divided into 10 categories, each of which contains 100 photographs. Africans, Beaches and Food are among the several categories. Every image in the Corel dataset is 384256 or 256,384 pixels in size. Figure 3 shows three images from every group, for a total of 30 images in this collection.

Table 4 shown gives the information regarding the time and accuracy of the same model built on different in-house clusters. The time and accuracy for each cluster setup is then compared based on the different modes used to create the model.

Table 3 Accuracy and time comparison on MNIST dataset using DDL with different in-house self-made clusters

MNIST	Accuray				Time			
	Normal	Synchronous	Aynchronous	Hogwild	Normal	Synchronous	Aynchronous	Hogwild
Single	0.96	N/A	N/A	N/A	5.47	N/A	N/A	N/A
1 + 4	N/A	0.87	0.94	0.26	N/A	25.61	21.53	19.75
1 + 15	N/A		0.10	0.10	N/A		40.79	35.58

Fig. 3 Corel-1 K samples (three images per category)

Table 4 Accuracy and time comparison of CBIR on Corel-1000 image dataset using DDL with different in-house self-made clusters

	Time			Accuracy		
Setup	Synchronous	Aynchronous	Hogwild	Synchronous	Aynchronous	Hogwild
1 + 4	303.8	2004.77	2031.85	0.18	0.12	0.18
1 + 15		2011.91	2017.57		0.11	0.19

Tables 5 and 6 give the comparison based on various performance metrics for 1 + 4 cluster and 1 + 15 cluster, respectively. The performance metrics used for comparison are APR, ARR, F-Score, ANMRR and TMRE. The performance metrics in each Tables 5 and 6 are compared to different modes built using the same cluster configuration.

Table 5 Performance metrics comparisons for 1 + 4 node in-house cluster

	APR	ARR	F-Measure	ANMRR	TMRE
Synchronous	42.74	26.82	29.260	0.650	918.16
Asynchronous	40.08	22.4	24.900	0.700	963.71
Hogwild	42.13	28.01	29.920	0.650	828.18

Table 6 Performance metrics comparisons for 1 + 15 node in-house cluster

	APR	ARR	F-Measure	ANMRR	TMRE
Asynchronous	34.16	18.80	20.620	0.740	966.96
Hogwild	42.40	27.26	29.370	0.650	848.81

4 Conclusions and Future Scope

In this work, the DDL with three modes: Synchronous, asynchronous and Hogwild for CBIR is successfully performed. To measure the time advantage, the entire experimentation is done on two self-made in-house 'Hadoop and Spark' clusters: 1 + 4 and 1 + 15 nodes. Since the Corel-1000 dataset used is very small, the accuracies are very low. We are also able to perform the digit recognition on MNIST dataset on distributed environment. The same Hadoop and Spark' clusters are used for four of the image compression techniques: JPEG, LZW, Huffman and CCIT-3 in our laboratories.

Future scope. These accuracies can be increased by increasing the dataset size. We need to go a long way in this; DDL can be explored for other fields such as compression and digital olfaction.

References

1. Singha M, Hemachandran K (2012) Content based image retrieval using color and texture. Signal Image Process 3(1):39
2. Huang J, Kumar SR, Mitra M, Zhu WJ, Zabih R (1997) Image indexing using color correlograms. In: Proceedings of IEEE computer society conference on computer vision and pattern recognition. IEEE, pp 762–768
3. Chun YD, Kim NC, Jang IH (2008) Content-based image retrieval using multiresolution color and texture features. IEEE Trans Multimedia 10(6):1073–1084
4. Bhunia AK, Bhattacharyya A, Banerjee P, Roy PP, Murala S (2018) A novel feature descriptor for image retrieval by combining modified color histogram and diagonally symmet ric co-occurrence texture pattern, arXiv preprint arXiv:1801.00879
5. Ojala T, Pietikainen M, Maenpaa T (2002) Multiresolution gray-scale and rotation invariant texture classification with local binary patterns. IEEE Trans Pattern Anal Mach Intell 24(7):971–987
6. Zhang B, Gao Y, Zhao S, Liu J (2009) Local derivative pattern versus local binary pattern: face recognition with high-order local pattern descriptor. IEEE Trans Image Process 19(2):533–544
7. Verma M, Raman B, Murala S (2015) Local extrema co-occurrence pattern for color and texture image retrieval. Neurocomputing 165:255–269
8. Murala S, Maheshwari RP, Balasubramanian R (2012) Local tetra patterns: a new feature descriptor for content-based image retrieval. IEEE Trans Image Process 21(5):2874–2886
9. Heikkilä M, Pietikäinen M, Schmid C (2006) Description of interest regions with center-symmetric local binary patterns. In: Computer vision, graphics and image processing, Springer, Berlin, pp 58–69
10. Haralick RM, Shanmugam K, Dinstein IH (1973) Textural features for image classification. IEEE Trans Syst Man Cybern 6:610–621

11. Clausi DA (2002) An analysis of co-occurrence texture statistics as a function of grey level quantization. Can J Remote Sens 28(1):45–62

12. Hu RX, Jia W, Ling H, Zhao Y, Gui J (2013) Angular pattern and binary angular pattern for shape retrieval. IEEE Trans Image Process 23(3):1118–1127

13. Hu R, Barnard M, Collomosse J (2010) Gradient field descriptor for sketch based retrieval and localization. In: 2010 IEEE international conference on image processing, pp 1025–1028

14. Mathew SP, Balas VE, Zachariah KP (2015) A content-based image retrieval system based on convex hull geometry. Acta Polytechnica Hungarica 12(1):103–116

15. Osowski S (2002) Fourier and wavelet descriptors for shape recognition using neural networks—a comparative study. Pattern Recogn 35(9):1949–1957

16. Rui Y, Huang TS, Chang SF (1999) Image retrieval: Current techniques, promising directions, and open issues. J Vis Commun Image Represent 10(1):39–62

17. Smeulders AW, Worring M, Santini S, Gupta A, Jain R (2000) Content-based image retrieval at the end of the early years. IEEE Trans Pattern Anal Mach Intell 22(12):1349–1380

18. Kokare M, Chatterji BN, Biswas PK (2002) A survey on current content based image retrieval methods. IETE J Res 48(3–4):261–271

19. Zheng L, Yang Y, Tian QSIFT, CNN SM (2018) A decade survey of instance retrieval. IEEE Trans Pattern Anal Mach Intell 40(5):1224–1244

20. Liu P, Guo JM, Wu CY, Cai D (2017) Fusion of deep learning and compressed domain features for content-based image retrieval. IEEE Trans Image Process 26(12):5706–5717

21. Ye F, Xiao H, Zhao X, Dong M, Luo W, Min W (2018) Remote sensing image retrieval using convolutional neural network features and weighted distance. IEEE Geosci Remote Sens Lett 15(10):1535–1539

22. Swati ZNK, Zhao Q, Kabir M, Ali F, Ali Z, Ahmed S, Lu J (2019) Content-based brain tumor retrieval for MR images using transfer learning. IEEE Access 7:17809–17822

23. Qayyum A, Anwar SM, Awais M, Majid M (2017) Medical image retrieval using deep convolutional neural network. Neurocomputing 266:8–20

24. Noel C, Osindero S, Dogwild! Distributed Hogwild for CPU & GPU

25. Elephas: distributed deep learning with Keras & Spark, https://github.com/max-pumperla/elephas

26. Wang JZ (2020) Modeling objects, concepts, aesthetics and emotionsin big visual data. http://wang.ist.psu.edu/docs/home.shtml. Accessed 19 Nov 2020

Automated Detection of Type 2 Diabetes with Imbalanced and Machine Learning Methods

G. Anirudh and Upasana Talukdar

1 Introduction

Diabetes is one of the most common chronic diseases affecting around 415 million people around the world. Early diagnosis and prediction of diabetes can suppress its effects and can prevent long-term complications. In the past few years, literature reported many works on the prediction of diabetes using machine learning algorithms, tested on PIMA dataset,[1] one of the most widely used diabetes datasets in literature [1–3]. However, such datasets are imbalanced. Class imbalance problem can be defined as having an unequal distribution of the data. Such a problem poses a challenge in detecting and extracting diabetic patterns. Because of the dominance of one class, existing machine learning algorithms may fail to detect diabetic cases accurately. Nnamoko and Korkontzelos [3] proposed a two-step data pre-processing approach on PIMA Dataset, where the first step identified the outliers using the Interquartile Range (IQR) algorithm and the second step employed Synthetic Minority Oversampling Technique (SMOTE).

This paper aims to find the best machine learning model for predicting diabetes with an imbalanced source. In this process, this research work presents rigorous experimentation in three categories: category 1: experiments with classification algorithms, category 2: experiments with ensemble methods, and category 3: experiments with imbalanced data pre-processing (different undersampling, oversampling, and

---

[1]https://www.kaggle.com/uciml/pima-indians-diabetes-database.

G. Anirudh (✉)
Department of Data Science and Analytics, Central University of Rajasthan, Ajmer, Rajasthan, India
e-mail: ganirudhani90@gmail.com

U. Talukdar
Department of Computer Science and Engineering, Indian Institute of Information Technology Guwahati, Guwahati, India

© The Author(s), under exclusive license to Springer Nature Singapore Pte Ltd. 2023
R. Doriya et al. (eds.), *Machine Learning, Image Processing, Network Security and Data Sciences*, Lecture Notes in Electrical Engineering 946,
https://doi.org/10.1007/978-981-19-5868-7_3

combination techniques) and classification algorithms. Undersampling, oversampling, and combination are the techniques to adjust the class distribution of data. Undersampling down-sizes the majority class by removing observations, oversampling over-sizes the minority class by adding observations, while in combination methods, the data is oversampled and then the transformed data is undersampled.

The performance of the solutions has been evaluated using six different metrics: $F1$-score, Precision, Recall, Area Under Receiver Operating Characteristic curve (AUROC), Area Under Precision-Recall curve (AUPR), and Classification Accuracy (Accuracy). Experimental results show that the amalgamation of imbalanced data pre-processing methods improves the performance of traditional machine learning classifiers achieving the best accuracy as 98.49%. The results are compared with the existing methods in the literature. The proposed model yields better performance in terms of accuracy as compared to all other existing methods. Besides, we examined the validity of our proposed model in other domains (not related to healthcare) with the credit card dataset that exhibits high-class imbalance.

2 Related Works

The health sector has been showing impeccable growth in terms of technology, with the use of machine learning and deep learning. Few notable contributions are, detection of lung cancer [4, 5], dermatoscopic melanocytic skin lesion segmentation [6], lung segmentation [7, 8], and diabetes detection [1–3]. One common problem with methodologies for dealing with such data is the class imbalance. Literature reported many ways to tackle the class imbalance problem in various domains. Common approaches for handling class imbalance are undersampling and oversampling techniques or a combination of both.

Undersampling: Different methods under undersampling techniques can be categorized as *a. Methods that select the samples to keep*: Near Miss [9], and Condensed Nearest Neighbor Rule [10], *b. Methods that select the samples to delete*: Tomek Links [11], and Edited Nearest Neighbors [12], *c. Combinations of keep and delete methods*: One-Sided Selection [13], and Neighborhood Cleaning Rule [14].

Oversampling: In the similar way, oversampling methods can be categorized into different methods: a. Synthetic Minority Oversampling Technique [15], b. Borderline-SMOTE [16], c. Borderline-SMOTE SVM [17], d. Adaptive Synthetic Sampling (ADASYN) [18], where (b), (c) and (d) are extensions of (a).

Combination of Undersampling and Oversampling: In the Combination family, we combine oversampling methods and undersampling to make it more effective. A few examples of effective combinations are: (i) SMOTE and Tomek Links [19], and (ii) SMOTE and Edited Nearest Neighbors [20].

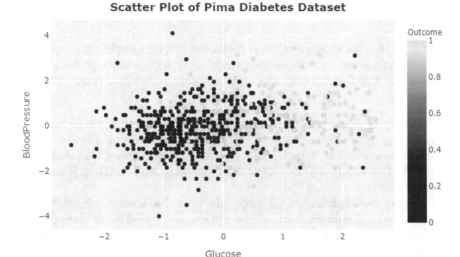

Fig. 1 Scatter plot of PIMA dataset

3   Materials and Methods

3.1   Dataset Description

PIMA dataset[2] is used in this paper for analysis. It has a total of 768 samples with 9 features. The class ratio of diabetic to non-diabetic is 0.34:0.66 (see Fig. 1). The yellow dots and the blue dots in the scatter plot represent the diabetic cases and non-diabetic cases.

3.2   Feature Engineering

The data contains 0 as a measurement for certain features. The pregnancy column in the dataset containing 0 indicates that the woman is 0 times pregnant. Age and Diabetes Pedigree Function are continuous attributes. Apart from Outcome, Age, Diabetes Pedigree Function, and Pregnancies, the rest of the features containing 0 are assumed to be missing observation. The assumed missing values are replaced with the median since the median is not affected by extreme values.

---

[2] https://www.kaggle.com/uciml/pima-indians-diabetes-database.

3.3   Experimental Setup

This paper reported rigorous experimentation to tackle the class imbalance problem and adopted various state-of-the-art methodologies to attain better performance in the prediction of diabetic cases. The experiments were conducted in three different categories.

- **Category 1—Experiments with traditional machine learning algorithms**: In this category, five different supervised classification algorithms are employed on our dataset, which includes Logistic Regression (LR), Support Vector Machine (SVM), Decision Tree (DT), K-Nearest Neighbour (KNN), and Deep Neural Network (DNN).
- **Category 2—Experiments with ensemble machine learning algorithms**: In this category, five different ensemble algorithms are applied to our dataset, which includes Bagging, Random Forest, AdaBoost, Gradient Boosting, and XGBoost.
- **Category 3—Experiments with imbalanced data pre-processing and traditional machine learning methods**: Here, to tackle the class imbalance problem different undersampling techniques, oversampling techniques, and a combination of both have been employed before feeding it to the machine learning algorithms. The undersampling techniques like Random Undersampling (RU), Near miss-1 [9], Near miss-2 [9], Tomek Links [11], Edited Nearest Neighbors (ENN) [12], and One-Sided Selection [13] are employed. On the other hand, oversampling techniques like Random Oversampling (RO), Synthetic Minority Oversampling Technique (SMOTE) [15], Borderline SMOTE-1 [16], Borderline SMOTE-2 [16], SVM-SMOTE [17], and Adaptive Synthetic Sampling (ADASYN) [18] are employed in this study. From the experiments with undersampling and oversampling methodologies, the two best oversampling and undersampling methods are picked up. The combination of the two methods is then investigated.

4   Experimental Results and Discussions

4.1   Category 1: Experiments with Traditional Machine Learning Methods

Five supervised classification algorithms were applied that include Logistic Regression (LR), Support Vector Machine (SVM), Decision Tree (DT), K-Nearest Neighbour (KNN), and Deep Neural Network (DNN), with class weights as 0.34 and 0.66 for class 0 and class 1, respectively.

In the KNN, $k = 7$ is taken as with $k = 7$ kNN performed best. For DNN, the architecture is built with 3 layers with 5, 8, and 1 unit of nodes, and Rectified Linear Unit (ReLU) is used as activation function We have used Adam optimizer, with batch size 32, and the number of epochs 20.

Table 1 Performance of traditional machine learning algorithms

Algorithm	AUROC	AUPR	F1-score	Precision	Recall	Accuracy
Logistic Regression (LR)	0.85	0.73	0.72	0.8	0.80	0.79
K-Nearest Neighbour (KNN) (7)	0.75	0.64	0.58	0.70	0.71	0.70
Support Vector Machine (SVM)	0.85	0.72	0.72	0.79	0.79	0.79
Decision Tree (DT)	0.65	0.65	0.57	0.58	0.56	0.68
Deep Neural Networks (DNN)	0.77	0.46	0.46	0.74	0.72	0.71

Table 2 Performance of ensemble methods

Algorithm	AUROC	AUPR	F1-score	Precision	Recall	Accuracy
Bagging	0.78	0.67	0.51	0.72	0.72	0.72
Random Forest	0.82	0.72	0.64	0.75	0.76	0.75
AdaBoost	0.77	0.64	0.60	0.73	0.74	0.74
Gradient Boosting	0.80	0.68	0.64	0.75	0.76	0.75
XGBoost	0.82	0.71	0.65	0.76	0.77	0.76

The performance of different classification algorithms has been illustrated in Table 1. It is seen that, in terms of all the six evaluation metrics, LR performed best while SVM performed second best. DNN also gave a comparable performance in terms of AUROC, Precision, Recall, and Accuracy. However, in terms of AUPR and F1-score, DNN performed worst. Besides that, DNN requires further fine-tuning of hyper-parameters and implementing it after an appropriate pre-processing technique is computationally expensive, requires a large amount of memory, and computational source than LR, KNN, SVM, and DT. Hence, we eliminated DNN from the list of classification algorithms for further analysis.

4.2 Category 2: Experiments with Ensemble Machine Learning Methods

To evaluate the performance of ensemble methods on imbalanced data, this study includes experiments with five different ensemble algorithms: Bagging, Random Forest, AdaBoost, Gradient Boosting, and XGBoost. The results are given in Table 2 in terms of all the six evaluation metrics. It is seen from the results that XGBoost performed best in terms of all the evaluation metrics except AUPR, while Random Forest performs best in terms of AUPR and second best in terms of remaining metrics.

4.3 Category 3: Experiments with Imbalanced Data Pre-processing and Traditional Machine Learning Methods

This category of experimentation includes the amalgamation of imbalanced data pre-processing and machine learning methods. A variety of undersampling and oversampling techniques were examined to process the data. The undersampling techniques like RU, Near miss-1, Near miss-2, Tomek Links, ENN, and OSS are employed. On the other hand, oversampling techniques like RO, SMOTE, Borderline SMOTE-1, Borderline SMOTE-2, SVM-SMOTE, and ADASYN are applied in the study. The two best oversampling and undersampling methods are picked up, and their combination is investigated.

The pre-processed data is then classified using traditional machine learning algorithms that include LR, KNN, SVM, and DT.

Undersampling Techniques The sampling strategy, one of the parameters in undersampling techniques, is defined as the ratio of the total number of samples in the minority class to the total number of samples in the majority class after re-sampling. However, for the present dataset, the minority class contains 268 instances, and the majority class contains 500 instances. Ideally, the denominator can take any value in the range of [268, 500]. The sampling strategy cannot be below 0.53 (268/500) for the current dataset. It can take any value in the range of [0.53, 1]. When the value is 1, the class ratio will be balanced to 0.5:0.5. However, doing so will reduce the number of samples from 768 to 536. But we aimed to remove only those samples which were affecting the models initially. Keeping these constraints in mind and the size of the data, we tuned this parameter to 0.625. The number of samples after down-sampling is 694, with the class ratio of diabetic to non-diabetic being 0.39:0.61. Table 3 presents the results when the data was pre-processed with under-sampling methods. It was seen from the table that ENN performed best in terms of all evaluation metrics with all the machine learning algorithms, whereas Near miss-1 performed second best in terms of AUPR.

Oversampling Techniques In oversampling, a sampling strategy is defined as the ratio of the total number of samples in the minority class after re-sampling to the total number of samples in the majority class. The numerator can take any value in the range of [268, 500]. Therefore in our dataset, the parameter can take any value in the range of [0.53, 1]. Since the data is small, we compromised ourselves for maximum redundancy. This redundancy of information from the minority group will balance the instances of two classes in the dataset and thereby gives better results. We tuned the parameter to 1. All the minority instances will now be upsampled to the proportion of the majority class. The total number of samples after upsampling is 1000, with the class ratio of diabetic to non-diabetic being 0.5:0.5. Table 4 presents the results when the data is pre-processed with oversampling methods. It is seen from the table that RO gives the best performance in terms of all the evaluation metrics except Recall with all the machine learning algorithms, whereas SMOTE performed best in terms of Recall.

Table 3 Performance of different machine learning methods with undersampling techniques

Undersampling methods	ML algorithm	AUROC	AUPR	F1-score	Precision	Recall	Accuracy
RU	LR	0.86	0.80	0.66	0.76	0.76	0.76
	KNN (7)	0.82	0.72	0.59	0.70	0.70	0.70
	SVM	0.85	0.79	0.66	0.77	0.76	0.76
	DT	0.70	0.72	0.62	0.73	0.73	0.73
Near miss-1 (Neighbour = 3)	LR	0.81	0.85	0.75	0.73	0.73	0.74
	KNN (7)	0.75	0.81	0.69	0.70	0.69	0.69
	SVM	0.80	0.85	0.75	0.73	0.73	0.73
	DT	0.60	0.72	0.62	0.60	0.60	0.60
Near miss-2 (Neighbour = 3)	LR	0.82	0.79	0.70	0.69	0.69	0.69
	KNN (7)	0.79	0.83	0.74	0.73	0.73	0.73
	SVM	0.79	0.82	0.69	0.69	0.69	0.69
	DT	0.69	0.79	0.73	0.70	0.70	0.70
Tomek Links	LR	0.84	0.73	0.65	0.76	0.77	0.77
	KNN (7)	0.84	0.70	0.67	0.77	0.77	0.77
	SVM	0.85	0.74	0.63	0.75	0.75	0.75
	DT	0.72	0.71	0.65	0.74	0.73	0.73
ENN (Neighbours = 3)	LR	0.92	0.93	0.82	0.82	0.82	0.82
	KNN (7)	0.93	0.93	0.87	0.87	0.87	0.87
	SVM	0.92	0.93	0.83	0.83	0.83	0.83
	DT	0.82	0.87	0.84	0.82	0.82	0.82
OSS	LR	0.80	0.84	0.71	0.75	0.72	0.72
	KNN (7)	0.73	0.76	0.72	0.71	0.71	0.70
	SVM	0.73	0.78	0.72	0.7	0.7	0.69
	DT	0.72	0.78	0.72	0.72	0.72	0.72

Combination Methods After experimenting with different oversampling and undersampling techniques, we picked up the two best undersampling and oversampling methods in terms of AUPR and combined them. AUPR is not affected in the case of moderate to a high-class imbalance of the data and can also provide accurate predictions [21]. With undersampling, we observed that ENN (KNN and DT) surpassed all the remaining methods in terms of all the evaluation metrics. Apart from ENN, Near miss-1 (LR) performs second best and achieved greater than 80% with three classifiers in terms of AUPR. With oversampling, Random oversampling (KNN and DT) performs best in terms of AUROC, AUPR, F1-score, Precision, Accuracy, and better in terms of Recall. SMOTE (KNN) performs best in terms of Recall and second best in terms of AUPR. Hence, we made 4 combinations: RO + ENN, RO + Near miss-1, SMOTE + Near miss-1, and SMOTE + ENN. Figures 2 and 3 show the scatter plot after employing the aforesaid four combinations using the first two features. The yellow dots and the blue dots in the scatter plot represent the diabetic

Table 4 Performance of different machine learning methods with oversampling techniques

Oversampling methods	ML algorithm	AUROC	AUPR	F1-score	Precision	Recall	Accuracy
RO	LR	0.81	0.76	0.73	0.74	0.74	0.74
	KNN (7)	0.91	0.91	0.8	0.81	0.79	0.78
	SVM	0.82	0.78	0.73	0.74	0.74	0.73
	DT	0.79	0.84	0.80	0.80	0.79	0.79
SMOTE	LR	0.82	0.77	0.73	0.75	0.74	0.73
	KNN (7)	0.86	0.82	0.77	0.69	0.88	0.75
	SVM	0.82	0.76	0.74	0.75	0.75	0.74
	DT	0.75	0.79	0.74	0.76	0.75	0.74
Borderline SMOTE-1	LR	0.76	0.69	0.65	0.67	0.67	0.66
	KNN (7)	0.84	0.78	0.78	0.80	0.76	0.76
	SVM	0.78	0.70	0.70	0.71	0.70	0.69
	DT	0.73	0.78	0.72	0.74	0.74	0.73
Borderline SMOTE-2	LR	0.78	0.70	0.68	0.65	0.71	0.69
	KNN (7)	0.81	0.74	0.75	0.76	0.73	0.73
	SVM	0.78	0.70	0.67	0.68	0.67	0.66
	DT	0.70	0.76	0.70	0.71	0.7	0.70
SVM-SMOTE	LR	0.80	0.74	0.71	0.73	0.73	0.73
	KNN (7)	0.85	0.82	0.77	0.78	0.76	0.76
	SVM	0.82	0.75	0.73	0.75	0.74	0.73
	DT	0.77	0.81	0.77	0.78	0.77	0.77
ADASYN	LR	0.81	0.75	0.71	0.71	0.71	0.70
	KNN (7)	0.79	0.74	0.74	0.74	0.72	0.71
	SVM	0.81	0.75	0.73	0.73	0.72	0.71
	DT	0.75	0.80	0.74	0.75	0.75	0.75

cases and non-diabetic cases, respectively. It is seen that the ratio of diabetic and non-diabetic cases improves as compared to Fig. 1.

Table 5 presents the results of traditional machine learning algorithms pre-processed by the aforesaid combined methods. KNN with $k = 3$ is used, as with $k = 3$, the model achieves the highest performance.

It is seen from Table 5 that SMOTE + ENN gives the best performance in terms of all evaluation metrics with all the classifiers, while SMOTE + ENN + KNN gives the highest performance. The combination (SMOTE + ENN) is further investigated with different ensemble machine learning methods (see Table 6). It is seen that the performance of the ensemble methods improves with the combination of these two imbalanced pre-processing techniques achieving the highest Accuracy of 96% with Random Forest.

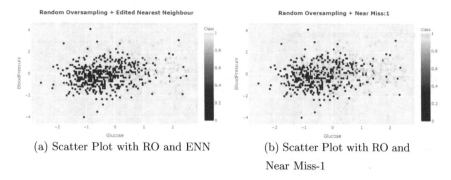

(a) Scatter Plot with RO and ENN

(b) Scatter Plot with RO and Near Miss-1

Fig. 2 Scatter plot of Pima Indian dataset with RO and two best undersampling methods

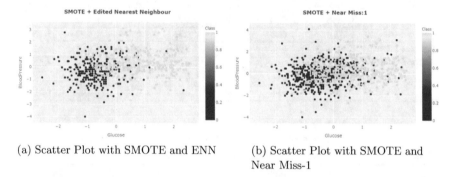

(a) Scatter Plot with SMOTE and ENN

(b) Scatter Plot with SMOTE and Near Miss-1

Fig. 3 Scatter plot of Pima Indian dataset with SMOTE and two best undersampling methods

4.4 Comparison with Previous Studies

The comparison is also carried out with the state-of-the-art methods (see Table 7). The results present that our approach produced better accuracy as compared to past studies. Naz and Ahuja [2] obtained comparable accuracy with Deep Learning (98.07%) as compared to our work. However, Deep Learning is computationally extensive to train. Some of the studies listed in Table 7 have evaluated their performance in terms of other metrics. In particular, Nanni et al. [22] evaluated their performance in terms of $F1$-score, G-mean, and AUROC while Raghuwanshi and Shukla [23] presented in terms of G-mean and AUROC. In terms of $F1$-score and AUROC, our model performs best as compared to both studies. Zahirnia et al. [24] presented in terms of feature cost and misclassification cost and Wei et al. [25] evaluated with sensitivity, $F3$ and G-mean diabetes dataset.

Table 5 Performance of different machine learning methods with the combination of undersampling and oversampling techniques

Methods	ML algorithm	AUROC	AUPR	F1-score	Precision	Recall	Accuracy
RO + ENN (Sample size: 757)	LR	0.94	0.88	0.81	0.88	0.87	0.87
	KNN (8)	0.99	0.99	0.94	0.96	0.96	0.96
	SVM	0.93	0.88	0.80	0.87	0.87	0.87
	DT	0.93	0.91	0.90	0.93	0.92	0.92
RO + Near miss-1 (Sample size: 1000)	LR	0.84	0.83	0.75	0.76	0.76	0.75
	KNN (3)	0.88	0.89	0.82	0.84	0.81	0.80
	SVM	0.84	0.83	0.74	0.75	0.75	0.75
	DT	0.79	0.83	0.80	0.80	0.79	0.79
SMOTE + Near miss-1 (Sample size: 1000)	LR	0.81	0.80	0.69	0.70	0.70	0.70
	KNN (3)	0.85	0.84	0.78	0.78	0.75	0.75
	SVM	0.80	0.79	0.71	0.72	0.72	0.71
	DT	0.72	0.78	0.72	0.72	0.72	0.72
SMOTE + ENN (Sample size: 602)	LR	0.96	0.97	0.88	0.88	0.87	0.86
	KNN (3)	0.99	1	0.98	0.99	0.98	0.98
	SVM	0.96	0.97	0.90	0.89	0.88	0.88
	DT	0.95	0.95	0.93	0.92	0.92	0.91

Table 6 Performance of ensemble methods with SMOTE + ENN

Algorithm	AUROC	AUPR	F1-score	Precision	Recall	Accuracy
Bagging	0.98	0.99	0.95	0.94	0.94	0.94
Random Forest	0.98	0.99	0.97	0.96	0.96	0.96
AdaBoost	0.98	0.99	0.95	0.93	0.93	0.93
Gradient Boosting classifier	0.98	0.99	0.95	0.94	0.94	0.94
XGBoost	0.98	0.98	0.94	0.93	0.93	0.93

5 Conclusion and Future Directions

The experiments portrayed in the paper proved that the imbalanced data processing methods lead to greater performance. To attain this, we investigated the effects of different imbalanced data processing methods and machine learning algorithms based on classification performance metrics. Results present that SMOTE + ENN gave the best performance on the PIMA Indian dataset. These results are also better as compared to the previous studies carried out on the Pima Indian dataset. However, not all the studies on diabetes prediction available in the literature are based on the same dataset, so we identified those with the same dataset and compared results. Future work would include investigation with different unsupervised methods and semi-supervised methods.

Table 7 Comparison with previous studies in terms of accuracy

Author/article	Year	Method	Best accuracy (%)
Kumari and Chitra [26]	2013	SVM	0.78
Iyer et al. [27]	2015	NB	0.79
Chen et al. [28]	2017	K-means and DT	0.90
Ramezani et al. [29]	2018	Logistic adaptive network-based fuzzy inference system	0.88
Haritha et al. [30]	2018	Firefly and cuckoo search algorithms	0.81
Zhang et al. [31]	2018	Feedforward NN	0.82
Nnamoko and Korkontzelos [3]	2020	C4.5 (IQRd + SMOTEd)	0.89
Naz and Ahuja [2]	2020	DL, ANN, SVM, and DT	0.98 (DL)
Maulidina et al. [32]	2021	Backward elimination and SVM	0.85
Our work		SMOTE + ENN + KNN	0.98

References

1. Benbelkacem S, Atmani B (2019) Random forests for diabetes diagnosis. In: 2019 international conference on computer and information sciences (ICCIS). IEEE, pp 1–4
2. Naz H, Ahuja S (2020) Deep learning approach for diabetes prediction using pima Indian dataset. J Diab Metab Disord 19(1):391–403
3. Nnamoko N, Korkontzelos I (2020) Efficient treatment of outliers and class imbalance for diabetes prediction. Artif Intell Med 104:101815
4. Sahu SP, Londhe ND, Verma S (2019) Pulmonary nodule detection in CT images using optimal multilevel thresholds and rule-based filtering. IETE J Res 1–18
5. Sahu SP, Londhe ND, Verma S, Singh BK, Banchhor SK (2021) Improved pulmonary lung nodules risk stratification in computed tomography images by fusing shape and texture features in a machine-learning paradigm. Int J Imaging Syst Technol 31(3):1503–1518
6. Singh L, Janghel RR, Sahu SP (2021) Slicaco: an automated novel hybrid approach for dermatoscopic melanocytic skin lesion segmentation. Int J Imaging Syst Technol
7. Sahu SP, Kumar R, Londhe ND, Verma S (2021) Segmentation of lungs in thoracic CTs using K-means clustering and morphological operations. In: Advances in biomedical engineering and technology. Springer, pp 331–343
8. Sahu SP, Agrawal P, Londhe ND et al (2017) A new hybrid approach using fuzzy clustering and morphological operations for lung segmentation in thoracic CT images. Biomed Pharmacol J 10(4):1949–1961
9. Mani I, Zhang I (2003) KNN approach to unbalanced data distributions: a case study involving information extraction. In: Proceedings of workshop on learning from imbalanced datasets, vol 126
10. Hart P (1968) The condensed nearest neighbor rule (corresp.). IEEE Trans Inf Theory 14(3):515–516
11. Tomek I et al (1976) Two modifications of CNN
12. Laurikkala J (2001) Improving identification of difficult small classes by balancing class distribution. In: Conference on artificial intelligence in medicine in Europe. Springer, pp 63–66
13. Kubat M, Matwin S et al (1997) Addressing the curse of imbalanced training sets: one-sided selection. In: ICML, vol 97. Citeseer, pp 179–186

14. Laurikkala J (2001) Improving identification of difficult small classes by balancing class distribution. In: Conference on artificial intelligence in medicine in Europe. Springer, pp 63–66

15. Chawla NV, Bowyer KW, Hall LO, Kegelmeyer WP (2002) SMOTE: synthetic minority oversampling technique. J Artif Intell Res 16:321–357

16. Han H, Wang WY, Mao BH (2005) Borderline-SMOTE: a new over-sampling method in imbalanced data sets learning. In: International conference on intelligent computing. Springer, pp 878–887

17. Tang Y, Zhang YQ, Chawla NV, Krasser S (2008) SVMs modeling for highly imbalanced classification. IEEE Trans Syst Man Cybern Part B (Cybern) 39(1):281–288

18. He H, Bai Y, Garcia EA, Li S (2008) ADASYN: adaptive synthetic sampling approach for imbalanced learning. In: 2008 IEEE international joint conference on neural networks (IEEE world congress on computational intelligence). IEEE, pp 1322–1328

19. Batista GE, Bazzan AL, Monard MC et al (2003) Balancing training data for automated annotation of keywords: a case study. In: WOB, pp 10–18

20. Batista GE, Prati RC, Monard MC (2004) A study of the behavior of several methods for balancing machine learning training data. ACM SIGKDD Explor Newsl 6(1):20–29

21. Saito T, Rehmsmeier M (2015) The precision-recall plot is more informative than the ROC plot when evaluating binary classifiers on imbalanced datasets. PLoS ONE 10(3):e0118432

22. Nanni L, Fantozzi C, Lazzarini N (2015) Coupling different methods for overcoming the class imbalance problem. Neurocomputing 158:48–61

23. Raghuwanshi BS, Shukla S (2019) Class imbalance learning using underbagging based kernelized extreme learning machine. Neurocomputing 329:172–187

24. Zahirnia K, Teimouri M, Rahmani R, Salaq A (2015) Diagnosis of type 2 diabetes using cost-sensitive learning. In: 2015 5th international conference on computer and knowledge engineering (ICCKE). IEEE, pp 158–163

25. Wei X, Jiang F, Wei F, Zhang J, Liao W, Cheng S (2017) An ensemble model for diabetes diagnosis in large-scale and imbalanced dataset. In: Proceedings of the computing frontiers conference, pp 71–78

26. Kumari VA, Chitra R (2013) Classification of diabetes disease using support vector machine. Int J Eng Res Appl 3(2):1797–1801

27. Iyer A, Jeyalatha S, Sumbaly R (2015) Diagnosis of diabetes using classification mining techniques. arXiv preprint arXiv:1502.03774

28. Chen W, Chen S, Zhang H, Wu T (2017) A hybrid prediction model for type 2 diabetes using k-means and decision tree. In: 2017 8th IEEE international conference on software engineering and service science (ICSESS). IEEE, pp 386–390

29. Ramezani R, Maadi M, Khatami SM (2018) A novel hybrid intelligent system with missing value imputation for diabetes diagnosis. Alex Eng J 57(3):1883–1891

30. Haritha R, Babu DS, Sammulal P (2018) A hybrid approach for prediction of type-1 and type-2 diabetes using firefly and cuckoo search algorithms. Int J Appl Eng Res 13(2):896–907

31. Zhang Y, Lin Z, Kang Y, Ning R, Meng Y (2018) A feed-forward neural network model for the accurate prediction of diabetes mellitus. Int J Sci Technol Res 7(8):151–155

32. Maulidina F, Rustam Z, Hartini S, Wibowo V, Wirasati I, Sadewo W (2021) Feature optimization using backward elimination and support vector machines (SVM) algorithm for diabetes classification. J Phys Conf Ser 1821:012006

Deep Transfer Learning and Intelligent Item Packing in Retail Management

Mohammad Alodat

1 Introduction

Traditional vending system is known as time-consuming system as it relays on barcode mark by scanning to facilitate management of products every item on retail market [1]. Barcode marks are used in automatic identification of commodities. So it is suitable for the prepacked products, but not suitable for plant products packing service that uses weight. Traditional packaged vending system is product packaging service without technological interference inside retail market. Product packaging service, which is adding a barcode to plant products that do not contain a barcode after weighing while the shopper is waiting [1, 2]. This paper was created to help shorten the waiting period of customers while dealing with sold products of fruits and vegetables. The stages of the packing service start in succession with take weight, product recognition, calculation of costs, labeling with barcodes and ends with the packaging service. Retailers face more consumption of material resources and manpower with current traditional packing vending system, because product management depends on a number of points: (a) classification by descriptive categories that depend on complex shapes and varying colors. (b) Intuitively is based on guesswork and opinion based on experience. (c) Human memory preservation to sort and extract the barcode for each item. Managing the product in this way leads to increase in the complexity of tasks result in prone to narrow margins of errors and data deletion that cause an increase in cost and wasting time to retailer. Consumers face obstacles with current traditional packing vending system, such as (1) there is no confidence in the correctness of the provider estimate of the cost of the product. (2) Customers have increasing pressures on their available time. Product packaging service classification and sorted manually based on human processing is a challenge since it is visually similar. There

M. Alodat (✉)
Sur University College, Sur 440 411, Sultanate of Oman
e-mail: Dr.maalodat@suc.edu.om

© The Author(s), under exclusive license to Springer Nature Singapore Pte Ltd. 2023   41
R. Doriya et al. (eds.), *Machine Learning, Image Processing, Network Security and Data Sciences*, Lecture Notes in Electrical Engineering 946,
https://doi.org/10.1007/978-981-19-5868-7_4

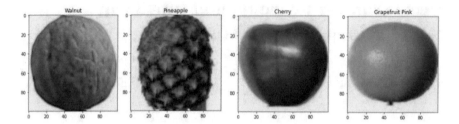

Fig. 1 Selection of visualization items products

are two categories of human visual classification, namely (a) descriptive categories use human eye to identify plant items products, as shown in Fig. 1. They are either a category similar such as berries raspberries and blueberries or a category of the same type has external features, multidimensional and constantly changing such as ellipsoid, heart and oval. (b) Categories intuitively described after ignore effects of size [3].

2 Methodology

This paper used Python libraries in Jupyter Notebook since they are simple to use. The dataset used in this research was collected from a variety of sources; we combined public datasets with our own dataset, as follows: (1) In Sultanate of Oman, a set of 463 photographs was collected from three retail stores during a time period from 26th of June to 26th of September 2021. (2) An open-source dataset called Fruits-360 from Kaggle and GitHub that is available online. It contains 81 item and 41322 images that can be found by following the references links [4–6]. (3) Six volunteers were randomly chosen from retail market, to distinguish between what was bought which is eighteen items before packing service. Cross-validation is a technique for splitting a dataset into a training dataset and a validation dataset in order to acquire a better understanding. We used a dataset that was retrieved from training and validation to validate the model's performance. The entire dataset which is 81 products was distributed in 17 layers as follows: training 41785/validation 13877/test 2500 images. Some examples of products 492/156/55 images of cherry, 492/164/9 images for lemon, 738/246/166 images for tomato. Many studies have been carried out to demonstrate the effectiveness of the proposed CNN model in detecting items in real time. In terms of training time and accuracy in ILSRVC 2012, multiple comparisons with many state-of-the-art models reveal that the examined MobileNetV2 performs well. The following was the work flow: (1) the step of feature extraction, which is divided into two parts, (a) to avoid destroying any information during training, all layers were frozen in the model. (b) New trainable layers should be added. (2) Unfreezing is used to perform fine-tuning on the entire model. (3) Throughout both stages, (a) use the new model to run our dataset. (b) Resized the photographs to fit a neural network and used data augmentation to standardize them [7].

3 Architecture CNN

CNN includes parameters in this study to improve recognition accuracy. Body or feature transforms, as well as head or classifier, are internal layers. The body is divided into the following sections: By applying 32 filters to the convolution layer, a feature map (activation map) is created (feature map), and its size is 3×3. The pooling layer is followed by the production bottleneck layer, which is 8×8 in size. The flatten layer now forms the first layer of complete connection (ANN), which includes 4096 neurons, and the head stage begins. The learning rate of the gradient descent optimizer was set to 0.001. Softmax classifier and 81 neurons make up the final layer of the entire connection (ANN). In this Fig. 2, each box represents a layer in our design and the operation it performs.

4 Recognition

In this paper, the employment of computer vision technologies in the process of product identification and classification instead of traditional packaged vending systems, referred to as intelligent items packing service system, is referred to as recognition on plant items products before packaging service. This system combines convolutional neural network, deep learning and web application with a single camera and introducing touch screen technologies [8, 9]. This system provides support to all stakeholders in order to facilitate the management of the retail market and improve the shopping experience of consumers, (a) retailer assistance in transforming the shopping experience to improve customer service and make it more pleasurable than other retailers. (b) Consumers who are integrated with this system benefit from it because it allows them to make purchases without feeling pressured time. In this study, a shopper's (customer's) opinion of a retail market and its retailers (providers) when using an intelligent goods packing service system is referred to as a shopping experience. It creates augmented reality that allows retailers (providers) and customers (shoppers) to form smart partnerships that seek mutual satisfaction [10, 11]. The smart partnership's contributions are as follows: (a) The smart partnership influences intent decisions to re-shop or return to the retail market. (b) A smart partnership improves efficiency, which leads to an increase in sales, resulting in profits in the retail market. (c) Competitiveness is achieved through smart partnerships because of increased service quality. (d) Smart partnership is the strong motive to adopt technical infrastructure improvements. (e) To achieve the maximum shopping productivity, smart partnerships provide understanding of consumer trends, wants and behaviors, as well as gaining their loyalty and satisfaction. In this study,

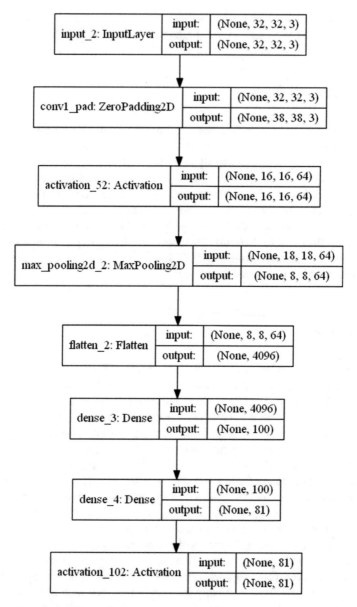

Fig. 2 MobileNetV2 architecture pre-trained models

shopping productivity is defined as the ability to save time/effort, make informed purchases, save money and enjoy shopping [1, 11]. The intelligent goods packaging service system's mechanism will take the place of the current traditional packaged vending system, which will deal with products and give barcode during weight. The following are the steps of the intelligent recognition on plant items products packing service, in order of, first take the item's weight product. Second, real-time identification of the item on the pan using convolutional neural networks and deep learning techniques. Third, after detecting the product, the system displays information and recommendations regarding the items on a touch screen for the provider. Fourth, the provider must confirm the information without relying on memory. Fifth, after receiving confirmation, the system calculates expenses, prints a label with the relevant barcode and completes the packing service. The purpose of this research is to improve plant item product classification in traditional packaged vending systems during take weight by incorporating artificial intelligence and machine learning techniques, such as: 1. Plant item products are difficult to detect and comprehend, which leads to inaccurate categorization for the following reasons: such as citrus, which comprises oranges and grapefruits, has similar categories, making it difficult to distinguish them within groupings. (b) A diverse and ever-changing category of the same plant species. Improving the CNN architecture to tackle the challenges of identifying and recognizing plant products and convolutional neural network training [12].

5 Transfer Learning

Some researchers have utilized transfer learning to take features learnt on one problem and apply them to a different problem, such as the team ImageNet, whose goal is to obtain image archives. Their models were made open source to test for picture categorization as part of the ImageNet large-scale visual recognition challenge (ILSVRC). Since 2010, the ImageNet team has held an annual reciprocal competition between them, where research teams evaluate their computer vision algorithms for various image identification tasks [13, 14]. We constructed a convolutional neural networks (CNN) model that analyzes images in order to facilitate detection and recognition of items products using transfer learning from a pre-trained network [15, 16]. Drawbacks of CNN are that it needs more time to train and more parameters to reach better recognition accuracy, which makes it more complicated. CNN has the following internal layers: (1) The convolution layer produces a feature map (activation map) by executing the 32 filters (feature map), which is 3×3 in size. (2) Pooling layer leads to the production of pooled feature map by executing maxpooling, its size is 2×2, which is called bottleneck layer. (3) Flatten layer leads to the production of first layer of full connection (ANN). CNN each layer contains multi-stage operation, as follows: (a) activation function rectifier (ReLU) to allow only the positive values and make all negative values to be zero. (b) Filter (feature detector): is filters or weights, and this weight values have a spatial relationship. (c) Training is the process of iteratively optimizing the weights and biases to improve the learning rate. Learning rate mean amount of jumps equals 0.001; this technique is called the gradient descent optimizer. (d) In this research, the last layer of full connection (ANN) has Softmax classifier and one neuron, where the input neuron count is 81 [17]. The CNN training network requires large datasets, and even if the data is obtained, training network takes a long time. To overcome the limitations of the CNN model, we reuse learnt feature maps (weights trained) and apply it to image of items products of packing service, which is called deep transfer learning (DTL). DTL stands for pre-trained Keras applications of CNN canned architectures with weights, often known as off-the-shelf. DTL speeds up training by avoiding retraining the network from scratch, improving feature extraction precision and dealing with tiny datasets [18]. We employed feature extraction, the Keras library and TensorFlow 2.0 with tf.keras in this article, as well as pre-trained networks such as Xception, ResNet50, ResNet, InceptionV3 and MobileNetV2 models [19–21]. CNN training requires a large quantity of annotated data to classify an image of a product, and the quality of the annotation is typically critical. We would develop deep transfer learning using five pre-trained CNN networks in the following steps: The first step (a) input size (width = 75x height = 75x channels = 3) was used. (b) Using ImageNet-trained pre-loaded weights (by setting weights= "imagenet"). (c) Pre-load one of the five pre-trained networks (by setting include top = False) that does not include the classification layers at the top. The second step: Freezing is the freezing of the bottleneck layer and feature extractions which is the last layer before the convolutional flattening process. Freeze and retrain the classifier to improve the performance of CNN by setting model.trainable = False. Once freezing the feature extractor, backpropagation only affects the classifier parameters. The third step fine-tuning phase is an alternative to immediately training a network, in which the network is initialized with a pre-trained classification network and subsequently trained for a new task. It involves unfreezing the model by adding layers during training and using the updated weights in the top layers (by setting model.trainable = True) [22].

6   Result and Discussion

6.1   Performance Evaluation

The MobileNetV2 CNN model is compared to ResNet50, ResNet50V2, Xception and VGG19, which are state-of-the-art deep learning models. As demonstrated in Table 1, after fine-tuning, our model in MobileNetV2 and Xception models achieves 100 % accuracy on the training and validation sets [23]. On the training set, the ResNet50V2 model achieves 100 percent accuracy, but only 0.961 on the validation set. In MobileNetV2, ResNet50V2 and Xception, the model roughly obtains 98, 96 and 61 percent accuracy on the validation set in the freezing stage. After the finetuning stage, the Xception model was essentially identical to MobileNetV2, but it was eliminated since the validation loss was substantially higher than the test loss (5.170 %), indicating the presence of some overfitting.

To test the performance, objective metrics were used like precision, recall, accuracy and F1-score. The accuracy of the VGG19 model has the worst performance, with precision = 0.054 correct predictions, as shown in Table 2. The MobileNetV2 and ResNet50V2 models have the best accuracy, with precision of 1.00 and 0.970,

Table 1 Accurate performance of deep learning transfer

Performance			Fine-tuning			Freezing	
		Train	Validation	Test	Train	Validation	Test
ResNet50	Accuracy	0.612	0.603	0.544	0.611	0.652	0.565
	Loss	5.958	6.093	7.073	5.968	5.343	6.790
ResNet50V2	Accuracy	1.000	0.961	0.743	0.988	0.968	0.713
	Loss	0.000	0.311	3.101	0.001	0.110	3.704
Xception	Accuracy	1.000	1.000	0.661	0.612	0.613	0.544
	Loss	0.000	0.000	5.170	5.944	6.093	7.073
MobileNetV2	Accuracy	1.000	1.000	0.660	1.000	0.980	0.677
	Loss	0.000	0.000	0.701	0.000	0.060	4.173
VGG19	Accuracy	0.636	0.653	0.556	0.615	0.603	0.544
	Loss	5.167	5.314	5.997	5.901	6.093	7.073

respectively. On the MobileNetV2 model, an average precision of 0.990 percent was achieved, a recall of 0.985 percent and an F1-score of 0.987 percent for the Item#5. In terms of classifying plant items packing services, the MobileNetV2 model surpasses the other five pre-trained networks models.

The freezing phase of the MobileNetV2 model as well as learning curves for training and validation/loss accuracy are shown in Fig. 3.

Table 2 Comparison of the performance of the five models pre-trained network

Confusion matrix		Item1	Item2	Item3	Item4	Item5
	Precision	0.000	0.000	0.230	0.000	0.058
ResNet50	Recall	0.000	0.000	1.000	0.000	0.250
	f1-score	0.000	0.000	0.380	0.000	0.094
	Precision	0.970	1.000	1.000	0.810	0.946
ResNet50V2	Recall	1.000	1.000	0.630	1.000	0.908
	f1-score	0.980	1.000	0.770	0.900	0.914
	Precision	0.000	0.000	0.000	0.340	0.086
Xception	Recall	0.000	0.000	0.000	1.000	0.250
	f1-score	0.000	0.000	0.000	0.510	0.127
	Precision	1.000	1.000	1.000	0.960	0.990
MobileNetV2	Recall	1.000	1.000	0.940	1.000	0.985
	f1-score	1.000	1.000	0.970	0.980	0.987
	Precision	0.000	0.000	0.000	0.340	0.054
VGG19	Recall	0.000	0.000	0.000	1.000	0.250
	f1-score	0.000	0.000	0.000	0.510	0.094

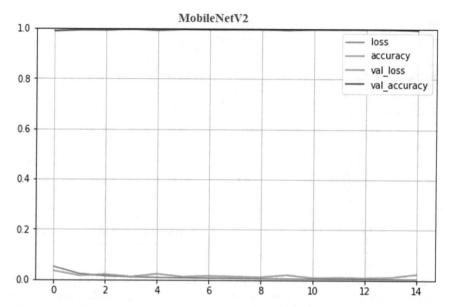

Fig. 3 Loss and accuracy curves

Evaluation results of the MobileNetV2 model in fine-tuning stage from pre-trained networks, using the confusion matrix performance of validation data, are shown in Fig. 4. The number of correct predictions is represented by the diagonal elements, whereas the number of incorrect predictions is represented by the other elements.

We utilize a curve connected with validation data called the receiving operating characteristics (ROC) for the best and worst MobileNetV2 models, respectively, to validate the ability to classify items packaging service. We were able to display a vertical line using cross-validation learning curves in the last levels of fine-tuning, as shown in Fig. 5.

6.2 Classify Before Packaging Service

Pre-trained MobileNetV2 models were used with fine-tuned items packing service recognition with six volunteers in retail market, to distinguish between eighteen items packing service. In our model (MobileNetV2), error rate is 0.06, and packing vending system's error rate is 0.72. Our model is pre-trained MobileNetV2 model with fine-tuned that matched the actual product for all shoppers except shopper #6 which we could not classify, as shown in Fig. 6.

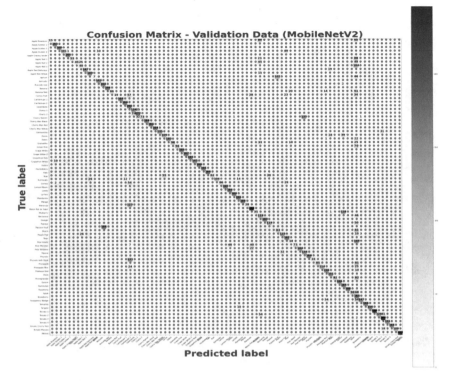

Fig. 4 Multi-class confusion matrix (81-class confusion matrix)

7 Conclusion

Our results demonstrated that deep transfer learning (DTL) of MobileNetV2 model pre-trained network is the most efficient of the models. Intelligent items packing service system was able to 1. facilitate managing complex tasks when classifying plant products packaging service, 2. create luxury for the customer and retailer, where customer can get commodities quickly without queuing, 3. positively affect the shopping experience and purchase behavior, leading to improved purchase support without wasting time in queues, and 4. The retailer has been able to sustain competition and introducing shopping pleasure to consumers. Our program in this research was able to identify plant items products packing service and could be accurately classified using convolutional neural network, deep learning and unsupervised machine learning. In the future: recognition in the fruit test without the participation of the provider, which is the capacity to eat fruits and vegetables, identify fruits and count them.

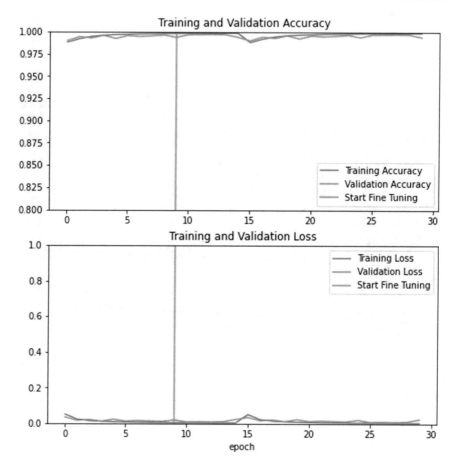

Fig. 5 Vertical line of fine-tuning

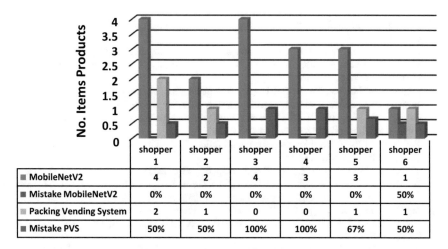

	shopper 1	shopper 2	shopper 3	shopper 4	shopper 5	shopper 6
■ MobileNetV2	4	2	4	3	3	1
■ Mistake MobileNetV2	0%	0%	0%	0%	0%	50%
▩ Packing Vending System	2	1	0	0	1	1
■ Mistake PVS	50%	50%	100%	100%	67%	50%

Fig. 6 Recognition with six volunteers in retail market

Acknowledgements I would like to express my gratitude to Sur University College administration for their continuing support and encouragement in doing this study.

Compliance with Ethical Standards The author declares that there is no conflict of interest and no fund was obtained. Institution permission and Institution Review Board (IRB) were taken from Sur University College. Written informed consent was obtained from all individual participants included in the study. The researcher explained the purpose and the possible outcomes of the research. Participation was completely voluntary, participants were assured that they have rights to withdraw at any time throughout the study, and non-participation would not have any detrimental effects in terms of the essential or regular professional issues or any penalty. Also participants were assured that their responses will be treated confidentially.

Ethical Approval This research paper contains a survey that was done by participants as per their ethical approval. "All procedures performed in studies involving human participants were in accordance with the ethical standards of the institutional and/or national research committee and with the 1964 Helsinki declaration and its later amendments or comparable ethical standards."

References

1. Priporas C-V, Stylos N, Fotiadis AK (2017) Generation Z consumers' expectations of interactions in smart retailing: a future agenda. Comput Hum Behav 77:374–381
2. Xia K et al (2021) An intelligent self-service vending system for smart re-tail. Sensors 21(10):3560
3. Feldmann MJ et al (2020) Multi-dimensional machine learning approaches for fruit shape phenotyping in strawberry. GigaScience 9(5):giaa030
4. Fruits 360 Dataset on GitHub. https://github.com/Horea94/Fruit-Images-Dataset. Last visited on 01 Nov 2021) 1, 10
5. Fruits 360 Dataset on Kaggle. https://www.kaggle.com/moltean/fruits. Last visited on 01 Nov 2021) 1, 10

6. Mureşan H, Oltean M (2017) Fruit recognition from images using deep learning. arXiv preprint arXiv:1712.00580
7. Alodat M (2021) Analyzing CT scan images using deep transfer learning for patients with Covid-19 disease. In: International conference on medical imaging and computer-aided diagnosis. Springer, Singapore
8. Albawi S, Mohammed TA, Al-Zawi S (2017) Understanding of a convolutional neural network. In: 2017 international conference on engineering and technology (ICET). IEEE
9. Chang C-S, Lee Y-C (2020) Ultrasonic touch sensing system based on lamb waves and convolutional neural network. Sensors 20(9):2619
10. Wei Y et al (2020) Deep learning for retail product recognition: Challenges and techniques. Computat Intell Neurosci (2020)
11. Yilmaz K, Temizkan V (2020) Smart shopping experience of customers using mobile applications: a field research in Karabuk/Turkey. Gaziantep Univ J Soc Sci 19(3):1237–1254
12. Lefkimmiatis S (2018) Universal denoising networks: a novel CNN architecture for image denoising. In: Proceedings of the IEEE conference on computer vision and pattern recognition
13. Sarang P, Deep dive in tf. keras. Artificial neural networks with tensor- flow 2. Apress, Berkeley, CA, pp 71–132
14. Russakovsky O et al (2015) Imagenet large scale visual recognition challenge. Int J Comput Vision 115(3):211–252
15. Alodat, M, Abdullah I (2018) Surveillance rapid detection of signs of traffic services in real time. J Telecommun Electron Comput Eng (JTEC) 10(2–4):193–196
16. Zhuang F et al (2020) A comprehensive survey on transfer learning. In: Proceedings of the IEEE 109.1, pp 43–76
17. Sim Y et al (2020) Deep convolutional neural network–based software improves radiologist detection of malignant lung nodules on chest radiographs. Radiology 294(1):199–209
18. Xie M et al. (2016) Transfer learning from deep features for remote sensing and poverty mapping. In: Proceedings of the AAAI conference on artificial intelligence, vol. 30(1)
19. Alodat M (2020) Predicting student final score using deep learning. In: Advances in computer, communication and computational sciences. Springer, Singapore, pp 429–436
20. Chollet F (2016) Building autoencoders in keras. The Keras Blog
21. Nguyen G et al (2019) Machine learning and deep learning frameworks and libraries for large-scale data mining: a survey. Artif Intell Rev 52(1):77–124
22. Baykal E et al (2020) Transfer learning with pre-trained deep convolutional neural networks for serous cell classification. Multimedia Tools Appl 79(21):15593–15611
23. Dai W et al (2020) A flower classification approach with mobileNetV2 and transfer learning. In: Proceedings of the 9th international symposium on computational intelligence and industrial applications (ISCIIA2020), vol. 31. Beijing, China

Prediction of Polycystic Ovarian Syndrome Using Machine Learning Techniques

Asis Kaur Baweja and M. Kanchana

1 Introduction

Polycystic ovarian syndrome is a condition in which a woman's hormones are out of balance. Women with PCOS tend to have higher amounts of male hormone or androgen in their body. This condition also leads to lower levels of female hormones or progesterone along with formation of cysts on the ovaries. As a direct repercussion of this, the menstrual cycle of the patient stops or becomes unpredictable. Unwanted body hair, facial hair and high risk of diabetes and blood pressure are few of the other addendums. Few speculated causes of PCOS are high insulin level as well as other hereditary affiliations. There is no particular medical test that can decisively predict PCOS. Doctors usually recommend surplus tests like blood tests to measure your hormone levels, blood sugar, and cholesterol. Ultrasound can check ovaries for cysts, look for tumours, and measure the lining of the uterus but none of these tests are sufficient for determining PCOS. A few other facts that catalysed this research were, every one in four Indian women has PCOS yet it has an undeticatibility rate of 75%. Current methods of prediction are time consuming, costly and unreliable. If not detected at the right age, PCOS can lead to cardiovascular diseases, ovarian cancer and infertility.

Current machine learning approaches use the results of these medical tests as input feature vectors in order to determine the susceptibility of a person having this condition. These methods might increase the accuracy of prediction by clubbing the results of various medical tests but it fails in reducing the cost as well as time

A. K. Baweja (✉) · M. Kanchana
School of Computing, SRM Institute of Science and Technology, Kattankulathur,
Tamil Nadu 603203, India
e-mail: ab8161@srmist.edu.in

M. Kanchana
e-mail: kanchanm@srmist.edu.in

associated with diagnosis. The objective of this work is to increase the prediction accuracy by taking a unique approach in feature selection and predicting PCOS on the basis of few rudimentary symptoms that patients tend to have.

2   Literature Survey

In [1], the author states that our knowledge on the topic of PCOS is sparse; thus, a detailed analysis has been conducted that discusses its current status in the world. Environmental factors as well as hereditary aspects are major catalyses of this condition. 30% of infertility cases that occur in women are a direct consequence of PCOS. In [2], the author highlights the need of generating awareness about PCOS as a majority of women remain undiagnosed even after having sufficient access to health-care providers. Only three to ten per cent of women are diagnosed even though the expected number of cases is much higher.

In Polycystic Ovarian Syndrome: Diagnosis and Management [3, 4] projects the redundancy of current methods of detection. A majority of doctors deem women with irregular cycles as patients of PCOS even though 20% of the PCOS patients have synchronized cycles. Doctors take into consideration signs of IR syndrome when testing for PCOS. IR depends on weight gain although studies show that 30% of woman who have PCOS aren't obese. A cross-sectional study of polycystic ovarian syndrome among adolescent and young girls in Mumbai, India [4], states that only 10.7% PCOS tested patients have high androgen levels, which otherwise is considered a key element in diagnosis determination. The Rotterdam ESHRE/ASRM-sponsored PCOS Consensus Workshop Group [5–9] classify PCOS as a metabolic and reproductive disorder, if not treated at the right time this seldom culminates into long term diseases like type-2 diabetes, ovarian and breast cancer. In USA, women of reproductive age who tend to have severe weight gain issues, acne, hair problems and irregular periods have PCOS. Recent studies have shown that due to weak immunity, women with PCOS are more susceptible to COVID virus along with cardio-metabolic diseases [10]. The Complementary and Alternative Medicine for Polycystic Ovary Syndrome: A Review of Clinical Application and Mechanism [11] as well as [12] talk about the lack of any coherent method of treatment; these recent research papers further shed light on the necessity of prediction as it is the first step of treating any disease.

In [13–16], PCOS prediction has been done using symptoms associated with it as well as several lab results which include blood tests, insulin test and ultrasound. Procuring the results of these medical tests is a time consuming and costly affair. Secondly once the results of these tests are in hand, doctors can analyse them at one glance and understand if the ovaries have cysts or not, this later helps in PCOS diagnosis. Some key conclusions that can be drawn from this survey are that there is no coherent method for detecting PCOS at the moment. The current methods are not reliable. PCOS prediction can be done successfully to a great extent on the basis of some rudimentary symptoms associated with it.

3 Proposed Methodology

Figure 1 describes the architectural flow of proposed work. The first step is cleaning the data, filling the missing columns and taking mandatory steps to ensure data is not skewed before moving to analysis and training. Not all features are taken into account at the time of training. In the feature selection step, redundant fields are dropped from the dataset. Before training, it is necessary to make sure that all features have the same scale, the features which do not lie in the range of 0–1 are normalized. Dataset is trained, and a comparative study is done using five eminent algorithms, decision trees, support vector machines, Naive Bayes, logistic regression and multilayer perceptron in the above mentioned order. A detailed analysis of best model, i.e. MLP technique, is done. Results obtained from all the models are critiqued, and an inference is drawn in the concluding section of the paper.

Fig. 1 Flow of proposed work

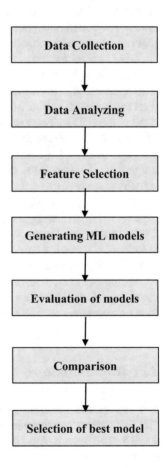

3.1 Dataset Description and Feature Selection

Polycystic ovary syndrome (PCOS) [6] dataset from Kaggle is used in this comparative study of various predicting models. The dataset consists of information of five hundred forty patients and it is collected from ten hospitals of Kerala in India. A totality of thirty nine features are a part of this dataset which have supposed connotations of associativity with PCOS. A vast majority out of these thirty nine features can only be procured by conducting lab test. These lab tests are costly and time consuming in nature. According to the traditional methods of prediction, a doctor after analysing these medical tests decides if the patient is having PCOS or not; thus, the medical results once obtained diminish the requirement of an AI based predictor analogous to the ones in paper [13]. Our aim in this paper is to exclude these features at the time of training. Thus, in the first iteration of feature selection, we have manually discarded features like Anti-Mullerian-Hormone test (AMH test) and ultrasound results and boiled down our dataset to a set of ten rudimentary symptoms of PCOS that can be gauged by any individual on their own without assistance.

Table 1 shows the list of the ten features selected after the first iteration of feature selection along with some necessary statistical information. In the second iteration of feature selection, a univariate linear regression test is performed. This linear model tests the individual effect of each of many regresses. Figure 2 and Table 2 provide a visual as well as tabular representation of feature score accumulated with the help of f_regression in sklearn; this method assigns the feature score to all attributes on the basis of their p values. In null hypothesis significance testing, the p-value is nothing but the probability of obtaining test results at least as extreme as the results actually observed, given the assumption that the null hypothesis is correct. Out of above mentioned ten parameters, an inference can be drawn that the first feature 'Age' is not contributing much to our target output as its importance score in Table 2 is relatively low. Hence, we can drop this feature at the time of training. Another prominent observation based on Fig. 2 is that 'BMI' is the most important symptom of PCOS. Hence, measures taken to control weight can become a useful aspect in combating PCOS. According to Fig. 2 apart from BMI, skin darkening and hair loss can also play an eminent role in determining PCOS, whereas other features like fast food consumption, regular exercise and weight gain are relatively trivial.

3.2 Normalization

It is evident from column min and max of Table1. That 'Age' and 'BMI' have a different scale when compared to other features. Their values do not lie in between 0 and 1. The feature 'Age' is discarded in the second iteration of feature extraction due to low importance score; so before training the ML model feature, 'BMI' is normalized using Eq. (1) and its scale is converted into 0 to 1.

Table 1 List of selected features

S. No	Feature	Count	Mean	Std	Min	Max
1	Age (yrs)	540	31.32	5.71	1.00	48.00
2	BMI	540	24.90	11.65	13.38	277.47
3	Cycle (R/I)	540	0.29	0.45	0.00	1.00
4	Weight gain (Y/N)	540	0.41	0.49	0.00	1.00
5	hair growth 1 (Y/N)	540	0.34	0.47	0.00	1.00
6	Skin darkening (Y/N)	540	0.35	0.47	0.00	1.00
7	Hair loss	540	0.42	0.49	0.00	1.00
8	Pimples (Y/N)	540	0.38	0.48	0.00	1.00
9	Fast food (Y/N)	540	0.41	0.49	0.00	1.00
10	Regular exercise (Y/N)	540	0.24	0.43	0.00	1.00

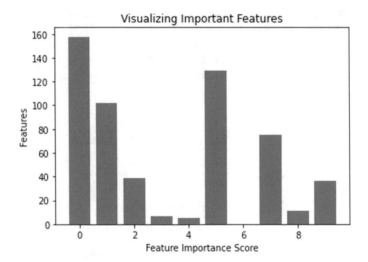

Fig. 2 Feature importance chart

$$x_{\text{scaled}} = \frac{x - x_{\min}}{x_{\max} - x_{\min}} \tag{1}$$

3.3 Results and Discussion

In order to train various models, the dataset is divided into 80:20. The first part is the training set whereas the second part is the test set which will help in analysing the accuracy of all the models. All the models are compared using four parameters,

Table 2 Importance score of features

S. No	Feature	Importance score
1	BMI	157.693
2	Hair loss	101.733
3	Cycle (R/I)	38.834
4	Weight gain (Y/N)	6.799
5	Hair growth (Y/N)	5.390
6	Skin darkening (Y/N)	129.199
7	Age (yrs)	0.019
8	Pimples (Y/N)	74.914
9	Fast food (Y/N)	11.229
10	Regular exercise (Y/N)	36.601

precision, recall, F1_ Score and accuracy. The exactness of a particular classifier can be measured using precision as in Eq. (2). The efficiency of a classifier in correctly predicting positive instances is recall as specified in Eq. (3). The count of actual occurrences of an individual class is support. The harmonic mean of precision and recall is known as F1 score, and the formula for calculating F1 score is mentioned in Eq. (4).

$$\text{Precision} = \frac{\text{True positive}}{(\text{True positive} + \text{False positive})} \quad (2)$$

$$\text{Recall} = \frac{\text{True positive}}{(\text{True positive} + \text{False negative})} \quad (3)$$

$$F1 = \frac{2 * (\text{Precision} * \text{Recall})}{(\text{Precision} + \text{Recall})} \quad (4)$$

The five selected models for comparative study are CART, SVM, Naive Bayes, logistic regression and MLP. Classification and regression tree is an algorithm that takes Gini impurity index as the splitting criteria for building a decision tree. Support vector machines and robust ML algorithm are efficient in solving classification problems by plotting examples in a n-dimensional space and segregating them on basis of appropriate hyperplane. Naive Bayes is a simple algorithm that functions on Bayes theorem of probability. Logistic regression uses a purely statistical linear approach for classifying a given dataset. Mishra and Srivastava [17] One of the most common supervised learning algorithms is multi-layer perceptron that learns a function on the basis of the provided dataset by taking all the features present in it as inputs. The MLP model considered in this paper has three hidden layers consisting of 5, 8, 5 neurons respectively. Activation function used is ReLU, and the optimizer is Adam. ReLU is selected over other functions like sigmoid since it is not prone to vanishing gradient problems [18]. Adam optimizer gave best results as it combines the abilities of RMSProp and stochastic gradient descent [19]. The initial learning rate is 0.001, and the value of hyperparameters is 0.9, respectively.

Figure 3 and Table 3 give the list of five models that were taken into consideration for the purpose of comparative analysis. The results obtained on the test set using all these models are jotted down in Table 3; Fig. 3 shows the bar graph comparing precision, recall, f1 score and accuracy of all models. It is evident from the results mentioned in Table 3 as well as Fig. 3 that the best results were obtained using MLP. Highest accuracy was 93%. Logistic regression was a close second in terms of all parameters. Although the decision tree successfully delivered sufficient accuracy, its recall score was the lowest i.e. 0.73. Thus, it would not be taken into account in future as chances of overfitting are high in this model. Performance of Naive Bayes and SVM was moderate in all respects. In medical oriented research studies, it is important to judge models on the basis of several parameters like precision, recall and f1 score rather than simply focusing on accuracy. The reason for this is that we need to come up with such a model that does not give us false positives. Figure 3 shows that the models considered in this paper have given above 75% results in all fields. For the purpose of further analysis, tenfold cross validation was applied on all models. To ensure fair evaluation, each model is configured with the same random seed so that the same splits to the training data are performed and that each algorithm is evaluated in precisely the same way.

Figure 4 and Table 4 represent the box and whiskers plot obtained from tenfold cross validation of five models. Although the average accuracy of MLP, logistic regression as well as SVM is similar, MLP and logistic regression are considerably better models than SVM. This inference is drawn from the fact that their outliers shown in Fig. 4 are less widespread than those of SVM. CART and Naive Bayesian models failed to give satisfactory results; Fig. 4 shows that the average accuracy of CART and NB is 82% apart from this the outliers of NB are widespread; hence, they can be neglected in future research works of the same topic. MLP has given best

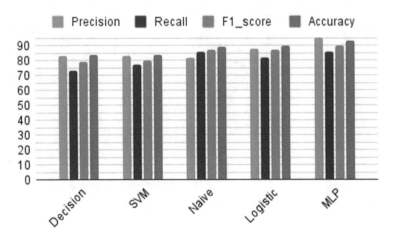

Fig. 3 Comparative analysis of various algorithms

Table 3 Comparative analysis of various algorithms

Models	Precision	Recall	F1 Score	Accuracy
Decision tree/CART	0.83	0.73	0.79	0.84
SVM	0.83	0.77	0.80	0.84
Naive Bayes	0.82	0.86	0.87	0.89
Logistic regression	0.88	0.82	0.87	0.90
MLP	0.95	0.86	0.90	0.93

results as it has the tendency of adding non-linearity to a dataset. Due to this ability, it is able to capture the minute nuances of complex as well as noisy datasets; this is the major reason why it outperformed other proposed algorithms on all parameters. MLP is also more adaptable than other algorithms and thus is capable of catering further changes like increasing and decreasing the number of features in future study.

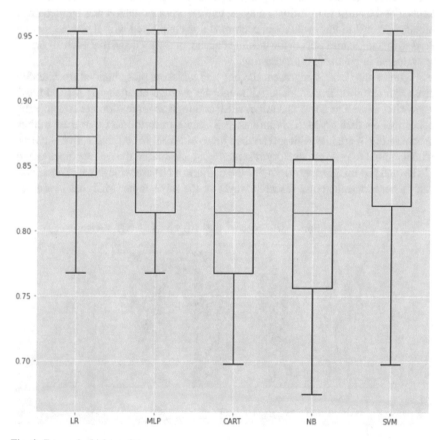

Fig. 4 Box and whiskers plot

Table 4 Tenfold cross validation score

Model	Average accuracy
Logistic regression	0.867865
MLP	0.858457
Decision tree (CART)	0.825233
Naive Bayes (NB)	0.829831
SVM	0.859831

Table 5 Comparison of proposed system with other existing methods

References no	Features extracted	Classifiers used	Classification accuracy obtained (%)
18	Follicles on ovaries	CNN	85
19	Follicles on ovaries	SVM-RBF Kernel	82.55
20	Follicles on ovaries	KNN-Euclidean distance	78.81
1	Ten features including follicles on ovaries	Logistic regression	92
Proposed work	Nine features excluding follicles on ovaries	MLP	93

Table 5 presents the comparison of the proposed system with other existing methods. In the papers [14], PCOS is predicted using CNN and deep neural networks by follicle detection on ultrasound images [15, 16]. Also use ultrasound images for predicting PCOS using SVM and KNN respectively. Research shows that follicle detection is neither appropriate nor the sole criteria for PCOS diagnosis; this claim can be verified by an in depth study of [3, 4]. Secondly, cysts can easily be detected by doctors by manually looking at the ultrasound images. Hence, real-time projects based on these papers will have little utility. In [13] PCOS has been detected using follicles detection as well as some symptoms that patients generally have. The futility of real-time application based on [13] is again a point of concern. In this paper, the best MLP model has not only outperformed existing research but has also been successful in achieving these results after eliminating redundant parameters.

4 Conclusion and Future Work

A comparative study was conducted to find out the best algorithm that can predict polycystic ovarian syndrome. Out of the five algorithms tested, best is MLP which has an accuracy of 93%; results of logistic regression were also noteworthy. MLP gave splendid results in all parameters considered in comparative study. Thus, in future, this model can be integrated in a website for PCOS prediction. Since this model makes accurate predictions only on the basis of simple features, it can overcome the bottleneck of traditional methods of prediction and can easily reduce the time and cost associated with diagnosis.

References

1. Barthelmess EK, Naz RK (2014) Polycystic ovary syndrome: current status and future perspective. Front Biosci-Elite 6(1):104–119, Jan 2014
2. Wolf W, Wattick R, Kinkade O, Olfert M (2018) Geographical prevalence of polycystic ovary syndrome as determined by region and race/ethnicity. Int'l J Environ Res Publ Health 15:2589
3. Sheehan MT (2004) Polycystic ovarian syndrome: diagnosis and management. Clin Med Res 2(1):13–27. https://doi.org/10.3121/cmr.2.1.1
4. Joshi B et al (2014) A cross-sectional study of polycystic ovarian syndrome among adolescent and young girls in Mumbai, India. Indian J Endocrinol Metab 18(3):317–24. https://doi.org/10.4103/2230-8210.131162
5. The Rotterdam ESHRE/ASRM-sponsored PCOS consensus workshop group, Revised 2003 consensus on diagnostic criteria and long-term health risks related to polycystic ovary syndrome (PCOS). Hum Reprod 19(1):41–47, Jan 2004
6. Polycystic ovary syndrome (PCOS) dataset from kaagle.com
7. Diamanti-Kandarakis E, Dunaif A (2012) Insulin resistance and the polycystic ovary syndrome revisited: an update on mechanisms and implications. Endocr Rev 33(6):981–1030
8. Pasquali R, Stener-Victorin E, Yildiz BO et al (2011) PCOS Forum: research in polycystic ovary syndrome today and tomorrow. ClinEndocrinol (Oxf) 74(4):424–433. https://doi.org/10.1111/j.1365-2265.2010.03956.x
9. Rojas J, Chávez M, Olivar L, Rojas M, Morillo J, Mejías J, Calvo M, Bermúdez V (2014) Polycystic ovary syndrome, insulin resistance, and obesity: navigating the pathophysiologic labyrinth. Int J Reprod Med 2014(17):2014, Article ID 719050
10. Subramanian A, Anand A, Adderley NJ, Okoth K, Toulis KA, Gokhale K, Sainsbury C, O'Reilly MW, Arlt W, Nirantharakumar K (2021) Increased COVID-19 infections in women with polycystic ovary syndrome: a population-based study. Eur J Endocrinol 184(5):637–645. Accessed 2 Aug 2021
11. Jia L-Y, Feng J-X, Li J-L, Liu F-Y, Xie L-Z, Luo S-J, Han F-J (2021) The complementary and alternative medicine for polycystic ovary syndrome: a review of clinical application and mechanism. Evid -Based Complement Altern Med 2021, 12. Article ID 5555315
12. El Hayek S, Bitar L, Hamdar LH, Mirza FG, Daoud G (2016) PolyCystic ovarian syndrome: an updated overview. Front Physiol 7:124. Published 2016 Apr. https://doi.org/10.3389/fphys.2016.00124
13. Tanwani N (2020) Detecting PCOS using machine learning. Int J Mod Trends Eng Sci 7(1):15–20
14. Sumathi M, Chitra P, Sakthi Prabha R, Srilatha K (2021) Study and detection of PCOS related diseases using CNNet al 2021. IOP Conf Ser Mater Sci Eng 1070 012062
15. Deepika V (2019) Applications of artificial intelligence techniques in polycystic ovarian syndrome diagnosis. J Adv Res Technol Manage Sci 01(03), Nov 2019, ISSN: 2582–3078
16. Purnama B, Wisesti UN, Adiwijaya FN, Gayatri A, Mutiah T (2015) A classification of polycystic Ovary Syndrome based on follicle detection of ultrasound images. In: 2015 3rd International conference on information and communication technology (ICoICT), pp 396–401. https://doi.org/10.1109/ICoICT.2015.7231458

17. Mishra M, Srivastava M (2014) A view of artificial neural network. In: 2014 international conference on advances in engineering & technology research. Unnao, India, pp 1–3
18. Nwankpa C, Ijomah W, Gachagan A, Marshall S (2020) Activation functions: comparison of trends in practice and research for deep learning. Dec (2020) Book
19. Kingma D, BJ Adam (2014) A method for stochastic optimization. In: International conference on learning representations Dec-(2014)

Medical Image Fusion for Diagnosis of Alzheimer Using Rolling Guidance Filter and Parameter Adaptive PCNN

K. Vanitha, D. Satyanarayana, and M. N. Giri Prasad

1 Introduction

Alzheimer's disease is an attained disorder of impairment of behavioral and cognitive data that definitely interfuse with occupational and social functioning. The functions of brain are more affected as there is more advance in disease, and it seems most difficult to cut back the destructive process [1]. As the disease has no cure, and its advancement has been slowed down, only early diagnosis is the best thing. The earliest stage of disorder progression called mild cognitive impairment has amnesia as symptom. Next stage of Alzheimer's disease is moderate and severe [2]. Alzheimer's screening is done by utilizing neuro-imaging modalities like MRI, CT, PET, SPECT, etc. In early cases of disorder, CT scans are mostly helpful in finding the changes with respect to structure. MRI scan provides more prominent measurement of brain structures, which are used for treatment to slow down the advancement of disorder [3]. The scans related to functional modalities PET and SPECT are most important and have been widely useful in testing process of drugs and analyzing their whole information. The scans related to modalities PET and SPECT are taken as multi-spectral images, whereas the MR and CT have been considered as panchromatic images, giving us most changing information useful for early diagnosis [4]. Multi-spectral integration of CT with MRI, MRI with PET and SPECT scans is an emerging technique used in disorder findings and treatment. Multimodal image fusion simply defined as superimposition of the complementary features that are acquired from neuro-imaging modalities to produce a composite image. This process fetches both spatial and spectral features from source modalities [5, 6]. Hence, the proposed work

K. Vanitha (✉) · M. N. G. Prasad
JNTU College of Engineering and Technology, Ananthapuramu, India
e-mail: vanithakamarthi@gmail.com

D. Satyanarayana
RGM College of Engineering and Technology, Nandyal, India

focuses in development of most effective MMIF method in spatial domain to provide us more significant data for analysis and early detection of stages of disorders. So many MMIF schemes have been mentioned in over last few years. Still, the resultant image used to analyze disorder stages suffers from loss of energy, information, and finer details, blurring of edges, blocky artifacts, color distortions. Hence, simultaneous edges preservation, extraction of all scale details, and removal of small textures without affecting the loss of information are required. This is possible by using rolling guidance filter. PA-PCNN also utilized to process detail parts to compensate finer details loss. Thus, MMIF scheme based on RGF using PA-PCNN is introduced in this article to overcome the above problems.

2 Related Work

The way of using rolling guidance filter RGF to decompose the source medical image pairs into base and detail parts is explained and is mathematically given in detail within this section.

2.1 Rolling Guidance Filter (RGF)

Zhang et al. [7] introduced simple, easy, and faster edge aware filter called rolling guidance filter (RGF) to smoothen images and extract saliency. It is simply based on a rolling guidance with smoothing control over fine scale of all detail components. RGF has fast convergence and iterative implementation process. The advantage of RGF is that it easily differentiates all structures of an image in different scales even though the model of noise or details are not known performs the removal, recovery, and preservation operations. The structures related to large scale have been preserved, small scale has been removed, and edges are recovered. First, source image is smoothened using Gaussian filter (GF) then applied with joint bilateral filter (JBF) to produce RGF output image. GF removes small textures without edges blurring, whereas JBF iteratively recovers the edges. Consider I as source image then applied with Gaussian filter GF, output image is given as

$$\text{GF(p)} = \frac{1}{X_P} \sum_{q \in M(p)} \exp\left(\frac{-\|(p-q)\|^2}{2\sigma^2}\right) I(q)$$

where

(p, q) Image pixel positions
σ Deviation of GF
$M(p)$ Window with center p of GF
GF (p) Output image

The output of GF acts as input to JBF, and its output is given as

$$J' = \mathrm{GF}(p), J^{i+1} = \text{output of JBF at i}^{\text{th}}\text{ iteration}$$

$$J^{i+1}(p) = \frac{1}{X_P} \sum_{q \in M(p)} \exp\left(\frac{-\|(p-q)\|^2}{2\sigma^2} - \frac{\|J^i(p) - J^i(q)\|^2}{2\sigma_r^2}\right) I(q)$$

where σ_r = range weights controlling factor and.

Xp = normalization factor.

Finally, combining the above two steps into one results as following equation, J^i = constant = C

$$J^{i+1}(p) = \frac{1}{X_P} \sum_{q \in M(p)} \exp\left(\frac{-\|(p-q)\|^2}{2\sigma^2}\right) I(q)$$

2.2 Parameter Adaptive PCNN (PA-PCNN)

PCNN does not need any training process. Moreover, setting of decay coefficients, different amplitudes, and linking strength is the key challenge in PCNN [8]. The adaptive version of PCNN called PA-PCNN model is suggested by Chen essentially recommended for segmenting of images [9]. In this paper, we are also arguing that it works effectively for MMIF. PA-PCNN is applied to merge the obtained high-frequency coefficients from FPDE decomposition. Actually, target image pixel intensity is used as input to segmentation using SPCNN. PCNN transmits the coefficient information from one to others, so that the information from all pixels gets coupled and has been utilized. In the integration of coefficients related to high frequency, absolute values of each coefficient are utilized as measure. On the basis of above-specified deliberations, it has been clear that the fusion of medical images problem exhibits great similarity with respect to segmentation, which provokes us to use the same for selection of most prominent coefficients (Fig. 1).

Figure 1 shows the PA-PCNN model architecture, and its parameters are described in detail, see reference [10].

$$F_{kl}[x] = H_{kl}$$

$$L_{ij}[x] = V_L \sum_{ij} W_{ijkl} Y_{ij}[x-1]$$

$$U_{kl}[x] = e^{-\alpha_f} U_{kl}[x-1] + F_{kl}[x-1](1 + \beta L_{kl}[x-1])$$

$$E_{kl}[x] = e^{-\alpha_e} E_{kl}[x-1] + V_E Y_{kl}[x]$$

$$Y_{kl}[x] = \begin{cases} 1, & U_{kl}[x] > E_{kl}[x-1]; \\ 0, & \text{otherwise} \end{cases}$$

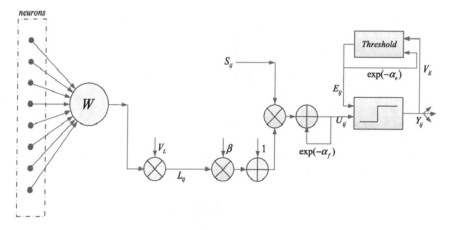

Fig. 1 PA-PCNN model architecture

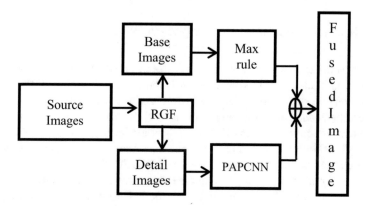

Fig. 2 Proposed MIF block diagram

The whole number of firing times are calculated by including the last step at each iteration end.

$$T_{ij}[x] = T_{ij}[x - 1] + Y_{ij}[x]$$

3 Proposed Method

MIF can be implemented by using RGF decomposition, finding final base and detail components, their linear combination, and its schematic is shown in Fig. 2.

Algorithm:

Step 1: Each medical image pair is applied with RGF so that the base, detail components are extracted using the following equations.

$$I_{1B}(p, q) = \text{RGF}(I_1(p, q))$$
$$I_{1D}(p, q) = I_1(p, q) - I_{1B}(p, q)$$
$$I_{2B}(p, q) = \text{RGF}(I_2(p, q))$$
$$I_{2D}(p, q) = I_2(p, q) - I_{2B}(p, q)$$

Step 2: The base components I_{1B} (p, q), I_{2B} (p, q) are integrated using the below equation:

$$F_B(p, q) = \begin{cases} I_{1B}(p, q), \ I_{1B}(p, q) > I_{2B}(p, q) \\ I_{2B}(p, q), \ \text{otherwise} \end{cases} \tag{1}$$

Step 3: The detail components I_{1D} (p, q), I_{2D} (p, q) are integrated using the below equation:

$$F_D(p, q) = \begin{cases} I_{1D}(p, q), \ \text{if } T_1[N] \geq T_2[N] \\ I_{2D}(p, q), \qquad \text{otherwise} \end{cases} \tag{2}$$

where $T_1[N]$ and $T_2[N]$ are whole firing times of each detail component
Step 4: Output: Fused image

$$F(p, q) = F_B(p, q) + F_D(p, q) \tag{3}$$

4   Experimental Results

Experiments were carried out on medical images of persons affected with Alzheimer taken from [11], see Fig. 3. The effectiveness of our technique is verified on 4 pairs of neuro-imaging medical modalities, which includes all the four combinations of CT, MRI, T1, T2-weighted MRI, PET, and SPECT. The list of methods which have been utilized for comparison are ADF [12], GF [13], FPDE [14], LatLRR [15], CS-MCA [16]. The objective measures utilized to assess performances of above-mentioned schemes are deviation (SD), feature-based Q_P, Q_G and information Q_{TE}, Q_{NCIE}, Q_{MI}, and human perception metric Q_{CB}, see references [10, 17] for more particulars such as equations, definitions, and calculations (Fig. 4).

From the resultant images of distinct methods, the observations made are like this. The fused image of ADF is totally blurred, as it suffers from contrast reduction. In the same manner, FPDE also suffers from spatial degradation. Also visual distortions have been introduced near edges using GF. These shortcomings have been overcome

Fig. 3 Medical image pairs used for experiment

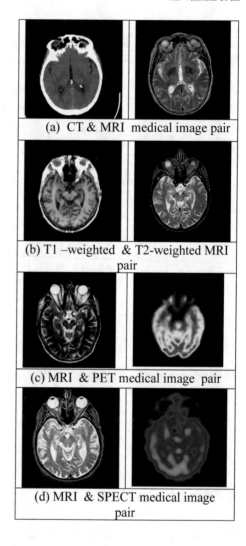

(a) CT & MRI medical image pair

(b) T1 –weighted & T2-weighted MRI pair

(c) MRI & PET medical image pair

(d) MRI & SPECT medical image pair

by using LatLRR, as it mainly aims to extract the parts related to low frequency and salient features in a greater way. CS-MCA can be able to extract the components easily, but some regions are not very clear due to some pixel distortions. Our method uses RGF, which not only extract all scale of details but also removes small textures without affecting the edges. The major highlights of our method such as edge preservation and details extraction in view of all scale give us an accurate detection of disorder problems at all stages (Table 1).

Our method has mean 66.37, deviation 84.13, Q_{IE} 0.813, Q_{MI} 1.01, Q_{TE} 0.697, Q_G 0.74 which are bolded because these values are highest among other schemes. Even though Q_P and Q_{CB} are high for GF, still visual quality is very poor. These values reflect the robustness of our method (Fig. 5).

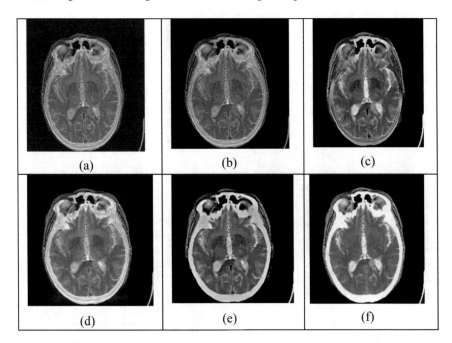

Fig. 4 Fused Images of existing and proposed methods for CT & MRI **a** ADF, **b** FPDE, **c** GF, **d** LatLRR, **e** CS-MCA, **f** proposed

Table 1 Objective assessment of MMIF methods for CT and MRI

	ADF	FPDE	GF	Latent LRR	CS-MCA	Proposed
M	0.14	0.25	0.10	0.18	0.021	**56.02**
SD	0.207	0.384	0.302	0.252	0.144	**77.27**
Q_{IE}	0.805	0.809	0.803	0.807	0.802	**0.811**
Q_{MI}	0.619	0.888	0.217	0.647	0.038	**0.941**
Q_{TE}	0.316	0.361	**0.395**	0.372	0.367	0.359
Q_G	0.722	**0.752**	0.502	0.577	0.454	0.453
Q_P	**0.494**	0.227	0.189	0.429	0.154	0.391
Q_{CB}	0.666	0.658	0.622	0.579	0.637	**0.679**

From the resultant images of distinct methods, the observations made are like this. The fused image of ADF is totally blurred, as it suffers from contrast reduction. In the same manner, FPDE also suffers from spatial degradation. Also visual distortions have been introduced near edges using GF. These shortcomings have been overcome by using LatLRR, as it mainly aims to extract the parts related to low frequency and salient features in a greater way. CS-MCA can be able to extract the components easily, but some regions are not very clear due to some pixel distortions. Our method uses RGF, which not only extract all scale of details but also removes small textures

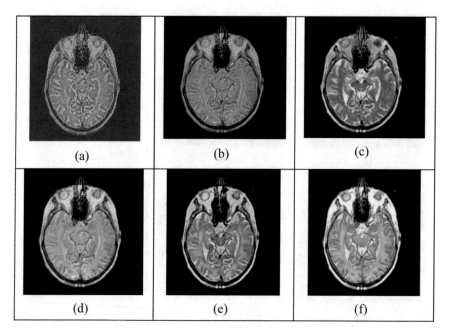

Fig. 5 Fused Images of existing and proposed methods of MRI & MRI **a** ADF, **b** FPDE, **c** GF, **d** LatLRR, **e** CS-MCA, **f** proposed

without affecting the edges. The major highlights of our method such as edge preservation and details extraction in view of all scale give us an accurate detection of disorder problems at all stages (Table 2).

Our method has mean 60.08, deviation 82.11, Q_{IE} 0.814, Q_{MI} 1.095, Q_{TE} 0.734, Q_G 0.805 which are bolded because these values are highest among other schemes. Even though Q_P and Q_{CB} are high for GF, still visual quality is very poor. These values reflect the robustness of our method (Fig. 6).

Table 2 Objective assessment for MRI-T1 and MRI-T2

	ADF	FPDE	GF	Latent LRR	CS-MCA	Proposed
M	42.75	42.98	45.95	0.219	48.27	**60.08**
SD	61.81	58.3	65.03	0.28	69.37	**82.11**
Q_{IE}	0.807	0.808	0.809	0.81	0.812	**0.814**
Q_{MI}	0.667	0.722	0.792	0.684	0.758	**1.095**
Q_{TE}	0.709	0.718	0.324	0.379	0.316	**0.734**
Q_G	0.456	0.681	0.789	0.345	0.744	**0.805**
Q_P	0.193	0.167	**0.687**	0.301	0.524	0.409
Q_{CB}	0.189	0.219	**0.729**	0.558	0.696	0.319

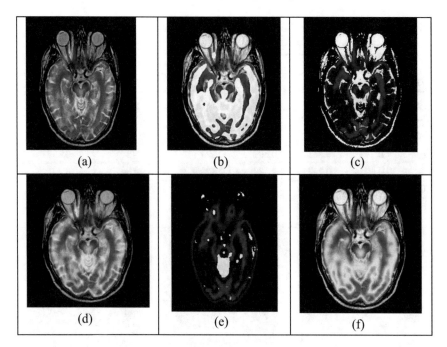

Fig. 6 Fused Images of existed and proposed methods of MRI & PET **a** ADF, **b** FPDE, **c** GF, **d** LatLRR, **e** CS-MCA, **f** proposed

Figure 3 shows the case of a man-71 old, suffered from memory disorders since eight months before screening. His MR and PET scan have confirmed the Alzheimer's disease by observing his brain affected regions. With respect to visual perception, fused image of other methods such as FPDE, GF, and CS-MCA is not good. Color distortions and artifacts are clearly visible in fused images of ADF, LatLRR. Our method works well for color images, which gives almost complete information of all details. Thus, the regions with affected disorder can be found to detect the stage and plan for treatment. Our method outperforms with respect to visual detection of disorders at all stages (Table 3).

Our method has mean 56.02, deviation 77.27, Q_{IE} 0.811, Q_{MI} 0.941, Q_{CB} 0.679 which are bolded because these values are highest among other schemes except Q_P, Q_G, and Q_{TE}. Q_P is high for ADF, Q_G is high for FPDE, and Q_{TE} is high for GF, but the affected regions showing disorder are not found clearly in order to detect the stage of disease (Fig. 7).

Figure 3 shows the case of a woman-75 yr old with the visual hallucinations problem. Slowly, she has been faced difficulties in scenes identification which have been known previously for her. ADF output image gives details but suffers from contrast problem. FPDE fused contains blocky artifacts, which leads to very low quality. GF provides not clear details, because of color distortions. LatLRR produces good amount of textures, salient, and fine details but it does not gives good quantitative

Table 3 Objective assessment of MMIF methods for MRI and PET

	ADF	FPDE	GF	Latent LRR	CS-MCA	Proposed
M	0.14	0.25	0.10	0.18	0.021	**56.02**
SD	0.207	0.384	0.302	0.252	0.144	**77.27**
Q_{IE}	0.805	0.809	0.803	0.807	0.802	**0.811**
Q_{MI}	0.619	0.888	0.217	0.647	0.038	**0.941**
Q_{TE}	0.316	0.361	**0.395**	0.372	0.367	0.359
Q_G	0.722	**0.752**	0.502	0.577	0.454	0.453
Q_P	**0.494**	0.227	0.189	0.429	0.154	0.391
Q_{CB}	0.666	0.658	0.622	0.579	0.637	**0.679**

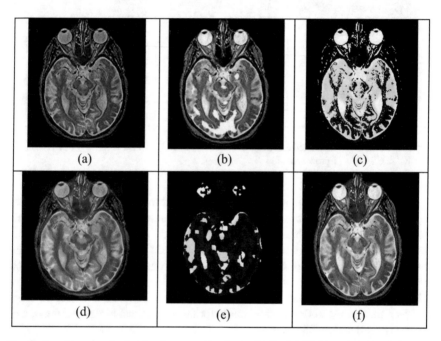

Fig. 7 Fused Images of existed and proposed methods of MRI & SPECT **a** ADF, **b** FPDE, **c** GF, **d** LatLRR, **e** CS-MCA, **f** proposed

values. CS-MCA is suitable for merging CT and MRI but not for MRI-PET, MRI-SPECT image pairs. It fails to give visually clear features, which are helpful in taking decision about the stage of Alzheimer. Our method exhibits greater benefits when compared with all the before mentioned techniques (Table 4).

Our method has mean 68.55, deviation 79.46, Q_{IE} 0.817, Q_{MI} 0.93, Q_{TE} 0.454, Q_G 0.276, and Q_P 0.63; some are bolded because these values are highest among other schemes. Even though Q_G 0.811 and Q_{CB} 0.705 are high for FPDE, visually,

Table 4 Objective assessment for MRI and SPECT

	ADF	FPDE	GF	Latent LRR	CS-MCA	Proposed
M	0.19	0.266	0.237	0.244	0.059	**68.55**
SD	0.23	0.331	0.425	0.270	0.236	**79.46**
Q_{IE}	0.80	0.816	0.803	0.808	0.803	**0.817**
Q_{MI}	0.62	0.902	0.349	0.611	0.085	**0.930**
Q_{TE}	0.32	0.387	**0.454**	0.412	0.415	0.407
Q_G	0.72	**0.811**	0.325	0.367	0.284	0.276
Q_P	0.56	0.516	0.122	0.436	0.107	**0.630**
Q_{CB}	0.66	**0.705**	0.537	0.496	0.499	0.675

the image is not good. Our method outperforms with respect to objective metrics, so much useful in finding disorders at all stages of Alzheimer.

5 Conclusion

Rolling guidance filter-based decomposition is presented for medical image fusion. Firstly, each source image is disintegrated into base, detail images, respectively, using RGF. Detail components are integrated with the help of PA-PCNN. Due to the speedy convergence of PA-PCNN, a great number of structural details are selected which leads to higher efficacy. A result demonstrates that image obtained has rich information with respect to fine details, structure retention. Hence, Alzheimer's disease can be analyzed with the clear study of fused image containing changes in brain with respect to structure and function.

Acknowledgements Declared none.

Funding
None.

Conflict of Interest
The authors declare no conflict of interest, financial, or otherwise.

Ethics Approval and Consent to Participate
Not applicable.

Human and Animal Rights
No animals/humans were used for studies that are the basis of this research.

Consent for Publication
Not applicable.

Availability of Data and Materials
The authors confirm that the data supporting the findings of this research are available within the article.

References

1. Ortiz A, Fajardo D, Górriz JM, Ramírez J, Martínez-Murcia FJ (2014) Multimodal image data fusion for Alzheimer's Disease diagnosis by sparse representation. In: InMed, pp 11–18
2. Bhateja V, Moin A, Srivastava A, Bao LN, Lay-Ekuakille A, Le DN (2016) Multispectral medical image fusion in Contourlet domain for computer based diagnosis of Alzheimer's disease. Rev Sci Instrum 87(7):074303
3. James AP, Dasarathy BV (2014) Medical image fusion: a survey of the state of the art. Inf Fusion 19:4–19
4. Fatmael-Zahra A-G (2016) Current trends in medical image registration and fusion. Egypt Inform J 17(1):99–124
5. Li S, Kang X, Fang L et al (2017) Pixel-level image fusion: a survey of the state of the art". Inf Fusion 33:100–112
6. Tirupal BCM, Srinivas Kumar S (2020) Multimodal medical image fusion techniques—a review. Curr Sign Transduction Ther
7. Zhang Q, Shen X, Xu L, Jia J (2014) Rolling guidance filter. In: European conference on computer vision. Springer, Cham, pp 815–830
8. Jiao K, Xu P, Zhao S (2018) A novel automatic parameter setting method of PCNN for image segmentation. In: 2018 IEEE 3rd international conference on signal and image processing (ICSIP). IEEE, pp 265–270
9. Yin M, Liu X, Liu Y, Chen X (2018) Medical image fusion with parameter-adaptive pulse coupled neural network in nonsubsampled shearlet transform domain. IEEE Trans Instrum Meas 68(1):49–64
10. Jagalingam P, Hegde AV (2015) A review of quality metrics for fused image. Aquat Procedia 4:133–142
11. www.med.harvard.edu/AANLIB/
12. Bavirisetti DP, Dhuli R (2016) Fusion of infrared and visible sensor images based on anisotropic diffusion and Karhunen-Loeve Transform. IEEE Sens J 16(1):203–209, 1 Jan 2016
13. Bavirisetti DP, Xiao G, Liu G (2017) Multi-sensor image fusion based on fourth order partial differential equations. In: International conference on information fusion. Xi'an, pp 1–9
14. Li S, Kang X, Hu J (2013) Image fusion with guided filtering. IEEE Trans Image Process 22:2864–2875
15. Li H, Wu XJ (2018) Infrared and visible image fusion using Latent Low-Rank Representation, arXiv:1804.08992
16. Liu Y, Chen X, Ward RK, Wang ZJ (2019) Medical image fusion via convolutional spaarsity based morphological component analysis. IEEE Signal Process Lett 26(3):485–489
17. Liu Z et al (2012) Objective assessment of multi resolution image fusion algorithms for context enhancement in night vision: a comparative study. In: IEEE transactions on pattern analysis and machine intelligence, vol. 34(1), pp. 94–107

Effectiveness of Ensemble Classifier Over State-Of-Art Machine Learning Classifiers for Predicting Software Faults in Software Modules

Mansi Gupta⊕, Kumar Rajnish⊕, and Vandana Bhattacharya⊕

1 Introduction

We now live in a modern digital era where software applications are required for the majority of our daily and commercial operations. This transition did not occur over the course of a day or week; rather, it began more than two decades ago. Software application reliability is directly related to program quality; the greater the quality, the more dependable the software [1]. Customers and developers have traditionally prioritized high-quality software at a reasonable cost, yet errors are unavoidable owing to the huge size and complexity of necessary systems [2]. Software testing is one of the most important tasks in the software development life cycle since it guarantees that high-quality software [3, 4] is delivered. It has also been stated that software testing consumes a significant amount of resources during the development life cycle, necessitating the creation of a cost-effective and efficient process for locating and fixing errors. Software fault prediction (SFP) is a viable solution to this problem, ensuring excellent software quality while working with limited resources. With this methodology, software modules that are expected to be faulty may be fully examined in comparison to modules that are predicted to be non-faulty. Since the previous two decades, machine learning techniques have been frequently utilized to anticipate software defects. These methods are divided into three categories: (1) supervised, (2) unsupervised, and (3) hybrid. The classes in supervised learning are known ahead of time. These learning approaches require pre-classified data (training data) for training, during which classification rules are developed and then applied to previously unknown data (test data). Although classes are unknown in unsupervised learning, these approaches utilize specific algorithms to investigate and discover the structure of data. Hybrid learning, also known as semi-supervised learning, combines both supervised and unsupervised approaches naïve Bayes [5],

M. Gupta (✉) · K. Rajnish · V. Bhattacharya
Department of Computer Science and Engineering, BIT Mesra, Ranchi, India
e-mail: jv.mansi@gmail.com

J48, decision tables (DTs), and random tree (RT) classifiers have all been shown to be effective in predicting faults. On three versions of eclipse datasets, this study investigates and contrasts these supervised machine learning and ensemble classifiers [6–11]. Also, the goal of this study is to help improve the prediction of software modules that are prone to faults by using ensemble algorithms (AdaBoost, gradient boosting machine, and XGBoost) [12].

2   Related Works

Extensive research work has been done out in SFP in recent years for the precise prediction of faults in the early stages of development. The researchers used many machine learning methodologies, and variety of metric measurements to try to enhance the model's performance. The most current research that are relevant to our work are covered in this section.

Laradji et al. [13], presented a two-variant (with and without feature selection) ensemble learning method to give robustness to both data imbalance and feature redundancy with efficient feature selection. The performance of the GFS selection technique, the correlation-based method with its two versions, Fisher's criteria, Pearson's correlation, and the suggested average probability ensemble (APE) learning model (W-SVMs and random forests were used as baseline classifiers) are all taken into account in the experimental design. Eventually, the proposed APE model's classification performance was assessed using six publicly accessible software defect datasets. Finally, the improved version of the suggested model, which coupled APE with greedy forward selection, achieved significantly better AUC values for each dataset. Balogun et al. [14], by using the analytic network process (ANP) multi-criteria decision approach, their research measured the performance of single classifiers (SMO, MLP, kNN, and decision tree) and ensembles (bagging, boosting, stacking, and voting) in software defect prediction. The results demonstrate that ensemble techniques can improve classification outcomes in SDP, with the Boosting method providing the best results. Matloob et al. [15], in their study a software fault prediction framework was offered which used feature selection and ensemble learning approaches. The proposed framework was applied to six publicly accessible NASA MDP datasets. First, for each dataset, the performance of all search techniques inside the framework is compared, and the method with the best score in each performance metric is identified. Second, the suggested framework's findings are compared to the results of ten well-known supervised classification algorithms using all search strategies. The suggested framework outperformed all existing classification methods.

The author in [16] created a majority vote based feature selection algorithm (MVFS) for determining the most important software metrics. The method's central idea was to use a cooperation of feature rankers to discover the most significant software metrics. Experiments indicated that the suggested strategy was able to identify the most important software metrics for improving defect prediction accuracy.

Elahi et al. [17] compared decision trees, logistic regression, naive Bayes, multinomial naive Bayes, and K closest neighbor to the performance of current average ensemble methods such as voting and stacking. Different resampling approaches, such as SMOTE, random under sampling, and random over sampling, are used to address the problem of class imbalance. When compared to alternative ensemble methods, the experimental findings demonstrated that the model averaging technique outperformed. Mangla et al. [18], they presented a sequential ensemble approach for predicting software problems. The performance of the proposed model was assessed using a variety of error measures, including average absolute error, average relative error, and prediction. The obtained findings are positive, indicating that the suggested model is competent.

The author in [9] provided an alternate method for selecting base classifiers for a parallel heterogeneous ensemble. The basic idea was to trim out underperforming classifiers, resulting in a more effective heterogeneous ensemble. To solve this problem, the disparities in efficacy across the ensemble's basic classifiers are used to identify weak classifiers. When compared to other state-of-the-art methodologies, the experimental study proved the effectiveness and superiority of the suggested methodology. Elahi et al. [19], in their study dataset was preprocessed in two stages before the model was trained. After that, four base learners were utilized, and their outputs were ensembled using the model averaging approach. The suggested approach's outcomes were also compared to an existing method for dealing with unbalanced data. Experiments have shown that the suggested approach outperforms the capability of prediction.

3 Methodology

Experiments are carried out in our study utilizing Google Colaboratory notebook, using Python 3.6.9. The following are the proposed work goals:

1. To investigate the effect of ensemble learning technique on Eclipse datasets.
2. Then comparing the performance of ensemble learning technique with other State-of-art machine learning techniques.

3.1 State-Of-Art Classifiers

We utilized four classifiers in this study: J48, decision table, random Tree, and naive Bayes (NB). They were chosen because they have a wide acceptance in the literature for software failure prediction. Using k-fold cross validation ($k = 10$), each of these classifiers is trained and evaluated on the SFP datasets.

3.2   Ensemble Learning Technique

Ensemble techniques are a type of machine learning approach that integrates many base models to create a single optimum prediction model. The objective of each machine learning task is to identify a single model that predicts our desired outcome. Rather than creating a single model and hope it is the best/most accurate predictor possible, ensemble techniques consider a large number of models and average them to generate a single final model. Popular machine learning algorithms like XGBoost, gradient boosting, and AdaBoost are among the approaches used in ensemble learning.

In a nutshell, ensemble learn may sometimes enhance the outcomes of your machine learning by an order of magnitude.

3.3   Boosting and Boosting Algorithms

Boosting is a sequential procedure in which each successive model seeks to fix the preceding model's mistakes on subsets of the data. The models that follow are reliant on the prior model. The boosting algorithm combines a group of weak learners to create a strong learner and improve the overall performance.

Working of boosting is explained below (Fig. 1):

1. The original dataset is divided into subsets.
2. At first, all data points are given the same weight.
3. This subset is used to build a foundation model.
4. This model is applied to the entire dataset to produce predictions.
5. The actual and anticipated numbers are used to compute the errors.
6. Higher weights are assigned to observations that are erroneously anticipated.
7. On the dataset, a new model is constructed, and predictions are produced.

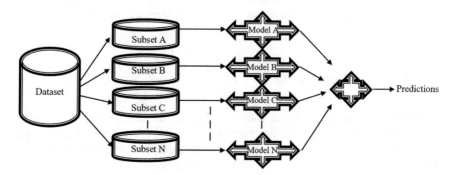

Fig. 1 Working of boosting algorithms

8. Multiple models are produced in the same way, each one fixing the faults of the preceding model.
9. The final model (strong learner) is the weighted mean of all the weak learner models on the whole dataset.

3.3.1 AdaBoost

AdaBoost, or adaptive boosting, is one of the most basic boosting algorithms. Modeling is usually done with decision trees. Multiple sequential models are produced, each one correcting the previous model's faults. AdaBoost provides weights to the observations that are erroneously predicted, and the following model strives to properly forecast these values.

3.3.2 Gradient Boosting (GBM)

Gradient boosting machine learning (GBM) is another ensemble machine learning method that may be used to solve both regression and classification problems. GBM employs the boosting approach, which entails merging several weak learners into a single strong learner. Each succeeding tree in the series is constructed on the mistakes calculated by the preceding tree, with regression trees serving as the base learner.

3.3.3 XGBoost

The gradient boosting technique is enhanced with XGBoost (extreme Gradient Boosting). XGBoost is nearly ten times quicker than other gradient boosting algorithms and has a strong predictive power. It also features several regularization techniques that prevent overfitting and boost overall performance. As a result, the approach is also known as "regularized boosting."

Decision trees with boosted gradient are used in XGBoost, which improves speed and performance. It is largely reliant on the target model's computational speed and performance. Gradient boosted machines are slow to install because model training must be done in a certain order.

4 Results and Discussion

4.1 Datasets

In this study, we have used publically available Eclipse version dataset (Eclipse 2.0, Eclipse 2.1, and Eclipse 3.0). The original Eclipse dataset for all the versions have 202 features. For our study, we have considered 30 features (features with

Table 1 Characteristics of the eclipse datasets

Dataset	Name	Granularity	Features	Instances
Eclipse bug dataset	Eclipse 2.0	File	30	6729
	Eclipse 2.1	File	30	7888
	Eclipse 3.0	File	30	10,593

high feature importance). These features were selected using random forest feature selection technique (Table 1).

4.2 Evaluation Parameters

This section summarizes the experimental results obtained after executing a series of experiments. The suggested framework's outputs are assessed using a variety of metrics, including F-measure/F1-Score, accuracy, precision, and recall. These values are derived from the confusion matrix's parameters. Confusion matrix of size 2*2 is used for binary classification with actual and predicted values on its either axis. It is used to measure the performance of a classification model. Confusion matrix structure is shown below (Fig. 2).

where,

TN is True Negative, FN is False Negative, FP is False Positive, and TP is True Positive

Description about F-measure/F1-Score, Accuracy, Precision, Recall and other evaluation parameters such as True Positive Rate (TPR), True Negative Rate (TNR), False Positive Rate (FPR), and False Negative Rate (FNR) used in this research work.

Precision indicates how many of the instances that were accurately predicted turned out to be positive.

$$\textbf{Precision} = (\textbf{TP})/(\textbf{TP} + \textbf{FP})$$

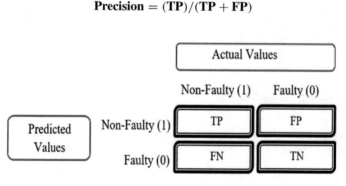

Fig. 2 Confusion matrix

Recall indicates how many of the actual positive cases our model was able to properly anticipate.

$$\text{Recall} = (TP)/(TP + FN)$$

The **F1-score** is a method for examining both recall and precision at the same time. It employs harmonic mean, penalizing extreme values more severely.

$$F1 - Score = (2 * \text{Precision} * \text{Recall})/(\text{Precision} + \text{Recall})$$

The **Accuracy** is used to determine the percentage of values that are properly categorized. It indicates how frequently our classifier is correct.

$$\text{Accuracy} = (TP + TN)/(TP + TN + FP + FN)$$

True Positive Rate (TPR) is known as sensitivity and recall. It is the ratio of true positive and totally positive.

$$TPR = TP/(FN + TP)$$

True Negative Rate (TNR) is known as specificity. It is the ratio of true negative and total negative.

$$TNR = TN/(TN + FP)$$

False Positive Rate (FPR) is known as **Type I error**. It is the ratio of false-positive and total negative.

$$FPR = FP/(TN + FP)$$

False Negative Rate (FNR) is known as **Type II error. It is the ratio of false-negative and totally positive**.

$$FNR = FN/(FN + TP)$$

4.3 Results and Analysis

Tables 2, 3 and 4 presents the performance metrics of all state-of art models and ensemble learning models used over the three datasets. Table 5 presents the confusion matrix analysis for all the three Eclipse datasets.

Table 2 Performance comparison for the eclipse 2.0 dataset

Eclipse 2.0					
Classifier type		Precision	Recall	F-Measure	Accuracy
State-of Art	Naïve Bayes	0.84	0.76	0.79	76.68
	Decision Table	0.82	0.85	0.81	85.80
	J48	*0.85*	0.86	0.82	85.51
	Random Tree	0.78	0.83	0.80	83.23
Ensemble learning	AdaBoost	*0.85*	*0.87*	0.83	86.69
	GBM	*0.85*	*0.87*	0.84	86.56
	XGBoost	*0.85*	*0.87*	*0.92*	**87.11**

Italics means corresponding highest values

Table 3 Performance comparison for the eclipse 2.1 dataset

Eclipse 2.1					
Classifier type	Algorithm	Precision	Recall	F-measure	Accuracy
State-of Art	Naïve Bayes	0.85	0.78	0.81	78.11
	Decision Table	0.87	*0.89*	0.85	88.90
	J48	0.78	0.88	0.83	88.32
	Random Tree	0.81	0.87	0.84	87.15
Ensemble Learning	AdaBoost	*0.89*	*0.89*	*0.89*	89.17
	GBM	0.87	*0.89*	0.85	89.09
	XGBoost	0.85	*0.89*	0.84	**89.19**

Italics means corresponding highest values

Table 4 Performance comparison for the eclipse 3.0 dataset

Eclipse 3.0					
Classifier type	Algorithm	Precision	Recall	F-measure	Accuracy
State-of Art	Naïve Bayes	0.83	0.75	0.78	75.83
	Decision Table	0.83	0.85	*0.85*	85.19
	J48	0.82	085	0.81	84.69
	Random Tree	0.77	0.83	0.79	83.13
Ensemble learning	AdaBoost	0.80	0.85	0.79	85.23
	GBM	0.82	0.85	0.81	85.24
	XGBoost	*0.84*	*0.86*	0.82	**85.98**

Italics means corresponding highest values

Table 5 Confusion matrix analysis for eclipse dataset

Algorithm	Eclipse 2.0				Eclipse 2.1				Eclipse 3.0			
	TPR	TNR	FPR	FNR	TPR	TNR	FPR	FNR	TPR	TNR	FPR	FNR
Naïve Bayes	0.33	0.87	0.12	0.66	0.24	0.91	0.09	0.75	0.32	*0.92*	*0.07*	0.67
Decision table	0.56	0.86	0.13	0.43	*0.67*	0.89	0.10	*0.32*	0	0.85	0.14	0
J48	0.57	0.82	0.11	0.40	0	0.88	0.11	0	1	0.84	0.15	0
Random tree	0.31	0.86	0.13	0.68	0.18	0.89	0.10	0.81	0.30	0.86	0.13	0.69
AdaBoost	0.67	0.87	0.12	0.32	0	0.89	0.10	0	0.52	0.85	0.14	0.47
GBM	0.68	0.87	0.12	0.31	0.63	0.89	0.10	0.36	0.60	0.86	0.13	0.40
XGBoost	*0.71*	*0.92*	*0.07*	*0.28*	0.53	*0.93*	*0.06*	0.46	*0.65*	0.86	0.13	*0.34*

Italics means corresponding highest values

In Table 2, XGBoost gave the best accuracy result of 87.11% followed by AdaBoost and GBM with 86.69% and 86.56%, respectively. Based on F-measure, the ensemble methods performed better than single classifiers with XGBoost with 0.92 followed by AdaBoost and GBM with 0.84 and 0.83, respectively. Recall is high for all the three ensemble classifier with the value 0.87, whereas precision is good for AdaBoost, GBM, XGBoost, and J48 with the value 0.85.

In Table 3, XGBoost gave the best accuracy result of 87.19% followed by AdaBoost and GBM with 89.17% and 89.09% respectively. Based on F-measure, recall, and precision the ensemble method AdaBoost performed better than other classifiers with the value 0.89.

In Table 4, XGBoost gave the best accuracy result of 85.98 followed by GBM and AdaBoost with 85.24 and 85.23, respectively. Based on precision and recall, the ensemble methods performed better than single classifiers. But, the decision table classifier gave best result in case of F-measure with the value 0.85.

For a higher performance, TPR and TNR should be high, whereas FNR and FPR should be low. From Table 5, it is observed that in all the three ensemble classifier TPR and TNR is higher and FNR and FPR is low. When ensemble classifiers are compared with other classifiers then it is observed that in Eclipse 2.0, XGBoost has high TPR and TNR and low FNR and FPR. Similarly, in Eclipse 2.1, decision tree have high TPR and low FNR, also XGBoost have high TNR and low FPR. In Eclipse 3.0, naïve Bayes have high TNR and low FPR, also XGBoost have high TPR and low FNR. So, by analyzing confusion matrix it can be concluded that ensemble classifier XGBoost outperforms in most of the cases.

Figures 3, 4, 5 and 6 displays the performance comparison of all state-of-art classifier and ensemble classifier in terms precision, recall, f-measure, and accuracy. Almost in all the cases, ensemble classifiers outperformed all the other classifiers in predicting software fault in Eclipse dataset.

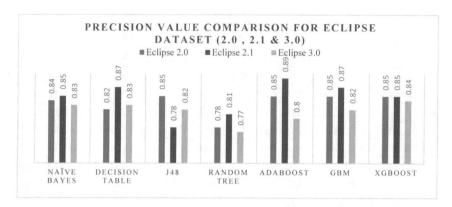

Fig. 3 Precision value comparison of different ML models on Eclipse 2.0 dataset

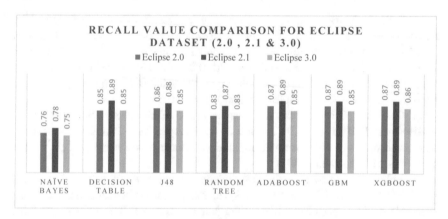

Fig. 4 Recall value comparison of different ML models on Eclipse 2.0 dataset

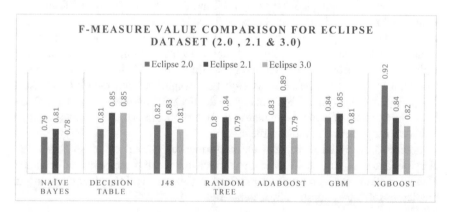

Fig. 5 F-Measure value comparison of different ML models on Eclipse 2.0 dataset

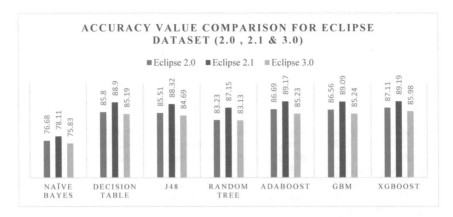

Fig. 6 Accuracy value comparison of different ML models on Eclipse 2.0 dataset

5 Conclusion and Future Scope

In this paper, an attempt has been made to test the efficiency of ensemble classifiers over state-of art classifiers in predicting software faults. For study, experiments are carried out utilizing Google Colaboratory notebook, using Python 3.6.9. A comparative analysis has been made between naïve Bayes, decision Table, J48, random tree, AdaBoost, GBM, and XGBoost. Accuracy, F1 scores, precision, and recall are four frequently used measures for performance assessment. From Table 2, it is observed that for Eclipse 2.0, XGBoost performed well for all performance measures. From Table 3, we can conclude that accuracy is good for XGBoost and AdaBoost performed well in terms of precision, recall, and f-measure. Similarly, from Table 4, for Eclipse 3.0 dataset, XGBoost gave high results for accuracy, precision, and recall, whereas decision table performed better in terms of f-measure. From Table 5, it is observed that in all the three ensemble classifier TPR and TNR is higher and FNR and FPR is low. So, it can be concluded that ensemble techniques can improve classification outcomes in SFP as compared to other classifiers, with the XGBoost method providing the best results in most of the cases.

In terms of future scope, we extend our work by incorporating other feature selection techniques for selecting features from Eclipse dataset. Also, the fault prediction will be made by using deep learning models such as convolutional neural network (ConvoNet), recurrent neural network (RNN), and long short-term memory (LSTM).

References

1. Moeyersoms J, Junqu E, Dejaeger K, Baesens B, Martens D (2015) Comprehensible software fault and effort prediction: a data mining approach. J Syst Softw 100:80–90 (Feb 2015)
2. Jiang Y, Cukicc B, Menzies (2007) Fault prediction using early lifecycle data. In: Proceedings of 17th IEEE international symposium on software reliability. Sweden, pp 237–246

3. Azeem N, Usmani S (2011) Defect Prediction Leads to High Quality Product. J Softw Eng Appl 4(11):639–645
4. Gao K, Khoshgoftaar TM, Wang H, Seliya N (2011) Choosing software metrics for defect prediction: an investigation on feature selection techniques. Softw Practice Experience 41(5):579–606
5. Perreault L, Berardinelli S, Izurieta C, Sheppard J (2017) Using classifiers for software defect detection. In: 26th international conference on software engineering and data engineering. Sydney, 2–4, 2–4 Oct 2017
6. Alsaeedi A, Khan MZ (2019) Software defect prediction using supervised machine learning and ensemble techniques: a comparative study. J Softw Eng Appl 12(05):85–100
7. Rathore SS, Kumar S (2020) An empirical study of ensemble techniques for software fault prediction. Appl Intell 51(6):3615–3644
8. Pandey SK, Mishra RB, Tripathi AK (2020) BPDET: An effective software bug prediction model using deep representation and ensemble learning techniques. Expert Syst Appl 144:113085
9. Alshdaifat E, Malak Al-H, Aloqaily A (2021) Effective heterogeneous ensemble classification: an alternative approach for selecting base classifiers. ICT Express 7(3):342–349, Sep 2021
10. Ansari AA, Iqbal A, Sahoo B (2020) Heterogeneous defect prediction using ensemble learning technique. In: Artificial intelligence and evolutionary computations in engineering systems, pp 283–293
11. Aljamaan H, Alazba A (2020) Software defect prediction using tree-based ensembles. In: 16th ACM international conference on predictive models and data analytics in software engineering, Nov 2020
12. Mehta S, Patnaik KS (2021) Improved prediction of software defects using ensemble machine learning techniques. Neural Comput Appl 33(16):10551–10562
13. Laradji IH, Alshayeb M, Ghouti L (2015) Software defect prediction using ensemble learning on selected features. Inf Softw Technol 58:388–402
14. Balogun AO, Bajeh AO, Orie VA, Yusuf-Asaju AW (2018) Software defect prediction using ensemble learning: an ANP based evaluation method. FUOYE J Eng Technol 3(2), Sep 2018
15. Matloob F, Aftab S, Iqbal A (2019) A framework for software defect prediction using feature selection and ensemble learning techniques. Int J Mod Educ Comput Sci 11(12):14–20
16. Borandag E, Ozcift A, Kilinc D, Yucalar F (2019) Majority vote feature selection algorithm in software fault prediction. Comput Sci Inf Syst 16(2):515–539
17. Elahi E, Kanwal S, Asif AN (2020) A new ensemble approach for software fault prediction. In: 2020 17th international Bhurban conference on applied sciences and technology (IBCAST), Jan 2020
18. Mangla M, Sharma N, Mohanty SN (2021) A sequential ensemble model for software fault prediction. Innovations Syst Softw Eng Mar 2021
19. Elahi E, Ayub A, Hussain I (2021) Two staged data preprocessing ensemble model for software fault prediction. In: 2021 international Bhurban conference on applied sciences and technologies (IBCAST), Jan 2021

A Machine Learning Approach for Detection of Breast Cancer in Women Using Advanced GLCM

L. Kanya Kumari⊙ and B. Naga Jagadesh⊙

1 Introduction

Our body contains a huge number of cells that are assigned specific jobs. The cells die if they are worn out or damaged, and the new cells are automatically generated. If the cells grow abnormally, it will lead to cancer [1]. There are nearly 120 types of cancers. The most common cancers are breast cancer, cervical cancer, kidney cancer, and lung cancer, etc. [2]. A computer-aided diagnosis (CAD) uses image processing techniques, computer software's, and efficient tools to retrieve medical information [3]. So, an automated CAD system is required for mammogram classification [4]. The main modules in any CADx system are image acquisition, feature extraction, and classification. The system starts with acquiring images, and then, the features are retrieved using the feature extraction technique. These extracted features are classified using different classifiers. Many CAD systems are proposed by different researchers to improve the BC detection rate. The problem with the existing CAD systems is low classification accuracy which is a research gap from the literature. To improve the accuracy, a novel intelligent system is proposed which extracts texture, intensity, and shape information from mammogram image classification as intensity and shape of the tumor are also important including texture to detect the abnormalities [5]. These features are given to artificial neural networks (ANN) to classify images into normal or abnormal, and the results are compared with KNN, SVM, and RF. Designing an optimal neural network is critical because of optimal parameters

L. Kanya Kumari (✉)
Department of Computer Science & Engineering, Koneru Lakshmaiah Education Foundation, Vaddeswaram, Guntur District, Andhra Pradesh, India
e-mail: kanyabtech@yahoo.com

B. Naga Jagadesh
School of Computer Science and Engineering, VIT-AP University, Amaravathi, Andhra Pradesh, India

R. Doriya et al. (eds.), *Machine Learning, Image Processing, Network Security and Data Sciences*, Lecture Notes in Electrical Engineering 946,
https://doi.org/10.1007/978-981-19-5868-7_8
89

which can be decided based on different experiments. The proposed CAD system aims at diagnosing mammograms in a better way. The key points in our proposed methodology are as follows:

1. Acquire the images from MIAS dataset.
2. Texture-, shape-, and intensity-based features are retrieved by using AGLCM.
3. These features are classified by ANN classifier, and the results are compared with other classifiers and the state-of-the-art methods [9, 15, 19].

The remaining paper discusses the following: Sect. 2 designates literature work; the proposed framework is described in Sect. 3 that contains subsections: feature extraction and classification. The experimental results are presented in Sect. 4, and the conclusion is mentioned.

2   Related Work

Recently, researchers have focused on BC detection by using mammograms. This section discusses a few CAD systems that are developed by researchers in recent years.

The authors [6] used a shape-based feature extraction technique and evolved that the features in the image are dependent on the pre-segmented images to analyze the medical images. The authors [7] have extracted texture features from mammograms. They applied the gray-level co-occurrence matrix (GLCM) and then segmented it to identify the part affected by the disease. In [8], the authors concentrated on detecting microcalcifications in mammogram images and they extracted textual, statistical, and structural features. They concluded that pre-processing is requisite to extract the features to reduce noise, sharpen edges, and remove backgrounds which lead to better feature extraction. They concluded that the spherical wavelet transforms with an SVM classifier gives better results [9].

The authors [10] used Bethezata General Hospital database and a public dataset called MIAS. For feature extraction, they employed GLCM, Gabor filters, and CNN. The authors concluded that Gabor and CNN features with MLP classifier outperform well for mammogram classification.

In [11], the images in the DDSM dataset images were pre-processed by Gaussian filtering for smoothening purposes. GLCM and gray-level run length matrix (GLRLM) methods were used for feature extraction and given to the neural network with backpropagation. Performance was measured with receiver operating characteristic curve (ROC). They achieved sensitivity and specificity as 98%, 97.8%, respectively.

The authors segmented the images using the region growing technique [12]. In this, more features were extracted by using shape, statistical features, and wavelet transform. These features were fed to multi-layer perceptron, and the performance was measured using ROC and AUC.

The authors [13] designed a model called the CLAHE image enhancement technique to increase the contrast. A modified fuzzy C-means clustering was used for classification. In [14], DDSM images were classified using an SVM classifier based on taxonomic diversity and distinctness texture features, and 98.88% accuracy was achieved. In [15], the authors used several pre-processing techniques and Fourier transforms, and weighted Fourier Transforms were used for feature extraction, PCA for feature selection, and SVM for classification and concluded that they have achieved better results than other state-of-the-art methods.

The authors [16] have classified DDSM mammogram images based on the features like circularity, root mean square slope, fractal dimension and root mean square slope. The extracted features were fed to ANN, KNN, and SVM, and it was concluded that SVM with root mean square slope (RMS) gives better accuracy than compared to other classifiers. The authors concluded that it was not possible to select one technique as the best feature extraction for finding breast tissues [17]. They extracted local binary patterns and curvelet transforms features for better features, and similar features were removed by statistical ANalysis Of VAriance called ANOVA. The selected features were given as input to polynomial classifier (PL), decision tree, and random forest and concluded that PL gives better results than other classifiers to classify DDSM images.

The authors [18] extracted texture-based and statistical-based features and were given as input to SVM and RF and concluded that RF gives better results.

The authors [19] designed a methodology for mammogram classification. They have used CLAHE as a pre-processing technique and histogram of oriented gradients (HOG) for feature extraction, and RF is used as a classifier. They obtained a classification accuracy of 66%.

From the above literature, it is observed that to classify mammogram images, feature extraction and machine learning algorithms are important. So, we proposed a novel CAD system that extracts texture-, intensity-, and shape-based features called AGLCM. Because of this, the AGLCM approach is proposed for mammogram classification to classify into normal or abnormal using classification algorithms.

3 Proposed Methodology

The CAD system proposed in this paper is a 3-step process: image acquisition, feature extraction, and classification. The framework is depicted in Fig. 1.

Initially, the mammogram images are taken as input. Features are extracted using AGLCM and classified using ANN classifier.

Fig. 1 Proposed CAD system framework for mammogram classification

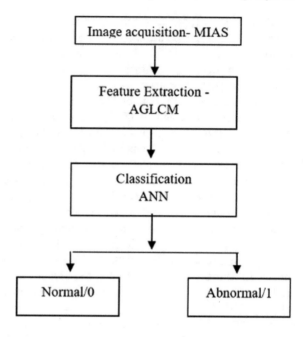

3.1 *Image Acquisition*

There are number of imaging techniques for breast cancer detection. They are like MRI magnetic resonance imaging (MRI), positron emission tomography (PET), X-ray, CT-scan (computed tomography), and ultrasound. Among all these X-ray (mammograms) modality is good to detect BC in early stages. The dataset used for experiments is namely MIAS. This image dataset contains 322 Gy-scale images [20]. The dataset is partitioned into 70%, 30% training and testing data, respectively. The sample images from MIAS dataset mdb006, mdb007, mdb008, and mdb009 are represented in Fig. 2.

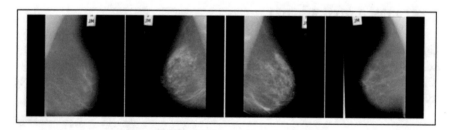

Fig. 2 Sample images from MIAS dataset

3.2 Advanced Gray-Level Co-occurrence Matrix

The MIAS mammogram image features are extracted based on the AGLCM approach. An AGLCM is a novel feature extraction technique that extracts texture-, intensity, and shape-based features as these are crucial to identify the abnormality in the tumor. The texture is a significant characteristic in a mammogram image. It is a spatial distribution of gray levels in an image. The texture shows both pixel values and its neighborhood. To extract the texture features, there are several techniques which are available in the literature. Among all, the gray-level co-occurrence matrix (GLCM) is a widely used technique in the prediction of BC [21]. A matrix form of gray values is represented called co-occurrence matrix (CM). The two adjacent pixels are separated by a distance 'd' and assume that the probability occurrence of gray-level pixel intensity 'i' (called reference pixel) in the adjacent pixel of intensity 'j' at a distance 'd' in 8 directions 'θ' ($0°, 45°, 90°, 135°, 180°, 225°, 270°,$ and $315°$) is calculated. But mostly the directions considered are ($0°$—horizontal, $45°$—bottom left to top right, $90°$—vertical, and $135°$—top left to bottom right). 8 directions of the co-occurrence matrix are represented in Fig. 3.

The block diagram of GLCM technique is represented in Fig. 4.

The GLCM features are calculated from co-occurrence matrices. The features calculated are energy, homogeneity, correlation, dissimilarity, and contrast. The energy feature measures the textual uniformity, i.e., pixel pair repetitions. Homogeneity measures the certainty of the dissemination of pixel values from the co-occurrence matrix. Correlation measures the dependency of gray levels which are present adjacently. Dissimilarity is the distance between the pair of pixels in the region of interest (ROI). Contrast measures the spatial frequency of an image. These are represented in the following Eqs. 1–5. The GLCM texture feature performs well in the early detection of breast cancer [22]. These 5 properties are calculated in 4

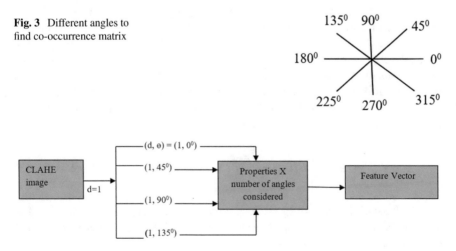

Fig. 3 Different angles to find co-occurrence matrix

Fig. 4 Block diagram of GLCM technique

different angles ($0°$, $45°$, $90°$, and $135°$) with distance $d = 1$ and obtained 20 feature vector. Including the GLCM texture feature, we also considered the image entropy. It is an intensity-based measure in any gray image. Low entropy value significance is that image is less contrast [23]. This is calculated using Eq. 6 and is added GLCM texture feature vector. So, a total of 21 features are extracted.

$$\text{Energy} = \sum_{u,v}^{n} p_{uv}^2 \quad \text{where } p_{ij} = \text{element } u, v(2 \text{ samples of intensities}) \quad (1)$$

$$\text{Homogeneity} = \sum_{u,v}^{n} \frac{P_{uv}}{1 + (u - v)^2} \tag{2}$$

$$\text{Correlation} = \sum_{u,v=1}^{n} \frac{(u - m)(v - m)}{s^2}, \text{ where } m \sum_{u,v=1}^{n} u P_{uv} \text{ and}$$

$$s^2 = \sum_{u,v=1}^{n} P_{uv}(1 - m)^2 \tag{3}$$

$$\text{Dissimilarity} = \sum_i \sum_j |u - v| p(u, v) \tag{4}$$

$$\text{Contrast} = \sum_{u,v=1}^{n} p_{uv}(u - v)^2 \tag{5}$$

$$\text{Entropy} = \sum_{u,v=0}^{n-1} -\ln(p_{uv}) p_{uv} \tag{6}$$

Including the above GLCM texture and intensity features, we also considered shape-based feature and is calculated by using Fourier descriptor (FD). An FD is a robust shape descriptor that describes the boundary of the shape of an image [24]. Shape description can be easily calculated using FDs. FD can be attained by using Fourier transform on a shape signature. Fourier transformation technique is proven as successful in the detection of BC, and these are invariable to translation, scaling, and rotation, and also this technique is useful to get the time–frequency spectrum [25, 26]. This can be represented in Eq. 7.

$$F(k) = \frac{1}{D} \sum_{x=0}^{D-1} C(i) \times e^{\left(\frac{-j2\pi xk}{D}\right)} \text{ where, } k = 0, 1, 2 \ldots D - 1 \tag{7}$$

The statistical analysis of FD is done by finding the mean of the descriptor. The mean of this FD is added to the above feature vector. The final 22 features vector is used for mammogram classification.

3.3 Classification

There are different machine learning algorithms for classification. In this paper, we used the ANN algorithm, and the results are compared with other techniques such as KNN, RF, and SVM [27]. ANN is the most powerful classification algorithm that behaves like human brain neurons [28]. Hence, it plays an important role in medical diagnosis [12]. A neural network (NN) is a graph that consists of nodes and is associated with edges. The edge in the network is associated with weight. By using these weights and bias values, an activation function is calculated. This is not only used for classification but also used for regression. A NN has three layers called the input layer, hidden layer, and output layer. The feature vector $(x_1, x_2 \ldots, x_n)$ is given to the input layer. These input and weights $(w_1, w_2, \ldots, w_n)$ are given as input to the hidden layers. The output layer generates the output-based weights and hidden units.

4 Experimental Results and Discussion

To validate our CAD model, we used Window 10 operating system, 4 GB RAM, i5 processor with 500 GB hard disk, and Python is used. The benchmark image dataset, namely MIAS, is used for our experiment. By using the AGLCM technique, 22 features are extracted. These features are represented in Table 1.

After extracting the AGLCM features, the classification experiments are done on the MIAS dataset using the ANN technique, and the results are compared with other techniques, namely KNN, SVM, and RF [29]. For these experiments, 70% of the MIAS images are considered as training and 30% as the testing data. These classifiers predict the class label of the image either normal or abnormal (0-normal and 1-abnormal). The success of the experiments is evaluated by a confusion matrix. Diagrammatically, the confusion matrix is represented in Table 2.

where TPS is the true positives that represents sick people are diagnosed correctly
   FPS is the false positives that represents healthy people are incorrectly diagnosed
   TNS is the true negatives that represents healthy people diagnosed correctly
   FNS is the false negatives that represents sick people diagnosed incorrectly

The important metrics calculated from the confusion matrix are sensitivity (also called recall), specificity, precision, accuracy, $f1$-score, and accuracy to measure the classifier performance [30]. These are calculated by using the Equations 8–12 as mentioned below.

$$\text{Sensitivity} = \frac{\text{TPS}}{\text{TPS} + \text{FNS}} \tag{8}$$

$$\text{Specificity} = \frac{\text{TNS}}{\text{FPS} + \text{TNS}} \tag{9}$$

Table 1 AGLCM features for MIAS mammogram images

Image number	Dissimilarity				Energy				Homogeneity			
	$\theta = 0°$	$\theta = 45°$	$\theta = 90°$	$\theta = 135°$	$\theta = 0°$	$\theta = 45°$	$\theta = 90°$	$\theta = 135°$	$\theta = 0°$	$\theta = 45°$	$\theta = 90°$	$\theta = 135°$
mdb006	6.596	7.446	6.375	6.588	0.371	0.372	0.377	0.372	0.498	0.494	0.531	0.498
mdb007	10.291	11.101	8.430	10.041	0.158	0.159	0.168	0.159	0.381	0.370	0.444	0.374
mdb008	4.798	5.337	4.201	4.639	0.394	0.395	0.402	0.395	0.653	0.648	0.694	0.652
mdb009	5.122	5.033	4.705	5.531	0.476	0.477	0.482	0.477	0.633	0.632	0.664	0.634

Image number	Correlation				Contrast				Entropy	Fourier descriptor mean
	$\theta = 0°$	$\theta = 45°$	$\theta = 90°$	$\theta = 135°$	$\theta = 0°$	$\theta = 45°$	$\theta = 90°$	$\theta = 135°$		
mdb006	0.977	0.974	0.983	0.978	230.558	265.601	170.309	220.205	35.8513	152.623
mdb007	0.957	0.957	0.98	0.962	550.177	551.748	260.235	489.901	44.046	163.07
mdb008	0.971	0.968	0.982	0.974	216.12	242.102	138.1	195.611	30.384	162.802
mdb009	0.976	0.979	0.985	0.975	200.333	174.658	131.527	213.355	28.99	157.133

Table 2 Confusion matrix

Category		Predicted class label	
		Predicted as having disease	Predicted as not having disease
Actual class label	Yes/patient having disease	TPS	FNS
	No/patient not having disease	FPS	TNS

Table 3 Performance of different classifiers

Feature extraction technique	Classifier	Sensitivity (%)	Specificity (%)	Precision (%)	F1-score (%)	Accuracy (%)
AGLCM	KNN	88.6	87.7	86.6	87.6	88.1
	SVM	88.3	86.0	84.4	86.3	87.0
	RF	90.0	91.4	91.8	90.9	90.7
	ANN	95.3	89.5	89.1	92.1	92.3

$$\text{Precision} = \frac{TPS}{TPS + FPS} \tag{10}$$

$$f1 - \text{score} = \frac{2 \times \text{Precision} \times \text{Senstivity}}{\text{Precision} + \text{Sensivity}} \tag{11}$$

$$\text{Accuracy} = \frac{TPS + TNS}{TPS + FPS + TNS + FNS} \tag{12}$$

where sensitivity is true positives rate, specificity is a total of true negatives, precision measures the accuracy of positive predictions, and $f1$-score is a harmonic mean of precision and sensitivity. The performance measures are evaluated for several classifiers such as KNN, SVM, RF, and ANN with AGLCM features. The results for AGLCM + KNN, AGLCM + SVM, AGLCM + RF, and AGLCM + ANN are 88.1%, 87.0%, 90.7%, and 92.3%, respectively. The experimental results are described in Table 3 and graphically in Fig. 5.

The above results shows that AGLCM features with ANN classifier performs well than other classifiers in mammogram classification.

5 Conclusion

In our study of research, an improved CAD system is proposed to meet the challenges in mammogram image classification. The proposed framework is a 3-step process.

Table 4 Comparative results with state-of-the-art methods

Reference No.	Feature extraction technique	Accuracy (%)
[9]	Spherical wavelet transform	88.8
[15]	Weighted type fractional-Fourier transform	92.16
[19]	Histogram of oriented gradients	66
Proposed method	Advanced GLCM	92.3

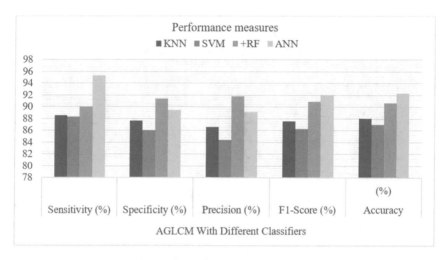

Fig. 5 Comparison of different classifiers with the proposed feature extraction technique. The results are also compared with the state-of-the-art methods represented in Table 4.

Initially, the mammogram images are acquired and the features are extracted using the AGLCM which extracts texture-, intensity-, and shape-based features. These features are given as input to the ANN. To estimate the effectiveness of the framework, the experiments are done on the MIAS dataset. The performance is measures using sensitivity, specificity, precision, $f1$-score, and accuracy. The better accuracy is obtained for the AGLCM feature extraction technique with ANN classifier. There are some future directions that may increase the accuracy. They are: the accuracy of our CAD system can be improved by pre-processing the images, apply the method on large databases, the optimal features are to be chosen from the extracted features for better classification by using meta-heuristic techniques.

References

1. Cancer.org. Last accessed 7 July 2021
2. Cancer.net. Last accessed 8 July 2021
3. Mohnaty, Rup S, Dash B et al (2019) Mammogram classification using contourlet features with forest optimization based feature selection approach. Multi med Tools Appl 78:12805–12834
4. Gupta S, Chyn PF, Markey MK (2006) Breast cancer cadx based on bi-rads descriptors from two mammographic views. Med Phys 33:1810–1817
5. Hossain T, Shishir FS, Ashraf M, Al Nasim MA, Muhammad Shah F (2019) Brain tumor detection using convolutional neural network. In: Proceedings of the 1st international conference on advances in science, engineering and robotics technology, pp 1–6
6. Liu J, Shi Y (2011) Image feature extraction method based on shape characteristics and its application in medical image analysis. In: Proceedings of the applied informatics and communication, pp 172–178
7. Pradeep S, Malliga L (2014) Content based image retrieval and segmentation of medical image database with fuzzy values. In: Proceedings of the international conference on information communication and embedded systems
8. Sharma M, Dubey R, Sujata, Gupta SK (2012) Feature extraction of mammograms. Int J Adv Comput Res 2:192–199
9. Ganesan K, Acharya UR, Chua K, Lim C, Thomas A (2013) Automated diagnosis of mammogram images of breast cancer using discrete wavelet transform and spherical wavelet transform features: A comparative study. Technology in cancer research & treatment. Int J Adv Comput Res 213:2–5
10. Debelee TG et al (2019) Classification of mammograms using texture and CNN based extracted features. J Biomimetics Biomater Biomed Eng 42:79–97
11. Punitha S, Amuthan A, Suresh Joseph K (2018) Benign and malignant breast cancer segmentation using optimized region growing technique. Future Comput Inform J 3:48–358
12. Danala G et al (2018) Classification of breast masses using a computer-aided diagnosis scheme of contrast enhanced digital mammograms. Ann Biomed Eng 46:1419–1431
13. Srivastava S et al (2014) A combined approach for the enhancement and segmentation of mammograms using modified fuzzy C-means method in wavelet domain. J Med Phys 39(3):169–83
14. de Oliveira FSS et al (2015) Classification of breast regions as mass and non-mass based on digital mammograms using taxonomic indexes and SVM. Comput Biol Med 57:42–53
15. Zhang Y-D et al (2016) Computer-aided diagnosis of abnormal breasts in mammogram images by weighted-type fractional Fourier transform. Adv Mech Eng 8(2):1–11
16. Beura S et al (2015) Mammogram classification using two dimensional discrete wavelet transform and gray-level co-occurrence matrix for detection of breast cancer. Neurocomputing 54(22):1–14
17. Peng W, Mayorga RV, Hussein EMA (2016) An automated confirmatory system for analysis of mammograms. Comput Methods Programs Biomed 125:134–144
18. Dong M, Lu X, Ma Y, Guo Y, Ma Y, Wang K (2015) An efficient approach for automated mass segmentation and classification in mammograms. J Digit Imaging 28(5):613–625
19. Bektaş B, Emre İE, Kartal E, Gulsecen S (2018) Classification of mammography images by machine learning techniques. In: 3rd international conference on computer science and engineering, pp 580–585
20. Suckling J et al (2015) The mammographic image analysis society digital mammogram database excerpta medica. In: International congress series, v1 21, pp 375–378
21. Parekh R (2012) Using texture analysis for medical diagnosis. IEEE MultiMedia 19(2):28–37
22. Sathish D et al (2016) Medical imaging techniques and computer aided diagnostic approaches for the detection of breast cancer with an emphasis on thermography—a review. Int J Med Eng Inform 8(3):275–299
23. Mahdi J (2015) Application of GLCM technique on mammograms for early detection of breast cancer

24. Wang P, Patel VM (2017) Extracting Fourier descriptors from compressive measurements. In: IEEE international conference on acoustics, speech and signal processing (ICASSP), pp 4755–4759
25. Tarique M, ElZahra F, Hateem A, Hasan M (2015) Fourier transform based early detection of breast cancer by mammogram image processing. J Biomed Eng Med Imag 2:17–31
26. Ahonen T, Matas J, He C, Pietikäinen M (2009) Rotation invariant image description with local binary pattern histogram Fourier features. In: Salberg AB, Hardeberg JY, Jenssen R (eds) Image analysis. Lecture notes in computer science, vol 5575. Springer, Berlin, Heidelberg
27. Breiman L (2001) Random forests. Mach Learn 45:5–32
28. Pratiwi M, Alexander, Harefa J, Nanda S (2015) Mammograms classification using gray-level co-occurrence matrix and radial basis function neural network. Proc Comput Sci 59:83–91
29. Janakiramaiah B, Kalyani G (2021) Dementia detection using the deep convolution neural network method. In: Hybrid computational intelligence for pattern analysis, trends in deep learning methodologies. Academic Press, pp 157–181
30. Kalyani G, Janakiramaiah B, Karuna A et al (2021) Diabetic retinopathy detection and classification using capsule networks. Complex Intell Syst

Sales Prediction Using ARIMA, Facebook's Prophet and XGBoost Model of Machine Learning

Sushila Ratre and Jyotsna Jayaraj

1 Introduction

Sales forecasting is the estimation of the number of sales expected for a future period of time [1]. According to the American Marketing Association sales forecast is "an estimate of sales, in dollar or physical units for a specified future period under a proposed marketing plan and under an assumed set of economic and other forces outside unit for which the forecast is made". The sales forecast may be for a specified product of for the entire product line or it can be for the market as a whole or any portion of it. The sales forecast serves as the foundation for sound budgeting. Sales forecasting is used to determine financial planning, working capital needs, plant growth, and other requirements. The sales forecast is used to schedule all manufacturing, including manpower, raw material purchases, and calculating the rate of output.

Predicting sales is a difficult job for researchers because it is a dynamic operation. It encompasses information from a variety of fields. The ability to forecast atmospheric parameters is difficult.

Time series data is usually used for estimation. A time series is a set of observable values of a single object taken at various points in time. With the advancement in data collection, massive volumes of data have been obtained, making manual processing difficult. This is where time series processing must be automated and new computational mechanisms must be used.

Present Address:
S. Ratre
Department of Computer Science and Engineering, Bharati Vidyapeeth Deemed University
Department of Engineering and Technology, Navi Mumbai, India
e-mail: sratre@bvucoep.edu.in

J. Jayaraj (✉)
Business Intelligence Unit, Axis Bank Ltd., Bangalore, India
e-mail: jyotsna.jayaraj@axisbank.com

There are generally two types of forecasting problems: short-term forecasting and long-term forecasting. This is based upon the nature of the industry for which we are making the forecasts. For example, the fashion industry necessitates short-term forecasting since new trends emerge regularly. In the case of steel plantation, long-term forecasting is possible since only a few industrial shifts must be taken into account over time. We should look at the Rossmann drug store chain's sales forecast in this context. Given the pharmaceutical industry is dynamic and is affected by developments in the field, we may infer that short-term forecasting is needed in this case.

2 Literature Review

2.1 Sales Forecasting Newspaper with ARIMA: A Case Study

The ARIMA model is more versatile in implementation and more precise in the accuracy of the simulative or predictive effects than the early Autoregressive (AR), Moving Average (MA) and Autoregressive Moving Average (ARMA) models. In the ARIMA model, a defined underlying process is created using observations from a time series to provide a good model that accurately depicts the process-generating mechanism. For a real case study of a newspaper business in Surakarta, the autoregressive integrated moving average (ARIMA) models were used to estimate the correct number of newspapers [2]. The maximum likelihood approach was used to find the model parameters. When predicting the number of newspapers, the ARIMA (1, 1, 0) model can be recommended.

2.2 Forecasting of Demand Using ARIMA Model

A time series approach to model and estimate demand in a food sector shows how past market data can be used to predict potential demand, as well as how these predictions impact the supply chain. Using the Box-Jenkins time series method, historical demand data was used to construct many autoregressive integrated moving average (ARIMA) models, and the best model was chosen on four output criteria: Akaike parameter, Schwarz Bayesian criterion, maximum probability, and standard error [3]. The chosen model was ARIMA (1, 0, 1).

2.3 Application of Facebook's Prophet Algorithm for Successful Sales Forecasting Based on Real-World Data

The proposed system demonstrated its ability to generate reasonably accurate monthly and quarterly sales predictions by testing its success in a real-world use case scenario: on a monthly basis, approximately 50% of the product portfolio can be forecasted with MAPE less than 30%, and on a quarterly basis, approximately 70% can be forecasted with MAPE less than 30% (of which 40% with MAPE less than 15) [4].

2.4 An Advanced Sales Forecasting System XGBoost Algorithm

Data mining techniques such as Linear Regression, Random Forest Regression, and XGBoost were analyzed. With efficacy being the way forward in many businesses today, the goal is to expand the solution to assist stores in improving productivity and increasing revenue by using Data Analysis. The weighted average of Random Forest yield and XGBoost yields a better result than individual estimates [5].

2.5 Retail Store Predictions

Linear regression, ridge regression, lasso regression, ensemble strategies, decision tree regression, and XGB regression are some of the sales forecasting models that were used in the research [6]. The Root Mean Square Error (RMSE) is used to calculate the prediction accuracy because of the nature of the problem. XGBoost is an excellent tool for building supervised regression models.

3 Proposed Methodology

The first step of data acquisition was done by accessing the pre-collected dataset of the Rossmann store dataset via Kaggle. The quantity and quality of the data determines the accuracy of our model.

Data preparation includes the wrangling of data and preparing it for training. From the Rossmann store dataset, missing values and outliers were removes. In this step, it is also common to visualize he data to understand relevant relationships between fields [7]. Data visualization and exploration of the Rossmann store dataset (Fig. 1).

Fig. 1 Steps in developing machine learning model

For this project, three models have been chosen to compare their performance: ARIMA Model, Prophet Model, and XGBoost Model. They are then trained, evaluated, hyper-parameter tuned and tested.

3.1 ARIMA Model

ARIMA, or Autoregressive Integrated Moving Average, is one of the most commonly used univariate time series data forecasting approaches. While the system can handle data with a trend, time series with a seasonal dimension are not supported.

SARIMA is an ARMA extension that allows for direct simulation of the seasonal portion of the sequence. Seasonal ARIMA (SARIMA) is an extension of ARIMA that specifically supports univariate time series data with a seasonal aspect.

It introduces three hyper-parameters for the seasonal portion of the series: autoregression (AR), differencing (I), and moving average (MA), as well as an additional parameter for the seasonality cycle. Selecting hyper-parameters for both the trend and seasonal elements of the series is needed when configuring a SARIMA.

There are three aspects of the trend that must be configured. They are the same as in the ARIMA model, and they are: 'p' as trend auto-regression order, 'd' as trend difference order and 'q' as trend moving average order.

Thus, the notation for an SARIMA model is: SARIMA(p, d, q)(P, D, Q)m.

As seen in Fig. 2, first the data is checked to determine whether the time series data has stationarity. Stationarity of data is observed when all mathematical properties such as mean, variance and autocorrelation structure remain constant over time. Rolling Mean Visualization and Dicky-Fuller Test were used to check stationarity.

To check the values, a grid search must be run to see which combination of 'p', 'q', and 'd' provides the lowest Akaike knowledge criterion (AIC), which shows how accurate statistical models are for a specific collection of data. The best model uses the lowest number of features to fit the data. Also, the best combination of parameters will give the lowest AIC score.

From the above grid search conducted the optimal parameter combination is ARIMA(1, 1, 1) × (0, 1, 1, 12)12—AIC:1806.2981906705384. Using these hyper-parameters, the model is fit (Fig. 3).

The Kernel Density Estimator (KDE) map closely follows the $N(0, 1)$ normal distribution plot, as shown in the above 'Histogram plus estimated density' figure. The ordered distribution of residuals follows a distribution that is identical to the regular distribution, as shown by the Normal Q–Q map. As a result, the model

Fig. 2 Steps in developing
an ARIMA model

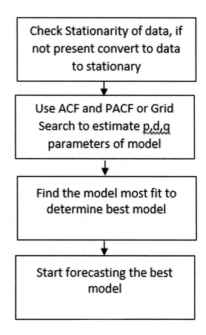

Check Stationarity of data, if
not present convert to data
to stationary

↓

Use ACF and PACF or Grid
Search to estimate p,d,q
parameters of model

↓

Find the model most fit to
determine best model

↓

Start forecasting the best
model

seems to be very successful. The standardized residual plot reveals no significant seasonality, which is supported by the Correlogram (autocorrelation) plot. The time series residuals have a low correlation with lagged versions of themselves, as seen by the autocorrelation map.

Figure 4 shows the final forecast visualization made by the model. From different combinations of parameters using grid search optimal parameter set was found to be: ARIMA(1, 1, 1) × (0, 1, 1, 12)12—AIC:1806.29 with an RMSE of 739.0611669336885.

3.2 Prophet Model

Prophet is a Facebook open-source platform for forecasting time series data that lets companies better interpret and anticipate the demand. It is based on a decomposable additive model in which non-linear patterns are fitted with seasonality and the effects of holidays are taken into account.

The model's general concept is similar to that of a generalized additive model. The Prophet Equation fits trend, seasonality and holidays. This is given by,

$$y(t) = g(t) + s(t) + h(t) + e(t). \tag{1}$$

where $g(t)$ refers to trend, $s(t)$ refers to seasonality, $h(t)$ refers to effects of holidays, $e(t)$ refers to the error term, and $y(t)$ refers to the forecast.

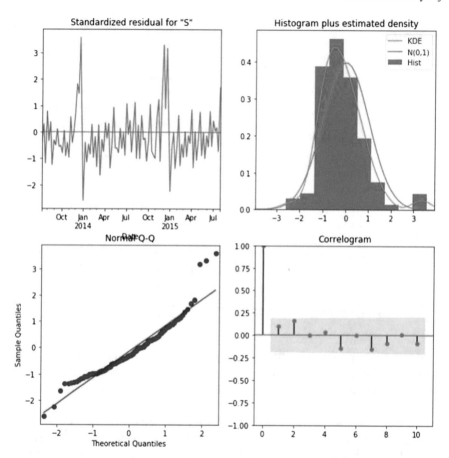

Fig. 3 Standardized residual for '*S*', histogram plus estimated density, normal *Q*–*Q*, correlogram for final SARIMA model

For the initial (baseline) model, the parameters will be set at the default parameters. The visualization of the forecast made by the initial model is shown in Fig. 5.

The RMSE value of the above initial model is 53782593196430.22 which too large. Hence, hyper-parameter tuning is done to try and reduce the RMSE value.

In the Prophet model, there are several criteria to choose from. One of the most relevant is 'holidays,' which helps the model to directly pass holidays when being trained. By observing whether there was a school or state holiday, a new 'holidays' data frame is generated. The three conditions that accompany tweaked are interval_width, growth and yearly_seasonality.

The visualization of the forecast made by the model after hyper-parameter tuning is shown in Figs. 6 and 7.

The baseline Prophet model used default parameters and resulted in RMSE of 53782649094881.14 and after hyper tuning, the value of RMSE is

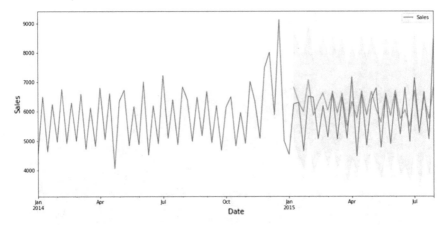

Fig. 4 Forecast by hyper-tuned ARIMA model

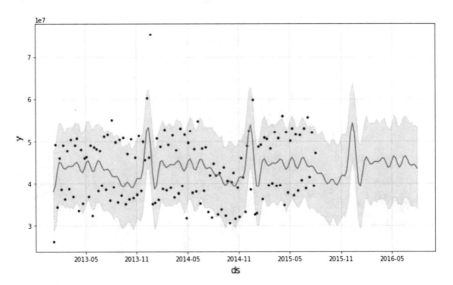

Fig. 5 Visualization of forecast by baseline prophet model

52478331938232.15. Even though the final model is performing better it is still performing very poorly when compared to ARIMA.

3.3 XGBoost Model

XGBoost is a decision tree-based ensemble Machine Learning technique that uses gradient boosting. XGBoost is a distributed gradient boosting library that has been

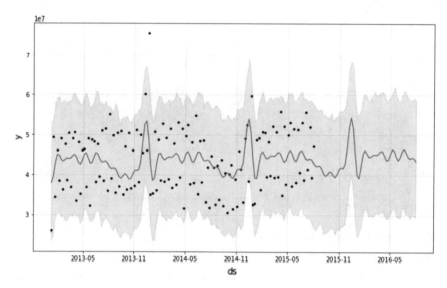

Fig. 6 Visualization of forecast by hyper-tuned prophet model

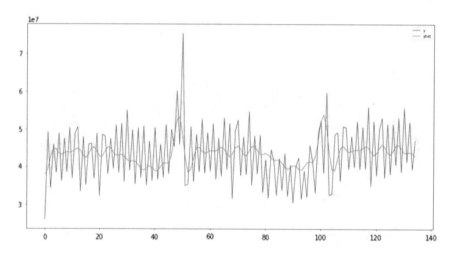

Fig. 7 Forecast by hyper-tuned prophet model

developed for performance, flexibility, and portability. It is known to do exceptionally well in all types of regression problems, despite not being explicitly developed for time series results.

The objective functions have two parts: training loss and regularization term, is a distinctive feature. This is given as:

$$\text{obj}(\theta) = L(\theta) + \Omega(\theta). \tag{2}$$

where L refers to the training loss function, and Ω refers to the regularization term.

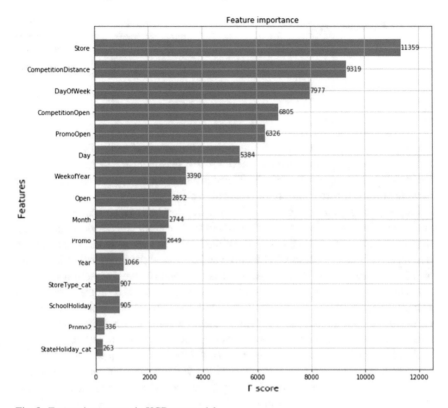

Fig. 8 Feature importance in XGBoost model

Default parameters are used for the baseline or initial model. It resulted in a Root Mean Squared Error of 1203.5497840781034.

To decrease the RMSE of XGBoost different values are passed for the hyperparameters in the XGBoost model. The parameters adjusted were eta, max_depth and gamma (Fig. 8).

4 Results

The Root Mean Squared Error (RMSE) is the square root of the average of squared deviations between expected and observable values. It is useful in cases where major errors are undesirable. Since the errors are squared before being averaged, significant errors are penalized. In this situation, RMSE is appropriate because we want to forecast sales with the least amount of error (i.e., penalize high errors) so that inventory can be better managed. Hence, RMSE was used to evaluate and validate the performance of various models used and the following results have been obtained (Fig. 9).

Fig. 9 Model comparison

	Model	RMSE
2	XGBoost	1171.255578716412
1	Prophet	53782593196430.22
0	SARIMA	739.0611669336885

SARIMA performed the best, followed by XGBoost, and finally Prophet, as seen in the table above. This is because SARIMA is a seasonal time series data-specific machine learning approach, while XGBoost is a general, though powerful, machine learning approach with a variety of applications.

Prophet is a popular option for quickly delivering forecasts because it does not entail a lot of technological knowledge. It is easy to put into practice on a large scale. Its poor performance in this area is most likely due to lack of data. It fits well for time series with heavy seasonal influences and historical data from several seasons. Prophet is tolerant of lost data and pattern changes, and it usually treats outliers well.

ARIMA is chosen as the final model to forecast sales based on the above study because it has the lowest RMSE and is well tailored to the needs of forecasting time series seasonal data. As a result, the final parameter combination is ARIMA(1, 1, 1) × (0, 1, 1, 12)12, which has an AIC of 1806.29 and an RMSE of 739.06.

However, there are some drawbacks to the ARIMA model that we must consider. It is computationally expensive because of the large data requirement and lack of convenient updating procedures. As we get new data, the entire modeling process will have to be repeated. In addition to this, the model tends to be unstable due to changes in observations and changes in model specifications.

5 Conclusion and Future Scope

Time series approaches to revenue analysis have some drawbacks. Here are some of them:

- To capture seasonality, historical data over a long time period is needed. However, historical data for a target variable is often unavailable, such as when a new product is introduced.
- Outliers and missing data are common in sales data. When using a time series technique, it is necessary to clean outliers and interpolate results.
- The presence of exogenous factors must be taken into account which have impact on sales.

The project's most intriguing aspect was that the group of stores with highest sales may not have the highest sale per customer. It is possible that this is due to the fact that certain shops carry small products that are needed on a regular basis. Another fascinating finding was that repeating a promotion does not result in increased sales. It is most likely that shoppers bought everything they could during the first discount sale.

To smooth the data, transformation techniques such as Moving Average, Log Transformation, and others may have been used to exclude seasonality and pattern to make the time series more stationary. After constructing the model, the results will be re-introduced to seasonality and pattern analysis. This may have led to a more accurate model with a lower RMSE. The SARIMAX model could have also been used, which takes exogenous variables into account. These are variables whose value is set outside of the model and imposed on it. In other words, variables that have an effect on a model but are not influenced by it. For instance, Competition Open, Promotion Open, and so on.

References

1. Matias AJ (2012) Budgeting and forecasting—the quick reference handbook, 1st edn. Matias Interactive Learning
2. Permatasari CI, Sutopo W, Hisjam M (2018) Sales forecasting newspaper with ARIMA: a case study. AIP Conf Proc 1931:030017
3. Fattah J, Ezzine L, Aman Z, el Moussami H, Lachhab A (2018) Forecasting of demand using ARIMA model. Int J Eng Bus Manage 10:184797901880867
4. ŽUnić E, Korjenić K, Hodžić K, ĐOnko D (2020) Application of Facebook's prophet algorithm for successful sales forecasting based on real-world data. Int J Comput Sci Inf Technol 12(2):23–36
5. Saradhi RP, Nelaturi N (2018) An advanced sales forecasting system using XGBoost algorithm
6. Pahadi T, Rani P, Verma A (2020) Retail store sale prediction. [Online]. Easychair.org
7. Guo Y (2018) The 7 steps of machine learning—towards data science. Medium. https://towardsdatascience.com/the-7-steps-of-machine-learning-2877d7e5548e

Modeling Concept Drift Detection as Machine Learning Model Using Overlapping Window and Kolmogorov–Smirnov Test

K. T. Jafseer, S. Shailesh, and A. Sreekumar

1 Introduction

Data from social media, sensors and various organizations have all generated large amounts of streaming data in recent years, necessitating the use of effective data analytics and machine learning approaches to help them make predictions and decisions. Data is streamed in particular, and it exceeds the memory and processing capacity of typical systems. As a result, streaming algorithms are built to handle data as it comes in, in real-time, and without storing enormous amounts of data in main memory.

The data distribution underlying the data may evolve dynamically over time. This phenomenon is known as concept drift, and it is a difficult problem that can affect a variety of application domains. If concept drift arises, the induced pattern of previous data may no longer be relevant to new data, resulting in inaccurate predictions and decisions. One of the most important aspects of streaming data analysis is the detection and handling of concept drift. Drifts can be incremental, abrupt, gradual, or reoccurring, depending on their speed, intensity, and frequency.

The main contribution of this work is to model concept drift detection as machine learning problem using the Kolmogorov–Smirnov hypothesis test with two overlapping sliding window samples that may change over time. For preserving the concept

K. T. Jafseer (✉) · S. Shailesh · A. Sreekumar
Department of Computer Applications, Cochin University of Science and Technology, Cochin, India
e-mail: jafsi@cusat.ac.in

S. Shailesh
e-mail: shaileshsivan@cusat.ac.in

S. Shailesh
Department of Computer Science, Cochin University of Science and Technology, Kalamassery, India

© The Author(s), under exclusive license to Springer Nature Singapore Pte Ltd. 2023
R. Doriya et al. (eds.), *Machine Learning, Image Processing, Network Security and Data Sciences*, Lecture Notes in Electrical Engineering 946,
https://doi.org/10.1007/978-981-19-5868-7_10

113

in the data stream, a set of relevant data points is carry forwarded from the current window W_t to the next window W_{t+1}. Then the machine learning model is developed to find out the drift in the concept of data stream.

2 Related Works

Concept drift is a significant challenge in streaming data analysis, and it has emerged as a major research topic. Many studies have been conducted on streaming data to tackle concept drift. According to Lu et al. [1] Concept drift is a process in which the statistical properties of a target domain change in an arbitrary manner over time. Schlimmer and Granger [2] was the first to propose it, intending to emphasize that noise data can transform into non-noise information at any time. Liu et al. [3] say that changes in hidden variables that cannot be measured directly could be the cause of these changes.

Gama et al. [4] proposed DDM, a statistical process control-based concept drift detection algorithm. This approach assumes that the classification error follows a Bernoulli distribution and detects concept drift using the confidence of the classification error and the error standard deviation. To adjust to the new data distribution, obsolete samples are removed when concept drift occurs.

Beana-Gracia et al. [5] presented the EDDM method, which is based on the estimated distribution of classification error distance. This approach can detect slow, gradual distribution changes. Bifet and Gavaldà [6] propose ADWIN2, a time and memory-efficient algorithm that computes the window size dynamically based on the rate of change in the data distribution and combines two learning algorithms, Naive Bayes (NB) and K-Means algorithms, and they tested these methods with both fixed-size and variable-size windows. As bounds on the rate of false positives and false negatives, this strategy ensures a good performance.

Based on Hoeffding's constraints, Fras-Blanco et al. [7] present a non-parametric drift detection approach. Moving average is used to detect abrupt concept drift, and weighted moving average is used to detect gradual concept drift. The Kolmogorov–Smirnov test is used by Dose Reis et al. [8] to develop an unsupervised online drift detection approach. The incremental algorithm for the Kolmogorov–Smirnov hypothesis test and the application of this algorithm to detect concept drift without the actual label are two contributions made by the authors in this work.

In the domain of concept drift, machine learning techniques are frequently utilized for a variety of goals. Sethi et al. [9] and Minku and Yao [10] introduced an ensemble learning-based concept drift detection approach that is model independent and employs the notion of unsupervised learning for unlabeled data. As a result, the model claims to have a good performance and a low false-positive rate.

Wu et al. [11] proposed a semi-supervised algorithm based on an evolved decision tree for tackling concept drift in an unlabeled data stream. When compared to several online algorithms on unlabeled data for both synthetic and real data, this yields a good performance. Widmer et al. [12] discuss a family of learning algorithms for flexible reaction to concept drift that takes advantage of situations where context reappear in a different way.

To detect concept drift, incremental learning models employ a variety of methods. Gama and Kosina [13] employ meta-learning techniques to detect concept drift in a dynamic environment, as well as the reoccurrence of context in unlabeled data. Cohen et al. [14] proposed a decision tree-based incremental learning algorithm for detecting concept drift in time-stamped data generated by a sensor network and automatically updating the model based on concept drift in a non-stationary data stream.

From all the literature we have done, both statistical methods and machine learning methods are utilized for detecting concept drift.

3 Proposed Methodology

The overall methodology of the proposed work is organized as three modules: windowing, labeling, and classification. The windowing module is use to split the data stream as overlapping batches. The window which contains at the instance 't' consider as W_t and the window which contains the data at instance '$t-1$' consider as W_{t-1}. These two windows are then passed to the labeling module, where the Kolmogorov–Smirnov hypothesis test is used to detect concept drift and the window is labeled. If there is a concept drift, the window will be labeled '*Drift*' else it will be labeled '*Not drift*'. For training the machine learning model, each window and its labels are saved in a folder.

Section 3.1 introduces the windowing module, whereas Sect. 3.2 explains the Kolmogorov–Smirnov test used in the labeling module. Section 3.3 demonstrates the learning module, which is used to anticipate whether or not the arriving window has exhibit concept drift.

3.1 Windowing Module

The input data for the suggested methodology should be streaming data. Windowing is one of various strategies for dealing with streaming data. Streaming data, window size, and loop back size are all input parameters for the window module. Window size and loop back size might have different lengths. We propose the overlapping sliding window method in this paper, which means that each window at the time 't' W_t. comprises a specified number (loop back size) of recent data points from the preceding window, W_{t-1}. The Kolmogorov–Smirnov two-sample hypothesis test is then used to detect concept drift (Fig. 1).

Automatic Labeling Algorithm:

> ***Input***: *Unlabeled streaming data X.*
> ***Parameters***: *window size and loop back length.*
> ***Output***: *The label for window W as 'drift' or 'not drift'*

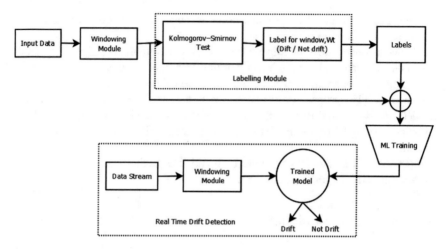

Fig. 1 The overall proposed model

Prev = []
X = []
Y = [0]

stream = DataStream (X, window size, loop back size)
While *(stream.has_next ()) do*
W = stream.get_next_window ()
    X.append (W)
    if *length of prev ≠ 0 then.*
        Result = KS_2Sample (prev, W)
        if *Result.pvalue < 0.01 and Result.statistics ≥ 0.7 then*
            y.append(1)
            Write drift detected at window W
      else
            y.append(0)
      end if
    end if
    prev = W
end while

See Fig. 2.

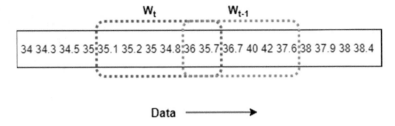

Fig. 2 Windowing

3.2 Kolmogorov–Smirnov Test

The two-sample Kolmogorov–Smirnov test is used to test whether two samples are the same distribution. We use the Kolmogorov–Smirnov test for detecting the concept drift. We employ two overlapping streaming data sliding windows. The most recent data points are in the first window W, while the prior data window is in the second window P.

The Kolmogorov–Smirnov test is a non-parametric test that accepts one-dimensional data without making any assumptions about the distribution underlying it. The absolute distance, $\text{dist}_{W,P}$ between two empirical cumulative distributions F_w and F_P is compared by,

$$\text{dist}_{W,P} = \sup_x |F_P(x) - F_W(x),$$

where $F(X) = 1/n \sum F(x) = \frac{1}{n} \sum_{j=1}^{n} I_{[-\infty, x]}(X_j)$ and

$I_{[-\infty, x]}(x_j)$ is an indicator function where $I_{[-\infty, x]}(x_j) = \begin{cases} 1, & X_j \geq x \\ 0, & \text{Otherwise} \end{cases}$

The $\sup(x)$ is the smallest required x for a condition to be valid. The null hypothesis is rejected with a significant value if the lower bound of maximum distance, i.e., $\text{dist}_{W,P}$ is greater than the test statistics. For two windows W and P of the same size, the test is reduced to,

$$\text{dist}_{W,P} > c(\alpha)\sqrt{\frac{n+n}{n*n}}$$

where α is the confidence level, n is the size of the windows

$\text{dist}_{W,P} = \sqrt{-\frac{1}{2}\ln\alpha}\sqrt{\frac{2}{n}} = \sqrt{-\frac{\ln\alpha}{n}}$, where $c(\alpha) = \sqrt{-\frac{1}{2}\ln\alpha}$.

$c(\alpha)$ is the critical value of the test with respect to the confidence level α.

Since the test is applied to all dimensions due to the one-dimensional distribution limitation, d tests must be performed on R^d at any moment t [15]. The Kolmogorov–Smirnov test will be excessively sensitive in a streaming scenario with potentially limitless data. The use of a large window size results in a high number of false

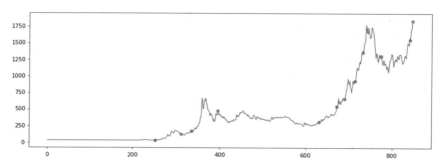

Fig. 3 Identified drift in gold price dataset

positives. As a result, we must choose a small window size (e.g., $n = 60$) that is statistically valid at the same time (Fig. 3).

3.3 Machine Learning Model for Concept Drift Detection

We also propose a model that uses the current window w_t and prior window w_{t-1} to forecast whether the arriving data window has drifted or not. For training the model, we use window W which is generated by concatenating two consecutive windows without overlapping (w_t, w_{t-1}) and the associated label, y. We can use the same windowing idea to predict the future once we have built the model (Fig. 4).

We divide the data into train and test sets, then convert them using standard scalar transformations. And compare the performance of various classification models (Logistic Regression, Support Vector Machine, K-Nearest Neighbors, Naïve Bayes, Decision Tree, and Random Forest) using this data set. The KNN model performs effectively and has a low false-positive rate in this context.

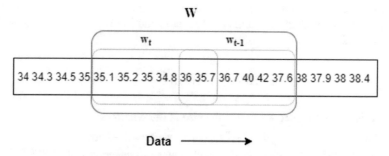

Fig. 4 Windowing for training the model

4 Results Analysis

4.1 Dataset

In this work, we have used three different data sets, the gold price dataset (Historical monthly gold prices data downloaded from DataHub), the SEA dataset (created using the SEA stream generator offered in scikit-multiflow), and the weather dataset (contains weather information collected between 1949 and 1999 in Bellevue, Nebraska [16]).

4.2 Logistic Regression

The most often used binary classification approach is logistic regression, which is based on the sigmoid function. The sigmoid function represents the characteristics of population expansion in ecology, with rapid growth and a maximum at the environment's carrying capacity. LR model estimates the probability of the default class (e.g., class 1) (Table 1).

4.3 Support Vector Machine

SVM is a type of machine learning algorithm that is used to solve classification and regression problems. The purpose of SVM is to use support vectors to generate a hyperplane between two classes (Table 2).

4.4 K-Nearest Neighbors

KNN may be used to solve classification and regression problems as well. KNN estimates the distance between all points in close vicinity to the unknown data and eliminates those with the smallest distances. As a result, it is also known as a distance-based algorithm (Table 3).

4.5 Naïve Bayes Classifier

The Nave Bayes method is a supervised learning algorithm for addressing classification problems that is based on the Bayes theorem. It analyses membership probabilities for each class, such as the likelihood that a certain record or data point belongs to that class. The most likely class is the one that has the highest probability (Table 4).

Table 1 Classification report of logistic regression classifier

Dataset	Gold price			SEA dataset			Weather		
Parameters	C = 1.0, penalty = 'l2', solver = 'lbfgs'			C = 1.0, penalty = 'l2', solver = 'lbfgs'			C = 1.0, penalty = 'l2', solver = 'lbfgs'		
Metrices	Precision	Recall	F1-score	Precision	Recall	F1-score	Precision	Recall	F1-score
0	0.73	0.89	0.80	0.86	0.98	0.92	0.96	0.99	0.98
1	0.67	0.40	0.50	0.70	0.19	0.30	0.80	0.29	0.42
Accuracy			0.71			0.86			0.96
Macro avg.	0.70	0.64	0.65	0.78	0.57	0.61	0.88	0.64	0.70
Weighted avg.	0.71	0.71	0.69	0.77	0.85	0.81	0.95	0.97	0.97

Table 2 Classification report of support vector machine classifier

Dataset	Gold price			SEA dataset			Weather		
Parameters	$C = 0.8$, kernel = 'linear'			$C = 0.8$, kernel = 'linear'			$C = 0.8$, kernel = 'linear'		
Metrices	Precision	Recall	F1-score	Precision	Recall	F1-score	Precision	Recall	F1-score
0	0.69	1.00	0.82	0.87	0.88	0.88	0.95	1.00	0.97
1	1.00	0.20	0.33	0.70	0.29	0.34	0.00	0.00	0.00
Accuracy			0.71			0.87			0.95
Macro avg.	0.85	0.60	0.58	0.78	0.57	0.61	0.47	0.50	0.49
Weighted avg.	0.80	0.71	0.65	0.79	0.84	0.79	0.90	0.95	0.92

Table 3 Classification report of KNN classifier

Dataset	Gold price			SEA dataset			Weather		
Parameters	Metric = 'minkowski', n_neighbors = 5, weights = 'uniform'			Metric = 'minkowski', n_neighbors = 5, weights = 'uniform'			Metric = 'minkowski', n_neighbors = 5, weights = 'uniform'		
Metrices	Precision	Recall	$F1$-score	Precision	Recall	$F1$-score	Precision	Recall	$F1$-score
0	0.96	0.99	0.97	0.96	0.99	0.98	0.98	0.99	0.98
1	0.80	0.26	0.38	0.80	0.29	0.42	0.80	0.44	0.57
Accuracy			0.96			0.96			0.98
Macro avg.	0.88	0.63	0.68	0.88	0.64	0.70	0.89	0.72	0.78
Weighted avg.	0.95	0.97	0.95	0.95	0.97	0.97	0.98	0.98	0.97

Table 4 Classification report of Naïve Bayes classifier

Dataset	Gold price			SEA dataset			Weather		
Parameters	Priors = none, var_smoothing = 1e-09			Priors = none, var_smoothing = 1e-09			Priors = none, var_smoothing = 1e-09		
Metrices	Precision	Recall	F1-score	Precision	Recall	F1-score	Precision	Recall	F1-score
0	0.67	0.89	0.76	0.80	0.98	0.87	0.96	0.49	0.65
1	0.50	0.20	0.29	0.60	0.12	0.19	0.06	0.62	0.11
Accuracy			0.64			0.79			0.50
Macro avg.	0.58	0.54	0.52	0.70	0.55	0.53	0.51	0.56	0.38
Weighted avg.	0.61	0.64	0.59	0.79	0.94	0.84	0.91	0.50	0.62

4.6 Decision Tree

A Decision Tree is a tree-structured classifier with core nodes that represent dataset attributes, branches that represent decision rules, and leaf nodes that indicate the conclusion. The purpose of employing a Decision Tree is to develop a training model that can use basic decision rules inferred from training data to predict the class or value of the target variable (Table 5).

4.7 Random Forest

Many decision trees make up a random forest algorithm. It predicts by averaging the output of various trees. The precision of the result improves as the number of trees grows. A random forest method overcomes the drawbacks of a decision tree algorithm. It reduces dataset overfitting and improves precision (Table 6 and Figs. 5, 6 and 7).

5 Conclusion

The technology advancements in the current scenario, lights wide scope in the area of streaming data analytics. The data stream becomes very common by the introduction of IoT, cyber-physical systems, and related domain and it can be viewed as unbounded continuous data elements or small batches may vary over time. In this work, we have modeled the concept drift detection as a machine learning problem by utilizing the Kolmogorov–Smirnov test which is used to determine the variation of two window samples. The proposed method utilizes the overlapping window to avoid information loss. For building the classifier we have applied various classification models with a different dataset. After implementing the method, it is found that the KNN model outperformed others and has a low false positive of 96%. The experiments conducted with different dataset reveals the efficiency and effectiveness of the proposed method. As a future scope, we claim deep learning techniques can be effectively used to detect and adapt the concept drift in real-time for real-world problems with improved efficiency.

Table 5 Classification report of decision tree classifier

Parameters	Gold price			SEA dataset			Weather		
	Criterion = 'gini', max_depth = none, max_features = none			Criterion = 'gini', max_depth = none, max_features = none			Criterion = 'gini', max_depth = none, max_features = none		
Metrices	Precision	Recall	F1-score	Precision	Recall	F1-score	Precision	Recall	F1-score
0	0.88	0.78	0.82	0.82	0.96	0.87	0.96	0.93	0.94
1	0.67	0.80	0.73	0.62	0.20	0.21	0.12	0.19	0.15
Accuracy			0.79			0.80			0.89
Macro avg.	0.77	0.79	0.78	0.72	0.58	0.54	0.54	0.56	0.54
Weighted avg.	0.80	0.79	0.79	0.80	0.93	0.85	0.91	0.89	0.90

Table 6 Classification report of random forest classifier

Datasets	Gold price			SEA dataset			Weather		
Parameters	Criterion = 'entropy', max_features = 'auto', n_estimators = 10			Criterion = 'entropy', max_features = 'auto', n_estimators = 10			Criterion = 'entropy', max_features = 'auto', n_estimators = 10		
Metrices	Precision	Recall	F1-score	Precision	Recall	F1-score	Precision	Recall	F1-score
0	0.78	0.78	0.78	0.80	0.98	0.87	0.87	0.96	0.93
1	0.60	0.60	0.60	0.60	0.12	0.19	0.21	0.12	0.19
Accuracy			0.71			0.79			0.80
Macro avg.	0.69	0.69	0.69	0.70	0.55	0.53	0.54	0.54	0.56
Weighted avg.	0.71	0.71	0.71	0.79	0.94	0.84	0.85	0.91	0.89

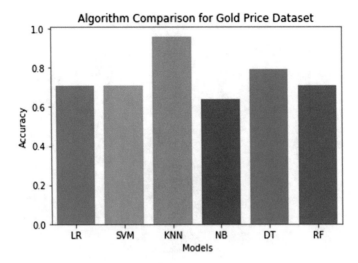

Fig. 5 Classification models' comparison report of gold price dataset

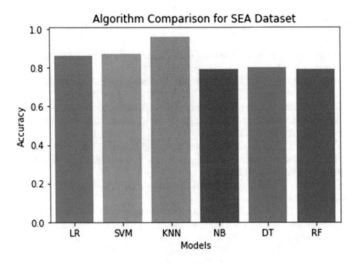

Fig. 6 Classification models' comparison report of SEA dataset

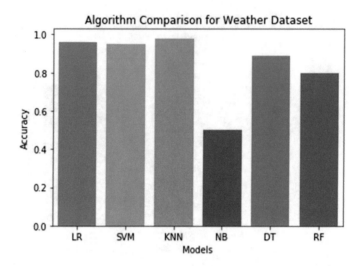

Fig. 7 Classification models' comparison report of Weather dataset

References

1. Lu N, Zhang G, Lu J (2014) Concept drift detection via competence models. Artif Intell 209:11–28
2. Schlimmer JC, Granger RH (1986) Incremental learning from noisy data. Mach Learn 1:317–354
3. Liu A, Song Y, Zhang G, Lu J (2014) Regional concept drift detection and density synchronized drift adaptation. University of Technology, Sydney, Australia, Faculty of Engineering and Information Technology, pp 2280–2286
4. Gama J, Medas P, Castillo G, Rodrigues P (2004) Learning with drift detection. Lecture notes computer science (including subseries lecture notes artificial intelligence lecture notes bioinformatics), vol 3171, pp 286–295
5. Baena-García M et al (2006) Early drift detection method. 4th ECML PKDD Int Work Knowl Discov Data Streams 6:77–86
6. Bifet A, Gavaldà R (2007) Learning from time-changing data with adaptive windowing. In: Proceedings of the seventh SIAM international conference on data mining, pp 443–448
7. Frías-Blanco I et al (2015) Online and non-parametric drift detection methods based on Hoeffding's bounds. IEEE Trans Knowl Data Eng 27:810–823
8. Dos Reis D, Flach P, Matwin S, Batista G (2016) Fast unsupervised online drift detection using incremental Kolmogorov-Smirnov test. In: Proceedings of the 22nd ACM SIGKDD international conference on knowledge discovery and data mining, pp 1545–1554
9. Sethi TS, Kantardzic M, Arabmakki E (2016) Monitoring classification blindspots to detect drifts from unlabeled data. Proceedings—2016 IEEE international conference on information reuse and integration, pp 142–151
10. Minku LL, Yao X (2012) DDD: a new ensemble approach for dealing with concept drift. IEEE Trans Knowl Data Eng 24:619–633
11. Wu X, Li P, Hu X (2012) Learning from concept drifting data streams with unlabeled data. Neurocomputing 92:145–155
12. Widmer G, Widmer G (1996) Learning in the presence of concept drift and hidden contexts. Mach Learn 23:69–101
13. Gama J, Kosina P (2014) Recurrent concepts in data streams classification. Knowl Inf Syst 40:489–507

14. Cohen L, Avrahami-Bakish G, Last M, Kandel A, Kipersztok O (2008) Real-time data mining of non-stationary data streams from sensor networks. Inf Fusion 9:344–353
15. Raab C, Heusinger M, Schleif FM (2020) Reactive soft prototype computing for concept drift streams. Neurocomputing 416:340–351
16. Elwell R, Polikar R (2011) Incremental learning of concept drift in nonstationary environments. IEEE Trans Neural Networks 22(10):1517–1531

Wearable Sensor-Based Framework for the Detection of Daily Living Activities Utilizing In-Depth Features

Updesh Verma, Pratibha Tyagi, and Manpreet Kaur

1 Introduction

Recognition of physical activity has various applications in a real-time scenario, such as personal health assistance, intrusion detection, entertainment, elderly care, and security [1, 2]. From the existing work of researchers, it has been seen that various methods have been adopted for activity recognition based on different sensor modalities such as vision, ambient sensor, wearable sensor, radar, and Wi-Fi signaling-based approaches. Other than wearable sensor-based approaches for activity recognition required a clear line of sight and distraction of signal with the subject's body and continuous maintenance and costly installation. Secondly, these have a limited range where recognition could be possible [3]. On the other hand, wearable sensor-based approaches can perform a recognition task in any place and any time without line-of-sight requirement and easy installation with low-cost sensors because of the advancements in miniature technologies. Different inertial measurement units (IMUs) [4] consisting of acceleration, gyroscope, and magnetometer sensors are utilized to convert human movement into electrical signal. These signals have a direct relationship with physical movements. Nowadays, machine learning and deep learning algorithms are in trend for activity recognition because this activity recognition problem is defined under classification problems [5].

Most of the researches in this field have given a promising result, but further, improvement is required due to some research challenges in physical activity recognition. Some major research challenges are (i) different persons perform the same activity in a varying manner. (ii) The same activity is performed differently at different times by the same person due to his or her mental status [6, 7]. (iii) The detection of

U. Verma (✉) · P. Tyagi · M. Kaur
Sant Longowal Institute of Engineering and Technology, Punjab, India
e-mail: updesh.verma01@gmail.com

similar types of activities (taking tea and taking water) and detection of complex activities (opening a fridge, ironing, brushing teeth, drinking, eating, watching TV, etc.) requires well-defined sensor placements and multimodal sensors [8]. (iv) Finding the best-suited sensor placements for detection of several activities with few numbers of sensors with sufficient wearing comfort of subjects, (v) effective features extraction techniques, and so on [9].

In this paper, the sensor data called physical activity monitoring of aging people (PAMAP2) and wireless sensor data mining lab (WISDM) datasets have been taken that consist of a combination of simple (walking, sitting, standing, etc.) and complex activities (ironing, rope jumping, vacuum-cleaning, etc.) [10]. The defined convolutional neural network (CNN) has accurately detected all the activities. This paper is divided into five sections; Sect. 2 is related to work where some previous research by researchers has been included which is related to the proposed work. Section 3 is the proposed methodology, where the mathematical part of the proposed methodology is elaborated. Section 5 described the results of the proposed work with the performance evaluation of different learning models and their recognition rate. This section also described the role of CNN features to mitigate the shortcomings of machine learning models. Section 6 is dedicated to a discussion where the results of different learning models are discussed, and some essential inferences have been drawn. The last section is for the conclusion and future work, where some concluding remarks for this model and modifications for further development are included.

2   Related Work

The machine learning approaches are required efficient feature extraction techniques because of the requirement of compelling features for distinguishing various physical activities. Efficient features have been extracted with the help of domain knowledge. On the other hand, deep learning models do not require feature extraction methods because they automatically extract the efficient features according to training and testing datasets. Machine learning models require a large amount of labeled data, which is rarely available. The difficulty to classify the activities of new subjects whose data are not included in the training session is observed in machine learning while performing real-time testing of the system. Deep learning models can accurately classify the activities of newcomers or an unknown person whose data are not included in the training phase of the model, and they do not require a large amount of labeled data. The unlabeled data can be used for real-time activity recognition.

2.1 Machine Learning Approaches

Dealing with the machine learning algorithms, concerned with selecting appropriate features, has immense importance for accurate classification of target class [11–15]—those feature vectors that are high in dimension require high-computational power and data acquisition cost. But low-dimensional feature vector provides the elimination of overfitting [16, 17]. The selection of all possible features from the dataset gives a better recognition rate, but it is impractical in computational cost. For that purpose, various feature selection methods with varying complexity have been proposed, and they classified existing feature selection methods into three parts, wrapper, embedded, and filter [13]. In preprocessing, the methods based on the filter for feature extraction are used without knowing the classifier. Mostly used methods based on filtering included Wilcoxon Mann Whitney test [18], chi-square test [19], t-test [20], Pearson correlation coefficient [21], mutual information [22], and principal component analysis [23]. Methods based on filter provided less computational cost, but cut-off point finding for effective feature selection with high ranking observed difficult due to noise interference. Wrapper methods generally demand high-computational costs, but these methods provide very efficient features for better classification accuracy. An exhaustive search of features is not feasible due to very high-computational cost, so extracting a subset of features is required. Many learning algorithms extract a subset from features based on some criterion, such as classification accuracy. Wrapper-based algorithms are divided into two parts, named greedy and stochastic. The most commonly used learning algorithm within the wrapper is the support vector machine (SVM). In greedy algorithms, sequential backward selection (SBS) and sequential forward selection (SFS) are generally used [24]. The popular and frequently used algorithms under stochastic are particle swarm optimization (PSO) [25], genetic algorithm (GA) [26], and ant colony optimization (ACO).

Embedded sensors such as accelerometers, gyroscopes, and magnetometers inside mobile phones were widely used for different activities recognition [27–29]. Five body-worn biaxial small sensors were placed on various body parts and used for activity recognition [30]. Seven body sensors were utilized to develop a body sensor system with wireless capability [31].

2.2 Deep Learning Approach

Different pattern analysis-based applications have been explored with artificial neural network (ANN) in the previous researches [32–34]. Pattern recognition analysis was performed by the deep neural network [35]. But the two major disadvantages have been observed with deep learning network, one described as overfitting and another one-time consuming training process. Furthermore, restricted Boltzmann machine (RBM) for deep learning was proposed under deep belief network (DBN) [33]. Usage of RBM in deep learning proved advantageous in terms of a quicker training process. Convolutional neural network (CNN) was proposed for further improvement in deep learning models. An increased discriminant power of CNNs compared to deep belief network (DBN) has attracted many researchers to explore different applications. Mostly, the visual pattern analysis has been done accurately with CNNs models. The CNNs consist of significant pooling, convolution, rectifier, tangent squashing, and normalization [33]. In physical activity recognition, DNNs, specifically CNNs, have achieved great success [36]. An accurate understanding of image topology by CNNs has allowed researchers for image-based classification through CNNs [37, 38]. When the saturation came in image-based CNN modeling, the researchers started implementing CNNs in other applications such as gesture recognition and human activity recognition [39, 40]. CNN consists of different layers like the pooling, fully connected, convolutional, and output. A convolutional layer is used for feature mapping with the help of convolution between different filters (kernels) and input data or output from the previous layer. The pooling layer is used for downsampling to decrease the computation of CNNs. In a fully connected model, all the nodes are connected to the nodes of the previous layers. Finally, the softmax function is used in the output layer in most of the previous research [41].

In the above literature review, it is observed that various machine learning algorithms are implemented by researchers for the detection of different daily living activities with suitable data processing steps depending on the type of activity. This paper presents a comparative analysis of these algorithms on 13 daily living activities, a novel approach toward activity detection with learning algorithms. Also, the most promising candidate CNN has been implemented, and its performance shows its capability to classify all the defined activities accurately.

3 Proposed Methodology

The first step toward classifying physical activities in this paper is to remove the unnecessary information, such as the columns like timestamp, heart rate, time, etc. This study is based on wearable sensors-based activity recognition, so only the acceleration, gyroscopic, and magnetometer are considered for activity information. In the second step, principal component analysis is applied to the preprocessed data to reduce the dataset's dimensions. In the third step, the standard scaling is used to scale the significant variations between different values to a limited range. The recognition accuracy has been improved. Next, to balance the dataset for giving equal weight to each activity, for that purpose, oversampling is applied. In the end, a fixed window technique is used to segment the balanced dataset, by which the fast computation is observed in the classification part of the whole process. At the classification end, the different machine learning algorithms are used to classify the target activities. Decision trees, support vector machines, Naïve Bayes, and random forest are demonstrated in the result section of this study. In the deep learning part, we have implemented the 2D convolutional neural network. This proposed deep

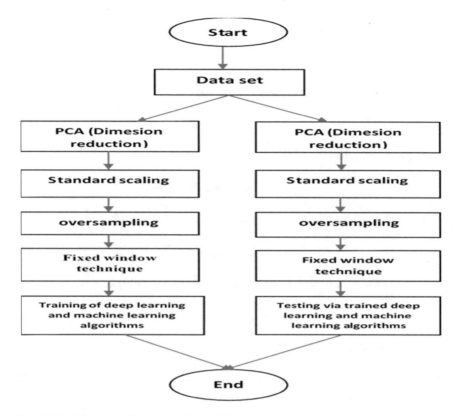

Fig. 1 Block diagram of the proposed methodology

learning algorithm is very efficient for classifying all the activities very accurately. The block diagram of the proposed methodology is shown in Fig. 1.

In the following section, short notes related to the mathematical analysis of the proposed methodology are given.

4 Data Preprocessing

The PAMAP2 dataset is taken from the UCI machine learning repository, used to model the physical activity recognition model [42]. The dataset is obtained by placing three inertial measurement units (IMU) on the wrist, chest, and ankle. Each IMU consists of two accelerometer data with three axes of different ratings, three-axis gyroscopic, and magnetometer data. The other data, such as orientation, heart rate, timestamp, etc., are removed for discarding unnecessary information, which results from a reduction in complexity. The different notations are given here for the sensors.

Acceleration from the IMU placed on the wrist of one rating is

$$A_{1w} = \left(a_{1wx}, a_{1wy}, a_{1wz}\right) \tag{1}$$

Gyroscopic data from IMU placed on the wrist are

$$G_w = \left(g_{wx}, g_{wy}, g_{wz}\right) \tag{2}$$

Magnetometer data from IMU placed on the wrist

$$M_w = \left(m_{wx}, m_{wy}, m_{wz}\right) \tag{3}$$

Acceleration from IMU placed on the wrist of the second rating

$$A_{2w} = \left(a_{2wx}, a_{2wy}, a_{2wz}\right) \tag{4}$$

Acceleration from the IMU placed on the chest of one rating is

$$A_{1c} = \left(a_{1cx}, a_{1cy}, a_{1cz}\right) \tag{5}$$

Gyroscopic data from IMU placed on the chest

$$G_c = \left(g_{cx}, g_{cy}, g_{cz}\right) \tag{6}$$

Magnetometer data from IMU placed on the chest

$$M_c = \left(m_{cx}, m_{cy}, m_{cz}\right) \tag{7}$$

Acceleration data from IMU placed on the chest of second rating is

$$A_{2c} = \left(a_{2cx}, a_{2cy}, a_{2cz}\right) \tag{8}$$

Acceleration data from IMU placed on ankle of one rating is

$$A_{1a} = \left(a_{1ax}, a_{1cy}, a_{1cz}\right) \tag{9}$$

Gyroscopic data from IMU placed on the ankle

$$G_a = \left(g_{ax}, g_{ay}, g_{az}\right) \tag{10}$$

Magnetometer data from IMU placed on the ankle

$$M_a = \left(m_{ax}, m_{ay}, m_{az}\right) \tag{11}$$

Table 1 Detected activities and their IDs

PAMAP2 dataset						WISDM dataset	
Activity ID	Activity	Activity ID	Activity	Activity ID	Activity	Activity ID	Activity
0	Transient	6	Cycling	13	Descending stairs	0	Downstairs
1	Lying	7	Nordic walking	16	Vacuum cleaning	1	Jogging
2	Sitting	9	Watching TV	17	Ironing	2	Sitting
3	Standing	10	Computer work	18	Folding laundry	3	Standing
4	Walking	11	Car driving	19	House cleaning	4	Upstairs
5	Running	12	Ascending stairs	20	Playing soccer	5	Walking
24	Rope jumping						

Acceleration data from IMU placed on ankle of the second rating

$$A_{2a} = (a_{2ax}, a_{2ay}, a_{2az}) \tag{12}$$

So that the actual data vector represented as

$$x = (A_{1w}, G_a, M_a, A_{2w}, A_{1c}, G_C, M_c, A_{2c}, A_{1a}, G_a, M_a, A_{2a}) \tag{13}$$

Equation 13 denotes that the data consists of high dimensions. No doubt, this data can provide accurate results, but the complexity of processing this data becomes very high. The principal component analysis is used to reduce the complexity of this recognition model because of its prominent use in the previous research [43–45]. The activities under consideration and their IDs are given in Table 1 for both datasets.

The component analysis is used to reduce the complexity of this recognition model because of its prominent use in the previous research [43–45]. The activities under consideration and their IDs are given in Table 1 for both datasets.

4.1 Principle Component Analysis

PCA represents the actual data vector in lower dimensions which exists in high dimensions in its actual form. The basics of PCA are to calculate the eigenvectors from the covariance matrix of data and approximate that data with the help of those top eigenvectors whose linear combination is possible. The t dimensional vector x

is defined in Eq. (13), where t, in this case, is 12. Each IMU contains three-axis acceleration of rating 1, 3 axis acceleration of rating 2, 3 axis gyroscope, and three-axis magnetometers, so the dimension of vector x is $12 \times 3 = 36$. If a total number of samples denoted by $i = 1, 2, 3 \ldots N$, then the vector represents a particular activity is defined as $X = \{x_1, x_2, \ldots x_N\}$. The value of the covariance matrix is defined as $Q = XX^T$. W is a linear transformation. The mathematical operation transforms t dimensional space to f dimension feature subspace where definitely $f \ll t$ relation is always followed. Now, the new value of the feature vector becomes y_i where $y_i = W^T x_i, i = 1, 2, 3 \ldots N$, and the column of W represents the eigenvector e_i and the value of $\lambda_i e_i = Q e_i$ where λ_i is the eigenvalue associated with the eigenvector e_i.

4.2 Standard Scaling (Standardization)

Scaling of features after applying PCA is done with standard scaling. Scaling is very important in preprocessing of data for classification accuracy at the end of the detection process. Because the features of sample data generally exist in varying numbers, and sometimes, their difference is huge. Many distance-based algorithms required standard features, such as K-nearest neighbors (KNNs) and support vector machine (SVM). In this paper, we have used a standard scaling that has been represented as follows:

$$Z = \frac{X - U}{S} \tag{14}$$

U is the mean, S is the standard deviation, and Z is the feature after standard scaling.

4.3 Data Balancing

The number of samples of data for each activity is obtained with varying numbers, by which the machine learning algorithms consider different activities with different weightage for classification. A large number of samples for a particular activity dominates on another low number of activity samples in the context of classification in artificial intelligence. So, data balancing is required for making the balancing of data for accurate classification of each activity. For that purpose, we have used an over-sampling technique, where each activity is balanced with equal samples by considering the reference of the activity with maximum samples [46]. Several samples per activity are shown in Fig. 2, and it also indicates that there is a considerable variation in samples between the activity ID numbers 0 and 24 for the PAMPA2 dataset

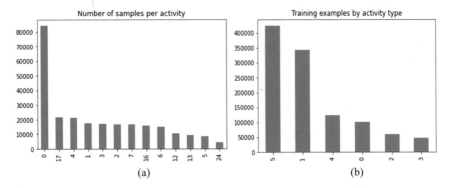

Fig. 2 **a** Number of samples per activity in the dataset for PAMAP2 dataset, **b** for WISDM dataset

(Fig. 2a) and in the same way for the WISDM dataset (Fig. 2b). So, there is a solid point to balance the data.

4.4 Sliding Window Technique

For data segmentation, the sliding window is used. The time-series data from wearable inertial sensors is divided into segments. The size of the window should be as large as it can match the duration of the activity. If the window size is too large, multiple activities can occur in one segment. If the window size is too small, then the complete activity cannot be recognized. The selection of the size of the window according to performed activity is an important aspect. Depending upon the application scenario, the size of the window has been chosen by the researchers from 0.08 s [47] to 2 s [48].

In some cases, it is up to 30 s [49]. In this study, we have taken the window size of 80 samples (0.8 s) and hope size (overlapping) of 40 samples (0.4 s). Figure 3 can help to understand how the sliding window works. Different activities are shown for the different durations. One window of fixed size and fixed hope size moving across each activity, activity number A_1 exactly matches with window w_1, but the other activities do not match. So, selecting a window is an essential aspect for an accurate assessment or classification of physical activities. We have used 50% overlap because of suggestions given by many studies [50].

5   Results

In this research, machine learning models recognize different physical activities consisting of the PAMAP2 and WISDM datasets. All the activities are coded in digits form because Python can understand the target variable in digits. For classification,

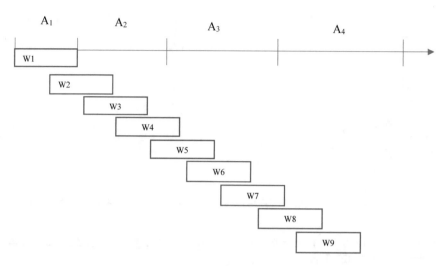

Fig. 3 Fixed sliding window approach for activity recognition [51]

data have been divided into training and testing sets. 40% of the data is used for testing, and the remaining 60% has been used for training. The performance evaluation parameters precision, accuracy, recall, and $F1$ score are considered for comparative analysis of the different algorithms. Deep learning 2D convolution neural network also used and analyzed at the end (Fig. 5).

Performance evaluation parameters:

$$\text{Precision} = \frac{\text{True Positive}}{\text{True Positive} + \text{False Positive}} \quad (15)$$

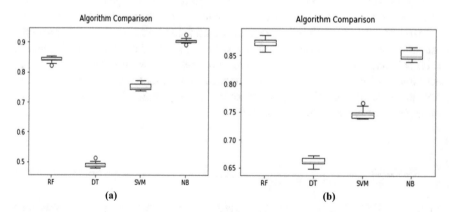

Fig. 4 Comparison of machine learning algorithms after k-fold validation (k–10) **a** for PAMAP2 dataset, **b** for WISDM dataset

Table 2 Classifier and their parameter settings

Classifier	Parameter settings
Random forest	n_estimators = 60, criterion = entropy, Max_features = Log2
Support vector machine	Kernel = sigmoid, Gamma = scale, Max_features = Log2, Degree = 3, Cache_size = 200
Decision tree	Criterion = Gini, splitter = Best, Random_scale = 100, Max_depth = 50, Max_features_leaf = 0, Max_sample_split = 2
Naïve Bayes	By default settings

$$\text{Accuracy} = \frac{\text{True Positive} + \text{True Negative}}{\text{True Positive} + \text{True Negative} + \text{False Positive} + \text{False Negative}} \tag{16}$$

$$\text{Recall} = \frac{\text{True Positive}}{\text{True Positive} + \text{False Negative}} \tag{17}$$

$$F1 \text{ score} = 2 \times \frac{\text{Precision} \times \text{Recall}}{\text{Precison} + \text{Recall}} \tag{18}$$

Different classification machine learning models and their performance analysis: The different parameter settings of some classifiers which are implemented in this paper are shown in Table 2.

5.1 Random Forest Classifier

We generate the bootstrapped sets from the original dataset for a growing number of trees and ensemble them together to make a different tree-based classifier, known as a random forest classifier. By increasing the number of trees of this model by which it can handle high-dimensional dataset. In our model, we have used 60 trees, and the performance is given in Fig. 5a and b in terms of classification report and confusion matrix, respectively. The report shows the different performance evaluation parameters for each activity. Table 2 shows the different parameter settings for random forest classifiers.

5.2 Support Vector Machine (SVM)

The idea by which the training data is divided as one of two categories and then finding the best solution to separate them, it can be a line, plane, and hyperplane, named as SVM. Figure 6a and b shows the classification report and confusion matrix for this model to detect physical activities which are defined under PAMAP2 dataset.

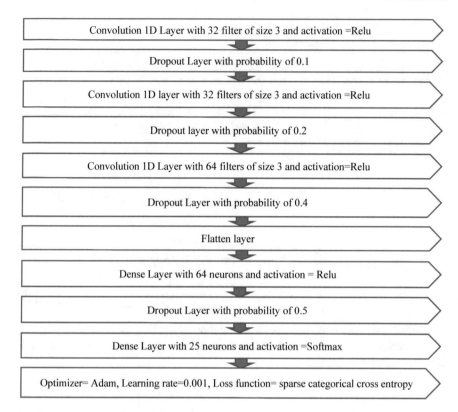

Convolution 1D Layer with 32 filter of size 3 and activation =Relu

Dropout Layer with probability of 0.1

Convolution 1D layer with 32 filters of size 3 and activation =Relu

Dropout layer with probability of 0.2

Convolution 1D Layer with 64 filters of size 3 and activation=Relu

Dropout Layer with probability of 0.4

Flatten layer

Dense Layer with 64 neurons and activation = Relu

Dropout Layer with probability of 0.5

Dense Layer with 25 neurons and activation =Softmax

Optimizer= Adam, Learning rate=0.001, Loss function= sparse categorical cross entropy

Fig. 5 Various layers of proposed CNN model

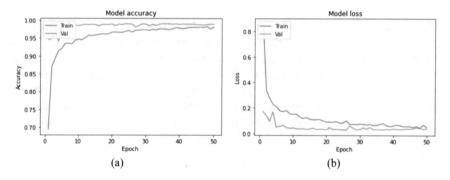

Fig. 6 Learning curves of CNN for **a** model accuracy and **b** model loss

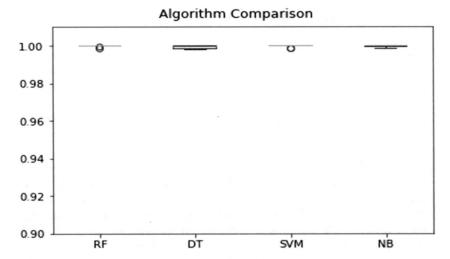

Fig. 7 Box plot for comparing different machine learning algorithms with CNN features

5.3 Naïve Bayes Classifier

Naïve Bayes classifier is not a single algorithm but a combination of algorithms of the same family based on the Bayes theorem. We have used Gaussian Naïve Bayes to classify different activities where every feature is treated independently for classifying a particular class of physical activity. The classification report with different parameters for performance evaluation of each activity addition with confusion matrix is given in Fig. 7a and b, respectively.

5.4 Decision Tree Classifier

A decision tree classifier is a learning algorithm that follows the multistage procedure for dividing the hard decision into many soft decisions. These collections of soft decisions are intended to provide an optimal decision to a particular classification problem.

The comparison of all implemented machine learning algorithms after k-fold validation where the value of $k = 10$ is shown in Fig. 4. The box plot shows that the Naïve Bayes classifier performed better than others in terms of precision and stability. The box plot shows minimum variations in the performance of Naïve Bayes during tenfold cross-validation, and the classifier can sustain at mean value. Random forest is also able to generate a recognition rate of a particular value very precisely. The decision tree classifier shows good precision but less accuracy for detecting physical activities. Support vector machine shows greater variation in accuracy score compared to others with moderate recognition rate.

5.5   Convolutional Neural Network

The deep learning algorithm, which is nothing but an artificial neural network, has gained a tremendous performance in machine learning problems in the last few decades. The powerful algorithm in the series of deep learning neural networks is a convolutional neural network due to its amazing performance in the previous studies. CNN, as its name suggests, is the linear mathematical operation called convolution between different matrixes. Different layers such as the pooling, non-linearity, fully connected, and convolution layers are part of its architecture. Two fully connected layers and a convolutional layer of CNN model demand parameters settings, but the non-linearity and pooling layer exist without parameters. CNN modeling has performed very well with the dataset of image, vision-based, and natural language processing. In this research, the first convolution layer of our 1D CNN modeling consists of 16 filters with the size of 3, the second convolution layer consists of 32 filters, and the third convolution layer consists of 64 filters of the same size as in the convolution layer 1 with activation function rectified linear activation function (ReLU). The ReLU activation function is used for passing the input data of positive values to the next layer. The next flatten layer is used to convert the data into a one-dimensional vector. A dense layer of 64 neurons is connected as a deep network layer, and another dense layer of 25 neurons with softmax activation function is also connected. The learning curve of CNN for model accuracy plotted for validation value and training value is shown in Fig. 6a. Model loss plotted for validation and training loss is shown in Fig. 6b. In Fig. 5, the various layers of the CNN model have been described.

Tables 3 and 4 describe the performance of all the machine learning algorithms and CNN for each activity in the form of precision, recall, and $F1$ score.

Tables 5 and 6 shows the recognition rate of different machine learning algorithms and deep learning model.

5.6   Extraction of CNN Features for the Training of Machine Learning Models

Hand-crafted features could not represent the data of a particular activity due to the lack of domain knowledge. Experts who have a good knowledge of the domain can define effective hand-crafted features. Deep learning features are very effective in representing the data of a particular activity due to their layered structure. In this section, the importance and effectiveness of deep learning features are observed by implementing the activity recognition model using those machine learning models defined earlier, trained with the features of implemented CNN. The modeling of CNN is defined above now. Weights are taken from different layers and features extracted by training these weights. These features are used for training the different machine learning algorithms, performance is evaluated with the help of recognition

Table 3 Performance evaluation of different machine learning algorithms and deep learning model for PAMAP2 dataset

Activity	PAMAP2 dataset														
	Support vector machine			Naïve Bayes			Decision tree			Random forest			CNN		
	Precision	Recall	F1 score	Precision	Recall	F1 score	Precision	Recall	F1 score	Precision	Recall	F1 score	precision	Recall	F1 score
0	0.02	0.02	0.02	0.02	0.33	0.04	0.73	0.72	0.73	0.79	1.00	0.89	0.99	1.00	1.00
1	1.00	0.91	0.95	1.00	0.99	0.99	0.98	0.98	0.98	1.00	0.99	1.00	1.00	1.00	1.00
2	0.96	0.91	0.94	1.00	0.87	0.93	0.83	0.82	0.82	1.00	0.96	0.98	1.00	1.00	1.00
3	0.76	0.84	0.80	0.98	0.93	0.95	0.62	0.62	0.62	1.00	0.97	0.99	1.00	1.00	1.00
4	0.65	0.55	0.60	0.94	0.88	0.91	0.33	0.30	0.32	0.93	0.75	0.83	0.98	0.93	0.96
5	0.72	0.78	0.75	0.93	0.92	0.92	0.28	0.26	0.27	0.64	0.67	0.65	1.00	0.99	1.00
6	0.91	0.86	0.89	0.98	0.90	0.94	0.44	0.44	0.44	0.97	0.76	0.85	1.00	1.00	1.00
7	0.67	0.72	0.70	0.99	0.91	0.95	0.27	0.27	0.27	0.65	0.64	0.64	0.99	1.00	0.99
12	0.68	0.68	0.68	0.98	0.94	0.96	0.27	0.27	0.27	0.56	0.70	0.62	0.93	0.98	0.95
13	0.76	0.74	0.75	0.98	0.94	0.96	0.17	0.18	0.17	0.50	0.81	0.62	1.00	0.98	0.99
16	0.91	0.86	0.88	1.00	0.82	0.90	0.47	0.53	0.50	1.00	0.94	0.97	1.00	1.00	1.00
17	0.93	0.91	0.92	1.00	0.90	0.95	0.66	0.65	0.66	1.00	0.97	0.98	1.00	1.00	1.00
24	0.82	0.89	0.85	0.98	0.92	0.95	0.47	0.52	0.49	0.99	0.88	0.93	0.99	1.00	1.00

Table 4 Performance evaluation of different machine learning algorithms and deep learning model for WISDM dataset

Activity	WISDM dataset																	
	Support vector machine			Naïve Bayes			Decision tree			Random forest			CNN		
	Precision	Recall	F1 score	Precision	Recall	F1 score	Precision	Recall	F1 score	Precision	Recall	F1 score	precision	Recall	F1 score
0	0.75	0.70	0.72	0.86	0.62	0.72	0.42	0.41	0.41	0.70	0.63	0.66	0.94	1.00	**1.00**
1	0.91	0.90	**0.90**	1.00	0.95	**0.97**	0.69	0.69	0.69	1.00	0.98	**099**	1.00	1.00	**1.00**
2	1.00	1.00	**1.00**	1.00	1.00	**1.00**	0.96	0.95	**0.96**	1.00	1.00	**1.00**	1.00	1.00	**1.00**
3	0.99	0.76	**0.86**	1.00	1.00	**1.00**	0.95	0.95	**0.95**	1.00	1.00	**1.00**	1.00	1.00	**1.00**
4	0.52	0.74	0.61	0.82	0.80	0.81	0.36	0.36	0.36	0.59	0.66	0.62	0.95	0.94	**0.94**
5	0.38	0.41	0.39	0.46	0.87	0.60	0.63	0.66	0.64	0.97	1.00	**0.98**	1.00	1.00	**1.00**

Table 5 Recognition rate of different classifiers of different activities for the PAMAP2 dataset

Activity ID	Activity	Random forest classifier (%)	Support vector machine (%)	Naïve Bayes (%)	Decision tree (%)	Convolutional neural network (%)
0	Transient	83.0	1.3	2.0	76.0	**99.0**
1	Lying	**100.0**	**100.0**	**100.0**	98.0	**100.0**
2	Sitting	**100.0**	**100.0**	**100.0**	86.0	**100.0**
3	Standing	**94.0**	70.0	**98.0**	60.0	**100.0**
4	Walking	**94.0**	65.0	**94.0**	33.0	**98.0**
5	Running	61.0	70.0	**87.0**	26.0	**100.0**
6	Cycling	**96.0**	**89.0**	**98.0**	41.0	**100.0**
7	Nordic Walking	62.0	68.0	**99.0**	25.0	**99.0**
12	Ascending stairs	54.0	66.0	**98.0**	25.0	**93.0**
13	Descending stairs	47.0	73.0	**98.0**	15.0	**100.0**
16	Vacuum cleaning	**100.0**	**91.0**	**100.0**	45.0	**100.0**
17	Ironing	**100.0**	94.0	**100.0**	73.0	**100.0**
24	Rope jumping	**100.0**	80.0	**94.0**	56.0	**99.0**

Table 6 Recognition rate of different classifiers of different activities for the WISDM dataset

Activity ID	Activity	Random forest classifier (%)	Support vector machine (%)	Naïve Bayes (%)	Decision tree (%)	Convolutional neural network (%)
0	Downstairs	61.13	69.65	61.96	40.53	**95.0**
1	Jogging	**98.49**	**89.80**	**94.96**	69.39	**100.0**
2	Sitting	**100.0**	**99.88**	**99.88**	95.25	**100.0**
3	Standing	**100.0**	76.15	**100.0**	95.00	**100.0**
4	Upstairs	63.80	74.47	**80.16**	35.59	**93.63**
5	Walking	**99.69**	41.08	**87.22**	66.17	**99.88**

rate, and results are compared with the previously obtained results. Tables 7 and 8 show the performance evaluation in terms of precision, recall, and $F1$ score of different machine learning algorithms after being trained with CNN features.

Tables 9 and 10 show the recognition rate of different machine learning algorithms after training with CNN features on both datasets.

Table 7 Performance evaluation of different machine learning algorithms with deep CNN features for PAMAP2 dataset

Activity	PAMAP2 dataset											
	Support vector machine			Naïve Bayes			Decision tree			Random forest		
	Precision	Recall	F1 score	Precision	Recall	F1 score	Precision	Recall	F1 score	Precision	Recall	F1 score
0	1.00	1.00	1.00	1.00	1.00	1.00	1.00	1.00	1.00	1.00	1.00	1.00
1	1.00	1.00	1.00	1.00	1.00	1.00	1.00	1.00	**1.00**	1.00	1.00	1.00
2	1.00	1.00	1.00	1.00	1.00	1.00	1.00	1.00	1.00	1.00	1.00	1.00
3	1.00	1.00	1.00	1.00	1.00	1.00	1.00	1.00	1.00	1.00	1.00	1.00
4	0.99	0.98	0.98	0.99	1.00	0.99	1.00	0.98	0.98	0.99	0.99	0.99
5	0.98	0.97	0.98	0.98	0.97	0.98	0.98	0.97	0.97	0.98	0.98	0.98
6	0.97	1.00	0.98	1.00	0.99	0.99	0.99	0.99	0.99	0.98	0.99	0.98
7	0.98	0.98	0.98	0.97	0.98	0.98	0.98	0.98	0.98	0.98	0.98	0.98
12	0.97	0.98	0.98	0.98	0.98	0.98	0.97	0.97	0.97	0.98	0.98	0.98
13	0.99	0.97	0.98	0.99	0.98	0.98	0.97	0.98	0.98	0.99	0.98	0.99
16	1.00	1.00	1.00	1.00	1.00	1.00	1.00	0.99	1.00	1.00	1.00	1.00
17	1.00	1.00	1.00	1.00	1.00	1.00	1.00	1.00	1.00	1.00	1.00	1.00
24	0.99	1.00	0.99	1.00	0.99	1.00	0.99	1.00	0.99	0.99	1.00	0.99

Table 8 Performance evaluation of different machine learning algorithms with deep CNN features for WISDM dataset

Activity	WISDM dataset											
	Support vector machine			Naïve Bayes			Decision tree			Random forest		
	Precision	Recall	F1 score	Precision	Recall	F1 score	Precision	Recall	F1 score	Precision	Recall	F1 score
0	0.94	0.95	0.94	0.93	0.95	0.94	0.93	0.96	0.95	0.93	0.96	0.94
1	1.00	1.00	1.00	1.00	1.00	1.00	1.00	1.00	1.00	1.00	1.00	**1.00**
2	1.00	1.00	**1.00**	1.00	1.00	**1.00**	1.00	1.00	**1.00**	1.00	1.00	**1.00**
3	1.00	1.00	1.00	1.00	1.00	**1.00**	1.00	1.00	**1.00**	1.00	1.00	**1.00**
4	0.95	0.94	0.94	0.95	0.93	0.94	0.96	0.93	0.94	0.96	0.92	0.94
5	1.00	1.00	1.00	1.00	1.00	1.00	1.00	1.00	1.00	1.00	1.00	**1.00**

Table 9 Recognition rate of different classifiers for different activities with CNN features

Activity ID	Activity	Random forest classifier with CNN features (%)	Support vector machine with CNN features (%)	Naïve Bayes with CNN features (%)	Decision tree with CNN features (%)
0	Transient	100	100	100	99.88
1	Lying	100	100	100	100
2	Sitting	100	100	100	100
3	Standing	100	100	100	99.64
4	Walking	97.86	97.50	99.64	97.86
5	Running	97.39	97.27	97.39	97.15
6	Cycling	99.64	99.76	99.05	99.28
7	Nordic walking	97.62	97.74	98.45	97.98
12	Ascending stairs	98.45	98.45	97.62	97.15
13	Descending stairs	98.10	97.39	97.98	98.45
16	Vacuum cleaning	99.88	99.88	99.88	99.40
17	Ironing	100	100	100	100
24	Rope jumping	99.76	99.76	99.40	99.76

Table 10 Recognition rate of different classifiers for different activities with CNN features for WISDM dataset

Activity ID	Activity	Random forest classifier with CNN features (%)	Support vector machine with CNN features (%)	Naïve Bayes with CNN features (%)	Decision tree with CNN features (%)
0	Transient	96.28	95.22	95.40	96.16
1	Lying	100.0	100.0	100.0	100.0
2	Sitting	100.0	100.0	100.0	100.0
3	Standing	100.0	100.0	100.0	100.0
4	Walking	92.40	93.52	93.28	92.75
5	Running	99.88	99.88	99.88	99.76

Tables 5, 6, 9, and 10 show the comparison of the recognition rate of different machine learning classifiers without CNN features and with CNN features, respectively, on both the datasets for each activity. It is clear from observation that CNN features have improved the recognition rate significantly, which is not seen before in the research of physical activity detection. Figures 4 and 7 show a box plot for performance comparison of different classifiers without and with CNN features, respectively, tenfold cross-validation carried out in this comparison, and box plots show that the machine learning models with CNN features achieved significant improvement in terms of sustainability and accuracy. The bar plot in Fig. 8 shows the comparison of the mean accuracy of each algorithm, where blue and red bars show the mean accuracy of algorithms with CNN features and without CNN features, respectively.

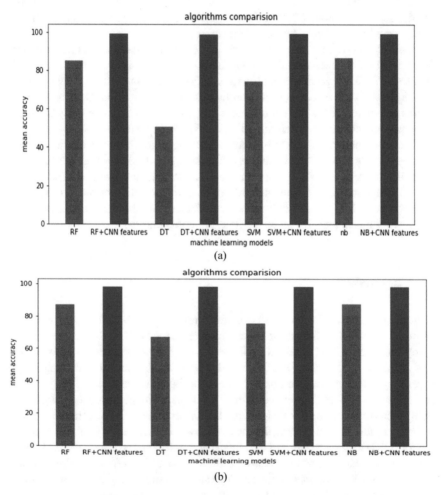

Fig. 8 **a** Comparison of different machine learning algorithms with CNN features and without CNN features for PAMAP2 dataset and **b** for WISDM dataset

6 Discussion

If it is considered that the $F1$ score above 0.85 is justifiable for detecting physical activities on both datasets. In that sense, as shown in Table 3, the Naïve Bayes classifier performed better for the PAMAP2 dataset. Other classifiers performed very well for some activities but not for others. Table 4 shows that none of the classifiers can detect all the activities with a good $F1$ score for the WISDM dataset. Nevertheless, random forest performed well than others. The table also shows that the deep learning model CNN performed much better and detected all the activities with a very high $F1$ score for both datasets.

Tables 5 and 6 show the recognition rate of different machine learning and deep learning model for each activity of both datasets, respectively. Suppose it can be said that above 85% is a good recognition rate. In that case, it is estimated that the Naïve Bayes classifier can detect most of the activities with a recognition rate of above 85%. In this parameter (recognition rate) also, CNN gives a very accurate recognition rate of approximately 100% for all the activities of both datasets.

The shortcomings of all the machine learning algorithms are eradicated with the methodology described in this paper. Tables 7 and 8 show that after learning from the features extracted from the CNN layer, machine learning models have gained momentum in performance, where most of the activities are detected with approximately $1.0\,F1$ score. In the same way, Tables 9 and 10 indicate approximately 100% recognition rates for all the activities of both datasets.

7 Conclusion

It is seen from the above discussion that fine-grained features of the CNN model are proved very effective for performance enhancement of different machine learning algorithms. The model obtained by the learning of these features is observed very fast, accurate, and robust. The improved version of the machine learning model gives very accurate results on both datasets. Decision tree classifier gives its worst performance for both datasets but with CNN features its performance gained very high enhancement and after that, it can classify accurately all the activities of both datasets. Figure 8a and b show the mean accuracy of different algorithms with and without CNN features in terms of the plot of bar graph, and it is observed that blue bars gained high-mean accuracy over the algorithms without CNN features. Hand-crafted features which were defined in the previous studies were time consuming, complex, and required domain knowledge for crafting the features. Now, deep features are easy to extract and have the high representative capability by which learning of algorithms has been improved. Two datasets are taken in this study which have a similar type of activities, real-time data is required for real-time activity recognition for future work. Ensemble methods for modeling deep learning models could be taken by which more complex activities can be detected.

Conflict of Interest There is no conflict of interest.

References

1. Gu F, Khoshelham K, Valaee S, Shang J, Zhang R (2018) Locomotion activity recognition using stacked denoising autoencoders. IEEE Internet Things J 5(3):2085–2093. https://doi.org/10.1109/JIOT.2018.2823084

2. Wang J, Chen Y, Hao S, Peng X, Hu L (2019) Deep learning for sensor-based activity recognition: a survey. Pattern Recogn Lett 119:3–11. https://doi.org/10.1016/j.patrec.2018.02.010

3. Yu S, Chen H, Brown RA (2018) Hidden Markov model-based fall detection with motion sensor orientation calibration: a case for real-life home monitoring. IEEE J Biomed Heal Inform 22(6):1847–1853. https://doi.org/10.1109/JBHI.2017.2782079

4. Townsend D, Knoefel F, Goubran R (2011) Privacy versus autonomy: a tradeoff model for smart home monitoring technologies. In: Proceedings of the annual international conference of the IEEE engineering in medicine and biology society. EMBS, pp 4749–4752. https://doi.org/10.1109/IEMBS.2011.6091176

5. Gani MO et al (2019) A light weight smartphone based human activity recognition system with high accuracy. J Netw Comput Appl 141:59–72. https://doi.org/10.1016/j.jnca.2019.05.001

6. John D, Sasaki J, Staudenmayer J, Mavilia M, Freedson PS (2013) Comparison of raw acceleration from the genea and actigraph^{TM} GT3X + activity monitors. Sensors (Switzerland) 13(11):14754–14763. https://doi.org/10.3390/s131114754

7. Montoye AHK et al (2018) Raw and count data comparability of hip-worn ActiGraph GT3X+ and link accelerometers. Med Sci Sports Exerc 50(5):1103–1112. https://doi.org/10.1249/MSS.0000000000001534

8. Blanke U, Schiele B (2010) Remember and transfer what you have learned—recognizing composite activities based on activity spotting

9. Bulling A, Blanke U, Schiele B (2014) A tutorial on human activity recognition using body-worn inertial sensors. ACM Comput Surv 46(3):1–33. https://doi.org/10.1145/2499621

10. Khan A, Hammerla N, Mellor S, Plötz T (2016) Optimising sampling rates for accelerometer-based human activity recognition. Pattern Recogn Lett 73:33–40. https://doi.org/10.1016/j.patrec.2016.01.001

11. Blum AL, Langley P (1997) Artificial intelligence selection of relevant features and examples in machine. Artif Intell 97(1–2):245–271

12. Gheyas IA, Smith LS (2010) Feature subset selection in large dimensionality domains. Pattern Recogn 43(1):5–13. https://doi.org/10.1016/j.patcog.2009.06.009

13. Singh KP, Basant N, Gupta S (2011) Support vector machines in water quality management. Anal Chim Acta 703(2):152–162. https://doi.org/10.1016/j.aca.2011.07.027

14. Preece SJ, Goulermas JY, Kenney LPJ, Howard D (2009) A comparison of different feature generation methods in activity classification.pdf 56(3):871–879

15. Guyon I, Gunn S, Nikravesh M, Zadeh LA (2008) Feature extraction: foundations and applications, vol 207. Springer

16. Liu Y, Zheng YF (2006) FS_SFS: a novel feature selection method for support vector machines. Pattern Recogn 39(7):1333–1345. https://doi.org/10.1016/j.patcog.2005.10.006

17. Famili A, Shen WM, Weber R, Simoudis E (1997) Data preprocessing and intelligent data analysis. Intell Data Anal 1(1):3–23. https://doi.org/10.3233/IDA-1997-1102

18. Liao C, Li S, Luo Z (2006) Gene selection for cancer classification using Wilcoxon rank sum test and support vector machine. In: 2006 international conference on computational intelligence and security ICCIAS 2006, vol 1, pp 368–373. https://doi.org/10.1109/ICCIAS.2006.294156

19. Jin X, Xu A, Bie R, Guo P (2006) Machine learning techniques and chi-square feature selection for cancer classification using SAGE gene expression profiles. Lecture notes computer science (including subseries lecture notes artificial intelligence lecture notes bioinformatics), vol 3916 LNBI, pp 106–115. https://doi.org/10.1007/11691730_11

20. Hua J, Tembe W, Dougherty ER (2008) Feature selection in the classification of high-dimension data. Department of Electrical & Computer Engineering, Texas A & M University, College Station, TX 77843, USA, pp 1–2

21. Biesiada J, Duch W (2007) Feature selection for high-dimensional data—a Pearson redundancy based filter. Adv Soft Comput 45:242–249. https://doi.org/10.1007/978-3-540-75175-5_30

22. Peng H, Long F, Ding C (2005) Feature selection based on mutual information: criteria of max-dependency, max-relevance, and min-redundancy. IEEE Trans Pattern Anal Mach Intell 27(8):1226–1238. https://doi.org/10.1109/TPAMI.2005.159

23. Rocchi L, Chiari L, Cappello A (2004) Feature selection of stabilometric parameters based on principal component analysis. Med Biol Eng Comput 42(1):71–79. https://doi.org/10.1007/BF02351013

24. Peng J-X, Ferguson S, Rafferty K, Kelly PD (2011) An efficient feature selection method for mobile devices with application to activity recognition. Neurocomputing 74(17):3543–3552. https://doi.org/10.1016/j.neucom.2011.06.023

25. Wang X, Yang J, Teng X, Xia W, Jensen R (2007) Feature selection based on rough sets and particle swarm optimization. Pattern Recogn Lett 28(4):459–471. https://doi.org/10.1016/j.patrec.2006.09.003

26. Coley DA (1999) Writing a genetic algorithm. In: An introduction to genetic algorithms for scientists and engineers, pp 93–112. https://doi.org/10.1142/9789812386359_0005

27. Sun L, Zhang D, Li B, Guo B, Li S (2010) Activity recognition on an accelerometer embedded mobile phone with varying positions and orientations. In: International conference on ubiquitous intelligence and computing, pp 548–562

28. Ayu MA, Mantoro T, Matin AFA, Basamh SSO (2011) Recognizing user activity based on accelerometer data from a mobile phone. In: ISCI 2011—2011 IEEE symposium on computers & informatics, pp 617–621. https://doi.org/10.1109/ISCI.2011.5958987

29. Lau SL, David K (2010) Movement recognition using the accelerometer in smartphones. In: 2010 future network and mobile summit, pp 1–9

30. Bao L, Intille SS (2004) Activity recognition from user-annotated acceleration data BT—UbiComp 2002: ubiquitous computing. In: UbiComp 2002 Ubiquitous Computer, vol 3001, Chapter 1, pp 1–17

31. Yang AY, Iyengar S, Sastry S, Bajcsy R, Kuryloski P, Jafari R (2008) Distributed segmentation and classification of human actions using a wearable motion sensor network. In: 2008 IEEE computer society conference on computer vision and pattern recognition workshops (CVPRW). https://doi.org/10.1109/CVPRW.2008.4563176

32. Uddin MZ, Khaksar W, Torresen J (2017) Facial expression recognition using salient features and convolutional neural network. IEEE Access 5:26146–26161. https://doi.org/10.1109/ACCESS.2017.2777003

33. Uddin MZ, Hassan MM, Almogren A, Alamri A, Alrubaian M, Fortino G (2017) Facial expression recognition utilizing local direction-based robust features and deep belief network. IEEE Access 5:4525–4536. https://doi.org/10.1109/ACCESS.2017.2676238

34. Kiranyaz S, Ince T, Gabbouj M (2016) Real-time patient-specific ECG classification by 1-D convolutional neural networks. IEEE Trans Biomed Eng 63(3):664–675. https://doi.org/10.1109/TBME.2015.2468589

35. Cornacchia M, Ozcan K, Zheng Y, Velipasalar S (2017) A survey on activity detection and classification using wearable sensors. IEEE Sens J 17(2):386–403. https://doi.org/10.1109/JSEN.2016.2628346

36. Ferrari A, Micucci D, Mobilio M, Napoletano P (2020) On the personalization of classification models for human activity recognition. IEEE Access 8:32066–32079. https://doi.org/10.1109/ACCESS.2020.2973425

37. Zhang Y, Gao J, Zhou H (2020) Breeds classification with deep convolutional neural network. In: ACM international conference on machine learning and computing, pp 145–151. https://doi.org/10.1145/3383972.3383975
38. Yann L, Yoshua B (1995) Convolutional networks for images, speech, and time-series 4:2571–2575
39. Kim SY, Han HG, Kim JW, Lee S, Kim TW (2017) A hand gesture recognition sensor using reflected impulses. IEEE Sens J 17(10):2975–2976. https://doi.org/10.1109/JSEN.2017.2679220
40. Mario MO (2019) Human activity recognition based on single sensor square HV acceleration images and convolutional neural networks. IEEE Sens J 19(4):1487–1498. https://doi.org/10.1109/JSEN.2018.2882943
41. Kim KG (2019) Deep learning book review. Nature 29(7553):1–73
42. Reiss A, Stricker D (2012) Pamap2 physical activity monitoring data set. UCI ML repository
43. Turk M, Pentland A (1991) Eigedces for recognition. J Cogn Neurosci 3(1)
44. Moghaddam B, Pentland A (1997) Probabilistic visual learning for object representation for object representation 19(7):696–710
45. Kirby M, Sirovich L (1990) Application of the Karhunen-Loéve procedure for the characterization of human faces. IEEE Trans Pattern Anal Mach Intell 12(1):103–108. https://doi.org/10.1109/34.41390
46. Chen Y, Shen C (2017) Performance analysis of smartphone-sensor behavior for human activity recognition. IEEE Access 5:3095–3110. https://doi.org/10.1109/ACCESS.2017.2676168
47. Berchtold M, Budde M, Schmidtke HR, Beigl M (2010) An extensible modular recognition concept that makes activity recognition practical. Lecture notes computer science (including subseries lecture notes artificial intelligence lecture notes bioinformatics), vol 6359 LNAI, pp 400–409. https://doi.org/10.1007/978-3-642-16111-7_46
48. Wenfeng L, Longjin W, Daojin Y, Heng Y (2014) Fuzzy recognition of abnormal body behaviors based on motion feature analysis. J Huazhong Univ Sci Technol (Natural Sci Ed) 7:17
49. Tapia EM et al (2007) Real-time recognition of physical activities and their intensities using wireless accelerometers and a heart rate monitor. In: Proceedings—international symposium on wearable computers ISWC, pp 37–40. https://doi.org/10.1109/ISWC.2007.4373774
50. Chen Z, Zhu Q, Soh YC, Zhang L (2017) Robust human activity recognition using smartphone sensors via CT-PCA and online SVM. IEEE Trans Ind Inform 13(6):3070–3080. https://doi.org/10.1109/TII.2017.2712746
51. Ma C, Li W, Cao J, Du J, Li Q, Gravina R (2020) Adaptive sliding window based activity recognition for assisted livings. Inf Fusion 53:55–65. https://doi.org/10.1016/j.inffus.2019.06.013

Implementing Robotic Path Planning After Object Detection in Deterministic Environments Using Deep Learning Techniques

R. Gayathri, V. Uma, and Bettina O'Brien

1 Introduction

Robotic path planning [13] or motion planning is the most defining feature of a robot. It can be understood as the ability to navigate in an environment in which it is either previously used to or new to. Motion planning is used to define a number of successive configurations in an environment which leads the robot from a start position to a goal state. The problem of navigation [21] can be integrated into four categories such as perception, localization, motion control and path planning. Perception is one of the most significant capabilities of robots which visualizes the environment and are capable of capturing every activity along the way. Localization is the process of identifying the location of the robot in the environment. It can be done in terms of other obstacles present in the environment as well. One such localization algorithm is simultaneous localization and mapping (SLAM) [11]. Motion control is the problem of identifying the next action for a robot based on the present state of the environment. Path planning defines trajectories and provides a collision-free path for the robot to navigate.

Path planning algorithms can be categorized as deterministic or non-deterministic state algorithms, which can also be referred to as global and local path planning respectively. The robots in the deterministic environment takes advantage of knowing the environment before execution of a task, whereas in a non-deterministic type, the

R. Gayathri (✉)
Department of Computer Science, Rajiv Gandhi National Institute of Youth Development (RGNIYD), Ministry of Youth Affairs and Sports, Government of India, Sriperumbudur, Chennai, India
e-mail: gayathrir339@gmail.com

V. Uma · B. O'Brien
Department of Computer Science, Pondicherry University, Puducherry, India

© The Author(s), under exclusive license to Springer Nature Singapore Pte Ltd. 2023
R. Doriya et al. (eds.), *Machine Learning, Image Processing, Network Security and Data Sciences*, Lecture Notes in Electrical Engineering 946,
https://doi.org/10.1007/978-981-19-5868-7_12

robot explores and perceives a changing environment. Thus, the robot avoids collision with known obstacles and estimates feasible paths using various path planning algorithms [7, 13]. The traditional path planning algorithm builds a map or blueprint of the environment ahead of time, thereby generating the shortest path towards the goal. Later, neural networks [20] were used to train the robot to understand its environment and plan a path accordingly. Given a set of environmental images, a model could be built so as to train on images to perceive the environment [3, 14] and generate paths for an input image [20].

Object detection [15, 17, 22], an important aspect in neural networks, has been made possible using various models like convolutional neural network (CNN) [24], recurrent neural network (RNN), long short-term memory (LSTM) and so on. The metrics and hyperparameters can be tuned in such a way as to increase the efficiency of the model, so that a collision-free optimized path can be generated. In this paper, three sampling-based path planning algorithms, probabilistic RoadMap (PRM), rapidly exploring random trees (RRT) and bidirectional-RRT (Bi-RRT) are implemented after detecting obstacles in an environment.

The overview of the paper is defined as such. Section 2 discusses about the related work regarding the gradual improvement in the methods of implementing path planning techniques using neural network models. Section 3 deals with the methodologies used to process images, identify and detect objects as well as generation of paths. Our proposed work involves a CNN model [9] along with three sampling-based path planning algorithms [4, 18] to navigate the robot in a deterministic environment. In Sect. 4, experimental setup, the results obtained using sampling-based algorithms are defined. Section 5 depicts the implementation comparison of methods and its graphical analyses. Finally, in Sect. 6, the paper concludes the aim of the proposed technique and presents the future proceedings.

2   Related Study

In general, path planning algorithms can be branched into sampling-based, node-based, mathematical model, bio-inspired-based and multi-fusion-based methods [5]. Figure 1 depicts the branches of path planning algorithms. Node-based planning is a search mechanism which explores a set of nodes starting from an initial node and finds an optimal path based on decomposition process. Some of the traditional node-based algorithms are Dijkstra, A^*, D^*, etc. Mathematical model-based path planning is completely based on the kinematics and dynamics of the physical space where the robot navigates.

This paper aims at comparing PRM, RRT and Bi-RRT sampling-based algorithms [2] after differentiating the obstacle and free space using a CNN model. In sampling-based method, there are active and passive techniques [13]. In active method, given the start and goal points, the agent randomly finds ways by generating sampling points along the path towards the goal, whereas in passive method, the whole search space is given along with the goal and the agent creates a roadmap towards the goal.

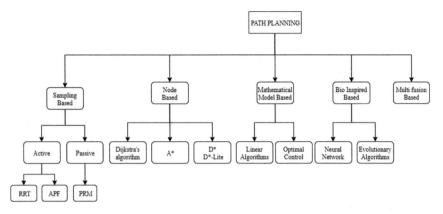

Fig. 1 Methods in path planning

Rapidly exploring random tree (RRT) and artificial potential fields (APF) are two notable active path planning algorithms. RRT algorithm generates random tree-like structural feasible paths from the start to goal points, among which the shortest path is selected [6]. Probabilistic RoadMap (PRM) [4] is a passive path planning method, where the outcome is based on high probability and sample points are generated to construct a graph. PRM has a local planner connects two points x and y in the Configuration-space (C-space) if there is no obstacles in that edge and a roadmap method to construct a map of the environment. A probabilistic planner is used and works in offline and online modes. In offline, the planner learns about the environment and constructs a roadmap, whereas in online mode, a graph is generated from the roadmap and the planner queries an optimal path for the robot. Bidirectional RRT (Bi-RRT) [18] algorithm works similar to RRT but generates random paths from both the start and goal positions.

Object detection [1], a core challenge in computer vision, detects objects from images which involves computer vision and deep learning strategies, particularly in facial detection [10] and image recognition [8] applications. Bio-inspired-based path planning is a method which is inspired by the natural behaviour of individuals. For instance, inspired by the human neural system, artificial neural network (ANN) [21] was invented. Robotic path planning which requires a deep understanding and learning about the environment is implemented using various architectures of CNN [23, 24]. For the past few years, CNN has proved to be a reliable method for object detection and classification [12] due to its speed and accuracy. Detection of objects has been possible with both deep learning and OpenCV [2]. You Only Look Once (YOLO) [14, 19] detects objects with higher accuracy but does not identify objects in a group. A deep learning single neural network, Single Shot MultiBox Detector (SSD) [16], is a straightforward and easy model for training smaller-sized data.

3 Proposed Methodology

The proposed model defines a method in which the obstacles in the given image are detected after which path planning is done by excluding the regions where detection is performed. In some instances, certain obstacles are not considered to be obstacles by the basic motion planning algorithms. Hence, paths were generated over such undetected obstacles. Thus, the proposed model is segmented into two modules, object detection and path generation phases. Figure 2 depicts the architecture of the proposed path planning strategy.

3.1 Object Detection

This phase identifies and localizes obstacles in digital images. The obstacle detection model used is a MobileNet deep CNN architecture with a Single Shot MultiBox Detector (SSD) framework. The SSD framework is similar to a VGG16 CNN model, used to localize objects, whereas the MobileNet architecture is made up of seventeen blocks used to classify images with labels. Together, object detection is done by replacing VGG16 with MobileNet. SSD is proved to precisely bound boxes for objects with high accuracy.

The model is trained with a sample environmental images, which includes both grayscale and coloured obstacles. Figure 3 shows some sample environmental images in which the obstacle shapes are emphasized, used for training and testing. This environment map provides the random position of fixed set of obstacles in varying shapes. The hurdles to overcome in the environment are that performing safely and robustly when negotiating tight spaces in map, like obstacles or edges. Further, a method is proposed to understand the real-time information about the obstacles of varying shapes and to detect the obstacle-free space. This is used in generating the collision-free waypoints and finding an optimal path. In the traditional path planning strategy, the obstacles that are sketched in Fig. 3a are not been identified or detected.

The proposed work is based on transfer learning in which the model is not trained from the scratch, rather it uses the pre-trained weights of the SSD detection using coco dataset. The performance of SSD framework is directly proportional to object

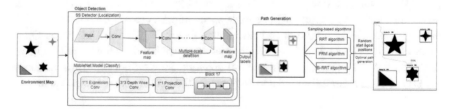

Fig. 2 Proposed architecture

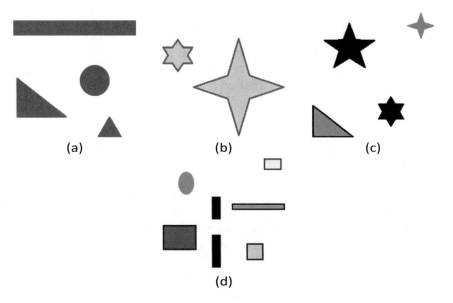

Fig. 3 **a, b** Sample train images and **c, d** Sample test images

sizes and does not fare too well on object categories with small sizes. Therefore, MobileNet architecture is used to resize certain parts of the image which helps the network to identify and learn features for small object categories.

The basic block of the MobileNet architecture has a 1×1 expansion layer, a 3×3 depthwise layer and a 1×1 projection layer. The expansion convolution augments the channel numbers of the input image. The depthwise convolution filters reduce the channels after which the filtered values are combined to give new learned features. The projection layer projects images with increased channel numbers and dimensions. The outcome of this phase is an image with bounding boxes around all the obstacles.

3.2 Path Generation

In this phase, the collision-free trajectory is generated by the sampling-based path planners such as RRT, PRM and Bi-RRT. The principle use of this method is to generate a random sample in the environment in the form of nodes, cells or in other forms in order to achieve a feasible path. This algorithms requires prior knowledge of the environment in finding a path.

During navigation, the path planner takes into account the geometric constraints of obstacles in order to reach the desired target point. The area explored by the algorithms is the area occupied by the free space. The obstacle detection-based sampling-based algorithms generate an optimal path towards the goal and improve the exploration efficiency, thereby reducing the computational over-head.

Initially, for each algorithm, for different start and goal positions, all possible feasible paths towards the goal are generated, out of which the optimal path is identified. Out of these, Bi-RRT and PRM have proved to produce the best paths in terms of time and distance, respectively.

4 Implementation and Analyses

The proposed model is implemented using a custom-made environmental image dataset with obstacles. All the images have a resolution of 500×500 pixels. We use the labeling annotator to label the images with ground truth boxes. The corresponding XMLs are converted into CSV format after splitting the training and test images. Then, the TFRecords are generated for both the train and test images.

The aim of this method is to perform obstacle detection on these images and generate all the possible obstacle-free paths. Amongst this, the optimal shortest path is found. The model has a single class called 'obstacle' with L2 regularizer, ReLU 6 activation, learning rate as 0.004 and RMSprop optimizer. Figure 4 depicts obstacle detection performed of three sample test images.

The obstacle detection model is implemented with a pre-trained SSD MobileNet model that uses a single GPU with hyperparameters 1500 epochs, 50 evaluation steps and batch size 12 set as such. This model is trained with the environment map with bounding boxes. As the number of training epochs increases, the test loss decreases. This is shown in Fig. 5.

The performance of obstacle detection model is measured in terms of mean average precision (mAP), recall, $F1$-score and frames per second (fps). The overall object labels from the area under precision and recall curve is calculated by mean average precision (mAP) which is the average of APs. This is shown in Eq. (4). Frames per second are the number of frames that can be processed per second.

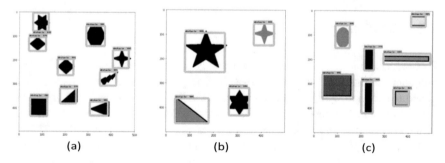

Fig. 4 Obstacle detection under different scenarios

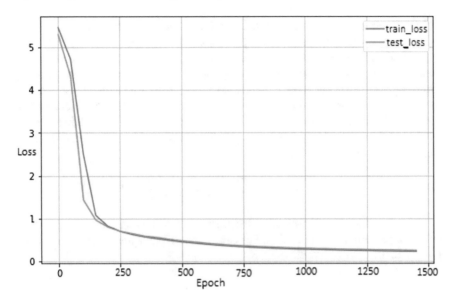

Fig. 5 Training curves of the loss function

$$\text{Precision} = \frac{\text{TP}}{\text{TP} + \text{FP}} \tag{1}$$

$$\text{Recall} = \frac{\text{TP}}{\text{TP} + \text{FN}} \tag{2}$$

$$F1 - \text{score} = \frac{2PR}{P + R} \tag{3}$$

$$\text{mAP} = \frac{1}{N} \sum_{i=1}^{N} AP_i \tag{4}$$

Table 1 shows that the number of parameters, mean average precision (mAP), recall and $F1$-score as well as their per-frame inference speed. SSD MobileNet architecture obtains high $F1$-score, processing speed and mAP due to depthwise separable convolutions which drastically reduces the number of parameters in the network.

Table 1 Number of parameters, mAP, recall, $F1$-score and processing speed of object detection approach

Model	Backbone	Parameters	mAP	Recall	$F1$-score	Speed (fps)
SSD	MobileNet	7.5M	84.6	80.11	90.38	95

Path generation for sampling-based algorithms RRT, PRM and Bi-RRT are done using octave at different start and goal positions in the environment. Negative coordinates would not be accepted and for such positions, an exception 'coordinates lies on obstacles' is shown. For each random sampling method, multiple paths are found by exploring the environment, out of which the optimal path is generated. In addition to the shortest path, the execution time in milliseconds and the distance in terms of the number of nodes along the path are calculated. The distance of the path between the two coordinate points (x_1, y_1) and (x_2, y_2) is calculated using the Euclidean distance. This formula is given in Eq. (5).

$$\text{Distance}(d) = \sqrt{(x_2 - x_1)^2 + (y_2 - y_1)^2} \tag{5}$$

The execution time is estimated the time taken to compute the solution from an initial position to goal position. For each method, paths are generated for many sample environments, out of which one is depicted.

5   Comparative Analysis

Tables 2, 3 and 4 show a comparison of RRT, PRM and Bi-RRT path generation algorithms for a sample environment, after obstacle detection. Clearly, from these table, we capture that all methods provide an optimal path in a certain measure, but the bidirectional-RRT algorithm provides an optimal path in a much lesser time.

Table 2 Path generated by RRT in sample environment

Start Goal	Exploration	Optimal path	Runtime (sec) Distance(m)
	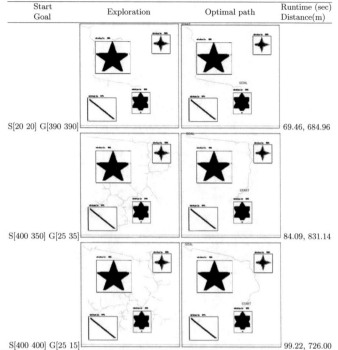		
S[20 20] G[390 390]			69.46, 684.96
S[400 350] G[25 35]			84.09, 831.14
S[400 400] G[25 15]			99.22, 726.00

We computed the path length and run time of each environment. The results are shown in Table 5. From the obtained results, we found that Bi-RRT yields minimum time when compared with the other two approaches. PRM results in minimum distance due to more obstacle-free space in the environment but it has taken maximum time to search the optimal path due to the number of vertices in the roadmap parameter.

Figure 6a and b depicts the time and distance metrics for three different source S and goal G given by the three path generation algorithms.

6 Conclusion and Future Directions

The aim of this paper is to provide a path planning approach using deep learning, in which the obstacles are identified in the environment and detected using SSD framework. Then, path planning is performed using three sampling-based algorithms

Table 3 Path generated by PRM in sample environment

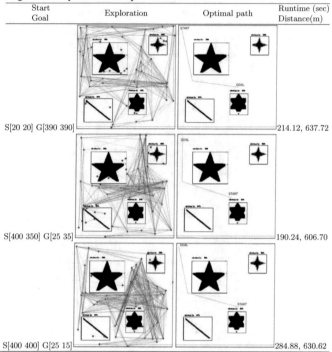

Start Goal	Exploration	Optimal path	Runtime (sec) Distance(m)
S[20 20] G[390 390]			214.12, 637.72
S[400 350] G[25 35]			190.24, 606.70
S[400 400] G[25 15]			284.88, 630.62

and comparative analyses is performed for each method's time and distance metrics. The results are tabulated, and Bi-RRT proves to be the best out of the three methods. The future work is this paper is to include semantic features in obstacles and to identify obstacles in terms of the semantic labels.

Table 4 Path generated by Bi-RRT in sample environment

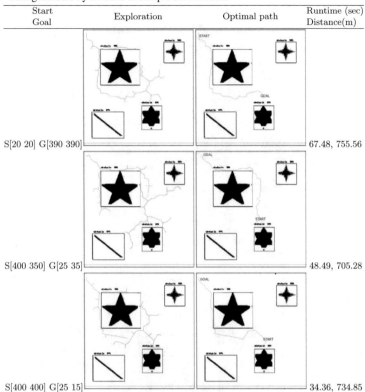

Start Goal	Exploration	Optimal path	Runtime (sec) Distance(m)
S[20 20] G[390 390]			67.48, 755.56
S[400 350] G[25 35]			48.49, 705.28
S[400 400] G[25 15]			34.36, 734.85

Table 5 Comparison of each method with respect to execution time and path length

Performance metrics	RRT	PRM	Bi-RRT
Avg. execution time (s)	84.25	229.74	50.11
Avg. distance (m)	747.36	625.01	731.89

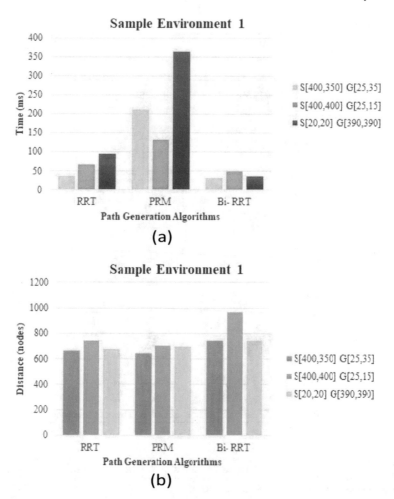

Fig. 6 Comparison of performances of various algorithms in difference start and goal positions with respect to **a** execution time **b** distance covered

References

1. Ahmed SM, Tan YZ, Lee GH, Chew CM, Pang CK (2016) Object detection and motion planning for automated welding of tubular joints. In: 2016 IEEE/RSJ international conference on intelligent robots and systems (IROS). IEEE, pp 2610–2615
2. Chandan G, Jain A, Jain H et al (2018) Real time object detection and tracking using deep learning and openCV. In: 2018 international conference on inventive research in computing applications (ICIRCA). IEEE, pp 1305–1308
3. Duguleana M, Mogan G (2016) Neural networks based reinforcement learning for mobile robots obstacle avoidance. Expert Syst Appl 62:104–115
4. Faust A, Oslund K, Ramirez O, Francis A, Tapia L, Fiser M, Davidson J (2018) PRM-RL: long-range robotic navigation tasks by combining reinforcement learning and sampling-based

planning. In: 2018 IEEE international conference on robotics and automation (ICRA). IEEE, pp 5113–5120

5. Gayathri R, Uma V (2019) Performance analysis of robotic path planning algorithms in a deterministic environment. Int J Imaging Robot 19(4):83–108

6. Gayathri R, Uma V, Bettina O (2021) Unified robot task and motion planning with extended planner using ROS simulator. J King Saud Univ Comput Inf Sci

7. Geraerts RJ (2006) Sampling-based motion planning: analysis and path quality

8. He K, Zhang X, Ren S, Sun J (2016) Deep residual learning for image recognition. In: Proceedings of the IEEE conference on computer vision and pattern recognition, pp 770–778

9. Howard AG, Zhu M, Chen B, Kalenichenko D, Wang W, Weyand T, Andreetto M, Adam H (2017) Mobilenets: efficient convolutional neural networks for mobile vision applications. arXiv preprint arXiv:1704.04861

10. Jiang H, Learned-Miller E (2017) Face detection with the faster R-CNN. In: 2017 12th IEEE international conference on automatic face & gesture recognition (FG 2017). IEEE, pp 650–657

11. Khairuddin AR, Talib MS, Haron H (2015) Review on simultaneous localization and mapping (slam). In: 2015 IEEE international conference on control system, computing and engineering (ICCSCE). IEEE, pp 85–90

12. Krizhevsky A, Sutskever I, Hinton GE (2017) Imagenet classification with deep convolutional neural networks. Commun ACM 60(6):84–90

13. LaValle SM (2006) Planning algorithms. Cambridge University Press

14. Li G, Ma Y (2018) A deep path planning algorithm based on CNNs for perception images. In: 2018 Chinese automation congress (CAC). IEEE, pp 2536–2541

15. Li X, Wang S (2017) Object detection using convolutional neural networks in a coarse-to-fine manner. IEEE Geosci Remote Sens Lett 14(11):2037–2041

16. Liu W, Anguelov D, Erhan D, Szegedy C, Reed S, Fu CY, Berg AC (2016) SSD: single shot multibox detector. In: European conference on computer vision. Springer, pp 21–37

17. Orozco-Rosas U, Picos K, Montiel O, Sepu´lveda R, D´ıaz-Ram´ırez VH (2016) Obstacle recognition for path planning in autonomous mobile robots. In: Optics and photonics for information processing X, vol 9970. International Society for Optics and Photonics, p 99700X

18. Qureshi AH, Ayaz Y (2015) Intelligent bidirectional rapidly-exploring random trees for optimal motion planning in complex cluttered environments. Robot Auton Syst 68:1–11

19. Redmon J, Divvala S, Girshick R, Farhadi A (2016) You only look once: unified, real-time object detection. In: Proceedings of the IEEE conference on computer vision and pattern recognition, pp 779–788

20. Szegedy C, Toshev A, Erhan D (2013) Deep neural networks for object detection. In: Advances in neural information processing systems, pp 2553–2561

21. Tai L, Li S, Liu M (2017) Autonomous exploration of mobile robots through deep neural networks. Int J Adv Rob Syst 14(4):1729881417703571

22. Tripathi S, Dane G, Kang B, Bhaskaran V, Nguyen T (2017) LCDet: Low-complexity fully-convolutional neural networks for object detection in embedded systems. In: Proceedings of the IEEE conference on computer vision and pattern recognition workshops, pp 94–103

23. Zhao ZQ, Zheng P, Xu ST, Wu X (2019) Object detection with deep learning: a review. IEEE Trans Neural Networks Learn Syst 30(11):3212–3232

24. Zhiqiang W, Jun L (2017) A review of object detection based on convolutional neural network. In: 2017 36th Chinese control conference (CCC). IEEE, pp 11104–11109

SDDSCNet: Siamese-Based Dilated Depthwise Separable Convolution Neural Network with Wavelet Fusion for Change Detection

Parmeshwar S. Patil, Prathmesh R. Bhosale, Raghunath S. Holambe, and Laxman M. Waghmare

1 Introduction

Change detection (CD) through high-resolution satellite imagery is critical for human society's long-term survival. Change detection is advantageous in the civil and environmental disciplines, as it provides for a better understanding of natural resources and man-made infrastructures. It plays a key role in government policy decisions. This approach is typically used in urban planning and environmental monitoring to assess natural impacts on the land surface as well as planetary trends. The goal of this study is to identify minor differences between bi-temporal satellite images of the same region. Change detection algorithms in the literature often take one of two approaches. First, they use pixel-based analysis [1], which divides the bi-temporal images into predetermined different classes and then uses pixel-by-pixel correlation to create the change map. Change map is created pixel to pixel from the original satellite image pairs using basic operations such as subtraction, stacked change map, and logarithmic ratio [2]. The second method is object-based analysis; it is not the same as pixel-based approaches. Object-based methods are not the same as pixel-based approaches. Rather of comparing pixels individually, these methods aggregate

P. S. Patil (✉) · R. S. Holambe · L. M. Waghmare
Shri Guru Gobind Singhji Institute of Engineering and Technology, Nanded,
Maharashtra 431606, India
e-mail: patilparam25@gmail.com

R. S. Holambe
e-mail: rsholambe@sggs.ac.in

L. M. Waghmare
e-mail: lmwaghmare@sggs.ac.in

P. R. Bhosale
Indian Institute of Technology Kharagpur, Kharagpur, West Bengal 721302, India
e-mail: bhosale1prathmesh@gmail.com

© The Author(s), under exclusive license to Springer Nature Singapore Pte Ltd. 2023
R. Doriya et al. (eds.), *Machine Learning, Image Processing, Network Security and Data Sciences*, Lecture Notes in Electrical Engineering 946,
https://doi.org/10.1007/978-981-19-5868-7_13

pixels in an image into nearby semantic objects. The differences are then emphasized using object-by-object comparisons [3, 4].

The features considered for CD approaches are very hand-designed and poor in the image illustration, as explained previously. As a reason, deep learning is increasingly being used to extract features straight from source imagery. The generated feature data are the most stable and robust. For identifying changes between optical and SAR images. In [5], author has developed an asymmetric convolution coupling network (SCCN). By translating the retrieved feature into feature space, a change detection map is produced in this method. The optimal coupling method, which only relies on the unchanging pixels, has been used to train and learn the SCCN network. For improving change detection accuracy, with the k-nearest technique, in [6] presented shallow convoluted 4-level siamese model. On the other hand, the knn only add if their set k-level is inside the scale. As a result, it is incorrect to analyze the modified and changed pixels of unbalanced data. (FC-EF) fully convolutional with early fusion network, (FC-Siam-concatenat), and (EF-Siam-difference) models were provided by the author in [7]. These fully convolutional networks were trained from start to finish without any post-processing. The results' spatial precision was enhanced by employing skip connection on these siamese networks, but the fundamental disadvantage of the skip connection network is the significantly reduced time for convergence [8]. To minimize the training parameters, in [9] in place of the typical UNet, the author constructed a (DDSCN) deep depthwise separable convolution network, which is somewhat effective than the original convolution technique. The approaches described before can be characterized as supervised [6, 10, 11] or, unsupervised [5, 12–15].

The ground truth (GT) labeled data can not be used by unsupervised algorithms. As a result, they are generally trained on specific assumptions; nevertheless, in landsat imagery, characteristics in the unsupervised model are analytically and dimensionally transformed due to imbalanced and actively overlying samples [6]. It could be a difficult task for unsupervised techniques in this situation. On the other part, if labeled GT samples are accessible for training, it may provide a great deal of information for decision-making. The fundamental purpose of this research is to evaluate the accuracy of informational difference images created with a siamese-based dilated DWconv network and the original UNet structure on satellite images out of the same location. In addition, the designed project intends to:

- In this paper, designed a lightweight siamese-based dilated DWconv (SDDSC-Net) for CD, which minimize the computational complexity of the network and increases the accelerate the segmentation task. This study uses a UNet decoder network based on DWconv to reconstruct soft activation maps with optimal use of relevant data. The DWconv layer is employed to reduce the number of multiplications while assure change detection exactness.
- This paper designed the dense dilated DWconv (DDWconv) center part in proposed method, which necessarily expand the susceptible area of network to capture context information and assuring the accuracy of the semantic segmentation task.

- The UDWT post-processing fusion approach is being utilized to combine the binary output of a proposed siamese model for better image interpretation. By using the undecimated wavelet transform and its restoration, the diverse information problem is defeated and the stability to get more information difference image with improved viewing aspect [16].

The rest of the paper is structured as follows: Sect. 2 describes the dataset. Section 3 describes the proposed technique, training parameter, and methodology. Section 4 describes the experimental data, and discussion is presented. After Sect. 5, there comes a conclusion.

2 Dataset Description

This study utilizes the SZATKI AirChange Dataset to develop the designed architecture and evaluate the algorithm. This dataset was used in [6, 9, 11, 17]. This benchmark dataset is made up of three pairs of registered satellite images that were captured over a large span of time and under a different of unusual conditions. The informative indexes were SZADA, ARCHIVE, and TISZADOB and include 7, 5, and 1 image pairs with a 23-year lag time, respectively. The GTs were manually annotated by the experts. Each image is 952×640 size with 1.5 m per pixel resolution and a binary change label. The third image of the TISZADOB and the first images of the SZADA dataset were used to test our model. In addition, we compared and assessed our methodology using the (OSCD) Onera Satellite Change Detection imagery data [11]. The remote sensing scientific community suggested the OSCD dataset, which is an available and standardized approach for measuring the adaptability of CD application. For this dataset, 24-locations with around 600×600 size with resolutions of 10 m and varied degrees of urban development changes were chosen from around the world (14 image for training and 10 images for testing, for a total of 24 training image pairs). The natural color images for every region on each pair were physically contrasted to create labeled GT. This dataset is more adapted for the application of supervised methods to the change detection problem (Fig. 1).

The designed architecture's backbone is a change detection encoder–decoder-based UNet framework with fixed input and output image data dimensions [18]. We downscale each image from the top-left to the bottom-right corner to 112×112 pixels in order to create overlaying down-scaled patches for training and testing purpose, with regions clipped to be 40% overlaying and some space at the top-left and bottom-right to remove each gaps. Because the pixels might be covered a large area in different scaled images, the proportion of overlapping does not have to be high to produce good results. Instead, it is indeed possible that they will cause misunderstandings. The percentage of overlapping is chosen. Training, validation, and testing data are split 70%:10%:20% accordingly, in this paper. To reinforce cropped training patches, where each cropped patch is rotated by 90°, 180°, and 270° vertically, horizontally, and flipped. The experiment involved a total of 1045

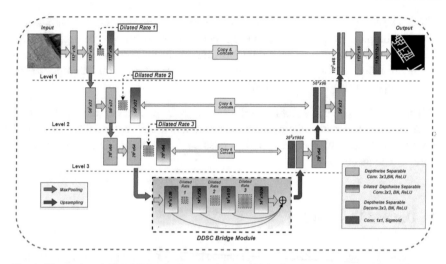

Fig. 1 The designed SDDSCNet: in the encoder, the original convolution layers are replaced by DWconv and employing n as a dilated rate with level increases. Dilated-based DWconv layer is used at every layer of an encoder for extracting different scale-related features which enlarge the receptive field of the network. Dilated rate with DWconv linearly increased as the layer increases in the DDWconv center part to ensuring the accuracy of the segmentation network. ReLU activation with Learning rate = 0.0001 and batch normalization are activated in the network

augmented images. This technique effectively expands the variety of training data available to the model. It is worth noting that the sets used for train, validation, and test are really not overlapped, indicating that the preliminary results are genuine. For testing and training, we used the SZATKI AirChange and the OSCD Benchmark dataset in our proposed method.

3 Proposed Method

3.1 UNet Structure with Original Convolution

Specially, an UNet is designed for the semantic segmentation task, which contains encoder, center part, and decoder path [18]. Using numerous convolution layers and maximum pooling, the encoder of the UNet converts input images into feature representations. The image is successively downsampled, and the resolution of the image is decreased to extract rich information from the source image. The CNN architectures downscaling the resolutions of the source input to determine the resulting output map. Reconstructing the original size segmentation result from a reduced resolution feature map is a difficult task. Deconvolution is used in the decoder to up-sample the encoder's feature maps, restoring and improving object information

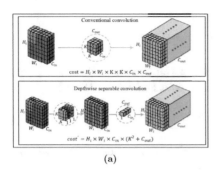 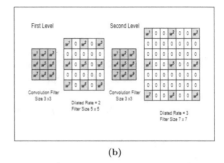

(a)   (b)

Fig. 2 **a** A notional example of original convolution and DWconv operation. **b** Illustration design: one convolutional kernel with its dilated kernel size

during the processing. UNet concatenates and transposes enriched features content from encoder levels to feature information in decoder levels.

3.2 DWconv-Depthwise Separable Convolution

The DWconv replaces conventional convolution with two convolutions: pointwise convolution and depthwise convolution [19]. We make the depthwise operation to get a one kernel for each input depth. In pointwise operation, we perform a normal 1×1 filter on the depthwise convolution to obtain a combined output of the depthwise convolution. Figure 2a shows the approach of depthwise separable and standard convolution process.

Examine, one kernel per input depth in depthwise operation is defined as:

$$X_{(p,q,r)} = \sum_{m,n} F_{m,n,r} * Y_{(p+m-1),(q+n-1),r} \tag{1}$$

where depthwise operation kernel F of dimension $F \times F$, rth channel in Y is multiply with rth kernel in F to produce the rth channel of X output map.

To calculate the two convolution cost, consider that two convolutions examine on the activation map L^i of resolution $H^i \times W^i \times C^{in}$ and get a output map L^{out} of resolution $H^i \times W^i \times C^{out}$. Equation (2) explains the computation calculation of the original convolution with filter dimension $F \times F$.

$$\text{Standard}_{\text{cost}} = H^i \times W^i \times F \times F \times C^{in} \times C^{out} \tag{2}$$

The computation calculation of DWconv is the sum of depthwise and pointwise layer exercise. Firstly, divide the source image into the number of depth C^{in} and kernel F into individual depth, and then perform with the corresponding depth with a $F \times F$ of kernel dimensions. The computation calculation of the example is as shown:

$$\text{cost}_{\text{depth}} = H^i \times W^i \times C^{\text{in}} \times F \times F \times 1 \tag{3}$$

Further, 1×1 filter (pointwise convolution) performs with C^{out} kernels getting output for depthwise convolution. The computation calculation is defined as:

$$\text{cost}_{\text{point}} = H^i \times W^i \times C^{\text{in}} \times 1 \times 1 \times C^{\text{out}} \tag{4}$$

now, the computation cost of DWconv is the combination of Eqs. 3 and 4, which is formulated as:

$$\text{Depthwise}_{\text{cost}} = H^i \times W^i \times C^{\text{in}} \times (F^2 + C^{\text{out}}) \tag{5}$$

from standard parameter and DWconv parameter, we derive the final computation cost which is shown below:

$$\frac{\text{Depthwise}_{\text{cost}}}{\text{Standard}_{\text{cost}}} = \frac{H^i \times W^i \times C^{\text{in}} \times (F^2 + C^{\text{out}})}{H^i \times W^i \times C^{\text{in}} \times F \times F \times C^{\text{out}}}$$
$$= \frac{1}{C^{\text{out}}} + \frac{1}{F^2}$$

Accordingly, the DWconv reduces the parameter calculations by F^2 times than the original convolution's parameter. $F = 3$ of DWconv is utilized in SDDSCNet, to minimize the training parameters of the network to 9 times that of the original UNet. This is very computational cost effective and speed up the change detection segmentation.

3.3 Dilated Convolution Operation

Dilated convolution permits us to significantly expand the region of interest of filters to include a considerable amount of context without raising the number of parameters or computations [20]. Figure 2b gives the detailed view of dilated convolution filter. The author uses the multiple convolution with increasing dilated rate fashion to use dilated convolution to extract features from several scales. Suppose, dilated rate r in dilated convolution added zeros $r - 1$ in the filter weights, the $F \times F$ filter enlarges the scale in the following manner which is formulated as:

$$F \times F = [F + (F - 1)(r - 1)] \times [F + (F - 1)(r - 1)] \tag{6}$$

Particularly, the number of non-zero filter weights is the same as the standard values which put the parameter cost constant. The dilated convolution effectively

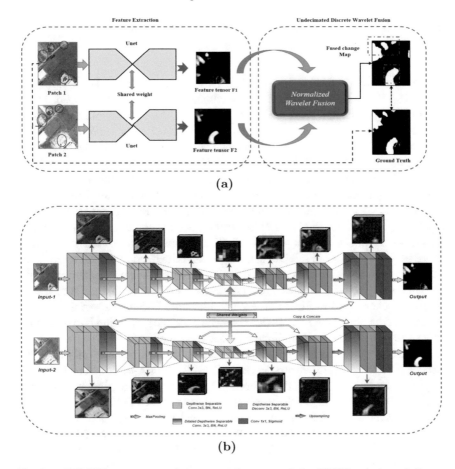

Fig. 3 **a** SDDSCNet structure and post-processing approach for UDWT-undecimated discrete wavelet transform. **b** SDDSCNet layer-by-layer extracting features representation using a UNet structure

increases the related region of network to capture context information and assure the accuracy of the segmentation task. Dilated convolution and DDWconv center part is conventional to extract most relevant information than original UNet. For attention purposes, Fig. 3b defines the rich feature maps which are derived by SDDSCNet. It is shown that the information capture by SDDSCNet is more negotiable than the original UNet. The suggested design outperformed typical approaches with expanded filters and compact layers, resulting in a considerable reduction in computing efficiency.

3.4 SDDSCNet with Dilated-Based Depthwise Separable Convolution for Change Detection

An encoder path, decoder path, and bridge network compensate a UNet-based network [18]. It is a different format that is commonly utilized for change detection semantics segmentation. As demonstrated in Fig. 1. This paper explores a advance another UNet; it consists often of a siamese UNet based on dilated DWconv, abbreviated as SDDSCNet. It is prompted by the foundation of the UNet construction, which is built on dilated-based DWconv, and which, when compared to ordinary UNet designs, fundamentally improves on the compact layers with much less parameterization, limited computational performance, and design input. By demonstrating, this SDDSCNet architecture, that takes the overlaying downscaled patches of its input images, it solves the issue of not having enough training data and learning the algorithm. This improves the individual's cross-uniformity's ability to identify minor possible changes in satellite data. In [6], in the extraction of features task, the siamese design has a superior description. We employ a siamese framework in the proposed study, which contains two structures with the same composition. One of the two patches is fed as input into each architecture. The systems of the siamese designs, on the other extreme, provide the same weighting, enabling it to collect the very same information from multiple inputs in an equitable way [21].

An encoder path, a decoder path, and a DWconv center part comprise the SDDSC-Net design. The encoder route is made up of 3 levels of upper-to-down encoders with varying convolutional feature dimensions. Every dilated convolution layer's receptive fields increase sharply as the levels go up in the encoder. In Fig. 1, 3×3, 5×5, and 7×7 is the dilated filter size of the 1st, 2nd, and 3rd level with 3×3, 5×5, and 7×7 are the filter size, respectively. DWconv linearly increases the dilated rate as layer goes on increases in the DDWconv center part, which enable the architecture to capture related feature and assure the accuracy of the network. The extracted features are upsampled in the decoder part, which then performs DWconv with 50% of the dimensions after recombining the concurrent image features as from encoder. BN-Batch normalization and ReLU activation with Learning rate $= 0.0001$ are employed to every layers in the architecture. We have 18-convolutional layers in total, compared to 23-convolutional layers in the UNet, which is demonstrated in Fig. 1. The framework is represented by a layer-by-layer extracting features feature maps as illustrated in Fig. 3b. The proposed architecture depends on the siamese-based dilated DWconv with UDWT-undecimated discrete wavelet transform fusion which is given in Fig. 3.

3.5 Details of Training Parameter

An Adam-adaptive moment estimation optimizer is utilized in the training phase as a version of the SGD-stochastic gradient descent optimizer with a batch of 16 images. This work uses binary crossentropy as a loss-function to train the proposed framework. The Adam optimizer was chosen since it only requires a few setting parameters [22]. To decrease the probability of generalization throughout the training procedure, this study used data augmentation techniques such as horizontal and vertical flips, contrast, and brightness. For 100 epochs, the model was trained. The abovementioned parameters were chosen based on their excellent experimental results. The proposed architecture performance can be enhanced further by customizing the training algorithm's parameters.

3.6 UDWT-Undecimated Discrete Wavelet Transform Fusion

Fusion of image is a strategy for integrating information from multiple source to create a restored image with a large amount of data. Fusion of image can result in an effectively outcome that is useful for image analysis [23]. The fusion rule is used to integrate feature maps F_1 and F_2 from Fig. 3b, to create a change information image. For fusion, there are numerous wavelet approaches described in the literature. These are used to merge data from several image sources [23]. For fusion, The DWT-discrete wavelet transform is generally adapted for information fusion. In both the geographical and temporal aspects, DWT employs a different-level multi-dimensional study of images, outcome in a much transformed result [24]. DWT is convenient for image squeezing purpose; however, when it comes to data analysis, it does not provide an accurate solution. The limitation of DWT is that it does not translate uniformly, which has a variety of effects in the final image. As a result, UDWT is appropriate for image study [16]. UDWT uses the original bank of filters of DWT, but the output is not down-sampled. Therefore, all sub-bands are the equal size as the standard resolution. Because there is no downscaling, the output image is less degraded by noise, shift invariant, and suppress the diverse pixel problem [25]. The different dimensional study of I^i source input is a 2-level procedure employing UDWT decomposition, where i is the set of features. The image is first decomposed using a t-level UDWT algorithm. $I^i_{t,\text{LL}}, I^i_{t,\text{LH}}, I^i_{t,\text{HL}}, I^i_{t,\text{HH}}$ are the four sub-bands obtained at each level, with $k = 1, 2, \ldots t$ where H and L stand for high- and low-pass kernels. By combining the kernel L with the rows and columns, the low-frequency sub-band $I^i_{t,\text{LL}}$ is obtained. The other three sub-bands of high-frequency are created by applying a H or L filter to the column first, and then a H or L filter to the row. Equations (7) to (10) can be used to generate the UDWT decomposition as follows:

$$I^i_{t+1,\text{LL}}(x, y) = \sum_{u=0}^{N_{t,\text{L}-1}} \sum_{v=0}^{N_{t,\text{L}-1}} \text{L}_t(u)\text{L}_t(v)I^i_{t,\text{LL}}(x + u, y + v) \tag{7}$$

$$I^i_{t+1,\text{LH}}(x, y) = \sum_{u=0}^{N_{t,\text{L}-1}} \sum_{v=0}^{N_{t,\text{H}-1}} \text{L}_t(u)\text{H}_t(v)I^i_{t,\text{LL}}(x + u, y + v) \tag{8}$$

$$I_{t+1,\mathrm{HL}}^{i}(x, y) = \sum_{u=0}^{N_{t,\mathrm{H}-1}} \sum_{v=0}^{N_{t,\mathrm{L}-1}} \mathrm{H}_t(u) \mathrm{L}_t(v) I_{t,\mathrm{LL}}^{i}(x+u, y+v) \qquad (9)$$

$$I_{t+1,\mathrm{HH}}^{i}(x, y) = \sum_{u=0}^{N_{t,\mathrm{H}-1}} \sum_{v=0}^{N_{t,\mathrm{H}-1}} \mathrm{H}_t(u) \mathrm{H}_t(v) I_{t,\mathrm{LL}}^{i}(x+u, y+v) \qquad (10)$$

$I_{0,\mathrm{LL}}^{i} = I^{i}$, where $N_{t,\mathrm{L}}$ and $N_{t,\mathrm{H}}$ are the dimensions of the low-pass filter L_t and high-pass filter H_t. The number of images is i. In this work, the one level decomposition UDWT is applied after the feature extraction. The fusion rule is used to create the altered image. SDDSCNet, which contains change information data, is used to extract the feature maps F_1^{i} and F_2^{i}. By refer to fusion rule, which is stated in Eq. (11) this data are being collected in order to build an accurate change map. Using Eqs. (7) to (10), UDWT decomposition on F_1^{i} and F_2^{i} feature maps yields four sub-bands for each. The low-frequency sub band represents the input image's essential properties, and as a result, it displays the changing information of two source inputs. The fusion rule in Eq. (11) is used to merge the low-frequency sub-bands. The output of fusion is determined by the level of decomposition; however, the number of layers of decomposition does not necessarily imply that great results will be achieved; rather, they can lead to misinterpretation. As a result, it is based on the spatial degree of the statistics in the image. The level of decomposition is chosen. A decomposition of single level is used in proposed technique. Equation (11) is obtain to fuse the low-frequency $(F_1^{i})_{\mathrm{LL}}$ and $(F_2^{i})_{\mathrm{LL}}$ coefficients.

$$I_{\mathrm{fu}}^{i} = \alpha \times (F_1^{i})_{\mathrm{LL}} + \beta \times (F_2^{i})_{\mathrm{LL}} \qquad (11)$$

$$\alpha = \frac{\min\left(|(F_1^{i})_{\mathrm{LL}}|, |\tilde{I}_{\mathrm{LL}}|\right)}{\max\left(|(F_2^{i})_{\mathrm{LL}}|, |\tilde{I}_{\mathrm{LL}}|\right)} \qquad (12)$$

$$\beta = 1 - \alpha \qquad (13)$$

$$\tilde{I} = \frac{\left((F_1^{i})_{\mathrm{LL}} + (F_2^{i})_{\mathrm{LL}}\right)}{2} \qquad (14)$$

$\tilde{I}_{\mathrm{LL}}$ is the coefficient of low-frequency mean value of the output maps F_1^{i} and F_2^{i} and I_{fu}^{i} is the fused information image. The low-frequency sub-bands $(F_1^{i})_{\mathrm{LL}}$ and $(F_2^{i})_{\mathrm{LL}}$ represent complementary information, which implies that some changes detected in sub-band of low-frequency $(F_1^{i})_{\mathrm{LL}}$ may not be apparent in sub-band of low-frequency $(F_2^{i})_{\mathrm{LL}}$ and vice versa. A result, by combining these sub-bands of low-frequency, the whole change data result can be obtained. Using α and β values, maintain the concentus of wavelet in the image fusion. To avoid the fused image's excessive range, the wavelet coefficients in the image fusion are modified in standard range by α and β normalizing values.

Table 1 Comparison of Evaluation Matrices, parameters, inference time, and IoU between Proposed Method with Existing Methods (comparison results of proposed method with other methods are marked in bold)

Methods	Parameters	Inf. time (s)	Dataset											
			Szada/1				Tiszadob/3				OSCD-3 ch.			
			Pre.	Rec.	F1scr	IoU	Pre.	Rec.	F1scr	IoU	Pre.	Rec.	F1scr	IoU
FC-EF [7]	–	1.72	87.6	91.1	84.3	0.85	43.5	68.7	52.1	0.83	61.9	78.6	80.1	0.81
DSCN [6]	–	1.81	56.0	64.2	71.8	0.87	89.7	75.5	82.2	0.79	88.7	91.2	72.9	0.85
UNet [26]	7,760,961	1.48	71.6	73.2	81.6	0.90	86.3	82.1	78.9	0.81	91.3	89.4	82.2	0.91
Sim-UNet [26]	15,521,922	1.23	**89.1**	79.2	81.1	0.94	86.1	**93.2**	82.6	0.93	76.4	81.5	82.7	0.93
DDSCN [9]	1,512,097	1.20	75.2	81.4	79.3	0.96	68.8	75.9	81.7	0.89	86.5	**93.2**	89.1	0.91
SDDSCNet (proposed)	**881,724**	**1.18**	85.9	**92.6**	**85.3**	**0.97**	**90.7**	90.5	**86.4**	**0.95**	**92.6**	89.2	**88.9**	**0.98**

4   Results

In this part, the demonstrated results of proposed method are presented in order to examine the method's validity. The proposed methodology was evaluated by using two publicly accessible benchmark change detection datasets. The AirChange (AC) [12] and the OSCD-Onera Satellite Change Detection dataset [11] are the two datasets. OSCD is mainly composed of multispectral satellite images, whereas AC is composed of RGB colored images, as mentioned in Sect. 2. From the OSCD (RGB images) and Tiszadob-3, and Szada-1, images from the AirChange dataset, the proposed network is truly evaluated. The precision results of change detection are measured using three evaluation criteria. The first is precision (Pre), which is the proportion of TP-true positive among all corrected pixels. The second metric is recall (Rec) that is the TP amount of pixels among the all GT data, and the third is F1-score ($F1scr$), which is the percentage mean of accuracy and recall. Intersection over union (IoU) is a new indication added to the mentioned 3-evaluation metrics for the identification of CD outcome to measure the achievement of our proposed approach. The IoU is a fundamental indicator for calculating the overlap percent between the original input to the predicted resulting map, and it is defined as follows:

$$IoU = \frac{TP}{TP + FP + FN}$$

False-negative, true-positive, and false-positive pixels are represented by FN, TP, FP, respectively. Table 1 summarizes the results of this paper's comparison of several models for this segmentation of change detection assignment. The proposed method's performance is compared to that of existing standard convolution methods. On the

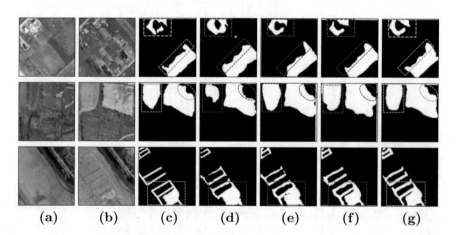

(a)   (b)   (c)   (d)   (e)   (f)   (g)

Fig. 4 The Szada/1, Tiszadob/3, and OSCD-3 ch. datasets were used to produce the illustrations. Display the two image pairs in **a**, **b**. **c** GT. **d** Standard UNet result. **e** Sim-UNet result. **f** DDSCN's result. **g** The proposed method result

OSCD and Tiszadob/3, and Szada/1 of the AirChange dataset, the Unet [26], siamese Unet (Sim-Unet) [26], and (DDSCN) [9] based on DWconv methods were optimized for evaluation. The trainable parameters and execution (inference) time on test image of our method are compared to the given mentioned state-of-the-art methods in this paper. Table 1 summarizes the computed outcomes. On the test dataset, SDDSCNets' parameters and the prediction time (inf. time (s)) of our method are fewer than the other approaches. Although our design outperforms in other comparison matrices, the proposed method determines that feature and parameter complexity are significantly reduced. Less parameter of architecture can better fit in the trainable process and so produce accurate results on the test images. Figure 4 illustrates a summary of results from the Tiszadob/3, Szada/1, and OSCD-3 ch. datasets. Higher IoU is achieved using the proposed approach. In the identification of small changes in landsat imagery, proposed method outperforms other compared state-of-arts in terms of evaluation as well as change map representation and interpretation, as shown in Fig. 4.

5 Conclusion

For remotely sensed images, this paper demonstrates an UNet with encoder–decoder structure (SDDSCNet) which is based on dilated DWconv network that requires few parameters and computation. With the application of the post-processing strategy, the suggested method defeats comparison methods in terms of inference speed and IoU in the detection of urban changes. From input image pairings, the developed architecture with shared weights extracts complex, robust, and abstract features. We applied the post-processing approach as UDWT fusion, which results in a superior visual quality change map that is suitable for visual perception. The presented lightweight SDDSCNet architecture, in particular, decreases the model's computational cost and increasing the execution time of semantic segmentation task. After that, we compared our method to state-of-the-art algorithms and examined at how original convolution and dilated-based DWconv methods impacted on the performance of detection of changes. The outcomes of the architecture show that proposed network defeat existing networks and improves the accuracy of change detection output. The proposed algorithm may be improved in future by employing transfer learning approach and optimized parameter improvement.

References

1. Ghaderpour E, Pagiatakis SD, Hassan QK (2021) A survey on change detection and time series analysis with applications. Appl Sci 11(13):6141
2. Bovolo F, Bruzzone L (2005) A detail-preserving scale-driven approach to change detection in multitemporal SAR images. IEEE Trans Geosci Remote Sens 43(12):2963–2972
3. Bock M, Xofis P, Mitchley J, Rossner G, Wissen M (2005) Object-oriented methods for habitat mapping at multiple scales—case studies from Northern Germany and Wye Downs, UK. J Nat Conserv 13:75–89

4. Wang B, Choi S, Byun Y, Lee S, Choi J (2015) Object-based change detection of very high resolution satellite imagery using the cross-sharpening of multitemporal data. IEEE Geosci Remote Sens Lett 12(5):1151–1155

5. Liu J, Gong M, Qin K, Zhang P (2016) A deep convolutional coupling network for change detection based on heterogeneous optical and radar images. IEEE Trans Neural Netw Learn Syst 29(3):545–559

6. Zhan Y, Fu K, Yan M, Sun X, Wang H, Qiu X (2017) Change detection based on deep siamese convolutional network for optical aerial images. IEEE Geosci Remote Sens Lett 14(10):1845–1849

7. Daudt RC, Le Saux B, Boulch A (2018) Fully convolutional siamese networks for change detection. In: 2018 25th IEEE international conference on image processing (ICIP). IEEE, pp 4063–4067

8. Heidary F, Yazdi M, Dehghani M, Setoodeh P (2021) Urban change detection by fully convolutional siamese concatenate network with attention. arXiv preprint arXiv:2102.00501

9. Liu R, Jiang D, Zhang L, Zhang Z (2020) Deep depthwise separable convolutional network for change detection in optical aerial images. IEEE J Sel Top Appl Earth Obs Remote Sens 13:1109–1118

10. Hussain M, Chen D, Cheng A, Wei H, Stanley D (2013) Change detection from remotely sensed images: from pixel-based to object-based approaches. ISPRS J Photogramm Remote Sens 80:91–106

11. Daudt RC, Le Saux B, Boulch A, Gousseau Y (2018) Urban change detection for multispectral earth observation using convolutional neural networks. In: IGARSS 2018–2018 IEEE international geoscience and remote sensing symposium. IEEE, pp 2115–2118

12. Benedek C, Szirányi T (2009) Change detection in optical aerial images by a multilayer conditional mixed Markov model. IEEE Trans Geosci Remote Sens 47(10):3416–3430

13. Noh H, Hong S, Han B (2015) Learning deconvolution network for semantic segmentation. In: Proceedings of the IEEE international conference on computer vision, pp 1520–1528

14. Gao Y, Gao F, Dong J, Wang S (2019) Change detection from synthetic aperture radar images based on channel weighting-based deep cascade network. IEEE J Sel Top Appl Earth Obs Remote Sens 12(11):4517–4529

15. de Jong KL, Bosman AS (2019) Unsupervised change detection in satellite images using convolutional neural networks. In: 2019 international joint conference on neural networks (IJCNN). IEEE, pp 1–8

16. Starck J-L, Fadili J, Murtagh F (2007) The undecimated wavelet decomposition and its reconstruction. IEEE Trans Image Process 16(2):297–309

17. Singh A, Singh KK (2018) Unsupervised change detection in remote sensing images using fusion of spectral and statistical indices. Egypt J Remote Sens Space Sci 21(3):345–351

18. Ronneberger O, Fischer P, Brox T (2015) U-net: convolutional networks for biomedical image segmentation. In: International conference on medical image computing and computer-assisted intervention. Springer, pp 234–241

19. Iandola FN, Han S, Moskewicz MW, Ashraf K, Dally WJ, Keutzer K (2016) SqueezeNet: AlexNet-level accuracy with 50x fewer parameters and <0.5 mb model size. arXiv preprint arXiv:1602.07360

20. Gashi D, Pereira M, Vterkovska V (2017) Multi-scale context aggregation by dilated convolutions machine learning-project

21. Zhang Z, Vosselman G, Gerke M, Tuia D, Yang MY (2018) Change detection between multimodal remote sensing data using siamese CNN. arXiv preprint arXiv:1807.09562

22. Kingma DP, Ba J (2014) Adam: a method for stochastic optimization. arXiv preprint arXiv:1412.6980

23. Pohl C, Van Genderen JL (1998) Review article multisensor image fusion in remote sensing: concepts, methods and applications. Int J Remote Sens 19(5):823–854

24. Bruzzone L, Prieto DF (2000) Automatic analysis of the difference image for unsupervised change detection. IEEE Trans Geosci Remote Sens 38(3):1171–1182

25. Celik T, Ma K-K (2010) Multitemporal image change detection using undecimated discrete wavelet transform and active contours. IEEE Trans Geosci Remote Sens 49(2):706–716
26. Ji S, Wei S, Lu M (2018) Fully convolutional networks for multisource building extraction from an open aerial and satellite imagery data set. IEEE Trans Geosci Remote Sens 57(1):574–586

Evaluation of Customer Care Executives Using Speech Emotion Recognition

Battula Pragati, Chandana Kolli, Diksha Jain, A. V. Sunethra, and N. Nagarathna

1 Introduction

The human–machine interface is commonly used in many systems today. When two people converse with each other, the inherent emotion in the conversation by the two parties can be understood. Speech emotion recognition (SER) is the process of attempting to detect human emotion and emotional states through speech. Since emotions are subjective, speech emotion recognition is difficult [1].

There has been an increasing interest in designing human–machine interfaces that are more adaptable and sensitive to a user's emotion and behavior in the previous several decades. In this regard, using emotion in speech synthesis and recognizing emotion in speech play an essential role in attempting to increase the naturalness of human–machine interaction (HMI) [2]. As emotions play a key role in decision making and better judgment, recognition of emotions can be useful in mental health counseling, banking, customer support centers, robotics engineering, psychiatric diagnosis, call redistribution in helpline centers, audio/video surveillance, clinical

B. Pragati (✉) · C. Kolli · D. Jain · A. V. Sunethra · N. Nagarathna
BMS College of Engineering, Bull Temple Rd, Basavanagudi, Bangalore, Karnataka 560019, India
e-mail: pragatibattula@gmail.com

C. Kolli
e-mail: kllchandana@gmail.com

D. Jain
e-mail: diksha7354@gmail.com

A. V. Sunethra
e-mail: sunethraav25@gmail.com

N. Nagarathna
e-mail: nagarathna.cse@bmsce.ac.in

investigations, web-based learning, entertainment, computer games and commercial applications [3–5].

Consumer-centric enterprises have identified the potential of using SER technology to analyze customer emotions. A call center executive responds to customer calls and provides information on the various facets of the services offered by the organization they represent. The supervisors generally track the calls and identify if any agent failed to please a customer. The number of calls received at a typical call center is extremely high, making monitoring of these calls incredibly difficult for a supervisor. The price involved in human supervising these calls is also very high. Therefore, from a business perspective, automated monitoring of these calls for identifying the emotional characteristics is a major challenge.

We propose a speech emotion recognition system to evaluate the performance of customer care executives in a call center. This is achieved by identifying emotional characteristics present in the speech of the customer. This will help the company enhance their business choices, customer engagement, and operational performance.

The related work in the area of speech emotion recognition is covered in the ensuing section.

2   Related Work

Various approaches and datasets have been used in prior research on speech emotion recognition. For emotion classification, several of them employ various neural networks and classifiers.

In [6–8], the authors have mentioned the following factors, which make emotion identification from the discourse of the speaker exceedingly tedious: (a) In view of the presence of various sentences, speakers, conversing styles, speaking pace, and accosting fluctuation; speech features get influenced. (b) Various emotions might be identified from the same emotion. (c) Every emotion may relate to the various segments of the expressed utterance. Hence, it is hard to separate these parts of an expression. (d) Emotional speech relies on the speaker and his or her environment and community. In [9], the author has proposed speech emotion recognition in call centers using criteria that represent the four basic features of speech: intonation, voice quality, loudness and rhythm to recognize affect in speech.

In [10], the authors have shared how people and machines recognize emotions in speech with respect to call centers. The current work, on the other hand, can only distinguish between two states: agitation and quiet. In [11], the authors have proposed a system for detection of unsatisfied customer calls using deep learning with a precision of 64.4% at the recall of 30%. They claim that their precision is 18% better than a baseline built using traditional classification algorithms. [12] Introduced the SER system using recurrent neural networks (RNN), which accounts for the extended contextual effect on emotional speech as well as the uncertainty of emotional labeling.

In [13], the authors have focused on speaker independent performance. Though the ensemble classification improves the overall performance slightly, the computational efforts are increased considerably. The authors of [14] have used convolutional neural network (CNN), RNN and time distributed CNN. They noticed that they received higher accuracy while using long short-term memory (LSTM) network layers. Of the three, they achieved highest accuracy with the time distributed CNN. Gunawan et al. [15] helped us to understand the various algorithms that can be used in the field of speech analysis. They have also proposed a system that uses MFCC for feature extraction and deep forward neural networks for classification. In [16], the authors have created twelve isolated Hindi words repository. Principal component analysis is performed on speech features generated by HFCC analysis and used Bayes' decision rule. Authors from [17] have utilized the HTK toolkit to recognize Hindi isolated words in 2013. LPC and MFCC are the feature extraction techniques they utilized.

Our work concentrates on language independent recognition of emotion in speech using three different datasets to achieve an accurate and flexible system. This automates supervision of the customer care executives and supplements the existing feedback system.

3 Implementation

We propose a two-layer framework to detect the emotion of the customers, which utilizes the spectral acoustic features of the speech. The customer's speech is classified into one of the five emotions: angry, sad, disgust, neutral, happy, using a multi-layer perceptron (MLP) classifier.

Speech emotion recognition is achieved by selecting a suitable speech database, followed by pre-processing of these audio files. Figure 1 shows the proposed speech emotion recognition system where we extract five spectral features, namely mel-frequency cepstral coefficients (MFCC), mel-spectrogram, chroma, tonnetz and spectral contrast from the preprocessed input audio files. The extracted features are fed into the classifier for training which can recognize the following emotions: anger, disgust, sad, neutral, and happy. The selection of these emotions is based on the relevance to the call center scenario. To test our model, features from an unknown audio file are extracted, fed into the trained model to predict the emotion and measure the accuracy.

The dataset, audio features and classifier used in our work are further explained in the following sections.

3.1 Dataset Description

In the field of emotion detection, an appropriate selection of speech databases (corpora) plays a vital role. Our model can be used for performance evaluation,

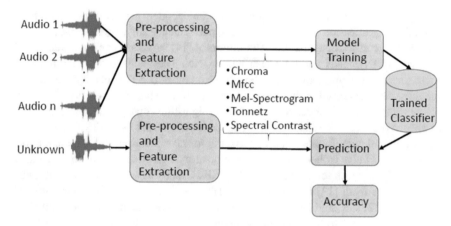

Fig. 1 Proposed speech emotion recognition system

for any language that the customer care executive and customer use for communication, as we are not dealing with the semantic features of speech. For a successful emotion recognition system, a context-rich emotional speech database is desired. The following are three types of corpora that are used for building a speech schema as we infer from [18–20]:

Elicited emotional speech database. By creating an artificial emotional condition, this type of database is extracted from the narrator. As there is increased variation in the actual words used, elicited speech data is less suitable for training on acoustic variance between speakers.

Actor-based speech database. This form of speech dataset is gathered from experienced and qualified performers. It is very simple to collect this form of data, and a broad range of emotions is present in the corpora.

Natural speech database. This kind of data set is unscripted or conversational. The relative lack of structure and unpredictability of this database makes it difficult to train on.

The datasets used in our implementation are actor based and is an amalgamation of audio files from Ryerson Audio-Visual Database of Emotional Speech and Song (RAVDESS), Emotional Database (Emo-DB), and Toronto Emotional Speech Set (TESS). We also used a custom dataset which contains some unbalanced noisy audio files. This amalgamated dataset is divided into eighty percent training and twenty percent testing set.

RAVDESS contains audio files generated by 24 actors. It is a gender-balanced database, and the audio files are present in North American accent. The audio files in TESS were generated by two female actors. Emo-DB, also known as Berlin speech emotion database, is an actor-based database. It is a gender-balanced database as well with five actors from each gender. Gender balanced datasets are used; as in a

Table 1 Speech databases used

Database	Samples	Number of speakers		Emotions
		Male	Female	
TESS	2800	0	2	Fear, pleasant surprise, anger, disgust, happiness, neutral and sadness
RAVDESS	2452	12	12	Sad, disgust, calm, angry, fearful, happy and surprise
Emo-DB	535	5	5	Neutral, anger, sadness, fear, disgust and joy

real-world scenario, customer care executives respond to the calls of both males and females [3]. Table 1 gives an overview of the speech corpus used in our system.

This dataset is preprocessed, and features are extracted from the same which is explained in the next section.

3.2 Pre-processing and Feature Extraction

In a call center scenario, we have access only to the speech/audio of the customer for analysis of their underlying emotion. As mentioned in [13], the speech signal includes a vast number of valuable details that represent the characteristics of sentiment, such as stuttering, age, gender and the identity of the speaker. When it comes to distinguishing between speakers' speech, feature representation plays a big influence. From [21, 22], the authors mentioned that the speech features can be used to discern the difference between many emotional gestures. A speech signal can consist of both acoustic features (of or relating to the sense of hearing, the organs of hearing, sound or sound science) and linguistic features (any attribute used to classify a phoneme or word) where either or both can be used to understand the emotion. The authors of [2, 23, 24] indicated that the most widely used spectral acoustic features for SER are prosodic features (pitch, intensity, duration), spectral features (bandwidth and formant location), cepstral features (MFCC) and often voice quality features (shimmer, jitter, harmonic-to-noise ratio).

We focus on the acoustic features of speech by extracting the following spectral features: chroma, tonnetz, spectral contrast, mel-frequency cepstral coefficients (MFCC) and mel-spectrogram. Since we are dealing with acoustic features, our model can be utilized for performance evaluation in any language that the customer service executive and customer communicate in.

Before the features are extracted, the dataset used for training and testing is sampled at a frequency rate of 16 kHz and mono-audio channel. As a part of the pre-processing step, framing and windowing are performed on the speech signal. Generally, speech is a non-stationary signal, but for the purpose of processing, it is assumed to be stationary and framing is performed on speech signals on small time

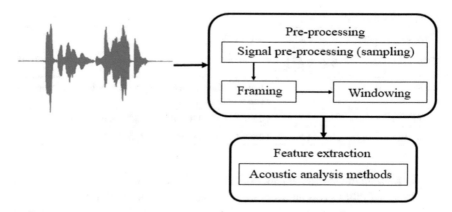

Fig. 2 Pre-processing and feature extraction process

intervals. This is followed by windowing which is used to coordinate spectral infiltration of the signal and intersection as a result of overlap. After pre-processing, speech features are extracted for each audio file. Figure 2 illustrates the pre-processing and feature extraction process where first the input audio files are sampled, framed and windowed. The five acoustic features as mentioned in Table 2 are extracted for the resulting audio files.

For our work, we extracted the spectral acoustic features of speech using the Python library Librosa, to train and test the model. Librosa is a popular package for analyzing music and audio, which provides functions to extract spectral features.

Once all the features are extracted for the entire dataset, they are given as an input to the classifier.

3.3 Classification

Classifier detects the emotions expressed by the customers. We use a multi-layer perceptron (MLP) classifier which is a feed forward neural network augmentation. The input layer receives the extracted features. The output layer is responsible for prediction and classification. MLP is a feedforward network where data flows from input layer to the output layers with 'n' number of hidden layers in between. In the MLP model used, the number of input neurons is equal to the number of features extracted, the number of output neurons is equal to the number of emotions recognized.

Figure 3 shows the multi-layer perceptron classifier used in our system.

The main task of the classifier is to determine the customer's hidden emotion. The model is trained with the speech features—mel-frequency cepstral coefficients, mel-spectrogram, chroma, tonnetz and spectral contrast. We recorded the numerical

Table 2 Spectral features used

Feature	Number of features	Description
MFCC	40	Windowing the signal, using the DFT, obtaining the log of the magnitude, warping the frequencies on a MEL scale, and finally using the inverse DCT are all part of the MFCC feature extraction approach.
Mel-spectrogram	128	Mel-spectrograms are spectrograms that show how sounds on the mel scale are visualized. A logarithmic transformation of a signal's frequency is the mel scale. The underlying notion behind this transformation is that sounds of equal distance on the mel scale are perceived by humans as being of the same distance.
Chroma	12	The twelve distinct pitch classes each of the 12 semitones in an octave C, C#, D..., B are referred to as chroma features or chromagrams. The average energy of each semitone is represented by each bin in the chroma spectrogram.
Spectral_contrast	7	The energy contrast is calculated for each sub-band by comparing the mean energy in the highest quantile (peak energy) to the mean energy in the bottom quantile (bottom energy).
Tonnetz	6	The tonnetz is a pitch space defined by a network of melodic contributions. On a large Euclidean plane, close symphony relationships are shown as small separations.

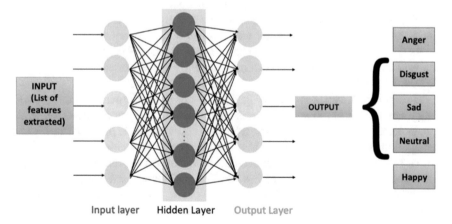

Fig. 3 Multi-layer perceptron

values of each feature in two-dimensional arrays for training. These arrays are fed into the MLP classifier as input.

The MLP uses backpropagation, to make weight and bias adjustments relative to the error. The input data is acted upon and processed by the hidden layer where the rectified linear unit function was employed as the activation function. The maximum recognition rate is obtained with 300 neurons in the hidden layer. There is no significant improvement in the recognition rate on further increase in the number of neurons in the hidden layer. It also increased the computational complexity, thus resulting in a longer processing time.

The model can recognize the ranges of customer's speech parameter values that correspond to angry, disgust, sad, neutral and happy emotions. We have chosen these emotions as the customers dialing the customer care executives generally express these emotions. When we provide the model an unknown test dataset as an input, it samples the data, extracts the features and predicts the emotion according to the training data. The model's results are explained in the next section.

4 Results

In our system, 193 features were extracted for each of the 3933 input audio files using Librosa Python library. The MLP classifier with learning rate for weight updates equal to adaptive and activation function being rectified linear unit function was used. The overall training score and testing accuracy score obtained for the model were 0.9539 and 0.8284, respectively. This accuracy score is calculated by taking the ratio of the number of correct predictions to the total number of predictions.

As shown in Fig. 4, the loss value decreases as the model begins to learn. When the validation score did not improve more than tolerance for optimization equal to 0.000001 for 10 consecutive epochs, the training is terminated.

The confusion matrix shown in Fig. 5 represents the performance of our classification model. The emotion disgust was identified with 74% recognition rate, while emotion neutral has 80% recognition rate, emotion angry and happy have the highest recognition rates with 96% and 81% respectively. Emotion sadness was identified with a 79% recognition rate. These accuracies help in performance evaluation of the call center executives in a precise manner. The addition of more audio files of less recognized emotions will add diversity to the dataset. This will increase the accuracy of our model making it more general by virtue of being trained on more audio samples.

We compare our result with five different setups for speech emotion recognition, namely LSTM-based RNN, SVM, AAE and TDNN-LSTM with 12 layers. We observe that our approach of MLP with a single hidden layer of 300 neurons gives best accuracy of 82.84%. Table 3 summarizes the approaches along with their respective features extracted, classifiers, databases used and accuracies of their outcome.

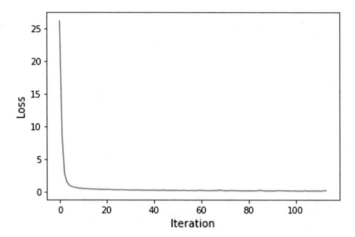

Fig. 4 Loss curve

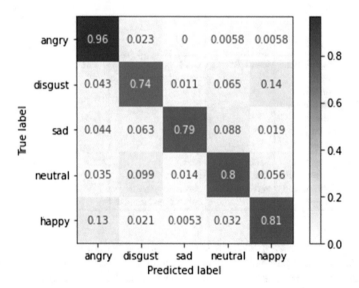

Fig. 5 Confusion matrix

5 Conclusion

Speech emotion recognition from human speech is undergoing rapid research as it contributes to better human–machine interactions. Our speech emotion recognition system consists of a speech emotion database, feature extraction module and MLP classifier. The quality of pre-processing has a big impact on a model's performance. This paper demonstrates that MLPs are extremely effective in classifying speech signals.

Table 3 Comparison of various SER models results

Reference	Emotions	Database	Features extracted	Classifiers	Accuracy (%)
[25]	Neutral, sadness, happiness, anger	IEMOCAP	MFCC + chromagram-based + time spectral	Stacked LSTM-based RNN	71.04
[26]	Anger, neutral, disgust, sadness, Joy, fear	Emo-DB + EESDB	MFCC	SVM	79.5 (Emo-DB), 60.7 (EESDB)
[27]	Angry, neutral, happy, sad	IEMOCAP	Energy based + spectral + prosodic	AAE	57.88
[28]	Happiness, neutral, sad, angry	IEMOCAP	MFCC	TDNN-LSTM with 12 layers	Weighted accuracy: 70.6 Unweighted accuracy: 60.7
[29]	Calm, sad, neutral, happy, surprise, angry, fearful, disgust	RAVDESS	CWT, prosodic coefficients	SVM	60.10
Proposed model	Angry, happy, sad, neutral and disgust	TESS, RAVDESS and emo-DB	MFCC, mel-spectrogram, chroma, spectral contrast and tonnetz	MLP	82.84

Using our proposed speech emotion recognition system to evaluate the performance of customer care executives at call centers, we reduce the manual effort that goes into evaluating the executives at low cost. Since this process is automated, the supervisors can direct their efforts toward other crucial tasks while the executives feel accountable and engage in improving customer satisfaction and retaining the customer base. This method is independent of languages and does not necessitate any changes to the implementation to shift between languages. The results show that speech recognition is feasible, and that MLPs can be utilized for any task involving voice recognition and demonstrating the accuracy of each emotion contained in the speech.

Our system does not eliminate background noise which can hamper the quality of customer's speech. Emotions are subjective and expression of emotions can vary from person to person which can make the recognized emotion ambiguous.

6 Future Work

In addition to speech, other body gestures such as facial articulation or movement of the body can be used for recognizing emotions. Dealing with whispered and over-lapping speech can be implemented as they are common in telephonic conversations. Therefore, the identification of emotions using machine learning still has different obstacles to address and work on.

References

1. Khalil RA, Jones E, Babar MI, Jan T, Zafar MH, Alhussain T (2019) Speech emotion recognition using deep learning techniques: a review. IEEE Access 7:117327–117345. https://doi.org/10.1109/ACCESS.2019.2936124
2. Bojani M, Deli V, Karpov A (2020) Call redistribution for a call center based on speech emotion recognition. MDPI Appl Sci
3. Singh N, Singha K, Agarwal P, Das D (2020) A review paper on emotion recognition. Int J Eng Appl Sci Technol 04:472–483. https://doi.org/10.33564/IJEAST.2020.v04i12.083
4. Zvarevashe K, Olugbara O (2020) Ensemble learning of hybrid acoustic features for speech emotion recognition. MDPI Algorithms 13:70
5. Basu S, Chakraborty J, Bag A, Aftabuddin M (2017) A review on emotion recognition using speech. In: 2017 International conference on inventive communication and computational technologies (ICICCT)
6. Koolagudi K, Shashidhar G, Rao S (2012) Emotion recognition from speech: a review. Int J Speech Technol 15. https://doi.org/10.1007/s10772-011-9125-1
7. Ayadi ME, Kamel MS, Karray F (2011) Survey on speech emotion recognition: features, classification schemes, and databases. Patt Recogn 44: 572–587
8. Ingale AB, Chaudhari DS (2012) Speech emotion recognition. Int J Soft Comput Eng (IJSCE) 2(1):235–238
9. Fernandez R (2004) A computational model for the auto-matic recognition of affect in speech. PhD Thesis, MIT Media Arts and Sciences
10. Petrushin VA (1999) Emotion in speech: recognition and application to call centers. In: Proceedings of ANNIE
11. Cong P, Wang C, Ren Z, Wang H, Wang Y, Feng J (2016) Unsatisfied customer call detection with deep learning, pp 1–5. https://doi.org/10.1109/ISCSLP.2016.7918385
12. Lee J, Tashev I (2015) High-level feature representation using recurrent neural network for speech emotion recognition. In: 16th Annual conference of the international speech communication association
13. Schuller B et al. (2005) Speaker independent speech emotion recognition by ensemble classification. In: 2005 IEEE international conference on multimedia and expo, IEEE
14. Lim W, Jang D, Lee T (2016) Speech emotion recognition using convolutional and recurrent neural networks. In: 2016 Asia-Pacific signal and information processing association annual summit and conference (APSIPA), IEEE
15. Gunawan T, Hanifah A, Kartiwi M (2018) A review on emotion recognition algorithms using speech analysis. Indonesian J Electr Eng Info 6:12–20. https://doi.org/10.11591/ijeei.v6i1.409
16. Baranwal N, Tripathi S, Nandi GC (2014) A speaker invariant speech recognition technique using HFCC features in isolated Hindi words. Int J Comput Intell Stud 3(4):277–291
17. Tripathy S, Baranwal N, Nandi GC (2013) A MFCC based Hindi speech recognition technique using HTK toolkit. In: 2013 IEEE second international conference on image information processing (ICIIP-2013), IEEE, pp 539–544

18. Deshmukh RR, Shaikh RA, Gadhe RP, Waghmare VB, Shrishrimal PP (2015) Emotion recognition from speech: a survey. Int J Sci Eng Res 6:632–635
19. Adigwe A, Tits N, Haddad KE, Ostadabbas S, Dutoit T (2018) The emotional voices database: towards controlling the emotion dimension in voice generation systems
20. Gunawan TS, Alghifari MF, Morshidi MA, Kartiwi M (2018) A review on emotion recognition algorithms using speech analysis. Indonesian J Electr Eng Inf (IJEEI) 6(1):12–20
21. Özseven T (2018) A novel feature selection method for speech emotion recognition. Appl Acoust
22. Lalitha S, Madhavan A, Bhushan B, Saketh S (2014) Speech emotion recognition. International Conference on Advances in Electronics Computers and Communications 2014:1–4. https://doi.org/10.1109/ICAECC.2014.7002390
23. Gupta P, Rajput N (2007) Two-stream emotion recognition for call center monitoring. pp 2241–2244
24. Hinton G, Deng L, Yu D, Dahl G, Mohamed A, Jaitly N, Senior A (2012) Deep neural networks for acoustic modeling in speech recognition. IEEE Sign Process Maga
25. Tripathi S, Beigi H (2018) Multi-modal emotion recognition on IEMOCAP dataset using deep learning. arXiv: 1804.05788. [Online]. Available: https://arxiv.org/abs/1804.05788
26. Wang K, Su G, Liu L, Wang S (2020) Wavelet packet analysis for speaker-independent emotion recognition. Neurocomputing 398:257–264
27. Sahu S, Gupta R, Sivaraman G, AbdAlmageed W, Espy-Wilson C (2018) Adversarial auto-encoders for speech based emotion recognition. arXiv:1806.02146. [Online]. Available: https://arxiv.org/abs/1806.02146
28. Sarma M, Ghahremani P, Povey D, Goel NK, Sarma KK, Dehak N (2018) Emotion identification from raw speech signals using DNNs. In: Proceedings interspeech, pp 3097–3101
29. Shegokar P, Sircar P (2016) Continuous wavelet transform based speech emotion recognition. In: 2016 10th International conference on signal processing and communication systems (ICSPCS), pp 1–8

Deep Convolutional Neural Network Approach for Tomato Leaf Disease Classification

Surabhi Lingwal, Komal Kumar Bhatia, and Manjeet Singh

1 Introduction

Plant disease [1] symptoms need to be detected at an early age since they are the major factor responsible for the shortage in food production and supply. Manual examination of plant disease identification is an exhaustive and error-prone task that should be automated as the data is growing rapidly. Therefore, plant disease identification and detection process are getting automated through the involvement of pattern recognition and machine learning for easy handling and spotting of disease [2]. This will allow for better monitoring of plant health and quality for improved productivity. Visual traits such as color, shape, and texture from plant images can be used for the health monitoring of plants. Machine learning techniques allow for feature extraction [1] as the preprocessing step followed by the classification process to classify the images to their correct classes. While on the other hand, the deep learning process allows for automatic feature extraction from a large set of images. Thus, deep learning is emerging as a solution for various agriculture problems [3]. It is being employed for crop quality analysis from the images which can be used for plant disease identification. Deep learning allows several hidden layers that could improve the accuracy rate and produces better results due to the automatic feature extraction process as compared to the handcrafted features extraction process in machine learning [4]. Several machine learning and deep learning techniques have been employed earlier for the plant disease classification [1]. They have been used for plants detection and identification [5–7] based on features like leaf shape, texture,

S. Lingwal (✉) · K. K. Bhatia
Computer Engineering, J C Bose University of Science and Technology, YMCA, Faridabad, Haryana, India
e-mail: surabhi.lingwal@gmail.com

M. Singh
Computer Applications, J C Bose University of Science and Technology, YMCA, Faridabad, Haryana, India

© The Author(s), under exclusive license to Springer Nature Singapore Pte Ltd. 2023 199
R. Doriya et al. (eds.), *Machine Learning, Image Processing, Network Security and Data Sciences*, Lecture Notes in Electrical Engineering 946,
https://doi.org/10.1007/978-981-19-5868-7_15

lamina, etc. Plant disease classification has been performed using machine learning based on visual attributes [1, 2, 8]. With the introduction of deep learning, the accuracy of the classification process has improved over the earlier machine learning results [9]. Convolutional neural network is the most largely used technique for image data; therefore, it is considered a well-suited model for plant disease identification and classification. CNN has been employed for plant disease classification [10] through different ways such as MobileNet [3, 11], SVM [12], and EfficientNet [13]. Transfer learning is also playing a major role in plant disease classification due to the unavailability of the large dataset as needed for deep learning for correct classification. The standard CNN-based models trained on the standard large dataset is being employed for transfer learning where the output layer get replaced with the number of output classes of the user dataset [14–21].

2 Literature Review

CNN has been employed in the literature for plant disease identification and classification. The author [22] has employed 7 classes of tomato leaves, where 6 are infected and 1 is a healthy image group from the PlantVillage dataset. The comparison has been performed on AlexNet and VGG16 net. KNN and C5.0 models have been employed to classify healthy and diseased leaves [23]. The paper has employed conditional generative adversarial network (C-GAN) to generate synthetic images, and then the DenseNet-121 model is used to detect the tomato leaf diseases [15]. The paper [21] has applied CNN-based transfer learning and adopted different optimizers to validate the results. The author has applied CNN for tomato leaf disease identification carrying nine diseases [24]. CNN and three pre-trained models VGG16, InceptionV3, and MobileNet have been used for tomato disease classification [25]. Powdery mildew disease has been identified using three machine learning techniques k-nearest neighbor (kNN), support vector machine (SVM), and Naïve Bayes (NB) [26]. Thus, considering the results of the transfer learning approach for the unbalanced and limited data the paper has employed four transfer learning models for the given problem and dataset available. The results are also compared with a CNN model developed from scratch for plant disease identification and classification. The results are compared to identify the model with the best accuracy and minimum loss. The work is being conducted on a tomato leaf disease dataset covering different diseases adopted from the plant village dataset. The dataset comprises 9 different types of tomato leaf diseases and 1 healthy set of images. The paper is being organized as: Sect. 1 entails the Introduction, Sect. 2 covers the Literature Review. Section 3 deals with the Materials and Methods that include the different classifiers involved, the flow chart of the work performed, and the data collection. Section 4 illustrates the Experimentation and Results achieved under the research process. Finally, the Conclusion is given in Sect. 5.

3   Method and Materials

3.1   Deep Learning-Based Image Classifiers Applied for Process

DenseNet: DenseNet [27] is a densely connected convolutional neural network, successful in reducing the vanishing gradient problem. It is identified as a model useful for feature propagation and reuse that reduces the number of parameters. DenseNet utilizes the dense blocks to form a dense connection connecting the layers with matching features map sizes. It processes the input from the preceding layers to the subsequent layers including its feature map.

Inception V3: Inception V3 [28] belongs to GoogLeNet architecture that works on ImageNet data. The network makes use of residual network along with Inception architecture composed of pooling and convolutional layer. 1 * 1 convolutional layer helps in the computational requirements.

ResNet50: ResNet50 [29] belongs to the residual network. It is also called as deep residual model because of the much deeper network than that of the VGG model. The architecture is composed of different residual blocks with 3 * 3 filters. A deep residual network was introduced because of the nonlinearity of CNN layers suffering from the problem of vanishing gradient.

VGG-16: VGG-16 is one of the most popular transfer learning methods used for image classification. VGG-16 was trained on the ImageNet dataset containing 1 crore 40 lakh images covering 1000 different labels. It was developed by Visual Graphics Group (VGG) at Oxford [30]. The model is used to transfer the knowledge by applying the already trained weights on the standard dataset to other classification problems. The original class labels of the output are replaced by the class labels defined in the problem. VGG-16 contains the layers of a normal CNN model: convolutional layer, max-pooling layer, and fully connected layer.

CNN model built from scratch: The model is developed from scratch including five convolutional layers, four max-pooling layers with a dropout of 0.25, the learning rate of 0.0001, and two dense layers with softmax function for the output classes.

3.2   Work Flow

The entire workflow for the classification of plant disease is given in Fig. 1. Initially, the images are preprocessed and augmented. These resized images are further labeled to produce the different classes. These labeled images are divided into training, test, and validation set. The training set images are used for developing the model with the help of an algorithm. The developed model is applied to the test data for checking the classification accuracy of the model. The final pre-trained model is further validated using the validation or unknown data. A similar procedure is being applied to all the other transfer learning models. Finally, all the models are compared for accuracy and loss.

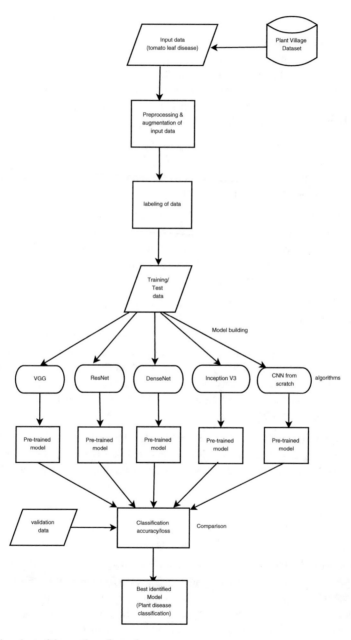

Fig. 1 Flowchart of the work performed

(a) target_spot   (b) mosaic_virus   (c) Yellow_Leaf_curl

(d) early_blight   (e) healthy   (f) bacterial_spot   (g) Late_blight

(h) Leaf_Mold   (i) Septoria_spot   (j) Spider_mites

Fig. 2 Different tomato leaf diseases considered for the experimentation

3.3 Data Collection

The research has been conducted for tomato disease classification where the data was collected from the PlantVillage dataset [14]. The dataset is composed of 9 different tomato diseases and one healthy set of tomato leaves. The total collection of images are split into a ratio of 70:20:10 where 70% of data is reserved for training, 20% is reserved for the test, and 10% is reserved for validation. The data belonging to different classes is unbalanced. The sample images under the different classes are as shown in Fig. 2.

4 Experimentation and Results

The process is implemented using Python 3.7 with NVIDIA GPU processor in combination with OpenCV, Keras, and CuDNN libraries. The experimentation is performed

Table 1 Metrics evaluating the efficiency of models

Model	Training loss	Training accuracy	Validation loss	Validation accuracy
Densenet	0.5712	0.9748	67.6174	0.4408
Inception V3	1.5943	0.8940	0.0000e+00	0.4714
ResNet	0.7837	0.9829	169.4404	0.0659
VGG 16	0.0886	0.9694	0.0619	0.9084
CCN from scratch	0.5641	0.8001	0.3837	0.8366

with four transfer learning models and a base CNN model built from scratch. The result of the experimentation is given in Table 1 that illustrates the different model's evaluation metrics in terms of training and test accuracy. Also, the categorical cross-entropy loss is calculated during the training and test time. Total 25 epochs are considered for the training after which the results get saturated. The models are trained with a batch size of 32 and a learning rate of 0.0001. The experimentation has been performed on five deep learning models: CNN built from scratch, DenseNet, Inception v3, ResNet50, and VGG-16. These models are initially trained on ImageNet data, and later, the layers of output classes are replaced with our dataset with 10 output classes. The training and test results derived under the different models experimented with are shown graphically in Fig. 3. The first two graphs (a) and (b) give the training and validation accuracy derived under the DenseNet model which depicts that the validation accuracy and validation loss are poor in both cases. Similar is the case of the Inception V3 model represented by the curve of training and test accuracy along with training and test loss produced during the processing of the model. It can be seen from the table that the VGG-16 and CNN models developed from scratch perform better than the other three models. VGG-16 gains the maximum validation accuracy and minimum validation loss followed by the CNN model developed from scratch. While on the other side DenseNet121, Inception-v3 and ResNet50 perform poorly on the dataset. The results are further validated with the help of confusion matrix. The confusion matrix of the test set data based on the predicted output and actual output derived under the different models is shown in Fig. 4a–d where the top row and leftmost column give the output classes. It can be seen from the four confusion matrices that VGG-16 gives the maximum correct classes between the predicted and actual output resulting in maximum accuracy. The results derived in the paper are compared with the other methods employed in the existing papers. The comparative analysis between the different models used in the paper and the other methods employed in the existing papers is given in Table 2.

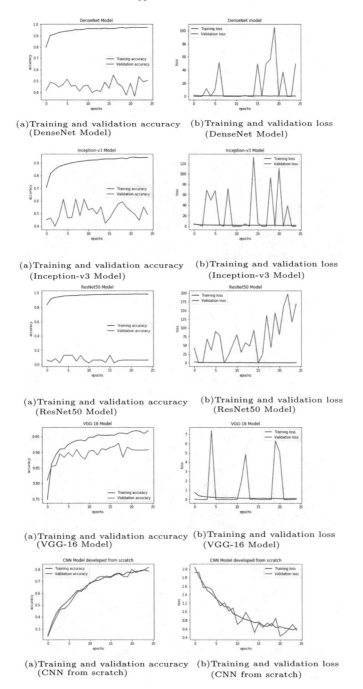

(a) Training and validation accuracy (DenseNet Model)

(b) Training and validation loss (DenseNet Model)

(a) Training and validation accuracy (Inception-v3 Model)

(b) Training and validation loss (Inception-v3 Model)

(a) Training and validation accuracy (ResNet50 Model)

(b) Training and validation loss (ResNet50 Model)

(a) Training and validation accuracy (VGG-16 Model)

(b) Training and validation loss (VGG-16 Model)

(a) Training and validation accuracy (CNN from scratch)

(b) Training and validation loss (CNN from scratch)

Fig. 3 Graphs illustrate the training and test accuracy and training and test loss produced under the different experimented models

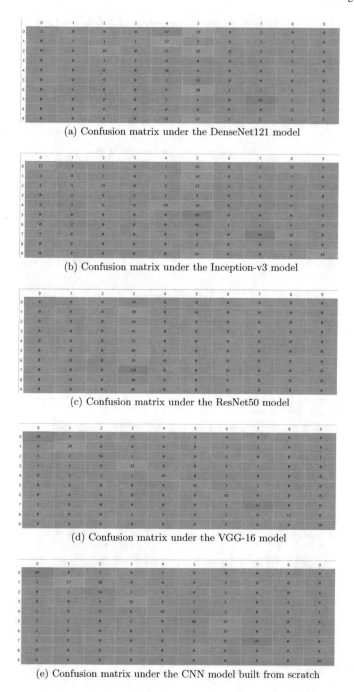

(a) Confusion matrix under the DenseNet121 model

(b) Confusion matrix under the Inception-v3 model

(c) Confusion matrix under the ResNet50 model

(d) Confusion matrix under the VGG-16 model

(e) Confusion matrix under the CNN model built from scratch

Fig. 4 Confusion matrix derived for the test set under the different models based on the classification results. The top row and the first column signifies the number of classes as the output

Table 2 Comparison of techniques employed for tomato leaf disease classification

Paper	No. of classes	Classification	Best techniques	Accuracy model (%)
[24]	9	CNN, AlexNet, GoogLeNet, InceptionV3	InceptionV3	99.18
[21]	9	D-CNN (transfer learning-based CNN)	D-CNN	99.5
[25]	10	CNN, VGG16, InceptionV3, and MobileNet	CNN	91
[22]	7	AlexNet, VGG-16	AlexNet	91.2
Our model	10	CNN, DenseNet121, ResNet50, Inception-V3, VGG-16	VGG-16	90.84

5 Conclusion

The paper has successfully illustrated the process of plant disease identification and classification on tomato leaves carrying 10 different classes. The image dataset under the different classes contains unbalanced data that somehow affects the results of classification. The paper performs the learning process with four different well-established transfer learning models, these are DenseNet 121, Inception-V3, ResNet 50, VGG-16, and CNN model developed from scratch. The results have revealed that VGG-16 has shown promising results on the dataset followed by a self-developed CNN model. The test accuracy and categorical cross-entropy loss achieved under the VGG-16 model are best among all the other implemented models with 90% test accuracy and 0.06% validation loss. This, followed by the CNN model built from scratch that attains 83% test accuracy and 0.3% validation loss. The future work will include more classes and a balanced dataset. The future work will be covering the image segmentation of the infected region.

References

1. Kaur S, Pandey S, Goel S (2019) Arch Comput Methods Eng 26(2):507
2. Shrivastava VK, Pradhan MK (2021) J Plant Pathol 103(1):17
3. Kamal K, Yin Z, Wu M, Wu Z (2019) Comput Electron Agric 165:104948
4. Lee SH, Chan CS, Wilkin P, Remagnino P (2015) 2015 IEEE international conference on image processing (ICIP). IEEE, pp 452–456
5. Agarwal G, Belhumeur P, Feiner S, Jacobs D, Kress WJ, Ramamoorthi R, Bourg NA, Dixit N, Ling H, Mahajan D et al (2006) Taxon 55(3):597
6. Yanikoglu B, Aptoula E, Tirkaz C (2014) Mach Vis Appl 25(6):1369
7. Liu N, Kan J et al (2016) J Beijing For Univ 38(3):110
8. Mokhtar U, Ali MA, Hassanien AE, Hefny H (2015) Information systems design and intelligent applications. Springer, pp 771–782

9. Ghazi MM, Yanikoglu B, Aptoula E (2017) Neurocomputing 235:228
10. Lingwal S, Bhatia KK, Singh M (2021) Proceedings of integrated intelligence enable networks and computing. Springer, pp 651–658
11. Ashwinkumar S, Rajagopal S, Manimaran V, Jegajothi B (2021) Mater Today Proc
12. Thaiyalnayaki K, Joseph C (2021) Mater Today Proc
13. Atila Ü, Uçar M, Akyol K, Uçar E (2021) Ecol Inform 61:101182
14. Barbedo JGA (2018) Comput Electron Agric 153:46
15. Abbas A, Jain S, Gour M, Vankudothu S (2021) Comput Electron Agric 187:106279
16. Sravan V, Swaraj K, Meenakshi K, Kora P (2021) Mater Today Proc
17. Subetha T, Khilar R, Christo MS (2021) Mater Today Proc
18. Chen J, Chen J, Zhang D, Sun Y, Nanehkaran YA (2020) Comput Electron Agric 173:105393
19. Sharma P, Berwal YPS, Ghai W (2020) Inf Process Agric 7(4):566
20. Thenmozhi K, Reddy US (2019) Comput Electron Agric 164:104906
21. Thangaraj R, Anandamurugan S, Kaliappan VK (2021) J Plant Dis Prot 128(1):73
22. Rangarajan AK, Purushothaman R, Ramesh A (2018) Procedia Comput Sci 133:1040
23. Xie C, Yang C, He Y (2017) Comput Electron Agric 135:154
24. Brahimi M, Boukhalfa K, Moussaoui A (2017) Appl Artif Intell 31(4):299
25. Agarwal M, Singh A, Arjaria S, Sinha A, Gupta S (2020) Procedia Comput Sci 167:293
26. Bhatia A, Chug A, Singh AP, Singh RP, Singh D (2021) Indian Phytopathol 1–6
27. Brahimi M, Arsenovic M, Laraba S, Sladojevic S, Boukhalfa K, Moussaoui A (2018) Human and machine learning. Springer, pp 93–117
28. Wang A, Zhang W, Wei X (2019) Comput Electron Agric 158:226
29. Chen K, Pang J, Wang J, Xiong Y, Li X, Sun S, Feng W, Liu Z, Shi J, Ouyang W et al (2019) Proceedings of the IEEE/CVF conference on computer vision and pattern recognition, pp 4974–4983
30. Simonyan K, Zisserman A (2014) arXiv preprint arXiv:1409.1556

Cognitive Load Classification During Arithmetic Task Using Single Convolution Layer-Based 2D-CNN Model

Aman Anand Rai and Mitul Kumar Ahirwal

1 Introduction

Cognitive load (CL) also called mental workload (MWL) is the quantitative measure of mental effort required to complete a task [1]. It is used in many fields like driver health assessment, educational program review, mental state analysis of airplane dispatchers and pilots [2]. An optimal CL is required for better performance, and if it exceeds a certain limit, it can cause mental fatigue. Mental fatigue causes loss in employee performance, and for finding an optimal CL, some assessment or measure for CL is required. CL can be measured using various methods [3] like traditional manual questionnaire process, physiological signals like electroencephalogram (EEG) [4], electrocardiogram (ECG), galvanic responses [5], and eye movement tracking [6].

EEG signals are used to measure the activity of the brain due to change in electrical voltage because of synaptic excitations of dendrites. EEG signals are classified into 5 categories based on their frequency band. CL can be measure through EEG, and it is also the cheapest way. But EEG has some limitations of its own as it easily gets affected by artifacts/noises. These artifacts can be removed from the signal using various signal processing and filtering methods [7–9].

Many studies have been done for MWL assessment using EEG signals. CL assessment is used for evaluating multimedia resources for education [10]. It is highly beneficial especially in the time of pandemic when the mental health is of utmost importance. Mental fatigue can lead to road accidents while driving, and therefore, CL must be kept in check for reducing loss of lives on roads. In [11], CL was measured while driving and multitasking to find optimal value of CL. Mathematical cognitive task and visual search task are performed by drivers while changing lanes. EEGs are

A. A. Rai (✉) · M. K. Ahirwal
Maulana Azad National Institute of Technology, Bhopal, India
e-mail: amananandrai@gmail.com

used to classify driver fatigue [12]. From literate review, it is observed that the field of CL and MWL assessment is very importance for society, and it is also related to almost all the tasks which engages brain [13, 14] like emotion detection [15, 16], mental stress identification [17, 18]. At present, the recent trend of research is the use of CNN and other deep learning models to solve classification problems. The detailed review of deep learning models application on EEG signals for classification is provided in [19]. Therefore, in this paper, an attempt has been done to classify mental state of subject based on their CL while performing mental arithmetic task.

Novelty of this paper is that for the first time, 2D-CNN model is utilized on the EEG dataset of mental arithmetic calculations. For this, one dimensional EEG signal is reshaped into two dimensional matrix as input to 2D-CNN. EEG dataset which has data for mental arithmetic task is used [20]. During recording of EEG signals, subjects are performing series of subtractions in their brain (mentally). The subjects performing this task were labeled as good counter (GC) and bad counter (BC) based on the accuracy of result of subtraction. Two dimensional convolutional neural network (2D-CNN) model is used for classification of GC and BC, and input to CNN is EEG signal.

The rest of the paper is arranged as follows: Sect. 2 provides details about the method used for the classification of data. It also has sub-parts that explain the dataset and preprocessing, the architecture of the neural network used, and performance evaluation metrics for the models. Section 3 explains the results obtained from the different models, and in Sect. 4, conclusions derived and future scope have been provided.

2 Methodology

2.1 Dataset and Pre-processing

The dataset comprises 36 recording of multichannel EEG corresponding to 36 subjects at the time of mental arithmetic task. Out of 36 subjects, 26 are GC, and 10 are BC.

The EEG signal is recorded with the help of a device, named Neurocom Monopolar EEG 23-channel system. There are 23 electrodes in the device for different channels of EEG data. 19 channels are selected out of these 23 channels, namely Fp1, Fp2, F3, F4, F7, F8, T3, T4, C3, C4, T5, T6, P3, P4, O1, O2, Fz, Cz, and Pz.

The subjects are labeled as good counter and bad counter based on the results of arithmetic task performed by them. The arithmetic task involves the series of subtractions of 4-digit number and 2-digit numbers. The EEG signals are recorded for 61 s with a sampling frequency of 500 Hz. The shape of the matrix for a single subject is 19 * 31,000. The shape of the matrix is reshaped. The new shape of the matrix is 760 * 775 where each channel's signal is divided into 40 equal parts and arranged consecutively to form the new shape. This is done to make shape of the matrix symmetric.

2.2 Architecture of CNN

The CNN used consists of a single unit comprising six components which include the convolution layer, max pooling layer, batch normalization layer, dropout layer, flatten layer, and dense layer. The details of these layers are given below:

Convolution Layer:

Convolution layer is the most important part of the CNN architecture. In our architecture, 2D-CNN is used. The activation function used is rectified linear unit (ReLU). It is used to find features from images which are 2D matrices. The parameters are number of filters, size of filter, and stride length used to extract different features from the 2D input matrix. Model used in this paper consists of 3×3 filter (kernel) size. The kernel size must be odd.

Max Pooling Layer:

The pooling layer is used to reduce the dimension of the feature map obtained as output of convolution layer and thus reduces the computation. Max pooling is used in the architecture which finds out the max of the feature map window. Window size can be adjusted as per model requirement.

Batch Normalization Layer:

This layer is used to normalize the input of the data and stabilize the learning process along with reducing the number of epochs for training.

Dropout Layer:

This layer is used to reduce overfitting in training process. It randomly ignores a certain amount of neurons which is known as the dropout rate.

Flatten Layer:

This layer is used to reshape the dimension of output obtained from the previous layer into a 1D array. This process is called as flattening.

Dense Layer:

It is the normal fully connected layer as used in artificial neural network (ANN). The activation function used is this layer can be changed. Sigmoid, softmax, and ReLU are some example of activation function.

Figure 1 represents the architecture of CNN model developed in this study along with the number of parameters for input and output of each layer.

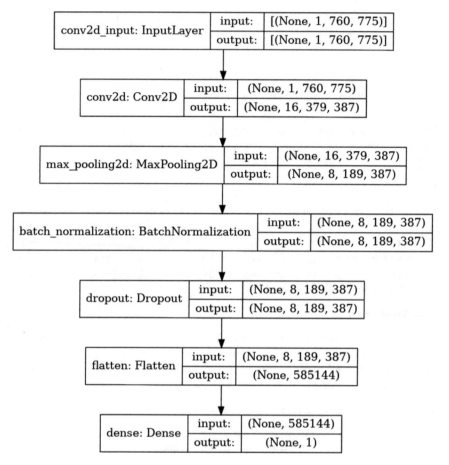

Fig. 1 Architecture of the CNN used for classification

2.3 Performance Measures

There are different performance measures used to compare the different architectures of CNN, such as accuracy, precision, recall, area under curve, and F1-score.

(i) Accuracy (ACC): This is the ratio of correct predictions and total number of predictions, and accuracy is obtained by Eq. (1),

$$ACC = (TP + TN) \big/ (TP + TN + FP + FN), \tag{1}$$

(ii) Precision (PR)/(Positive Predictive Value (PPV)): This is the ratio of true positive and total predictions in predicted positive, and it is simply calculated by Eq. (2),

$$PR = TP/(TP + FP), \qquad (2)$$

(iii) Recall (RC) or Sensitivity: This is the ratio of true positive and total predictions in actual positive, and it is simply calculated by Eq. (3),

$$RC = TP/(FN + TP), \qquad (3)$$

(iv) Area Under Curve (AUC): This is the area under the curve for receiver operating characteristic which is curve of true positive rate (TPR) or recall (RC) vs false positive rate (FPR) at different classification thresholds. RC is calculated by Eq. (3), and FPR is calculated by Eq. (4),

$$FPR = FP/FP + TN, \qquad (4)$$

(v) F1-score: This is parameter based on the previous above parameters, and it is calculated as Eq. (5),

$$F1 = 2 * \big((PR * RC)/(PR + RC)\big), \qquad (5)$$

3 Results and Analysis

The validation results with training–testing split of ratio 70:30 are obtained. Results of single convolution layer-based 2D-CNN architecture with other layers shown in Fig. 1 with different numbers of filters and stride size are listed in Tables 1, 2 and 3. In Table 1, the details of the performance measures for the architecture with numbers of filters 32 and different stride size are present. Similarly, the results for numbers of filters 16 and 8 for different stride size are present in Tables 2 and 3. It is observed that the best accuracy is obtained when number of filters is 16, and stride size is 2. In Fig. 2, the comparison of average performance measures for different numbers of filters is shown. It is done to analyze the affect variation in number of filters in performance, and it is observed that 16 gives the best output.

In Table 4, the average result for the optimal numbers of filters 16 and stride size 2 is shown when leave-one-subject-out validation technique.

Table 1 Performance measures for numbers of filters 32 in the architecture

Stride size	Accuracy (%)	Precision (%)	Recall (%)	AUC (%)	F1-score (%)
1	94.44	96.15	96.15	93.07	96.15
2	88.88	100.00	84.61	92.30	91.66
3	86.11	95.65	84.61	88.84	89.79
4	94.44	92.85	100.00	94.61	96.29

Table 2 Performance measures for numbers of filters 16 in the architecture

Stride size	Accuracy (%)	Precision (%)	Recall (%)	AUC (%)	F1-score (%)
1	94.44	96.15	96.15	93.07	96.15
2	97.22	96.29	100.00	94.80	98.11
3	88.88	100.00	84.61	91.53	91.66
4	94.44	96.15	96.15	92.88	96.15

Table 3 Performance measures for numbers of filters 8 in the architecture

Stride size	Accuracy (%)	Precision (%)	Recall (%)	AUC (%)	F1-score (%)
1	88.88	100.00	84.61	92.30	91.66
2	94.44	96.15	96.15	94.80	96.15
3	94.44	96.15	96.15	94.61	96.15
4	94.44	96.15	96.15	94.23	96.15

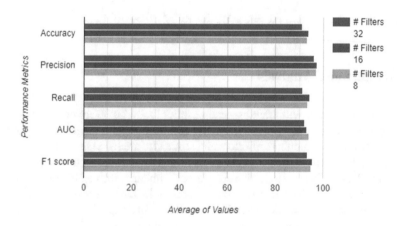

Fig. 2 Average performance measures for different numbers of filters

Table 4 Results of leave-one-subject-out validation for 16 filters and stride size 2

Stride size	Accuracy (%)	Precision (%)	Recall (%)	F1-score (%)
2	94.44	72.22	72.22	72.22

4 Conclusion and Future Scope

In this study, a single convolution layer-based 2D-CNN architecture is used. This architecture also consists of a max pooling layer, a batch normalization layer, a flatten layer, and a dense layer. Total 36 subjects are classified into good counter and bad counter based on the EEG signals recorded during mental task. The various parameters of CNN like no. of filters, kernel size, and stride length are varied to find the optimum architecture which gives the best performance. The best accuracy of 97.22% is achieved for kernel size 3, no. of filters 16, and stride size 2 when using hold-out validation. The same architecture when used with leave-one-subject-out validation gives accuracy of 94.44%. In future, this work will be extended using data augmentation techniques for generating new data samples in order to make number of samples balanced in both the classes.

References

1. Gevins A (1997) High-resolution EEG mapping of cortical activation related to working memory: effects of task difficulty, type of processing, and practice. Cereb Cortex 7(4):374–385
2. Plechawska-Wójcik M, Tokovarov M, Kaczorowska M, Zapała D (2019) A threeclass classification of cognitive workload based on EEG spectral data. Appl Sci 9(24):5340
3. Paas F, Tuovinen J, Tabbers H, Van Gerven PWM (2003) Cognitive load measurement as a means to advance cognitive load theory. Educ Psychol 38:63–72
4. Antonenko P, Paas F, Grabner R et al (2010) Using electroencephalography to measure cognitive load. EducPsychol Rev 22:425–438
5. Hossain D et al. (2019) Cognitive load measurement using galvanic skin response for listening tasks. In: 2019 4th International conference on electrical information and communication technology (EICT), Khulna, Bangladesh, pp 1–4
6. Fowler A, Nesbitt K, Canossa A (2019) Identifying cognitive load in a computer game: an exploratory study of young children, 2019 IEEE conference on games (CoG), London, United Kingdom, pp 1–6
7. Ahirwal MK (2020) Analysis and identification of EEG features for mentalstress. In: 8th International conference on frontiers of intelligent computing: theory and applications (FICTA), NIT Karnataka, Surathkal, India, Jan 2020 (In Press)
8. Ahirwal MK, Kumar A, Singh GK (2013) EEG/ERP Adaptive noise canceller design with controlled search space (CSS) approach in cuckoo and other optimization algorithms. IEEE/ACM Trans Comput Biol Bioinf 10(6):1491–1504
9. Ahirwal MK, Kumar A, Singh GK (2016) Study of ABC and PSO algorithms as optimized adaptive noise canceller for EEG/ERP. Int J Bio-Inspired Comput 8(3):170–183
10. B. Wang, F. Wu and S. Zhang, 2010, Reflections on the Control of Cognitive Load in Multimedia Learning, 2010 Second International Conference on Multimedia and Information Technology, Kaifeng, pp. 14–16.
11. Putze F, Jarvis J, Schultz T (2010) Multimodal recognition of cognitive workload for multi-tasking in the car. In: 20th international conference on pattern recognition, Istanbul, pp 3748–3751
12. Hu J (2017) Automated detection of driver fatigue based on Adaboost classifier with EEG signals. Front Comput Neurosci 11
13. Sega S, Iwasaki H, Hiraishi H, Mizoguchi F (2011) Applying qualitative reasoning to a driver's cognitive mental load. In: IEEE 10th International conference on cognitive informatics and cognitive computing (ICCI-CC'11), Banff, AB, pp 67–74
14. Rai AA, Ahirwal MK (2020) Electroencephalogram based cognitive load classification during mental arithmetic task, In: ADCOM 2020: 26th annual international conference on advanced computing and communications (In Press)
15. Ahirwal MK, Kose MR (2020) Audio-visual stimulation based emotion classification by correlated EEG channels. Heal Technol 10(1):7–23
16. Ahirwal MK, Kose MR (2021) Development of emotional decision-making model using EEG signals. In: Bhateja V, Peng SL, Satapathy SC, Zhang YD (eds) Evolution in computational

intelligence. Advances in intelligent systems and computing, vol 1176. Springer, Singapore. https://doi.org/10.1007/978-981-15-5788-0_27

17. Ahirwal MK (2021) Analysis and identification of EEG features for mental stress. In: Bhateja V, Peng SL, Satapathy SC, Zhang YD (eds) Evolution in computational intelligence. Advances in intelligent systems and computing, vol 1176. Springer, Singapore. https://doi.org/10.1007/978-981-15-5788-0_19

18. Ahirwal MK, Kumar A, Singh GK (2021) Biomedical signals. In: Computational intelligence and biomedical signal processing. SpringerBriefs in Electrical and Computer Engineering, Springer, Cham. https://doi.org/10.1007/978-3-030-67098-6_1

19. Craik A, He Y, Contreras-Vidal JL (2019) Deep learning for electroencephalogram (EEG) classification tasks: a review. J Neural Eng 16(3):031001

20. Zyma I, Tukaev S, Seleznov I, Kiyono K, Popov A, Chernykh M, Shpenkov O (2019) Electroencephalograms during mental arithmetic task performance. Data 4(1):14

Plant Leaf Diseases Detection Using Deep Learning Algorithms

Vikki Binnar and Sanjeev Sharma

1 Introduction

The Indian economy is based on agriculture. The many climates of India assure the availability of a wide range of fresh vegetables and fruits. According to the Agricultural and Processed Food Products Export Development Authority (APEDA), it ranks second in the world for vegetable and fruit output [1]. Agriculture's massive commercialisation has had a devastating impact on our environment. Chemical pesticides have accumulated in our environment such as soil, rivers, atmosphere, wildlife, and even human beings. For more sustainable and proper agriculture, as well as to avoid wasteful waste of time, money, and other resources, quick and precise detection of plant leaf diseases is critical [2].

Many times, plants have infections with no obvious signs; hence, enhanced analytical methods for such plant leaf diseases are unavoidable. However, many indications of plant leaf disease are visible, and today's standard procedure is for an experienced plant pathologist to identify the disease by optical examination of infected plant leaves. However, due to the large diversity of plants, many plant diseases brought on by climate change, and the rapid spread of illnesses to new areas, even expert pathologists are unable to detect some diseases [3, 4]. An automated system that can help us diagnose plant diseases based on visual symptoms and the look of the plant might be a valuable tool for amateur farmers [5]. Farmers will benefit from this technology since it will inform them at the correct moment, before the disease spreads across a big region. Artificial intelligence-based devices that can identify a wide spectrum of illnesses on their own are increasingly routinely used. In the preceding

V. Binnar (✉) · S. Sharma
Indian Institute of Information Technology Pune, Pune, India
e-mail: vikkibinnar20@ece.iiitp.ac.in

S. Sharma
e-mail: sanjeevsharma@iiitp.ac.in

© The Author(s), under exclusive license to Springer Nature Singapore Pte Ltd. 2023   217
R. Doriya et al. (eds.), *Machine Learning, Image Processing, Network Security and Data Sciences*, Lecture Notes in Electrical Engineering 946,
https://doi.org/10.1007/978-981-19-5868-7_17

decade, a number of machine learning models were used to identify and categorise plant leaf diseases [6]. A support vector machine (SVM) was used to identify and describe illnesses seen in sugar beets using spectral plant indexes. After executing texture-based feature extraction and colour-based feature extraction, AlHairy et al. employed K-means to segment the ill areas obtained by the preliminary methods, and then classified those regions using artificial neural networks (ANN). Another study used the SVM algorithm to detect and identify two separate viruses that cause disease and display symptoms on tomato leaves.

Deep neural network structure includes many processing layers and neurons that efficiently execute high-complexity tasks like image and speech recognition for vast amounts of input [7, 8]. It is extremely common to employ deep learning algorithms in the detection and categorisation of diseases using medical pictures. The deep learning (DL) approach was employed in this study, which is the industry standard for picture categorisation.

Convolutional neural networks are a specialised network design for high dimensional and rather large data images (CNNs). In this project, I use four models such as the simple sequential model, AlexNet, Inception V3, and MobileNet, and compare and contrast all four models to determine which is the best model for detecting plant leaf disease.

The rest of the paper is organised as follows: Sect. 2 discusses the literature review. Section 3 discusses the materials and procedures used in the planned study. Section 4 discusses the experiments and their outcomes. Finally, the work in Sect. 4 is coming to a close.

2 Literature Review

We explored some important literature on plant leaf disease detection using various methodologies in this paper.

The author of this study characterises it as a wheat illness in-field automatic diagnostic system based on a deep learning technique, i.e. deep instance based learning, that achieves an integration of detection for simply image-level annotation for training images in uncontrolled conditions [9]. Wheat Disease Database 2017, a replacement in-field image dataset for wheat disease, is also gathered to test the efficiency of our technology. Using two distinct CNN models, VGG FCN S and VGG FCN VD16, with average accuracy rate of 97.95% and 95.12%, respectively, over fivefold cross-validation on Wheat Disease Database 2017, VGG-CNN-S and VGG-CNN-VD16 outperformed the outcomes of 93.27% and 73.00%, respectively. The suggested approach beats traditional CNN models on identification accuracy with a comparable amount of parameters, while preserving precise positioning according to disease regions, according to experimental data. It may be integrated into a real-time mobile application to aid in the detection of agricultural diseases.

In this study, the authors highlighted and reviewed forty research studies that employ deep learning techniques and implement them to a variety of plant problems

[10]. Analyse the agricultural challenges, the precise models and frameworks utilised, the sources of data, nature, and pre-processing, and the actual quality attained as per the metrics used at each task under consideration [11, 12]. This paper compared deep learning approaches to other current popular techniques in terms of regression and classification ability and concluded that deep learning delivers superior accuracy to the other methods.

The author employed deep neural networks to recognise plant diseases; in this paper, CNN capabilities could be emphasised by using more real and diverse image datasets [13]. Although CNN skills could be reinforced through employing better credible and diversified visual datasets, deep neural networks were used to identify plant illnesses in this study. Plant-village datasets were utilised to images acquired online in this research. There were 54303 images in all. This research was conducted utilising the GoogleNet architecture and a pretrained CNN. The total accuracy is 82%, with accuracy ranging from 75 to 100% for each crop.

The author of this paper recommends combining basic leaf pictures of normal and infected plants, as well as convolution neural network models built using deep learning methods, to identify and diagnose plant illnesses [14]. The model was trained using an accessible data including more than 87k pictures of twenty five different plants of fifty-eight different plant disease categories. In detecting the corresponding plant disease, the accuracy reached a 99.53% success rate. Because of its great accuracy, the model is an excellent advising or early warning tool.

Plant disease identification in Malus domestica was described in this work using a K-mean clustering, texture, and colour analysis [15]. It categorises and recognises many plant diseases. It makes advantage of the texture and colour elements that may be found in both the normal and afflicted areas.

Durmus et al. use pretrained CNN architectures AlexNet and SqueezeNet to identify diseases in tomato leaves in this study [16, 17]. In this study, the author uses an ANN and multiple image processing algorithms to develop a method for identifying plant illness [18, 19]. An ANN classifier-based approach is used for classification, which gives excellent outcomes with a detection accuracy of 91% [20]. An ANN-based classification that identifies illnesses based on a combination of textures, colours, and features.

3   Materials and Methods

We are employing a convolution neural network (CNN) to identify plant leaves disease, and it's fast becoming the industry standard for picture categorisation. Here, we are using four models such as AlexNet, simple sequential model Inception-v3, MobileNet mode. For implementation, gather the dataset first and then divide it into train and test, typically 80% for training and 20% for validation. Deep learning methods are then trained from scratch or with transfer learning approaches, and training/validation graphs are created to determine the algorithms' relevance. Then, for the categorisation of plant disease pictures, efficiency measures are utilised, and

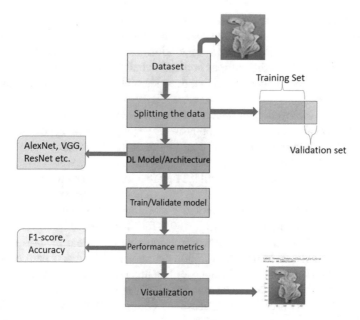

Fig. 1 Flow graph

finally, visualisation methodologies are used to identify images. Figure 1 represents the flow diagram of the work.

3.1 Datasets

We used the Kaggle-available new plant diseases dataset, which is open-source and simple to use. Around 87,500 RGB photos of normal and ill or diseased crop leaves are organised into thirty-eight categories in this database [21]. While the directory structure is kept, the entire dataset is divided into an 80/20 training and validation set. Later, a new collection containing thirty-three test images is created for prediction purposes. The fourteen plant species depicted are orange, peach, bell pepper, potato, raspberry, soybean, squash, strawberry, apple, blueberry, cherry, corn, grape, and tomato. Figure 2 represents the summary of dataset images.

3.2 Deep Learning Models

AlexNet Model AlexNet is an eight-layer model with learnable parameters. With a 224-pixel input image, the AlexNet architecture includes five convolution layer and three fully connected layers, and a Softmax layer. The AlexNet architecture employed

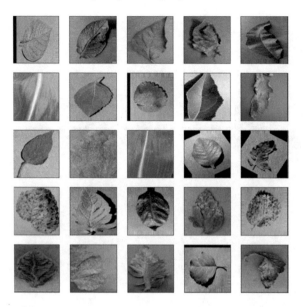

Fig. 2 Summary of dataset images

in this work has a fully connected layer (FC-8) that is coupled to the Softmax layer with 39 neurons. RGB images are used as input to the model. The activation function used in all stages is Relu. In total, there were three dropout levels. The activation function used in the output layer is Softmax. Figure 3 represents the architecture of the AlexNet mode.

Simple Sequential Model It contains four layers with learnable features, and RGB images are used as input. It has three fully connected layers and two convolution layers with max-pooling. At all levels, the activation function Relu is used. One dropout layer was utilised. The activation function used in the output layer is Softmax. There are 62.3 million parameters in this architecture. Figure 4 represents the architecture of the simple sequential model.

MobileNet model The input to the MobileNet model is RGB pictures, and the model comprises 27 convolutions layers. There are 13, 3 × 3 depthwise convolution layers in the model. There are three layers in total: one average pool layer, one fully

Fig. 3 Architecture represents AlexNet model

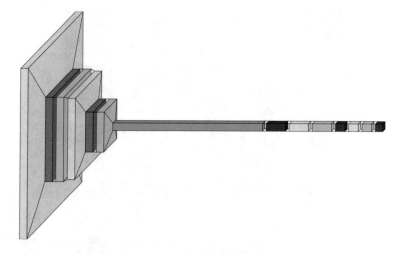

Fig. 4 Architecture represents simple sequential model

Fig. 5 Architecture represents MobileNet model

connected layer, and one Softmax layer. In MobileNet, 1×1 convolution takes up 95% of the time. There are 4.2 million parameters in it. Andrew G. Howard and other Google researchers created this approach. Figure 5 represents the architecture of the MobileNet model.

Inception V3 The Inception V3 model is a 48-layer neural network that exceeds VGGNet significantly. It was a 1st Runner Up in the ILSVRC for image classification in 2015. It has 23,851,784 parameters and has a reduced error rate. Figure 6 represents the architecture of the Inception V3 model.

4 Experiments and Results

4.1 Software Environment

Due to insufficient computing capabilities, it is difficult to train the classification model locally on the majority of ordinary PCs. As a result, we take use of the

Fig. 6 Architecture represents Inception V3 model

processing power provided by Google Colab notebook, which rapidly and easily links us to a free TPU instance. We bring in all of the libraries such as Numpy, Keras, Os, Sklearn, and Matplotlib. We will need to process the data and create the categorisation model.

4.2 Hardware Requirements

We need laptop/computer which has at least dual core CPU with 2.10 GHz processor, minimum of 3GB ram is required, and at least, a 32-bit operating system is required. If we have GPU, then it will train our model in less time as compared to normal time required for training the model without GPU.

4.3 Metrics Used

We used following metrics to check the performance of models.

Accuracy The accuracy of a classification model is a criterion used to compare it to other classification models.

The formula for finding the accuracy is:

$$\text{Accuracy} = \frac{\text{True Negative} + \text{True Positive}}{\text{True Positive} + \text{False Positive} + \text{True Negative} + \text{False Negative}}$$

Precision The ratio of true positives to total predicted positives is calculated. The accuracy of a classification model gives us how accurate the predicted positives are in terms of percentage.

The formula for finding the precision is:

Table 1 Training hyperparameters

Training parameters	Simple sequential Model	AlexNet Model	Inception V3 model	MobileNet Model
Learning rate	0.1	0.1	0.001	0.001
Batch size	32	32	128	128
Optimiser	RMSprop	SGD	Adam	Adam
Epochs	20	20	20	20
Horizontal/vertical flip-ping	Yes	Yes	Yes	Yes
Zoom range	0.2	0.2	0.2	0.2

$$\text{Precision} = \frac{\text{True Positive}}{\text{True Positive} + \text{False Positive}}$$

4.4   Parameters Setup

We used data augmentation to increase learning efficiency and prevent overfitting in the network, and we trained our dataset using AlexNet, simple sequential, MobileNet, Inception-v3 models, and our model used 20 epochs. It is worth mentioning that we did not resize the images for training or testing since we did not want to lose the infection's little amount of data. Table 1 shows the training hyperparameters we used.

4.5   Calculation of Results

Prakanshu et al. conducted an experiment on new plant diseases dataset with 38 classes [22]. On the test dataset, they achieved an accuracy of 88%. In our paper, we compare four deep learning models such as simple sequential model, AlexNet model, Inception V3 and, MobileNet model and try to find out best suitable model for plant leaf disease detection. We achieved the best result for the MobileNet architecture with training and validation accuracy of 99.07% and 97.52% respectively. In Table 2, we compare all the four models training and validation accuracy. In Fig. 7, we show the graph of training and validation loss and in Fig. 8, we show the graph of training and validation accuracy. Here, orange line represents the validation data and the blue line represents the training data. Figure 9, shows the confusion matrix of all the models.

Table 2 Comparison of all the four models

Accuracy	Simple sequential Model	AlexNet Model	Inception V3 model	MobileNet Model
Training accuracy (%)	75.61	59.83	96.15	99.07
Validation accuracy (%)	76.27	62.32	94.08	97.52

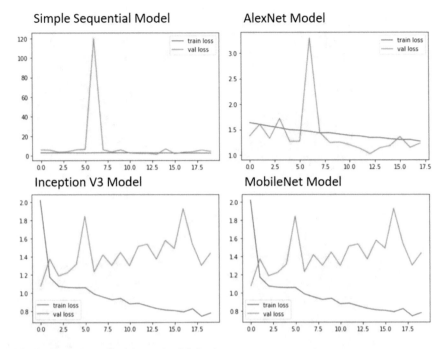

Fig. 7 Comparison of training and validation losses

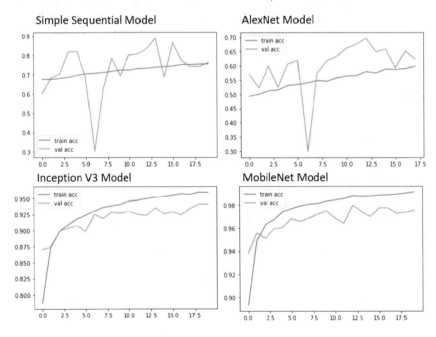

Fig. 8 Comparison of training and validation accuracy

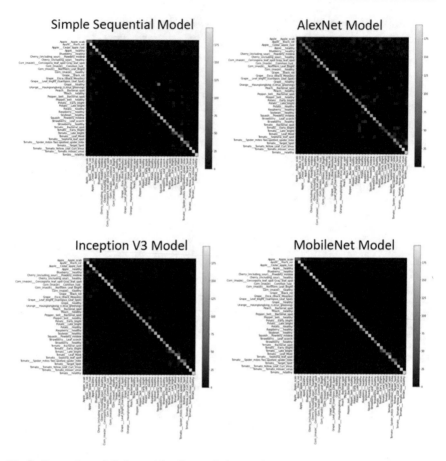

Fig. 9 Comparison of all the models using confusion matrix

5 Conclusion and Future Scope

5.1 Conclusion

It is extremely difficult to classify plant diseases using digital images. Deep learning approaches, specifically CNNs, appear to be capable of tackling the majority of the technical issues related with plant disease categorisation.

5.2   Future Work

Here, we train model for plant leaf detection only. In future, we can work on how it will provide information of disease and also provide solution for this particular disease(recommend pesticide). We can also make user-friendly android application. Farmers will benefit from this technology since it will inform them at the correct moment, before the disease spreads over a vast region, and it will also propose pesticides for certain diseases.

References

1. http://www.apeda.gov.in/apedawebsite/index.html: Agricultural and processed food products export development authority (2017)
2. Nalawade R, Nagap A, Jindam L, Ugale M (2020) Agriculture field monitoring and plant leaf disease detection, pp 226–231
3. Bhagat M, Kumar D, Mahmood R, Pati B, Kumar M (2020) Bell pepper leaf disease classification using CNN. Expert systems with applications, pp 1–5
4. Sardoˇgan M, Tuncer A, Ozen Y (2018) Plant leaf disease detection and classification based on CNN with lvq algorithm. In: 2018 3rd International conference on computer science and engineering (UBMK), pp 382–385
5. Nandhini S, Suganya R, Nandhana K, Varsha S, Deivalakshmi S, Thangavel SK (2021) Automatic detection of leaf disease using CNN algorithm, pp 237–244
6. Trivedi J, Shamnani Y, Gajjar R (2020) Plant leaf disease detection using machine learning, pp 267–276
7. Dalal T, Singh M (2021) Review paper on leaf diseases detection and classification using various CNN techniques, pp 153–162
8. Ajra H, Nahar MK, Sarkar L, Islam MS (2020) Disease detection of plant leaf using image processing and CNN with preventive measures, pp 1–6
9. Lu J, Hu J, Zhao G, Mei F, Zhang C (2017) An in-field automatic wheat disease diagnosis system 142:369–379
10. Kamilaris A, Prenafeta-Bold FX (2018) Deep learning in agriculture: a survey 147:70–90
11. Bhattacharya S, Mukherjee A, Phadikar S (2020) A deep learning approach for the classification of rice leaf diseases, pp 61–69
12. Gajjar R, Gajjar N, Thakor VJ, Patel NP, Ruparelia S (2021) Real-time detection and identification of plant leaf diseases using convolutional neural networks on an embedded platform 147:1432–2315
13. Ferentinos K (2018) Deep learning models for plant disease detection and diagnosis 145:311–318
14. Barbedo J (2019) Plant disease identification from individual lesions and spots using deep learning 180:96–107
15. Singh V, Misra A (2017) Detection of plant leaf diseases using image segmentation and soft computing techniques 4:41–49
16. Durmuˌs H, Gunes E, Kirci M (2017) Disease detection on the leaves of the tomato plants by using deep learning, pp 1–5
17. Kibriya H, Rafique R, Ahmad W, Adnan S (2021) Tomato leaf disease detection using convolution neural network, pp 346–351
18. Bin L, Zhang Y, He D, Li Y (2017) Identification of apple leaf diseases based on deep convolutional neural networks 10:11–24

19. Naik D, Shaikh R, Shetti S, Kanakaraddi S, Jahagirdar S, Hubli B (2015) Detection and quantification of disease in cabbage using clustering and RGB colour features 14:2–20
20. Lee SH, Chan CS, Mayo SJ, Remagnino P (2017) How deep learning extracts and learns leaf features for plant classification 71:1–13
21. http://www.kaggle.com/vipoooool: New plant diseases data-set
22. Srivastava P, Mishra K, Awasthi VVKS, Pal PK (2021) Plant disease detection using convolutional neural network 691–698

Performance Comparison of the Classifiers for Betel Vine Disease Prediction

S. Aneesh Fathima⬭ and M. Nandhini⬭

1 Introduction

India is an agricultural country, with farming employing 70% of the population. Agriculture has a vital role in human life. Betel vine is one of the horticultural crops having high export value, mostly cultivated in the South Asian region. In the betel plant, heart-shaped deep green leaves are the most significant parts that represent the crop yield with high aesthetic and commercial values. Cultivation of the betel vine is labor-intensive, and it is mostly done in South Asian countries. Betel leaf disease management is one of the necessities of betel vine cultivation. The betel vine has a lifespan of roughly 2–3 years in most cases. Betel leaves have a significant risk of disease infection during their short life span, and this must be regulated to increase the farmer's productivity. Hence, the design and development of the smart system for betel vine cultivation are required to detect and diagnose the diseases in advance. Image processing is the process of applying operations on a visual image in order to improve it or extract usable information from it. It is a sort of signal processing in which the input is an image and the output is an image or image-related elements or characteristics. Digital image processing is a multidisciplinary field which employs computer algorithms from Computer vision, Data mining, Artificial intelligence, and Machine learning to perform image processing which aid in analyzing and understanding the image-rich domain. Image classification is one of the difficult tasks of image processing because of the complexity of image contents.

S. A. Fathima (✉) · M. Nandhini
Government Arts College, Udumalpet, Tamilnadu, India
e-mail: anejul89@gmail.com

S. A. Fathima
Sri GVG Visalakshi College for Women, Udumalpet, Tamil Nadu, India

M. Nandhini
Government Arts and Science College for Women, Puliakulam, Coimbatore, Tamilnadu, India

In this work, the images of the betel vine plant are captured and basic pre-processing techniques such as edge detection-based segmentation and scaling are performed to retrieve the betel leaf images with good resolution. Further, the features of the image are extracted using SqueezeNet [1], an image embedding technique. Iandola et al. [1] proposed a small Convolution Neural Network (CNN) architecture SqueezeNet which attains good precision with $50 \times$ fewer parameters compared to AlexNet. The classifiers require input data to be in the numeric form. A feature is an individual measurable property of a phenomenon being observed. Image embedding technique converts image contents into vectors of numeric values. In this work, SqueezeNet is used to extract features from the images. SqueezeNet is basically a small CNN deep model architecture for image recognition trained on ImageNet. The pre-trained model on ImageNet is less than 5 MB in size, making it ideal for use in a real-world application. Feature selection techniques are used in order to retain the significant and eliminate insignificant features. ANOVA, Chi-square $\left(\chi^2\right)$, Fast Correlation-based Filter (FCBF), Gain Ratio (GR), Gini Index (GI), Information Gain (IG), Relief-F (ReF), and Principal Component Analysis (PCA) are the most popular pre-processing techniques widely used for significant feature selection. Classification is one of the predictive data mining techniques used to predict/detect the class of the unseen samples using the trained examples. In literature, Linear classifiers (LR, NB, SGD), Kernel estimation algorithm (SVM), Tree-based model (DT, RF), KNN [2], and NN are efficient classifiers that offer significant results for most of the real-time applications. This work aims in analyzing the performance of the above mentioned eight classifiers over the extracted features. Further significant features are hauled out using eight feature selection approaches. To improve the performance of the classifiers, significant features obtained using feature selection techniques are used for disease detection. It is found that classifier built using LR over the significant feature set obtained using ReF gives 87% accuracy which is higher than other combinations. The LR algorithm proves to be the best classifier in classifying the betel leaf disease compared to other classifiers in terms of AUC, classifier accuracy, F1-score, precision, and recall.

Section 2 surveys contemporary works carried in the domain of disease classification using image processing and predictive data mining techniques. Section 3 describes the methodology used for image classification, algorithms, and pre-processing approaches that are used in this paper. Results are analyzed briefly in Sect. 4. Section 5 concludes the research work.

2   Literature Review

Hossain et al. [3] suggested that the disease found at an early stage can be cured by proper treatment and pruning of the affected leaves. In this paper, SVM classifier is used to recognize the diseases and it has got an accuracy of 93%, and the neural network achieves 91% accuracy. In their work, eleven features are analyzed for disease detection. Potato leaves are analyzed to detect diseases in [4]. Millions of images are classified with the help of SGD and SVM in [5]. For image classification, Hsu et al. [6] introduced a new paired local observation-based Naïve Bayes classifier. Das et al. [7] describes a method for detecting, quantifying, and classifying leaf disease using digital photographs. The major characteristic parameters such as background, shape, and size are used. SVM, RF, and ANN are applied, and the results are compared. FCM clustering is used to find the affected regions of leaf disease. Texture features are extracted from HSV images to train the classifier. From the results, it is found that the ANN classifier gives the best accuracy than the other algorithms. Image features were extracted pixel-by-pixel and turned into a database-like table where data mining techniques may use to explore [8]. Transductive Support Vector Machine-based classification to detect leaf disease using shape and texture features is performed in [9]. Color and texture features of soil images are extracted, and further, Latent Dirichlet Allocation and Artificial Neural Network classification techniques are also applied for disease detection. Data mining algorithms are used to detect disease in [10]. The major steps such as pre-processing feature extraction and image mining and evaluation are also applied yet it has the issues in classification accuracy/speed. The performance of the machine learning algorithms such as NB, RF, DT, SVM, and LR are compared with respect to accuracy in [11].

Citrus leaf disease detection system consisting of phases such as image pre-processing, segmentation, feature extraction, and finally classification of diseases is proposed in [12]. A deep learning framework using Keras/Tensor Flow is used, and it achieves a classification accuracy of 89%. Disease prediction is a growing field in Asian countries. Segmentation and classification are used for disease prediction. Tomato pests and their diseases are detected in [13]. Object recognition, image indexing and retrieval, association rules mining, image classification, and clustering are used in [14]. In [15], only color and texture features are used for the image-based classification. The proposed classifier produces 88.89% accuracy for grape leaf disease detection. In addition, the accuracy of the classifier is increased by using pre-processing techniques such as Resizing, Thresholding, and Gaussian filtering. SVM, Artificial Neural Network (ANN), and Regression to detect crop disease, soil moisture, and crop growth monitoring in [16]. Image processing algorithms are used to detect leaf rot disease in [17]. The amount of severity helps to regulate pesticide management and thereby reduce the cost of appropriate treatment. Segmentation is performed using a k-means clustering algorithm, and neural network-based classification is applied to detect brinjal leaf disease [18]. Several agricultural applications employ diverse image processing techniques. The automatic detection of plant diseases is designed to find diseases in leaves, stem, and fruits [19]. Paddy crop leaf disease classification system is designed to provide suggestions to the farmers [20]. Color, texture, and size of the image are considered as image features in [21]. Computer-aided system was developed for the identification of diseases in brinjal leaves [22]. The technique was proposed by Vijayakumar and Arumugam [23] to discover foot rot disease in betel vines caused by the fungus *Phytophthora parasitica*. Throughout the crop growing, diseases such as leaf spot, leaf rot, and powdery mildew plague the betel plant, causing significant losses for farmers [24].

The symptoms of cotton leaf spot images are described, and the diseases are categorized using NN in [25]. The pest recommendation to control disease is done using the boundary, shape, color, and texture features. Imaging, weed detection, and fruit grading techniques are described in [26]. In [27], a method for leaf disease detection is proposed with the help of an artificial neural network. Bacterial Leaf Spot and stem leaf disease detection and classification are performed using the SVM and Gaussian mixer model [28]. Leaf spot disease is identified using image processing technique [29]. Neural network classifier is used for classification, and K-means clustering is used for image segmentation. Rice leaf diseases such as leaf smut, bacterial leaf blight, and brown spot were detected in [30]. K-Nearest Neighbor, J48 (Decision Tree), Naïve Bayes, and Logistic Regression classifiers are used in this work. It is found that decision tree has performed best with 97% accuracy.

3 Proposed Work

This work proposes a betel leaf disease detection system using digital image processing and predictive data mining algorithms. From the field study, betel leaf images are captured and preprocessed. Due to its high dimensionality, classifying multimedia data can be difficult, and pre-processing plays an important role in structuring image data. Feature selection is used to decrease the features for training the classifiers such as KNN, DT, SVM, SGD, RF, NN, NB, and LR. AUC, accuracy, F1-score measure, precision, and recall are some of the evaluation measures used to assess the performance of the eight classifiers.

The dataset for analysis may not be readily available for analysis; hence, there is a necessity for data collection. Figure 1 represents the betel vine images captured in the field. Captured leaves are taken as the training dataset for this work. Experiments are conducted using 100 leaf images with 50 infected and 50 healthy. Images captured may not be in the quality expected for pre-processing; hence, it is improved by image scaling techniques. In order to handle images efficiently, image embedding via the SqueezeNet technique is applied over the leaf images to extract important features. The extracted features are then used to train classifiers in order to build a disease detection system that is effective. In addition, the classifier performance is improved by using feature selection techniques such as ANOVA, χ^2, FCBF, GR, GI, IG, ReF, and PCA. Classification algorithms such as KNN, DT, SVM, SGD, RF, NN, NB, and LR are applied over the dataset, and the classifier performance is compared based on measures like AUC values, accuracy, F1-score, precision, and recall. Figure 2 describes the workflow of the proposed methodology.

(a) Leaf spot   (b) Leaf rot   (c) Powdery Mildew   (d) Healthy

Fig. 1 **a–c** Infected leaves, **d** healthy leaf

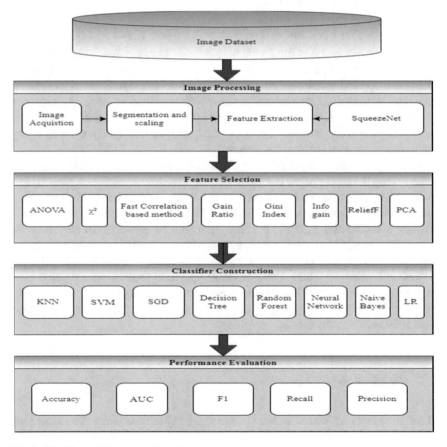

Fig. 2 Workflow of the proposed work

3.1 Dataset

Datasets are integral parts of the classification algorithms. The classification algorithms rely heavily on datasets. High-quality labeled training datasets are essential for supervised and semi-supervised machine learning algorithms, but they are difficult and expensive to create since class labeling the data takes a long time. In this work, primarily dataset consists of pictures, i.e., images. Betel leaf images are captured from the field. 50 healthy and 50 infected leaf images are taken for the experimentation.

3.2 Image Pre-processing

Real-world data is frequently insufficient, inconsistent, and/or devoid of confident patterns or trends, and it is filled with inaccuracies. Data pre-processing may be an evidenced technique of solving real-world problems. Pre-processing refers to the alterations applied to the dataset before giving it to the classification algorithms. This usually achieves a higher result, especially for the image datasets. In this work, classification algorithms make use of 100 images as the training dataset. The captured images contain noise, in order to improve the quality of the input images, cropping, and scaling is performed over the images.

Edge-based segmentation [8] is applied to crop the captured betel leaf image. It helps to crop the heart-shaped betel leaf. Further, image scaling [6] is applied to scale all images to a uniform size which enhances the quality of the captured images. Then, the images are labeled as healthy or infected. Labeled images cannot be fed directly into the classification algorithms; hence, it should be converted to tabular/vector format. The image characteristics are extracted by SqueezeNet approach, an image embedding technique, and the extracted features are articulated in tabular/vector format with numeric values. Using SqueezeNet, 1000 features are extracted from each image. Hence, the 1000 features from every image represent a vector in the dataset. Similarly, for 100 images, 1000 features are stored, forming 100 vectors with 1000 values in the dataset.

3.3 Feature Selection

In machine learning, classification is done using features/variables. The higher the number of features, the harder to work/visualize the training set. Also, most of the features are redundant and insignificant. Further real-time problems often deal with the high-dimensional dataset. Henceforth, it is necessary to eliminate insignificant dimensions and retain good ones. Feature selection attempts to realize a subset of the input variables (also known as features or attributes). Feature selection methods focused to reduce the number of input features to those that are believed to be most significant to a classifier in order to perform prediction. The selection of features is self-employed in any machine learning algorithm. The following feature selection techniques are used in this work for finding relevant features.

ANOVA. ANalysis Of VAriance (ANOVA) is a statistical method used to select the significant features of the dataset by analyzing the nature of one or more response variables/features among classification groups under diverse conditions. It examines the impact of one or more features by comparing the means of different samples and the relative variance between them. The p-values are used to rank the important features with small values, and the sorted numbers of features are used for further processing.

Chi-square (χ^2). The χ^2 test is a statistical method for determining whether two variables are independent. It calculates the difference between the expected (e) and observed (o) counts. χ^2 statistic is used to compare actual and discovered knowledge as given in (1).

$$\chi^2 = \sum(f_o - f_e)/f_e \tag{1}$$

where f_o is the discovered frequency and f_e is the anticipated frequency.

Fast Correlation-based Filter (FCBF). FCBF selects features that have a strong correlation with the target feature but little connection with other features in a classifier-independent manner. The correlation is based on symmetrical uncertainty. It is divided into two steps, the first of which is used to rank the input features utilizing the symmetric ambiguity with respect to the goal output. This stage is used to exclude features that have a ranking score that is less than a predetermined threshold. The second stage is a redundancy analysis, which aims to select the most important possibilities from the relevant set gathered in the first stage.

Gain Ratio (GR). GR is a feature ranking approach that is used to rank data attributes. Low-ranking attributes are filtered out, resulting in smaller data subsets. It produces better results than information gain since it considers the number of branches.

Gini Index (GI). The Gini coefficient, often known as the Gini Index, is a statistic that measures the disparity between two variables values. The more dispersed the data is, the higher its index value is. Alternatively, half of the relative mean absolute difference can be used to determine the Gini coefficient.

Information Gain (IG). IG is completely based on the decrease of entropy after a dataset is split on an attribute. The entropy must be calculated for each branch. IG conjointly remarked as Mutual information helps to live with the dependence between the 2 variables.

In a classification task, it is used to determine the degree of dependence between the feature and the target variable. The information gain is a measurement of purity. It shows the estimated amount of data required to determine whether or not a new incident should be categorized as a disease. Another measure of impurity is entropy (the opposite). It is outlined for a binary category with class values a/b as given in (2)

$$\text{Entropy} = -P(a) * \log(P(a)) - P(b) * \log(P(b)) \tag{2}$$

Relief-F (ReF). It is a feature selection method based on filters that is extremely sensitive to feature relationships. This method was designed to solve binary classification issues involving discrete or numerical features. It assigns each attribute a score, which may subsequently be used to rank and select the highest-scoring qualities for feature selection.

Principal Component Analysis (PCA). PCA is a linear dimensionality reduction approach. The data's correlation matrix is formed, and the matrix's Eigen vectors are computed. PCA can recover a significant portion of the original data variance. PCA's main goal is to minimize the dimensionality of a dataset containing numerous variables that are connected with each other, either strongly or weakly, while preserving the differences in the dataset to the greatest extent possible. It will be done the same way, by transforming the variables into a new set of orthogonal and ordered variables known as principal components (PCs), with the amount of variance retained in the original variables reducing as the order increases. Because the principal components are the Eigen vectors of a variance matrix, they are orthogonal.

3.4 Classifier Construction

Supervised learning use mapping function $Y = f(X)$ to predict the output variables (Y) with respect to the input variables (X). These algorithms forecast variables based on the input variables within the dataset. Classification, a supervised learning algorithm, finds or discovers a model/function that helps to separate the data into multiple categorical classes, i.e., discrete values. Although there are numerous classification algorithms available, it is impossible to determine one is superior to the others. It is dependent on the application and the nature of the data collection supplied.

For the experimentation, the benchmark algorithms KNN, DT, SVM, SGD, RF, NN, NB, and LR available in Orange 3.22 (Visual programming software package for Data visualization, Machine learning, Data mining, and Data analysis) are used. Performance evaluation and comparison are carried out based on the findings.

K-Nearest Neighbor (KNN). K-Nearest Neighbor is used for many real-world classification problems that do not require any training process. The entire dataset is used for predicting/classifying new data. When a new data value is given, it calculates the distance from the new data value to all other values in the dataset depending on the K value; it identifies the nearest neighbors in the dataset. The Euclidian measure is used for calculating the distance as a metric and the value for K is set as 4, since there are four classes of images such as healthy and infected with three subgroups (leaf rot, leaf spot, and powdery mildew).

Decision Tree (DT). A tree is a basic method that divides data into nodes based on purity of class. It is the parent of Random Forest. Like its name suggests, it creates classification models in the shape of a tree-like structure. The targeted result is already known in supervised learning. Both categorical and numerical data can be analyzed using DT. It divides the dataset into subsets according to the most important attribute in the dataset. In the decision tree, the dataset is divided into homogeneous and non-overlapping sections. It uses a top-down approach, with the top area presenting all of the observations in one place before splitting into two or more branches, each of which splits further. Because it only considers the current node and ignores future nodes, this method is also known as a greedy method. After a decision tree has been constructed, many nodes may reflect outliers or noisy data. Tree pruning is a technique for removing unwanted branches from a tree. As a result, the accuracy of the classification model improves. The decision tree algorithms will continue to run until they reach a limit, such as a certain number of observations. In this work, the tree is constructed as a tree with a minimum of four leaves in an instance. Parameters such as 'split' and the 'maximum tree depth' are set as ' < 5' and '100.'

Random Forest (RF). RF may be a multipurpose machine learning technique efficient of acting each regression and classification tasks. It is a kind of ensemble learning technique, wherever a bunch of weak models mixes to make a robust model. Random Forest has a tendency to grow multiple trees as a hostile one tree in the CART model. The forest chooses the category holding the chief votes (over all the trees within the forest). It has the power to handle massive information set with a higher spatial property. It will handle thousands of input variables and establish the most vital variables. In this work, parameters such as the number of trees are set as 10, and the split value is set as ' < 5.'

Support Vector Machine (SVM). SVM is a classification algorithm. It constitutes the umbrella of machine learning and majorly used in classification problems. This approach plots every information item in the n-dimensional area to some extent, with the value of each feature representing the coordinate. It achieves categorization by locating the hyper-plane that clearly distinguishes the two classes. In this work, the SVM model is constructed with parameters such as cost, kernel, and iteration limit set as 1.00, RBF, and 100. Radial Base Function kernel is a function whose valuation depends on the length from the root or from some juncture.

Stochastic Gradient Descent (SGD). SGD is a method for improving the effectiveness of an objective function with proper smoothness properties by repeating the process. SGD can be thought of as a stochastic approximation of gradient descent optimization because it evaluates the method using random sampling or shuffling. It computes the gradient of the parameters using a few training examples. In this SGD model, parameters such as the classification loss function are set as Hinge, the learning rate is fixed as constant with the initial rate of 0.0100 and then the number of iteration is set as 1000.

Neural Network (NN). Neural networks are based on the learning process in human brains. It has function parameters that allow the machine to learn. Artificial Neural Networks (ANNs) are composed of simple components called neurons that take a real value, multiply it by weight, and then pass it through a non-linear activation function. The network may learn very complex functions by establishing numerous layers of neurons, each of which gets a portion of the input variables and then passes on its results to the following layers. When given enough computational capacity, a NN may hypothetically find the nature of whatever function. It is especially useful for high-dimensional situations with complicated attribute relationships and multifaceted functions that connect input and output features. The NN uses iterative learning process in which the input values are changed each times rows are presented in the network. Important decisions are decided by the number of elements in each layer. NN model is constructed with 1000 and 100 neurons in the input and hidden layers. ReLU with the solver Adam, an optimization algorithm, is used for activation function. The maximum number of iteration is set as 200.

Naïve Bayes (NB). A probabilistic classifier is NB. It is based on the conditional probability distribution, which describes the likelihood of assigning a class given a collection of characteristics. All classes conditional probabilities will be calculated. It will believe that all features are independent of one another since it is ignorant. It will be assumed that there is no correlation between any features and that their contribution to class prediction is unaffected by other factors. Bayes Theorem is used to calculate the conditional probabilities using (3).

$$P(\text{Class}|\text{Feature set}) = \frac{P(\text{Feature set}|\text{Class}) \times P(\text{Class})}{P(\text{Feature set})} \tag{3}$$

The probability $P(\text{Class}|\text{Feature set})$ is also referred to as the posterior probability. $P(\text{Feature set})$ is called evidence since it is the probability of the record/observation containing the set of features. $P(\text{Feature set}|\text{Class})$ is called the likelihood of being an image with the set of features belongs to the diseased or healthy class. The whole dataset is taken as a feature matrix. The size of each row (vector) in the dataset is set as 1000.

Logistic Regression (LR). LR is basically a statistical method used for binary classification, and it uses the technique for analyzing the dependency of a binary result on one or more independent variables. It is a supervised classification algorithm with the target variable and a set of features/inputs variables having only discrete values. This model is constructed with a regulation type as Ridge ($L2$) with a strength value set as 1.

3.5 Performance Evaluation

Evaluating a classifier is the main task of constructing a successful classification model. The assessment measures aid to distinguish the performance of the classifiers. 10 Cross-fold validation is performed to check the performance of each classifier. The following are the performance metrics used to evaluate the classifier.

AUC. A binary classifier's performance can be measured by the area under the curve (AUC). This is typically used in classification analysis to discover which of the existing options supersede the classes. AUC represents the degree or measure of separability, while Receiver Operating Characteristics (ROC) is a probability curve. When comparing the ROC curves and AUC, the greater the AUC, the better the classifier in distinguishing between infected and diseased cases.

Accuracy. Accuracy is the familiar metric employed for estimating classification models. Informally, accuracy is the fraction of predictions in a model that learned precisely (4).

$$Accuracy = \frac{TP + TN}{Total\ no.\ of\ samples} \tag{4}$$

Here, TP = True Positives, TN = True Negatives.

Precision. Precision, also known as the positive predictive value, is the percentage of truly positive outcomes. It can be calculated with the help of (5).

$$Precision = \frac{TP}{TP + FN} \tag{5}$$

Here, TP = True Positives, FN = False Negatives. Precision is an excellent measure to resolve when the costs of False Positives (FP) are high.

Recall. Recall/Sensitivity calculates the total number of the actual positives the classifier captures in the course of tagging it as Positive (True Positive). When there is a large cost associated with False Negative, one of the classifier metrics that helps to select the optimal model is Recall. This is calculated using (6).

$$Recall = \frac{TP}{P} \tag{6}$$

Simply, it is the number of right positive outcomes divided by the total number of samples.

F1-score. F1-score (also F-score or F1-measure) is a metric for determining the accuracy of an assessment. The precision and recall are taken into account when calculating the score. The F1-score is the harmonic mean of precision and recall, with the best value being 1 and the worst being 0.

4   Results and Discussions

In this investigational study, the entire dataset consisting of all the 1000 features is used for constructing classification models using eight classifiers such as KNN, DT, SVM, SGD, RF, NN, NB, and LR. Performances of the eight classifiers are shown in Table 1.

From Table 1, it is observed that more or less KNN, NN, and LR classifiers yield similar results for all the performance evaluation measures. These three classifiers found to be better than the DT, SVM, SGD, RF, and NB. On an overall, LR achieves top values for all the measures. Figure 3 depicts the performance comparison of the eight classifiers without feature selection.

Table 1 Performance (%) of the classifiers over the original dataset

Classifiers	Performance measures				
	AUC	Accuracy	F1-Score	Precision	Recall
KNN	87.7	83	83	83	83
DT	67.7	69	69	69.1	69
SVM	90	82	82	82.1	82
SGD	82	82	82	82	82
RF	82.6	73	72.9	73.2	73
NN	91.6	83	83	83	83
NB	84.1	79	79	79.1	79
LR	91.9	83	83	83	83

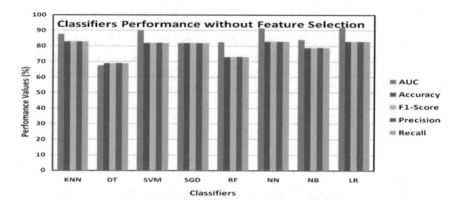

Fig. 3 Performance comparison of classifiers without feature selection

To improve the performance of the classifier, feature selection methods are used to reduce the dataset's dimensionality. ANOVA, χ^2, FCBF, GR, GI, IG, ReF, and PCA are used in this work. The nature and theory behind each method are explained in Sect. 3. Tables 2, 3 and 4 show the performance of the eight classifiers in combination with eight feature selection techniques.

The ReF outperformed the other feature selection methods according to the AUC values (Table 2). Furthermore, the feature selection methods significantly improve the performance of the eight classifiers. In terms of AUC values, Fig. 4 compares the performance of classifiers and feature selection methods.

With respect to the classifier accuracy values (Table 3), the again, ReF proved to be a better method than the other feature selection methods. Further, on comparing with the original performances, accuracy values of the eight classifiers are significantly improved by the use of feature selection methods. The same is illuminated in Fig. 5.

It is observed from Table 4 that ReF achieves better F1-scores for almost all classifiers except NN classifier. Figure 6 illustrates the performance comparison of the eight classifiers in combination of feature selection methods in terms of F1-score

Table 2 AUC values (%) of the eight classifiers using feature selection techniques

Classifiers	Feature selection techniques							
	ANOVA	χ^2	FCBF	GR	GI	IG	ReF	PCA
KNN	87.9	87.7	89.1	87.7	89.6	89.1	89.9	82.4
DT	70.2	71	71.6	71	71.6	71.6	75.2	72.3
SVM	90.3	49.3	90.4	50.1	90.8	90.6	92.4	86.3
SGD	78	50	81	48	82	82	87	77
RF	86.4	67.7	84.3	72.8	89.4	84.6	86.1	76.6
NN	92	30.2	92.4	30.2	92.4	92.1	92.5	89.3
NB	83.7	74	85.1	74	85.1	85.1	85.1	80.3
LR	90.8	91.2	90.8	91.2	90.7	90.8	92.5	86.9

Table 3 Accuracy values (%) of the eight classifiers with feature selection techniques

Classifiers	Feature selection techniques							
	ANOVA	χ^2	FCBF	GR	GI	IG	ReF	PCA
KNN	83	83	83	83	83	83	86	77
DT	71	69	73	69	73	73	75	68
SVM	81	48	83	48	82	83	84	79
SGD	78	50	81	48	82	82	87	77
RF	79	65	78	66	80	71	78	67
NN	82	33	87	33	85	84	85	78
NB	79	64	82	64	82	82	82	73
LR	83	85	84	85	84	84	85	77

Table 4 F1-Score values (%) of the eight classifiers with feature selection techniques

Classifiers	Feature selection techniques							
	ANOVA	χ^2	FCBF	GR	GI	IG	ReF	PCA
KNN	83	83	83	83	83	83	85.9	76.9
DT	71	69	73	69	73	73	75	67.8
SVM	81	48	83	48	82	83	84	79
SGD	78	49.3	81	48	82	82	87	77
RF	80	64.8	77.9	66	79	70.9	79	66.6
NN	82	32.7	87	32.7	85	84	85	78
NB	79	64	82	64	82	82	82	73
LR	83	85	84	85	84	84	85	77

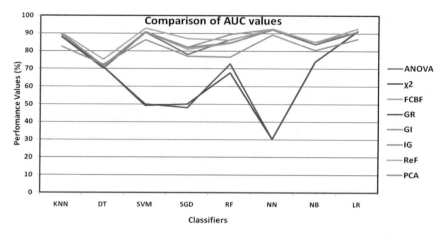

Fig. 4 Comparison of AUC values (%) with feature selection techniques

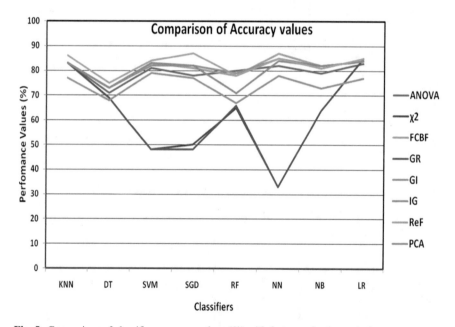

Fig. 5 Comparison of classifier accuracy values (%) with feature selection techniques

values. ReF works better for almost all classifiers except NN classifier. Similarly, the eight classifiers with feature selection produce same results for precision and recall measures. ReF produces better precision and recall values for all combinations except NN.

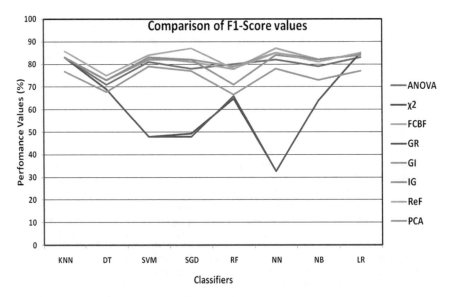

Fig. 6 Comparison of F1-Score values (%) with feature selection techniques

From the experimentation, it is found that feature selection methods gave good results for all the eight classifiers. Especially, ReF achieves top result for all the classifiers; hence, it is proved to be the best method among eight feature selection methods. Among the eight classifiers, Logistic regression outperforms the other algorithms.

Finally, using feature selection methods adds flavor to all eight classifiers, i.e., feature selection methods significantly improve the performance of the classifiers. In terms of AUC, accuracy, F1-score, precision, and recall, the combination of ReF and Logistic regression outperforms the other combinations.

5   Conclusions and Future Work

Culminations of image processing and predictive data mining techniques are applied to create a system for the identification and classification of betel vine leaf diseases. Contemporary classification algorithms such as KNN, Decision Tree, SVM, SGD, Random Forest, Neural network, Naïve Bayes, and Logistic regression are applied over the extracted 1000 features to build efficient classifiers for betel vine disease detection. Out of the eight classifiers, Logistic regression achieves the best result with the 91.9% AUC value. In addition, the decision tree classifier produces poor results in terms of AUC values, accuracy, and F1-score. Feature selection is used to enrich the obtained results by reducing the size of the extracted features. Based on the experimentation, it is found that the performance of the classifiers using significant features has appreciably higher than the classifiers without feature selection. ReF outperformed the other feature selection methods in terms of AUC values, accuracy, and F1-score out of eight feature selection methods. On the whole, it is found that the combination of ReF and Logistic regression achieves AUC value of 92.5% which is higher than the other combinations.

References

1. Iandola FN, Moskewicz MW, Ashraf K, Han S, Dally WJ, Keutzer K (2016) SqueezeNet. arXiv
2. Buttrey SE, Karo C (2002) Using k-nearest-neighbor classification in the leaves of a tree. Comput Stat Data Anal 40:27–37
3. Hossain MS, Mou RM, Hasan MM, Chakraborty S, Abdur Razzak M (2018) Recognition and detection of tea leaf's diseases using support vector machine. In: Proceedings-2018 IEEE 14th international colloquium on signal processing and its application, CSPA 2018, pp 150–154
4. Patil P, Yaligar N, Meena S (2018) Comparision of performance of classifiers-SVM, RF and ANN in potato blight disease detection using leaf images. In: 2017 IEEE International conference on computational intelligence and computing research, ICCIC 2017, pp 1–5
5. Do T-N (2014) Parallel multiclass stochastic gradient descent algorithms for classifying million images with very-high-dimensional signatures into thousands classes. Vietnam J Comput Sci 1:107–115
6. Hsu SC, Chen IC, Huang CL (2016) Image classification using pairwise local observations based Naive Bayes classifier. In: 2015 Asia-Pacific signal and information processing association annual summit and conference, APSIPA ASC 2015, pp 444–452
7. Das A, Dey A, Sharma M (2018) Leaf disease detection. quantification and classification using digital image processing 8:423–432
8. Lu KC, Yang DL (2009) Image processing and image mining using decision trees. J Inf Sci Eng 25
9. Sabareeswaran D, Guna Sundari R (2017) A hybrid of plant leaf disease and soil moisture prediction in agriculture using data mining techniques. 7169–7175
10. Pandey S, Khetwat S (2017) A survey paper on image classification and methods of image mining. Int J Comput Appl 169:10–12
11. Pranckevičius T, Marcinkevičius V (2017) Comparison of naive bayes, random forest, decision tree, support vector machines, and logistic regression classifiers for text reviews classification. Balt J Mod Comput 5:221–232
12. Meena Prakash R, Saraswathy GP, Ramalakshmi G, Mangaleswari KH, Kaviya T (2018) Detection of leaf diseases and classification using digital image processing. In: Proceedings of 2017 international conference on innovations in information, embedded and communication systems, ICIIECS 2017, pp 1–4
13. Shijie J, Peiyi J, Siping H, Haibo Sl (2017) Automatic detection of tomato diseases and pests based on leaf images. In: Proceedings-2017 Chinese automation congress, CAC 2017, pp 2537–2510
14. Shukla SV, Vala JA (2016) A survey on image mining, its techniques and application. Int J Comput Appl 133, pp 12–15
15. Padol PB, Yadav AA (2016) SVM classifier based grape leaf disease detection. Conference on Advances in Signal Processing, CASP 2016:175–217
16. Mucherino A, Papajorgji P, Pardalos PM (2009) A survey of data mining techniques applied to agriculture, 121–140
17. Dey AK, Sharma M, Meshram MR (2016) Image processing based leaf rot disease, detection of betel vine (Piper BetleL.). Proc Comput Sci 748–754
18. Anand R, Veni S, Aravinth J (2016) An application of image processing techniques for detection of diseases on brinjal leaves using k-means clustering method. In: 2016 International conference on recent trends in information technology, ICRTIT 2016, pp 1–6

19. Francis J, Anto Sahaya Dhas D, Anoop BK (2016) Identification of leaf diseases in pepper plants using soft computing techniques. In: Presented at the (2016), pp 168–173
20. Sushma B, Suraksha IS (2016) Disease prediction of paddy crops using data mining and image processing techniques. Int J Adv Res Electr Electron Instrum Eng 5
21. Chouhan P, Tiwari M (2015) Image retrieval using data mining and image processing techniques. IJIREEICE 3
22. Subramani B, Arumugam S, Ragupathy B (2019) Computer aided classification and detection of leaf disease using ANN. Int J Innov Technol Explor Eng 8
23. Vijayakumar J, Arumugam S (2013) Certain investigations on foot rot disease for betelvine plants using digital imaging technique. In: Proceedings-2013 international conference on emerging trends in communication, control, signal processing and computing applications, IEEE-C2SPCA 2013, pp 1–4
24. Jane NS, Deshmukh A, Joshi M (2014) Review of study of different diseases on betelvine plant and control measure. Int J Appl Innov Eng Manag 3:560–563
25. Revathi P, Hemalatha M (2014) Classification of cotton leaf spot diseases using image processing edge detection techniques. IEEE proceedings of the international conference on emerging trends in science engineering and technology: recent advancements on science and engineering innovation, INCOSET 2012:169–173
26. Vibhute A, Bodhe SK (2012) Applications of image processing in agriculture: a survey. Int J Comput Appl 52
27. Raphel MR, Prabhakaran R, Thamilarasi C (2020) Automatic leaf parameter monitoring and analysis of irrigation system in agriculture using machine learning technique. Int J Res Adv Dev
28. Hasan MZ, Zeba N, Malek A, Reya SS (2021) A leaf disease classification model in betel vine using machine learning techniques. In: International conference on robotics, electrical and signal processing techniques, pp 362–366
29. Usha Kumari C, Jeevan Prasad S, Mounika G (2019) Leaf disease detection: feature extraction with k-means clustering and classification with ANN. In: Proceedings of the 3rd international conference on computing methodologies and communication, ICCMC 2019, pp 1095–1098
30. Ahmed K, Shahidi TR, Irfanul Alam SM, Momen S (2019) Rice leaf disease detection using machine learning techniques. In: 2019 International conference on sustainable technologies for industry 4.0, STI 2019, pp 1–5

Enhanced Object Detection in Floor Plan Through Super-Resolution

Dev Khare, N. S. Kamal, H. B. Barathi Ganesh, V. Sowmya, and V. V. Sajith Variyar

1 Introduction

Design thinking in architecture, engineering and construction (AEC) is adapting to new methods in artificial intelligence (AI) at a rapid pace. The process optimization capabilities of AI are fueling the need for automation of complex processes in the construction industry. There are many reasons for this: the need for critical testing of inferences before the project moves into stages where designs become concrete, a more general approach for influencing floor plan designs, and building architecture based on primary data; not biased by employee experience. A centralized database of relevant information comprising of regional interests and metrics would help formulate better inferences for design selection than just relying on individual expertise. However, the main challenge in this process lies in the data representation from sources like computer-aided design (CAD) tools, building information modelling (BIM) software, etc. [1]. For sketch-type data, data representation becomes very cumbersome as the information contains vector objects and geometric entities; for

Data and code at https://github.com/rbg-research/Floor-Plan-Detection.git.

D. Khare · H. B. Barathi Ganesh · V. Sowmya (✉) · V. V. Sajith Variyar
Center for Computational Engineering and Networking (CEN), Amrita School of Engineering, Amrita Vishwa Vidyapeetham, Coimbatore, India
e-mail: v_sowmya@cb.amrita.edu

H. B. Barathi Ganesh
e-mail: aiss@rbg.ai

V. V. Sajith Variyar
e-mail: vv_sajithvariyar@cb.amrita.edu

N. S. Kamal · H. B. Barathi Ganesh
RBG.AI, Resilience Business Grids LLP, SREC Incubation Center, Coimbatore, Tamil Nadu, India
e-mail: kamal@rbg.ai

floor plan data, this is a big hurdle recently realized by Kalervo et al. resulting in the creation of the CubiCasa5k corpus [2]. CubiCasa5k is a corpus containing five thousand floor plan images and labels that segment floor plan images to find the polygons representing rooms, walls, and various icons in a floor plan like doors and windows. This process uses convolutional neural networks (CNNs), which influenced most of the research works in computer vision.

Segmentation of floor plans needs to be precise for an end-to-end application. After observing the segmentation results of the empirical model for floor plans of various sizes, we concluded that there is a need for the CubiCasa approach to incorporate image enhancement as an essential preliminary step. Before digitization, architects used to scan building plans manually resulting in different image qualities for different projects. Now, architectural drawings come in the form of vector images where everything is in a scalable format. Since a large chunk of floor plan images that are retrieved from web data have varying sizes, a workable data pipeline for floor plan images requires the use of image enhancement before storing the data into a database. Super-resolution is one such method used for image enhancement and is approached differently for various use cases. The process mainly varies with the type of image; for example, enhancing a facial appearance would require a more comprehensive approach with millions of variables and repeated steps. To address the question of end-to-end automation of floor plan image data to 3D building models, we explore this idea with experimental image enhancement results and its influence on floor plan object detection.

2 Literature Review

Automating floor plan image annotation was first looked at by Liu et al. [3]. The approach proposed in the paper uses a network inspired by the ResNet-152 architecture. The problem is subdivided into three sections that are solved simultaneously; this makes the neural network a multitasking CNN. The multitasking aspect becomes clear after looking at the innovative use of junction point orientations in the form of heatmaps. This means of point detection allow for precise detection of the wall skeleton in floor plan images. The main drawback of this implementation was lack of data used for training, and this was solved by the creation of the CubiCasa5k data set. The neural architecture used by Kalervo et al. [2] contains multiple ResNet blocks, similar to [3]. Their network uses a loss function containing room losses, icon losses, and a specially defined heatmap loss (containing junction point data) resulting in a multi-component output [2]. The future of building design estimation lies in the ability of models to manipulate core conceptual ideas in the design, like the size of rooms based on estimates of the number of people or the type of walls based on the region's cultural influences, logistical constraints, etc. The first step to achieving such feats is creating a successful base model for parametrizing floor plans, 3D point clouds for buildings, etc. [4].

A major use case for floor plan annotation is that of 3D building reconstruction. In 2019, an overview of the state-of-the-art methods for converting 2D images to 3D was given by Han et al. [5]. The paper brought to notice a lot of exciting approaches for solving the 3D reconstruction problem. One such method was combining loss functions that measure different types of loss metrics in the model; this is a powerful approach commonly used for 3D reconstruction [5]. 3D reconstruction is highly dependent on the available data. Reconstruction of 3D point clouds of buildings with complex designs, carried out by Zhang and Huang [6], is a recent achievement in this field that uses 2D building section data for its inference. Super-resolution in this implementation takes care of data loss when the sections are passed through the proposed network, enhancing the overall prediction accuracy. Training the proposed network on CAD models of building reconstructions meant that simple slicing operations were sufficient for section data creation. Another approach recently explored by Yu et al. [7] used topological heatmaps to reconstruct buildings directly from satellite images. This implementation used the WHU corpus to extract topological heatmaps as labels for training [7–10]. A lot of these works rely on the output data being in a point cloud format which contains no information about the actual shape of the building. Floor plan wall annotation, in [3], retrieves polygonal information that is editable in nature; using these polygons for 3D reconstruction takes a simple extrusion, making this approach more feasible [3]. Another advantage of using floor plan data is the volume of data on the web that can be used to fine-tune such models. This brings us to the question of image quality.

The use of image enhancement as a preliminary step to classification or segmentation problems is applicable for many computer vision use cases [11]. Super-resolution networks are CNN-based networks that are trained on high-resolution images to serve the purpose of noise free image interpolation [12, 13]. Image enhancement is essential for precise segmentation of floor plans; this was made very clear in the application by Han et al. The use of a super-resolution framework called SRCNN enhances sectional 2D data for more precision on target output in their work [6]. There are multiple frameworks for super-resolution that exist. In 2017, enhanced deep super-resolution network (EDSR) was the state-of-the-art approach to super-resolution; the method used a standard ResNet-based architecture and improved on several problems in model structure [14]. In 2021, the latest methods involve generative adversarial networks (GAN's) and probabilistic graphical models. Saharia et al. have improved the existing techniques with their iterative refinement method for image super-resolution [15]. By incorporating a Markov chain to add a parametrized Gaussian noise to a low-resolution image (upsampled by bi-cubic interpolation), a posterior probability is defined to iteratively denoise Gaussian noise resulting in a high-resolution image. In this work, the denoising step uses a modified UNet architecture with a loss function that is made aware of this Gaussian diffusion process. The model surpasses all prior state-of-the-art super-resolution methods; however, the process is highly time-consuming for larger images. Therefore, it is not recommended to use the method in [15] for floor plan use cases as the desired high-resolution image is quite large.

For a use case involving floor plan images, there are faster networks that perform super-resolution with minimal drop in quality. In 2016, Shi et al. [16] have used an efficient sub-pixel layer in their architecture for real-time single image video enhancement. Similarly, Dong et al. [17] worked on a faster version of the existing SRCNN by removing the process of bi-cubic interpolation before model evaluation; their network used an hourglass CNN instead of direct up-scaling to achieve this. Another notable work, by Lai et al. [18], on a Laplacian pyramid-based CNN architecture (LapSRN) outperforms both [16, 17] in performance. The use of local skip connections and shared network parameters for different up-scaling factors makes this one of the most versatile networks for super-resolution.

3   Methodology

The application of deep learning in object detection can be challenging given the time constraints and system requirements. For the task of floor plan annotation, we have assumed that this process need not be real time. Since we are performing an end-to-end conversion, the main objective here is to enhance accuracy without constraints on time and computing power. To do handle this, we experiment a novel multi-component module that performs image enhancement followed by the object detection. As mentioned earlier, CubiCasa5k is a corpus that contains five thousand annotated floor plans for the use of training a multitask CNN. From this corpus, we select ninety low-resolution floor plans and observe the increase in performance after super-resolution. Since CubiCasa5k is a robust corpus with varying sizes, we can hope for some improvement in performance of low-resolution floor plans.

3.1   Preliminary Step

This work performs super-resolution for image enhancement before detecting floor plan icons and room types; stacking super-resolution frameworks with the CubiCasa architecture results in a multi-component module that does just this. The networks chosen for super-resolution here are EDSR, ESPCN, FSRCNN, and LapSRN [14, 16–18]. For the inference, we need a quantifiable measure that could help us make a conclusive statement on improving performance by using super-resolution as a preliminary step. For this, the accuracy scores have to be based on ground truth scaled by the same factor chosen for super-resolution; the CubiCasa5k corpus provides ground truth in scalable vector graphics (SVG) format making this possible.

3.2   Wall/Room Detection

Annotations are of three types here; rooms, icons, and junction points. Junction point information results in a heatmap that contains a mapping of junction point orienta-

Fig. 1 Junction points colour coded based on mapping to different labels

tions for walls, icons, windows, and doors. The predicted heatmaps are thresholded
to retrieve the exact junction point locations. For this application, loss functions
(defined by [3]) are used to optimize three segmentation problems. Icon, room, and
heatmap losses were set up to improve the accuracy of a common goal: room and
icon polygon detection. The class labels for all three tasks were manually annotated.
The junction points are colour coded based on their connections to rooms and icons.
The CubiCasa5k data set has ground truth information that comes in SVG format. It
contains an archive of polygon types of which 12 are rooms (including walls) and 11
are icons (including doors and windows). A mapping is made to separate 21 junction
points into their respective heatmaps; it contains 13 wall junction orientations, 4 icon
corner orientations, and 4 window/door orientations (Fig. 1).

3.3 Post-processing

The multitask CNN used for object detection in this paper uses many post-processing
techniques. The junction points retrieved from respective heatmaps get connected
based on geometric orientations. Specifically for wall detection, the process results

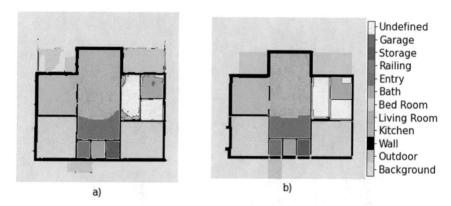

Fig. 2 **a** Segmented rooms, **b** room polygons after post-processing

in a wall skeleton. The algorithm considers junction point triplets for definition. After this, a prunning step, defined to consider self-intersecting polygons and incorrectly classified regions, makes the polygon detection more precise by using the segmentation maps as means for refinement. In Fig. 2, for the room values alone, we show the how the room detection looks with and without post-processing.

4   Results and Discussion

The model architecture in [2] is stacked with various SR models (refer Sect. 3.1) to provide further insight into the functioning of this model; a comparative study is done on the SR inference latencies and performance metrics of the SR stacked models.

4.1   *Inference Latency*

EDSR, ESPCN, FSRCNN, and LapSRN [14–17] can upscale any image by a factor of 2, 3, or 4. However, with the up-scaling factor comes an exponential rise in

Table 1 Execution time (in seconds) of SR networks chosen

Image size	EDSR	ESPCN	LapSRN	FSRCNN
690 × 769	215.431	0.340	2.245	0.320
896 × 890	323.201	0.509	4.136	0.490
1130 × 1016	353.921	0.797	4.907	0.686
1449 × 1373	745.119	1.357	8.501	1.253

computational time as the number of network parameters is greater for large scaling factors. The surge in computational time can also come from large input image sizes, so we have limited the use of super-resolution to images of size less than 800 × 800 pixels for this application. Despite these modifications, on observation we find that EDSR is much slower than the other methods used in this paper. This is because EDSR contains 43 million learnable parameters which is considerably higher compared to ESPCN, FSRCNN, and LapSRN. This is given in Table 1.

For the inference step, we found it fit to do a performance test on the influence of image enhancement (pre-processing) on object detection. The experiment was set up by stacking the super-resolution frameworks in series and then performing a scaling operation on the ground truth annotations for quantifying the results. For testing this process, we have used 90 images from the CubiCasa5k corpus selected at random. We have chosen micro average as the performance metric in measuring the overall accuracy of the segmentation. Micro average precision, recall, and $F1$ scores are helpful for testing the performance with data containing imbalanced class objects. Experiments were run on an AWS server with NVIDIA T4 Tensor Core GPU having 320 Turing Tensor cores, 2560 CUDA cores, and 16 GB of memory. Intel(R) Xeon(R) Platinum 8259CL CPU with a clock speed of 2.50 GHz, 32 GB RAM(DDR4), and 8 vCPUs.

4.2 Results

The multi-component module performed room detection with higher accuracy than that of when using CubiCasa5k model alone. Since wall detection is mapped to room detection, we can say that there is improvement in the junction point detection and post-processing. But the same cannot be said about icon detection. There is a slight performance drop in icon detection after performing super-resolution. We can attribute this to the fact that the icon heatmaps contain lesser no of points for each floor plan. For icon detection, there is more dependence on the data used for pre-training. A major point to look at is that for images where icon junction point detection fails,

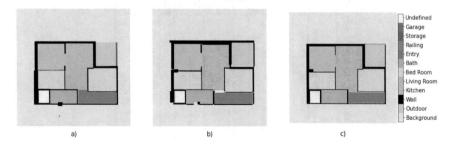

Fig. 3 Comparison of a sample result with ground truth; **a** original image, **b** pre-processed with EDSR, **c** ground truth

Table 2 Room detection comparison of SR methods with original

	ESPCN			EDSR			FSRCNN			LapSRN			Original		
	Precision	Recall	F1-score	Precision	Recall	F1-score	Precision	Recall	F1-score	Precision	Recall	F1-score	Precision	Recall	F1-score
Background	0.638	0.704	0.636	0.638	0.703	0.637	0.638	0.703	0.635	0.640	0.702	0.636	0.560	0.522	0.521
Outdoor	0.532	0.537	0.459	0.542	0.537	0.458	0.542	0.536	0.469	0.554	0.535	0.469	0.282	0.593	0.227
Wall	0.170	0.189	0.170	0.169	0.187	0.169	0.169	0.188	0.168	0.170	0.189	0.170	0.093	0.122	0.088
Kitchen	0.336	0.482	0.304	0.336	0.483	0.304	0.338	0.483	0.304	0.346	0.485	0.309	0.153	0.650	0.142
Living room	0.551	0.550	0.459	0.529	0.554	0.450	0.532	0.549	0.448	0.528	0.551	0.448	0.230	0.503	0.185
Bed room	0.481	0.558	0.449	0.470	0.557	0.437	0.481	0.557	0.448	0.467	0.555	0.435	0.287	0.708	0.238
Bath	0.233	0.411	0.199	0.232	0.410	0.198	0.245	0.410	0.210	0.221	0.412	0.199	0.159	0.901	0.148
Entry	0.270	0.457	0.253	0.269	0.456	0.251	0.268	0.453	0.251	0.278	0.460	0.255	0.207	0.924	0.207
Railing	0.601	0.417	0.331	0.567	0.417	0.330	0.589	0.420	0.332	0.615	0.418	0.331	0.491	0.615	0.353
Storage	0.494	0.577	0.438	0.494	0.577	0.438	0.493	0.577	0.437	0.495	0.576	0.438	0.479	0.887	0.455
Garage	0.942	0.948	0.904	0.931	0.948	0.904	0.943	0.948	0.905	0.943	0.948	0.905	0.910	0.989	0.910
Undefined	0.240	0.418	0.207	0.239	0.416	0.210	0.239	0.415	0.208	0.240	0.416	0.208	0.183	0.779	0.159
Micro avg	0.460	0.460	0.460	0.461	0.461	0.461	0.459	0.459	0.459	0.460	0.460	0.460	0.305	0.305	0.305

Table 3 Icon detection comparison of SR methods with original

	ESPCN			EDSR			FSRCNN			LapSRN			Original		
	Precision	Recall	F1-score	Precision	Recall	F1-score	Precision	Recall	F1-score	Precision	Recall	F1-score	Precision	Recall	F1-score
No icon	0.939	0.931	0.935	0.939	0.931	0.935	0.939	0.931	0.935	0.939	0.931	0.935	0.950	0.933	0.941
Window	0.155	0.115	0.109	0.132	0.115	0.097	0.134	0.116	0.099	0.151	0.113	0.106	0.095	0.115	0.025
Door	0.049	0.048	0.036	0.050	0.047	0.037	0.049	0.048	0.036	0.049	0.050	0.038	0.015	0.447	0.015
Closet	0.214	0.226	0.159	0.212	0.228	0.159	0.213	0.227	0.158	0.212	0.224	0.157	0.106	0.617	0.094
Electrical appliance	0.112	0.196	0.119	0.114	0.204	0.122	0.113	0.199	0.120	0.115	0.202	0.122	0.082	0.626	0.070
Toilet	0.168	0.228	0.117	0.157	0.227	0.106	0.174	0.220	0.099	0.169	0.228	0.117	0.182	0.898	0.159
Sink	0.134	0.161	0.081	0.111	0.161	0.079	0.130	0.160	0.081	0.135	0.160	0.081	0.159	0.761	0.159
Sauna bench	0.458	0.591	0.465	0.457	0.591	0.464	0.459	0.587	0.463	0.456	0.588	0.462	0.455	0.939	0.452
Fire place	0.911	0.866	0.843	0.911	0.866	0.843	0.911	0.867	0.844	0.911	0.867	0.844	0.920	0.966	0.909
Bathtub	0.966	0.933	0.910	0.966	0.933	0.910	0.966	0.933	0.910	0.966	0.933	0.910	0.989	1.000	0.989
Chimney	1.000	0.978	0.978	1.000	0.978	0.978	1.000	0.978	0.978	1.000	0.978	0.978	1.000	1.000	1.000
Micro avg	0.875	0.875	0.875	0.875	0.875	0.875	0.875	0.875	0.875	0.874	0.874	0.874	0.886	0.886	0.886

post-processing time raises by a huge amount. In these cases, there are a lot of icon points detected. The post-processing algorithm removes self-intersecting polygons and fine-tunes the results based on segmentation maps. Since the time taken to remove self-intersecting polygon is dependent on the number of icons detected, for failure cases, the number of icons detected rises exponentially. After super-resolution, the failure becomes even more catastrophic as there are even more polygons detected. Another point is that of polygon splitting. After super-resolution, there are chances of polygons not joining properly to form the wall skeleton. This can be seen in Fig. 3b (Tables 2 and 3).

5   Conclusion and Future Work

The multi-component module used in this paper was successful in improving the performance of icons and rooms in the CubiCasa5k framework. The best improvement in accuracy for the data set chosen is 39.47%; EDSR is the SR model used in this case. EDSR also showed the best result from all the super-resolution methods with a 12.17% improvement on average. The improvement with LapSRN is 12.01% on average but it is 82.76 times faster than EDSR, which makes up for the slight drop in performance. It is evident that LapSRN would be the best SR approach for practical use cases. On the context of time, for an end-to-end application, there is some uncertainty. Existing post-processing methods rely too much on the junction point search. This causes huge computation times for junction point failure cases where the search for self-intersecting polygons becomes a combinatorially expensive process. There is definitely a need for better post-processing methods to use the segment information more efficiently.

In the context of performance, we have used a scaling factor of 2 for all the methods presented here. There is a possibility that detection can improve even further with LapSRN and a higher scaling factor. However, it is clear that the stacked super-resolution method has to be used during training to alter the dimensions of low-resolution images. This could enhance the overall performance of the network and push it to a wider range of use cases.

References

1. Raghavi V, Gowtham R (2019) AI based semantic extensibility and querying techniques for building information model. In: 2019 international conference on intelligent computing and control systems (ICCS). IEEE, pp 1497–1501
2. Kalervo A, Ylioinas J, Häikiö M, Karhu A, Kannala J (2019) Cubicasa5k: a dataset and an improved multi-task model for floorplan image analysis. In: Scandinavian conference on image analysis. Springer, Cham, pp 28–40
3. Liu C, Wu J, Kohli P, Furukawa Y (2017) Raster-to-vector: revisiting floorplan transformation. In: Proceedings of the IEEE international conference on computer vision, pp 2195–2203

4. Chaillou S (2019) AI + architecture. Masters thesis, Harvard University: Self
5. Han X-F, Laga H, Bennamoun M (2021) Image-based 3D object reconstruction: state-of-the-art and trends in the deep learning era. IEEE Trans Pattern Anal Mach Intell 43(5):1578–1604. https://doi.org/10.1109/TPAMI.2019.295488
6. Zhang H, Huang Y (2021) Machine learning aided 2D-3D architectural form finding at high resolution. In: Proceedings of the 2020 DigitalFUTURES. Singapore, pp 159–168
7. Yu D, Ji S, Liu J, Wei S (2021) Automatic 3D building reconstruction from multi-view aerial images with deep learning. ISPRS J Photogramm Remote Sens 171:155–170. https://doi.org/10.1016/j.isprsjprs.2020.11.011
8. Liu J, Ji S (2020) A novel recurrent encoder-decoder structure for large-scale multi-view stereo reconstruction from an open aerial dataset. In: Proceedings of the IEEE/CVF conference on computer vision and pattern recognition, pp 6050–6059
9. Yao Y, Luo Z, Li S, Fang T, Quan L (2018) MVSNet: depth inference for unstructured multi-view stereo. In: Proceedings of the European conference on computer vision (ECCV), pp 767–783
10. Yao Y, Luo Z, Li S, Shen T, Fang T, Quan L (2019) Recurrent MVSNet for high-resolution multi-view stereo depth inference. In: Proceedings of the IEEE conference on computer vision and pattern recognition, pp 5525–5534
11. Harichandana M, Sowmya V, Sajithvariyar VV, Sivanpillai R (2020) Comparison of image enhancement techniques for rapid processing of POST flood images. Int Arch Photogramm Remote Sens Spat Inf Sci 44:45–50
12. Nair DP, John AM, Varshini ERA, Arunima D, Gopakumar G (2021) Performance analysis of deep learning architectures for super resolution. J Phys Conf Ser 1917(1):012002
13. Sujee R, Padmavathi S (2018) Pyramid-based image interpolation. In: 2018 international conference on computer communication and informatics (ICCCI). IEEE
14. Lim B, Son S, Kim H, Nah S, Mu Lee K (2017) Enhanced deep residual networks for single image super-resolution. In: Proceedings of the IEEE conference on computer vision and pattern recognition workshops, pp 136–144
15. Saharia C, Ho J, Chan W, Salimans T, Fleet DJ, Norouzi M (2021) Image super-resolution via iterative refinement. arXiv preprint arXiv:2104.07636
16. Shi W, Caballero J, Huszár F, Totz J, Aitken AP, Bishop R, Rueckert D, Wang Z (2016) Real-time single image and video super-resolution using an efficient sub-pixel convolutional neural network. In: Proceedings of the IEEE conference on computer vision and pattern recognition, pp 1874–1883
17. Dong C, Loy CC, Tang X (2016) Accelerating the super-resolution convolutional neural network. In: European conference on computer vision, Oct 2016. Springer, Cham, pp 391–407
18. Lai WS, Huang JB, Ahuja N, Yang MH (2018) Fast and accurate image super-resolution with deep Laplacian pyramid networks. IEEE Trans Pattern Anal Mach Intell 41(11):2599–2613

Attention-Based Bitemporal Image Deep Feature-Level Change Detection for High Resolution Imagery

Nitesh Naik, K. Chandrasekaran, M. Venkatesan, and P. Prabhavathy

1 Introduction

Change detection (CD) being the trend and challenging area in remote sensing is used to determine the differences in a set of multitemporal images of the same area [1]. With the advancements in the remote sensing domain, the data which are multispectral and multitemporal are widely available with different spatial and temporal resolutions. Bitemporal images are a set of images which are being taken of the same area with pre-change and post-change data to identify the differences on the land surfaces in form of changed or unchanged feature space. CD techniques are applied in a variety of fields like environmental assessment [2], land cover mapping [3], disaster monitoring [4], and urban expansion [5]. In the literature, various approaches have been proposed to determine the changes between bitemporal images. Generally, these CD methods can be categorized into four types.

1. Based on Image arithmetic—these are the methods which generates image difference maps by directly performing the comparison of pixel values by the application of threshold values to carry out the classification of pixels into changed and unchanged category. Arithmetic-based operations like image differencing [6], image rationing [7], image regression [8], and change vector analysis [9] are traditionally used for comparison of the images.
2. Based on Image transformation—these methods also termed as feature extraction, perform the transformation of combinations of image spectral data into

N. Naik (✉) · K. Chandrasekaran · M. Venkatesan
Department of Computer Science and Engineering, National Institute of Technology Karnataka, Surathkal, India
e-mail: nn.197cs004@nitk.edu.in

P. Prabhavathy
School of Information Technology and Engineering, Vellore Institute of Technology, Vellore, India

© The Author(s), under exclusive license to Springer Nature Singapore Pte Ltd. 2023   259
R. Doriya et al. (eds.), *Machine Learning, Image Processing, Network Security and Data Sciences*, Lecture Notes in Electrical Engineering 946,
https://doi.org/10.1007/978-981-19-5868-7_20

a precise feature domain to emphasize the change pixels and restrain the ones which are unchanged. This methods perform the transformation of the spectral combinations of the images into a particular feature domain to discriminate among the changed pixels. Various algorithms like PCA [10] are being utilized for dimensionality reduction, the major drawback being the dependence of the statistical properties of the images which are under consideration and possibility of easily being affected by the unbalanced data factor. A classical method [11] which is known for its application of distinct weights to a given set of observations and huge weights are allocated to the observation which depicts smaller changes, but the only drawback being, this method ignores the considerable internal relationship among the bitemporal bands.

3. Based on post-classification—this is the most popular supervised method for CD in which the bitemporal images are masked/labeled individually and classified. The extraction of the change areas is done by performing comparison of the results directly in terms of classification [12]. This methods usually omit the differences in CD which arise from the raw images at different instants of time making it highly sensitive to the outcomes of classification.

4. Advance image processing-based methods like Wavelet transformation and Markov random fields.

The first two methods are categorized as unsupervised methods and the post-classification being a supervised method, the arithmetic and transformation-based techniques fail to attain convincing outcomes on the images of higher resolution that completely relies on the empirical algorithms for high end extraction of features. Multiple errors produced by the application of methods based on pixel-level like image differencing, unresolved segmented objects derived from object-based methods, and with respect to post-classification, the misclassification errors related to bitemporal images may drastically affect the CD results at the end. In the upcoming years, the unconventional rise in the remote sensing information and the extensive application of high computing power has enhanced innumerable development in deep learning (DL), making exceptional attainments in multiple areas of science and engineering. The image analysis being the most complex task, as it is related to multiple texture features and finer resolution details of the image contributes to new challenges and opportunities for the change detection task.

There are multiple architectures used for extraction of deep features in the object and pixel-based methods with deep learning methods like convolution neural network [13], deep belief network [14], and stacked denoising autoencoder [15]. In [16] they proposed a UNet ++ with the combination of dense skip connections and recurrent neural networks to capture the spatiotemporal information. Deep feature-based methods were also discussed in [17], which uses deconvolutional network and fully CNN in [18, 19]. In [20], they incorporated 3D fully convolutional network with long short-term memory networks. A BiDatenet architecture was proposed in [21] to inculcate temporal information in bitemporal images by blending LSTM and UNet structure. Metric-based learning has also provided immense contributions in the area of CD, like [22] proposed a Siamese convolutional neural network for determination of the difference between two deep features.

The error propagation issues are still existing in this methods. More distinguishing features are of great importance to alleviate pseudochanges that represents false alarms being produced by the inclusion of disturbances by some external parameters among the bitemporal images such as illumination and differences in the scale. The contribution of these methods based on deep features that transform the bitemporal data into higher level feature space and the deep-level features is considered as the component of analysis. This unique method amalgamates feature extraction and difference evaluation network for the production of the change map in an effective manner. In view of the above, a deep supervised-based difference evaluation network (DSDEN) for CD in high resolution bitemporal images is proposed. Highly representative multiscale attributes from multiple levels of bitemporal images are being extracted by pretrained VGG16 feature extractor network. The extracted features are fed to the deeply supervised difference evaluation network in a sequential manner for performing CD. Convolutional block attention module (CBAM) is incorporated for differentiating the features in more unique form in spatial and channel-wise manner to combine the raw deep features and features of the difference image for effective generation and reconstruction of the change map.

2 Methodology

In this section, an overview of our proposed architecture is first provided, after which each component of the architecture will be explained in detail.

2.1 Outline

The methodology of the proposed method is depicted in Fig. 1. It consists of three components known as the feature extractor, CBAM module (channel-based attention module), and deep supervision. The multiscale features from the bitemporal sets of images are being extracted by utilizing the representative features for CD. As per the feature pairs of the bitemporal images, the CBAM module is incorporated to generate the features in an effective manner by using spatial and channel attention blocks which contributes to the production of the distance map represented in Fig. 6 with black as unchanged and white as changed. Deep supervision is performed to provide assistance to the hidden layers in reproducing additional useful features. Let T_1 and T_2 represent bitemporal images of the same area at different instants of times K_1 and K_2, while the labels are as shown in Fig. 5. The architecture can be explained as follows:

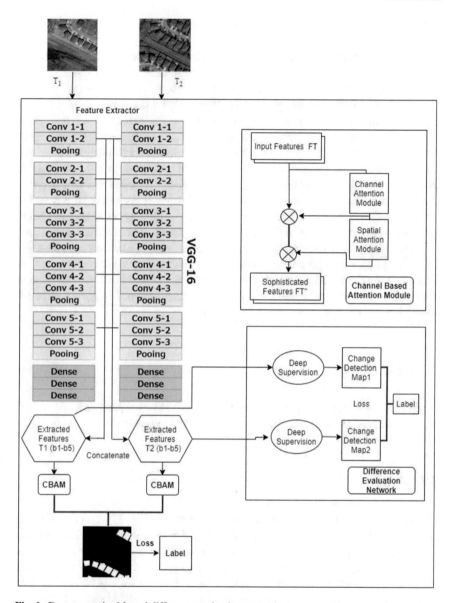

Fig. 1 Deep supervised-based difference evaluation network

1. The feature extractor is fed with images KT_1 and KT_2 with the weight sharing component, which will produce a series of spatiotemporal feature vectors ranging from FA_z^1 to FA_z^4 where $z = T_1, T_2$.

2. The feature pairs consisting of same dimension are combined by the vectors which belong to the same time stamp; the features FT_1 and FT_2 are made more distinctive with the inclusion of the CBAM block. It computes the distance map between the two features, wherein the loss is computed as per the distance map D and the label.
3. Subsequently, the absolute values calculated among the two features Fabs = $FA_{T_1}^m - FA_{T_2}^m$, $i = 1, 2$ are being fed to the deep supervision component to generate the two intermediate change maps CDM1 and CDM2, and the loss is calculated as per the maps and the annotated label.
4. Eventually, the loss computed in both are merged to accommodate training of the model accurately.

2.2 Feature Extractor

The feature extractor is tuned to a VGG16 network with the inclusion of two branches which shares the weight to carry out the process of extraction of features from bitemporal images. As seen in Figs. 2 and 3, the T_1 image and the T_2 image structures and parameters are used and shared with each other with the use of pretrained network. Both the features are combined in an effective way to contribute to the attention component with the inclusion of both the high as well as low raw image features. The combination of both the features is done in an effective manner in a way to all the layers before pool5 of the VGG16 are being utilized to construct the network and provide as a backbone to the difference evaluation network. This VGG16 will extract the features from the given image, namely B, representing blocks as

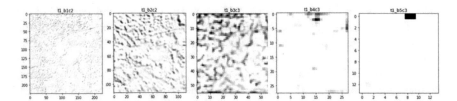

Fig. 2 Representation of the extracted features from T_1

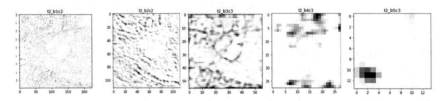

Fig. 3 Representation of the extracted features from T_2

B1_Conv1, B1_Conv2, B2_Conv1, B2_Conv2, B3_Conv1, B3_Conv2, B3_Conv3,

B4_Conv1, B4_Conv2, B4_Conv3, B5_Conv1, B5_Conv2, B5_Conv3. An image of dimensions 224×224 is the input to the VGG16 model which is diminished and preprocessed version of the dataset. Figures 2 and 3 show the required extracted features are being stored in variables like t1_b1c2, t1_b2c2, t1_b3c3, t1_b4c3, t1_b5c3 and t2_b1c2, t2_b2c2, t2_b3c3, t2_b4c3, and t2_b5c3.

The successive abstraction with application of convolutional, maxpooling, and stacked layers at the extensive level in the images T_1 and T_2 perceives larger reception of the field and contains overall information in a compact manner. Hence, B5_Conv3 serves as the primary input to the difference evaluation network for the production of the initial change tensor map which is dense and universal in size. Initial layers in DEN (i.e., B4_conv3, B3_conv3, B2_conv2, and B1_conv2) which consist of information regarding the low-level structure of the bitemporal images which is incorporated with skip connections to the layers of the deep neural network consisting of similar scales in a way to aggregate the image features of the single-handed bitemporal images.

2.3 Difference Evaluation Network

The difference evaluation network consists of four deep supervision components named as brch_1, brch_2, brch_3, brch_4, where brch is branch used to start its operations with the deep raw features of the images. The application of the three layers of two-dimensional convolution over the combination of deep image features known as t1_b5c3 and t2_b5c3 is used to produce the feature maps of the difference image globally with inclusion of compact sizes. The concatenated features of the layers from brch_5 are used to represent the final change tensor. Thereafter, a spatial attention component from CBAM is included to perform the extraction of the spatial dimension to fetch the spatial attention maps. The processed feature maps of the difference image are being up-sampled with transposed 2D convolutions to perform the operation of enlarging the feature maps to revert back to the resolution of the actual input raw images. The up-sampled subtracted image features are mixed with features at the low level, i.e., t1_b4c3 and t2_b4c3 from the deep learning layers in order to retrieve details of fine-grained image and better labels of the change objects. While we perform the amalgamation of this two parameters as discussed above, it may lead in difficulty for training the model.

To overcome this issue in an efficient way, a channel attention module is being called to concentrate on channels which are pertinent to the final generation as compared to the irrelevant channels. The channel-based attention module CBAM consists of two components known as spatial attention module and channel attention module as shown in Fig. 4. The channel-based attention operation is being incorporated in all the branches for extraction of the low as well as high features of the deep learning layers. The spatial attention component is being included to expand

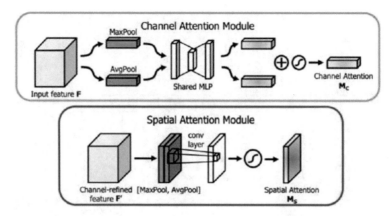

Fig. 4 Channel and spatial attention modules

the calculated distances among the pixels which are changed and unchanged. In this manner, the merging of deep features of raw images with the features of difference image is extracted in a sequential manner to generate the fine-grained change map.

3 Experiments and Results

The datasets and the brief explanation of the implementation and metrics for evaluation are being discussed here. The experimental outcomes with the change tensors are also being analyzed in a detailed manner.

3.1 Dataset

The LEVIR-CD dataset [23] as shown in Fig. 5 is composed of 637 high resolution image pairs of 0.5/m pixel with a size of 1024 × 1024 pixels which are being collected from Google Earth. This set of bitemporal images is captured from 20 various regions that consist of several cities of Buda, Dripping Springs, Austin, Manor, Bee Cave, Kyle, Lakeway, Pflugervilletx, Texas of the USetc. Each image pair is cut into 256 × 256 pixel patches without overlapping. Figure 5 demonstrates the geospatial dissemination of the dataset and also an enlarged image patch. Every region consists of various sizes and consists of multiple number of patches of images. The capture time for the data lies between 2002 and 2018.

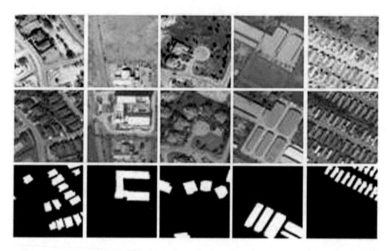

Fig. 5 Chosen samples (256 × 256) cropped images from LEVIR-CD. Each column denotes one sample, comprising the image pair (rows 1 and 2) and label (the last row, white representing change and black as no change)

3.2 Implementation Details

We made use of the keras library of Python for conducting our experiments. The batch size of the proposed network was being set to 4 for the processing. The Adam optimizer was incorporated into the network with learning rate of 0.0001 on our dataset. The kernel size in the spatial attention component was set to 7, and the reduction ratio in the channel attention was set to 8. The margin values in the loss function carried a value, and the threshold value for segmentation was set to one for the distance map. The loss function used is the dice losses for the proposed method. All the experiments were carried out on RTX 3080 of NVDIA GeForce to perform the acceleration in training the model.

3.3 Comparison and Evaluation of the Dataset

To evaluate the performance of our method, we made use of four metrics like precision, $F1$-score, recall, overall accuracy, and intersection over union (IOU). To demonstrate the effectiveness of our approach, two prominent CD methods were used for comparison from the existing literature.

1. Siamese Concatenation Fully Convolutional Network (SC-FCN): This approach [18] is based on the deep learning architecture of UNET in which the input bitemporal set of images is merged as multibands to be provided as input. The skip

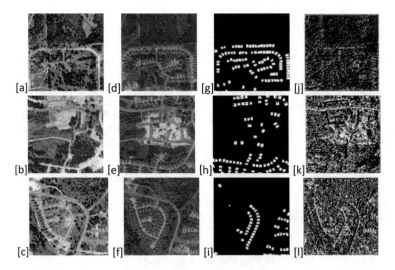

Fig. 6 **a–c** T_1 **d–f** T_2 **g–i** ground truth **j** SC-FCN **k** BiDateNet **l** proposed

connections are being incorporated for spatial information recovery by successfully transferring the multiscale features via the Siamese encoder successfully to the decoder.

2. BiDateNet: This method [21] is used as a fusion of UNet with FCN architecture that includes skip connections with long short-term memory for enhanced temporal flow inspection among the bitemporal images.

The change maps of all the bitemporal images applied with the existing methods are as shown in Fig. 6a–c is the T_1 image, and (d–f) is the T_2 image. The ground truth is shown in (g–i) with the change maps in (j) SC-FCN method (k) BiDateNet method and (l) proposed method of (DSDEN). A brief comparison between existing models is provided in Table 1. As seen in Table 2, which provides us with the summary of all the evaluation parameters, i.e., precision being lower in the existing methods, recall and $F1$ also not showing higher values with improper changes in the change maps and overall accuracy of the proposed method being the highest among others. The intersection over union (IOU) values also signify better changes in the proposed method. All this values show that the proposed method has performed well on the dataset providing us with accurate changes in pixels denoted as white and the black representing as unchanged.

4 Conclusion

In this article, we have presented a method named DSDEN for bitemporal images. The spatial information and the channel-based assessment is carried out by the CBAM

Table 1 Comparison with existing models

Existing models	Limitations	Proposed model (Advantage)
Encoder–decoder using UNet ++ [16]	Semantic information among the change areas not identified	Change detection at feature level using deep representation and change analysis among the features with attention modules leads to effective generation of change map for bitemporal imagery
Deconvolutional network based on stacking contraction and expansion blocks Fully convolutional networks [17]	Majority of the elements in the pooling area are of high magnitude for maxpooling operation The distinguishing features may vanish once the maximum pooling procedure is completed	
Recurrent 3D fully convolutional networks [20]	Use of fully connected layers are computationally expensive due to large number of parameters	
Fully convolutional network with long short-term memory [21]	LSTM may take longer time to train leading to overfitting of the parameters for change detection	

Table 2 Evaluation of various methods on LEVIR-CD dataset

		Performance measures (%)				
		Overall accuracy	Precision	Recall	$F1$	IOU
Methods	SC-FCN	90.36	92.34	68.75	78.81	67.82
	BidateNet	92.37	94.52	71.72	81.55	74.78
	DSDEN (proposed)	94.62	95.61	80.84	87.60	80.01

component which helps to learn the change map which is being obtained directly from the deep image features with the inclusion of feature extractor using a pretrained network. A loss function is also incorporated to blend this two components into the process of training. Experimental results show that DSDEN performs well on the LEVIR-CD dataset as compared to the other CD methods. The improved change maps demonstrate the detail changes happened over the years at a particular location thus contributing to the effectiveness of the proposed approach. In future, we would consider more complex scenarios with the inclusion of information concerned with semantic and dynamic data to overcome the above limitations.

References

1. Singh A (1989) Review article digital change detection techniques using remotely-sensed data. Int J Remote Sens 10(6):989–1003
2. Chen C-F, Son N-T, Chang N-B, Chen C-R, Chang L-Y, Valdez M, Centeno G, Thompson CA, Aceituno JL (2013) Multi-decadal mangrove forest change detection and prediction in Honduras, central America, with Landsat imagery and a Markov chain model. Remote Sens 5(12):6408–6426
3. Bruzzone L, Serpico SB (1997) An iterative technique for the detection of land-cover transitions in multitemporal remote-sensing images. IEEE Trans Geosci Remote Sens 35(4):858–867
4. Koltunov A, Ustin SL (2007) Early fire detection using non-linear multitemporal prediction of thermal imagery. Remote Sens Environ 110(1):18–28
5. Wang F, Jun Xu Y (2010) Comparison of remote sensing change detection techniques for assessing hurricane damage to forests. Environ Monit Assess 162(1):311–326
6. Singh A (1986) Change detection in the tropical forest environment of northeastern India using Landsat. Remote Sens Trop Land Manage 44:273–254
7. Todd WJ (1977) Urban and regional land use change detected by using Landsat data. J Res US Geol Surv 5(5):529–534
8. Jackson RD (1983) Spectral indices in N-space. Remote Sens Environ 13(5):409–421
9. Johnson RD, Kasischke ES (1998) Change vector analysis: a technique for the multispectral monitoring of land cover and condition. Int J Remote Sens 19(3):411–426
10. Deng JS, Wang K, Deng YH, Qi GJ (2008) PCA-based land-use change detection and analysis using multitemporal and multisensor satellite data. Int J Remote Sens 29(16):4823–4838
11. Nielsen AA (2007) The regularized iteratively reweighted mad method for change detection in multi-and hyperspectral data. IEEE Trans Image Process 16(2):463–478
12. Chen W, Bo D, Cui X, Zhang L (2017) A post-classification change detection method based on iterative slow feature analysis and Bayesian soft fusion. Remote Sens Environ 199:241–255
13. Zhang H, Gong M, Zhang P, Linzhi S, Shi J (2016) Feature-level change detection using deep representation and feature change analysis for multi-spectral imagery. IEEE Geosci Remote Sens Lett 13(11):1666–1670
14. El Amin AM, Liu Q, Wang Y (2017) Zoom out CNNs features for optical remote sensing change detection. In: 2017 2nd international conference on image, vision and computing (ICIVC). IEEE, pp 812–817
15. Lei Y, Liu X, Shi J, Lei C, Wang J (2019) Multiscale superpixel segmentation with deep features for change detection. IEEE Access 7:36600–36616
16. Peng D, Zhang Y, Guan H (2019) End-to-end change detection for high resolution satellite images using improved UNet++. Remote Sens 11(11):1382
17. Alcantarilla PF, Stent S, Ros G, Arroyo R, Gherardi R (2018) Street-view change detection with deconvolutional networks. Auton Robots 42(7):1301–1322
18. Daudt RC, Le Saux B, Boulch A (2018) Fully convolutional Siamese networks for change detection. In: 2018 25th IEEE international conference on image processing (ICIP). IEEE, pp 4063–4067
19. Long J, Shelhamer E, Darrell T (2015) Fully convolutional networks for semantic segmentation. In Proceedings of the IEEE conference on computer vision and pattern recognition, pp 3431–3440
20. Song A, Choi J, Han Y, Kim Y (2018) Change detection in hyperspectral images using recurrent 3D fully convolutional networks. Remote Sens 10(11):1827
21. Papadomanolaki M, Verma S, Vakalopoulou M, Gupta S, Karantzalos K (2019) Detecting urban changes with recurrent neural networks from multitemporal sentinel-2 data. In: IGARSS 2019–2019 IEEE international geoscience and remote sensing symposium. IEEE, pp 214–217
22. Liu X, Zhou Y, Zhao J, Yao R, Liu B, Zheng Y (2019) Siamese convolutional neural networks for remote sensing scene classification. IEEE Geosci Remote Sens Lett 16(8):1200–1204
23. Chen H, Shi Z (2020) A spatial-temporal attention-based method and a new dataset for remote sensing image change detection. Remote Sens 12(10)

Prostate Cancer Grading Using Multistage Deep Neural Networks

Ramya Bygari, K. Rithesh, Sateesh Ambesange, and Shashidhar G. Koolagudi

1 Introduction

In men, a walnut-sized gland, called the prostate, is located below the bladder and in front of the rectum, surrounding the urethra. The prostate produces and stores fluid that helps to make semen. A tumor, benign or cancerous, is formed when normal healthy cells in the prostate change and grow out of control. Prostate cancer is marked by an uncontrolled (malignant) growth of cells in the tissues of the prostate gland. Prostate cancer is the second most commonly occurring cancer in men and the fourth most commonly occurring cancer overall, with approximately 1.2 million cases each year [1]. The median age at diagnosis of carcinoma of the prostate is 66 years, and every one in 9 men are diagnosed approximately. The evaluation of prostate cancer is based exclusively on the structural pattern of the tumor, i.e., the Gleason patterns [2]. There is not only a high incidence to mortality ratio, but also the patients with prostate cancer run a fear of over-diagnosis and over-treatment. Prostate cancer is highly treatable in the early stages. Hence, there arises a strong need for accurate assessment of patient prognosis. The pathologist assigns a Gleason score after inspection of the cancer morphology. This score serves as a prognostic marker for the prostate cancer patients. The accuracy of the grade assigned correlates to the expertise of the pathologist. Unfortunately, such proficiency is not broadly available and suffers from intra- and inter-observer variability [3, 4]. Therefore, transcribing expert-level Gleason grading will aid prostate cancer diagnosis.

R. Bygari (✉) · K. Rithesh · S. Ambesange · S. G. Koolagudi
National Institute of Technology Karnataka, Surathkal, India
e-mail: 16co239.ramya@nitk.edu.in

© The Author(s), under exclusive license to Springer Nature Singapore Pte Ltd. 2023   271
R. Doriya et al. (eds.), *Machine Learning, Image Processing, Network Security and Data Sciences*, Lecture Notes in Electrical Engineering 946,
https://doi.org/10.1007/978-981-19-5868-7_21

2 Grading

Grading the tissues is one of the popular ways of identifying and distinguishing the cancerous cells and their severity from the normal cells. There are two widely known grading systems used in medical imaging: the Gleason score and the ISUP grading.

2.1 Gleason Score

Gleason score [2] is a grading technique developed early in oncology, and it has been subjected to many changes since then. It was first used by Donald Gleason in 1966 for his research in the field of prostatic adenocarcinoma. In 1974, after undergoing a few changes in the scoring system, it was accepted globally as a category 1 prognostic parameter.

From 1974 to date, it has faced several changes and betterment's, and the Gleason score used today categorizes the tissue into familiar patterns:

– Pattern 1: The normal, well-differentiated cells, characterized by uniform shape and boundary structure.
– Pattern 2: Well-differentiated cells but with slight variation in shape and boundary structure.
– Pattern 3: Not-so-well-differentiated cells with huge differences in cell structure, infiltrative margins of growth detected.
– Pattern 4: Highly irregular in structure with a lot of pale cells and tumor cells.
– Pattern 5: Carcinoma with almost no differentiation.

Figure 1 demonstrates how Gleason scores operate for cancerous and normal cells, the normal cells represented by similar-shaped cells and the cancerous cells shown as irregular cells.

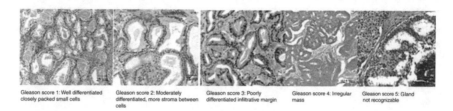

Gleason score 1: Well differentiated closely packed small cells
Gleason score 2: Moderately differentiated, more stroma between cells
Gleason score 3: Poorly differentiated infiltrative margin
Gleason score 4: Irregular mass
Gleason score 5: Gland not recognizable

Fig. 1 Gleason scores for different cells. The cells ranging from normal to carcinogenic moving from left to right

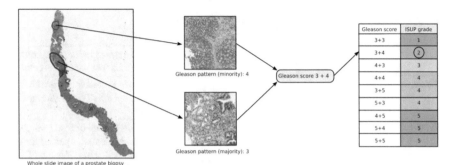

Fig. 2 Calculation of ISUP scores from the biopsy of a tissue. The usage of Gleason scores for ISUP score calculation is also shown

2.2 ISUP Grading

As research in oncology grew, so did the need of better grading of the cells, and subsequently new and improved grading systems emerged. In 2006, a conference took place under ISUP and found a new grading system called the International Society of Urologic Pathologists (ISUP) grading system [5].

- Instead of looking at just one area of a tissue for determining the score, two largest areas in the tissue containing similar cells (similar in their morphology) are observed.
- The Gleason score of both these regions is considered, and their sum is taken to get the ISUP grade.

Figure 2 shows how ISUP grades are calculated from a biopsy of a tissue using the Gleason scores of two most prominent regions of the tissue. Table 1 has the mapping of all the possible Gleason score sums and their corresponding ISUP scores.

3 Literature Survey

Previous works deployed conventional machine learning approaches, such as, feature engineering for prostate cancer detection [7–9]. Gradually, researchers switched to usage of deep learning-based methods for the detection of prostate cancer [10]. Most of the existing research emphasizes on segmentation of prostate cancer images [11, 12]. Recently, research has transitioned to prostate cancer grading, and there has not been substantial research done on the same.

Bulten et al. [13] developed a system using 5834 biopsies from 1243 patients. A segmented image is generated using UNet [14] to classify whether the biopsy is benign or malignant. The segmented image is further used to obtain a normalized ratio of epithelial tissue corresponding to the normalized volume percentages of

Table 1 Mapping between Gleason scores and ISUP grading [6]

ISUP grade	Gleason score	Definition
Grade 1	2–6	Well-formed tissues, very little or no signs of cancerous cells
Grade 2	3 + 4 = 7	Glands well-developed with a minor patch of poorly formed cells
Grade 3	4 + 3 = 7	Poorly formed or fused cells forming the major part of the gland, with a minor patch of well-formed cells
Grade 4	4 + 4 = 8	Only poorly formed/fused/cribriform glands
	3 + 5 = 8	Well-developed cells forming the majority of the glands, but the minor patch has deformed/lacking cells
	5 + 3 = 8	Predominantly lacking glands and a smaller component of well-formed glands
Grade 5	9–10	Complete lack of development of gland, filled with under-developed cells

each growth pattern. This paper does not describe the distribution of patients across different grades, where if skewness exists in data, it can hinder the training of the UNet. The paper also uses hard-coded normalized value percentage to determine the biopsy patch's final grade, which does not handle exceptional biopsies such as where the tumors are concentrated in one particular region of the biopsy.

Nagpal et al. [15] developed a deep learning system (DLS) is proposed that consists of two stages. The first is a regional classification followed by a whole-slide Gleason grade group classification. Small image patches are produced that are fed into a convolutional neural network (CNN). The CNN classifies each patch into one of four classes: non-tumor or Gleason pattern 3, 4, or 5. A heatmap is generated indicating the categorization of each patch. A nearest neighbor classifier is used in the second stage that is fed the heatmap output from the first stage to classify the grade group of each slide. However, a nearest neighbor classifier can be sensitive to the scale of data and irrelevant features. VGG-16 convolutional neural network and ordinal class classifier with J48 as the base classifier is used for grading by Lucas [16]. The training data used in [16] are imbalanced for grade 4 and grade 5; hence, the features extracted using VGG-16 may not be an accurate representation of the grade 4 and grade 5 cancer. This paper proposes a novel architecture that involves no manual intervention and seeks to address the problems discussed in the above papers.

4   Methodology

As mentioned earlier, the machine learning approach (in particular, a combination of Image Processing techniques) is used to analyze and score the histopathological images with the help of the ISUP grading system. Artificial intelligence (AI) model pipeline is devised which takes in the image and gives out the ISUP scores.

The AI Model pipeline of scoring the images involves:

1. Segmenting the image to obtain a mask for the images, highlighting the potential cancerous regions.
2. Overlaying the masks over the images to highlight the regions over the original image.
3. Classifying the highlighted regions into the ISUP score classes.

4.1   Segmentation

Segmentation comprises the first part of the AI model pipeline, which focuses on segmenting the image different color code for the most important, most relevant parts. The input is a raw histopathological image from the dataset, and the output is a mask corresponding to the input image. The weights of each pixel correspond to their relevance for the classification.

Need for this section: The prostate cells (which might contain the carcinogenic cells) make up a tiny part of the image (as observed in the dataset), while the majority of the image has a white background. Feeding the raw images directly to a classifier model would mean that the classifier sees the whole image as a white blob with just a tiny percentage of other pixels. This would result in the model generalizing all the images as a white blob and grouping all the images in just one class (this is called an under-fitting problem). To avoid this, additional data are sent for the classifier model highlighting the region in the image for the model to classify the image based on focused part of image. This additional information is provided by the mask given out by this segmentation model.

Model specifications: UNet model is used for segmentation. (Figure 3 shows the structure of UNet model.) The model consists of two parts—a constructive/encoding path that breaks down the image to only a semantic understanding (with the help of convolution layers) and an expansive/decoding path that constructs the mask using the broken-down semantic meaning of the image and the original image itself.

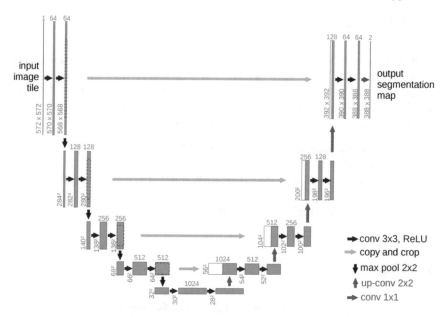

Fig. 3 Structure of UNet model used for segmentation [14]

4.2 Overlay

The overlay is a vital step before the data is fed from the segmentation pipeline to the classifier. The mask obtained from the segmentation model is overlaid on the raw image. This image-mask merge is then fed to the classifier model.

Need for this section: At the end of the segmentation component, two images correspond to the same data point—the original histopathological image and the mask generated by the segmentation model. The classifier needs these images to effectively categorize the data point under one of the ISUP score classes. And the best approach would be to merge the images so that the model can focus on one image and classify.

4.3 Classification and Explainable AI

The final and essential component of the AI pipeline is classification. It takes in the image-mask overlaid and gives out the ISUP grade class for the image.

Model specifications: For the classifier, two variants are chosen for two different purposes:

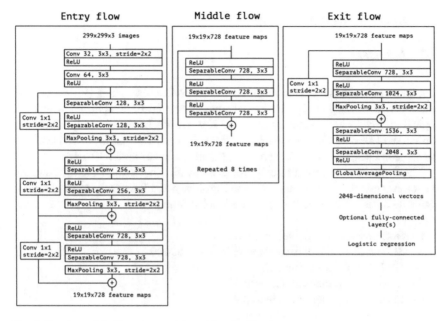

Fig. 4 Structure of the Xception model used for classification

- Model 1: An ensemble of Xception, Resnet, Efficient Net models. This combination of three individual image classifier models gave us the best performance (in terms of accuracy), and so, this ensemble model will be used in the AI pipeline.
- Model 2: An Xception model. This was the best stand-alone model out of all the image processing models considered for classification, and this model will be used to obtain the GradCam visualization of the images. Gradcam visualization helps us in understanding the key regions in the images that influenced the decision of the model in classification. Model decision explanation is essential for doctors to believe in the result of the model. Explainable AI models essential in AI healthcare diagnosis space.

Figure 4 shows the structure of the Xception model used. The performance of these two models, along with its competitor models, is summarized in the next section.

The ISUP grades are used as the decision classes of the classifier. Proposed model can also predict the Gleason scores by changing the last couple of layers and training the deep learning model using a technique called transfer Learning. The transfer learning mechanism improves the performance Gleason scores prediction model and reduce the training time.

5   Experiments and Results

5.1   Dataset

The dataset chosen is from the Prostate cANcer graDe Assessment (PANDA) Challenge hosted in Kaggle [17]. The dataset contains around 10,000 labeled histopathological images from two data sources: the **Karolinska Institute** and the **Radboud University Medical Center**, each having 5000 images. The masks are also available for these images, showing which parts of the image led to the ISUP grade.

These masks aren't used directly for classification because of the difference in the masks between the two data sources (Karolinska and Radboud). Masks from the Radboud dataset have masks with pixels labeled from 0 to 5:

0—Background (non tissue) or unknown
1—Stroma (connective tissue, non-epithelium tissue)
2—Healthy (benign) epithelium
3—Cancerous epithelium (Gleason 3)
4—Cancerous epithelium (Gleason 4)
5—Cancerous epithelium (Gleason 5).

And the masks from the Karolinska dataset have pixels labeled 0–2:

0—Background (non tissue) or unknown
1—Benign tissue (stroma and epithelium combined)
2—Cancerous tissue (stroma and epithelium combined).

Due to the nature of the masks being different, both the masks cannot be used together for classification.

5.2   AI Training Pipeline

The AI pipeline has two models: the segmentation model and the classification model.

Segmentation: The role of the segmentation model is to highlight the relevant parts of the image for the classifier to predict on these regions. To train the model, only the Radboud dataset is selected, and the masks from the Radboud dataset are used as the expected output for the Radboud images. This is because the masks from the Radboud dataset gave us more information about the images than the Karolinska dataset (6 values per pixel in Radboud masks as opposed to just 3 values per pixel in Karolinska masks).

Classification: After training the segmentation model, the segmentation model is used to generate the masks for both Karolinska and Radboud datasets. Now, both

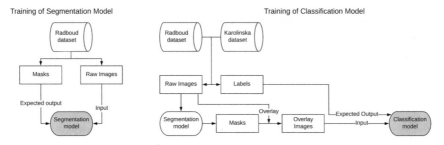

Fig. 5 The steps involved in training proposed model. The blue box highlighted in the flow is the model trained in that flow

the datasets have similar mask structures and can be both used to train the classifier model. The mask is overlaid on the images, passes it to the model for classification, and uses the labels of these images as the expected prediction classes to train the model.

Figure 5 shows these training steps in a graphical form. And since the classification model is trained in the way the pipeline actually flows, the classifier's performance is, in fact, the performance of the entire pipeline.

5.3 Parameters and Metrics

The parameters listed here are the best values found during hyper-parameter tuning of the model.

Segmentation: In the **U-Net model** selected for segmentation, the kernels used are [64, 128, 256, 512], and the activation selected is **ReLU** (Rectified Linear Unit). **Adam** optimizer suited the best among other optimizers, and **Categorical Cross-entropy** was chosen as the loss metric during the training of the model. The performance metric used for the model is **Accuracy**.

Classification: The **Ensemble of Xception, ResNet-50 and EfficientNet-b7** was chosen for classification, and the activation selected is **ReLU** (Rectified Linear Unit), same as in the segmentation model. **Adam** optimizer again turned out to be the best optimizer for the ensemble, with **Categorical Cross-entropy** as the loss metric during the training process. **Accuracy** is chosen as the performance metric.

5.4 Performance Comparison

Segmentation: A comparison of the performance of the selected model (UNet) with top 4 other standard segmentation models is compiled in Table 2.

Table 2 Performance compilation of segmentation models

Segmentation model	Accuracy
LadderNet	91.15
Mask-RCNN	92.46
FastFCN	92.63
Gated-SCNN	93.03
U-Net	**93.67**

Table 3 Performance compilation of classifier models

Classifier model	Accuracy
DenseNet	88.55
RESNET-50	89.09
VGG-16	89.43
EfficientNetb0	89.79
Xception	**90.35**

Table 4 Performance compilation of ensemble combinations of classifier models

Ensemble combination	Accuracy
VGG-19, RESNET-50, Inception-V3	90.51
Xception, Inception-V3, VGG-16	90.86
Xception, Inception, Resnet-50	91.02
VGG-19, RESNET-50, EfficientNet-b7	91.47
Xception, Resnet-50, EfficientNet-b7	**92.38**

The UNet model has given out an accuracy of **93.67**% outperforming other segmentation models used for a similar purpose. Even though the various models used are derivatives of the UNet architecture, they could not beat the performance of the basic UNet model. This is because the complexity of the derived models has resulted in over-fitting, decreasing the performance significantly from their peak.

Classification: Two sets of performances were measured for the classification model—one with the standard models and the other with the different ensemble combinations tried out. Of which top 5 results are compiled in each measurement set, summarized in Tables 3 and 4.

Table 3 shows that Xception model outperforms other classification models, giving an accuracy of **90.35**, and Table 4 shows that the ensemble of Xception, Resnet-50, and EfficientNet-b7 is the best among the various combinations, with the accuracy of **92.38**.

Fig. 6 GradCam visualization of images using the Xception model. From left: the histopathological image in ISUP grade 1 (1); the GradCam visualization of the image in ISUP grade 1 (2); the histopathological image in ISUP grade 3 (3); the GradCam visualization of the image in ISUP grade 3 (4); the histopathological image in ISUP grade 5 (5); the GradCam visualization of the image in ISUP grade 5 (6)

5.5 Explainable AI: GradCam Visualization

GradCam images give us additional information of the regions that the model has focused on to classify the images. And since the grading of the images is based on cancerous regions in the tissue, the GradCam images tell the tissue regions where the cells are present for that grade.

GradCAM heatmap generated for the Xception classification as it is the best scoring stand-alone model. Figure 6 is a collection of three pairs of the raw image, and its GradCam visualization from three different ISUP grades (Grade 1, Grade 3, and Grade 5, from left to right).

The red regions of the visualization are the most focused region implying their contribution in the final segmentation. The GradCAM visualization hints about which part of image influenced in decision of classification model. Specialist doctors will understand the decision of classification model, when heatmap generated through GradCAM is superimposed over the cancer image. Proposed model, not only ensemble the classification, but add another path of diagnosis with explainability using GradCam.

6 Conclusion

Prostate cancer grading is handicapped by the lack of sufficient trained clinicians and intensive manual procedures. Moreover, the manual procedure is error prone and time-consuming. The delay in procuring results or the inaccuracy in the diagnosis of prostate cancer and can increase mortality. A pipeline of segmentation and classification models with an overlay section is proposed in this paper to overcome this drawback. This pipeline has an accuracy of 92.38%, and the GradCam visualization of the images has revealed the regions in the image concentrated with the cells influencing the classification, indicating that the cancerous cells could be populated in this region. The explainability of model using GradCam helps doctors to understand what influenced the decision. The future scope of research is to enhance the performance of segmentation, which enhances classification performance and improves data augmentation to address images not learned effectively.

References

1. Bray F, Ferlay J, Soerjomataram I, Siegel RL, Torre LA, Jemal A (2018) Global cancer statistics 2018: GLOBOCAN estimates of incidence and mortality worldwide for 36 cancers in 185 countries. CA Cancer J Clin 68(6):394–424. https://doi.org/10.3322/caac.21492. Epub 12 Sept 2018. Erratum in: CA Cancer J Clin 70(4):313. PMID: 30207593

2. Epstein JI (2010) An update of the Gleason grading system. J Urol 183(2):433–440. https://doi.org/10.1016/j.juro.2009.10.046. Epub 14 Dec 2009. PMID: 20006878

3. Allsbrook W, Mangold K, Johnson M, Lane R, Lane C, Amin M, Bostwick D, Humphrey P, Jones E, Reuter V, Sakr W, Sesterhenn I, Troncoso P, Wheeler T, Epstein J (2001) Interobserver reproducibility of Gleason grading of prostatic carcinoma: urologic pathologists. Hum Pathol 32:74–80. https://doi.org/10.1053/hupa.2001.21134

4. Egevad L, Ahmad AS, Algaba F, Berney DM, Boccon-Gibod L, Compérat E, Evans AJ, Griffiths D, Grobholz R, Kristiansen G, Langner C, Lopez-Beltran A, Montironi R, Moss S, Oliveira P, Vainer B, Varma M, Camparo P (2013) Standardization of Gleason grading among 337 European pathologists. Histopathology 62(2):247–256. https://doi.org/10.1111/his.12008. PMID: 23240715

5. Leenders I (2020) The 2019 international society of urological pathology (ISUP) consensus conference on grading of prostatic carcinoma. Am J Surg Pathol 44(8)

6. Revisiting prostate biopsy with 2014 ISUP modified Gleason score and Gleason grade—a cross section study—scientific figure on ResearchGate. Available from: https://www.researchgate.net/figure/2014-ISUP-Gleason-score-and-Gleason-grade-groups-15_tbl1_329964806

7. Swiderska-Chadaj Z, de Bel T, Blanchet L et al (2020) Impact of rescanning and normalization on convolutional neural network performance in multi-center, whole-slide classification of prostate cancer. Sci Rep 10:14398. https://doi.org/10.1038/s41598-020-71420-0

8. Komura D, Ishikawa S (2018) Machine learning methods for histopathological image analysis. Comput Struct Biotechnol J 16:34–42

9. Pinckaers H, Bulten W, Laak J, Litjens G (2021) Detection of prostate cancer in whole-slide images through end-to-end training with image-level labels. IEEE Trans Med Imaging 1

10. Campanella T (2019) Clinical-grade computational pathology using weakly supervised deep learning on whole slide images. Nat Med 25(8):1301–1309

11. Ing N, Ma Z, Li J, Salemi H, Arnold C, Knudsen BS, Gertych A (2018) Semantic segmentation for prostate cancer grading by convolutional neural networks. In: Medical imaging 2018: digital pathology. SPIE, pp 343–355

12. Ing N, Ma Z, Li J, Salemi H, Arnold C, Knudsen B, Gertych A (2018) Semantic segmentation for prostate cancer grading by convolutional neural networks. In: Medical imaging 2018: digital pathology, pp 105811B

13. Bulten W, Pinckaers H, Boven H, Vink R, Bel T, Ginneken B, Laak J, Kaa C, Litjens G (2020) Automated deep-learning system for Gleason grading of prostate cancer using biopsies: a diagnostic study. Lancet Oncol 21(2):233–241

14. Ronneberger O, Fischer P, Brox T (2015) U-Net, convolutional networks for biomedical image segmentation

15. Nagpal K, Foote D, Liu Y, Chen PH, Wulczyn E, Tan F, Olson N, Smith J, Mohtashamian A, Wren J, Corrado G, MacDonald R, Peng L, Amin M, Evans A, Sangoi A, Mermel C, Hipp J, Stumpe M (2019) Development and validation of a deep learning algorithm for improving Gleason scoring of prostate cancer. npj Digit Med 2:48

16. Lucas H (2019) Deep learning for automatic Gleason pattern classification for grade group determination of prostate biopsies. Virchows Arch 475(1):77–83
17. Kaggle.com (2021) Prostate cANcer graDe Assessment (PANDA) challenge | Kaggle. [Online]. Available at: https://www.kaggle.com/c/prostate-cancer-grade-assessment/data

Analyzing Wearable Data for Diagnosing COVID-19 Using Machine Learning Model

Manpreet Kaur Dhaliwal⑩, **Rohini Sharma**⑩, **and Naveen Bindra**⑩

1 Introduction

The term "epidemic" refers to an increase in the number of cases of a disease in a short period. According to the US Centers for Disease Control and Prevention, "An epidemic is defined as an increase in the number of illness cases in a geographic area beyond what is normally expected." In most cases, the surge in cases occurs rapidly. In the last, two decades, the world has confronted five epidemics. In the year 2003, Severe Acute Respiratory Syndrome (SARS) [1], in 2009, novel Influenza A (H1N1) virus [2], then the Middle East Respiratory Syndrome (MERS) in 2012 [3], Ebola outbreak in 2014–2016 [4], and the deadliest among these, Severe Acute Respiratory Syndrome Coronavirus 2 (SARS-CoV-2) which was first identified in December 2019. All are infectious diseases that are transmitted by the direct transmission of disease-causing microorganisms from one person to another. A healthy person gets infected, when an infected person kisses, embraces, touches, coughs, or sneezes at them. The outbreak of COVID-19 was confirmed in 220 countries, more than 246 million people worldwide were infected, and the deaths toll reached around 5 million [5]. It affected the whole human civilization physically, mentally, socially, and economically. However, technology plays an important role during a pandemic. Chamola et al. [6] discussed how numerous Internet of Things (IoT) technologies support the battle against COVID-19. Smart thermometers connected

M. K. Dhaliwal (✉) · R. Sharma
Department of Computer Science and Applications, Panjab University, Chandigarh, India
e-mail: preet2016@pu.ac.in

R. Sharma
e-mail: rohini@pu.ac.in

N. Bindra
Postgraduate Institute of Medical Education and Research, Chandigarh, India
e-mail: naveenjb@hotmail.com

© The Author(s), under exclusive license to Springer Nature Singapore Pte Ltd. 2023   285
R. Doriya et al. (eds.), *Machine Learning, Image Processing, Network Security and Data Sciences*, Lecture Notes in Electrical Engineering 946,
https://doi.org/10.1007/978-981-19-5868-7_22

to mobile apps trace people with high fever in the region. Autonomous vehicles are used for delivering meals and medical supplies. Internet of Medical Things facilitates remote patient monitoring. IoT buttons are used to maintain the cleaning standard. Apart from this, wearable devices, mobile apps, drones, and robots have an extensive impact on the fight against the pandemic. Singh et al. [7] discussed that IoT-based applications during COVID-19 help in the superior treatment, timely diagnosis, error-free reports, inexpensive treatment, timely control, monitoring of disease, interconnected hospitals, rapid screening, telehealth consultation, smart tracing of infected patients, wireless health care, informing medical staff during an emergency, etc.

Early detection of the disease is the need of an hour. The current world population is around 7.9 billion [8] and WHO recommendation of doctor–patient ratio is 1:1000. In India, the ratio is 1:1456 [9] which is the world's second-largest populous country. Similarly, in Indonesia, ratio is 0.5:1000, in South Africa 0.8:1000, and China, the ratio is 2.2:1000 [10]. India does not have enough resources in terms of manpower, hospitals, beds, emergency wards, etc., to handle a huge population. In this scenario, technology can play an important role. With the help of wearable devices, diseases can be predicted in advance using the characteristic features extracted from wearable devices data, patients can be monitored remotely and reduce the transmission rate of infectious disease. It can help patients in early detection, save resources, decrease the cost of treatment, and burden on healthcare workers. In this study, we are analyzing the wearable dataset of COVID-19 patients for prior detection of the disease using heart rate, heart rate variability and steps indicators. Our results show that biometric devices data can help us in the prediction of COVID-19 disease in advance.

The constitution of this article is as follows. Section 2 discusses the available related studies. In Sect. 3, research problem is discussed on which this study is based. Section 4 presents the detailed discussion of the research question formulated in Sect. 3. Limitations of the study are explored in Sect. 5. Section 6 presents the conclusion of the paper.

2   Related Studies

Wearable or wearable technology is a sensor-based device that can be worn by the users for tracking physiological changes in the body. The devices can send or receive the data using an Internet connection. During the first three months of 2021, the global wearables market surged 34.4% to reach 104.6 million devices, the fastest for any first trimester [11]. Islam et al. [12] explored the benefits of wearables, including how they can be used to monitor patients remotely, minimize transmission rates among doctors and health care workers and identify who is in a critical state. The wearable respiratory systems and symptoms monitoring systems are also discussed which can be used to help COVID-19 affected people. Seshadri et al. [13] provided in-depth knowledge about the various wearables available in the market and metrics necessary for the COVID-19 detection. Researchers suggested the development of an early detection algorithm that can detect and alert users before signs and symptoms appear.

Wu et al. [14] projected a 7-day early prediction of Acute Exacerbations of Chronic Obstructive Pulmonary Disease (AECOPD) on 67 subjects using wearable devices, home air quality sensing devices, mobile app and questionnaires. Prediction performance is evaluated using various machine learning models like a deep neural network, random forest, K nearest neighbor, decision tree, linear discriminant analysis and adaptive boosting model. Furthermore, researchers concluded that biometric technologies can anticipate AECOPD in the subsequent days with 92.1% accuracy. Li et al. [15] concluded that the onset of Lyme disease, inflammation and risk of type 2 diabetes can be identified using wearable sensors.

Few studies are available on the pre-symptomatic prediction of COVID-19 also, using wearable devices. According to Mishra et al. [16] smartwatch data can be used to predict COVID-19 before symptom onset using heart rate, sleep, and the daily number of steps data. To prove this, MyPHD app is used for data collection from Fitbit, Apple, and Garmin devices. Thirty-two individuals' data are used for an experiment from the 5262 enrolled participants. The Cusum method, which is based on cumulative statistics, is used for the real-time detection of COVID-19, and 63% of cases are detected before the symptom onset. Quer et al. [17] used digital engagement and tracking early control and treatment (DETECT) app to collect data from smartwatches, activity trackers and self-reported symptoms. Sleep, activity and resting heart rate indicators are used. The authors concluded that sensor-based data and self-reported data if used jointly will predict COVID-19 patients more accurately before undergoing testing.

Marinsek et al. [19] used an achievement app linked to a Fitbit device and questionnaire for data collection and to identify if the patient had COVID-19 or influenza. Chest discomfort, difficulty breathing and loss of smell are more prevalent in COVID-19 as compared to flu illness. Furthermore, it is concluded that steps count decreased and RHR elevated in COVID-19 patients. In Natarajan et al. [20] both the self-reported symptoms and Fitbit smartwatch data are used to predict the hospitalization of patients. Respiration rate, heart rate and heart rate variability are used as indicators and logistic regression classifier which is used to predict hospitalization. Researchers concluded that heart rate variability is decreased, and respiration rate, heart rate are increased due to illness.

A home-based patient monitoring unit is developed by Motta et al. [21] that provides remote monitoring of patients SpO2, body temperature, beats per minute and peak expiratory flow. This home-based system is connected to a hospital unit that continuously tracks for any abnormalities and responds to them immediately. This method economizes the hospital resource and allows for early detection of individuals who are rapidly worsening and require immediate attention. The authors observed that SpO2 decreases and BPM increases in COVID-19. Hirten et al. [22] enrolled 297 healthcare workers from Mount Sinai Hospital; iPhone and questionnaire data are used to predict COVID-19 before its diagnosis using heart rate variability metrics. Significant changes were observed in heart rate variability metrics by the researchers, 7 days before and after, in infected patients as compared to uninfected patients. Zhu et al. [23] proposed a paradigm for anticipating the COVID-19 trend ahead of time using wearable devices data. Sleep, activity and heart rate indicators are used to anticipate trends using the Huami wearable gadget.

According to Wong et al. [25] use of wearables assists us in the early prediction of COVID illness. The researcher used the cohort of 200–1000 asymptomatic quarantine persons who have close contact with COVID-19 patients for early detection of disease using wearable biosensors on their arms. Biosensor-generated data are transferred in real time to the Biovital sentinel mobile app. The app data are processed by a cloud-based multivariate physiology analytics engine. Doctors review the data, and if needed, further diagnostic tests are performed. Smarr et al. [26] launched the tempredict study to collect fever data of 50 subjects using the Oura ring wearable device and self-reported symptoms. In this study, researchers concluded that prediction of disease onset is possible using wearable devices.

Hassantabar et al. [27] proposed a framework CovidDeep for daily detection of COVID-19. The framework is based on medical sensors that reduce the overall cost of clinical testing. Data are collected from the smartwatch; pulse oximeter and blood pressure monitor and deep neural network models are applied on the data that achieved 98.1% accuracy. Miller et al. [28] performed a study on 271 individuals who are experiencing COVID-19 symptoms but not clinically verified. Gradient boosted classifier is used to predict the COVID-19 infection before the symptom onset date or during the first few days of the symptom onset using respiration rate indicator.

From the above description, it is clear that the use of wearable sensors based data for predicting respiratory disease in general and COVID-19, in particular, is still in its infancy. It is also clear that heart rate, sleep, steps, respiration rate, heart rate variability and SpO2 in conjunction with the self-reported symptoms are good indicators for advanced prediction of disease using a machine learning model. More research work is required in this area. As, it has a lot of scope due to the benefits it offers.

3   Research Problem

The use of wearable technology can change the whole scenario of health care, especially for detecting infectious diseases like COVID-19 before the actual test is conducted. Few studies arouse [16, 17, 20, 21, 25, 26] hope of promising medical use of wearables. In this study, we use the physiological features data which can be collected easily using wearables, study and analyze their importance and contribution in detecting COVID-19 before symptoms appear. The following questions have been devised to conduct the study:

RQ1 What are characteristic physiological features that can be used for early detection of COVID-19?

RQ2 Is it possible to predict COVID-19 before the actual symptom appears?

4   Dataset Used

In the majority of studies, data collected by researchers are not shared with third parties. After a rigorous scan on the internet, a freely available wearable devices dataset is found for COVID-19. The data are available at https://github.com/Welltory/hrv-covid19 [29]. These data are collected by the using Welltory app which is freely available for research. Welltory is a smart fitness and health app that utilizes the camera on your smartphone or data from your Apple Watch to provide you with detailed body diagnostics. To aid in the fight against the pandemic outbreak, Welltory started an open research project to investigate diagnostic patterns of coronavirus disease. Infected people are encouraged to join this study by using the Welltory app to track their symptoms, heart rate variability, and data from wearables like the Apple Watch, Garmin or Fitbit. Researchers from University College London, Johns Hopkins University, Harvard Medical School and other institutions have also used the Welltory app in several peer-reviewed studies [30].

4.1   Characteristic Physiological Features

There are nine tables in this dataset, blood_pressure.csv, heart_rate.csv, sleep.csv, surveys.csv, hrv_measurements.csv, participants.csv, scales_description.csv, wearables.csv and weather.csv. All the tables contain a user code column that uniquely identifies all the participants. The diagram view of all the tables is provided in Fig. 1.

There is total nine tables with numerous features but few of them are chosen because most of the values are missing or not contributing to the advanced detection of COVID-19. A few observations about the dataset tables are given below:

- **Participant table** presents general information of participant. A total of 185 participants from 25 countries participated and contributed data as shown in Fig. 2, and most are from Russia and the USA. The maximum participant's age range is 24–44, and female participants are more than male as shown in Fig. 3.
- In the **wearables table**, the features are resting_pulse, steps_count, SpO2, body temperature, etc., but almost all the values are missing except step_counts. So, only this feature is considered for further analysis.
- In the **sleep table**, sleep data of only 10 participants are available. When the sleep data of these ten participants are plotted, it is realized that data of only a few days are available in a scattered form which is not useful for prediction.
- **Blood pressure table** has data of only 28 participants that are also not contributing to prediction because it does not show any changes it follows the same pattern.
- **Heart Rate table** contains heart rate readings during rest or activity with the date and time of the day. Every user recorded 3–4 readings per day. Few of them recorded data every minute. So, it generated a large amount of data but those participants are very few.

Fig. 1 Diagram view of all the tables present in the dataset

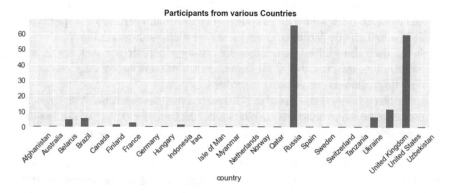

Fig. 2 Participants from various countries

Fig. 3 Male female ratio of participants

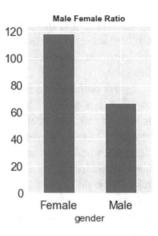

- **Weather table** contains the weather information on a particular date like average temperature, humidity and pressure, etc., which is not useful at the participant level
- **Scale table** provides information about the intensity of symptom means if the user is suffering from fever, then its fever is very mild, mild, moderate, severe or extremely severe, etc.
- **Survey table** contains detailed information about the participant's health conditions like if the patient has anxiety, confusion, pain, cough, heart disease, etc., with dates.

After analyzing all the tables in the dataset, it is concluded that for many features either the values are missing or the amount of data is not sufficient to perform analysis. For three features, heart rate, heart rate variability and steps counts data are available which are used for analysis. In heart rate variability, two sub-features considered are standard deviation of the inter-beat interval of normal sinus beats (SDNN) and beats per minute (bpm). In this study, heart rate, HRV and steps count physiological features are used for the early detection of COVID-19.

Before analyzing, the stationarity of data is checked using augmented Dickey fuller test (ADF). After executing this test, it will return test statistics and critical values. If test statistics is less than the critical value, then data is stationary otherwise non-stationary and it is difficult to model non-stationary data. After stationarity check, the dataset is preprocessed using resampling and scaling techniques. In the first step, resampling is performed as the dataset is nonuniform. Resampling is the process of converting a dataset recorded in some period to another like to summarize and accumulate the time series data into new time like hourly data into minute data. Resampling generates a uniform time sampling on the actual dataset [31]. On the selected features, minute sampling is performed over heart rate and heart rate variability and day sampling is performed on steps data.

Secondly, scaling is performed on the dataset. The information gathered contains features of various scales and dimensions. The modeling of the dataset is affected by the different scales which results in the biased output. Standardization is a data-scaling process that converts statistical data distributions into mean zero and standard deviation one distribution [32]. Standard scaler method of sklearn library is used in this study.

Lastly, outliers are detected. Outliers are data points that are unusual in comparison to other data points. There are various anomaly detection methods like DBScan, isolation forest, local outlier factor and elliptic envelope method. In this study, elliptic envelope method is used for outlier detection. Elliptic envelope considers that the data are normally distributed and construct an ellipse around the data, identifying any observation inside the ellipse as an inlier and outside as an outlier. Contamination refers to an outlier in the dataset [33]. In this study, contamination value is taken as 0.1. After preprocessing is done, data values are visualized using the Matplot library of Python. The following are the features selected for the study with visualization results.

Heart rate represents the number of times a heart beats in a minute or a given time interval. Heart rate variability (HRV) is the changes in the time intervals between successive heartbeats, known as inter-beat intervals (IBIs). The IBI of normal sinus beats (SDNN) standard deviation is measured in milliseconds. SDNN levels can be used to predict morbidity and mortality [24]. There are many reasons for heart rate elevation like infection, fever, heart problems, certain medication, atrial fibrillation or ventricular tachycardia, asthma or other breathing trouble [36]. Lung disease can also increase the heart rate. When you are unwell, your adrenaline levels rise, causing your heart to rush. The heart also beats faster when there is less oxygen in the blood [37]. Apart from this, [15, 16, 19, 20, 25] also concluded that heart rate or beats per minute value is elevated before and after the COVID-19 symptom onset date. Heart rate variability is reduced in patients suffering from chronic obstructive pulmonary disease (COPD) [22, 34, 35]. COPD is defined as a respiratory illness that can be barred and preserved. In [20, 25, 27], researchers considered heart rate variability as a primary indicator for the COVID-19 detection. In [15, 18–20], researchers concluded that steps count is altered during the onset of the symptom. Below, every physiological feature selected for the study with visualization results is discussed:

- Heart Rate

Heart rate is a very important indicator and is elevated before the onset of illness [15, 16, 18, 19, 25] concluded the elevation of heart rate before and after the symptom onset date. After analyzing the visualized result, this study also concluded that heart rate is elevated a few days before and after the onset of COVID-19.

After the preprocessing of the dataset, 40 participant's records are left and these 40 participants are those whose heart rate readings of at least 7–8 days are available. Of these 40 participants, symptom onset date for four participants is not available and 16 participants' data is very scattered. So, those participants are discarded. At last, 19 participants are left for further analysis and results are given in Table 1. And a plot for user code 295ed96279 is shown in Fig. 4.

Table 1 Detailed view of participants heart rate data

No. of participants	User code	Result
09	01bad5a519, 1942df1c47, 5efbee746a, 78cc008261, aa036185e3, d40dc56a36, f9edcb7056, fde84801d8, 1ed25f66e9	After symptom date heart rate is remain elevated for 16–25 days
2	3acfbb328e, 9871ee5e7b	Heart rate started elevating 3–4 days before symptom appears
5	295ed96279,7ba5381254, 1c2e6b2eb, b523b4512b, cdf7848d2b	Heart rate is elevated 4–7 days before and after symptoms appear
3	1ce1d77659,856d41cc60, c174f32d88	These user codes do not show any abnormal behavior in heart rate as a sign of disease

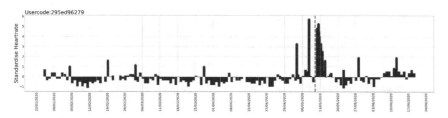

Fig. 4 Standardized heart rate relative to dates and red line represent the symptom date

- Beats Per Minute

Beats per minute or pulse rate terms are synonymously used by researchers to represent heart rate. We have plotted BPM and heart rate individually because bpm is taken from the HRV_measurements table and heart rate is taken from the heart_rate table. BPM increases when a patient suffers from an infectious disease. In this study, 10 participants out of 36 are considered in other cases symptom onset date is not available or data is very scattered. Results obtained for the participants are shown in Table 2. A plot for user code 295ed96279 is shown in Fig. 5, where bpm is increasing 5 days before the symptom appears. The red vertical dashed line represents the symptom onset date, and small red dots on the bars represent anomalies in the data.

- Standard deviation of the inter-beat interval of normal sinus beats

SDNN is a feature from heart rate variability measurement. In this study, ten participants are considered because of the non-availability of other users' data. Results are shown in Table 3. A plot for user code a1c2e6b2eb is shown in Fig. 6, where SDNN value is decreasing before and after symptom date. The red vertical dashed line represents the symptom onset date and small red dots on the bars represent anomalies in

Table 2 Detailed view of participants BPM data

No. of participants	User code	Result
03	01bad5a519, aa036185e3, fde84801d8	After symptom date BPM is elevated for 14–20 days
2	3acfbb328e, 9871ee5e7b	Beats per minute increased 3–4 days before symptom appears
4	c174f32d88, 295ed96279, fcf3ea75b0, a1c2e6b2eb	BPM is elevated 5–7 days before and after symptoms appear
1	f9edcb7056	Not showing any anomalous behavior after symptom date

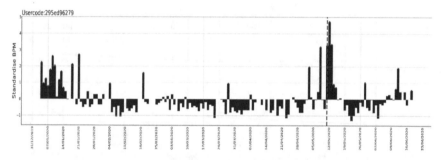

Fig. 5 Standardized BPM relative to dates and red line represent the symptom date

the data. It is concluded from visualized results that SDNN value decreases a few days before and after the COVID-19 symptom appear.

- Steps

In this study, 17 participants out of 29 are considered as in other cases either symptom onset date is not available or before and after symptom onset data is not available. Results are shown in Table 4, and a plot for user code 01bad5a519 is shown in Fig. 7. It is concluded that steps count is a very good indicator for early disease identification.

Table 3 Detailed view of participants SDNN data

No. of participants	User_Code	Result
04	01bad5a519, aa036185e3, fde84801d8, 295ed96279	After symptom date SDNN is decreasing means patient is still suffering from disease
1	3acfbb328e	SDNN is decreased 7 days before symptoms appear
4	1ce1d77659, a1c2e6b2eb, c174f32d88, fcf3ea75b0	SDNN values decreasing 4–7 days before and after symptom starts
1	f9edcb7056	Not showing any anomalous signs in data

Fig. 6 Standardized SDNN relative to dates and red line represent the symptom date

Table 4 Detailed view of participants steps data

No. of participants	User code	Result
3	aa036185e3, fde84801d8, d40dc56a36	Steps count shown downward trend in 12–20 days after symptoms appear
2	b523b4512b, c174f32d88	Steps count is increased before symptoms date but decreased after symptoms date
10	01bad5a519, 42a99d8248,985083f4d, 5d200bd1c6,5efbee746a,6be5033971,7ba5381254, 9871ee5e7b, ebf2c3cb63, fcf3ea75b0	Downward trend in steps count 7–10 days before and after symptom date
1	e8240b51a2	Not showing any anomalous behavior in steps data
1	f922e9b06c	Downward trend in steps count 3 days before symptoms date

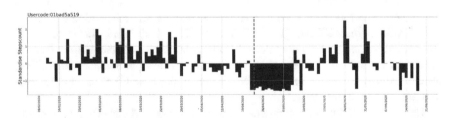

Fig. 7 Standardized steps relative to dates with their user code and red line represent the symptom date

From the results explained above, it is concluded that it is possible to predict COVID-19 using data collected from wearable devices. As we discussed in Sect. 4.1 the features chosen and then in detail discussed and plotted every feature data. It is clear that prediction before a symptom appears is possible. However, there are many limitations of this study.

5 Limitations of This Study

There are various limitations to our research.

- First, the dataset size is very small. Only 185 subjects participated in this study, and after preprocessing, only 36 participants were left.
- The data collection process is nonuniform. Participants are collecting data as per their convenience, and the uniformity of time has not been adhere to.
- For confirming COVID-19, a molecular or rapid antigen test is performed. However, it is not clear in the dataset, which test is performed for the confirmation of COVID-19 and symptom onset date is given by participants themselves and not verified by some medical practitioner.
- Data are not uniform; the young-age population is more than old-age population. Till date, it has been established that old-age population is more prone to COVID-19 infection but the dataset utilize has lesser number of old age population. Moreover, most of the participants are from Russia and US countries.

6 Conclusion

This study is an attempt to verify if the prediction of a respiratory disease, i.e., COVID-19, is possible using wearable technology before the actual onset of symptoms. There are not many datasets available to carry out the study in public domain. There have been few studies which analysis the dataset. After analyzing the dataset and visualizing results thoroughly, it is concluded that features like heart rate, heart rate variability and step count collected from wearable devices can help in the presymptomatic prediction of disease in symptomatic and asymptomatic carriers before the clinical test. These findings required further studies because of the small size of the dataset used in this study.

This is not a clinical study; only the data are analyzed and visualized with regard to varied patterns observed in patients. This is helpful in alerting patients to consult doctor and take precautions before lab test is conducted. However, this disease is to be confirmed with a laboratory test only. We cannot stop epidemics, but we can control them with the help of technology.

References

1. Severe Acute Respiratory Syndrome (SARS). https://www.who.int/health-topics/severe-acute-respiratory-syndrome#tab=tab_1. Last accessed 11 August 2021
2. 2009 H1N1 Pandemic (H1N1pdm09 virus) | Pandemic Influenza (Flu) | CDC. https://www.cdc.gov/flu/pandemic-resources/2009-h1n1-pandemic.html. Last accessed 1 August 2021
3. Middle East respiratory syndrome coronavirus (MERS-CoV). https://www.who.int/news-room/fact-sheets/detail/middle-east-respiratory-syndrome-coronavirus-(mers-cov). Last accessed 1 August 2021
4. Ebola virus disease. https://www.who.int/health-topics/ebola#tab=tab_1. Last accessed 1 August 2021
5. Coronavirus cases worldwide by country | Statista. https://www.statista.com/statistics/104 3366/novel-coronavirus-2019ncov-cases-worldwide-by-country/. Last accessed 30 Oct 2021
6. Chamola V, Hassija V, Gupta V, Guizani M (2020) A comprehensive review of the COVID-19 pandemic and the role of IoT, drones, AI, blockchain and 5G in. X:1–35. https://doi.org/10. 1109/ACCESS.2020.2992341.
7. Singh RP, Javaid M, Haleem A, Suman R (2020) Internet of things (IoT) applications to fight against COVID-19 pandemic. Diabetes Metab Syndr 14:521–524. https://doi.org/10.1016/J. DSX.2020.04.041
8. World Population Clock: 7.9 Billion People (2021)—Worldometer. https://www.worldomet ers.info/world-population/. Last accessed Last accessed 2 August 2021
9. The doctor-population ratio in India is 1:1456 against WHO recommendation | Deccan Herald. https://www.deccanherald.com/business/budget-2020/the-doctor-population-ratio-in-india-is-11456-against-who-recommendation-800034.html. Last accessed Last accessed 2 August 2021
10. Health resources—Doctors—OECD Data. https://data.oecd.org/healthres/doctors.htm#indica tor-chart. Last accessed 2 August 2021
11. Samsung pips Xiaomi to grab 2nd spot in global wearables market | Business Standard News. https://www.business-standard.com/article/technology/samsung-pips-xiaomi-to-grab-2nd-spot-in-global-wearables-market-121052900563_1.html. Last accessed 16 August 2021
12. Islam M, Mahmud S, Rabiul LJM, Sheikh I (2020) Wearable technology to assist the patients infected with novel coronavirus (COVID–19). SN Comput Sci 1:1–9. https://doi.org/10.1007/ s42979-020-00335-4
13. Seshadri DR, Davies EV, Harlow ER, Hsu JJ, Knighton SC, Walker TA, Voos JE, Drummond CK (2020) Wearable sensors for COVID-19: a call to action to harness our digital infrastructure for remote patient monitoring and virtual assessments 2:1–11. https://doi.org/10.3389/fdgth. 2020.00008
14. Wu CT, Li GH, Huang CT, Cheng YC, Chen CH, Chien JY, Kuo PH, Kuo LC, Lai F (2021) Acute exacerbation of a chronic obstructive pulmonary disease prediction system using wearable device data, machine learning, and deep learning: development and cohort study. JMIR mHealth uHealth 9. https://doi.org/10.2196/22591
15. Li X, Dunn J, Salins D, Zhou G, Zhou W, Schüssler-Fiorenza Rose SM, Perelman D, Colbert E, Runge R, Rego S, Sonecha R, Datta S, McLaughlin T, Snyder MP (2017) Digital health: tracking physiomes and activity using wearable biosensors reveals useful health-related information. PLOS Biol 15:e2001402. https://doi.org/10.1371/JOURNAL.PBIO.2001402
16. Mishra T, Wang M, Metwally AA, Bogu GK, Brooks AW, Bahmani A, Alavi A, Celli A, Higgs E, Dagan-Rosenfeld O, Fay B, Kirkpatrick S, Kellogg R, Gibson M, Wang T, Hunting EM, Mamic P, Ganz AB, Rolnik B, Li X, Snyder MP (2020) Smartwatch data. Nat Biomed Eng 4. https://doi.org/10.1038/s41551-020-00640-6
17. Quer G, Radin JM, Gadaleta M, Baca-motes K, Ariniello L, Ramos E, Kheterpal V, Topol EJ, Steinhubl SR (2021) Wearable sensor data and self-reported symptoms for COVID-19 detection. Nat Med 27. https://doi.org/10.1038/s41591-020-1123-x

18. Menni C, Valdes AM, Freidin MB, Sudre CH, Nguyen LH, Drew DA, Ganesh S, Varsavsky T, Cardoso MJ, El-Sayed Moustafa JS, Visconti A, Hysi P, Bowyer RCE, Mangino M, Falchi M, Wolf J, Ourselin S, Chan AT, Steves CJ, Spector TD (2020) Real-time tracking of self-reported symptoms to predict potential COVID-19. Nat Med 26:1037–1040. https://doi.org/10.1038/s41591-020-0916-2
19. Shapiro A, Marinsek N, Clay I, Bradshaw B, Ramirez E, Min J, Trister A, Wang Y, Althoff T, Foschini L (2021) Characterizing COVID-19 and influenza illnesses in the real world via person-generated health data. Patterns 2:100188. https://doi.org/10.1016/j.patter.2020.100188
20. Natarajan A, Su HW, Heneghan C (2020) Assessment of physiological signs associated with COVID-19 measured using wearable devices. npj Digit Med 3. https://doi.org/10.1038/S41746-020-00363-7
21. Motta LP, Paulo P, Borguezan BM, Bo N, Luis J, Gonc L, Ferraz MR, Mogami R, Acatauassu R (2021) An emergency system for monitoring pulse oximetry, peak expiratory flow , and body temperature of patients with COVID-19 at home : development and preliminary application. PLoS One 2:1–19. https://doi.org/10.1371/journal.pone.0247635
22. Hirten RP, Danieletto M, Tomalin L, Choi KH, Zweig M, Golden E, Kaur S, Helmus D, Biello A, Pyzik R, Charney A, Miotto R, Glicksberg BS, Levin M, Nabeel I, Aberg J, Reich D, Charney D, Bottinger EP, Keefer L, Suarez-Farinas M, Nadkarni GN, Fayad ZA (2021) Use of physiological data from a wearable device to identify SARS-CoV-2 infection and symptoms and predict COVID-19 diagnosis: observational study. J Med Internet Res 23:1–14. https://doi.org/10.2196/26107
23. Zhu G, Li J, Meng Z, Yu Y, Li Y, Tang X, Dong Y, Sun G, Zhou R, Wang H, Wang K, Huang W (2020) Learning from large-scale wearable device data for predicting the epidemic trend of COVID-19 2020
24. Shaffer F, Ginsberg JP (2017) An overview of heart rate variability metrics and norms. Front Public Heal 5:258. https://doi.org/10.3389/FPUBH.2017.00258/BIBTEX
25. Wong CK, Ho DTY, Tam AR, Zhou M, Lau YM, Tang MOY, Tong RCF, Rajput KS, Chen G, Chan SC, Siu CW, Hung IFN (2020) Artificial intelligence mobile health platform for early detection of COVID-19 in quarantine subjects using a wearable biosensor: protocol for a randomised controlled trial. BMJ Open 10:1–5. https://doi.org/10.1136/bmjopen-2020-038555
26. Smarr BL, Aschbacher K, Fisher SM, Chowdhary A, Dilchert S, Puldon K, Rao A, Hecht FM, Mason AE (2020) Feasibility of continuous fever monitoring using wearable devices. Sci Rep 10:1–11. https://doi.org/10.1038/s41598-020-78355-6
27. Hassantabar S, Stefano N, Ghanakota V, Ferrari A, Nicola GN, Bruno R, Marino IR, Hamidouche K, Jha NK (2021) CovidDeep : SARS-CoV-2/COVID-19 test based on wearable medical sensors and efficient neural networks 1–11
28. Miller DJ, Capodilupo JV, Lastella M, Sargent C, Roach GD, Lee VH, Capodilupo ER (2020) Analyzing changes in respiratory rate to predict the risk of COVID-19 infection. PLoS ONE 15:1–10. https://doi.org/10.1371/journal.pone.0243693
29. GitHub—Welltory/hrv-covid19: COVID-19 and Wearables Open Data Research. https://github.com/Welltory/hrv-covid19. Last accessed 11 August 2021
30. Our story—Welltory, https://welltory.com/our-story/. Last accessed 11 August 2021
31. Resampling—Pandas 1.3.4 documentation. https://pandas.pydata.org/docs/reference/resampling.html. Last accessed 16 August 2021
32. How to use StandardScaler and MinMaxScaler transforms in Python. https://machinelearningmastery.com/standardscaler-and-minmaxscaler-transforms-in-python/. Last accessed 16 August 2021
33. Machine learning for anomaly detection: elliptic envelope | by Mahbubul Alam | Towards data science. https://towardsdatascience.com/machine-learning-for-anomaly-detection-elliptic-envelope-2c90528df0a6. Last accessed 16 August 2021
34. Camillo CA, Pitta F, Possani HV, Barbosa MVRA, Marques DSO, Cavalheri V, Probst VS, Brunetto AF (2008) Heart rate variability and disease characteristics in patients with COPD. Lung 186:393–401. https://doi.org/10.1007/s00408-008-9105-7

35. Roque AL, Valenti VE, Massetti T, Da Silva TD, Monteiro CBDM, Oliveira FR, De Almeida Junior ÁD, Lacerda SNB, Pinasco GC, Nascimento VG, Granja Filho LG, De Abreu LC, Garner DM, Ferreira C (2014) Chronic obstructive pulmonary disease and heart rate variability: a literature update. Int Arch Med 7:1–8. https://doi.org/10.1186/1755-7682-7-43
36. How's your heart rate and why it matters?—Harvard Health. https://www.health.harvard.edu/heart-health/hows-your-heart-rate-and-why-it-matters. Last accessed 17 August 2021
37. Ask the doctor: racing heart and pneumonia—Harvard Health. https://www.health.harvard.edu/heart-health/racing-heart-and-pneumonia. Last accessed 17 August 2021

Comparative Analysis of Classification Methods to Predict Diabetes Mellitus on Noisy Data

Uppalapati Padma Jyothi, Madhavi Dabbiru, Sridevi Bonthu, Abhinav Dayal, and Narasimha Rao Kandula

1 Introduction

Diabetes mellitus is a set of metabolic illnesses marked by chronic hyperglycemia caused by insulin production, insulin action, or both [1]. Diabetes is a serious health concern that can lead to a variety of long-term problems, including renal, cardiovascular, and neuropathic disorders. Many of these issues can lead to higher healthcare costs, as well as an increased chance of ICU stay and mortality [2].

Around 422 million people worldwide have diabetes, with the majority living in low and middle-income countries, and 1.6 million deaths are directly attributed to diabetes per year. Both the composition of cases and the frequency of diabetes have been progressively increasing over the last several decades [3].

The Middle East and North Africa regions have the highest prevalence of diabetes in adults (10.9%) whereas the Western Pacific region has the highest number of adults diagnosed with diabetes and has countries with the highest prevalence of diabetes (37.5%). India has the second-highest number of diabetes patients aged 20–79 years as of 2019. The true number of diabetes in India is estimated to be approximately

U. P. Jyothi (✉) · S. Bonthu · A. Dayal · N. R. Kandula
Vishnu Institute of Technology, Bhimavaram, A.P., India
e-mail: padmajyothi64@gmail.com

A. Dayal
e-mail: abhinav.dayal@vishnu.edu.in

M. Dabbiru
Dr. L. Bullaya College of Engineering, Vishakapatnam, A.P., India
e-mail: dmadhavi@lbce.edu.in

40 million [4]. Around 8.5% of the adult population is diagnosed with diabetes[1] independent of the gender. To predict diabetes mellitus, data mining techniques are commonly utilized for prediction at an early stage [5, 6] and also for knowledge discovery from biomedical data.

Diabetic individuals with COVID-19 infection have a advanced threat to be admitted to the ICU and show a higher mortality threat during the illness [7]. Monitoring diabetes situations of ICU admitted cases continously is veritably important, and testing it by traditional ways is a tedious job.

Checking diabetes for the ICU admitted cases is necessary as the extensive data indicate that in cases with or without a previous diagnosis of diabetes is associated with an increased threat of complications and mortality rate [8]. As per the norms of medical associations, it is obligatory to check the position of diabetes in all ICU admitted cases before pacing to the next step.

The WiDS Datathon 2021,[2] a world-wide team at Standford focuses on patient health, with main emphasis on the chronic condition of diabetes. It has collected the data from MIT's Global Open Source Severity of Illness Score (GOSSIS) initiative. The main objective of this work is to findout whether a patient admitted to an ICU has been previously diagnosed with data mining or not using the data gathered during first 24 h of patient intensive care [9]. The importance of diabetes prediction through computation is to identify which external factors are influencing more like age, BMI, blood glucose levels, and others. The data mining approaches are used for the prediction of diabetes mellitus, but the main problem is the model may not be adaptive for all the diabetic datasets. In order to overcome these and improve algorithms, ensembling models can also be included for increasing the performance of the model.

This is a binary classification problem with 2 classes (0 and 1) for classification of diabetic mellitus patients using factors:

Labels: let $Y = 0$ for diabetic patient and $Y = 1$ for non-diabetic patient.

Model:

$$f(x) = W^{T}X + b \tag{1}$$

Decision rule:

$$\text{Assign } x \text{ to } Y = \begin{cases} 1 \text{ if } f(x) \geq 0 \\ 0 \text{ if } f(x) < 0 \end{cases} \tag{2}$$

Our approach to the women in data science challenge of 2021 uses traditional classification algorithms and also different ensemble models like XGBoost [10, 11] and LightGB [12, 13] after performing data preprocessing. The presented approach is one of the best performing one in the challenge.

---

[1] https://www.who.int/news-room/fact-sheets/detail/diabetes.

[2] https://www.kaggle.com/c/widsdatathon2021.

The rest of the paper is structured as follows. Section 2 presents the former important work carried out in the prediction of diabetics complaint, Sect. 3 introduced the data and highlights the main strengths and weakness of the data, Sect. 4 covers the experimentation done. Section 5 preents the results and conversations corridor. The paper concludes in Sect. 6 with future scope of the work.

2 Related Work

Formerly, diabetic prediction used to be done very easily as the number of parameters to consider is reasonable. Machine learning can assist people in making a primary judgment about diabetes mellitus according to their daily physical examination data, and it can serve as a guide for croakers [14, 15]. Now, if we need to work to predict with a machine learning system, selection of valid features and classification system is the major problem. Various classification algorithms like Naïve Bayes, logistic regression, K-nearest neighbors, decision tree, random forest, and support vector machine.

Wu et al. [16] proposed a novel algorithm which is a hybrid technique combination of improved K-means clustering and logistic regression on the PIMA dataset and achieved good accuracy. Azrar et al. [17] compared different data mining algorithms like decision tree, Naïve Bayes, and K-nearest neighbors by using the PID dataset for early prediction of diabetes. Perveen et al. [18] worked with bagging, AdaBoost, and J48 decision tree on the dataset CPCSSN. Evaluation of results indicates that the AdaBoost ensemble method performs better than bagging as well as a stand-alone J48 decision tree. Also suggested that other data mining techniques like logistic regression, Naïve Bayes can also be incorporated as base learners in the framework of ensembles.

Kandhasamy and Balamurali [19] worked with data samples from UCI repository and compared different machine learning classifiers. According to their study before preprocessing, the J48 decision tree acquired better accuracy than KNN, Random forest, and Support Vector Machine. After removing the noisy data they obtained good results with the classification algorithm Random Forest and KNN. Viloria et al. [20] worked with the diagnosis of diabetes mellitus of different data samples based on the inputs of the patients by considering only a few factors like age, BMI and blood glucose. The authors used a Support vector machine, an effective custom classifier dYG for prediction. An accuracy of 99.2% was achieved for Columbian patients for other datasets of patients only 65.6%. It's clear the results are mainly based on the patient ethnic condition. Harz et al. [21] worked with the artificial neural networks for predicting diabetes using Just Neural Network technique using a back propagation algorithm. The authors used a Neural Network with one input layer of 16 inputs, one hidden layer, and one output layer of 1 output on a dataset collected from UCI repository and achieved 87.3% of accuracy.

Tigga and Garg [22] experimented with two different data samples like questionnaires collected online and offline from 18 questions on health, family background and also lifestyle. The other is the PIMA Indian Diabetes database. On both data, the authors experimented with different classification techniques like KNN, Naive Bayes, logistic regression, random forest, support vector machine, and decision tree. Among all these, random forest yield better results. Naz and Ahuja [23] tested different classification techniques on the PIMA Indian Diabetes dataset and observed that the accuracy ranges in between 90 and 98%. In order to increase the better result, they worked with deep neural networks and acquired an accuracy of 98.07%.

Maniruzzaman et al. [24] used three types of partition protocols (K2, K5, and K10) have also espoused and repeated these protocols into 20 trials for testing the performance of various classifiers of machine learning; individual classifiers achieved nearly 90% accuracy. The authors combined logistic regression and random forest to improve the performance and as a result they achieved 94.25% accuracy and 0.95 area under the curve. Hasan et al. [25] worked with different models of machine learning and also ensembling models including AdaBoost (AB), XGBoost (XB) and multilayer perceptron (MLP). As the traditional methods don't yield better results, combinations of different ensembling models are used, among them, the AB + XB gives better accuracy.

There is no model trained on patients data gathered at intensive care. Our work mainly focuses on predicting Diabetic Mellitus on this data. Our approach is training baseline followed by ensembling models and to present comparative analysis of all the techniques.

3 Exploratory Data Analysis

The first step in doing any machine learning project is to understand the data. The more we explore the data the better results would be. To understand more about the data, data analysis is carried out. The data regarding the details and data of patients who are admitted to the hospital. Different observations like weight, height, age, BMI, Ethnicity, and lab test reports are also recorded in that dataset.

The dataset contains 130,157 rows and 181 columns. It is too overwhelming to understand the dataset which contains 181 columns. Among those features, there are many unique classes for each object of the column. As shown in Table 1, more unique classes are available for hospital_admit_source which is 15, most of the features are of multi-class.

One observation is among all the 181 columns, few variables like age, gender and ethnicity are influencing the target variable when compare with other variables. The table illustrates what is the impact of each feature on the target variable. As it is a medical dataset it took a while to categorize the attributes. The dataset is categorized into 5 groups after careful examination of the dataset (Table 2).

Table 1 Unique classes in each column

Feature	Number of unique classes
Ethnicity	6
Gender	2
Hospital_admit_source	15
ICU_admit_source	5
ICU_stay_type	3
ICU_type	8

Table 2 Variables, which are showing major influence on the target variable

Feature	Category	Diabetes	
		Yes	No
Age	<50	2.92	17.34
	50–60	3.79	14.03
	60–70	5.75	16.31
	70–80	5.57	15.45
	>80	3.06	11.89
Gender	Male	11.84	42.33
	Female	9.77	35.99
Ethnicity	Caucasian	15.83	61.18
	Hispanic	0.95	2.92
	African American	2.80	7.88
	Asian	0.41	1.27
	Native American	0.22	0.47

1. Data about the patient like age, weight, height, BMI
2. Data about the hospital and icu's like hospital_id, icu_id etc.
3. h1_features
4. d1_features
5. Others.

Here h1_features and d1_features are the columns whose names are starting with h1 and d1, respectively. These are some domain-related names. Others containing remaining columns like leukemia, lymphoma, and AIDS.

One important observation from Fig. 1, female diabetic patients based on the age is not more than male patient. But, the special case, female patients whose age is in between 20 and 40 are having more percent of diabetic compare to male. The reason is the female during maternity stage their is high chance of getting diabetic based on health issues and family background.

The very next thing we started looking at in the dataset is whether the data were balanced or not. The main objective of this project is to determine whether an individual admitted to ICU will have diabetes mellitus from the details of the patient. This

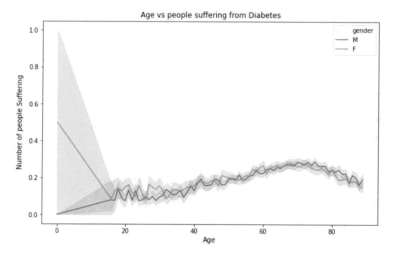

Fig. 1 Age versus people suffering from diabetic mellitus

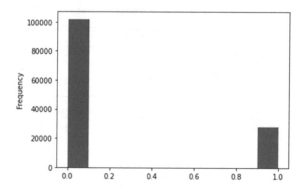

Fig. 2 Imbalanced dataset

is a binary classification problem, and the target column is diabetes_mellitus. From Fig. 2, we can see that our dataset contains more number of records of the patient who doesn't have diabetes_mellitus, i.e., 78.3% compare to the patient having diabetes is 21.6%. So, after looking at this, we can say that our dataset is imbalanced concerning the target.

Another problem we generally encounter while dealing with datasets is NA values. In the dataset, 34% of the cells out of 130,157 × 181 cells are NA values. It is not a negligible percentage. The percentages of NA values of all five categories are represented in the pie chart. In the dataset of 90% of NA values are in the d1_features category and h1_features category.

The possible conclusion from the exploratory data analysis is, we need to impute NA values properly and also need to balance the dataset. There are few challenges with the dataset we got for competition.

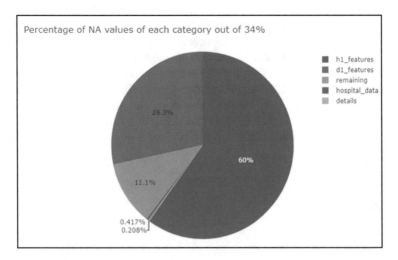

Fig. 3 Missing values

1. It has 181 features divided into demographics, APACHE covariate, APACHE comorbidity, vitals, labs, labs blood gas categories and a target variable with the name diabetes mellitus. Every category provided details of features like unit of measure, description, example, etc.
2. The training dataset is half-empty. Few features with significant correlation like h1_bun_min, h1_bun_max, h1_creatinine_min, h1_creatinine_max, h1_glucose_ min, h1_glucose_max, h1_diasbp_invasive_min have more than 75 k Null values. We decided to drop them as they may not play role in training.
3. Missing values: From Fig. 3, h1_features and d1_features are having more missing values.
4. Handling missing values: The features we have selected have a correlation threshold of more than 0.1. Most of the selected features are related to glucose concentration and blood pressure resulted from the medical tests.

4 Methodology

Data preprocessing is one of the crucial modules in any machine learning task. It is a process of removing or dropping the unnecessary or irrelevant data from the dataset to ensure better performance. For performing data preprocessing, the programming language used is Julia [26, 27]. Julia is a dynamic programming language that supports high-speed mathematical computation, easy to use, and is also more flexible. It also supports hardware that includes TPUs and GPUs mostly on every cloud.

The percentage of Nan's (missing values) in training data is 61.33, whereas for the testing data, 61.41. 34% of cells are having missing values in the complete dataset. As the percent of missing values is more in the dataset.

The dataset which is chosen is imbalanced. The challenge is that out-of-box classifiers like logistic regression and random forest trends to discard the rare class during the training phase. To handle imbalanced data using different techniques like resampling, cross-validation, ensemble different resampled datasets, or using an improved model. In this paper, we used different ensemble models to manage imbalanced data.

4.1 Modeling

The dataset is collected from the Kaggle Web site of the WIDS 2021 competition. Data preprocessing is performed using Julia programming to remove unnecessary features and also deal with missing values. Splitting of data is done for training and testing. We experimented with different algorithms to build a predictive model for diabetes mellitus. They are logistic regression [28], K-nearest neighbors, random forest [29], XGBoost [10], and LightGBM [12]. Finally, the test data are given for testing the results of the above algorithms. The performance is evaluated with some statistical metrics like accuracy, precision, recall, and ROC-AUC. The methodology adopted is summarized in Fig. 4.

Logistic Regression: Regression methods have become an integral component of any data analysis concerned with describing the relationship between a response variable and one or more explanatory variables [28]. Consider the logistic regression of the data points (x_i, y_i) here the x is the set of features like BMI, gender, ethnicity,

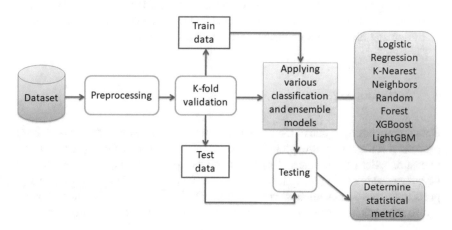

Fig. 4 Flowchart of the methodology

and others where output y is binary outcome diabetic or not. The logistic regression models assign a probability between 0 and 1 for the given input x.

$$\frac{1}{1 + e^{-(WX+b)}} \tag{3}$$

Also referred as sigmoid function $\sigma(x)$ as it takes real value and maps to range [0, 1].

Random Forest: The random forest is set of many decision trees. Model chooses the best tree among all the possible decision trees. The converged forest contains B^* number of trees for predicting diabetes and $\gamma^*(\tau)$ denote the weight of tree τ in the converged forest. If $p^*_{(\tau)}(c)$ denotes the probability of class label, predicted by tree τ for the input test data, then the actual class label (c^*) for the input test data is given for every tree by equation. The result is a tree with maximum class label, i.e., diabetic or non-diabetic.

$$c^* = \text{argmax}_c \sum_{\tau=1}^{B^*} \text{gamma}(\tau) \, P^*\tau(c) \tag{4}$$

KNN: K-nearest neighbors are a non-parametric classification algorithm which is used to classify the diabetic dataset into diabetic class and non-diabetic. Classifies new case labels based on a similarity measure like manhattan distance, Euclidean distance, and many other are available. K is the number of neighbors, based on K-value the classification is done.

XGBoost: (eXtreme Gradient Boosting) is one of the best classifiers in machine learning that uses a gradient boosting framework for its better performance and computing speed. It is an ensemble technique where new models are added to increase its performance. The diabetic dataset is an unbalanced one; we can optimize using gradient boosting algorithm by tree pruning, regularization, parallel processing, and handling missing values to overcome overfitting of data.

LightGBM: Light Ggadient boosting machine is a gradient boosting algorithm that used tree-based learning. It includes gradient boosting decision tree (GBDT) or gradient-based one-sided sampling (GOSS) which are used for prediction. GBDT—forms a strong classifier model from various weak classifiers to increase the performance of the model. GOSS—will avoid the significant portion of the data part which has small gradients and only use the remaining data to estimate the overall information gain. This section discusses in detail each of the steps mentioned in Fig. 1.

5 Results

The work checks five classification techniques for diabetes mellitus. All the classifiers are trained and tested, and recorded results are presented in Table 3. To find out which classifier performs well on this kind of noisy dataset, a comparison among all the 5 classifiers is made. To compare the classifiers, five evaluation metrics were adopted. They are area under the curve—receiver operating characteristics (AUC-ROC), accuracy, precision, recall, and F1-score. These metrics are calculated using the below equations. The ROC is a probability that plots TPR and FPR at various threshold values, and AUC is the measure of the ability to distinguish between the classes.

$$\text{Accuracy} = \frac{\text{TP} + \text{TN}}{\text{TP} + \text{TN} + \text{FN} + \text{FP}}$$

$$\text{Precision} = \frac{\text{TP}}{\text{TP} + \text{FP}}$$

$$\text{Sensitivity} = \text{Recall} = \text{True positive rate} = \frac{\text{TP}}{\text{TP} + \text{FN}}$$

$$\text{Specificity} = \text{False positive rate} = \frac{\text{TN}}{\text{TN} + \text{FP}}$$

$$F\text{1-Score} = \frac{2 * (\text{Precision} * \text{Sensitivity})}{\text{Precision} + \text{Sensitivity}}$$

From the table, it is evident that accuracy, precision, recall and F1-score are above 82% for XGBoost and LightGBM methods, and ROC-AUC is 83% for random Forest. Logistic regression and KNN classifers have obtained smaller values for the metrics. The ensembling methods like XGBoost and LightGBM are performing well on the dataset with more columns and more missing values. One can adopt ensembling methods for this kind of prediction tasks.

Table 3 Comparsion of performance

Algorithm	Accuracy	ROC	Precision	Recall	F1-score
Logistic regression	0.780	0.649	0.70	0.78	0.69
K-nearest neighbors	0.530	0.530	0.73	0.78	0.72
Random forest	0.780	0.831	0.70	0.78	0.69
XGBoost	0.834	0.704	0.82	0.83	0.82
LightGBM	0.838	0.708	0.83	0.84	0.83

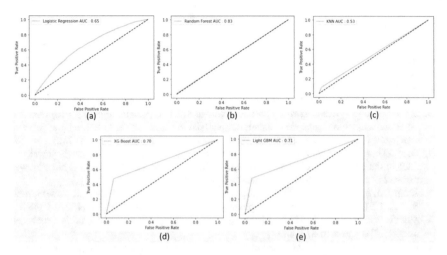

Fig. 5 AUC-ROC curves **a** logistic regression, **b** random forest, **c** KNN, **d** XGBoost, **e** LightGBM

Figure 5 represents the AUC curves of all the five models. The higher the AUC, the better the model is at distinguishing between patients with diabetic complaint or no complaint. Among all the figures, It is very clear that random forest has good AUC and distinguishes well between the classes.

6 Conclusion and Future Work

This work describes how diabetes mellitus prediction for ICU admitted patients as part WiDS competition is solved based on the data available on previous records of the patients and the laboratory test reports obtained in the past 24 h. The supplied data were high dimensional, unbalanced, and with a lot of missing values. A winning solution which gains 83% accuracy was obtained by doing rigorous exploratory data analysis, preprocessing, and training several models. The accuracy of the classification models like logistic regression, random forest, KNN, XGBoost, and LightGBM was computed and compared. The ensemble methods like XGBoost and LightGBM are performing well for the dataset. The classification methods adopted to solve this challenge are classical machine learning algorithms. This work can be extended by training neural network models on this as neural networks are also proving good in handling tabular data.

References

1. American Diabetes Association (2014) Diagnosis and classification of diabetes mellitus. Diabetes Care 37(Supplement 1):S81–S90
2. Anand RS et al (2018) Predicting mortality in diabetic ICU patients using machine learning and severity indices. In: AMIA summits on translational science proceedings 2018, p 310
3. Sarwar N, Gao P, Seshasai SR, Gobin R, Kaptoge S, Di Angelantonio et al (2010) Diabetes mellitus, fasting blood glucose concentration, and risk of vascular disease: a collaborative meta-analysis of 102 prospective studies. Emerging risk factors collaboration. Lancet 375:2215–2222
4. Over 30 million have now been diagnosed with diabetes in India. The CPR (crude prevalence rate) in the urban areas of India is thought to be 9 per cent (2021) Diabetes. https://www.diabetes.co.uk/global-diabetes/diabetes-in-india.html
5. Alam TM, Iqbal MA, Ali Y, Wahab A, Ijaz S, Baig TI, Hussain A, Malik MA, Raza MM, Ibrar S, Abbas Z (2019) A model for early prediction of diabetes. 16:100204. ISSN 2352-9148
6. Sun YL, Zhang DL (2019) Machine learning techniques for screening and diagnosis of diabetes: a survey. Teh Vjesn 26:872–880
7. Roncon L et al (2020) Diabetic patients with COVID-19 infection are at higher risk of ICU admission and poor short-term outcome. J Clin Virol 127:104354
8. Dhatariya K, Corsino L, Umpierrez GE (2000) Management of diabetes and hyperglycemia in hospitalized patients. Updated 30 Dec 2020. In: Feingold KR, Anawalt B, Boyce A et al (eds) Endotext [Internet]. MDText.com, Inc., South Dartmouth (MA). Available from: https://www.ncbi.nlm.nih.gov/books/NBK279093/
9. Mujumdar A, Vaidehi V (2019) Diabetes prediction using machine learning algorithms. Procedia Comput Sci 165:292–299. ISSN 1877-0509
10. Chen T, Guestrin C (2016) XGBoost: a scalable tree boosting system. In: Proceedings of the 22nd ACM SIGKDD international conference on knowledge discovery and data mining
11. Ogunleye A, Wang Q-G (2020) XGBoost model for chronic kidney disease diagnosis. IEEE/ACM Trans Comput Biol Bioinform 17(6):2131–2140. https://doi.org/10.1109/TCBB.2019.2911071
12. Ke G et al (2017) LightGBM: a highly efficient gradient boosting decision tree. Adv Neural Inf Process Syst 30:3146–3154
13. Rufo DD et al (2021) Diagnosis of diabetes mellitus using gradient boosting machine (LightGBM). Diagnostics 11(9):1714
14. Lee BJ, Kim JY (2016) Identification of type 2 diabetes risk factors using phenotypes consisting of anthropometry and triglycerides based on machine learning. IEEE J Biomed Health Inform 20:39–46. https://doi.org/10.1109/JBHI.2015.2396520
15. Kavakiotis I, Tsave O, Salifoglou A, Maglaveras N, Vlahavas I, Chouvarda I (2017) Machine learning and data mining methods in diabetes research. Comput Struct Biotechnol J 15:104–116. https://doi.org/10.1016/j.csbj.2016.12.005
16. Wu H, Yang S, Huang Z, He J, Wang X (2018) Type 2 diabetes mellitus prediction model based on data mining. Inform Med Unlocked 10:100–107
17. Azrar A, Ali Y, Awais M, Zaheer K (2018) Data mining models comparison for diabetes prediction. Int J Adv Comput Sci Appl 9
18. Perveen S, Shahbaz M, Guergachi A, Keshavjee K (2016) Performance analysis of data mining classification techniques to predict diabetes. Proc Comput Sci 82:115–121
19. Kandhasamy JP, Balamurali SJPCS (2015) Performance analysis of classifier models to predict diabetes mellitus. Procedia Comput Sci 47:45–51
20. Viloria A et al (2020) Diabetes diagnostic prediction using vector support machines. Procedia Comput Sci 170:376–381
21. Harz HH et al (2020) Artificial neural network for predicting diabetes using JNN. Int J Acad Eng Res (IJAER) 4(10)
22. Tigga NP, Garg S (2020) Prediction of type 2 diabetes using machine learning classification methods. Procedia Comput Sci 167:706–716

23. Naz H, Ahuja S (2020) Deep learning approach for diabetes prediction using PIMA Indian dataset. J Diab Metab Disord 19(1):391–403
24. Maniruzzaman M et al (2020) Classification and prediction of diabetes disease using machine learning paradigm. Health Inf Sci Syst 8(1):1–14
25. Hasan MK et al (2020) Diabetes prediction using ensembling of different machine learning classifiers. IEEE Access 8:76516–76531
26. Bezanson J et al (2017) Julia: a fresh approach to numerical computing. SIAM Rev 59(1):65–98
27. Gao K et al (2020) Julia language in machine learning: algorithms, applications, and open issues. Comput Sci Rev 37:100254
28. Zou X et al (2019) Logistic regression model optimization and case analysis. In: 2019 IEEE 7th international conference on computer science and network technology (ICCSNT). IEEE
29. Biau G (2012) Analysis of a random forests model. J Mach Learn Res 13(1):1063–1095

A Robust Secure Access Entrance Method Based on Multi Model Biometric Credentials Iris and Finger Print

Pranay Yadav, Nishant Chaurasia, Kamal Kumar Gola,
Vijay Bhasker Semwan, Rakesh Gomasta, and Shivendra Dubey

1 Introduction

Biometric technology are becoming more relevant in today's world for securing access to several locations. Among the many domains where biometrics have extensive are using are network login sharing, digital data security, e-commerce, Internet access, ATM or credit card usage, physically security systems, personal phone and passports and identification of corpses in criminal investigations. Biometric data could be used in conjunction with Identity cards but also passwords to provide an extra layer of protection in specific situations. Pattern recognition underpins any biometric system; it takes biometric information from a person, derives a key selection of characteristics from the input, then compares that set against a templates set of

P. Yadav
Department of Research and Development, Ultra Light Technology (ULT), Bhopal, Madhya
Pradesh 462023, India

N. Chaurasia
Department of Computer Science and Engineering, S V Polytechnic College, Bhopal, Madhya
Pradesh 462002, India

K. K. Gola (✉)
Department of Computer Science and Engineering, College of Engineering Roorkee (COER),
Roorkee, Uttarakhand 247667, India
e-mail: kkgolaa1503@gmail.com

V. B. Semwan
Department of CSE, MANIT, Bhopal, Madhya Pradesh, India

R. Gomasta
Department of Research and Development, Navigator Technologies, Bhopal, Madhya Pradesh,
India

S. Dubey
Senior IT Faculty, iNurture Education Solution Pvt. Ltd, Bangalore, Karnataka 560052, India

© The Author(s), under exclusive license to Springer Nature Singapore Pte Ltd. 2023   315
R. Doriya et al. (eds.), *Machine Learning, Image Processing, Network Security and Data
Sciences*, Lecture Notes in Electrical Engineering 946,
https://doi.org/10.1007/978-981-19-5868-7_24

features in the database [1]. In the last decade there are many researchers are working in this area in Himanshu Purohit et.al presented a features fusion-based multi modal secure human authentication method modified region growing algorithm for features extraction and optimal feature level fusion gray wolf optimization for classification of features. This presented method shows accuracy of 91.6% [2]. Teena Joseph et.al. presented a multi model-based biometric authentication system for enhancement of cloud security, in which used three different biometric credentials finger print, palm and iris after that apply XOR between features then implement MD5 hashing algorithm for data encryption. The accuracy of presented work is 94.54% [3]. Sakthi Prabha presented a single model based automatic access control system based on finger print biometric system. For features extraction used a wavelet transform algorithm. The presented system is convenient to the users in banking sector. The testing of system is made by criteria finger print biometric vascular biometrics interfacing PIC16F877A with RF module [4]. Elhoseny et al. presented a multi model based biometric system for personal identification. In this presented method use iris as well as fingerprint as a biometric credentials. This presented work accuracy is 99.86% [5]. Yadav et al. presented a multi model-based biometric system in which used three biometric credentials, fingerprint, palm print and iris. For the combination of the features use matching score fusion method. The result of presented method obtained is 95.23% in multi model in case unimodel fingerprint, palm print and iris, obtained is 72.73, 65.57, and 80% [6]. In this similar way most of the researchers are used unimodel as well as multi model biometric system for secure physical access system. But now a day multi model based biometric credentials system is successful as compare to unimodel system due to indomitable cyber-attacks. There are many attacks first one involves presenting a fake biometric, second one is feature extractor module replaced with a Trojan horse program that functions according to its designer's specifications [7].

In the next section discuss the different type of biometric system as well as different recognition techniques. Section 3 discuss the proposed method. Simulation of proposed method and results of proposed method discuss in Sect. 4. In Sect. 5 nut shall of this research article.

2 Type of Biometric System

In this section discuss the different type of biometric system. There are two type of single model biometric system and multi model biometric fusion system.

2.1 Single Modal Bio System

Single biometrics feature (physiological or behavioral characteristic) is used in the single modal biometrics for identify individuals. Fingerprints, biometric traits, eye

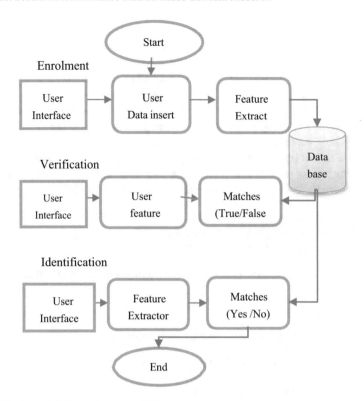

Fig.1 Single modal biometric system [10]

patterns, ear styles, face expressions, and other biometric traits identifiers are examples of physiological biometric identifiers. Voice, signature, writing habits, and other behavioral indicators serve as behavioral identifiers. While recognize a person's characteristics, the system should be able to tell whether someone is authentic or if they are a fraud [8].

Single modal biometric systems need to cope with variety of issues like noisy information, intra-class variations, non-universality, spoof attacks, restricted degrees of freedom and into liable fault degrees. A numeral of these inadequacies is shown by organizing multi modal biometric schemes that combinations resistant conferred by multiple sources of bio information of data base [9] (Fig. 1).

2.2 Multi Modal Biometric System

There are many drawbacks to biometrics systems that employ always one sense. These drawbacks include inaccurate sensor readings, non-universality, and/or a lack of distinctiveness in the biometric feature. The accuracy of the system may be improved by taking into account various qualities based on different scores [11]. Fusion at the feature extraction level, matching score level, or decision level is feasible in a multi-biometric approach using distinct biometric attributes. Consolidating feature level fusion is problematic because distinct modalities may employ selected features that are unavailable or incompatible [12]. Because of the limited quantity of information accessible at this level, fusion is too stiff at the decision-making level. Integrating matching scores is thus recommended owing to the simplicity with which matching scores can be accessed. An detailed data fusion would be divided into three sections: pre-mapping fusion; middle-mapping fusion; and late fusion in pre-mapping fusion; sensors as well as uniqueness level fusion in pre-mapping fusion [13]. There are three main types of sensor-level combination [14] (Fig. 2):

(1) A single sensor with several instances,
(2) A large number of sensors within a class,
(3) A variety of sensors between classes.

Gimmick level combination can be predominantly sorted out in two classes:

(1) Intra-class
(2) Between class.

Intra-class is again grouped into four subcategories:

(a) Same sensor-same gimmicks,
(b) Same sensor-distinctive peculiarities,
(c) Different sensors-same gimmicks,

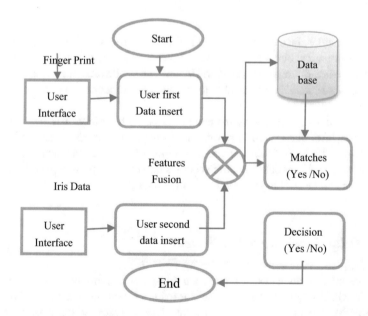

Fig. 2 Multi modal biometric system [15]

(d)   Different sensors-diverse peculiarities [8].

2.3   *Fingerprint Recognition*

Each unique finger impression of every individual is thought to be one of a kind, even the Twins additionally have diverse unique mark. Unique mark acknowledgment is the most acknowledged biometric acknowledgment prepare. Fingerprints have been utilized from long time for recognizing people. Fingerprints comprise of edges and wrinkles on the surface of a unique mark [16]. Fingerprints are characterized into six groups: (a) curve, (b) core, (c) right circle, (d) left loop, (e) delta and (f) twin circle as appeared in taking after Fig. 3 [17].

A run of the mill unique finger impression acknowledgment framework having distinctive stride which comprise of an examining gadget, a component extraction part, and an examination part where a distinguishing proof confirmation result is taken. In Fig. 4 represent the working if finger print recognition system.

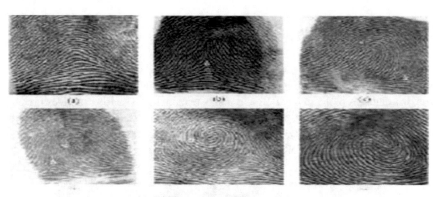

(a) Different type of Finger print

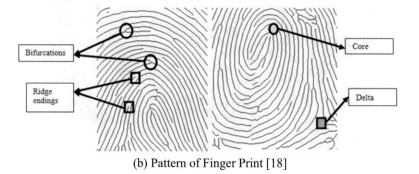

(b) Pattern of Finger Print [18]

Fig. 3   Different patterns of fingerprints [17]

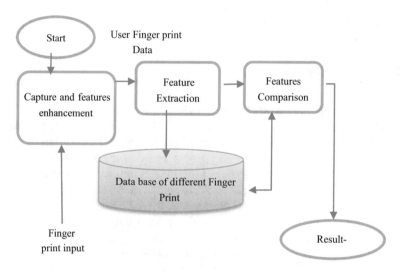

Fig. 4 Working of fingerprint recognition system [17]

2.4 Iris Recognition

The iris is the hued ring around the understudy of each individual and like a snowflake, no two are the same. Everyone is extraordinary iris. Figure 5 indicates what is mean by iris. Iris cameras perform location of a man's personality. The iris examines prepare begin to get something on film. It joins PC vision, measurable surmising, design acknowledgment and optics. The iris is the hued ring around the understudy of each person and like a snow flake; everyone is exceptional [17, 19].

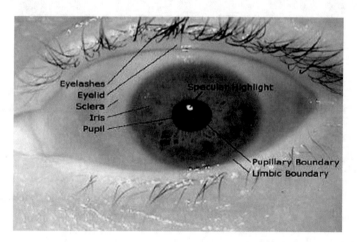

Fig. 5 Information about eye [17]

3   Proposed Method

The proposed multi model biometric system is design to improve the biometric-based security system enhancements. The proposed system is used to detect the unauthentic access of fake persons. Secure access is the common problem in the protected places. For improve the security system multi model biometric system play an important role, first create the data base of the persons present in secured of both biometric finger print as well as iris. In the proposed work calculate the matching percentage of biometric properties from one person to other person. For the calculation of accuracy required both data training and testing data sets. In the first part of proposed method create training data set and in the second part apply image processing for authentic access and unauthentic access. Process shown in steps.

3.1   Training and Data Set Creation

Figure 6 shows the flow chart of steps data set creation and feature excretion of different user biometric information also the take some unauthentic persons for checking the false detection.

Steps of training data set creation.

Step 1—First collect the different user finger print biometric and iris images biometric which contain different properties.

Step 2—Apply feature execration techniques of these biometric information of different user and create a training data set.

3.2   Biometric Finger Print and Iris Matching Proposed Algorithm

Step 1—Query Image Selection:

First select the biometric information in the form of image from different data sets of users. The data set is the combination of the different type of biometric finger print images.

Step 2—Calculate the Minutiae of the query image. After that selection of image, apply this image into the preprocessing block (Fig. 7).

Figure 8 shows the thinned image, for the thinned image calculate the binary image of the query image used by morphology processing functions.

Step 3—Algorithm the Iris Matching

First Load testing image—Click on the load image then open this window for selected the iris print. Click on testing image and further proceed on the image (Figs. 9 and 10).

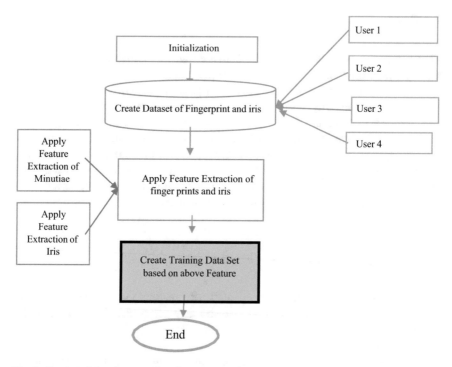

Fig. 6 Create training data set using feature extraction

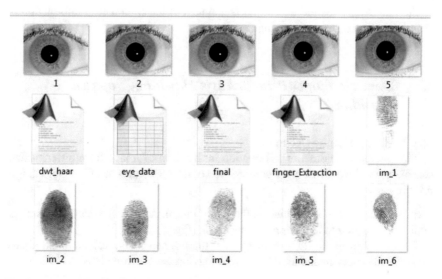

Fig. 7 Select of biometric-based finger print from the different users

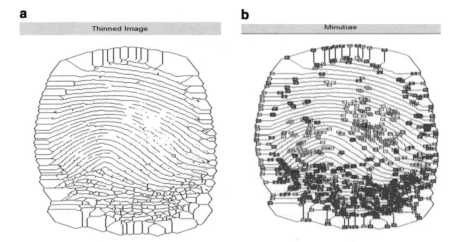

Fig. 8 **a** and **b** Shows the minutiae of the query image

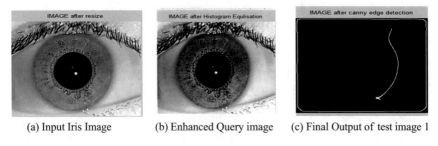

(a) Input Iris Image   (b) Enhanced Query image   (c) Final Output of test image 1

Fig. 9 Output of the test image for iris recognition

Algorithm for authentic person data base creation
Begin.

1. For n = 1: Number of person
      Binary form of the image. // im2bw (input image)
2. Apply Morphological Operation//(binary image, 'thin',Inf);
3. Now search the ridge end finding of the thin image
      //[ridge_xridge_y] =find (ridge==2); Fig. 8b
4. after that find out the bifurcation finding—[Bifurcation x bifurcation y] = find (bifurcation = 4);
      len=length(bifurcation_x);
5. Store the Minutiae of image of memory. Create data file
6. Desire = bifurcation; //Figure print data set creation process
7. **Iris Data set creation** // collection iris image from sensor
8. Apply prepossessing re-sizing & gray conversion
9. Apply DWT Harr Transform // Inbuilt Lib. Dwt_harr

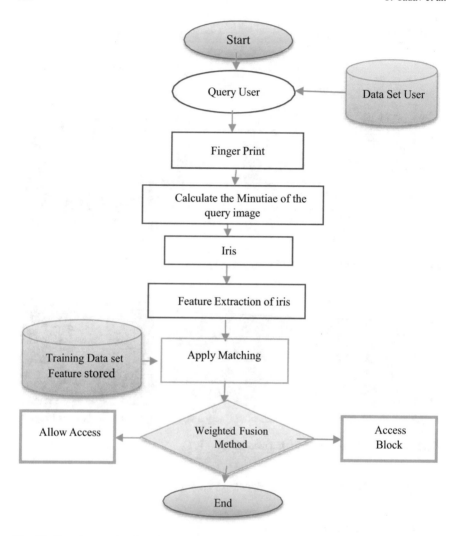

Fig. 10 Complete process flow chart

10. Apply Histogram of High Low outcome of DWT
11. Apply Gaussian filtering for noise filter
12. Apply Edge Detection Gaussian filter iris image
13. Obtain Edge information of iris image
14. Final obtain a numeric value of edge and also the edge data of iris.
15. End // Apply same process for all input data and create data base of authentic persons

Algorithm for authentic person matching and mismatching from created data base, Begin.

1. Load Record // server connected data base
2. Person enter fingerprint sensor send data for server
3. Calculate Minutiae and bifurcation
4. Apply Query for Search Matching Minutiae
5. If (input Minutiae == Minutiae match in server database)
6. Display ('fingerprint matched with person ...')
7. Else ('fingerprint mismatched with person try again')
8. Process again two try left
9. If (input person == finger print matched successfully)
10. Apply iris matching → input person iris sensor data collection send to database.// Load iris data
11. Apply iris features calculation == Match with input iris
12. If (iris accuracy (input) > 95)
13. Apply Weighted features Fusion (Iris & fingerprint match)
14. Message display ('Welcome', 'OK'). // Entrance Open
15. Else message display ('iris not matched with finger print ', 'Fraud', 'error') End

4 Simulation and Result

For the simulation of the proposed method use a matrix laboratory (MATlab) software platform. The result of proposed method for different dataset images of iris and finger print detection in different data sets [17, 20] by using images processing shown in this section. The performance of the proposed algorithm is tested for data set Sokoto-Coventry-finger print-dataset that is shown in Fig. 11. Basic configuration of our system is: Processor: Intel (R) Quad Core (VM) i5–3110 Central Processing unit @, 2.40 GHz with 4GB RAM: System type: 64-bit Operating System. MATLAB-based simulation result shows good result of matching iris and finger print matching.

(a)   (b)   (c)   (d)   (e)   (f)

Fig. 11 Fingerprint data set [17]

Result Parameters

There are different result parameters in finger print matching and iris detection like percentage of matching with other person. Therefor correct person identifications the major task of the proposed work. Second result parameter is affected regions matching from different person and the last one is accuracy for that perform features matching between different iris images with the help of features matching.

Classification

The major task of proposed work is separate by machine learning the iris [20] and fingerprint [17] recognition and classification method by using image processing and soft computing techniques.

Accuracy

Multi model bio matrix system is the tedious task for researchers. Finger Print Region Matching detection a detected is a true positive (TP) whereas a real negative (TN) is a unmatched detection of the person detected.

$$Accuracy = \frac{(TP + TN)}{S} \tag{1}$$

Data Sets

There are different deceases data set available for the finger print as well as iris detection. Finger Print Data Set [17] and Iris deceases data set [20].

In Fig. 11 shows the different imagers finger print data set images. In Fig. 11 shows only six image of this finger prints.

In Fig. 12 shows the iris data set.

Matching of finger and iris

Step 1—Enter User Bio matrix information—For show the result analysis of the multi modal bio matrix system. First select the any one bio matrix information that is finger print (Figs. 13, 14, 15 and 16).

Apply matching from data set.

As Table 1 clearly that the both data are matching with 100% with user three it means that access allow for user 3 (Fig. 17).

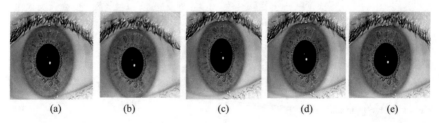

(a)   (b)   (c)   (d)   (e)

Fig. 12 Iris data set [20]

Fig. 13 Select the finger print bio matrix information

Fig. 14 Select 3rd user
finger print

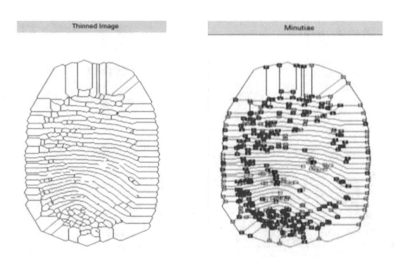

Fig. 15 Thinned image and minutiae of the user 3 finger

Case 2 When the Bio Matrix Not Matched the User (Figs. 18 and 19):

1. User 2 Finger print of user 2

2. User 3 Iris print of user 2

   Finger print matched with User—2
   Iris Matched accuracy = 11.92 22.44 **100.00** 14.11 14.69
   Here the iris matched with the user 3 and finger print of user 2 that why access in deny (Table 2).

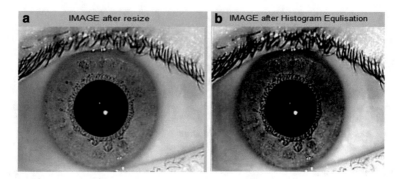

Fig. 16 **a** Taking of iris of user **b** histogram of the iris

Table 1 Matching percent of iris and finger print form different user

U-1	U-2	U-3	U-4	U-5
11.9263	22.4426	100.000	14.1174	14.6973

Fig. 17 User both biometric credentials iris and finger print successful matched using weighted features fusion method

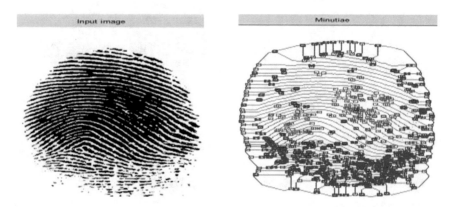

Fig. 18 Shows the biometric fingerprint of user 2

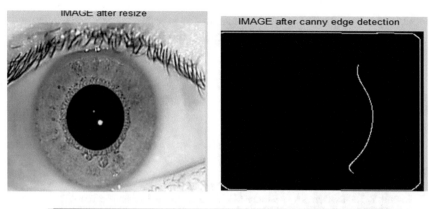

Fig. 19 Mismatched of biometric credentials iris and finger print

Table 2 Discuss result comparison of proposed method with previous method

References/year	Model	Biometric credential	Algorithm	Result parameter
Proposed/[2021]	Multi model	Finger print and iris	Fingerprint features minutiae of image and iris DWT high low canny edge, weighted fusion features	Accuracy = 96.89%

5 Conclusion

There would be a multi model identification of the person in this research, which was provided. In order to address the drawbacks of single model biometrics, we created a multi-biometric system. The accuracy of the fingerprint and iris biometric systems used here is greater than that of the other two. The suggested method has a 96.4% accuracy rate. According to the system's design, it creates a fusion at the matching score level as quickly as possible. For each of the three different characteristics, a score is given. These numbers reflect how similar the features are to one another. In order to merge the results, the weighted fusion method is used. According to the findings, a multi modal system is more exact than a single modal system. Also, talk about why a multi model system is necessary to improve the existing single model system. Also, in multi model system, compare the many multi model systems that have been implemented over the previous decade.

References

1. Xu Y, Fei L, Zhang D (2015) Combining left and right palmprint images for more accurate personal identification. IEEE Trans Image Process 24(2)
2. Purohit H, Ajmera PK (2021) Optimal feature level fusion for secured hu man authentication in multimodal biometric system. Mach Vis Appl 32(1):1–12
3. Joseph T, Kalaiselvan SA, Aswathy SU, Radhakrishnan R, Shamna AR (2020) A multi-modal biometric authentication scheme based on feature fusion for improving security in cloud environment. J Ambient Intell Humanized Comput 1–9
4. Sakthi Prabha R (2019) Automatic physical access control system based on biometric identification by wavelet transform algorithm. Int J Recent Technol Eng (IJRTE) 7(6):659–673
5. Elhoseny M, Elkhateb A, Sahlol A, Hassanien AE (2018) Multi-modal biometric personal identification and verification. In: Advances in soft computing and machine learning in image processing. Springer, Cham, pp 249–276
6. Yadav P, Sharma S, Tiwari P, Dey N, Ashour AS, and Gia Nhu N (2018) A modified hybrid structure for next generation super high speed communication using TDLTE and Wi-Max. In: Internet of things and big data analytics toward next-generation intelligence. Springer, Cham, pp 525–549
7. Patil AP, Bhalke DG (2016) Fusion of fingerprint, palmprint and iris for person identification. In: International conference on automatic control and dynamic optimization techniques (ICACDOT). IEEE
8. Zhang D, Kong W-K, You J, Wong M (2003) Online palmprint identification. IEEE Trans Pattern Anal Mach Intell 25(9)
9. Aggarwal A, Verma MK (2016) Multimodal biometric systems—a survey. Int J Adv Res Comput Sci Softw Eng 6(3)
10. Li X, Miao C, Liu T, Yuan C (2011) Theoretical analysis and experimental study on multimodal biometric. IEEE
11. Sumalatha KA, Harsha H (2014) Biometric palmprint recognition system—a review. Int J Adv Res Comput Sci Softw Eng 4(1)
12. Usharani V, Saravanan SV (2014) Multi modal biometrics using palmprint and palmvein. J Theor Appl Inf Technol 67(1)
13. Zheng S, Shi W-Z, Liu J, Zhu G-X, Tian J-W (2007) Multisource image fusion method using support value transform. IEEE Trans Image Process 16(7)
14. Iwasokun GB, Akinyokun OC (2014) Fingerprint singular point detection based on modified Poincare index method. Int J Sign Process Image Process Pattern Recogn 7(5):259–272
15. Gupta A, Malage A, More D (2014) Feature level fusion of face, palm vein and palm print modalities using discrete cosine transform. In: IEEE international conference on advances in engineering & technology research (ICAETR—2014)
16. Karthikeyan T, Sumathi TK (2015) Implementation of biometric personal identification based on normalized approach of fusion technique. Int J Adv Inf Arts Sci Manage (IJAIASM) 4(8)
17. https://pureportal.coventry.ac.uk/en/publications/sokoto-coventry-fingerprint-dataset
18. Sharma S, Yadav P (2014) Removal of fixed valued impulse noise by improved trimmed mean median filter. In: 2014 IEEE international conference on computational intelligence and computing research. IEEE, pp 1–8

19. Paithane AN, Bormane DS, Patil U (2016) Novel algorithm for feature extraction and feature selection from electrocardiogram signal. Int J Comput Appl 134(9):6–9
20. https://www4.comp.polyu.edu.hk/~csajaykr/IITD/Database_Iris.htm 21 Nov 2016

Region Classification for Air Quality Estimation Using Deep Learning and Machine Learning Approach

Sumneet Kaur Bamrah, Shruti Srivatsan, and K. S. Gayathri

1 Introduction

Air comprises a mixture of gases. Clean, dry air consists primarily of 78% N_2 and 21% O_2 by volume. The remaining 1% is a mixture of other gases, mostly Ar (0.9%), along with trace amounts of CO_2, CH_4, H_2, He and more. Impure air comprises higher levels of chemical pollutants which harm the environment and its beings [1]. In order to detect the quality of air and classify it, a numerical value is used which is known as air quality index (AQI). It ranges between 0 and 500 and has 6 categories associated with it.

There are multiple factors which cause pollution and affect the quality of air [2]. It is important to closely monitor, identify the sources of the major pollutants so that control measures can be drawn accordingly. The six major air pollutants are CO, NOx, SO_2, O_3, PM, Pb, also known as criteria pollutants. Table 1 highlights the direct impacts of such harmful pollutants on the health of individuals. The Environmental Protection Agency (EPA) designates permissible limits and has set acceptable concentrations of such pollutants. These values are essential to compute the AQI.

In order to collect samples of such data, it is crucial to identify the sources of the criteria pollutants. Industrial and vehicular emissions are a superior contributor to air

S. K. Bamrah (✉) · S. Srivatsan
Department of Computer Science and Engineering, Sri Venkateswara College of Engineering, Sriperumbudur, Tamil Nadu, India
e-mail: sumneetbamrah@gmail.com

S. Srivatsan
e-mail: shrutisrisvce@gmail.com

K. S. Gayathri
Department of Information Technology, Sri Sivasubramaniya Nadar College of Engineering, Kalavakkam, Tamil Nadu, India
e-mail: gayathriks@ssn.edu.in

© The Author(s), under exclusive license to Springer Nature Singapore Pte Ltd. 2023
R. Doriya et al. (eds.), *Machine Learning, Image Processing, Network Security and Data Sciences*, Lecture Notes in Electrical Engineering 946,
https://doi.org/10.1007/978-981-19-5868-7_25

Table 1 Criteria pollutants and their effects on health

Pollutant	Health impact
CO	Cause chest problems, hamper vision, reduce mental and physical capabilities
NOx, O_3	Affects lung functions, cause inflammation and irritation in breathing passages
NO_2	Causes pulmonary oedema
SO_2	Causes asthma diseases, eye and throat irritation
PM	Causes breathing difficulties
Pb	Causes learning disabilities, seizures

pollution in cities. Rural regions rely on traditional mechanisms for cooking which are accountable as well [3]. Air quality stations are widely installed in urban regions that readily capture the critical values on a timely basis whereas rural regions do not have the same facility available. It becomes challenging to estimate the quality of air in smaller cities, towns and regions farther.

Identification of the sources of pollution is a wide field in itself. Climate and geography are underlying factors which contribute to air pollution and affect the overall quality of air [4]. The movement of air impacts and influences air pollutants. Temperature, wind patterns, cloudiness, humidity, precipitation, wildfires, wind-blown dust and emissions from vegetation associated with air pollution are widely explored in scientific studies.

Characteristics of a region also play a major role in air pollution. Areas surrounded by forests, wetlands and mountains show different patterns in air quality monitoring since the quality of air is better in comparison to a crowded city, urban area. Forests carry important functions that enhance the air quality. They prevent pollution of areas by absorbing toxic materials and slowing down air movements. Greenhouse gases such as CO_2 are emitted less into the atmosphere. Plains that have hollow terrain structure have an area that blocks airflow. This causes a rise in air pollution levels during the winter months. Mountainous terrain is subject to influence the quality of air as well.

Urban and rural regions have unique air quality patterns. Distinct factors are taken into consideration whilst evaluating the levels of pollution. It is pertinent to be able to understand the relevant features of each region whilst estimating the air quality levels. Pollution control is keen on capturing the status of ambient air and its quality in both urban and rural regions. Consistent and persistent efforts are taken by the authorities at varied levels to address the issue. There are different methods to capture and monitor air quality data in urban and rural regions that include governmental monitoring stations, satellites and low-cost sensors [5–7].

Experts capture the essential data and further analyse the same. Scientists understand how the air pollutants disperse and chemically react in the atmosphere. They use complex techniques to simulate the processes and build air quality models. This information is further extended for air quality management strategies by officials. Newer and sophisticated methods are being developed and adapted. Deep learning techniques are applied to locate the sources of pollution, detect areas of high pollution levels and predict future pollutant concentrations. It offers the benefit of feature extraction and transformation.

Air pollution and its management is based on numerous factors. Most regions are monitored using the available resources by the concerned authorities. Greater number of air quality monitoring stations are installed and maintained in urban regions in comparison to rural regions leading to overall scarcity of labelled data [1, 8]. Satellite images are used as an additional resource to capture essential details of pollutants, climate and geography of the various regions. Expert and domain knowledge is required to analyse the different and unique forms of data. Machine and deep learning are primarily used to identify the pollutant sources, distinguish between urban and rural regions in order to estimate the air quality. Policy-makers require a holistic approach in order to take decisions for the overall management of air pollution.

It is challenging to have a standardised system that is able to detect air quality and pollution levels at all times. There are practical and technical limitations involved whilst capturing essential information. Experts rely on different techniques to observe, monitor and apply the relevant information. The objective of this study is to use different models for classification of regions. Urban and rural regions have their individual characteristic features involved whilst estimating the air quality. It is pertinent to be able to clearly classify the regions and further understand the local features that cause air pollution in the respective region. Standard deep learning techniques have been applied for the primary task of classification of the regions. A machine learning model is used on related pollutant and meteorological data to estimate the AQI for urban and rural regions.

Section 2 focusses on existing studies performed for air quality management and air quality estimation. In Sect. 3, the proposed work is introduced showcasing the application of deep learning for region classification. The experimental setup is briefed in Sect. 4 discussing the modules used and their performances. Conclusion and future work is presented in Sect. 5.

2 Literature Review

Air pollution levels and AQI patterns vary based on the region whilst considering the relevant geographical and terrain features. The quality of air is distinct in urban and rural regions [9, 10]. Most studies focus on urban regions [5, 11]. There are several challenges in compilation and analysis of urban data for fine-grained areas [6]. Climate directly and indirectly influences the levels of pollution and quality of air [12]. Important pollutant and meteorological data are captured by air quality monitoring machines. Urban regions capture the essential information more effectively in comparison to rural regions as the number of monitoring stations are limited geographically [13]. Semi-supervised learning is a preferred approach. A large variety of features are considered whilst estimating the quality of air and to determine the core issues of air pollution [5].

Researchers utilise sensors as an alternative. Low-cost sensors are used to monitor pollution and meteorological data on smaller scales in rural regions. Sophisticated air quality monitoring systems devices are built at mid-levels to assist in air pollution monitoring and control [7]. With the constant rising levels of pollution in urban cities, it is not uncommon for people to rely on customised air purifier systems available.

Air quality models are built after careful assessment by experts and scientists. Some of the modelling techniques are receptor modelling, source apportionment, dispersion modelling [14]. This process enables policy-makers to understand the distribution of the various pollutants and their sources. Air pollution levels are indicated by AQIs. The generation of AQI is a complex process. There have been studies performed in India for the same.

Machine and deep learning techniques are applied and implemented to build air quality models and indicate pollution levels [9, 13].

AQI prediction is performed using different machine learning algorithms in [10]. Satellite images are being used to capture more detailed pollutant, meteorological and geographical features for air pollution analysis. OpenStreetMaps have a wide scope of applications whilst evaluating and analysing terrain features. Relevant images and data have been used in air quality management.

From the existing works, it can be identified that air pollution levels are predicted more frequently in urban regions. The availability of data is manageable whilst performing suitable experiments for the same [15]. It becomes even more challenging to capture data for rural regions which are required to estimate the air quality. Machine learning and deep learning offer their individual advantages whilst performing the estimation analysis [16]. In the studies performed, pollutant and meteorological data were widely considered. Air pollution levels are impacted by geography, whether the region is urban or rural.

Air quality and its management has largely been focussed on urban regions. The trend is shifting. There have been points of identification through expert studies that rural regions also contribute to the overall air pollution [17]. It is of utmost importance to clearly distinguish the regions and then further investigate the sources of pollution in the respective zones. In India, a National Air Quality Index is generated by the Central Pollution Control Board. The air pollution levels of different regions of the major cities are disseminated to the public. The information is represented by the corresponding AQI values computed. Being able to analyse the relevant data resourcefully requires innovative solutions [18]. Machine and deep learning are vastly applied by various engineers, scientists and researchers nationally and internationally to assist the policy-makers. It requires a holistic approach to have sufficient and accurate evidence in the overall process of air pollution management [14].

The objective of this paper is to identify regions as urban or rural using deep learning. This provides a basis to understand the overall distribution of the sources of pollutants. Further evaluation is performed using machine learning methods to generate air pollution levels for different regions using a collective feature set.

3 Proposed Work

Air pollution levels are identified by different mechanisms. It is pertinent to consider the aspect of distinguishing the regions as urban or rural. Both forms of air pollution are on the rise. Air quality monitoring machines capture the important pollutant and meteorological information for a given region without highlighting the region as urban or rural. In the proposed work, the task of classification of a region is performed using deep learning. Satellite images are compiled and labelled into urban and rural. Relevant feature extraction is performed automatically using several hidden layers (Fig. 1).

3.1 Proposed Region Classification Model Using Deep Neural Network

Deep neural networks comprise several input layers. Satellite images have a series of features which generate useful information for region classification. Manual selection of the features requires expert knowledge. Pollutants have several sources of emergence. There are several hidden layers included in the neural network that identify minor and minute details and generate the required output. A convolutional neural

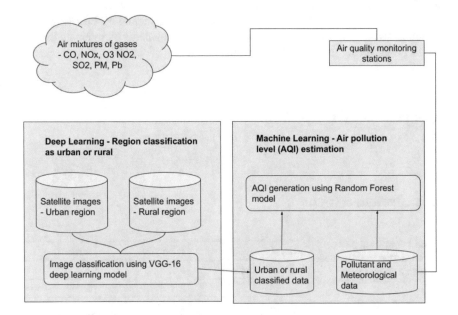

Fig. 1 Proposed architecture for the classification of a region as urban or rural

network offers the benefit of performing feature engineering with least human inter-vention. Classification of a region into urban and rural from imagery is an intricate and essential task for air pollution management. There are several deep learning models that have been pre-trained on huge data sets such as ResNet, Inception and VGG. VGG-16 is a convolutional neural network with 16 layers that have weights that are applied and provide the support for the required task of region classification.

3.2 Transfer Learning in Region Classification

The proposed model for classification of a region into urban or rural uses the pre-trained model of VGG-16, where the new layers of the model are trained without updating the weights of the layers in the model. The output of the last pooling layer is flattened, and fully connected layers are added. A dropout layer is added to prevent overfitting of the model. The architecture of VGG-16 is depicted in Figure 2. Table 2 highlights the overview of the different layers of the CNN model used.

The number of fully connected (FC) layers is 2. Sixteen weighted layers are included in the model. In addition, approximately, 140 million parameters are used in the learning process. The pre-trained weights used by the proposed deep learning model are ImageNet. It is considered as the standard measure to understand a model's performance during image classification tasks. By using ImageNet weights, the model takes fewer epochs to converge, optimising the time complexity. Whilst compiling the model, RMSProp optimizer is used to accelerate the process of opti-mization and to give a better final result. It uses step balancing by reducing the step for larger gradients and prevents vanishing.

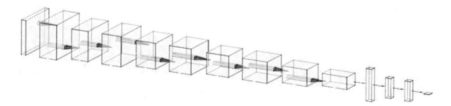

Fig. 2 Architecture of VGG-16

Table 2 Layers in the proposed deep learning model for region classification	Layer	Filter size	Stride
	Convolutional	3×3	1
	Maxpool	2×2	2
	Padding	2×2	2

3.3 AQI Estimation Using Ensemble Approach

Air pollution levels are estimated using machine learning techniques. Use of ensemble learning enables multiple decision trees to be combined as a stronger and effective learner in the estimation process. Random forest algorithm is applied, and random subsets of the chosen features are generated. This enables the process of generation of a relevant air quality model of pollution estimation. A comparative study is performed to prefer the ensemble learning approach.

4 Experimental Setup

In this paper, the list of modules includes,

– Data set collection for urban and rural regions
– Application of deep learning models for region classification
– Application of machine learning models for air pollution level estimation

4.1 Data Set Collection—Urban and Rural Regions

Tier-1, Tier-2, Tier-3 cities of India are used to formulate a list of urban regions. Regions surrounding villages, forest areas, water bodies, hill stations are considered as the baseline to accumulate the rural regions from the official website of the Census. All the images are downloaded from OpenStreetMaps. The steps used to capture the images are,

– In the search box, the region name was entered. Details of the regions are displayed in the results section.
– For an urban region, 'City', 'County', 'County boundary' options are preferred.
– In the case of rural regions, for a village, 'Village' option is chosen. For a mountainous region, 'Peak' or 'Hamlet' options are preferred. In case of water body presence, 'Stream' or 'Island' is used.
– The corresponding image generated is directly downloaded using the 'Share' option. Default settings are retained.

A set of 1000 images for both urban and rural regions in India are individually compiled and curated. A sample image used is showcased in Fig. 3.

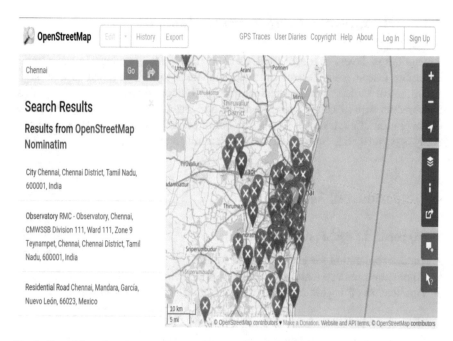

Fig. 3 Use of OpenStreetMaps to download an image for an urban region in India

4.2 Application of Deep Learning Models for Region Classification

The curated images are classified using deep learning. In order to understand the effectiveness of the classification process, a comparative study is done. Various standard deep learning models are analysed using the same data set. From Table 3, it can be inferred that VGG-16 and DenseNet have performed better than the other models. VGG-16 is preferred since it has fewer parameters to train and makes the code less complex when compared to the DenseNet model. The optimiser used in the proposed model is RMSProp along with binary cross-entropy as the loss function.

VGG-16 provides the most effective solution with an accuracy rate of 99.75%. The VGG-16 architecture is unique; instead of using many hyper-parameters, it focuses on convolution layers with 3×3 filter of stride 1 and consistently uses 2×2 filter with a stride of 2 as padding and maxpool layers.

Evaluation with a fixed data set uses resampling. The cross-validation procedure applied provides less bias. The deep learning models used in the classification process implemented K-fold validation. The value of 'k' is 3. The prior and post-results can be seen in Figs. 4 and 5. The training and validation accuracy levels are compared for the different models. Without the use of stratified K-fold cross-validation, MobileNetV2, VGG-16 and DenseNet architectures are able to maintain standard accuracy at similar levels.

Table 3 Experimental results of different deep learning models

Name of model	Optimizer	Loss function	Validation accuracy	Train accuracy	Mean K-fold validation accuracy	K-fold train accuracy
EfficientNetB5	RMSProp	Binary cross entropy	0.50	0.356	0.479	0.524
ResNet50	RMSProp	Binary cross entropy	0.50	0.448	0.470	0.524
MobileNetV2	RMSProp	Binary cross entropy	0.846	0.968	0.851	0.987
VGG-16	RMSProp	Binary cross entropy	0.86	0.93	0.841	0.997
DenseNet	RMSProp	Binary cross entropy	0.86	0.93	0.859	0.989

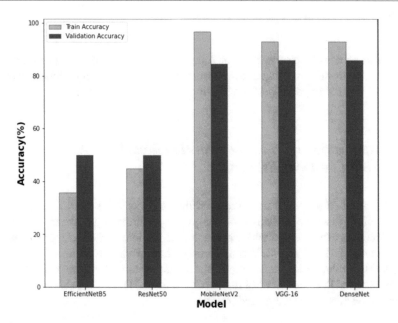

Fig. 4 Deep learning models performance before 3 cross-validation

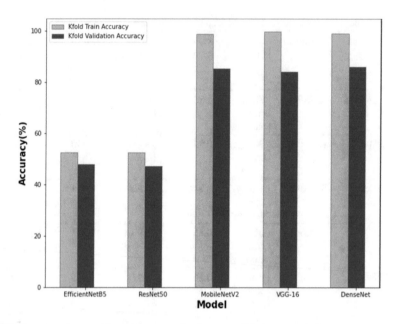

Fig. 5 Deep learning models performance after 3 cross-validation

In the process of 3 cross-validation training, the accuracy of the preferred models maintains a stronger and effective performance. Estimation of air pollution levels for an urban or rural region is performed using random forest model.

4.3 Application of Machine Learning Models for Air Pollution Level Estimation

The information garnered from the classification process is used to estimate the quality of air in a region. Regression analysis is performed on pollutant and meteorological data using an ensemble approach. The random forest technique generates an accuracy of 81% (Table 4). Various forms of data are used to estimate the air pollution levels. Pollutant and meteorological data are captured for a few cities from the official Central Pollution Control Board (CPCB) portal [19]. AQI values are captured from the National Air Quality Index portal [20].

5 Conclusion and Future Work

Air pollution management includes air quality estimation. The levels of pollution are on a steady rise and impact the lives of individuals. Identifying the diverse sources of

Table 4 Results of ensemble approach for estimation of air pollution levels

Metric	Linear regression	Decision trees	Support vector regression	Random forest
Accuracy score	0.79	0.66	0.22	0.81
Mean absolute error (MAE)	47.78	60.83	102.90	46.75
Mean squared error (MSE)	3718.74	6303.76	13,875.43	3588.01
Root mean squared error (RMSE)	60.98	79.39	117.79	59.90

pollution and their impact on pollution levels is challenging. An AQI value is representative of the pollution levels which may not consider the regional characteristics of a place. Urban and rural air pollution is different; the corresponding air quality patterns and AQIs are different. In the paper, deep learning is applied to classify a region as urban or rural. Satellite images are chosen and analysed on different models, and VGG-16-based model is preferred with an accuracy of 99.75%. Air pollution estimation is further performed using machine learning with the consideration of pollutant, meteorological, and geographic data. Random forest approach provides an accuracy of 81% when ensemble learning is applied for AQI estimation. After identification of a region, it assists in better assessment of air pollution levels. The approach can be extended by implementing different models for a wider range of cities and villages.

References

1. edx (2020) Air pollution: causes and impacts. Accessed 8 Nov 2020
2. World health organisation (2021) Ambient (outdoor) air pollution. Accessed 22 Sept 2021
3. Lee H-H, Iraqui O, Gu Y, Yim SH-L, Chulakadabba A, Tonks AY-M, Yang Z, Wang C (2018) Impacts of air pollutants from fire and non-fire emissions on the regional air quality in southeast Asia. Atmos Chem Phys 18(9):6141–6156. https://doi.org/10.5194/acp-18-6141-2018
4. Ravishankara AR, David LM, Pierce JR, Venkataraman C (2020) Outdoor air pollution in India is not only an urban problem. Proc Natl Acad Sci 117(46):28640–28644. ISSN 0027-8424. https://doi.org/10.1073/pnas.2007236117
5. Zheng Y, Liu F, Hsieh H-P (2013) U-air: when urban air quality inference meets big data. In: Proceedings of the 19th ACM SIGKDD international conference on knowledge discovery and data mining
6. Chen L, Cai Y, Ding Y, Lv M, Yuan C, Chen G (2016) Spatially fine-grained urban air quality estimation using ensemble semi-supervised learning and pruning. In: Proceedings of the 2016 ACM international joint conference on pervasive and ubiquitous computing, UbiComp'16. Association for Computing Machinery, New York, NY, USA, page 10761087. ISBN 9781450344616. https://doi.org/10.1145/2971648.2971725
7. Zheng K, Zhao S, Yang Z, Xiong X, Xiang W (2016) Design and implementation of LPWA-based air quality monitoring system. IEEE Access 4:3238–3245
8. Editorial team, carbon copy (2020) Study: air pollution levels in rural India almost as bad as metros. Accessed 26 Nov 2020

9. Lv M, Li Y, Chen L, Chen T (2019) Air quality estimation by exploiting terrain features and multi-view transfer semi-supervised regression. Inf Sci 483:82–95. ISSN 0020-0255. https://doi.org/10.1016/j.ins.2019.01.038
10. Bamrah SK, Saiharshith KR, S G (2020) Application of random forests for air quality estimation in India by adopting terrain features. In: 2020 4th international conference on computer, communication and signal processing (ICCCSP), pp 1–6
11. Qi Z, Wang T, Song G, Hu W, Li X, Zhang Z (2018) Deep air learning: interpolation, prediction, and feature analysis of fine-grained air quality. IEEE Trans Knowl Data Eng 30:2285–2297
12. Gu K, Qiao J, Lin W (2018) Recurrent air quality predictor based on meteorology and pollution-related factors. IEEE Trans Industr Inf 14(9):3946–3955. https://doi.org/10.1109/TII.2018.2793950
13. Hsieh H-P, Lin S-D, Zheng Y (2015) Inferring air quality for station location recommendation based on urban big data. In: Proceedings of the 21th ACM SIGKDD international conference on knowledge discovery and data mining, KDD'15. Association for Computing Machinery, New York, NY, USA, page 437446. ISBN 9781450336642. https://doi.org/10.1145/2783258.2783344
14. Fang X, Saito T, Park S, Li S, Yokouchi Y, Prinn RG (2018) Performance of back-trajectory statistical methods and inverse modeling method in locating emission sources. ACS Earth Space Chem 2(8):843–851. https://doi.org/10.1021/acsearthspacechem.8b00062
15. Janarthanan R, Partheeban P, Somasundaram K, Elamparithi PN (2021) A deep learning approach for prediction of air quality index in a metropolitan city. Sustain Cities Soc 67:102720
16. Liu N, Liu X, Jayaratne R, Morawska L (2020) A study on extending the use of air quality monitor data via deep learning techniques. J Clean Prod 274:122956
17. Gu Y, Zhang W, Yang Y, Wang C, Streets DG, Yim SHL (2020) Assessing outdoor air quality and public health impact attributable to residential black carbon emissions in rural china. Resour Conserv Recycl 159:104812
18. Chen Y, Wild O, Conibear L, Ran L, He J, Wang L, Wang Y (2020) Local characteristics of and exposure to fine particulate matter (PM2.5) in four Indian megacities. Atmos Environ X 5:100052
19. Central pollution control board
20. National air quality index

Neuroevolution-Based Earthquake Intensity Classification for Onsite Earthquake Early Warning

Siddhartha Sarkar⊙**, Anubrata Roy**⊙**, Bhargab Das, and Satish Kumar**⊙

1 Introduction

Earthquake being a complex process, and since there are multiple effects, viz., stress drop, interference, etc., involved, feature extraction is one of the essential steps toward developing the model to generate EEW. Effective onsite EEW is dependent on the reliability of warning in terms of warning lead time and accuracy. Warning accuracy can be increased if it reflects the probability of damage from the peak ground acceleration. Ensuing seismic intensity estimation in real time from the early p-wave signal is thus necessary. Artificial neural network (ANN) has emerged as a powerful tool in pattern recognition, signal classification, regression problems. ANN has also helped researchers develop various beneficial systems in the EEW aspect [1, 2].

A few countries, viz., Japan, Taiwan, Mexico, and the United States have operational EEW systems, while other nations actively experiment and prototype. The onsite approach has faster report times, close to the epicenter, and generally produces robust estimates of the local ground shaking, but typically, the earthquake source parameters are poorly determined; the regional approach is slower at small epicentral distances, but it can provide accurate estimates of location and magnitude though the quality of the ground motion prediction depends on the methodology [3]. Moreover, new methods for earthquake detection and location can provide information with one single triggering station.

Prevalent EEW methodologies have shown that earthquake location estimation controls magnitude estimation, which affects site-specific ground motion estimation,

S. Sarkar (✉) · A. Roy · B. Das · S. Kumar
Academy of Scientific and Innovative Research (AcSIR), Ghaziabad 201002, India
e-mail: ssarkar@csio.res.in

S. Sarkar · B. Das · S. Kumar
CSIR-Central Scientific Instruments Organization (CSIR-CSIO), Chandigarh 160030, India

on which reliability of EEW is solely dependent. Assumptions about the propagation models between source and warning sites are often simplified at the cost of accuracy. Moreover, most of the methodologies involve site-specific empirical relationships which depend upon the quantity, quality, and geographic resolution of seismic data. This imposes a limitation on many nations to carry on research and development of efficient EEW. In this context, research objectives are taken up to bridge the research gaps observed.

The training and modeling neural network is quite complex tasks to select the best features suitable for the training to provide optimal results. The initial synaptic weights of the network are often randomly generated. So, it is pretty laborious to find the weights that lead to global optimization, not partial. Slow convergence rate and oscillation effect result in overfitting or under fitting [4, 5]. Evolutionary computations like genetic algorithms, swarm optimization resolve this type of problem as these are meta-heuristic algorithms capable of solving such nonlinear dynamic issues [6, 7].

1.1 Evolutionary Computing Approach

Evolutionary computation is a family of algorithms used for real-world complex, complicated optimizations. Though its historical roots can be traced back to the late 50 s, it was not much practiced or applied due to the unavailability of powerful computational platforms [8, 9]. In general, there are two types of evolutionary computing: swarm intelligence and evolutionary algorithms.

Swarm Intelligence

These techniques are inspired by the collective cognitive behavior of a self-organized, decentralized group of animals such as ants, bees, lions, and wolf [10–12]. SI-based techniques are widely used in data mining, biomedical applications, signal processing, image processing, sophisticated applications areas, including micro-robot, navigation control, and control systems [13].

Colony optimization is a typical population-based meta-heuristic, probabilistic algorithm to solve complex optimization problems. While searching for food, building nests, ants, or bees go in different random ways, and while doing so, they leave their pheromones and mark their territories [14]. The more pheromone on a path means more sources of food available along the pathway. Thus, by a positive feedback-based scheme, they find their shortest way to food. Similar to the insects, there are sets of artificial insects in this algorithm that search for an optimized solution. The artificial insects incrementally build solutions by moving on a weighted graph. Based on a probabilistic model, artificial pheromones are determined, which is maintained, and the pheromone trail is updated by a heuristic function while searching for an optimal path [15–18].

On the other hand, particle swarm optimization (PSO) is stochastic and inspired by bird flocks or fish schools. Each particle or individual of the swarm discovers the optimal solution and, while finding, receives feedback from other particles of the population [19]. The particles have position and velocity, which changes while scouting for the optimal solution. While doing so, the particles move toward the best-positioned particle and further search for the best solution space [20, 21]. Due to computational advancements and the increasing number of databases, PSO is now used in different signal processing applications [21].

Genetic Algorithms (GA)

Genetic algorithms (GAs) and genetic programming (GP) are extensively used under evolutionary algorithms. Darwin's evolution approach inspires these algorithms. A randomly selected population is generated in these techniques, which undergo genetic operations, viz., crossover, mutation and produce a generation of offspring evolving towards finest candidate solutions [7, 22, 23]. Some basic attributes of GA, viz., population size, selection strategy, mutation probability, etc., are optimized empirically by the user. GP has been used along with AdaBoost for earthquake prediction [24].

Artificial neural network, support vector machine models are trained and adapted using PSO [25, 26]. There are several pieces of literature from which it can be inferred that PSO can be utilized for earthquake prediction and possible peak ground acceleration estimation for a specific region [5, 27, 28]. GA has been used to improve the weights of an ANN trained using the backpropagation technique to predict earthquakes [6].

Different seismic attributes are measured to predict the hazardous ground motion upfront to generate earthquake early warning. However, the ground motion estimation problem is a complex task due to the high variability of the ground medium compared to the availability of seismic data. Despite the complexity, ANN has been used for seismicity prediction [29], magnitude estimation [30], magnitude forecasting [31], and EEW [32, 33]. Seismic intensity is a critical factor that measures the probability of damage due to shaking of ground due to earthquake. Evolutionary algorithms are being used in research pertaining to earthquake, i.e., intensity estimation, fault clustering, structural engineering, etc. [28, 34–36]. However, the application of an ANN classifier developed using any evolutionary computing technique is not explored in the EEW regime.

Hence, in this article, a method is proposed for the seismic intensity-based warning classifier, which utilizes the peak ground acceleration values to map the earthquake events in light and strong categories. MMI scale is used for this intensity-based warning classification, where MMI > V events are taken as strong earthquake due to their moderate to heavy destructive nature [37]. The classifier is designed around MLP neural network, which trained using genetic algorithm for exploring the use of neuroevolutionary computing approach in onsite EEW system.

2 Methodology

Artificial neural networks (ANNs) are inspired from the biological systems of humans and based on the capability to mimic and learning ability of humans by establishing connections in the neurons in the brain. Like the human neurons, there are nodes in the neural networks that act as different layers like input, hidden, and output layers. Information is exchanged between the nodes. Each connection is from one node to another node is called weights. Now, each node is activated according to the activation function and a threshold parameter. The output can be formulated as,

$$z_i = \left(\sum x_i * w_{ij} + b \right) \tag{1}$$

z_i is the activated output; $T(.)$ is the activated function which introduces nonlinearity in the network; x_i is the input node; w_{ij} is the weight connecting node i and j; b is the added bias. The backpropagation technique adjusts weights according to the output by minimizing the error between the predicted output and the actual output by the networks [38]. However, it has several drawbacks due to the continuous searching and differentiability of the loss function [36, 37].

Multilayer perceptron (MLP) is the most trivial type of ANN with only feed-forward fully connected configuration without loops or feedbacks. Hence, MLP topology is used in the proposed methodology without pruning, dropout, and layer skipping possibility. However, the use of ReLU as activation functions in the hidden layer neurons achieves indirect deactivation of neurons by the effect of dying ReLU. Genetic algorithm is used to gain a more optimal meta-heuristic weight search instead of weight optimization using conventional gradient descent error backpropagation. The technique is termed as MLP-GANN and implemented using PyGAD [38]. The relevant neuroevolutionary parameters and MLP topology are shared in Table 2.

Neural Network Codification

The evolutionary algorithms-based ANN generation process is of three types: evolution of the weights, architectures, and learning rules [39]. In the proposed methodology, a predefined architecture of MLP, as shown in Fig. 1, is used only for the evolution of weights. Weights are serialized to form a string of real numbers, which is termed as the genotype or chromosome.

There are eleven features in the input layer as shown in Table 1, followed by two hidden layers with 12 and 6 neurons, respectively, and 2 output neurons for binary classification as shown in Fig. 1, which produces 216 genes or searchable parameters in individual neural networks for the evolution.

Number of Genes = Number of weights = $11 \times 12 + 12 \times 6 + 6 \times 2 = 216$

Fig. 1 MLP neural network with fully connected feedforward configuration

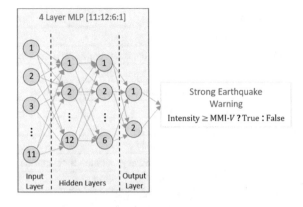

Table 1 Features used for MLP-based warning classifier

Feature type	Axes of the three-component accelerogram	Features
Peak ground acceleration (PGA)	Triaxial feature	Max (PGA$_{ud}$, PGA$_{ns}$, PGA$_{ew}$)
Cumulative absolute velocity (CAV) [40]	Up–down North–south East–west	CAV$_{ud}$ CAV$_{ns}$ CAV$_{ew}$
Binned average frequency (Hz)	Up–down East–west North–south	[1–2), [2–4), [4–8) [8–16), [16–32) [8–16), [16–32)

2.1 Neuroevolution

Genetic operators, viz., inheritance, mutation, selection, and crossover, are used for GA-based search of the approximate or optimal solution of weight matrix of the MLP neural network. The steps of evolving this MLP-based solution are shown in Fig. 2, inspired from evolutionary biology. Candidate neural networks constitute the population of solutions. The evolution is initialized from a randomly generated initial population. In each generation, every individual's fitness (quality) is evaluated by calculating the balanced accuracy of prediction. The genetic operators are applied to obtain a new, better population. Configurations of the genetic operators are shown in Table 2. The evolutionary steps are repeated until a fitness saturation criterion is met, or a maximum number of generations have been reached [41]. Two parents from the last generation are kept in the mating pool to introduce elitism and preserve individuals' diversity. Apart from a crossover-based search, a comparatively high rate of mutation (40%) is applied.

Table 2 MLP-GANN parameters

Neuroevolution Parameters		Values
GA	Number of individuals (chromosomes) in each generation	16
	Number of mating individuals	8
	Number of parents kept from last generation	2
	Crossover type	Single point
	Mutation type	Random
	Maximum mutation chance	40%
	Number of maximum generation for evolution	500
	Fitness function	Accuracy
MLP	Number of input features	11
	Number of hidden layers	2
	Number of perceptron in hidden layers	12, 6
	Number of output neurons	2
	Output classes of warning	Light, strong
	Activation functions in hidden layers	ReLU
	Activation function in output layer	Softmax
	Total Searchable Parameters (Fully connected layer weights)	216

2.2 Data

Location and occurrences of earthquakes are not yet predictable in advance. Hence, earthquake signal analysis relies on retrospective records. For this study, all the records from different seismic stations of NIED strong-motion Seismograph Network (K-Net) [41] from 1996 to 2006 have been used from 1459 earthquakes of 3–7.4 magnitudes. The waveform records are acceleration time-series of varying lengths in gal (cm/s^2), which were converted to the percentage of gravitational acceleration, g (i.e., %g) for coherence with the MMI scale [35]. The details of the dataset after generating class labels based on PGA values are shown in Table 3. As listed in Table 1, a set of features are extracted from 3 s feature windows sampled from the initial 4 s signal after p-wave arrival.

Dataset Balancing

The dataset is skewed initially, as shown in Table 3. The majority class, i.e., the light earthquake class, has 89.26% samples. Hence, the feature windows are oversampled from events having peak ground acceleration (PGA) greater than 9.2%g, which belongs to MMI > V, and the events from minority class are downsampled to strike a balance between the classes around 3.9%g, which produced a 1:1 ratio of samples from both the classes with a total of 20,000 samples. The distribution of PGA of feature windows from the unbalanced and balanced dataset is shown in Fig. 3.

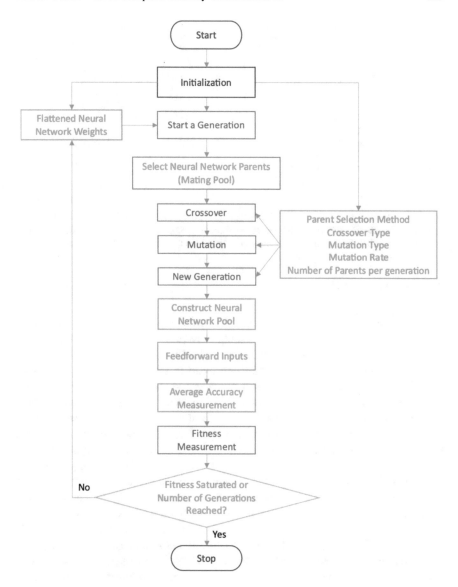

Fig. 2 Flowchart of neuroevolution

Table 3 Details of the dataset generated for the earthquake warning classification problem

Intensity classes	Warning	Intensity bracket (MMI [37])	PGA bracket (%g)	Damage potential	Number of earthquake records
Light	No	[II, V)	[0.17, 3.9)	None	16,251
Strong	Yes	[V, VIII)	[3.9, 50)	Very light to moderate/heavy	1955

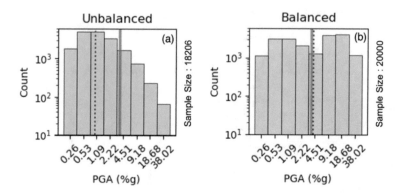

Fig. 3 Differential resampling around 3.9%g (green vertical solid line) to handle imbalanced classification: Sample distributions of the target variable, i.e., PGA, with respect to the 50th percentile (red dashed vertical line) of **a** unbalanced original earthquake dataset and **b** after balancing

3 Results and Discussion

The neuroevolution has been conducted for increasing training sample sizes from 200 to 18,000 out of a total of 20,000 samples as prepared in the last section using the stratified deferential resampling-based data balancing method as shown in Fig. 3.

The training samples are selected using uniform stratified sampling after shuffling. The remaining samples are used as the test set for respective training sizes. Classifier performances are again evaluated using macro means of precision, recall, and $f1$-scores as shown in Fig. 4a. It is observed that for the sample size of 4000, neuroevolution reached the saturation of fitness in only 28 generations for the reported run, which is significantly quicker than 81 generations, the following best number of generations to reach a saturated fitness. However, the 20% training sample size comprising 3641 of 18,206 samples of the unbalanced dataset took 290 generations to achieve a saturation of fitness for the reported run, as shown in Fig. 4b. The maximum precision of 0.94 is achieved for the sample size of 4000, with an $f1$-score of 0.89.

The fitness evolution with respect to generations for a sample size of 4000 is shown in Fig. 4a, which shows the fastest saturation of fitness. Hence, the confusion matrix parameters of the balanced dataset are calculated for the testing sample size 16,000, comprising the remaining samples, for detailed performance analysis, as shown in Fig. 4c. For the training sample size of 4000, the achieved training and testing accuracies are 91.07% and 90.02%, respectively. This difference shows a negative deviation of only 1.07% in training and testing accuracy, which shows the generalization of the learning.

The testing is done on a comparatively large test set comprising 80% samples while trained using only the remaining 20% samples, as shown in Fig. 4. After the proposed dataset balancing, the precision and recall increased from 64.09% and 46.68 to 94.47% and 85.01%, respectively. However, balanced accuracy on the test sample size of 80% improved from 71 to 90.02%.

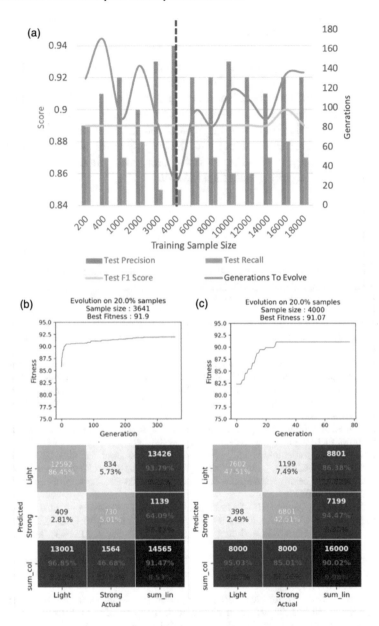

Fig. 4 **a** Warning classifier performance matrices (in the case of balanced dataset) with respect to training sample sizes and generations to achieve a saturation of fitness (blue line). The fitness evolution and corresponding confusion matrices from a testing sample size of 20% are shown for **b** unbalanced dataset (total 18,206 samples) and **c** balanced dataset (total 20,000 samples)

4 Conclusion

Earthquake early warning systems for onsite application are being adopted for the safety of vital installations, e.g., nuclear power plants, gas plants, high-rise buildings, and critical civil infrastructure. The developed MLP-GANN classifier with only two hidden layers and a reduced feature set is effective for implementation on an edge-processing device for strong earthquake detection without estimating source parameters, e.g., magnitude and location. The proposed early warning methodology is tested for providing severity-based warning, suitable for effective response in case of earthquakes of intensity greater than MMI-V.

References

1. Zhao Y, Takano K (1999) An artificial neural network approach for broadband seismic phase picking. Bull Seismol Soc Am 89:670–680
2. Günaydn K, Günaydn A (2008) Peak ground acceleration prediction by artificial neural networks for northwestern Turkey. Math Probl Eng 2008. https://doi.org/10.1155/2008/919420
3. Satriano C, Wu Y-M, Zollo A, Kanamori H (2011) Earthquake early warning: concepts, methods and physical grounds. Soil Dyn Earthq Eng 31:106–118. https://doi.org/10.1016/j.soildyn.2010.07.007
4. Orlic N, Loncaric S (2010) Earthquake-explosion discrimination using genetic algorithm-based boosting approach. Comput Geosci 36:179–185. https://doi.org/10.1016/j.cageo.2009.05.006
5. Stankiewicz J, Bindi D, Oth A, Parolai S (2013) Designing efficient earthquake early warning systems: case study of Almaty, Kazakhstan. J Seismol 17:1125–1137. https://doi.org/10.1007/s10950-013-9381-4
6. Zhang Q, Wang C (2008) Using genetic algorithm to optimize artificial neural network: A case study on earthquake prediction. In: Proceedings of the 2nd international conference on genetic and evolutionary computing WGEC, pp 128–131. https://doi.org/10.1109/WGEC.2008.96
7. Al-Sahaf H, Bi Y, Chen Q, Lensen A, Mei Y, Sun Y, Tran B, Xue B, Zhang M (2019) A survey on evolutionary machine learning. J R Soc New Zeal 49:205–228. https://doi.org/10.1080/03036758.2019.1609052
8. Back T, Hammel U, Schwefel H-P (1997) Evolutionary computation: comments on the history and current state. IEEE Trans Evol Comput 1:3–17. https://doi.org/10.1109/4235.585888
9. Fogel DB (2000) What is evolutionary computation? IEEE Spectr 37:26–32. https://doi.org/10.1109/6.819926
10. Mishra A, Agarwal C, Sharma A, Bedi P (2014) Optimized gray-scale image watermarking using DWT–SVD and firefly algorithm. Expert Syst Appl 41:7858–7867. https://doi.org/10.1016/j.eswa.2014.06.011
11. Horng M-H (2012) Vector quantization using the firefly algorithm for image compression. Expert Syst Appl 39:1078–1091. https://doi.org/10.1016/j.eswa.2011.07.108
12. Grosan C, Abraham A, Chis M (2006) Swarm intelligence in data mining
13. Chakraborty A, Kar AK (2017) Swarm intelligence: a review of algorithms. Model Optim Sci Technol 10:475–494. https://doi.org/10.1007/978-3-319-50920-4_19
14. Karaboga D, Akay B (2009) A survey: algorithms simulating bee swarm intelligence. Artif Intell Rev 31:61–85. https://doi.org/10.1007/s10462-009-9127-4
15. Gupta DK, Arora Y, Singh UK, Gupta JP (2012) Recursive ant colony optimization for estimation of parameters of a function
16. Birattari M, Pellegrini P, Dorigo M (2007) On the invariance of ant colony optimization. IEEE Trans Evol Comput 11:732–742. https://doi.org/10.1109/TEVC.2007.892762

17. Lafourcade M, Guinand F (2005) Ants for natural language processing, 22 p
18. Ojha VK, Abraham A, Snášel V (2015) ACO for continuous function optimization: a performance analysis. In: International conference on intelligent systems design and applications (ISDA), pp 145–150. https://doi.org/10.1109/ISDA.2014.7066253
19. Huang P, Xu Y (2006) PSO-based time-optimal trajectory planning for space robot with dynamic constraints. In: IEEE international conference on robotics and biomimetics. ieeexplore.ieee.org.
20. Bonyadi MR, Michalewicz Z (2017) Particle swarm optimization for single objective continuous space problems: a review. Evol Comput 25:1–54. https://doi.org/10.1162/EVCO_r_00180
21. Poli R (2008) Analysis of the publications on the applications of particle swarm optimisation. J Artif Evol Appl 2008:1–10. https://doi.org/10.1155/2008/685175
22. Tan KC, Feng L, Jiang M (2021) Evolutionary transfer optimization—a new frontier in evolutionary computation research. IEEE Comput Intell Mag 16:22–33. https://doi.org/10.1109/MCI.2020.3039066
23. Miikkulainen R, Forrest S (2021) A biological perspective on evolutionary computation. Nat Mach Intell 3:9–15. https://doi.org/10.1038/s42256-020-00278-8
24. Asim KM, Idris A, Iqbal T, Martínez-Álvarez F (2018) Seismic indicators based earthquake predictor system using genetic programming and AdaBoost classification. Soil Dyn Earthq Eng 111:1–7. https://doi.org/10.1016/j.soildyn.2018.04.020
25. Melgani F, Bazi Y (2008) Classification of electrocardiogram signals with support vector machines and particle swarm optimization. IEEE Trans Inf Technol Biomed 12:667–677. https://doi.org/10.1109/TITB.2008.923147
26. Shadmand S, Mashoufi B (2016) A new personalized ECG signal classification algorithm using block-based neural network and particle swarm optimization. Biomed Signal Process Control 25:12–23. https://doi.org/10.1016/j.bspc.2015.10.008
27. Mohais AS, Mohais R, Ward C, Posthoff C (2007) Earthquake classifying neural networks trained with random dynamic neighborhood PSOs. Proceedings of the GECCO 2007 genetic and evolutionary computation conference, pp 110–117. https://doi.org/10.1145/1276958.1276974
28. Ghasemi Nejad R, Ali Abbaspour R, Mojarab M (2021) Associating earthquakes with faults using cluster analysis optimized by a fuzzy particle swarm optimization algorithm for Iranian provinces. Soil Dyn Earthq Eng 140:106433. https://doi.org/10.1016/j.soildyn.2020.106433
29. Asim KM, Moustafa SS, Niaz IA, Elawadi EA, Iqbal T, Martínez-Álvarez F (2020) Seismicity analysis and machine learning models for short-term low magnitude seismic activity predictions in Cyprus. Soil Dyn Earthq Eng 130. https://doi.org/10.1016/j.soildyn.2019.105932
30. Adeli H, Panakkat A (2009) A probabilistic neural network for earthquake magnitude prediction. Neural Netw 22:1018–1024. https://doi.org/10.1016/j.neunet.2009.05.003
31. Rafiei MH, Adeli H (2017) NEEWS: a novel earthquake early warning model using neural dynamic classification and neural dynamic optimization. Soil Dyn Earthq Eng 100:417–427. https://doi.org/10.1016/j.soildyn.2017.05.013
32. Böse M, Wenzel F, Erdik M (2008) PreSEIS: a neural network-based approach to earthquake early warning for finite faults. Bull Seismol Soc Am 98:366–382. https://doi.org/10.1785/0120070002
33. Jozinović D, Lomax A, Štajduhar I, Michelini A (2020) Rapid prediction of earthquake ground shaking intensity using raw waveform data and a convolutional neural network. Geophys J Int 222:1379–1389. https://doi.org/10.1093/gji/ggaa233
34. Hason MM, Hanoon AN, Abdulhameed AA (2021) Particle swarm optimization technique based prediction of peak ground acceleration of Iraq's tectonic regions. J King Saud Univ Eng Sci. https://doi.org/10.1016/j.jksues.2021.06.004
35. Falcone R, Lima C, Martinelli E (2020) Soft computing techniques in structural and earthquake engineering: a literature review. Eng Struct 207:110269. https://doi.org/10.1016/j.engstruct.2020.110269

36. Zhang M, Cagnoni S (2018) Evolutionary computation and evolutionary deep learning for image analysis, signal processing and pattern recognition. In: GECCO 2018 companion—proceedings of the 2018 genetic and evolutionary computation conference companion, pp 1221–1257. https://doi.org/10.1145/3205651.3207859

37. Wald DJ, Quitoriano V, Heaton TH, Kanamori H (1999) Relationships between peak ground acceleration, peak ground velocity, and modified mercalli intensity in California. Earthq Spectra 15:557–564. https://doi.org/10.1193/1.1586058

38. Yong W (2021) Risk evaluation model and intelligent assessment of large scale sports events. ieeexplore.ieee.org

39. Rivero D, Dorado J, Rabuñal J, Pazos A (2010) Generation and simplification of artificial neural networks by means of genetic programming. Neurocomputing 73:3200–3223. https://doi.org/10.1016/j.neucom.2010.05.010

40. Sreejaya KP, Basu J, Raghukanth STG, Srinagesh D (2021) Prediction of ground motion intensity measures using an artificial neural network. Pure Appl Geophys. https://doi.org/10.1007/s00024-021-02752-9

41. Ashiru I, Czarnecki CA (1998) Evolving communicating controllers for multiple mobile robot systems. Microprocess Microsyst

Detection of Credit Card Fraud by Applying Genetic Algorithm and Particle Swarm Optimization

Debachudamani Prusti, Jitendra Kumar Rout, and Santanu Kumar rath

1 Introduction

Online financial transaction facilities help in eliminating the burden of completing a transaction without visiting the onsite branch of a bank [1, 2]. The usage of online transaction services viz., credit card transactions attract more number of users for a hassle free online experience, but simultaneously it also attracts the fraudulent customers with an intention of hijacking money from other account holders. The malicious users or the fraudsters pretend themselves as authorized users to steal the account as well as transaction information in an intelligent manner.

In this proposed research, attempt has been made to detect frauds in credit card transactions, so that the transactions can occur in a secured manner [3, 4]. Detection of malicious behavior is a subtle problem to find the original identity of card users, attempting to intrude into the online credit card transactions by customers. A good approach to identify the malicious activities, which reside among various credit card transactions, is to find the divergence that happens with continuous and frequent data transaction. Different approaches are applied in the past research methodologies with various techniques to identify the divergent behavior, i.e., supposed to be analyzed for better identification of the fraudulent transaction behaviors [5].

In this proposed study, the credit card frauds are analyzed by considering the financial transaction data of several financial institutions associated with the credit

D. Prusti (✉) · S. K. rath
Department of CSE, NIT Rourkela, Rourkela, India
e-mail: debaprusti@gmail.com

S. K. rath
e-mail: skrath@nitrkl.ac.in

J. K. Rout
Department of CSE, NIT Raipur, Raipur, India
e-mail: jitu2rout@gmail.com

© The Author(s), under exclusive license to Springer Nature Singapore Pte Ltd. 2023   357
R. Doriya et al. (eds.), *Machine Learning, Image Processing, Network Security and Data Sciences*, Lecture Notes in Electrical Engineering 946,
https://doi.org/10.1007/978-981-19-5868-7_27

cards. In the dataset, the fraudulent and legitimate classes are highly imbalanced. This higher imbalance between the two classes prompts the fraud detection system a very challenging job. Fraud detection technique can be conceptualized as a data mining technique with an objective to correctly predict the classification of online transactions as genuine or fraudulent. Basically, for classification problems, a good number of performance measures are specified and most are associated with correct number of cases, which can able to classify correctly.

Application of optimization techniques such as GA and PSO to detect the fraud in credit card transactions have been considered in this proposed approach [6–8]. The optimization techniques help to find various parameters, which is likely to be maximum or minimum (optimal) value of any target function. Optimization techniques are often applied with artificial neural network and SVM to evaluate the performance parameters for classification algorithms, since they provide certain coefficients that are often identified by trial and error method or by using the exhaustive search method.

Motivation of the study. This study is motivated to improve a credit card fraud detection solution that can optimize the chance of identifying the fraudulent transaction with better performance. Although the solution has been regarded as a successful one, still we consider that it can further be improved by taking the weighted values that can be better adjusted by considering the recent transaction behaviors and frauds occurred into it. The optimization methods such as GA and PSO help to improve the optimal values from the input by taking the various weight parameters.

2 Literature Survey

It has been observed in the literature that a good number of researchers as well as practitioners have presented their studies on fraud detection using several data mining and machine learning algorithms. The research includes random forest, support vector machine, regression analysis, artificial neural network applications, as these algorithms are very much helpful to classify the legitimate and fraudulent activities in the financial transactions. Panigrahi et al. [9] have suggested the methodology for fraud detection based on four components and are connected serially [9]. A set of abnormal and suspicious transactions are initially identified and later on Bayesian learning algorithm is considered to predict the fraudulent transaction.

Sanchez et al. [10] have represented several approaches and have applied association rule mining (ARM) method to characterize new card patterns for regular usage and identifying the ones that are not fitted to the suspicious patterns [10]. Mitchell [11] has commented about genetic algorithms in terms of evolutionary algorithms with an objective to obtain better solutions against the increase in time [11]. Aote et al. [12] have presented a detailed work on application of PSO along with its limitations [12]. Bratton and Kennedy [13] defined a standard PSO algorithm with the recent developments that help to improve the performance on standard measures to extend original PSO [13].

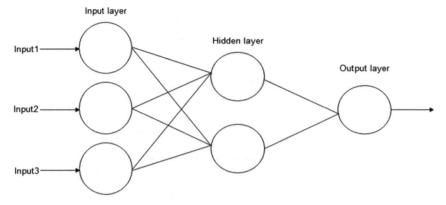

Fig. 1 Layers of neural network with single hidden layer

3 Artificial Neural Network Application

Artificial neural network (ANN) works in the similar way as a human brain does and it can be very well considered for detection of fraudulent transactions [14–16].

By using the previous one or two years data of various transactions, neural network is trained to identify a fixed pattern of using credit card by a specific customer. As shown in Fig. 1, the neural networks are trained in a multi-layered architecture style having one input layer, one output layer and at least one hidden layer. Except the input nodes, other nodes or neurons behave as activation function. It helps in mapping the input signals with the response variables.

4 Genetic Algorithm

The Genetic Algorithm as shown in Fig. 2 follows the procedure being inspired from the natural evolution [3, 17]. The whole objective is that with the evolution of generation, the survival chance of a stronger member in the population is greater than that of the weaker members. Starting with a number of initial given solutions, the genetic algorithm acts as the parent of current generation evolution. Crossover and mutation operators generate new solutions from these solutions. The unfit members are eliminated from the generation and more fit members are selected for the next generation as the parents. This process continues until a number of generations have passed and subsequently the best solution is obtained. But in some cases, genetic algorithm does not give any guaranty for identifying the global maxima and also there is chances to be trapped in local maxima.

GA with Neural Network. Hybridization of genetic algorithms with artificial neural networks present a better performance where GA is used to find the various performance parameters [17]. The main objective is how accurately GA and ANN

Fig. 2 Steps for applying
genetic algorithm

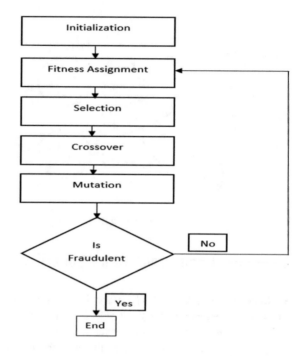

can be hybridized, i.e., how the neural network should be represented with the genetic
algorithm for a better predictive result.

In the initialization step, a large number of random individuals are generated to
begin the algorithm procedure. Then the empirical values of the parameters are evaluated, by applying artificial neural network according to the genome information.
After training with back-propagation, its performance is determined. Rather considering the individual's performance, the fitness evaluation considers a greater number
of cases. In order to generate small networks, few approaches consider about the
network size for the better evaluation of the parameters. Later, crossover and mutation replace the worst members of the population by creating new individuals. Initial
population is generated by randomizing weight matrices rather by randomizing the
chromosome strings allowing the initial weights to be distributed in a closed range.
The message or information in the neural network is encoded with neural network
algorithm within the genome of the genetic algorithm. Initially, the random individuals are generated and their parameters are evaluated based on the genome information. Finally, its performance values are determined empirically post training with
the back-propagation neural network algorithm.

5 Particle Swarm Optimization

Particle Swarm optimization (PSO) is one of the stochastic optimization techniques. Rather inspired by the natural evolution similar to other larger class of evolutionary algorithms like evolutionary strategies, genetic algorithms, genetic programming, PSO is mainly prompted from the stimulation of social behavior of the swarm particles in large group [18, 19]. PSO is based on sociological behavior and mainly inspired sociologically is visualized with bird flocking [20]. It is a kind of evolutionary algorithm similar to others, which is initialized with the population through random solutions.

The algorithm holds a swarm of particles, in which every particle tries to solve an optimization problem by providing a potential solution to the problem. Unlike other evolutionary algorithms, in PSO the individual's potential solution are passed through the problem space [21]. Let S be the swarm size and the particle i has several characteristics for obtaining the particle solution at each iteration. A swarm of particles is first initialized with the random position x_i and velocity v_i and the objective function $f(x)$ is calculated by considering the particles coordinates as input measures. The disadvantage of PSO is that it loses swarm diversity with low convergence rate during the iteration process.

5.1 Personal Best (p-best)

The p-best or particle best position is the individual best position P_i, of particle i. It is the best position of a particle that it visits (Prior value of x_i) and yields the fitness value which is regarded as highest. For any minimization method, if the position yields the smaller function value, then it is considered as having highest fitness. It denotes $f(x)$ as the objective function, should be minimized for the particle.

5.2 Global Best (g-best)

The robustness of g-best or global best is, it provides a faster rate of convergence at lower expense. This g-best particle has only a single best solution known as global best particle Pg among all the particles in the population or swarm. It behaves as an attractor and helps to pull the particles in the group toward it. Slowly all particles are being converged to g-best position. The swarm may converge in a premature manner unless updated regularly.

PSO algorithm mainly consists of three steps such as initialization, velocity updating and position updating.

Initialization. A swarm of particles are initialized randomly with positions and velocities in the problem space. Once the lower and upper limits of the decision variable are specified, the search space is getting confined. The coordinates are initialized with both positions as well velocities within a certain permissible range by fulfilling both equality and inequality constraints.

Velocity updating. The velocity of each particle in PSO is calculated using the distance traveled by the particle. It depends on the particle memory that is the previous best position and the swarm memory, which is the previous best solution. The velocity of each particle is updated by using the velocity updation equation by considering the particle memory and swarm memory.

$$v_i(t + 1) = wv_i(t) + c_1 r_1 [\hat{x}_i(t) - x_i(t)] + c_2 r_2 [g(t) - x_i(t)] \tag{1}$$

where

i	is considered for particle index
w	is the inertia weight to balance the local and global coefficient
c_1 and c_2	are considered as acceleration coefficients
r_1 and r_2	are random values generated with every velocity updation
$x_i(t)$	is the particle's position at time t
$\hat{x}(t)$	is the particle's individual best solution as of time t
$v_i(t)$	is the particle's velocity at time t
$g(t)$	is the swarm's best solution as of time t

Position updating. Between the successive iterations, the coordinates of all particles are updated according to the given equation:

$$x_i(t + 1) = x_i(t) + v_i(t + 1) \tag{2}$$

where $x_i(t + 1)$ is the new position, $x_i(t)$ is the previous position and $v_i(t + 1)$ is the new velocity.

PSO with Neural Network. PSO has a vast application area in evolutionary system to evolve artificial neural networks and other classification methods based on PSO algorithm [22, 23]. PSO-NN coordinates the architecture and the weights of neural network as shown in Fig. 3. PSO algorithm is used to predict the positioning errors, caused due to their geometric parameters [24]. A hybrid approach of PSO and NN training has been proposed in this research study for a better predictive result by considering different performance parameters for both training and testing. PSO-based NN is applied on the neurons of the neural network to optimize the parameter values and it helps to minimize the mean square error (MSE) iteratively. PSO helps for optimizing the weight matrices of the neural network and it is used to produce an output through an axon to another neuron. A correctly trained neural network is considered as an expert in categorizing the information that to be analyzed.

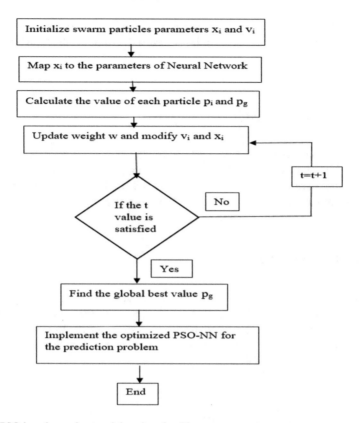

Fig. 3 PSO-based neural network learning algorithm

6 Result and Performance Analysis

To detect the fraudulent transactions, we have implemented both GA-based neural network as well as PSO-based neural network to find the prediction accuracy values and other performance parameters.

6.1 Dataset Used for Experiment

The optimal usage of dataset is a prior requirement to conduct the classification methodology. The size and volume of dataset most probably affect both training as well as testing data. Fraudulent classification data has been applied for the proposed classification model with optimization techniques has been retrieved from Kaggle website (https://www.kaggle.com/mlgulb/creditcardfraud). The dataset has a dimension of 31 columns and 284,807 rows. From it, 70% data instances are applied for training and remaining 30% for testing purpose. The predictive accuracy value and other evaluation metrics have been optimized with 70% training data and 30% testing data.

6.2 Experimental Setup

GA-based neural network and PSO-NN optimization algorithms have been implemented in Matlab platform version R2019a. During the implementation, the system configuration was noted as core i7 processor and 3.4 GHz clock speed. The secondary and main memory space were 1 TB and 8 GB, respectively.

6.3 Confusion Matrix

A confusion matrix helps to represent various evaluation metrics in a classification model. It shows the correct and incorrect classification samples with actual and predictive results in the test data. It is designed to count the number of all four results for the two-class classification and denoted as true positive, false positive, true negative and false negative.

6.4 Performance Parameters

Different performance metrics such as accuracy, sensitivity, precision, F-measure, specificity and mean square error (MSE) are evaluated by using the values in confusion matrix. The parameter values for the PSO-based neural network are compared by setting the iteration values and the predictive accuracy value is calculated and the mean square error value is observed with PSO-based neural network.

We have implemented Genetic algorithm and PSO with neural network technique and their performance parameters are critically analyzed. In the GA-based neural network the predictive accuracy is observed to be 89.91%. The genetic algorithm simulation result as shown in Fig. 4 represents the maximum instances lies between − 5 and + 5 values and few instances are sparse away.

In the PSO-based neural network, various performance parameters are critically evaluated by considering five phases with five different iterations and the mean square error is observed for each phase. We have considered the population or swarm size 100.

In Table 1, the experimental values of various performance parameters have been presented. They have been assessed by considering 70 and 30% of training and testing data, respectively. The performance measures are critically assessed for accuracy, sensitivity, specificity, precision, F-measure and mean square error. We have

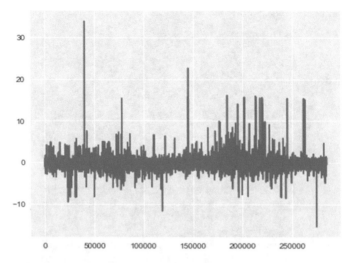

Fig. 4 Simulation result by implementing genetic algorithm

considered five different phases to find the result of various parameters. The prediction accuracy for phase 5 is observed to be 91.58%, which is significantly improved comparing to other four phases. The mean square error has been reduced in phase 5 and observed to be 0.67%. In PSO-based neural network technique, the optimized value of predictive accuracy with other performance measures have been achieved with reduced false alarm.

By using the PSO-based neural network the best cost is calculated in terms of mean square error value. From Figs. 5, 6, 7, 8 and 9, the X-label shows the total number of iterations and the Y-label shows the best cost value. In phase 1, phase 2, phase 3, phase 4, phase 5, we have taken the iterations 100, 200, 500, 1000 and 2000, respectively, having the population or swarm size 100. We observed that the best cost value in terms of mean square error value is reduced with more number of iterations. In phase 5, the MSE value is observed to be 0.67% when 2000 number of iterations are taken into consideration. Also, the predictive accuracy value is significantly increased and is observed to be highest, i.e., 91.58% when 2000 number of iterations are considered.

Table 1 Performance results for PSO-based neural network

Performance parameters	Phase 1	Phase 2	Phase 3	Phase 4	Phase 5
Accuracy	90.01	90.21	90.34	91.13	91.58
Sensitivity	91.11	90.06	91.05	90.00	91.69
Specificity	90.07	93.84	90.75	91.78	92.81
Precision	98.92	96.01	96.35	98.09	97.93
F-measure	95.29	94.85	94.92	95.36	95.50
MSE	5.46	3.03	1.45	1.07	0.67

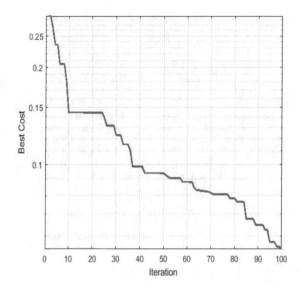

Fig. 5 Best cost is calculated with 100 iterations

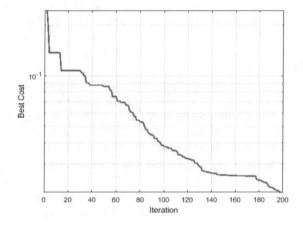

Fig. 6 Best cost is calculated with 200 iterations

7 Conclusion

In this proposed study, GA and PSO are employed along with neural network to make the learning process faster. The credit card fraud detection technique will be more efficient when the GA and PSO algorithms use the machine learning classification technique such as neural network. Among the GA-based neural network and PSO-based neural network, the latter has an improved prediction accuracy of 91.58%, when 2000 iterations are considered. The best cost is optimized with increasing the

Fig. 7 Best cost is calculated with 500 iterations

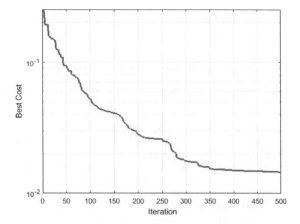

Fig. 8 Best cost is calculated with 1000 iterations

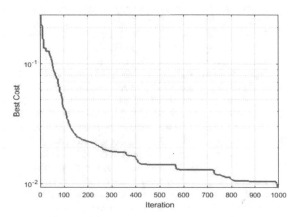

Fig. 9 Best cost is calculated with 2000 iterations

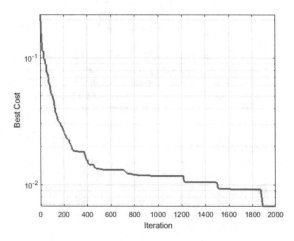

number of iterations and the mean square error value has been reduced to 0.67%, when the total number of iterations are 2000 considered.

References

1. Behdad M, Barone L, Bennamoun M, French T (2012) Nature-inspired techniques in the context of fraud detection. IEEE Trans Syst Man Cybern Part C (Appl Rev) 42(6):1273–1290
2. Gayathri C, Umarani R (2015) Efficient detection of financial fraud detection by selecting optimal ensemble architecture using optimization approaches. Indian J Innov Dev 4(8):1–9
3. Gadi MFA, Wang X, do Lago AP (2008) Credit card fraud detection with artificial immune system. In: International conference on artificial immune systems, pp 119–131. Springer, Berlin
4. Prusti D (2015) Efficient intrusion detection model using ensemble methods. PhD dissertation
5. Prusti D, Harshini Padmanabhuni SS, Rath SK (2020) Credit card fraud detection by implementing machine learning techniques. In: Safety, security, and reliability of robotic systems. CRC Press, Boca Raton, pp 205–216
6. Duman E, Hamdi Ozcelik M (2011) Detecting credit card fraud by genetic algorithm and scatter search. Exp Syst Appl 38(10):13057–13063
7. Alam S, Dobbie G, Riddle P, Asif Naeem M (2010) A swarm intelligence based clustering approach for outlier detection. In: IEEE congress on evolutionary computation, pp 1–7. IEEE
8. Shahreza ML, Moazzami D, Moshiri B, Delavar MR (2011) Anomaly detection using a self-organizing map and particle swarm optimization. Scientia Iranica 18(6):1460–1468
9. Panigrahi S, Kundu A, Sural S, Majumdar AK (2009) Credit card fraud detection: a fusion approach using Dempster–Shafer theory and Bayesian learning. Inf Fus 10(4):354-363
10. Sánchez D, Vila MA, Cerda L, Serrano JM (2009) Association rules applied to credit card fraud detection. Expert Syst Appl 36(2):3630–3640
11. Mitchell M (1998) An introduction to genetic algorithms. MIT press
12. Aote SS, Raghuwanshi MM, Malik L (2013) A brief review on particle swarm optimization: limitations & future directions. Int J Comput Sci Eng (IJCSE), 14(1):196–200
13. Bratton D, Kennedy J (2007) Defining a standard for particle swarm optimization. In 2007 IEEE swarm intelligence symposium, IEEE, pp 120–127
14. Brause R, Langsdorf T, Hepp M (1999) Neural data mining for credit card fraud detection. In: Proceedings 11th international conference on tools with artificial intelligence, pp 103–106. IEEE
15. Prusti D, Rath SK (2019) Fraudulent transaction detection in credit card by applying ensemble machine learning techniques. In: 2019 10th international conference on computing, communication and networking technologies (ICCCNT), pp 1–6. IEEE
16. Ghosh S, Reilly DL (1994) Credit card fraud detection with a neural-network. In: Proceedings of the twenty-seventh Hawaii international conference on system sciences, vol 3, 621–630. IEEE
17. Patidar R, Sharma L (2011) Credit card fraud detection using neural network. Int J Soft Comput Eng (IJSCE) 1:32–38
18. Zhang Y, Wang S, Lenan W, Huo Y (2010) PSONN used for remote-sensing image classification. J Comput Inform Syst 6(13):4417–4425
19. Kennedy J, Eberhart RC (1995) Particle swarm optimization. In: Proceedings of IEEE international conference on neural networks, Piscataway, NJ, pp 39–43
20. https://shodhganga.inflibnet.ac.in/bitstream/10603/181389/12/12_chapter%204.pdf, Particle swarm optimization
21. Elías A, Ochoa-Zezzatti A, Padilla A, Ponce J (2011) Outlier analysis for plastic card fraud detection a hybridized and multi-objective approach. In: International conference on hybrid artificial intelligence systems, pp 1–9. Springer, Berlin

22. Das M, Taylan, Canan Dulger L (2007) Off-line signature verification with PSO-NN algorithm. In: 2007 22nd international symposium on computer and information sciences, pp 1–6. IEEE
23. Zhang C, Shao H, Li Y (2000) Particle swarm optimization for evolving artificial neural network. In: Proceedings of the IEEE international conference on systems, man and cybernetics 2000, pp 2487–2490
24. Zhang JR, Zhang J, Lok TM, Lyu MR (2006) A Hybrid particle swarm optimization-back propagation algorithm for feedforward neural network training. Appl Math Comput 185:1026–1037

Traditional Indian Textile Designs Classification Using Transfer Learning

Seema Varshney, C. Vasantha Lakshmi, and C. Patvardhan

1 Introduction

Three fundamental requirements in human life are food, clothing, and shelter. While all three are important for life and living, clothing reflects the living culture and aesthetic sense of the age thoroughly. The fashion trends today are completely different from that of our past. The traditional costumes reflect the way of life in respective times. The traditional motifs that bring out the characteristics of the national heritage fabric give us a unique identity among various cultures [1].

Famous embroidery styles include 'Phulkari from Punjab,' 'Kashida from Kashmir,' 'Chikankari from Uttar Pradesh,' 'Kasuti from Karnataka,' 'Kantha from West Bengal,' 'Chamba rumal from Himachal Pradesh,' 'Pipli appliqué from Orissa,' and 'Sujani from Bihar' are some of the other famous embroidery styles which have given recognition to their places of origins. 'Resist-dyed production technique' as against embroidered varieties are also used in traditional textiles like 'Bandhini of Gujarat,' Bandhas of Odisha, Pochampally Ikats (yarn resist-dyed) of Andhra Pradesh. The Bandhej (fabric resist-dyed) and Lehariya of Rajasthan, Patola of Gujarat, Bandhas of Odisha, Pochampally Ikats (yarn resist-dyed) of Andhra Pradesh. The origin of the technique and the procedure again varies from region to region. Another technique employed in textile production is printing using hand-carved wooden blocks. Examples of printed textiles include Bagru and Sanganeri prints of

S. Varshney (✉) · C. Vasantha Lakshmi
Department of Physics and Computer Science, Dayalbagh Educational Institute, Agra, India
e-mail: seema@dei.ac.in

C. Vasantha Lakshmi
e-mail: vasanthalakshmi@dei.ac.in

C. Patvardhan
Department of Electrical Engineering, Dayalbagh Educational Institute, Agra, India
e-mail: cpatvardhan@dei.ac.in

© The Author(s), under exclusive license to Springer Nature Singapore Pte Ltd. 2023
R. Doriya et al. (eds.), *Machine Learning, Image Processing, Network Security and Data Sciences*, Lecture Notes in Electrical Engineering 946,
https://doi.org/10.1007/978-981-19-5868-7_28

Rajasthan, Kalamkari prints from Andhra Pradesh, Madhubani from Bihar, Warli from Maharashtra, etc. Such is the huge variety and diversity of Indian textiles.

For such a diverse Indian Textile Industry, creativity and innovation has to be an integral part. Currently, it is up to textile designers as to how they make creative new designs while adhering to the traditional motifs, techniques, and styles of the respective regions. Fashion designers try to contemporize traditional designs. The industry is caught in a changing landscape with two problems being most prominent.

- The traditional design process is extremely skill-oriented with the human worker being the designer and the implementer of the design as well. The designers learn the skills painstakingly and their productivity is pretty much limited with not much technical support. The art component is extremely high, and the quality and quantity both depend on the individual designer concerned. Demand for larger variety is insatiable and individual designers find it hard to bring in more variety because of limited skills and training.
- The onslaught of technology has made time to market the crucial deciding factor between success and failure. New designs are supposed to be brought to market as fast as possible with the early bird getting the advantage in a winner takes all situation.

Therefore, there is a need for an automated traditional textile design classification system so that the productivity of the textile industry business can be improved. It is necessary to meet the needs of customers as well as to preserve our traditional art heritage form.

For pattern recognition, deep learning techniques, namely convolutional neural networks (CNN), can be used [2–4]. As an alternative to training from the ground up, transfer learning has great potential. It is so because, in this, a network trained on one task is fine-tuned and implemented to another but related task [5, 6]. Transfer learning revolves around the idea of extraction of labeled data or knowledge from related domains. It is done to help a machine learning algorithm such that to achieve elevated performance in the domain of interest. Two prominent ways can be followed for the application of transfer learning—as a feature generator or as a baseline [7–9]. In a pre-trained network, the parameters are modified in line with the required task when used as a baseline. Although when utilized as a feature generator, the features are filtered from the input and then deployed to train a new classifier.

In this paper, an attempt is made to design an effective and efficient approach for Indian traditional textile designs classification problems using Transfer learning. Two competitive pre-trained networks: InceptionResNetV2 and VGG16 are experimented with to try and obtain the top-performing network. The major difficulty was the non-availability of a ready database of images of traditional Indian textiles. Efforts were, therefore, made to create one from scratch, and this database was used for the purpose at hand. Specifically, the following experiments were performed.

- A database of seven Indian Traditional Textile classes (Batik, Chikankari, Ikat, Kalamkari, Kashida, Madhubani, and Warli) images was created using images collected from various sources.

- Experiments were performed for three different training–testing data splits to determine the best split for obtaining the best classification results.
- For every experiment, fine-tuning is attempted layer-wise as well as with a logistic regression classifier.

This is the first reported attempt for the classification of traditional Indian textiles. The work is intended to decrease the time of creating new designs for meeting the ever-growing demand for fabric designs in the market. It also helps the e-commerce industry as well as the shoppers to search for traditional designs.

2 Prior Art

Deep learning-based models have emerged as the best performers in many fields for image classification and object recognition [10]. The CNN, which is a deep learning model, is widely regarded as the state-of-the-art model for image classification. One of its usages was as the base structure by ILSVRC-2014 top achievers [11]. It has been shown to refine results in other problems of image classification like Batik classification [12]. To increase the image classification's performance on small datasets, 'CNN-based methods' have different strategies: either by data augmentation or by transfer learning. Wang and Perez [13] investigated the effectiveness of data augmentation in image classification. Agastya et al. proved data augmentation approach in deep learning improved the accuracy in classification problems [14].

Machine learning and image processing methods have been utilized to identify fabric pattern designs [15, 16]. A handmade embroidery pattern recognition system was developed by Jimoh et al. on a new validated database [17]. Olawale et al. developed a Model for African Traditional Fabrics Analysis and Recognition system using a two-level classification scheme [18]. Fabric weaving patterns can be identified using machine learning techniques [19–21]. Some researchers have experimented with some improved approaches like using convolution neural networks to match large-scale clothes styles and patterns with comprehensive annotation [22]. Gultom et al. classified batik classes using a multi-layer perceptron (MLP) classifier on the VGG16 pre-trained network, and it performed better than SIFT and SURF approaches [23].

No work has been reported on traditional Indian textile designs. This work is intended to fill this gap.

3 Methodology

Here in this work, the two renowned pre-trained CNN models: VGG16 and Inception-ResNetV2, are used, for transfer learning by logistic regression classifier and by layer-wise fine-tuning. Training of both models is done on ImageNet dataset which contains millions of images pertaining to 1000 classes. The InceptionRes-NetV2 network is 164 layers deep and its input image size is 299-by-299. Moreover, for a wide range of images, it has learned rich feature representations. Whereas VGG16 is 16 layers deep and its input image size is 224-by-224. Both VGG16 and InceptionResNetV2 are frequently used pre-trained CNN models because of their exhaustive architecture. Furthermore, when it came to the 2014 ImageNet Large Scale Visual Recognition Challenge (ILSVRC-2014), VGG16 achieved the first place in localization and the second place in classification. One of the significant revelations of VGG16 is generalization on the various other datasets including Caltech-256, Caltech-101, PASCAL VOC 2007, and PASCAL VOC 2012 [11, 24]. 'InceptionRes-NetV2' is a variant of 'Inception-v1' which is in actual 'The Inception deep convolutional architecture' incepted as GoogLeNet in Szegedy et al. [25]. It is a high-cost hybrid Inception version, with conspicuously better-quality recognition performance [26]. In this work, as a feature generator, the pre-trained network explained above is utilized in view of all the activations before the last entirely associated layer in the network. Additionally, to study a new classifier for the classification ground, these activations are used as features vectors. In this context, to make the final decision, logistic regression (LR) is exploited as a new classifier.

Moreover, both the mentioned pre-trained networks are also fine-tuned layer-wise. Here, the entire layered structure from a previously learned model was selected and the last fully connected layer was detached, which brings a chance for each of the 1000 classes in the ImageNet and substitutes it with a layer that changes the classification stage up to our requirement. This means we could take all the low-level and high-level information that the pre-trained network has trained on the ImageNet and implement to our problem. For this, we start our network with the weights from the ImageNet and then fix all the convolutional and max-pooling layers such that not to alter their weights, leaving behind only the completely connected ones free. The impact of size of the training–testing data is also accounted for the behavior of fine-tuned layer-wise and by logistic regression classifier network.

3.1 Dataset

The traditional textile designs database was created for seven traditional classes, i.e., Batik, Chikankari, Ikat, Kalamkari, Kashida, Madhubani, and Warli of India. The colored images of individual traditional classes were collected, from various sources. Every class consists tentatively of the same number of images. This dataset includes a total of 1046 images. Images were cleaned, cropped, enhanced, resized and compressed during the pre-processing processes. Joint Photographic Enhanced Graphic Format (JPEG) images were saved in 1200 × 1200 pixels with the JPEG tool and compressed. Data samples in the data set are depicted in Fig. 1.

Fig. 1 Textile design images from traditional textile design dataset with four classes. **a** Batik, **b** Kalamkari, **c** Madhubani, and **d** Warli

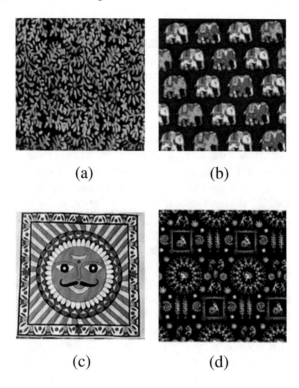

(a) (b)

(c) (d)

4 Results and Discussion

Here, we have shown that our results are coherent for the traditional Indian Textile Designs Classification application. The dataset prepared is used for both fine-tuning layer-wise and fine-tuning logistic regression classifier CNNs. A similar configuration is used for all experiments: HP Z6 G4 Workstation with Intel(R) Xeon(R) Silver 4208 CPU @2.10 GHz 2.10 GHz (2 processors), NVIDIA QUADRO RTX 6000 GPU, Windows 10, 256 GB RAM.

We investigate the potential of layer-wise finely tuned CNNs in the context of textile design images classification as an alternative to fine-tuned logistic regression classifier. Along with the selection of the best hyperparameter, each experiment is run 30 times. Layers from an earlier trained model were carefully chosen. To avoid destroying any information during subsequent training rounds, layers were frozen and then some new layers are added over these frozen ones. It seems that they learned to predict based on old features on our dataset.

According to the researchers, image classifiers need a great deal of fine-tuning to be accurate. In order to achieve optimal performance, shallow tuning or updating of the final few layers of the convolutional algorithm is found to be enough in many applications.

To assess the classification behavior of the fine-tuned CNN approaches, the training data and testing data are separated from the entire dataset. This method of separating data, in neural networks, is a common practice for performance analysis. To figure out the impact of the size of training–testing data is related to network behavior—three separating ways are utilized viz (90%:10%, 80%:20%, 70%:30%).

With the application of these three splitting ways, experiments are accomplished for both fine-tuned approaches. Precision, recall, and F1 score for each class individually are the terms in which the experimental outcomes are assessed. After each experiment, the average results of the seven classes are calculated to make assessment easier. Furthermore, the presentation of classification values is authenticated using the receiver operating characteristic (ROC) analysis and area under the curve (AUC), as illustrated in Fig. 2. In the present work, we maintain the pre-trained network weights, on the hypothesis that they are already quite proficiently trained. Tables 1 and 2 present the outcomes gained from the transfer learning layer-wise and by logistic regression classifier of InceptionResNetV2, and VGG16 on the Indian Traditional Textile Design dataset.

According to Table 1, it is evident that fine-tuning Inception ResNetV2 Layer-wise substantially improves performance in comparison to VGG16. However, because of the extremely large size of the network, inadequate performance may arise. In addition to decreasing the capacity of the network, freezing some layers may lead to over-fitting. We obtain performance gain by fine-tuning the additional trainable layers with the best parameters on top of the frozen layers of the pre-trained networks. Further, in performance assessment for the layer-wise fine-tuning and by LR classifier fine-tuning, InceptionResNetV2 showed a better performance than the VGG16 network as demonstrated in Tables 1 and 2.

As shown in Fig. 2, the receiver operating characteristic (ROC) curves and area under the curves (AUCs) of layer-wise and logistic regression classifier networks are equated when training and testing are split by 90%:10%. As can be seen in Tables 1 and 2, the layer-wise Inception ResNetV2 (AUC-96.03%) and VGG16 (AUC-93.64%) performed better than the pre-trained logistic regression classifier InceptionResNetV2 (AUC-95.18%), and VGG16 (AUC-93.21%) by a small amount. Both the networks exhibited good results after a 90% :10% split of the training – testing data; however, the condition is slightly unlike for pre-trained fine-tune layer-wise VGG16 which presented the same performance for the 80%:20% split in the training– testing data. The nonconformity of VGG16 from the normal trend is on account of its more sensitivity toward Batik, Chikankari, Ikat, Kalamkari, Kashida, Madhubani, and Warli during 70% of training and 30% of testing data split. As a conclusion, it has been verified that the layer-wise transfer learning style ends up in a remarkable outcome about transfer learning by LR classifier over the textile designs, even if the training dataset is restricted in size.

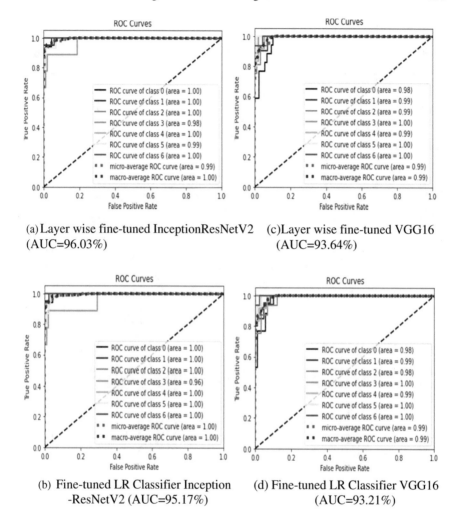

(a) Layer wise fine-tuned InceptionResNetV2 (AUC=96.03%)

(c) Layer wise fine-tuned VGG16 (AUC=93.64%)

(b) Fine-tuned LR Classifier Inception -ResNetV2 (AUC=95.17%)

(d) Fine-tuned LR Classifier VGG16 (AUC=93.21%)

Fig. 2 Traditional textile design classification ROC analysis curve for 90%:10% training–testing split

5 Conclusions and Future Directions

Traditional Indian textile designs are very rich and varied and reflect the culture of the area in which they are popular. They have heritage value, and it is imperative that attempts must be made to preserve them. Unfortunately, the number of artisans is dwindling for these forms of art because of the onslaught of mechanization and low productivity of the handmade textiles. The art has to be learned painstakingly and creating new designs in sync with the market trends is again a time taking task. Any

Table 1 Traditional textile design classification performance evaluation using fine-tuning by layer-wise pre-trained network (InceptionResNetV2, and VGG16)

Model name	Hyper-parameter learning rate = lr Drop_out = drop Neurons = nr	Train-test data splitting (%)	Class-type	Precision	Recall	F-score	Correctly identified images	Accuracy (%)	AUC (%)
Inception Res-NetV2	lr = 0.0001 Drop = 0.2, 0.2 nr = 15,361,536	**90–10**	Batik	1.00	0.88	0.94	98/105	**93.33**	**96.03**
			Chikankari	0.90	0.95	0.93			
			Ikat	0.94	1.00	0.97			
			Kalamkari	0.80	0.89	0.84			
			Kashida	0.92	1.00	0.96			
			Madhubani	1.00	0.80	0.89			
			Warli	0.94	1.00	0.97			
			Avg/Total	0.94	0.93	0.93			
		80–20	Batik	1.00	0.83	0.91	192/210	91.43	94.67
			Chikankari	0.94	0.94	0.94			
			Ikat	0.89	0.94	0.91			
			Kalamkari	0.89	0.77	0.83			
			Kashida	0.87	0.96	0.92			
			Madhubani	0.94	0.94	0.94			
			Warli	0.87	0.96	0.92			
			Avg/Total	0.92	0.91	0.91			
		70–30	Batik	0.91	0.72	0.81	280/314	89.17	93.49
			Chikankari	0.88	0.92	0.90			
			Ikat	0.94	0.93	0.93			

(continued)

Table 1 (continued)

Model name	Hyper-parameter learning rate = lr Drop_out = drop Neurons = nr	Train-test data splitting (%)	Class-type	Precision	Recall	F-score	Correctly identified images	Accuracy (%)	AUC (%)
			Kalamkari	0.88	0.78	0.82			
			Kashida	0.80	0.98	0.88			
			Madhubani	0.92	0.92	0.92			
			Warli	0.91	0.97	0.94			
			Avg/Total	0.89	0.89	0.89			
VGG16	lr = 0.0002 Drop = 0.3 nr = 1024,1024	90–10	Batik	0.81	0.76	0.79	93/105	88.57	93.64
			Chikankari	0.90	0.90	0.90			
			Ikat	0.82	0.88	0.85			
			Kalamkari	0.82	1.00	0.90			
			Kashida	0.91	0.83	0.87			
			Madhubani	0.93	0.93	0.93			
			Warli	1.00	0.94	0.97			
			Avg/Total	0.89	0.89	0.89			
		80–20	Batik	0.83	0.83	0.83	186/210	88.57	93.33
			Chikankari	0.97	0.83	0.90			
			Ikat	0.90	0.82	0.86			
			Kalamkari	0.83	0.86	0.84			
			Kashida	0.81	0.89	0.85			
			Madhubani	0.92	1.00	0.96			
			Warli	0.93	0.96	0.95			

(continued)

Table 1 (continued)

Model name	Hyper-parameter learning rate = lr Drop_out = drop Neurons = nr	Train-test data splitting (%)	Class-type	Precision	Recall	F-score	Correctly identified images	Accuracy (%)	AUC (%)
			Avg/Total	0.89	0.89	0.89			
		70–30	Batik	0.86	0.84	0.85	274/314	87.26	92.67
			Chikankari	0.92	0.92	0.92			
			Ikat	0.91	0.76	0.83			
			Kalamkari	0.81	0.83	0.82			
			Kashida	0.74	0.90	0.81			
			Madhubani	0.94	0.92	0.93			
			Warli	0.93	0.95	0.94			
			Avg/Total	0.88	0.87	0.87			

Bold signifies the most suitable values obtained through different parameters

Table 2 Traditional textile design classification performance evaluation using fine-tuning by logistic regression classifier pre-trained network (InceptionResNetV2, and VGG16)

Model name	Hyper-parameter tolerance = tol	Train-test data splitting (%)	Class-type	Precision	Recall	F-score	Correctly identified images	Accuracy (%)	AUC (%)
Inception Res-NetV2 + LR	tol = 0.0002	**90–10**	Batik	1.00	0.88	0.94	97/105	**92.38**	**95.18**
			Chikankari	0.90	0.95	0.93			
			Ikat	0.88	0.94	0.91			
			Kalamkari	0.88	0.78	0.82			
			Kashida	0.92	1.00	0.96			
			Madhubani	0.93	0.87	0.90			
			Warli	0.94	1.00	0.97			
			Avg/Total	0.93	0.92	0.92			
		80–20	Batik	0.96	0.86	0.91	190/210	90.48	94.25
			Chikankari	0.92	0.94	0.93			
			Ikat	0.94	0.91	0.92			
			Kalamkari	0.89	0.77	0.83			
			Kashida	0.85	1.00	0.92			
			Madhubani	0.94	0.85	0.89			
			Warli	0.84	0.96	0.90			
			Avg/Total	0.91	0.90	0.90			
		70–30	Batik	0.92	0.84	0.88	278/314	88.54	93.25
			Chikankari	0.87	0.92	0.89			
			Ikat	0.98	0.91	0.94			
			Kalamkari	0.83	0.81	0.82			

(continued)

Table 2 (continued)

Model name	Hyper-parameter tolerance = tol	Train-test data splitting (%)	Class-type	Precision	Recall	F-score	Correctly identified images	Accuracy (%)	AUC (%)
			Kashida	0.78	0.95	0.86			
			Madhubani	0.91	0.84	0.88			
			Warli	0.90	0.93	0.91			
			Avg/Total	0.89	0.89	0.89			
VGG16 + LR	tol = 0.02	90–10	Batik	0.81	0.76	0.79	92/105	87.62	93.21
			Chikankari	0.89	0.85	0.87			
			Ikat	0.82	0.88	0.85			
			Kalamkari	0.75	1.00	0.86			
			Kashida	0.91	0.83	0.87			
			Madhubani	0.93	0.93	0.93			
			Warli	1.00	0.94	0.97			
			Avg/Total	0.88	0.88	0.88			
		80–20	Batik	0.85	0.79	0.82	182/210	86.66	92.01
			Chikankari	0.91	0.89	0.90			
			Ikat	0.88	0.85	0.86			
			Kalamkari	0.77	0.77	0.77			
			Kashida	0.77	0.86	0.81			
			Madhubani	0.91	0.91	0.91			
			Warli	0.93	0.96	0.95			
			Avg/Total	0.87	0.87	0.87			

(continued)

Table 2 (continued)

Model name	Hyper-parameter tolerance = tol	Train-test data splitting (%)	Class-type	Precision	Recall	F-score	Correctly identified images	Accuracy (%)	AUC (%)
		70–30	Batik	0.85	0.81	0.83	270/314	85.99	91.83
			Chikankari	0.88	0.92	0.90			
			Ikat	0.91	0.80	0.85			
			Kalamkari	0.79	0.83	0.81			
			Kashida	0.72	0.80	0.76			
			Madhubani	0.92	0.90	0.91			
			Warli	0.93	0.95	0.94			
			Avg/Total	0.86	0.86	0.86			

Bold signifies the most suitable values obtained through different parameters attempt at developing technology for the preservation of these art forms is, therefore, the need of the hour.

In this work, an attempt has been to create a database of traditional Indian textiles designs and use transfer learning with CNNs for classifying the textile images. Two pre-trained networks (InceptionResNetV2, and VGG16) are employed for fine-tuning layer-wise and by LR classifier. The fine-tuned layer-wise pre-trained InceptionResNetV2 yielded the best performance with 93.33% accuracy, and 96.03% area under the ROC curve (AUC). This work can be extended toward the development of content-based retrieval of similar designs to aid the designer in creating new designs and verifying their novelty and, ultimately, toward automatic designs using learnings from evolutionary art and creative AI.

References

1. Upadhyay MN, Gandhi I (1966) Handicrafts of India, Andhra Pradesh book distributors
2. Le Cun Y, Bengio Y, Hinton G (2015) Deep learning. Nature 521:436–444
3. Hoffer E, Ailon N (2015) Deep metric learning using triplet network. In: International workshop on similarity-based pattern recognition
4. Irsoy O, Alpaydın E (2019) Continuously constructive deep neural networks. IEEE Trans Neural Netw Learn Syst 31:1124–1133
5. Ellis HC (1965) The transfer of learning
6. Pan SJ, Yang Q (2009) A survey on transfer learning. IEEE Trans Knowl Data Eng 22:1345–1359
7. Sharif Razavian A, Azizpour H, Sullivan J, Carlsson S (2014) CNN features off-the-shelf: an astounding baseline for recognition. In: Proceedings of the IEEE conference on computer vision and pattern recognition workshops
8. Azizpour H, Sharif Razavian A, Sullivan J, Maki A, Carlsson S (2015) From generic to specific deep representations for visual recognition. In: Proceedings of the IEEE conference on computer vision and pattern recognition (CVPR) workshops
9. Gopalakrishnan K, Khaitan SK, Choudhary A, Agrawal A (2017) Deep convolutional neural networks with transfer learning for computer vision-based data-driven pavement distress detection. Constr Build Mater 157:322–330
10. Rawat W, Wang Z (2017) Deep convolutional neural networks for image classification: a comprehensive review. Neural Comput 29:2352–2449
11. Simonyan K, Zisserman A (2014) Very deep convolutional networks for large-scale image recognition. arXiv preprint arXiv:1409.1556
12. Wicaksono AY, Suciati N, Fatichah C, Uchimura K, Koutaki G (2017) Modified convolutional neural network architecture for batik motif image classification. IPTEK J Sci 2
13. Perez L, Wang J (2017) The effectiveness of data augmentation in image classification using deep learning. arXiv preprint arXiv:1712.04621
14. Agastya IMA, Setyanto A (2018) Classification of Indonesian batik using deep learning techniques and data augmentation. In: 2018 3rd international conference on information technology, information system and electrical engineering (ICITISEE)
15. Zhang R, Xin B (2016) A review of woven fabric pattern recognition based on image processing technology. Res J Textile Apparel
16. Loke KS (2017) Automatic recognition of clothes pattern and motifs empowering online fashion shopping. In: 2017 IEEE international conference on consumer electronics-Taiwan (ICCE-TW)
17. Jimoh KO, Odéjobí OÀ, Folárànmí SA, Aina S (2020) Handmade embroidery pattern recognition: a new validated database. Malaysian J Comput 5:390–402

18. Olawale JB, Ajayi AO (2013) A model for African fabrics analysis and recognition. Int J Comput Appl 975:8887
19. Pan R, Gao W, Liu J, Wang H (2010) Automatic recognition of woven fabric patterns based on pattern database. Fibers Polym 11:303–308
20. Jing J, Xu M, Li P, Li Q, Liu S (2014) Automatic classification of woven fabric structure based on texture feature and PNN. Fibers Polym 15:1092–1098
21. Boonsirisumpun N, Puarungroj W (2018) Loei fabric weaving pattern recognition using deep neural network. In: 2018 15th international joint conference on computer science and software engineering (JCSSE)
22. Liu Z, Luo P, Qiu S, Wang X, Tang X (2016) Deepfashion: powering robust clothes recognition and retrieval with rich annotations. In: Proceedings of the IEEE conference on computer vision and pattern recognition
23. Gultom Y, Arymurthy AM, Masikome RJ (2018) Batik classification using deep convolutional network transfer learning. Jurnal Ilmu Komputer dan Informasi 11:59–66
24. Wang P, Cottrell GW (2015) Basic level categorization facilitates visual object recognition. arXiv preprint arXiv:1511.04103
25. Szegedy C, Liu W, Jia Y, Sermanet P, Reed S, Anguelov D, Erhan D, Vanhoucke V, Rabinovich A (2015) Going deeper with convolutions. In: Proceedings of the IEEE conference on computer vision and pattern recognition
26. Russakovsky O, Deng J, Su H, Krause J, Satheesh S, Ma S, Huang Z, Karpathy A, Khosla A, Bernstein M et al (2015) Imagenet large scale visual recognition challenge. Int J Comput Vis 115:211–252

Classification of Electrocardiogram Signal Using Hybrid Deep Learning Techniques

Ishu Garg, Saroj Kumar Pandey, Rekh Ram Janghel, and Anupam Shukla

1   Introduction

According to various reports by global health organizations as well as WHO, primarily, cardiovascular diseases are responsible for the majority of deaths across the globe. Annually, the number of deaths recorded from cardiac diseases is more than deaths resulting due to any other disease. Eighty-five percent of the deaths among these thirty-one percent are due to strokes and heart attacks. Generally, seventy-five percent of cardiac deaths occur globally at places with lower income groups or middle ones [1]. As of 2015, 82% of the 17 million deaths which were premature in nature occurred in countries with income groups from lower and middle section of society. These were mainly due to non-communicable diseases, and the remaining ones were caused due to heart abnormalities. Cardiac arrhythmias and their long-term effect are the main reasons of CVDs which if ignored result in fatal issues. Arrhythmias are generally found when there is problem in electrical conduction of impulses to the heart and the coordination of heartbeats is irregular.

When the heart rate is either too slow or too fast, the resulting condition is called Arrhythmia. It is basically a rhythm conduction disorder and there is a crucial significance of Arrhythmias in ECG abnormalities [2]. Fatal heart arrhythmias and other

I. Garg (✉) · A. Shukla
IIIT Pune, Pune, India
e-mail: ishugarg567@gmail.com

S. K. Pandey
GLA University Mathura, Chaumuhan, India
e-mail: saroj.pandey@gla.ac.in

R. R. Janghel
NIT Raipur, Raipur, India
e-mail: rrjanghel.it@nitrr.ac.in

abnormalities which pose great harm should be and can be identified using Electro-cardiography (ECG), where the electrical impulse and activities of a patient's heart are detected by the help of electrodes which are put on the chest part of the patient's body [3]. Generally, ECG sessions to record data last for a long time and the clinicians and doctors study and assess the waveforms to detect whether the patient is under any potential health risk or not and if any heart abnormalities are present or not [4]. This complete procedure consumes a lot of time. Henceforth, detection of heart arrhythmias in medical field is very critical for timely diagnosis by the doctors and clinicians.

In our proposed study, we have evaluated our proposed technique on the conventional database, i.e., MIT-BIH which pertains to AAMI/ANSI standardization for performance calculations. In this paper, we have put forward a novel deep learning neural network which is a combination of Convolutional Neural Network (CNN)—Long Short-Term Memory (LSTM) model on ECG signal [5, 6]. In the proposed study, initially input building takes place where the heartbeat is divided into four input layers. Initially, three inputs are convolved and fed to the max pooling layer following which the developed time-dependent data is fed to the LSTM network. Subsequently, fully connected dense layers are employed and the resulting output is joined with RR intervals features, which are the fourth input layer and eventually the result is fed to the last fully connected layer where Softmax is employed as the activation function to classify the ECG signal into four types of heartbeats as per the ANSI/AAMI standards.

2 Related Work

In [7], Chen et al. has used electrocardiogram signal classification method which is based on the projected and dynamic features. Discrete Cosine Transform is used for row transformation in the derivation of projected features. SVM classifier is employed for clustering the heartbeats into the different classes. Here, the dynamic features are the three weighted RR intervals. Li et al. in [8] has used Random forests (RF) and Wavelet Packet Entropy (WPE) with respect to AAMI standards to classify the ECG signals. Wavelet Packet Decomposition (WPD) is used to decompose the ECG signals, entropy is calculated from decomposed coefficients, and eventually, the random forests are applied for classification of ECG signal.

Matthews et al. in [9] has employed a deep learning mechanism using RBM and DBN using only single-lead ECG. This study has used a lower sampling rate, and the features used are simple to perform the classification of ECG signals. In [10], Sellami et al. has used deep CNN along with batch-weighted loss function for the imbalanced classes to perform classification on the ECG signals. The author has even used multiple heartbeats for a better ECG signal classification.

In [11], Can Ye et al. has used a new mechanism for heartbeat classification using an amalgamation of dynamic as well as morphological features. Wavelet transformation along with independent component analysis is used for the derivation of morphological features. Dynamic features are computed using RR interval information. Eventually, after the concatenation of the two distinct types of features namely morphological and dynamic, SVM is used for the ECG Arrhythmia signal classification. Chazal et al. in [12] has employed a method where twelve configuration feature sets are compared from two ECG leads and the mentioned feature sets were derived from morphology of ECG signals, RR interval features, and the heartbeat intervals. A statistical classifier was used which was based on supervised learning and utilized its advantages.

3 Material and Method

In Fig. 1, architectural diagram of our proposed model is depicted. In the diagram, the steps involved for ECG signal classification are clearly mentioned and depicted diagrammatically. After the initial heartbeat detection, the heartbeat is divided into four input layers. The three input layers are taken as input for three convolutional layers separately. The resulting output from the above layers is then conjoined, and constructed time series is fed to the LSTM network. Subsequently, the result from the LSTM layer is flattened and result is then fed to two fully connected dense layers. With the two fully connected dense layers' output, the fourth input layer of RR intervals is concatenated and then fed to the last fully connected layer where Softmax is employed as the activation function to give the output. The output from the network is then evaluated, and other metrics are calculated.

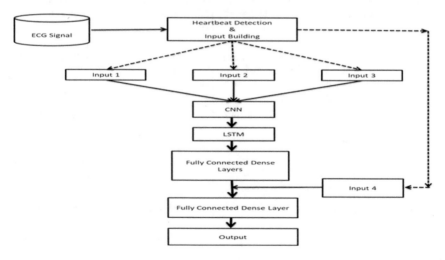

Fig. 1 Architectural diagram of CNN-LSTM model

3.1   ECG MIT-BIH Arrhythmia Database

This paper employs the use of MIT-BIH dataset [5]. The MIT-BIH database used for arrhythmia classification holds forty-eight records of half an hour each. In our study, the whole MIT-BIH database is segregated into two sections so as to think about the outcomes from the past works. The whole MIT-BIH dataset is divided into Train dataset (DS1) and Test dataset (DS2) for patient-specific classification [1]. Each database contains information from 22 records.

Train records	101, 106, 108, 109, 112, 114, 115, 116, 118, 119, 122, 124, 201, 203, 205, 207, 208, 215, 220, 223, 230
Test records	100, 103, 105, 111, 113, 117, 121, 123, 200, 202, 210, 212, 213, 214, 219, 221, 222, 228, 231, 232, 233, 234

With reference to the division of records above, we see that there are two sections, one is the training dataset and the other is the testing dataset. Here, for proper and efficient training of the model we use the training dataset while the validation or testing dataset is employed to affirm, check, and find out the performance metrics of the CNN-LSTM model (Table 1).

Table 1   The relation between ECG heartbeat labels to AAMI Standards

ANSI-AAMI classes	N Beat	S Beat	V Beat	F Beat	Q Beat
ECG MIT-BIH database classes	Normal (N)	Aberrated atrial premature beats (a)	Ventricular escape beats (E)	Fusion of normal and ventricular beats (F)	Unclassified beats (U)
	Left bundle branch block (L)	Supraventricular premature beats (S)	Premature ventricular contraction (V)		Paced beats (P)
	Right bundle branch block (R)	Atrial premature (A)			Fusion of normal and paced beats (f)
	Aterial escape (e)	Contraction nodal premature beats (J)			
	Nodal escape (j)				

3.2 Heartbeat Detection

Since majority of information in an ECG signal are centered around the R-peak, the R-peak locations are used as fiducial points (FP). Using information from these fiducial points help retain the characteristics of the raw signal, hence the signal is not distorted. For our ECG signal classification, the segment starting from 0.4 s prior to the R-peak to 0.5 s following the R-peak is taken as a complete heartbeat. In the convolution layers, different strides are taken and the heartbeat is segregated into 3 parts. The first section is divided between $FP - 0.4$ s and $FP - 0.15$ s. The second region has signal information varying from $FP - 0.15$ s to $FP + 0.15$ s, while the third region comprises the signal between $FP + 0.15$ s and $FP + 0.5$ s. Henceforth, the three segments are of length 90, 108, and 126, respectively. The fourth input in the form of RR intervals is fed to the network after the application of 2 fully connected dense layers. The RR interval features comprise anterior RR interval, posterior RR interval, local average RR interval, and average RR interval of the recording [1]. These four RR interval features along with the normalized values from the first three features, which are nothing but resulting ratios of them to average RR interval, comprise a total of seven features which form up the fourth input.

3.3 Classification Model

3.3.1 Convolutional Neural Network

Convolutional Neural Network (CNN) is one of the widely employed Deep Learning networks which are more or less based on connected feed forward neural network. It is a deep neural network, and there exists a weight sharing mechanism in CNN for the convolutional kernel. But the network is inspired by time delay neural network and the weight sharing mechanism is limited. CNN is extremely powerful in extracting implicit features without any feature extraction process. The combination of convolution layer, polling layer, and fully connected layer forms up the convolutional neural network [13, 14].

The core structure of CNN is the convolutional layer. In this layer, feature extraction process is automated and it is based on weight sharing and local connection. It also helps in dimensionality reduction. Convolution operations in this layer take place between the inputs and the kernels. On increasing CNNs depth, they could result in finding better targeted results and obtaining better approximation in features along with an increased complexity. The second layer or the pooling layer is a subsampling layer. The work of this layer is to reduce the dimensions of the convolved extracted features. The virtue of pooling layer in being invariant against input's local linear transformations significantly enhances the generalization of the network. In pooling operation, a time window is set and the maximum or the average value of the neurons is found in the same period.

The fully connected layers are responsible for conducting the final classification decision. Generally, the first fully connected layer takes all inputs from feature extraction and analysis process and applies weights to predict the result while the fully connected output layer calculates the final label probabilities [15, 16]. This layer is more or less like the traditional multilayer perceptron.

3.3.2 Long Short-Term Memory Network

LSTM is a special type of Recurrent Neural Networks (RNN). LSTMs are capable to learn long-term dependencies. They were introduced by Hochreiter and Schmidhuber and perform extremely well in vanishing gradient problem. LSTMs cell is a specifically designed logic unit which are extremely helpful in retaining information over longer time periods, i.e., prediction of text sequence data [4]. LSTM network can maintain a constant error, and this helps them to learn longer for many time steps and even do back propagation through layers. The structure of the memory block is such that it contains forget gate, input gate, and output gate.

Forget Gate: It deletes all the information that is redundant and no longer in use for the task completion. This helps in optimizing the model performance.

$$f_t = \text{sigmoid}(W_f^T h_{t-1} + U_f^T x_t + b_f) \tag{1}$$

where t is the time, x_t is the input vector at t, and h_{t-1} is memory block's output at time $t-1$. Here, the activation function used is sigmoid and W_f and U_f are weight vectors while b_f is the bias vector [1].

Input Gate: This gate is used to add information to the cells and henceforth even control what information is added to the memory.

$$i_t = \text{sigmoid}(W_i^T h_{t-1} + U_i^T x_t + b_i) \tag{2}$$

where t is the time, x_t is the input vector at t, and h_{t-1} is memory block's output at time $t-1$. Here, the activation function used is sigmoid and W_i and U_i are weight vectors while b_i is the bias vector.

Output Gate: This gate is used to decide what information is sent to the next step and henceforth also decides the information that is outputted [1].

$$O_t = \text{sigmoid}(W_o^T h_{t-1} + U_o^T x_t + b_o) \tag{3}$$

3.4 Working of the Proposed Deep CNN-LSTM Model

The deep neural network is a combination of Convolutional Neural Network (CNN) and Long Short-Term Memory Network (LSTM). The layer structure, i.e., in the order of layers, convolutional layer is the first layer followed by the pooling layer and the concatenating layer. After this, the time series generated input is fed to the LSTM layer and the output is flattened and used as an input for a series of two fully connected layers and the output is joined with fourth input of RR intervals. Subsequently, the next layer is the fully connected layer with Softmax as the activation function after which the labeled classes are the output. The ECG signal under study is one dimensional and hence 1-D CNN is used. Initially, the CNN is used to extract the implicit features where the embedding is performed. The three inputs of dimensions 90 * 1, 108 * 1, and 126 * 1 are initially sent to the convolutional layer after which the output is fed to the max pooling layers. Initially, the inputs are convolved with 32 kernels each of size 13 * 1 with Leaky ReLU employed as the activation function. The convolution layers have different strides of 2, 1, and 2, respectively, and the dimensions of output are 39 * 32, 96 * 32, and 57 * 32, respectively. Subsequently, the max pooling layer is employed where the output dimensions vary as 19 * 32, 48 * 32, and 28 * 32, respectively.

The outputs from max pooling layer are then concatenated and fed as a time sequence to the LSTM network. The size for this layer input is 95 * 32. Further, the output from the LSTM layer is flattened to a size of 3040 * 1 and two fully connected layers are then employed in the network. The first fully connected layer has 333 units and the output is fed to the second fully connected layer where 37 units are present. The output from the fully connected layer is concatenated with the RR interval features, which make up the fourth input unit and this input unit is made up of four RR interval features namely, anterior RR, posterior RR, local RR, and average RR values and three normalized features from the initial three inputs. The activation function used in the above layers is Leaky ReLU. The concatenated input is then fed to the last fully connected layer of size 15 * 1 which is labeled into four classes. The activation function used for the last fully connected layer is the Softmax function, and Adam optimizer is used along with categorical cross entropy as the loss function. In our patient-specific scheme, the heartbeat is classified into four classes. Dropout is used to prevent over-fitting after LSTM layer and the first two fully connected layers with dropout probability of 0.5.

4 Experimental Results

For all distinguishing categories of ECG signal, the performance is evaluated of the proposed methodology. The performance of the model is based on metrics like specificity, sensitivity, and overall accuracy which are calculated with the help of true-positive, false-positive, true-negative, and false-negative values of the confusion matrix.

Sensitivity can be calculated as:

$$S_E = \frac{T_p * 100}{(T_p + F_n)} \tag{5}$$

Specificity can be calculated as:

$$S_p = \frac{T_N * 100}{(T_n + F_p)} \tag{6}$$

Accuracy can be calculated as:

$$\text{Accuracy} = \frac{(T_p + T_n) * 100}{(T_p + T_n + F_p + F_n)} \tag{7}$$

4.1 Experiment 1 (Patient Independent for Multiclass Classification)

In Fig. 1, we have diagrammatically shown the various layers of our architecture.

Based on that, in this experiment we have followed a patient-independent approach to classify the ECG signals into four classes. The overall accuracy along with the sensitivity and specificity of class N, S, V, and F is depicted in Table 2.

In patient-independent scheme, we have used the whole database and using random train-test split whole of the data is randomly segregated into training and testing parts. The train-test ratio used for this experiment is 70–30. It implies that out of whole MIT-BIH dataset 70% is used for training and 30% is used for validation of model. We have used 50 epochs for training the dataset.

In Table 2, it is clear that the model has predicted on 26,988 N type heartbeats, 823 S type beats, 2088 V type heartbeats, and 254 F type beats. Out of 26,988 Normal heartbeats, 26,588 are correctly classified while for V type only 1550 beats are correctly classified out of 2088. Due to very less samples of F beat, model has

Table 2 Confusion matrix for patient-independent data

Beat types	N	S	V	F
N	26,588	348	52	0
S	381	423	19	0
V	414	119	1550	5
F	236	3	14	1

Table 3 Performance of our classifier for patient-independent data

Overall accuracy		94.72%
Class N	SEN	98.51%
	SPC	83.15%
Class S	SEN	51.39%
	SPC	98.60%
Class V	SEN	74.23%
	SPC	98.05%
Class F	SPC	99.12%

Table 4 Performance of other method with our proposed model on patient-independent data

Authors	Proposed classifier	Overall accuracy (%)
Acharya et al. [17]	Deep CNN model	94.03
Martis et al. [18]	Three-layer feed forward NN-based classifier	94.52
Yildrim et al. [19]	CNN	91.33
Proposed work	*CNN-LSTM*	*94.72*

classified very few beats of F type correctly. S type beat is major cause of arrhythmia, and the model has predicted 423 S type beats correctly.

In Table 3, we have shown the metrics like accuracy, sensitivity (SEN), and specificity (SPC) for optimum results in the proposed work. The proposed deep CNN-LSTM model gets a good overall accuracy of 94.72% for patient-independent multiclass classification.

In Table 4, comparison on patient-dependent approach is shown of various studies. In [17], classification into five types of heartbeats is done using HOS features and a three-layered feed forward neural network is employed. Further in [19], 1-D CNN is used using 10 s ECG signal segments using end-to-end structure. Our proposed work has performed better as compared to the works as mentioned in Table 4 in terms of accuracy. The proposed model has achieved an accuracy of 94.72%.

4.2 Experiment 2 (Patient Specific for Multiclass Classification)

In this experiment, we use two datasets where one is employed for training (DS1) and other is used for testing (DS2) the data, i.e., a patient-specific regime is followed. The overall accuracy along with the sensitivity and specificity of class N, S, V, and F is depicted in Table 5. Since the major portion for cause of arrhythmias is because of S and V classes, their sensitivity and specificity are of high importance. In this experiment, we have used 50 epochs for training the dataset and 0.01 Leaky ReLu is used rather than 0.1.

Table 5 Confusion matrix for patient-specific/patient-oriented data

Beat types	N	S	V	F
N	43,507	130	538	2
S	1251	13	568	2
V	1192	13	2013	0
F	386	0	2	0

Table 6 Performance of our classifier for patient-specific/patient-oriented data

Overall accuracy		91.77%
Class N	SEN	98.48%
	SPC	75.14%
Class S	SEN	03.80%
	SPC	96.15%
Class V	SEN	62.56%
	SPC	97.31%
Class F	SPC	99.15%

In Table 5, it is clear that there are 44,177 N type heartbeats, 1834 S type beats, 3218 V type heartbeats, and 388 F type beats. Out of 44,177 Normal heartbeats, 43,507 are correctly classified while for V type only 2013 beats are correctly classified. Due to very less samples of F beat, model has not classified any beats of F type correctly.

In Table 6, we have shown the metrics like accuracy, sensitivity, and specificity for optimum results in the proposed work. The proposed deep CNN-LSTM model gets a good overall accuracy of 91.77%.

5   Discussion

Mathews et al. in [9] has employed a deep learning mechanism using Restricted Boltzmann machine and Deep Belief Networks using only single-lead ECG. The study has used a lower sampling rate and simple features to perform the classification of ECG signals. Our proposed model has shown good performance and efficiency in terms of accuracy as well the deep CNN-LSTM network is multi layered and gives accurate performance. In [10], Sellami et al. has used deep convolutional neural network along with batch-weighted loss function for the imbalanced classes to perform classification on the ECG signals. The author has even used multiple heartbeats for a better ECG signal classification. Our paper instead has used a combination of CNN and LSTM to extract features from raw data and provide a deep net to classify the ECG signals with a better accuracy.

In [11], Ye et al. has used a new mechanism for heartbeat classification using a combination of dynamic as well as morphological features. Wavelet transformation along with independent component analysis is used for feature extraction. The accuracy for subject oriented is around 86.4% where our deep CNN-LSTM model has outperformed the above model by getting a better accuracy. Chazal et al. in [12] has employed a method where twelve configuration feature sets are compared from two ECG leads and the mentioned feature sets were derived from morphology of ECG signals, RR interval features, and the heartbeat intervals. A statistical classifier was used which was based on supervised learning and utilized its advantages. Our proposed model gave a far better accuracy as compared to the morphology-based classification. Further, Sandeep et al. in [20] has used PSO and optimization techniques along with feature extraction for ECG signal classification. The accuracy and other metrics of our model are better than the accuracy achieved in the study (Fig. 2).

Overall as compared to all the studies mentioned in Table 7, the proposed Deep CNN-LSTM model gave a very good overall accuracy of 91.77% for patient-dependent/specific data. The model also performed significantly well for patient-independent multiclass classification and resulted in an accuracy of 94.72%. The heartbeat detection where the input building takes place helps in restoring the complete information from the raw ECG signal.

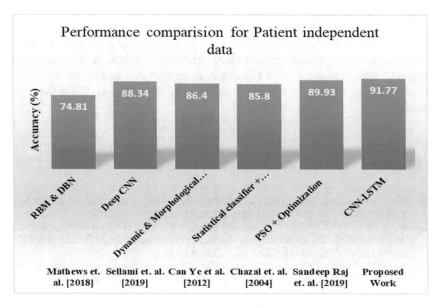

Fig.2 Performance comparison with CNN-LSTM Model

Table 7 Comparison table for patient-independent data

Authors	Proposed classifier	Overall accuracy (%)
Mathews et. al. [9]	RBM & DBN	74.81
Sellami et. al. [10]	Deep CNN	88.34
Ye et al. [11]	Dynamic and morphological features + SVM	86.4
Chazal et al. [12]	Statistical classifier + supervised learning	85.8
Raj et. al. [20]	PSO + optimization	89.93
Proposed work	*CNN-LSTM*	*91.77*

6 Conclusion

In this study, we used deep CNN-LSTM model for Patient-Specific Classification. After the heartbeat detection where the input is built by dividing into three regions and retaining the information of raw signal, the three inputs are fed to the layered network. Initially, the three inputs were used and their outputs from convolutional layer and max pooling layer were joined to be fed to the LSTM layer followed by fully connected dense layers and are then conjoined with the fourth RR interval feature input to go through final dense layer having Softmax as the activation function to output the labeled classes namely N, S, V, and F.

Results portray that this deep CNN-LSTM model can capture essential and useful information from the signals in their raw form, helping it to out-perform the previous developed and fully equipped and enhanced arrhythmia classifiers (using models like Support Vector Machine, Random Forest, or Deep Neural Network) that are mostly based on features of ECG for feature extraction and classification. The features are also handcrafted in nature.

References

1. Shi H, Qin C, Xiao D, Zhao L, Liu C (2020) Automated heartbeat classification based on deep neural network with multiple input layers. Knowl-Based Syst 188:105036
2. Pandey SK, Janghel RR (2021) Automated detection of arrhythmia from electrocardiogram signal based on new convolutional encoded features with bidirectional long short-term memory network classifier. Phys Eng Sci Med 44(1):173–182
3. Li J (2018) Detection of premature ventricular contractions using densely connected deep convolutional neural network with spatial pyramid pooling layer. arXiv preprint arXiv:1806. 04564
4. Pandey SK, Janghel RR (2021) Classification of electrocardiogram signal using an ensemble of deep learning models. Data Technol Appl 55:446–460
5. Pandey SK, Janghel RR (2019) Automatic detection of arrhythmia from imbalanced ECG database using CNN model with SMOTE. Austr Phys Eng Sci Med 42(4):1129–1139
6. Bienstock D, Shukla A (2019) Variance-aware optimal power flow: addressing the tradeoff between cost, security, and variability. IEEE Trans Control Netw Syst 6(3):1185–1196
7. Chen S, Hua W, Li Z, Li J, Gao X (2017) Heartbeat classification using projected and dynamic features of ECG signal. Biomed Signal Process Control 31:165–173

8. Li T, Zhou M (2016) ECG classification using wavelet packet entropy and random forests. Entropy 18(8):285
9. Mathews SM, Kambhamettu C, Barner KE (2018) A novel application of deep learning for single-lead ECG classification. Comput Biol Med 99:53–62
10. Sellami A, Hwang H (2019) A robust deep convolutional neural network with batch-weighted loss for heartbeat classification. Expert Syst Appl 122:75–84
11. Ye C, Vijaya Kumar BVK, Coimbra MT (2012) Heartbeat classification using morphological and dynamic features of ECG signals. IEEE Trans Biomed Eng 59(10):2930–2941
12. De Chazal P, O'Dwyer M, Reilly RB (2004) Automatic classification of heartbeats using ECG morphology and heartbeat interval features. IEEE Trans Biomed Eng 51(7):1196–1206
13. Pandey SK, Janghel RR (2019) Recent deep learning techniques, challenges and its applications for medical healthcare system: a review. Neural Process Lett 50(2):1907–1935
14. Bienstock D, Shukla A, Escobar M, Yang S, Yun S, Lokhov A, Deka D, Misra S, Vuffray M, Chertkov M (2017) Machine learning with PMU data. In: 2017 NASPI work group meeting, Gaithersburg, vol 9
15. Pandey SK, Janghel RR, Varma K (2020) Classification of ECG heartbeat using deep convolutional neural network. In: Machine learning for intelligent decision science, pp 27–47. Springer, Singapore
16. Shukla A (2015) A modified bat algorithm for the quadratic assignment problem. In: 2015 IEEE congress on evolutionary computation (CEC), pp 486–490. IEEE
17. Acharya UR, Fujita H, Lih OS, Hagiwara Y, Tan JH, Adam M (2017) Automated detection of arrhythmias using different intervals of tachycardia ECG segments with convolutional neural network. Inform Sci 405:81–90
18. Martis RJ, Rajendra Acharya U, Lim CM, Mandana KM, Ray AK, Chakraborty C (2013) Application of higher order cumulant features for cardiac health diagnosis using ECG signals. Int J Neural Syst 23(4):1350014
19. Yıldırım Ö, Pławiak P, Tan R-S, Rajendra Acharya U (2018) Arrhythmia detection using deep convolutional neural network with long duration ECG signals. Comput Biol Med 102:411–420
20. Raj S, Ray KC (2018) Sparse representation of ECG signals for automated recognition of cardiac arrhythmias. Exp Syst Appl 105:49–64

Fault Diagnosis in Wind Turbine Blades Using Machine Learning Techniques

Hema Sudheer Banala, Sudarsan Sahoo, Manas Ranjan Sethi, and Anup K. Sharma

1 Introduction

Wind energy is a plentiful renewable energy source that can be used as an effective energy source for power generation instead of conventional energy sources. We can use the wind's availability as an energy source with the help of wind turbines. Wind turbine development in the modern era has been very fast due to technological advancements, but it has also created a few obstacles [1]. It is critical to keep the operating turbine in good working condition to uphold its efficiency [2, 3]. There is always a need to reduce maintenance costs. As a result, detecting faults early on is critical in reducing shutdowns and increasing productivity. Wind energy is converted into electrical energy with the help of the wind turbine blades which rotate depending on the strength of the wind. These blades are frequently subjected to extreme climatic conditions, which cause several flaws not only in the blades but also in the entire system. Because of these flaws, the speed of rotation of the blades is reduced or even stops, lowering overall productivity. As the wind turbines are located in remote locations, evaluating the vibration of the blades online is difficult.

In a healthy state, all rotating systems have their type of vibrational signal, but when a fault occurs, the vibrational signal changes. Visual inspection is ineffective for analyzing these vibrational signals. We have a variety of techniques that assist us in analyzing these signals. On these types of signals, we can perform time, frequency and time–frequency analysis. We can find the statistical features to examine these signals in the time domain [4]. The fast Fourier transform allows us to analyze these signals in the frequency domain [5]. The continuous wavelet transform can be used to

H. S. Banala · S. Sahoo (✉) · M. R. Sethi · A. K. Sharma
NIT Silchar, Silchar, Assam 788010, India
e-mail: Sudarsan_iisc@yahoo.in

H. S. Banala
e-mail: banala_pg@ei.nits.ac.in

© The Author(s), under exclusive license to Springer Nature Singapore Pte Ltd. 2023   401
R. Doriya et al. (eds.), *Machine Learning, Image Processing, Network Security and Data Sciences*, Lecture Notes in Electrical Engineering 946,
https://doi.org/10.1007/978-981-19-5868-7_30

analyze the time and frequency of vibrational signals [6]. Advanced signal processing techniques, such as active noise cancelation, will aid in dealing with these types of signals to achieve better results [7]. Monitoring of the pitch faults in wind turbine blades was shown by Kusiak [8].

Machine learning techniques can be used for fault detection and classification as they can learn from the previous experiences and fit themselves to varying conditions, but we need proper data to separate faulty signals from good signals and classify different types of fault signals [9, 10]. The proposed work focuses on implementing this through the use of deep learning technique and machine learning technique.

The experimental work was carried out using the necessary sensors and data acquisition systems to obtain vibrational signals from a healthy blade and three blades with different types of faults. The measured vibrational signals were collected from the setup and used to derive statistical information.

This statistical information is used to train the artificial neural network and multiclass logistic regression algorithm. A two-layer feed-forward network with sigmoid function for hidden layer and Softmax for output layer can classify vectors arbitrarily well, provided there are enough neurons in its hidden layer which is implemented here for fault classification. The proposed work will determine whether the blades are in good or bad condition. If they are defective, we attempt to determine the nature of the defect. Figure 1 depicts the various steps for the current project.

2   Experimental Setup

The test was performed on a 50 W, 12 v horizontal axis wind turbine (HAWT) generator that was mounted against the wind source on a hardened platform with a 1000 mm exit. The wind source has a velocity varying from 5 to 15 m/s, which aids in the rotation of the wind turbine blades. For the data acquisition, the turbine's speed was kept constant at 700 RPM. Figure 2 depicts the experimental setup. A multichannel IEPE adapter is used along with a data acquisition model-WS-4601/U2-8 to acquire vibration signals. The accelerometers were mounted near the hub of wind turbine. Sensitivity of 500 and 100 mV/g IEPE accelerometers with a resonant frequency of 30 kHz were used for sensing the signals. A TNC-2 BNC cable connects the IEPE accelerometer, which ensures a solid and long-lasting connection. WS-DAQ data acquisition software is used for the experimental work. For feature extraction and deep learning techniques, MATLAB and Python were used.

3   Experimental Procedure

The experiment was accomplished using a horizontal axis wind turbine with three blades. At first, vibration signals from a wind turbine with healthy blades were collected. An accelerometer having a 12 kHz sampling frequency is used to collect

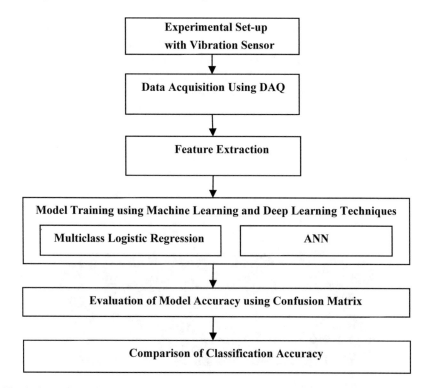

Fig. 1 Flow of work

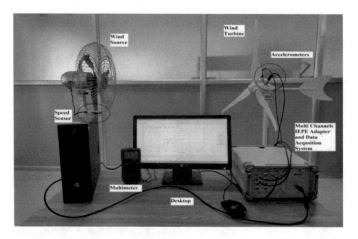

Fig. 2 Experimental setup

vibration signals. The sample length was set at 8190. For each of the four conditions of the wind turbine blade, a minimum of 100 samples were collected.

In the following stage, each of the defective blades is connected individually to obtain the required vibration signals as specified above. Figures 3, 4, 5 and 6 depict the good-condition blade along with defective blades which were put to use in the test.

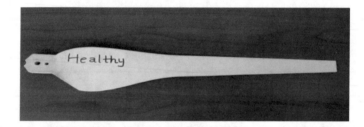

Fig. 3 Blade in good condition

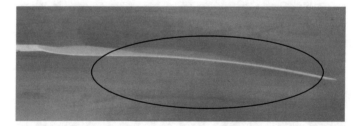

Fig. 4 Blade with a bend

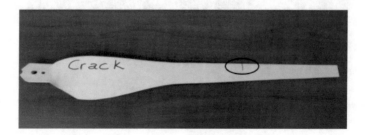

Fig. 5 Blade with crack

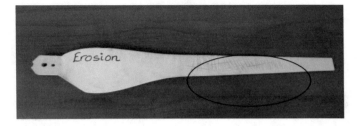

Fig. 6 Blade with erosion

4   Feature Extraction

The vibration signals for healthy and defective blade conditions are obtained from the data acquisition (DAQ) system. As the number of signal samples acquired is proportional to the blade's rotary motion, the time domain signals cannot be fed directly to the ANN and multiclass logistic regression algorithm. As a result, it is unable to serve as input to both of them directly for classification. However, before the classification process can begin, a few features must be extracted. In the feature extraction process, to serve as features, descriptive statistical features such as sample variance, kurtosis, range, mode, maximum, standard deviation, minimum, skewness, mean, standard error, median and sum were calculated for the vibrational signals. The statistical features were calculated for each case which are having 100 samples, and the features of a total of 400 samples were served as input to the artificial neural network and multiclass logistic regression algorithm.

Figure 7 shows the different types of vibration signals that are acquired from the wind turbine for different conditions of the blades. Type-0 indicates the blade is in good condition. Type-1 indicates the blade with a bend. Type-2 indicates the blade with a crack. Type-3 indicates the blade with erosion.

5   Implementation of Machine Learning Techniques

Machine learning techniques are widely used nowadays in different areas as they come up with different algorithms for classification, clustering, anomaly detection and regression. Multiclass logistic regression is one of the machine learning techniques which is employed here for fault detection and classification of wind turbine blades [11]. Logistic regression, in general, is an algorithm that predicts only between two classes, but the same can be implemented for multiclass as performed here. Multiclass logistic regression predicts multiple classes by a technique called one vs all. In this method, it first chooses one class and then groups all the others into a single second class to decide boundary, and this process is repeated for the remaining classes too. The statistical features obtained were used to train this algorithm by splitting

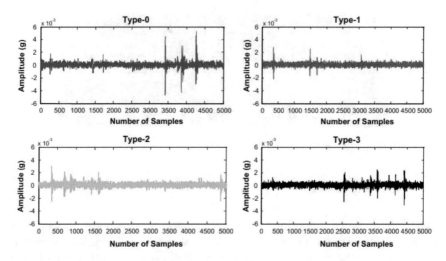

Fig. 7 Vibration signals of blades with different conditions at 700 rpm

Table 1 Comparison of statistical features for different vibration signals at 700 rpm

S. no.	Statical features	Blade in good condition	Blade with bend	Blade with crack	Blade with erosion
1	Skewness	0.43414000	1.04630000	− 0.15434000	0.49228000
2	Kurtosis	30.4144000	32.4218000	19.8612000	12.3742000
3	Variance	0.00000016	0.00000011	0.00000013	0.0000001
4	Crest factor	10.8979000	13.6671000	8.69350000	10.355100
5	Interquartile range	0.00036900	0.00033987	0.00038872	0.0003591
6	Entropy	0.03292500	0.01590300	0.03091300	0.0159030
7	Power	0.0000013	0.0000009	0.00000120	0.00000098
8	Mean	0.00005036	0.00009297	0.00011202	0.00011737
9	Standard deviation	0.0004097	0.0003379	0.00037127	0.00033026
10	Root mean square	0.00041274	0.00035048	0.00038776	0.00035046
11	Sum	0.20628000	0.3808100	0.45885000	0.48073000
12	Mode	0.00002428	0.0001310	0.00009229	0.00007286
13	Range	0.00919100	0.0073600	0.00693200	0.00574700
14	Minimum	− 0.00469000	− 0.0025700	− 0.0035600	− 0.0021000
15	Maximum	0.00449800	0.0047900	0.00337100	0.0036200

the whole data of 400 signals into 70 and 30%. Seventy percent of the data is used to train the algorithm, and the remaining is used to test it.

ANN comes under deep learning which is a part of the machine learning techniques. ANNs [12, 13] have proven to be effective algorithms for a variety of tasks such as classification, estimation and fault detection. It is simple to create ANNs for detecting faults and classify them due to their ability to deal with nonlinearities successfully and their benefits in real-time applications (Fig. 8).

The artificial neural network is trained by the evaluated statistical features. A two-layer feed-forward network with sigmoid as the activation function for the neurons of the hidden layer and SoftMax function is used at the neurons of the output layer. The ANN will be trained by using the scaled conjugate gradient backpropagation (Fig. 9).

Statistical features are served as input to the ANN; here, 15 statistical features from each signal were served as input to the network. This network is having 12 neurons in the hidden layer, and this is used to classify faults into 4 types. As we have to train the network, we have divided the data of 400 signals into three categories. Seventy percent of the data is used for training the network, 15 percent is used for validation, and the remaining percent is used for testing the ANN.

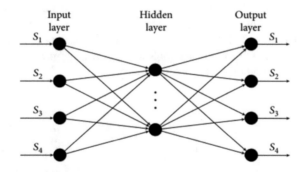

Fig. 8 Structure of ANN

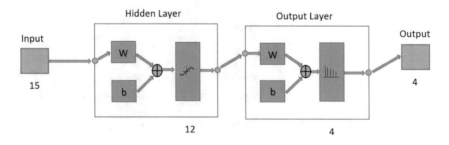

Fig. 9 Artificial neural network used for classification

6 Results

The results are evaluated for the rotating turbine at speed of 700 RPM for ANN and multiclass logistic regression algorithm. The confusion matrixes at different stages of training the ANN along with the confusion matrix of multiclass logistic regression algorithm are shown below. The accuracy can be calculated from the test confusion matrix by

$$\% \text{ Accuracy} = \frac{(\text{True positives} + \text{True negatives})}{\left(\begin{array}{l}\text{True negatives} + \text{False positives} \\ \quad + \text{False negatives} + \text{True positives}\end{array}\right)} \times 100 \qquad (1)$$

6.1 The Results Were Displayed with the Help of a Confusion Matrix

Figure 10 shows the test confusion matrix of the ANN. From that figure, it can get to known that the ANN can classify the blade faults efficiently. The accuracy of the ANN was found to be 85% for fault classification after testing it. Figure 11 shows the confusion matrix of the multiclass logistic regression algorithm after testing, and the accuracy was found to be 98.3% (Tables 2 and 3).

Fig. 10 Test confusion matrix of ANN

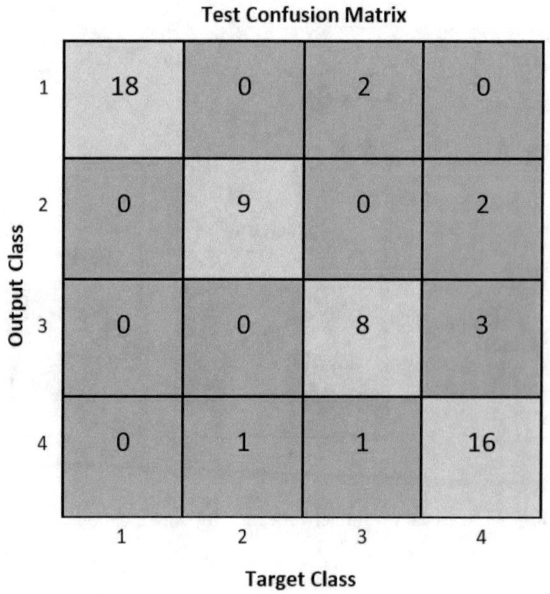

Fig. 11 Test confusion matrix of multiclass logistic regression

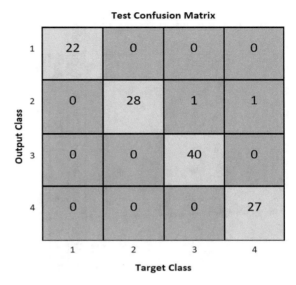

Test Confusion Matrix

Output Class

	1	2	3	4
1	22	0	0	0
2	0	28	1	1
3	0	0	40	0
4	0	0	0	27

Target Class

Table 2 Performance comparison of the machine learning techniques

S. no.	Machine learning techniques used	% classification accuracy
1	ANN	85
2	Multiclass logistic regression algorithm	98.3

7 Conclusion

The present work attempts to demonstrate the use of the artificial neural network and multiclass logistic regression algorithm for the diagnosis of the blade faults of wind turbines. The statistical features computed from the vibration data collected by the data acquisition unit serve as inputs to the ANN. The accuracy of the ANN was found to be 85%. While training the ANN, it took 23 epochs and the cross-entropy was found to be 1.37431. The accuracy can be improved by using different types of ANNs which are having other types of activation functions for the neurons and different types of output layers with several hidden layers. For the ANN used in this experimental work, different accuracies can be obtained by changing the number of neurons in the hidden layer and retraining the network. The accuracy of the multiclass logistic regression algorithm was found to be very high compared with the ANN used here. The same techniques can be implemented by performing feature selection after feature extraction to remove the redundant features which may help in improving the accuracy. The research can be expanded in the future to include other types of ANNs to build an overall fault detection system with high accuracy.

Table 3 Precision and recall values of various blades for the machine learning techniques

S. no.	Machine learning technique	Precision				Recall			
		Good blade	Bend blade	Crack blade	Erosion blade	Good blade	Bend blade	Crack blade	Erosion blade
1	ANN	90	81.81	72.72	88.88	100	90	72.72	76.19
2	Multiclass logistic regression	100	93.33	100	100	100	100	97.56	96.42

References

1. Liu WY, Tang BP, Han JG, Lu XN, Hu NN, He ZZ (2015) The structure healthy condition monitoring and fault diagnosis methods in wind turbines: a review. Renew Sustain Energy Rev 44:466–472. ISSN 1364-0321
2. Zhang P, Lu D (2019) A survey of condition monitoring and fault diagnosis toward integrated O&M for wind turbines. Energies 12:2801. https://doi.org/10.3390/en12142801
3. Ellabban O, Abu-Rub H, Blaabjerg F (2014) Renewable energy resources: current status, future prospects and their enabling technology. Renew Sustain Energy Rev 39:748–764. ISSN 1364-0321
4. Arockia D, Joshuva A, SugumaranV (2017) Fault diagnosis for wind turbine blade through vibration signals using statistical features and random forest algorithm. Int J Pharm Technol 9:28684–28696
5. Sahoo S, Das JK (2018) Bearing health monitoring and diagnosis using ANC based filtered vibration signal. J Eng Appl Sci 13:3587–3593
6. Kankar PK, Sharma SC, Harsha SP (2011) Fault diagnosis of ball bearings using continuous wavelet transform. Appl Soft Comput 11:2300–2312
7. Sahoo S, Jena DP, Panigrahi S (2014) Gear fault diagnosis using active noise cancellation and adaptive wavelet transform. Measurement 47:356–372
8. Kusiak A, Verma A (2011) A data-driven approach for monitoring blade pitch faults in wind turbines. IEEE Trans Sustain Energy 2(1):87–96
9. Gupta DL, Malviya AK, Singh S (2012) Performance analysis of classification tree learning algorithms. Int J Comput Appl 55(6):975–8887
10. Amarnath M, Sugumaran V, Kumar H (2013) Exploiting sound signals for fault diagnosis of bearings using decision tree. Measurement 46:1250–1256
11. Zhuo C (2015) The application of hierarchical clustering based logistic regression classification algorithm in coal area. In: International conference on intelligent transportation, big data and smart city, pp 834–836
12. Patan K (2008) Artificial neural networks for the modelling and fault diagnosis of technical processes, vol 377. Springer, Berlin
13. Specht DF (1991) A general regression neural network. IEEE Trans Neural Networks 2(6):568–576

Real-Time Detection of Vehicles on South Asian Roads

Rutuparn Pawar, Shubham Gujar, Suyash Chougule, Rutuja Pote, Dipti Pandit, and Yogesh Dandawate

1 Introduction

With an exponential increase in the number of vehicles, traffic monitoring has become a subject of immense importance. Regulation of traffic is essential since traffic congestion leads to a loss in productivity, adds to air pollution and leads to wastage of fuel which amounts to billions of dollars every year in major countries all over the world [1]. Intelligent traffic regulations with smart infrastructure are constantly being developed to help regulate traffic effectively. Vehicle detection and classification systems are an integral part of the traffic regulation infrastructure and

R. Pawar (✉) · S. Gujar · D. Pandit · Y. Dandawate
Department of Electronics and Telecommunication, Vishwakarma Institute of Information
Technology, Pune, Maharashtra, India
e-mail: rutuparn.17U253@viit.ac.in

S. Gujar
e-mail: gujar303shubham@gmail.com; shubham.21810749@viit.ac.in

D. Pandit
e-mail: dipti.pandit@viit.ac.in

Y. Dandawate
e-mail: yogesh.dandawate@viit.ac.in; yhdandawate@gmail.com

S. Chougule
Department of Mechanical Engineering, Vishwakarma Institute of Information Technology, Pune,
Maharashtra, India
e-mail: suyash.17u567@viit.ac.in

R. Pote
Department of Computer Science, Vishwakarma Institute of Information Technology, Pune,
Maharashtra, India
e-mail: rutuja.21810081@viit.ac.in

© The Author(s), under exclusive license to Springer Nature Singapore Pte Ltd. 2023   413
R. Doriya et al. (eds.), *Machine Learning, Image Processing, Network Security and Data
Sciences*, Lecture Notes in Electrical Engineering 946,
https://doi.org/10.1007/978-981-19-5868-7_31

have gained significant importance in recent years [2]. Video surveillance using low-cost CCTV camera-based systems and cloud infrastructure are being extensively researched since they require minimal modification of hardware for deployment which is ideal for large scale implementation.

Real-world applications of vehicle detection include traffic monitoring to prevent traffic congestion, vehicle speed measurement [3, 4] with number plate detection [5] for automated generation of traffic tickets, tracking emergency vehicles for improving ETA by effectively diverting traffic, and accident monitoring to alert first responders. Object detection applications related to road infrastructure include potholes detection [6], traffic sign and lane detection [7] which aid driver assistance systems, autonomous vehicles and the automated collection of road maintenance data [8]. Furthermore, traffic management agencies can make better decisions about road infrastructure and traffic management by using statistical analysis of traffic flow data generated by vehicle detection and counting.

Traffic in South Asian countries generally consists of vehicles such as bicycles, motorcycles, cars, busses, trucks, tempos and rickshaws. Cars, motorcycles and rickshaws are copious on roads in urban areas. Trucks, also known as lorry, are large vehicles used for transporting goods over long distances while tempos are small goods carrying vehicles used for transportation over short distances and are equivalent to mini trucks. Both trucks and tempos carry pipes, machinery, spools of metal sheets, sacks usually enclosed by a large canvas, logs, LPG gas cylinders and barrels in a quantity that can be accommodated in their cargo bed. The outer appearance of trucks in Southern Asia is customized by their owners by extensive use of decals and other decorative items making the detection much more challenging.

Auto-rickshaws or simply rickshaws are one of the primary modes of transportation for people living in urban areas of South Asian countries. They are small three-wheeled low power vehicles that have a sheet of plastic supported by metallic rods as a hood and do not have doors. Three-wheeled tempos look very similar to rickshaws making the detection more difficult. Furthermore, similar to trucks, the outer appearance of rickshaws is customized with decals and decorations by their owners. Occasionally, posters are pasted on the rear end of the rickshaw for additional income. The colour of the hood and the body of rickshaws vary from region to region. Commonly used colours for the hood and body of rickshaws include black, green, yellow, white, red and dark blue. Figure 1 illustrates the appearance of trucks, tempos and rickshaws. Additionally, a high resemblance exists in the outer appearance of vehicles found in all South Asian countries. Figure 2 illustrates the external appearance of vehicles in South Asian countries, namely India, Bangladesh, Nepal and Pakistan.

Meta deep convolutional neural networks have shown significant improvement in object detection. These networks have proven themselves to be highly effective and accurate at computer vision tasks such as image classification, object detection, object segmentation and many more [9]. Challenges in vehicle detection majorly involve lighting conditions due to the movement of the sun which creates shadows and/or strong reflections from the metallic surfaces of vehicles. Detection accuracy is affected by weather conditions such as rain, fog and snow as well as occlusion

Fig. 1 Some images of rickshaws (**a**) tempos (**b**) and trucks (**c**) from the dataset

Fig. 2 Make and model of vehicles in South Asian countries

which occurs extensively on a crowded road. Vehicle detection using deep learning can effectively address these challenges.

A model trained on the COCO [10] dataset can be used to recognize automobiles because some of the COCO dataset's classes can be categorized as vehicles but the model cannot efficiently detect vehicles because it was not explicitly trained for vehicle detection. Furthermore, since the model was also trained on classes that are not vehicles, the model detects unwanted objects and/or incorrectly classifies objects. For instance, rickshaws were sometimes incorrectly recognized as a car and at times as a toilet. Other unwanted detections were also obtained such as containers on a truck which were identified as a train. Though these predictions can be filtered using conditional logic, we are not effectively utilizing all the weights in the model. Training on classes of the COCO dataset that can be categorized as vehicles will yield a partial solution for detecting South Asian vehicles since the model trained on the COCO dataset is incapable of detecting rickshaws and tempos as a separate class. It is essential to detect all possible types for an effective analysis of traffic since different kinds of vehicles have different speeds and manoeuvrability.

To effectively detect vehicles in South Asia, we trained and tested various variants of the YOLO models on the images collected by extracting images from video feeds taken from cameras mounted near toll infrastructure, web-scraping websites containing the images and programmatically sorting images from the COCO and the IDD dataset. Due to the lack of images of trucks with different numbers of axles and high correlation in outer appearance, we propose a wheel detection-based axle counting algorithm that can be used to identify trucks with various number of axles. We trained and tested YOLO models for detecting the number of wheels in a cropped image containing a truck to determine the truck size thereby enabling better traffic analysis.

The paper is structured as follows. Section 2 discusses related research conducted in the field of vehicle detection. An overview of the dataset and the methods used to collect the images is delineated in Sect. 3. Sections 4 and 5 describe the methodology and the obtained results respectively, while Sect. 6 concludes the paper.

2 Related Work

Over the past two decades, significant studies have been conducted on vehicle detection [11, 12]. For the detection of vehicles, early strategies generally relied on background removal techniques, while current methodologies rely on deep learning. Ozkurt et al. [13] propose using three general approaches for vehicle detection which involve temporal difference, optical flow and background subtraction and conclude that background subtraction was the present best approach. Li et al. [14] employed a background and foreground removal coupled with Otsu's method for determining the optimal segmentation threshold for each frame of the surveillance video. Additional disturbances in the frames such as shadows were removed using morphology filters. In [15], Aqel et al. perform the detection of moving vehicles utilizing a background subtraction method where the background is modelled using temporal changes in intensity with a Gaussian model, and the vehicles in the ROI are identified based on the shape of the vehicle. Dubuisson et al. in [16] proposed a segmentation method for extracting the portions of the vehicle in an image. Three successive frames from the video are taken and blurred with an averaging mask to transform the edges to ramp edges. The vehicles are identified using a combined image made up of thresholded difference images obtained from the three images. Similar to Aqel et al. [15], Kafai et al. [17] used a Gaussian mixture model approach to detect moving vehicles which detected vehicles based on the likeliness of a pixel to belong to the background or the vehicle. They validate their approach by comparing it with the frame differencing approach. To deal with varying image backgrounds, Hsieh et al. [18] proposed using a background update mechanism to create a static background. They detect vehicles using image differences and track the vehicles by using the Kalman filter. Zhang et al. [19] implemented a real-time background subtraction and tracking to detect moving vehicles. In [20], Tseng et al. proposed a methodology for traffic density estimation for real-time surveillance of vehicles on a highway through detection, classification, tracking and counting. Techniques based on background removal are ineffective for detecting vehicles reliably since the background elements change due to lighting conditions and camera location resulting in decreased accuracy.

Deep learning-based vehicle detection methodologies have improved accuracy and performance. Vaddi et al. [21] performed recognition for Indian vehicles viz. bus, auto, truck and car for Indian road conditions using a support vector machine (SVM) classifier trained on a histogram of features obtained from the bag of features. SVM with RBF kernel was able to classify the latter mentioned vehicles with an accuracy of 90%. Their approach cannot effectively deal with occlusion and cannot robustly detect vehicles present on small scales. In [22], Mittal et al. propose using the Faster R-CNN model for vehicle detection. Faster R-CNN has higher accuracy than YOLOv3 but is too slow for real-time applications. Fachrie et al. [23] use YOLOv3 to perform detection followed by using the distance of the centroid of the bounding box to a virtual line along with the dynamics of detection to count the vehicles achieving an average counting accuracy of 97.72 and 91.90% for a 1080p video at 30 and 15 fps, respectively. The dataset they use consists of car, motorcycle, bus and truck images. Huang et al. [24] proposed a modification to YOLOv3 that resulted in a 3.86% increase in accuracy. The modification involved the use of distance IOU along with IOU and spatial pyramid pooling between the 5th and 6th convolution layer of YOLOv3. Oltean et al. [25] propose using YOLOv3 tiny for detection of vehicles found in the COCO dataset viz. car, truck and bus. The tiny variant was chosen to speed up the process of detection for real-time tracking. A tracking mechanism based on the dynamic movement of the centroid of the predicted boundary boxes is used to track and count the vehicles travelling on one or both lanes of the road. Chen et al. [26] perform vehicle detection using a YOLOv3 tiny modified for use in embedded systems so that an independent system for counting various types of vehicles can be created and deployed. The latter YOLOv3-based models were trained on the COCO dataset and hence provide a partial solution for detecting vehicles in South Asian countries.

We propose a methodology using two YOLO models for the detection and classification of vehicles on South Asian roads. The first YOLO model detects vehicles while the second YOLO model detects wheels to determine the number of axles in case the detected vehicle is a truck to further classify trucks. We use YOLO since it is a single-stage detection algorithm that provides fast prediction which is an essential trait required for real-time detection.

3 Dataset

We created a dataset consisting of images of seven vehicles, namely bicycles, motorcycles, cars, buses, rickshaws, tempos and trucks by extracting key frames from toll video feeds, subsetting similar datasets and web-scraping webpages. Since YOLO is a supervised learning algorithm and requires annotation, we annotated the images using an open-source tool named labelImg. The composition of the dataset is given in Table 1. We also created a dataset consisting of 850 images of trucks with their wheels in various positions and annotated the wheels using the labelImg tool. The following sections describe the methods we used to collect the images for the dataset.

3.1 Sub Setting the COCO and IDD Dataset

We collected images that contain bicycles, motorcycles, cars and/or buses from the Common Object in Context (COCO) dataset [10]. We then removed a small number of images that have rickshaws in them since we found that they were annotated as cars. Additionally, we also removed images taken during dusk and night, images that had vehicles mostly outside the image, images that were similar to vehicles such as images of toys and images that were taken from inside a vehicle. The appearance of trucks in Southern Asia differs from most images present in the COCO dataset; hence,

Table 1 Composition of the dataset

Dataset/source		COCO	IDD	Surveillance video key frames	Web scraped	Total
Number of images		10,547	2131	1326	719	14,723
Number of bounding boxes	Bicycle	4935	256	16	9	5216
	Motorcycle	5846	11,492	262	122	17,722
	Car	22,320	7553	677	195	30,745
	Bus	4069	1205	22	47	5343
	Truck	0	1757	1553	606	3916
	Tempo	0	2460	184	412	3056
	Rickshaw	0	5323	30	498	5851
Total number of bounding boxes		37,170	30,046	2744	1889	71,849

we refrain from using images containing trucks from the COCO dataset. Figure 3a shows a few images taken from the COCO dataset.

We also extracted images from the publicly available Indian Driving Dataset (IDD) [27] which contains images of Indian roads. The vehicles found in this dataset are motorcycle, bicycle, auto-rickshaw, car, truck, bus and caravan. Images containing truck, tempo and rickshaws were selectively sorted by a Python program using the manual annotations stored in XML files. We ignored other classes since images containing them are abundant in the COCO dataset. In addition to sorting the images, the program also converted the annotations to the YOLO format which required modifying the class id to match our dataset class ids and calculating the bounding box's centre coordinates along with the normalized height and width. Figure 3b shows a few images taken from the IDD dataset.

3.2 Frames from Surveillance Videos

We gathered surveillance videos from a toll station and extracted key frames from the videos using the ffmpeg tool. Images containing trucks, tempos and rickshaws were manually collected from the key frame images and annotated using the labelImg tool. Similar to the latter, we ignored other classes since there was an abundance of instances for those classes. Figure 3c shows a few images extracted from a video feed.

Fig. 3 Sample images from the dataset: **a** COCO, **b** IDD, **c** surveillance video frames, **d** web scraped images

3.3 *Web Scraping*

To counter the imbalance in the dataset, we scraped images containing trucks, tempos or rickshaws from the web using a Python program. The program fetched the webpage content from the internet using the entered URLs. The HTML code for the webpage was parsed to find image links. Once the image links were identified, they were extracted and stored in a text file. The text file was parsed, and the images were downloaded using the requests module. Some images that did not contain any one of the vehicles mentioned earlier or were too vague were manually removed. Similar to the collected images from surveillance videos, we annotated all the images scraped from the web using the labelImg tool. Figure 3d shows some images scraped from the internet.

4 Methodology

Object detection using deep learning has been a hot topic of research over the last two decades. Notable deep learning-based object detection methodologies include R-CNN [28], Fast R-CNN [29], Faster R-CNN [30], YOLO, SSD and many more [31]. R-CNN, Fast R-CNN and Faster R-CNN look at multiple regions in the image for detection making it computational inefficient. YOLO [32–34] is a family of one-stage object detection networks with later networks showing remarkable performance, accuracy and speed for object detection tasks. YOLO is based on a convolution neural network which segments an image into regions and then predicts boundary boxes along with the probabilities for each object. YOLO uses single pass approach making it possible to use them for real-time detection.

The input video feed is treated frame-wise. Two YOLO models are used for the detection of vehicles in the frame. The first YOLO model is trained on the vehicle dataset consisting of images collected using various methods and can effectively detect bicycles, motorcycles, cars, buses, trucks, tempos and rickshaws on South Asian roads. Whenever a frame is available, the frame is passed to the YOLO model to detect vehicles

$$y = mx + c \tag{1}$$

$$y_p - y(x_p) > 0 \tag{2}$$

$$y_p - y(x_p) < 0 \tag{3}$$

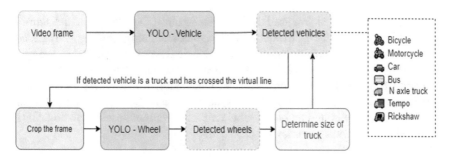

Fig. 4 Illustration of the proposed methodology

The second YOLO model is used to determine the number of axles in of a truck based on the number of wheels from a cropped region of the frame. The number of wheels is equal to the number of axles since wheels are mechanically connected to the axle hence a truck having N wheels is an N-axle truck. The second YOLO model is required since it is not possible to determine the type of truck with high accuracy by detection using the YOLO model of the earlier stage since there exists very low variation between trucks having different number of axles. The complete methodology has been illustrated in Fig. 4.

An essential consideration while classifying trucks based on the number of wheels is that the bounding boxes might be too small for effective detection of wheels. This is resolved by using a virtual line to determine if a frame is a statistically significant. The virtual line marks the boundary before or after which the wheel detection can be performed effectively depending on the direction of travel. The selection of a point whose position is consider for detecting boundary crossing is dependent on the orientation and position of the camera as well as the virtual line. Any one of the four bounding box corners or the centroid can be the point whose position is determined with respect to the virtual line. Equation 1 formulates the virtual line, while Eqs. 2 and 3 formulate the inequalities used to determine if a point (xp, yp) is before or after the virtual line. Additionally, a crop from the statistically significant frame for each vehicle can be used for further processing which may include number plate detection followed by optical character recognition, determining if the vehicle is an emergency vehicle and many more.

5 Experimentation and Results

We trained YOLOv3, YOLOv4, YOLOv3 tiny and YOLOv4 tiny on both the datasets. The images in the dataset were split into train and validation sets with a ratio of 80:20 to performed a fivefold cross-validation followed by aggregation of the results to compare the YOLO models. We trained the YOLO vehicle model for 15,000 epochs and the YOLO wheel model for 7000 epochs with a batch size of 64 on NVIDIA

Tesla P100 16 GB GPU. We used the K-means++ clustering algorithm to determine optimal anchor boxes for each training session since redefining the anchor boxes leads to improvement in accuracy [6]. Since the vehicle dataset is imbalanced, we scale each class's loss using a multiplier determined for each class based on the number of bounding boxes. Equation 4 formulates the calculation of multipliers for each class where m_i is the multiplier for class i, c is the list of number of bounding boxes and c_i is the number of bounding boxes for class i. The modified loss calculation aids in balancing the network accuracy for each class.

$$m_i = \max(c)/c_i \qquad (4)$$

The YOLOv4 model performed the best out of all the models we trained on the dataset and yielded a mAP of 71.05% while detecting vehicles on unseen test images. Scaling the individual class loss based on the number of bounding box instances resulted in better accuracy of the YOLO models. The detection speed of YOLO tiny models is faster, but their mAP is lower than their non-tiny counterparts. This can be attributed to the lower number of model parameters in the tiny models. The YOLOv4 tiny gave better accuracy than the YOLOv3 tiny with lower detection speed in case of vehicle detection. The YOLOv4 model gave a high accuracy of 94.33% when detecting wheels in the test image set making it ideal for determining the type of truck based on the number of wheels. A summary of the results can be found in Tables 2 and 3. The proposed method to determine the number of axles in case the detected vehicle is a truck gave an overall accuracy of 95 per cent when we use YOLOv4 for detecting the wheels. Figure 5 shows the detection of vehicles and wheels by respective YOLOv4 models.

We also performed tests on images from publicly available datasets using YOLOv4 to validate the model's usability for vehicle detection in Southern Asia. We have selected the YOLOv4 model since it has the highest detection accuracy. Table 4 summarizes the mAP for YOLOv4 while detecting vehicles from various South Asian countries. We hypothesize that the mAP for Bangladesh is comparatively lower since cycle rickshaws which were found in abundance were annotated as bicycles. Furthermore, the low mAP for Nepal can be explained by the fact that the images are tightly cropped and are in grayscale.

Table 2 mAP and detection speed for various YOLO models trained for detecting vehicles

YOLO variant	AP (%)							mAP (%)	Detection speed (FPS)
	Bicycle	Motorcycle	Car	Bus	Truck	Tempo	Rickshaw		
YOLOv3	45.19	47.77	47.19	69.43	74.07	62.70	66.23	58.94	48
YOLOv3 tiny	17.34	13.90	12.91	40.78	53.44	32.96	40.39	30.25	61
YOLOv4	58.50	63.73	67.69	79.68	81.40	71.28	75.28	71.08	36
YOLOv4 tiny	14.23	15.10	15.46	42.46	53.31	33.16	42.05	30.83	37

Table 3 mAP and detection speed for various YOLO models trained for detecting wheels

YOLO variant	mAP (%)	Detection speed (FPS)
YOLOv3	82.19	43
YOLOv3 tiny	75.08	57
YOLOv4	94.33	57
YOLOv4 tiny	80.72	57

Fig. 5 Detection of vehicles

Table 4 mAP for YOLOv4 while detecting vehicles from 4 South Asian countries

Country	Number of registered vehicle [35]	Dataset source	Short description of the dataset	YOLOv4 mAP (%)
India	210,023,289 (2015)	*Iitmhetra* [36]	Frames from a surveillance camera feed taken at a 2-s interval	72.72
Pakistan	18,352,500 (2016)	*pakistanvehicle*	Moderately sized cropped coloured images	52.63
Bangladesh	2,879,708 (2016)	*vehicle-detection-bangladeshi-roads*	Frames of a video taken from various locations	47.69
Nepal	2,339,169 (2014–15)	*vehicles-nepal*	Small tightly cropped grayscale images	36.37

6 Conclusion

YOLO models are capable of real-time detection of vehicles found in South Asian countries with high accuracy for various lighting and occlusion conditions as well as various vehicle body modifications. The YOLOv4 model performs best in terms of mAP for both vehicle and wheel detection. The tiny variants of the YOLO model can be used when an independent and less computationally capable system needs to be deployed for real-time detection. The proposed wheel-based axle determining method provides a high level classification of trucks which aids in better traffic analysis and will enhance other applications requiring the detection of vehicles.

Fine-tuning after deployment will help improve the accuracy of detection because the outer appearance of vehicles differs slightly in different geographical locations within South Asia. The detections for a short period of time after deployment can be can be manually reviewed and used for fine-tuning to a specific geographical region. Further research work includes the detection of niche vehicles such as tractors, cranes and many more. This research can be further extended to study the implementation of YOLO models on edge devices with cameras. An interesting direction of further research is using image to image translation models for the conversion of images taken during the night to day for detection of vehicles at night.

Acknowledgements We would like to thank Samiksha Gimonkar, Husain Fatepurwala, Paritosh Marathe, Atharva Sundge, Harsha Gupta and Niranjan Kakade for their contribution in creating the image datasets.

References

1. Davis N, Raymond Joseph H, Raina G, Jagannathan K (2017) Congestion costs incurred on Indian roads: a case study for New Delhi. arXiv preprint ar-Xiv:1708.08984
2. Yousaf K, Iftikhar A, Javed A (2012) Comparative analysis of automatic vehicle classification techniques: a survey. Int J Image Gr Signal Proces 4(9):52
3. Gauttam HK, Mohapatra RK (2019) Speed prediction of fast approaching vehicle using moving camera
4. Ranjit SSS, Anas SA, Subramaniam SK, Lim KC, Fayeez AFI, Amirah AR (2012) Real-time vehicle speed detection algorithm using motion vector technique
5. Babu RN, Sowmya V, Soman KP (2019) Indian car number plate recognition using deep learning. In: 2019 2nd international conference on intelligent computing, instrumentation and control technologies (ICICICT), vol 1, pp 1269–1272. IEEE
6. Dharneeshkar J, Aniruthan SA, Karthika R, Parameswaran L (2020) Deep learning based detection of potholes in Indian roads using YOLO. In: 2020 international conference on inventive computation technologies (ICICT), pp 381–385. IEEE
7. Danti A, Kulkarni JY, Hiremath PS (2012) An image processing approach to detect lanes, pot holes and recognize road signs in Indian roads. Int J Model Optim 2(6):658
8. Tabernik D, Skočaj D (2019) Deep learning for large-scale traffic-sign detection and recognition. IEEE Trans Intell Transp Syst 21(4):1427–1440
9. Khan A, Sohail A, Zahoora U, Qureshi AS (2020) A survey of the recent architectures of deep convolutional neural networks. Artif Intell Rev 53(8):5455–5516
10. Lin T-Y, Maire M, Belongie S, Hays J, Perona P, Ramanan D, Dollár P, Lawrence Zitnick C (2014) Microsoft coco: common objects in context. In: European conference on computer vision, pp 740–755. Springer, Cham
11. Ahmed W, Arafat SY, Gul N (2018) A systematic review on vehicle identification and classification techniques. In: 2018 IEEE 21st international multi-topic conference (INMIC), pp 1–6. IEEE

12. Hardjono B, Tjahyadi H, Rhizma MGA, Widjaja AE, Kondorura R, Halim AM (2018) Vehicle counting quantitative comparison using background subtraction, viola jones and deep learning methods. In: 2018 IEEE 9th annual information technology, electronics and mobile communication conference (IEMCON), pp 556–562. IEEE
13. Ozkurt C, Camci F (2009) Automatic traffic density estimation and vehicle classification for traffic surveillance systems using neural networks. Math Comput Appl 14(3):187–196
14. Li D, Liang B, Zhang W (2014) Real-time moving vehicle detection, tracking, and counting system implemented with OpenCV. In: 2014 4th IEEE international conference on information science and technology, pp 631–634. IEEE
15. Aqel S, Hmimid A, Abdelouahed Sabri M, Aarab A (2017) Road traffic: vehicle detection and classification. In: 2017 intelligent systems and computer vision (ISCV), pp 1–5. IEEE
16. Dubuisson M-P, Jain AK (1995) Contour extraction of moving objects in complex outdoor scenes. Int J Comput Vis 14(1):83–105
17. Kafai M, Bhanu B (2011) Dynamic Bayesian networks for vehicle classification in video. IEEE Trans Industr Inf 8(1):100–109
18. Hsieh J-W, Yu S-H, Chen Y-S, Hu W-F (2006) Automatic traffic surveillance system for vehicle tracking and classification. IEEE Trans Intell Transp Syst 7(2):175–187
19. Zhang L, Li SZ, Yuan X, Xiang S (2007) Real-time object classification in video surveillance based on appearance learning. In: 2007 IEEE conference on computer vision and pattern recognition, pp 1–8. IEEE
20. Tseng BL, Lin C-Y, Smith JR (2002) Real-time video surveillance for traffic monitoring using virtual line analysis. In: Proceedings, IEEE international conference on multimedia and expo, vol 2, pp 541–544. IEEE
21. Vaddi RS, Boggavarapu LNP, Anne K, Siddhartha V (2015) Computer vision based vehicle recognition on indian roads. Int J Comput Vis Signal Proces 5(1):8–13
22. Mittal U, Potnuru R, Chawla P (2020) Vehicle detection and classification using improved faster region based convolution neural network. In: 2020 8th international conference on reliability, Infocom technologies and optimization (trends and future directions) (ICRITO), pp 511–514. IEEE
23. Fachrie M (2020) A simple vehicle counting system using deep learning with YOLOv3 model. J RESTI (Rekayasa Sistem Dan Teknologi Informasi) 4(3):462–468
24. Huang Y-Q, Zheng J-C, Sun S-D, Yang C-F, Liu J (2020) Optimized YOLOv3 algorithm and its application in traffic flow detections. Appl Sci 10(9):3079
25. Oltean G, Florea C, Orghidan R, Oltean V (2019) Towards real time vehicle counting using yolo-tiny and fast motion estimation. In: 2019 IEEE 25th international symposium for design and technology in electronic packaging (SIITME), pp 240–243. IEEE
26. Chen S, Lin W (2019) Embedded system real-time vehicle detection based on improved YOLO network. In: 2019 IEEE 3rd advanced information management, communicates, electronic and automation control conference (IMCEC), pp 1400–1403. IEEE
27. Varma G, Subramanian A, Namboodiri A, Chandraker M, Jawahar CV (2019) IDD: A dataset for exploring problems of autonomous navigation in unconstrained environments. In: 2019 IEEE winter conference on applications of computer vision (WACV), pp 1743–1751. IEEE
28. Girshick R, Donahue J, Darrell T, Malik J (2014) Rich feature hierarchies for accurate object detection and semantic segmentation. In: Proceedings of the IEEE conference on computer vision and pattern recognition, pp 580–587
29. Girshick R (2015) Fast r-cnn. In: Proceedings of the IEEE international conference on computer vision, pp 1440–1448
30. Ren S, He K, Girshick R, Sun J (2015) Faster r-cnn: towards real-time object detection with region proposal networks. Adv Neural Inf Process Syst 28:91–99
31. Liu L, Ouyang W, Wang X, Fieguth P, Chen J, Liu X, Pietikäinen M (2020) Deep learning for generic object detection: a survey. Int J Comput Vis 128(2):261–318
32. Bochkovskiy A, Wang C-Y, Mark Liao H-Y (2020) Yolov4: optimal speed and accuracy of object detection. arXiv preprint arXiv:2004.10934

33. Benjdira B, Khursheed T, Koubaa A, Ammar A, Ouni K (2019) Car detection using unmanned aerial vehicles: comparison between faster r-cnn and yolov3. In: 2019 1st international conference on unmanned vehicle systems—Oman (UVS), pp. 1–6. IEEE
34. Redmon J, Farhadi A (2018) Yolov3: an incremental improvement. arXiv preprint arXiv:1804. 02767
35. Registered Vehicles Data by Country (2020) Global health observatory data repository. Retrieved July 10, 2021, from https://apps.who.int/gho/data/node.main.A995
36. Mittal D, Reddy A, Ramadurai G, Mitra K, Ravindran B (2018) Training a deep learning architecture for vehicle detection using limited heterogeneous traffic data. In: 2018 10th international conference on communication systems & networks (COMSNETS), pp 589–294. IEEE

Stock Market Prediction Using Ensemble Learning and Sentimental Analysis

Tinku Singh, Siddhant Bhisikar, Satakshi, and Manish Kumar

1 Introduction

The Stock market price prediction has attracted both the academic and the business world [1]. It is the act of attempting to assess the potential value of a publicly trading business stock or other financial instruments [2]. A better prediction of stock price could yield considerable benefit in the future. Learning about market trends becomes important since many people are associated with this field indirectly or directly. Stock markets are often nonparametric, nonlinear, noisy, and deterministic turbulent mechanisms. The main question is, how the historical data can be beneficial for prediction. The stock market data follow some patterns that can be identified using the historical data, it will help in forecasting the stock closing price. The patterns are not sufficient only for better prediction, since it does not consider the current market sentiments, for instance new foreign policies, diseases, socio-economic factors, and geographical factors that can affect the market. Inclusion of sentiments and people's opinion will help in better prediction.

The share price analysis reflects data from the financial time series. Market prices are highly volatile and dynamic, so we cannot expect consistent patterns. Time series nature of financial exchange information adds the unpredictability of a succession of reliance among the data sources. Most of the researches are using machine learning algorithms to create models with the time series data that can predict or forecast sequences or outcomes. The additional features (current market sentiments) along with historical data of share market will help to increase the accuracy of the models applied to them. Most of the people consider stock markets as highly risky for invest-

T. Singh (✉) · S. Bhisikar · M. Kumar
Indian Institute of Information Technology Allahabad, Prayagraj, India
e-mail: rsi2018006@iiita.ac.in

Satakshi
SHUATS Allahabad, Prayagraj, UP, India

© The Author(s), under exclusive license to Springer Nature Singapore Pte Ltd. 2023 429
R. Doriya et al. (eds.), *Machine Learning, Image Processing, Network Security and Data Sciences*, Lecture Notes in Electrical Engineering 946,
https://doi.org/10.1007/978-981-19-5868-7_32

ment and do not consider it suitable for trade and investments, while new investors often face the issue of when to invest in stocks. The calculation of seasonal variance and the study of the steady flow of any index will help both current and new investors to understand and make a decision to invest in the correct stock/share market.

In this paper, the focus is to predict the next day closing price of Nifty 50 stocks. Nifty 50 is NSE's expanded list involving the main 50 stocks from 13 areas. It tracks the market execution of biggest cap organizations stocks, this way it comprehensively mirrors the feeling of the Indian economy. The historical data for the five years from the year 2015 to 2019 has been used in the study. The dataset has been split in 80%: 20% for training and validation testing. As this is a time series prediction problem, the state-of-the-art deep learning and machine learning techniques such as LSTM, Auto-Regressive Integrated Moving Average (ARIMA), and ensemble approaches like XGBoost and weighted averaging have been be focused.

2   Literature Review

Various publication and journals have been explored for getting an idea about the recent development in the field of stock market price prediction. Jothimani et al. [1] found that by combining dissimilar data sources with the conventional technical indicators, an increase of more than 20% in the accuracy has been recorded. Using SVM and decision trees along with disparate data sources (data from Wikipedia, Google News, and stock data) with other indicators proves to be more accurate. Nan et al. [3] performed a sentimental analysis on news of the different trading companies to tackle the problems related to the lack of labeled data. The sentiment analysis and reinforcement learning model offered better profits than the models without sentiment analysis. The model used the open/close price of a day rather than the closing price and the volume of the last x days. Trade rules focused on ensemble models yield better ROI compared to the conventional Buy-and-Hold strategy. Moghaddam et al. [4] performed a detailed study on ANN to predict stock market prices with short-term stock and weekdays closing prices as inputs. Parmar et al. [5] studied a combination of regression and LSTM where regression has been used to minimize the error while LSTM remembers the result for the long run. The issue of selecting the training and testing data ratio is also discussed since it affects the accuracy of the model.

To make the predictions more accurate, real-time tweets from Twitter and sentimental analysis have been used and correlated with the results of RNN [6] using the dataset collected from Yahoo Finance Exchange and Bombay Stock Exchange over the period from the year 2004 to 2019. In study [7], a weighted ensemble of multiple regression, LSTM, and SVR learning method has been used for stock closing price Prediction for Yahoo Stock (1996–2016). Multiple regression achieved the highest accuracy while LSTM has the lowest accuracy. Stock market changes frequently, often the analysis of historical data alone is not sufficient to predict these changes. In study [8], the authors suggested an approach, using reinforcement learning, for the problem of algorithmic trading that combines concepts such as Q-learning, sentiment analysis, and function approximation.

Table 1 Training and testing timeline

Timeline	Data used for	Start date	End date
5-year	Training	1st Jan 2015	31st Dec 2018
	Testing	1st Jan 2019	31st Dec 2019
1-year	Training	1st Apr 2018	31st Mar 2019
	Testing	1st Apr 2019	30th Apr 2019

Most of the models for stock market price prediction have an overfitting nature, and they decide based on the predicted result if the stock will go boorish or bullish. In the study [9], a multilayer feedback network that uses various technical indicators along with principal component analysis (PCA) for the dimensionality reduction has been used for SPDR SP 500 ETF (ticker symbol: SPY) to predict the daily returns for the next day. The increase in the number of hidden layers for deep neural network avoids the overfitting issues and improves the classification accuracy over ANN classifier. The mean and standard deviation of the daily data termed as Sharpe ratio helps to identify the volatility situations. In the study [10], multilayer perceptron and stacked long short term memory have been used for National Stock Exchange dataset closing price prediction. MLP avoids overfitting problem using optimizer functions while LSTM overcomes the problem of vanishing gradient using a special unit to memory cells.

3 Dataset

The dataset will comprise three types of features: historical data, technical indicators (derived from historical data), and sentimental features for 50 stocks from the Nifty 50 index. Two timelines of 5 years and 1-year duration have been considered to understand the usefulness for the suitable number of lags for better prediction (Table 1).

3.1 Historical Features

Historical features include the opening price, closing price, high and low for the day, and volume of stocks traded on a particular day. All these values have been obtained by using Python scripts from Yahoo Finance [11].

3.2 Technical Indicators

Various technical indicators: Moving Average (MA), Moving Average-Convergence/ Divergence (MACD), Relative Strength Index (RSI), and Exponential Moving Average(EMA) have been studied. These indicators are used by the professionals of the stock market industry for stock market analysis. All the indicators value have been calculated using Python scripts.

1. Relative Strength Index (RSI): It is an indicator of momentum that measures the extent of the latest price shifts to determine the overbought or oversold status of the price for a stock or other commodity.
2. Moving Average (MA): It's a tool for the technical analysis that smooths out the closing price data by updating the average price constantly.
3. Stochastic Oscillators (%K): A stochastic oscillator is a thrust indicator that compares a particular security stock closing price over a certain period to a range of its values.
4. William (%R): It's a thrust indicator that ranges between 0 and − 100 and it indicates the stock overbought and oversold levels. To find the entry and exit points in the market, the Williams %R indicator can be used.
5. Moving Average-Convergence/Divergence (MACD): This shows the trend-following impulsion indicator used to show the relation of the security prices between two moving averages. It tends to be decided by taking away the 26-period Exponential Moving Average (EMA) from the 12-time frame EMA.
6. Average True Range (ATR): It is an unpredictability indicator used as a sign to exit a trade. ATR is calculated over 14 days of data. It is extracted from an average of the maximum value between current low, subtracted from current high, the absolute value of the present high subtracted from the previous close; and the absolute value of the present low subtracted from the previous close, summed over the 14 days.

3.3 Sentimental Features

The sentimental features such as number of hits on the Wikipedia pages of the company, number of mentions of the company in Google News are considered in this approach. Wikipedia page views of a company are fetched from a free online tool [12] in the comma separated value (CSV) format. Separate files for each company are downloaded and merged with the main dataset. We have a total of 12 features. The average number of working days in a year is 250 days. Thus, we have data of 250 * 5 (years) = 1250 * 12 (features). This is the data dimension for a single stock.

4 Methodology

The stock market data is of time series nature and state-of-the art machine learning algorithms in the area of time series forecasting will be effective for the prediction of stocks price. This study is focused on XGBoost, long short term memory(LSTM), Auto-Regressive Integrated Moving Average(ARIMA), and Support Vector Regression(SVR) models. The model varies based on the different timelines that help to find the suitable number of lags in the historical data for better prediction. This study has been performed on the 5-year and 1-year timelines. The 1-year timeline has been selected due to the availability of optimal entries for Google News Mentions and Wikipedia Page Hits. To select a stock for the prediction, it must have enough liquidity in terms of volume and also has good volatility for trading is a crucial task. Also considering the other sentiment features, the stock should be mentioned enough time in the news for bringing volatility. In this manner., two unpredictable stocks have been chosen with great edges—Housing Development Finance Corporation (HDFC) and Sun Pharmaceuticals. Both are Indian financial administrations organization situated in Mumbai, India.

Ensemble learning is an acknowledgment that in real-world circumstances, each model has limits and will make errors, considering these limitations, ensemble learning aims to deal with the model's strength and shortcomings, prompting the most ideal choice being taken in general. The ensemble of different models can increase the accuracy as various models fill out each other's drawbacks [13, 14]. The different ensemble of time series forecasting models has been studied to look for an increase in the prediction accuracy. In all the ensembles, the models have been combined in two sets, first set consists of ensemble of ARIMA with SVR, where ARIMA is used for time series analysis and SVR can properly manage the seasonality of the data. Another set comprises LSTM and XGBoost, LSTM is the state-of-the-art model for time series forecasting while XGBoost has excellent prediction accuracy because of the small base learners in the implementation. Weighted averaging of LSTM with XGBoost (WAVG-1), weighted averaging of SVR with ARIMA (WAVG-2), boosting LSTM with XGBoost (boosting-1) and boosting SVR with ARIMA (boosting-2) also been studied. Weighted averaging is an ensemble method where weightage is given to the output of various models [15]. The weightages are optimized further based on the error values between expected output and predicted output while blending of ensemble divides the training dataset into train and validation data.Boosting ensemble is a sequential process where each model predicts the output and next model tries to reduce the error in previous models output [16]. Considering the actual and predicted values, errors are calculated and minimized. The ensemble cannot be error-prone as different inputs need different weightages in the model. The models have been implemented with market data, combination of market data and technical indicators and lastly a combination of market data, technical indicators and sentimental features, i.e., Google News mentions and Wikipedia Pages Hits.

4.1   Proposed Methodology

Human thoughts have persistence, what we think, and understand do not get erased as soon as we move on to the next thought. This gives humans a better sense of subjective analysis. Simple and non-recurrent neural networks do not have this ability. This is where recurrent neural networks(RNN) come into the scene, with their loops allowing persistence of information. But in practice, the simple RNN are not best suited for dealing with long-term dependencies. LSTM networks are a type of RNNs that are used to handle such dependencies. They can process entire sequences of data. An LSTM network consists of a cell, an input gate, an output gate, and a forget gate [17]. XGBoost is among the most powerful machine learning algorithms that implement the gradient boosted decision trees. XGBoost relies on execution speed and model accuracy, and it performs better than already established implements of gradient tree boosting [18]. XGBoost is based on the ensemble of models, it offers the predictive power of multiple models while the resultant model gives weighted or means output from different models. XGBoost has an option of regularization to prevent overfitting since most tree-based algorithms do not handle the weighted data, it can effectively manage weighted data using quantile algorithms. XGBoost can maximize uses of available space on disk when a large dataset does not fit into memory.

For a dataset $\mathscr{D}$ with n records and m features $\mathscr{D} = (\mathbf{x}_i, y_i)(|D| = n, x_i \epsilon R_m, y_i \epsilon R)$, a tree ensemble model as can be seen in Fig. 1 uses $\mathcal{K}$ linear functions for the prediction of the output.

$$\hat{y}_i = \phi(\mathbf{x}_i) = \sum_{k=1}^{K} f_k(\mathbf{x}_i), \quad f_k \epsilon \mathcal{F} \tag{1}$$

where $\mathcal{F} = f(\mathbf{x}) = w_{q(\mathbf{x})}(q : R^m \rightarrow T, w \epsilon R^T)$ indicates the place for the regression trees. Here q indicates the tree structure that maps a record to the related leaf index. $\mathbf{T}$ indicates the number of leaves present in the tree while each f_k is related to a self-reliant tree structure q and weight of the leaves w. Each regression tree holds a score on every leaf dissimilar to the decision trees. w_i shows the score of the ith leaf. For instance, decision rules produced by q to classify within the leaves and to make the final decision by aggregating the score $\mathbf{w}$ of respective leaves. The minimization will help to formalize the objective of learning for the functions.

$$\mathcal{L}(\phi) = \sum_i l(\hat{y}_i, y_i) + \sum_k \Omega(f_k) \tag{2}$$

where $\Omega(f) = \gamma T + \frac{1}{2}\lambda ||w||^2$

Here $\mathcal{L}$ refers to the differential convex loss function that assesses the difference among the target variable y_i and predicted one $\hat{y}_i$. While Ω represents the penalty for the regressive function's complexity for the model. The overfitting can be avoided

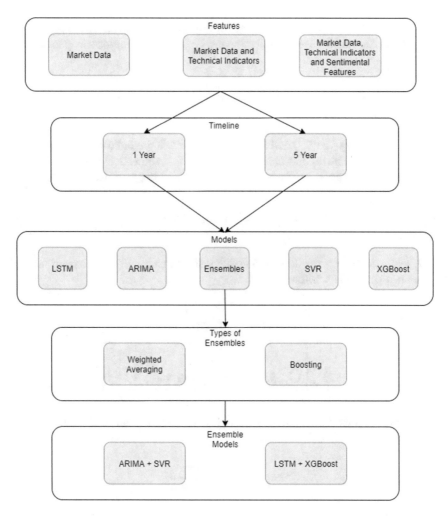

Fig. 1 Proposed methodology

with the help of regularization that smooth out the final adjusted weights. Regularization has been used to select the model that uses easy prognostic functions.

The ensemble model discussed in Eq. (2) uses the functions as a parameter, traditional optimization techniques will not help to optimize the in Euclidean space. rather, we have trained the model differently. Previously, let the prediction at tth iteration is $\hat{y}_i^t$ for ith instance, to achieve the objective of minimization, we will add f_t in Eq. (2).

$$\mathcal{L}^{(t)} = \sum_{i=1}^{n} l(y_i, \hat{y}^{(t-1)} + f_t(\mathbf{x}_i)) + \Omega(f_t) \qquad (3)$$

The function f_t as described in Eq. (2) improves our model. The second-order approximation can be used commonly for optimization purpose in general settings [19].

$$\mathcal{L}^{(t)} = \sum_{i=1}^{n} \left[l(y_i, \hat{y}^{(t-1)}) + g_i f_t(\mathbf{x}_i) + \frac{1}{2} h_i f_t^2(\mathbf{x}_i) \right] + \Omega(f_t) \tag{4}$$

where $g_i = \delta_{\hat{y}^{t-1}} l(y_i, \hat{y}^{(t-1)})$ and $h_i = \delta_{\hat{y}^{t-1}}^2 l(y_i, \hat{y}^{(t-1)})$ are indicating the first-order gradient statistics and second-order gradient statistics, respectively, on the loss function. The constant terms can be removed to achieve a simpler objective at the step t.

$$\tilde{L}^{(t)} = \sum_{i=1}^{n} \left[g_i f_t(\mathbf{x}_i) + \frac{1}{2} h_i f_t^2(\mathbf{x}_i) \right] + \Omega(f_t) \tag{5}$$

$I_j = i | q(\mathbf{x}_i) = j$ is the illustration set at leaf j. Equation (3) can be rewritten and Ω can be expended as follows

$$\tilde{L}^{(t)} = \sum_{i=1}^{n} \left[g_i f_t(\mathbf{x}_i) + \frac{1}{2} h_i f_t^2(\mathbf{x}_i) \right] + \gamma T + \frac{1}{2} \lambda \sum_{j=1}^{T} w_j^2$$

$$= \sum_{j=1}^{T} \left[\left(\sum_{i \in I_j} g_i \right) w_j + \frac{1}{2} \left(\sum_{i \in I_j} h_i + \lambda \right) w_j^2 \right] + \gamma T \tag{6}$$

To furbish up the formation q(**x**), the optimal weight w_j^* can be computed for the leaf j by

$$w_j^* = -\frac{\sum_{i \in I_j} g_i}{\sum_{i \in I_j} h_i + \lambda} \tag{7}$$

and the related optimal value can be calculated by

$$\tilde{L}^{(t)}(q) = -\frac{1}{2} \sum_{j=1}^{T} \frac{\left(\sum_{i \in I_j} g_i \right)^2}{\sum_{i \in I_j} h_i + \lambda} + \gamma T \tag{8}$$

The nature of a tree structure q can be measured using the scoring function given in Eq. (6). This score resembles the correctness score for assessing the decision trees, and it also infers a more extensive scope of target capacities. Figure 3a outlines, how this score can be determined since it is difficult to count all the conceivable tree structures q. A greedy approach that begins with a single leaf and iteratively adds branches to the tree is utilized all things considered. Let I_L and I_R represent the instance set after the split for the left and right nodes, respectively. Letting $I = I_L \cup I_R$, at that point the decrease in loss after the split is given by

Table 2 RMSE for stock market prediction based on 1-year timeline

S. No.	Models	Sunpharma			HDFC		
		MD	MD+TI	MD+TI+SF	MD	MD+TI	MD+TI+SF
1	SVR	7.34	8.025	8.94	32.65	26.54	31.54
2	ARIMA	6.12	9.54	9.37	37.51	27.21	34.77
3	LSTM	9.61	7.81	6.31	11.58	9.01	10.39
4	XGBoost	6.97	7.13	9.68	10.34	10.55	16.17
5	WAVG-1	9.18	5.52	4.84	9.48	5.41	6.96
6	WAVG-2	7.21	8.78	9.16	31.42	26.87	33.15
7	Boosting-1	10.11	9.58	10.01	15.93	16.72	16.4
8	Boosting-2	9.12	8.23	12.47	23.51	43.51	38.34

$$\mathcal{L}_{split} = \frac{1}{2} \left[\frac{\left(\sum_{i \in I_L} g_i\right)^2}{\sum_{i \in I_L} h_i + \lambda} + \frac{\left(\sum_{i \in I_R} g_i\right)^2}{\sum_{i \in I_R} h_i + \lambda} + \frac{\left(\sum_{i \in I} g_i\right)^2}{\sum_{i \in I} h_i + \lambda} \right] \tag{9}$$

This formula is usually used in practice for evaluating the split candidates.

5   Results and Discussion

The different models discussed in Sect. 4 have been deployed using the combinations of the market data (MD), technical indicators (TI), and sentimental features (SF) on HDFC and Sun Pharma's historical data. The RMSE for the forecasting on different models has been stored in Tables 2 and 3 for 1-year and 5-year timelines, respectively.

While using the market data as features for prediction on a 1-year timeline dataset, ARIMA shows the minimum RMSE, i.e., 6.12 among all the models, XGBoost is closer to that with 6.976 RMSE. In most of the cases, the sentiment features along with market data for prediction did not improve the accuracy by a significant factor except ensemble of weighted averaging of LSTM with XGBoost and boosting of SVR with ARIMA. The more information that affects the stock market, for instance, events of social or political interest and importance, has been included as the sentimental features along with market data and technical indicators to improve upon the models forecasting accuracy. The technical indicators in combination with sentiment features add value to most of the models, as the comparison between RMSE of different models using these features is less than their versions with only market data. It shows the fact that the traders can use the technical indicator and sentiments for better understanding of stocks predictions.

XGBoost performed well while using the market data for prediction purpose, as the RMSE resulted in its case is less than most of the models in the 1-year timeline data except the weighted averaging of LSTM and XGBoost (WAVG-1), output of the same can be seen in Fig. 2a. In the 5-year timeline, LSTM performed better among all that

Table 3 RMSE for stock market prediction based on 5-year timeline

S. No.	Models	Sunpharma			HDFC		
		MD	MD+TI	MD+TI+SF	MD	MD+TI	MD+TI+SF
1	SVR	13.42	12.75	16.84	24.95	28.54	29.54
2	ARIMA	9.006	9.62	9.35	52.67	39.74	28.541
3	LSTM	8.65	6.10	6.10	14.37	12.27	12.68
4	XGBoost	8.46	9.00	8.99	31.06	37.80	16.34
5	WAVG-1	8.82	12.37	12.82	12.36	13.27	13.49
6	WAVG-2	12.14	11.84	14.57	28.41	34.63	28.35
7	Boosting-1	8.98	8.97	8.98	16.10	15.79	15.81
8	Boosting-2	12.58	13.54	12.35	24.58	25.68	25.67

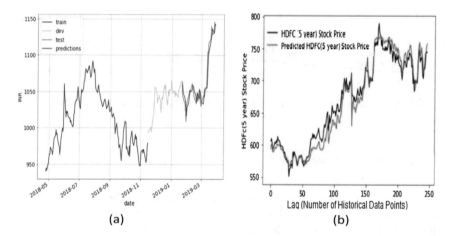

(a)   (b)

Fig. 2 Prediction of HDFC stock price: **a** 1-year timeline using WAVG-1 and **b** 5-year timeline using LSTM

shows the usefulness of XGBoost on smaller datasets while LSTM can understand underlying patterns better when applied on the large datasets. The sample output of LSTM on the HDFC dataset can be seen in Fig. 2b for a 5-year timeline. In XGBoost, *n_estimators* indicates the number of trees that should be allowed in an XGBoost algorithm for proper development of the module. More number of trees does not guarantee a better performing model as after a certain number of *n_estimators*, the model starts to produce the diminishing returns. *Max_deth* parameter in XGBoost has been used to fix the maximum depth of the tree the algorithm should reach. Low depth leads to missing out on important details in the data while higher depth leads to overfitting of the data, so finding a proper *max_depth* will help to improve upon the prediction accuracy.

In the HDFC closing price forecasting graph using XGBoost, shown in Fig. 3a, if *max_depth* is kept at the default value of 3, then the resulting RMSE is high compared to RMSE at *max_depth* of 5 that shows different stocks fits differently and

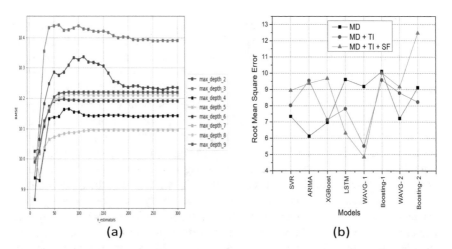

Fig. 3 **a** Prediction results of HDFC using XGBoost and **b** comparison of RMSE for different models

often hyperparameter tuning is required to fit the stock data onto a particular model as stock price react differently to individual news and other factors. So learning a projection path of every stock is different due to its reaction to varying hyperparameters. While for the Sun pharmaceuticals dataset varying *max_depth* and *n_estimators* leads to varying RMSE, at *max_depth* of 3 (default value), varying *n_estimators* after a certain point doesn't really change the RMSE much. So keeping a low *n_estimators* value with proper *max_depth* leads to a better trained model.

The ensembles of the models also provide good results in terms of low RMSE. In Fig. 3b, the comparison of results for SVR, ARIMA, XGBoost, LSTM, WAVG-1, WAVG-2, boosting-1, and boosting-2 have been shown. Among the ensembles, the weighted averaging ensemble using the models LSTM and XGBoost (WAVG-1) worked better, as both LSTM and XGBoost performed better individually as well. A weighted averaging ensemble of SVR and ARIMA(WAVG-2) worked better than the boosting ensemble of the same. Overall, LSTM and XGBoost performed better than SVR, ARIMA, and their ensembles for predicting the close price of both the stocks.

6 Conclusions and Future Work

LSTM and gradient boosting tree methods belong to two very different domains. XGBoost is useful for the scenarios when less data is available for training the model and overfitting should be avoided, while for the long patterns in the larger dataset, LSTM is the better choice. There are certain limitations of LSTM, for instance, time needed to train the model is significantly larger than usual, and it also has a high requirement of memory and is very likely to get over fit. The technical indicators and sentiment analysis have been included with models as wiki hits (including hits on each page related to the stock) of the last five years and news appearances of each stock of the last ten years. The weighted averaging of XGBoost with LSTM performed better among all the models in 1-year timeline for HDFC and Sun Pharma's stock price prediction while XGBoost is also a good choice for the same. In the 5-year timeline, LSTM is the best model for the prediction with the minimum RMSE while boosting of LSTM with XGBoost also provides the significant results in this case. The analysis of gradient boosting and weighted averaging along with different supervised learning models also provides the better results. Although, while testing the models on the dataset of different companies, the accuracy results vary, some of the companies' prediction results were desirably high while for the others it was comparatively low. The prediction result can be further improved by including features such as news sentiment analysis. There is also a further scope of improvement by ensemble or hybridizing these models with other models and ensembles and training it for higher epochs or other concerned parameters.

References

1. Weng B, Ahmed MA, Megahed FM (2017) Stock market one-day ahead movement prediction using disparate data sources. Exp Syst Appl 79:153–163
2. Corbet S, Lucey B, Urquhart A, Yarovaya L (2019) Cryptocurrencies as a financial asset: a systematic analysis. Int Rev Finan Anal 62:182–199
3. Nan A, Perumal A, Zaiane OR (2020) Sentiment and knowledge based algorithmic trading with deep reinforcement learning. arXiv preprint arXiv:2001.09403
4. Reddy AVM, Dinesh Y, Krishna V, Miranam S (2019) Stock market prediction using RNN and sentiment analysis
5. Parmar I, Agarwal N, Saxena S, Arora R, Gupta S, Dhiman H, Chouhan L (2018) Stock market prediction using machine learning. In: 2018 first international conference on secure cyber computing and communication (ICSCCC), pp 574–576. IEEE
6. Yao F, Wang Y (2020) Domain-specific sentiment analysis for tweets during hurricanes (DSSA-H): a domain-adversarial neural-network-based approach. Comput Environ Urb Syst 83:101522
7. Jothimani D, Yadav SS (2019) Stock trading decisions using ensemble-based forecasting models: a study of the Indian stock market. J Bank Finan Technol 3(2):113–129
8. Paspanthong A, Tantivasadakarn N, Vithayapalert W (2019) Machine learning in intraday stock trading. Stanford University
9. Banyal S, Goel P, Grover D (2020) Indian stock-market prediction using stacked LSTM and multi-layered perceptron. Int J Innov Technol Explor Eng
10. Mehta S, Rana P, Singh S, Sharma A, Agarwal P (2019) Ensemble learning approach for enhanced stock prediction. In: 2019 twelfth international conference on contemporary computing (IC3), pp 1–5. IEEE
11. Yahoo Finance. https://in.finance.yahoo.comquote
12. Wikipedia Hits. https://tools.wmflabs.org/pageviews/. Last accessed 30 Apr 2020
13. Zhang Z, Hong WC (2019) Electric load forecasting by complete ensemble empirical mode decomposition adaptive noise and support vector regression with quantum-based dragonfly algorithm. Nonlinear Dyn 98(2):1107–1136

14. Gavin B (2010) Ensemble learning. Encycl. Mach Learn 312:15–19
15. Card D, Zhang M, Smith NA (2019). Deep weighted averaging classifiers. In: Proceedings of the conference on fairness, accountability, and transparency, pp 369–378
16. Sagi O, Rokach L (2018) Ensemble learning: a survey. Wiley Interdiscip Rev Data Min Knowl Discov 8(4):e1249
17. Tensorflow Keras. https://www.tensorflow.org/api_docs/python/tf/keras. Last accesed 31 July 2020
18. Ke G, Meng Q, Finley T, Wang T, Chen W, Ma W et al (2017). Lightgbm: a highly efficient gradient boosting decision tree. In: Advances in neural information processing systems, pp 3146–3154
19. Ba J, Grosse R, Martens J (2016) Distributed second-order optimization using Kronecker-factored approximations

Multiple Feature-Based Tomato Plant Leaf Disease Classification Using SVM Classifier

Venkata Lalitha Narla and Gulivindala Suresh

1 Introduction

In developing countries like India, agriculture sector provides employment and food production [1]. Farmers have a lot of alternatives in selecting the right crops and pesticides for their plants. Crop damage would result in a significant loss of productivity, which would have a negative impact on the economy. Plants' leaves are the most vulnerable which exhibit disease symptoms first [2]. From the beginning of their life cycle until they are ready to be harvested, the crops must be monitored for illnesses. Initially, the plants were monitored for illnesses using the traditional naked eye observation. It is a time-consuming operation and requires expertise to manually inspect the crop fields. There are many instances where farmers lack a thorough understanding of their crops and the diseases that can impact them.

As the agriculture is the main source of food and human survival, it is required to protect the plants from various diseases. But, finding the disease of the plant affected is the major task for the farmer to take certain immediate actions to protect the entire crop. Currently, digital image processing (DIP) methods are widely explored in agriculture to ascertain the type of disease that crop is affected [3]. The primary goal of this paper is to use plant leaf photos to identify and classify diseases that afflict tomato plants. The main focus is to enhance the accuracy of the ability to detect disease in tomato plants. Related literature is reviewed in Sect. 2; various materials and methods are discussed in Sect. 3. Section 4 elucidates the proposed method. Experimentation with simulation results is presented in Sect. 5 followed by concluding remarks in Sect. 6.

V. L. Narla (✉) · G. Suresh
GMR Institute of Technology, Rajam, AP, India
e-mail: lalitha.nv@gmrit.edu.in

G. Suresh
e-mail: suresh.g@gmrit.edu.in

2 Related Works

Singh et al. present a method for image segmentation technique [1]. This algorithm helps in automatic identification of plant leaf disease by recognizing the symptoms of the disease. Economy of a country depends on the agricultural production. It is necessary to yield more products with minimum loss. As the diseases in plants are quite common, these diseases can be reduced by automatic plant leaf disease detection technique. This paper follows the genetic algorithm. Computational efforts are very less in this algorithm. This algorithm can be later used on other plants.

Ferentinos developed a convolution neural networks model [4] by which plant leaf disease is detected and sufficient diagnosis is suggested, through deep learning methodologies. This is performed on a database including 87,848 images of various plants. By observing the symptoms on the leaf, a certain diagnosis is suggested by the model. A deep learning model is established by considering convolution neural networks architecture for detecting the leaf disease of a certain plant. Dataset of plants from different geographic areas and cultivation conditions should be collected for training purposes for improvement of this model.

Jayme Garcia Arnal Barbedo suggests how the size and variety of datasets impact the deep learning technique [5] of plant leaf disease. Limited dataset for training shows effect on the techniques. Interference due to background in the image is a challenging factor. Small background, positive background, negative background, and mixed background are the types of interfering backgrounds. The major solution for plant pathology is CNN. Difference must be observed on these points: number of classes considered, similarities between images in training and testing, and characteristics of image background.

Kumar and Vani used convolutional neural network (CNN) which is a part of deep learning for classification of images of tomato leaves [6]. They trained a deep CNN using 14,903 plant village datasets. They modified the LeNet model which was the oldest architecture of CNN and applied data augmentation, regularization, and dropout techniques to avoid overfitting problem. LeNet and VGGNet networks are used for image classification and residual neural network (ResNet) for complex datasets. It has provided 91% test accuracy with VGGNet and is superior to remaining architectures, viz., LeNet, ResNet50, and Xception.

Khan et al. analyzed the severity of disease by capturing the images of the plant leaf and enhanced the features of images and classified using Support Vector Machine (SVM) technique [3]. Authors concluded that image processing was the efficient method for knowing the disease of a plant at the early stages.

Khan et al. implemented a method for diseases identification and recognition in apple leaves [7]. The method involves preprocessing, segmentation of disease spot, extracting the features, and followed by classification. Genetic algorithm is used for optimization of extracted features, and One-vs-All M-SVM is used for classification. Authors tested their algorithm on 3 types of diseases, namely black rot, rust, and scab.

Authors proposed a CNN deep learning (DL) approach for recognition of apple plant leaf disease [8]. They utilized GoogLeNet Inception structure with rainbow concatenation; a novel DL model for detection using CNNs is developed. This model is tested on 26,377 image dataset to recognize five types of general apple leaf diseases. This method achieved a detection accuracy of 78.80% mAP. Many number diseases of different plants can be trained using the same techniques in future.

Liang et al. developed a DL approach that offers the first ever computer-assisted strategy for estimating disease severity and classifying plant disease [9]. With a lower computational cost, the developed PD^2 SE-Net50 technique uses the ResNet50 model as the primary model and shuffle units to recognize plant species and classify plant diseases. Authors reported that this software can be further developed which can work with smart terminal devices for the benefit of entire agricultural applications and research.

Chen et al. present the automatic detection and diagnosis of the diseases of the plant in the field [10]. Initially, huge samples (images) of diseased plants are collected and labeled. Data augmentation methods are carried out on collected samples to produce enriched images. Processes like random rotation and flipping enlarge the images. The resulting images are aliased with INC-VGGN, and then, they are trained for the class prediction of the new images, i.e., real-time images of the plants in the field. This approach is tested on 500 rice images, 466 maize images.

Sun et al. worked on the northern leaf maize blight that affects the health of the maize plant [11]. They developed a detection method based on fusion of features obtained at different scales and CNNs. Dataset preprocessing, fine-tuning, and detecting are the three primary steps in this process. Preprocessing uses better retinex to overcome the limitation of low detection resulted due to high-intensity light. To decrease the search space of the classifier, an RPN network is used which identifies and removes the negative anchors. A detection module is designed which improves the detection ability of small target areas by fusing features at multiple scales.

Anjna et al. researched the diseases caused by the bacteria or fungus on the capsicum plants [2]. The disease symptoms for the plant can be distinguished by observing stem, leaf, or fruit. The image is collected, and preprocessing techniques like image resizing, color-space transformation, image enhancement, and histogram equalization have been implemented for better quality. Image is segmented into various parts to detect the affected part by using k-means clustering technique. The statistical features are obtained and given as input to the classifier, and they are classified using SVM method. This method is tested on 62 capsicum images which contains both healthy and infected images.

Argueso et al. presented the various methods to detect the various plagues and mitigate their effects on the crops [12]. They worked with few-shot learning techniques for the datasets acquired. The first step is the feature extraction by using v3 Inception CNN method, and then, the second step involves training the features by using SVM classifier. The training architecture basically uses Siamese network with different losses followed by network optimization and evaluation. For this study, 54,303 images are considered from the plant village dataset with 38 different categories of leaves.

Jadhav et al. worked on soybean plant diagnosis systems based on transfer learning techniques [13], viz., AlexNet and GoogleNet. The images in the dataset are preprocessed, and then, they are trained with CNN methods. GoogleNet uses three layers of CNN for the purpose of training the brightness and edge features. Conventional machine learning model training is used to improve detection accuracy. The developed method is trained with 649 diseased leaf images and 550 healthy images of the plants.

At the outset, several algorithms are developed including based on deep learning to improve the detection accuracy. However, there is still room for improvement in terms of detection accuracy, and an attempt is made to achieve this with multiple features & low feature dimension.

3   Preliminaries

All required materials to perform plant leaf disease classification are discussed in this section. Preprocessed tomato plant image is segmented using k-means algorithm first to find the infected region of the image. Three categories of features, viz., texture, shape, and color are extracted from the diseased segment and trained those features using classifier.

3.1   K-Means Algorithm

This algorithm attempts to combine similar data points into groups as shown in the fig. These similar data groups are called as clusters. Similarity of the two data points is calculated with their distance. K-means clustering [14] targets to arrange elements into "K clusters" in a manner that elements in a cluster are alike, and elements in the different clusters are dissimilar as shown in Fig. 1.

The distance between two points describes their similarity. The distance can be calculated in many ways. One of the most used distance metrics is the Euclidean distance. It is calculated using below equation. Euclidian distance (d) between pixels and centroid

Fig. 1 Grouping the unlabeled data into different labeled data

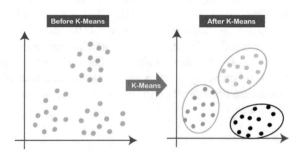

$$d = \sqrt{(C_{kx} - x_i)^2 + (C_{ky} - y_i)^2} \tag{1}$$

where $(C_{kx}, C_{ky})(C_{kx}, C_{ky})$ are centroids of clusters, (x_i, y_i) are chosen pixel points.

K-means clustering aims to reduce distances inside a cluster while increasing distances between clusters. If number of clusters are considered as "3" for the diseased plant image, then three clusters may be green portion of the image, background of the image, and diseased portion of the image.

3.2 Feature Extraction

The feature extraction involves obtaining texture features, shape features, and color features using gray-level co-occurrence matrix (GLCM), Hu invariants, and color moments, respectively. GLCM features [15] have been explored for various applications. Color moments [16] characterize color distribution in an image, and four color moments described in Eqs. 2–5 are computed for each channel of diseased image.

$$\text{Mean}(\mu) = \sum_{j=1}^{N} \frac{1}{N} p_{ij} \tag{2}$$

$$\text{Standard Deviation}(\sigma) = \sqrt{\frac{1}{N} \sum_{j=1}^{N} (p_{ij} - \mu)^2} \tag{3}$$

$$\text{Skewness}(s) = \sqrt[3]{\frac{1}{N} \sum_{j=1}^{N} (p_{ij} - \mu)^3} \tag{4}$$

$$\text{Kurtosis}(k) = \frac{1}{N} \sum_{j=1}^{N} \left[\frac{(p_{ij} - \mu)}{\sigma} \right]^4 \tag{5}$$

where N is the image size and $p_{ij} p_{ij}$ is the image pixel.

Hu moments [17] are good shape features because moments are not affected to rotation, translation, and scaling as it can detect the shape of the leaf even if the image is rotated or tilted. Equations for seven Hu moments are given below:

$$h_1 = \eta_{20} + \eta_{02} \tag{6}$$

$$h_2 = (\eta_{20} - \eta_{02})^2 + 4\eta_{11}^2 \tag{7}$$

$$h_3 = (\eta_{30} - \eta_{12})^2 + (3\eta_{21} - \mu_{03})^2 \tag{8}$$

$$h_4 = (\eta_{30} + \eta_{12})^2 + (\eta_{21} + \mu_{03})^2 \tag{9}$$

$$h_5 = (\eta_{30} - 3\eta_{12})(\eta_{30} + \eta_{12})\left[(\eta_{30} + \eta_{12})^2 - 3(\eta_{21} + \eta_{03})^2\right]$$
$$+ (3\eta_{21} - \eta_{03})(\eta_{21} + \eta_{03})\left[3(\eta_{30} + \eta_{12})^2 - (\eta_{21} + \eta_{03})^2\right] \tag{10}$$

$$h_6 = (\eta_{20} - \eta_{02})\left[(\eta_{30} + \eta_{12})^2 - (\eta_{21} + \eta_{03})^2\right]$$
$$+ 4\eta_{11}(\eta_{30} + \eta_{12})(\eta_{21} + \eta_{03}) \tag{11}$$

$$h_7 = (3\eta_{21} - \eta_{03})(\eta_{30} + \eta_{12})\left[(\eta_{30} + \eta_{12})^2 - 3(\eta_{21} + \eta_{03})^2\right]$$
$$- (\eta_{30} - 3\eta_{12})(\eta_{21} + \eta_{03})\left[3(\eta_{30} + \eta_{12})^2 - (\eta_{21} + \eta_{03})^2\right] \tag{12}$$

where $\eta_{ij} = \frac{\mu_{ij}}{\mu_{00}^{(i+j)/2+1}}$, $\mu_{ij} = \sum_x \sum_y (x - \overline{x})^i (y - \overline{y})^j I(x, y)$ and $(\overline{x}, \overline{y})$ are the centroid of the image $I(x, y)$.

4 Proposed Method

The principal objective of this work is to use plant leaf images to identify and classify diseases that afflict tomato plants. Initially, image contrast is improved and is translated into $l * a * b$ model. Segmentation is carried to identify diseased portion from the healthy portion of the image. Color, texture, and shape features are extracted and combined to form an effective feature vector to classify the disease category.

Algorithm for proposed tomato leaf disease detection is detailed below and is illustrated in Fig. 2.

Step 1: Select the folder containing the diseased images.

Step 2: Resize the image to 256×256.

Step 3: Enhance the contrast of the image.

Step 4: Represent the image into $l * a * b$ view.

Step 5: Apply k-means segmentation algorithm.

Step 6: Select the cluster image containing the diseased part as ROI.

Step 7: Extract the color features of the diseased part using color moments.

Step 8: Extract shape features of the disease using Hu moments.

Step 9: Extract the texture features using gray-level co-occurrence matrix.

Step 10: All these three sets of features are combined and used to train a classifier and further tested to detect the disease of an input leaf image.

Fig. 2 Process flow of the proposed method

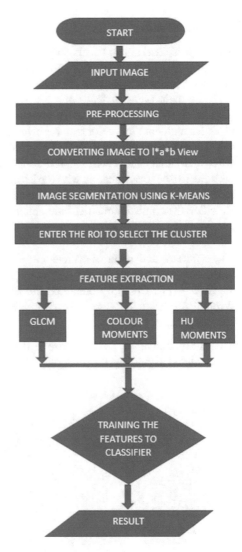

5 Simulation Results

The dataset includes a total 300 images of 6 diseases (Bacterial spot, early blight, late blight, leaf mold, Septoria leaf spot, yellow curl leaf) are acquired from PlantVillage dataset [18] in "JPEG" format. Each image of the disease is read from the dataset and is initially preprocessed by resizing into size of 256 × 256 and enhancing their contrast as shown in Figs. 3 and 4. After the preprocessing, every image in the dataset will be in the uniform size.

K-Means Results

The preprocessed image has undergone k-means algorithm with value "$k = 3$." So, the image has been segmented into 3 clusters having background, green part, and diseased portion as illustrated in Fig. 5.

Three main types of features are considered that are to be extracted from the diseased parts of the leaves, namely texture features using GLCM, shape features using Hu moments, and color features using color moments. The features like texture, color, and shape extracted from GLCM, color moments, and Hu's invariant moments are to be trained using classifier. The classification technique used is support vector machine (SVM) classification with the kernel as "RBF." The platform used for SVM technique is Python (Jupyter). When the dataset of the features is given to the SVM classifier, the confusion matrices are obtained, and their ROC curves are obtained.

Statistical Measures

The accuracy and other statistical measures can be calculated from the below formulae. True positives (TP): Correctly predicted the presence of disease. True negatives (TN): Correctly predicted the absence of disease. False positives (FP): Wrongly predicted that disease is present. False negatives (FN): Wrongly predicted that disease is not present.

Sensitivity: Sensitivity is a measure of the proportion of actual positive cases that got predicted as positive (or true positive). Sensitivity is also termed as recall.

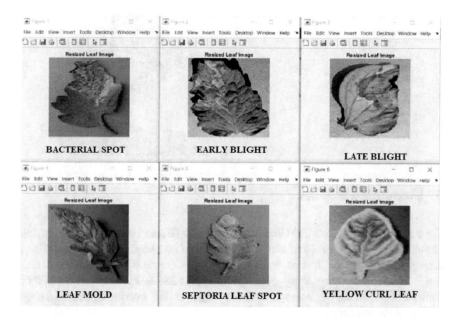

Fig. 3 Resized leaf image of 6 diseases

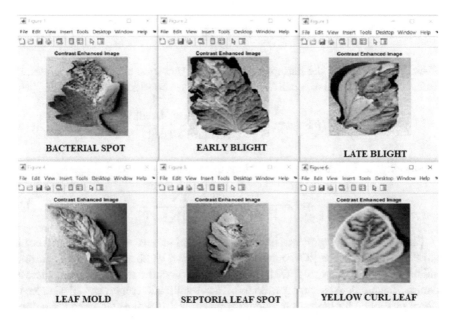

Fig. 4 Contrast enhanced images of 6 diseases

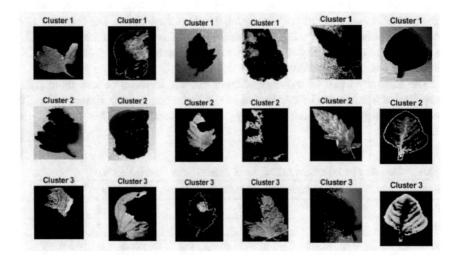

Fig. 5 K-means clustered (segmented) images of 6 different diseases

$$\text{Recall} = \frac{TP}{TP + FN} \tag{13}$$

Precision: It is the fraction of relevant instances among the retrieved instances.

$$Precision = \frac{TP}{TP + FP} \tag{14}$$

F1-Score: F1-score is the harmonic mean of the precision and recall. It is used to realize either precision or recall is more important to consider for the thesis.

$$F1\text{-}Score = \frac{2 \times Precision \times Recall}{Precision + Recall} \tag{15}$$

Accuracy: It is the fraction of predictions this model got right.

$$Accuracy = \frac{TP + TN}{TP + FN + TN + FP} \tag{16}$$

The classification report was obtained which includes accuracy, precision, recall, and F1-score. From the ROC curves, AUC score can be obtained. When the cross-validation technique with 5 folds is performed for the datasets of plant disease features, the predicted accuracy is 86.6%. The classification report and AUC score is shown in Table 2 for the various combinations of features of different combinations is given below.

ROC curve is the plot between the TPR (y-axis) and FPR (x-axis). The ROC curves of different combinations of features are given below. From the above observations, the accuracy of the prediction is maximum when all the features, i.e., texture, color, and shape of the image are taken into consideration. The area under the curve (AUC) is the measure of the ability of a classifier and is shown in Fig. 6. The higher AUC indicates better model performance.

The accuracy when all the three features are considered produced more accuracy than the other works which considered only one or two features. For the acquired dataset, the maximum accuracy produced is 86.66% and has three features considered.

Table 2 Classification report and AUC score of different features combinations

Features	Accuracy	Precision	Recall	F1-score	AUC-score
Color	75	75	74	0.74	0.641
Shape	51	53	51	0.51	0.664
Texture	75	75	75	0.75	0.503
Texture + shape	77	77	77	0.77	0.499
Shape + color	80	80	80	0.80	0.673
Color + texture	75	75	75	0.75	0.454
Texture + shape + color	86.6	86	86	0.86	0.565

Fig. 6 ROC curves of different combinations of features

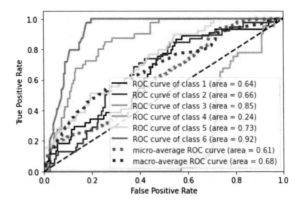

Table 3 Comparison of different approaches

Method	Accuracy (%)
8 shape features [19]	79.5
88 features [20]	73.33
Color and texture [21]	81.006
Proposed method	*86.66*

Comparative Analysis

The comparison table of different methods and the proposed method is given in Table 3. Each of the below mentioned methods is described in the literature survey which include their pros and cons.

The proposed method has highest accuracy as compared to the other methods because all the three features, i.e., color, texture, and shape of the images are considered, and the training of the classifier is done with the hand picking of every image of the acquired dataset.

6   Conclusion and Future Scope

The proposed method considered three features, viz., shape, texture, and color for classifier training, and an accuracy of 86.6% is obtained. This can be improved by growing the dataset size. Thus, using the image processing techniques for the disease detection saves the crops from spoilage and recommends the farmer to take necessary actions to save the crops. As the process completely goes on digitally, there will no need of collecting the sample leaves and making them into heaps as like traditional methods. Usage of these techniques provides an easier way to save the crops without the loss of crops. In future, accuracy can be improved by increasing the quantity of images present in the database. Deep learning models can be explored avoiding handcrafted features to obtain high accuracy. Hardware model can also be designed for disease identification to monitor the crops in real time.

References

1. Singh V, Misra AK (2017) Detection of plant leaf diseases using image segmentation and soft computing techniques. Inf Process Agric 4(1):41–49
2. Anjna MS, Singh PK (2020) Hybrid system for detection and classification of plant disease using qualitative texture features analysis. Procedia Comput Sci 167:1056–1065
3. Khan MS, Uandai SB, Srinivasan H (2019) Anthracnose disease diagnosis by image processing, support vector machine and correlation with pigments. J Plant Pathol 101(3):749–751
4. Ferentinos KP (2018) Deep learning models for plant disease detection and diagnosis. Comput Electron Agric 145:311–318
5. Barbedo JGA (2018) Impact of dataset size and variety on the effectiveness of deep learning and transfer learning for plant disease classification. Comput Electron Agric 153:46–53
6. Kumar A, Vani M (2019) Image based tomato leaf disease detection. In: 2019 10th international conference on computer networks and communication technologies ICCCNT 2019, pp 1–6
7. Khan MA, Lali MI, Sharif M, Javed K, Aurangzeb K, Haider SI, Altamrah AS, Akram T (2019) An optimized method for segmentation and classification of apple diseases based on strong correlation and genetic algorithm based feature selection. IEEE Access 7:46261–46277
8. Jiang P, Chen Y, Liu B, He D, Liang C (2019) Real-time detection of apple leaf diseases using deep learning approach based on improved convolutional neural networks. IEEE Access 7:59069–59080
9. Liang Q, Xiang S, Hu Y, Coppola G, Zhang D, Sun W (2019) PD2SE-Net: computer-assisted plant disease diagnosis and severity estimation network. Comput Electron Agric 157(December):518–529
10. Chen J, Chen J, Zhang D, Sun Y, Nanehkaran YA (2020) Using deep transfer learning for image-based plant disease identification. Comput Electron Agric 173(March):1–11
11. Sun J, Yang Y, He X, Wu X (2020) Northern maize leaf blight detection under complex field environment based on deep learning. IEEE Access 8:33679–33688
12. Argüeso D, Picon A, Irusta U, Medela A, San-Emeterio MG, Bereciartua A, Alvarez-Gila A (2020) Few-shot learning approach for plant disease classification using images taken in the field. Comput Electron Agric 175
13. Jadhav SB, Udupi VR, Patil SB (2020) Identification of plant diseases using convolutional neural networks. Int J Inf Technol
14. Dhanachandra N, Manglem K, Chanu YJ (2015) Image segmentation using k-means clustering algorithm and subtractive clustering algorithm. Procedia Comput Sci 54:764–771
15. Suresh G, Srinivasa Rao C (2020) Copy move forgery detection through differential excitation component-based texture features. Int J Digit Crime Forens 12(3):27–44
16. Patil JK (2011) Color feature extraction of tomato leaf diseases. Int J Eng Trends Technol 2(2):72–74
17. Alagumariappan P, Najumnissa Jamal D, Gughan NM, Bhaskar KB, Ramzan Ali AB, Vijay-alakshmi S (2020) Intelligent plant disease identification system using machine learning, pp 1–7
18. Hughes D, Salath M (2015) An open access repository of images on plant health to enable the development of mobile disease diagnostics. arXiv preprint arXiv 1511, 08060

19. Phadikar S (2012) Classification of rice leaf diseases based on morphological changes. Int J Inf Electron Eng 2(3):460–463
20. Prajapati HB, Shah JP, Dabhi VK (2017) Detection and classification of rice plant diseases. Intell Decis Technol 11(3):357–373
21. Sharma V, Mir AA, Sarwr DA (2020) Detection of rice disease using bayes' classifier and minimum distance classifier. J Multimed Inf Syst 7(1):17–24

A Methodological Review of Time Series Forecasting with Deep Learning Model: A Case Study on Electricity Load and Price Prediction

Ayush Sinha, Tinku Singh, Ranjana Vyas, Manish Kumar, and O. P. Vyas

1 Introduction

Adaptation of exact forecast strategy is the key to maximize profit among different domains, for example, in finance sector to forecast indices of stock markets or stock exchange courses [5], in business to manage human resource, inventory as well as correctly predict demand [14], predicting weather in meteorology, and in healthcare sector to monitor the proliferation of diseases [16]. Simultaneously, forecasting plays a crucial part in the control and management of electrical infrastructure plants and smooth electrical power exchange from transmission to distribution system [28]. The main motive of adapting forecasting strategy is to facilitate the experts in energy planning for understanding the effect of external covariates on the energy consumption pattern and thus design the pricing strategies and maintain the energy production chain [2]. On a temporal scale, the forecast can be of short or long-term type. The short-term forecast could be useful for the load balancing at micro-grid level and better price optimization, while long-term forecast is used for capacity expansion, revenue analysis, and return on investment studies [32]. Electrical load is stored in

A. Sinha (✉) · T. Singh · R. Vyas · M. Kumar · O. P. Vyas
Department of IT, Indian Institute of Information Technology, Allahabad, UP, India
e-mail: pro.ayush@iiita.ac.in

T. Singh
e-mail: rsi2018006@iiita.ac.in

R. Vyas
e-mail: ranjana@iiita.ac.in

M. Kumar
e-mail: manish@iiita.ac.in

O. P. Vyas
e-mail: opvyas@iiita.ac.in

© The Author(s), under exclusive license to Springer Nature Singapore Pte Ltd. 2023
R. Doriya et al. (eds.), *Machine Learning, Image Processing, Network Security and Data Sciences*, Lecture Notes in Electrical Engineering 946,
https://doi.org/10.1007/978-981-19-5868-7_34

the form of time series data that is mainly univariate in nature. However, combining this data with multiple covariates like price and weather makes it a multivariate.

Renewable resources are inexhaustible because they return to their original state or are regenerated quicker than they are decreased by their consumption. Since the human population, as well as its energy demand, are growing proportionally. Hence, to meet this growing need, renewable resources are emerged as the best choice as it is eco-friendly as well as eventually facilitates the objective to reduce the global warming and the greenhouse effect from the conventional sources such as oil, coal, and gas [4]. Renewable resources such as sunlight, wind, and biomass are used for energy generation in remote areas where grid electricity is absent. By using rooftop solar power plant, consumers can also send excess power to grid (net metering). Apart from these advantages, there are challenges which are to be sorted out regarding solar panel efficiency, irregular wind speed, and energy consumption in burning biomass. These challenges are driving force for research and development in this sector. This work highlights the use of deep learning methods to predict the short-term electrical load forecasting, thus is useful for optimal decision-making for agencies and corporations concerned with electricity production and distribution and optimize resource consumption for maximum benefit, both economically and environmentally.

As electricity has gradually evolved from a fixed price commodity to the one, traded freely on the market, it has been noted to have characteristics not usually seen in other commodities. This is due to multiple features which are unique to electricity such as a constant balance between its production and consumption (since alternating current cannot be stored) and highly varying peaks and lows due to multiple socio-economic phenomenons [40]. Owing to weather phenomenon as leading to variations in production and consumption of electricity, the price peaks have become more erratic and volatile [51]. Recently, with increased awareness of climate change owing to unsustainable fossil fuel consumption, there has been an effort to decrease our reliance on it. This has resulted to the maximum usage of Renewable Energy Sources (RES). While RES's contribution to sustainable energy production is unquestionable, there have been concerns regarding its unpredictable and volatile nature. As RESs largely depends on environmental factors, which themselves are unpredictable; the volatility and uncertainty in electricity prices have been exacerbated by increased usage of RES [26]. Nowadays, time series analysis is being extensively used in the area of research. We can see a variety of forecasting problems around us ranging from stock price prediction to weather forecasting, all, in some or the other way, deals with time series data. The paper focuses on uses of deep learning methods for the short-term electrical price and load forecasting. As an experimental proof, the data [13] is taken Fig. 1 and deep learning methods like LSTM, CNN has been performed and juxtapose it with the exiting statistical techniques is done for the electricity trading in the United States of America. Through such electricity trading regional entities, which are formed as aggregations of geographically clustered states, buy and sell electricity from each other, as per their individual supply and demand. This paper first introduces the process employed for the systematic review as explained in the next section, in the selection of research papers for this work. Equally, a brief description of some of the mostly used and accepted forecasting models is stated. As

Fig. 1 Selected locations for wholesale electricity and natural gas price hub as reported by inter-continental exchange [13]

each of the forecasting method has merits and demerits and no one is 100% suitable and correct, it becomes imperative to understand its limitations before consider it for use. A taxonomy is illustrated as the main outcome of this methodological review for the efficiency of prediction models. Finally, in the last, a discussion section explores some open questions evolved from this review.

2   Review Methodology

This work is the compilation of the critical review of academic research with main focus on electricity price and demand forecasting. A thorough approach is adopted for the paper selection. This section explains the systematic methodology followed for the review process. For this paper, a methodological review process has been adopted. So, along with the survey of the existing papers, the experimental proof is also stated in order to validate the outcome of the major algorithms widely accepted.

We adopted the systematic review protocol that differs from the normal review process in terms of incorporating vast literature exploration and meta-analysis of outcome, diminishing the consequence of chance and biases [42]. As per [19, 38], a systematic review process should adhere to well-elucidated protocol that eventually bring more clarity, repeatability, and rigor. We used well-rehearsed research question with specific key word like "electricity prediction model", "electricity forecasting models" or "electricity demand models". Initially, search result was limited to these

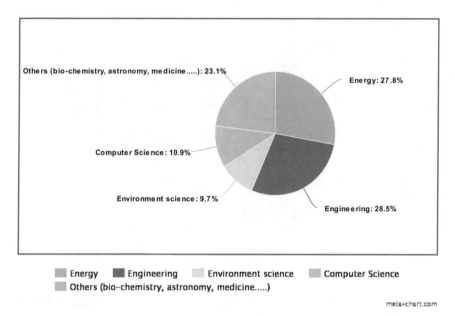

Fig. 2 Field's distribution through the papers

key word; then, citation databases and abstract of the reviewed literature is compiled. Initially, 1667 results were obtained Fig. 2. A statistical analysis showing the distribution of the outcomes through the area of study is presented. From the total results as 1667, 27.8% are from energy; 25.5% are from engineering; 8.6% from environment science and 10.8% from computer science. However, other domains are not pertinent to this review work and thus have been accordingly filtered.

3 Literature Review

The paper aims to cover the existing literature with the experimental support. This section is divided in to two segments; one is dedicated to electrical load forecasting, and another is for the electrical price forecasting. In the result and discussion section, we cover the experiment for both price and load prediction on univariate and multivariate dataset.

3.1 Electrical Load Forecasting

Authors proposed deep learning strategies, multi-layer neural network (MLNN) in [46] for time series prediction and apply these methods for prediction of electricity consumption pattern. However, the model highlighted that the neurons loss rate and very high processing time. In [22], authors analyzed the electrical price prediction with hybrid structured deep neural network (HSDNN) that is based on LSTM and CNN. Author also shows the accuracy of this model with existing benchmark algorithms. In [43], a combination of RNN and LSTM stated as gated recurrent units (GRUs) is proposed and compared the accuracy with SARIMA, Naive Bayes, and Markov chain. A new model proposed by Rohit et al. [11] named as back-propagation neural networks (BPNNs) for short-term load forecasting (STLF) that is used to minimize the forecasting errors. Authors proposed in [54] a algorithm based on SVM, SSA, and cuckoo search CS. For data preprocessing, SSA is used, and for forecasting, SVM and CS are used in this model, and accuracy of STLF is increased. For the training data validation, authors used in [6] the extra tree regressor (ETR) and recursive feature elimination (RFE) as embedded and wrapper methods, and for forecasting, LSTM-RNN is used. To overcome the problem of peak load and to reduce the electricity bill using tariff for consumer's for making the load shift from on-peak to the off-peak hours, in [41] utility-centric and consumer-centric algorithms are proposed. These algorithms are used for demand response (DR) scenario. In [20], the authors proposed the techniques for the feature selection and extraction that is being used, while data preprocessing step and consequently plays a major role in load forecasting. Chitsaz et al. developed an algorithm [9] for the energy storage and price prediction based on meta-learning approach for the preprocessing which facilitates better results. The proposed model termed as battery energy storage system (BESS) and is being used to achieve reliable price estimation and also suggested the price based on inter-hour calculation. Ruben et al. in [34] discussed the method for load estimation which varies from building to building based on clustering approach. The approach is based on k-means approach and cluster validity indices (CVIs) with Apache Spark's library. Authors predicted the accuracy of hourly demand in the different building of University of North Florida in [50]. Primarily, support vector regression (SVR) along with random forest (RF) is used for the comparison of the forecast accuracy based on different features: temperature, wind, day type, and humidity. In [24], based on data provided by Tunisian Power Company and PJM, authors use the classifiers as artificial neural networks (ANNs) and SVM to accurately forecast electrical load. However, for the feature extraction, regression tree (CART) and RF is used as a method.

3.2 Electrical Price Forecasting

In [23], authors proposed deep learning-based (DL) model, i.e., DNN, CNN, hybrid GRU-DNN structure, hybrid LSTM-DNN structure. The algorithm is then compared with 27 benchmark methods on a single dataset. However, due to limitation of a single dataset, one could not say that the algorithm performs better in all scenario. Wang et al. proposed [48] a composed framework use full for the feature selection criteria, extraction process, and dimensionality reduction by KPCA with GCA and forecast the energy price using support vector machine (SVM) as a classifier. However, the shortcoming of the model is the computational overhead that is increased due to use of very large dataset consist of different domains. In [49], authors used DNN and stacked denoising autoencoder (SDA) methods and later on compared the result with support vector machine(SVM), multivariate regression, and classical neural network. Lago et al. used functional analysis of variance and Bayesian optimization for feature selection to improve the prediction accuracy of energy trading price [23]. The authors also gave the way to compare the price of two interrelated market simultaneously. In [37], authors used the multivariate dataset instead of univariate for hourly price prediction. In addition to this, the risk of overfitting is also mitigated with dimensionality reduction techniques, but the comparison is only shown with the univariate modeling methods. Javaid et al. [29] predicted both price and load using DL-based model with DNN and LSTM and showed the accuracy of price prediction is not up to the mark. In [36] authors used probabilistic-based method called generalized extreme learning machine—(GELM) for the price prediction. For reducing the computational overhead, the bootstrapping method was used, but the algorithm did not perform well in case of large dataset. Oveis Abedinia et al. proposed a model [1] based on information theoretic criteria on feature selection and gave a hybrid filter-wrapper approach. In [17–30, 32–41], the authors tried to predict price and load both using a proposed a hybrid algorithm using least square support vector machine (LSSVM) as a feature selection technique. The major contribution of these papers was a modified quasi-oppositional artificial bee colony (QOABC) and an artificial bee colony optimization (ABCO) algorithm. Based on ANN, Keles et al. proposed a method [21] and found the optimal parameter for ANN using clustering algorithm. In [47], Wang et al. developed a neural network as dynamic choice artificial neural network (DCANN) used for the day-ahead pricing scenario. This model is a amalgamation of supervised and unsupervised machine learning methods that detect the bad samples and efficiently search the optimal input for learning. A hybrid model based on ANN was proposed [45].

Gamboa, J discussed the various deep learning models like ANNs, CNNs, RNNs, LSTMs for time series analysis as they have temporal dependencies that spawn two otherwise identical points belonging to different classes or predict different behavior. This would increase the difficulty of analysis. In these models, one stacks many independent neural network layers working together give better results than existing shallow structures [15]. A combination of convolutional neural networks and LSTMs were used in this paper to predict electricity prices. The performance is evaluated using mean squared error and root mean squared error. Kuo and Huang claim to produce improved results compared to zarlier methods of electricity price prediction by using latest deep learning architectures [22]. Ugurlu et al. used multi-layered gated recurrent units (MGRUs) as a new model for electricity price prediction. They used the data from Turkish electricity market and outperformed state-of-the-art statistical techniques using their multi-layered GRU architecture [43]. Bouktif et al. conducted a wide study on France's metropolitan electricity data. A number of machine learning algorithms and architectures were compared. Genetic algorithm was used to determine the optimal tag lag and number of layers for LSTM to be used in the model. They concluded that optimized LSTM outperformed all other machine learning algorithms for a complex time-dependant series [6]. Mujeeb et al. propose a deep neural network based on LSTMs that are proven to be a better approach than traditional data-driven algorithm due to the fact that its automatic feature learning ability is helpful in big data analysis where it is not affordable for humans to label and clean the data [30]. Peng et al. use the data from New South Wales, Germany, Austria, and France. It proposes the use of differential evolution algorithm for hyperparameter tuning of LSTM models being used so far to improve the results in terms of error. This model outperforms all previous results hence proving the viability of DE algorithm for hyperparameter tuning [33]. CNN can be applied with machine learning by viewing the multivariate time series as a sequence of space time images. The paper on Predictive Modeling of Electricity Trading Prices and the Impact of Increasing Solar Energy Penetration by Chakraborty and Shukla presents how predictive modeling may be done using standard machine learning models like SVM, random forests, and gradient boosted decision trees [8]. This research analyzes the daily electricity price at two major power trading hubs, namely the PJM West and Palo Verde. The data are analyzed over a 16 year period. The major highlighting factor was that as solar penetration increased in a region, solar irradiance became more dominant weather parameter instead of temperature. The solar irradiance is the output of light energy from the entire disk of the Sun, measured at the Earth. 16 years of daily data were available, and 75% of the daily data was used to train the model and 25% as a test set. Authors proposed a new ensemble-based deep learning model to accurately forecast time series. The deep learning model is based on AdaBoost algorithm, and kernel ridge regression uses as a meta-predictor [53]. Table 1 summarizes some of the major work from this literature survey section as:

4   Methodology for Dataset Generation and Data Preprocessing

This section would explain the details about the univariate and multivariate datasets used as an input to different statistical and deep learning models. The section discusses the process of making the multivariate time series dataset based on U.S. Energy Information Administration and combined it with typical meteorological year (TMY3) datasets. For the experiment with univariate datasets, we have taken six different and shown the efficacy of deep learning models in terms of its accuracy.

Table 1 Summary of literature review papers

Technique(s)	Objectives	Accomplishment(s)/ data source	Limitation(s)
Ensemble deep learning model [53]	Electrical price forecasting	Tested against three types of real-world data (wind speed, PM2.5 concentration and electricity price)	Computational efficiency and scalability of the model
Bidirectional LSTM in combination with ANN [35]	Electrical load forecasting for month ahead task	Month ahead hourly load forecasting	Not compare with publicly available data set
Comparative study between the Holt-Winters long-term and prophet forecasting models [3]	Electrical load forecasting and checking the model robustness	Established that Prophet model emerged as more resilient to noise, Data from year 2010 to 2020 belonging to the power plants located in Kuwait	Only two known model are studied
Multilayer NN [46]	Electrical price forecasting	Price forecasting with acceptable accuracy	computational time and loss rate is high
HSDNN (combination of CNN and LSTM) [22]	Electrical price forecasting	PJM (half an hour)	High computational time, no detail for short-term forecasting
Gated recurrent units (GRU) [43]	Electrical price forecasting	Day-ahead forecasting for Turkish electricity market	Increased overfitting problem, complex structure of neural network
Back propagation neural networks (BPNN) [11]	Short-term electricity load forecasting	Day-ahead Electric Reliability Council of Texas, USA	Increased complexity, High computational time
CS-SSA-SVM [54]	Electrical load Forecasting	Hourly, half hourly, non-working day and working day (New South Wales)	Very high computational time, model is complex, day-ahead load experiment is not done
LSTM-RNN [6]	Electricity load forecasting	Monthly and hourly data	Overfitting issue is not reduced, day-ahead load experiment is not done
CNN, DNN, LSTM [41]	Price prediction	Price prediction	Redundancy is not mitigated and the effect of dataset size is not handled
UC-DADR and CC-DADR algorithm [20]	Peak load is decreased and savings of consumer is increased	Pennsylvania-New Jersey-Maryland interconnection (PJM)	Reduced rate of fault tolerance, scalability of model not defined

(continued)

Table 1 (continued)

Technique(s)	Objectives	Accomplishment(s)/ data source	Limitation(s)
Battery based storage method [9]	Electrical price forecasting	Hourly data for Ontario's electricity	The model is not reliable and robust
Clustering validity indices (CVI's) [34]	Load consumption	Day advanced eight building data from University of Seoul, Korea	Very high computational time, exposure to limited dataset
Random forest and support vector regression (SVR) [50]	Electrical load forecasting	Hourly data for two educational buildings of North Central Florida	The model is not robust and efficient, exposure to limited dataset
ANN and SVM [24]	Electrical load forecasting	Day advanced Tunisian Power Company and PJM	Very high computational time
SVM, KPCA, DCA [48]	Electrical price forecasting	Predict price and uses hybrid feature selection	Dataset contains not relevant features that increase the computation overhead
DNN, SVM [49]	Short-term electrical price forecasting	Comparison among different models and forecast short-term electricity price	Only suitable for particular scenario, lack of robustness
DNN [23]	Electricity price forecasting	Improve the accuracy and perform feature selection through Bayesian optimization	Dimensionality reduction and redundancy are not under consideration
Multivariate model [37]	Electricity price prediction for hourly data	Used multivariate model, the risk of overfitting is reduced	Performance of model is not compared with state-of-the-art except the univariate models
DNN, LSTM [29]	Electricity price along with load prediction	Prediction of price and load both	Price prediction is less precise, impact of price on load is less evident
GELM [36]	Hourly price prediction	Forecast hourly price data, increase the computational speed through bootstraping techniques	Not scalable for large datasets, comparison with latest algorithms is not done
MI, IG [1]	Feature selection through hybrid algorithm	Increased accuracy by effective feature selection	Optimization is not done for the classifier, model becomes complex

(continued)

Table 1 (continued)

Technique(s)	Objectives	Accomplishment(s)/ data source	Limitation(s)
LSSVM, QOABC [17, 41]	Electrical price and load prediction	Price and load prediction with feature selection through conditional algorithm and modification in Artificial Bee Colony	Only fruitful of their specific defined scenario, benchmark dataset comparison is remaining
Artificial neural network (ANN) [21]	Finding best parameters for ANN	Optimized parameter for ANN and electricity price prediction	Overfitting problems are not taken in to account, computationally expensive
DCANN [47]	Day-ahead electrical price forecasting	Price forecasting and develop framework that automatically choose best neural network for different scenario	Very high computational time, optimization is not done
Hybrid neural network model [45]	Electrical price prediction	Price prediction over bench mark scheme	Feature extraction and selection are neglected

4.1 U.S. Energy Information Administration and TMY3—Multivariate Time Series Data

The U.S. Energy Information Administration is used as the source for actual trading prices; from there, we obtained several data files all of which contained some of the required information to this study. The U.S. Energy Information Administration hosts market data provided, republished and updated biweekly from data collected by the intercontinental exchange (ICE) [13]. The data posted under EIA's agreement with ICE represent eight major electricity hubs. Of these, our literature survey concluded that the PMJ West hub has sufficient data available (beginning in 2001) and so would be most suitable for the methods we wished to apply. Data for 2001 through to 12/31/2013 were available as a compressed bundle which contained daily values separated as per electricity hub. Apart from this, yearly files were available (until 2018) with data for all electricity hubs merged together. The process was to load each file into an individual pandas [27] dataframe, select values related to a single electricity hub and concatenate these data frames together and then with the data from 2001 to 2013. A dataset with 11 columns and 1 row for each working day in the period 2001–2018 was created:

- Price Hub, Trade date, Delivery Start Date
- Delivery End Date, High Price/MWh, Low Price/MWh

- Wtd Avg Price/MWh, Change, Daily Volume MWh
- Number of Trades, Number of Companies.

For the forecasting purpose in this study, the date and the weighted average price are the dominating features; rest of the features can be ignored. In addition to this, literature survey also directs toward the NSRDB [39] as a useful source for meteo-rological data. Initially, we were intrested in using the typical meteorological year (TMY3) datasets from Class-I weather station of each state within a hub's territory; the dataset for TMY3 [52] of year 2005 was missing therefore the data was selected from the NSRDB viewer Web interface [39]. However, as this would provide point-wise data, the data were taken from an arbitrarily chosen point near Pittsburgh.

The following features were available in this dataset: Year, Month, Day, Hour, Minute, DHI, DNI, GHI, Clearsky DHI, Clearsky DNI, Clearsky GHI, Cloud Type, Dew Point, Solar Zenith Angle, Fill Flag, Surface Albedo, Wind Speed, Precipitable Water, Wind Direction, Relative Humidity, Temperature, and Pressure.

According to the literature review, solar irradiance is the dominant feature to consider [8]. Global horizontal irradiance (GHI) is a measure of total solar irradiance at ground level; it is the sum of diffuse irradiance and direct normal irradiance. Thus, the key value needs to be included in the resulting dataset is GHI. The dataset thus obtained contained hourly values from the sensors; since the data for prices were available on a daily basis, GHI values are averaged for the period of 24 h and dataset is combined for the price data with the corresponding dates. After obtaining a pandas dataframe of dates, GHI values and weighted average price, the rows of the data frame were scanned, and the rows containing any unnamed values were dropped.The missing values will mislead the motive of predicting the next day trading price; therefore, the rows containing the NaN values in the price column are dropped. The resulting dataset contains price, and GHI values with 4256 records,the final dataset had the following features: GHI, Trade Date, and Wtd Avg Price $/MWh.

The following datasets were combined to get the final dataset:

1. Wholesale electricity data for the PJM West Hub provided by EIA: containing daily data on electricity prices, trading volume, etc., for the PJM West electricity trading hub [13]
2. SEDS dataset: This dataset is also provided by the US Energy Information Administration (EIA) and was used to extract the solar energy production esti-mates for the states covered by the PJM West hub from 2000 to 2013.
3. SP index daily price data, Yahoo nance: This dataset contains the daily prices of the SP IS equity index from 2000 to 2013.
4. PSM v3.0 data, National Solar Radiation Database: Data of weather parameters, like the direct normal irradiance, recorded by the different class 1 weather stations of 13 states under the PJM West hub's territory. As part of the dataset preparation rst the PSM data of the 13 states under the PJM [39]

West hub territory was extracted for different weather parameters of the class 1 weather stations in the 13 states. One weather station from each state is chosen as it is representative, and the weighted average for each weather parameter is computed

Table 2 List of features

S. no.	Feature name
1	High price of the day
2	Low price of the day
3	Wtd Avg price
4	Daily volume
5	Number of trades
6	Average DNI for the day
7	Mean temperature of the day
8	Average DHI
9	Mean pressure
10	Wind speed
11	Opening S & P index
12	Highest S & P price of the day
13	Lowest S & P price of the day
14	Closing S & P index price
15	Volume traded

based on that state's contribution to the total solar production for the hub. The weights were extracted from the SEDS dataset which contains the solar production estimates of each state from the years 1960–2017. For the estimation of weights, the data from 2000 to 2013 are used. The mean value of weather parameters for each date is calculated, as they values were available in 30 min interval gap for each day. In the next step, the data from the SP index, the wholesale electricity, and the PJM west were merged based on the timestamp, while the resulting data are merged with the processed PSM data obtained from the RST step. The features that were extracted are shown in Table 2.

The data thus obtained were cleaned further to remove any missing values and redundancies that might have persisted, and final data were normalized using the MinMaxScaler function from the sklearn library of Python.

4.2 Univariate Time Series Data

This section shows details of the datasets used for the study on univariatre time series data.

A. Fred Economic Data: This dataset is for Industrial Production: Electric and gas utilities and is provided by the Federal Reserve System US. It has monthly frequency. The Board of Governors of that system provided the dataset. The dataset contains the date and the demand column [18] Fig. 3.

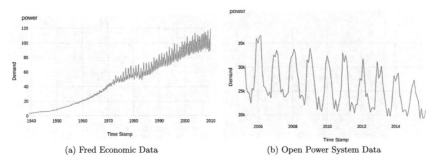

(a) Fred Economic Data   (b) Open Power System Data

Fig. 3 **a** Monthly dataset of demand for federal reserve system of US. **b** Hourly open power system dataset for 37 Europian countries [31]

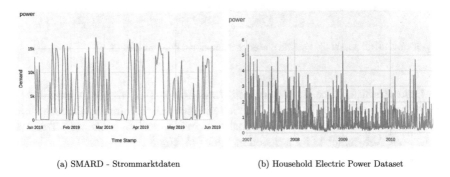

(a) SMARD - Strommarktdaten   (b) Household Electric Power Dataset

Fig. 4 **a** Electricity market data by Federal Network Agency, Germany [12]. **b** Household electric power data [31]

B. Open Power System Data: This is a time series dataset giving power load, wind, and solar power data consumption, resources, production prices, etc., in hourly manner. The data are available for 37 European countries, and it is provided by Open Knowledge Foundation. Various time series include electricity time consumption or the load, power system modeling, etc. Among the many columns, the one used is GB EAW load actual, so this column gives the total load for each day in England and Wales.It is published by National Grid [31].

C. SMARD—Strommarktdaten: A dataset provided by Federal Network Agency, Germany, contains the electricity market data. The dataset was created with the aim of improving transparency. The frequency of the taking data samples is daily. It contains the value of load for every 15 min per day [12] Fig. 4.

D. Household Electric Power Dataset: This dataset is provided by UC Irvine Machine Learning Repository Fig. 4. The dataset contains 2,075,259 instances for a single household with a sampling period of one minute which is located in France for a total period of 47 months. Nearly, 1.25% of the values are missing in the dataset. The dataset contains 9 columns out of which two, namely date and global reactive power, have been taken in consideration [10].

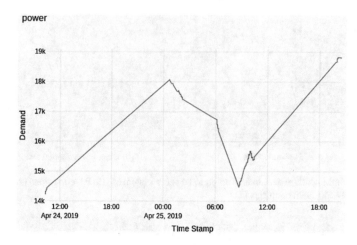

Fig. 5 Individual household electric power consumption dataset by UPPCL

E. Uttar Pradesh State Load Dispatch Data: This is a real-time data provided by Uttar State Load Dispatch Center. The Web site provides real-time data for schedule, draw, demand, total SSGS, UP Thermal Generation, deviation rate, etc. The data have been Web-scrapped for a period of 1 day [44] Fig. 5.

5 Result Discussion and Analysis

The data that do not follow the normal distribution leads to less accurate result from statistical methods like AR and ARIMA. The same argument is applicable to multivariate time series data where the joint probability distribution of covariates does not follow the normal distribution and it can't be said that data have independent and identically distribution property. Authors in [7] proposed a famous BDS test to check the nonlinearity in time series data. So, due to presense of nonlinearity, the deep learning-based technique like LSTM performs well since it captures the interdependence among covarites and good at multi-step forecasting [25].

This section addresses the results achieved by AR, ARIMA, LSTM, and CNN, starting with the quality parameters discussed in ?? with the help of different formulas used in for study. In Sect. 5.1, the analysis for multivariate time series has been performed, while Sect. 5.2 discusses the analysis of univariate time series analysis.

5.1 Multivariate Time Series

The multivariate time series analysis has been performed on the dataset discussed in Sect. 4.1. Trade Date, GHI, and Wtd Avg Price have been used for the analysis among them Wtd Avg Price is the target attribute for the prediction. The models used for the analysis are VAR, CNN, and LSTM. Auto-regression and auto-regression integrated moving average methods are not suitable for the forecasting of multivariate time series forecasting; therefore, these models are not included in the study for this dataset. Before applying any model in time series analysis, it is important to know on which lags the target variable is dependent. To find the suitable lags for the forecasting purpose, partial auto-correlation function (PACF) plot is used. PACF plot for the multivariate dataset can be seen in Fig. 6.

Multivariate dataset contains 4511 number of records, while the mean value of the target forecasting attribute (weighted avg price) is 50, and it has 23.44 deviation around the mean value. The statistical analysis for the same can be seen in Table 3.

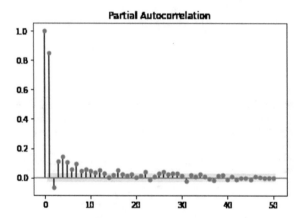

Fig. 6 Partial auto-correlation function of multivariate dataset

Table 3 Statistical analysis of multivariate dataset discussed in Sect. 4.1

Property	Weighted avg price $/mwh
Count	4511.000000
Mean	50.509370
std	23.448343
min	19.990000
25%	36.160000
50%	44.380000
75%	58.054800
max	366.910000

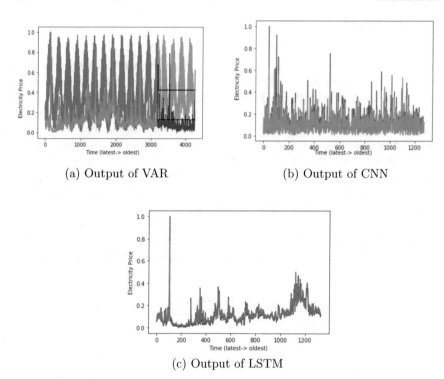

(a) Output of VAR   (b) Output of CNN

(c) Output of LSTM

Fig. 7 **a** Training data shown in blue, testing in orange and predicted in green for the normalized price. **b** Actual data shown in blue and predicted in orange for the normalized price. **c** Actual data shown in red and predicted in the green for the normalized price

Table 4 Aggregate score on predictions for next day electricity trading price

Model	Root mean square error (RMSE)
VAR	0.083
CNN	0.049
LSTM	0.032

The analysis of VAR, CNN, and LSTM on multivariate dataset can be seen in Fig. 7, and the results of the forecasting are displayed in Table 4. There is no the trend pattern in the dataset, and the standard deviation of the dataset is also low; therefore, all the models are showing the low RMSE between 0.032 and 0.083. The deep learning models CNN and LSTM are performing better than statistical model VAR. LSTM has the lowest RMSE, i.e., 0.032 among all the models.

Table 5 Statistical analysis of the datasets discussed in Sect. 4.2

Property	Energy production (FRED)	GB actual load (OPSD)	Demand (SMARD)	Global active power load (UCI)	Electricity demand in mW (UPSLDC)
Count	853	126	147	727	376
Mean	48.12	25,982	5149	0.810	16,404
std	32.53	4349	6281	0.912	1429
min	3.38	19,188	0	0.080	14,232
25%	16.45	22,509	113	0.268	15,288
50%	49.31	24,983	1275	0.392	15,683
75%	75.08	29,197	11,975	1.231	17,638
max	119.24	36,727	17,375	5.698	18,822

5.2 Univariate Time Series

The forecasting on the time series datasets discussed in Sect. 4.2 has been performed using AR, ARIMA, LSTM, and CNN models. Throughout the experiment, the statistical techniques for time series forecasting, i.e., AR and ARIMA, use the values (0, 1, 2) for p, (0, 1) for q and (0, 1, 2) for q, respectively. The statistical analysis for the datasets is shown in Table 5. Among the datasets for the study, FRED dataset shows the lowest standard deviation, while the OPSD and SMARD datasets are highly deviated with respect to the target forecasting attribute.

Before forecasting on the time series datasets, partial auto-correlation function (PACF) is used to know the suitable lags at time $t + 1$ for the forecasting purpose Fig. 8. PACF for the FRED dataset on energy prediction (target attribute) can be seen in Fig. 8a, the lags whose spikes are crossing the highlighted area on the X axis are suitable for the forecasting purpose.

The PACF plot for 50 lags on the OPSD dataset can be seen in Fig. 8b that shows the lags suitable for the forecasting purpose of the target attribute(demand) at a particular time $t + 1$. The mean value for the demand in SMARD dataset is 25,982 with the high standard deviation, i.e., 4349.

The analysis of AR, ARIMA, LSTM on FRED dataset can be seen in Fig. 9, and the results of the forecasting are displayed in Table 6. FRED dataset shows the trend pattern as can be seen from Fig. 9, and the standard deviation of the dataset is also low; therefore, among all the models, ARIMA performs better; it has the RMSE 5.193 that is lowest among all the models. The plot for the different models is as:

Figure 10 shows the analysis of different models on OPSD dataset. Among all the applied models LSTM results are more promising, RMSE for LSTM is 1035.05 while CNN shows the largest RMSE, i.e., 3357.54. The target attribute(demand) in time series dataset, OPSD has high deviation and it does not have any trend, therefore LSTM results have low root mean square error in compared to others. Similar study

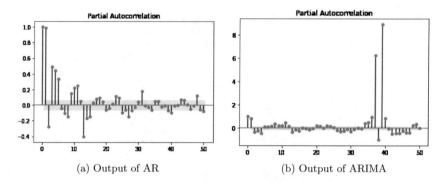

(a) Output of AR   (b) Output of ARIMA

Fig. 8 **a** Partial auto-correlation function of FRED dataset. **b** Partial auto-correlation function of SMARD dataset

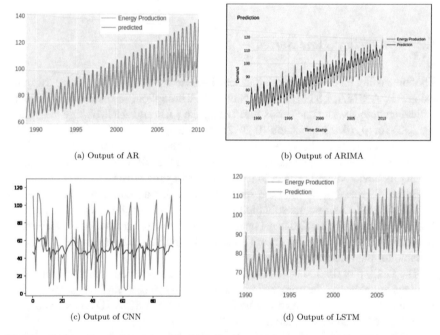

(a) Output of AR   (b) Output of ARIMA

(c) Output of CNN   (d) Output of LSTM

Fig. 9 **a** Output of auto-regression for FRED dataset energy production shown in orange color and predicted energy production in blue color. **b** Actual data shown in blue and predicted in orange for the normalized price. **c** Actual data shown in red and predicted in the green for the normalized price. **d** Actual data shown in blue and predicted in orange for the normalized price

Table 6 RMSE for different models used on univariate datasets

	FRED	OPSD	SMARD	UCI	UPSLDC
AR	8.247	1646.63	5870.88	0.702	1589.67
ARIMA	5.193	3710.96	5864.92	0.780	1780.71
LSTM	7.992	1035.05	5184.04	0.6526	334.54
CNN	3778.02	3357.54	5109.39	1.131	7369.47

(a) Output of AR

(b) Output of ARIMA

(c) Output of CNN

(d) Output of LSTM

Fig. 10 **a** Output of auto-regression for OPSD dataset energy production shown in blue color and predicted energy production in orange color. **b** Actual data shown in blue and predicted in orange for the normalized price. **c** Actual data shown in red and predicted in the green for the normalized price. **d** Actual data shown in blue and predicted in orange for the normalized price

is performed on the remaining datasets, root mean square error is calculated on SMARD, UCI and UPSLDC datsets using the statistical measurement methods like auto-regression, ARIMA, and deep learning methods like LSTM. The results of the study can be seen in Table 6.

The comparative study of AR, ARIMA, LSTM, and CNN has been performed on the datasets discussed in Sect. 4.2, and the results of the same can be seen in Fig. 11.

It is evident from the results shown in Table 6 and Fig. 11 that for all datasets except FRED, LSTM performs better as compared to other models.

Fig. 11 RMSE plot of different models on univariate datasets

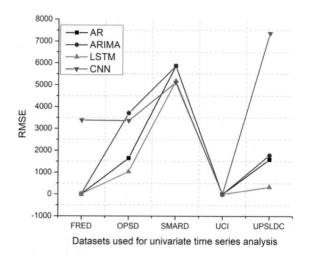

6 Conclusion and Future Work

This paper presents a methodological verification of different deep learning and statistical methods on uni- and multivariate time series datasets. Many criteria have been checked out as time series characteristics like trend and seasonality data preprocessing and error rate. Deep learning methods as LTSM, CNN, and regression techniques as ARIMA, VAR are applied to study their applicability for multivariate time series dataset of electrical load and price. The same set of models is also tested on five different univariate datasets and juxtaposes the results. Considering the vast use cases and the papers studied, we can say reasonably that it is good practice to assume the recurrence while forecasting. Regression models perform well in case of long-term prediction where the time series data are less periodic in nature. While in case of more complex multivariate time series data for electrical load and price in combination with covariates as weather, stocks, etc., deep learning methods are observed to be more use full. Additionally, it is shown that preprocessing and preanalysis of the input data is a good practice for better forecast. Preprocessing of time series data involves the smoothing, difference, and filling the missing values based on statistical measurements. Two generalized taxonomies are presented in this work; one is the outcome of different literature survey, and the second is the outcome of experiment done on deep learning and statistical algorithms. In case of model choosing by researchers working in this domain, one can refer to the first general taxonomy in terms of wide survey of papers and explore the model that fits in situation and then apply the model. In some scenario, researchers may directly benefited from the outcome of the experiment and choose an appropriate model as through the experiment, LSTMs are observed to be superior compare to CNNs, ARIMA, and VAR. We performed this analysis on data over a period of 18 years ranging from 2001 to 2018. This work may be expanded upon with a study on multiple codependent variables such as temperature, wind velocity, and humidity as well as other economical features such as daily trading prices of alternate, non-renewable electricity generation resources (e.g., gas), and aggregate economic trends through S&P 500 Index.

References

1. Abedinia O, Amjady N, Zareipour H (2016) A new feature selection technique for load and price forecast of electrical power systems. IEEE Trans Power Syst 32(1):62–74
2. Al-Ghandoor A, Jaber J, Al-Hinti I, Mansour I (2009) Residential past and future energy consumption: potential savings and environmental impact. Renew Sustain Energy Rev 13(6–7):1262–1274
3. Almazrouee AI, Almeshal AM, Almutairi AS, Alenezi MR, Alhajeri SN (2020) Long-term forecasting of electrical loads in kuwait using prophet and holt-winters models. Appl Sci 10(16):5627
4. Arent D, Pless J, Mai T, Wiser R, Hand M, Baldwin S, Heath G, Macknick J, Bazilian M, Schlosser A et al (2014) Implications of high renewable electricity penetration in the us for water use, greenhouse gas emissions, land-use, and materials supply. Appl Energy 123:368–377
5. Bianco V, Manca O, Nardini S (2009) Electricity consumption forecasting in italy using linear regression models. Energy 34(9):1413–1421
6. Bouktif S, Fiaz A, Ouni A, Serhani MA (2018) Optimal deep learning lstm model for electric load forecasting using feature selection and genetic algorithm: comparison with machine learning approaches. Energies 11(7):1636
7. Brock W, Dechert W, Lebaron B, Scheinkman J (1995) A test for independence based on the correlation dimension. Working papers, Wisconsin Madison—social systems
8. Chakraborty SV, Shukla SK (2019) Predictive modeling of electricity trading prices and the impact of increasing solar energy penetration. IEEE Milan PowerTech
9. Chitsaz H, Zamani-Dehkordi P, Zareipour H, Parikh PP (2017) Electricity price forecasting for operational scheduling of behind-the-meter storage systems. IEEE Trans Smart Grid 9(6):6612–6622
10. Dua D, Graff C (2019) UCI machine learning repository. University of California, Irvine
11. Eapen RR, Simon SP (2019) Performance analysis of combined similar day and day ahead short term electrical load forecasting using sequential hybrid neural networks. IETE J Res 65(2):216–226
12. Electricity Generation and Consumption in Germany (2019) Visualize market data SMARD version November 2019
13. Exchange I (2019) (ICE) U.S. Energy Information Administration, wholesale electricity and natural gas market data report
14. Field CB, Barros VR, Mastrandrea MD, Mach KJ, Abdrabo MK, Adger N, Anokhin YA, Anisimov OA, Arent DJ, Barnett J et al (2014) Summary for policymakers. In: Climate change 2014: impacts, adaptation, and vulnerability. Part A: global and sectoral aspects. Contribution of working group II to the fifth assessment report of the intergovernmental panel on climate change, pp 1–32. Cambridge University Press
15. Gamboa JCB (2017) Deep learning for time-series analysis. *arXiv preprint* arXiv:1701.01887
16. Generous N, Fairchild G, Deshpande A, Del Valle SY, Priedhorsky R (2014) Global disease monitoring and forecasting with Wikipedia. PLoS Comput Biol 10(11)
17. Ghasemi A, Shayeghi H, Moradzadeh M, Nooshyar M (2016) A novel hybrid algorithm for electricity price and load forecasting in smart grids with demand-side management. Appl Energy 177:40–59
18. Governors of the Federal Reserve System (US) (2019) Industrial production: electric and gas utilities retrieved from fred. Federal Reserve Bank of St, Louis

19. Higgins JP, Green S et al (2006) Cochrane handbook for systematic reviews of interventions [updated september 2006]. The Cochrane Library, vol 4
20. Jindal A, Singh M, Kumar N (2018) Consumption-aware data analytical demand response scheme for peak load reduction in smart grid. IEEE Trans Indus Electron 65(11):8993–9004
21. Keles D, Scelle J, Paraschiv F, Fichtner W (2016) Extended forecast methods for day-ahead electricity spot prices applying artificial neural networks. Appl Energy 162:218–230
22. Kuo P-H, Huang C-J (2018) An electricity price forecasting model by hybrid structured deep neural networks. Sustainability 10(4):1280
23. Lago J, De Ridder F, De Schutter B (2018) Forecasting spot electricity prices: deep learning approaches and empirical comparison of traditional algorithms. Appl Energy 221:386–405
24. Lahouar A, Slama JBH (2015) Day-ahead load forecast using random forest and expert input selection. Energy Convers Manage 103:1040–1051
25. Makridakis S, Spiliotis E, Assimakopoulos V (2018) Statistical and machine learning forecasting methods: concerns and ways forward. PloS One 13(3):e0194889
26. Martinez-Anido CB, Brin-kman G, Hodge B-M (2016) The impact of wind power on electricity prices. Renew Energy 94:474–487
27. McKinney W et al (2010) Data structures for statistical computing in python. In: Proceedings of the 9th python in science conference, vol 445, pp 51–56. Austin, TX
28. Mohandes M (2002) Support vector machines for short-term electrical load forecasting. Int J Ener Res 26(4):335–345
29. Mujeeb S, Javaid N, Akbar M, Khalid R, Nazeer O, Khan M (2018) Big data analytics for price and load forecasting in smart grids. In: International conference on broadband and wireless computing, communication and applications, pp 77–87. Springer
30. Mujeeb S, Javaid N, Ilahi M, Wadud Z, Ishmanov F, Afzal MK (2019) Deep long short-term memory: a new price and load forecasting scheme for big data in smart cities. Sustainability 11(4):987
31. OPSD (2019) Data package time series, version 2019-06-05. Retrieved from Federal Reserve Bank of St. Louis
32. Parlos AG, Oufi E, Muthusami J, Patton AD, Atiya AF (1996) Development of an intelligent long-term electric load forecasting system. In: Proceedings of international conference on intelligent system application to power systems, pp 288–292. IEEE
33. Peng L, Liu S, Liu R, Wang L (2018) Effective long short-term memory with differential evolution algorithm for electricity price prediction. Energy 162:1301–1314
34. Pérez-Chacón R, Luna-Romera JM, Troncoso A, Martínez-Álvarez F, Riquelme JC (2018) Big data analytics for discovering electricity consumption patterns in smart cities. Energies 11(3):683
35. Petrosanu DM, Pirjan A (2021) Electricity consumption forecasting based on a bidirectional long-short-term memory artificial neural network. Sustainability 13(1):104
36. Rafiei M, Niknam T, Khooban M-H (2016) Probabilistic forecasting of hourly electricity price by generalization of elm for usage in improved wavelet neural network. IEEE Trans Indus Inform 13(1):71–79
37. Raviv E, Bouwman KE, Van Dijk D (2015) Forecasting day-ahead electricity prices: utilizing hourly prices. Energ Econ 50:227–239
38. Righi AW, Saurin TA, Wachs P (2015) A systematic literature review of resilience engineering: research areas and a research agenda proposal. Reliab Eng Syst Saf 141:142–152
39. Sengupta M, Xie Y, Lopez A, Habte A, Maclaurin G, Shelby J (2018) The national solar radiation data base (nsrdb). Renew Sustain Energ Rev 89:51–60
40. Shahidehpour M, Yamin H, Li Z (2003) Market operations in electric power systems: forecasting, scheduling, and risk management. Wiley, New York
41. Shayeghi H, Ghasemi A, Moradzadeh M, Nooshyar M (2015) Simultaneous day-ahead forecasting of electricity price and load in smart grids. Energ Convers Manage 95:371–384
42. Tranfield D, Denyer D, Smart P (2003) Towards a methodology for developing evidence-informed management knowledge by means of systematic review. Br J Manage 14(3):207–222

43. Ugurlu U, Oksuz I, Tas O (2018) Electricity price forecasting using recurrent neural networks. Energies 11(5):1255
44. UPSLDC (2019) UP generation summary
45. Varshney H, Sharma A, Kumar R (2016) A hybrid approach to price forecasting incorporating exogenous variables for a day ahead electricity market. In: 2016 IEEE 1st international conference on power electronics, intelligent control and energy systems (ICPEICES), pp 1–6. IEEE
46. Wang H-Z, Li G-Q, Wang G-B, Peng J-C, Jiang H, Liu Y-T (2017) Deep learning based ensemble approach for probabilistic wind power forecasting. Appl Energ 188:56–70
47. Wang J, Liu F, Song Y, Zhao J (2016) A novel model: dynamic choice artificial neural network (dcann) for an electricity price forecasting system. Appl Soft Comput 48:281–297
48. Wang K, Xu C, Zhang Y, Guo S, Zomaya AY (2017) Robust big data analytics for electricity price forecasting in the smart grid. IEEE Trans Big Data 5(1):34–45
49. Wang L, Zhang Z, Chen J (2016) Short-term electricity price forecasting with stacked denoising autoencoders. IEEE Trans Power Syst 32(4):2673–2681
50. Wang Z, Wang Y, Zeng R, Srinivasan RS, Ahrentzen S (2018) Random forest based hourly building energy prediction. Energ Build 171:11–25
51. Weron R (2014) Electricity price forecasting: a review of the state-of-the-art with a look into the future. Int J Forecast 30(4):1030–1081
52. Wilcox S (2007) National solar radiation database 1991–2005 update: user's manual. Technical report, National Renewable Energy Laboratory (NREL), Golden, CO (United States)
53. Zhang S, Chen Y, Zhang W, Feng R (2021) A novel ensemble deep learning model with dynamic error correction and multi-objective ensemble pruning for time series forecasting. Inf Sci 544:427–445
54. Zhang X, Wang J, Zhang K (2017) Short-term electric load forecasting based on singular spectrum analysis and support vector machine optimized by cuckoo search algorithm. Electr Power Syst Res 146:270–285

Unexpected Alliance of Cardiovascular Diseases and Artificial Intelligence in Health Care

Rishika Anand, S. R. N. Reddy, and Dinesh Kumar

1 Introduction

Globally, most of the deaths are caused due to cardiovascular diseases as compared to other diseases. Approximately, 17.9 million of people died in 2016 from cardiovascular diseases, its 31% of all deaths occurred globally stated by WHO [1]. 85% of deaths are due to stroke and heart attacks out of these global figures. From last three to four years, most of the deaths from cardiovascular diseases occurred in middle and low-income countries. Approximately, 82% deaths occurred in middle and low-income countries from 17 million deaths in 2015 among which 37% is because of cardiovascular diseases [1].

Most of the behavioral parameters like unhealthy diet, use of tobacco, inactive lifestyle, obesity, and excess consumption of an alcohol can be considered to prevent a person from cardiovascular diseases using various strategies. People with hyperlipidemia, diabetes, and hypertension [1] require early detection of a cardiovascular disease, so that timely medicines and counseling can be provided to those patients. Various types of cardiovascular heart diseases like congenital heart disease, rheumatic heart disease, cardiomyopathy, heart failure, myocardial infection, carditis, thrombosis, heart arrhythmia, hypertensive heart disease, valvular heart disease, and aortic aneurysms are shown in Fig. 1.

Section 2 comprises of literature review. Section 3 discussed the proposed work. Section 4 comprises the results of proposed work followed by conclusion and future scope.

R. Anand (✉) · S. R. N. Reddy
Department of Computer Science and Engineering, Indira Gandhi Delhi Technical University for Women, Kashmere Gate, Delhi 110006, India
e-mail: rishika003phd19@igdtuw.ac.in

D. Kumar
Department of Pediatrics, Dr. Ram Manohar Lohia Hospital, Delhi, India

© The Author(s), under exclusive license to Springer Nature Singapore Pte Ltd. 2023
R. Doriya et al. (eds.), *Machine Learning, Image Processing, Network Security and Data Sciences*, Lecture Notes in Electrical Engineering 946,
https://doi.org/10.1007/978-981-19-5868-7_35

Fig. 1 Various
cardiovascular diseases

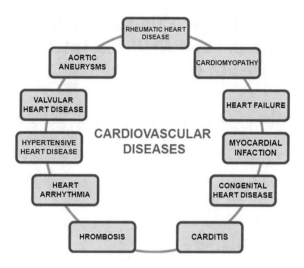

2 Literature Review

Various researchers devoted their work toward artificial intelligence to predict
cardiovascular disease. Heart disease is indicated by abnormal pulse rate, fatigue,
chest pain, and various other symptoms. Various risk factors like weight, sex, age,
smoking, obesity, diabetes, high blood pressure are associated to detect heart disease.
Numerous risks make it difficult for the physicians to detect type of cardiovascular
disease.

There are numerous technologies that are used to detect cardiovascular diseases.
Facial images are used to detect cardiovascular disease in a patient. Probabilistic
collaborative representation-based classifier is used to extract color features from
facial images to detect CVD [2]. Retinal fundus images can also be used to detect
cardiovascular disease with the help of deep learning techniques. Various parameters
such as age, gender, smoking status, systolic blood pressure, and major adverse
cardiac events are taken into consideration for this research [3]. Currently, most of
the cardiovascular surgeries are done by robots. While some researches show good
results of surgeries done by robots, still clinical efficacy, cost, and safety are the
major concern [4]. **Precision Medicine**: Remote health checkups and follow-ups,
counseling of disease in a real time, reminders for medication and early warnings
of disease are possible only because of artificial intelligence. AI can also use to
minimize the workload of the staff in healthcare sector by collecting the data through
voice [5]. **Clinical Predictions**: AI can be used to make precise predictions for
any disease as compared to the healthcare staff. Motwani in his research made a
deep learning-based model that will predict the risk of death for next five years [4]
for CHD patients. **Cardiac Imaging Analysis**: Currently, image analysis has taken
a new path in healthcare sector. Electrocardiogram (ECG), echocardiography, and
coronary angiography can be analyzed with the help of deep learning techniques [5].

Intelligent Robots: There are various surgical robots that can be used for surgery without the presence of any healthcare staff. Various surgeries like hysteromyoma resection and bladder replacement surgery are performed by these robots [4, 5].

Highly conceptual and reasonable problems are solved by human brain only. The mechanism is partially understood by the network. Hence, only, narrow insights are provided by the artificial intelligence [6]. Main aspect in implementing the concept of machine learning is that the model needs a large amount of data for training. But, most of the dataset are not available publicly, and small amount of dataset will inevitably affect the model performance. Differential diagnosis is one of the major issues which cannot be analyzed using AI. So, this will result in slow progress of AI in health care. Eventually, poor quality of data, human brain superficial knowledge, complex computational process and unreachability to traditional clinic workflow have led few controversies in healthcare applications of AI [7].

Artificial intelligence is everywhere from a long time. Currently, various artificial technologies can be used to detect cardiovascular diseases including cardiac image analysis, clinical prediction, and many more. Some of the researches that uses the concept of artificial intelligence for predicting cardiovascular diseases are described in Table 1. Various machine learning and deep learning algorithms are used to detect cardiovascular disease such as logistic regression, random forest, neural network, K-nearest neighbor, gradient-boosted trees, Naïve Bayes, decision tree, backpropagation neural network, deep learning, artificial neural network, convolution neural network, generative adversarial network, CAD, recurrent neural network, GRU, LSTM, BLSTM, support vector machine, ERF, deep neural network, CNN-UDRP, CART. Various datasets are freely available for doing the research on cardiovascular disease such as Cleveland heart disease, MIT-BIH Arrhythmia, Statlog (Heart), retinal fundus images, NIH PLCO, manual collection of data, UTHealth, Physio Net, PTB, HSS Corpus, NHANES Physical Activity and CVD Fitness and Framingham Heart Study. The maximum accuracy obtained by the research is 99.95 [8]. Basically, Cleveland heart dataset and MIT-BIH arrhythmia dataset are used to detect the cardiovascular disease, and the maximum accuracy gained by the researcher is 92% [9] and 97.98% [10]. There are some limitations in the various research performed previously; real-time analysis is not there [11]; size of the dataset is small for deep learning [3, 12, 13]; test group was different from training group [14]; noise is there [15]. The research discussed in Table 1 is categorized in two categories, i.e., sensor based and algorithm based. Sensor-based research consists either an IoT or IoT and ML/DL [16] integrated approach. Algorithm-based approach means the research is carried using machine learning or deep learning.

3 Proposed Work

Most of the researchers used Cleveland heart dataset [19] to monitor whether a patient is suffering from congenital heart disease or not. In this research, various deep learning algorithms and machine learning are applied to detect CVD.

Table 1 Cardiovascular disease detection

Research	Dataset	No. of classes	Algorithm used	Maximum accuracy (%)
[17]	Kaggle	2	Logistic regression, random forest, neural network, K-nearest neighbor	91.39
[10]	MIT-BIH Arrhythmia dataset	5	Gradient-boosted trees, random forest	97.98
[18]	Statlog (Heart) dataset	2	Backpropagation neural network	
[11]	Statlog dataset	2	Random forest, decision trees, and Naive Bayes	80.09
[19]	Cleveland Heart Disease Database	2	Logistic regression and neural network	84
[12]	Retinal fundus images from UK Biobank and EyePACS	2	Deep learning	72
[16]	–		Artificial neural network, convolutional neural network	
[8]	Southwest Hospital dataset	7	Deep learning and ECG analysis using deep learning	99.95
[20]	NIH PLCO dataset	2	Generative adversarial network	84.19
[14]	Manual data collection	2	Deep learning	73
[21]	Manual data collection	2	CAD detection algorithm	73
[22]	i2b2/UTHealth	2	CNN, RNN, GRU, LSTM, BLSTM	90.81
[23]	Cleveland dataset	2	SVM, LR, RF, GTB, ERF	82
[24]	Manual data collection	2	LR, SVM, RF, and GB	90.77
[9]	Cleveland Clinic Foundation	2	RF, DNN	92
[25]	Heart disease and heart disease risk prediction from UCI repository	2	NB, KNN, CNN-UDRP	82

(continued)

Table 1 (continued)

Research	Dataset	No. of classes	Algorithm used	Maximum accuracy (%)
[15]	Physio net database	5	RF, SVM, LSTM (2 and 4 hidden layers), BLSTM (2 and 4 hidden layers)	99.12
[26]	MIT-BIH and PTB database	5	Deep neural network	84
[27]	HSS corpus dataset	3	Recurrent neural network	47.9
[3]	Manual data collection	5	SVM, DNN, and KNN	87.2
[13]	Manual data collection	2	LR, CART, SVM, KNN	97
[28]	NHANES Physical Activity and CVD Fitness and Framingham Heart Study dataset	2	NB, DT, LR, KNN, RF, SVM, NN	98.5

3.1 Architecture of Proposed Work and Implementation

Architecture of proposed work I shown in Fig. 2. In this, patient data are there in the Cleveland dataset. Then, attributes are selected from dataset on which the preprocessing technique is performed. In this, exploratory data analysis (EDA) technique is used to do the analysis. Various classification algorithms such as ANN, AdaBoost, XGBoost, DT, RF, NB, SGD, KNN, LR, SVC are used to classify the patients suffering from cardiovascular disease. The algorithm which gives the maximum accuracy is selected for the prediction purpose.

3.2 Machine and Deep Learning Models

Artificial Neural Network: This algorithm is inspired by the human nervous system. A structure of this algorithm consists of edges and nodes as same as graph structure in which layered nodes are there, and these are connected by edge value, which signify a weight allotted to the connection. From various sets of inputs, weights are used to generate an output properly. Numerous architectures have been planned for neural networks such as convolutional neural networks, perceptron, deep learning, and radial basis function. In deep learning, there are additional layers which increase the number of weights significantly and require large numbers of computational effort, these layers are called hidden layers. Deep learning consists of convolutional

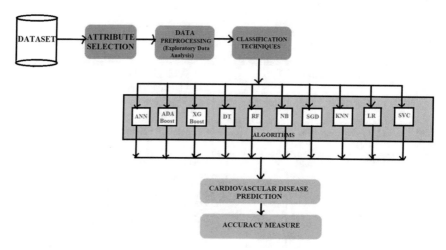

Fig. 2 Architecture of proposed work

networks which are inspired by animal cortex and have a significant role in analyzing the image.

Adaptive Boosting: In machine learning, AdaBoost is used as an ensemble method. In this, reassigning of weights can be done by using higher/new weights at each instance. It is used to reduce variance and biases in case of supervised learning. In this, learning rate increases sequentially. Except first, all the learners grow sequentially.

X-Gradient Boosting: Gradient boosting is based on the tree method. It uses vectors and gradients which increases the prediction rate. Stochastic gradient descent is an alternative to gradient boosting approach.

Decision Tree: It is a directed type tree. In this, the nodes with the edges are termed as an internal node. Other nodes which don't have edges are termed as leaves or terminal nodes. It classified the target based on features of the hierarchical decision set. Error is large in decision tree because of large variance.

Random Forest: Several decision trees are used to construct a single random forest. Firstly, numerous random samples are needed to build the database. This process is known as bootstrapping. Several decision trees can be made using variables (features) subsets of these new databases.

In the database, a new lesson is allotted to the group which has the largest decision trees by using the majority of votes method.

Naïve Bayes: To find out the conditional probability, Naïve Bayes algorithm is used. To categorize the element belonging to a particular category, conditional probability is used.

Stochastic Gradient Descent: In this, a system is linked with a random probability. In this, few samples are randomly selected for each iteration. In this, "batch" denotes the total sample number and is used to calculate gradient for every iteration.

K-Nearest Neighbor: Vector norm is a mathematical function. Various properties are satisfied by the vector norm and have a value ≥ 0. Difference between two vector norms is the approximate distance between those vectors. This norm is used by KNN to calculate distance between all these vectors to make the dataset/database. Then, k value is determined for each dataset vector which is closest to it. Vectors are included in a particular cluster by majority voting among neighbors.

Logistic Regression: This model predicts the output by estimation the probability based on input features/variables. If there is a slight change in the input values, then it will affect the final prediction.

3.3 Dataset

Kaggle is the most widespread platform that is used by the researchers to get dataset of various things. In this research, Cleveland dataset [19] is used to predict whether a patient is suffering from CVD or not. This dataset contains 303 patients' data. Fourteen feature columns are there which act as an input to predict CVD. Rows of data consist various attributes of a patient like chest pain, sex, age, fasting blood sugar, resting electrography, and cholesterol rate. The attributes in the dataset are listed in Table 2.

4 Results

In this research, various machine learning algorithms are used, such as artificial neural network, adaptive boosting, XGBoost, random forest, decision tree, stochastic gradient descent, Naïve Bayes, K-nearest neighbor, and logistic regression for detecting whether a person is suffering from cardiovascular disease or not. For analyzing the data, preprocessing is done to get the better results. In this, data are preprocessed, and various parameters such as chest pain, resting electrocardiography, exercise slope, number of vessels, and thalassemia are divided according to the value.

Figure 3 denotes the correlation plot of the preprocessed dataset. At epoch 500 and 800, artificial neural network gives maximum accuracy, i.e., 100% as compared to other epochs as shown in Fig. 4. Accuracy of all the epochs performed on the dataset is shown in Table 3. Various models are used, and the model which gives a maximum accuracy is ANN, AdaBoost, decision tree, and XGBoost, i.e., 100% as shown in Fig. 5. Accuracy of all the models used to detect whether a person is suffering from CVD or not is shown in Table 4. Previous versus proposed research on CVD using Cleveland heart dataset is presented in Table 5.

Table 2 Dataset details

S. no.	Attributes	Description	Value
1	age	Age of a patient	Age of a patient start from 29 and maximum age is 77
2	sex	Sex of a patient	1 signifies male, and 0 signifies the female
3	cp	Type of chest pain	1 signifies typical angina; 2 signifies atypical angina; 3 signifies non-anginal pain; 4 signifies asymptomatic
4	trestbps	Blood pressure in resting phase	Blood pressure of a patient start from 94 and maximum blood pressure is 200
5	chol	Serum cholesterol	Cholesterol of a patient start from 126 and maximum cholesterol is 564
6	fbs	Blood pressure in fasting phase	1 signifies true, and 0 signifies false
7	restecg	Electrocardiographic during resting	0 signifies normal; 1 signifies patients having ST-T wave abnormality; 2 signifies left ventricular hyperthrophy
8	thalach	Maximum heart rate	Heart rate ranges from 71 to 202
9	exang	Angina due to exercise	1 means true, and 0 means false
10	oldpeak	ST depression due to exercise	displays the value as float or integer
11	slope	exercise slope relative to rest	1 signifies upsloping; 2 signifies flat; 3 signifies down sloping
12	Ca	Number of vessels (0–3) colored by fluoroscopy	displays the value as float or integer
13	thal	Thalassemia	3 signifies normal; 6 signifies fixed defect, and 7 signifies reversable defect
14	target	Whether a person is having CVD or not	0 signifies that patient is not having CVD and 1 signifies that patient is having CVD

5   Conclusion and Future Scope

These days, cardiovascular diseases are getting complicated. People between the ages of 40–60 are mostly affected due to heart disease. CVD also affects teenagers with numerous heart diseases due to change in food habits and lifestyle. Manually, prediction of heart disease is difficult; hence AI come into the picture to predict CVD more accurately. In this research, various machine learning and deep learning techniques are used to diagnose whether a person is suffering from CVD or not. AdaBoost, XGBoost, ANN, and decision tree give the maximum accuracy, i.e., 100% in the proposed research whereas maximum accuracy achieved by the previous researchers is 96.04%. Especially, in the field of cardiac imaging and disease detection, deep

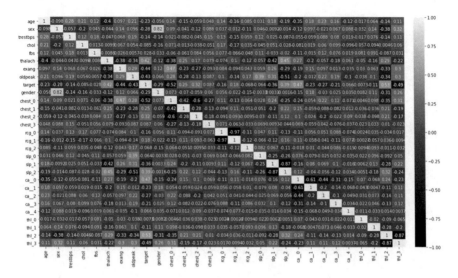

Fig. 3 Correlation plot

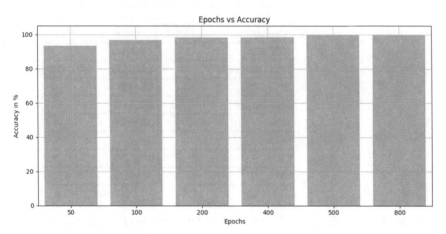

Fig. 4 Accuracy graph during various epochs

Table 3 Accuracy during various epochs	Epochs	Accuracy
	50	0.934426
	100	0.967200
	200	0.983607
	400	0.983607
	500	1.000000
	800	1.000000

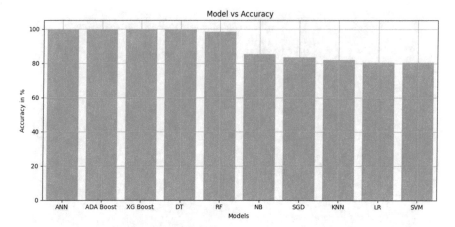

Fig. 5 Accuracy graph of various models

Table 4 Accuracy of various models	Model	Accuracy scores
	ANN	1.000000
	AdaBoost	1.000000
	XGBoost	1.000000
	Decision tree	1.000000
	RF	0.983607
	Naive Bayes	0.852459
	SGD	0.836066
	KNN	0.819672
	LR	0.803279
	SVC	0.803279

learning plays a major role. Telemedicine and mHealth are forming new networks between physicians and patients, converting passive health care into pervasive.

AI has touched all the areas of technologies. Some of the future trends of AI for cardiovascular area are as follows: **Consultations from Robots**: Presently, patients consult doctors if they have any health problem. The day is not far when they will book an appointment to take consultations from robots. **Virtual Reality in CVDs**: Virtual reality is a powerful tool that will give promising results to the user. This is very beneficial in cardiovascular areas as most of the diseases are not detected by the ultrasound, ECG, etc. This technique is very much beneficial for treating congenital heart disease [30]. **Wearable Technologies**: Patients with cardiovascular disease need monitoring all the time. Hence, there is a need for wearable technology so that the doctors will get their patients data timely. These wearable devices are used to measure heart rhythm, heart rate, thoracic fluid, and activity of the patient to avoid unfavorable conditions [31].

Table 5 Previous versus proposed research on CVD using Cleveland heart dataset

Research (year)	Algorithm used	Dataset used	Accuracy
Prediction of heart disease using ML [17] (2019)	LR, RF, NN, KNN	Cleveland dataset	91.39% accuracy by logistic regression
Heart disease prediction using neural network [12] (2017)	Logistic regression and neural network	Cleveland heart disease database	84%
Multi stage heart disease prediction using machine learning [19] (2020)	SVM, LR, RF, GTB, ERF	Cleveland dataset	LR gives high accuracy—82%
Heart disease prediction using deep neural networks and machine learning [21] (2020)	RF, DNN	Cleveland Clinic Foundation	DNN gives high accuracy—92%
Heart disease prediction using convolutional neural networks [22] (2018)	NB, KNN, CNN-UDRP	UCI repository	NB gives high accuracy—82%
Heart disease prediction using machine learning techniques[29] (2021)	DT, MLP, SVM, RF, Bayes net	Cleveland heart disease database	DT gives high accuracy—96.04%
Proposed	ANN, AdaBoost, XGBoost, DT, RF, NB, SGD, KNN, LR	Cleveland heart disease database	ANN, AdaBoost, DT, and XGBoost give high accuracy—100%

References

1. WHO (2020) Cardiovascular Diseases (CVDs). In: WHO. https://www.who.int/health-topics/cardiovascular-diseases#tab=tab_1. Accessed 14 Sep 2020
2. Shu T, Zhang B, Tang YY (2017) Effective heart disease detection based on quantitative computerized traditional Chinese medicine using representation based classifiers. Evid-Based Complement Altern Med. https://doi.org/10.1155/2017/7483639
3. Yaseen SGY, Kwon S (2018) Classification of heart sound signal using multiple features. Appl Sci (Switzerland). https://doi.org/10.3390/app8122344
4. Harky A, Chaplin G, Chan JSK et al (2020) The future of open heart surgery in the era of robotic and minimal surgical interventions. Heart Lung Circ 29:49–61
5. Johnson KW, Torres Soto J, Glicksberg BS et al (2018) Artificial intelligence in cardiology. J Am Coll Cardiol 71:2668–2679
6. Lonnerfors C (2018) Robot-assisted myomectomy. Best Pract Res Clin Obstet Gynaecol 46:113–119
7. Cacciamani GE, de Marco V, Sebben M, Rizzetto R (2018) Robot-assisted Vescica Ileale Padovana: a new technique for intracorporeal bladder replacement reproducing open surgical principles. Eur Urol. https://doi.org/10.1016/j.eururo.2018.11.037
8. Sharma M (2019) ECG and medical diagnosis based recognition & prediction of cardiac disease using deep learning. Int J Sci Technol Res 8:233–240
9. Ankireddy S (2020) A novel approach to the diagnosis of heart disease using machine learning and deep neural networks

10. Alarsan FI, Younes M (2019) Analysis and classification of heart diseases using heartbeat features and machine learning algorithms. J Big Data. https://doi.org/10.1186/s40537-019-0244-x
11. Fredrick David BH, Benjamin Fredrick David H, Antony Belcy S (2018) Heart disease prediction using data mining techniques. J Soft Comput 1824–1831. https://doi.org/10.21917/ijsc.2018.0254
12. Poplin R, Varadarajan A, Blumer K et al (2018) Prediction of cardiovascular risk factors from retinal fundus photographs via deep learning. Nat Biomed Eng 2:158–164. https://doi.org/10.1038/s41551-018-0195-0
13. Hossain E, Al-Mamun A (2019) Early heart attack prediction using machine learning technique
14. Kotanidis CP, Antoniades C (2020) Selfies in cardiovascular medicine: welcome to a new era of medical diagnostics. Eur Heart J 41:4412–4414
15. Singh S, Penzel T, Engineering E, Delhi N (2020) Irregularities using machine learning 438–442
16. Vemuri PK, Kunta A, Challagulla R et al (2019) Artificial intelligence and internet of medical things based health-care system for real-time maternal stress—strategies to reduce maternal mortality rate. Drug Invent Today 13:1126–1129
17. Mohan S, Thirumalai C, Srivastava G (2019) Effective heart disease prediction using hybrid machine learning techniques. IEEE Access 7:81542–81554. https://doi.org/10.1109/ACCESS.2019.2923707
18. Bakar WAWA, Man M, Awang WSW et al (2020) HDP: heart disease prediction tool using neural network. Int J Emerg Trends Eng Res 8:1794–1797. https://doi.org/10.30534/ijeter/2020/50852020
19. Maheswari KU (2017) Neural network based heart disease prediction. IJERT 5:1–4
20. Moradi M, Madani A, Karargyris A, Syeda-Mahmood TF (2018) Chest x-ray generation and data augmentation for cardiovascular abnormality classification. SPIE-Int Soc Opt Eng 57
21. Lin S, Li Z, Fu B et al (2020) Feasibility of using deep learning to detect coronary artery disease based on facial photo. Eur Heart J. https://doi.org/10.1093/eurheartj/ehaa640
22. Chokwijitkul T, Nguyen A, Hassanzadeh H, Perez S (2018) Identifying risk factors for heart disease in electronic medical records: a deep learning approach
23. Mahmoud M, Amen K, Zohdy M, Machine learning for multiple stage heart disease prediction
24. Yang X, Gong Y, Waheed N et al Identifying cancer patients at risk for heart failure using machine learning methods
25. Ambekar S, Phalnikar R (2018) Disease risk prediction by using convolutional neural network. In: Proceedings—2018 4th international conference on computing, communication control and automation, ICCUBEA 2018. https://doi.org/10.1109/ICCUBEA.2018.8697423
26. Islam Chowdhuryy MH, Sultana M, Ghosh R et al (2018) AI assisted portable ECG for fast and patient specific diagnosis. In: International conference on computer, communication, chemical, material and electronic engineering, IC4ME2 2018, pp 4–7. https://doi.org/10.1109/IC4ME2.2018.8465483
27. Amiriparian S, Schmitt M, Cummins N et al (2018) Deep unsupervised representation learning for abnormal heart sound classification. In: Proceedings of the annual international conference of the IEEE engineering in medicine and biology society, EMBS, pp 4776–4779. https://doi.org/10.1109/EMBC.2018.8513102
28. Rajliwall NS, Davey R, Chetty G (2019) Machine learning based models for cardiovascular risk prediction. In: Proceedings—international conference on machine learning and dataengineering, iCMLDE, pp 149–153. https://doi.org/10.1109/iCMLDE.2018.00034
29. Garg A, Sharma B, Khan R (2021) Heart disease prediction using machine learning techniques. IOP Conf Ser Mater Sci Eng 1022:93–96. https://doi.org/10.1088/1757-899X/1022/1/012046
30. Sacks LD, Axelrod DM (2020) Virtual reality in pediatric cardiology: hype or hope for the future? Curr Opin Cardiol 35:37–41
31. Pevnick JM, Birkeland K, Zimmer R et al (2018) Wearable technology for cardiology: an update and framework for the future. Trends Cardiovasc Med 28:144–150

A Novel Smartphone-Based Human Activity Recognition Using Deep Learning in Health care

Vaibhav Soni, Himanshu Yadav, Vijay Bhaskar Semwal, Bholanath Roy, Dilip Kumar Choubey, and Dheeresh K. Mallick

1 Introduction

In person-to-person contact and interpersonal relations, human activity recognition is important. Because it offers extensive knowledge about human actions, as well as difficult-to-extract information about a person's personality, psychological condition, and identity. One of the key issues of study in the scientific domains of machine learning and computer vision is human activity recognition, which has the ability to recognize people's daily life. Because of its numerous uses in health care, intelligent monitoring systems, smart homes, and rehabilitation, it is widely used, and in other disciplines, HAR has gotten a lot of attention.

The fast development of wearable and mobile technologies has eased their use in the field of healthcare. Monitoring real-time human behaviors, particularly activities of daily living of the elderly, is an important topic in smart healthcare, which may clearly improve medical rehabilitation and aged care utilizing wearable and mobile sensors.

Sensor-based HAR and vision-based HAR are the two main kinds of HAR. Sensor-based HAR emphasized sensor data of human motion recorded from smart sensors such as sound sensors, accelerometers, gyros, Bluetooth, and so on, whereas camera-based HAR focuses on human motion in videos and images format are taken from a

V. Soni (✉) · H. Yadav · V. B. Semwal · B. Roy
Department of Computer Science and Engineering, Maulana Azad National Institute of Technology, Bhopal, Madhya Pradesh, India
e-mail: vaibhavsoni@manit.ac.in

D. K. Choubey
Department of Computer Science and Engineering, Indian Institute of Information Technology, Bhagalpur, Bihar, India

D. K. Mallick
Department of Computer Science and Engineering, Birla Institute of Technology Mesra, Ranchi, Jharkhand, India

© The Author(s), under exclusive license to Springer Nature Singapore Pte Ltd. 2023   493
R. Doriya et al. (eds.), *Machine Learning, Image Processing, Network Security and Data Sciences*, Lecture Notes in Electrical Engineering 946,
https://doi.org/10.1007/978-981-19-5868-7_36

camera. Even though camera-based HAR has good results in recognizing actions of human, it has several drawbacks, including privacy concerns, being very expensive, and only covering a limited range of activities. Sensor-based HAR is becoming more popular these days due to privacy concerns as well as convenience. As a result, we will only discuss sensor-based systems in this paper.

In HAR, two types of recognition models are used: The first is based on traditional machine learning techniques, while the second is based on deep learning (DL) techniques. Many sensor-based HAR studios have used classic machine learning techniques such as decision tree (DT) [1, 2], random forests (RF) [3, 4], and support vector machine (SVM) [5, 6]. To screen out strongly representative features, all of these traditional techniques necessitate time-consuming and sophisticated feature engineering, feature selection, and dimensionality reduction. Deep learning takes the feature engineering phase-out of the equation, allowing researchers to focus on other factors of HAR, like power consumption in real-world applications.

1.1 Our Contribution

- A Bi-LSTM-CNN architecture is proposed on sensor raw data.
- In this architecture, sensor raw data is directly fed to the model with very few preprocessing steps.
- The proposed architecture utilized the capabilities of Bi-LSTM and CNN to capture long-term dependencies and also local feature in sensor raw data.
- The proposed architecture is validated using two publicly available datasets and got accuracy for WISDM and UCI-HAR datasets are 97.23, 96.89%, respectively.

2 Previous Work

In recent years, researchers have spent a lot of time looking at many sensing technologies, and a number of approaches for modeling and identifying human behavior, have been developed [7]. Early works employed decision trees, support vector machines (SVMs), and Naive Bayes to identify data acquired by sensors [8, 9].

Additionally, researchers have been experimenting with random undersampling, random oversampling, and ensemble learning methods. Ensemble learning [10] is a robust method for dealing with imbalanced data. The approach generally combines several different network classifiers and reduces statistical uncertainty (variance) and generalization errors. To develop a more accurate, fast, and stable HAR classifier using various sensor features, the authors in [3] used an ensemble learning method that combines several independent random classifiers. A classifier ensemble is formed by using multilayer perceptrons, J48 decision trees, and logistic regression in [11]. Their ensemble voting algorithm, which merged the strengths of three different models, was then applied and a variety of experiments were conducted to demonstrate its effectiveness.

Object detection [12, 13], classification [14, 15], natural language processing [16], and other domains have seen outstanding results using DL-based methods in recent years. Features can be learned automatically in DL frameworks without the requirement for any human interaction or effort. The authors of [17] used an accelerometer to collect motion data (arm motions) from four different human participants (triaxial). They developed a CNN model to predict arm motions. Wan et al. [18] built a HAR model based on smartphone sensors that use CNNs to identify a variety of human actions. The authors of [19] described a DL-based framework for identifying human actions in real time. To maintain information of time series data worldwide, CNN and statistical features were merged. The authors offer activity data which are weekly labeled gathered from wearable sensors using an attention-based HAR technique in [20]. To evaluate the interoperability of global and local features at the fully connected and convolutional layers, and utiized the attention submodules and also CNN pipeline. In [21], the authors proposed architecture for recognizing activity named a novel local loss architecture, which substitutes the baseline CNN's global loss with a local loss strategy. Using this approach, the sensor-based activity recognition framework requires significantly less memory. In addition, a CNN-based HAR approach for capturing scale invariance and local dependencies in mobile sensor data was established in [22].

Members of the DL family recurrent neural networks (RNN) also demonstrated their ability to handle sequential input. Traditional RNNs, on the other hand, are unable to learn long-term dependencies from sequential data [23]. The vanishing gradient problem has been handled using LSTM, a version of the RNN, and it is effective in handling long-term dependencies. By stacking five LSTM cells and using smartphone sensor data, the authors of [24] constructed a strong classifier for distinguishing distinct human activities. Hernández et al. [25] presented bidirectional LSTM-based HAR networks based on smartphone sensor data. In [26], they propose a connection in bidirectional that concatenates forward and backward states in a deep residual LSTM for HAR. This experiment saw improvements in the spatial and temporal dimensions, as well as a higher recognition rate.

We present the Bi-LSTM-CNN, an innovative DNN for human activity recognition. This architecture can extract all the features and then classify them with very few parameters.

3 Dataset Description

Kwapisz et al. [27] generated the WISDM dataset, which comprises six daily activities. A total of 30 subjects participated in capturing the UCI-HAR dataset consists of six activities. There are some distinctions between these two. The WISDM dataset has the most samples and is also the most imbalanced. The WISDM dataset captured using accelerometer sensor, and on the other hand, UCI-HAR dataset captured using accelerometer as well as gyroscope sensor.

3.1 WISDM

For the WISDM dataset, Fig. 1 presents the number of total samples connected with every activity. The distribution of WISDM is imbalanced. Walking is the most popular mode of transportation, accounting for 38.6% of all trips while standing accounts for only 4.4%. It is made up of 36 different subject recordings. During specific daily tasks, the participants carried a mobile in the pocket of the front leg. In smartphones, there is some sensors built-in, one is an accelerometer that is used for capturing data with 20 Hz sampling rate.

3.2 UCI-HAR

In UCI-HAR dataset, Fig. 2 presents the number of total samples connected with every activity. Thirty people between the ages of 19–48 were included in the UCI-HAR dataset [28]. During the recording, each subject followed an activity program. They wore a smartphone with inertial sensors on their waists. Walking, standing, upstairs, sitting, downstairs, and laying are among the 6 activities included in the UCI-HAR dataset. These 6 daily routine activities were utilized as input samples in this work because of the low percentage of postural shifts. The trials were video filmed for labeling the raw data. The researchers recorded 3-axial angular velocity and 3-axial acceleration data at a frequency 50 Hz.

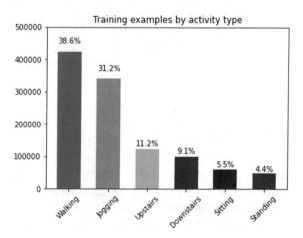

Fig. 1 No. of samples for each activity type for WISDM dataset

Fig. 2 No. of samples for each activity type for UCI-HAR dataset

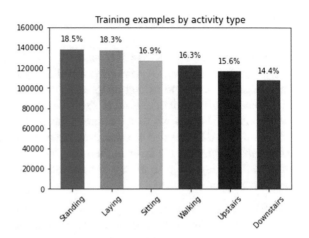

4 Proposed Methodology

4.1 Data Preprocessing

To enrich the suggested approach and enhance the model's performance, preprocessing of the sensor raw data is necessary.

Interpolation and Handling missing values The datasets we used are actual, and the sensors worn by subjects are wireless. As an outcome, some information may be missing throughout the data collection steps, in which case NaN/0 is generally used to signify the missing data. This study solves the problem by employing the linear interpolation algorithm.

Normalization When huge values from channels are used to train models, it may result in a poor training result. As a result, the input data must be normalized to the 0 to 1 range, as illustrated in Eq. (1):

$$X_j = \frac{X_j - X_{j\,min}}{X_{j\,max} - X_{j\,min}}, (j = 1, 2, 3, 4 \ldots, m) \tag{1}$$

Here, m is the number of the channels, the maximum values of the jth channel is $X_{j\,max}$, and the minimum values of the jth channel is $X_{j\,min}$.

Segmentation An end-to-end system is described in this work for HAR. Data sequences are supplied into this model. It is made up of brief time series that have been derived from raw data acquired from sensors. Throughout the data collection steps, data were continuously recorded. To maintain the temporal relationship between data points, data acquired by motion sensors were segmented using a sliding window of 50% overlap rate. WISDM and UCI-HAR both have a 128-sliding window length. For UCI-HAR and WISDM, the total number of features is 9,3, respectively.

4.2   Proposed Architecture

Figure 3 shows the Bi-LSTM-CNN model's flow diagram. There are eight layers in total. In the first layer, 64 neurons in a Bi-LSTM are used to process the prepro-cessed data. It is used to extract temporal layers, and it is followed by two further convolutional layers that are used to extract spatial information. The first conv1D layer contains 64 filters, with a kernel size of three. The second conv1D layer contains 32 filters, with a kernel size of three. And there is a max-pooling layer in between. The output from conv1D layer is then sent to fully connected (FC) output layer through flatten layer with a softmax as a activation function which classify the result over the number of classes.

Bi-LSTM Layer Bidirectional LSTMs are an LSTM type that could be utilized to improve model's overall performance in sequence classification problems, where the sequence of timesteps is known, and bidirectional LSTMs can train two LSTM on the input instead of one.

Bi-LSTM gets information in both horizontal and vertical directions, in horizontal it gets past and future information, and in vertical, it gets information from the lower layer. In Fig. 3, there are forward layer ($H^{\rightarrow}$) and backward layer ($H^{\leftarrow}$). At time t, the hidden layer and the input layer are defined as follows:

$$H_t^{\rightarrow} = g(U_{H \rightarrow} x_t + W_{H \rightarrow} H_t^{\rightarrow} + b_{H \rightarrow}) \tag{2}$$

$$h_t^{\leftarrow} = g(U_{H \leftarrow} x_t + W_{H \leftarrow} H_{t-1}^{\leftarrow} + b_{H \leftarrow}) \tag{3}$$

$$y_t = g(V_{H \rightarrow} H_t^{\rightarrow} + V_{H \leftarrow} H_t^{\leftarrow} + b_y) \tag{4}$$

where, W, U, and V are weight matrices and b is bias vector and g denotes input, output, and forgot gates, and y denotes output set.

Convolutional Layers In CNN layer, convolution kernels are used to convolve the input signals in CNN's convolutional layers. It functions as a filter and is activated by the following nonlinear function:

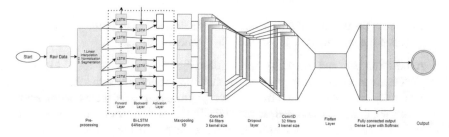

Fig. 3 Block Diagram of the proposed Bi-LSTM-CNN architecture

$$a_{i,j} = f\left(\sum_{p=1}^{P}\sum_{q=1}^{Q} w_{p,q}.x_{i+p.j.q} + b\right) \tag{5}$$

Here, $a_{i,j}$ represents the activation and $w_{p,q}$ represents the pXq weight matrix of the kernel, the activity of the top neurons connected to the neuron (i,j) is represented by $x_{i+p.j+q}$, the bias value is represented by b, and f is a nonlinear function.

5 Experiments and Results

Using two frequently used public datasets, we assessed the Bi-LSTM-CNN model's generalization ability and accuracy. A sliding window of fixed length is widely used for segmenting the continuous recordings of sensor inputs. The accuracy and generalization ability of the Bi-LSTM-CNN model were evaluated using two commonly used public datasets in this paper. They were all constantly recorded, and a popular way for segmenting sensor data is to employ a sliding window of fixed length. The sliding window is set to 128 and the step-size is 64. The database for the UCI-HAR dataset was created by recording 30 participants conducting six activities. The training set was made up of 22 subjects' recordings, while the test set was made up of the rest. The WISDM dataset consists of 36 recordings from six different activities. Table 1 illustrates the total instances of the training set and the testing set acquired after segmentation on both datasets.

5.1 Model Implementation

Keras, a Python-based high-level neural networks API that may operate on Tensor-Flow, CNTK, or Theano, is used to create the proposed architecture. TensorFlow is utilized as the backend in the tests (Table 2).

Table 1 Instances of both dataset

	WISDM	UCI-HAR
Training set	13,654	7319
Test set	3036	3069

5.2 Performance Measure

Data on human activities recorded in natural settings are frequently skewed [32]. The WISDM refers to unbalanced datasets. The results might be excellent, if the classifier forecasts every instance as a most class and evaluates the model's performance based on overall classification accuracy. As a result, evaluating the model's performance in this manner is improper. In the information retrieval community, the F-measure (F1 score) incorporates false negatives and false positives, as well as two measures generated from the number of correctly identified samples, called as precision and recall, respectively. As a result, the F1 score is frequently a better predictor of performance than accuracy. Precision and recall are computed using the formulas TP/(TP+FP) and TP/(FN+TP), where FP and TP represent the number of false and true positives, respectively, FN represents the number of false negatives. The F1 score compensates for class imbalance by weighting classes according to their proportion of samples. The F1 score is calculated as follows:

$$F_1 = \sum_i 2 * w_i \frac{\text{Precision}_i.\text{recall}_i}{\text{Precision}_i + \text{recall}_i} \tag{6}$$

where $w_i = n_i/N$ signifies the fraction of class I samples, n the sample size in that class, and N the total sample size. Two publicly accessible datasets were utilized to properly evaluate the performance of the suggested model. Table 4 demonstrates the confusion matrices created when the architecture was predicted using the WISDM datasets, respectively. Table 3 gives the total accuracy, precision, recall, and F1 score for both datasets. For the WISDM dataset, the Bi-LSTM-CNN model has a high

Table 2 Hyper-parameters used

Stage	Hyper-parameter		Selected values
Data preprocessing	Step_size		64
	Window_size		128
	Bi-LSTM		64 neurons
	Bi-LSTM		64 neurons
	Max-pooling		
Architecture	CONV1D	Filters	64
		Kernel size	3
	CONV1D	Filters	32
		Kernel size	3
Training	Optimizer		Adam
	Batch size		32
	Learning rate		0.001
	No. of epochs		250

Table 3 Performance measure of proposed model

	WISDM (%)	UCI-HAR (%)
Accuracy	97.23	96.89
Precision	97.24	96.85
Recall	97.21	96.91
F1 score	97.22	96.88

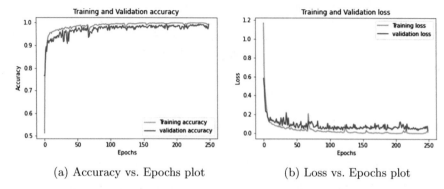

(a) Accuracy vs. Epochs plot   (b) Loss vs. Epochs plot

Fig. 4 Accuracy versus epochs and loss versus epochs plot for WISDM dataset

Table 4 Confusion matrix of Classification for WISDM dataset

Activities	Walk	Jog	Up	Down	Sit	Stand
Walk	468	0	28	0	0	0
Jog	9	428	34	0	0	0
Up	3	0	417	0	0	0
Down	1	3	0	393	89	5
Sit	3	0	0	74	455	0
Stand	0	0	0	0	0	537

Table 5 Accuracy comparison of models for the both datasets

Model	UCI-HAR (%)	WISDM (%)
CNN-LSTM [29]	94.80	94.28
LSTM-CNN [30]	95.78	95.85
CNN-Bi-LSTM [31]	96.37	96.05
Bi-LSTM-CNN (proposed)	96.89	97.23

degree of accuracy, while for the UCI-HAR dataset, it has a decent level of accuracy (Fig. 4; Table 5).

5.3 Conclusion

In this study, a unique combination of Bi-LSTM and CNN models is proposed with 97.23% accuracy and 96.89% for 6 basic activities with the WISDM and UCI-HAR datasets, respectively. Compared to other state-of-the-art methods, our model demonstrates significant improvements in terms of various performance metrics. The proposed architecture can be enhanced with ensemble techniques for better accuracy. Ensemble techniques with the proposed architecture can be used as our future work to improve the performance. Further, some imbalancing techniques can be adopted for balancing some imbalanced datasets such as WISDM. For future works, we suggest working on tiny machine learning (TinyML) technique using Arduino board or raspberry pi.

References

1. Xu H, Li J, Yuan H, Liu Q, Fan S, Li T, Sun X (2020) Human activity recognition based on Gramian angular field and deep convolutional neural network. IEEE Access 8:199393–199405
2. Pärkkä J, Cluitmans L, Ermes M (2010) Personalization algorithm for real-time activity recognition using PDA, wireless motion bands, and binary decision tree. IEEE Trans Inform Technol Biomed 14:1211–1215
3. Feng Z, Mo L, Li M (2015) A Random Forest-based ensemble method for activity recognition. In: 2015 37th annual international conference of the IEEE Engineering in Medicine and Biology Society (EMBC), pp 5074–5077
4. Uddin M, Uddiny M (2015) A guided random forest based feature selection approach for activity recognition. In: 2015 international conference on electrical engineering and information communication technology (ICEEICT), pp 1–6
5. Chen Z, Zhu Q, Soh Y, Zhang L (2017) Robust human activity recognition using smartphone sensors via CT-PCA and online SVM. IEEE Trans Indus Inform 13:3070–3080
6. Abidine B, Fergani L, Fergani B, Oussalah M (2018) The joint use of sequence features combination and modified weighted SVM for improving daily activity recognition. Pattern Anal Appl 21:119–138
7. Chen L, Nugent C, Wang H (2011) A knowledge-driven approach to activity recognition in smart homes. IEEE Trans Knowl Data Eng 24:961–974
8. Jain A, Kanhangad V (2017) Human activity classification in smartphones using accelerometer and gyroscope sensors. IEEE Sens J 18:1169–1177
9. Fullerton E, Heller B, Munoz-Organero M (2017) Recognizing human activity in free-living using multiple body-worn accelerometers. IEEE Sens J 17:5290–5297
10. Gupta A, Semwal V (2020) Multiple task human gait analysis and identification: ensemble learning approach. In: Emotion and information processing, pp 185–197
11. Catal C, Tufekci S, Pirmit E, Kocabag G (2015) On the use of ensemble of classifiers for accelerometer-based activity recognition. Appl Soft Comput 37:1018–1022
12. Dewangan D, Sahu S (2021) PotNet: Pothole detection for autonomous vehicle system using convolutional neural network. Electron Lett 57:53–56
13. Dewangan D, Sahu S (2020) Deep learning-based speed bump detection model for intelligent vehicle system using raspberry Pi. IEEE Sens J 21:3570–3578
14. Chen L, Wang R, Yang J, Xue L, Hu M (2019) Multi-label image classification with recurrently learning semantic dependencies. Vis Comput 35:1361–1371
15. Dewangan D, Sahu S (2021) RCNet: road classification convolutional neural networks for intelligent vehicle system. Intell Serv Robot 14:199–214

16. Zhu R, Tu X, Huang J (2020) Using deep learning based natural language processing techniques for clinical decision-making with EHRs. In: Deep learning techniques for biomedical and health informatics, pp 257–295
17. Panwar M, Dyuthi S, Prakash K, Biswas D, Acharyya A, Maharatna K, Gautam A, Naik G (2017) CNN based approach for activity recognition using a wrist-worn accelerometer. In: 2017 39th annual international conference of the IEEE Engineering in Medicine and Biology Society (EMBC), pp 2438–2441
18. Wan S, Qi L, Xu X, Tong C, Gu Z (2020) Deep learning models for real-time human activity recognition with smartphones. Mob Netw Appl 25:743–755
19. Ignatov A (2018) Real-time human activity recognition from accelerometer data using convolutional neural networks. Appl Soft Comput 62:915–922
20. Wang K, He J, Zhang L (2019) Attention-based convolutional neural network for weakly labeled human activities' recognition with wearable sensors. IEEE Sens J 19:7598–7604
21. Teng Q, Wang K, Zhang L, He J (2020) The layer-wise training convolutional neural networks using local loss for sensor-based human activity recognition. IEEE Sens J 20:7265–7274
22. Zeng M, Nguyen L, Yu B, Mengshoel O, Zhu J, Wu P, Zhang J (2014) Convolutional neural networks for human activity recognition using mobile sensors. In: 6th international conference on mobile computing, applications and services, pp 197–205
23. Bengio Y, Simard P, Frasconi P (1994) Learning long-term dependencies with gradient descent is difficult. IEEE Trans Neural Netw 5:157–166
24. Ullah M, Ullah H, Khan S, Cheikh F (2019) Stacked lstm network for human activity recognition using smartphone data. In: 2019 8th European workshop on visual information processing (EUVIP), pp 175–180
25. Hernández F, Suárez L, Villamizar J, Altuve M (2019) Human activity recognition on smartphones using a bidirectional lstm network. In: 2019 XXII symposium on image, signal processing and artificial vision (STSIVA), pp 1–5
26. Zhao Y, Yang R, Chevalier G, Xu X, Zhang Z (2018) Deep residual bidir-LSTM for human activity recognition using wearable sensors. Math Probl Eng
27. Kwapisz J, Weiss G, Moore S (2011) Activity recognition using cell phone accelerometers. ACM SigKDD Explor Newsl 12:74–82
28. Reyes-Ortiz J, Oneto L, Sama A, Parra X, Anguita D (2016) Transition-aware human activity recognition using smartphones. Neurocomputing 171:754–767
29. Mutegeki R, Han D (2020) A CNN-LSTM approach to human activity recognition. In: 2020 international conference on artificial intelligence in information and communication (ICAIIC), pp 362–366
30. Xia K, Huang J, Wang H (2020) LSTM-CNN architecture for human activity recognition. IEEE Access 8:56855–56866
31. Challa S, Kumar A, Semwal V (2021) A multibranch CNN-BiLSTM model for human activity recognition using wearable sensor data. Vis Comput pp 1–15 (2021)
32. Ronao C, Cho S (2016) Human activity recognition with smartphone sensors using deep learning neural networks. Exp Syst Appl 59:235–244

An Enhanced Deep Learning Approach for Smartphone-Based Human Activity Recognition in IoHT

Vaibhav Soni, Shashank Jaiswal, Vijay Bhaskar Semwal, Bholanath Roy, Dilip Kumar Choubey, and Dheeresh K. Mallick

1 Introduction

Human activity recognition using smartphone sensor data is a time-series classification task that is used for predicting the activity or movement of a human body (e.g., jogging, walking, climbing upstairs, etc. The key methodology in HAR is the sliding window method, which involves moving a certain length analysis window along the signal sequence to retrieve frames. Previously, a lot of work has been done on HAR using manually crafted features. Manually constructed features depend on trial and error. Deep learning models provide automatic feature extraction and gradually create features obtaining a high level of representation, having more judicious capability than the hand-crafted features.

With the increase in the use of sensor technology in smart devices like smartphones, smartwatches, etc., the popularity of sensor-based HAR has grown and is widely used without compromising the privacy of subjects. For improving the activity recognition accuracy, researchers have looked into the significance of various sensing technologies in HAR.

Medical professionals can examine a patient's fitness state depending on activity level in a medical healthcare system, and suggest everyday workouts to help people live healthier lives. Understanding human activity profiles can also help with

V. Soni (✉) · S. Jaiswal · V. B. Semwal · B. Roy
Department of Computer Science and Engineering, Maulana Azad National Institute
of Technology Bhopal, Bhopal, Madhya Pradesh, India
e-mail: vaibhavsoni@manit.ac.in

D. K. Choubey
Department of Computer Science and Engineering, Indian Institute of Information Technology
Bhagalpur, Bhagalpur, Bihar, India

D. K. Mallick
Department of Computer Science and Engineering, Birla Institute of Technology Mesra,
Ranchi, Jharkhand, India

© The Author(s), under exclusive license to Springer Nature Singapore Pte Ltd. 2023   505
R. Doriya et al. (eds.), *Machine Learning, Image Processing, Network Security and Data
Sciences*, Lecture Notes in Electrical Engineering 946,
https://doi.org/10.1007/978-981-19-5868-7_37

sports training, athlete rehabilitation, injury identification, and disease detection [1]. Furthermore, the information gathered from detected activities could be used to improve the safety of individuals in the smart transport system and manufacturing contexts. There is a large range of applications for activity recognition in mobile applications—like employee monitoring, health tracking, and fitness, context-based advertising. Customization of behavior based on the current activities can be done using context-aware applications. For example, in [2–4] for recognizing movements such as running and walking, researchers have used the smartphone accelerometer. With advancement, mobile sensing area users are enabled to monitor their exercise patterns and sleep patterns [5], monitor individual commute behaviors [6], emotional state tracking [7], or even measure time spent for queuing in retail stores.

1.1 Our Contribution

- A BiGRU-CNN architecture is proposed on sensor-based raw data.
- The sensor base raw data is directly fed to the model with minimum preprocessing.
- To extract long-term dependencies along with local features in sensor raw data, the proposed architecture used the characteristics of BiGRU and CNN.
- The proposed architecture is validated using two publicly available datasets and acquired an accuracy of 97.94% for WISDM dataset and 96.15% for UCI-HAR dataset.

2 Literature Review

Over the last few years, researchers have conducted numerous studies to investigate various sensing technologies and methodologies for recognizing and modeling human activity [8]. To categorize data obtained from sensor devices, previous research primarily concentrated on classic machine learning (ML) techniques such as support vector machine (SVM), Naive Bayes, decision tree, and so on [9, 10].

In [9], for collecting accelerometer and gyroscope data characteristics, the centroid feature was utilized to create a Fourier descriptor and a gradient histogram. The authors Jain et al. recognized the activities of two public datasets using two classifiers, k-nearest neighbor (KNN) and support vector machine (SVM). For constructing a monitoring system, Jalloul et al. [11] have used six inertial measurement units. Following analysis of the network, the authors created a feature set using statistical tests, after which they classified the activities using a random forest (RF) classifier, achieving an overall accuracy of 84.6%.

According to a recent survey on deep learning methods for HAR using sensor technologies falls into three main categories. The first category of architecture is one containing RNN model only [12–15]. The second category of architecture is one containing the CNN model only and can be divided into sub-types data driven and model driven.[16] Data-driven models use CNN on sensor-produced raw data directly. In the model-driven method, first data is preprocessed to form a grid-like structure then CNN is used on it. Recent work focuses on the hybrid model of CNN which contains a combination of CNN layers along with a fusion layer merging the features extracted by different models. The third category of architecture uses both CNN and RNN models. [17] Restricted Boltzmann machine and autoencoders are other techniques used in HAR.

Various studies by researchers also show that the problem exists with image recognition [18], where for recognizing handwriting by extracting different types of features as compared to recognizing faces. A vast number of deep learning methods have been developed and effectively deployed on recognition problems as preprocessing technologies have advanced [19, 20]. These methods allow for automatic feature extraction without the need for any prior subject expertise. In [21], Ronald et al. have proposed CNN-LSTM architecture and have acquired a good accuracy on UCI-HAR dataset and iSPL internal dataset. The authors of [22] built a multi-task RNN model using inertial sensor data for identifying human activity. Xia et al. [23] built a DL-based framework LSTM-CNN with global average pooling layer and batch normalization layer before softmax layer that uses sensor raw data for identifying human actions.

In this paper, an enhanced architecture is proposed for recognizing activities in several application domains based on bidirectional gated recurrent units and convolutional neural networks (BiGRU-CNN).

3 Dataset Description

The two datasets used in the study are publicly available. There are several slight differences between the two datasets that can be noticed. The UCI-HAR dataset has a record of 30 subjects. The WISDM dataset has a larger number of samples compared to UCI-HAR. Both datasets are recorded using smartphone sensors under controlled environmental conditions.

3.1 UCI-HAR Dataset

The UCI-HAR dataset [24] is developed by recording the activities of 30 subjects between the ages of 19 and 48. The subjects that took part in the dataset recording were instructed to follow a set of activity guidelines. The subjects wore a smartphone (Samsung Galaxy S II) embedded with an inertial sensor around their waist. Walking upstairs (Up), downstairs (Down), laying (Lay), walking (Walk), standing (Std), and sitting (Sit) are the daily activities used in the UCI-HAR dataset. Data on the accelerometer and gyroscope are collected at a constant rate 50 Hz during the data

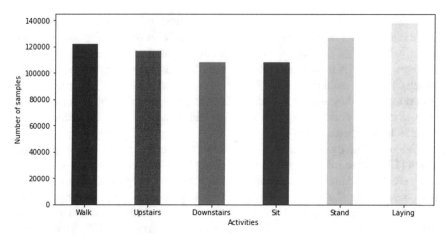

Fig. 1 Activities for UCI-HAR dataset

collecting process. The number of records in the UCI-HAR dataset is 748406, and the details of the dataset are shown in Fig. 1.

3.2 WISDM Dataset

The WISDM dataset [3] contains a total data record of 1098209 samples, Fig. 2 shows the proportion of the total number of samples linked with every activity. It's worth noting that the WISDM dataset is quite imbalanced. Walking accounts for 38.6% of all records, while standing accounts for only 4.4% of all records. A total of 36 people are involved in the study. These participants kept their smartphones in their front leg pockets while carrying out their routine activities. An accelerometer with 20 Hz sampling rate and built-in motion sensors are utilized in smartphones. Jogging (Jog), downstairs (Down), upstairs (Up), walking (Walk), sitting (Sit), and standing (Stand) are the six activities that are recorded using a smartphone. To assure data quality, the data gathering was supervised by an experienced individual.

4 Data Preprocessing

The raw data collected using smartphone sensors must be preprocessed before being fed into the proposed architecture with a particular dimension of data to increase the accuracy of model.

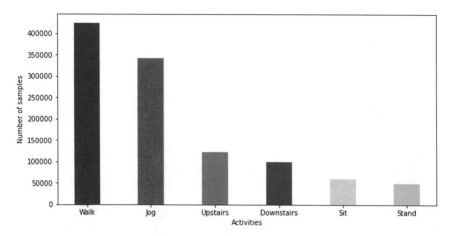

Fig. 2 Activities for WISDM dataset

4.1 Linear Interpolation

The sensors used for collecting the above mentioned realistic datasets are wireless because of which during the collection process some data may be lost, and the lost data is generally represented with $NaN/0$. To solve the problem of missing values, linear interpolation algorithm is used in the proposed work.

4.2 Scaling and Normalization

Training bais can be caused by directly training models with huge values from channels. To prevent training bais, the input data is required to be normalized in the range of 0–1, as follows:

$$X_i = \frac{X_i - X_i \min}{X_i \max - X_i \min}, (i = 1, 2, \ldots, m) \tag{1}$$

In the above equation, m is channel quantity, and $x_i \max$; $x_i \min$ are the largest and least values of the ith-channel, respectively.

4.3 Segmentation

A holistic human activity detection model is created using the data sequence, which is a short time series of raw data obtained from smartphone sensors. The data was constantly gathered throughout the data collection process. A sliding window with a 50% overlap rate is used to partition the data received by smartphone sensors for maintaining the temporal relationship among the data points in HAR. The window size in the WISDM and UCI-HAR datasets is 128.

5 Proposed Methodology

Smartphone sensor data is used in the BiGRU-CNN model for activity recognition. It does not involve any hand-crafted feature extraction technique, and the feature extraction is done automatically by deep learning techniques, and the data used is in raw form and requires nominal preprocessing.

In this model, layers of CNN extract features, whereas BiGRU layers capture dependencies, capturing the diversity of data. The model consists of two layers of BiGRU and a double layer of CNN with filter sizes of 64 and 32.

Experiments are utilizing two separate human activity datasets, UCI-HAR and WISDM, are used to validate the model. UCI-HAR and WISDM datasets had accuracy scores of 96.15% and 97.94%, respectively.

5.1 Bidirectional Gated Recurrent Unit

In bidirectional gated recurrent unit, there are two sequences, first is forward sequence that uses GRU architecture in forward direction, and in second sequence, GRU is used in backward direction and the combination forms two hidden layer states.

GRU is a more advanced type of RNN. To overcome the vanishing gradient issue of a standard RNN, GRU uses the update and reset gates. The data that should be transferred to the output is characterized by two vectors in general. They are special in that they can be trained to remember past information without having to wash it away over time or remove extraneous information.

The model stated in this paper uses two layers of BiGRU each having a unit value of 64. The activation function used is Leaky Relu for each CNN layer. There is flattening layers after CNN layers.

5.2 Convolutional and Max Pooling Layers

CNN is well-known for its ability to learn distinct patterns from speech and graphics [25]. Convolution kernels are used to convolve the inputs of CNN's convolutional layer. It functions as a filter, with a nonlinear activation function, as shown below:

$$a_{i,j} = f\left(\sum_{m=1}^{M}\sum_{n=1}^{N} w_{m,n}.x_{i+m.j.n} + b\right) \tag{2}$$

where $a_{i,j}$ is an identical activation, $w_{m,n}$ represents the $m \times n$ convolution kernel's weight matrix, $x_{i+m.j.n}$ represents the upper neurons activation connected to the neuron (i, j), b represents bias value, and function f is nonlinear. In this paper, for calculating feature maps, the convolutional layers uses leaky rectified linear units (leaky ReLU) , and definition of its nonlinear function is as follows:

$$f(t) = 1(t < 0)(\alpha t) + 1(t \geq 0)(t) \tag{3}$$

where α is a constant.

The number of hidden features that can be mined in the input data grows as the count of convolution kernels grows.

The porposed architecture is shown in Fig. 3.

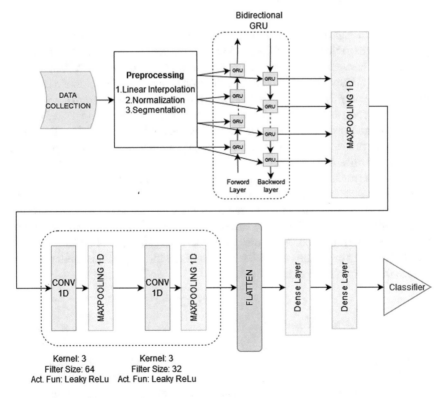

Fig. 3 Proposed BiGRU-CNN architecture

6 Experiments and Results

Two public datasets are utilized to assess the accuracy and generalization ability of the BiGRU-CNN architecture in the proposed work. A specified length sliding window is employed to partition the data from smartphone sensors, and the information is recorded continuously. The window measures 80 time units long with a 40 unit step size. The UCI-HAR dataset was created by recording 30 participants performing six different activities. The training data was produced using the recordings of 22 subjects, while the test set was produced using the recordings of the remaining 8 subjects. The WISDM dataset consisted of 36 participants participating in six different activities. The training data is made up of sensor records of 30 participants, while the test set is made up of recordings of the remaining 6 subjects, entirely separating the two portions.

6.1 Model Implementation

The network structure proposed is built using Keras a neural network API built using Python and is capable to run on TensorFlow. TensorFlow is used as a backend in this experiment. The classification and training of the model are done on a PC that has a 2-core Xeon 2.2 GHz with 13 GB RAM. The PC used in the experiment contains a 64-bit Windows operating system. The gradient was transferred backward from the Softmax activation function to the CNN layer, and the model was completely supervised during training. Weights and biases are set using values selected at random. The difference between the actual and probability distributions is calculated using cross-entropy. In this study, the difference between true and anticipated values is calculated using the mean square error function. The optimizer is Root Mean Squared Propagation, or RMSProp, an AdaGrad modification of gradient descent that employs a decreasing average of partial gradients in the adaption of the size of step for every parameter. In the training phase, the size of the batch is set to 80 and the epochs count is set to 250 for better performance. A learning rate with a default value of 0.001 is utilized to raise the fitting capability, and the sequence of the training data is randomized to increase the performance of the model.

6.2 Performance Measure

In natural environments, while collecting human activity data some imbalance often occurs. The WISDM dataset mentioned above is not properly balanced. The outcome is very accurate when the classifier treats each instance as a majority class and judges the model's effectiveness based on total classification accuracy. As a result, the overall classification accuracy cannot be used to assess performance. The F-measure ($F1$ score) accounts for both false negatives and positives, and combining the two metrics depending on the total number of samples successfully identified, known as "precision" and "recall". As a result, the $F1$ score is a better predictor of performance than accuracy.

Precision is represented as:

$$\frac{\text{True Positive}}{\text{True Positive} + \text{False Positive}} \tag{4}$$

Recall is represented as:

$$\frac{\text{True Positive}}{\text{True Positive} + \text{False Negative}} \tag{5}$$

By grading classes depending on their share of samples, the $F1$ score balances out class disparities. The $F1$ score is represented as follows:

$$F_1 = \sum_i 2 * w_i \frac{\text{precision}_i * \text{recall}_i}{\text{precision}_i + \text{recall}_i} \tag{6}$$

where $w_i = n_i/N$ is the ratio of samples of class i, where n_i is count of samples in the ith class and N is the total number of samples.

6.3 Evaluation of Two Datasets

Two publicly available datasets are used to validate the capability of the proposed architecture. The classification confusion matrix generated when using the WISDM dataset's test set is shown in Fig. 4.

Table 1 gives different performance matrices like accuracy, $F1$ score, precision, and recall for UCI-HAR and WISDM datasets.

Figure 5a shows the plots of accuracy while training and validation for WISDM dataset using the proposed BiGRU-CNN architecture. Figure 5b shows the plots of loss while training and validation for WISDM dataset using the proposed BiGRU-CNN architecture.

Accuracy comparison of the proposed architecture with known state-of-the-art methods are given in Table 2 for the two datasets.

6.4 Conclusion

This research proposes a unique deep neural network for HAR that combines BiGRU layers with CNN layers. The fully-connected layer is the focus of CNN's weight parameters. The raw data acquired from smartphone sensors is fed into BiGRU

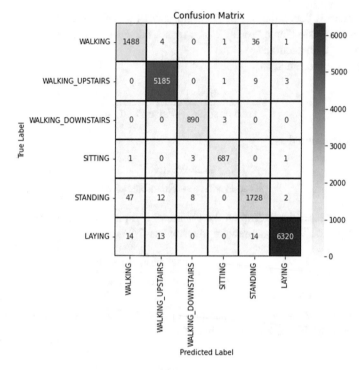

Fig. 4 Classification confusion matrix for WISDM dataset

Table 1 Performance measures for proposed architecture

Model	UCI-HAR (%)	WISDM (%)
Accuracy	96.15	97.94
$F1$ score	96.17	97.95
Precision	96.13	97.95
Recall	96.15	97.94

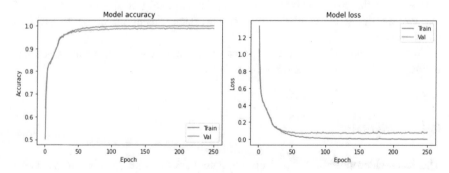

Fig. 5 Accuracy plot and loss plot for the proposed model

Table 2 Accuracy comparison of the proposed architecture

Model	UCI-HAR (%)	WISDM (%)
CNN [26, 27]	92.71	93.32
LSTM [28]	92.10	95.78
CNN-LSTM [21]	94.80	94.28
BiGRU-CNN (proposed)	96.15	97.94

layers followed by CNN layers in the proposed architecture, allowing it to understand the temporal dynamics on multiple time scales based on the learned parameters of GRU for improved accuracy. Since BiGRU uses two layers of GRU architecture, so it increases the cost of overall architecture. The two public datasets, UCI-HAR and WISDM, were used in the experiment to validate the proposed model's generalization ability and effectiveness. The accuracy attained for UCI-HAR and WISDM datasets are 96.15% and 97.94%, respectively.

References

1. Kim E (2020) Interpretable and accurate convolutional neural networks for human activity recognition. IEEE Trans Indus Inf 16:7190–7198
2. Lara O, Labrador M (2012) A mobile platform for real-time human activity recognition. In: 2012 IEEE consumer communications and networking conference (CCNC). pp 667–671
3. Kwapisz J, Weiss G, Moore S (2011) Activity recognition using cell phone accelerometers. ACM SigKDD Expl Newslett 12:74–82
4. Consolvo S, McDonald D, Toscos T, Chen M, Froehlich J, Harrison B, Klasnja P, LaMarca A, LeGrand L, Libby R et al (2008) Activity sensing in the wild: a field trial of ubifit garden. In: Proceedings of the SIGCHI conference on human factors in computing systems. pp 1797–1806
5. Reddy S, Mun M, Burke J, Estrin D, Hansen M, Srivastava M (2010) Using mobile phones to determine transportation modes. ACM Trans Sens Netw (TOSN) 6:1–27
6. Rachuri K, Musolesi M, Mascolo C, Rentfrow P, Longworth C, Aucinas A (2010) Emotion-Sense: a mobile phones based adaptive platform for experimental social psychology research. In: Proceedings of the 12th ACM international conference on ubiquitous computing. pp 281–290
7. Wang Y, Yang J, Chen Y, Liu H, Gruteser M, Martin R (2014) Tracking human queues using single-point signal monitoring. In: Proceedings of the 12th annual international conference on mobile systems, applications, and services pp 42–54
8. Chen L, Nugent C, Wang H (2011) A knowledge-driven approach to activity recognition in smart homes. IEEE Trans Knowl Data Eng 24:961–974
9. Jain A, Kanhangad V (2017) Human activity classification in smartphones using accelerometer and gyroscope sensors. IEEE Sens J 18:1169–1177
10. Fullerton E, Heller B, Munoz-Organero M (2017) Recognizing human activity in free-living using multiple body-worn accelerometers. IEEE Sens J 17:5290–5297
11. Jalloul N, Porée F, Viardot G, L'Hostis P, Carrault G (2017) Activity recognition using complex network analysis. IEEE J Biomed Health Inf 22:989–1000
12. Guan Y, Plötz T (2017) Ensembles of deep lSTM learners for activity recognition using wearables. In: Proceedings of the ACM on interactive, mobile, wearable and ubiquitous technologies 1:1–28

13. Inoue M, Inoue S, Nishida T (2018) Deep recurrent neural network for mobile human activity recognition with high throughput. Artif Life Robot 23:173–185
14. Li H, Shrestha A, Heidari H, Le Kernec J, Fioranelli F (2019) Bi-LSTM network for multimodal continuous human activity recognition and fall detection. IEEE Sens J 20:1191–1201
15. Hammerla N, Halloran S, Plötz T (2016) Deep, convolutional, and recurrent models for human activity recognition using wearables. ArXiv Preprint ArXiv:1604.08880
16. Ma H, Li W, Zhang X, Gao S, Lu S (2019) AttnSense: multi-level attention mechanism for multimodal human activity recognition. IJCAI :3109–3115
17. He J, Zhang Q, Wang L, Pei L (2018) Weakly supervised human activity recognition from wearable sensors by recurrent attention learning. IEEE Sens J 19:2287–2297
18. Tang Y, Salakhutdinov R, Hinton G (2012) Robust boltzmann machines for recognition and denoising. In: 2012 IEEE conference on computer vision and pattern recognition. pp 2264–2271
19. Hochreiter S, Schmidhuber J (1997) Long short-term memory. Neural Comput 9:1735–1780
20. Fahim M, Fatima I, Lee S, Park Y (2013) EFM: evolutionary fuzzy model for dynamic activities recognition using a smartphone accelerometer. Appl Intell 39:475–488
21. Mutegeki R, Han D (2020) A CNN-LSTM approach to human activity recognition. In: 2020 international conference on artificial intelligence in information and communication (ICAIIC). pp 362–366
22. Martindale C, Christlein V, Klumpp P, Eskofier B (2021) Wearables-based multi-task gait and activity segmentation using recurrent neural networks. Neurocomputing 432:250–261
23. Xia K, Huang J, Wang H (2020) LSTM-CNN architecture for human activity recognition. IEEE Access 8:56855–56866
24. Reyes-Ortiz J, Oneto L, Sama A, Parra X, Anguita D (2016) Transition-aware human activity recognition using smartphones. Neurocomputing 171:754–767
25. Ronao C, Cho S (2016) Human activity recognition with smartphone sensors using deep learning neural networks. Exp Syst Appl 59:235–244
26. Wan S, Qi L, Xu X, Tong C, Gu Z (2020) Deep learning models for real-time human activity recognition with smartphones. Mob Netw Appl 25:743–755
27. Ignatov A (2018) Real-time human activity recognition from accelerometer data using convolutional neural networks. Appl Soft Comput 62:915–922
28. Chen Y, Zhong K, Zhang J, Sun Q, Zhao X, et al (2016) LSTM networks for mobile human activity recognition. In: Proceedings of the 2016 international conference on artificial intelligence: technologies and applications, Bangkok, Thailand. pp 24–25

Classification of Indoor–Outdoor Scene Using Deep Learning Techniques

Bagesh Kumar, Harshit Gupta, Shriyash Pravin Ingale, and O. P. Vyas

1 Introduction

The importance of scene classification can be observed in scene understanding. A scene contains numerous things, situations, and activities. Although considered separate from visual perception, scene comprehension differentiates goals as well as the location of goals within a scene [1]. Scene recognition (SR) [2–4] is data and image processing that encompasses various techniques and procedures, which incorporate picture subtitling under a single word. The computer vision problem of scene classification is a significant issue. More and more people are demanding greater organization and a return to picture databases as digital images advance quickly and more online storage space becomes available. Improve scene categorization by employing a range of approaches and boost processing efficiency by creating different indoor–outdoor categories. It is standard practice to divide a picture into smaller blocks and treat each block separately, to make use of the image for classification. Scenic comprehension has a major influence on computer vision since it allows you to observe, evaluate, and understand scenes that give rise to new fields of research. To discover the most essential details and designate them to a certain category, the many qualities of artificial intelligence are needed. The feature attribute that has the biggest

B. Kumar (✉) · H. Gupta · S. P. Ingale · O. P. Vyas
IIIT Allahabad, Allahabad, India
e-mail: pse2016001@iiita.ac.in

H. Gupta
e-mail: rsi2020501@iiita.ac.in

S. P. Ingale
e-mail: mit2019032@iiita.ac.in

O. P. Vyas
e-mail: opvyas@iiita.ac.in

© The Author(s), under exclusive license to Springer Nature Singapore Pte Ltd. 2023
R. Doriya et al. (eds.), *Machine Learning, Image Processing, Network Security and Data Sciences*, Lecture Notes in Electrical Engineering 946,
https://doi.org/10.1007/978-981-19-5868-7_38

impact is that the feature value, and picture category, must be fixed firmly. A categorization system's accuracy is derived from the descriptive power of the characteristics that are selected. Feature extraction and selection strategies are employed to enhance overall efficiency while simultaneously increasing the sensitivity, comprehensibility, and accessibility of the acquired knowledge. The critical step is to extract features and organize them into categories. Neural networks, which are based on artificial neural networks, tried to mimic the structure and function of the human brain by drawing on deep learning [5].

Basic [6, 7] scene classification, image retrieval, image processing, and robot application have all suggested indoor–outdoor scene classification problems for over 20 years. However, there is no agreement on which scene classification method is capable of producing flawless scene classifications across different environments. A large-scale image dataset has been built, while machine learning technology, especially deep learning-based techniques produces impressive computer vision performance. This allows us to provide researchers with valuable guidance and advice about solving the indoor–outdoor scene classification problem [8].

Deep learning [9, 10] is carried out using supervised learning algorithms and algorithms that need a hierarchical nonlinear transformation of input data for model building, which are then used to build a statistical model of output. ML is increasingly used by researchers. It has been applied in several applications, including the detection of different types of images, the evaluation of multimedia concepts, and the mining of text documents. For all these purposes, DL, or representational learning, is applied by various machine learning algorithms. Data analysis DL has advanced at a greater rate and to a higher degree in many aspects, for instance, natural language processing, picture recognition, or voice enhancement, as compared to traditional learning methods. Using [11, 12], a deep DL architectural design of a CNN, a unique CNN DL architecture, has been successful in solving many computer vision problems, including numerous image recognition issues. Due to the extreme deep structure, an image-domain convolution layer can capture and generalize filter processes resulting in very abstract and efficient features. CNN's approach for DL is the most efficient. CNN's [13] pooling and convolution layers are different layer types. Input data filters with well-designed designs form part of the CNN layers. Deep learning trains with a large amount of data and, while training, discovers the strength and distortion of the model. The further testing network models are equipped with these weights. When a new network model is ready, the new network model may be implemented [14].

Transfer learning (TL) is employed to facilitate the transfer of knowledge between different subject domains, using a deep network. Nontechnical interactions enable us to experiment with transfer learning in the real world. The TL technique involves building up knowledge by solving a problem and then applying that information to tackle another related issue. The notion of transfer learning involves reusing or transferring previously learned knowledge to learn new tasks, and it boosts the performance of a strengthening agent significantly [15].

The rest of the paper is structured in the following manner: Sect. 2 contains relevant published work. Section 3 introduces the VGG-19 Deep CNN Model. Section 4 summarizes and explores the model simulation's findings. In Sect. 5, the outcome and further work are outlined.

2 Literature Review

Several new effective approaches have emerged in the last several years for classifying indoor and outdoor scenes. In [16], the authors have proposed an effective scene categorization technique for three various classes using scene objects detection. Use the specified weighting matrix to categorize a picture into one of three types (i.e., indoor, nature, and city). The approach suggested obtained 92% of the verification accuracy and improved by over 2% compared to current CNN models.

In [17], a new scene categorization technique is suggested employing self-monitored gated self-attention generative adversarial networks (GANs) with a loss of similarity. Experimenting with AID and NWPU-RESISC45 datasets indicates that the technique suggested achieves superior performance in comparison with the current unsupervised methods of categorization. The work proposed in [18] shows that a modified ResNet is successful for addressing both color and depth picture classification problems. By doing a classification experiment on several kinds of publicly accessible datasets of outdoor and indoor scenes that also include matching depth maps, the team evaluates the effectiveness of their classification method. In the vast majority of situations, the recommended technique delivers almost perfect performance in terms of color and depth, concerning datasets. The researchers also provide a good comparison to other state-of-the-art techniques. Study in [19] suggests a novel classification model utilizing both CNN and MLP approaches, to their fullest potential. Despite fully connected layers, the features are produced using pretrained CNN. It was found that compared to the best existing techniques, the suggested technique will enhance recognition accuracy. The suggested segmentation approach in [20] gives a unique statistical multi-object segmentation approach that incorporates robust scene model learning with object segregation to identify individual items in a scene. The unique characteristics are taken from these separated items, and this results in employing a linear support vector machine (SVM) for recognition. This final feature addition provides a multi-layer perceptron with scene recognition weights. Their method was proven to be superior to current industry standards. The suggested system works in robotic vision, GPS-based location finder, and security and sports autonomous vision systems.

The study in [21] proposed an ensemble technique based on SVM for picture scene categorization. Studies showed that the scene classification issue can be effectively applied by our technique, as well as performance can be increased with some stability. To improve classification pictures into their class, AlexNet-based transfer learning [22] has been suggested in this research. From the publicly accessible SUN397 dataset, 12 classes were picked, with 6 of them being indoor classes and the remaining 6 being outdoor classes. Classes taken indoors and outdoors are isolated from one other, and then a model is built to compare their outcomes. The model performed well in indoor classes, having an accuracy of 92%, and also in outdoor classes, where it had an accuracy of 98%.

In the work [23], the utilization of cellular network data to conduct the ensemble learning of indoor–outdoor classification for a typical urban area. Key performance indicators (KPIs) are used to identify the variables. This process is known as signal extraction. These factors contribute to the growth and division of decision trees by the Gini index of sample characteristics. Next, the decision trees are put together to form the ensemble learning system, which increases the capability of classifying the features. The accuracy of the ensemble model is demonstrated by the self-validation findings, which indicate the model has excellent (1% out-of-bag error) categorization for indoor and outdoor settings. Another reason for using conspicuous variables in early training is that the variables are given considerable weight in the training. The reconfigured model, built on fewer variables and learners with a lower capability for error, also outperforms conventional machine learning approaches in terms of accuracy and relative computation time. The proposed deep CNN technique [24] on a publicly huge dataset with many state-of-the-art CNN models. The test results show that the approach presented is successful in extracting high-level category characteristics for the HRRS categorization scenario. The proposed random-scale stretched CNN (SRSCNN) technique [25] multiply classifies a picture for voting on the label. Results obtained with two datasets, i.e., UC Merced, Google SIRI-WHU datasets, demonstrate improved performance than standard scene categorization algorithms. In [26], an adaptive CNNs classification technique of the video scene. Research findings demonstrate that the approach described in this study can resolve the challenge of categorization of the video image with a complicated environment. A model is proposed in [27] that does not have to build several binary models, but has a single model that predicts distinct labels' probabilistic threshold values and utilized them for their respective labels to turn the probabilities into presence and class/label absence. This approach leads to greater accuracy and takes less time than previous ways.

In this work, [28] a unique technique is intended to harvest the discriminatory scene categorization information. The planned MIT 67 Indoor and Scene 15 database offers various state-of-the-art approaches. In [29], a detailed analysis of the many aspects that impact classification results, including size as well as descriptor quality, is done in this work to reduce the gap between theoretical techniques and real-world solutions. To implement this strategy, they undertake a comprehensive study of the RGB-D sensor's visual and depth data to look for approaches that will enable real-time indoor scene categorization. The visual and depth information sources are acquired by accurately identifying and integrating the various visual and depth inputs.

In [30], the work is being studied, three off-shelf CNN models include AlexNet, VGGNet, and GoogleNet. Extensive tests using a publicly accessible field usage dataset of 21 classes as well as similarities with other advanced techniques show that deep CNN features are useful for scene categorization of remote sensing pictures at spatial precision. The work [31] begins with an efficient pipeline by proposing to compute the GIST vector of a picture in the first step. The feedforward neural network for the classification task has a large training dataset fed into it. Classification accuracy has been proven to be superior to several state-of-the-art methods.

The final classification pipeline was deployed on an Amazon EC2 server to address computational constraints on mobile devices and run live on the Amazon Elastic Compute Cloud (EC2) virtual machine instance. A quick binary coding approach [32] for successfully generating the global discriminatory picture scene representations characteristic. Two datasets tests show that the suggested FBC achieves satisfactory recognition accuracy and considerably quicker computing speed simulation results show scene classification algorithms.

The work [33] suggests an approach produces improved classification accuracy efficiency. This study is being assessed using IITM-SCID2, a dataset comprising 15 datasets comprising 3442 pictures gathered on the web by researchers. An unsupervised feature learning approach [34] is suggested for the categorization of high-resolution picture scenes. Experimental examination of remote sensing pictures at high resolution reveals the usefulness and efficiency of the suggested approach. In [35] Multi-scale concentrated circular-structured BOVW technique employing various land-use categorization characteristics is proposed. Public land-use classification datasets results show that the suggested approach is superior to many of the previous BOVW methods and is ideal for resolving the problem of land-use scene categorization.

A technique is suggested in [36] that delivers improved classification detection accuracy of around 81.5% when the number of training pictures is reduced. IITM-SCID 2 (information extraction image database), as well as 2011 pictures from the web, are evaluating the suggested approach. To get a stronger scene characterization, [37] provides mid-level data. Tests showed that it delivers equivalent results with the use of low-level characteristics while utilizing mid-level. In combination with low-level functionality, the categorization performance is enhanced. In this paper [38], integrate holistic and object-based scene categorization techniques. The synergetic technique suggested is capable of benefiting from both approaches. Various holistic and object-based state-of-the-art techniques are described. Studies having on a commonly recognized dataset show improved combinatory better performance results.

This work [39] tries to identify these higher degree structures mechanically by locating meaningful object groupings using MDL. We then utilize these components for the categorization of the picture and illustrate which we can obtain better accuracy with them. In [40], a novel method for the alternative optimization of the conventional SVM solver as well as kernel parameters for the sample, either through linear programming (for l l-standard) (for l p-norm). Tests on both naturals generated encumbered indoor datasets show the performance and competitiveness of their method. The work [41] is a new categorization technique based on a combination of low-level and semantic modeling strategies. The test findings demonstrate that the suggested strategy is competitive with previous techniques across three frequently used datasets.

The usefulness of human key performance indicators is explored in [42] for categorizing indoor–outdoor pictures to increase the efficiency of a machine indoor–outdoor classification is seen to enhance by 4% the classification of 10,000 indoor and 10,000 outdoor photographs that have never been viewed. Their tests also show that edge gist is much more characteristic than picture gist for interior situations. In [43] A NN learning effective indoor–outdoor categorization method. Effective image (aggregate) feature extraction based on picture color, entropy, DCT parameters and edge orientations was created to ease the system architecture. The trained classifiers show high accuracy.

3   Research Methodology

A. **Problem Statement**

We take a look at the basic problem of scene classification in the context of indoor–outdoor scene classification. They previously utilized AlexNet DCNN for indoor–outdoor scene classification. The model's depth is shallow, making it difficult to learn from the images in the collection. Better outcomes are produced with more time. It is possible to place more layers and maximum size filters into AlexNet.

To face this situation, we have utilized a deep CNN model capable of distinguishing between distinct scenes and picture activations with the support of VGG16 deep CNN scene comprehension and classification. The Visual Geometry Group's alternate collection, the AlexNet, was born from the collection known as the Visual Geometry Group at Oxford and, as a result, bears the name VGG. VGG, on the other hand, utilizes ideas from prior work to enhance them, and thus implements DCNN layers to enhance the use of the VGG. It was created and developed in 2012 by a group of like-minded individuals.

B. **Proposed Methodology**

In this work, our first and most important step was to use the dataset images of the SUN367 and Places365 Datasets. These datasets are made up of 59,906 images. We need to preprocess before use both datasets because these are in raw format. Once this is done, we have done all the preprocessing on the dataset, and it includes the following process: removing noise and missing values, normalization, feature selection, and transformations. Data augmentation is now required. Because the trained network will have preset parameters for input pictures, data augmentation is necessary. Following that, we will boost the picture data. This is the approach that is employed to grow a dataset by introducing additional variant images. Initially, we have provided our extensions with their ImageDataGenerator objects, which they then use to generate their training, test, and validation datasets. After we have made advances in augmented picture data use it. Then, uploaded these enhanced picture data into the CNN or VGG-19 pertained model for training, after which we have used CNN or VGG-19 pertained model for target detection and positioning, also known as VGG-19 for training.

(1) *Data Preprocessing*

The procedure of preprocessing data is an important part of any data processing system before it is used in deep learning algorithms. In this approach, the processes of cleaning, normalization, feature selection, and transformation are all incorporated. The model input requires a clean picture dataset to provide good results. A further example is in CNN, which used fully connected layers where every picture needed to be of the same type. We can use preprocessing to minimize model training time, too [45].

(2) *Data augmentation (DA)*

Data augmentation plays a key part in the suggested process's enhanced efficiency. To train deep CNN models, a large range of labeled data is required. The results from a model developed with insufficient data often do not generalize well when tested on the training set. Using the tool Image DA, which deliberately creates data from versions, we may increase the amount of the training dataset. Deep learning models of neural networks can result in more knowledgeable models and methods that can provide several versions of pictures that expand the capabilities of accurate models. Deep learning network library Keras has an ImageDataGenerator class that allows you to contribute image data to models [46].

- **Image Data Generator**

  Mostly with the Keras ImageDataGenerator class, we can achieve a similar result. An increase in real time is seen when the ImageDataGenerator produces picture data batches. ImageDataGenerator is used in Keras for image augmentation. The major advantage of using Keras ImageDataGenerator is that images in real time may be generated. This indicates that as the model's training proceeds, it can generate dynamically expanded pictures to improve the overall model [47].

(3) *Convolutional Neural Network (CNN)*

CNN is a reliable DL technique for managing large volumes of data quickly. A CNN is composed of three layers: an input layer, a hidden layer, and an output layer. CNN may have hundreds of hidden layers if the hidden layer of a standard NN is one or two layers. Process feature extraction is one of the two major elements of process management. In this scenario, the convolutional layers, max batch normalization, linear correction units, and dropouts are together referred to as the extraction feature. Unlike the softmax FCL classifier, the classifier component is a layer with softmax FCL [48].

(4) *Neural network model VGG-19*

VGG-19 deep CNN is employed as a model for preprocessing. It has better in-network depth in comparison with classic CNN. It employs a framework alternating with several includes the number and nonlinear activation layers which would be stronger than a single convolution [49]. VGG-19 is an enhanced CNN with pretrained layers and good knowledge of the form, color, and structure of a picture. VGG-19 is quite deep and has been trained in millions of different images that have complex classification problems.

VGG19 Network

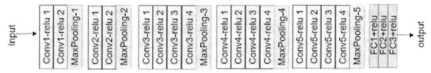

Fig. 1 VGG-19 network model architecture

The variables of the pretrained model optimize models' variables of CL by finalizing the transfer learning approach and resolving the classification problem of wear masks (Fig. 1).

C. Proposed Algorithm

Input: Places365 and SUN397 dataset
Output: Indoor–outdoor scene classification

Strategy:
step1 Collect the input images from the dataset
step2 Preprocess the data to remove the missing value and noisy data
step3 Perform data augmentation on processes data
step4 Trained the model on augmented data
step5 Apply CNN or VGG-19 model with different layer setting
step6 Set all layers with their parameters and batch size
step7 Use ReLu activation function with each layer by $g(z) = \max\{0, z\}$
where $g()$ mathematically using the max$()$ function over the set of 0.0 and the input z
step8 Calculate softmax activation function with a dense layer for classification problem

$\text{Softmax}(z_i) = \frac{\exp(z_j)}{\sum_j \exp(z_i)}$

where z_i are the scores inferred by the net for each class in C.
step9 Use the categorical cross-entropy loss function to calculate the loss of an example by

computing the following sum: $\text{Loss} = -\sum_{i=1}^{\text{output size}} y_i * \log \hat{y}_i$

where $\hat{y}_i$ is the i-th scalar value in the model output, y_i is the corresponding target value, and the output size is the number of scalar values in the model output.
step10 Test the model.
step11 Obtain predicted results.

D. Proposed Flow Chart

See Fig. 2.

Fig. 2 Flowchart of the
proposed methodology

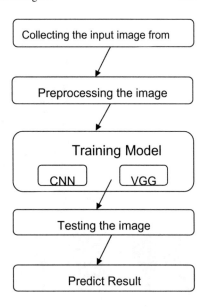

4   Results and Discussion

This work has been carried out with the help of the Python programming language as well as the target platform was Jupiter notebook.

A. Dataset Description

Here, we summarize two publicly available datasets for indoor/outdoor scene classification.

(1) **Places365 dataset**

Scene classification is the focus of the Places365 [50] dataset. It is made up of 10 million pictures divided into 434 scene classifications. The dataset comes in two versions: Places365-Standard, which has 1.8 million train as well as 36,000 validation images from $K = 365$ scene classes, or Places365-Challenge-2016, which has 6.2 million extra images in the training set, such as 69 new scene classes (for a total of 8 million train images from 434 scene classes).

(2) **SUN397 dataset**

The data provided for public usage may be found in the SUN397 dataset. (Xiao et al. [44]). Included in the dataset are 108,753 pictures, 397 categories, and 134 properties, which were used to the SUN benchmark. The number of photos found in each category might fluctuate between one hundred and one thousand images. It has been proposed at least that this rule may not apply to locations before SUN397 because of its great size. With a large number of categories in

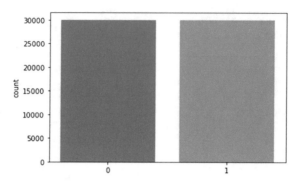

Fig. 3 Distribution of dataset

Fig. 4 Samples of images from a dataset with label

this dataset, together with the training data that is restricted (50 pictures per category), this dataset presents a significant challenge. While other standards do exist, this is the most generally accepted scene classification standard for the industry. We have tested seven different sizes, ranging from 196 × 196 to 196 × 196 scaled pictures (Figs. 3 and 4; Table 1).

B. **Performance Measures**

To assess the dependability of the suggested model, the following measurements are implemented:

1. **Accuracy**: It is a degree of closeness to the true value.

$$\text{Accuracy} = \frac{\text{TP} + \text{TN}}{\text{TP} + \text{TN} + \text{FN} + \text{FP}} = \frac{\text{TP} + \text{TN}}{\text{P} + \text{N}}$$

Table 1 Parameters information

Parameters	value
Dataset	Places365 and SUN397
Loss function	Binary crossentropy
Optimizer	Adam
Batch size	128
Images	59,906
Classes	2
Neural network model	VGG-19
Epoch	50

2. **Precision**: It is the degree to which an instrument or process will repeat the same value.

$$\text{Precision} = \frac{TP}{TP + FP}$$

3. **Recall**: It is a fraction of related documents that are fruitfully retrieved.

$$\text{Recall} = \frac{TP}{TP + FP}$$

4. **F1-score**: The result is a delicate and harmonic ratio of precision and recall.

$$F_\beta = \frac{\left(1 + \beta^2\right)(\text{Precision} \; - \; \text{Recall})}{\beta^2 * (\text{Precision} + \text{Recall})}$$

C. Experimental Outcomes

This section represents an analysis of the result obtained by the proposed and base model. The figures, confusion matrices, graphs, and tables for indoor and outdoor scene classes are shown in the Figs. 5, 6, 7, 8, 9 10, 11 and 12.

Figure 5 represents a line graph for indoor/outdoor CNN model training and validation accuracy. This process continues up to 50 epochs. It shows training 98% and validation 90% accuracy and also shows the training and validation loss.

The diagonal of the matrix represents the figure that is classified correctly into their respective labels. The actual categories are represented in rows, and the predicted label is indicated by columns.

According to Fig. 7, it can be found that after 50 epochs, the VGG-19 model can get better indoor/outdoor image results. The dataset is then divided into 99% for the training and 89% for validation.

Figure 11 represents a line graph for indoor/outdoor model accuracy. This process continues up to 50 epochs. It shows training and validation accuracy and also shows the training and validation loss.

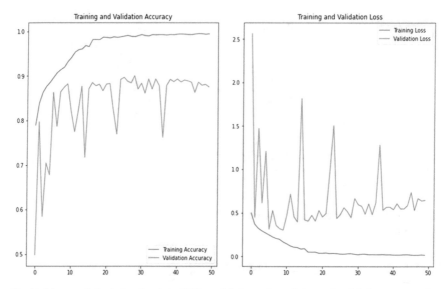

Fig. 5 Line graph for indoor/outdoor CNN model shows the training and validation accuracy for places365 dataset

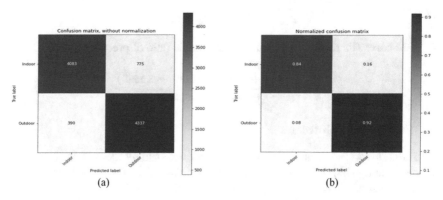

Fig. 6 Confusion matrix without normalization and with normalization for indoor/outdoor CNN model for places365 dataset

The confusion matrix above demonstrates that the model performs precisely for the images it has already been trained on and is detailed in Fig. 12.

According to Table 2, the suggested indoor/outdoor images are supported by various important performance metrics, such as accuracy. To determine the effectiveness of the proposed method, a performance study is performed to compare CNN versus VGG-19. The models provided training and validation accuracy, as well as the model's loss, are presented (Figs. 13 and 14; Table 3).

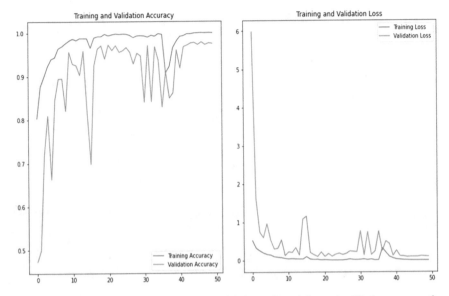

Fig. 7 Line graph for indoor/outdoor CNN model shows the training and validation accuracy for SUN365 dataset

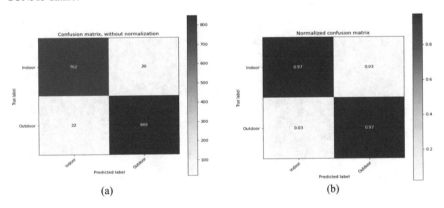

Fig. 8 Confusion matrix without normalization and with normalization for indoor/outdoor CNN model for SUN365 dataset

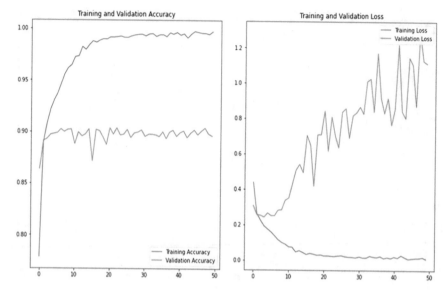

Fig. 9 Line graph for indoor/outdoor VGG-19 model shows the training and validation accuracy for places365 dataset

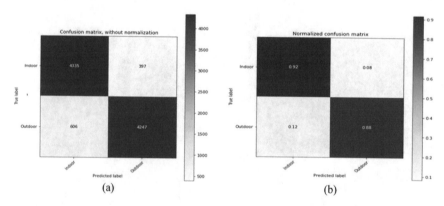

Fig. 10 Confusion matrix without normalization and with normalization for indoor/outdoor VGG-19 model for places365

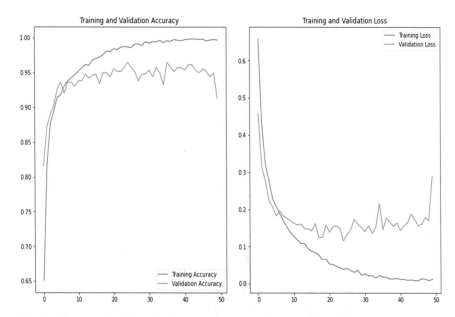

Fig. 11 Line graph for indoor/outdoor model accuracy for SUN365 dataset

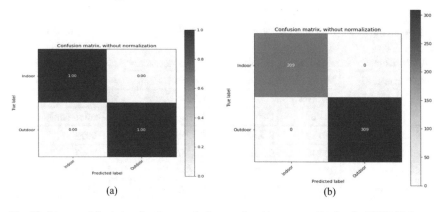

Fig. 12 Line graph for indoor/outdoor confusion matrix without normalization for SUN365 dataset

Table 2 Comparison table of accuracy, loss, val_loss and val_accuracy for places365 dataset

Parameters	Model preformation for binary classification			
	AlexNet		CNN	VGG-19
	Indoor	Outdoor	Indoor–outdoor	Indoor–outdoor
Training acc	0.9139	0.9686	0.9946	0.9986
Validation acc	0.5246	0.5431	0.8756	0.9126
Training loss	0.2482	0.1008	0.0150	0.0073
Validation loss	2.4624	2.5717	0.6456	0.2897

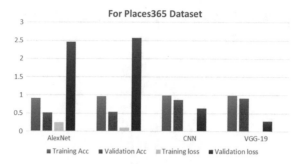

Fig. 13 Comparison of accuracy, loss, val_loss and val_accuracy for places365 dataset

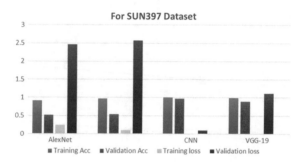

Fig. 14 Comparison graph of accuracy, loss, val_loss, and val_accuracy for SUN365 dataset

Table 3 Comparison table of accuracy, loss, val_loss, and val_accuracy for SUN365 dataset

Parameters	Model preformation for binary classification			
	AlexNet		CNN	VGG-19
	Indoor	Outdoor	Indoor–outdoor	Indoor–outdoor
Training acc	0.9139	0.9686	0.9999	0.9972
Validation acc	0.5246	0.5431	0.9746	0.8959
Training loss	0.2482	0.1008	0.0015	0.0092
Validation loss	2.4624	2.5717	0.1008	1.1131

5   Conclusion

A significant amount of research has been done over the decades to explore the concept of indoor–outdoor scenes, our understanding; all of the research was focused on a VGG-16, where both indoor and outdoor images are labeled. However, geometry comprehension is a major challenge when it comes to comprehending visual imagery and larger picture problems in computer graphics. While earlier years have seen the emergence of numerous indoor classifications systems, each with a very specific set of strict standards, we are now starting to see new systems emerge. We have successfully created deep CNNs in this study. This research is focused on improving the prediction accuracy by employing the CNN and VGG-19 model as a transfer learning model. These novel techniques were suggested for classifying pictures. Using the Places365 and SUN397 indoor–outdoor datasets, these algorithm's findings are tested and show that the approach presented is better than the existing technology for classifying scenes.

6   Future Work

Creating a new CNN architecture from the ground up for indoor–outdoor scene recognition that identifies both indoor and outdoor classes with great efficiency is also of interest. Deep learning is effective in several computer vision tasks. However, the best way to describe the outdoor indoor situation is still a mystery. As a result, diverse researchers must focus on the indoor–outdoor scene classification challenge, particularly from neurobiology and machine learning researchers, for further investigation. In the future, we will develop an I/U dataset based on existing databases. We would also use a deep learning model to test the results and compare them to past research.

References

1. Pawar PG, Devendran V (2019) Scene understanding: a survey to see the world at a single glance. https://doi.org/10.1109/ICCT46177.2019.8969051
2. Matei A, Glavan A, Talavera E (2020) Deep learning for scene recognition from visual data: a survey. https://doi.org/10.1007/978-3-030-61705-9_64
3. Xie L, Lee F, Liu L, Kotani K, Chen Q (2020) Scene recognition: a comprehensive survey. Pattern Recognit. https://doi.org/10.1016/j.patcog.2020.107205
4. Priya Singla RM (2020) Scene recognition using significant feature detection technique. Int J Innov Technol Explor Eng. https://doi.org/10.35940/ijitee.c8653.019320
5. Shariff SU, Basavanna MGG (2020) Fruit categorization and disease detection using Ml raspberry Pi based fruit categorization and quality maintenance with disease detection using Ai and machine learning 9(11):219–227
6. Aarthi S, Chitrakala S (2017) Scene understanding-a survey. https://doi.org/10.1109/ICCCSP.2017.7944094

7. Clouse HS, Bian X, Gentimis T, Krim H (2014) Multi-level scene understanding via hierarchical classification. https://doi.org/10.1109/ICIP.2014.7025194
8. Tong Z, Shi D, Yan B, Wei J (2017) A review of indoor-outdoor scene classification. https://doi.org/10.2991/caai-17.2017.106
9. Zeng D et al. (2021) Deep learning for scene classification: a survey
10. Patel TA, Dabhi VK, Prajapati HB (2020) Survey on scene classification techniques. https://doi.org/10.1109/ICACCS48705.2020.9074460
11. Lee Y, Lim S, Kwak IY (2021) CNN-based acoustic scene classification system. Electron 10(4):1–16. https://doi.org/10.3390/electronics10040371
12. Liu Y, Zhong Y, Qin Q (2018) Scene classification based on multiscale convolutional neural network. IEEE Trans Geosci Remote Sens. https://doi.org/10.1109/TGRS.2018.2848473
13. Guo D, Xia Y, Luo X (2020) Scene classification of remote sensing images based on saliency dual attention residual network. IEEE Access. https://doi.org/10.1109/ACCESS.2019.2963769
14. Li Y, Zhang H, Xue X, Jiang Y, Shen Q (2018) Deep learning for remote sensing image classification: a survey. Wiley Interdisc Rev Data Min Knowl Discovery. https://doi.org/10.1002/widm.1264
15. Weiss K, Khoshgoftaar TM, Wang DD (2016) A survey of transfer learning. J Big Data. https://doi.org/10.1186/s40537-016-0043-6
16. Yeo WH, Heo YJ, Choi YJ, Park SJ, Kim BG (2021) Scene classification algorithm based on semantic segmented objects. https://doi.org/10.1109/ICCE50685.2021.9427672
17. Guo D, Xia Y, Luo X (2021) Self-Supervised GANs with similarity loss for remote sensing image scene classification. IEEE J Sel Top Appl Earth Obs Remote Sens. https://doi.org/10.1109/JSTARS.2021.3056883
18. Kumari S, Jha RR, Bhavsar A, Nigam A (2020) Indoor–Outdoor scene classification with residual convolutional neural network. https://doi.org/10.1007/978-981-32-9291-8_26
19. Shawky OA, Hagag A, El-Dahshan ESA, Ismail MA (2020) Remote sensing image scene classification using CNN-MLP with data augmentation. Optik (Stuttg). https://doi.org/10.1016/j.ijleo.2020.165356
20. Rafique AA, Jalal A, Kim K (2020) Statistical multi-objects segmentation for indoor/outdoor scene detection and classification via depth images. https://doi.org/10.1109/IBCAST47879.2020.9044576
21. Akodad S, Bombrun L, Xia J, Berthoumieu Y, Germain C (2020) Ensemble learning approaches based on covariance pooling of CNN features for high resolution remote sensing scene classification. Remote Sens. https://doi.org/10.3390/rs12203292
22. Yashwanth A (2019) A novel approach for indoor-outdoor scene classification using transfer learning. 5(2):1756–1762
23. Zhang L, Ni Q, Zhai M, Moreno J, Briso C (2019) An ensemble learning scheme for indoor-outdoor classification based on KPIs of LTE network. IEEE Access. https://doi.org/10.1109/ACCESS.2019.2914451
24. Han W, Feng R, Wang L, Gao L (2018) Adaptive spatial-scale-aware deep convolutional neural network for high-resolution remote sensing imagery scene classification. https://doi.org/10.1109/IGARSS.2018.8518290
25. Liu Y, Zhong Y, Fei F, Zhu Q, Qin Q (2018) Scene classification based on a deep random-scale stretched convolutional neural network. Remote Sens. https://doi.org/10.3390/rs10030444
26. Ye O, Li Y, Li G, Li Z, Gao T, Ma T (2018) Video scene classification with complex background algorithm based on improved CNNs. https://doi.org/10.1109/ICSPCC.2018.8567752
27. Rout AR, Bagal SB (2018) Natural scene classification using deep learning. https://doi.org/10.1109/ICCUBEA.2017.8463727
28. Sun H, Chen Y, Chen W, Huang Z (2017) Scene classification with the discriminative representation. https://doi.org/10.1109/ICMIP.2017.66
29. Romero-González C, Martínez-Gómez J, García-Varea I, Rodríguez-Ruiz L (2017) On robot indoor scene classification based on descriptor quality and efficiency. Expert Syst Appl. https://doi.org/10.1016/j.eswa.2017.02.040

30. Cheng G, Ma C, Zhou P, Yao X, Han J (2016) Scene classification of high resolution remote sensing images using convolutional neural networks. https://doi.org/10.1109/IGARSS.2016.7729193
31. Tahir W, Majeed A, Rehman T (2016) Indoor/outdoor image classification using GIST image features and neural network classifiers. https://doi.org/10.1109/HONET.2015.7395428
32. Hu F, Wang Z, Xia GS, Luo B, Zhang L (2015) Fast binary coding for satellite image scene classification. https://doi.org/10.1109/IGARSS.2015.7325814
33. Raja R, Roomi SMM, Dharmalakshmi D (2015) Robust indoor/outdoor scene classification. https://doi.org/10.1109/ICAPR.2015.7050698
34. Fu M, Yuan Y, Lu X (2015) Unsupervised feature learning for scene classification of high resolution remote sensing image. https://doi.org/10.1109/ChinaSIP.2015.7230392
35. Zhao LJ, Tang P, Huo LZ (2014) Land-use scene classification using a concentric circle-structured multiscale bag-of-visual-words model. IEEE J Sel Top Appl Earth Obs Remote Sens. https://doi.org/10.1109/JSTARS.2014.2339842
36. Raja R, Roomi SMM, Dharmalakshmi D, Rohini S (2013) Classification of indoor/outdoor scene. https://doi.org/10.1109/ICCIC.2013.6724252
37. Liu Y, Li X (2013) Indoor-outdoor image classification using mid-level cues. https://doi.org/10.1109/APSIPA.2013.6694294
38. Chen Z, Chi Z, Fu H, Feng D (2012) Combining holistic and object-based approaches for scene classification. https://doi.org/10.1109/ISCID.2012.25
39. Sadovnik A, Chen T (2012) Hierarchical object groups for scene classification. https://doi.org/10.1109/ICIP.2012.6467251
40. Han Y, Liu G (2011) Efficient learning of sample-specific discriminative features for scene classification. IEEE Signal Process Lett. https://doi.org/10.1109/LSP.2011.2170165
41. Zhou L, Hu D (2011) Scene classification combining low-level and semantic modeling strategies. https://doi.org/10.1109/ICDMA.2011.265
42. Pavlopoulou C, Yu SX (2010) Indoor-outdoor classification with human accuracies: Image or edge gist? https://doi.org/10.1109/CVPRW.2010.5543428
43. Tao L, Kim YH, Kim YT (2010) An efficient neural network based indoor-outdoor scene classification algorithm. https://doi.org/10.1109/ICCE.2010.5418764
44. Xiao ATJ, Hays J, Ehinger K, Oliva A (2020) SUN database: scene categorization benchmark. IEEE Conf Comput Vis Pattern Recognit [Online]. Available: https://vision.princeton.edu/projects/2010/SUN/
45. Ramya S, Reshma S, Manogna VD, Saroja YS, Gandhi GS (2019) Accident severity prediction using data mining methods. Int J Sci Res Comput Sci Eng Inf Technol. https://doi.org/10.32628/cseit195293
46. Joshus M (2020) Image data augmentation using Keras ImageDataGenerator. https://medium.com/featurepreneur/image-data-augmentation-using-keras-imagedatagenerator-1cee60255ea8
47. Bhandari A (2020) Image augmentation on the fly using Keras ImageDataGenerator. https://www.analyticsvidhya.com/blog/2020/08/image-augmentation-on-the-fly-using-keras-imagedatagenerator/
48. Setiawan W, Utoyo MI, Rulaningtyas R (2019) Classification of neovascularization using convolutional neural network model Telkomnika Telecommun Comput. Electron Control. https://doi.org/10.12928/TELKOMNIKA.v17i1.11604
49. Xiao J, Wang J, Cao S, Li B (2020) Application of a novel and improved VGG-19 network in the detection of workers wearing masks. https://doi.org/10.1088/1742-6596/1518/1/012041
50. Kai Z (2020) Places365. https://www.kaggle.com/benjaminkz/places365/metadata

Prediction of the Reference Evapotranspiration Data from Raipur Weather Station in Chhattisgarh using Decision Tree-Based Machine Learning Techniques

Abhishek Patel and Syed Taqi Ali

1 Introduction

Water is an important input in agriculture. Farmers rely on rainwater and different water resources (such as ponds, canals, and rivers) for irrigation purposes. Due to climate change and population growth, water resources are decreasing. There must be alternate ways to satisfy agricultural water demand. One way is to improve water management by controlling the irrigation process using technology [1].

Reference evapotranspiration (ET_0) is a loss of water from the soil surface by evaporation and from the crop by transpiration. ET_0 is an essential part of a hydrological cycle [2]. Many factors affect the ET_0, including solar radiation, wind speed, temperature, humidity, and sunshine duration.

Several empirical methods have been used for ET_0 estimation [3]. Hargreaves-Samani equation [2] takes minimum temperature (T_{min}) and maximum temperature (T_{max}) as inputs, whereas Turc method [4] takes T_{min}, T_{max}, and shun shine duration (SSH) as input. On the other hand, Blaney-Criddle and FAO56-Penman-Monteith [2, 5] equations accept all six inputs along with solar radiation. Few more conventional methods were used earlier to estimate ET_0. Blaney-Criddle and FAO56-Penman-Monteith [6, 7] have been proven to be better methods because both accept more inputs than other methods. Empirical methods need a lot of things to be considered carefully when estimating ET_0 [8]. ML-based methods showed better performance than the conventional techniques [8–10].

The emergence of artificial intelligence (AI) and machine learning (ML) has shown great importance in predicting ET_0 with limited climatic data. Quite a variety

A. Patel (✉) · S. T. Ali
Department of Computer Science and Engineering, Visvesvaraya National Institute of Technology, Nagpur, Maharashtra, India
e-mail: mrabhi.patel@gmail.com

S. T. Ali
e-mail: sta@cse.vnit.ac.in

© The Author(s), under exclusive license to Springer Nature Singapore Pte Ltd. 2023   537
R. Doriya et al. (eds.), *Machine Learning, Image Processing, Network Security and Data Sciences*, Lecture Notes in Electrical Engineering 946,
https://doi.org/10.1007/978-981-19-5868-7_39

of researches have been published so far, which proved that ML algorithms to predict ET_0 are more efficient than conventional approaches. Torres et al. [11] have implemented ET_0 forecasting using multivariate relevance vector machine algorithm and artificial neural network (ANN)-based multilayer perceptron. Granata [12] used support vector machine (SVM) to predict actual evapotranspiration at Central Florida, with a humid subtropical climate.

ANN-based deep learning neural network (DNN) models such as radial basis function neural network (RBFNN), convolutional neural network (CNN), and multilayer ANN (MLANN) for modeling ET_0 have been developed [9, 13, 14]. Majhi and Naidu [10] have implemented differential evolution RBFNN and particle swarm optimization-based RBFNN (RNFPSO) hybrid methods using a different combination of inputs. In recent researches, deep learning methods such as long short term memory (LSTM) perform better and more accurately than other ML algorithms [15, 16].

Present study focus on tree-based models applied in the meteorological data of Raipur station in Chhattisgarh collected from the India Meteorological Department (IMD) [17]. Key goals of this paper are i. develop tree-based ML models to predict ET_0 and evaluate them and ii. validate the results obtained with ANN-based models applied on the dataset based on the same weather station.

This paper is organized into the following sections. Section 1 is the introduction of the problem, literature review, and motivation for the experiment. Section 2 is a detailed description of the study site and dataset. Section 3 discusses the data cleaning, feature selection criteria, decision tree-based ML methods used in the experiment and evaluation criteria used. Section 4 discusses the results obtained. Section 5 summarizes the research, and lastly, references are mentioned.

2 Study Site and Dataset

2.1 Study Site

Raipur station is geographically located almost at the center of the Chhattisgarh state in India. Station latitude is 21° 14′, and the longitude is 81°40′. It is situated in the central Chhattisgarh plain. Raipur district has a maximum temperature of 44.3 °C and a minimum of 12.5 °C. Mean Sea Level (MSL) height of the station is 295–298 m. The total average rainfall in the district is 1370 mm. This information is tabulated in Table 1.

2.2 Dataset

Meteorological data of Raipur weather station in Chhattisgarh, India is collected from the IMD [17]. It includes 5556 records from the year 2001–2017. Parameters

Table 1 Description of dataset

Perameter	Raipur station
Latitude	21° 14'
Longitude	81° 40'
Altitude	295–298
Number of records	5556
Training data size	5000
Testing data size	556

Table 2 Description of climatic variables from Raipur weather station

Variable	Max	Min	Range	Mean	SD	CV
ET_0	37.1	0.3	36.8	3.89	2.19	0.58
T_{max}	70.1	17.6	52.5	32.98	5.22	0.15
T_{min}	99.6	3.8	95.5	20.75	6.59	0.29
RH_1	100	18	82	79.46	17.94	0.21
RH_2	100	4	96	43.42	23.61	0.52
WSP	21.1	0	21.1	4.9	3.46	0.71
SSH	88	0	88	6.85	4.71	0.73

Table 3 Correlation matrix of all variables

	T_{max}	T_{min}	SSH	WSP	RH_1	RH_2	ET_0
ET_0	−0.027	0.030	0.067	−0.044	0.108	0.080	1.000
RH_1	−0.839	−0.334	−0.275	−0.270	1.000	0.627	0.108
RH_2	−0.502	0.341	−0.694	0.289	0.627	1.000	0.080
SSH	0.270	−0.353	1.000	−0.421	−0.275	−0.694	0.067
T_{min}	0.565	1.000	−0.353	0.650	−0.334	0.341	0.030
T_{max}	1.000	0.565	0.270	0.324	−0.839	−0.502	−0.027
WSP	0.324	0.650	−0.421	1.000	−0.270	0.289	−0.044

are ET_0 in mm, T_{max} in Degrees C, T_{min} in Degrees C, daily relative humidity (RH_1) in % at 0700 h hours IST, daily relative humidity (RH_2) in % at 1400 h IST, mean wind speed (WSP) in KMPH, and SSH in hours.

Table 2 also gives other information of variables, i.e., minimum, maximum, range, mean, standard deviation (SD), and coefficient of variance (CV). Table 3 gives the correlation matrix of all variables, and Fig. 1 shows the scattered plot of ET_0 with other variables. From the Table 3 and Fig. 1, it is observed that the correlations of ET_0 with most of the variables are significantly less.

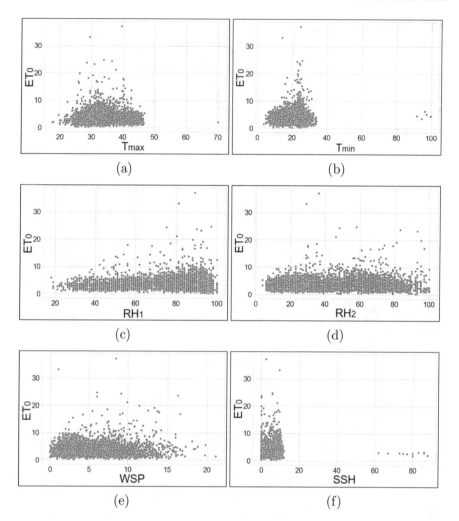

Fig. 1 Scattered graph of ET_0 with meteorological parameters: **a** T_{max}, **b** T_{min}, **c** RH_1, **d** RH_2, **e** WSP, and **f** SSH

3 Methods

3.1 Preprocessing

Dataset may be manipulated or mutated due to various reasons, which may cause outliers in the dataset. It may cause loss of information in the dataset [18]. So, data cleaning starts with the handling of outliers using the quantile method. Furthermore, lots of null values are also there in the dataset. There may be many reasons behind this, such as instruments not working, data being doubtful, and lack of communication with the concerned office, which may result in biased prediction [19]. It is handled by filling with the previous valid entry row wise. Every feature is measured using different units, so features have different ranges. To bring the numeric values to a common scale, normalization is applied using the standard z-score normalize method. The formula for z-score is given by

$$z = \frac{x_i - \mu}{\sigma} \tag{1}$$

where x_i is the ith observation, μ is the mean of the variable, and σ is the SD of that variable.

3.2 Input Variables Selection

Among all input variables, we have selected two sets of features for model development. The first selection is based on ease of availability of data. Temperature can easily be measured at a low cost. So one feature set is temperature based only. It takes two input variables as an input, i.e., T_{max} and T_{min} called featureset-1. Second model is considering all six input variables named as featureset-2.

3.3 Decision Tree-Based Machine Learning Techniques

The decision tree (DT) method is an important predictive modeling tool. It is a supervised ML technique used both for classification and regression problems. Dataset is divided into smaller subsets, and forms like a tree structure with decision nodes and leaf nodes. Decision making is based on comparing the record with the current node, starting from the root. It is an easy to understand and time saving method as it requires less effort for data preparation.

Random forest (RF) ensembles several DTs, which are assigned different samples of data chosen randomly. Different training sets supplied to different DTs produce different outputs. These outputs are ranked, and the highest rank is selected as a final output, whereas ExtraTrees regression (ET) is a similar ensemble method as RF. Prediction output is produced by averaging all the outputs from various DTs.

Gradient boosting regression (GBR) is an ML model used for regression and classification problems. It uses gradient descent to reduce the error. It is a week prediction ensemble model. It constructs the model by combining simple models (weak learners) sequentially to get a final model. It uses DTs as simple learners.

3.4 Performance Evaluation Criteria

Performance measures such as mean absolute error (MAE), mean square error (MSE), and root mean square error (RMSE) between predicted values of ET_0 (ET_{pr}) and observed values of ET_0 (ET_{ob}) are used to measure the performance of the proposed ML models. MAE is a simple way to assess the quality of the predicted value. It is a mean of all the differences between observed values and corresponding predicted values. The formula of MAE is given by

$$\text{MAE} = \frac{1}{n} \sum_{i=1}^{n} |ET_{pr} - ET_{ob}| \tag{2}$$

MSE is another simple tool for performance evaluation. It is an average of the square of all the differences between ET_{pr}, and ET_{ob}. The formula of MSE is given by

$$\text{MSE} = \frac{1}{n} \sum_{i=1}^{n} (ET_{pr} - ET_{ob})^2 \tag{3}$$

The square root of MSE is termed as RMSE. It shows the concentration of data around the line of best fit. The formula of RMSE is given by

$$\text{RMSE} = \sqrt{\frac{1}{n} \sum_{i=1}^{n} (ET_{pr} - ET_{ob})^2} \tag{4}$$

4 Results and Discussions

Table 4 gives the prediction results of the four tree-based models using performance measures (MAE, MSE, and RMSE) for meteorological data of Raipur station from

Table 4 Performance of all models for both feature sets

	Model	MAE	MSE	RMSE
Featureset-1	GBR	1.1708	1.9684	1.4029
	RF	1.2549	2.4325	1.5594
	ET	1.3217	2.7567	1.6601
	DT	1.4712	3.4804	1.8648
Featureset-2	ET	1.0972	1.8073	1.3441
	RF	1.1087	1.8214	1.3493
	GBR	1.1383	1.8744	1.3690
	DT	1.4791	3.5529	1.8844

Table 5 Comparison of RMSE obtained with artificial neural network-based models

	Experiment	Model	RMSE value
Featureset-1	Naidu and Majhi [9]	hargreaves	6.22
		MLANN1	4.10
		RBFNN1	3.19
	Majhi and Naidu [10]	RBFDE1	2.98
		RBFPSO1	2.98
		RBFNN1	3.22
		MLANN1	3.23
		Hargreaves	6.13
	Our experiment	BGR	**1.40**
		RF	1.56
		ET	1.66
		DT	1.86
Featureset-2	Naidu and Majhi [9]	Blaney-criddle	6.99
		MLANN1	1.76
		RBFNN1	1.43
	Majhi and Naidu [10]	RBFDE4	**0.36**
		RBFPSO4	0.43
		RBFNN4	0.82
		MLANN4	1.29
		Blaney-criddle	7.20
	Our experiment	ET	1.34
		RF	1.35
		GBR	1.37
		DT	1.88

MLANN multilayer artificial neural network and *RBFNN* radial basis function neural network

the IMD. A commonly recommended, value of $k = 10$ is applied for the k-fold cross-validation in all models [20]. Each feature set results are arranged in ascending order of RMSE. The table gives that in featureset-1, GBR performed better than the other models in terms of all criteria. The prediction result improves if the second feature set is selected with all variables.

In featureset-1, GBR is the best performer. Values obtained are further refined by applying bagging. It helps to reduce variance within a noisy dataset. MAE value improved from 1.1708 to 1.6660 (SD = 0.0159), MSE value enhanced from 1.9684 to 1.9599(SD = 0.0514) and RMSE enhanced from 1.4029 to 1.3996 (SD = 0.0178).

Similarly, in featureset-2, ET is the best performer. The result of MAE is obtained as 1.0972 (SD = 0.0193). MSE is enhanced from 1.8073 to 1.7754 (SD = 0.0529), and RMSE is improved from 1.3441 to 1.3323 (SD = 0.0199) after applying bagging.

For validating the results obtained in this experiment, RMSE values are compared with ANN-based models given in Table 5 for the dataset based on the same weather station. Empirical methods need lots of effort and time to calculate ET_0, whereas

ML-based methods can predict it more efficiently. Our experiment performed well in featureset-1 but is a little bit lacking in featureset-2. In featureset-1, RMSE = 1.40 is the lowest value achieved by GBR, but in featureset-2, RBFDE4 gives the lowest RMSE value as 0.36.

5 Conclusion

The present experiment is conducted to test the ability of tree-based ML methods. Four tree-based models are developed for the Raipur weather station in Chhattisgarh, India with two input feature sets. The experiment revealed that featureset-2 is performing better than featureset-1 in all evaluation criteria. The RMSE value of this experiment is also compared with ANN-based ML methods. Temperature is the readily available parameter that is used in featureset-1. Decision tree-based methods may be a better choice for the places where the weather stations are not collecting all parameters rather than considering all variables.

Acknowledgements The authors wish to express their gratitude to the IMD, Pune, India for access to the weather station data.

References

1. Jain SK (2012) India's water balance and evapotranspiration. Current Sci 102(7):964-967 (2012). https://www.jstor.org/stable/24084532
2. Allen RG, Pereira LS, Raes D, Smith M (1998) FAO irrigation and drainage paper 56. FAO-Food Agricult Org UN 56(97):e156
3. Melo GLD, Fernandes ALT (2012) Evaluation of empirical methods to estimate reference evapotranspiration in Uberaba, State of Minas Gerais. Brazil Engenharia Agrícola 32(5):875–888. https://doi.org/10.1590/S0100-69162012000500007
4. Turc L (1961) Evaluation des besoins en eau d'irrigation, évapotranspiration potentielle. Ann Agron 12:13–49
5. Doorenbos J, Pruitt WO (1977) Guidelines for predicting crop water requirements. FAO Irrigation and Drainage paper, vol 56
6. Rajasekhar, Siddhardha, Prasad MA, Kumar PS, Kumar NR (2015) Comparison of different methods for estimating potential evapotranspiration in a regional area of Andhra Pradesh. Int J Earth Sci Eng 8(2):149–152
7. Fernandes LC, Paiva CM, Filho OCR (2012) Evaluation of six empirical evapotranspiration equations-case study: Campos dos Goytacazes/RJ. Revista Brasileira de Meteorologia 27(3):272–280. https://doi.org/10.1590/S0102-77862012000300002
8. Abdullah SS, Malek MA (2016) Empirical Penman-Monteith equation and artificial intelligence techniques in predicting reference evapotranspiration: a review. Int J Water 10(1):55–66. https://doi.org/10.1504/IJW.2016.073741
9. Naidu D, Majhi B (2019) Reference evapotranspiration modeling using radial basis function neural network in different Argo-climatic zones of Chhattisgarh. J Agrometeorol 21(3):316–326

10. Majhi B, Naidu D (2021) Differential evolution based radial basis function neural network model for reference evapotranspiration estimation. SN Appl Sci 3(1):1–19. https://doi.org/10.1007/s42452-020-04069-z

11. Torres AF, Walker WR, McKee M (2011) Forecasting daily potential evapotranspiration using machine learning and limited Climatic Data. Agricult Water Manage 98(4):553–562. https://doi.org/10.1016/j.agwat.2010.10.012

12. Granata F (2019) Evapotranspiration evaluation models based on machine learning algorithms-a comparative study. Agricult Water Manage 217:303–315. https://doi.org/10.1016/j.agwat.2019.03.015

13. Ferreira LB, Cunha FFD (2020) New approach to estimate daily reference evapotranspiration based on hourly temperature and relative humidity using machine learning and deep learning. Agricult Water Manage 234:106–113. https://doi.org/10.1016/j.agwat.2020.106113

14. Manikumari V, Murugappan (2020) Modelling of reference Evapotransipration using climatic parameters for irrigation scheduling using machine learning. ISH J Hyd Eng. https://doi.org/10.1080/09715010.2020.1771783

15. Ayaz A, Rajesh M, Singh SK, Rehana S (2021) Estimation of reference evapotranspiration using machine learning models with limited data. AIMS Geosci 7(3):268–290. https://doi.org/10.3934/geosci.2021016

16. Ferreira LB, Cunha FFD (2020) Multi-step ahead forecasting of daily reference evapotranspiration using deep learning. Comput Electron Agricult 178. https://doi.org/10.1016/j.compag.2020.105728

17. India Meteorological Department (IMD), Ministry of Earth Sciences, Government of India. https://mausam.imd.gov.in/

18. Wada K (2020) Outliers in official statistics. Jpn J Stat Data Sci 3(2):669–691. https://doi.org/10.1007/s42081-020-00091-y

19. Hochreiter S, Schmidhuber J (1997) Long short-term memory. Neural Comput 9(8):1735–1780. https://doi.org/10.1162/neco.1997.9.8.1735

20. Refaeilzadeh P, Tang L, Liu H (2009) Cross-validation. Springer, US, pp 532-538. https://doi.org/10.1007/978-0-387-39940-9-565

Application of 1-D Convolutional Neural Network for Cutting Tool Condition Monitoring: A Classification Approach

Sonali S. Patil, S. S. Pardeshi, Nikhil Pradhan, Abhishek D. Patange, and Jay Shah

1 Introduction

The performance of any machining activity is usually assessed by surface finish of workpiece which is mainly driven by condition of the cutting tool [1]. Cutting tool removes excessive material while producing desirable surface roughness [2]. Tool Condition Monitoring (TCM) assists early detection of wear/faults, which in turn increase productivity and reduce downtime [3]. As far as turning is considered, material is removed from rotating workpiece with the help of single cutting tip/edge which is fitted on tool post of lathe machine [4]. Failure of cutting tool mainly occurs because of change in input parameters such as speed, feed and depth of cut of machining that leads excessive friction, rubbing, generation of heat to name a few [5]. To avoid this, there is need for a state-of-the-art tool condition monitoring scheme and expected to assist self-monitoring which seems to be important aspect of Industry 4.0. Prediction of tool life as remaining useful life is considered as characterization of overall process whereas condition monitoring requires categorization of tool state as healthy and faulty thus this investigation is established on classification approach.

Abundant research related to TCM is available—Starting from conventional methods to the application of modern machine learning-based techniques. Some of the conventional methods involve signal and image processing in different domains

S. S. Patil (✉) · S. S. Pardeshi · N. Pradhan · A. D. Patange · J. Shah
College of Engineering Pune, Wellesley Road, Shivajinagar, Pune, Maharashtra 411005, India
e-mail: sonalipatilmech@gmail.com

S. S. Pardeshi
e-mail: ssp.mech@coep.ac.in

N. Pradhan
e-mail: pradhannr18.mech@coep.ac.in

J. Shah
e-mail: shahjo18.mech@coep.ac.in

© The Author(s), under exclusive license to Springer Nature Singapore Pte Ltd. 2023   547
R. Doriya et al. (eds.), *Machine Learning, Image Processing, Network Security and Data Sciences*, Lecture Notes in Electrical Engineering 946,
https://doi.org/10.1007/978-981-19-5868-7_40

such as time, frequency and time-frequency followed by statistical analysis. Later use of machine learning-based techniques was established. Ozel and Nadgir presented use of neural networks for monitoring flank wear with a variety of states of cutting. In this method, a piezoelectric type dynamometer was utilized to measure forces at the designated cutting states [6]. During turning operations, the wear of replaceable carbide units was measured by Abu-Zahra and Yu by using discrete wave transformations of ultrasound waves and multilayer perceptron architecture was designed to find correlations using wave packets [7]. Devillez et al. suggested white light interferometry as a method to measure wear craters on several replaceable attachments on cutting tools [8]. Scheffer et al. provided a comparison between using Hidden Markov Models and Neural Networks to predict tool faults and stated the advantages and disadvantages of both the methods [9]. Rmili et al. reviewed multiple signal processing methods which were based on the analysis of time and frequency domains to understand several signs of cutting tool conditions. The results provided initial elements of real-time online TCM systems [10]. Elangovan et al. demonstrated a data mining technique to examine the condition of the tool from the vibrational data acquired from sensors. The results of the histogram characteristics and the statistical characteristics which were obtained by employing Bayes Net and Naïve Bayes algorithms were compared to get better results [11]. Fang et al. proposed a method in which discrete wavelet transform was employed along with Fast Fourier transform to analyze vibrations occurred in accordance with the tool edge wear. To measure the vibrations, a dynamometer along with an amplifier and a data acquisition system was used. Along with the vibrations, the multiple components of force were also analyzed [12]. A counter propagative neural network method was suggested by Liu and Jolley in which three axis cutting forces were used to obtained indexes. These indexes were processed by the neural network as input features to get the desired result [13]. Madhusudana et al. described a monitoring system using vibration data collected through accelerometer. This data is then analyzed and extracted statistically. The extracted data, with the help of machine learning techniques, is used to provide an understanding of the machine tool condition [14]. Satishkumar and Sugumaran used Nested dichotomy classifiers to determine the duration of the useful life. Vibration features were extracted statistically and were classified using class various dichotomy classifiers [15]. Zhang et al. explained the utility of deep learning for sequential behavioral data processing and Markov transition field in online fraud detection [16]. Wang proved that multivariate time series forecasting is apt for deep neural networks approach [17]. Yang et al. briefed about how convolutional neural network is used for sensor classification by using time series as two-dimensional color images [18]. Courageous investigations based on use of decision tree, random forest, logistic model, Bayes models, bagging and boosting, etc. has been successfully presented for monitoring tool condition during face milling operation [19–26].

The need for tool condition monitoring systems in the manufacturing domain is evident. A brief review summarized here shows that research related to TCM from conventional methods to machine learning-based techniques has good efficiency however when its deployment is considered, it lacks practicability. First of all, conventional methods require costlier instruments and a human resource with knowledge of signal signatures. On the other hand machine learning-based methods work well on small datasets and within the same data distribution however when a high noise environment, versatile operating conditions and cross-domain machining is considered, it still lacks key steps of generalizing unknown tool faults. In an attempt to address these, Deep Learning-based scheme is gaining significant attention. In this paper, healthy and faulty tools are classified using convolution neural networks 1-D CNN and hyper-parameter tuning is used to enhance accuracy.

2 Machining and Data Collection

Figure 1 depicts the various components used in the experimental arrangement. A traditional Lathe machine was used for the turning process. The workpiece was held in the chuck and the tool post holds the cutting tool.

A micro-electro-mechanical (MEM) accelerometer (Analog ADXL335) was used in the setup to acquire the vibrational data. The sensitivity of the accelerometer was 330 mV/g. The sensor was fixed to the tool post using an adherent. The accelerometer is connected to an Arduino ATmega 2560 microcontroller to transfer data. The data was stored in MS-Excel by transferring data from the Arduino Software using the parallax DAQ software.

To perform machining operation and collect vibration data, the machining speed was set to 88 meters per minute, the feed rate was 0.1 millimeters per revolution, and the cut depth was 0.2 mm. The turning operation was done with various incorporated defects (nose wear, crater wear, flank wear and notch wear) after performing turning with a healthy tool. Figure 2 shows acceleration response for different tool conditions (healthy and faulty).

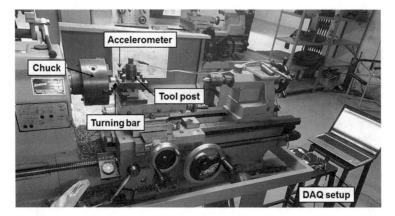

Fig. 1 Experimental setup

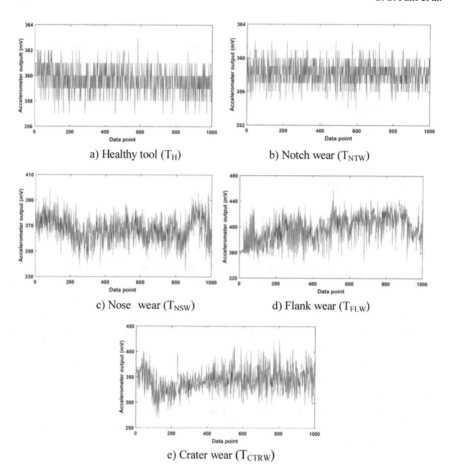

a) Healthy tool (T$_H$)

b) Notch wear (T$_{NTW}$)

c) Nose wear (T$_{NSW}$)

d) Flank wear (T$_{FLW}$)

e) Crater wear (T$_{CTRW}$)

Fig. 2 Acceleration response

3 Data Augmentation

Deep neural networks require large amounts of data to yield better results. Data augmentation was used to create a broader dataset to minimize the losses and increase the accuracy of the model. The scale of augmentation was balanced to tackle the issue of over-fitting. In this work raw data without manual feature extraction was used. Here, 1500 vibration data points were extracted and 125 fragments of 1500 data points were used as input features. Therefore 1500 input features for a fragment of every condition were considered. The data was augmented from 125 fragments to 1100 fragments for every tool wear condition.

4 2-D Convolution Neural Networks

There are three layers for CNN, namely, convolution layer, pooling layer and fully connected layers. Additionally, dropout layer and activation function are two important parameters of CNN. The layered details of Convolution Neural Network is shown in Fig. 3.

4.1 Layers in CNN

The first layer known as Convolution layer is used to identify different features from input images. Here, convolution is performed between input images and the predefined size filter. The filters need to slide over the input image based on that dot product should be taken for input image and filter position at that moment. The output of this product is known as feature map. The second layer of CNN is pooling layer. The computational costs can be reduced by decreasing the convolved feature map size. This operation can be done by decreasing the connections between layers and operates on each feature map without any dependency. There are different methods pooling operations. The average pooling is the average of the elements of the predefined image. The total sum of the elements in the predefined section is computed in sum pooling. The pooling layer is the strong connection between convolution layer and fully controlled layer. The Fully Connected (FC) layer is the combination of weights and biases of neurons. Two different layer neurons are connected through fully connected layer. Flattened input image from the previous layer is fed to FC layer. The vectored image modifications takes place for few layers and classification will be activated. Over-fitting can occur when all features are connected through FC layers. The negative impact of over-fitting is creating wrong impact about model's performance on a new set of data. The solution is drop out of layer. 40% of the nodes are dropped out randomly on passing dropout of 0.4.

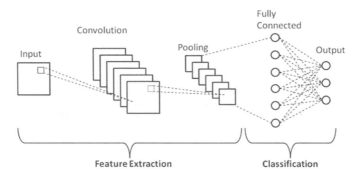

Fig. 3 Layered details of convolution neural network

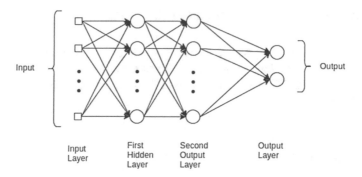

Fig. 4 Multi-layer perceptron architecture

4.2 Activation and Loss Functions

The most important function of CNN model is activation function, i.e., a learning function. This function will decide which information in the model should fire at the end of the model. Even it can add non linearity in the model. Most popular activation functions are SoftMax, tanH, ReLU and Sigmoid Functions. The error function is conventionally known as loss function which can be used to estimate the loss of the model and weights can be used to minimize loss for next evolution. The Multi-Layer Perceptron architecture is shown in Fig. 4.

5 1-D Convolution Neural Network

The 2-D Convolution Neural Network is generally used for image and video data. However 1-D Convolution Neural Network requires simple array operations rather than matrix operation. Figure 5 shows 1-D CNN Architecture.

Fig. 5 1-D CNN architecture

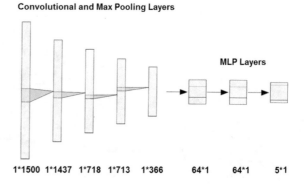

Table 1 Details of convolutional layers

Layer	Filters	Filter size	Activation	Size	Strides
Convolutional layer 1	64	6	Relu	NA	NA
Batch normalization	NA	NA	NA	NA	NA
Max pooling 1	NA	NA	NA	3	2
Convolutional layer 2	64	6	Relu	NA	NA
Batch normalization	NA	NA	NA	NA	NA
Max pooling 2	NA	NA	NA	3	2

Table 2 Fully connected layers

Layer	Perceptrons	Activation
Input	64	Relu
Hidden layer	64	Relu
Output	5	Softmax

1-D Convolution Neural Network with a smaller number of hidden layers and neurons can solve more complex problems compared to 2-D network. The hardware requirement of 1-D network is much simpler than 2-D network, which can reduce computational time and cost. In the above architecture 3 CNN layers are used with 2 MLP layers which can provide better performance for more complicated data.

6 Hyper Parameter Tuning

Hyper parameters include various parameters such as number of convolutional layers, max pooling and batch normalization layers. Within each layer, aspects such as number of filters, their size, activation function, size and strides may vary. Details are presented in Tables 1 and 2, respectively.

7 Results and Discussion

A variety of CNN architectures were used based on commonly used CNN architectures and custom designed architectures. Initially, the architectures AlexNet, ResNet-50, VGG16 and LeNet-5 were used. These architectures were utilized to get an understanding of the size of the CNN architecture to be used while custom designing the architecture for the methodology. AlexNet comprises 5 convolutional layers and exhibited an accuracy of 18.5%. VGG16 comprises 13 convolutional layers and exhibited an accuracy of 23.81%. ResNet-50 comprises 48 convolutional layers and exhibited an accuracy of 21%. LeNet-5 comprises 2 convolutional layers and exhibited an accuracy of 66%. Therefore, it was understood that with greater number of convolutional layers, the precision of the classifier was considerably low. However, LeNet-5, with only 2 convolutional layers, exhibited an accuracy of 66%. As the size of the dataset was not too big, over-fitting was occurring when a large number of convolutional layers were used. Based on the fact that LeNet- 5 displayed the greatest accuracy, a number of custom designed architectures with 2 convolutional layers were used. In these architectures, the parameters like filter size, number of filters, strides, padding, pooling layers, MLP layers and activation functions were varied in an attempt to get the highest possible accuracy. The augmented data was divided into 70:30 training testing ratio. In the confusion matrices, the numbers 0, 1, 2, 3, 4 represent the tool conditions defective, new, flank wear, nose wear and notch wear, respectively. The truth values are represented on the y-axis and the predictions by the model are represented on the x-axis. The confusion matrix in Fig. 6a is the representation of the performance of 1-D CNN model on 70% training data of the augmented data. The model gave an accuracy of 100% on the augmented training data. The confusion matrix in Fig. 6b is the representation of the performance of 1-D CNN model on 30% testing data of the augmented data. The model gave an accuracy of 99.04% on the augmented testing data. The confusion matrix in Fig. 6c is the representation of the performance of 1-D CNN model on a blind dataset. The defective wear condition as well as the new and notch wear conditions accurately classified 10 out of 10 inputs. The flank wear condition was precisely predicted 8 out of 10 times. The model predicted the nose wear condition with the least accuracy. Out of 50, the model made 44 correct predictions which is an accuracy of 88%. In Fig. 6a fully correct classification has been represented as there is no misclassification between healthy and faulty tool and even there is no misclassification among faulty configurations as well. This shows that the collected vibration data and augmented data both adequately reflect the tool state. Moreover, when test split of the augmented data was considered, the confusion matrix in Fig. 6b shows that misclassification exist only in flank and crater wear. This might be because in real-time machining the flank wear might have extended to crater wear due to change in input parameters. Otherwise no misclassification was observed in healthy and any of faulty configurations of tool. Similarly while evaluating independent blind data, misclassification was observed in flank, nose and crater wear as shown in Fig. 6c due to variation in input parameters the flank wear extends to nose and crater wear and that has been reflected in classification. Here in case of blind data also, proposed framework has performed well as there was no misclassification in healthy and other faulty configurations of tool.

8 Conclusion and Futuristic Directions

Application of 1-D Convolutional Neural Network (CNN) has been appropriately exemplified in this paper for classifying vibration datasets correlating to cutting tool state as healthy or faulty. The time-dependent response of acceleration representing

Fig. 6 Confusion matrices
for classification

True class	T_H	784	0	0	0	0
	T_{NTW}	0	770	0	0	0
	T_{NSW}	0	0	783	0	0
	T_{FLW}	0	0	0	782	0
	T_{CTRW}	0	0	0	0	818
		T_H	T_{NTW}	T_{NSW}	T_{FLW}	T_{CTRW}

Predicted class

a) Confusion matrix for training split of the augmented data

True class	T_H	342	0	0	0	0
	T_{NTW}	0	338	0	0	0
	T_{NSW}	0	0	325	0	0
	T_{FLW}	0	0	8	332	0
	T_{CTRW}	0	8	0	0	335
		T_H	T_{NTW}	T_{NSW}	T_{FLW}	T_{CTRW}

Predicted class

b) Confusion matrix for test split of the augmented data

True class	T_H	10	0	0	0	0
	T_{NTW}	0	10	0	0	0
	T_{NSW}	0	0	8	2	0
	T_{FLW}	2	0	0	6	2
	T_{CTRW}	0	0	0	0	10
		T_H	T_{NTW}	T_{NSW}	T_{FLW}	T_{CTRW}

Predicted class

c) Confusion matrix for testing of independent blind data

machining vibrations is observed as periodic and cyclic as a result of characteristic tool failure and five different configurations and has suitably been supported for health monitoring considering the present framework. The classification results achieved considering training, testing and blind folds indicate that the methodology is proficient of tool health monitoring. Manual feature extraction was successfully eliminated with the help of this new 1-D network technology since manual feature extraction increases computational time and complexity of the system. This system shall assist edge-old systems to upgrade themselves to be smarter within fewer resources. This deep learning-based classification scheme shall ensure effective use of the cutting tool. The aforesaid strategies will be investigated in future research in order to decrease the amount of experimental effort necessary. It would be feasible to eliminate the requirement for data augmentation with a larger and more comprehensive dataset. This might also help with the development of a more precise classifier. Additionally, future research should be directed toward deployment and real-time implementation of this methodology in the industry.

References

1. Patange AD, Jegadeeshwaran R (2021) Review on tool condition classification in milling: a machine learning approach. Mater Today Proc 46(2):1106–1115
2. Patil SS, Pardeshi SS, Patange AD, Jegadeeshwaran R (2021) Deep learning algorithms for tool condition monitoring in milling: a review. J Phys Conf Ser IOP Publishing 1969(012039)
3. Tambake NR, Deshmukh BB, Patange AD (2021) Data driven cutting tool fault diagnosis system using machine learning approach: a review. J Phys Conf Ser IOP Publishing 1969(012049)
4. Khade HS, Patange AD, Pardeshi SS, Jegadeeshwaran R (2021) Design of bagged tree ensemble for carbide coated inserts fault diagnosis. Mater Today Proc 46(2):1283–1289
5. Khairnar A, Patange A, Pardeshi S, Jegadeeshwaran R (2021) Supervision of carbide tool condition by training of vibration-based statistical model using boosted trees ensemble. Int J Performability Eng 17(2):229–240
6. Özel T, Nadgir A (2002) Prediction of flank wear by using back propagation neural network modeling when cutting hardened H-13 steel with chamfered and honed CBN tools. Int J Mach Tools Manuf 42(2):287–297
7. Abu-Zahra N, Yu G (2003) Gradual wear monitoring of turning inserts using wavelet analysis of ultrasound waves. Int J Mach Tools Manuf 43(4):337–343
8. Devillez A, Lesko S, Mozer W (2004) Cutting tool crater wear measurement with white light interferometry. Wear 256(1–2):56–65
9. Scheffer C, Engelbrecht H, Heyns PS (2005) A comparative evaluation of neural networks and hidden Markov models for monitoring turning tool wear. Neural Comput Appl 14:325–336
10. Rmili W, Serra R, Ouahabi A, Kious M (2006) Tool wear monitoring in turning process using vibration measurement. In: 13th International congress on sound and vibration, Vienna, Austria
11. Elangovan M, Ramachandran KI, Sugumaran V (2010) Studies on Bayes classifier for condition monitoring of single point carbide tipped tool based on statistical and histogram features. Expert Syst Appl 37(3):2059–2065
12. Ning F, Pai PS, Mosquea S (2011) Effect of tool edge wear on the cutting forces and vibrations in high-speed finish machining of Inconel 718: an experimental study and wavelet transform analysis. Int J Adv Manuf Technol 52:65–77
13. Liu TI, Jolley B (2015) Tool condition monitoring (TCM) using neural networks. Int J Adv Manuf Technol 78:1999–2007
14. Madhusudana CK, Kumar H, Narendranath S (2016) Condition monitoring of face milling tool using K-star algorithm and histogram features of vibration signal. Eng Sci Technol Int J 19(3):1543–1551
15. Satishkumar R, Sugumaran V (2016) Estimation of remaining useful life of bearings based on nested dichotomy classifier–a machine learning approach. Int J Eng Technol 8(1):339–349
16. Zhang R, Zheng F, Min W (2018) Sequential behavioral data processing using deep learning and the Markov transition field in online fraud detection. Math Comput Sci 1808(05329):1–5. https://arxiv.org/pdf/1808.05329.pdf
17. Wang K (2016) Intelligent predictive maintenance (IPdM) system-industry 4.0 scenario. WIT Trans Eng Sci 113(10):259–268
18. Yang CL, Chen ZX, Yang CY (2019) Sensor classification using convolutional neural network by encoding multivariate time series as two-dimensional colored image. Sensors 20(1):168, 1–15
19. Bajaj NS, Patange AD, Jegadeeshwaran R, Kulkarni KA, Ghatpande RS, Kapadnis AM (2022) A Bayesian optimized discriminant analysis model for condition monitoring of face milling cutter using vibration datasets. J Nondestr Eval Diagn Progn Eng Syst ASME 5(2):1–13. https://doi.org/10.1115/1.4051696
20. Patange AD, Jegadeeshwaran R (2021) A machine learning approach for multipoint tool insert health prediction on VMC. Measurement 173(108649):1–16. https://doi.org/10.1016/j.measurement.2020.108649

21. Shewale MS, Mulik SS, Deshmukh SP, Patange AD, Zambare HB (2019) Novel machine health monitoring system, advances in intelligent systems and computing, vol 828. Springer, Singapore, pp 461–468. https://doi.org/10.1007/978-981-13-1610-4_47
22. Nalavade SP, Patange AD, Prabhune CL, Mulik SS, Shewale MS (2019) Development of 12 channel temperature acquisition system for heat exchanger using MAX6675 and arduino, Lecture notes in mechanical engineering, vol 1. Springer, Singapore, pp 119–125. https://doi.org/10.1007/978-981-13-2697-4_13
23. Patange AD, Jegadeeshwaran R, Dhobale NC (2019) Milling cutter condition monitoring using machine learning approach. Mater Sci Eng IOP Publishing Ltd, UK 624(1):1–7
24. Mulik SS, Patange AD, Jegadeeshwaran R, Rahegaonkar AA, Pardeshi SS (2020) Development and experimental assessment of a fluid flow monitoring system using flow sensor and Arduino interface, Lecture notes in mechanical engineering, Springer, Singapore, pp 115–122. https://doi.org/10.1007/978-981-15-6619-6_12
25. Patange AD, Jegadeeshwaran R (2020) Application of Bayesian family classifiers for cutting tool inserts health monitoring on CNC milling. Int J Prognostics Health Manage 11(2):1–13
26. Dhobale N, Mulik S, Jegadeeshwaran R, Patange A (2021) Supervision of milling tool inserts using conventional and artificial intelligence approach: a review. Sound Vib 55(2):87–116

Image Processing and Computer Vision

Wireless Surveillance Robot for Industrial Application

Rishabh Singh, Anjali Kushwah, Preeti Warrier, and Shraddha Oza

1 Introduction

Surveillance has a significant role in security. In Industrial areas, continuous monitoring is required, making the job monotonous and strenuous. Security guards may get bored and become careless, compromising security. Using a robot for constant monitoring of an area will improve surveillance efficiency and ensure the safety of human resources as the robot can be operated from anywhere. Robots are usually miniature so that they can enter tunnels, mines, and tiny holes in buildings and even have the capability to survive in a harsh and challenging climate for a lifelong time without any harm [12]. Nowadays, a mobile robot with a camera is popularly used for surveillance. The camera used in making the robot can move to different locations. These sorts of robots are more flexible than fixed cameras. Primarily used surveillance robots are wheel-based robots. The wheel-based robots are more worthy of the leveled platform. With the advent of wireless communication and the Internet, the videos captured by a robot can be seen remotely on a PC/laptop.

The majority of private security forces are using Internet protocol Camera-based installation instead of the analog camera. Analog cameras are conventional cameras that are used in CCTV. It sends video with the help of cable to VCR and DVR. In the modern era, we also use a hybrid system consisting of both analog and IP camera-based installation. This is because IP-based system provides better picture quality, and it is also beneficial in terms of mobility, stability, and flexibility. An IP camera is a digital video camera that controls data and gives image data output through an IP network. Unlike analog cameras, they do not require a recording device. Here we are using an IP camera to store the videos over the Internet [11].

The purpose of this paper was to build a small, land-based surveillance robot that can be controlled over Internet communication through Raspberry Pi 3 Model B from

R. Singh (✉) · A. Kushwah · P. Warrier · S. Oza
Army Institute of Technology, Pune, Maharashtra, India
e-mail: rishabhsingh_16592@aitpune.edu.in

© The Author(s), under exclusive license to Springer Nature Singapore Pte Ltd. 2023   561
R. Doriya et al. (eds.), *Machine Learning, Image Processing, Network Security and Data Sciences*, Lecture Notes in Electrical Engineering 946,
https://doi.org/10.1007/978-981-19-5868-7_41

anywhere. This robot continuously watches its surroundings, sends live streaming to an authorized person, and helps detect, track, and chase the object. Furthermore, it can be operated in an entire internet zone with a PC/laptop.

2 Related Work

Ahmed et al. [3] implemented substitutes for locks and fingerprint sensors in security systems, especially for a physically challenged person. First, the person in front of the camera was corroborated by the webcam. Then, through face detection and recognition algorithm, it authenticates the person, whether owner or outsider. The individual whose status is correct will only be permitted to go through the entrance. However, this project may fail when the owner changes his look.

Kumar et al. [4] implemented the border surveillance system using computer vision. First, a digital webcam is used for surveillance. Then, object detection is executed using the OpenCV library of python. If any human is detected, then this system will check whether the human is known or unknown. If the person is known, it will continue surveillance; else, it will send an alert signal at the receiver end.

Mohammed et al. [5] discussed a system for identifying suspicious activity while live streaming in their paper. Twilio API immediately alerts the user via SMS, including an image of suspicious activity captured. In addition, the system always sets up the flask server, which allows only authorized users to access the data.

Kumar et al. [6] implemented Innovative city surveillance systems, which drive over the battery. The standard library OpenCV is used to perform face detection, alignment, and improvement. Face identification is implemented by getting the required features using Local Binary Pattern. Because of the increased feature reduction, it is ideal for all image identification applications used in IoT-based surveillance equipment.

These days, security at home is equally important. Therefore, people usually need low-cost and effective surveillance systems. Sabri et al. [7] executed a low-cost multi-unit surveillance system that can regulate several webcams to identify and monitor the object. The camera is connected to a Camera Serial Interface port. The software program focuses on a deep neural network-based method that has been tuned using the saliency approach, a deep-learning technique.

Rao et al. [9] works on the robot's movement, which can also be controlled by a designed web browser using python language. This paper implemented a movable surveillance camera using the Internet of Things (IoT) and Raspberry Pi 3 Model B. Furthermore, the created web page can establish a server on Raspberry Pi 3 Model B.

Hashib et al. [10] implemented a security system to detect the humans and backpacks entering the room where this system is placed. When a human or bag is scanned, it saves the image and sends it via email. Additionally, alarm security is provided by the glowing bulb.

Rao et al. [11] implemented surveillance using Raspberry Pi 3 Model B with an Internet connection. Whenever there is movement in the surveillance area, it will be recorded and sent to the user's system.

Zhang et al. [12] performed indoor security systems consisting of a remote Internet-based network connection and a local wireless sensor network. The individual coming through the doorway can be detected by sensors, which will alert the jumping robot. The robot will leap into the surveillance area of the sensor and take a picture, which will then be sent to the user.

Rakesh et al. [10] implemented surveillance systems in a Zigbee protocol-based cellular network. It is linked to a BeagleBoard Single Board Computer (SBC)-based surveillance management platform. When flames or invader action is identified, the program sends text messages to cellular phones as a notification and activates the burglar alarm.

This paper implements surveillance in industrial areas with object detection, object tracking, and chasing the object with obstacle handling. All the algorithms are executed using the python programming language

3 Proposed Design

The proposed surveillance system consists of a Raspberry Pi 3 Model B module interfaced with Ultrasonic sensors, a webcam, and an Ethernet port for Internet connectivity. We are using the VNC server remotely to access the webcam for the images or videos of the desired locations. After acquiring images, we use open CV to join several frames to form a video for live streaming. Data acquired by the surveillance bot the enemy. The recorded videos are saved on cloud computing services. The system also drives motors with the help of Motor driver IC $L298N$ as described in Fig. 1.

4 System Description

All the hardware used in this system is described in Fig. 2.
The objectives of this model are:

- Surveillance
- Object detection and tracking
- Object chasing and obstacle handling.

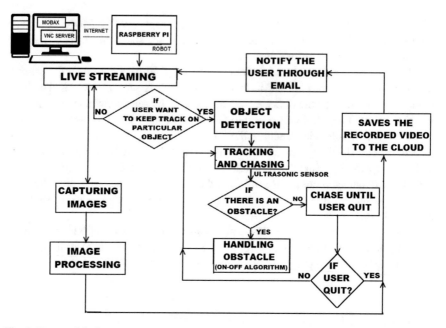

Fig. 1 Proposed design

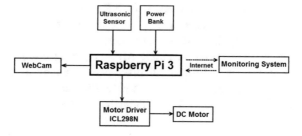

Fig. 2 Block diagram

4.1 Surveillance

The camera captures a stream of frames which are RGB images. The individual frames are the output as NumPy array of the frame.

These frames are then added to the double-ended queue (deque) for future use. By storing the image into deque, we can speedily get the recently captured frames from the front of the dequeue and older frames from the rear.

Deque allows computation of movement over several frames and can be adjusted or restricted to the size of the frames storing in the deque. Restriction of the deque is necessary because Raspberry Pi 3 Model B only has limited memory space. However, we have also used Cloud computing services for storing the data.

4.2 Object Detection and Tracking

Only surveillance is not enough for security; keeping a close watch on the object is also necessary. Object detection helps in focusing the object by marking it with a yellow circle around the object.

The problem occurs when the object moves rapidly or changes direction in every short period of time. Here Tracking comes into the picture. Tracking the object improves the ability of the robot to chase the target effortlessly. So here we are executing object detection and tracking with a YOLO algorithm as described in Algorithm 1.

4.3 Object Chasing and Obstacle Handling

If the authorized user has a suspicion about someone or wants to track something unusual, he can click on the object, and the robot will start chasing that object until the user presses the space bar key.

Now wherever the object moves, the robot will follow its path. With the help of a webcam connected further to the Motor, the Motor will also work accordingly and track the object as the object moves.

If the user wants to quit tracking the particular object and wants the robot to do some other task, then he will press "space bar." After pressing the space bar, it will stop chasing that object and wait for the following command by the user. We have used IR sensors to handle the obstacle while tracking the object. If the target, the robot is tracking disappears, it will send the signal through raspberry pi, and the user will receive the signal via the VNC server. The user will handle further action. Algorithm 2 is used to handle the barriers.

5 Experiment

A fully customized application was developed for video streaming surveillance systems using Raspberry Pi 3. Steps followed while achieving this are described as follow:

5.1 Activation of VNC Server

A basic login page was designed using Mobax to get the user enrolled. Since this is a fully authorized system, users need to log in to the VNC server to access the Raspberry Pi 3 Model B desktop, as shown in Fig. 3. Once the user gets signed in, a

---

Algorithm 1: Object Detection and Tracking

---

1 Load the COCO class labels, YOLO model was trained on;
2 Initialize a list of colors to represent each possible class label;
3 Route the YOLO weights and model configuration;
4 Load our YOLO object detector trained on COCO dataset and determine only the *output* layer names that we need from YOLO;
5 Read and loop the current frame from the Video stream;
6 **while** *True* **do**
7   **if** *No frame* **then**
8   Break; // Video Ends
9   **else**
10   Initialize our confidences, class IDs, and lists of detected bounding boxes, respectively;
11   **for** *Output* **do**
12   **for** *Detection in output* **do**
13   Extract the class ID and confidence (i.e., probability) of the current object detection;
14   Filter out weak predictions by ensuring the detected probability is greater than the minimum probability;
15   **if** *Confidence > args["confidence"]* **then**
16   Calculate width and height of frame;
17   Determine x,y coordinate of objects;
18   **end**
19   Apply non-maxima suppression to suppress weak, overlapping bounding boxes;
20   **if** *len(idxs) > 0* **then**
21   **for** *i in idxs.flatten()* **do**
22   Extract and draw the bounding box coordinates;
23   **end**
24   **end**
25   Check if the video writer is None;
26   **if** *writer is None* **then**
27   Initialize our video writer;
28   Some information on processing single frame;
29   **end**
30   **end**
31   **end**
32   **end**
33   Write the output frame to disk;
34 **end**
35 **if** *keyPressed == 'q'* **then**
36   break;
37 **end**
38 Release the camera and close all windows;

Algorithm 2: Obstacle Handling

---

1 **for** *distance* $<=$ *threshold* **do**
2   Stop;
3   Rotate 45° toward right;
4   move forward by distance d;
5   Rotate 90° toward left;
6   move forward by distance d ;
7   Rotate 45° toward right;
8   Search for the object;
9   **if** *robot finds the object* **then**
10   chase the object;
11   **else**
12   send signal to user;
13   wait for user's instruction;
14   **end**
15 **end**
16 Go forward and go to step 1 again

Fig. 3 VNC sever login and authentication

local room layout VNC server is displayed to easily switch to wherever he wants to provide security and access live video streaming.

5.2 Live Streaming

Multiple image frames are captured and joined together to form a video. According to the controls defined by the authorized user, live streaming video is observed by the authorities using the Internet, as is shown in Fig. 4.

The robot's movement is supervised by the motor driver IC used to command the wheels and is connected to Raspberry Pi 3 Model B and a webcam. So, for example, if a user wants to keep track of a particular object, he can move the robot closer to it and click on the image of the object.

Fig. 4 Live streaming

Once the robot detects the object, if we press "t", the robot will start tracking the object.

Now wherever the object moves, the robot will follow its path. With the help of a webcam, the motor will also work accordingly and track the object as the object moves.

If the user wants to quit tracking the particular object and wants the robot to do some other task, he will press "q". After pressing "q", it will quit chasing that object and wait for the next command by the user.

User can also handle the movement of the robot by pressing the keys "w," "s", "d", "a", and the space bar key to move the robot forward, backward, right, left, and stop, respectively.

5.3 Image Processing

Surveillance at night or in dark places is one of the significant challenges for humans. This robot does not skip an opportunity to discover, detect, track and chase the unusual event irrespective of the environment.

Further, if the user finds any abnormal activity in the dark, which may not be apparent to human eyes, he can capture pictures and perform image processing on them, as shown in Fig. 5.

5.4 Object Detection and Tracking

The system implemented and described here is capable of detecting and tracking a given object. The idea is, once the user clicks on the object, it will continuously track it until the user quit. The algorithm is implemented in python.

Fig. 5 Original image compared with contrast image

Fig. 6 Object detection and tracking

The system will first detect the particular object whose Hue Saturation Value(HSV) is mentioned in the code.

Once detected, it will track the object as it moves around the video by using its preceding positions as it moves. Here, it will use an (x, y) graph plot, store the object's previous position, and make a contrail that follows its path, as shown in Fig. 6.

6 Performance

The image capturing quality was tested against different webcam positions. During the tests, it was observed and concluded that the design of the robot was improved by setting the camera right in the middle of the robot. Furthermore, it stabilized the robot by keeping the center of gravity lower by reducing the camera's height according to the user's need, as shown in Fig. 7.

Further after complete implementation, testing is performed to get the accuracy of the robot to detect objects in various areas and under various conditions. Testing is done on more than 600 objects, and the percentage of objects detected is plotted

Image and video captured when webcam is not placed at center of gravity

Image and Video captured when camera is placed at center of gravity

Fig. 7 Web cam positions and its effect on image quality

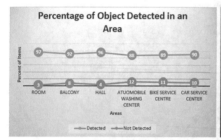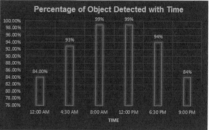

Fig. 8 Accuracy of object detection

against the different places and times of the day. The plot is shown in Fig. 8. As observed, the robot's accuracy in detecting objects is greater than 92%, which proves our robot is reliable and can be used for further developments.

7 Results

After training and testing, the proposed Wireless Surveillance robot shows promising results. The accuracy and its measure of precision for the data are collected using the following formulae:

- Calculating Accuracy
  Let,
  Accuracy in each observation be μ_x, where $x = 1, 2, 3, \ldots n$

$$\mu_x = 100\%\text{-Error Rate} \tag{1}$$

$$\text{Error Rate} = \frac{|\text{ Observed Value - Actual Value}|}{\text{Actual Value}} * 100 \tag{2}$$

Table 1 Accuracy and measure of precision

Experiment	Accuracy (%)	Precision (%)
Object detection in an area	92.00	(92 ± 3.41)
Object detection with respect to time	92.17	(92.17 ± 6.20)

$$\mu = \frac{\sum_{x=1}^{n} (\mu_x)}{n} \tag{3}$$

- Calculating its measure of precision

$$s = \frac{\text{Number of objects detected in an area}}{\text{Total Number of objects}} * 100 \tag{4}$$

$$\sigma = \sqrt{\frac{\sum (s - \mu)^2}{n}} \tag{5}$$

where,

Observed Value is Number of objects detected in an area.
Actual Value is Total Number of objects in an area.
μ is Overall accuracy of object detection
σ is Standard deviation
s is Percentage of object detected
n is Number of responses

The reported accuracy of object detection of the robot concerning area is 92%, which means that out of every 100 distinct object at different places, 92 distinct objects are detected, tracked as well as chased by the robot appropriately, and its measure of precision came out to be (92 ± 3.41)%.

The reported accuracy for object detection concerning the different times of the day is 92.17% i.e., out of every 100 distinct object at different times of the day, approximately 92 distinct objects were appropriately detected, tracked as well as chased by the robot and its measure of precision came out to be (92.17 ± 6.20)% (Table 1).

8 Conclusion

In this paper, a wireless surveillance robot for Industrial application is proposed. An algorithm is designed for the robot to detect the object and track its path by making "contrail" using its previous image and storing them with help of deque. With the help of this robot, we can monitor the real-time scenario of hazardous areas without any human source interference. The surveillance robot gives us live streaming video, image processing, object detection, and tracking according to the command given by the user on a PC/laptop through internet communication. It can also save and store the captured data with the name "Frame" in the cloud for future analysis.

9 Future Scope

This paper can be further used for military purposes to keep track of movements in specific areas. Its capabilities include fast communication, negligible human interference, multiple object tracking, and chasing as well as monitoring hazardous areas for safety and debugging. It can be used for guarding a designated area that has been designed for an assigned task. It can also be developed into a weapon if a Laser Gun is added to it. It can also be developed into a rover for space missions like Chandrayan-2, searching for life and water on the planet.

References

1. Ahmed HM, Rasheed RT (2020) A raspberry Pi real-time identification system on face recognition. In: 2020 1st information technology to enhance e-learning and other application (IT-ELA, pp 89–93. IEEE
2. Kumar D, Aadarsh S, Kumar H (2020) Border surveillance system using computer vision. In: 2020 6th international conference on advanced computing and communication systems (ICACCS), pp 623–628. IEEE
3. Mohammed JA, Paul A, Kumar A, Cherukuri J (2020) Implementation of human detection on raspberry Pi for smart surveillance. In: 2020 IEEE international conference for innovation in technology (INOCON), pp 1–8. IEEE
4. Kumar M, Raju KS, Kumar D, Goyal N, Verma S, Singh A (2021) An efficient framework using visual recognition for IoT based smart city surveillance. In: Multimedia tools and applications. Springer, New York
5. Sabri ZS, Li Z (2021) Low-cost intelligent surveillance system based on fast CNN. PeerJ Comput Sci 7:e402
6. Rao BN, Sudheer R, Sadhanala MA, Tibirisettti V, Muggulla S (2020) Movable surveillance camera using IoT and raspberry Pi. In: 2020 11th international conference on computing, communication and networking technologies (ICCCNT), pp 1–6. IEEE
7. Hashib H, Leon M, Salaque AM (2019) Object detection based security system using machine learning algorithm and raspberry Pi. In: 2019 international conference on computer, communication, chemical, materials and electronic engineering (IC4ME2), pp 1–4. IEEE
8. Rao BN, Sudheer R (2020) Surveillance camera using IoT and raspberry Pi. In: 2020 2nd international conference on inventive research in computing applications (ICIRCA), pp 1172–1176. IEEE
9. Zhang J, Song G, Qiao G, Meng T, Sun H (2011) An indoor security system with a jumping robot as the surveillance terminal. IEEE Trans Consum Electron 57(4)
10. Rakesh VS, Sreesh PR, George SN (2012) An improved real-time surveillance system for home security system using BeagleBoard SBC, Zigbee and FTP webserver. In: 2012 annual IEEE India conference (INDICON), pp 1240–1244. IEEE

11. Yang M-J, Jo YT, Wu D, Goh KH (2009) Cost effective IP camera for video surveillance. In: 2009 4th IEEE conference on industrial electronics and applications, pp 2432–2435. IEEE
12. Kim K, Bae S, Huh K (2010) Intelligent surveillance and security robot systems. In: 2010 IEEE workshop on advanced robotics and its social impacts, pp 70–73. IEEE

An Iterative Posterior Regularized NMF-Based Adaptive Wiener Filter for Speech Enhancement

Sivaramakrishna Yechuri and Sunny Dayal Vanambathina

1 Introduction

Numerous applications of signal processing, speech enhancement of noisy speech signals from various non-stationary interferences are strenuous work, and it is still an open challenge. Many statistical-based approaches are proposed for speech enhancement [1]. The benefit of statistical-based techniques is no need to consider any prior information. In these methods, we assume that both noise and speech signals are stationary. The performance of statistical approaches is poor under the non-stationary background noise conditions. Template-based techniques make use of specific sorts of prior speech or noise information. Typical statistics or patterns found from a speech or noise database can be used as prior knowledge. NMF is one of the most widely used approaches in this category. Under non-stationary conditions, the signals of speech and audio can be handled efficiently by using the NMF approach [2–4]. Since there is no restriction on assuming the nature of noise, those methods are more robust for non-stationary noise environments. The advantage of this method is that it uses both the statistical-based method and the template-based method. However, the output of the Wiener filter method becomes distorted since their model has no updates. The proposed method updates the model iteratively. In the machine learning and signal processing fields, NMF has held an eminent position over the last two decades. NMF is used in many applications, including spectral unmixing [4], face recognition [5], remote sensing image classification [6], and visual data mining [7], automatic speech recognition [8], and hearing assistive systems [9–11].

S. Yechuri (✉) · S. D. Vanambathina
School of Electronics Engineering, VIT-AP, Amaravati, India
e-mail: sivaramakrishna.20phd7163@vitap.ac.in

S. D. Vanambathina
e-mail: sunny.dayal@vitap.ac.in

In [12], frameworks impose general subspace constraints on NMF by augmenting the original objective function with two additional terms. In [13], the strategy of speech enhancement is to develop noise reduction filters to improve the level of accuracy in microcontroller speech recognition. Xiao et al. [14] exploited the embedded priors of speech and noise acoustic models used for speech enhancement. In [15], an NMF-based adaptive Wiener filtering noise reduction (NR) method regulates the source estimation errors of the Wiener filter and improves the speech quality by adjusting the base vector weights based on estimated noise and speech levels. The majority of the proposed NMF-based approaches that have improved the quality of speech contain the additional term regularization of the log-likelihood function (LLF) of the observed data. Defining the right penalty in the given latent model is one of the most important steps for incorporating the user-annotation constraint. The posterior regularization (PR) terms can be used to obtain the user annotations [16]. These annotations are incorporated into latent variable models in several ways, for instance, by using the regularization functions and expectation maximization (EM) algorithms. The authors of [16] propose using constraints based on user interaction, i.e., users need to manually select sources on the display of time–frequency sound. The spectrograms might be overlapping when the number of sources is large. It is very difficult to differentiate the sources manually. In such scenarios, it is inefficient to use the user interaction-based constraints approach.

To avoid the above-discussed problems, we propose a combination of an iterative posterior regularized NMF-based adaptive Wiener filter, and in the proposed method, first, construct the posterior model using the prior probabilities to adaptively update the penalties of the speech signal and noise signal contributions, and second, construct an adaptive Wiener filter method, utilizing the genetic algorithm to derive the adaptive factor (α) based on the estimated SNR level for the Wiener filter gain. The adaptive factor minimizes the estimation errors of the Wiener filter and improves the speech quality by adjusting the base vector weights based on estimated noise and speech levels. This kind of conjunction technique can provide a reasonable solution to the problem of single-channel speech enhancement when the resultant models fit the statistical features of the observed signals well enough.

The rest of the paper is organized as follows. In Sect. 2, the basic concepts of regularized NMF and adaptive Wiener filtering are discussed. In Sect. 3, a detailed explanation of the proposed iterative posterior regularized NMF-based adaptive Wiener filter method is given. In Sect. 4, the analysis of the result is discussed. Finally, Sect. 5 is the conclusion of the proposed work.

2 Regularized NMF and Adaptive Wiener Filtering

The noisy speech signal denotes $x(n)$ have n sample, and it consists as the sum of clean speech denotes $s(n)$ and noise distortion denotes $d(n)$.

$$x(n) = s(n) + d(n), \tag{1}$$

To obtain the spectral magnitude of the noisy speech spectrogram, first, apply the windowing technique to divide the noisy speech into a "t" number of parts, and each part has the same number of samples and the magnitude spectrum of each part. The noisy speech signal is estimated using the short-time Fourier transform (STFT) of the noisy speech signal represented as

$$|X(f, t)| = |S(f, t)| + |D(f, t)|, \tag{2}$$

where f indicates the bin of frequencies and t indicates the number of frames.

The magnitudes are found from the $|X(f, t)|$ and are represented in a matrix $X \in \mathbb{R}_+^{f \times t}$ of nonnegative elements. NMF is utilized for decomposition of multivariate data, to pursue the matrix factorization and divide X into a sum of multiplication of two smaller size nonnegative matrices, i.e., W and H.

$$X = WH = \sum_{Z=1}^{R} W_Z H_Z, \tag{3}$$

where the matrix $W = [w_1, w_2, ...w_R] \in \mathbb{R}_+^{f \times R}$, represents the columns containing the basis vectors and the matrix $H = [h_1^T, h_2^T, ...h_R^T,] \in \mathbb{R}_+^{R \times t}$ collects their respective weights, and R denotes the latent component number.

Mean square error (MSE) is used for the objective function minimization using Eq. (4), W and H obtained by reiterating the multiplicative update using Eqs. (5) and (6):

$$D(W, H) = \|X - WH\|_F^2, \tag{4}$$

$$W \leftarrow W. * \frac{ZH^T}{IH^T}, \tag{5}$$

$$H \leftarrow H. * \left(W^T Z\right), \tag{6}$$

$$Z = \frac{X}{\sum(WH)\Theta\Lambda}, \tag{7}$$

where Λ is penalties and ". *" is element-wise multiplication. The spectral magnitude of noise and clean speech is assumed as

$$X_N \approx W_N H_N, \tag{8}$$

$$X_S \approx W_S H_S, \tag{9}$$

The standard regularized NMF was performed to update the four base matrices iteratively using the multiplicative Eqs. (5) and (6). Finally, express estimated the noise and speech as

$$X'_S \approx W_s H_S, \tag{10}$$

$$X'_N \approx W_N H_N, \tag{11}$$

2.1 Adaptive Wiener

The adaptive Wiener method's [15] gain function is written as

$$\hat{G} = \frac{\widehat{X'_S}}{\alpha * \widehat{X'_S} + (1 - \alpha) * \widehat{X'_N}}, \tag{12}$$

where α is represented as an adaptive factor. When the testing conditions of the input SNR level are known, α can be predefined directly. Specifically, the scalar α is a weighting factor for reflecting the power ratio between the clean and noisy signals [15].

To avoid voice distortion, the maximum utilized value is 1 when the input SNR is larger than 20 dB. To prevent noise-induced disruptions, the lowest usable value is 0.05 when the input SNR is less than -5 dB. The equation of can be written as

$$\alpha = \begin{cases} 0.05, \, x \leq -5 \text{ dB} \\ 0.95x \frac{P(x) - p(-5 \text{ dB})}{P(20 \text{ dB}) - P(-5 \text{ dB})} + 0.05, & 20 \text{ dB} \geq x \geq -5 \text{ dB} \\ 1, x \geq 20 \text{ dB} \end{cases} \tag{13}$$

where x represented as input SNR. The input SNR value is calculated based on the X'_s and X'_N, which were obtained from the NMF. The P(x) is constructed using Eq. (13) is

$$p(x) = ax^2 + bx + c, \tag{14}$$

where the coefficients of a, b, and c are determined from the genetic algorithm (GA) [17]. The above polynomial function is compared with other polynomials; it provides good sound quality. GA utilized the bio-inspired operation; it consists of the following as crossover, mutation, and selection operations to provide a better solution for searching.

3 Iterative Posterior Regularized NMF-Based Adaptive Wiener Filter Method

The detailed block diagram of the proposed iterative posterior regularized NMF-based adaptive Wiener filter is shown in Fig. 1. The proposed method's key objective is to use an adaptation approach to alter the source models based on the actual features of the signals observed in the mix. The statistical prior information of the proposed method noise and speech signals is robust, and the user notations are replaced [16]. The prior distributions for magnitudes of noise and speech guide penalties that regularize the matrix factorization issue. Noise comes out from the mixture of many small unconstrained factors. So, the central limit theorem said that the mixture increases the resultant contribution Gaussian. In addition to the regime of non-asymptotic, the inequality of entropy power is a guarantee to increment the entropy power of finite mixture [18]. The Gaussian distribution model is powerful for the distorted signal since it has the highest entropy for the statistics of the first and second order.

The magnitude of noise samples is assumed to be chosen from the Gaussian distribution with scale parameter σ. The maximum likelihood function is fitted to the observed values is

$$f(x, \sigma) = \frac{x}{\sigma^2} e^{\frac{-x^2}{2\sigma^2}}, \tag{15}$$

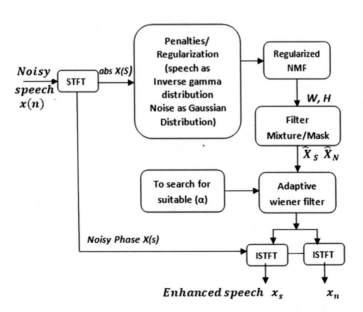

Fig. 1 Block diagram for iterative posterior regularized NMF-based adaptive Wiener filter

where $x \geq 0$ and $\sigma^2 = \frac{1}{2N} \sum_{i=1}^{N} x_i^2$

Equation (15) can be rewritten as

$$f(x; \sigma) = e^{\log\left(\frac{x}{\sigma^2}\right)} e^{\frac{-x^2}{2\sigma^2}} = e^{\log\left(\frac{x}{\sigma^2}\right) - \frac{x^2}{2\sigma^2}}, \tag{16}$$

Apply the negative logarithm on Eq. (16), we get

$$-\log(f(x; \sigma)) = -\log\left(e^{\log\left(\frac{x}{\sigma^2}\right) - \frac{x^2}{2\sigma^2}}\right) = \frac{x^2}{2\sigma^2} - \log\left(\frac{x}{\sigma^2}\right), \tag{17}$$

The regularization (penalty) term taken as prior distribution for noise magnitude of the signal is defined as

$$\Lambda_N = \Lambda_{S1} = -\log(f(x; \sigma)) = \frac{x^2}{2\sigma^2} - \log\left(\frac{x}{\sigma^2}\right), \tag{18}$$

The magnitude of the sample speech is equal to super-Gaussian [19], An inverse gamma distribution [20] is employed to adjust the shape and scale parameters. So, the speech signal magnitudes are distributed suitably to the inverse gamma; probability density function is defined as

$$f(x; \alpha, \beta) = \frac{\beta^\alpha}{\Gamma(\alpha)} \left(\frac{1}{x}\right)^{1+\alpha} e^{\left(\frac{-\beta}{x}\right)}, \tag{19}$$

where $x \geq 0$, shape parameter $\alpha \geq 0$, and scale parameter $\beta \geq 0$.

Apply the negative logarithm on Eq. (19), to get the regularization value of speech sample

$$\Lambda_{Sp} = \Lambda_{S2} = -\log(f(x; \sigma, \beta)) = \frac{\beta}{x} - \log\left(\frac{\beta^\alpha}{\Gamma(\alpha)} \left(\frac{1}{x}\right)^{\alpha+1}\right), \tag{20}$$

Algorithm 1: Iterative posterior regularized NMF-based adaptive Wiener filter.

Procedure

$\Lambda X \mathbb{R}_+^{f \times t}$ % Observed data

$\Lambda_S \in \mathbb{R}_+^{f \times t}, \quad S \in \{1 \dots N_S\}$ % Λ_S -penalties

$\Lambda_{S(NEW)} = 0,$

$\Lambda_{S1} = \Lambda_{N(OLD)} = \frac{x^2}{2\sigma^2} - log\left(\frac{x}{\sigma^2}\right), \tag{21}$

$\Lambda_{S2} = \Lambda_{Sp(OLD)} = \frac{\beta}{x} - log\left(\frac{\beta^\alpha}{\Gamma(\alpha)} \left(\frac{1}{x}\right)^{1+\alpha}\right), \tag{22}$

Reiteration

Algorithm 1: Iterative posterior regularized NMF-based adaptive Wiener filter.

For all s do

$$\hat{\Lambda}_{s(OLD)} \leftarrow \exp(\Lambda_S), \tag{23}$$

$$\hat{\Lambda}_s = (1 - \mu)\Lambda_{S(OLD)} + \mu\Lambda_{S(NEW)}, \% \text{ Update penalties using LMS} \tag{24}$$

$$\Lambda_{S(OLD)} = \Lambda_{S(NEW)}, \tag{25}$$

$$X_S \leftarrow X. * \hat{\Lambda}_S, \tag{26}$$

End For

$$\Gamma \leftarrow \sum_S (W_s H_s). * \hat{\Lambda}_S, \tag{27}$$

For all s do

$$Z_s \leftarrow \frac{X_S}{\Gamma}, \tag{28}$$

$$W_s \leftarrow W_s. * \frac{Z_s H_s^T}{1 H_s^T}, \tag{29}$$

$$H_s \leftarrow H_s. * \left(W_s^T Z_s\right), \tag{30}$$

End For

% Reconstruction

For all s do

$$M_s \leftarrow \frac{W_s H_s}{WH}, \%computefilter \tag{31}$$

$$\hat{X}_s \leftarrow M_s. * X, \% \text{ Filter Mixture} \tag{32}$$

$$\hat{G} = \frac{\widehat{X'_S}}{\alpha * \widehat{X'_S} + (1-\alpha) * \widehat{X'_N}}, \%\text{Adaptive gain} \tag{33}$$

$$\Lambda_{s_1} = \Lambda_{N(OLD)} = \frac{\hat{X}_{s_1}^2}{2\sigma^2} - log\left(\frac{\hat{X}_{s_1}}{\sigma^2}\right),$$

$$\Lambda_{S_2} = \Lambda_{SP(OLD)} = \frac{\beta}{\hat{X}_{S_2}} - log\left(\frac{\beta^\beta}{\Gamma(\alpha)}\left(\frac{1}{\hat{X}_{s_2}}\right)^{\alpha+1}\right),$$

$$\Lambda_{S(NEW)} = -\exp\left(\Lambda_{s(OLD)}\right), \tag{34}$$

% $\Lambda_{s(OLD)}$ represents both Λ_{SP} and Λ_N

$$x_s \leftarrow ISTFT\left(\hat{G}, \angle G, P\right), \tag{35}$$

End For

Until Convergence

Return Time-domain signals

The proposed adaptive iterative posterior regularized NMF method is summarized in Algorithm 1. It assures that the iteration operation descends using the majorization-minimization method [21] or the stationary point can converge [22]. This proposed method can be regarded as an upgrade version of PR and Wiener filter techniques, an adaptive iterative method that utilizes the prior probabilities to construct the posterior model for the noise and speech contributions and user notations restored by an automatic iterative procedure, and adaptive Wiener filter regulates the estimation errors based on adaptive factor.

In Algorithm 1, the penalties Λ_{SP} and Λ_N are magnitudes of speech and noise samples, respectively, assumed to be of inverse gamma and Gaussian distribution. Apply the negative exponential on the negative logarithms of the penalty terms Λ_{SP} and Λ_N, therefore the penalties suit corresponding PDFs, based on the small step size of the least mean squared method to improve the penalties. The observed noise and speech data are separately multiplied with each updated penalty [23].

The new posterior regularization is obtained utilizing the Eqs. (30) and (31). Basis of W and H is adaptively updated using Eqs. (29) and (30). Ms computed the filter matrix using Eq. (31). Adaptive Wiener gain is calculated based on adaptive factor α using the Eq. (33). Inverse STFT employed on the adaptive Wiener filter output with the input mixture phase to get the improved speech signal in the time domain using the Eq. (35). In Algorithm 1, subscript s represents the rows or columns of the corresponding matrix of the assigned source and the matrix of ones represents 1 with suitable dimensions.

4 Experimental Results

We conducted several experiments to get the high-level quality of source enhancement using different NMF methods. Samples for various speech and noise signals are collected from NOIZEUS. In NOIZEUS, various algorithms will be used to evaluate the speech enhancement algorithms [24]. A database consisting of audio source samples of males and females which have a sampling rate of 8 kHz will be considered. Hanning window is applied to speech signal consisting of noise to divide each window length of 1024 samples which will be in the time domain. STFT is used to convert each window sample from the time domain to the frequency domain which uses an overlap of 75%. Out of the available magnitude spectrum, 200 samples of speech and noise are considered which form the basis vectors. An experimental implementation is performed by taking into account the different input SNR's conditions (-3, 0, 5, and 10 dB). The inverse gamma distribution is applied to produce speech and noise penalties Λ_{sp}, Λ_n. This proposed method has the advantage that the priors are adaptively updated iteratively. The μ value is assumed to be 0.001. This iteration of the algorithm takes place until it converges.

The objective evaluations were performed on the noisy speech signal $x(n)$ in presence of three non-stationary noises (babble, street, restaurant) and one stationary noise signal (white noise) at different input SNR, of $-3, 0, 5,$ and 10 dB. The proposed method was compared with Euclidean NMF (EUC-NMF) [2], the constrained version of NMF (CNMF) [4], adaptive Wiener NMF (AW-NMF) [15], and PR-NMF [16]. Averaged values of PESQ [25], STOI [26], and SDR [27] metrics were used to evaluate the performance of the suggested approach. Higher value shows better performance for PESQ, STOI, and SDR.

The values of PESQ, STOI, and SDR of the various NMF examined are shown in Tables 1, 2, and 3. The experimental findings demonstrate that the proposed technique outperforms the existing benchmark methods in terms of the PESQ, STOI, and SDR indices.

5 Conclusion

For single-channel speech enhancement, an iterative posterior regularized NMF-based adaptive Wiener filter algorithm is suggested. The magnitude spectra of noise and speech are modeled employing Gaussian and inverse gamma distributions. To regularize the NMF cost function, the appropriate log-likelihood functions are utilized as penalties. The suggested regularization of multiplicative updating methods is used to compute the estimate of basis and weight matrices. To regulate the noise estimation error, an adaptive Wiener filter is used. The adaptive wiener gain depends on the adaptive factor, which is calculated using a genetic algorithm. The experimental results show that the proposed speech enhancement approach outperforms previous benchmark approaches in terms of PESQ, STOI, and SDR values.

Table 1 Proposed method compared with existing methods in terms of SDR values at different input SNR in presence of different noise conditions

Input SNR	Noise type	EC-NMF [2]	CNMF [4]	PR-NMF [22]	AW-NMF [21]	Proposed method
−3	White	0.63	0.75	1.02	1.25	2.01
0		1.13	1.29	1.57	1.92	2.98
5		2.21	2.56	2.84	3.12	4.36
10		2.36	2.89	2.96	3.32	4.71
−3	Babble	0.29	0.36	0.45	0.75	1.46
0		1.23	1.36	1.45	2.56	3.05
5		1.65	1.75	1.89	2.67	3.32
10		1.89	1.95	2.14	2.86	3.53
−3	Street	0.98	1.26	1.49	1.68	2.47
0		0.62	0.86	1.29	1.73	2.31
5		1.32	1.65	1.94	2.61	3.91
10		1.45	1.98	2.12	2.85	3.98
−3	Restaurant	0.65	0.78	0.81	0.98	1.15
0		1.19	1.34	1.47	1.72	2.33
5		1.36	1.49	1.68	2.34	2.95
10		1.84	1.83	2.16	2.69	3.67

Table 2 Proposed method compared with existing methods in terms of STOI values at different input SNR in presence of different noise conditions

Input SNR	Noise type	EC-NMF [2]	CNMF [4]	PR-NMF [22]	AW-NMF [21]	Proposed method
−3	White	0.451	0.512	0.542	0.589	0.63
0		0.462	0.526	0.561	0.611	0.67
5		0.489	0.561	0.595	0.636	0.70
10		0.512	0.547	0.576	0.649	0.69
−3	Babble	0.414	0.515	0.543	0.56	0.58
0		0.51	0.529	0.541	0.584	0.64
5		0.487	0.534	0.56	0.61	0.67
10		0.495	0.581	0.595	0.63	0.69
−3	Street	0.427	0.524	0.557	0.57	0.60
0		0.452	0.496	0.524	0.579	0.62
5		0.471	0.486	0.534	0.584	0.66
10		0.483	0.497	0.547	0.597	0.68
−3	Restaurant	0.398	0.496	0.514	0.564	0.60
0		0.419	0.486	0.543	0.593	0.64
5		0.431	0.469	0.497	0.576	0.68
10		0.481	0.546	0.598	0.625	0.84

Table 3 Proposed method compared with existing methods in terms of PESQ values at different input SNR in presence of different noise conditions

Input SNR	Noise type	EC-NMF [2]	CNMF [4]	PR-NMF [22]	AW-NMF [21]	Proposed method
−3	White	0.62	0.86	0.91	1.14	1.55
0		0.79	0.91	1.21	1.36	1.59
5		0.81	1.16	1.31	1.48	1.80
10		0.76	0.88	0.99	1.27	1.79
−3	Babble	0.87	0.94	1.27	1.34	1.69
0		0.67	0.96	1.37	1.61	1.90
5		0.84	0.97	1.29	1.68	2.11
10		0.94	1.21	1.42	1.64	1.89
−3	Street	0.79	0.94	1.29	1.49	1.81
0		0.74	0.89	1.31	1.51	1.81
5		0.68	0.76	0.94	1.34	1.69
10		0.81	0.88	0.97	1.47	1.86
−3	Restaurant	0.83	0.98	1.28	1.62	1.98

(continued)

Table 3 (continued)

Input SNR	Noise type	EC-NMF [2]	CNMF [4]	PR-NMF [22]	AW-NMF [21]	Proposed method
0		0.94	1.04	1.41	1.68	1.95
5		0.99	1.20	1.37	1.69	1.85
10		0.91	1.18	1.33	1.57	1.83

References

1. Ephraim Y, Malah D (1984) Speech enhancement using a minimum-mean square error short-time spectral amplitude estimator. IEEE Trans Acoust Speech Signal Process 32(6):1109–1121
2. Lee D, Seung HS (2001) Algorithms for non-negative matrix factorization. In: Advances in neural information processing systems, pp 556–562
3. Févotte C, Bertin N, Durrieu JL (2009) Nonnegative matrix factorization with the Itakura-Saito divergence: With application to music analysis. Neural Comput 21(3):793–830
4. Berry MW, Browne M, Langville AN, Pauca VP, Plemmons RJ (2007) Algorithms and applications for approximate nonnegative matrix factorization. Comput Stat Data Anal 52(1):155–173
5. Chen WS, Zhao Y, Pan B, Chen B (2016) Supervised kernel nonnegative matrix factorization for face recognition. Neurocomputing 165–181
6. Han M, Liu B (2015) Ensemble of extreme learning machine for remote sensing image classification. Neurocomputing 149:65–70
7. Babaee M, Tsoukalas S, Rigoll G, Datcu M (2016) Immersive visualization of visual data using nonnegative matrix factorization. Neurocomputing 173:245–255
8. Su Y-C, Tsao Y, Wu J-E, Jean F-R (2013) Speech enhancement using generalized maximum a posteriori spectral amplitude estimator. In: Proceedings ICASSP, pp 7467–7471
9. Lai Y-H, Su Y-C, Tsao Y, Young ST (2013) Evaluation of generalized maximum a posteriori spectral amplitude (GMAPA) speech enhancement algorithm in hearing aids. In: Proceeding IEEE International Symposium Consumer Electronics (ISCE), pp 245–246
10. Chen F, Hu Y, Yuan M (2015) Evaluation of noise reduction methods for sentence recognition by mandarin-speaking cochlear implant listeners. Ear Hearing 36(1):61–71
11. Chen J, Wang Y, Yoho SE, Wang D, Healy EW (2016) Large-scale training to increase speech intelligibility for hearing-impaired listeners in novel noises. J Acoust Soc Amer 139(5):2604–2612
12. Liu Y, Liao Y, Tang L, Tang F, Liu W (2016) General subspace constrained non-negative matrix factorization for data representation. Neurocomputing 173:224–232
13. Chan KY, Nordholm S, Yiu KFC, Togneri R (2013) Speech enhancement strategy for speech recognition microcontroller under noisy environments. Neurocomputing 118:279–288
14. Xiao X, Lee P, Nickel RM (2009) Inventory-based speech enhancement for speaker dedicated speech communication systems. In: IEEE international conference on acoustics, speech and signal processing, IEEE, pp 3877–3880
15. Lai YH, Wang SS, Chen CH, Jhang SH (2019) Adaptive wiener gain to improve sound quality on nonnegative matrix factorization-based noise reduction system. IEEE Access 43286–43297
16. Bryan, N. J., & Mysore, G. J.: An Efficient Posterior Regularized Latent Variable Model for Interactive Sound Source Separation. In ICML (3). pp. 208–216. (June 2013).
17. Holland JH (1992) Adaptation in natural and artificial systems: an introductory analysis with applications to biology, control, and artificial intelligence. MIT Press, Cambridge, MA, USA
18. Cruces S, Cichocki A, Amari S (2004) From blind signal extraction to blind instantaneous signal separation: criteria, algorithms, and stability. IEEE Trans Neural Netw 15(4):859–873

19. Erkelens JS, Hendriks RC, Heusdens R, Jensen J (2007) Minimum mean-square error estimation of discrete Fourier coefficients with generalized Gamma priors. IEEE Trans Audio Speech Lang Process 15(6):1741–1752
20. Kounades-Bastian D, Girin L, Alameda-Pineda X, Gannot S, Horaud R (2016) An inverse-gamma source variance prior with factorized parameterization for audio source separation. In: IEEE international conference on acoustics, speech and signal processing (ICASSP), pp. 136–140
21. Cichocki A, Cruces S, Amari SI (2011) Generalized alpha-beta divergences and their application to robust nonnegative matrix factorization. Entropy 13(1):134–170
22. Lin CJ (2007) On the convergence of multiplicative update algorithms for nonnegative matrix factorization. IEEE Trans Neural Netw 18(6):1589–1596
23. Sunnydayal, Kumar K, Cruces S (2016) An iterative posterior NMF method for speech enhancement in the presence of additive Gaussian noise. Neurocomputing 312–315
24. NOIZEUS: A noisy speech corpus for evaluation of speech enhancement algorithms: http://ecs.utdallas.edu/loizou/speech/noizeus/
25. Hu Y, Loizou PC (2008) Evaluation of objective quality measures for speech enhancement. IEEE Trans Audio Speech Lang Process 16(1):229–238
26. Vincent E, Gribonval R, Févotte C (2006) Performance measurement in blind audio source separation. IEEE Trans Audio Speech Lang Process 14(4):1462–1469
27. Taal CH, Hendriks RC, Heusdens R, Jensen J (June 2010) A short-time objective intelligibility measure for time-frequency weighted noisy speech. In: IEEE international conference on acoustics, speech and signal processing, pp 4217–4217

ADASemSeg: An Active Learning Based Data Adaptation Strategy for Improving Cross Dataset Breast Tumor Segmentation

Arnab Kumar Mishra, Pinki Roy, Sivaji Bandyopadhyay, and Sujit Kumar Das

1 Introduction

Breast cancer is the most common type of cancer among women, with above 2 million reported cases in the year 2020 itself, according to the World Health Organization[1]. Such kind of statistics suggests that the application of ideas stemming from the recent advancements in machine learning (ML) and deep learning(DL) must be studied so that adequate data-driven decision support can be provided to the involved medical professionals. Recently, several researchers have considered the problem of automatic breast cancer detection and classification by analyzing breast ultrasound(BUS) images, as it is a non-invasive and non-radioactive imaging modality with relatively easy access [1–3]. Although several such sophisticated approaches are present in the current literature on BUS tumor detection and classification, one severe limitation still exists in all of these works regarding the deployment of trained ML and DL models in a new diagnostic setting with different ultrasound machines and radiologists. This limitation is that a model trained on data samples from one center often fails to attain the same levels of high efficiency when tested on data samples from a new and different center. This is primarily because the data distribution in the new center might be very different from the one on which the predictive model has been previously trained, as the ultrasound imaging system might be different, radiologists are different, and also significant levels of operator bias might be present as supported by the previous research works [4, 5]. In this work, we propose a novel active learning (AL)-based strategy ADASemSeg to solve this problem. The main idea is to actively interact with an Expert/Oracle to effectively adapt a BUS tumor segmentation model to new settings.

---

[1] https://www.who.int/news-room/fact-sheets/detail/breast-cancer.

A. K. Mishra (✉) · P. Roy · S. Bandyopadhyay · S. K. Das
Department of CSE, National Institute of Technology Silchar, Silchar, Assam 788010, India
e-mail: arnab.mishra.1992@gmail.com

The recent developments in the areas of artificial intelligence (AI), machine learning (ML), and computer vision(CV) have revolutionized the field of medical diagnosis by providing adequate data-driven approaches for automatic disease detection [6–12]. With respect to the problem of BUS tumor detection also, similar advances have been observed especially using the encoder–decoder-based semantic segmentation approaches. The authors in [13] have proposed to solve the problem of breast US tumor segmentation with the help of three CNN-based networks, patch-based LeNet, UNet, and transfer learning based on FCN-AlexNet. The FCN-AlexNet-based approach was found to be the best for the segmentation task according to F1-score-based evaluation. In [14], the authors have proposed a modified UNet-based approach, where apart from the original BUS images, visual saliency maps are also provided as input. With this approach, the authors obtained impressive dice similarity scores(> 0.9) on a privately collected dataset. Another modified UNet model for BUS tumor segmentation has been proposed by the authors in [15], where several components like residual skip connections, attention gate modules, and dilated convolutional layers are incorporated in the UNet architecture. With these modifications, above 80% segmentation performances were observed on a privately collected dataset. In [16], the authors have considered the problem of detecting small tumors in BUS images by having multiple paths in a UNet like architecture, with each path having different convolutional kernel sizes. With this multi-path approach, the authors obtained impressive intersection over union (IoU) scores of 0.85 and 0.7 on two publicly available datasets. However, none of the above techniques focuses on improving the cross dataset training and inference related problem. In fact, the authors of [13] have also stated in their work that training in one dataset and testing in another reduces performance significantly. Since solution to such a problem is critical to deploy learned models in real diagnostic scenarios, appropriate data adaptation strategies need to be developed. This is where the field of active learning (AL) can be beneficial since it deals with data adaptation-based ML approaches where labeled data is scarce. This idea of an AL-based solution to the data scarcity problem has been explored up to some extent for related problems like skin lesion detection [17] and prostate MRI segmentation [18]. In a recent medical image segmentation work [19], the authors have applied query-by-committee-based active learning approach for performing segmentation of hippocampus MRI scans and pancreas CT scans. The idea of active learning-based brain tumor segmentation has been explored in [20], where uncertainty driven learning strategies are proposed which are able to obtain impressive data labeling cost reduction. The researchers in [21] studied the importance of segmentation uncertainty in the process of label efficient active learning, where the importance of active learning for reducing labeling cost is highlighted. However, the data adaptation problem specifically for BUS tumor segmentation has not yet been explored by the previous works. Motivated by such observations from the literature review, we proposed a novel AL-based data adaptation approach, which can deal with the data adaptation problem in a cross dataset/center setting.

More specifically, an active data adaptation-based semantic segmentation (ADASemSeg) strategy is proposed in this work, where a large-sized labeled BUS tumor segmentation dataset is considered as the source dataset where the initial model building is to be performed, and a smaller unlabeled dataset is considered as a target dataset to which the model needs to be adapted. This target dataset represents a different data distribution from the source dataset, and it can be assumed to correspond to a different diagnostic center and its imaging setup. The main idea of ADASemSeg is to actively interact with a domain expert (radiologist) for a few rounds of a small number of ground truth labeling of informative samples that are representative of the target data distribution, and the model is currently confused about. The model can be updated with such an iterative adaptation approach to achieve significantly better performances on the target data distribution. The following points can summarize the main contributions of this work.

- A novel strategy ADASemSeg is proposed in this work for cross dataset/center BUS tumor segmentation, which employs an active learning-based approach.
- A bootstrapping and mutual dice loss-based uncertainty quantification approach is proposed in ADASemSeg, which can help select Oracle query samples with high segmentation uncertainty.
- A tumor segmentation-specific sample representativeness scoring approach is proposed that can help select Oracle query samples with high representativeness of the entire target data distribution with respect to the task of tumor segmentation.

The rest of the paper is organized as follows. Firstly, in Sect. 2, some background knowledge is provided on encoder–decoder-based semantic segmentation approaches and also the ideas behind the active learning process. Followed by this, in Sect. 3, the dataset descriptions and proposed methodology are presented in rigorous detail. After this, the experimental setup is discussed concisely in Sect. 4. The experimental results and discussion are presented next in Sect. 5. Finally, the paper is concluded in Sect. 6, with a summary of the findings and potential future research directions.

2 Background

2.1 Semantic Segmentation

The problem of semantic segmentation of images can be seen as a mapping problem from an input image to an output segmentation map that highlights the regions/objects of interest present in the input image. More formally, given an input image $\mathbb{R}^{H \times W \times C}$, the goal is to generate a mask image $\mathbb{R}^{H \times W \times C'}$ by learning a mapping $f : \mathbb{R}^{H \times W \times C} \rightarrow \mathbb{R}^{H \times W \times C'}$ where the number of channels in the input image(C) and the generated mask(C') may or may not be identical. The recent advances in DL have shown that encoder–decoder-based semantic segmentation approaches work quite well in various domains. The main idea of these encoder–decoder like architectures in that the input image is passed through several layers of 2D convolution and pooling operations to arrive at an abstract representation of the input image that can capture the key concepts present in the image. This is called the encoding stage. Considering the goal to learn the mapping f, the encoding stage produces a latent representation of the form $\mathbb{R}^{H' \times W' \times C''}$ where typically the following inequalities hold- $H' < H$, $W' < W$, and $C < C'' > C'$. After this, the decoding stage makes use of transpose convolution and upsampling layers (and possible direct skip connections from encoding layers) to get the final segmentation map $\mathbb{R}^{H \times W \times C'}$. This entire process can be learned in an end-to-end manner by optimizing the loss between the predicted and desired maps with the help of a training dataset. Several effective encoder–decoder-based semantic segmentation models have been proposed in the CV literature [22–25], out of which the popular UNet model [22] is utilized as the underlying predictive model for ADASemSeg.

2.2 Active Learning

Active learning (AL) is a field of ML that deals with the problem of lack of labeled data. Often the process of data labeling is very time-consuming and expensive for many domains, which is especially true for the medical imaging field. To deal with such scenarios, AL approaches can be utilized where the main idea is that active interactions with domain experts can be included in the model training phase so that predictive modeling can be performed for more critical and informative samples. This also allows for better generalization of the model with minimal sample complexity.

Given access to a dataset $D_1 = \{(x_1, y_1), (x_2, y_2), \ldots, (x_p, y_p), x_{p+1}, \ldots x_{p+q}\}$, where p is usually very small, the goal of AL is to carry out a few rounds r of expert interactions in the form of Oracle query on k(budget) selected informative samples from the subset $\{x_{p+1}, x_{p+2}, \ldots, x_{p+q}\}$ for ground truth labeling. The samples labeled in round r_i are then to be considered as part of the supervised set of samples. The selection of k samples in r_i for Oracle query typically depends on two factors, predictive uncertainty(U) and sample representativeness(R). For each unlabeled sample $x_j \in D_1$, a query worthiness score is calculated as specified by a function $S(x_j) = g(R(x_j), U(x_j))$ where $g(\bullet)$ is a function that combines the uncertainty and representativeness of x_j in some specific manner. The U part tells AL how uncertain the current model is about its prediction on x_j and the R part tells AL how representative is x_j of the entire set of data points in D_1 according to the current model. With this worthiness measure $S(x_j)$, the unlabeled samples can now be ranked in the decreasing order to select the top k for Oracle query. Once these samples are labeled, D_1 is modified to include these new labels for the corresponding samples. A new predictive model is then trained on the new D_1 to arrive at an improved model. This process can be repeated r times to arrive at better and better models iteratively. This approach has shown to do quite well in several medical imaging problems, a detailed discussion for which can be found at [26].

3 Data and Methods

3.1 Dataset Description

Two publicly available datasets are utilized in this work to evaluate the proposed active data adaptation approach experimentally. The labeled source dataset considered for this work is the BUSI dataset [27], which consists of 487 benign and 210 malignant BUS samples along with their ground truth tumor segmentation masks. This source dataset is to be used for the initial model building before adaptation. On the other hand, the UDIAT dataset [13] consisting of 110 benign and 53 malignant samples is considered as the target dataset to which the semantic segmentation model is to be adapted to. Some of the representative samples from both the datasets, along with their tumor segmentation masks, are shown in Fig. 1. The selection of these two datasets for experimentation is especially appropriate for the current work due to the following reasons:

- Both the datasets have been collected in different diagnostic centers (BUSI: Baheya Hospital Egypt; UDIAT: UDIAT Diagnostic Centre of the Parc Taulí Corporation, Sabadell, Spain).
- The BUS samples have been collected using different types of ultrasound systems (BUSI: LOGIQ E9 ultrasound system; UDIAT: Siemens ACUSON Sequoia C512 system).
- Different radiologists with potentially different levels of expertise were involved in the ground truth segmentation mask generation process.
- Baseline experimentations show that when deep semantic segmentation model training is performed on the BUSI dataset and is directly used the trained model for inference on the UDIAT dataset samples, a significant reduction in segmentation performance can be observed($\sim 20\%$).

3.2 Proposed Methodology

An active data adaptation-based semantic segmentation (ADASemSeg) approach is proposed in this work to improve the BUS tumor segmentation performance in a cross dataset setting. ADASemSeg makes use of AL-based ideas to actively adapt to a new data distribution for performing encoder–decoder-based semantic segmentation. The high-level workflow diagram of ADASemSeg is depicted in Fig. 2.

The ADASemSeg approach is iterative in nature, where an initial model trained on a source dataset(D_s) is adapted to a target dataset (D_t) round-after-round by improving the dataset it learns from via AL. Before the start of AL rounds, only the original D_s is used for model building; however, in each round, the source dataset gets modified to include a few intelligently selected Oracle labeled samples from D_t. In each round, the models trained on the current D_s help determine which samples from

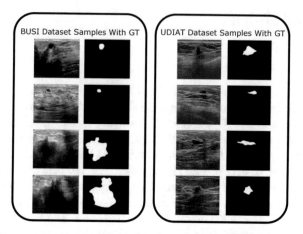

Fig. 1 Some BUS samples along with their ground truth (G.T.) from the BUSI and UDIAT datasets

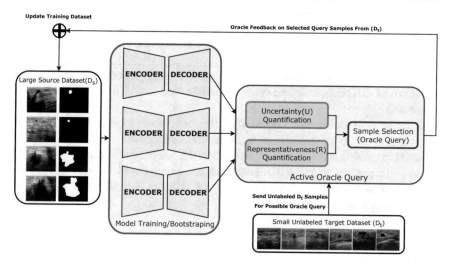

Fig. 2 High-level overview of the proposed ADASemSeg approach

D_t the models are highly under-confident about and how representative these samples are of the entire data distribution of D_t. Based on such assessment, the top k (budget) samples with the highest Oracle query worthiness scores are selected for ground truth (G.T) labeling by the Oracle. These newly labeled samples are then added back to D_s so that a better predictive modeling can be performed in the next round. The entire step-by-step process of ADASemSeg approach is depicted in algorithm 1.

Algorithm 1: ADASemSeg Algorithm

Input : Labeled Source Dataset: $D_s = \{(x_1^s, y_1^s), (x_2^s, y_2^s), \ldots, (x_n^s, y_n^s)\}$
Unlabeled Target Dataset: $D_t = \{x_1^t, x_2^t, \ldots, x_m^t\}$
ADASemSeg budget per round: k
ADASemSeg total no. of rounds: r

Output: Final semantic segmentation model ϕ adapted from D_s to D_t via ADASemSeg

1 **for** i *in range* 1 *to* r **do**

2 | Train 3 different models ϕ_1, ϕ_2 and ϕ_3 on 3 different train/val. splits of D_s

3 | totalScores = [ ] /* To store oracle query worthiness scores for each sample.   */

4 | **for** *each sample* $x_j^t \in D_t$ **do**

5 | | $y_{1j}^t = \phi_1(x_j^t); y_{2j}^t = \phi_2(x_j^t); y_{3j}^t = \phi_3(x_j^t)$

   | | /* Uncertainty(U) quantification using Dice loss.   */

6 | | $U = \frac{(Dice(y_{1j}^t, y_{2j}^t) + Dice(y_{1j}^t, y_{3j}^t) + Dice(y_{2j}^t, y_{3j}^t))}{3}$

   | | /* For Representativeness(R) quantification, find vectorized latent representations of x_j^t from Encoder parts, via ϕ_1^{Enc}, ϕ_2^{Enc} and ϕ_3^{Enc} */

7 | | $l_{1j}^t = \phi_1^{Enc}(x_j^t); l_{2j}^t = \phi_2^{Enc}(x_j^t); l_{3j}^t = \phi_3^{Enc}(x_j^t)$

8 | | cosScores = [ ] /* To store cosine similarity scores against every other sample   */

9 | | **for** *each sample* $x_p^t \in D_t$ *where* $x_p^t \neq x_j^t$ **do**

10 | | | $l_{1p}^t = \phi_1^{Enc}(x_p^t); l_{2p}^t = \phi_2^{Enc}(x_p^t); l_{3p}^t = \phi_3^{Enc}(x_p^t)$

11 | | | cosScores.append($\frac{(Sim(l_{1j}^t, l_{1p}^t) + Sim(l_{2j}^t, l_{2p}^t) + Sim(l_{3j}^t, l_{3p}^t))}{3}$)

12 | | **end**

13 | | $R = Average(cosScores)$

14 | | totalScores.append($\frac{(U+R)}{2}$)

15 | **end**

16 | Sort all samples $x_j^t \in D_t$ in decreasing order of scores according to totalScores.

17 | Pick top k samples and query Oracle for ground truths.

18 | Update D_s with these newly labeled samples.

19 **end**

20 Return final model ϕ trained on the updated D_s after r rounds.

From the ADASemSeg algorithm, it can be seen that to determine the predictive uncertainty(U) of a sample, the idea of bootstrapping on different training subsets of D_s and prediction on D_t is used, followed by an averaging of the mutual dice loss of individual model predictions. This calculation ensures that the differences among predictions by models trained on separate training subsets are captured, which is essentially the predictive uncertainty of the sample. Two examples of uncertainty scoring are depicted in Fig. 3, where the scores obtained for a sample with very high predictive uncertainty and also a sample with very low predictive uncertainty are shown in the first and the second rows, respectively.

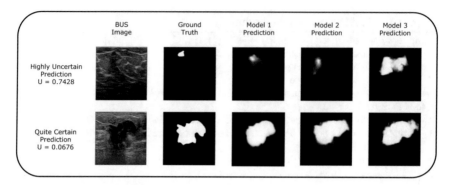

Fig. 3 Uncertainty quantification example

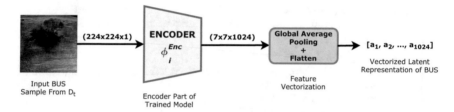

Fig. 4 Extraction of vectorized latent representation of BUS from Encoder part(ϕ_i^{Enc}) of trained model (ϕ_i)

Apart from uncertainty quantification, quantifying a sample's representativeness(R) is also very important. We need to select samples that are the most similar to the other samples in D_t, and the G.T labels for such samples can prove to be highly informative for data adaptation. This representativeness quantification is performed in this work by first passing the input image x_j^t through the individual models and extracting the encoder part's vectorized latent representation as shown in Fig. 4. Once these vectorized representations are available for each sample in D_t, we can find the cosine similarity-based representativeness of each sample with respect to every other sample in D_t. Finally, R is computed by taking the average of all cosine similarity scores as shown in Algorithm 1. The overall worthiness scoring can then be performed by taking the average of U and R for each sample, and top k samples that are the most uncertain and the most representative of D_t can be chosen for Oracle query. In the next round, the modified D_s can be used for model training, which now consists of some intelligently selected labeled samples from D_t as well.

At the end of r rounds, a final model ϕ can be trained on the updated D_s, which can be used for inference. We hypothesize that this model ϕ can make efficient predictions on unseen samples from the data distribution of D_t since it has adapted itself to this target distribution via active learning.

4 Experimental Setup

The entire experimental setup has been mentioned in a point-by-point manner below:

- For the purpose of experimentally evaluating the data adaptation capabilities of the proposed ADASemSeg approach, we have considered the BUSI dataset as the source dataset(D_s) on which the initial model training is performed and the UDIAT dataset as the target dataset(D_t) to which we want to adapt the predictive model.
- The encoder–decoder architecture considered in this work is the popular UNet model [22], with a ResNet34 backbone. The model training is performed using an Adam optimizer(lr = 0.001) for 500 epochs with an early-stopping patience of 100 epochs and training batch size of 16.
- All the performance evaluation is performed with the help of 20% randomly chosen test samples from D_t. The reported results are averaged over five such randomly sampled test sets of D_t.
- For bootstrapping, the three model $\phi_1, \phi_2,$ and ϕ_3 are trained on 3 different 80–20 train/validation splits of the samples in D_s.
- The experimental results are shown for $r = 1, 2, \ldots, 5$ and $k = 3, 4, 5$, in terms of dice similarity scores.
- The proposed approach (henceforth called as ADASemSeg-(U+R)) is compared against several baselines which are described below:

  - **No ADASemSeg**: This is a baseline which corresponds to the direct test set inference of model learned on the original D_s, without any ADASemSeg rounds.
  - **ADASemSeg-(Random)**: In this baseline, the data adaptation is performed by picking random k samples in each round. No uncertainty and representativeness quantification are performed here.
  - **ADASemSeg-(U)**: This baseline performs ADASemSeg by picking the top k samples with the most predictive uncertainty in each round. No representativeness quantification is taken into account here.
  - **ADASemSeg-(R)**: This baseline considers only representativeness quantification for picking top k samples in each round of ADASemSeg.

5 Results and Discussion

The round-wise average test dice similarity scores for the proposed approach with $k = 5$ is given in Table 1, along with No ADASemSeg and ADASemSeg-(Random) baselines. From the table, it is clear that the proposed approach can help improve the performance on the target dataset, achieving an average improvement of $\sim$25% and $\sim$12% compared to No ADASemSeg and ADASemSeg-(Random) approaches, respectively. Moreover, it can be observed that with just one round of active learning, the proposed approach can achieve $\sim$12% improvement on the segmentation task.

Table 1 Round-wise segmentation performances of the proposed approach($k = 5$), compared to simple baseline models

	Round-wise dice scores					Final scores
	Round1	Round2	Round3	Round4	Round5	
No ADASemSeg	–	–	–	–	–	0.4763
ADASemSeg-(Random)	0.4899	0.5237	0.5518	0.5697	0.6003	0.6003
ADASemSeg-(U+R)	**0.6026**	**0.6483**	**0.6583**	**0.6787**	**0.7261**	**0.7261**

Fig. 5 Segmentation dice score results for ADASemSeg variants for budget $k = 5$

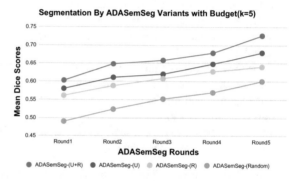

Fig. 6 Segmentation dice score results for ADASemSeg variants for budget $k = 4$

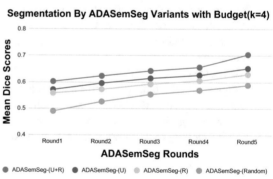

The round-wise test set performance comparisons of proposed ADASemSeg-(U+R) approach with other baselines are shown in Figs. 5, 6, and 7 for budget $k = 5, 4$, and 3, respectively. The improvements in mean dice scores in quite evident from these line charts across all the different budgets.

Some of the key observations from these figures are mentioned below:

- Having larger budget gives better data adaptation performance on the target dataset.
- Having more rounds of active learning makes the ADASemSeg process more effective in adapting to the target dataset.

Fig. 7 Segmentation dice score results for ADASemSeg variants for budget $k = 3$

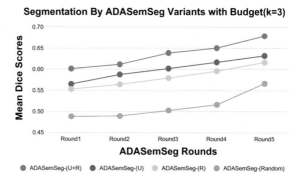

- Individually, ADASemSeg-(U) performs better data adaptation than ADASemSeg-(R), suggesting that uncertainty quantification is more important than representativeness quantification. However, when both of them are combined in ADASemSeg-(U+R), much better performances can be observed.
- Even with very few rounds and small budgets, significant improvements can be observed, demonstrating the proposed approach's usefulness.

A quick formal analysis of Algorithm 1 shows that if there are r rounds and m samples in D_t train set, then the time complexity of Algorithm 1 is $O(rm^2)$. However, this does not reflect the actual time taken in practice since several factors need to be taken into account like-

- Usually both r and m will be a very small.
- Training deep semantic segmentation models for bootstrapping is dependent upon the training epochs and other such settings.
- The calculation of U and R values also involves model predictions which might themselves be time taking.

Because of these reasons, we also present the average time taken in practice for one round with the help of Table 2. As given in the table, for a D_t train set of size ~100, the proposed approach takes ~36 min on an average per round. The majority of the time taken is due to the model training involved in the bootstrapping step. This time calculation heavily depends on the implementation system configuration. As all the experimentations in this work are performed on a publicly available single GPU system provided by Kaggle[2], with more powerful systems, this total time can be reduced significantly. Nevertheless, the actual inference on the samples from target data distribution is still quite fast, since the entire ADASemSeg process can be performed in offline mode and is a one-time expense for adapting to the new setting. In real diagnostic settings, such a one-time expense is acceptable if the model can be effectively adapted to the new environment for accurate and fast future inference.

Some of the sample test time predictions by the proposed approach are presented in Fig. 8, which shows its adaptive power as compared to the No ADASemSeg baseline.

---

[2] www.kaggle.com.

Table 2 Average per round time taken by ADASemSeg-(U+R) process

Steps per round	Time taken(s)
ϕ_1 training	545.83
ϕ_2 training	537.15
ϕ_3 training	542.13
Uncertainty quantification	0.55
Representativeness quantification	561.28
Total	2186.93

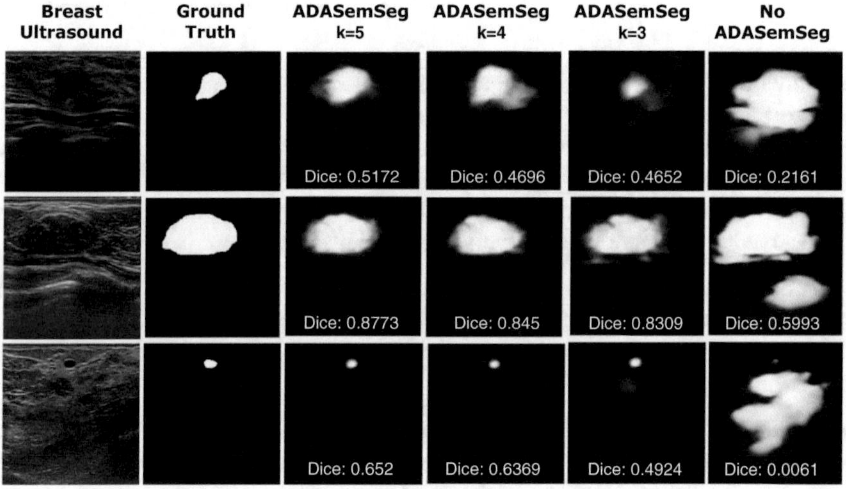

Fig. 8 Sample round 5 predictions of proposed approach compared to random approach

From the figure, it can be seen that across all the different budgets, at the end of round 5, the proposed approach can produce very accurate tumor segmentations and outperform the baseline significantly.

From the experimental results above, it can be concluded that the proposed ADASemSeg strategy can achieve significant improvements(12–25%) over the non-adaptive baselines. This is primarily due to the active interactions with the Expert/Oracle during the active learning rounds. The importance of uncertainty and representativeness quantification has also been identified through experimental evaluation, as due to such assessment of the unlabeled BUS images, appropriate query samples can be selected for expert labeling. With the help of such intelligently performed active interactions, the proposed approach can adapt to the target setting more effectively.

Comparing the performance of the proposed approach against other semantic segmentation approaches cannot be performed fairly as we did not find any attempt by the previous researchers to improve cross dataset breast tumor segmentation performance from BUSI to UDIAT data distributions. However, a few of the related works [13, 16] did show that their proposed BUS tumor segmentation approaches had reduced performances when the training was done on one dataset and testing was done on a different dataset. Our proposed ADASemSeg approach will be able to deal with this problem effectively, because it is a very generic strategy that can help any semantic segmentation model adapt to a new data distribution. Although only UNet-based model is considered for experimentation in this work, the ADASemSeg strategy can be applied to any of the more sophisticated segmentation approaches. Such kind of a generic approach, therefore, has a very high potential applicability in real diagnostic settings.

6   Conclusion

The problem of cross dataset/center data adaptation is considered in this work with respect to the BUS tumor segmentation task. An active learning-based data adaptation approach ADASemSeg is proposed in this work to perform better cross dataset BUS tumor segmentation. The main idea of ADASemSeg is to perform active interactions with an Expert/Oracle, who can be queried for ground truth labels for a few intelligently selected samples from the target data distribution. Experimental analysis on two publicly available datasets suggests that with ADASemSeg, nearly 25% dice score improvements can be observed on an average compared to directly using a model that has not been adapted to the new distribution. Moreover, intelligently selecting Oracle query samples can improve the adapted segmentation performance by nearly 12% as compared to a random choice of query samples. The generic nature of the proposed approach suggests that it can be utilized along with any sophisticated deep semantic segmentation model, and better data adaptation can be achieved.

Further research works can be carried out to study the robustness of the proposed approach by considering other semantic segmentation models and datasets for a more detailed experimental study.

Acknowledgements We thank Dr. Moi Hoon Yap, Reader in Computer Vision, Manchester Metropolitan University, Department of Computing, Mathematics and Digital Technology, John Dalton Building, Chester Street, Manchester M1 5GD, one of the Principal Investigators of the Breast Ultrasound Lesions Dataset (Dataset B) [13] for providing access to the UDIAT dataset for the purpose of academic research.

References

1. Mishra AK, Roy P, Bandyopadhyay S, Das SK (2021) Breast ultrasound tumour classification: a machine learning-radiomics based approach. Expert Syst:e12713. https://doi.org/10.1111/exsy.12713

2. Moon WK, Lee YW, Ke HH, Lee SH, Huang CS, Chang RF (2020) Computer-aided diagnosis of breast ultrasound images using ensemble learning from convolutional neural networks. Comput Methods Programs Biomed 190:105361. https://doi.org/10.1016/j.cmpb.2020.105361

3. Sadad T, Hussain A, Munir A, Habib M, Ali Khan S, Hussain S, Yang S, Alawairdhi M (2020) Identification of breast malignancy by marker-controlled watershed transformation and hybrid feature set for healthcare. Appl Sci 10(6):1900. https://doi.org/10.3390/app10061900

4. Park CS, Kim SH, Jung NY, Choi JJ, Kang BJ, Jung HS (2015) Interobserver variability of ultrasound elastography and the ultrasound BI-RADS lexicon of breast lesions. Breast Cancer 22(2):153–160. https://doi.org/10.1007/s12282-013-0465-3

5. Kim SH, Kang BJ, Choi BG, Choi JJ, Lee JH, Song BJ, Choe BJ, Park S, Kim H (2013) Radiologists' performance for detecting lesions and the interobserver variability of automated whole breast ultrasound. Korean J Radiol 14(2):154–163. https://doi.org/10.3348/kjr.2013.14.2.154

6. Mishra AK, Das SK, Roy P, Bandyopadhyay S (2020) Identifying COVID19 from chest CT images: a deep convolutional neural networks based approach. J Healthc Eng 2020. https://doi.org/10.1155/2020/8843664

7. Das Das SK, Roy P, Mishra AK (2021) Recognition of ischaemia and infection in diabetic foot ulcer: a deep convolutional neural network based approach. Int J Imag Syst Technol. https://doi.org/10.1002/ima.22598

8. Das SK, Roy P, Mishra AK (2021) DFU_SPNet: a stacked parallel convolution layers based CNN to improve diabetic foot ulcer classification. ICT Express. https://doi.org/10.1016/j.icte.2021.08.022

9. Das SK, Roy P, Mishra AK (2021) Fusion of handcrafted and deep convolutional neural network features for effective identification of diabetic foot ulcer. Concurrency Comput Pract Experience: e6690. https://doi.org/10.1002/cpe.6690

10. Das SK, Roy P, Mishra AK (2021) Deep learning techniques dealing with diabetes mellitus: a comprehensive study. In: Health informatics: a computational perspective in healthcare. Springer, Singapore, pp 295–323. https://doi.org/10.1007/978-981-15-9735-0_15

11. Jain D, Mishra AK, Das SK (2021) Machine learning based automatic prediction of Parkinson's disease using speech features. In: Proceedings of international conference on artificial intelligence and applications. Springer, Singapore, pp 351–362. https://doi.org/10.1007/978-981-15-4992-2_33

12. Kumar Das S, Kumar Mishra A, Roy P (2018) Automatic diabetes prediction using tree based ensemble learners. In: Proceedings of international conference on computational intelligence and IoT (ICCIIoT)

13. Yap MH, Pons G, Martí J, Ganau S, Sentís M, Zwiggelaar R, Davison AK, Marti R (2017) Automated breast ultrasound lesions detection using convolutional neural networks. IEEE J Biomed Health Inf 22(4):1218–1226. https://doi.org/10.1109/JBHI.2017.2731873

14. Vakanski A, Xian M, Freer PE (2020) Attention-enriched deep learning model for breast tumor segmentation in ultrasound images. Ultrasound Med Biol 46(10):2819–2833. https://doi.org/10.1016/j.ultrasmedbio.2020.06.015

15. Zhuang Z, Li N, Joseph Raj AN, Mahesh VG, Qiu S (2019) An RDAU-NET model for lesion segmentation in breast ultrasound images. PloS one 14(8):e0221535. https://doi.org/10.1371/journal.pone.0221535

16. Shareef B, Xian M, Vakanski A, (2020) Stan: small tumor-aware network for breast ultrasound image segmentation. In, (2020) IEEE 17th international symposium on biomedical imaging (ISBI), pp 1–5. IEEE. https://doi.org/10.1109/ISBI45749.2020.9098691

17. Shi X, Dou Q, Xue C, Qin J, Chen H, Heng PA (2019) An active learning approach for reducing annotation cost in skin lesion analysis. In: International workshop on machine learning in medical imaging, pp 628–636. Springer, Cham. https://doi.org/10.1007/978-3-030-32692-0_72

18. Mahapatra D, Buhmann JM (2016) Visual saliency-based active learning for prostate magnetic resonance imaging segmentation. J Med Imag 3(1):014003. https://doi.org/10.1117/1.JMI.3.1.014003

19. Nath V, Yang D, Landman BA, Xu D, Roth HR (2020) Diminishing uncertainty within the training pool: active learning for medical image segmentation. IEEE Trans Med Imag. https://doi.org/10.1109/TMI.2020.3048055
20. Hassan M, Das S, Dipu SA (2021) An active-learning based training-schedule for biomedical image segmentation on deep neural networks. PhD dissertation, Brac University
21. Czolbe S, Arnavaz K, Krause O, Feragen A (2021) Is segmentation uncertainty useful? In: International conference on information processing in medical imaging, pp 715–726. Springer, Cham. https://doi.org/10.1007/978-3-030-78191-0_55
22. Ronneberger O, Fischer P, Brox T (2015) U-net: convolutional networks for biomedical image segmentation. In: International conference on medical image computing and computer-assisted intervention, pp 234–241. Springer, Cham. https://doi.org/10.1007/978-3-319-24574-4_28
23. Long J, Shelhamer E, Darrell T (2015) Fully convolutional networks for semantic segmentation. In: Proceedings of the IEEE conference on computer vision and pattern recognition, pp 3431–3440. https://doi.org/10.1109/cvpr.2015.7298965
24. Chaurasia A, CulurcielloLinknet E, (2017) Exploiting encoder representations for efficient semantic segmentation. In, (2017) IEEE visual communications and image processing (VCIP), pp 1–4. IEEE. https://doi.org/10.1109/VCIP.2017.8305148
25. Lin TY, Dollár P, Girshick R, He K, Hariharan B, Belongie S (2017) Feature pyramid networks for object detection. In: Proceedings of the IEEE conference on computer vision and pattern recognition, pp 2117–2125. https://doi.org/10.1109/CVPR.2017.106
26. Budd S, Robinson EC, Kainz B (2021) A survey on active learning and human-in-the-loop deep learning for medical image analysis. Med Image Anal 102062. https://doi.org/10.1016/j.media.2021.102062
27. Al-Dhabyani W, Gomaa M, Khaled H, Fahmy A (2020) Dataset of breast ultrasound images. Data in Brief 28:104863. https://doi.org/10.1016/j.dib.2019.104863

Dense Disparity Map Generation for Images Captured by Lunar Rover Navigation Camera

Yukti Khosla, U. Rachna, Y. Narendra Reddy, Shikha Tripathi, Amit Maji, and Jayanta Laha

1 Introduction

Lunar rovers are used to perform various in-situ scientific experiments. This entails a rover to understand the terrain accurately so that it can traverse to scientifically interesting areas without running into obstacles. This requires sensing the position and height of the obstacles accurately. To locate the obstacles concerning the rover, depth computation is inevitable. Depth can be estimated using active and passive methods. The active methods include lidar, laser-based, depth camera, and time of flight camera methods. The passive methods use stereo cameras. The power consumption by the active methods is much more than passive methods. Passive methods only require a normal camera to be setup in a stereo setup. This makes the use of passive methods more feasible and, therefore, the same has been used in this analysis. Images captured by a single camera can only provide two-dimensional information. Three-dimensional reconstruction from the two-dimensional data available is to be estimated by using a stereo camera. A point in the world coordinate will appear in the left and right camera with different horizontal coordinates but the same vertical coordinate. The difference in the horizontal coordinate is called disparity. Using this disparity, depth can be computed. There are four steps to compute disparity. The first one is cost computation. Followed by cost aggregation. The third step is disparity computation using minimum cost and finally, disparity refinement is done. Disparity maps have been generated by making use of local, semi-global and global methods in the past. Local methods allow for fast processing time, however, lead to inaccurate disparity maps. Global methods are very efficient in estimating the disparities but are

Y. Khosla · U. Rachna · Y. Narendra Reddy · S. Tripathi (✉)
PES University, Bengaluru, Karnataka, India
e-mail: shikha.eee@gmail.com

A. Maji · J. Laha
Laboratory for Electro -Optics Systems, Indian Space Research Organization, 1st Cross, 1st Stage, Peenya Industrial Estate, Bengaluru 560058, India

© The Author(s), under exclusive license to Springer Nature Singapore Pte Ltd. 2023   603
R. Doriya et al. (eds.), *Machine Learning, Image Processing, Network Security and Data Sciences*, Lecture Notes in Electrical Engineering 946,
https://doi.org/10.1007/978-981-19-5868-7_44

unsuitable for real-time applications due to their long processing time. In this work, a good quality disparity map is generated for the available dataset replicating the surface of the moon using Semi-Global Matching(SGM). Comparison of disparity maps produced by the methods mentioned above has been performed and evaluated on the Middlebury stereo vision dataset [1]. The contents of this paper have been organized as follows, Sect. 2 contains the literature survey, Sect. 3 brings out the methodology used, Sect. 4 contains the results and evaluation, Sect. 5 contains the conclusions and future directions.

2 Literature Review

In the work reported in [2], a dense stereo matching method for planetary rovers has been proposed. The KITTI dataset [3] and stereo images of the Chang'e-3 rover have been used for this analysis. A pixel-wise disparity search range is restricted to a few pixels at coarse levels. This method is useful at depth discontinuities, low texture regions, and occlusion regions. The method proposed in [4] uses an adaptive window to perform stereo matching on real stereo images. An initial estimate of the disparity is produced statistically. The disparity is then calculated iteratively until the algorithm converges. An assumption that the intensities within a window follow a zero-mean gaussian white distribution when the center pixel is considered is made. The work demonstrated in [5], proposes an FPGA-based embedded system for stereo vision. The matching cost is computed for each pixel in the reference and candidate image. Each reference pixel is compared to each candidate pixel in terms of a dissimilarity metric computed by aggregating the matching costs within an aggregation window of fixed radius. The datasets used for this analysis were Middlebury benchmarks Tsukuba, Venus, Teddy, and Cones. The mentioned interfaces require additional costly hardware peripherals and initialization procedures resulting in complex systems with resource-consuming FPGA designs involving external memories and CPUs. Local stereo matching methods are area-based and have very fast processing speeds suitable for real-time applications [6]; however, their accuracy is low. Pixels in the reference image are matched by looking at neighboring pixels in the corresponding match image within a window. In this analysis, comparisons between different compatible stereo algorithms like SAD, SSD, NCC, SAD by derivatives, and non-parametric census transform are presented. Computation of disparity map, both grayscale, and color are performed on the Middlebury Stereo Dataset by making use of Ground Truth disparities. Evaluation of accuracy is done on the Middlebury dataset using RMS error and BAD PIXEL match as quality metrics. The method proposed in [7] uses a belief propagation-based global method in real-time to obtain top-notch results. The algorithm contains two parts. The correlation volume computation constructs the data term and the belief propagation updates the smoothness term to minimize the energy. The performance efficiency is attributed to parallelism in the hardware enabling a speedup of 45 times as compared to the CPU implementation. The runtime of a belief propagation algorithm based on adaptively updating pixel cost is linear to the number of iterations. Due to a large number of iterations, implementation on real-time applications is infeasible. Unlike general belief propagation methods, the runtime of this algorithm converges by a large amount. The results were obtained for the Middlebury dataset. The work reported in [8] is aimed at establishing a method for stereo processing using SGM based on mutual information. Matching based on mutual information is proposed by combining 1D constraints to form a single 2D constraint. The refinement procedures work comparatively better in presence of occlusion and outliers in the map. Deep learning methods have become extensively popularized in recent years. They have also been made use of in stereo matching to obtain results with high accuracy and inference speed. FADNet [9] is a Fast and Accurate Disparity estimation Network that makes use of the DispNetC architecture, Scene Flow and KITTI 2015 are used to evaluate the performance of this network. Another method proposed by Sun et al. [10] called Disp R-CNN computes disparity only for specific pixels containing objects of interest instead of the entire image hence leading to a faster runtime. Wang et al. [11] proposed a SMAR-Net based on generative adversarial learning which consists of a disparity regressor and left image generator in a two-stage network by minimizing content loss and adversarial loss. Deep learning methods require GPU utilization and hence prove to be infeasible for real-time applications. The need for a large number of ground truth data for training these huge networks poses a limitation, despite the generation of pseudo-ground truth images in [10, 11]. Although local stereo matching methods have been widely used for their fast processing speeds, the SGM method provides results with a much-improved accuracy, but with slightly higher processing times. Global methods require the usage of external memory and GPU due to their high computational load and hence are unsuitable for real-time applications. Implementation of SGM can be done on FPGA efficiently. In the proposed work SGM has been used for computing the disparity map of lunar surface images in real-time. Such an attempt for images captured by the lunar rover has not been carried out so far.

3 Methodology

Figure 1 illustrates the workflow in the form of a block diagram.

3.1 Camera Calibration

Calibration of Stereo cameras is crucial to perform image rectification. There are two types of camera calibrations parameters; intrinsic camera parameters and extrinsic camera parameters. Intrinsic camera parameters provide us with the internal properties of the camera. These parameters include focal length, optical center, aspect ratio, distortion coefficients, and shear constant. Extrinsic camera parameters talk about external parameters of the camera; these parameters are important because they give

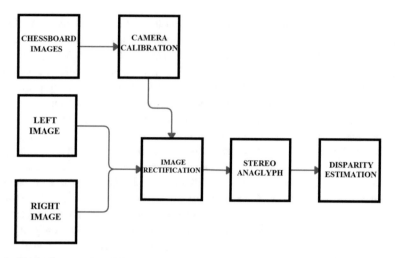

Fig. 1 Block diagram of workflow

Fig. 2 Left and right
checkerboard image pair

us the exact baseline distance between the cameras. Fifteen pairs of left and right
chessboard images in various positions and tilts obtained from the Indian Space
Research Organization (ISRO) were used for calibration. The size of the checkerboard pattern was 30 mm. The left and right checkerboard image pairs are illustrated
in Fig. 2.

The calibration algorithm assumes a pinhole camera model:

$$\left(w \, [\, x \ y \ 1 \,] = [\, X \ Y \ Z \ 1 \,] \ [\, Rt \,]^T \ K \right) \tag{1}$$

where
(X, Y, Z): world coordinates of a point
(x, y): coordinates of the corresponding image point
w : arbitrary scale factor
K: camera intrinsic matrix
R: matrix representing the 3D rotation of the camera
t: translation of the camera relative to the world coordinate system
T: Transpose of the matrix

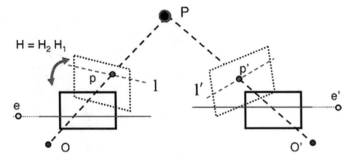

Fig. 3 Epipolar geometry and epipolar geometry rectified

3.2 Image Rectification

Image rectification is a process that projects multiple images onto the same image surface. It helps correct a distorted image into a standard coordinate system. It ensures that the images appear as though they have been taken only at a horizontal displacement.

There are two methods of computing image rectification, without using camera calibrations and making use of camera calibrations. In this analysis, image rectification has been performed making use of camera calibrations to avoid distortions. Image rectification makes use of camera parameters to derive transformation matrices that perform the projective transformation on the left and right images using the fundamental camera matrix. This results in rotation of the left and right images to have axes parallel to the baseline axis. The second transformation results in the perfect alignment of the image optical axes with the baseline axis. We finally scale both the images to the same image resolution. A reduced search space is obtained to find the corresponding pixel match in the left and right images.

In Fig. 3, O and O' represent the centers of the left and right camera lenses and P is the 3D point of interest. We focus on p and p' which are the projections of the point P onto the camera planes. The darkened boxes represent the rectified left and right image planes after undergoing projective transformations. The resulting epipolar lines e and e' are now parallel to the horizontal axis.

3.3 Stereo Anaglyph

Stereo Anaglyph is a special type of image which allows our eyes to perceive three-dimensional information using two-dimensional images when viewed through a special glass. It is obtained by superimposing the images taken from stereo cameras with different fields of view and printed in monochrome colors, usually red and cyan. Thus, each eye sees different images which makes the brain automatically perceive depth.

Fig. 4 Stereo Anaglyph
before rectification with a
100.06-pixel difference

Image rectification can be better visualized by observing the stereo anaglyphs of the image pairs as shown in Figs. 4 and 5. The maximum disparity and minimum disparity used for Figs. 4 and 5 are 304 and 16 respectively.

3.4 Disparity Estimation

Disparity refers to parallax or the difference in location of an object point due to the horizontal separation of the eyes. This can be realized by focusing on an object with one eye closed and immediately switching to the other eye. It can be seen that there is a slight motion in the location of the object while doing so. Stereo cameras are separated horizontally along the same axis while capturing the image of the same scene. The concept described above can be directly applied to stereo cameras as well. The disparity can be defined as the pixel difference between the corresponding points in the reference and match image. This difference can be made use of to derive the depth information of a scene or object whose image is captured by stereo cameras. When correspondence has been established for all points in an image, a disparity map can be obtained with each point representing the apparent pixel difference of corresponding points in the two images.

Local Methods of Disparity Estimation The sum of absolute differences (SAD) is a similarity metric that is used to calculate the degree of similarity between two images. It is done so by taking the absolute difference in the intensities of all the pixels in one image and its corresponding pixels in the other. These differences are then summed. The sum of squared differences (SSD) is a variation of the sum of absolute differences with an additional step. Calculation of the same is done by taking the squared difference of the intensity values assumed by each pixel in one image and its corresponding pixel in the other. These squared differences are then summed.

Normalized Cross-Correlation (NCC) is another metric that is used to calculate the degree of similarity between two images in comparison. It is a parametric method that depends on the actual values of intensities held by the pixels in the image; however, the main advantage of this method is that it performs well in the presence of illumination changes. This is because normalization is performed in this method before comparison between images. Hence, the range of all pixels is confined to $[-1, 1]$.

Semi-Global Matching (SGM) SGM is a stereo matching algorithm that lies in between local and global methods used to obtain the disparity map for a rectified stereo image pair. Pixel-wise matching can be performed using many methods, from simple intensity-based matching to matching using Mutual Information. All these methods try to find the correspondence for every pixel based on a similarity measure. The matching cost is calculated for a base image pixel p and its corresponding match pixel q in the matched image which is expected to lie on the epipolar line for rectified images. The method used by the authors for pixel-based matching cost computation is the Census Transform.

Census Transform is a non-parametric image transformation that associates with each pixel of a grayscale image, a binary string based on a specific criterion. The transformation does not depend directly on the intensity values associated with each pixel but on the relative ordering of its intensities under a fixed-size window. Census Transform is given by [8].

$$C(p, \, p')) = \begin{cases} 0 \text{ if } p > p' \\ 1 \text{ if } p < p' \end{cases} \tag{2}$$

Hamming Distance is used as a distance metric/inverse similarity metric between any two-bit strings resulting from Census Transform. In practical implementation, the Census Transform outputs of the left and right rectified images are pixel-wise XOR'd and the set bits are counted to generate matching cost. The objective of cost aggregation is to minimize the energy term. Due to noise, wrong pixel cost calculation could be lower than correct pixel cost calculation. Hence, additional constraints are added to increase smoothness (term 2 and term 3) [8].

$$E(D) = \sum_{p} C(p, D_p) + \sum_{q \in N_p} P_1 T[|D_p - D_q| = 1] + \sum_{q \in N_p} P_2 T[|D_p - D_q| > 1] \tag{3}$$

The first term corresponds to the sum of all pixel matching costs which have the disparity as D. The second and third terms are penalty terms. The second term corresponds to the penalty when disparity changes by 1 pixel and the third term correspond to the penalty when the difference in disparity is greater than 1. Using a lower penalty for disparity changes of 1 pixel ensures adaptation on curved surfaces. A higher penalty for larger changes in disparity preserves discontinuities. Therefore,

$$P2 \geq P1.$$

Minimization of the Energy function along the rows can be minimized using Dynamic Programming. However, this would lead to very large constraints in one direction combined with weaker constraints in other directions. To solve this issue, aggregation of costs is done in one direction from all 8 directions equally (NE, N, NW, W, SW, S, SE, E). The cost can be defined by a recursive function computed using Eq. 4 [8].

$$
\begin{aligned}
L_r(p, d) = C(p, d) + \min(&L_r(p - r, d), L_r(p - r, d - 1) \\
&+ P1, L_r(p - r, d + 1) + P1, \min_i L_r(p - r, i) + P2) \\
&- \min_k L_k(p - r, k)
\end{aligned}
\tag{4}
$$

4 Results

The major problem faced while capturing images of the lunar surface is that of illumination. The low lighting conditions make the process of estimating depth difficult. Navcam makes use of visible light while capturing the stereo image pair. Similar low illumination conditions have been created by the authors in the laboratory and made use of to ensure the generation of efficient disparity maps.

Occlusion problems in stereo vision restrict the generation of good disparity maps. The occlusion problem is faced when regions behind objects are visible only in one field of view and are hidden in the other. This leads to uncertainty in the value of disparity for occluded pixels resulting in holes. To overcome this, the occluded pixels must first be detected after performing a thorough left-right consistency check. The proposed method has been tested and verified on the experimental data.

4.1 Quantitative Analysis on the Standard Dataset

Comparison of the algorithms has been performed using root mean squared error for the disparity maps obtained using NCC and SGM algorithm with the true disparity values available.

Root mean square error is calculated as:

$$
\mathbf{RMSE} = \sqrt{\frac{1}{n} \sum_{i=1}^{n} (Y_i - y_i)^2}
\tag{5}
$$

RMSE = root mean squared error
n = no of data point
Y_i = observed values
y_i = predicted values

Fig. 5 Stereo Anaglyph
after rectification with the
95.00-pixel difference
between an object as seen in
the left and right image

The results have been calculated only for those pixels in the true disparity which do not have a 0 value. The maximum disparity range used to obtain the disparity map for SGM is 64. Normalization of the ground truth and disparity image is done by using the maximum disparity value. The first 64 pixels in the left image have no corresponding match, leading to holes in the obtained disparity map. The first 64 pixels in the ground truth image are neglected while performing root mean squared error comparison.

The disparity maps obtained on the Cones dataset can be seen in Fig. 6. The results obtained are shown in Table 1. The proposed method works best in cases of occlusion which is the aim of this paper. The standard Middlebury datasets show little to no occluded pixels in their images, however, a significant decrease in the root mean square error can be seen in the case of Teddy images using the proposed method.

4.2 Qualitative Analysis

Topographic conditions similar to those on the lunar surface have been mimicked in the laboratory while capturing stereo image pairs for experimentation. Disparity maps for the ISRO dataset using the SGM algorithm can be seen from Figs. 7, 8 and 9.

Table 1 Root mean square error of the disparity map generated on the Middlebury dataset in pixels (px)

Technique	Cones (px)	Teddy (px)
NCC [6]	6.727	7.053
Segment tree [12]	4.663	4.164
Non-local [12]	4.385	3.878
Guided filter [12]	2.919	3.662
SGM [8]	2.512	2.758
Modified-SGM (proposed method)	2.761	2.29

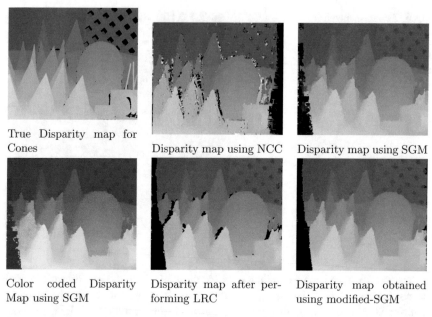

True Disparity map for
Cones

Disparity map using NCC

Disparity map using SGM

Color coded Disparity
Map using SGM

Disparity map after per-
forming LRC

Disparity map obtained
using modified-SGM

Fig. 6 Disparity maps obtained on Cones dataset

Left Rectified image for
set1

Disparity map using SGM

Color-coded disparity
map using SGM

Fig. 7 Set 1

4.3 Occlusion Handling for a Wide-Baseline Stereo Camera (Modified-SGM)

The process involves discarding pixels in both the left and right disparity maps
which do not hold the same disparity values due to wrong matches from occlusion
and mismatch. Hole filling can then be performed by finding for each hole, the first
pixel on the left and the first pixel on the right with a valid disparity value, and then
replacing the discarded pixel with their minimum(min(left, right)). The resulting

Left Rectified image for set2

Disparity map using SGM

Color-coded disparity map using SGM

Fig. 8 Set 2

Left Rectified image for set3

Disparity map using SGM

Color-coded disparity map using SGM

Fig. 9 Set 3

map has been refined further using Weighted Median Filtering. Figure 10 shows the disparity maps for occlusion handling cases using the method stated above.

It has been observed that the proposed procedure computes the disparity with minimum error while taking care of occlusion problems using a normal stereo camera setup. This can be used on-board thus giving the disparity real-time to the lunar rover to position itself and navigate through an appropriate path with a significant reduction in computation and cost.

5 Conclusion and Future Directions

The quantitative analysis performed on the disparity maps obtained proves that the SGM method generates the disparity map with the least error. Therefore, SGM has been used to generate the disparity map from the dataset obtained from ISRO with an additional down-sampling step. Qualitative analysis has been done on the dataset as obtaining ground truth for real scene images was not feasible. Good quality images have been produced as can be seen in Sect. 4. The maximum and the minimum dis-

| Left Rectified image for set 1 | Disparity map after performing LRC | Final disparity map obtained using modified-SGM |

Fig. 10 Results obtained

parity considered are 304 and 16 respectively. A high disparity value is necessary to obtain accurate and efficient results for objects of interest; objects closer to the camera plane. The left-right consistency check has been performed to get rid of mismatched and occluded pixels followed by hole filling. The current method of generating disparity maps involves offline computation as the rover has low computational power. The proposed method is suitable for real-time computation and enables FPGA implementation for on-board disparity map generation.

The work could be enhanced by making use of images of the moon captured in real-time. Global methods could not be implemented as GPU utilization was a constraint. A larger disparity search range could have been considered for more accurate results but the search time would increase proportionally. A larger search space could be considered for an application that is not required to be implemented in real-time. Stereo cameras cannot handle occlusion. In the future, a combination of stereo cameras and lidar-based cameras can help to overcome this problem.

Acknowledgements The authors would like to thank ISRO for helping and supporting the project.

References

1. Middlebury Dataset. https://vision.middlebury.edu/stereo/data/. Last accessed 19 July 2021
2. Raajan NR, Ramkumar M, Monisha B, Jaiseeli C, Prasanna Venkatesan S (2021) Disparity estimation from stereo images. Procedia Eng 38:462–472. (International Conference on Modelling Optimization and Computing)
3. Kitti Dataset. Available online. http://www.cvlibs.net/datasets/kitti/. Last accessed on 29th July 2021
4. Kanade T, Okutomi M (1994) A stereo matching algorithm with an adaptive window: theory and experiment. IEEE Trans Pattern Anal Mach Intell 16(9):920–932. https://doi.org/10.1109/34.310690

5. Perri S, Frustaci F, Spagnolo F, Corsonello P (2018) Design of real-time FPGA-based embedded system for stereo vision. In: 2018 IEEE international symposium on circuits and systems (ISCAS), pp 1–5. https://doi.org/10.1109/ISCAS.2018.8351886

6. Tabssum T, Charles P, Patil AV (2016) Evaluation of disparity map computed using local stereo parametric and non-parametric methods. International conference on automatic control and dynamic optimization techniques (ICACDOT) 2016:104–109. https://doi.org/10.1109/ICACDOT.2016.7877560

7. Nistér D (2006) Real-time global stereo matching using hierarchical belief propagation. In: 2006 Proceedings of the British machine vision conference, Vol. 6. Edinburgh, UK, pp 989–998. https://doi.org/10.5244/C.20.101

8. Hirschmuller H (2008) Stereo processing by semiglobal matching and mutual information. IEEE Trans Pattern Anal Mach Intell 30(2):328–341. https://doi.org/10.1109/TPAMI.2007.1166

9. Wang Q, Shi S, Zheng S, Zhao K, Chu X (2020) FADNet: a fast and accurate network for disparity estimation. arXiv:2003.10758

10. Sun J et al (2020) Disp r-cnn: stereo 3d object detection via shape prior guided instance disparity estimation. In: Proceedings of the IEEE/CVF conference on computer vision and pattern recognition

11. Wang C et al (2021) Self-supervised multiscale adversarial regression network for stereo disparity estimation. IEEE Trans Cybern 51(10):4770–4783. https://doi.org/10.1109/TCYB.2020.2999492

12. Zhang K, Fang Y, Min D, Sun L, Yang S, Yan S (2017) Cross-scale cost aggregation for stereo matching. IEEE Trans Circ Syst Video Technol 27(5):965–976. https://doi.org/10.1109/TCSVT.2015.2513663

Threat Detection in Self-Driving Vehicles Using Computer Vision

Umang Goenka, Aaryan Jagetia, Param Patil, Akshay Singh, Taresh Sharma, and Poonam Saini

1 Introduction

As technology is advancing very fast nowadays; therefore, whatever is relevant to the market today becomes irrelevant for tomorrow. Self-driving cars are the future and a very convenient and easy-to-use mode of transportation; however, the only reason that refrains people from adopting the same is its safety parameter. The concern includes if the car will be as safe as a traditional car and secondly, it can detect the threats accurately as well as alert the system proactively. To answer these questions, a substantial amount of research has been carried out in this field focusing on various approaches. Accidents have been on a surge in recent years and are constantly increasing over the years as the number of automobiles is increasing. The WHO in its recent report published in June 2021 [1], mentions some key facts which include that road accident deaths are around 1.4 million, GDP loss is in the range of 3%, and also, the most vulnerable age group is 5–29. Moreover, India has suffered a loss of between 1.17 lakh crores and 2.91 lakh crores in 2019 due to road accidents. India, which owns nearly 1% of global vehicles, contributes to around 11% of annual deaths in accidents [2]. Thus, having an automated system of vehicles that follow all the safety guidelines can be an effective solution to this problem as well.

The main objective of our work is to identify the threats and make the vehicle self-aware. The problem will be analyzed by taking into consideration various factors and varying the parameters such as *depth estimation* and *region of interest* (RoI) to

U. Goenka · A. Jagetia (✉)
Indian Institute of Information Technology, Lucknow, India
e-mail: lit2019033@iiitl.ac.in

P. Patil
Sardar Patel Institute of Technology, Mumbai, India

A. Singh · T. Sharma · P. Saini
Punjab Engineering College, Chandigarh, India

© The Author(s), under exclusive license to Springer Nature Singapore Pte Ltd. 2023
R. Doriya et al. (eds.), *Machine Learning, Image Processing, Network Security and Data Sciences*, Lecture Notes in Electrical Engineering 946,
https://doi.org/10.1007/978-981-19-5868-7_45

achieve the best possible accuracy of the model. Adopting such a system will allow immediate response to threats using neural networks and computer vision. Moreover, we can directly use the model to deploy a system on cars that works in real-time and can detect accidents and provide indications that could help in reducing fatal injuries. The dataset has been sequentially analyzed, combined, and tested using the best-suited algorithm such as YOLO which uses the COCO dataset.

The paper is divided into four sections as follows:

1. Sect. 2 details an extensive literature survey of past studies.
2. Sect. 3 describes the flow of the proposed model and its implementation.
3. Sect. 4 presents the results and analysis of the proposed approach under varying parameters.
4. Sect. 5 mentions the conclusion, limitations, and future scope.

2 Background and Related Work

In this section, we present the literature review, summarize, and analyze the work related to accident/threat detection in automated vehicles.

Deeksha Gour et al. [3] proposed an artificial intelligence-based traffic monitoring system that can detect the occurrence of accidents of vehicles in live camera feeds and detect collision of these moving objects. Further, the emergency alerts are immediately sent to the nearby authority for necessary actions. The paper focuses on the Yolo algorithm that is capable of detecting accidents and also it can run on CPU-based devices such as laptops or mobile phones. Here, the authors do not consider the actual distance of the vehicle from the camera which is an important parameter and can result in false signals being sent to vehicles moving in other lanes.

Ibrahim and Hassan [4] presented the work which focuses on detecting the cars using YOLO and further assigning the cars into lanes using a real-time computer vision algorithm. For the proposed approach, the authors have divided the road into three sections, namely left, right, and emergency lanes which is the main region of focus to run the algorithm. This work suffers from limitations like the model could focus on car detection only and not other obstructions that may hinder the road. Also, image processing is done to consider only the car's lane and ignore all the obstructions that fall in the peripheral vision of the driver.

Dogru and Subasi [5] proposed a system that detects the event of accidents by collecting necessary information like vehicle position, speed, and other related abnormal activities from neighboring vehicles and process the same using machine learning tools to detect possible accidents in the future. The study aims to analyze traffic behavior and consider vehicles that move differently than current traffic behavior, as a possible accident case. The authors implemented a clustering algorithm to detect accidents; however, the problem is unsolvable with their approach when the road is curved as the data values will vary accordingly, and this factor is not considered.

Rana et al. [5] presented a paper on accident detection and severity pre- diction with the help of machine learning and computer vision. The principal focus of the project is to detect the vehicles using the YOLO model and then perform watershed image segmentation using computer vision along with random forest classifier. The project primarily focuses on alerting the drivers about the accident-prone areas and further reducing the chain of accidents rather than focusing on the driver's path.

Khandbahale et al. [6] published a paper in which the authors used an embedded system within the vehicle. If the obstacle lies in the front, then the microcontroller can communicate inside the system and alert the driver, in case, any factor enters a non-safe zone. The main drawback is that sensors can be too costly and may not work correctly in rainy conditions.

Varsha Goud et al. [7] exhibited some research for accident detection using an accelerometer. With signals from an accelerometer, a severe accident can be recognized. According to this project report, whenever a vehicle meets with an accident, the vibration sensor will immediately detect the signal, or if a car rolls over, a micro-electro-mechanical system (MEMS) sensor will alert the system. The limitation comes in the form of costly sensors as well as the threat detection is possible only up to a certain distance.

Kalyani et al. [8] proposed a model which can detect any accident on occurrence using vibrations and will send a message to a number. The hardware is used in the accident detection technique wherein at the time of an accident a vibration sensor is triggered due to vibration, the GPS module is then fetched and the location of the incident is sent as a message to the provided mobile number with the help of GSM module that is inbuilt into the particular system. The main problem here is that hardware is not always reliable and can cause a delay in predicting the nature of an accident.

Kattukkaran et al. [9] presented the idea of using an accelerometer. Here, the accelerometer in the vehicle senses the tilt of the vehicle and the heartbeat sensor on the user's body senses the abnormality of the heartbeat to understand the seriousness of the accident. Thus, the system made the decision and sent the information to the smartphone, through Bluetooth. However, the Bluetooth range is very limited and heartbeat is not a suitable measurement for accident verification because it is subjective to interpretation.

Jianfeng et al. [10] published a work in which a classification and recognition method is used for analyzing the severity of road traffic accidents based on rough set theory and support vector machine (SVM). The authors classified the data based on attributes in humans, vehicles, roads, environment, and accidents. The main shortcoming is that SVM is found to be limited while analyzing objects and instance segmentation during detection and hence the instance classification is hindered.

Gluhakovi´c et al. [11] proposed a method for vehicle detection near an autonomous vehicle. The authors used YOLO v2 which employs identity mapping, concatenating feature maps from a previous layer to capture low-level features. As YOLO v2's architecture lacks in capturing a few important elements, we use Yolo v3 which uses residual blocks with no skip connections and no upsampling, thus, resulting in improvised modeling.

3 Methodology

This section proposes a four-step model for obstacle detection on the road using computer vision and neural networks. The camera mounted on the windshield records the video which is simultaneously executed on the deep learning algorithms. As an output from the proposed model, we successfully outline the obstacle with a red boundary and ensure to proactively alert the system about a potential threat on the road.

3.1 System Overview

The subsection briefly explains the model assumptions followed by broader steps of the proposed approach.

Model Assumptions:

1. The camera must be mounted on the windshield.
2. Focal length of the camera.
3. Speed must be provided while the vehicle is moving.

Broader Steps:

Step 1: Region of Interest and Lane Detection

The initial step is to identify the region of interest of the image by varying the parameters used for determining the horizon and also take some help from the lane detection algorithm.

Step 2: Object Detection using YOLO

Followed by identifying the main area to focus on, we will detect the obstacles in our region and also find their proximity from our region of interest so that we can anticipate any danger beforehand. In case there is a real danger, it is outlined with a red boundary.

Step 3: Distance of the obstacle from camera

Next, we will calculate the distance of the object from our camera. Although there are many multi-regression techniques to identify the same, we have used regression technique along with real-time data to calculate the model equation.

Step 4: Calculating Safety

For identifying the safety parameter, we used a popular two-second rule technique [12]. We will make use of the distance calculated in the previous step and the speed of our car to measure safety.

3.2 System Architecture

The subsection will discuss a detailed description of the steps of the proposed model. The workflow for the same has been shown in Figure 1.

Lane Detection and Region of Interest

In case, there are lines already drawn on the road, an advanced lane detection algorithm may be used. However, in the absence of lines, we may use an appropriate estimation method in order to calculate the horizon and then configure the lane.

(i) **Lane Detection**: Given an image as shown in Fig. 2a, the following steps are essential to determine the exact lane of the car:

Step 1: *Eliminating the distortions from the image:* The image is transformed into two-dimensional objects to eliminate two sorts of distortions, i.e., radial and tangential. We have used Pythons' OpenCV library for the following purpose (Fig. 2b).

Step 2: *Processing color channels:* Here, we obtain a binary image that contains the lane by applying filters on it (Fig. 2b). For filtering, the three threshold criteria have been used; (i) lightness threshold to remove the edges formed by shadows; (ii) using saturation channel threshold to extract white lanes; (iii) hue for the line colors.

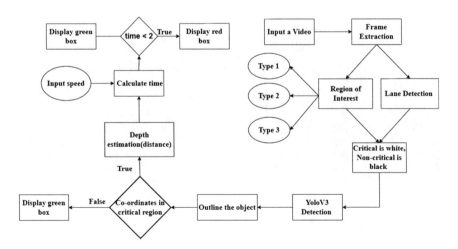

Fig. 1 System workflow

(a) Initial Image   (b) Filter

Fig. 2 Initial image and filter

Step 3: *Birds eye view:* Here, we wrap the image to have a top view of the lane. This helped us to effectively run our algorithm and fit a curve on lane pixels.

Step 4: *Finding left and right lane pixels:* We fit these pixels in a two-degree polynomial. The value of the pixel is 0 and 1. We get peaks where the color is white and the rest of the time it is 0. From the peaks, the position of the lanes can be easily identified.

Step 5: *Sliding window:* From the base position of the left and right lines, we create a sliding window that is placed around the center of the line. This window finds and tracks the line to the top of the frame (Fig. 3a).

Step 6: *Determining the lane curvature:* A derivative function has been used to calculate the radius of curvature of the road [13].

Step 7: *Drawing the lane boundaries:* Finally, after executing the above steps, we will draw these white points on the white part which represents the lane on the original image (Fig. 3b).

(a) Sliding Window   (b) Final Image

Fig. 3 Sliding window and final Image

Algorithm 1 Lane Detection

1: #Calibrate and correct distortions
2: undist = cv2.undistort(input image, mtx, dist, None, mtx)
3: #process gradients and color channels for creation of binary image that consists of lane pixels.
4: thresh_img = ColorThreshCombined(undist, s_thresh, l_thresh, v_thresh, b_thresh)
5: #Birds eye view
6: warpped_img = PerspectiveTransform(thresh_img, src_pts, dst_pts, False)
7: #process gradients and color channels for creation of binary image that consists of lane pixels
8: #Finding the lines
9: left_fit,right_fit,lines_img,mean_curverad,position = find_lines_video(warpped_img)
10: #unwarp the image back to the original perspective
11: inv_matrix, unwarpped_img = InvertPerspective(warpped_img, src_pts, dst_pts)

(ii) **Region of Interest**: In case, there are no lanes on the road (which is common in many middle and small-income countries), our algorithm may not perform accordingly. In order to address the issue, we used geometric logic to identify the region of interest by varying the parameters. The fact is that a road in front of our eyes converges at infinity. Such a region is to be selected in a manner that the results must be accurate and can detect a threat quickly.

Using this logic, we divided the region into two parts initially, one is above and the other is below the horizontal line A as mentioned in Fig. 4. The part which is above the line A in Fig. 4 is not of major concern majority of the road lies in the region below line A. We are dividing the upper and lower part into a 45:55 split. If the center of the detected object is found in the upper part, it is rejected. Further, the parameters are varied to determine whether an object is a threat or not. Three such possibilities have been configured in Fig. 4.

1. The blue line in the figure above represents the first region of interest. It is the largest among all three and will detect most of the obstacles. The limitation is that some obstacles in certain situations may not be detected which do not pose a real danger.

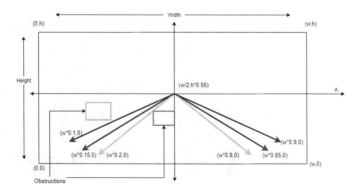

Fig. 4 Region of interest

2. The red line is a medium-sized region of interest and it may detect most of the objects. The final results are described in the next session.
3. The green line is the smallest of all and is least prone to detecting false danger; the only challenge is whether it will detect all the threats beforehand.

Algorithm 2 Region of Interest

1: masked_image = np.zeros_like(InputImage)
2: cv2.fillPoly(masked_image, RegionPoints, color = (255,255,255))

Determining the obstacles using YOLO:

YOLO [14] is the real-time object detection system that uses the COCO dataset from Darknet for training. This trained model will be able to detect vehicles from the roads in the working environment. Unlike classifier-based approaches, YOLO with the help of a loss function is trained and directly corresponds to detection performance and the whole model is trained together. YOLO outperforms the more accurate Fast RCNN as R-CNN takes about 2–3 s to predict an object in an image and hence is not feasible for real-time object detection. With the help of YOLO, we can train the whole object detection model with a single neural network.

YOLO when combined with several algorithms, such as lane detection, depth estimation, and computer vision can increase the likelihood to attain the desired threat detection or warning as mentioned in Fig. 7. YOLO turns out to be ideal since it's robust, powerful, and quick object detection (Fig. 5).

Algorithm 3 YOLO Detection

1: #configure Convolutional neural network using configuration and weights file with CPU related executions
2: neural_network = cv2.dnn.readNetFromDarknet('yolov3.cfg','yolov3.weights')
3: neural_network.setPreferableBackend(cv2.dnn.DNN_BACKEND_OPENCV)
4: neural_network.setPreferableTarget(cv2.dnn.DNN_TARGET_CPU)

Fig. 5 Yolo detection image

Table 1 Variation of area as the distance changes

Area (pixel^2)	Distance (m)
440,380	2
239,598	3
137,138	4
96,657	5
67,626	6
47,294	8
33,631	10
25,479	11
12,168	16

Distance of the obstacle from camera

In this section, we conducted an experiment to estimate the relationship and generate an equation between distance from the front camera of the car to anyother obstruction detected in front of us in the danger region, where the selection of ROI/lane detection has been explained in the previous section.

As you can see in Table 1, we choose mainly two parameters and conduct our experiment solely on these parameters.

(i) Area (pixel^2): The area occupied in the image by obstruction (Refer Fig. 6). Here, the yellow box around the car rightly displays the area that is occupied by the car.
(ii) Distance (m): The distance between the object and the front camera.

In Table 1, we placed a car at various distances from the car, captured a picture from that point, and took nine different sets of photos. After capturing the image, our next step was to write a program that detects the car using YOLO and returns the coordinates of the car around which we not only draw a bounding box but also calculate the area and display it (Fig. 6).

For readings in Table 1, we parked a car at different distances from another car, captured a picture from one point, and took 9 sets of photos. After cap-turing the image, we modeled our approach to detect the car using YOLO and returned the coordinates of the car around. Using this, we can draw a bounding box and calculate the area as well. Thereafter, a graph is plotted with the retrieved values wherein the x-axis depicts the area and y-axis depicts the distance. Finally, we chose a function which is the best fit for our observed values, i.e., the power function which generated an equation $Y = 4319.3x^{-0.589}$. Afterward, we integrate this in our system by just calculating the area of all the objects that are detected in the danger region, and further substituting that value in the generated equation which, in turn, gives the distance of the object from the car, which was the primary objective.

Fig. 6 Depth image

2m From Camera   8m From Camera

16m From Camera

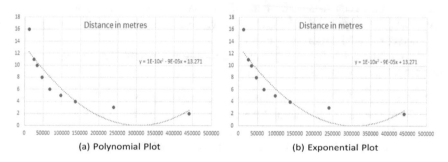

(a) Polynomial Plot   (b) Exponential Plot

Fig. 7 Graph of depth estimation equations

Calculating the safety standards between two objects

After calculating the objects in the region of interest and their distance from the camera, it is to identify whether the object is the real danger. For this, we follow the two-second rule, commonly used in many western and European countries. According to the rule, if a vehicle crosses point A, the vehicle following it must pass point A only after 2 s. Refer Fig. 7.

Algorithm 4 Calculating safety with the help of depth estimation and the 2-s rule

---

if Object_Lies_in_critical_region(CenterOfObject **then**
   depth_of_object = DepthEstimation(height,width)
   time = depth_of_object/input_speed
   if Time < 2 **then**
     DANGER!!!
   else
     SAFE!

---

4 Observations and Results

In this work, we consider two important parameters to be varied for accuracy, namely, *region of interest* and *depth estimation*. In order to calculate the accuracy, we downloaded the dataset [15] and used 500 videos of a car being driven, wherein 250 videos showed the car crash and the remaining 250 videos showed no car crash. The length of each video is 10–15 s on an average. Further, each video is fetched as an input in our system and later on checked if the system correctly displayed the red bounding box/ blue bounding box, i.e., the two classification of output which is to ensure if a vehicle is under a threat. The classification of region of interest (ROI) in our work is as:

4.1 Region of Interest

(i) *Type 1*: It is the biggest of all the three types having the base coordinates at 0.1 *w and 0.9 * w, respectively, (Blue line).

ii) *Type 2*: It is medium in size and has base coordinates at a distance 0.7 * w apart at 0.15 * w and 0.85 * w, respectively, (Red line).

iii) *Type 3*: The smallest of all has its base coordinates at 0.2 * w and 0.8 * w, respectively (green line).

Three ROI's and their accuracy

In Table 2, the accuracy in Type 1 ROI is comparatively less as the angle is more; therefore, it unnecessarily detects and run the algorithm on outliers. The accuracy of Type 3 is less than the accuracy of Type 2 mainly because the angle is very narrow, and hence, it is unable to detect the cars that are in the peripheral vision of the camera, thereby, eliminating objects in vicinity of the car. Therefore, we can conclude that the accuracy is best among the three in Type 2.

The reason behind the calculations of this type of results was mainly to understand how varying angles in ROI could play a significant role in establishing the system.

Three ROI's and their frames

The analysis in Table 3 can help us to understand how quickly an output will be generated and display the results to the user. Here, the frame delay is calculated in the output of the video, and the results are obtained by providing 250 video inputs which fall under category 1, i.e., the car crashes. Thereafter, we find the number of

Table 2 Comparison of accuracy in different region of interest	Region of interest	Accuracy (in %)
	Type 1	71.42
	Type 2	82.65
	Type 3	79.59

Table 3 Comparison of average and median in different region of interest

Region of interest	Frame delay (average)	Frame delay (median)
Type 1	10.71	7
Type 2	11.41	8
Type 3	12.35	10

frames until the system is able to find the object and generate a result for the first time for all 250 videos and calculate the average and median for the same.

Type 1 is having the largest angle, and it would naturally generate results faster as it will detect the objects quicker. Similarly, the angle becomes shorter in

Type 2, thereby, resulting in more average frame delay as compared to Type 1. The frame delay is comparatively the most in Type 3 as the angle is the shortest; therefore, it takes more time than other techniques to actually detect an object and generate results. The comparison can be made in only those videos where all the three regions of interest give accurate results, so the test dataset videos were reduced to around 250. The average frames per video is 38.

4.2 Depth Estimation

As mentioned briefly in sect. 3, we carried our own experiment and noted the observations. Afterward, we plotted the data on a scatter plot and finally made two best fit equations. Firstly, by using a two-degree polynomial expression followed by an exponential expression. Refer Table 4.

Here, we found out that the polynomial expression gave a less accurate result (75.79%) as compared to exponential (82.65%) as shown in Fig. 8a and b, respectively. One of the reasons might be that in a certain range (250000–400000), the polynomial expression exhibits a very less distance and resulted in detecting some vehicles which were not a problem or threat. Also, the expression indicates a big distance for a very large area which can also be a possibility of less accuracy to some extent.

Table 4 Comparison of accuracy using different equations

Equation	Accuracy using ROI 2 (%)
Polynomial ($y = 1\text{E}{-}10x^2 \text{-} 9\text{E}{-}05x + 13.721$)	75.61
Exponential ($y = 4319.3x^{-0.589}$)	82.65

5 Conclusion and Future Scope

Automated cars are the need of the hour. However, the main hindrance is reliability and safety. With this research work, we aimed to focus on obstacle detection techniques. Our proposed system was divided into four sections, i.e., finding the lane/ROI, detecting the cars, calculating the distance using various depth estimation techniques, and calculating safety. During this process, ROI having coordinates 0.7 w apart at 0.15 and 0.85 w along with an exponential equation for depth estimation resulted in positive threat detection with 82.65% accuracy. For future work, we will focus on improvement of the accuracy as well as ensure that the model learns and reacts to more complex situations like threats from behind and sideways. Also, some complex cases of curvature can be considered for reduced delay in threat identification and notification.

References

1. World Health Organization (online website), Road traffic injuries Accessed: August 2021. [Online]. Available: https://www.who.int/news-room/fact-sheets/detail/road-traffic-injuries
2. Financial (online website), Road accidents in India have socio- economic cost of upto Rs 2.91 lakh crore Accessed: October 2021. [Online]. Available: https://www.financialexpress. com/auto/industry/road-accidents-in-india-have-socio-economic-cost-of-usd-15–71–38–81- bn-bosch-deaths-fatalities/2356726/
3. Gour D, Kanskar A (2019) Optimised YOLO: algorithm for CPU to detect road traffic accident and alert system. Int J Eng Re s Technol (IJERT) 8(10)
4. Ibrahim AM, Hassan RM (2020) Real-time collision warning system based on computer vision using mono camera. In: 2nd Novel intelligent and leading emerging science conference (NILES). https://doi.org/10.1109/NILES50944.2020.9257941
5. Dogru N, Subasi A (2012) Traffic accident detection by using machine learning methods. In: International symposium on sustainable development 2(March)
6. Rana V, Joshi H, Parmar D, Jadhav P, Kanojiya M (2019) Accident detection using machine learning algorithm. Int Res J Eng Technol (IRJET) 08(10)
7. Khandbahale C, Pawar N, Rathod J, More K (2019) Multi object detection in vehicle for accident prevention and safety assistance using embedded system-implementation paper. Int J Eng Res Technol 08(05):18
8. Goud V (2012) Vehicle accident automatic detection and remote alarm device. Int J Reconfigurable Embed Syst (IJRES) 1(2):2012. https://doi.org/10.11591/ijres.v1i2.493
9. Kalyani T, Monika S, Naresh B, Vucha M (2019) Accident detection and alert system. Int J Innov Technol Exploring Eng (IJITEEE) ISSN: 2278-3075. https://doi.org/10.22214/ijraset. 2019.5568
10. Kattukkaran N, George A, Mithun Haridas TP (2017) Intelligent accident detection and alert system for emergency medical assistance. IEEE International conference on computer communication and informatics. 10.1109/ ICCCI.2017.8117791
11. Two second rule. Available: https://en.wikipedia.org/wiki/Two-secondrule
12. Advanced lane detection algorithm. Available: https://cacheop.medium.com/advanced-lane- detection-for-autonomous-cars-bff5390a360f
13. Redmon J, Divvala S, Girshick R, Farhadi A (2016) You only look once: unified, real-time object detection. In: IEEE Conference on computer vision and pattern recognition (CVPR). https://doi.org/10.1109/CVPR.2016.91

14. YOLO COCO darknet. Available: https://pjreddie.com/darknet/yolo/
15. Xi J, Guo H, Tian J, Liu L, Liu H (2019) A classification and recognition model for the severity of road traffic accidents. SAGE J 11(5)

Natural Language Processing

KDC: New Dataset for Kannada Document Categorization

R. Kasturi Rangan⑩ and B. S. Harish⑩

1 Introduction

Never-lasting demand for the creation of multilingual digital world made Internet no more monolingual. Yet even today many Indian regional languages are less resourced. Due to these extremely low resources, the natural language processing tasks on regional languages are arduous. Hence, regional language resources are still in demand for various natural language processing tasks. On the other hand, some of the regional languages have their own legacy of more than thousand years. Preservation of these languages is essential, so availability of these regional languages on digital platform is must. According to the People's linguistic Survey of India, there are 780 languages and dialects in India. Among them, 150 could vanish in next 50 years [22, 25]. UNESCO identified 191 Indian languages as vulnerable. These statistics demands the presence of regional languages in digital.

As per Ethnologue, India is a home to many natural languages. Among the list of 22 scheduled languages in Indian constitution, Kannada is one of the major south Indian languages having legacy since from fifth century. Due to the complexity in Kannada scripts, there are challenges in digitalizing the scripts. Hence, there are fewer digital resources for Kannada. Similarly, many Indian regional languages have lesser digital resources. Despite this, researchers worked on their own dataset by proposing machine learning algorithms for various language processing tasks. More recent studies on the state of the art in language processing tasks like machine

R. Kasturi Rangan (✉)
Department of Information Science & Engineering, Vidyavardhaka College of Engineering, Mysuru, India
e-mail: rkrangan@vvce.ac.in

B. S. Harish
Department of Information Science & Engineering, JSS Science & Technology University, Mysuru, India
e-mail: bsharish@jssstuniv.in

© The Author(s), under exclusive license to Springer Nature Singapore Pte Ltd. 2023
R. Doriya et al. (eds.), *Machine Learning, Image Processing, Network Security and Data Sciences*, Lecture Notes in Electrical Engineering 946,
https://doi.org/10.1007/978-981-19-5868-7_46

633

translation, named entity recognition, document categorization, and sentiment analysis, for Indian regional languages are found in [9, 11]. These surveys report novel performances of language processing methods based on pattern recognition strategies.

Natural language text categorization is the process of approximating an unknown category assignment function $F : D \times L \rightarrow \{0, 1\}$, where D represents the set of documents and L is the set of predefined categories/Labels. Text analysis and its categorization can be performed at document level, paragraph level, or sentence level [14]. Especially for document level, large data resources with respect to regional languages are in high demand.

In categorizing Indian languages, authors of [8] proposed a fuzzy rule inference system for the Bangla web text categorization and obtained result of 98.63%. As Bangla is also a less resourced Indian regional language, authors build their own dataset of 10,300 articles with 8 categories. Similarly, Dhar et al. [7] proposed TF-IDF-ICF (Term Frequency-Inverse Document Frequency-Inverse Class Frequency), a new feature selection method for Bangla text categorization, and claimed an accuracy of 98.87%. Further authors in [5, 6] experimented on 4000 and 1960 Bangla documents, and they achieved 98.03% and 97% of accuracy using Multi-Layer Perceptron (MLP) and dimensionality reduction techniques, respectively.

Further, authors in [24] experimented on 1680 Gujarati documents and obtained an accuracy of 88.96% using naïve bayes classifier. Digamberrao and Prasad [10] worked on author identification task for Marathi language articles. They considered only 15 articles of 5 Marathi authors. Authors in [21] experimented on 200 Marathi documents belonging to 20 different categories and found LINGO (Label Induction Grouping) clustering algorithm performed efficiently on their own dataset. Similar experiments on Punjabi poetry texts are carried out in [26]. They worked on 2034 poems of 4 different categories and obtained an accuracy of 76.02% using SVM (Support Vector Machine). Recently, [1, 17, 18] worked on categorizing Hindi documents on their own datasets created. Table 1 presents the author-built dataset information on various Indian regional languages, used for the task of regional document classification.

1.1 Previous Work on Other Kannada Datasets

As there is raise in demand of regional languages, research community concentrated on resource creation in digital platform for respective regional languages for various online tasks. Even for Kannada language, there is a need to create resources for various language processing tasks. Authors in [14] used a custom-built corpus called Technology for Development of Indian Languages (TDIL) which is a comprehensive Kannada text resource, developed by Central Institute of Indian Languages (CIIL). Further, they also experimented on the dataset built by fetching Kannada Wikipedia text. In [14], sentence level text classification is achieved. Similarly, summarization of categorized text document in Kannada language is experimented in [13] based on

Table 1 List of authors built Indian regional languages' datasets

Author details	Language	Number of documents	Categories
Bafna and Saini [1]	Hindi	697	4
Pal and Patel [17]	Hindi	122	3
Pal and Patel [18]	Hindi	55	9
Dhar et al. [8]	Bangla	10,300	8
Dhar et al. [7] Dhar et al. [6]	Bangla	4000	8
Dhar et al. [5]	Bangla	1960	5
Rakholia and Saini [24]	Gujarati	1680	6
Digamberrao and Prasad [10]	Marathi	15	5
Patil and Bogiri [21]	Marathi	200	20
Narhari and Shedge [15]	Marathi	200	8
Kaur and Saini [26]	Punjabi	2034	4
Rajan et al. [23]	Tamil	754	8
Deepamala and Kumar [4]	Kannada	600	6

sentence ranking technique. Authors in [13] built their own dataset from Kannada webdunia webpages. At paragraph level, authors of [12] worked on 1791 Kannada text paragraphs. These paragraphs are categorized into 4 classes and belong to CIIL developed TDIL corpus. The authors in [4] presented a dataset consisting of 600 webpage Kannada Text documents for classification task, and they have 6 categories in the corpus. Caryappa et al. [2] and Parameswarappa et al. [20] worked on algorithms to collect the Kannada web contents to build corpus and automatically check Kannada grammar, respectively.

2 A Dataset for Kannada Document Classification

Authors in [3] presented the action plan and initiatives taken by the Indian government to build corpus for Indian Languages which thereby encourage the regional language resource creations. Among Indian regional languages, Kannada language lacks in digital resources. The low resource condition drives the researchers to build their own corpus for various language processing tasks. This Kannada documents' dataset consists of 1007 documents which are collected from various sources. Documents of this dataset are collected by two means; one is through the Kannada news articles which are available on Internet and another way is by digitalizing

Table 2 New Kannada dataset and its characteristics

Label	Categories	No. of documents	No. of lines	No. of terms	No. of characters	Avg. No. of lines per document	Avg. No. of terms per line
1	Space and Science	70	3219	36,332	263,893	45.98	11.28
2	Politics	244	13,836	136,035	989,346	56.70	9.83
3	Crime	55	2390	27,584	200,692	43.45	11.54
4	Sports	60	2406	30,343	203,424	40.10	12.61
5	Economics	50	2106	25,143	412,617	42.12	11.93
6	Entertainment	100	6538	57,488	412,617	65.38	8.79
7	Health	28	1520	13,993	108,666	54.28	9.20
8	Stories and other articles	400	22,266	210,777	1,514,256	55.66	9.46

the hard copy of Kannada articles using optical character recognition technique. In the proposed dataset, there are eight different categories: Space and Science, Politics, Crime, Sports, Economics, Entertainment, Health, and Stories/Other articles. The documents are labeled manually based on the contents. This dataset is multilabel and unbalanced because document's count for each category is different. The total number of terms in the corpus is 537,695. The detail statistics of the dataset is presented in Table 2.

2.1 Main Challenges in Creating the Dataset

The documents are collected from online publicly available news articles and by digitalizing the hard copy of Kannada articles. This is done to ensure that the samples would be realistic. Each document consists of more than 500 words on an average and labeled with respect to its category.

The main challenge in this work is to obtain the data, especially from online news articles, because of less availability of publicly available articles. The online source links are (a) https://www.kannadaprabha.com, (b) https://kannada.oneindia. com, (c) https://kannada.asianetnews.com/india-news, (d) https://www.udayavani. com, and (e) https://kanaja.karnataka.gov.in/. Further challenge is to preprocess the documents. The challenges encountered in the processing of Kannada news articles are (a) Incorrect Spellings of terms and (b) Presence of multilingual words. The sample of this is presented in Fig. 1, where few English terms are present and incorrect spelling of Kannada term are also observed.

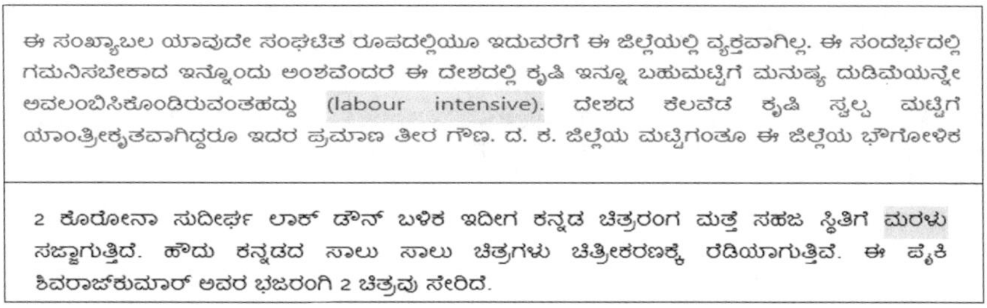

ಈ ಸಂಖ್ಯಾಬಲ ಯಾವುದೇ ಸಂಘಟಿತ ರೂಪದಲ್ಲಿಯೂ ಇದುವರೆಗೆ ಈ ಜಿಲ್ಲೆಯಲ್ಲಿ ವ್ಯಕ್ತವಾಗಿಲ್ಲ. ಈ ಸಂದರ್ಭದಲ್ಲಿ ಗಮನಿಸಬೇಕಾದ ಇನ್ನೊಂದು ಅಂಶವೆಂದರೆ ಈ ದೇಶದಲ್ಲಿ ಕೃಷಿ ಇನ್ನೂ ಬಹುಮಟ್ಟಿಗೆ ಮನುಷ್ಯ ದುಡಿಮೆಯನ್ನೇ ಅವಲಂಬಿಸಿಕೊಂಡಿರುವಂತಹದ್ದು (labour intensive). ದೇಶದ ಕೆಲವೆಡೆ ಕೃಷಿ ಸ್ವಲ್ಪ ಮಟ್ಟಿಗೆ ಯಾಂತ್ರೀಕೃತವಾಗಿದ್ದರೂ ಇದರ ಪ್ರಮಾಣ ತೀರ ಗೌಣ. ದ. ಕ. ಜಿಲ್ಲೆಯ ಮಟ್ಟಿಗಂತೂ ಈ ಜಿಲ್ಲೆಯ ಭೌಗೋಳಿಕ

2 ಕೊರೋನಾ ಸುದೀರ್ಘ ಲಾಕ್ ಡೌನ್ ಬಳಿಕ ಇದೀಗ ಕನ್ನಡ ಚಿತ್ರರಂಗ ಮತ್ತೆ ಸಹಜ ಸ್ಥಿತಿಗೆ ಮರಳು ಸಜ್ಜಾಗುತ್ತಿದೆ. ಹೊಸ ಕನ್ನಡದ ಸಾಲು ಸಾಲು ಚಿತ್ರಗಳು ಚಿತ್ರೀಕರಣಕ್ಕೆ ರೆಡಿಯಾಗುತ್ತಿವೆ. ಈ ಪೈಕಿ ಶಿವರಾಜ್ಕುಮಾರ್ ಅವರ ಭಜರಂಗಿ 2 ಚಿತ್ರವು ಸೇರಿದೆ.

Fig. 1 Spelling mistakes (correct spelling: ಮರಳಲು[Maraḷalu]) and multilingual words in dataset

On the other hand, documents are also collected by digitalizing the Kannada articles using OCR technique. The Google lens application is used in scanning the articles. The sources of document collection are from some of the monthly Kannada magazines like Kasturi, Mayura, and Arogya Darpana. The difficulty faced in scanning hard copy is fabrication of terms, i.e., some Kannada characters were recognized as other language characters [19]. This is due to the similarity of strokes of some Kannada characters as other language characters. The OCR will be ambiguous in digitalizing such scanned characters; hence, there will be fabrication of characters in scanned documents. For example, in Fig. 2, the highlighted characters are fabricated, i.e., Kannada characters are digitized as Telugu characters. Similarly, if many terms are fabricated, then those terms will be forming noise and deceive the language processing tasks.

Further, the challenges of spelling mistakes and presence of multilingual words are also part of this type of document collection.

ಅಗ್ನಿವೇಶನು ತನ್ನ ಹೆಸರಿನಿಂದಲೇ ರಚಿಸಿರುವ ಅಗ್ನಿವೇಶತಂತ್ರವು ಅತ್ಯಂತ ವಿಸ್ತಾರವಾಗಿಯೂ, ಗಂಭೀರ ವಿಷಯಗ ನ್ನೊಳಗೊಂಡಿರುವ ದಾಗಿಯೂ, ವಿಭಾಗರಹಿತವಾಗಿಯೂ, ಇದ್ದುದರಿಂದ ಚರಕಮಹರ್ಷಿಯು ಲೋಕಕಲ್ಯಾಣಾರ್ಥವಾಗ ವಿಸ್ತೃತ ವಿಷಯವನ್ನು ಸಂಕ್ಷೇಪಿಸಿ ಸಂಕ್ಷಿಪ್ತ ವಿಷಯವನ್ನು ವಿಸ್ತರಿಸಿ ನಿದಾನ, ವಿಮಾನ, ಶಾರೀರ, ಇಂದ್ರಿಯ, ಚಿಕಿತ್ಸಾ, ಕಲ್ಪ, ಸಿದ್ಧಿ, ಎಂಬ ಎಂಟು ಸ್ಥಾನಗಳನ್ನಾಗ ವಿಭಾಗಿಸಿ ಸಂಸ್ಕರಿಸಿದನು.

ಅಗ್ನಿವೇಶನು ತನ್ನ ಹೆಸರಿನಿಂದಲೇ ರಚಿಸಿರುವ ಅಗ್ನಿವೇಶತಂತ್ರವು ಅತ್ಯಂತ ವಿಸ್ತಾರವಾಗಿಯೂ, ಗಂಭೀರ ವಿಷಯಗ ನ್ನೊಳಗೊಂಡಿರುವ ದಾಗಿಯೂ, ವಿಭಾಗರಹಿತವಾಗಿಯೂ, ಇದ್ದುದರಿಂದ ಚರಕ ಮಹರ್ಷಿಯು ಲೋಕಕಲ್ಯಾಣಾರ್ಥವಾಗಿ ವಿಸ್ತೃತ ವಿಷಯವನ್ನು ಸಂಕ್ಷೇಪಿಸಿ ಸಂಕ್ಷಿಪ್ತ ವಿಷಯವನ್ನು ವಿಸ್ತರಿಸಿ ನಿದಾನ. ವಿಮಾನ. ಶಾರೀರ. ಇಂದ್ರಿಯ. ಚಿಕಿತ್ಸಾ. ಕೆಲ್ಪ. ಸಿದ್ಧಿ. ಎಂಬ ಎಂಟು ನ್ಯಾನಗಳನ್ನಾಗಿ ವಿಭಾಗಿಸಿ ಸಂಸ್ಕರಿಸಿದನು.

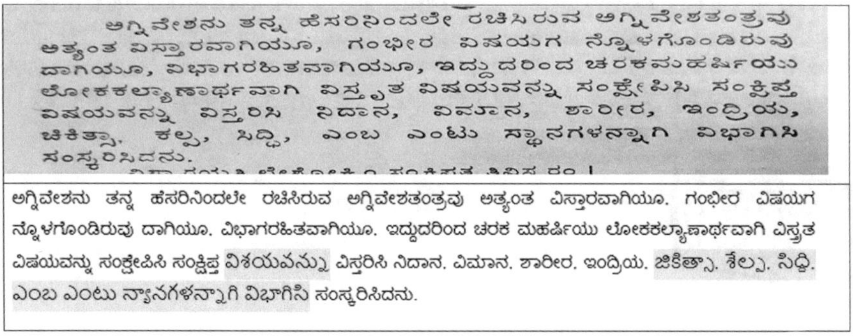

Fig. 2 An example of Kannada characters digitized as Telugu characters

3   Methodology Used to Validate the New Dataset

A newly created dataset is evaluated empirically using various classifiers. The general steps followed to carry out the automatic Kannada text categorization are shown in Fig. 3.

3.1   Tokenization

The initial step after the collection of raw datasets is preprocessing and tokenization. During preprocessing, numbers, punctuations, and few terms of less importance are removed. At first, regular expressions are used to remove the numbers and punctuations. Later, the threshold of higher and lower term frequency is obtained empirically. Based on these thresholds, terms are removed by considering them as less important. Tokenization is the process of splitting the entire documents into set of terms. This is achieved based on delimiters existing between the terms. Each term is called as a token. Generally, Natural Language Tool Kit (NLTK) library is used for tokenization [16].

3.2   Unicode Encoding

Due to limited 8-bit encoding, non-English characters are not able to represent by ASCII values; hence, Unicode came into existence. Encoding is the process of revamping the Unicode characters into a sequence of bytes. To overcome the loss of agglutination of characters in representing Kannada terms, a numeric representation of each term based on Unicode encoding is performed. Table 3 depicts an example of Unicode encoding for a Kannada term (Term: ಹಸಿರು; Transliteration: Hasiru).

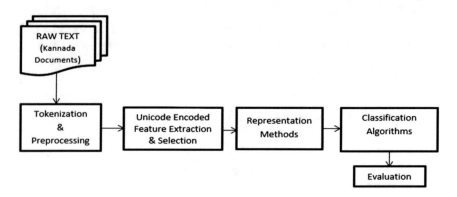

Fig. 3   Generic architecture of automatic Kannada text categorization

Table 3 An example for a numeric representation of each term based on Unicode encoding

Characters	ಹ	ಸ	ಿ	ರ	ು
Unicode standard values	\u0CB9	\u0CB8	\u0CBF	\u0CB0	\u0CC1
Encoding (UTF-16)	b'\xff\xfe\xb9\x0c\xb8\x0c\xbf\x0c\xb0\x0c\xc1\x0c'				
Decimal representation	394720271698498249767 3215743				

3.3 Vector Space Model

The digital text should be represented in a computationally appropriate form. In vector space model, documents are considered as vectors and each term's weight is calculated using either term frequency or term frequency-Inverse document frequency. TF-IDF weight represents the relevance of the term to a document and specifically IDF (Inverse Document Frequency) is a good index of a term in classification. Set of terms $T \in dj$ document and $T = \{t1, t2, t3, \ldots tk\}$ contains (k) unique terms. These unique terms represent the respective text document. Each (ti) has weight (wti) and calculated using TF (dj, ti), or TF-IDF (dj, ti), statistical measure. TF-IDF consists of TF(ti) and IDF(ti).

$$\text{IDF}(ti) = \log\left(\frac{N}{\mathrm{d}f(ti)}\right) \qquad (1)$$

$$wt(ti, dj) = \text{TF} * \text{IDF} \qquad (2)$$

In Eq. (1), N is the total number of documents and $\mathrm{d}f(ti)$ is the frequency of documents containing term (ti). In Eq. (2), $wt(ti, dj)$ represents the TF-IDF weight for each term. All documents in this new dataset are represented in vector space.

3.4 Classifiers

As a further step, the classification algorithms are applied on the new Kannada document dataset. From literature survey, among various classifiers, predominantly used classifiers like K-Nearest Neighbor (K-NN), Multinomial Naïve Bayes (MNB), Decision Tree (DT), and Support Vector Machine (SVM) are applied. Further, the neural networks and Multilayer Perceptron (MLP) classifier are also applied. The architecture of MLP consists of one hidden layer with 100 neurons, maximum epochs are set to 50, "ReLU" activation function in neurons, and the learning rate is fixed to 0.001.

To avoid the bias in the distribution of documents for training and testing sets, K-fold validation is performed for the entire dataset. K-fold makes every document to be part of both testing and training sets in any of the folds/distribution, i.e., given dataset samples are randomly divided into "K" equal divisions. Among these divisions, $K-1$ divisions will be taken for training and remaining will be used for testing the model. This process continues for "K" number of experiments. From K-fold experiments mean accuracy is calculated. Kannada document dataset is multilabel and unbalanced, i.e., in dataset every category consists of different number of documents. Hence, stratified K-fold validation is performed.

4   Experiments and Results

The benchmarking dataset is analyzed with the formerly mentioned machine learning algorithms. The experimentation results are presented to measure the reach and range of the benchmark dataset built, with well-known state-of-the-art classifiers.

Formerly, the documents are tokenized at word level and preprocessed by removing the numbers, punctuations. Further, the low and high frequency terms are also removed due to less significance, and frequency threshold values are computed empirically.

The Kannada documents are categorized using the classifiers like K-NN, SVM, DT, Multinomial NB, and MLP. Stratified K-fold validation is performed, as dataset is unbalanced and multilabel. In K-fold, parameter called "K" refers to the number of groups that a given data sample is to be split into. For an example, if $K = 2$ then the dataset is divided into 2 folds, that is 1007 documents are divided into 503 and 504 documents' sets. Later, each of it will be part of training and testing set. Further mean accuracy of those K-fold experiments is calculated. The following are the benchmarking experiments conducted.

4.1   K-Nearest Neighbor Classifier

This classifier is called as "Slow Learner," because it finds similarity with all the training samples using distance metrics for each test sample. The performance obtained when the K-Nearest Neighbor (K-NN) classifier is applied on Kannada documents at various K-fold experiments is as shown in Figs. 4 and 5. In Fig. 4, $k = 3$, i.e., the nearest neighbor value is 3 and 2, 3, 5, and tenfolds are considered for experimentation. The mean of threefold validation is 93.93%, which is better than all other experiments. Similarly, in Fig. 5, with $k = 5$ nearest neighbor value the mean of threefold validation is 94.03%. It is better than all other K-fold experiments.

Fig. 4 K-NN ($k = 3$) classifier results on Kannada document dataset

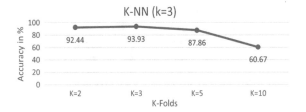

Fig. 5 K-NN ($k = 5$) classifier results on Kannada document dataset

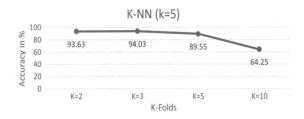

Fig. 6 SVM classifier results on Kannada document dataset

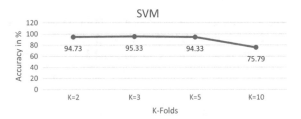

4.2 Support Vector Machine

In support vector machine, the documents are categorized by inducing hyperplane. This hyperplane's orientation and position depend on the supportive document vectors in document vector space. In Fig. 6, the results of 2, 3, 5, and tenfold experiments performed using Support Vector Machine (SVM) classifier are presented. The K-fold experiment ($K = 3$) mean accuracy result obtained is 95.33%, and it is the best among other K-fold results. The higher value of "K" leads to less biased model, but due to large variance it leads to over-fit. Due to over-fitting, fivefold and tenfold experiments obtained lesser accuracy.

4.3 Multinomial Naïve Bayes Classifier

Naïve Bayes classifier categorizes the documents based on Bayes' theorem. The Naïve word states that features in the dataset are mutually independent, i.e., occurrence of one feature does not affect the probability of occurrence of another feature.

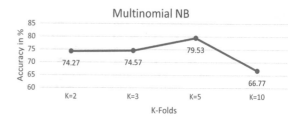

Fig. 7 Multinomial Naïve Bayes classifier results on Kannada document dataset

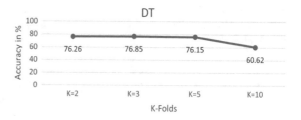

Fig. 8 Decision tree classifier results on Kannada document dataset

The Multinomial Naïve Bayes algorithm is used for the Kannada document categorization. Among K-fold validation experiments on proposed dataset, $(K = 5)$ fivefold validation accuracy is higher, i.e., 79.53% when compared to other K-fold's results.

4.4 Decision Tree

In Decision Tree (DT) classifier, data is continuously split at every node based on the decision rules. The performance of Decision Tree classifier over proposed Kannada document dataset is presented in Fig. 8. Among all K-fold's experiments, $K = 2$, $K = 3$, and $K = 5$ results are almost close but $K = 3$ experiment's performance is slightly higher, i.e., 76.85% than other K-fold's results.

4.5 Multilayer Perceptron

The next set of experiments are conducted using neural network architecture. As formerly mentioned, Multilayer Perceptron (MLP) neural network classifier is chosen for Kannada document categorization. The documents are divided into 70:30 ratio for training and testing sets, respectively. After preprocessing, totally 704 documents are trained. Initially, we consider one hidden layer with 100 neurons, 50 iterations, and "ReLU" (Rectified linear unit) as an activation function. ReLU function avoids sparsity, and Eq. 3 presents the functioning of "ReLU." Due to single hidden layer, this architecture is called as "vanilla" neural network. This vanilla architecture of neural network yields 92.07% accuracy. Similarly, another experiment with 150 neurons and 100 convergence iterations yields 98.01%; further with increase in neurons results

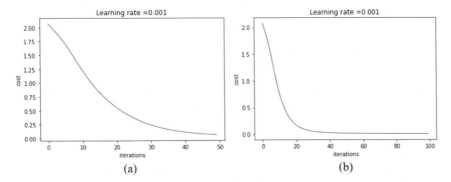

Fig. 9 The cost versus iteration graph **a** 100 neurons **b** 150 neurons

the same accuracy. The error-cost versus iteration graphs of both experiments are presented in Fig. 9.

$$f(x) = x^+ = \max(0, x) \tag{3}$$

5 Conclusion

A new dataset for Kannada document categorization, including both online and digitized documents, is proposed in this paper. The online documents are collected from various publicly available news webpages. The digitized documents are scanned with optical character recognition technique. There are 8 different categories of the documents and are all asymmetrical, i.e., number of documents per category is different.

The well-known state-of-the-art classifiers are used in experiments to benchmark the dataset. Among all the K-fold experimented classifiers, the SVM classifier in K = threefold experimentation yields best result, i.e., 95.33% mean accuracy. On the other hand, neural network especially vanilla multilayer perceptron network achieved better results than K-fold experimented results, i.e., 98.01% for 150 neurons in the hidden layer. However, in neural network classifier, the features considered for classification are higher than other classifiers. Hence, there is a scope for obtaining better results with new feature engineering techniques.

This new Kannada document dataset will elicit new corpus for developing optimized feature engineering techniques, new representation models for Kannada documents, and new algorithms for language processing tasks. The challenges mentioned like tackling the terms with mistakes in their spellings, multilingual tokens, tokenization, and other linguistic challenges need to be addressed. The results reported from benchmarking experiments could serve as a baseline for further research in Kannada document categorization.

References

1. Bafna PB, Saini JR (2020) On exhaustive evaluation of eager machine learning algorithms for classification of Hindi verses. Int J Adv Comput Sci Appl
2. Caryappa BC, Hulipalled VR, Simha JB (2020) Kannada grammar checker using LSTM neural network. In: 2020 international conference on smart technologies in computing, electrical and electronics (ICSTCEE). IEEE, pp 332–337
3. Choudhary N (2021) LDC-IL: the Indian repository of resources for language technology. Lang Resour Eval 1–13
4. Deepamala N, Kumar PR (2014) Text classification of Kannada webpages using various pre-processing agents. In: Recent advances in intelligent informatics. Springer, Cham, pp 235–243
5. Dhar A, Dash NS, Roy K (2018a) Application of TF-IDF feature for categorizing documents of online Bangla web text corpus. In: Intelligent engineering informatics. Springer, Singapore, pp 51–59
6. Dhar A, Dash NS, Roy K (2018b) Categorization of Bangla web text documents based on TF-IDF-ICF text analysis scheme. In: Annual convention of the Computer Society of India. Springer, Singapore, pp 477–484
7. Dhar A, Dash NS, Roy K (2018c) Classification of Bangla text documents based on inverse class frequency. In: 2018 3rd international conference on internet of things: smart innovation and usages (IoT-SIU). IEEE, pp 1–6
8. Dhar A, Mukherjee H, Dash NS, Roy K (2020) Automatic categorization of web text documents using fuzzy inference rule. Sādhanā 45(1):1–22
9. Dhar A, Mukherjee H, Dash NS, Roy K (2020b) Text categorization: past and present. Artif Intell Rev 1–48
10. Digamberrao KS, Prasad RS (2018) Author identification using sequential minimal optimization with rule-based decision tree on Indian literature in Marathi. Proc Comput Sci 132:1086–1101
11. Harish BS, Rangan RK (2020) A comprehensive survey on Indian regional language processing. SN Appl Sci 2(7):1–16
12. Jayashree R, Murthy KS, Anami BS (2013) Performance analysis of naïve Bayesian methods for paragraph level text classification in the Kannada language. In: International conference on human-computer interaction. Springer, Berlin, Heidelberg, pp 435–439
13. Jayashree R, Srikanta MK, Anami BS (2012) Categorized text document summarization in the Kannada language by sentence ranking. In: 2012 12th international conference on intelligent systems design and applications (ISDA). IEEE, pp 776–781
14. Jayashree R, Srikantamurthy K, Anami BS (2015) Sentence level text classification in the Kannada language—a classifier's perspective. Int J Comput Vision and Robotics 5(3):254–270
15. Narhari SA, Shedge R (2017) Text categorization of Marathi documents using modified lingo. In: 2017 international conference on advances in computing, communication and control (ICAC3), IEEE, pp 1–5
16. NLTK Website (2021) https://www.nltk.org/_modules/nltk/tokenize/regexp.html
17. Pal K, Patel BV (2020a) Automatic multiclass document classification of Hindi poems using machine learning techniques. In: 2020 international conference for emerging technology (INCET). IEEE, pp 1–5
18. Pal K, Patel BV (2020b) Model for classification of poems in Hindi language based on Ras. In: Smart systems and IoT: innovations in computing. Springer, Singapore, pp 655–661
19. Pal U, Chaudhuri BB (2004) Indian script character recognition: a survey. Pattern Recogn 37(9):1887–1899
20. Parameswarappa S, Narayana VN, Bharathi GN (2012) A novel approach to build Kannada web corpus. In: 2012 international conference on computer communication and informatics. IEEE, pp 1–6
21. Patil JJ, Bogiri N (2015) Automatic text categorization: Marathi documents. In: 2015 international conference on energy systems and applications. IEEE, pp 689–694

22. People Linguistic Survey (2012) http://peopleslinguisticsurvey.org/
23. Rajan K, Ramalingam V, Ganesan M, Palanivel S, Palaniappan B (2009) Automatic classification of Tamil documents using vector space model and artificial neural network. Expert Syst Appl 36(8):10914–10918
24. Rakholia RM, Saini JR (2017) Classification of Gujarati documents using Naïve Bayes classifier. Indian J Sci Technol 10(5):1–9
25. Reuters Blog (2013) http://blogs.reuters.com/india/2013/09/07/india-speaks-780-languages-220-lost-in-last-50-years-survey/
26. Kaur J, Saini JR (2020) Designing Punjabi poetry classifiers using machine learning and different textual features. Int Arab J Inf Technol 17(1):38–44

The Ties that Matter: From the Perspective of Similarity Measure in Online Social Networks

Soumita Das and Anupam Biswas

1 Introduction

Significant advancements in the usage of Online Social Networks (OSNs) have flooded the Internet with unprecedented volume of connections. The users of OSNs make connections based on common interests and backgrounds. With the rapid growth of connections in the cyberspace, the OSNs have become dynamic in nature. In order to emphasize the evolution of these networks, it is necessary to determine probability of a social connection between two users. This is extensively referred as the link prediction problem [1–6]. Links are predicted through similarity between two users based on various features. Recently, local similarity measures have gained a lot of attention because of it's accuracy and low time complexity. Some of the local similarity measures include common neighbors (CN) [6], Jaccard index [7], Adamic Adar (AA) [8], resource allocation (RA) [9], Sorensen [10], Salton Index (SA) [11], mutual information (MI) [12], preferential attachment [13], measure by Ghorban-zadeh et al. [14] and so on. Local similarity measures based on node degree and common neighbors information have been explored by Martínez et al. [4]. However, conventional local similarity measures such as common neighbors, Adamic Adar, resource allocation, resource allocation considering common neighbor interactions fails to normalize it's similarity score. In fact, such measures could not make a distinction between edge scores for directed edges. Aghabozorgi et al. [15] proposed a local measure based on a combination of common neighbors and triadic structures blocks to obtain similarity between two users but their approach is not practical for

S. Das (✉) · A. Biswas
Department of Computer Science and Engineering, National Institute of Technology,
Silchar 788010, Assam, India
e-mail: wingsoffire72@gmail.com

A. Biswas
e-mail: anupam@cse.nits.ac.in

© The Author(s), under exclusive license to Springer Nature Singapore Pte Ltd. 2023   647
R. Doriya et al. (eds.), *Machine Learning, Image Processing, Network Security and Data Sciences*, Lecture Notes in Electrical Engineering 946,
https://doi.org/10.1007/978-981-19-5868-7_47

large networks due to high time complexity. The local measure presented by Li et al. [16] is based on future common neighbors, where neighbors are classified into three classes.

Finding similarity between connected nodes can be used to detect group of similar nodes commonly referred as a community. Particularly, community detection algorithms based on local similarity have low time complexity [17–19]. Intuitively, these algorithms are mostly seed expansion oriented where at first seed nodes are selected based on certain criterion and then communities are expanded by adopting similarity measure. For instance, (α, β) algorithm explores the role of Jaccard Index in the detection of communities [20], another community detection approach incorporates random walk to traverse neighborhood information matrix [21, 22]. Moreover, local similarity can also be deployed in label propagation algorithm [23, 24]. Next, it is very important to validate the performance of the local similarity measures. To achieve this, we have selected a similarity based community detection method, namely Closeness Similarity driven Information Diffusion-based community detection (CSID) [25]. We incorporated our proposed local similarity measure, i.e., Neighborhood Density-based Edge Similarity (NDES) to generate communities. Next, the communities are evaluated in two perspectives: quality and accuracy. Quality metrics are used to determine the structural feasibility of detected communities by considering connectivity within and outside a community. However, accuracy metrics are deployed to evaluate the accuracy of the detected communities by comparing with ground-truth [26]. Different quality and accuracy metrics are available to evaluate the goodness and correctness of detected communities, respectively. We have evaluated NDES measure on CSID algorithm by considering several small real-world datasets, popular local simiarity measures, accuracy metrics and quality metrics. Comparative analysis of the results obtained would assist to infer the quality and accuracy of our proposed measure.

In this paper, a novel asymmetric edge similarity measure has been presented. The proposed measure considers neighborhood density to compute edge similarity. The contributions of this paper are as follows:

- Introduced a novel Neighborhood Density-Based Edge Similarity measure considering common neighborhood information.
- This is a normalized similarity score. This normalization part is important to reduce redundancy and improve score accuracy.
- Edge similarity score obtained by implementation of our proposed measure is asymmetric. Therefore, it is possible to compute edge similarity score for directed graphs as well.
- Evaluation of communities obtained by incorporation of our proposed similarity measure on a certain community detection algorithm suggests that proposed similarity measure gives comparatively good results both in terms of accuracy and quality.
- Time complexity is less compared to the representative local similarity measures.

The organization of the paper is as follows: Sect. 2 defines the proposed local similarity measure, Sect. 3 gives a literature review about existing local similarity measures, Sect. 4 presents a detailed discussion about our proposed approach, Sect. 5 discusses about the experimental analysis part and Sect. 6 is about conclusion.

2 Problem Definition

Given a simple graph $G(V, E)$ where V indicates set of nodes, E indicates set of edges. Each edge refers to a connection between node pairs $\{x, y\}$ where $x, y \in V$. The problem of edge similarity measure $s_{x,y}$ is to find proximity between connected node pairs based on local connectivity pattern. It is generally influenced by attributes such as neighbors, common neighbors and degree of the nodes under consideration because nodes share strong connections only with those nodes with which it shares tight neighborhood. The greater the value contributed by these attributes, higher is the $s_{x,y}$ score.

Often, similarity scores of all edges are computed to predict link establishment. Mostly, local similarity based problems consider common neighbors to determine $s_{x,y}$ scores and are symmetric in nature. Moreover, most of the existing measures are not normalized. It is to be mentioned here that normalization is important to reduce redundancy and improve accuracy. We introduce the notion of neighborhood density, information (see Sect. 4) in addition to common neighbors. Neighborhood density plays a significant role to derive the similarity between connected nodes because highly similar entities are densely connected with their neighboring entities. Additionally, it is not compulsory for both the nodes sharing a connection to have the same affinity toward each other. Therefore, we have introduced the information measure to normalize our proposed method. Thus, for a given graph G, the new local similarity measure utilizes common neighbor, neighborhood density and information to compute the similarity score.

3 Related Work

In general, link prediction methods are classified into three categories: similarity based algorithms, maximum-likelihood based algorithms and probabilistic models [2]. Similarity based algorithms are based on computation of the similarity score s_{xy} between node pairs (x, y). Higher $s_{x,y}$ value indicates higher probability of link establishment. In maximum-likelihood-based algorithms, the link establishment is calculated based on a series of rules. However, in probabilistic models, an abstract network model is generated to determine link establishment. Out of these algorithms, similarity based algorithms are comparatively simple and have low time complexity and therefore, applicable on large-scale networks as well. Recently, local similarity based measures received a lot of attention due to it's low time complexity, effectiveness and relative accuracy in social networks.

To explore the local similarity measures, let us first formalize some of the mostly used terms. Suppose, we have a graph $G(V, E)$ comprising n number of nodes and m number of edges. For a node say $x \in V$, set of neighbors and degree of node x is represented by $\Gamma(x)$ and $| \Gamma_x |$, respectively. If we assume $\{x, y\}$ to be a connected node pair where $x, y \in V$, then set of common neighbors and number of common neighbors between nodes x and y is indicated by $\Gamma(x) \cap \Gamma(y)$ and $| \Gamma(x) \cap \Gamma(y) |$, respectively. Union of node x and node y indicated by $\Gamma(x) \cup \Gamma(y)$ and k indicates largest node degree of graph G. Some of the existing local similarity measures are summarized as follows:

Adamic Adar: It is a measure to calculate the similarity between two web pages which is defined by [8],

$$s_{xy} = \sum_{z \in \Gamma(x) \cap \Gamma(y)} \frac{1}{\log(\Gamma(z))} \tag{1}$$

From Eq. (1), it is inferred that this is not a normalized measure and is symmetric. It's time complexity is $O(nk^3)$.

Preferential Attachment: It is defined by [13],

$$s_{xy} = | \Gamma_x | \times | \Gamma_y | \tag{2}$$

From Eq. (2), it is inferred that it is not a normalized similarity score and is symmetric. It's time complexity is $O(nk^3)$.

Resource Allocation: Both Adamic Adar and resource allocation measures penalizes common neighbors having high degree. However, RA gives better efficiency for networks having high average degrees. RA is defined by [9],

$$s_{xy} = \sum_{z \in \Gamma(x) \cap \Gamma(y)} \frac{1}{\Gamma(z)} \tag{3}$$

From Eq. (3), it can be derived that it not a normalized measure and is symmetric. It's time complexity is $O(nk^3)$.

Salton Index: It is also referred as cosine measure and is defined by [11],

$$s_{xy} = \frac{| \Gamma(x) \cap \Gamma(y) |}{\sqrt{| \Gamma_x | \times | \Gamma_y |}} \tag{4}$$

Equation (4) indicates that it is a normalized similarity score and is symmetric. It's time complexity is $O(nk^3)$.

Jaccard Coefficient: It is defined by [7],

$$s_{xy} = \frac{|\ \Gamma(x) \cap \Gamma(y)\ |}{|\ \Gamma(x) \cup \Gamma(y)\ |} \tag{5}$$

Eq. 5 indicates that it is a normalized similarity score and is symmetric. It's time complexity is $O(nk^3)$.

Discussion: In this paper, we have developed a novel edge similarity measure called NDES to estimate the proximity of vertices in a network. Existing similarity measures do not address the directionality and time complexity aspect properly. NDES has been developed to address the above mentioned issues. The NDES approach utilizes neighborhood density score to analyze similarity shared by connected node pairs. Here, neighborhood density is used to identify density of connections shared by connected node pairs. This is beneficial in this context because larger number of connections between connected node pair indicates higher similarity between nodes under consideration.

4 Proposed Approach

In this section, we shall discuss about our proposed local edge similarity measure which is based on density of connections shared by an edge with it's neighbors. To do so, at first, we formalize some basic concepts such as neighborhood density, number of common neighbors and degree of node that are used to design our proposed edge similarity measure. Additionally, we have designed a new information quantification formula to compute information possessed by a node for normalizing our edge similarity measure. As the information attached with connected nodes may be different, so the edge similarity score given by our proposed method is asymmetric.

4.1 Preliminaries

- Neighborhood density: For a connected node pair $\{x, y\}$, neighborhood density is used to compute the density of it's neighbors. This neighborhood density score is utilized to measure the connection similarity of the node pair under consideration. Let us assume that we have connected node pair $\{x, y\}$ where $x, y \in V$, then neighborhood density is indicated by $\rho_{x,y}$. Higher $\rho_{x,y}$ value indicates greater connection similarity score.
- Number of common neighbors: OSN users have a tendency to bond more with other users who are known to them. These acquaintances are identified by the connectivity information which gives the number of common neighbors shared by node pair. Here, the number of common neighbors shared by a node pair $\{x, y\}$ is

indicated by $|\Gamma(x) \cap \Gamma(y)|$. It is used to compute the similarity score associated with the node pair. The greater the number of common neighbors shared by node pair, larger is the similarity score of the corresponding node pair.

- Degree of node: It reflects the number of connections associated with a node. It plays a vital role to determine the relationship between node pairs connected by an edge. For instance, if the degree of node (say, x) indicated by $|\Gamma_x|$ is one, then it is evident that node x shares maximum similarity with it's associated edge.
- Information I_x: It indicates the amount of information related to node x in an undirected and unweighted network G. If connected nodes possess equal amount of information, it indicates that they are surrounded by the same set of entities and hence are similar.

4.2   Neighborhood Density-Based Edge Similarity

We have designed an edge strength measure, namely Neighborhood Density-based Edge Similarity (NDES) considering neighborhood density of the edge for better comprehension of the similarity shared by connected nodes. Suppose, we have connected node pair $\{x, y\}$, where $x, y \in V$, then we use the term $e_{x,y}$ to represent the edge shared by nodes x and y. The similarity score of node pair $\{x, y\}$ is based on common neighborhood computation. In this context, common neighborhood computation is defined in terms of neighbors between nodes x and y. Higher common neighborhood score indicates greater interaction frequency and hence higher similarity. We need to consider following cases for common neighborhood computation.

Case a. Nodes x and y do not have any common neighbor, i.e., $|\Gamma(x) \cap \Gamma(y)| = \phi$, then common neighborhood score of connected node pair $\{x, y\}$ is defined by,

$$\rho_{x,y} = \begin{cases} 1, & \text{if } |\Gamma_x| = 1 \text{ or } |\Gamma_y| = 1 \\ 0, & \text{if } |\Gamma_x| > 1 \text{ or } |\Gamma_y| > 1 \end{cases} \tag{6}$$

Case b. Nodes x and y share one or more than one common neighbor, i.e., if $|\Gamma(x) \cap \Gamma(y)| >= 1$, then common neighborhood score of connected node pair $\{x, y\}$ is defined by,

$$\rho_{x,y} = |\Gamma(x) \cap \Gamma(y)| + |\Gamma(x) \cap \Gamma(z)| + |\Gamma(y) \cap \Gamma(z)| + |\sigma_{xy}| + |\Gamma(w) \cap \Gamma(z)|,$$
$$\forall w, z \in (\Gamma(x) \cap \Gamma(y)) \text{ if } e_{w,z} \in E, \ w \neq z. \tag{7}$$

Equation (7) consists of five parts. Here, the first term $|\Gamma(x) \cap \Gamma(y)|$ indicates the common neighbors that is shared by nodes x and y, symbols $|\Gamma(x) \cap \Gamma(z)|$ and $|\Gamma(y) \cap \Gamma(z)|$ in the second and third term indicates the number of common neighbors that is shared by nodes x and y with common neighbor of x and y, respectively, forth term $|\sigma_{xy}|$ indicates the number of connections shared by the common neighbors of

x and y, fifth term $| \Gamma(w) \cap \Gamma(z) |$ indicates the number of common neighbors that is shared by common neighbors of x and y. Next, after the common neighborhood score $\rho_{x,y}$ have been computed for all the edges, we try to address the directionality aspect associated with an edge by computing the information possessed by a node say x as I_x which is defined as,

$$I_x = \max_{y \in \Gamma(x)} \rho_{x,y} \tag{8}$$

Equation (8) indicates that information possessed by node x is equal to the maximum neighborhood density score that x shares with it's neighboring nodes. Next, NDES score of connected node pair $\{x, y\}$ is computed by,

$$\text{NDES}(x, y) = \frac{\rho_{x,y}}{I_x} \tag{9}$$

And NDES score of an edge (y, x) is computed by the following equation,

$$\text{NDES}(y, x) = \frac{\rho_{x,y}}{I_y} \tag{10}$$

If $\rho_{x,y} = 0$, then NDES $(x, y) = 0$.

4.3 Time Complexity

It is inferred from NDES measure discussion that it comprises three parts. In the first part, finding common neighbors takes $O(n)$ time complexity. Next, in the second part, time complexity of finding possible connections among common neighbors and number of common neighbors that is shared by connected common neighbors is around $O(nk^2)$ where k refers to maximum degree of the network. In the third part, the time complexity associated with finding information associated with all the nodes is $O(n)$. Therefore, total time complexity associated with NDES is $O(nk^2)$. It is to be mentioned here that our method need not be applied in complete graphs because it won't be meaningful to find similarity scores of node pairs in completely connected graphs. Therefore, total time complexity is $O(nk^2)$.

5 Experimental Analysis

In this section, the strategy for evaluating the performance of NDES is detailed. We have selected a community detection algorithm, namely Closeness Similarity driven Information Diffusion-based community detection (CSID) and substituted their similarity measure, namely Closeness Similarity Measure [25] with popular local simi-

Table 1 Comparative summarization of local similarity measures

Similarity	Normalized/ not normalized	Symmetric/ asymmetric	Time complexity
NDES	Normalized	Asymmetric	$O(nk^2)$
Salton index	Normalized	Symmetric	$O(nk^3)$
Jaccard coefficient	Normalized	Symmetric	$O(nk^3)$
Adamic Adar	Not normalized	Symmetric	$O(nk^3)$

larity measures such as Salton Index [11], Jaccard Index [7], Adamic Adar [8] and our proposed similarity measure, namely NDES one by one as given in Table 1 to perform the comparative analysis. The communities obtained by incorporating these measures are evaluated in two directions: accuracy and quality to infer about the efficiency and effectiveness of our proposed similarity measure. We have considered accuracy metrics to evaluate correctness of detected communities using Normalized Mutual Information (NMI), Adjusted Random Index (ARI) and Normalized $F1$-Score (NF1). Furthermore, quality metrics are used to evaluate structural feasibility of detected communities which in turn is used to comparatively evaluate the goodness of our selected and proposed similarity measures. We have selected quality metrics based on internal connections such as modularity, external connections such as cut_ratio, expansion and combination of the internal and external connections such as conductance [27]. Next, we have selected some publicly available datasets from SNAP [28] repository. The quality and accuracy results obtained by incorporation of each of the similarity measures on CSID on several small real-world datasets such as strike network, karate network, riskmap network and dolphin network having ground-truth are presented in this section.

5.1 Result Analysis

As a matter of primary importance, we have investigated efficiency of proposed measure in terms of accuracy with respect to several popular similarity measures. The comparative graphical results with respect to accuracy of NDES measure on several real-world datasets are presented in Fig. 1. From these subfigures, it is inferred that NDES gives comparatively good accuracy results on all the representative datasets. Though the accuracy have not been achieved fully, we have accomplished our goal better in comparison with other similarity metrics. Furthermore, we have also analyzed quality-related aspects during this analysis. As can be observed from Figs. 2, 3, 4 and 5, NDES gives the best modularity score out of all the selected similarity measures on all the representative datasets which indicates goodness of NDES in terms of internal connections. Next, comparative analysis with respect to cut_ratio and expansion shows that NDES gives comparatively good performance with respect

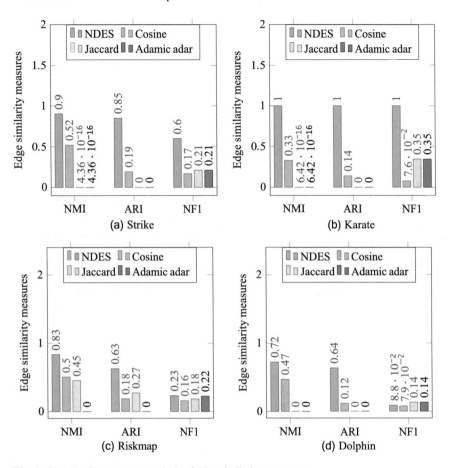

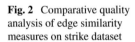

Fig. 1 Comparative accuracy analysis of edge similarity measures

Fig. 2 Comparative quality analysis of edge similarity measures on strike dataset

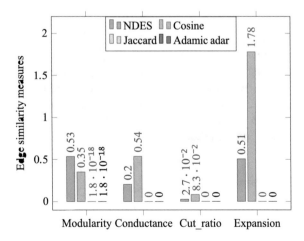

Fig. 3 Comparative quality
analysis of edge similarity
measures on Karate dataset

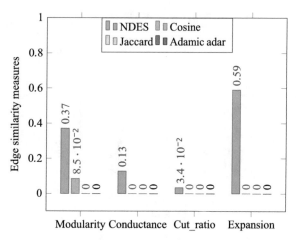

Fig. 4 Comparative quality
analysis of edge similarity
measures on Riskmap dataset

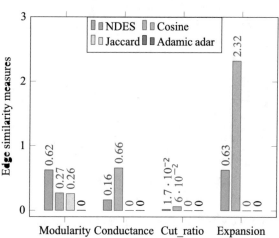

to external connections. Additionally, as can be seen from these figures, the results given by Jaccard index and Adamic Adar are zero and hence is negligible and therefore, not considered for analysis. Similarly, the comparative analysis of NDES with respect to conductance shows the goodness of NDES with respect to combination of internal and external connections. Therefore, it can be concluded that neighborhood density and information concept adopted by NDES is effective and efficient in determining similarity between connected nodes.

Fig. 5 Comparative quality analysis of edge similarity measures on Dolphin dataset

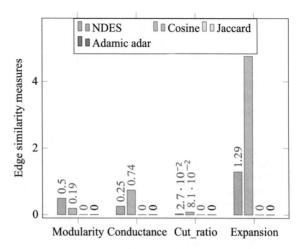

6 Conclusion

In this paper, we developed a neighborhood density-based asymmetric similarity measure called NDES considering both dense and sparse networks. It utilizes neighborhood density information associated with the connected node pairs to compute edge similarity score. An application of our proposed similarity measure for community detection in OSNs have been shown. For this, we have substituted the similarity measure of our selected community detection technique with NDES. Experiments on several small real-world datasets show that NDES achieves best accuracy and quality among Salton Index, Jaccard Coefficient and Adamic Adar. In addition to this, NDES has least time complexity in comparison with the baseline similarity measures. In the future works, we shall perform extensive experiments on large networks to evaluate performance of NDES.

References

1. Palla G, Derényi I, Farkas I, Vicsek T (2005) Uncovering the overlapping community structure of complex networks in nature and society. Nature 435(7043):814–818
2. Lü L, Zhou T (2011) Link prediction in complex networks: a survey. Physica A Stat Mech Appl 390(6):1150–1170
3. Al Hasan M, Zaki MJ (2011) A survey of link prediction in social networks. In: Social network data analytics. Springer, pp 243–275
4. Martínez V, Berzal F, Cubero J-C (2016) A survey of link prediction in complex networks. ACM Comput Surv (CSUR) 49(4):1–33
5. Dunlavy DM, Kolda TG, Acar E (2011) Temporal link prediction using matrix and tensor factorizations. ACM Trans Knowl Discov Data (TKDD) 5(2):1–27
6. Liben-Nowell D, Kleinberg J (2007) The link-prediction problem for social networks. J Am Soc Inf Sci Technol 58(7):1019–1031

7. Jaccard P (1901) Étude comparative de la distribution florale dans uneportion des alpes et des jura. Bull Soc Vaudoise Sci Nat 37:547–579
8. Adamic LA, Adar E (2003) Friends and neighbors on the web. Soc Netw 25(3):211–230
9. Zhou T, L ü L, Zhang Y-C (2009) Predicting missing links via local information. Euro Phys J B 71(4):623–630
10. Sorensen TA (1948) A method of establishing groups of equal amplitude in plant sociology based on similarity of species content and its application to analyses of the vegetation on Danish commons. Biol Skar 5:1–34
11. Salton G, McGill MJ (1983) Introduction to modern information retrieval. Mcgraw-Hill
12. Tan F, Xia Y, Zhu B (2014) Link prediction in complex networks: a mutual information perspective. PloS one 9(9):e107056
13. Barabâsi A-L, Jeong H, Néda Z, Ravasz E, Schubert A, Vicsek T (2002) Evolution of the social network of scientific collaborations. Phys A Stat Mech Appl 311(3-4):590–614
14. Ghorbanzadeh H, Sheikhahmadi A, Jalili M, Sulaimany S (2021) Ahybrid method of link prediction in directed graphs. Exp Syst Appl 165:113896
15. Aghabozorgi F, Khayyambashi MR (2018) A new similarity measure for link prediction based on local structures in social networks. Physica A Stat Mech Appl 501:12–23
16. Li S, Huang J, Zhang Z, Liu J, Huang T, Chen H (2018) Similarity-based future common neighbors model for link prediction in complex networks. Sci Rep 8(1):1–11
17. Jiang Y, Jia C, Yu J (2013) An efficient community detection method based on rank centrality. Phys A Stat Mech Appl 392(9):2182–2194
18. Li Y, Jia C, Yu J (2015) A parameter-free community detection methodbased on centrality and dispersion of nodes in complex networks. Phys A Stat Mech Appl 438:321–334
19. Wang T, Wang H, Wang X (2015) A novel cosine distance for detecting communities in complex networks. Phys A Stat Mech Appl 437:21–35
20. Eustace J, Wang X, Cui Y (2015) Community detection using local neighborhood in complex networks. Phys A Stat Mech Appl 436:665–677
21. Zhou H (2003) Distance, dissimilarity index, and network community structure. Phys Rev E 67(6):061901
22. Clauset A (2005) Finding local community structure in networks. Phys Rev E 72(2):026132
23. Bagrow JP, Bollt EM (2005) Local method for detecting communities. Phys Rev E 72(4):046108
24. Raghavan UN, Albert R, Kumara S (2007) Near linear time algorithm to detect community structures in large-scale networks. Phys Rev E 76(3):036106
25. Das S, Biswas A (2021) Community detection in social networks using local topology and information exchange. In: 2021 international conference on intelligent technologies (CONIT). IEEE, Hubli, pp 1–7
26. Das S, Biswas A (2021) Deployment of information diffusion for community detection in online social networks: a comprehensive review. IEEE Trans Comput Soc Syst 8(5):1083–1107
27. Chakraborty T, Dalmia A, Mukherjee A, Ganguly N (2017) Metrics for community analysis: a survey. ACM Comput Surv (CSUR) 50(4):1–37
28. SNAP Datasets: Stanford large network dataset collection. http://snap.stanford.edu/data. Accessed 27 Sep 2021

Comparative Study of Abstractive Summarizers (Sequence2Sequence Models)

Vijay Karunakaran and Manoj Das

1 Introduction

The world is getting smarter as the technology is being developed. These days smart people with more knowledge are valued more than just being smarter. To gain more knowledge in a smarter way, we need to have the grasp of many things in shorter amount of time, there comes the need for summarizer. With the help of text summarizer, we can get the summary of articles, reviews, lessons, websites and so on, and this can help us gaining more knowledge in shorter time. An automatic text summarizer will be of great use in the future, as the text data is getting accumulated day by day. Thus, researchers make a lot of studies on automatic text summarizer, to develop more reliable and efficient text summarizer. The text summarizer is majorly of two categories,

1. Extractive Text Summarizer,
2. Abstractive Text Summarizer.

The extractive text summarizer, as the name suggests, it summarizes the text paragraphs by extracting out most important lines of the paragraph, here the summary is a part of the text paragraph. While in abstractive summarizer, the summary would be the essence of the text paragraph, where a new meaningful sentence is generated, it is more likely a human way of summarizing the text.

In this paper, both extractive and abstractive summarizers are discussed in more detail, with the intuition behind each of the methods. For extractive summarizer, we use text-rank algorithm and for abstractive summarizer, we try out two deep learning models, that make use of Long-Short Term Memory (LSTM) and Bidirectional LSTM units. This has been elaborately discussed in methodology section of

V. Karunakaran (✉) · M. Das
ABV -IIITM, Gwalior 474015, India

© The Author(s), under exclusive license to Springer Nature Singapore Pte Ltd. 2023   659
R. Doriya et al. (eds.), *Machine Learning, Image Processing, Network Security and Data Sciences*, Lecture Notes in Electrical Engineering 946,
https://doi.org/10.1007/978-981-19-5868-7_48

this paper. The way we implement such algorithms are provided in implementation section, and we also compare and analyze both of the models that are being discussed in this paper (Compare and Analyze).

2 Literature Review

There are hundreds of studies on text summarization techniques, in [1], the authors reviewed many different methods for summarizing and checked whether those methods results in extractive or abstractive, and they were more specific about Arabic text Summarizer. On studying [2, 3] we get idea on various extractive summarization methods like statistical approaches, graph-based approaches and machine learning approaches, wherein machine learning approach can be of clustering or classification methods, further which can also be extended with neural networks. One of the most popular [4] graph-based ranking algorithms which is generally applied to text summarization is called TextRank [5] is inspired from PageRank [6] algorithm which is also a backbone of Google Search engine, which was designed for web link analysis. Before even getting to all of such algorithms, we need to understand various techniques in Natural Language Processing for Text Preprocessing [7] which is the base of any of the computations on text data. In [8], the author examines the effect of text preprocessing techniques on text classification and concludes that the accuracy of the classification significantly varies on text preprocessing techniques.

With the help of tokenization from any input text, the words can be converted to input units of text classification models, which then turned out to have an efficient Word2Vec [9] representation. As our goal fully focused on text summarization techniques, a pretrained multiword embeddings can be used to preprocess the text data [9]. The reference paper [10] is an evidence that the Natural Language Generated Abstractive summarizer outperforms the ranking-based extractive summarizer especially with controversial text data. And typically, an abstractive text summarizer fall under Seq2Seq models [11] as the size of the input sequence varies from the size of the output sequence. The unidirectional encoder–decoder architecture might not perform as good as bidirectional Long-Short Term Memory (LSTM) architecture with attention-based mechanism with multi-sentence text to produce short summaries [12]. The objective of the paper is to study the differences between LSTM architectures with and without attention mechanism by comparing the ROUGE scores.

3 Methodology

3.1 Text Preprocessing

In the text data preprocessing, all the paragraphs are converted to individual sentences. These sentences undergo few steps,

- remove punctuations, numbers and special characters,
- make alphabets lowercase letters,
- remove the stopwords (words like is, was, am, in, the).

After cleaning the text by the above-mentioned steps, the cleaned text are tokenized by the Natural Language Toolkit (NLTK) [13]. Further these tokens are made to sentence vectors with the help of word embeddings.

3.2 Word Embeddings

Word embedding is the vectorial representation of the text, where each of the word is represented by a feature vector, and the values of the vector represents the syntactical and semantic feature of the word. These word embeddings help the abstractive summarizer, by mapping the word vectors with corresponding word vectors that gives the similar meaning of the words and retains the original meaning of the summary. In Natural Language Processing (NLP), these word embeddings [14] are frequently used; therefore, researchers developed few readymade word embeddings such as Global Vectors (GloVe), Word2Vec, FastText and few more. GloVe word embedding is a pretrained word embedding which was created by Standford University, where unsupervised algorithms make use of some statistical information present in the occurrences of the words in the text, which then outputs a matrix with meaningful substructures. Word2Vec is another model that helped in faster training of word embeddings for larger datasets. There are two methods for Word2Vec model, first is skipgram and second is continuous bag of words (CBOW) [14]. Current word is predicted with the help of next-next words in the case of CBOW method, whereas in skip-gram method current word is used to predict the next-next words [9].

3.3 Extractive Summarizer

Extractive summarizer is typically a concept of arranging the sentences from most important to the lesser important sentences from a given text paragraph. Here the summary would be some top most important sentences. This summarizer assumes that if any sentence contains the words with highest degree (here degree refers the frequency of the word in the entire text), essentially that sentence has to describe the purpose of the text. To extract out such top most important sentences, the text-rank algorithm [5] suits the best. After text preprocessing, the similarity matrix is made. The number sentences are the order of the matrix, and every element of similarity matrix represents the similarity scores of two sentences. The score is measured as the number of words that are common to both the sentences. Further, this similarity matrix is made to a weighted graph with similarity scores as edge weights. And then graph-based ranking algorithm [4] is applied and the sentences are arranged in ascending order of their ranks.

3.4 Abstractive Summarizer

Unlike extractive summarizer where it gives the summary text from the given text, an abstractive summarizer generates new sentences as summary of the text, which is similar to human tasks. And it is known that deep learning simulates the human brain, thus for abstractive summarizers, various deep learning techniques [15] are used such as recurrent and convolution neural networks (RNN,CNN) and sequence2sequence models.

3.4.1 Recurrent Neural Network (RNN)

A recurrent neural network in deep learning is one of the technique which is used to process the sequence of data one step at once and outputs the next sequence based on the previous sequence [16]. This technique is applied when the output depends on the previous outputs, for example when teaching the machine to find a pattern of a sequence of numbers then the machine should have the knowledge of the output for the previous numbers in that sequence. The same technique is applied even for the cases of text.

3.4.2 Long-Short Term Memory (LSTM)

With the RNN model, the weights of each neuron changes while training the sequences and finally can predict the next part of the sequences, but it does not have the capacity to remember the past elements of the sequence. However, to build up a model that works well with a real-time data like text, speech, etc., a component of memory is required in a model while training the data. Here comes the LSTM architecture in use. LSTM also solves the issue of vanishing gradient and error back-flow problems [17]. As shown in the Fig. 1, each LSTM cell has these four gates at its main components, input, output, memory and forget gates.

In the input gate, the data is fed at a given timestep is the output of preceding timestep. The input vector for the foremost LSTM cell is a vector of random values or generally consists of zeroes. The forget gate takes output of the last few cells, current

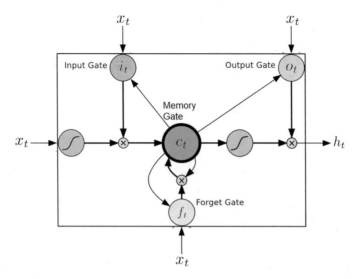

Fig. 1 LSTM Architecture

input data, last memory cell data and bias as its input, and it determines whether it should remember the previous state. The memory gate is the component where the information is aggregated from the previous states along with the new data. Finally, the output gate of the LSTM cell decides the quantity of new information which was generated by the memory gate of the current cell, which has to be given to the next LSTM cell.

3.4.3 Encoder–Decoder

Keeping the LSTM units as base, the encoder–decoder architecture is used for solving a enormous amount of sequence2sequence problems especially when the lengths of input and output are significantly different [18]. In the Encoder–Decoder architecture, at the encoder part, for any LSTM unit, the vector representations of the live input words (Xi) and also the output of the LSTM cells of all preceding words are fused together and given to the succeeding LSTM unit.

As the Fig. 2 shows the vector form of the word X3, the outputs from first LSTM cell and second LSTM cell are fused and given as a input to the third LSTM unit. After providing and processing all the word vectors of the input text, the output is produced from the endmost LSTM unit of the Encoder is forwarded to the Decoder in a vector form often known with a name the context vector [19]. Along with the context vector, that is given to the foremost LSTM unit of the Decoder, a symbol <SOS>which refers start of the sequence is also taken to produce the initial word of the summary (assume Y1, as seen in Fig. 2). Upon this condition, Y1 is given as a input vector to the succeeding decoder LSTM unit. Each developed output word is

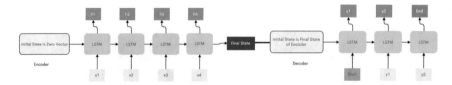

Fig. 2 Encoder–decoder architecture

forwarded to the succeeding decoder LSTM cell as its input to predict the next-next words of the summary. The endmost produced word is the end of the output string <EOS>symbol. Before making the final summary, each of the output vector (like Y1,Y2,etc.) from the decoder is taken in the form of a distributed depiction prior to evaluating the efficiency of the model.

3.4.4 Attention Mechanism

In the above-mentioned Encoder–Decoder model, the encoder transforms the complete input sequence of word vectors within a fixed-length vector of word vectors and later the decoder outputs the final string (summary). This works only in case of short sequence of inputs as the Decoder is focusing at the complete input data for developing the summary. So, it is difficult for the encoder to store and remember the long sequences into fixed-length vectors. Therefore, the efficiency of a Normal Encoder–Decoder model decreases exponentially when the length of the input sequence increases [12, 19]. Thus, we bring the concept of attention mechanism in abstractive text summarizations and many other NLP tasks.

The attention mechanism is generally implemented at every output vector of the encoder to compute the weight connecting the output vector and the corresponding input vector, and the sum of these weights is unit. The main purpose of utilizing weights to the word vectors is to determine which input vector must acquire the attention for the corresponding output vectors. The weighted mean of the preceding hidden states of the Decoder in each timestep is computed after forwarding every input vector and given to the Softmax layer together with the preceding LSTM cell's output [20].

3.4.5 Evaluation

It is very important to evaluate our model's performance based on the output that is being generated. Recall-Oriented Understudy for Gisting Evaluation (ROUGE) [21] a text similarity metric extensively used for text summarizing. ROGUE was specifically introduced for text summarizer. It has some different types. ROGUE-n types are rooted on ngram co-occurrence. ROGUE-L an another type which is rooted in longest common subsequence in the test output and the actual output. Ideally, only this evaluation metric alone cannot decide the performance of the model. But for a comparative analysis, this kind of evaluation is sufficient enough.

4 Implementations

4.1 Datasets

There are more than 48 datasets of various platform that are available over Internet that are made specifically for text summarization. In this paper, two different datasets are for two deep learning models (Table 1).

4.2 Training

After the text preprocessing is performed as discussed in the Sect. 3, the data is split in 90:10 ratio as train and test data, where 90% is used in training and 10 percent in testing for both of the datasets. Then we decide the maximum fixed length of the textual data and summary data, after which we use padding in order to make the length of the textual data and summary data to the fixed maximum length (Table 2).

Both of these datasets have quite a good number of data instances, hence we used Tensor Processing Unit (TPU) provided by Kaggle platform. Both these models

Table 1 Datasets used

Dataset	Model used	Total no of instances	No of instances used
Amazon food fine review	Encoder–decoder	568,454	100,000
WikiHow (large-scale data)	Encoder–decoder (with attention mechanism)	215,365	215,365

Table 2 After preprocessing fixing the lengths of text and summary

Dataset	Model used	Max length of text	Max length of summary
Amazon food fine review	Encoder–decoder	80	10
WikiHow (large-scale data)	Encoder–decoder (with attention mechanism)	70	20

V. Karunakaran and M. Das

Fig. 3 Model-1 (Amazon dataset without attention layer)

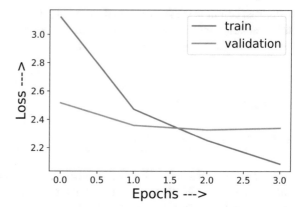

Fig. 4 Model-2 (WikiHow dataset with attention layer)

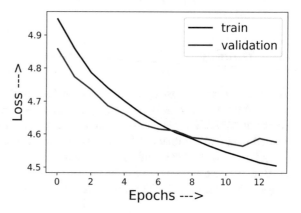

were prepared to train for 50 epochs but as we included EarlyStopping, that prevents the model from overfitting the training data, the model automatically tends to stop training after some number of epochs. The major difference between both the models is that for WikiHow dataset, the model employs attention mechanism which is an extra embedding layer added as compared with the normal Encoder-Decoder model used for Amazon food fine review. Fig. 3 shows the training and validation loss to the corresponding epoch number for model-1 (Amazon food fine review). Fig. 4 shows training and validation loss to the corresponding epoch number for model-2 (WikiHow). As, it can be observed the model-1 which is without attention mechanism has greater validation loss during the training, while the model-2 with attention layer trains well and the validation loss decreases with the number of epochs trained. This shows the model-2 trains very well with the dataset.

Table 3 ROUGE scores

Dataset	Model used	ROUGE-1	ROUGE-2	ROUGE-L
Amazon food fine review (Model-1)	Encoder–decoder	0.1000	0.0200	0.1000
WikiHow (Model-2)	Encoder–decoder (with attention mechanism)	0.2774	0.0479	0.2595

5 Results

It is necessary to observe the accuracy of the model after training for which we have already kept the test data aside. By using this test data, we evaluate both the models, by ROUGE scores. Before that we take a sample of data from test dataset and feed it to our trained model, first to the encoder of the model, which would give output from the last hidden layers, which then be fed to the decoder of the model and get the final output as tokens, which is a vector representation of words. These tokens are further converted to the text of words. Next comes the comparison of the words in predicted summary and test summary by using ROUGE scores. In the model-1 which uses Amazon dataset and without attention mechanism, the scores are very less as compared to model-2 which is with attention mechanism. The Rouge-1 scores represent Unigram that describes the number of single words match between the generated summary and the actual summary from the dataset. Similarly, Rouge-2 scores represent the Bigram that describes about the two word matches. And Rouge-L scores represent the longest common subsequence match between the actual and generated summaries. It's observed that all the three types of scores are better for model-2 which has attention mechanism (Table 3).

6 Comparative Analysis

It is clearly observed from the ROUGE scores, that the model-2 encoder–decoder with attention mechanism model generates better summaries when compared with model-1 encoder–decoder without attention mechanism. However, it may not be generalized for any given datasets. Here, we used two different models for two different datasets. It may happen that for a dataset whose length of text and summaries are small, yet model-1 out performs model-2. But we can surely generalize that for the datasets where the length of text is larger, then attention-based model will give a better result than a model without attention mechanism.

7 Future Improvements

There are better models for abstractive text summarizer which has been used as web apps or mobile apps, so for the future improvements, we may need to try out recent models and improve further. However, our goal is only to compare the normal encoder–decoder model and the model with attention mechanism, even this comparison can be performed in a much better way. By taking a dataset with the text length smaller than the datasets that we used, and train the both the models with the same dataset. This work can result in better comparison of the models, in case of smaller text dataset, same can be performed with larger text length dataset. Further, for evaluating the models, BLEU scores can be used which is a better evaluation metric as compared to ROUGE score [22]. These works mentioned above will result in getting a deep insights on both the models by understanding their behavior in training and testing.

8 Conclusion

Abstractive text summarizer should be considered as a hot domain in RNN, every now and then researchers are publishing a paper on text summarizer. Achieving a text summarizer that can mimic human made summarizer might not be easy, yet a lot of improved models on transfer learning [23] gives a better version of text summarizer. However, there is no generalized model for text summary, as there are many categories like summarizer for single sentence, multiple sentences and multiple documents. One of model might out perform in a category and might under perform in another category. Still a lot more study might need to be performed on basic models and improve further, in order to make innovative model which could be a combined models that can bring us generalized text summarizer.

References

1. Abualigah L, Bashabsheh MQ, Alabool H, Shehab M (2020) Text summarization: a brief review. https://doi.org/10.1007/978-3-030-34614-0_1
2. Al-Taani AT (2017) Automatic text summarization approaches. In: 2017 international conference on Infocom Technologies and Unmanned Systems (Trends and Future Directions) (ICTUS), pp 93–94. https://doi.org/10.1109/ICTUS.2017.8285983
3. Babar S, Tech-Cse M (2013) Rit. Text summarization: an overview
4. Mihalcea R (2004) Graph-based ranking algorithms for sentence extraction, applied to text summarization. In: ACL
5. Mihalcea R, Tarau P (2004) TextRank: bringing order into text. EMNLP
6. Brin S, Page L (1998) The anatomy of a large-scale hypertextual web search engine. Comput Netw 30:107–117
7. Camacho-Collados J, Pilevar MT (2017) On the role of text preprocessing in neural network architectures: an evaluation study on text categorization and sentiment analysis

8. Uysal AK, Gunal Serkan (2014) The impact of preprocessing on text classification. Inf Process Manag 50:104–112. https://doi.org/10.1016/j.ipm.2013.08.006

9. Mikolov T, Sutskever I, Chen K, Corrado GS, Dean J (2013) Distributed representations of words and phrases and their compositionality. Adv Neural Inf Process Syst 26

10. Carenini G, Cheung JCK (2008) Extractive vs. NLG-based abstractive summarization of evaluative text: the effect of corpus controversiality

11. Shi T, Keneshloo Y, Ramakrishnan N, Reddy CK (2021) Neural abstractive text summarization with sequence-to-sequence models. ACM/IMS Trans Data Sci 2(1), Article 1:37. https://doi.org/10.1145/3419106

12. Suleiman D, Awajan A (2020) Deep learning based abstractive text summarization: approaches, datasets, evaluation measures, and challenges, mathematical problems in engineering. 2020(Article ID 9365340):29. https://doi.org/10.1155/2020/9365340

13. Loper E, Bird S (2002) NLTK: the natural language toolkit. CoRR. cs.CL/0205028. https://doi.org/10.3115/1118108.1118117

14. Mikolov T, Chen K, Corrado G, Dean J (2013) Efficient estimation of word representations in vector space. In: Proceedings of workshop at ICLR

15. Wang H, Zeng D (2020) Fusing logical relationship information of text in neural network for text classification. Math Prob Eng 2020, Article ID 5426795:16. https://doi.org/10.1155/2020/5426795

16. Graves A (2013) Generating sequences with recurrent neural networks

17. Hochreiter S, Schmidhuber J (1997) Long short-term memory. Neural Comput 9:1735–80. https://doi.org/10.1162/neco.1997.9.8.1735

18. Vinyals O, Bengio S, Kudlur M (2015) Order matters: sequence to sequence for sets

19. Lopyrev K (2015) Generating news headlines with recurrent neural networks

20. Chopra S, Auli M, Rush AM (2016) Abstractive sentence summarization with attentive recurrent neural networks, pp 93–98. https://doi.org/10.18653/v1/N16-1012

21. Lin C-Y (2004) ROUGE: a package for automatic evaluation of summaries. In: Proceedings of the ACL workshop: text summarization braches out 2004:10

22. (Graham Y (2015) Re-evaluating automatic summarization with BLEU and 192 shades of ROUGE (pp 128–137). https://doi.org/10.18653/v1/D15-1013

23. Keneshloo Y, Ramakrishnan N, Reddy CK (2018) Deep transfer reinforcement learning for text summarization

Comparative Analysis of Lexicon-Based Emotion Recognition of Text

Anima Pradhan, Manas Ranjan Senapati, and Pradip Kumar Sahu

1 Introduction

Human emotions are classified into two types: verbal and non-verbal. Verbal emotions are expressed in the form of speech, sounds, or texts, whereas non-verbal emotions come through facial expression, body movement, or hand gestures. Understanding the emotions of a person by analysing his/her feelings or thoughts written in texts is quite a challenging task. This is because most of the time emotional words are not used to express the emotions. Hence the system needs to analyse the texts, interpret, and predict the perception of concepts to identifying human emotions such as joy, anger, and fear

Human–computer interaction plays a significant role in recognizing emotions in the text [1, 2]. Nowadays various social networking sites, such as news, blogs, and discussing forum allows people to share views as emotions, sentiments, and opinions. Quite a few researchers are of the opinion that recognizing emotions is a more important task than identifying sentiment polarity. More than one emotion may be categorized into the same sentiment polarity, i.e. positive, negative, or neutral that can influence the sentence differently. For example, "I was scar" (FEAR) and "The morning newspaper has not arrived yet" (ANGER) come under the negative polarity. Both sentences convey different types of information to the decision-makers from the perspective of emotions [3]. Therefore, researchers have proposed emotion recognition task using emotion-word lexicon decisions [4] and machine learning methods [5].

The emotional analysis is a fine-grained model and is known as a natural evolution of sentiment analysis. Several articles have been written about sentiment analysis with a limited amount of work focusing on emotion recognition from texts. Emo-

A. Pradhan (✉) · M. R. Senapati · P. K. Sahu
Department of Information Technology, Veer Surendra Sai University of Technology, Burla, Odisha, India
e-mail: animap2011_phdit@vssut.ac.in

© The Author(s), under exclusive license to Springer Nature Singapore Pte Ltd. 2023
R. Doriya et al. (eds.), *Machine Learning, Image Processing, Network Security and Data Sciences*, Lecture Notes in Electrical Engineering 946,
https://doi.org/10.1007/978-981-19-5868-7_49

tion recognition has many applications such as stock prediction [6], advertisement or product recommender systems [7], political speech [8] influenced by people's emotions, marketing strategies [9] of a company based on consumer's emotions, etc. Generally, there are three labels, namely positive, negative, or neutral to represent sentiments. However, at the same time for emotions, a distinct number of representations exist such as "Plutchik's wheel of emotions" [10] with eight emotions (joy, surprise, trust, sadness, fear, anger, anticipation, and disgust) or "Ekman's" [11] six emotions (sadness, fear, happiness, disgust, anger, and surprise). "WordNet-Affect (WNA)" [12] and "NRC word-emotion lexicon" [13] include handcrafted emotion lexicons which associates between words and emotions identified by "Plutchik" and "Ekman".

Though various number word-emotion lexicons have been developed for English, the size of emotion lexicons is still small than sentiment lexicons. Another challenging task is to create high-quality and high-precision emotion lexicons for the researchers."Depechemood" is one of the largest emotion lexica, which generate numerical scores for various emotion automatically. Later, an extended version of "Depechemood", is developed known as "Depechemood++ (DM++)", to improve the performance in terms of coverage and precision using simple techniques. Here the data is directly feed into the lexicon and it interprets associated emotions to score automatically rather than to only label them.

Therefore, "DM++" is focused on emotion recognition on textual information and compares the performance with another emotion lexicon "NRC", which is also publicly available on the web. To extract emotions, techniques of "Natural Language Processing (NLP)" are applied and implemented on Python language version 3.6.

The organization of this paper is as follows. In Sect. 2, related work on "machine learning" and "lexicon-based" approach for emotion recognition is presented. In Sect. 3, detail of our research method for automatic emotion classification is explained. Result is evaluated in Sect. 4 and conclusion of the paper is presented in Sect. 5.

2 Related Work

In this section, a review of the research effort to detect emotions made by different researchers is presented. Based on the two popular techniques, the review is divided into a "machine learning" and "lexicon-based approach". In a machine, it depends on the availability of the word-emotion pair in the respective lexicon [14], whereas the domain-independent nature of "lexicon-based approaches" makes it training dependent.

2.1 Machine Learning Approach

"Machine learning approaches", such as supervised and unsupervised learning depend on the various classifiers. "Plutchik's wheel of emotions" is classified using different classifiers ("Logistic Regression", "Bayesian", "Support Vector Machines (SVM)", and "Random Forest"), and their performances are compared [5]. Another study compared three machine learning classifiers, "SVM", "Decision Tree", and "Naive Bayes" to a lexicon-based approach ("NRC lexicon"). Some studies demonstrated the results using the "Naive Bayes" classification algorithm in emotion detection [15, 16]. Other studies classified emotions using the "SVM machine learning classification algorithm" [13, 17–19].

2.2 Lexicon-Based Approach

"Lexicon-based approaches" use single or multiple lexical resources to detect emotions. The most popular lexicon "WordNet Effect" was developed [16] by tagging effective synsets with "Ekman's" six basic emotions with its meaning in English "WordNet". It contains 2874 synsets and 4787 words. Though the "WordNet effect" is of limited size, its quality is good as it was created and validated manually. "NRC Emotion lexicon", the largest annotated emotion lexicon [20], contains 14,200 unigram words obtained from Google n-gram corpus accompanied by "Plutchik's eight emotions". "DepecheMood" [21] was created automatically by extracting social media data from "rappler.com", which were crowd annotated news articles accompanied "Rappler's Mood meter" that allowed the users to share their feelings/emotions about the articles they are reading. The lexicon consists of 37K words with seven emotion scores (afraid, inspired, sad, angry, annoyed, don't care, happy, and amused)."DepecheMood++" is a high-precision/high coverage lexicon and extended version of "DepecheMood" used in domain-specific tasks [22].

3 Automatic Emotion Classification

Here, a brief description of the process on how to collect, annotate the data set, and compare the publicly available lexicons and to apply NLP techniques on "NRC" and "DepecheMood++" is given.

3.1 Data Source

International Survey on Emotion Antecedents and Reactions (ISEAR) sentence-label emotion data set consists of 7666 sentences is used in the experiment. It is the collection of news headlines from news websites and newspapers. This data set consists of seven emotion classes: joy, disgust, anger, fear, shame, surprise, and sadness. The data set which is in a CSV file and labelled with emotions is extracted using Pandas dependency. The extracted data is then used to show the average percentage of votes for each emotion. Here, Joy has a higher percentage of votes as reported in Table 1.

First, the emotion matrix $Emotion\_matrix$ is built using "DepecheMood++" emotion lexicon, which provides the voting percentage of each sentence in the eight emotion labels: happy, angry, amused, don't care, afraid, annoyed, inspired, and sad. Then, each document is Part of Speech (PoS) tagged and the nouns, adjectives, and verbs are extracted, which are later lemmatized and the lists of lemmas feed into the lexicon to compute the emotion score for each emotion label.

Mathematically, it was written as follows:

Let D be a set of documents represented as follows: $Dn = \{d1, d2, ...dn\}$ where n is total number of documents, $E(Di) = \{$basic emotion assigned to document$\}$ and $Em = \{e1, e2, ...em\}$ be the list of emotion labels represented as follows: ["AFRAID" ,"AMUSED","ANGRY" ,"ANNOYED" ,"DONT_CARE" ,"HAPPY", "INSPIRED" ,"SAD"].

Based on "Rappler's mood meter", the lexicon contains eight mood-related words. The technique is applied on the data set which consists of seven emotion classes. Out of the eight mood-related word used in "Rappler's mood meter", four words like happy, angry, sad, and afraid are replaced with joy, anger, sadness, and fear for its applicability on the dataset is being used. The rest of the four emotions Amused, Annoyed, Don't Care, and Inspired are discarded as it is not available in the data set that is being used in the experiment. Even though the emotion words are discarded but still the technique has assigned some emotion score because another similar word is used in the sentence. A part of the matrix generated by this process is given in Table 2.

Table 1 Average percentage of votes for each emotion in dataset

Emotion	Votes	Emotion	Votes
Joy	0.145	Sadness	0.140
Fear	0.144	Disgust	0.142
Anger	0.143	Shame	0.142
Guilt	0.140		

Table 2 An excerpt of the *Emotion_matrix*

Sent_id	AFRAID	AMUSED	ANGRY	ANNOYED	DON'T_CARE	HAPPY	INSPIRED	SAD
doc_id_01	**0.074**	0.146	**0.115**	0.138	0.125	**0.095**	0.214	**0.091**
doc_id_01	**0.079**	0.138	**0.110**	0.128	0.159	**0.101**	0.171	**0.114**
doc_id_03	**0.091**	0.128	**0.116**	0.122	0.116	**0.084**	0.215	**0.127**
doc_id_04	**0.103**	0.141	**0.134**	0.131	0.131	**0.108**	0.127	**0.14**
doc_id_05	**0.084**	0.164	**0.107**	0.132	0.124	**0.097**	0. 0.207	**0.084**

The bold value signify the probability value of common emotions in both the dataset and Rappler's mood meter

4 Evaluation

Experiments on the data set is performed using several benchmark algorithms. For all the experiments, the data labelled with Joy, Angry, Sadness, and Fear are considered.

The correlation between the emotion score extracted from *Emotion_matrix* is compared with the predicted score for the ISEAR data set using "Pearson's correlation". The result obtained from the correlation analysis is given in Table 3. It can be verified that for "NRC" correlation score is low for emotions like fear and anger, whereas it is high for joy and sad. Similarly, for "DM++", all the four emotions correlation score are high. The result shows that "DM++" outperformed the "NRC". To carry out the classification for the each emotion, emotion scores are normalized between 0 to 1 using the formula given below:

$$e' = \frac{(e - \min(e))}{(\max(e) - \min(e))} \tag{1}$$

The normalized emotion score is then converted into a binary representation. If the score is more than 0.5, changed into 1 otherwise 0. For evaluation, F1-Measure is employed, and the results obtained are given in Table 4.

The classification accuracy for the corpus using "Naive Bayes'", "Logistic Regression", "Support Vector Machine", and "Gaussian Naive bayes" as applied on "DM++" and "NRC" lexicons is given in Table 5. The accuracy of PoS@token and lemma is compared with a popular word lexicon "NRC".

Table 3 Pearson correlation score between predicted and word lexicon

Emotion	DM++ @Lemma	DM++ @PoS	NRC @token
Fear	0.129	**0.280**	0.047
Anger	0.134	**0.205**	0.085
Joy	0.199	**0.304**	0.228
Sad	0.242	**0.289**	0.141

Table 4 F1-Measure results for emotion classification

Emotion	DM++@Lemma	DM++@PoS	NRC@token
Fear	0.382	**0.339**	**0.339**
Anger	0.419	**0.432**	0.429
Joy	0.496	**0.525**	0.394
Sad	**0.534**	0.453	0.529

The bold value signify the highest F1-Measure

Table 5 Comparison of classification results in terms of accuracy over all emotions, NB, LR, SVM, KNN and GNB using DM++ and NRC word lexicon

Lexicon	Accuracy				
	NB	LR	SVM	KNN	GNB
DM++@lemma	0.26	0.43	0.39	0.53	0.43
DM++@PoS_token	0.30	**0.48**	**0.45**	**0.57**	**0.47**
NRC token	**0.40**	0.40	0.40	0.17	0.39

The bold value signify the highest accuracy

5 Conclusion

Emotion detection is one of the important fields for researchers in various applications. There are several works that have been proposed in emotion detection from audio and facial information. On the other hand, emotion detection from textual information is an interesting and novel research area. Therefore, a lexicon-based emotion detection system is focused to identify emotions from text. In an emotion recognition task, two word-emotion lexicons "NRC" and "Depechemood++" have shown their skills in identifying emotions from ISEAR data set. The classification accuracy was considered to evaluate the performance of five machine learning algorithms like "Naive Baye's", "Logistic Regression", "K-Nearest Neighbours", "Support Vector Machine", and "Gaussian Naive Bayes" classifiers. The experimental results based on the ISEAR corpus indicate that there are some distinct differences between the performances of the "DM++" and "NRC" lexicons. The performance of "NRC" is better in "NB", whereas "Depechemood++" performed better in "LR", "SVM", "KNN", and "GNB" algorithm.

References

1. Abdul-Mageed M, Ungar L (2017) Emonet: fine-grained emotion detection with gated recurrent neural networks. In: Proceedings of the 55th annual meeting of the association for computational linguistics, vol 1: Long papers, pp 718–728
2. Alm CO, Roth D, Sproat R (2005) Emotions from text: machine learning for text-based emotion prediction. In: Proceedings of the conference on human language technology and empirical methods in natural language processing, pp 579–586

3. Raghunathan R, Pham MT (1999) All negative moods are not equal: motivational influences of anxiety and sadness on decision making. Organ Behav Hum Decis Process 79(1):56–77
4. Meo R, Sulis E (2017) Processing affect in social media: a comparison of methods to distinguish emotions in Tweets. ACM Trans Internet Technology (TOIT) 17(1):1–25
5. Mohammad SM, Turney P (2013) Crowdsourcing a word-emotion association lexicon. Comput Intell 29(3):436–465
6. Bollen J, Mao H, Zeng X (2011) Twitter mood predicts the stock market. J Comput Sci 2(1):1–8
7. Mohammad SM, Yang TW (2013) Tracking sentiment in mail: how genders differ on emotional axes. In: Proceedings of the 2nd workshop on computational approaches to subjectivity and sentiment analysis. Association for computational linguistics, pp 70–79
8. Pang B, Lee L (2008) Opinion mining and sentiment analysis. Found Trends Inf Retrieval 2(1–2):1–135
9. Bougie R, Pieters R, Zeelenberg M (2003) Angry customers don't come back, they get back: the experience and behavioral implications of anger and dissatisfaction in services. J Acad Mark Sci 31(4):377–393
10. Plutchik R (1994) The psychology and biology of emotion. HarperCollins College Publishers
11. Ekman P (1992) An argument for basic emotions. Cogn Emotion 6(3–4):169–200
12. Strapparava C, Valitutti A (2004) Wordnet affect: an affective extension of wordnet. In Lrec, vol 4, pp 1083–1086
13. Mohammad SM, Zhu X, Kiritchenko S, Martin J (2015) Sentiment, emotion, purpose, and style in electoral tweets. Inf Process Manag 51(4):480–499
14. Koumpouri A, Mporas I, Megalooikonomou V (2015) Evaluation of four approaches for "Sentiment Analysis on Movie Reviews" The Kaggle competition. In: Proceedings of the 16th international conference on engineering applications of neural networks (INNS), pp 1–5
15. Krishnan H, Elayidom MS, Santhanakrishnan T (2017) Emotion detection of Tweets using Naïve Bayes Classifier. Int J Eng Technol Sci Res 4(11):457–462
16. Strapparava C, Mihalcea R (2008) Learning to identify emotions in text. In: Proceedings of the 2008 ACM symposium on applied computing, pp 1556–1560
17. Li W, Xu H (2014) Text-based emotion classification using emotion cause extraction. Expert Syst Appl 41(4):1742–1749
18. Roberts K, Roach MA, Johnson J, Guthrie J, Harabagiu SM (2012) EmpaTweet: annotating and detecting emotions on Twitter. In: Lrec, vol 12, pp 3806–3813
19. Mike T, Kevan B, Georgios P, Di C, Arvid K (2010) Sentiment in short strength detection informal text. J Am Soc Inf Sci Technol 61(12):2544–2558
20. Luyckx K, Vaassen F, Peersman C, Daelemans W (2012) Fine-grained emotion detection in suicide notes: a thresholding approach to multi-label classification. Biomed Inf Insights 5(Suppl. 1):61–69
21. Staiano J, Guerini M (2014) Depechemood: a lexicon for emotion analysis from crowd-annotated news. In: Proceedings of the 52nd annual meeting of the association for computational linguistics, association for computational linguistics, pp 427–433
22. Araque O, Gatti L, Staiano J, Guerini M (2019) Depechemood++: a bilingual emotion lexicon built through simple yet powerful techniques. IEEE Trans Affect Comput 13(1):496–507

A Comprehensive Understanding of Text Region Identification and Localization in Scene Imagery Using DL Practices

Ritu Devi and Bijendra Kumar

1 Introduction

Automatic extraction of textual information from visual media plays a crucial role in the field of machine-based vision analysis. Text regions embedded in the surrounding images communicate viable information. The evolution of potent machine vision practices and the generation of a huge amount of visual data over the last few years lead to tremendous development in text region identification and localization approaches. Many growing applications like robotic navigation, scene text erasing, blind auxiliary, and others prerequisite the development of a robust and efficient text region detector. Despite significant STD research achievements, experts are still striving to build a robust and real-time solution due to the following challenging aspects: (1) The text is spread across the image, locating textual information that may vary in size/scale, aspect ratio, shape (irregular shaped), font, color, texture, and orientation is a tedious task. (2) The background detail includes text-like outliers such as windows, bricks, foliage, and other elements that make text discrimination difficult. (3) Additional challenges may include an intractable lighting situation, extremely low contrast, non-uniform illumination, and a cluttered background. The presence of multiple scripts in natural scene images makes recognition tasks more challenging because their style and scripting vary.

Classical approaches explored hand-made features extensively. And integrating image processing tasks with conventional machine learning-based techniques improved the results considerably. Researchers have been able to reap the benefits

R. Devi (✉) · B. Kumar
Netaji Subhas University of Technology, New Delhi, India
e-mail: ritu.co18@nsut.ac.in

B. Kumar
e-mail: bizender@nsut.ac.in

R. Doriya et al. (eds.), *Machine Learning, Image Processing, Network Security and Data Sciences*, Lecture Notes in Electrical Engineering 946,
https://doi.org/10.1007/978-981-19-5868-7_50

of automation in a few or all parts of the learning framework since the development of DL techniques, allowing them to focus on more target-specific difficulties.

1.1   Problem Overview

Reading textual information from scene images/documents consists of two sub-parts: text detection and text recognition. Detection/Localization of text from native surrounding images depicts the detection and verification of text instances followed by locating them using bounding boxes around them. The detection task can be illustrated as shown in Fig. 1 based on observations from current DL-based techniques. It may include the following subtasks:

Image Pre-processing: Image quality is enhanced to make it easier to discern text features from their surroundings, resulting in fewer false text detections.

Feature Generation and Selection: In conventional feature learning, time-consuming, handcrafted features are engineered, which are more prone to outliers. But with the advancement of deep neural network techniques, features from data are learned automatically. The researchers can either use transfer learning to employ the pre-trained architecture for feature production or build and train a network from the ground up for their problem domain.

Candidate Proposal Generation: The proposal lists candidates who are likely to have text regions in the images. The proposals can be generated based on pre-designed bounding boxes (i.e., anchors), simple clustering, and others.

Prediction Model: The feature generated from the backbone model will feed into the prediction model. The model is then trained and learned to predict the adjusted offset by calculating the loss functions among predicted and ground truth coordinates. These learned weights are then employed in inference to determine the efficiency of the model.

Post-processing: Some of the approaches utilized this step to further refine accuracy of anticipated bounding boxes. It may include text binarization, non-max suppression, morphological operations, and so on.

The processes outlined above may differ based on the problem-solving component selected by researchers. We looked at and summarized contemporary techniques

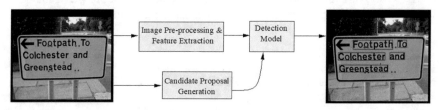

Fig. 1 Visualization of the process of text instance detection and localization in scene image. The example is taken from ICDAR2013 [1]

reported in the recent five to six years for this study. The following is a breakdown of the paper's structure: The classification of existing methodologies published in the literature presented in Sect. 2. Sections 3 and 4 describe the feature extraction and detection models utilized. Section 5 includes the numerous available datasets and evaluation protocol. Finally, in Sect. 6, conclusion and future aspects in the mentioned domain are discussed.

2 Previous Work

The STD approaches can be conventional machine learning-based approaches and deep learning-based approaches.

2.1 Before Deep Learning Era

The text detection task in conventional system was based on handcrafted complex feature generation and selection techniques that required complex pre- and post-processing procedures to refine the process. Connected component analysis (CCA) [2–8] and sliding window (SW) [9–12]-based techniques are the two types of methodology [13]. Initially, researcher had utilized primary features such as color, gradients, and textures for text/non-text candidate discrimination in an image. These low-level features were then combined to distinguish the text components in complex environment that include stroke, regions, points, and others. Stroke width transform (SWT) [14], maximally stable extremal regions (MSER) [15], HOG, and other hybrid features have shown to be successful in extracting text characteristics in increasingly complex scenarios.

CCA-Based: MSER and SWT are prominent and efficient candidate component extraction mechanisms and are used in literature extensively. Due to the enormous text-like outliers produced by these approaches, the model needs sophisticated filtering capable classifiers to discriminate the text from the non-text component. These approaches are computationally efficient, but they may not handle a vast diversity of text in the complex scene images.

SW-Based: Generally, these approaches are categorized as texture-based and supervised in nature where the textual information is predicted by shifting the varying size sub-windows across an image comprehensively. These methods are computationally inefficient and by their very nature, slow.

To improve the resilience and accuracy of text region detection and localization systems, hybrid methods [16, 17] integrate and take the benefit from different features representing varying characteristics of the text. Huang et al. [16] proposed a robust approach by combining the MSER and sliding window methods. The convolutional neural network (CNN) classifier is used by the author to extract high-level semantic information to discriminate between text and non-text components. In summary, the traditional method supported horizontal or nearly horizontal text detection effectively but having complex implementation with high time-consuming pre- and post-processing steps leads less robust system.

2.2 DL-Based Methodologies

With the evolution of neural network, schemes and large-scale data availability with the high-processing feasible devices made the feature learning task automated. Which reduced the researcher's overhead for producing complex features manually that motivate them to explore the problem in more accurate and robust manner to deal with various challenges associated with the problem domain. In literatures, text region extraction problem may be solved either by using regression-based mechanism or segmentation-based mechanism. Some researcher takes the benefit from both methodologies called hybrid approaches.

Regression-based approaches: These kinds of approaches cast the text detection task as general object detection scheme by inspiring from the existing frameworks [18–22] for feature extraction and bounding box predictions. These approaches are mainly anchor-based and focused on horizontal and multi-oriented text. Some of the popular approaches proposed based on pre-designed anchor boxes are [23–25]. Recently, authors are focusing on anchor free approaches [26–29] to target the diversity of text in complex environment. Author in [30] had analyzed the anchor-based regression with a point-specific regression and adopted the direct regression that predicts offset from a given point in direct and straightforward way. He adopted FCN followed by a recalled NMS as a post-processing step to address the arbitrary-oriented text region identification. The rotation region proposal network (RRPN) [23] proposed an approach that regresses bounding boxes precisely to fit into text regions with different orientations. A new aspect had introduced by connectionist text proposal network (CTPN) that integrates a backbone network VGG16 with RNN to locate sequential nature text instances. It provides a method for creating vertical text proposals that can be easily adapted to different scripts, including cursive text. The arbitrary-oriented scene text regions had detected in [31] by proposing the rotational R-CNN approach.

Although, regression-based schemes are popular for multi-oriented detection of text object, but it require complex pre-defined fixed size bounding boxes which difficult to tune during training. And having structural limitation to capture all possible shapes that may fail to deal with curved text or irregular shaped text (Table 1).

Segmentation-based approaches: Prominently, these algorithms utilized to localize the free-form text instances accurately by casting the STD problem as semantic segmentation task. In semantic segmentation, pixels are arranged in an interpretable way to segment the various text blocks/regions in an image and instance segmentation treats the multiple instances of the same class individually by introducing a new learning head called mask. The segmentation-based algorithms may

Table 1 Regression-based text detection approaches

Method	Year	Backbone/diction model	Pre-key contribution
CTPN [25]	2016	VGG16/Faster R-CNN	Anchor-based approach that localize multi-scale text lines in ambiguous environment by integrating with recurrent mechanism
SSTD [32]	2017	VGG16/SSD	Single-stage detector with text regional attentional and hierarchical inception components to enhance localization accuracy
DDR [30]	2017	FCN	Point-specific regression approach adopted followed by recalled NMS to identify irregular shaped text
SegLink [24]	2017	VGG16/SSD	Focused on oriented text segment by partitioning text line into segments and links
R2CNN [31]	2017	VGG16/Faster R-CNN	Rotational R-CNN proposed to detect arbitrary-oriented text
EAST [29]	2017	VGG16/FCN	Simplified the network pipeline that directly estimate the arbitrary-oriented text
TextBox ++ [33]	2018	VGG16/SSD	Focused on multi-oriented text
RRPN [23]	2018	VGG16/Faster R-CNN	Proposed angle-specific proposals to identify multi-oriented text
RRD [34]	2018	VGG16/SSD	Different branches introduced for rotation insensitive classification and rotation-sensitive regression to address multi-orientation
AF-RPN [28]	2019	VGG16/Faster R-CNN	Acquainted anchor-free RPN to identify multi-oriented text
SPCNet [35]	2019	ResNet50/Mask R-CNN	Irregular shaped text detection by reducing false positive and flexible boxes introduced
PuzzleNet [36]	2020	ResNet/FPN	Focused on segment-based proposal to predict irregular shaped text
ContourNet [27]	2020	ResNet50	Focused on minimization of false positive using texture information in horizontal and vertical direction and large-scale text using adaptive RPN
FC2RN [26]	2021	ResNet50 + FPN	Anchor-free corner detection-based mechanism to identify multi-oriented large text instances accurately
Cao et al. [37]	2021	EfficientNet18/BiFPN	Proposed bidirectional FPN to improve the results

differ in the manner that they segregates the text pixels into the individual text instances.

Methods in [38, 39] had utilized fully convolutional network (FCN) [40] model for pixel-specific identification of text. Wordsup [41] acquainted the character-based labeling issue and adopted a weakly-supervised framework that exploits the word-based annotations. TextSnake proposed in [42] was designed to handle free-form text instances based on symmetric axis. Author in [43] proposed an approach inspired from [41] to localize individual character regions accurately and finding affinity between them. Multi-scale expansion of kernel utilized by [44] to address the irregular shaped text region detection as well as cohesive text instances separation issues faced in the previous approaches using ResNet as a backbone with feature pyramid network (FPN) prediction model. To balance the speed and accuracy of the text detection pipeline, [45] equipped the lightweight segmentation network that is ResNet18 with a feature pyramid enhancement module (FEPM) followed by feature fusion module (FFM). The author proposed a differential binarization (DB) component that is fully differentiable and can be optimized during learning to ameliorate the performance of segmentation task in [46]. ResNet18/50 utilized as a backbone architecture pre-trained on SynthText dataset and then fine-tuned on the other real-world available datasets. Ye et al. [47] acquainted the issues associated with irregular shaped text and exploit the inter- and intra-dependency in text instances properties using collaborative learning.

The complex pixel-level computation makes segmentation-based techniques more flexible to capture arbitrary shape text. It often needs post-processing steps which makes it computationally expensive. Sometimes, it may fail to separate adhesive text instances accurately.

Hybrid Approaches: It integrates the characteristics from above two approaches to address the problems that are unsolved by individual schemes. Some of the popular approaches are [27–29, 48]. In [29], the text identification pipeline had simplified by using a single network to approximate the text orientation represented by quadri-lateral/rectangular boundaries directly. A strategy to cope with false positives and the large-scale variation problem in scene images has been acquainted by the author in [27]. And focused on minimization of false positives using texture information in the horizontal and vertical direction and large-scale text using adaptive RPN. To tackle the sticky variable-shaped text identification problem, a multi-perspective lightweight learning framework was introduced that simplified the model. Some works use a combination of methodologies to optimize the outcome in complex circumstances. However, improving detection accuracy necessitates the development of a novel framework, which may lengthen overall processing time due to the additional processing stages (Table 2).

Table 2 Segmentation-based text detection approaches

Method	Year	Backbone/diction model	Pre-key contribution
STDH [38]	2016	VGG16/FCN	Localizing global and local-level textual information using holistic prediction of multi-level and multi-scale features
MOTD [39]	2016	VGG16/FCN	Utilized two FCN, one for salient map estimation and another for character centroid to minimize false result
WordSup [41]	2017	VGG16/FCN	Character-based labeling issue addressed and a weakly-supervised framework adopted
TextSnake [42]	2018	VGG16/U-Net	Designed to handle free-form text instances based on symmetric axis
PixelLink [49]	2018	VGG16/FCN	Focused on very close text instances via intance-aware segmentation
CRPN [50]	2019	VGG16/Faster R-CNN	DeNet utilized anchor-free corner-based proposal to estimate locations and estimate links among them using LinkDirection
CRAFT [43]	2019	VGG16/U-Net	Improved localization accuracy by extracting character-based regions and estimating affinity among them
PSENet [44]	2019	ResNet/FPN	Multi-scale kernel proposed to address the arbitrary shaped and cohesive text instances issues
PAN [45]	2019	ResNet18/FPEM + FFM	Explore the tradeoff among speed and accuracy and proposed a lightweight framework for arbitrary shaped text
SBD [51]	2019	RestNet/Mask R-CNN	Addressed label confusion issue and integrate SBD into mask R-CNN to enhance detection performance
TextField [52]	2019	VGG16/FCN	Addressed irregular shaped text issue and proposed direction field followed by some post-processing steps
DB [46]	2020	ResNet/FPN	Proposed a fully differentiable component that can be optimized during learning that optimize result
CTRNet [53]	2021	ResNet50/FPN	Focused on label design using cognition aware technique and omit the need of text kernel segmentation
I3CL [47]	2021	ResNet/Mask R-CNN	Utilized the inter- and intra-dependency in text instances properties using collaborative learning

(continued)

Table 2 (continued)

Method	Year	Backbone/diction model	Pre-key contribution
MT [48]	2021	ResNet/FPN	Introduced a simple light-weight model to detect cohesive irregular shaped text instances

3 Feature Extraction Model

CNN is a type of artificial neural network that has a variety of applications, including machine vision and optical character recognition (OCR). It may be used to learn or extract features from scene imagery, as well as classify text regions. These traits are being used to identify information in their problem area, such as text component categorization, localization, detection, and recognition. CNN is prominently used for feature learning as compared to other neural network because: (1) It necessitates fewer connections between neurons. (2) By pooling kernel weights, the number of parameters can be reduced. (3) Down-sampling allows the network to lower the dimensionality of the image. Convolutional layer and pooling layer are the most basic components of a CNN model. The kernels for expressing various features are followed by activation functions and bias in the convolutional layer. In general, loss functions and optimization have been employed to learn the model as needed. Momentum, Adam, and gradient descent are often used optimization techniques in the literature.

The term "convolution" first introduced in [54] where a simple CNN model named as "LeNet" has been implemented to recognize the handwritten zip code. The CNN became the more popular in 2012 among research community after winning a "ImageNet large-scale visual recognition challenge (LSVRC)" competition by AlexNet [55]. The success of AlexNet attracts the researchers to explore it in various ways that improves the performance. A variety of successor models have been acquainted such as VGGNet [56], ResNet [57], DenseNet [58], MobileNet [59], and their improved versions that may vary in number of layers like wider, deeper, and lighter. A detail evolution of CNN can be referred in [60]. The feature extraction procedure can be accomplished with the help of a pre-trained model that has been trained on a huge dataset. The objective behind transfer learning is to freeze some layers or parameters and then retrain the remaining layers according to the issue domain. The fully connected/head layer is often removed and trained using a domain-specific dataset. This trend is useful when resources are limited, such as when the dataset is small, and there are not enough processing units to train a network. If this is not the case, a model can be trained from start.

4 Prediction Model

In past few years, the general object detection frameworks have been widely explored and tailored as per the needs of specific domain. These frameworks may include fast R-CNN [18], faster R-CNN [22], SSD [21], YOLO [61], and DenseBox [20] have been widely used to address the text detection problem and substantially outperform the traditional bottom-up text detection approaches. The candidate text proposals are generated and feed into the prediction model to produce the adjusted prediction offsets by calculating overlapped ratio between candidate proposal and ground truth. Detection may be at character-level, word- level, or text-line level. These models cast the text or components of text as a general object and tailored the existing framework as per the problem domain. The researchers investigate and adapt these detectors, which could include single-stage and double-stage detectors. Single-stage detectors [21, 61] are typically faster but less precise than double-stage detectors fast, faster, and mask.

Another framework includes pixel-specific segmentation network [40, 62] which is frequently used for dense estimation to anticipate text at the pixel level. These networks pixel-by-pixel categorize text regions and provide pixel-by-pixel score maps for prediction, allowing text candidates to distinguish from non-text candidates. After that, the anticipated labeled pixels are aggregated to find the intended outcomes.

5 Benchmark Datasets

Several standard datasets containing scene text images acquired in the specified heterogeneous complex environment are available online. In Table 3, we have summarized the prominently used datasets for the detection tasks covering the different challenging aspects. It includes *orientation* that can be horizontal [1, 63, 64] or multi-oriented [65–68], number of training and testing images, text instances per image, *annotations* that may be at char/word/text-line level, *multi-lingual text instances* [66, 69], and *curved text instances* [70, 71]. Table 3 lists the characteristics of a few well-known datasets.

The standard evaluation practice is a crucial part of any algorithm to identify the efficiency of the system. The most common metrics used in literature are precision (P), recall (R), and f-measure. PASCAL Eval and DetEval are the popular ones used for the detection task. In DetEval, intersection over union (IoU) is determined by calculating precision and recall as: precision = AI/AP, AP denotes the predicted bounding box area recall = AI/AGT. where AGT denotes the bounding box area for ground truth, and AI denotes the intersected area between AGT and AP. And in PASCAL, IoU can be calculated as IoU = AI/AU. AU denotes the union. The compatibility criteria between anticipated and given bounding boxes vary between the designed protocols. The compatibility criteria include one-to-one, one-to-many,

Table 3 Some of the popular accessible datasets

Dataset (Year)	Train/test images	Characteristics/annotation	Orientation/language
ICDAR11 (2011) [64]	229/255	Char/Word	Horizontal, English
MSRA-TD500 (2012) [68]	300/200	Text line	Multi-oriented
ICDAR13 (2013) [1]	229/233	Char/Word	Horizontal, English
ICDAR15 (2015) [65]	1000/500	Word	Multi-oriented, English
COCO-Text (2016) [67]	43,686/20000	Word	Multi-oriented, English
SynthText (2016) [63]	858,750	Char/Word	Horizontal, English
ICDAR RCTW (2017)	8034/4229	Text line	Multi-oriented, Chinese
Total-Text (2017) [70]	1225/300	Word/Text line	Curved, English/Chinese
ICDAR17MLT (2017) [66]	900/900	Word, min word 3 Char	Multi-oriented, multi-lingual
CTW1500 (2019) [71]	1000/500	Word/Text line	Curved, English
ICDAR19MLT (2019) [69]	1000/1000	Word	Multi-oriented, multi-lingual
SynthText3D (2020) [72]	10,000	Word	Multi-oriented, English

many-to-one, and many-to-many mappings among predicted and actual bounding boxes.

6 Conclusions and Future Perspective

In the paper, we have outlined and discussed the most recent strategies for DL-based scene text detection and localization. We briefly discussed the available frameworks for the classification and detection of text in scene imagery. According to the findings, academics have been focusing their efforts in recent years on solving a more specialized and exceedingly difficult problem, such as multi-oriented, arbitrarily shaped, coherent, and extended text instances. And, despite their outstanding performance in this domain, these DL-based algorithms necessitate high-processing devices and substantial datasets to train the model for more precise recognition and localization. Researchers have developed a lightweight architecture that includes additional processing components to reduce computational time, and albeit accuracy may be compromised in some cases.

Some of the significant future views in this sector that need to be explored include (1) extraction of textual content from complex backgrounds with occlusion, low-quality images with multilingual, calligraphic typefaces, and odd characters as text instances, all of which are not well covered in current datasets, still need a lot of work. (2) Large, annotated datasets are required for training the DL-based frameworks, yet data annotation remains time-consuming and expensive. Creating a large dataset with diverse views, such as multi-orientations, multiple languages, and irregular shapes, is a major challenge. (3) Implementing STD technology into smart handheld devices can considerably assist people's day-to-day chores and is a promising future development path. However, the performance of portable devices, which cannot achieve real-time levels while maintaining adequate detection accuracy, limits the majority of current options. As a result, real-time STD appears to be a viable future growth path.

References

1. Karatzas D, Shafait F, Uchida S, Iwamura M, i Bigorda LG, Mestre SR, Mas J, Mota DF, Almazan JA, De Las Heras LP (2013) ICDAR 2013 robust reading competition. In: 2013 12th international conference on document analysis and recognition. IEEE, pp 1484–1493
2. Busta M, Neumann L, Matas J (2015) Fastext: efficient unconstrained scene text detector. In: Proceedings of the IEEE international conference on computer vision, pp 1206–1214
3. Cho H, Sung M, Jun B (2016) Canny text detector: fast and robust scene text localization algorithm. In: Proceedings of the IEEE conference on computer vision and pattern recognition, pp 3566–3573
4. Huang W, Lin Z, Yang J, Wang J (2013) Text localization in natural images using stroke feature transform and text covariance descriptors. In: Proceedings of the IEEE international conference on computer vision, pp 1241–1248
5. Neumann L, Matas J (2010) A method for text localization and recognition in real-world images. In: Asian conference on computer vision. Springer, pp 770–783
6. Yao C, Bai X, Liu W, Ma Y, Tu Z (2012a) Detecting texts of arbitrary orientations in natural images. In: 2012 IEEE conference on computer vision and pattern recognition. IEEE, pp 1083–1090
7. Yi C, Tian Y (2011) Text string detection from natural scenes by structure-based partition and grouping. IEEE Trans Image Process 20(9):2594–2605
8. Yin X-C, Yin X, Huang K, Hao H-W (2013) Robust text detection in natural scene images. IEEE Trans Pattern Anal Mach Intell 36(5):970–983
9. Coates A, Carpenter B, Case C, Satheesh S, Suresh B, Wang T, Wu DJ, Ng AY (2011) Text detection and character recognition in scene images with unsupervised feature learning. In: 2011 international conference on document analysis and recognition. IEEE, pp 440–445
10. Lee J-J, Lee P-H, Lee S-W, Yuille A, Koch C (2011) Adaboost for text detection in natural scene. In: 2011 International conference on document analysis and recognition. IEEE, pp 429–434
11. Mishra A, Alahari K, Jawahar C (2012) Scene text recognition using higher order language priors. In: BMVC-British machine vision conference. BMVA
12. Pan Y-F, Hou X, Liu C-L (2010) A hybrid approach to detect and localize texts in natural scene images. IEEE Trans Image Process 20(3):800–813

13. Ye Q, Doermann D (2014) Text detection and recognition in imagery: a survey. IEEE Trans Pattern Anal Mach Intell 37(7):1480–1500
14. Epshtein B, Ofek E, Wexler Y (2010) Detecting text in natural scenes with stroke width transform. In: 2010 IEEE computer society conference on computer vision and pattern recognition. IEEE, pp 2963–2970
15. Matas J, Chum O, Urban M, Pajdla T (2004) Robust wide-baseline stereo from maximally stable extremal regions. Image Vis Comput 22(10):761–767
16. Huang W, Qiao Y, Tang X (2014) Robust scene text detection with convolution neural network induced MSER trees. In: European conference on computer vision. Springer, pp 497–511
17. Yi C, Tian Y (2012) Localizing text in scene images by boundary clustering, stroke segmentation, and string fragment classification. IEEE Trans Image Process 21(9):4256–4268
18. Girshick R (2015) Fast R-CNN. In: Proceedings of the IEEE international conference on computer vision, pp 1440–1448
19. He K, Gkioxari G, Doll´ar P, Girshick R (2017a) Mask R-CNN. In: Proceedings of the IEEE international conference on computer vision, pp 2961–2969.
20. Huang L, Yang Y, Deng Y, Yu Y (2015) DenseBox: unifying landmark localization with end to end object detection. arXiv preprint arXiv:1509.04874
21. Liu W, Anguelov D, Erhan D, Szegedy C, Reed S, Fu C-Y, Berg AC (2016) SSD: single shot multibox detector. In: European conference on computer vision. Springer, pp 21–37
22. Ren S, He K, Girshick R, Sun J (2015) Faster R-CNN: towards real-time object detection with region proposal networks. Adv Neural Inf Process Syst 28:91–99
23. Ma J, Shao W, Ye H, Wang L, Wang H, Zheng Y, Xue X (2018) Arbitrary-oriented scene text detection via rotation proposals. IEEE Trans Multimedia 20(11):3111–3122
24. Shi B, Bai X, Belongie S (2017) Detecting oriented text in natural images by linking segments. In: Proceedings of the IEEE conference on computer vision and pattern recognition, pp 2550–2558
25. Tian Z, Huang W, He T, He P, Qiao Y (2016) Detecting text in natural image with connectionist text proposal network. In: European conference on computer vision. Springer, pp 56–72
26. Qin X, Zhou Y, Guo Y, Wu D, Wang W (2021) FC 2 RN: a fully convolutional corner refinement network for accurate multi-oriented scene text detection. In: ICASSP 2021–2021 IEEE international conference on acoustics, speech and signal processing (ICASSP). IEEE, pp 4350–4354
27. Wang Y, Xie H, Zha Z-J, Xing M, Fu Z, Zhang Y (2020) Contournet: taking a further step toward accurate arbitrary-shaped scene text detection. In: Proceedings of the IEEE/CVF conference on computer vision and pattern recognition, pp 11753–11762
28. Zhong Z, Sun L, Huo Q (2019) An anchor-free region proposal network for faster R-CNN-based text detection approaches. Int J Doc Anal Recogn (IJDAR) 22(3):315–327
29. Zhou X, Yao C, Wen H, Wang Y, Zhou S, He W, Liang J (2017) East: an efficient and accurate scene text detector. In: Proceedings of the IEEE conference on computer vision and pattern recognition, pp 5551–5560
30. He W, Zhang X-Y, Yin F, Liu C-L (2017c) Deep direct regression for multi-oriented scene text detection. In: Proceedings of the IEEE international conference on computer vision, pp 745–753
31. Jiang Y, Zhu X, Wang X, Yang S, Li W, Wang H, Fu P, Luo Z (2017) R2CNN: rotational region CNN for orientation robust scene text detection. arXiv preprint arXiv:1706.09579
32. He P, Huang W, He T, Zhu Q, Qiao Y, Li X (2017b) Single shot text detector with regional attention. In: Proceedings of the IEEE international conference on computer vision, pp 3047–3055
33. Liao M, Shi B, Bai X (2018) Textboxes++: a single-shot oriented scene text detector. IEEE Trans Image Process 27(8):3676–3690
34. Liao M, Zhu Z, Shi B, Xia G-S, Bai X (2018b) Rotation-sensitive regression for oriented scene text detection. In: Proceedings of the IEEE conference on computer vision and pattern recognition, pp 5909–5918

35. Xie E, Zang Y, Shao S, Yu G, Yao C, Li G (2019) Scene text detection with supervised pyramid context network. In: Proceedings of the AAAI conference on artificial intelligence, vol 33, pp 9038–9045
36. Liu H, Guo A, Jiang D, Hu Y, Ren B (2020) Puzzlenet: scene text detection by segment context graph learning. arXiv preprint arXiv:2002.11371
37. Cao D, Dang J, Zhong Y (2021) Towards accurate scene text detection with bidirectional feature pyramid network. Symmetry 13(3):486
38. Yao C, Bai X, Sang N, Zhou X, Zhou S, Cao Z (2016) Scene text detection via holistic, multi-channel prediction. arXiv preprint arXiv:1606.09002
39. Zhang Z, Zhang C, Shen W, Yao C, Liu W, Bai X (2016) Multi-oriented text detection with fully convolutional networks. In: Proceedings of the IEEE conference on computer vision and pattern recognition, pp 4159–4167
40. Long J, Shelhamer E, Darrell T (2015) Fully convolutional networks for semantic segmentation. In: Proceedings of the IEEE conference on computer vision and pattern recognition, pp 3431–3440
41. Hu H, Zhang C, Luo Y, Wang Y, Han J, Ding E (2017) Word-sup: exploiting word annotations for character based text detection. In: Proceedings of the IEEE international conference on computer vision, pp 4940–4949
42. Long S, Ruan J, Zhang W, He X, Wu W, Yao C (2018) Textsnake: a flexible representation for detecting text of arbitrary shapes. In: Proceedings of the European conference on computer vision (ECCV), pp 20–36
43. Baek Y, Lee B, Han D, Yun S, Lee H (2019) Character region awareness for text detection. In: Proceedings of the IEEE/CVF conference on computer vision and pattern recognition, pp 9365–9374
44. Wang W, Xie E, Li X, Hou W, Lu T, Yu G, Shao S (2019a) Shape robust text detection with progressive scale expansion network. In: Proceedings of the IEEE/CVF conference on computer vision and pattern recognition, pp 9336–9345
45. Wang W, Xie E, Song X, Zang Y, Wang W, Lu T, Yu G, Shen C (2019b) Efficient and accurate arbitrary-shaped text detection with pixel aggregation network. In: Proceedings of the IEEE/CVF international conference on computer vision, pp 8440–8449
46. Liao M, Wan Z, Yao C, Chen K, Bai X (2020b) Real-time scene text detection with differentiable binarization. In: Proceedings of the AAAI conference on artificial intelligence, vol 34, pp 11474–11481
47. Ye J, Zhang J, Liu J, Du B, Tao D (2021) I3cl: intra-and inter-instance collaborative learning for arbitrary-shaped scene text detection. arXiv preprint arXiv:2108.01343
48. Yang C, Chen M, Yuan Y, Wang Q (2021) MT: multi-perspective feature learning network for scene text detection. arXiv preprint arXiv:2105.05455
49. Deng D, Liu H, Li X, Cai D (2018) PixelLink: detecting scene text via instance segmentation. In: Proceedings of the AAAI conference on artificial intelligence, vol 32
50. Deng L, Gong Y, Lin Y, Shuai J, Tu X, Zhang Y, Ma Z, Xie M (2019) Detecting multi-oriented text with corner-based region proposals. Neurocomputing 334:134–142
51. Liu Y, Zhang S, Jin L, Xie L, Wu Y, Wang Z (2019b) Omni-directional scene text detection with sequential-free box discretization. arXiv preprint arXiv:1906.02371
52. Xu Y, Wang Y, Zhou W, Wang Y, Yang Z, Bai X (2019) Textfield: learning a deep direction field for irregular scene text detection. IEEE Trans Image Process 28(11):5566–5579
53. Cui C, Lu L, Tan Z, Hussain A (2021) Conceptual text region network: cognition-inspired accurate scene text detection. arXiv preprint arXiv:2103.09179
54. LeCun Y, Bottou L, Bengio Y, Haffner P (1998) Gradient-based learning applied to document recognition. Proc IEEE 86(11):2278–2324
55. Krizhevsky A, Sutskever I, Hinton GE (2012) Imagenet classification with deep convolutional neural networks. Adv Neural Inf Process Syst 25:1097–1105
56. Simonyan K, Zisserman A (2014) Very deep convolutional networks for large-scale image recognition. arXiv preprint arXiv:1409.1556

57. He K, Zhang X, Ren S, Sun J (2016) Deep residual learning for image recognition. In: Proceedings of the IEEE conference on computer vision and pattern recognition, pp 770–778
58. Huang G, Liu Z, Van Der Maaten L, Weinberger KQ (2017) Densely connected convolutional networks. In: Proceedings of the IEEE conference on computer vision and pattern recognition, pp 4700–4708
59. Howard AG, Zhu M, Chen B, Kalenichenko D, Wang W, Weyand T, Andreetto M, Adam H (2017) MobileNets: efficient convolutional neural networks for mobile vision applications. arXiv preprint arXiv:1704.04861
60. Li Z, Liu F, Yang W, Peng S, Zhou J (2021) A survey of convolutional neural networks: analysis, applications, and prospects. IEEE Trans Neural Networks Learn Syst
61. Redmon J, Divvala S, Girshick R, Farhadi A (2016) You only look once: unified, real-time object detection. In: Proceedings of the IEEE conference on computer vision and pattern recognition, pp 779–788
62. Noh H, Hong S, Han B (2015) Learning deconvolution network for semantic segmentation. In: Proceedings of the IEEE international conference on computer vision, pp 1520–1528
63. Gupta A, Vedaldi A, Zisserman A (2016) Synthetic data for text localisation in natural images. In: Proceedings of the IEEE conference on computer vision and pattern recognition, pp 2315–2324
64. Shahab A, Shafait F, Dengel A (2011) ICDAR 2011 robust reading competition challenge 2: reading text in scene images. In: 2011 international conference on document analysis and recognition. IEEE, pp 1491–1496
65. Karatzas D, Gomez-Bigorda L, Nicolaou A, Ghosh S, Bagdanov A, Iwamura M, Matas J, Neumann L, Chandrasekhar VR, Lu S et al (2015) ICDAR 2015 competition on robust reading. In: 2015 13th international conference on document analysis and recognition (ICDAR). IEEE, pp 1156–1160
66. Nayef N, Yin F, Bizid I, Choi H, Feng Y, Karatzas D, Luo Z, Pal U, Rigaud C, Chazalon J et al (2017) ICDAR2017 robust reading challenge on multi-lingual scene text detection and script identification—RRC-MLT. In: 2017 14th IAPR international conference on document analysis and recognition (ICDAR), vol 1. IEEE, pp 1454–1459
67. Veit A, Matera T, Neumann L, Matas J, Belongie S (2016) Coco- text: dataset and benchmark for text detection and recognition in natural images. arXiv preprint arXiv:1601.07140
68. Yao C, Bai X, Liu W, Ma Y, Tu Z (2012b) Detecting texts of arbitrary orientations in natural images. In: 2012 IEEE conference on computer vision and pattern recognition. IEEE, pp 1083–1090
69. Nayef N, Patel Y, Busta M, Chowdhury PN, Karatzas D, Khlif W, Matas J, Pal U, Burie J-C, Liu C-l et al (2019) ICDAR2019 robust reading challenge on multi-lingual scene text detection and recognition—RRC-MLT. In: 2019 international conference on document analysis and recognition (ICDAR). IEEE, pp 1582–1587
70. Ch'ng CK, Chan CS (2017) Total-text: a comprehensive dataset for scene text detection and recognition. In: 2017 14th IAPR international conference on document analysis and recognition (ICDAR), vol 1. IEEE, pp 935–942
71. Liu Y, Jin L, Zhang S, Luo C, Zhang S (2019) Curved scene text detection via transverse and longitudinal sequence connection. Pattern Recogn 90:337–345
72. Liao M, Song B, Long S, He M, Yao C, Bai X (2020) SynthText3D: synthesizing scene text images from 3D virtual worlds. Sci China Inf Sci 63(2):1–14

TCRKDS: Towards Integration of Semantic Intelligence for Course Recommendation in Support of a Knowledge Driven Strategy

Harsh Shaw, Gerard Deepak, and A. Santhanavijayan

1 Introduction

E-learning has always been an area which needs constant improvement, with introduction to various platforms and courses introduced now and then it becomes quite a task for someone to find the relevant course, topic, task or material he/she wants to learn, recommendation system which is being known to us for a while is becoming a popular technique to suggest relevant courses, topics, e-books, contents etc. to users based on their history of selection or even record of other users for the same course, known as personalized learning since this is the semantic web era hence a need for knowledge-centric driven approach is evitable for such problems.

During the COVID, when all the educational institutes were closed, hence not only contents and e-books but also video tutorials, blogs, articles and online MOOC courses played a vital role in communicating education to learners. There were many approaches in past to personalize the recommendations for catering to the educational needs for a user, be that a classical method of clustering, Data mining, Association rules or Ontology-based approaches. In this paper, a semantic knowledge-based Deep learning approach has been proposed for course recommendation and compared with baseline models.

Motivation: There was a need for semantic-based approaches since the present era is of web 3.0, owing to the explosion of data on the world wide web, non-semantic approaches or classical approaches become insufficient and do not yield

H. Shaw · A. Santhanavijayan
Department of Computer Science and Engineering, National Institute of Technology
Tiruchirappalli, Tiruchirappalli, India

G. Deepak (✉)
Manipal Institute of Technology Bengaluru, Manipal Academy of Higher Education, Manipal,
India
e-mail: gerard.deepak.christuni@gmail.com

© The Author(s), under exclusive license to Springer Nature Singapore Pte Ltd. 2023   693
R. Doriya et al. (eds.), *Machine Learning, Image Processing, Network Security and Data Sciences*, Lecture Notes in Electrical Engineering 946,
https://doi.org/10.1007/978-981-19-5868-7_51

effective results when the density of data is very high so for a highly dense cohesive environment like the semantic web there is a need for the semantically inclined course recommending mechanism to improve the retrieval of content, entities, also the diversity that should be counted while computing the recommendation plays a vital role in generating course which is being dealt in the paper.

Contribution: An RDF generation has been incorporated for the unique categories obtained from the Dataset. A metadata-based approach has been proposed for semantically enriched course recommendation. LSTM is used for classification then knowledge is provided by incorporating the entities from WebChild, google knowledge-based API and Aristo Tuple for enriching the entities density approach, and then the semantic similarity is measured using concept similarity, normalized compression distance, deviance information criterion and the percent of precision, accuracy, F-measure and nDCG is increased compared to the baseline approaches.

Organization: The remaining part of the paper is organized as follows. Section 2 depicts the related works. Section 3 depicts the proposed architecture. Section 4 presents the implementation. Section 5 depicts the results and performance evaluation. The paper is concluded in Sect. 6.

2 Related Works

Gulzar et al. [1] proposed a Query classification based Course Recommendation System supported by ontologies and accounts for user's learning area of interest as well while recommending the course. Gulzar et al. [2] in proposed. Ontology Supported Hybrid Recommender System With Threshold Based Nearest Neighbourhood Approach Lin et al. [3] paper's on Intelligent Recommendation System for Course Selection in Smart Education used SLIM (sparse linear method) methodology for top-N course recommendation by using expert knowledge and sparseness regularization in the computation. Sulaiman et al. [4] proposed a model where a course recommendation system was developed using the fuzzy logic approach he used the fuzzy rule technique to calculate each user skill/interest using Mamdani fuzzy inference system method.

Singh et al. [5] paper eliminate problems such as cold start and sparsity by using an ontology-based approach. The Ontology is modeled using prot´eg´e and visualized online using Graphical Ontology Editor OWLGrEd. Hence, it achieved a precision of 95%, but the only drawback was that it was domain-specific since it used ontology under the hood. Zhang et al. [6] proposed hierarchical reinforcement learning for course recommendation in MOOCs to handle the diverse historic selection of courses for a user using a hierarchical approach which revises user profile and tune model to recent interest. Zhou et al. [7] in their paper proposed a novel method for full path personalized learning recommendation taking feature similarity metrics on learners, where they clustered the users and performed LSTM on the data. Zhang et al. [8]

showed MCRS in their paper which is based on distributed computation framework, which is an improvement to the Apriori algorithm. Aher et al. [9] proposed different approaches, namely ADTree classification algorithm, Simple K-means algorithm, Apriori association rule algorithm and five different methods as well. Huang et al. [10] showed an ontology-based approach for course recommendation around 2013. In [11–21], several ontological models in support of the literature of the proposed approach have been depicted.

3 Proposed System Architecture

Figure 1 depicts phase 1 of the architecture of hybridized approach. It considers the user's current navigation as well as the web usage data of the user. Web-based data of the user comprises of the historical user visits which help in as well as a course requirement of the user is recorded in the user's current navigation and also the proposed approach considers the search query, but the search query is an optional entity in the proposed approach if the search query is not given then only the web data and user navigation is taken into account any web usage data and search query is subject to preprocessing such as tokenization, lemmatization, stop word removed and named entity recognition, all preprocessing of the user requirement are refurbished.

The ontology for English literature for medieval literature has been modelled by crawling several standard classics, the title as well as English literature syllabus ranging from undergraduate and PG courses around the world;ontology is modelled based on the domains pertaining to the syllabi. It is to be noted that 15% of ontology is manually modelled various the remaining the 85% is made using OntoCollab, so the manually as well as OntoCollab model ontologies are subject to verification by expert and are subject to RDF generation again the RDF is generated from the world wide web using the SPARQL endpoint via RDF distiller and OntoCollab, the reason for generating is because a large majority of the current, as well as the archived content on the WWW, should be included into the framework, as a result, RDF is generated to intensify the knowledge and further enrich the knowledge.

The ontology for the English literature and RDF is still insufficient and further concentration of entities can be done using the three standard API: Google knowledge-based API, WebChild and Aristo tuple knowledge-based. The reason for using three API is mainly due to the fact that google knowledge-based API has a hierarchical subgraph which tends to increase the depth, whereas aristo tuple is a set of relevant tuples which are collected to increase the quantity in terms of entities, so google knowledge increases depth and aristo, as well as the web child, increases the exploratory knowledge by concentrating the entities. All the three Google Knowledge-based API have direct access, whereas SPARQL endpoints via agents are retained to intensify the auxiliary knowledge into the approach so using the entity is populated as well as generating RDF as well as the ontology which

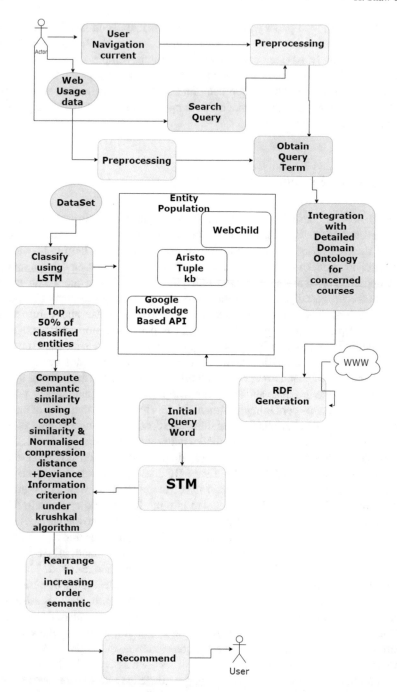

Fig. 1 Proposed architecture of TCRKDS for knowledge centric course recommendation

is included for the user obtained query term. All of these are used as a feature for classifying the dataset using the LSTM to yield the top 15% of the classified entity.

At the end of the first phase of the hybrid intelligent architecture for course recommendation for English literature as a domain of choice the user's query is enriched, populated and classified using the LSTM in order to yield the top 15% of the entity. The integration of query terms with the ontologies is done using the concept similarity, so the similarity threshold is set to 0.5 in order to integrate the query term as well as the ontology. By computing the similarity between the query term and the ontologies, ontology integration takes place with a threshold of 0.5. The phase 2 of the architecture of the hybrid intelligent architecture inputs the 50% of the classified instances from the dataset which is obtained from phase 1 as well as the initially preprocessed query words which is again subject to structured topic modelling (STM) it is used to uncover the hidden topics from the WWW. This is further subjected to the topic model on query words as well as the top 50% classified instances are subject to computation of semantic similarity in this case using two things one is concept similarity, other is normalized compression distance and deviance information criterion under Kruskal algorithm which serves as the meta-heuristic algorithm for the optimization of the initial solution into a more recommendable solution set so first of what happens in the first phase the semantic similarity is computed using semantic similarity and the normalized compression distance, for concept similarity we have vertices and 0.5 as threshold and normalized compression distances as 0.75 as threshold for deviance computation with a deviation size of 0.25 is computed between the entities and the classified and the STM passed entity of the initial query words in order to get the initial solution, this set is again optimized using the Kruskal algorithm.

4 Implementation

The proposed framework was implemented using python anaconda as IDE, OWL ontologies were converted into RDF, RDF was generated using OntoCollab. OntoCollab was used for automatic generation of ontology Google Knowledge API, and WebChild cloud was accessed via API whereas the AristoTuple was accessed via an agentDataset used here is kaggle https://www.kaggle.com/siddharthm1698/course racourse-dataset Coursera course Dataset, however, the dataset lacks the English literature courses, as a result, several English literature courses from Coursera, Udemy etc. have been incorporated, apart from this course the course task from several other universities have been crawled from the syllabus and the English literature courses are crawled based on the syllabus the categories are indexed on each particular courses, structure is also incorporated into the dataset along with several categories and the dataset is modified and populated with 70% more content when compared to the

Kaggle Coursera dataset comprising of courses pertaining to English literature are also the open course systems from MIT courseware from all top universities from the USA which has an open library and open syllabus are crawled and get into the dataset.

Algorithm 1: An algorithm for implementation proposed Architecture

---

Input Input used here for the framework are Dataset with course era courses
Output Output will be highly relevant courses proposed for a particular user using proposed framework
Step 1: Data is preprocessed using, Lowercasing, Stemming
, Lemmatization, Stopword processing
Step 2: D.Tokenize(); D.lemmatize(); ds.WordNet.Lemmatize(); ds.Wordnet.Tokenize(); ds.WordNet.StopWordElimination(); ds.TolowerCase(); ds.NER(); **Step 3**: Ts = ds.Tokenize(); Ts.Lemmatize();
Step 4: if(ls.Ts = = StopWord)
Eliminate Ts.current()
Step 5: RDF generation using
WebChild
AristoTuple
Google knowledge Api
Step 6: HashSet C = Ts.current();
Step 7: obtain unique categories Metadata Generation classify using LSTM obtain top 25%
Step 8: Compute similarity score using concept similarity Normalized compression Distance, Deviance Information Criterion, ANOVA concept similarity
Step 9: Rearrange in increasing order concept similarity
Step 10: Recommend Course

---

5 Results and Performance Evaluation

From Table 1, we can see that the proposed architecture has performed better than the baseline approaches on various parameters such as with User Selection, precision, recall, accuracy, F-Measure, false discovery rate (FDR) and nDCG are used as the metrics, which is depicted in Eqs. (1)–(5), respectively, so the reason for choosing these measure are due to the fact that they quantify the relevance of results, whereas the FDR quantify the number of false discoveries found in the results, nDCG quantifies the diversity in the results recommendation system is quite appreciable if it delivers diversity as well as relevant results that's the reason why nDCG is used as a metric proposed. TCRKDS is based line with five different models, namely CRQCA [1], Ontologies + TBNNA [2], SLIM [3], CSFLA [4] and FACRS:TCR [5]. It is evident from the table that TCRKDS has Precision of 96.81%, Avg Recall of 98.47%, Average 97.64%, F-Measure 97.63%, FDR 0.04, nDCG 0.99 hence the new architecture has performed better than the baseline approaches in term of all the metrics

Table 1 Performance comparison for TCRKDS on various metrics

Approach	Average precision (%)	Average recall (%)	Accuracy (%)
CRQCA [1]	82.23	84.05	83.14
Ontologies + TBNNA [2]	88.04	91.83	89.93
SLIM [3]	80.19	83.98	82.08
CSFLA [4]	81.16	85.88	83.52
FACRS:TCR [5]	92.17	94.03	93.19
Proposed TCRKDS	**96.81**	**98.47**	**97.64**

$$\text{Precision} = \frac{\text{Retrieved} \cap \text{Relevant}}{\text{Retrieved}} \tag{1}$$

$$\text{Recall} = \frac{\text{Retrieved} \cap \text{Relevant}}{\text{Relevent}} \tag{2}$$

$$\text{Accuracy} = \frac{\text{Precision} + \text{Recall}}{2} \tag{3}$$

$$F - \text{measure} = \frac{2 \cdot \text{Precision} \cdot \text{Recall}}{(\text{Precision} + \text{Recall})} \tag{4}$$

$$\text{FDR} = 1 - \text{Precision} \tag{5}$$

CRQCA [1] is a query classification approach, in this model N-gram classification technique is incorporated, however, the usage of Ingram makes it weak and naive as a result it yield comparably lower values for the given metrics and high FDR, also the Ingram is not able to process diversity Ontologies + TBNNA [2] is a threshold that improves the Precision, Recall, F-Measure as compared to the CRQCA [1] the reason is that ontologies provide lateral augmented knowledge however the nDCG is also very high when compared to other baseline models hence it can be improvised incorporation of a better learning model, classification model, decision-making model will definitely make the model more productive, use of ontology alone it is a static ontology which is modelled and using the approach this alone increases the metrics but there is a high scope of improving SLIM [3] (Sparse Linear Method) is a matrix format, matrix derivation scheme wherein matrix factorization is to be used which can increase the overall complexity of the model, hence there is always a scope of improvement (Table 2).

CSFLA [4] model is a fuzzy logic approach, Mamdani fuzzy inference was used, so fuzzy rules derivation has to be done and fuzzy rules will be generated; however, fuzzy the approach is quite not dependable, however, it has better precision, accuracy, recall and F-measure. Reason is that fuzzy techniques are approximate hence they

Table 2 F-measure, FDR and nDCG comparison

Approach	F-measure (%)	FDR	nDCG
CRQCA [1]	83.10	0.18	0.82
Ontologies + TBNNA [2]	89.89	0.12	0.95
SLIM [3]	82.04	0.20	0.81
CSFLA [4]	83.45	0.19	0.82
FACRS:TCR [5]	93.09	0.18	0.95
Proposed TCRKDS	97.63	0.04	0.99

don't compute accurate results. Hence, a semantic approach can always improve such models. FACRS:TCR [5] uses ontology which is modelled and visualized using a graphical ontology editor, however the approach solves the cold start problem, sparsity, first-rater and scalability and other problems significance level was considered to be less than 0.05 however the main issue is this is a static ontology which recommends what it has and evaluates what is recommended. Hence this approach has a very high the precision of 92.17%, Recall 94.03%, Average 97.64%, F-Measure of 93.09%, etc. but it fails to incorporate dynamic and relevance into the system.

Proposed TCRKDS is a deep learning integrated with semantic knowledge derivation paradigm, where LSTM is used for classification which is deep learning powerful classifier, so as a result, inferencing load becomes very low. The usage of RDF generation and also the current ontology as well as the user clicks tends to increase the knowledge instilled into the framework. The real-world knowledge is incorporated by means of RDF, ontologies which has been generated by worldwide web context and ontology of course tends to increase the consequences of the intensification of knowledge. Apart from this, entity knowledge enrichment is achieved via WebChild, Aristo tuple and Google knowledge-based API. Combination of these three ensures that deviation is minimized by the increment and enhancement of entities, which are relevant to the framework, domain in which the framework works. As a result, approach performs much better because of the intensification of the knowledge at every stage. Also, semantic similarity comparison is done by incorporation of concept similarity, normalized compression distance and deviation information criterion under the Kruskal algorithm. Concept similarity and Normalized compression are semantic similarity models with a specified threshold, whereas deviance is a criterion based on step deviation criterion, and as well as Kruskal algorithm is used to derive the final recommendable optimized solution set from the initially recommended relevant population set as a result the proposed algorithm is much better than baseline models, another most important part is STM (Structured topic modelling) has also being instilled for further topic integration which has been missed out as a result of a there is always a knowledge derivation scheme. Hence the proposed approach is better than the baseline approaches on every metric.

6 Conclusions

A novel approach for course recommendation has been proposed which uses semantic knowledge populated with entities from WebChild, Aristo tuple, Google knowledge API, LSTM to classify top 50% of classified entities, obtain query term from user and later on integration with detailed domain ontology for concerned courses for, RDF generation computing semantic similarity from the classified entities and finally recommend course Methodology Proposed TCRKDS has showed better performance than the baseline approaches clearly, where the classical method of using CRQCA [1], Ontologies + TBNNA [2], SLIM [3], CSFLA [4], FACRS:TCR [5] was outperformed by a considerable difference, hence an knowledge centric approach infused with machine learning paradigm (LSTM) and a semantic similarity score is generated which produces final Course for the User, we achieve an Recall of 96.81%, Precision of 98.47%, Accuracy of 97.64%, F-Measure 97.63%, FDR of 0.04 and nDCG of 0.99 .

References

1. Gulzar Z, Leema AA (2018) Course recommendation based on query classification approach. Int J Web Based Learn Teach Technol (IJWLTT) 13(3):69–83
2. Gulzar Z, Raj LA, Leema AA (2019) Ontology supported hybrid recommender system with threshold based nearest neighbourhood approach. Int J Inf Commun Technol Educ (IJICTE) 15(2):85–107
3. Lin J, Pu H, Li Y, Lian J (2018) Intelligent recommendation system for course selection in smart education. Proc Comput Sci 129:449–453
4. Sulaiman MS, Tamizi AA, Shamsudin MR, Azmi A (2020) Course recommendation system using fuzzy logic approach. Indonesian J Electr Eng Comput Sci 17(1):365–371
5. Singh P, Ahuja S, Jaitly V, Jain S (2020) A framework to alleviate common problems from recommender system: a case study for technical course recommendation. J Discrete Math Sci Crypt 23(2):451–460
6. Zhang J, Hao B, Chen B, Li C, Chen H, Sun J (2019) Hierarchical reinforcement learning for course recommendation in MOOCs. In: Proceedings of the AAAI conference on artificial intelligence, vol 33, pp 435–442
7. Zhou Y, Huang C, Hu Q, Zhu J, Tang Y (2018) Personalized learning fullpath recommendation model based on LSTM neural networks. Inf Sci 444:135–152
8. Zhang H, Huang T, Lv Z, Liu S, Zhou Z (2018) MCRS: a course recommendation system for MOOCs. Multimedia Tools Appl 77(6):7051–7069
9. Aher SB, Lobo L (2012) Best combination of machine learning algorithms for course recommendation system in e-learning. Int J Comput Appl 41(6)
10. Huang C-Y, Chen R-C, Chen L-S (2013) Course-recommendation system based on ontology. In: 2013 International conference on machine learning and cybernetics, vol 3. IEEE, pp 1168–1173
11. Deepak G, Teja V, Santhanavijayan A (2020) A novel firefly driven scheme for resume parsing and matching based on entity linking paradigm. J Discrete Math Sci Crypt 23(1):157–165
12. Santhanavijayan A, Naresh Kumar D, Deepak G (2019) A novel hybridized strategy for machine translation of Indian languages. In: International conference on soft computing and signal processing. Springer, Singapore, pp 363–370

13. Surya D, Deepak G, Santhanavijayan A (2021) KSTAR: a knowledge based approach for socially relevant term aggregation for web page recommendation. In: International conference on digital technologies and applications. Springer, Cham, pp 555–564
14. Roopak N, Deepak G, Santhanavijayan A (2020) HCRDL: a hybridized approach for course recommendation using deep learning. In: International conference on intelligent systems design and applications. Springer, Cham, pp 1105–1113
15. Adithya V, Deepak G, Santhanavijayan A (2021) OntoBlogDis: a knowledge-centric ontology driven socially aware framework for influential blogger discovery. In: International conference on emerging trends and technologies on intelligent systems. Springer, Singapore, pp 37–47
16. Rithish H, Deepak G, Santhanavijayan A (2021) Automated assessment of question quality on online community forums. In: International conference on digital technologies and applications. Springer, Cham, pp 791–800
17. Arulmozhivarman M, Deepak G (2021) OWLW: ontology focused user centric architecture for web service recommendation based on LSTM and whale optimization. In: European, Asian, Middle Eastern, North African conference on management & information systems. Springer, Cham, pp 334–344
18. Manoj N, Deepak G (2021) ODFWR: an ontology driven framework for web service recommendation. In: Data science and security. Springer, Singapore, pp 150–158
19. Srivastava RA, Deepak G (2021) PIREN: prediction of intermediary readers' emotion from news-articles. In: Data science and security. Springer, Singapore, pp 122–130
20. Varghese L, Deepak G, Santhanavijayan A (2021) A fuzzy ontology driven integrated IoT approach for home automation. In: International conference on digital technologies and applications. Springer, Cham, pp 271–277
21. Nandhakishore CS, Deepak G, Santhanavijayan A (2022) Conceptualization, visualization, and modeling of ontologies for elementary kinematics. In: Advanced computing and intelligent technologies. Springer, Singapore, pp 15–23

Network Security and IoT

Developing MCDM-Based Technique to Calculate Trustworthiness of Advertised QoE Parameters in Fog Computing Environment

Shefali Varshney, Rajinder Sandhu, and P. K. Gupta

1 Introduction

With the advancement in technology, the Internet of Things (IoT) has become a platform that provides connectivity with several objects like animals, buildings, machines, etc. However, these devices generate a large amount of data and have several restrictions of memory usage, storage capacity and battery power. Therefore, these devices use cloud storage for further processing of data and provide the results in real time to the various end users.

IoT-based smart applications send their request to access services of the Fog environment and provide better quality of experience (QoE) to the end users as shown in Fig. 1. These IoT-based smart applications further increase the use of network and computational requirements [1]. Use of Fog computing reduces the issue of delay-sensitive applications and improves the processing and storage capabilities at the network edge [2]. These Fog computing environment consists of various Fog nodes and Fog service providers (FSP) that helps in analysing the incoming data from various IoT-based devices and provides low latency, location awareness, high scalability and real-time interactions [3].

In contrast to cloud computing, Fog computing environment supports low latency, location awareness, high scalability and real-time interactions. However, there is a disadvantage of use of Fog computing while allocating required the resources to the end user [4]. The smart applications requesting services from the Fog resources must satisfy the demand of the end users. If the Quality of Experience (QoE) of the smart applications does not match with the Fog resource, then the smart application will not be trusted by the end users and gets rejected for further use. Here, the QoE of the end user with the use of smart application plays an essential role in need of the

S. Varshney (✉) · R. Sandhu · P. K. Gupta
Department of Computer Science and Engineering, Jaypee University of Information Technology, Solan, India
e-mail: pkgupta@ieee.org

© The Author(s), under exclusive license to Springer Nature Singapore Pte Ltd. 2023   705
R. Doriya et al. (eds.), *Machine Learning, Image Processing, Network Security and Data Sciences*, Lecture Notes in Electrical Engineering 946,
https://doi.org/10.1007/978-981-19-5868-7_52

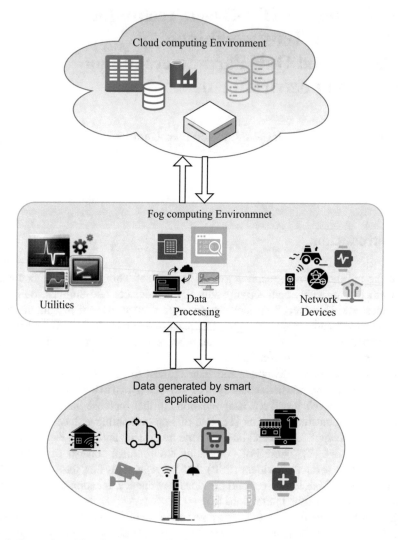

Fig. 1 Processing of data from smart applications in Fog computing environment

services provided by the respective application [5]. Smart applications requesting the resources from Fog computing environment need to be processed on a priority basis [6]. This evaluation is required because there are a huge number of smart applications that require immediate response for their better performance which results into poor application placement in that Fog computing environment [7].

In this paper, we have proposed a Multi-Criteria Decision Making (MCDM)-based framework to overcome from this issue by calculating the trustworthiness of the QoE parameters. The trust evaluation of various QoE parameters is considered as a criteria selection problem [8]. The proposed framework implements the MCDM-based technique known as TOPSIS for evaluating the trust of various QoE parameters for smart applications. In the TOPSIS-MCDM method, the criteria weights are carefully decided because the method's performance depends on the criteria weights. This paper presents an easier approach that calculates the trust of advertised QoE parameters of smart applications by applying MCDM technique.

The paper is organized into different sections as follows. Section 2 represents the paper studied that focuses on the trust evaluation of QoE parameters for smart applications. Section 3 describes about the proposed framework for evaluation of trust of smart applications using QoE parameters. Section 4 presents the performance analysis of the proposed framework. Section 5 concludes the paper.

2 Related Work

This section discusses an extensive review of service selection in the cloud and the Fog computing environment. Here, various studies have been categorized that discusses the service selection using MCDM technique for allocation of resources to the smart applications. In 2021, Baranwal et al. [8] have presented an approach for selection of Fog Orchestrator Node (FON). The poor selection of FON may lead to a decline in performance. The authors have explained the proposed algorithm by applying it to a state of the art that results in better application placement. The proposed approach selects an appropriate FON in order to improve the overall performance of IoT. Zang et al. [9] have proposed a QoE aware framework for cloud service ranking-based on the Markov chain model. This model incorporates QoE metrics to enhance the rank results. In addition, the authors have proposed a technique that represents the prediction model for calculating the reliability of the ranks. Jatoth et al. [10] proposed a novel Grey TOPSIS integrated with AHP to assign ranks to cloud services on the basis of quantified QoS parameters. The authors had analysed the proposed technique in terms of adequacy under change in alternatives, sensitivity analysis, handling of uncertainty and adequacy to support group decision making. Hussain et al. [11] have proposed a novel integrated approach known as Methodology for Optimal Service Selection (MOSS). This technique comprises five steps which are helpful in better selection of cloud services. The authors have had considered both QoS and QoE for the selection of best cloud service. However, after completion of all the five stages of the proposed model, it is found to be more practical and useful. Al-khafajiy et al. [12] have presented a COMITMENT method that works with the help of QoS and quality of history measures. The quality of history measures has been considered from the earlier direct and indirect interactions of the Fog nodes in the Fog computing environment. The proposed approach is helpful in identifying the interactions among the Fog nodes by 66% and reduces the response time by 15s. Ciszkowski et al. [13] have used a fuzzy analytical hierarchy process (fuzzy-AHP) technique to prioritize and identified the trust parameters in the Fog computing environment. The results indicate that the QoS is a best prioritized parameter that a service requester uses for evaluating the trust level of service provider. In contrast, the quality of security (QoSec) has been ranked with the worst-ranked. The framework also ranks the social relationships as the most trustworthy parameter.

Kumar et al. [14] have proposed a framework to access the cloud services-based on the QoS criteria value using fuzzy environment. They have used the fuzzy-AHP method for evaluating the weights of the criteria, TOPSIS technique for calculating the final rank of the cloud service. Skarlat et al. [15] have presented a visionary Fog computing framework in which they have provided the solution for the problem of service placement of various IoT-based applications using QoS attributes. The authors have proposed a genetic algorithm-based solution to resolve the issue and discussed the service execution to reduce the network communication delay. Yu et al. [16] have considered the case of both single and multiple applications which was NP-hard problems. The authors have proposed the schemes for both the cases, such as for single application, a fully polynomial-time optimisation scheme has been proposed. Mahmud et al. [17] have proposed a policy for integrated Fog and cloud environments. The profit aware application placement policy has been prepared using integer linear programming model. The prposed model enhances the profit regularly and makes sure of the QoS during placement of applications. Mahmud et al. [18] have proposed a QoE aware application placement policy that prefers the application placement request with the respective the user expectations. The proposed policy was evaluated using the iFogSim simulator. The obtained experimental results improve the network congestion, service quality, data processing time and resource affordability. Murtaza et al. [19] have presented a new concept of smart layer between the Fog nodes and the IoE devices in order to integrate an intelligent task scheduling technique based on QoS parameters. The performance is recorded simultaneously, and the authors have also presented an optimal approach that allocates the best suitable Fog resource to the smart applications.

3 Proposed Framework

The proposed framework provides a suitable Fog environment for the placement of smart application to advertise its services as shown in Fig. 3. There are several QoE parameters that improves the performance of the smart applications. The proposed technique considers the network bandwidth (NB), time to finish (TF), total number of cores required (TNoC) and storage (S), as QoE parameters [18]. The major steps of the proposed TOPSIS-MCDM technique, as shown in Fig. 2 for calculating the trust of the QoE parameters values for smart applications, can be summarized as per following: [20].

- Firstly, the MCDM problem is identified that requires a priority list of ranks [21].
- In next step, the technique considers QoE parameters, i.e. network bandwidth, time to finish, total number of cores and storage defines the criteria of the alternatives.
- Further, it calculates the priority-wise weights for the considered alternative.

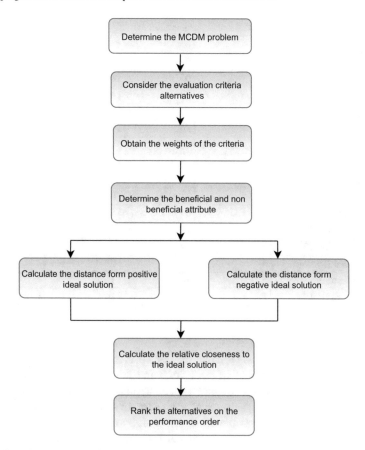

Fig. 2 Steps involved in MCDM-TOPSIS Technique

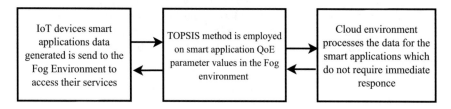

Fig. 3 Proposed MCDM-based Framework

- The next step is to specify the beneficial and non-beneficial criteria among the considered set of criteria.
- Now we calculate the distance from the beneficial and non-beneficial criteria.
- Lastly, the relative closeness of the ideal solution is evaluated, and on the basis of this relative closeness, the ranks are provided to the alternatives.

Table 1 QoE parameter values taken for smart applications

Smart aplication	NB	TF	TNoC	S
Smart application 1	3	95	1	2
Smart application 2	4	95	6	4
Smart application 3	2	73	4	1
Smart application 4	3	47	10	2
Smart application 5	2	89	1	1
Smart application 6	2	46	2	2
Smart application 7	5	25	5	1
Smart application 8	4	10	3	4
Smart application 9	5	82	6	1
Smart application 10	3	65	8	2
Smart application 11	3	13	5	4
Smart application 12	4	99	8	4
Smart application 13	4	57	2	1
Smart application 14	5	84	1	4
Smart application 15	2	72	19	8

Here, we have used various QoE parameters, i.e. Network Bandwidth(NB), Time to Finish(TF), Total Number of Cores(TNoC) and Storage(S), to evaluate the proposed framework. TOPSIS technique has been applied on the data values as given in Table 1. Here, Table 1 lists the set of values for 15 smart applications.

Further, Table 2 represents the obtained result by using the TOPSIS technique on various values as listed in Table 1. The performance score has been evaluated for 15 smart applications along with their ranks. Table 2 represents the ranks of all the smart applications as calculated by using various QoE parameters. In Table 2, a small subset of the smart application is shown among 99 other instances for a better understanding of the applications. The weights have been considered for the evaluation of the TOPSIS technique are $NB = 0.1150, TF = 0.0645, TNoC = 0.5956$ and $S = 0.2246$.

4 Performance Analysis

The performance of the proposed framework is done with the help of TOPSIS-MCDM technique which is implemented in Python. This framework simulates the smart applications QoE parameters consisting a subset of 99 smart applications values. The QoE parameters considered for the evaluation of smart applications are NB, TF, TNoC and S. The MCDM-TOPSIS technique has been applied on a sample data set which is created with the help of Poisson distribution and consists of 99 parameter values. Here we have used the Intel CORE $i5$ processor with 8 GB RAM to perform

Table 2 Ranks of smart applications using TOPSIS technique

S. No.	Smart application	Relative closeness	Rank
1	Smart application 1	0.03948	97
2	Smart application 2	0.13241	45
3	Smart application 3	0.08908	68
4	Smart application 4	0.19662	20
5	Smart application 5	0.03565	99
6	Smart application 6	0.05758	88
7	Smart application 7	0.11211	54
8	Smart application 8	0.08878	69
9	Smart application 9	0.12719	48
10	Smart application 10	0.16102	35
11	Smart application 11	0.11774	51
12	Smart application 12	0.16614	32
13	Smart application 13	0.05792	87
14	Smart application 14	0.06194	83
15	Smart application 15	0.36602	7

experiment about the trust worthiness of the smart applications. Here, Fig. 4 shows the QoE parameter values of the created data set for all the smart applications. This figure shows the three QoE such as network bandwidth and total core required and storage. However, Fig. 5 shows the values for time required to finish for a smart application. For better trust evaluation of smart application on the basis of QoE parameters, MCDM-TOPSIS technique has been applied. This proposed technique evaluates the smart applications through all the steps as shown in Fig. 2. In this paper, a small set of 15 smart applications have been considered for evaluation on the basis of TOPSIS technique that provide an insight about the trust worthiness of QoE parameters of the smart applications.

Further, Table 2 represents the trust generated on the smart application QoE parameters values and shows the performance score and ranks of the applications that depicts the trustworthy nature of the smart applications. Here, the smart application $SA15$, has the highest rank and is considered as the most trustworthy application that request the resources from the Fog computing environment. The performance analysis shows that the smart application $SA15$ is the most trustworthy application with rank 7 in comparison with the other smart applications.

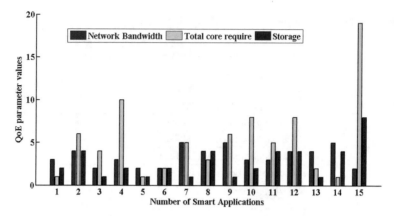

Fig. 4 QoE parameter values considered for smart applications

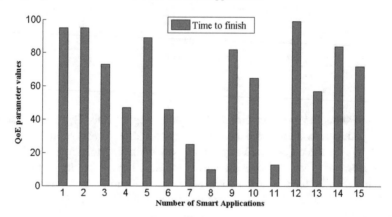

Fig. 5 Time required to finish for a smart application

5 Conclusion

The issue of trust on the smart applications QoE parameters needs to be addressed on a regular basis to enhance the performance of the applications. In this paper, a MCDM-TOPSIS-based trust evaluation framework has been discussed that considers the values of the QoE parameters and provides evaluated trust using their ranks. The proposed framework is based on the performance monitoring of the smart application when they request resources from the FSP. The various QoE parameters enclose the quality of experience offered by the FSP. The proposed framework generates the trust on the smart applications. The criteria considered for the ranking of the smart applications is lower the rank higher will be the trust value and vice versa. These trust values of the smart application will be helpful in further communication of services to the Fog computing environment for processing. In future work, research can be done on revising the trust of smart applications for improvement of their performance.

References

1. Guerrero C, Lera I, Juiz C (2019) Evaluation and efficiency comparison of evolutionary algorithms for service placement optimization in fog architectures. Future Gener Comput Syst 97:131. https://doi.org/10.1016/j.future.2019.02.056
2. Skarlat O, Nardelli M, Schulte S, Dustdar S (2017) Towards qos-aware fog service placement. In: 2017 IEEE 1st international conference on fog and edge computing (ICFEC) (IEEE), pp 89–96. https://doi.org/10.1109/ICFEC.2017.12
3. Sharma P, Gupta P (2021) QoS-aware CR-BM-based hybrid framework to improve the fault tolerance of fog devices. J Appl Res Technol 19(1):66. https://doi.org/10.22201/icat.24486736e.2021.19.1.1493
4. Varshney S, Sandhu R, Gupta P (2019) QoS-aware CR-BM-based hybrid framework to improve the fault tolerance of fog devices. In: International conference on advances in computing and data sciences. Springer, Berlin, pp 711–723. https://doi.org/10.1007/978-981-13-9942-8_66
5. Lin Y, Wang X, Zhou T (2014) Survey on quality evaluation and control of online reviews. J Softw 25(3):506. https://doi.org/10.13328/j.cnki.jos.004517
6. Varshney S, Sandhu R, Gupta P (2021) QoE-based resource management of applications in the fog computing environment using AHP technique. In: 2021 6th international conference on signal processing, computing and control (ISPCC) (IEEE), pp 669–673. https://doi.org/10.1109/ISPCC53510.2021.9609479
7. Varshney S, Sandhu R, Gupta P (2020) QoE-based multi-criteria decision making for resource provisioning in fog computing using AHP technique. Int J Knowl Syst Sci (IJKSS) 11(4):17. https://doi.org/10.4018/IJKSS.2020100102
8. Baranwal G, Vidyarthi DP (2021) FONS: a fog orchestrator node selection model to improve application placement in fog computing. J Supercomput 1–28. https://doi.org/10.1007/s11227-021-03702-x
9. Zhang Y, Liu H, Deng B, Peng F (2014) A reliable QoE-aware framework for cloud service monitoring and ranking. In: Proceedings of the 2013 international conference on electrical and information technologies for rail transportation (EITRT2013), vol II. Springer, Berlin, pp 401–409. https://doi.org/10.1007/978-3-642-53751-6_43
10. Jatoth C, Gangadharan G, Fiore U, Buyya R (2019) SELCLOUD: a hybrid multi-criteria decision-making model for selection of cloud services. Soft Comput 23(13):4701. https://doi.org/10.1007/s00500-018-3120-2
11. Hussain A, Chun J, Khan M (2020) A novel customer-centric Methodology for Optimal Service Selection (MOSS) in a cloud environment. Fut Gener Comput Syst 105:562. https://doi.org/10.1016/j.future.2019.12.024
12. Al-Khafajiy M, Baker T, Asim M, Guo Z, Ranjan R, Longo A, Puthal D, Taylor M (2020) COMITMENT: a fog computing trust management approach. J Parallel Distrib Comput 137:1. https://doi.org/10.1016/j.jpdc.2019.10.006
13. Ciszkowski T, Mazurczyk W, Kotulski Z, Hossfeld T, Fiedler M, Collange D (2012) Towards quality of experience-based reputation models for future web service provisioning. Telecommun Syst 51(4):283. https://doi.org/10.1007/s11235-011-9435-2
14. Kumar RR, Shameem M, Kumar C (2021) A computational framework for ranking prediction of cloud services under fuzzy environment. In: Enterprise information systems, pp 1–21. https://doi.org/10.1080/17517575.2021.1889037
15. Skarlat O, Nardelli M, Schulte S, Borkowski M, Leitner P (2017) Optimized IoT service placement in the fog. Serv Oriented Comput Appl 11(4):427. https://doi.org/10.1007/s11761-017-0219-8
16. Yu R, Xue G, Zhang X (2018) Application provisioning in fog computing-enabled internet-of-things: a network perspective. In: IEEE INFOCOM 2018-IEEE conference on computer communications. IEEE, pp 783–791. https://doi.org/10.1109/INFOCOM.2018.8486269
17. Mahmud R, Srirama SN, Ramamohanarao K, Buyya R (2020) Profit-aware application placement for integrated fog–cloud computing environments. J Parallel Distrib Comput 135:177. https://doi.org/10.1016/j.jpdc.20

18. Mahmud R, Srirama SN, Ramamohanarao K, Buyya R (2019) Quality of Experience (QoE)-aware placement of applications in fog computing environments. J Parallel Distrib Comput 132:190. https://doi.org/10.1016/j.j

19. Murtaza F, Akhunzada A, ul Islam S, Boudjadar J, Buyya R (2020) QoS-aware service provisioning in fog computing. J Netw Comput Appl 165:102674

20. Varshney S, Sandhu R, Gupta PK (2021) Multicriteria decision-making in health informatics using IoT. In: IoT-based data analytics for the healthcare industry. Academic Press Elsevier, pp. 105-121. https://doi.org/10.1016/B978-0-12-821472-5.00014-4

21. Lai YJ, Liu TY, Hwang CL (1994) Topsis for MODM. Eur J Oper Res 76(3):486. https://doi.org/10.1016/0377-2217(94)90282-8

Data Clustering Approach on the Basis of Data Sensitivity for Implementation of Secure Cloud Computing Environment

Rajdeep Singh📵 and R. K. Pateriya

1 Introduction

In present scenario, cloud computing facilitates the ease of sharing resources based on the external locations (servers) instead of from the local locations (servers) [1]. But despite of several advantages including the positive delivery of resources and impactful services, privacy is the major concern [2–7]. Cloud provides have to show the user requirements, data usage, data storage limitations, and it should ensure the secure relation based on the data visibility to maintain the data integrity and data transparency [1].

Data breaches possibility is higher in cloud computing environment as the number of users, and the traffic on the communication relay is so high [4]. So, there are lots of privacy issues and protection mechanism breaches which will affect the data continuation in the same area with user centric control on the data.

Along with the aforesaid, security mechanisms incorporated in cloud computing environment are implemented uniform for every set of data. The novelty of this work lies in the process of data clustering based on the data size as it will be helpful in determining the data security as per the cluster levels, which in future will help us to implement hybrid security algorithm, as per requirement.

2 Related Work

In 2018, Abdullah and Bakar [8] discussed the role of cloud computing in supporting the virtualization synergy for the adoption of the cloud computing. They have

R. Singh (✉) · R. K. Pateriya
Department of Computer Science & Engineering, Mewar University, Chittorgarh, Rajasthan, India
e-mail: rajdeepsinghji@gmail.com

© The Author(s), under exclusive license to Springer Nature Singapore Pte Ltd. 2023   715
R. Doriya et al. (eds.), *Machine Learning, Image Processing, Network Security and Data Sciences*, Lecture Notes in Electrical Engineering 946,
https://doi.org/10.1007/978-981-19-5868-7_53

suggested that the privacy is the important concern in the security preservation of the data storage. Author expounds the security requirements in the cloud computing environment. They have discussed and analyzes the risk-adaptable access control (RAdAC). They have also proposed two-factor authentication scheme in RAdAC for the privacy-preserving perspective.

In 2018, scalability of cloud computing environment is suggested by Kumar and Rathore [9]. They have suggested the isolation of the virtual machines for secure resource pooling. They have suggested hypervisors for the secure isolation. Authors illustrate the hypervisor as a chunk of software. It plays its role among the guest VMs and the physical hardware. Security is a noteworthy concern when numerous occupants dealing with the equivalent machine. As more and more organizations are migrating themselves to the cloud computing environment, so as the vulnerability of information is increasing. Security vulnerabilities are identified with the virtualization in distributed computing, and its feasible counter measures are exhibited.

In 2018, Li et al. [10] discussed the security aspect in the cloud computing. They have suggested that because of the dynamic and uncertain nature of the cloud platform the security state of cloud computing may be affected. They have constructed a linear regression AdaBoost learning and predicting algorithm for the security observance of the cloud computing. Their results showed that their proposed method has the capability of predicting the hidden security state.

In 2018, Markandey et al. [11] illustrate the collaboration of clouds and big data. They have also concerned about the data leaking from the online platform. Their main aim is to implement cloud storage security strategy. These procedures are joined with the results of existing information by considering the security dangers and client information on distributed storage and move toward the suitable security system, which depends on properties of distributed storage framework.

In 2018, Giannakou et al. [12] discussed the security and virtualization infrastructure of cloud computing. They have addressed the issues related to the security monitoring systems. It is based on the network intrusion detection systems.

In 2018, Qing et al. [13] discussed about the private cloud. The venture data security framework needs to incorporate the data security development into the foundation development. Endeavor private cloud arrange security circumstance is a precise, generally speaking circumstance the board designing issues, and any private cloud vulnerabilities may prompt loss of motion of the whole organize.

In 2018, Elliott et al. [14] discussed the use of containers and containerizing services. They have suggested some names like Docker, Kubernetes, and LXC. They have presented a container management approach for the rapid live migration. They have discussed this in the host condition for private, public, or hybrid clouds. They have also provided a container management vision which includes the security and resiliency.

In 2018, Chung et al. [15] discussed about searchable encryption (SE). They have suggested that the SE can help in the security vulnerability by making index into cipher text. They have presented a security proxy. It is based on the wildcard SE construction. In 2018, Sun et al. [16] discussed about the cyber-resiliency. They have suggested that it is important for providing essential functions for the enterprise network. They have discussed about the capability and suggested it can be measured by the supported missions and business processes.

In 2018, Lee et al. [17] discussed about the third-party data centers. They have suggested that the cloud utilizes this. They have also listed the example as the Heroku. They have explored that it also supports several programming languages. It is useful for Web application deployment model. For security issue, they have applied advanced encryption standard (AES) for the data security in Heroku. Their approach is efficient in the data delay time.

In 2018, Esposito et al. [18] discussed the progressive shift of data and services to the cloud. They have studied the blockchain technology in terms of protecting the healthcare data hosted within the cloud. They have also described the different associated challenges.

Gordin et al. [19], in 2018, expound the use and applicability of several cloud like Google, Amazon EC2, and Microsoft Azure. They have suggested that the security is mainly maintained by issuing companies in the public cloud. But in terms of private clouds, it is a concern. They have performed a security analysis in the private cloud. Their study elaborates the security threats found on multi-tenant environment along with the solutions.

In 2018, Salunke et al. [20] proposed to store the data authentically in the cloud. So, the author proposed the requirement of data security. They have applied a technique for the anonymous authentication for stored data on cloud. Their approach is capable in the user's identity preservation. Their main aim is to prevent the unauthorized users. They have implemented their approach in Java with MySQL database.

Surbiryala et al. [21], in 2018, illustrate the changes in cloud computing from the client and server side. They have suggested that the physical location is unknown to many of the users. They have also not aware of the storing of their data on backup servers. For these problems, they have proposed a framework based on the reconstruction of the data from the deleted servers.

In 2018, Manzoor et al. [22] discussed the usage of the cloud proliferates. They have targeting to achieve the holistic cloud threat analysis. It has been done by designing a novel multi-layer cloud model, using Petri nets in the cloud operations. They have also conducted threat modeling to identify threats. It has been done for different layers of the cloud computing operations. Our approach also provides the threat analysis to infer the cloud attack surface.

In 2018, Srinivasan et al. [23] discussed about the logistic services. It has been done through the cloud-based logistics services. They have proposed a robust security framework. It is for the purpose of the cloud-based logistics services. They have implemented this model for the long-term benefits. It is for the business enterprises. It also improves the overall cloud-based logistics services security.

Nhlabatsi et al. [24] analyzed the security risk assessment in the cloud computing environment. They have suggested that it is a challenging task. The dangers confronted by every customer may shift contingent upon their security necessities. The cloud supplier may likewise apply nonexclusive alleviation systems that are not destined to be viable in upsetting explicit dangers for various customers. They have proposed a threat-specific risk assessment framework. Their risk assessment process has three phases. Their framework is for the benefit for the security risk assessment challenges in the cloud computing environment.

Mthunzi et al. [25] discuss the limitless scalability and virtual resources scaling. They have suggested the main focus is the virtualization technology where the core area is the virtual machines. They have evaluated the security framework in terms of virtual machines. Their work shows that their approach is capable in extracting the VM communication sequences from trigger scenarios.

In 2018, Zhang et al. [26] discussed the anomalous behaviors of cloud services and the impact based on these services. They have presented a practical robust anomaly detection system. It is for the large-scale cloud called PerfInsight. In their approach, first, the potential trends have been detected automatically. Then, they have used an entropy-based feature selection mechanism. It is for the detection efficiency. Their results show that their approach has the capability of reducing the cardinality of models.

Torkura et al. [27] illustrated the cloud storage brokerage systems. Authors suggested that the security risk assessment is important for the cloud storage brokers (CSBs). They have analyzed a threat modeling schema. It has been used for the analysis for identifying the security threats and risks in cloud brokerage systems. Their schema working mechanism is done through by generating attack trees, attack graphs, and data flow diagrams. For supporting the schema, they have presented the common configuration scoring system (CCSS). They have demonstrated the efficiency by devising CCSS base scores.

In 2018, Tang et al. [28] discussed about securing cloud storage services. It has been done through the trusted blockchain. They have suggested that ChainFS hardens the cloud storage security against forking attacks. They have implemented ChainFS system on Ethereum and S3FS. Their results show low overhead.

In 2019, Xu et al. [29] discuss about the balancing of service openness and security control. They have presented the theoretical discussion in this regard. It is based on Nash equilibrium. They have considered two conditions based on the quantitative assessment. They have derived complete service openness investment based on their analysis. Based on this, they have provided the optimal strategy for coordinating investment in both service and security.

Sharma et al. [30] expounded the cloud computing as the repository. Author suggested that the security of the data is needed as the data has been migrated from another medium. Author also proposed the use of multi-encryption technique from the perspective of security of the data and privacy protection.

3   Method

Figure 1 shows the overall system structure. The system structure is capable of text and image data selection and uploading. The categorization of the sensitivity is based

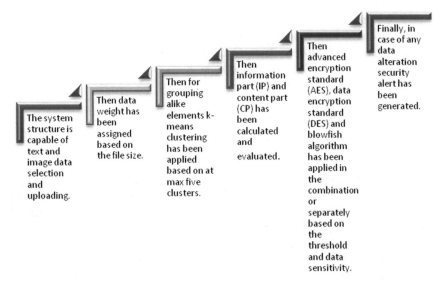

Fig. 1 Overall system structure

on the 10 attributes, and it has been selected on the basis of the size and information of data. These attributes are nothing but occurrences of different keywords in the content of data. We have considered 10 attributes for our work for the sake of simplicity. More attributes can also be considered, but it will incur more time for the process. Afterward, for clustering of similar elements, K-means clustering algorithm is applied which clusters the data in maximum of 5 clusters. Then information part (IP) and content part (CP) have been calculated and evaluated. It is helpful for the input set creation, and it has been applied in the combination or separately based on the threshold and data sensitivity. It has been updated for the data labeling, and the data has been ready for the security analysis.

Then k-means clustering has been applied on the weight matrix obtained from the previous phase. In this phase, the text and image data will be clustered based on the weight matrix. In our framework, maximum five clusters can be generated for the alikeness measure and checking. It will be helpful in data sensitivity analysis and based on the CP-based threshold will be applied for the data security.

Algorithm 1

Step 1: Weight values for the initial centroids.

   Step 2: The next weights have been evaluated based on these staring centroids.

   Step 3: Euclidean distance has been applied for the similarity measurement:

$$D((x, y), (a, b)) = \sqrt{(x - a)^2 - (y - b)^2}$$

Step 4: The addition of weight and their recalculation has been done till the epoch.

   Step 5: Closet cluster has been selected and assigned.

Step 6: It has been repeated till the similarity occurrences.

Step 7: Clusters have been generated.

In this paper, 3 steps of overall proposed system structure have been implemented. Implementation of hybrid security using multiple encryption algorithms will be the part of future scope of this work.

4 Results and Discussion

Data weight assignment has been processed for data preprocessing and weight assignment. Text and image data have been considered for experimentation. The maximum size considered in our approach is 60000 KB. Data has been accepted in the form of text and images. The weight values of different attributes are considered on the scale of 1–10. We have given the name from D1–D10.

For experimentation, different random samples have been considered and accepted for result calculation and comparison. In our framework, k-means algorithm has been applied for cluster formation based on the alike sensitivity or weight. There are at max five clusters. It is depending on the user selection for the formation of the cluster. It has been formed and divided for the grouping and division. Then, IP and CP have been calculated and evaluated. IP has been calculated based on the total attributes which follow the threshold level which is generated automatically. CP shows the total value generated based on the complete attribute accumulated based on the scale. Based on the IP and CP, sensitivity of the data has been generated.

Table 1 shows the data weight value for 10 random samples. It has been inputted for the k-means process for the clustering of the data. The data considered here is randomly selected, and then, three clusters have been formed. Figure 2 shows the overall time comparison.

Table 1 Data weight value for 10 random samples

ID	D1	D2	D3	D4	D5	D6	D7	D8	D9	D10
1	89	56	69	55	82	70	66	72	80	100
2	26	20	27	23	30	15	21	19	20	30
3	93	62	57	92	66	79	73	69	71	100
4	52	71	88	96	73	73	66	100	86	100
5	83	52	59	99	82	61	61	61	88	100
6	71	79	74	58	84	76	78	73	82	100
7	72	76	42	50	60	41	40	43	43	80
8	66	59	75	100	54	97	81	72	64	100
9	19	20	15	30	23	19	19	16	18	30
10	61	60	57	52	62	71	90	95	88	100

Table 2 Cluster 1 for 10 random samples

ID	D1	D2	D3	D4	D5	D6	D7	D8	D9	D10
1	89	56	69	55	82	70	66	72	80	100
6	71	79	74	58	84	76	78	73	82	100
7	72	76	42	50	60	41	40	43	43	80
10	61	60	57	52	62	71	90	95	88	100

Table 3 Cluster 2 for 10 random samples

ID	D1	D2	D3	D4	D5	D6	D7	D8	D9	D10
2	26	20	27	23	30	15	21	19	20	30
9	19	20	15	30	23	19	19	16	18	30

Table 4 Cluster 3 for 10 random samples

ID	D1	D2	D3	D4	D5	D6	D7	D8	D9	D10
3	93	62	57	92	66	79	73	69	71	100
4	52	71	88	96	73	73	66	100	86	100
5	83	52	59	99	82	61	61	61	88	100
8	66	59	75	100	54	97	81	72	64	100

Table 2 shows the cluster 1 for 10 random samples mentioned above, which is obtained after applying K-means clustering. It is those set of data having similar data sensitivity.

Table 3 shows the cluster 2 for 10 random samples, which is obtained after applying K-means clustering. It is those set of data having similar data sensitivity.

Table 4 shows the cluster 3 for 10 random samples, which is obtained after applying K-means clustering. It is those set of data having similar data sensitivity.

Similarly, the data weight value for 15 and 20 random samples is taken into consideration via different clients. The data is considered as input to K-means clustering algorithm, which in turn divides this data into different clusters. The data considered here is randomly selected, and then, 3–5 clusters have been formed.

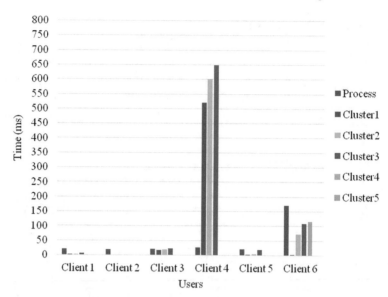

Fig. 2 Overall time comparison

In Fig. 2, it is clearly visible graphically, the time incurred (in ms) in the process of clustering data from different client, according to data sensitivity. The more sensitive data will take more time in clustering process, and less sensitive data will take less time. The decision of implementing set of encryption algorithm lies on this criteria.

5 Conclusion

First of all, on the basis of size of the file and segment content, weight values are assigned. It has been preprocessed based on random attribution scaling. Attribute weight scale is based on the scale of 1–100. The attributes scaling is on the scale of 1–10. It has been prepared for partitioning based on the content alikeness and sensitivity of the data. For clustering, k-means algorithm has been applied with $k = 5$ at max as per the user partitioning requirement. Two types of data structure have been considered. Text and images have been considered. Then, IP and CP will be calculated and evaluated. It has been evaluated and calculated for data sensitivity analysis. There are total four sensitivity and threshold levels in our approach. The time result and categorization show the effectiveness of our approach. Further, in future work, this categorization of data will be used to apply multiple levels of encryption schemes, which will in turn save time and provide secure environment. This work can also be expanded by considering different data formats. Along with the same, the effectiveness of work can also be validated with other standard encryption techniques.

References

1. Larus JR (2011) The cloud will change everything. In: ACM SIGARCH computer architecture news, vol 39(1), pp 1–2
2. Xiao Z, Xiao Y (2012) Security and privacy in cloud computing. IEEE Commun Surv Tutorials 15(2):843–859
3. Annane B, Ghazali O, Alti A (2019) A new secure proxy-based distributed virtual machines management in mobile cloud computing. Int J Adv Comput Res 9(43):222–231
4. Tari Z (2014) Security and privacy in cloud computing. IEEE Cloud Comput 1(1):54–57
5. Dalin G, Radhamani V (2018) IRIAL—an improved approach for VM migrations in cloud computing. Int J Adv Technol Eng Explor 5(44):165–171
6. Wei L, Zhu H, Cao Z, Dong X, Jia W, Chen Y, Vasilakos AV (2014) Security and privacy for storage and computation in cloud computing. Inf Sci 258:371–386
7. Dubey AK, Dubey AK, Namdev M, Shrivastava SS (2012) Cloud-user security based on RSA and MD5 algorithm for resource attestation and sharing in java environment. In: 2012 CSI sixth international conference on software engineering (CONSEG). Indore, India, pp 1–8
8. Abdullah S, Bakar KA (2018) Security and privacy challenges in cloud computing. In: IEEE, 2018 cyber resilience conference (CRC). Putrajaya, Malaysia, pp 1–3
9. Kumar V, Rathore RS (2018) Security issues with virtualization in cloud computing. In: IEEE, International conference on advances in computing, communication control and networking (ICACCCN). Greater Noida, India, pp 487–491
10. Li Z, Liu L, Zhang Y, Liu B (2018) Learning and predicting method of security state of cloud platform based on improved hidden Markov model. In: IEEE, 3rd international conference on smart city and systems engineering (ICSCSE). Xiamen, China, pp 600–605
11. Markandey A, Dhamdhere P, Gajmal Y (2018) Data access security in cloud computing: a review. In: IEEE, 2018 international conference on computing, power and communication technologies (GUCON). Greater Noida, India, pp 633–636
12. Giannakou A, Rilling L, Morin C, Pazat JL (2018) SAIDS: a self-adaptable intrusion detection system for IaaS clouds. In: IEEE, ACM. Proceedings of the 18th IEEE/ACM international symposium on cluster, cloud and grid computing. Washington, DC, USA, pp 354–355
13. Qing L, Boyu Z, Jinhua W, Qinqian L (2018) Research on key technology of network security situation awareness of private cloud in enterprises. In: IEEE, 3rd international conference on cloud computing and big data analysis (ICCCBDA). Chengdu, China, pp 462–466
14. Elliott D, Otero C, Ridley M, Merino X (2018) A cloud-agnostic container orchestrator for improving interoperability. In: IEEE, 11th international conference on cloud computing (CLOUD). San Francisco, CA, USA, pp 958–961
15. Chung SM, Shieh MD, Chiueh TC (2018) A security proxy to cloud storage backends based on an efficient wildcard searchable encryption. In: IEEE, 8th international symposium on cloud and service computing (SC2). Paris, France, pp 127–130
16. Sun X, Liu P, Singhal A (2018) Toward cyberresiliency in the context of cloud computing [resilient security]. IEEE Secur Priv 16(6):71–75
17. Lee BH, Dewi EK, Wajdi MF (2018) Data security in cloud computing using AES under HEROKU cloud. In: IEEE, 27th wireless and optical communication conference (WOCC). Hualien, Taiwan, pp 1–5
18. Esposito C, De Santis A, Tortora G, Chang H, Choo KK (2018) Blockchain: a panacea for healthcare cloud-based data security and privacy? IEEE Cloud Comput 5(1):31–37
19. Gordin I, Graur A, Potorac A, Balan D (2018) Security assessment of open stack cloud using outside and inside software tools. In: IEEE, International conference on development and application systems (DAS). Suceava, Romania, pp 170–174
20. Salunke PM, Mahale VV (2018) Secure data sharing in distributed cloud environment. In: IEEE, 2nd international conference on I-SMAC (IoT in social, mobile, analytics and cloud) (I-SMAC). Palladam, India, pp 262–266

21. Surbiryala J, Agrawal B, Rong C (2018) Improve security over multiple cloud service providers for resource allocation. In: IEEE, 1st international conference on data intelligence and security (ICDIS). Texas, USA, pp 145–148
22. Manzoor S, Zhang H, Suri N (2018) Threat modeling and analysis for the cloud ecosystem. In: IEEE, International conference on cloud engineering (IC2E). Orlando, FL, USA, pp 278–281
23. Srinivasan K, Gupta T, Agarwal P, Nema A (2018) A robust security framework for cloud-based logistics services. In: IEEE, International conference on applied system invention (ICASI). Piscataway, NJ, pp 162–165
24. Nhlabatsi A, Hong JB, Kim DS, Fernandez R, Fetais N, Khan KM (2018) Spiral ^ SRA: a threat-specific security risk assessment framework for the cloud. In: IEEE, International conference on software quality, reliability and security (QRS). Lisbon, Portugal, pp 367–374
25. Mthunzi SN, Benkhelifa E, Alsmirat MA, Jararweh Y (2018) Analysis of VM communication for VM-based cloud security systems. In: IEEE, Fifth international conference on software defined systems (SDS). Barcelona, Spain, pp 182–188
26. Zhang X, Meng F, Xu J (2018) PerfInsight: a robust clustering-based abnormal behavior detection system for large-scale cloud. In: IEEE, 11th international conference on cloud computing (CLOUD). San Francisco, CA, USA, pp 896–899
27. Torkura KA, Sukmana MI, Meinig M, Cheng F, Meinel C, Graupner H (2018) A threat modeling approach for cloud storage brokerage and file sharing systems. In: IEEE, IEEE/IFIP network operations and management symposium. Taipei, Taiwan, pp 1–5
28. Tang Y, Zou Q, Chen J, Li K, Kamhoua CA, Kwiat K, Njilla L (2018) ChainFS: blockchain-secured cloud storage. In: IEEE, 11th international conference on cloud computing (CLOUD). San Francisco, CA, USA, pp 987–990
29. Xu J, Liang C, Jain HK, Gu D (2019) Openness and security in cloud computing services. Assessment methods and investment strategies analysis. IEEE Access 7:29038–29050
30. Sharma Y, Gupta H, Khatri SK (2019) A security model for the enhancement of data privacy in cloud computing. In: IEEE, Amity international conference on artificial intelligence (AICAI). Dubai, UAE, pp 898–902

An Approach for Energy-Efficient Resource Allocation Through Early Planning of Virtual Machines to Servers in Cloud Server Farms

P. Kumar, S. Vinodh Kumar, and L. Priya

1 Introduction

As a result of the Internet's massive success and the rapid advancement of computing and volume advancements, computing assets have become more affordable, viable, and all-around accessible. This innovative initiative has resulted in the acceptance of a new computer model known as cloud computing. Cloud computing is a relatively new category of Internet-based services that has arisen in recent years. Grid computing, utility computing, and autonomic computing are just a few of the computing paradigms and innovations that make up cloud computing. Cloud as a model for delivering universal, advantageous, on demand network induction to a typical pool of adjustable processing assets that can be provisioned and communicated with little effort or specialist co-op communication. It enables the client to pay-per-use lease or share computing equipment. The cloud is a massive pool of instantly and effectively accessible virtualized computing resources that also serves as a platform for application development and various types of services. The pool can be powerfully reconfigured to change in accordance with competing responsibilities in terms of load balancing, scalability, and elasticity, allowing for optimal resource utilization.

One of the most essential characteristics of cloud computing is the ability to distribute and de-administer cloud resources for cloud customers on demand. A service-level agreement (SLA) is a contract between a service provider and its clients that details the services the provider will deliver and the service standards to which the provider must adhere. Customers and service providers agree on specific characteristics of the service, such as quality, availability, and responsibility. The goal of the cloud service is to meet client service-level agreements (SLAs) while

P. Kumar (✉) · S. Vinodh Kumar · L. Priya
Rajalakshmi Engineering College, Chennai, India
e-mail: kumar@rajalakshmi.edu.in

© The Author(s), under exclusive license to Springer Nature Singapore Pte Ltd. 2023
R. Doriya et al. (eds.), *Machine Learning, Image Processing, Network Security and Data Sciences*, Lecture Notes in Electrical Engineering 946,
https://doi.org/10.1007/978-981-19-5868-7_54

reducing functional expenses during the period spent allotting and de-assigning assets from server farms. Load balancing is accomplished utilizing virtual machine (virtual machine) movement, which chips away at the highest point of virtualization innovation. Virtual machine relocation in cloud server farms also enables reliable and responsive asset provisioning. Consolidating virtual machines or workloads is an efficient way to maximize asset utilization while lowering energy consumption. Cloud computing also entails reducing energy use in order to improve overall energy efficiency. According to estimates, the cost of cooling and controlling server farms accounts for 53% of total activity utilization [1]. According to one study, server farms in the United States consumed more than 1.5% of total energy produced in 2006, with that percentage expected to rise to 20% in the future [2]. Subsequently, service providers are predominantly worried about the decrease in energy utilization. Server consolidation [3] and energy mindful undertaking planning [4] are two distinct ways to address the issue by merging the assignments into fewer machines and turning off or putting into rest mode unused machines. As a result, overall data center resource utilization is improved, and power consumption is reduced. Consider a scenario in which there are ten hosts. It can be seen that all hosts are in use, with usage ranging from 25 to 55%. We can move a few workloads from one host to another using workload consolidation so that the target host is not overcrowded. We were able to put five hosts into power-saving mode while leaving five others running, with utilization varying from 60 to 75%. Business clouds make use of large-scale server farms and work in an integrated manner, achieving high sensitivity and lowering ongoing costs. It also necessitates a significant initial investment in the development of server farms and increases energy utilization [5]. The small-sized server farms are more ideal than huge-sized server farms for reasons like (a) a little server farm burns through less force compared with an enormous server farm;consequently, an incredible and exorbitant cooling framework doesn't need and (b) more modest-sized server farms are more affordable to set up and they are better geologically appropriated when contrasted with bigger-sized server farms. The actual assets, like CPU centers, data transmission, and disk storage, should be cut and divided between virtual machines.

In cloud server farms, over provisioning of assets is a typical wonder, as cloud ensures limitless asset provisioning through elasticity, reliability, and availability. Amazon, Google, and Microsoft, for example, are sending massive amounts of server farms all over the world to meet the rapidly expanding capacity interest of clients. They have roughly more than 1 million servers between them in their server farms. As an outcome, a tremendous amount of energy is devoured by these immense server farms to run the servers and keep the cooling framework working. Thus, enormous scope server farms are more costly to support, just as they have additional consequences for the climate because of high energy utilization. The issue of asset and energy failure is tended to with the utilization of virtualization advancing. Virtualization advancements permit the formation of different virtual machines on a solitary actual server, each virtual machine totally disconnected from the other, addressing a runtime environment. Virtualization advances additionally permit live movement of virtual machines [6], starting with one machine, then onto the next, and along these lines, further developing asset use. Power consumption can be diminished by transforming inactive actual machines into power-saving modes to save energy while fulfilling a client's execution requirements.

2 Related Work

Energy utilization is one of the significant concerns distinguished by numerous analysts, in the cloud environment. It is recommended to change every one of the inactive servers to suspend or wind down mode. Yet, this might raise different issues like tradeoff in execution, infringement of SLA, the expense of reconfiguration, and figuring/correspondence cost during virtual machine relocation. So, to resolve these issues, it is prescribed to monitor server use and responsibility migration. Furthermore, by developing a competent method, there will be an improvement in asset utilization and energy utilization. Verma et al. [7] viewed the trial of power as a careful, one-of-a-kind situation of usage as a major issue. Canisters are viewed as a variable in terms of size and cost. Live migration is used for virtual machine development, starting with one host and progressing to the next at a typical arranging stretch. Regardless, the creators do not discuss the SLA. Prakash et al. [8] propose optimized energy utilization in deployment and forecast (OEUDF) to reduce energy consumption in the cloud. Makers propose two stages of instruments: first, computing the best data-gathering to energy path (ODEP) to pass on and orchestrate the virtual machines; and second, computing the situation to design the work interaction. Makers have created power/energy models and proposed an estimation method that uses directed acyclic graphs (DAG).

Lee and Zomaya [9] recognized the problem of underutilized resources consuming energy. Makers propose that latent resources be put into rest/power-saving mode to maximize resource use while reducing energy consumption. Two task association heuristics, ECTC and MaxUtil, for determining energy, have been presented. It is proposed that a computation be used to join the obligations using cost work (separate for ECTC and MaxUtil). Manufacturers pledged to reduce energy use, as well as utility prices and their carbon footprint. Beloglazov et al. [10] presented a method for identifying overloaded and under-loaded servers by carefully putting up upper and lower utilization borders. Makers recommend transferring some virtual machines from this host to avoid SLA infringement if the host client excels as far as possible (SLAV). If utilization falls below the lowest possible level, all virtual machines on this underutilized host must be transferred, and the host must be shut down to save energy. In any event, no formal technique or process for determining the upper and lower margin has been provided. Wu et al. [11] propose a booking calculation with a dynamic voltage frequency scaling (DVFS) procedure to improve asset utilization and thus reduce overall energy utilization. The key concept is determining loads for each virtual machine and allocating a virtual machine to the work based on the weight (in expanding requests). Creators guarantee the strategy's effectiveness in reducing energy consumption based on experimentation results.

Song et al. [12] use virtualization for dynamic resource segmentation according to the obligation's requirements and work on the number of dynamic hosts to achieve energy viability in the cloud server ranch. The estimation of variable thing size holder squeezing (VISBP) has been proposed as a model for resource dispersal subject to the major difficulty of free online repository. As long as the gathering (of virtual machines and PMs) requirements are followed, VISBP can handle an acceptable sized assortment. When the movement and weight offset in troublesome places show differently than the current estimate, the makers ensure improved execution. In any case, all PMs are treated as homogeneous, and the application's cardinal limitation may be the unit cutoff. The problems of growing cloud system use while limiting total cost were perceived by Lee et al. [13]. Makers focused on resource allocation for the board and virtual machine, and provided an execution assessment-based resource assignment method (using the best fit strategy). The creators claimed that by providing the computation and subsequent experiments, they were able to distribute virtual machines to the best central location, promoting resource use. Workload consolidation to achieve higher resource utilization and energy efficiency in cloud data center has been proposed by Patel and Patel [14]. Responsibility union is a notion that restricts the number of dynamic servers in a server farm without compromising client requirements or the presentation of tasks. In general, the course of responsibility combination includes (a) selecting a small number of virtual machines from over utilized has and attempting to put them on different has so that this source has becomes normal and the target hosts are not over utilized, and (b) selecting all virtual machines from underutilized has and attempting to put them on different has so that target hosts are not over utilized, and turning off these underutilized hosts.

3 Proposed Work

The objective of this paper is to address the executives' asset use and energy use in cloud computing. Saving energy might result in a compromise in execution. As a result, depending on the client's requirement for quality of service (QoS) [14], an adaptable choice for energy utilization by the client is dependent on their execution requirement.

The proposed system architecture is displayed in Fig. 1. It shows that cloud clients are on top and they present their prerequisites to the cloud service provider (CSP) through the online interface. In the base, the cloud server farm involves various actual machines as registering components. These actual machines are given as virtual machines for the execution of errands. Each actual machine is composed of different virtual machines. Each host has a hypervisor (otherwise called a "Virtual Machine Monitor"), which is responsible for dealing with and managing all the virtual machines on the host. The planning part deals with virtual machine booking for the host, and the home specialist monitors the situation with all the virtual machines and the status of the execution of errands. The widespread specialist monitors the whole status of the server farm by totaling data from every one of the home specialists.

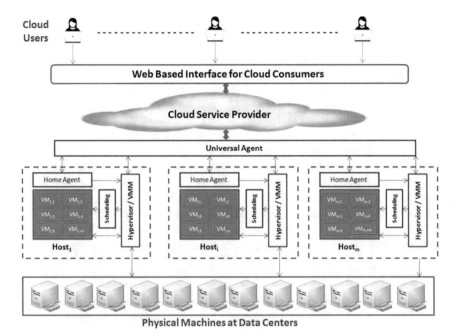

Fig. 1 Cloud system architecture

Workload consolidation has been identified as a process that can be divided among four sub-processes.

3.1 Early Planning

The most generally used method of installing virtual machines on servers can be divided into two parts: (i) initial virtual machine mapping on servers during the startup stage; and (ii) virtual machine assurance, development, and placement during the cementing stage. Early planning of virtual machines to servers assumes an imperative part in energy utilization in impending time cycles and ensuing tasks in the cloud environment. On the off chance that the underlying planning isn't productive, ensuing activities might prompt pointless virtual machine relocations, which may thus bring about an expansion in movement costs and SLA infringement. Proficient planning of something very similar during the beginning planning will keep (a) the quantity of the live host as negligible as could possibly be expected and (b) the live host as occupied as conceivable by effectively using them.

The trial is completed with a changing number of virtual machines and hosts to grasp the present starting preparation of virtual machines on servers in CloudSim. There are minimal drawbacks to the present early-on virtual machine location method. In any event, the strategy reliably allocates all of the virtual machines to open hosts. During the basic stage, it does not consider the stack of a single host while putting a virtual machine on the host. This resulted in a number of changes in the blend time and, as a result, a degradation in the system's execution. Second, each host can support up to two virtual machines. This restriction limits the number of virtual machines that can be installed on open hosts, and from time to time, distributions of virtual machines that are more than twofold in number seem to behave differently with respect to host size. Third, while setting up a virtual machine on it and commencing preparation, the default technique does not consider a cutoff. It merely determines whether the true host has sufficient capacity to meet the virtual machine's requirements. It doesn't function when it comes to selecting a suitable host for a certain virtual machine, taking into account the host's capacity, usage, existing weight, and so on. As a result, the goal of this research is to identify these concerns and conduct tests using established appropriation methodologies such as the default technique, least strategy, top strategy, earliest technique, and backpack approach.

(a) Default technique: For the most part, this method correctly assigns all virtual machines to accessible hosts. The following are a few examples to help you understand the practical scenario, using various virtual machines and the number of hosts as boundaries. It is typical that the host has sufficient capacity to meet the virtual machine's requirements.

> Instance 1: Regardless of the host limit or utilization, coordinated planning would be done with a total number of virtual machines of 500 and a total number of hosts of 500.
> Instance 2: The total number of virtual machines is 500; the total number of hosts is 250: Each host will receive two virtual machines.
> Instance 3: The total number of virtual machines is 750; the total number of hosts is 250: Even if the hosts have the capacity to accommodate more virtual machines, after distributing two virtual machines per host, the remaining 250 virtual machines would remain unallocated.
> Instance 4: The total number of virtual machines is 400, and the number of hosts is 250: Initially, 250 virtual machines would be distributed among 250 hosts based on a balanced strategy. With one virtual machine already disbursed, 150 virtual machines would be allocated to 150 hosts. As a result, 150 hosts will have two virtual machines each, while 100 hosts will have one virtual machine each.

> As a result, the default methodology disregards the single host constraint when establishing a virtual machine on it in the first phase. It simply guarantees that the genuine host has adequate resources to provide the virtual machines with what they need. It doesn't function when it comes to selecting the best host for a specific virtual machine based on the host's capacity, usage, weight, and other factors. This causes a lot of changes in the time it takes to blend and, as a result, contamination in the overall system's execution. Finally, because each host has two focuses, there can be all things considered ridiculous two virtual machines on each host during initial preparation.

This barrier limits the number of virtual machines that can be placed on accessible hosts, and it manifests itself to a large extent when virtual machines are assigned that are more than two times the size of the hosts.

(b) Least strategy: The least strategy method chooses the host with the maximum raised breaking point for any virtual machine to be propagated on available hosts. A virtual machine of 500 MIPS, for example, must be installed on a host. 500 MIPS, 1000 MIPS, 1500 MIPS, and 2000 MIPS are the open host possibilities. The least strategy approach technique would place a 500 MIPS necessary virtual machine on a host with a limit of 2000 MIPS. This will free up the most space on the host when the virtual machine duty is completed, increasing the chances of obliging one more virtual machine in the host'fs farthest reaches. In any case, this method slows down the production of small openings by as much as MIPS on the server; the disadvantage is that if a virtual machine with higher requirements emerges later, it won't be obligated because the host with the most resources is now involved.

(c) Top strategy: When allocating virtual machines to existing hosts, the top strategy method chooses the host with the least MIPS limit that can hold the required virtual machines. A virtual machine with 500 MIPS is necessary, for example, to be installed on a host. 400 MIPS, 600 MIPS, 1000 MIPS, and 1500 MIPS are the available host options. The top system strategy would place a 500-MIPS-essential virtual machine on a 600-MIPS-capable host. Although this strategy makes use of accessible hosts, it is computationally slower when it comes to finding a true host for a virtual machine. It is possible that it will frequently create small, insufficient air pockets of unutilized MIPS.

(d) Earliest technique: The earliest strategy methodology picks first has its encounters adequately huge to fulfill the virtual machine need for any virtual machine to be designated on available hosts. A virtual machine with 500 MIPS necessary, for example, to be installed on a host. 400 MIPS, 1000 MIPS, 600 MIPS, and 2000 MIPS are the open host options. The earliest methods methodology would place a virtual machine using 500 MIPS on a host with a limit of 1000 MIPS. However, while this method is more powerful in terms of finding a suitable host for a virtual machine, it results in inefficient assignment of existing host limit, as the excess idle constraint of host after designation becomes waste if it is unreasonably more modest, and as a result, virtual machine requests with greater essential cannot be satisfied.

(e) Backpack technique: It's a problem with combinatorial upgrades. Choose the mix of virtual machines to remember for a host from a large number of virtual machines, each with its own essential, so that the hard and fast need for virtual machines isn't actually or comparable to the host's capacity, and as far as feasible is just as broad as could truly be expected. Rather of seeking for the necessary for each virtual machine as in the previous situations, this method looks for an open decision for all expected mixes of virtual machines for a particular host. The computation of combinatorial advancement using backpack is shown as calculation Sect. 3.2.

3.2 *Algorithm*

Input: PossibleHost (For virtual machine Assignment), virtual machines_to_Transfer

Result: Designated virtual machines_to_Transfer, Host Selected

Sort PossibleHost and virtual machines_to_Transfer list in descending order based on consumption

for eachHost Selected in PossibleHost do

        Assign Backpack [virtual machines_to_Transfer.length][virtual machines_to_Transfer.length] = 0

        Assign ConsumptionDifference [virtual machines_to_Transfer. length] = 0

        Assign Total virtual machines_to_TransferOnHost [virtual machines_to_Transfer.length] = 0

for J = 0 to virtual machines_to_Transfer.length with increment 1 do

        OutstandingHostConsumption = Tu - U(Host Selected)

  for K = 0 to virtual machines_to_Transfer.length with increment 1 do

        if U(virtual machines_to_Transfer(K)) < OutstandingHostConsumption Backpack [J][K] = 1

Outstanding Host Consumption = OutstandingHostConsumption - (virtual machines_to_Transfer(K))

Total virtual machines_to_TransferOnHost[J]++

ConsumptionDifference[J] = OutstandingHostConsumption

Add all virtual machines to Selected virtual machines_to_Transfer for migration with lowest_ConsumptionDifference

Update the list of PossibleHost

Update virtual machines_to_Transfer list

return Selected virtual machines_to_Transfer, Host Selected

The backpack approach seeks out the finest optimum mix of virtual machines with the goal of relegating the greatest number of virtual machines possible, with the ensuing host utilization remaining high and low for a long time. Furthermore, this solution would reduce the size of the powerful host as little as possible, reducing future migrations, lowering energy consumption, and promoting SLA.

4   Results and Discussion

Cloud computing environment should provide a perspective on limitless processing assets to clients. To evaluate the proposed calculations, a massive scope of virtualized server farm foundation is required. However, it is quite difficult to complete a substantial degree in order to investigate a recognized establishment that it is necessary to survey and examine the recommended calculations. Diversions have since been enjoyed as a means of evaluating the presentation of planned work and

Table 1 Selection of virtual machine and host for experimentation (small in size) during early planning

Trials	T1	T2	T3	T4	T5	T6	T7
Virtual machine	22	22	22	22	22	22	22
Host	8	10	12	14	16	19	20

Table 2 Percentage of underutilized host during early planning (small in size) using cloudsim

Trials	T1	T2	T3	T4	T5	T6	T7
Default	2	2	3	3	3	4	4
Least	2	18	29	33	49	50	54
Earliest	18	32	42	47	50	55	56
Top	19	35	44	49	52	57	58
Backpack	22	37	47	51	55	59	61

ensuring the repeatability of assessments. The CloudSim [15] tool compartment has been chosen as a recreation stage.

To comprehend the impact of beginning planning (of virtual machines on servers) on the energy utilization of server farms, a progression of experimentation with existing default strategy and different methodologies, including dynamic writing computer programs, was conducted [16]. The results of the experiments imply that there has been some progress in the default planning strategy used by CloudSim. A movement of experiments with an arrangement of blends of different hosts and virtual machines with changed MIPS limits were coordinated [17]. Because the cloud is inherently active, with various proportions of hosts and virtual machines sent to a server farm, the trials are divided into two social occasions: (a) for few hosts and virtual machines, and (b) for incalculable hosts and virtual machines which is shown in Tables 1 and 2.

Figure 2 shows the underutilized after introductory planning of various methods. Regardless of the number of virtual machines, the default procedure is used on all hosts open in server ranches. A basic number of hosts remain unused, which will be abandoned in the following stages and the virtual machines on them will be relocated to other hosts. This cycle is long, and unending development could result in SLA encroachment. The degree of unutilization rises when the backpack is shown differently than it is in the default configuration [18]. This indicates that there is still more capacity that might be converted to a power-saving mode, resulting in increased energy adequacy. Therefore, one more virtual machine segment methodology is recommended to be used rather than the default procedure during the starting preparation of virtual machines to reduce planning time and SLA encroachment.

Cloud server farms are lively environments, and the quantity of hosts and virtual machines is colossal in size. From now on, incalculable hosts and virtual machines are seen as experimentation. Table 3 shows the quantity of virtual machines and hosts in the server farm, which is huge in size.

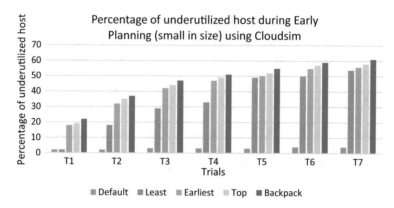

Fig. 2 Underutilized hosts after early planning (small in size) of different techniques

Table 3 Selection of virtual machine and host for experimentation (large in size) during early planning

Trials	T1	T2	T3	T4	T5	T6	T7
Virtual machine	22	50	100	500	1000	1500	2000
Host	12	40	65	350	760	1200	1800

Figure 3 shows values of exploratory outcomes for various portion strategies like default, least, top, earliest, and backpack technique. The names of the operations are highlighted in the X-pivot, and the Y-hub displays various underutilized rates. The results are shown in Table 4, which demonstrates that the degree of underutilization has improved from the default system to Backpack, implying that the strategies retain a greater number of hosts underutilized even after spreading the existing weight among the hosts. These underutilized hosts can be reprogrammed to regulate the energy-saving mode, resulting in increased energy viability. Along these lines, SLA insurance will be achieved indirectly.

Figure 4 shows the average resource underutilization per active host during early planning. The X-pivot illustrates the method used, and the Y-hub delineates the normal, underutilized MIPS per dynamic host in a cloud server farm.

From Fig. 4, the graph observed that the measure of underutilization per dynamic host decreased from the default technique to the backpack technique. Hence, the backpack technique improves the usage of accessible dynamic hosts. Therefore, higher resource utilization is achieved with the existing default technique.

The research outcomes, which are shown in Table 5, show that effective planning during beginning designations keeps the quantity of disconnected hosts as extreme as possible, which thusly brings about less energy utilization.

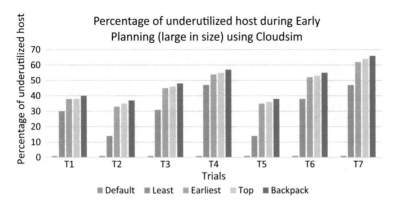

Fig. 3 Underutilized hosts after early planning (large in size) of different techniques

Table 4 Percentage of underutilized host during early planning (large in size) using cloudsim

Method	T1	T2	T3	T4	T5	T6	T7
Default	1	1	1	1	1	1	1
Least	30	14	31	47	14	38	47
Earliest	38	33	45	54	35	52	62
Top	38	35	46	55	36	53	64
Backpack	40	37	48	57	38	55	66

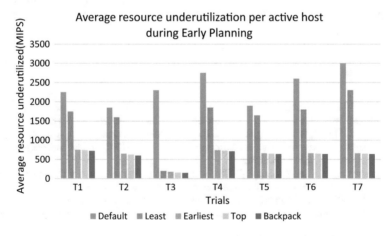

Fig. 4 Average resource underutilization per active host during early planning

Table 5 Average resource underutilization per active host during early planning

Method	T1	T2	T3	T4	T5	T6	T7
Default	2250	1850	2300	2750	1900	2600	3000
Least	1750	1600	200	1850	1650	1800	2300
Earliest	750	650	180	740	660	660	660
Top	740	625	160	725	650	650	650
Backpack	720	600	150	710	640	640	640

5　Conclusion

Effective designation of virtual machines on a host will support a decrease in total energy utilization for server farms, without compromising general activity and without disregarding SLAs in cloud environments. One of the critical features for resolving the issue of energy utilization in a cloud server farm is the underlying planning of virtual machines. Backpack is used as the initial virtual machine arrangement for combinatorial development. The proposed calculations are assessed through recreations of an enormous scope analysis arrangement utilizing responsibility follows from in excess of 1000 PlanetLab virtual machines. Through the reenactment result, we could accomplish an upgrade in the energy effectiveness of the server farm without compromising the SLA. In the future, the proposed calculations can be reached from reproduction arrangement to ongoing server farm climate, for example, OpenStack with more intricate responsibility models like Markov chains.

References

1. Hamilton J (2009) Cooperative expendable micro-slice servers (CEMS): low cost, low power servers for internet-scale services. In: Conference on innovative data systems research (CIDR)
2. Li B, Li J, Huai J, Wo T, Li Q, Zhong L (2009) Enacloud: an energy-saving application live placement approach for cloud computing environments. In: IEEE international conference on cloud computing, pp 17–24. IEEE
3. Srikantaiah S, Kansal A, Zhao F (2008) Energy Aware Consolidation for Cloud Computing. In: Proceedings of power aware computing and systems, vol 10, pp 1–5
4. Vasić N, Barisits M, Salzgeber V, Kostic´ D (2009) Making cluster applications energy-aware. In: ACDC. Proceedings of the 1st workshop on automated control for datacenters and clouds, pp 37–42
5. Kumar P, Anand S (2016) Multi criteria based task scheduling in cloud environment. Asian J Res Soc Sci Humanit 6(11):659–675, ISSN: 22497315
6. Clark C, Fraser K, Hand S, Hansen J, Jul E, Limpach C, Pratt I, Warfield A (2005) Live migration of virtual machines. In: ACM proceedings of the 2nd conference on symposium on networked systems design & implementation, vol 2, pp 273–286
7. Verma A, Ahuja P, Neogi A (2008) pMapper: power and migration cost aware application placement in virtualized systems. In Proceedings of the 9th ACM/IFIP/USENIX international conference on middleware, pp 243–264

8. Prakash P, Kousalya G, Vasudevan SK, Sangeetha KS (2015) Green algorithm for virtualized cloud systems to optimize the energy consumption. In: Artificial intelligence and evolutionary algorithms in engineering systems, Springer, pp 701–707
9. Lee YC, Zomaya AY (2012) Energy efficient utilization of resources in cloud computing systems. J Supercomput 60(2), pp 268–280
10. Beloglazov A, Buyya R (2010) Energy efficient resource management in virtualized cloud data centers. In: Proceedings of the 2010 10th IEEE/ACM international conference on cluster, cloud and grid computing, IEEE Computer Society, pp 826–831
11. Wu CM, Chang RS, Chan HY (2014) A green energy-efficient scheduling algorithm using the DVFS technique for cloud datacenters. J Future Gener Comput Syst 37:141–147
12. Song W, Xiao Z, Chen Q, Luo H (2014) Adaptive resource provisioning for the cloud using online bin packing. IEEE Trans Comput 63(11):2647–2660
13. Lee HM, Jeong YS, Jang (2014) Performance analysis based resource allocation for green cloud computing. J Supercomput 69(3):1013–1026
14. Patel N, Patel H (2020) Energy efficient resource allocation during initial mapping of virtual machines to servers in cloud datacenters. Int J Distrib Sys Technol
15. Calheiros RN, Ranjan R, Beloglazov A, De Rose CA, Buyya R (2011) CloudSim: a toolkit for modeling and simulation of cloud computing environments and evaluation of resource provisioning algorithms. J Softw Pract Experience 41(1):23–50
16. Huang J, Wu K, Moh M (2014) Dynamic virtual machine migration algorithms using enhanced energy consumption model for green cloud data centers. In: IEEE international conference on high performance computing & simulation (HPCS). IEEE, pp 902–910
17. Kumar P, Anand S (2013) An approach to optimize workflow scheduling for cloud computing environment. J Theoret Appl Inf Technol 57(3):617–623
18. Ghamkhari M, Mohsenian-Rad H (2013) Energy and performance management of green data centers: a profit maximization approach. IEEE Trans Smart Grid 4(2):1017–1025
19. Chen H, Zhu X, Guo H, Zhu J, Qin X, Wu J (2015) Towards energy-efficient scheduling for real-time tasks under uncertain cloud computing environment. J Syst Softw 99:20–35
20. Yang CT, Liu JC, Huang KL, Jiang FC (2014) A method for managing green power of a virtual machine cluster in cloud. Futur Gener Comput Syst 37:26–36
21. Kumar P, Anand S (2012) Priority based workflow task scheduling in cloud computing environments. Aust J Basic Appl Sci 8(17):532–539
22. Patel N, Patel H (2016) A comprehensive assessment and comparative analysis of simulations tools for cloud computing. Int J Eng Comput Sci 5(11):18972–18978

negSPUC: Trees-Based Single-Phase High-Utility Itemset Mining Algorithm with Negative Profit Values

B. Anup Bhat, S. V. Harish, and M. Geetha

1 Introduction

Mining patterns of interest from transaction databases have been ushered to seek answer to a trivial question:*"What set of items are purchased frequently by customers on their visit to the supermarket store?"* The resulting patterns called frequent patterns or frequent itemsets form the basis for several tasks such as association rule mining and recommendation systems. In frequent itemset mining, the measure of interestingness frequency of appearance of an itemset is determined by support count, s. A transaction T is deemed to support an itemset X if all the items that form X are purchased in T. However, the support count is solely based on the occurrence of an itemset and does not take into account the quantity or the profit of the item. In order to accommodate such factors, a more specific form of mining task called the high-utility itemset mining has been evolved. The measure of utility depends on the objective of the mining task. Conventionally, utility is measured in terms of the revenue generated by the items that appear in a transaction. Although, the profit bears a positive value, more often than not certain items are sold on a loss due to various reasons. For example, during cross-selling, a slow moving item could be sold freely along with some fast moving items to increase its sales or promote it. In such a scenario, the entire itemset could be a HUI despite having an item sold at loss or negative utility. Hence, mining should accommodate both the positive as well as negative utility values to enumerate complete set of HUIs.

Most algorithms to mine HUIs with positive utilities employ upper bounds on utility such as transaction utility (TU) or transaction weighted utility (TWU) to prune the combinatorial search space. Recently, a single-phase trees-based algorithm called single-phase utility computation (SPUC) to mine HUIs has been proposed [1]. SPUC

B. Anup Bhat · S. V. Harish (✉) · M. Geetha
Department of Computer Science and Engineering, Manipal Institute of Technology, Manipal
Academy of Higher Education, Manipal, India
e-mail: harish.sv@manipal.edu

© The Author(s), under exclusive license to Springer Nature Singapore Pte Ltd. 2023   739
R. Doriya et al. (eds.), *Machine Learning, Image Processing, Network Security and Data Sciences*, Lecture Notes in Electrical Engineering 946,
https://doi.org/10.1007/978-981-19-5868-7_55

leverages a prefix tree called the utility count tree (UCT) and another compressed tree called the string utility tree (SUT) to guide enumeration of candidate HUIs and determination of utility without database rescan. This algorithm has displayed significantly better performance than the existing IHUP [2], UP-Growth [3] and UP-Growth+ [4] algorithms. SPUC employs two over estimations—path utility and overestimated utility—for eliminating candidates. However, these over estimations do not necessarily hold when negative utility values are encountered rendering an incomplete set of HUIs. Hence, algorithms such as high-utility itemsets with negative item values (HUINIV)-Mine [5], faster high-utility itemset miner with negative unit profits (FHN) [6, 7] redefine these measures. HUINIV-Mine uses an apriori-like approach and hence involves numerous database scans. Also, filtering a large number of candidate HUIs adversely affects the performance of the algorithm. Hence, in this study, the SPUC algorithm that overcomes the drawbacks of HUINIV-Mine with the following advantages has been proposed:

- Through a single database scan, two trees, viz. utility count tree (UCT) and string utility tree (SUT) are constructed. All the items are accommodated in these trees to ensure completeness. Further, the redefined over estimations of utility stored in the UCT holds even when items bear negative profit values. Further, SUT achieves better compaction where each node represents a transaction of the database unlike UCT. Also, this facilitates utility computation without any need for additional database scan.
- For efficient search space exploration, the nodes in the trees store redefined overestimations. Thus, in conjunction with the pruning strategies employed in SPUC, the negative single-phase utility computation (negSPUC) is proposed for efficient mining.
- On real and synthetic data sets, negSPUC demonstrates significant improvement in comparison with HUINIV-Mine.

The remainder of the paper is organised as follows: Sect. 2 introduces preliminary concepts and existing algorithms. In Sect. 3, UCT and SUT are discussed, followed by the negSPUC algorithm. Experimental evaluation is described in Sect. 3.3 and the paper concludes with Sect. 4.

2 Background

Consider a transaction database D that records customer purchases of a hypothetical supermarket store selling n distinct items from $I = \{i_1, i_2, ...i_n\}$. Each purchase is represented by a transaction T_d in D that enlists set of items purchased. As depicted in Table 1b, each pair (i_x, q_x) suggests i_xth item was bought in q_x quantities. Further, the unit profit for every item is recorded in Table 1a. In this example, items 2 and 5 have negative unit profits.

Table 1 Sample database

(a) Profit table	
Item	1 2 3 4 5 6 7
Profit	5 −2 1 2 −3 5 1

(b) Transaction table	
TID	Transaction
T_1	{(3,1)(5,1)(1,1)(2,5)(4,3)(6,1)}
T_2	{(3,3)(5,1)(2,4)(4,3)}
T_3	{(3,1)(1,1)(4,1)}
T_4	{(3,6)(5,2)(1,2)(7,5)}
T_5	{(3,2)(5,1)(2,2)(7,2)}

Definition 1 Utility of an item i in transaction T_d, denoted by $u(i, T_d)$ follows the notion of revenue and is the product of quantity q_x with unit profit $p(i)$.

Definition 2 Utility of an itemset X in transaction T_d, i.e. $u(X, T_d)$ is $\sum_{i \in X \wedge X \subseteq T_d} u(i, T_d)$.

Definition 3 Utility of an itemset X in D denoted by $u(X)$, is defined as

$$u(X) = \sum_{X \subseteq T_d \wedge T_d \in D} u(X, T_d) \tag{1}$$

e.g.
$u(\{2\}, T_2) = 4 \times -2 = -8$
$u(\{1, 5\}) = u(\{1, 5\}, T_1) + u(\{1, 5\}, T_4) = 2 + 4 = 6$

Definition 4 An itemset X is deemed to be a high-utility itemset (HUI) if $u(X) \geq min\_util$, where min_util is the minimum utility input by the user. A HUI X can contain items that have either positive or negative utility. However, if all the items have negative utilities, then it can not be a HUI (as $min\_util > 0$).
For example, when min_util is set to 15, the HUIs from the database in Table 1 along with their utilities are {{1} = 20, {1, 3, 4} = 20, {3, 4} = 19, {1, 4, 6} = 16, {1, 3} = 28, {1, 4} = 18, {1, 3, 7} = 21, {3, 7} = 15, {1, 7} = 15, {1, 3, 4, 6} = 17, {1, 3, 5, 7} = 15}. It can be seen that although the item 5 has a negative profit, it still appears in one of the HUIs.

Definition 5 Redefined transaction utility of a transaction T_d, i.e. $RTU(T_d)$ is determined by accumulating the utilities of only those items appearing in the transaction with positive profits, i.e. $RTU(T_d) = \sum_{i \subseteq T_d \wedge p(i) > 0} u(i, T_d)$. For example, $RTU(T_1) = u(\{3\}, T_1) + u(\{1\}, T_1) + u(\{4\}, T_1) + u(\{6\}, T_1) = 1 + 5 + 6 + 5 = 17$

Definition 6 Redefined transaction weighted utility of an itemset X, i.e. $RTWU(X)$ is determined by accumulating RTU of all the transactions in D where X is supported, i.e. $RTWU(X) = \sum_{X \subseteq T_d \wedge T_d \in D} TU(T_d)$. For example, $RTWU(\{1, 4\}) = RTU(T_1) + RTU(T_3) = 17 + 8 = 25$

Definition 7 An itemset X is deemed to be a high-transaction weighted utility itemset (HTWUI), provided $RTWU(X) \geq min\_util$. Also, all the HUIs are HTWUIs and an HTWUI may or may not be a HUI.

Property 1 (RTWU Downward Closure Property) For any HTWUI X, all of its subsets shall be HTWUIs. Also, if an itemset X is not a HTWUI, then none of its supersets can be HTWUIs.

Definition 7 and the RTWU Downward Closure Property are employed in HUINIV-Mine to enumerate all the candidate HUIs through multiple database scans. The final phase prunes the itemsets that do not have at least one item with positive utility and outputs the complete set of HUIs with an additional database scan.

2.1 Related Work

As per Definition 3, the utility measure is not downward closed. As a result, the algorithms to mine HUIs resort to formulate utility upperbounds and overestimations. One such measure called transaction weighted utility (refer Definition 6) was put forward by Liu et al. [8, 9]. In this study, the authors employed TWU to prune the combinatorial search space by enumerating candidate itemsets level-wise. In the first phase, with k-passes of the database, k-HTWUIs which are potential HUIs were enumerated. The next phase involved $(k + 1)$th scan to determine the actual utility of these potential HUIs. Since this study, several algorithms have been proposed to reduce the database scans [10, 11] and mine HUIs efficiently by transforming the database into tree [2, 4, 12, 13] or list [14, 15] structures.

Algorithms based on tree structures prune the 1-itemsets that are not HTWUI and insert the remaining items of the transaction into a prefix tree after sorting them in a predetermined order. Using a bottom-up pattern-growth approach similar to the FP-Growth [16], a recursive mining procedure is then invoked that outputs all the candidate itemsets. During this task, different pruning strategies based on TU, TWU, path utilities are employed to enhance the mining performance. Recently, another trees-based algorithm called SPUC that eliminates the second phase was proposed using a prefix and transaction-based compact tree structures. However, the overestimations used for pruning fail when the transaction database contains items with negative profits.

In HUINIV-Mine algorithm, Chu et al. proposed the measure of $RTWU$ based on RTU that prevented the negative utility items to be considered during the calculation (Refer Definitions 6 and 7). The algorithm employed an approach similar to the two-phase algorithm to mine HUIs level-wise. After the completion of the first phase, the candidate itemsets that did not contain at least one item with positive profit value were filtered out. An efficient algorithm based on fast high-utility miner (FHM) called the FHN [6, 7] was proposed by Fournier-Viger et al. to accommodate negative profit items. The utility list structure employed in FHM was modified to separately store the positive and negative utility values in positive-negative-utility (PNU)-list. By modifying the pruning strategies developed in FHM, the authors demonstrated the superiority in performance of FHN over HUINIV-Mine.

In the present study, negSPUC algorithm has been proposed to handle the negative profit items when mining HUIs. In this regard, the modifications to UCT and SUT are detailed in Sect. 3.1; the algorithm is then provided in Sect. 3.2.

3 Methodology

Items with negative unit profits such as that shown in sample database Table 1 is a plausible scenario in retail marketing. The SPUC algorithm mines a complete set of HUIs provided the unit profit of items is a positive value. To cater high-utility negative itemset mining, in the following subsections, UCT and SUT are modified to ensure complete enumeration of HUIs.

3.1 Utility Count Tree and String Utility Tree

UCT stores the item id, count and the utility value along the path in the tree in its nodes. Thus, it has a node per item of a transaction. In order to promote prefix sharing, the items are arranged in ascending order prior to inserting in to the tree and the utility and count fields get updated appropriately. In order to avoid the content of the third field called $nodeUtility$ being underestimated when items with negative values are encountered, the corresponding value is kept to 0. For example, after reading T_1 and sorting the items in ascending order, a node is constructed for every item and inserted such that the consecutive items get added as child nodes (refer Fig. 1). A node corresponding to item 1 has the following values in its fields: $\langle 1, 1, 5 \rangle$. Then, item 2 gets inserted as child of this node with contents: $\langle 2, 1, 0 \rangle$. Note that the utility field is 0 as item 2 has a negative profit. Subsequently, the remaining items get inserted. A header list is also constructed that contains the items and indexes into the tree pointing at the first occurrence of the corresponding item. Also, $nodelink$ connects nodes bearing the same item id as shown in Fig. 1.

SUT stores per transaction information in its node. It has three fields that store items, RTU along with corresponding item utilities of a transaction. The items and utility values are stored as a string with a delimiter such as x. This also ensures prefix sharing, i.e. any other incoming transaction that contains items that are substrings of an already inserted transaction, then it gets inserted as its child node. For example, a node for T_1 contains: $\langle 1x2x3x4x5x6, 17, 5x - 10x1x6x - 3x5 \rangle$. Also, as shown

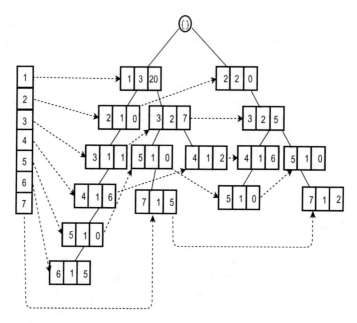

Fig. 1 UCT with modified *nodeUtility* field for database in Table 1

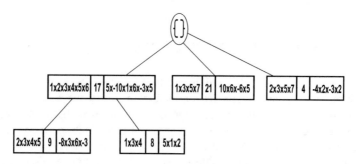

Fig. 2 SUT modified for database in Table 1

in Fig. 2, it contains two child nodes representing transactions T_2 and T_3 as all the items in these two are completely contained in T_1.

Both the trees are complete, i.e. they do not discard any items during the construction phase. Also, they ensure prefix sharing facilitating compact representation.

3.2 negSPUC Algorithm

The general framework for mining is based on pattern-growth approach. The steps are enumerated as follows:

1. The header list of the UCT is scanned from the bottom; all the prefix paths corresponding to the suffix item under consideration are collected via the node links. These prefix paths form the conditional pattern base (CPB) of this item.
2. For each prefix path, the subsets that contain the suffix item are generated as these are the valid patterns to be explored.
3. For the subsets generated, the utility is calculated from the SUT. Intuitively, it suffices to check only for the occurrence of the suffix item in any node of SUT. If this is the case, then the itemsets are checked. Depending on this, the utility is updated or the search follows with the next itemset. Also, the child nodes of the current node are visited.

The following pruning strategies are incorporated at Step 1 and Step 2, respectively.

1. If the accumulated path utilities for an item does not exceed min_util, then no subsets generated from the CPB of the item shall be a HUI. The details of the proof are provided in [1]. Hence, the item can be pruned and the search can proceed with the next item in the header list. Path utility for a path is ascertained by adding up the $nodeUtility$ fields. For example, consider items 6 and 2. From Fig. 1, the CPB of 6 contains only one prefix path-$\langle 1, 2, 3, 4, 5, 6 \rangle$ with path utility of 32. Similarly, for 2, the two prefix paths in its CPB- $\langle 1, 2 \rangle$ and $\langle 2 \rangle$ have path utilities of 20 and 0, respectively. If the min_util was set to 30, while item 2 gets pruned, i.e. no subsets from any of its prefix paths for further examination shall be generated. However, as the path utility of 6 exceeds the min_util, subsets from its path that contain 6 shall be generated.

   Consider the scenario where the $nodeUtility$ contents were not redefined. If $min\_util = 13$, then path utility for {5} shall be 1 and hence $CPB(\{5\})$ shall not be further explored. However, the itemset {1, 3, 5} with utility of 13 which is a HUI shall be missed. Hence, redefining these overestimates as mentioned in Sect. 3.1 is imperative.

2. If the overestimated utility of a subset formed for a given suffix item is not at least min_util, then it cannot be a HUI and hence pruned. The overestimated utility (OU) for an item in the CPB is the sum of the $nodeUtility$ fields of the different path it occurs in. For example, consider mining with suffix item 4 and min_util of 20. Sum of its path utilities amounts to 67 and exceeds min_util. Hence, its CPB needs to be explored to generate possible subsets with 4 as suffix. Particularly, it suffices to generate subsets from path {1, 2, 3, 4}. The overestimated utility of the items in of this path with respect to the CPB is recorded in Table 2. Itemsets and their OUs are also given in Table 3. As the OU of itemsets {4} and {2, 4} does not exceed min_util, they are pruned. Only the utility of remaining items will be determined from SUT.

After applying the above pruning strategies, the utility of the remaining itemsets is computed using the SUT. If the same example of mining with suffix item 4 is continued, as given in Table 3, except for {4} and {2, 4}, all other itemsets utilities are to be calculated. All the nodes of the SUT may not contain the itemsets that are suffixed on 4. Hence, instead of checking for the entire itemset, a node is checked

Table 2 OU of items in CPB of 4

Item	OU
1	40
2	0
3	13
4	14

Table 3 OU of subsets from CPB of 4

Itemset	OU
{4}	14
{3, 4}	27
{2, 4}	14
{1, 4}	54
{1, 3, 4}	67
{2, 3, 4}	27
{1, 2, 3, 4}	67

Table 4 Utility of subsets from CPB of 4

Itemset	$\langle 1 \times 2 \times 3 \times 4 \times 5 \times 6 \rangle$	$\langle 2 \times 3 \times 4 \times 5 \rangle$	$\langle 1 \times 3 \times 4 \rangle$
{3, 4}	7	(9)16	(3)19
{1, 4}	11	(0)11	(7)18
{1, 3, 4}	12	(0)12	(8)20
{2, 3, 4}	-3	(1)-2	(0)-2
{1, 2, 3, 4}	2	(0)2	(0)2

for presence of 4. If so, all the itemsets in the list are checked for the presence in the current node. When the first node in the SUT is encountered, it contains the suffix item 4. Hence, all the itemsets are checked for their presence. If we consider the itemset, {1, 3, 4}, then all these itemsets are present in the first node of the SUT. Hence, its utility is obtained from the utility fields. This is a trivial operation as the utility values in this field follow the same indices as the items stored in the item field. So the utility of {1, 3, 4} is computed as $5 + 1 + 6 = 12$. In a similar manner, the utilities of other itemsets if present get updated. Subsequently, the child node of this node gets visited. In this case, if we consider the right child of the node, the utilities of the itemsets {1, 4}, {3, 4} and {1, 3, 4} get updated. Table 4 captures the utility of these itemsets updated after visiting the first node and its child nodes. The values in the braces denote the utility value for this itemset in the current node being considered.

The detailed steps of the negSPUC algorithm incorporating the pruning strategies illustrated above are provided in Algorithm 1. UCT, SUT and min_util are input

---

Algorithm 1 negSPUC algorithm

Input: $UCT, SUT, minUtil$
Output: HUIs
1: $HashMap\ hash\_item\_utilities(List\_Integer\ itemset, Integer\ utility)$
2: **for each** item i from the bottom of H **do**
3:   $CPB(i) \leftarrow$ Get all the prefix paths of i and calculate path utility
4:   **if** sum of the path utilities $>= minUtil$ **then**
5:     **for each** prefix path, $p \in CPB(i)$ **do**
6:       $itemset\_list \leftarrow$ generate subsets from the items in p that include i
7:       **for each** itemset X in $itemset\_list$ **do**
8:         **if** $OU(X) < minUtil$ **then**
9:           $itemset\_list \leftarrow itemset\_list \setminus X$
10:         **end if**
11:       **end for**
12:       Call MINE($itemset\_list, SUT.root$)
13:     **end for**
14:   **end if**
15: **end for**

---

to this algorithm. The header table is examined from the rear end so as to collect the prefix paths of each item via the node links (*line 3*). Along with this, the path utility is also determined by adding the $nodeUtility$ fields of the different items that form the prefix path. Once the CPB is constructed, thus the path utilities are summed up and checked against min_util (Pruning Strategy 1 *line 4*). If this condition is met, then each prefix path gets evaluated and subsets from each path that contain the suffix item shall be generated (*line 6*). Then, for each of the subsets generated, OU is calculated and itemsets whose OU is not at least min_util shall not be considered further (*lines 8 and 9*). For the remaining itemsets, the utility is computed using the MINE algorithm (*line 12*). As the SUT stores the utility of the items in the thrid field, accessing its nodes via the presence of suffix ensures faster utility computation [1].

3.3 Experimental Evaluation

The source code implementation of HUINIV-Mine [5] in Java provided by SPMF was extensively used for experimental evaluation [17]. Table 5 records the data sets used for comparing the proposed negSPUC algorithm with HUINIV-Mine. The items with negative profit values were chosen at random and the total number approximated to $20\% * |I|$. Fig. 3 displays the execution time of negSPUC and HUINIV-Mine. negSPUC clearly outperforms HUNINV-Mine, especially at lower thresholds. Despite construction of two tree structures eliminates the second phase of calculating the utility values of candidate itemsets, at higher thresholds, the execution time is almost similar to that of HUINIV-Mine. However, the variation in execution time across different thresholds is very less in the case of negSPUC across the chosen range of min_util. On the contrary, HUINIV-Mine mining time is very sensitive to

Table 5 Data sets characteristics

Data set	$|D|$	$|I|$	T	Density(%)
Foodmart	4141	1559	4.4	0.28
Liquor	9284	2626	2.7	0.001
s1	10000	1000	5.5	0.054
s2	10000	50000	5.5	0.016
s3	10000	100000	5.4	0.013

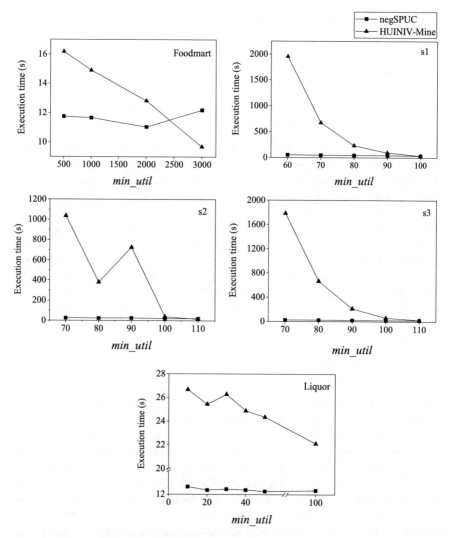

Fig. 3 Execution time across various data sets

Fig. 4 Execution time after
scaling synthetic data sets

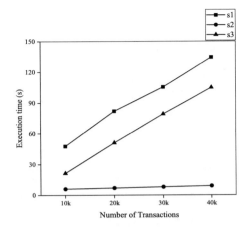

changes in the thresholds. This can be attributed to the candidate enumerated that decreases considerably with increased threshold. negSPUC with its pruning strategies explores the search space efficiently. Hence, it displays a stable performance.

Scalability of negSPUC on the synthetic data sets was also evaluated by adding 10000 transactions in every step. As seen from Fig. 4, across all the data sets, the execution time for mining increased linearly between the database insertions. As both the designed trees exploit the prefix feature either with respect to items in the transaction or entire transaction, the construction converges faster. Also, with the elimination of candidate generation phase, negSPUC achieves linear scalability.

4   Conclusion

Mining high-utility itemsets provides for a framework that accommodates business objectives in terms of utility measure. When transaction databases are considered, a HUI can always contain an item which was sold at a loss. Hence, it becomes important to consider such items in mining rather than discarding them. In the current study, negSPUC was proposed to handle both the cases of items with positive or negative profit values. In conjunction with two pruning strategies based on path and overestimated utilities, the mining performance was enhanced. In future, this study shall be extended to mine high on-shelf utility itemsets and mine HUIs in a distributed environment.

References

1. Bhat BA, Harish SV (2021) A single-phase algorithm for mining high utility itemsets using compressed tree structures. ETRI J
2. Ahmed CF, Tanbeer SK, Jeong BS, Lee YK (2009) Efficient tree structures for high utility pattern mining in incremental databases. IEEE Trans Knowl Data Eng 21(12):1708–1721
3. Tseng V, Wu C, Shie B, Yu P (2010) UP-growth: an efficient algorithm for high utility itemset mining. Discovery Data Min 253–262. http://dl.acm.org/citation.cfm?id=1835839
4. Tseng VS, Wu CW, Fournier-Viger P, Yu PS (2016) Efficient algorithms for mining high utility itemsets from transactional databases. IEEE Trans Knowl Data Eng 28(1):54–67
5. Chu CJ, Tseng V, Liang T (2009) An efficient algorithm for mining high utility itemsets with negative item values in large databases. Appl Math Comput 215(2):767–778
6. Fournier-Viger P (2014) Fhn: efficient mining of high-utility itemsets with negative unit profits. In: Luo X, Yu JX, Li Z (eds) Advanced data mining and applications. Springer International Publishing, Cham, pp 16–29
7. Lin JW, Fournier-Viger P, Gan W (2016) Fhn: an efficient algorithm for mining high-utility itemsets with negative unit profits. Knowl Based Syst 111:283–298
8. Liu Y, Liao WK, Choudhary A (2005) A two-phase algorithm for fast discovery of high utility itemsets. In: Proceeding PAKDD'05 proceedings of the 9th Pacific-Asia conference on Advances in knowledge discovery and data mining, pp 689–695
9. Liu Y, Liao WK, Choudhary A (2005) A fast high utility itemsets mining algorithm. In: Proceedings of the 1st international workshop on utility-based data mining. UBDM '05, Association for Computing Machinery, New York, NY, USA, pp 90-99. https://doi.org/10.1145/1089827.1089839
10. Anup Bhat B, Harish SV, Geetha M (2018) A dynamic itemset counting based two-phase algorithm for mining high utility itemsets. In: 2018 15th IEEE India Council International Conference (INDICON), pp 1–6
11. Lan G-C, Hung T-P, Tseng V (2012) An efficient gradual pruning technique for utility mining. Int J Innov Comput Inf Control 8(7):5165–5178 (2012). http://www.ijicic.org/ijicic-11-04070.pdf
12. Ahmed CF, Tanbeer SK, Jeong B, Lee Y (2011) HUC-prune: an efficient candidate pruning technique to mine high utility patterns. Appl Intell 34(2):181–198. https://doi.org/10.1007/s10489-009-0188-5
13. Lin CW, Hong TP, Lu WH (2011) An effective tree structure for mining high utility itemsets. Expert Syst Appl 38(6):7419–7424. https://doi.org/10.1016/j.eswa.2010.12.082
14. Fournier-Viger P, Wu CW, Zida S, Tseng VS (2014) Fhm: faster high-utility itemset mining using estimated utility co-occurrence pruning. In: International symposium on methodologies for intelligent systems. Springer, Berlin, pp 83–92
15. Liu M, Qu J (2012) Mining high utility itemsets without candidate generation. In: Proceedings of the 21st ACM international conference on Information and knowledge management, pp 55–64
16. Han J, Pei J, Yin Y, Mao R (2004) Mining frequent patterns without candidate generation: a frequent-pattern tree approach. Data Min Knowl Discov 8(1):53–87. https://doi.org/10.1023/B:DAMI.0000005258.31418.83
17. Fournier-Viger P (2021, January) SPMF an open-source data mining library, developer's guide. https://www.philippe-fournier-viger.com/spmf/index.php?link=developers.php

LoRa-Based IoT Architecture Using Ant Colony Optimization for Intelligent Traffic System

Sarita Simaiya, Umesh Kumar Lilhore, Jasminder Kaur Sandhu, Jyoti Snehi, Atul Garg, and Advin Manhar

1 Introduction

One of the most significant reasons for mortality globally is traffic fatalities. Traveling has grown with one of the most stressful aspects of daily life. Even though traveling should give an excellent option as personal vehicles, this has been discovered that daily individuals feel not only negative emotion but also anger and frustration as little more than a result of heavy traffic jams [1]. Given the massive quantity of automobiles operating on the roadways together in particular locations in a restricted number of intervals zones, traffic jams are frequently one of the leading reasons for major and minor traffic crashes [2]. The method utilizes smart and connected communication systems, transportation theories, and machine learning methods to generate a rapid and responsive system. Higher resource consumptions, poor scalability, and scalability are three main problems in developing an ITM system.

S. Simaiya · J. Snehi · A. Garg
Chitkara University Institute of Engineering & Technology, Chitkara University, Rajpura, Punjab, India
e-mail: Jyoti.snehi@chitkara.edu.in

A. Garg
e-mail: atul.garg@chitkara.edu.in

U. K. Lilhore (✉)
Department of CSE, KIET Group of Institutions Delhi-NCR, Ghaziabad, India
e-mail: umeshlilhore@gmail.com

J. K. Sandhu
Institute of Engineering, Chandigarh University, Mohali, India
e-mail: jasmindersandhu@gmail.com

A. Manhar
JECRC University, Jaipur, India
e-mail: advin.manhar@jecrc.edu.in

© The Author(s), under exclusive license to Springer Nature Singapore Pte Ltd. 2023
R. Doriya et al. (eds.), *Machine Learning, Image Processing, Network Security and Data Sciences*, Lecture Notes in Electrical Engineering 946,
https://doi.org/10.1007/978-981-19-5868-7_56

751

Intelligent traffic management has a comprehensive list of advantages. It minimizes the number of pollutants released by automobiles daily by giving drivers the fastest routes, resulting in lower fuel usage. First, from the standpoint of vehicles, traffic jams relieve them of their daily stress. Whenever a medicinal emergency strikes, this proposed system will help save people by prioritizing the ambulances and traumatic center, allowing them to get to the victims as quickly as possible [3]. Finally, intelligent transportation technology can help detect and prevent criminality. Intelligent analytics, which measures the smart city using security cameras, make these contributions feasible. There are already numerous studies in the domain of intelligent traffic control systems. However, most of them have mainly concentrated on techniques that have made numerous obstacles and flaws, as described in Sect. 2 [4].

Considering the disadvantages of the conventional transportation management system earlier discussed, it is evident that there must be a significant necessity to expand its performance by incorporating intelligence to facilitate dynamic and adaptation. As a result, it can assist in the decrease of traffic congestion, lowering journey time and carbon. Conventional transportation management systems have been proven around for centuries [5].

This study presents modified cross-layer LoRa architecture as transmitting information in the anticipated intelligent traffic management structure to improve traffic jams and offer greater driving comfort for the drivers. This research suggests an ant colony optimization focused on vehicular traffic, with a highly competitive environment based on accumulating substances en pathway [6]. The critical characteristic of ACO, which is used in transportation planning, is the concentration of pheromone reserve and upgrading characteristics. ACO significantly outperformed all other optimization techniques, including ABC, used in vehicular management and control using intelligent ant colony-based systems [7].

Each of these issues is addressed by the proposed approach:

- This research aims to make usage LoRa innovation because of its long-range communication and minimal energy requirements.
- Existing methods encounter data rate restriction; the system implementation attempts to remove the data rate transfer restriction.
- The cross-layer communication framework has been developed.
- The approach has been introduced to address the constantly appearing problem of scalability.
- This proposed architecture makes it possible to create a novel process or alter an existing one dependent on the transportation principal's shifting requirements.
- Finally, develop an ACO-based intelligent traffic management system, which also utilizes the features of LoRa architecture [8].

The complete research article is divided into various sections covering various sections. Section 1 covers the introduction of the research; the section covers related work in intelligent traffic management; Sect. 3 covers the architecture of the proposed system (ACO with LoRa); Sect. 4 covers the simulation results and analysis. Section 5 covers the conclusion and future work.

2 Related Work

The research article [9] suggested a deductive research logic detector to identify the vehicle types. These detectors are established primarily on expressways. So, when objects pass over through the continuous loop plane, a transformation in the activated impedance is noted. This modification denotes the motion of a new vehicle over the circuit detector and therefore archives the volume of traffic passing on a particular road.

The research article [10] illustrated a metallic sensor predicated vehicular sensing technology that utilized electromagnets to recognize the geomagnetic field modifications. Heavy trucks typically cause more fluctuation in actual magnetic measurements; all such detectors are usually helpful for identifying their existence. The research article [11] devised and introduced a motion-based traffic categorization. The sound waves created whenever the moving vehicle migrated over the activity tracker sensors were detected by this framework.

In [12], researchers have discussed an integrated illustration computation-focused vehicular detection approach. Therefore, processing techniques provide an effective solution for identifying the roads on the road. In the research article [13], the communication system, technique for finding are trained to detect the trends about the physical structure of a heavy vehicle, a ridiculously low Webcam equipped on the crossings and many other places can sometimes underperform to acknowledge the appropriate volume of traffic regularly.

The research article [14] suggested an ant colony [ACO] method for retrieving alternatives to issues connected to share configurations. The congestion is prevented by the direction of intelligent sensors and is likely to increase the demand. The research [15] suggested a geographic data and base station self-centered arrangement to address the difficulties of selfish greed. The intermediate nodes are consolidated with geographical data to select a correct routing protocol.

The research [16] proposed a neighborhood and perception reward system to encourage a self-centered terminal to participate in message transmission. Under this system, every base station can preserve, inform, and demonstrate prestige for confirmation only when needed. The crucial element in this system is the generosity feature that starts kicking out malicious nodes.

3 Proposed System Architecture

We can employ LoRa's long-range communication rate inside an ITMS due to the technology's extended communication capacity. The proposed scheme architecture addresses the scale and performance issues that an ITMS faces. ACO is a deterministic methodology that finds the best solution.

The behavior and attitude of ant colonies are searching the shortest route among their colony and food source. It is a meta-heuristic optimization innovation. The route is observed by analyte deposits whenever the ants travel at irregular intervals.

Architecture of Proposed ACO with LoRa

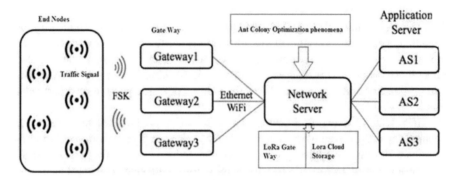

Fig. 1 The architecture of proposed (ACO with LoRa Method)

Another pheromone receipt on a route enhances the possibility of the route being accompanied. The selected solution depends on the highest pheromone reserve from the initial node, and the route is evaluated for optimal solutions.

The proposed cross-layer framework for an intelligent traffic management system predicated on ant colony with LoRa is represented in Fig. 1. The presence of a cross-layer separates this architectural style from the conventional LoRa stack. In research [26], conventional architecture structures restrict overall effectiveness, particularly in Wi-Fi networks. The disadvantage of traditional stacks is that the algorithm cannot change the set parameters.

The implementation of the proposed method is a novel approach in using LoRa to enhance current transport systems. Among the most appealing aspects of this proposed architecture is its flexibility in development and operation. When the suggested project is implemented, both administration and customers will access the information and determine the level of traffic and congestion [27].

ACO is a methodology predicated on the attitude of the ant colonies in determining the relatively short route from an origin to the meals. An ant colony is often used to identify the optimized route to the destination. Data mainly move from a transmitter to the receiver in a dynamic routing process. Ants are also based on similar dynamic phenomena, and they always dump a definite quantity of pheromone on their route, which helps them in the recollection process [28].

The artificial ants used as automobiles are guided by a prediction principle that uses pheromone deposit densities and searches to select solution elements. When an ant has formed an alternative, the ant analyzes the entire report so that the methodology can determine how often pheromones accumulate for the next phase. The prediction principle directs ant mobility through a location decision strategy based on pheromone deposit, collapse, and heuristic data.

ACO is used to solve urban transportation optimization issues. Automobiles are simulated as ant colonies from either an origin across the transportation system in this issue. Pheromone reserves along the defined route estimate the pathways. Image and pheromone sensors are used to monitor the entire path. Regardless of the pheromone reserve, all left available pathways are open when approaching a cross-junction, whether four or three ways [29].

The traffic's maximum queue length determines the permission for all other pathways. The pheromone sensors estimate the queue length to determine which path has the highest pheromone deposit value. Weights are assigned to simulated ants as vehicles based on their heavy, medium, or light type. The pheromone intensity weights are assumed to be 2, 1, and 0.5. For projections for the future, all pheromone upgrades or scheduled details are saved in a server. The vehicles' permitted pathways are graphically simulated, whether they are in a four-way or triple-bond junction (Y or T) [30].

Algorithm 1: LoRa and ACO-Based Method for Intelligent Traffic Control

Input: Ants A = [A1..........,An], Traffic Path = [P1, P2.............., Pn], Ql = Queue Length for storing record, Dl = Time delay, Vn = Vehicle in the queue
TD = Time Delay, P_intensivity = intensity value for phenomena

Output: Queue is complete or with maximum volume and time t

1. *Set the initial value of pheromone routes for each route to NULL.*
2. *The emergence of ant colonies for each route from p1pn.*
3. *Instance 1: Cross expressway*
   a) Except for pedestrian crosswalks, almost all left pathways have always been accessible.
   b) For pathways, one to n, create ant mobility labeled by alarm pheromone fund.
   c) Upgrade pheromone significance throughout all pathways.

$$T Dij = [1 - P\_intensivity]T Dij + \Delta T Dij \quad (1)$$

   d) Traffic mobility is proposed based on the pheromone benefit.
   e) On motion, pheromones benefit filtration.
   f) We are prioritizing a route based on assumptions.

$$P_{intensivity}{}_{ij}^{k}(TD) = \frac{|T Dij(T D)|T D^{\alpha} * N Dij^{\beta}}{\sum T Dij} \quad (2)$$

Algorithm 1: LoRa and ACO-Based Method for Intelligent
Traffic Control

   g) Repeat till the pheromone frequency crosses the threshold.
     significance.
    h) Continue to step 3 until all paths have been round-robin
  optimized.
  4.   Instance 2: repetition steps 3 & 4 for the "Y" and "T"
  junctions.
  5.   Computation of the time spent waiting for each of the
  multiple crossing
     processes.
  6. Stop.

4 Simulation Results and Discussion

We have collected data to validate the proposed LoRa ACO-based method from
multiple agencies [17, 22]. The information included a traffic population count
on Major Highways in the southern region, including around 450 road crossings.
The proposed (ACO with LoRa) and existing ACO methods are implemented in
the MATLAB traffic simulator. The virtual environment variables are the automo-
bile category, qualify of vehicles, the density of pheromone reserve, decay factor,
the primary concern, wait period for each waiting line, and the waiting times. The
research methodology yields an indicator per each vehicle's waiting times, collected
through the ant colony optimization with the LoRa method. Figure 2 shows the
simulation phenomena of traffic system.

**The following predictions are created in the proposed ACO with the LoRa
technique:**

- There are three different waiting times in each path and a similar number of
  queues.
- Automobiles will be positioned according to a selection of paths in each waiting.
- The direction of sensing devices peruses monitoring of pheromone reserve.
- The data received from sensors are accumulated in a server system for fast
  processing and approval for congestion control. Crosswalks path is also taken
  into account.

The simulation-included ACO optimization with LoRa includes:

- There is no need to optimize if the pheromone deposit intensity is similar. In most
  cases, all paths are given a one-minute time limit [31].
- Suppose the pheromone intensity varies significantly or is unequal in one or more
  paths, in that case, time is optimized by deducting the less pheromone path's

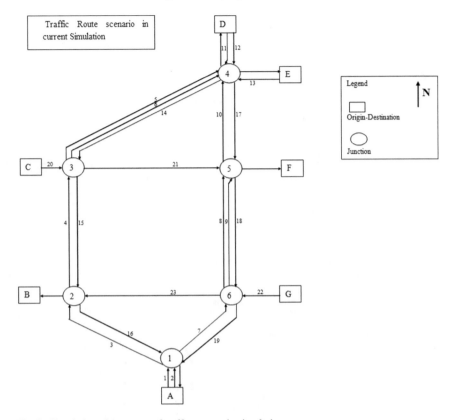

Fig. 2 Simulation phenomena of traffic system in simulation

passage time and assigning it to the needy paths. All four paths are optimized when there are pedestrians.

- When a primary consideration vehicle enters, the route's pheromone significance is restored; the existing prioritized vehicle is given the highest value, and the route is returned to its previous state.

Figure 3 shows the experimental results time versus phenomena deposit intensity for proposed ACO with LoRa method for various lanes from (Lane 2 to Lane 6). Traffic management becoming real-time utilization, the model is simulated on an intelligent computer system adopting the LoRa and ant colonies method characteristics. A demographic breakdown linking all the paths in various directions represents all the road vehicles. A threshold completely seals of pheromone deposits in a single carriageway is used, allowing all enclosed traffic to pass along uniquely.

Figure 4 shows ACO versus (ACO with LoRa) performance comparison simulation results. The experimental results show the strength of the proposed method (ACO with LoRa) compared to the existing LoRa method.

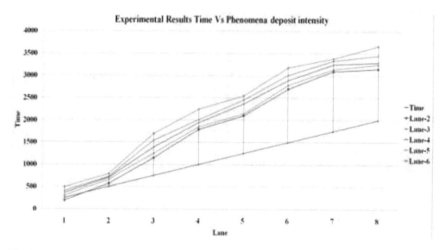

Fig. 3 Experimental results time versus phenomena deposit intensity

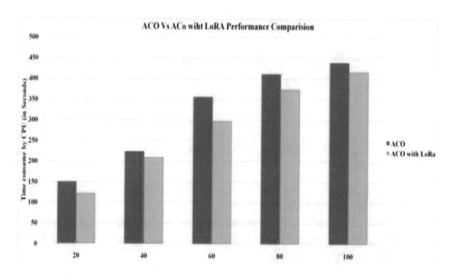

Fig. 4 Simulation results for ACO versus (ACO with LoRa) performance comparison

5 Conclusion and Future Work

In the proposed ACO-LoRa approach, we finally concluded via our investigation and analysis that ACO with LoRa methods is highly suitable for controlling and managing massive traffic in metropolitan areas considering the dynamic nature of transportation planning. It is effective because ants function as intelligent objects, and the pheromone reserve is linked to motion. The methodology as well takes priority to ambulances in a traffic intersection. This proposed ACO with the LoRa

Table 1 Comparison of existing research methods

Refere nces	Methodology	Key points	Challenges
[16]	Machine learning	Monitors, Road traffic, Smart traffic light, Congestion, Apply classification of vehicle	Typical to detect heavy traffic volume
[17]	Deep learning	Vehicle image classification, Traffic volume detection	Unable to work when vehicle changing lane
[18]	Infrared (Active mode)	Vehicle communication traffic control	Typical to detect heavy traffic volume
[19]	ANN method	Vehicle congestion, road accident detection	Unable to work when vehicle changing Lane
[20]	Inductive repetition	Detect traffic parameters	Typical to detect heavy traffic volume
[21]	Magnet strong sensor (MSS)	Worked using WSM, Traffic communication	Unable to work when vehicle changing lane
[22]	UV sensor	Vehicle volume detection	Typical to detect heavy traffic volume
[23]	Image process	Vehicle image analysis helps in traffic management	Unable to work when vehicle changing lane
[24]	Infrared (Passive mode)	Vehicle speed management	Expensive
[25]	CNN method	Can help in detecting various lanes, traffic density	Typical to detect heavy traffic volume

algorithm has obtained more than 90% precision in the experiment. Further, with the investigation, we assume the developed scheme can be an acceptable option for intelligent transportation planning.

In future work, we consider administrators and developers test platforms to maximize the effectiveness and expertise of this proposed system in the actual world circumstance. We also anticipate the model's precision to be maintained to be used irrespective of the test script.

References

1. Dewangan DK, Sahu SP (2021) Deep learning-based speed bump detection model for intelligent vehicle system using raspberry pi. IEEE Sens J 21(3):3570–3578
2. Moghaddam K, Balali V (2021) Evaluation of multi-class multi-label machine learning methods to identify the contributing factors to the severity of animal-vehicle collisions. Int J Traffic Transp Eng 11:120–136. https://doi.org/10.7708/ijtte2021.11(3).01

3. Hassan A (2021) Integration of internet of things (IoT) in health care industry: an overview of benefits, challenges, and applications. In: Data science and innovations for intelligent systems. CRC Press, Boca Raton
4. Jardines A (2021) Convection indicator for pre-tactical air traffic flow management using neural networks. Mach Learn Appl 5:100053–100053
5. Trivedi NK (2021) COVID-19 pandemic: role of machine learning & deep learning methods in diagnosis. Int J Curr Res Rev 150–155
6. Jin J (2021) An end-to-end recommendation system for urban traffic controls and management under a parallel learning framework. IEEE Trans Intell Transp Syst 22:1616–1626
7. Liu Y (2021) Thresholds based image extraction schemes in big data environment in intelligent traffic management. IEEE Trans Intell Transp Syst 22:3952–3960
8. Ganapathy (2021) Design of algorithm for IoT-based application: case study on intelligent transport systems. Internet Things 12(3):227–249
9. Reddy PS (2021) Traffic rules violation detection using machine learning techniques. In: 2021 6th International conference on communication and electronics systems (ICCES), vol 7, no 11, pp 1024–1032
10. Sandamali GGN (2021) A safety-aware real-time air traffic flow management model under demand and capacity uncertainties. IEEE Trans Intell Transp Syst 1–14
11. Nguyen-An H (2021) IoT traffic: modeling and measurement experiments. Internet Things 2:140–162
12. Akhter S (2020) A SUMO based simulation framework for intelligent traffic management system. J Traffic Logist Eng 1–5
13. Gunantara N (2020) The characteristics of multi-criteria weight on ad-hoc network with ant colony optimization. Int J Commun Antenna Propag 10:249
14. Ermakov E (2020) Analysis of road accidents in Smolensk region. Fire Emerg Prev Elimin 3:40–45
15. Guleria K (2020) Breast cancer prediction and classification using supervised learning techniques. J Comput Theor Nanosci 17:2519–2522
16. Song M (2020) Intelligent control method for traffic flow at urban intersection based on vehicle networking. Int J Inf Syst Change Manag 12:350–359
17. Lilhore UK (2020) A hybrid tumour detection and classification based on machine learning. J Comput Theor Nanosci 17:2539–2544
18. Lilhore UK (2020) An efficient load balancing method by using machine learning-based VM distribution and dynamic resource mapping. J Comput Theor Nanosci 17:2545–2551
19. Jeong MK (2019) A study on current state and development plan of driving assistance center for the people with disabilities. J Korean Soc Occup Ther 27:51–65
20. Toledo TD, Torrisi N (2019) Encrypted DNP3 traffic classification using supervised machine learning algorithms. Mach Learn Knowl Extr 1:384–399
21. Malviya DK (2018) Survey on security threats in cloud computing. Int J Trend in Sci Res Dev 3:1222–1226
22. Tiwari S (2018) Artificial neural network and genetic clustering-based robust intrusion detection system. Int J Comput Appl 179:36–40
23. Choi J (2018) Analysis of mutual understanding about dangerous driving behaviors between male and female drivers by co-orientation model. J Korea Inst Intell Transp Syst 17:32–45
24. Kwon SM (2017) Analysis of pedestrian-thrown distance pattern by pedestrian-vehicle collision position. J Korea Inst Intell Transp Syst 16:90–100
25. Shrivas, P (2017) Genetic approach based image retrieval by using CCM and textual features. In: 2017 6th International conference on reliability, infocom technologies and optimization (Trends and future directions) (ICRITO) pp 1–12
26. Laxmi P (2016) Ant colony optimization for optimum service times in a Bernoulli schedule vacation interruption queue with balking and reneging. J Ind Manag Optim 12:1199–1214
27. Raghuwanshi V, Lilhore U (2016) Neighbor trust algorithm (NTA) to protect VANET from denial of service attack (DoS). Int J Comput Appl 140:8–12

28. Ochiai J, Kanoh H (2014) Hybrid ant colony optimization for real-world delivery problems based on real-time and predicted traffic in a wide-area road network. Comput Sci Inf Technol 4(7):555–565
29. Al-Kandari A (2013) Comparative study between traffic control methods using simulation software. Int J Mach Learn Comput 3:424–429
30. Karungaru S (2013) Road traffic signs recognition using genetic algorithms and neural networks. Int J Mach Learn Comput 313–317
31. Datta P, Sharma B (2017) A survey on IoT architectures, protocols, security and smart city-based applications. In: 8th International conference on computing, communication and networking technologies (ICCCNT), pp 1–5

Energy Saving Techniques for Cloud Data Centres: An Empirical Research Analysis

Arif Ahmad Shehloo, Muheet Ahmed Butt, and Majid Zaman

1 Introduction

Over the previous decade people, devices and businesses have turn into data factories which are pumping-out improbable amounts of data each day to the web. Approximately, 90% of overall data existing over Internet has been generated since 2016 at 2.5 quintillion data bytes per day, as stated by IBM Marketing Cloud study [1].

Google Inc.'s MapReduce parallel processing model has received great attention due to its capabilities involving higher scalability, failure recovery, and programming simplicity [2]. By the overgrowing need to analyse the large data sets, MapReduce has become a conventional programming model. Apache Hadoop appears to be frequently used open-source MapReduce implementation. Yahoo! first industrialised it and is now largely spreads through production clusters for business purposes [3]. Apache Hadoop inspects the underlying system's hardware complexities and offers a high-level framework optimised for the execution of large-scale data sets. In addition, it offers applications with more scalability and reliable storage of data on a given cluster. As a result of these capabilities, Apache Hadoop has found widespread applications in various fields, such as social networking, business intelligence, bioinformatics, and health care. [4].

Apache Hadoop is a highly realistic approach to distributed computing, but it currently suffers from various performance and energy efficiency issues. Given that

A. A. Shehloo (✉)
Research Scholar, Mewar University, Rajasthan, India
e-mail: arif4aziz@gmail.com

M. A. Butt
P.G. Deparment of Computer Science, University of Kashmir, Srinagar, India
e-mail: ermuheet@gmail.com

M. Zaman
Directorate of IT & Support System, University of Kashmir, Srinagar, India
e-mail: zamanmajid@gmail.com

© The Author(s), under exclusive license to Springer Nature Singapore Pte Ltd. 2023   763
R. Doriya et al. (eds.), *Machine Learning, Image Processing, Network Security and Data Sciences*, Lecture Notes in Electrical Engineering 946,
https://doi.org/10.1007/978-981-19-5868-7_57

Hadoop acceptance is expanding beyond batch jobs (such as off-line log scrutiny) to online processing of data, a greater emphasis on improving Hadoop scheduling is expected [5]. Previous research has primarily focused on improving Hadoop cluster efficiency by reducing job processing time, minimising the impact of task failures, balancing task processing growth, and so on. However, data centres use vast quantities of energy seems to have become a critical issue in recent years. Which, in today's era of green computing, has made energy conservation a vital subject of interest [6]. The United States Department of Energy (DOE) reported in a study on data centre energy usage that data centres consumed approximately 70×109 (70 billion) kWh of energy in 2014. According to the current report, data centre energy use increased by about 4% from 2010 to 2014, 24% from 2005 to 2010, and nearly 90% from 2000 to 2005. Expected energy consumption indicates an increase of 4% from 2014 to 2020, with the same rate as the last five years. On the basis of current trend estimations, U.S data centres are expected to consume about 73×109 (73 billion) kilowatt-hours of energy in 2020 [7].

The Apache Hadoop system is commonly used in data centres to analyse large quantities of data. Optimising Hadoop's energy consumption has been identified as a critical issue, with numerous scheduling strategies based on nature and non-nature-oriented architectures have been developed to address this issue. The main objective of this study is:

1. To examine the nature and non-nature-oriented energy-efficient methodologies often employed in cloud data centres. Moreover, classify them into node management, virtualisation and consolidation, task scheduling, data placement, and infrastructure change categories with the discussion about the rationale of each category, along with its strengths and weaknesses.
2. For computation and I/O-intensive workloads, examine the CPU energy consumption of three commonly used cloud workload scheduling algorithms: FIFO, fair, and capacity to see if the energy usage among the three schedulers differs significantly between two types of workloads and different job sizes.

The findings and futuristic perspective provided in this study may be helpful to the researchers interested in optimising cloud data centre energy consumption.

2 Background

Hadoop is a widely accepted open-source platform for analysing and interpreting petabyte-scale data volumes. Hadoop was developed by Doug Cutting, as a part of Apache Nutch project (a web-based search engine). Hadoop is a distributed large-scale batch processing system used for massive data processing and storing. Additionally to facilitating scalability, the system can detect and handle failures. Furthermore, Hadoop facilitates data availability by storing and managing numerous

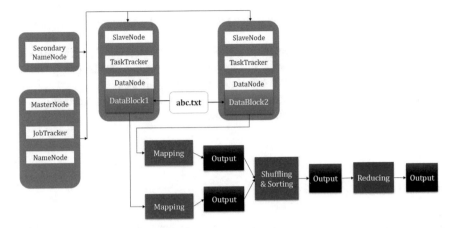

Fig. 1 Hadoop framework architecture

data replicas through cluster nodes in a Hadoop data centre. Hadoop is composed of two major modules: MapReduce and Hadoop distributed file system (HDFS) [4]. Figure 1 depicts a simplified diagram of the Hadoop framework architecture.

Cloud data centres include a series of carefully structured physical machines (servers and networking devices) running VMs. In some instances, the data centre infrastructure is rich in resources to ensure overall service efficiency and availability [5]. In addition, about 30% of servers or physical machines (PMs) in cloud data centres are often idle and mostly use 10–15% of existing resources and thus contributes to increased energy usage [27].

Energy efficiency is an acceptable NP-hard challenge in a cloud computing environment, and numerous scheduling strategies based on both nature-inspired and non-nature-oriented architectures have been developed [8]. This paper divided all the strategies into 5 categories: node management, virtualisation and consolidation, task scheduling, data placement, and infrastructure change.

2.1 Motivation

The processing of large amounts of data has become increasingly popular in the recent years. Hadoop's ecosystem offers data scientists a versatile and easy-to-use way to schedule and implement comprehensive big data analytics processes. Nevertheless, most big data analytics processes consume a considerable amount of energy because they are extremely time intensive [5]. Optimising Hadoop-based data analytics processes is crucial, with the result became a key reason for writing this paper. The novel contributions of this paper include:

1. Various categories identified in the paper may aid in improving Hadoop's energy efficiency.
2. The comparison of energy usage among the three schedulers enables us to discover how energy consumption varies between two types of workloads and job sizes, which eventually helps to improve Hadoop's energy efficiency.
3. Several perspectives and future insights are presented in the paper that can be used to improve Hadoop's energy efficiency.

3   Literature Review

Lowering data centre energy costs leads to improved cloud computing. The following subsections discuss practical methods for lowering data centre energy consumption based on the categories, including node management, virtualisation and consolidation, task scheduling, data placement, and infrastructure changes.

3.1   Node Management

For systems that are either homogeneous or heterogeneous, dynamic node management is a widely used technique for conserving energy. A series of hardware-level policies are used to maximise energy efficiency on worker nodes, such as moving servers into low-energy states, shutting down servers, and dynamically adjusting CPU performance (using DFS and DVFS).

Dynamic voltage and frequency scaling (DVFS) has been introduced as a viable alternative for lowering a CPU's energy consumption [9]. Scaling the supply voltages of compute nodes in a DVFS-enabled cluster allows them to operate at various frequencies [10]. DVFS technique finds its application in large and high end data centres, to get maximum energy saving and to realise high reliability/availability [11]. The technique has numerous implementations and performs in accordance with the providential policies. For instance, [12, 13] discuss the technique for scheduling individual tasks on a processing unit with DVFS support, [14, 15] develops a DVFS-enabled multi-processor scheduling technique for dependent tasks.

Li et al. [16] investigated the effect of CPU temp and frequency on the device's energy consumption. Consequently, the author proposes a model in addition to the frequency scaling technique, which exuberantly scales the CPU frequency as per the predictable value of power to accomplish power capping. Nevertheless, while performing the scaling decisions, the technique makes no contemplation of server workload. This limitation over CPU frequency may result overload and task failure in highly employed servers.

Ibrahim et al. [17] scrutinised the impact of five different frequency scaling governors on various jobs performing on the given Hadoop cluster, including Pi, Sort, and Grep. The experimental results demonstrate that the governors employed in the experiment do not accurately contemplate their design purpose and may even become ineffective while minimising the energy consumption. As a result, it is difficult for any governor to generate an optimum solution that will increase efficiency while decreasing energy usage for a given Hadoop data centre. Correspondingly, [18] also experimented to minimise energy consumption by exploiting the DVFS in the Hadoop cluster. They discovered that the defined parameters have a greater impact on a Hadoop framework's energy consumption and performance.

To optimise the Hadoop system's energy efficiency, [19] suggested a cluster segregation scheme in which a given cluster is split into hot and cold zones. A machine usually goes into the sleep or standby mode, when it is taken in to the cold zone. The author recommends that at least 70 per cent of the total number of cluster machines must be placed in the hot zone. However, the technique does not take into consideration the energy efficiency of cluster machines/servers.

Krish et al. [20] suggested a strategy for scheduling Map/Reduce jobs in a diversified environment that ensures distinct worker nodes are clustered into distinct subclusters. Following the submission of a job, the proposed strategy computes the energy consumed during its operation on each subcluster and routes it to the most energy-efficient one. The scheduler ensures energy-efficient resource utilisation, but ignores the fact that the system will eventually be unable to maintain its current level of energy efficiency as workload increases or decreases.

To review the MapReduce workload, [21] proposed Berkeley EnergyEfficient MapReduce (BEEMR) as a novel scheme to minimise the energy consumption of a given Hadoop system. Experimental results illustrate that BEEMR diminishes the energy consumption of given Hadoop system by 50%. However, activities like power state transition and data portioning causes excessive workload in data processing stage.

3.2   Virtualisation and Consolidation

Techniques of virtualisation and consolidation are aimed at resolving resource allocation and energy usage issues based on three decision queries, which include (i) when to relocate a specific virtual machine, (ii) where to relocate the virtual machine, and (iii) which physical machine to deactivate in order to decide the optimum resource allocation that results in the least amount of resource and energy usage.

3.2.1   Virtualisation

Virtualisation is a cloud data processing function that delivers a virtualised version of a server, storage device, network resource, or operating system. This entails the portability of high-level services and sharing of physical resources.

Javanmardi et al. [22], Shojafar et al. [23] proposed a scheduling scheme that combines the concept of fuzzy set theory with the genetic algorithm to optimise the cloud data centre resource scheduling. The authors improved the genetic algorithm by integrating fuzzy theory to reduce the time taken to make the best decision. The method provides efficient results by taking into account the execution-cost as well as the total execution time of data centre resources.

Sharma et al. [24] developed a hybridised approach by combining DVFS and GA to lower a data centre's energy consumption, improve resource utilisation, and achieve solution convergence. Despite the fact that the hybrid model achieves its objectives, energy savings are marginal owing to the solution's slow convergence.

In Hadoop cloud data centre, MapReduce jobs may vary in their resource usage and time of execution. Looking at this aspect, [25] built a resource handling approach for MapReduce applications in virtualised cloud computing systems. Simulated findings suggest that this resource assignment strategy dramatically increases energy efficiency by about 15–25%. However, the heterogeneity that often occurs in a cloud computing system was not taken into consideration in this work.

Eugen et al. [5] recognised that virtualisation dramatically increases resource usage but can also result in a decline in performance.

Sharma et al. [26] proposed a two-phase hybrid scheduling algorithm, labelled as HybridMR, for data centres having both physical as well as virtual machines to take advantage of both of them. Experimental assessment reveals that, relative to the native cluster, HybridMR offers 45% increase in resource usage and about 43% in energy savings, with a minimum penalty for performance.

3.2.2 Consolidation

The consolidation strategy employs real-time virtual machine (VM) relocation to integrate VMs in a systematic manner, allowing for the removal of overused physical machines (PMs) and migration to underused PMs. The benefit of applying this approach is that it significantly improves the resource and energy utilisation of data centre servers.

For cloud data processing centres, [27] suggested ant colony optimisation for virtual machine consolidation (VMC-ACO). This method makes use of a vector algebra-based variant of the ant colony optimisation. It supposes a homogeneous environment and classifies resources such as CPU, memory, and network I/O as vital to the data centre's energy efficiency. VMC-ACO makes use of the most recent ant colony optimisation version and handles each VM-PM mapping as a solution constituent.

Li et al. [28] proposed a tweaked particle swarm optimisation (MPSO) strategy for integrating virtual machines (VMs) to avoid getting stuck in a loop of local optima. Although the proposed solution decreases energy usage, the findings seem insufficient due to the omission of memory and network components.

For energy-efficient cloud computation, [29] introduced an ant colony optimisation-based consolidation algorithm that could be used with a virtual machine.

The strategy intends to boost data centre energy efficiency by grouping virtual machines together into a smaller set of functional physical machines. However, it lacks the network part of the data centre.

To address the issue of virtual machine placement (VMP), [30] proposed an improved heuristic strategy that puts an emphasis on energy efficiency and resource waste management. The proposed strategy (MinPR) significantly decreases overall energy consumption by decreasing the amount of active compute nodes and promoting the use of energy-efficient ones.

3.3 Task Scheduling

Depending on the volume of data being handled and system characteristics, a submitted job is partitioned into Map/Reduce-tasks. The required task scheduler assigns these Map/Reduce-tasks to the processing nodes (both virtual and physical machines). Because of the varying task resource requirement and cluster heterogeneity, the scheduling policy significantly impacts the task's energy efficiency. Job profiling is one of the policies for gathering the requisite information that could be used to optimise the Hadoop cluster's energy efficiency.

Shah et al. [31] developed a scheme for reducing MapReduce operations' energy consumption. The proposed approach is a phase-level energy-efficient MapReduce scheduler that delegates Map/Reduce-tasks to nodes based on the optimal node availability. According to the findings, the proposed solution uses less energy than current heuristic methods and has a shorter runtime.

Yigitbasi et al. [32] acknowledged that the conventional method for determining the volume of tasks to be performed in the Hadoop data centre could result in resource waste. To conclude, the author suggested a technique for deciding the optimum number of tasks to initiate. However, the consistency of the system is limited to a few categories of jobs and needs a substantial amount of training data sets. One more downside of this study is a lack of analysis of the diversity among servers.

Cluster nodes vary dramatically in their power behaviours. [33] executed MapReduce workloads on two distinct homogeneous clusters comprised of energy-efficient and high-performance hardware. To conclude, the author recommended EESched, an energy-efficient scheduler. The scheduler tends to delegate the reduce-task to a low-power node with an I/O bound workload as part of the reduce-task. However, the author does not go into detail on how to balance energy efficiency and data locality.

Wen [34] independently designed energy utilisation methods for transmitting data and performing the task. The scheduler in this framework begins by enabling/ disabling a group of nodes that are bound to the resource requirements of a particular job and the data centre's workload at the instant. However, the proposed scheme does not factor in data locality.

Zhao et al. [35] proposed a robust energy-efficient task scheduling method that uses a waking up threshold and sleep delay function to meet data centre response requirements, thus lowering cloud computing energy demand. In addition, the author constructed a cost function for balancing multiple performance metrics and enhanced the genetic algorithm used to determine the optimal parameter combination.

3.4 Data Placement

The Hadoop file system (HDFS) is capable of storing the input and output data for MapReduce jobs as well as their instantaneous results. However, statistics show that reading, writing, and shuffling operations in MapReduce consume more than 10% of the total energy consumed by a particular data node [36]. Typically, energy optimisation in data placement focuses on lowering transportation costs for data by placing data blocks on appropriate nodes.

Scalability is an essential aspect of Hadoop. Hadoop contains a process called balancer, which is configured to redistribute HDFS data blocks while scaling. Nevertheless, the default re-balancing process needs to be optimised in efforts to realise energy-efficient data placement. In this context, [37] designed a flexible and efficient Hadoop system with a data re-balancing policy. The proposed system stabilises the average workload of each individual node and rack during scale-down process by transferring data from the nodes to be removed to the remaining nodes. There are distinct thresholds for each node and the cluster-wide average workload in the system. These can be configured optimally, but regular changes in the workload can often and needlessly cause re-balancing.

By default, the HDFS data placement strategy is "rack aware" but assumes that the cluster is homogeneous. In fact, in a heterogeneous set-up, the default replication and data placement configurations are likely to result in workload inequity and disc space waste. [38] resoled this issue by developing and implementing SLDP, a novel optimised data placement scheme. The suggested scheme considers the rate at which the data block is accessed. The energy efficiency of the device is improved by dynamically scaling the proportion of working nodes in response to the SLDP's data placement strategy.

Song et al. [39] suggested a rational modulo-based data placement algorithm (DPA) to minimise node inactivity in MapReduce systems for energy savings. The primary objective of this study is to avoid the increased expense of data loading. Nonetheless, the processes of data replication have not been taken into account by the authors.

Leverich and Kozyrakis [40] refined the Hadoop data centre's data placement policy by placing the main focus on reduction in energy cost and consumption. The novel data placement policy is based on a group of data centre nodes known as the Covering Set (CS). Covering Set (CS) stores at least one data replica on each node/server of the set. However, no any specific policy has been provided by the author to construct a particular covering set. Additionally, we believe that adaptive change in the covering set will boost the Hadoop data centre's energy efficiency and thus performance.

Kim et al. [41] suggested the PACS technique for locating a covering set within a given Hadoop system. When searching the nodes for a covering set, the technique takes cluster heterogeneity into account. Additionally, the technique also gives preference to the nodes having high energy efficiency. However, it ignores the computing ability of nodes.

3.5　Infrastructure Change

Data centres can also become more energy-efficient by changing their infrastructure. Data centre operators may be able to achieve this if they upgrade their server computers, cooling systems, and switch to advanced software designed to operate the data centre at maximum efficiency. As a result, energy consumption is kept to a minimum.

Today, energy consumption is taken into account when developing the software packages, drivers, and module kernels. They add value by allowing users to access the system's current state and energy usage [42]. [43] ran the same applications on different builds of Windows and Linux and found that the energy consumption varied significantly. A computer's operating system (OS) is the critical component that controls all of the device's operations. Operating systems use varying quantities of energy and can be optimised for energy efficiency depending on their genre [44].

Consolidating and sharing scarce resources, rather than having multiples per cluster rack, are another way to save energy. When fewer computing machines are used in the data centre, this technique has proven to be very effective in lowering power consumption [45]. Using the minimal criticality strategy, tasks from underutilised machines may be redirected to other computing machines, enabling them to execute at maximum potential [46]. As a result, only a limited amount of device is required, leading to a lower energy consumption. Similarly, replacing existing servers with blade/rackmount servers improves energy efficiency by using approximately 10% less energy than traditional servers [47]. It should be noted that effective restructuring not only allows the entire workload to be accomplished with the fewest resources available, but, it also ensures that each resource is utilised efficiently.

4　Experiment

The purpose of workload schedules currently is to improve job execution time. Nonetheless, it results in energy waste because the same tasks can be performed with limited resources when deployed on small clusters, while meeting service-level agreements (SLAs) constraints. Therefore, clusters can be made more energy-efficient by distributing workload among a small number of clusters according to their size and type, rather than by optimising response times. In this paper, we experiment with CPU energy consumption on Hadoop benchmark data sets using three of the most commonly used scheduling algorithms in cloud data centres: FIFO, fair, and capacity scheduler to see if the energy usage among the three schedulers differs significantly between two types of workloads and different job sizes. The data were collected in order to conduct both small and large size experiments using Wordcount and Terasort workloads.

4.1 Set-up

The experimentation model included the use of 4 heterogeneous machines (virtual): one operated as the MasterNode, and the other 3 as SlaveNodes. The MasterNode and SlaveNodes are equipped with quad-core processor (Core i7) running at 3.4GHz clock speed and 32GB of RAM. Using First-In First-Out (FIFO) scheduler, capacity scheduler, and fair scheduler, we calculate the different forms of energy usage costs associated with Wordcount and Terasort job metrics. As part of our experiments, we utilised Ubuntu Server x64, installed within a kernel-based virtual machine (KVM) environment on top of the Windows operating system. To determine power measurements associated with each job metrics for different Hadoop schedulers, we used Powertop [48]. Figure 1 shows the model for measuring energy.

4.1.1 Workloads involved in small size experiments

- Workload consisting of 20 Map-Tasks and 10 Reduce-Tasks.
- Workload consisting of 24 Map-Tasks and 12 Reduce-Tasks.
- Workload consisting of 28 Map-Tasks and 14 Reduce-Tasks.

4.1.2 Workloads listed below are included in large size experiments

- Workload consisting of 180 Map-Tasks and 220 Reduce-Tasks.
- Workload consisting of 270 Map-Tasks and 420 Reduce-Tasks.
- Workload consisting of 320 Map-Tasks and 540 Reduce-Tasks.

4.2 Findings and Interpretation

4.2.1 Small size Experiments

For the FIFO scheduler, capacity scheduler, and fair Scheduler, the energy consumed by three small size jobs with the fewest tasks was evaluated. During the evaluation, a limited number of tasks are selected to restrict the count of Map/Reduce-tasks under

Fig. 2 Energy measuring model

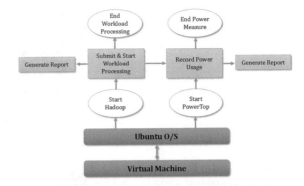

Fig. 3 Energy usage for Terasort problem with least number of tasks

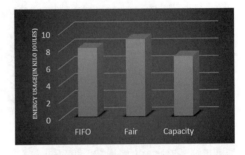

Fig. 4 Energy usage for Wordcount problem with least number of tasks

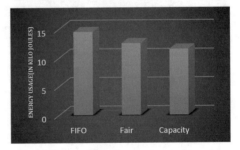

30. Figures 1 and 2 display the energy usage values associated with the First-In First-Out (FIFO) scheduler, capacity scheduler, and fair scheduler for the 2 separate workload groups. The findings indicate that, for both Wordcount and Terasort job types, the capacity scheduler significantly lowers the energy demand of a Hadoop data centre. It may be due to the capacity scheduler's ability to deploy Map and Reduce-tasks more effectively.

4.2.2 Large size Experiments

To determine the energy efficiency of First-In First-Out (FIFO) scheduler, capacity scheduler, and fair scheduler, 3 wide jobs with a diverse set of tasks were tested.

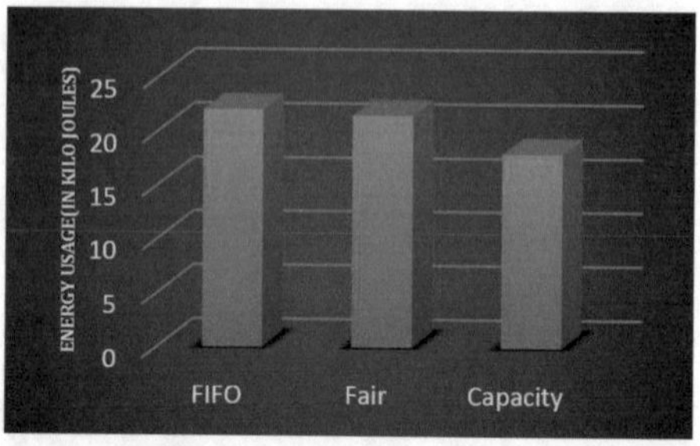

Fig. 5 Energy usage for
Terasort problem with large
number of tasks

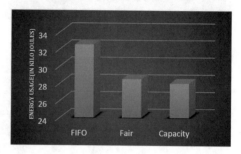

Fig. 6 Energy usage for
Wordcount problem with
large number of tasks

Figures 3 and 4 illustrate the amount of energy used by these three schedulers for
Terasort and Wordcount workload types. The figures show that, in contrast to other
schedulers, the capacity scheduler consumes substantially less energy (Figs. 5 and
6).

5 Discussion

To solve the energy efficiency issue in cloud computing, we discussed different scheduling policies with different categories. For each category, we discussed
scheduling techniques that focus on energy consumption and resource efficiency.
In addition to the futuristic perspective provided in Section-7 of the paper, we see
that virtualisation and consolidation techniques are efficient with little or no network
overhead. Their system design is based on when and where to relocate a specific
virtual machine and which physical machine to deactivate, for optimum resource
allocation, leading to efficient resource and energy use. Table 1 compares several
virtualisation policies in terms of implementation, resource utilisation, energy efficiency, total execution time, and load balancing.

Table 1 Comparative analysis

Algorithm	Implementation	Resource utilisation	Energy efficiency	Total execution time	Load balancing
Chen et al. [21]	Nature oriented	•	•	•	•
Shojafar et al. [23]	Nature oriented	•	•	•	•
Sharma et al. [24]	Nature oriented	•	•	○	•
Cardosa et al. [25]	Non-nature oriented	•	•	○	○
Sharma and Reddy [26]	Non-nature oriented	•	•	○	•
Ferdaus et al. [27]	Nature oriented	•	•	○	○
Li et al. [28]	Nature oriented	•	•	○	•
Farahnakian et al. [29]	Nature oriented	•	•	○	○
Azizi et al. [30]	Non-nature oriented	•	•	•	○

6   Possible Directions for Future Research

As a result of our extensive research, we discovered the various possible research opportunities that have yet to be reviewed:

1. It is worthwhile to look into the effectiveness of energy savings methods. The majority of evaluations of the results obtained from energy-efficient schemes require performance stability or consistency, since a large proportion of nature-oriented methodologies are heuristic in nature. As a result, the balance of these methodologies in relation to the production environment warrants further investigation. Furthermore, the majority of methodologies are analysed on a variety of workloads in a simulated system. Besides, the energy efficiency of a given nature/non-nature-inspired methodology is heavily reliant on the system design in which it is implemented. As a matter of fact, prior to simulation and implementation, it is necessary to conduct a theoretical analysis of the design preferences for a particular problem.

2. SLA violations are inherent in VM migration, as a result of the inevitable temporary service interruption caused during the migration process. Furthermore, virtual machine (VM) migration appears to increase network traffic and energy usage. Existing VM consolidation algorithms do not take into account the overhead

associated with VM migration. To address this issue, it is critical to incorporate a proactive strategy that limits VM migration while maintaining an acceptable rate of SLA violations.

3. Different VMs co-hosted on a particular physical machine (PM) exhibit a range of resource consumption patterns. As a result, no single optimised technique is applicable to all PMs, despite current predictive VM consolidation algorithms employing a common optimised technique for all PMs. Consequently, there appears to be an unfilled research-gap.

4. The main determinants of energy demand for MapReduce-tasks are energy efficiency and data locality. However, when scheduling tasks, we must choose between energy efficiency and data locality. On the one hand, starting a non-local task on an energy-efficient device might not be the best choice because input-data transfer may be expensive. Contrary to this, if we focus exclusively on data locality and begin executing a given task on a low-energy computer, the execution would consume a large amount of energy despite the lack of data transfer. As a result, we must first develop a computational model for calculating the task's cost, which includes both the energy used to perform the task and the energy used to transmit the data.

5. The majority of VM feature selection techniques only implement virtual machine CPU requirements while ignoring network bandwidth, memory, and storage drive I/O requirements. Moreover, [27] claim, choosing a VM solely on the basis of CPU utilisation will eventually lead to CPU saturation and no significant increase in utilisation, while placing other types of resources underutilised. So, it is necessary to identify a single convergence point that represents the approximate resource demand of a diverse range of resources.

7 Conclusion

Task scheduling, which aims to minimise cluster energy consumption while maintaining service-level agreements, is becoming more critical as more cloud-based applications leverage MapReduce to analyse massive volumes of data. The study looked at both nature and non-nature-oriented energy saving techniques that are widely used in cloud computing data centres. The reviewed techniques were evaluated on the basis of their functionality in order to determine their corresponding levels of energy efficiency. Furthermore, analyses of the methodologies confirmed that SLAs are violated while reducing the data centre energy demand. Finally, based on previous research, we expand on our findings and discuss futuristic perspective in the area for maximising cloud data centre energy efficiency.

Most MapReduce-tasks are however scheduled using FIFO schedulers, which allows jobs to be completed faster. In doing so, however, the jobs are scheduled across a variety of machines without considering energy costs. To achieve SLA goals, small clusters could be used to schedule workloads in an effort to reduce energy costs. Based on the comparison study and experimentation results, the capacity scheduler exhibited better efficiency in terms of energy usage than FIFO and fair. Tests conducted using benchmarks on both large- and small-scale workloads. However, further tests are needed on other systems and cloud platforms to confirm the accuracy of our measurements.

References

1. IBM Marketing Cloud "10 Key Marketing Trends for 2017" ,
2. Dean J, Ghemawat S (2004) MapReduce: simplified data processing on large clusters. In: OSDI'04: sixth symposium on operating system design and implementation, San Francisco, CA, pp 137–150
3. Apache Hadoop technolog. https://developer.yahoo.com
4. The Apache Hadoop Project. https://hadoop.apache.org
5. Eugen F, Ramakrishnan L, Morin C (2015) Performance and energy efficiency of big data applications in cloud environments: a Hadoop case study. J Parallel Distrib Comput 80–89
6. Lang W, Patel JM (2010) Energy management for MapReduce clusters. In: Proceedings of VLDB Endowment, pp 129–139
7. Shehabi A, Smith SJ, Sartor DA et al (2016) United States data center energy usage report. Lawrence Berkeley National Laboratory, Berkeley, California. LBNL-1005775
8. Fister I Jr, Yang X-S, Fister I, Brest J, Fister D (2013) A brief review of nature-inspired algorithms for optimization. Elektrotehniski Vestnik 80(3):1–7
9. Hsu C-h, Feng W-c (2005) A feasibility analysis of power awareness in commodity-based high-performance clusters. In: IEEE international conference on cluster computing, pp 1–10
10. von Laszewski G, Wang L, Younge AJ, He X (2009) Power-aware scheduling of virtual machines in DVFS-enabled clusters. In: IEEE international conference on cluster computing and workshops, pp 1–10
11. Feng W-c, Ching A, Hsu C-H (2007) Green supercomputing in a desktop box. In: IEEE international parallel and distributed processing symposium, pp 1–8
12. Yao F, Demers A, Shenker S (1995) A scheduling model for reduced CPU energy. In: Proceedings of IEEE 36th annual foundations of computer science, pp 374–382
13. Manzak A, Chakrabarti C (2003) Variable voltage task scheduling algorithms for minimizing energy/power. IEEE Trans Very Large Scale Integr (VLSI) Syst 270–276
14. Wei G-Y, Kim J, Liu D, Sidiropoulos S, Horowitz MA (2000) A variable-frequency parallel I/O interface with adaptive power-supply regulation. IEEE J Solid-State Circ 1600–1610
15. Gruian F, Kuchcinski K (2001) LEneS: task scheduling for low-energy systems using variable supply voltage processors. In: Proceedings of the ASP-DAC 2001. Asia and South Pacific Design Automation Conference 2001 (Cat. No.01EX455), pp 449–455
16. Li S, Abdelzaher T, Yuan M (2011) TAPA: temperature aware power allocation in data center with Map-Reduce. In: International green computing conference and workshops, pp 1–8
17. Ibrahim S, Phan T-D, Carpen-Amarie A, Chihoub H-E, Moise D, Antoniu G (2016) Governing energy consumption in Hadoop through CPU frequency scaling: an analysis. Future Gener Comput Syst 219–232
18. Ibrahim S, Moise D, Chihoub HE, Carpen-Amarie A, Bougé L, Antoniu G (2014) Towards efficient power management in MapReduce: investigation of CPU-frequencies scaling on power efficiency in Hadoop. In: Pop F, Potop-Butucaru M (eds) Adaptive resource management and scheduling for cloud computing. ARMS-CC 2014. Lecture notes in computer science, vol 8907. Springer, Cham
19. Kaushik RT, Bhandarkar M (2010) GreenHDFS: towards an energy-conserving storage-efficient. Hot Power

20. Krish KR, Iqbal MS, Rafique MM, Butt AR (2014) Towards energy awareness in Hadoop. In: Fourth international workshop on network-aware data management, pp 16–22

21. Chen Y, Alspaugh S, Borthakur D, Katz R (2012) Energy efficiency for large-scale MapReduce workloads with significant interactive analysis. Association for Computing Machinery, pp 43–56

22. Javanmardi S, Shojafar M, Amendola D, Cordeschi N, Liu H, Abraham A (2014) Hybrid job scheduling algorithm for cloud computing environment. In: Proceedings of the fifth international conference on innovations in bio-inspired computing and applications IBICA 2014. Advances in intelligent systems and computing, vol 303. Springer, Cham

23. Shojafar M, Javanmardi S, Abolfazli S et al (2015) FUGE: a joint meta-heuristic approach to cloud job scheduling algorithm using fuzzy theory and a genetic method. Cluster Comput 18:829–844

24. Sharma NK, Reddy GRM (2015) Novel energy efficient virtual machine allocation at data center using Genetic algorithm. In: 3rd international conference on signal processing, communication and networking (ICSCN), pp 1–6

25. Cardosa M, Singh A, Pucha H, Chandra A (2011) Exploiting spatio-temporal tradeoffs for energy-aware MapReduce in the Cloud. In: 2011 IEEE 4th international conference on cloud computing, pp 251–258

26. Sharma B, Wood T, Das CR (2013) HybridMR: a hierarchical MapReduce scheduler for hybrid data centers. in: IEEE 33rd international conference on distributed computing systems, pp 102–111

27. Ferdaus MH, Murshed M, Calheiros RN, Buyya R (2014) Virtual machine consolidation in cloud data centers using ACO metaheuristic. In: Silva F, Dutra I, Santos Costa V (eds) Euro-Par 2014 parallel processing. Euro-Par 2014. Lecture notes in computer science, vol 8632

28. Li H, Zhu G, Cui C (2016) Energy-efficient migration and consolidation algorithm of virtual machines in data centers for cloud computing. Computing 98:303–317

29. Farahnakian F, Ashraf A, Pahikkala T, Liljeberg P, Plosila J, Porres I, Tenhunen H (2015) Using ant colony system to consolidate VMs for green cloud computing. IEEE Trans Serv Comput 8:187–198

30. Azizi S, Zandsalimi M, Li D (2020) An energy-efficient algorithm for virtual machine placement optimization in cloud data centers. Cluster Comput 23:3421–3434

31. Shah M, Shukla PK, Pandey R (2016) Phase level energy aware map reduce scheduling for big data applications. In: International conference on signal processing, communication, power and embedded system (SCOPES), pp 532-535

32. Nghiem PP, Figueira SM (2016) Towards efficient resource provisioning in MapReduce. J Parallel Distrib Comput 95:29–41

33. Yigitbasi N, Datta K, Jain N, Willke T (2011) Energy efficient scheduling of MapReduce workloads on heterogeneous clusters. Association for Computing Machinery, GCM '11

34. Wen Y-F (2016) Energy-aware dynamical hosts and tasks assignment for cloud computing. J Syst Softw 115:144–156

35. Zhao W, Wang X, Jin S, Yue W, Takahashi Y (2019) An energy efficient task scheduling strategy in a cloud computing system and its performance evaluation using a two-dimensional continuous time Markov chain model. Electronics 8

36. Wirtz T, Ge R (2011) Improving MapReduce energy efficiency for computation intensive workloads. International Green Computing Conference Proceedings and Workshops, pp 1–8

37. Maheshwari N, Nanduri R, Varma V (2012) Dynamic energy efficient data placement and cluster reconfiguration algorithm for MapReduce framework. Future Gener Comput Syst 28:119–127

38. Xiong R, Luo J, Dong F (2015) Optimizing data placement in heterogeneous Hadoop clusters. Cluster Comput 18:1465–1480

39. Song J, He H, Wang Z et al (2018) Modulo based data placement algorithm for energy consumption optimization of MapReduce system. J Grid Comput 16:409–424

40. Leverich J, Kozyrakis C (2010) On the energy (in)efficiency of Hadoop clusters. Assoc Comput Mach 44:61–65

41. Kim J, Chou J, Rotem D (2011) Energy proportionality and performance in data parallel computing clusters. Springer, pp 414–431
42. Blanquicet F, Christensen K (2008) Managing energy use in a network with a new SNMP power state MIB. In: 33rd IEEE conference on local computer networks (LCN), pp 509–511
43. Michael Am, Krieger K (2010) Server power measurement. United States Patent
44. Meisner D, Gold BT, Wenisch TF (2009) PowerNap: eliminating server idle power. Assoc Comput Mach 37:205–216
45. Bianzino AP, Chaudet C, Rossi D, Rougier J-L (2012) A survey of green networking research. IEEE Commun Surv Tutorials 14:3–20
46. Jiang D, Zhang P, Lv Z, Song H (2016) Energy-efficient multi-constraint routing algorithm with load balancing for smart city applications IEEE Internet Things J 3:1437–1447
47. Emerson Network Power (2010) Energy logic: reducing data center energy consumption by creating savings that cascade across systems. White Pap. https://01.org/sites/default/files/page/powertop_users_guide_201412.pdf
48. Linux, Linux powertop. https://01.org/powertop

Preliminary Conceptions of a Remote Incoercible E-Voting Scheme

Nazia Jahan Khan Chowdhury⑩, **Shinsuke Tamura**⑩, and **Kazi Md. Rokibul Alam**⑩

1 Introduction

This paper describes the concepts of a new e-voting scheme that is being developed. It accepts remote voters and freely chosen write-in ballots while satisfying all essential requirements of voting systems, namely accuracy, privacy, verifiability, coercion resistance, fairness and robustness [1]. In the remainder, the scheme is called secret key coercion resistance voting scheme (*SK-CRVS*).

Many schemes had been developed already [1], but satisfying requirements about coercion resistance are difficult, and they cannot protect remote voters or freely chosen write-in ballots from coercers. In addition, they require volumes of computations to make tallied results verifiable. Where to protect voter V from coercers, voting schemes must hide V's vote in the tallied results even from V. Besides, they must prevent randomization, simulation and forced abstention attacks [1]. To accept remote voters and write-in ballots while efficiently satisfying the other requirements, *SK-CRVS* adopts *CR-SVRM* and secret key anonymous tag-based credentials [2] accompanied by check codes, where *CR-SVRM* is the combination of revised simplified verifiable re-encryption mix-net (*R-SVRM*) [3] and confirmation numbers (*CNs*) [4] and conceals correspondences between voters and their votes from anyone as usual mix-nets do. But different from usual mix-nets, verification terms in it together with *CNs* make *CR-SVRM* verifiable without examining individual mix-servers.

N. J. K. Chowdhury (✉) · K. Md. R. Alam
Department of Computer Science and Engineering, Khulna University of Engineering & Technology (KUET), Khulna 9203, Bangladesh
e-mail: naziajkc@cse.kuet.ac.bd

S. Tamura
Graduate School of Engineering, University of Fukui, Fukui 910-8507, Japan
e-mail: tamura@dance.plala.or.jp

Secret key anonymous tag-based credentials make voters anonymous, and together with check codes, protect even remote voters and freely chosen write-in ballots from simulation, forced abstention and randomization attacks. Namely, voter V obtains multiple credentials and casts votes with check codes that accompany the credentials. But only one credential V obtained is accompanied by a valid check code, and other credentials with invalid check codes are fake ones. Then, because votes accompanied by invalid check codes are not counted and only V knows (i) credentials, (ii) the number of credentials and (iii) the validities of credentials it obtains, V can protect itself from simulation and forced abstention attacks even when it is at remote sites by showing fake credentials to coercers. Randomization attacks are also prevented even if write-in ballots exist because check codes attached to votes for inferior candidates are not examined, where inferior candidates are ones that did not obtain the pre-specified number of votes and election results do not depend on votes for them, i.e. no one can know the validity of the vote if it is for a candidate unique to it.

2   Related Works

Many existing e-voting schemes are not coercion resistance [3–9]. For example, although schemes in [3, 4, 9] were developed based on CNs or R-$SVRM$ as same as SK-$CRVS$, they cannot protect voters from forced abstention or simulation attacks without inconvenient constraints. Developing coercion resistant schemes becomes difficult further when remote voters or freely chosen write-in ballots exist.

Namely, although homomorphic encryption-based schemes, which do not decrypt individual votes, efficiently satisfy requirements about privacy [10, 11], they cannot accept write-in ballots. On the other hand, mix-net based ones can accept write-in ballots theoretically, but practically, it is difficult to protect voters from coercers when write-in ballots or remote voters exist. For example, schemes in [10, 12] exploit fake credentials as same as SK-$CRVS$ does, but coercers can easily identify their votes in election results if they are unique. In addition, because voters in these schemes can generate an arbitrary number of fake credentials, remote voters may cast an infinite number of votes. Another scheme proposed in [5] uses blockchain technology.

In the same way, a scheme in [8] cannot accept write-in ballots or protect remote voters from simulation attacks, although trackers, which are unique to voters as CNs are, make it end to end verifiable. The scheme proposed in [6] deploys homomorphic signcryption. Paper-based visual cryptographic voting schemes [7] cannot accept remote voters either because paper sheets must be handled by election authorities. But they satisfy requirements about everlasting privacy because votes are concealed physically. They also can easily convince voters that votes are handled correctly, because they do not include complicated cryptographic operations. About the ever-lasting privacy, although a scheme in [13] achieves it based on the pure cryptographic approach, still it is difficult to accept remote voters, i.e. voters require their private channels.

3 Cryptographic Tools

The cryptographic tools are as follows. Here, the mix-net consists of P-mix-servers $M_1, \ldots, M_P$, and each mix-server M_i encrypts integer v to $E_{Y*}(k, v) = \{g^k$ (mod Q), vY_*^k (mod Q)}, by secret integer k under ElGamal encryption scheme, where entity B is an agent of the mix-servers. Q and g are a public large prime number and a generator, X_i and $Y_i = g^{X_i}$ (mod Q) are secret decryption and public encryption keys of M_i, $Y_* = Y_1 Y_2 \ldots Y_P = g^{X_1 + \cdots + X_P}$ (mod Q). Provided that Q_* is a prime number, Q is constructed as $Q = 2Q_* + 1$ to define set $A_* = \{a^i$ (mod Q): $i = 1, \ldots, Q_* - 1\}$ so that the order of all elements in A_* becomes equal to Q_* (notation (mod Q) is omitted in the followings).

3.1 Confirmation Numbers (CNs)

CNs are unique registered integers $\{C_1, \ldots, C_N\}$, and mix-servers re-encrypt each C_n to $E_{Y*}(l_{n*}, C_n) = \{g^{l_{n*}}, C_n Y_*^{l_{n*}}\}$ and shuffle them. Thus, no one can link $E_{Y*}(l_{n*}, C_n)$ to C_n unless all mix-servers conspire [4]. Here $l_{n(i)}$ is a secret integer of each M_i, $l_{n*(i)} = l_{n(1)} + \cdots + l_{n(i)}$ and $l_{n*} = l_{n*(P)}$; hence, no one knows l_{n*}. CNs are encrypted as below.

1. B generates integers $\{C_1, \ldots, C_N\}$ to disclose them publicly.
2. M_i receives $E_{Y*}(l_{n*(i-1)}, C_n)$ from M_{i-1}, encrypts it to $E_{Y*}(l_{n*(i)}, C_n) = (g^{l_{n*(i-1)}} g^{l_{n(i)}}, C_n Y_*^{l_{n*(i-1)}} Y_*^{l_{n(i)}})$ and shuffles the encryption results to forward to M_{i+1}. As a result, M_P discloses $E_{Y*}(l_{n*}, C_n)$.

About the correctness of encryption results, an efficient verification scheme is being developed while using the facts that CNs are unique and known.

3.2 CR-SVRM

CR-SVRM conceals links between pairs $\{v_n, A_n\}$ ($1 \leq n \leq N$) and their encryption forms. But instead of $\{v_n, A_n\}$, mix-servers encrypt and shuffle quadruplet $< v_n, A_n, E_{Y*}\{(l_{n*}, C_n), (\delta_{n*}, \ddot{\upsilon}_n)\} >$, where C_n is a confirmation number assigned to $\{v_n, A_n\}$, $\ddot{\upsilon}_n$ is a verification term calculated as $\ddot{\upsilon}_n = (v_n^{\sigma_1} C_n A_n^{\sigma_2})^\lambda$, and λ, σ_1, σ_2 are sums of mix-servers' secret integers; therefore, no one knows their values. Then together with C_n, $\ddot{\upsilon}_n$ ensures correct generations, encryptions and decryptions of quadruplets including the integrity of pair $\{v_n, A_n\}$.

In detail, decryption form $\{v_n, A_n, C_n, \ddot{\upsilon}_n\}$ of quadruplet $< v_n, A_n, E_{Y*}\{(l_{n*}, C_n), (\delta_{n*}, \ddot{\upsilon}_n)\} >$ is consistent only when $\ddot{\upsilon}_n = (v_n^{\sigma_1} C_n A_n^{\sigma_2})^\lambda$ and C_n is a registered integer unique to it. Therefore, anyone that does not know λ, σ_1 or σ_2 cannot forge consistent quadruplets, i.e. anyone can detect the dishonestly handled quadruplets without examining individual mix-servers when λ, σ_1, σ_2 are disclosed. Quadruplet $< v_n, A_n, E_{Y*}\{(l_{n*}, C_n), (\delta_{n*}, \ddot{v}_n)\} >$ is constructed as below so that no one can know pair $\{\alpha, \alpha^{\sigma1\cdot\lambda}\}$ or $\{\alpha, \alpha^{\sigma2\cdot\lambda}\}$ for any α (pairs $\{g, g^{\sigma1}\}$ and $\{g, g^{\sigma2}\}$ are disclosed).

1. V_n sends encryption form of pair $\{v_n, A_n\}$ with $E_{Y*}(l_{n*}, C_n)$ to B and mix-servers.
2. Each M_i calculates pair $E_{Y*}\{(\sigma_{1(i)}, v_n^{\sigma1(i)}), (\sigma_{2(i)}, A_n^{\sigma2(i)})\}$ by using secret integers $\sigma_{1(i)}, \sigma_{2(i)}$ to send it to B.
3. B calculates the product of pairs sent from mix-servers as $E_{Y*}\{(\sigma_1, v_n^{\sigma1}), (\sigma_2, A_n^{\sigma2})\}$ and constructs $E_{Y*}(s_{n*}, \ddot{v}_n = v_n^{\sigma1}C_nA_n^{\sigma2})$ to send it to mix-servers, where $\sigma_1 = \sigma_{1(1)} + ... + \sigma_{1(P)}$, $\sigma_2 = \sigma_{2(1)} + ... + \sigma_{2(P)}$ and $s_{n*} = \sigma_1 + \sigma_2 + l_{n*}$.
4. Each M_i calculates $E_{Y*}(s_{n*}\lambda_i, \ddot{v}_n^{\lambda i})$ by using secret integer λ_i to send to B.
5. B calculates verification term $E_{Y*}(\delta_{n*} = s_{n*}\lambda, \ddot{v}_n)$ as the product of encryption forms sent from mix-servers and constructs quadruplet $< v_n, A_n, E_{Y*}\{(l_{n*}, C_n), (\delta_{n*}, \ddot{v}_n)\} >$, where $\lambda = \lambda_1 + ... + \lambda_P$ and $\ddot{v}_n = \ddot{v}_n^{\lambda}$.

After that, quadruplets are encrypted while being shuffled and decrypted by mix-servers, and finally each M_i discloses $\sigma_{1(i)}, \sigma_{2(i)}, \lambda_i$ so that anyone can confirm that B and mix-servers honestly encrypted and decrypted quadruplets.

3.3 Check Codes and Encrypted Unknown Integer Pairs

A check code (CC) is a pair $\{G_n, \underline{G}_n\}$ of integers in set A_*, and it is valid when $\underline{G}_n = G_n^{\pi}$ holds for integer π. But π is calculated as $\pi = \pi_1 + ... + \pi_P$ based on secret integer π_i of each mix-server M_i, therefore no one can know π, i.e. no one except the holder of $\{G_n, \underline{G}_n\}$ can determine whether $\{G_n, \underline{G}_n\}$ is valid or not.

Here, CCs are attached to votes so that votes cast by coercers are regarded as invalid, and must satisfy an additional requirement, i.e. no one can identify the vote accompanied by CC in tallied results by tracing CC. This requirement can be satisfied by transforming $\{G_n, \underline{G}_n\}$ to $E_{Y*}\{(r_n, \Omega_nG_n), (\underline{r}_n, \Omega_n^{\pi}\underline{G}_n)\}$ while using unknown integer pair (UI-pair) $\{\Omega_n, \Omega_n^{\pi}\}$. Namely, $\{\Omega_n, \Omega_n^{\pi}\}$ is encrypted to $E_{Y*}\{(r_n, \Omega_n), (\underline{r}_n, \Omega_n^{\pi})\}$ by multiple mix-servers (i.e. r_n and $\underline{r}_n$ are sums of mix-servers' secret integers), and no one can link $E_{Y*}\{(r_n, \Omega_nG_n), (\underline{r}_n, \Omega_n^{\pi}\underline{G}_n)\}$ to decrypted pair $\{\Omega_nG_n, \Omega_n^{\pi}\underline{G}_n\}$ in the tallied results. Nevertheless, $\{\Omega_nG_n, \Omega_n^{\pi}\underline{G}_n\}$ is valid (i.e. $(\Omega_nG_n)^{\pi} = \Omega_n^{\pi}\underline{G}_n$) only when $\{G_n, \underline{G}_n\}$ is valid. In addition, $\{G_n, \underline{G}_n\}$ is attached to credential $T(G_n, Z_n)$ as will be discussed later, and G_n in $\{G_n, \underline{G}_n\}$ must coincide with that in $T(G_n, Z_n)$ must coincide with G_n in credential $T(G_n, Z_n)$, therefore anyone cannot forge valid CCs.

Encrypted UI-pairs can be generated by combining secret integers of individual mix-servers as below.

1. Each M_i defines secret integer $\Omega_{n(i)}$ in set A_* ($1 \leq n \leq N$), encrypts each $\Omega_{n(i)}$ to $E_{Y*}(r_{n(i, 0)}, \Omega_{n(i)})$ by using secret integer $r_{n(i, 0)}$, and sends $E_{Y*}(r_{n(i, 0)}, \Omega_{n(i)})$ to M_1.

2. Mix-servers jointly re-encrypt and shuffle $E_{Y*}(r_{n(i,\,0)}, \Omega_{n(i)})$ to $E_{Y*}\{(r_{n(i)}, \Omega_{n(i)}),$
   $(\underline{r}_{n(i)}, \Omega_{n(i)}{}^{\pi})\}$ $(1 \le i \le P, 1 \le n \le N)$ by using secret integers $r_{n(i,\,p)}$ and π_p of
   each M_p, and disclose the results publicly, where $r_{n(i)} = r_{*n(i,\,P)}$, $r_{*n(i,\,p)} = r_{n(i,\,0)}$
   $+ r_{n(i,\,1)} + \dots + r_{n(i,\,p)}$ and $\underline{r}_{n(i)} = \pi_1 \cdot r_{*n(i,\,1)} + \dots + \pi_P \cdot r_{*n(i,\,P)}$.
3. B calculates $E_{Y*}\{(r_n, \Omega_n), (\underline{r}_n, \Omega_n{}^{\pi})\}$ as the product of $E_{Y*}\{(r_{n(1)}, \Omega_{n(1)}), (\underline{r}_{n(1)},$
   $\Omega_{n(1)}{}^{\pi})\}, \dots, E_{Y*}\{(r_{n(P)}, \Omega_{n(P)}), (\underline{r}_{n(P)}, \Omega_{n(P)}{}^{\pi})\}$ for each n, where $r_n = r_{n(1)} + \dots$
   $+ r_{n(P)}$ and $\underline{r}_n = \underline{r}_{n(1)} + \dots + \underline{r}_{n(P)}$.

Honest calculations of secret integer pairs can be verified by calculating $E_{Y*}\{(r_n,$
$\Omega_{*i}), (\underline{r}_n, \Omega_{*i}{}^{\pi})\}$ as the product of $E_{Y*}\{(r_{1(i)}, \Omega_{1(i)}), (\underline{r}_{1(i)}, \Omega_{1(i)}{}^{\pi})\}, \dots, E_{Y*}\{(r_{N(i)},$
$\Omega_{N(i)}), (\underline{r}_{N(i)}, \Omega_{N(i)}{}^{\pi})\}$ for each i, decrypting it to pair $\{\Omega_{*i}, \Omega_{*i}{}^{\pi}\}$ and confirming
that the pair is consistent, i.e. $\Omega_{*i}{}^{\pi}$ is calculated from Ω_{*i} and π. Namely, if $\{\Omega_{n(i)},$
$\Omega_{n(i)}{}^{\pi}\}$ is not consistent, one of $\{\Omega_{*1}, \Omega_{*1}{}^{\pi}\}, \dots, \{\Omega_{*P}, \Omega_{*P}{}^{\pi}\}$ becomes inconsistent.
Here, consistency of each $\{\Omega_{*i}, \Omega_{*i}{}^{\pi}\}$ can be examined without knowing π while
exploiting non-interactive zero-knowledge proofs (NZKPs) [14].

3.4   Secret Key Anonymous Tag Based Credentials

Voters can show their eligibility without revealing them when anonymous tag-based
credentials (*CDs*) [15] are used. But eligibility of voters is examined only by election
authorities. Therefore, public keys in [15] can be replaced with secret keys, and to
make the scheme efficient, *SK-CRVS* uses secret key anonymous tag based *CDs*
while simplifying the credential structure proposed in [2].

Credential $T(G, Z)$ issued by authority B to entity V is constructed as $T(G, Z) = (G^{R+Z})^d$. About integers $\{d, R\}$, they are secret signing/verification key and secret
integer of B, respectively, and common to all credentials. Integers $\{Z, G\}$ are unique
to $T(G, Z)$, and Z is a secret of V but G is publicly known. Also, G is in set A_*, i.e.
$G = a^\beta$, and only B knows β.

To convince B that it is a holder of $T(G, Z)$, V shows $T(G, Z)^w = (G^{R+Z})^{d \cdot w} = T(G^w, Z)$ by using secret integer w so that B cannot link $T(G, Z)$ to $T(G^w, Z)$, where
V is a legitimate holder of $T(G^w, Z)$ when V knows integers $\{G_x, G_y, G_\beta, \Gamma\}$ that
satisfy $G_x = G_\beta{}^R$ and $G_y = G_\beta{}^\Gamma$, and $G^{w(R+Z)d}$ is calculated from $G_x G_y$ by using
signing key d (it can be proved that $G_\beta = G^w$, $\Gamma = Z$). Then as same as in [2], no
one except B can forge $T(G, Z)$ and only V that knows Z can use $T(G, Z)$. Here, $T(G, Z)$ and $T(G^w, Z)$ are identical because it is trivial to construct $\{G^{w \cdot R}, G^{w \cdot Z}, G^w, Z\}$
from $\{G^R, G^Z, G, Z\}$.

The followings are procedures in which B issues credential $T(G, Z)$ with check
code $\{G, G^\pi\}$ to V and verifies it. Here, to simplify the issuing procedure, B calculates
$\{G^Z, G^R, G^\pi\}$ together with $U = a^{\beta(U)}$ in A_* in advance, and U is publicly disclosed
to be used for calculating used seals explained later, but $\beta(U)$ is an integer no one
knows. About G^Z, it is calculated as $G^Z = G^{Z1} \cdot G^{Z2} \dots G^{ZP}$ from secret integer Z_i
of each M_i, and M_i discloses Z_i only in forms such as G^{Zi}, therefore no one except
V can know Z. Uniqueness of Z can be maintained by calculating Δ^Z for publicly

known integer Δ and discarding Z when Δ^Z appeared before. B issues $T(G, Z)$ as below.

1. V requests B a credential while showing itself.
2. If V is eligible, B informs V of $\{G, D_Z = G^Z, D_R = G^R, T(G, Z) = G^{(R+Z)d}, D_\pi = G^\pi\}$. At the same time, each M_i informs V of Z_i.
3. V calculates $Z = Z_1 + \ldots + Z_P$ and confirms that $D_Z = G^Z$, and while exploiting NZKPs, examines relations $\{D_R = G^R, T(G, Z) = G^{(R+Z)d}, D_\pi = G^\pi\}$ without knowing $\{R, d, \pi\}$. Then if the relations hold, V accepts credential $T(G, Z)$ and check code $\{G, \underline{G} = D_\pi\}$. Otherwise, it requests a credential again.

The verification procedure proceeds as below.

1. V generates secret integer w, calculates $\{G^w, G_x = G^{w \cdot R}, G_y = G^{w \cdot Z}, T(G, Z)^w = T(G^w, Z), \underline{C} = \underline{G}^w, U_* = U^Z\}$ and conducts NZKPs to convince B that $\{G_y, U_*\}$ are calculated from $\{G^w, U\}$ by using same integer Z without disclosing Z.
2. When the NZKPs at step 1 were successfully completed, B conducts NZKPs to convince V whether $G_* = G^{w \cdot R}$ and $T(G^w, Z) = (G_x G_y)^d$ hold or not without disclosing R or d. Then, if $G_* \neq G^{w \cdot R}$, $T(G^w, Z) \neq (G_x G_y)^d$ or U_* appeared before (i.e. $T(G, Z)$ was used before as explained later), B rejects $T(G^w, Z)$. Otherwise, B accepts $T(G^w, Z)$ and memorizes check code $\{G^w, \underline{C}\}$.
3. When $T(G^w, Z)$ is rejected but V does not agree with the rejection, B conducts NZKPs to convince V that the NZKPs at step 2 were honestly conducted.

Where B cannot intentionally accept ineligible V if commitments and responses of the NZKPs in step 1 and 2 are disclosed publicly. Anyone cannot forge a consistent CC either, because G^w in $T(G^w, Z)$ is used to comprise pair $\{G^w, \underline{G}^w\}$. About U_*, because V must calculate it as U^Z, U^Z is unique to $T(G, Z)$ and only V knows Z; it can be used as a used seal, an evidence that V had used $T(G, Z)$. But without additional means, B may terminate the interaction between V without providing services, because the used seal U^Z was shown already.

4 SK-*CRVS*

SK-*CRVS*, which consists of N voters $V_1, \ldots, V_N$, registration manager B, and P (≥ 2) mix-servers $M_1, \ldots, M_P$, accepts remote voters and write-in ballots while satisfying all essential requirements of e-voting systems. As mentioned before, it exploits fake credentials as same as many recent schemes do. Namely, voter V_n obtains multiple credentials together with check codes, and by one of them, it proves its eligibility without disclosing itself and casts its vote together with the accompanying check code. But, among multiple credentials, only one credential is valid which is accompanied by a valid check code, i.e. other credentials are fake ones, and votes accompanied by invalid check codes are not counted. Besides, only V_n knows credentials and the number of credentials it obtained and their validities, and votes are encrypted and shuffled so that even V_n cannot identify its vote. Then by

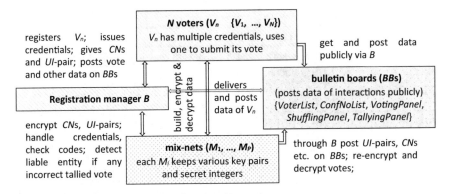

Fig. 1 Major interactions among involved entities

ID	Signature		CN	Encrypted CN		UI-pair	Used seal
V_n	V_n's signature		C_n	$E_{Y^*}(l_{m^*}, C_m)$		$E_{Y^*}\{(r_p, \Omega_p),(\underline{r}_p, \Omega_p^n)\}$	U^{Zn}

a) *VoterList*   b) *ConfNoList*

Vote	Used seal		Vote
$E_{Y^*}\{(s_n, v_n),\ (r_n, \underline{G}_{\Omega(n)}),\ (\underline{r}_n,$ $\underline{G}_{\Omega(n)}),\ (l_{n^*}, C_n),\ (s_n{*}\lambda, \ddot{u}_n)\}$	$\{U^{Zn}, \underline{U}^{Zn}\}$, NZKPs		$E_{Y^*}\{(k_{n^*}, v_n),\ (t_{n^*}, \underline{G}_{\Omega(n)}),\ (m_{n^*}, \underline{G}_{\Omega(n)}),\ (u_{n^*}, C_n),$ $(\delta_{n^*}, \ddot{u}_n)\}$

c) *VotingPanel*   d) *ShufflingPanel*

Vote	CN	Check code
$\{v_n, \ddot{u}_n\}$	C_n	$\{G_{\Omega(n)}, \underline{G}_{\Omega(n)}\}, D_{\pi(n)},$ NZKP

e) *TallyingPanel*

Fig. 2 Configurations of bulletin boards

giving fake credentials to coercers, even remote voters are protected from simulation and forced abstention attacks. Because check codes attached to votes for inferior candidates are not examined, randomization attacks are also prevented even when write-in ballots exist.

SK-CRVS consists of preparation, registration, voting, tallying and vote correction stages shown in the following sub-sections and exploits bulletin boards (*BBs*) [1] *VoterList*, *ConfNoList*, *VotingPanel*, *ShufflingPanel* and *TallyingPanel* shown in Fig. 2. Figure 1 summarizes interactions among entities, and Table 1 shows used notations.

4.1 Preparation Stage

Registration manager *B* and mix-servers prepare *CNs*, *UI*-pairs, credentials, check codes and publicly known integers $\{U, \underline{U}\}$ used for calculating 1st and 2nd used seals. Where no one can be assumed as honest in election systems; therefore integers

Table 1 List of notations

Notation	Description
V_n, v_n	n-th voter and a candidate (freely) chosen by V_n $(1 \le n \le N)$
B, M_i	Registration manager and i-th mix-server $(1 \le i \le P)$
$X_i, Y_i, X_*, Y_*, E_Y(k, v)$	$\{X_i, Y_i = g^{X_i}\}$ are secret decryption and public encryption keys of M_i, $X_* = X_1 + \ldots + X_P$, $Y_* = Y_1 \ldots Y_P = g^{X_*}$, $E_Y(k, v) = \{g^k, vY^k\}$
A_*	$A_* = \{a^i \pmod{Q} : i = 1, \ldots, Q_* - 1\}$, where Q_* and Q are prime numbers and $Q = 2Q_* + 1$
$\{d, R, \pi, \sigma_1, \sigma_2, \sigma_3, \lambda\}$	Integers and no one knows them, *i.e.* they are calculated as $d = d_1 + \ldots + d_P$, $R = R_1 + \ldots + R_P$, $\pi = \pi_1 + \ldots + \pi_P$, $\sigma_q = \sigma_{q(1)} + \ldots + \sigma_{q(P)}$ $(q = 1, 2, 3)$, $\lambda = \lambda_1 + \ldots + \lambda_P$, where $\{d_i, R_i, \pi_i, \sigma_{1(i)}, \sigma_{2(i)}, \sigma_{3(i)}, \lambda_i\}$ are secret integers of each M_i, and d is a joint signing key of mix-servers
$C_n, E_{Y*}(l_{n*}, C_n)$	CN assigned to V_n and its encryption form
$T(G_n, Z_n)$	Credential issued to V_n, where integer G_n is in A_*
$\{G_n, \underline{G}_n\}$	Check code accompanying $T(G_n, Z_n)$, and it is valid when $G_n{}^\pi = \underline{G}_n$
Ω_n	Unknown integer to transform $\{G_n, \underline{G}_n\}$ to $\{\Omega_n G_n, \Omega_n{}^\pi \underline{G}_n\}$, where Ω_n is in A_*
$U^{Z_n}, \underline{U}^{Z_n}$	1st and 2nd used seals calculated by $T(G_n, Z_n)$, where $\{U, \underline{U}\}$ are in A_*

$\{d, R, \pi, \sigma_q \ (q = 1, 2, 3), \lambda\}$ are constructed as sums of secret integers of each M_i so that no one can know their values. Below is the preparation procedure.

1. Jointly with mix-servers, B defines integers $\{U = a^{\beta(U)}, \underline{U} = a^{\beta(\underline{U})}\}$ in set A_* so that no one can know $\beta(U)$ or $\beta(\underline{U})$ and discloses $\{U, \underline{U}\}$ publicly.
2. B generates $\{C_1, \ldots, C_{N*}\}$ $(N_* > N)$ as CNs, and for each n, mix-servers encrypt C_n to $E_{Y*}(l_{n*}, C_n)$ and calculate encrypted UI-pair $E_{Y*}\{(r_n, \Omega_n), (\underline{r}_n, \Omega_n{}^\pi)\}$ to be disclosed on *ConfNoList*.
3. B and mix-servers prepare integers for each V_n so that V_n at the registration stage can construct credentials $T(G_{(n, j)}, Z_{(n, j)})$ and check codes $\{G_{(n, j)}, \underline{G}_{(n, j)}\}$ $(1 \le j \le J)$.

Here among J-credential and check code pairs prepared for V_n, relation $\underline{G}_{(n, j)} = G_{(n, j)}{}^\pi$ holds only when $j = 1$, i.e. $T(G_{(n, j)}, Z_{(n, j)})$ is a fake credential for $j \ge 2$. But coercers may know valid credentials if B knows credentials it issues; therefore step 3 is conducted through the credential preparation procedure below.

3.1. Each M_p generates integer $\Lambda_{(n, i, p)}$ and discloses it for each i.
3.2. B decomposes $\{\underline{T}_n, G_{*n}\}$ into $\{\underline{T}_n(1), \ldots, \underline{T}_n(P)\}$ and $\{G_{*n}(1), \ldots, G_{*n}(P)\}$, and sends $\{\underline{T}_n(i), G_{*n}(i)\}$ with $\{\underline{T}_n, G_{*n}\}$ to M_i for each I, where $\underline{T}_n = \underline{T}_n(1) \cdot \ldots \cdot \underline{T}_n(P)$, $G_{*n} = G_{*n}(1) \cdot \ldots \cdot G_{*n}(P)$ and each $\underline{T}_n(i)$ is defined as $\underline{T}_n(i) = \Lambda_{(n, i, 1)} + \ldots + \Lambda_{(n, i, P)}$ for $i \ne P$; therefore $\underline{T}_n(P) = \underline{T}_n / \{\underline{T}_n(1) \cdot \underline{T}_n(2) \cdot \ldots \underline{T}_n(P-1)\}$.
3.3. Each M_i calculates pair $\{\underline{T}_n(i)^{w*(n, i)}, G_{*n}(i)^{w*(n, i)}\}$ by secret integer $w_*(n, i)$ $(\ne w(n, i))$ to send it to other mix-servers.

3.4. Each M_p calculates pair $\{\underline{T}_n(i)^{w*(n,\,i)\cdot w(n,\,p)}, G_{*n}(i)^{w*(n,\,i)\cdot w(n,\,p)}\}$ for each i from the pair sent by M_i to send the result to M_i.

3.5. From pairs calculated at step 3.4, M_i calculates $\{\underline{T}_n(i)^{w*(n,\,i)\cdot w(n)},\allowbreak G_{*n}(i)^{w*(n,\,i)\cdot w(n)}\}$ $(w_{(n)} = w_{(n,\,1)}+\ldots+w_{(n,\,P)})$ to send them to other mix-servers.

3.6. M_p calculates pair $\{\underline{T}_n(i)^{w*(n,\,i)\cdot w(n)\cdot dp}, G_{*n}(i)^{w*(n,\,i)\cdot w(n)\cdot \pi p}\}$ for each i and sends it back to M_i.

3.7. While using $w_{*(n,\,i)}^{-1}$, from the pair at step 3.5 and pairs at step 3.6, M_i calculates $\{\underline{T}_n(i)^{w(n)}, \underline{T}_{*n}(i)^{w(n)} = \underline{T}_n(i)^{w(n)\cdot d}, G_{*n}(i)^{w(n)}, \underline{G}_{*n}(i)^{w(n)} = G_{*n}(i)^{w(n)\cdot \pi}\}$ and memorizes $\{Z_{(n,\,i)}, \underline{T}_n(i)^{w(n)}, \underline{T}_{*n}(i)^{w(n)}, G_{*n}(i)^{w(n)}, \underline{G}_{*n}(i)^{w(n)}\}$.

3.8. B jointly with mix-servers calculates commitments and responses of NZKPs for convincing voters at the registration stage that $T(G_n, Z_n)$ and $\{G_n, \underline{G}_n\}$ are calculated correctly by using $\{d, R, \pi\}$ without disclosing them. Then, B memorizes the commitments and responses.

At step 3.6, because check code $\{G_{(n,\,j)}, \underline{G}_{(n,\,j)}\}$ is invalid for $j > 1$, each M_p defines an arbitrary values as that of $G_{*n}(i)^{w*(n,\,i)\cdot w(n)\cdot \pi p}$ when $j > 1$. About step 3.8, it reduces computation volumes required for B in the registration stage to calculate commitments and responses of the NZKPs, where the computation volume in this stage is not critical because elections do not start yet.

4.2 Registration Stage

Voter V_n at this stage obtains credentials and check codes from registration manager B, where V_n and B interact face to face at a registration office to prevent others from impersonating V_n. Also each mix-server M_i constructs $I_v(i)$ in advance as a set of integers randomly selected from $\{2, 3, \ldots, J\}$. In the voter registration procedure, below $\{\underline{T}_n(i)^{w(n)}, \underline{T}_{*n}(i)^{w(n)}, G_{*n}(i)^{w(n)}, \underline{G}_{*n}(i)^{w(n)}\}$ in the preparation stage are renamed $\{T_n(i), T_{*n}(i), G_n(i), \underline{G}_n(i)\}$ to simplify notations.

1. V_n shows itself to B.
2. If V_n is eligible, B selects J-credentials prepared in the preparation stage, and for each credential, each M_i informs V_n of 5-tuple $\{Z_{(n,\,i)}, T_n(i), T_{*n}(i), G_n(i), \underline{G}_n(i)\}$, where only the 1st credential is valid, also M_i does not send the tuple, if the credential is the j-th one and j is included in set $I_v(i)$.
3. For each credential, V_n calculates $\{Z_n = Z_{(n,\,1)} + \ldots + Z_{(n,\,P)}, T_n = T_n(1) \ldots T_n(P), T_{*n} = T_{*n}(1) \ldots T_{*n}(P), G_n = G_n(1) \ldots G_n(P), \underline{G}_n = \underline{G}_n(1) \ldots \underline{G}_n(P)\}$. After that it calculates $\{G_n^{Z_n}, G_n^R = T_n/G_n^{Z_n}\}$ and confirms that T_{*n} is consistent without knowing $\{R, d\}$ while exploiting NZKPs. V_n also confirms $\underline{G}_n = G_n^{\pi}$ without knowing π when T_{*n} is the 1st credential. Then if they are confirmed, V_n accepts $\{Z_n, T_n, T_{*n}, G_n, \underline{G}_n\}$ and puts its signature on *VoterList* as a receipt. But if V_n cannot obtain the predefined number of credentials or check codes, it requests credentials again, where each M_i deletes the specified number of elements from $I_v(i)$ if necessary.

Then, V_n can conceal its credentials from others. Because no one knows all sets $I_v(i)\,(1 \le i \le P)$, only V_n can know the number of credentials it obtains. Also, provided that at least one mix-server is honest, ineligible V_n cannot obtain credentials. Here, B or mix-servers do not need to calculate commitments or responses of the NZKPs.

4.3   Voting Stage

Voter V_n puts its vote on *VotingPanel* possibly at a remote site via 2 sub-stages.

Voter Acceptance. By showing credential $T(G_n, Z_n)$, anonymous V_n obtains $E_{Y*}(l_{n*}, C_n)$ and *UI*-pair through the voter acceptance procedure, where even B may intentionally accept inconsistent $T(G_n, Z_n)$ and terminate the voting stage incompletely. Commitments and responses of NZKPs calculated at steps 1 and 2 and disclosed in the used seal parts of *VotingPanel* in the vote construction stage prevents B from accepting illeigitimate credentials, i.e. anyone can confirm that those credentials were honestly verified. Used seal pair $\{U_*, \underline{U}_*\}$ at step 2, which is consistent when U_* and $\underline{U}_*$ are calculated by a same credential, prevents incomplete terminations of the stage, i.e. although V_n calculated U_* already, it calculates $\underline{U}_*$ after its vote is successfully put on *VotingPanel*.

The voter acceptance procedure is below.

1. V_n decomposes $T(G_n, Z_n)$ into $\{G_x = G_n{}^R, G_y = G_n{}^{Zn}\}$, calculates $U_* = U^{Zn}$ and shows 6-tuple $\{G_n, \underline{G}_n, G_x, G_y, T(G_n, Z_n), U_*\}$ to B and mix-servers. Then, V_n conducts NZKPs to convince B that $\{G_y = G_n{}^{Zn}, U_* = U^{Zn}\}$ without disclosing Z_n.
2. When $\{G_y, U_*\}$ were successfully examined at step 1, B jointly with mix-servers conducts NZKPs and rejects V_n's request if $G_x \ne G_n{}^R$, $T(G_n, Z_n) \ne (G_x G_y)^d$ or consistent $\{U_*, \underline{U}_*\}$ exists on *VotingPanel* (i.e. V_n's vote was put on *VotingPanel* already). Otherwise, B gives unassigned $E_{Y*}(l_{n*}, C_n)$ and $E_{Y*}\{(r_n, \Omega_n), (\underline{r}_n, \Omega_n{}^\pi)\}$ on *ConfNoList* to V_n, and B puts U_* on BB corresponding to $E_{Y*}(l_{n*}, C_n)$. But, if U_* exists already, B gives $< E_{Y*}(l_{n*}, C_n), E_{Y*}\{(r_n, \Omega_n), (\underline{r}_n, \Omega_n{}^\pi)\} >$ which is accompanied by U_*.
3. V_n that receives CN and *UI*-pair constructs encrypted check code $E_{Y*}\{(r_n, G_{\Omega(n)} = G_n \Omega_n), (\underline{r}_n, \underline{G}_{\Omega(n)} = \underline{G}_n \Omega_n{}^\pi)\}$ from $\{G_n, \underline{G}_n\}$ and $E_{Y*}\{(r_n, \Omega_n), (\underline{r}_n, \Omega_n{}^\pi)\}$. If its request was rejected but V_n does not agree with the rejection, B jointly with mix-servers conducts NZKPs to convince V_n that the NZKPs in step 2 were conducted honestly.

Then, V_n can obtain $E_{Y*}(l_{n*}, C_n)$ and *UI*-pair anonymously, if and only if it is a holder of a consistent CD, where V_n does not need to change forms of $T(G_n, Z_n)$ or $\{G_n, \underline{G}_n\}$, because only V_n knows them.

Vote Construction. To be put on *VotingPanel*, a vote of voter V_n accepted in the previous sub-stage is constructed through the procedure for *CR-SVRM* in Sect. 3.2. Here, the vote includes freely chosen candidate v_n, check code $E_{Y*}\{(r_n, G_{\Omega(n)}), (\underline{r}_n,$

$\underline{G}_{(\Omega n)}$)}, CN $E_{Y*}(l_{n*}, C_n)$ and verification term $\ddot{\upsilon}_n$, which is calculated as $\ddot{\upsilon}_n = (v_n{}^{\sigma 1} C_n G_{\Omega(n)}{}^{\sigma 2} \underline{G}_{\Omega(n)}{}^{\sigma 3})^\lambda$. Also, to conceal v_n from others, V_n encrypts v_n to $E_{Y*}(s_n, v_n)$ by secret integer s_n, i.e. the vote is 5-tuple $\{E_{Y*}\{(s_n, v_n), (r_n, G_{\Omega(n)}), (\underline{r}_n, \underline{G}_{\Omega(n)}), (l_{n*}, C_n), (s_n*\lambda, \ddot{\upsilon}_n)\}$. This means that the decrypted tuple is consistent when $\ddot{\upsilon}_n = (v_n{}^{\sigma 1} C_n G_{\Omega(n)}{}^{\sigma 2} \underline{G}_{\Omega(n)}{}^{\sigma 3})^\lambda$ holds and C_n is a registered CN unique to it.

In the above, B and mix-servers may calculate verification term $\ddot{\upsilon}_n$ dishonestly, in addition anyone can forge consistent 5-tuple as the product of existing tuples while exploiting the homomorphism of ElGamal encryption scheme. *SK-CRVS* detects these dishonesties in the tallying stage and identifies liable entities in the vote correction stage. The vote construction sub-stage proceeds as follows.

1. V_n encrypts v_n to $E_{Y*}(s_n, v_n)$, and sends quadruplet $E_{Y*}\{(s_n, v_n), (r_n, G_{\Omega(n)}), (\underline{r}_n, \underline{G}_{\Omega(n)}), (l_{n*}, C_n)\}$ to mix-servers and B.
2. Each M_i calculates triplet $E_{Y*}\{(s_n \cdot \sigma_{1(i)}, v_n{}^{\sigma 1(i)}), (r_n \cdot \sigma_{2(i)}, G_{\Omega(n)}{}^{\sigma 2(i)}), (\underline{r}_n \cdot \sigma_{3(i)}, \underline{G}_{\Omega(n)}{}^{\sigma 3(i)})\}$, and B calculates $E_{Y*}(s_{n*}, \ddot{\upsilon}_n = v_n{}^{\sigma 1} C_n G_{\Omega(n)}{}^{\sigma 2} \underline{G}_{\Omega(n)}{}^{\sigma 3})$ from triplets calculated by mix-servers, where $s_{n*} = s_n \cdot \sigma_1 + r_n \cdot \sigma_2 + \underline{r}_n \cdot \sigma_3 + l_{n*}$.
3. Each M_i calculates $E_{Y*}(s_{n*}\lambda_i, \ddot{\upsilon}_n{}^{\lambda i})$, and B calculates verification term $E_{Y*}(s_{n*}\lambda, \ddot{\upsilon}_n = \ddot{\upsilon}_n{}^\lambda)$. Then, B constructs 5-tuple $E_{Y*}\{(s_n, v_n), (r_n, G_{\Omega(n)}), (\underline{r}_n, \underline{G}_{\Omega(n)}), (l_{n*}, C_n), (s_n*\lambda, \ddot{\upsilon}_n)\}$ and puts the 5-tuple on *VotingPanel*.
4. If the first 4 terms in the 5-tuple are correct, V_n calculates $\underline{U}^{Zn}$ to send them to B and conducts NZKPs to convince B that $\{U^{Zn}, \underline{U}^{Zn}\}$ are calculated from $\{U, \underline{U}\}, Z_n$.
5. B puts pair $\{U_*, \underline{U}^{Zn}\}$ and commitments and responses of the NZKPs in the voter acceptance stage in the used seal part corresponding to the 5-tuple on *VotingPanel*.

Then, V_n can conceal v_n from others, and it is ensured that the first 4 terms of V_n's vote are correctly put on *VotingPanel*.

4.4 Tallying Stage

To conceal links between voters and votes in tallied results, mix-servers re-encrypt, shuffle and then decrypt votes on *VotingPanel* to disclose the results on *TallyingPanel*. Also, incorrectly handled votes are detected, and to discard invalid votes, check code $\{G_{\Omega(n)}, \underline{G}_{\Omega(n)}\}$ in each decryption result $\tilde{V}(v_n) = \{v_n, G_{\Omega(n)}, \underline{G}_{\Omega(n)}, C_n, \ddot{\upsilon}_n\}$ is examined if it is for a non-inferior candidate. The tallying procedure proceeds as follows.

1. Mix-servers re-encrypt and shuffle 5-tuples $E_{Y*}\{(s_n, v_n), (r_n, G_{\Omega(n)}), (\underline{r}_n, \underline{G}_{\Omega(n)}), (l_{n*}, C_n), (s_n*\lambda, \ddot{\upsilon}_n)\}$ $(1 \leq n \leq N_*)$ on *VotingPanel* and disclose the results on *ShufflingPanel*.
2. Mix-servers decrypt each re-encrypted 5-tuple on *ShufflingPanel* to $\tilde{V}(v_n) = \{v_n, G_{\Omega(n)}, \underline{G}_{\Omega(n)}, C_n, \ddot{\upsilon}_n\}$ and disclose the result on *TallyingPanel*.
3. After all votes were decrypted, mix-servers decrypt unassigned encrypted CNs to construct set $\hat{C}$ that consists of all assigned CNs.

4. Each M_i discloses secret integers $\{\sigma_{1(i)}, \sigma_{2(i)}, \sigma_{3(i)}, \lambda_i\}$ to reveal $\{\sigma_1, \sigma_2, \sigma_3, \lambda\}$.
5. B determines $\hat{V}(v_n)$ is inconsistent, if $\ddot{v}_n \neq (v_n{}^{\sigma 1} C_n G_{\Omega(n)}{}^{\sigma 2} \underline{G}_{\Omega(n)}{}^{\sigma 3})^{\lambda}$, or C_n in $\hat{V}(v_n)$ is not unique to it or not included in $\hat{C}$.
6. For each consistent $\tilde{V}(v_n)$, if it is not for an inferior candidate, each M_i calculates $G_{\Omega(n)}{}^{\pi i}$ and sends it to B.
7. B calculates $D_{\pi(n)} = G_{\Omega(n)}{}^{\pi}$. Then, jointly with mix-servers it conducts NZKPs to convince anyone that $D_{\pi(n)}$ was honestly calculated without disclosing any π_i and puts commitments and responses of the NZKPs in the check code part corresponding to $\tilde{V}(v_n)$ on *TallyingPanel*. But if $D_{\pi(n)} \neq G_{\Omega(n)}{}^{\pi}$, B asks mix-servers to go back to step 6.

4.5   Vote Correction Stage

This stage is incorporated in step 5 of the tallying procedure, and identifies liable mix-servers for inconsistent 5-tuple $\tilde{V}(v') = \{v', G', \underline{G}', C', \ddot{v}'\}$, corrects $\tilde{V}(v')$ by tracing $\tilde{V}(v')$ back to *VotingPanel*. Once M_i liable for $\tilde{V}(v_n)$ is identified, mix-servers are asked to re-encrypt and/or decrypt the 5-tuple corresponding to $\tilde{V}(v_n)$ again.

5   Preliminary Evaluation

5.1   Satisfied Requirements

SK-CRVS satisfies all essential requirements of e-voting systems, e.g. requirements, those about verifiability and coercion resistance are satisfied as below.

Coercion resistance: Because anyone cannot link votes on *VotingPanel* and *Tallying-Panel*, coercers that are coercing voter V_n cannot identify V_n's vote on *TallyingPanel*. Simulation and forced abstention attacks are also prevented because coercers do not know credentials, number of fake credentials or validity of individual credentials V_n obtained. In addition, randomization attacks are impossible, i.e. check codes accompanying votes for inferior candidates are not examined.

Verifiability: All encrypted votes are disclosed and inconsistent votes and liable entities are identified; then correct election results are recalculated without re-election.

5.2   Computation Volumes and Comparisons

To evaluate volumes of computations, numbers of exponentiations (*exps*) and hash values (*hashes*) required in each stage were estimated while assuming implementations of NZKPs tentatively as shown in Table 2. Here, the preparation and the vote

Table 2 Computation volumes and a comparison between proposed *SK-CRVS* and *CRVS* [10]

Stages	V_n		B		Each M_i	
	SK-CRVS	CRVS	SK-CRVS	CRVS	SK-CRVS	CRVS
Registration (per credential)	7-*exps* 3-*hashes*	11 + 5-*exps* 3 + 2-*hashes*	–	–	–	–
Voter acceptance (per voter)	3-*exps* 1-*hash*	3-*exps* 1-*hashes*	8-*exps* 3-*hashes*	8-e*xps* 3-*hashes*	2-*exps*	2-exps
Vote construction (per vote)	4-*exps* 1-*hash*	≥ 24-*exps* 4-*hashes*	2-*exps* 1-*hash*	≥ 6-*exps* 4-h*ashes*	8-*exps*	12-exps
Tallying (per vote)	–	–	6-*exps* 1-*hash*	≥ 8P-*exps*	8-*exps*	≥ 10-exps

correction stages were ignored. The table also shows numbers of *exps* and *hashes* required by the scheme proposed in [10] that accepts remote voters as a comparison. As shown in the table, *SK-CRVS* is more efficient than [10].

6 Conclusions

Concepts of *SK-CRVS* were reported. It accepts remote voters and freely write-in ballots while satisfying all essential requirements of e-voting schemes. Also, preliminary evaluation results showed it is efficient as other recent e-voting schemes are. As future works, procedures in individual stages must be improved and interactions among entities for implementing NZKPs must be clarified. Also, volumes of computations and communications must be evaluated while developing a prototype system.

References

1. Sampigethaya K, Poovendran R (2006) A framework and taxonomy for comparison of electronic voting schemes. Comput Secur 25(2):137–153
2. Tamura S (2018) A scheme for self-issuable e-cash systems. LAMBERT (2018)
3. Tamura S et al (2015) An incoercible E-voting scheme based on revised simplified verifiable re-encryption mix-nets. Inf Secur Comput Fraud 3(2):32–38
4. Alam KMR, Tamura S, Taniguchi S, Yanase T (2010) An anonymous voting scheme based on confirmation numbers. IEEJ Trans EIS 130(11):2065–2073
5. Zhou Y, Liu Y, Jiang C, Wang S (2020) An improved FOO voting scheme using blockchain. Int J Inf Secur 19(3):303–310

6. Fan X, Wu T, Zheng Q, Chen Y, Alam M, Xiao X (2020) HSE-Voting: a secure high-efficiency electronic voting scheme based on homomorphic signcryption. Futur Gener Comput Syst 111:754–762
7. Moran T, Naor M (2010) Split-ballot voting: Everlasting privacy with distributed trust. ACM Trans Information Syst Secur 13(2):1–43
8. Ryan P, Rønne PB et al (2016) Selene: voting with transparent verifiability and coercion-mitigation. In: International Conference on F. cryptography and data security, pp 176–192
9. Alam KMR, Tamura S et al (2021) An electronic voting scheme based on revised-SVRM and confirmation numbers. IEEE Trans Dependable Secure Comput 18(1):400–410
10. Araujo R et al (2016) Remote electronic voting can be efficient, verifiable and coercion-resistant. In: International conference on F. cryptography and data security, pp 224–232
11. Rønne PB et al (2019) Coercion-resistant voting in linear via fully homomorphic encryption: towards a quantum-safe scheme. arXiv preprint arXiv:1901.02560
12. Juels A, Catalano D, Jakobsson M (2005) Coercion-resistant electronic elections. In: Proceding of the 2005 ACM workshop on privacy in the electronic society, pp 61–70
13. Demirel D, Graff JVD (2012) A publicly-verifiable mix-net with everlasting privacy towards observers. In: Proceeding of IACR cryptology ePrint archive
14. Bayer S, Groth J (2012) Efficient zero-knowledge argument for correctness of a shuffle. Adv Cryptol - EUROCRYPT, pp 263–280
15. Tamura S, Taniguchi S (2014) Enhancement of anonymous tag based credentials. Inform Secur Comput Fraud 2(1):10–20

Evaluating Data Migrations with Respect to Interoperability in Hybrid Cloud

S. M. Barhate and M. P. Dhore

1 Introduction

Cloud computing is a big revolution in the field of computing in which infrastructure, platforms and software are provided in the form of services to the users. The end user accesses these services through the middleware say Internet from channel of servers which redirect the requests to specific server. The servers help to store, process and use data over the Internet. The industry is shifting toward cloud technology to get ideal machine usage, i.e., ideal throughput, response time, cut cost, etc. [1, 2]

Virtualization is the technology which helps in effective utilization of resources. It separates the physical resources, thereby extending the power by creating multiple virtual machines. When multiple virtual machines are created, we can very efficiently make use of resources with very less waiting time and more throughput.

Interoperability means ease of moving of the workloads between private and public clouds without any vendor lock-in situation. It just does not mean the transfer of data between the clouds but adjusting of workload within the clouds also. When there are multiple virtual machines available for efficient resource provisioning, then we have to switch among virtual machines to get better access to different resources. This switching can be among homogeneous or heterogeneous cloud environment. So data migration can be considered as a very important issue of interoperability [3, 4].

S. M. Barhate (✉)
DECS, RTM Nagpur University Nagpur, Nagpur, Maharashtra 440033, India
e-mail: lncs@springer.com

M. P. Dhore
SSESA'S College, RTM Nagpur University Nagpur, Nagpur, Maharashtra 440035, India

© The Author(s), under exclusive license to Springer Nature Singapore Pte Ltd. 2023   795
R. Doriya et al. (eds.), *Machine Learning, Image Processing, Network Security and Data Sciences*, Lecture Notes in Electrical Engineering 946,
https://doi.org/10.1007/978-981-19-5868-7_59

2 Background

There are some obstacles to cloud computing in which interoperability is considered as the most important but understudied issue. NIST, OMG, DMTF has proposed various use cases for interoperability. On summing up all the used cases, we find the following four use cases as the most affecting ones as far as the consumer–provider relation in cloud computing is concerned.

1. **User Authentication**: A user who has established with a cloud provider can use same identity with another cloud provider.
2. **Workload Management**: A workload being executed in one cloud provider can be migrated and executed in other cloud provider also.
3. **Data Migration**: A data of one cloud provider can be migrated to another cloud provider if need be.
4. **Load Balancing**: Different tools and techniques should be used to manage the workload among different cloud providers [5].

So from the above four used cases, the paper considers data migration use case with respect to interoperability by proposing hybrid cloud model.

3 Related Work

In [6], authors have considered CPU utilization and power consumption by enabling virtual machine migration. They implemented four power models on IAAS environment and evaluated the best model for energy efficiency. In [7], authors state that when there is increase in cloud computing services the QOS parameters should also be changed. They consider QOS parameters based on three strategies evaluation, comparison and trustworthiness of the services to be analyzed and also the QOS parameters are analyzed with the help of scheduling algorithms. In [8], the authors focus upon cloud resource management considering it as the key factor cloud development. The paper states that poor resource utilization leads to underutilization and wastage of resources like high-speed CPU, costly storage, etc. The paper proposes to use bin packing algorithm which deploys best-fit algorithm to obtain results and compared to select best algorithm for efficient use of resources. In [9], the authors have made use of cloud federation approach to increase resource utilization have presented an approach to reduce power consumption for IaaS providers by choosing the most appropriate host and allocating the best virtual machine which leads to satisfy users requests, save energy and reduce the cost of resources.

4　Research Aim

The paper aims to address the interoperability issues that can exist in hybrid cloud. While the interoperability is being thought off, the following key research questions arise as follows:

1. How hybrid cloud is modeled?
2. How the cloudburst is implemented between private and public cloud?
3. Which data migration techniques are involved?
4. How data migration takes place in homogenous and heterogeneous clouds?
5. What is impact of using hybrid cloud with respect to interoperability?
6. Performance metrics affected by data migration.

5　Existing Methodologies

Hybrid cloud model is a powerful agglomeration of private as well as public clouds, thereby increasing the power an advantages of cloud computing. This combination is powerful as we are exploring the scalability and cost effectiveness of public cloud and security of private cloud as well. The idea behind using the hybrid cloud is first the data would be sent to private cloud, and as the threshold reaches, the data is forwarded to public cloud so that the service provisioning is continuous [10, 11].

In cloud environment, there are many of data centers, and hence, the virtual machines need to be migrated among these data centers for better resource provisioning. The logic stands here is there are various virtual machines working in parallel above a physical machine. The need of data migration arises when the a virtual machine is overutilized, and hence, the user request needs to be migrated to other virtual machine which is underutilized to maintain the workload and thereby implementing better resource utilization and less power consumption. In case of interoperability, the data has to migrated to some other virtual machine or some other data centre even, as the need be. But while this data migration is carried out, there are two technologies which are implemented as follows:

1. Distribution
2. Consolidation.

These technologies are implemented in order to reduce the power consumption while the data is migrated in homogenous or heterogeneous cloud environment [8–10].

The power consumption is calculated by using the following formula:

$$\textbf{Energy Consumption} = \frac{\textbf{Wattshost} * \textbf{Userhour}}{\textbf{1000}} \tag{1}$$

Fig. 1 Before consolidation

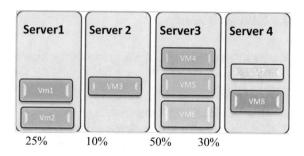

Fig. 2 After consolidation

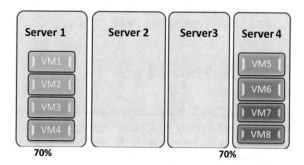

Thus, the energy consumption is calculated by energy consumption of host in watts and time taken by user in hours. There are various power management techniques as follows:

1. Provisioning.
2. **Consolidation**.
3. **Distribution.**

We are considering consolidation with respect to data migration. Consolidation is a technique in which power consumption reduction is managed by reducing the underutilized physical servers by consolidating the underutilized virtual machines and switching of the unused machines. Consolidation implements VM migration and VM placement as a strategy to manage power consumption.

VM migration can either be for energy consumption reduction or be for efficient resource utilization. Thus, there is swapping of virtual machines among underutilized physical servers, thereby shutting down the unused ones (Figs. 1 and 2).

6 Simulation of Data Migration in Hybrid Cloud

Direct implementation and modeling of hybrid cloud is very difficult and expensive in real cloud environment so we chose to use CloudSim Simulator for simulation of

Table 1 Provider parameters

Parameters	Values
No. of data centers	3
No. of hosts	3
VM scheduling policy (const)	Time Shared
Processing Elements	4
MIPS/PE	2400
Cloudlets per min	250
Avg. length of Cloudlets	50,000

Table 2 VM parameters

Parameters	Values
No. of VM	5
Avg. image size	1000
Avg RAM	512 MB
Avg. bandwidth	100,000

performance evaluation of data migration in terms of resource utilization and energy consumption.

The paper analyses two different case studies as follows:

Case 1 : The simulation is carried out in 3 data centers with 2 hosts each and 5 customers with 5 virtual machines each. Thus, the environment we considered was **homogenous environment** [12] (Tables 1 and 2; Graphs 1 and 2; Fig. 3).

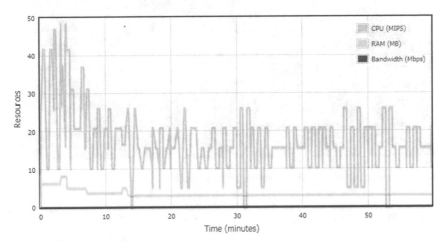

Graph 1 Overall resource utilization of Case 1

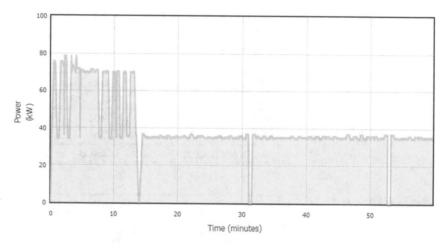

Graph 2 Overall power consumption of Case 1

Fig. 3 Snapshot of data migration technique used in Case 1

Case 2: Where there are four data centers with three hosts in DC1 and DC2 and five customers with ten virtual machines each. Thus, the environment we considered was **heterogeneous**.

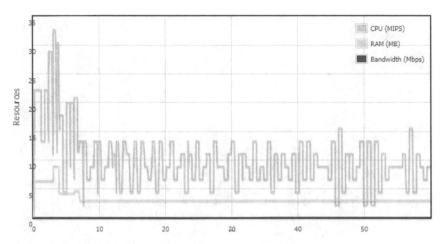

Graph 3 Overall resource utilization of Case 2

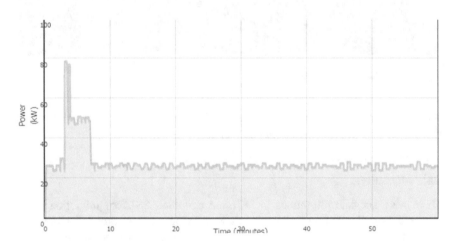

Graph 4 Overall power consumption of Case 2

The provider and VM parameters are as in Case 1. We again collect the performance metrics in the form of overall resource utilization and overall power consumption. The graphs for the same are as follows (Graphs 3 and 4; Fig 4):

7 Results and Discussion

From the above simulation results, we got the graphs for overall resource utilization and overall power consumption of the hybrid cloud while the data migrations are taking place within homogenous and heterogeneous hosts respectively. First, the

Fig. 4 Snapshot of data migration in case 2

consumer request goes to private cloud, and when the threshold is reached, the resource request is redirected to public cloud.

Observations of Case 1:

Data Migrations:

There were six data migrations in DC1 out of which first four migrations were implementing distribution technique and done to increase resource utilization, and the other two were of type consolidation done to reduce power consumption.

Resource Utilization:

The environment was homogenous; the highest value of resource utilization was 45 resources in first ten minutes, and the overall resource consumption was maintained at 20 resources. We could also notice that the RAM utilization increased during first ten minutes and then maintained to be stable.

Power Consumption:

The power consumption in Case 1 reached highest peak at 80 KW in first 10 min, and then, it got reduced and maintained to 38 KW thereafter.

Observations of Case 2:

Data Migrations:

In this case, there were 13 data migrations out of which first 8 were of type distribution and other 5 were of type consolidation.

Resource Utilization:

The environment was homogenous; the highest value of resource utilization was 32 resources in first ten minutes, and the overall resource consumption was maintained at 14 resources. We could also notice that the RAM utilization increased during first ten minutes and then maintained to be stable.

Power Consumption:

The power consumption in Case 2 reached highest peak at 80 KW in first 10 min, and then, it got reduced and maintained to 30 KW thereafter.

8   Conclusions

Interoperability remains an understudied issue in cloud computing. This paper has evaluated the data migration in interoperability under the performance metrics like resource utilization and power consumption. The paper concludes that data migration reduces power consumption where the resource utilization in the form of RAM utilization and other resources also increases substantially. The paper also evaluated the data migration techniques in detail and hence can be concluded the distribution and consolidation techniques are implemented while migrating between different clouds. The paper on evaluation has come to a**n important conclusion that the power consumption and resource utilization are directly proportional**.

The study of data migration with respect to different power models is kept as a future work.

References

1. "CSCC Interoperability and portability for cloud computing a guide," www.cloud-council.org
2. Grance T, Mell P (2009) The NIST definition of cloud computing. National Institute of Standards and Technology, Information Technology Laboratory, 7 Oct 2009
3. Sotiriadis S et al (2013) The inter-cloud meta-scheduling (ICMS) framework. In: IEEE conference on advanced information networking and applications
4. Machado GS, Hausheer D, Stiller B, Considerations on interoperability of and between cloud computing standards
5. Lewis GA (2012) Role of standards in cloud computing interoperability. CMU- SEI 2012
6. Jena S,Vijayraja V, Sahu AK (2016) Performance evaluation of energy efficient power models for digital cloud. Indian J Sci Technol 9(48):2–7, Dec 2016

7. Amudhavel J et al (2016) An empirical analysis of QOS in cloud computing. Indian J Sci Technol 9(22), June 2016
8. Ngenzi A, Selvarani R, Nair S (2015) Dynamic resource management in cloud data cent ers for server consolidation. arXiv.org>cs> arXiv:1505.00577, May 2015
9. Bagheri B, Ghobaei-Arani M (2015) Resource management of IaaSproviders in cloud federation. Int J Grid Distrib Comput 8(5):327–336
10. Javadi B, Abawajy J, Buyya R (2012) Failure-aware resource provisioning for hybrid cloud infrastructure. J Parallel Distrib Comput 72(10):1318–1331
11. Barhate SM, Dhore MP (2015) Data migration issues in cloud computing: a survey. Spec Issue Int J Electron Commun Soft Comput Sci Eng. 360–363, ISSN: 2277-9477
12. Kertesz A, Dombi JD, Benyi A (2015) A pliant-based virtual machine scheduling solution to improve the energy efficiency of IaaS clouds. J Grid Comput 1–13

Secure Management of Digital Academic Certificates Using Blockchain Technology

Anindya Kumar Biswas⬛, Mou Dasgupta, and Sangram Ray

1 Introduction

The usability of blockchain technology is covered in an environment of hype, considering it a relatively newer perception. The foundation of modern cryptocurrencies, a realization, brought about by blockchain as it makes use of heavy cryptographic functions and is tamper resistant and does not depend on any central authority. In general, the underlying basics is that an assemblage of users exist who do not trust each other and also does not want to rely on any middle men for reliable negotiation of transactions. So, blockchain facilitates such a community to keep a record of activities/transactions in a distributed manner. Once published/recorded that particular activity can never be modified without getting caught. If there is any modification, it will be detected. So, it can be considered as a technology which is resilient to attempts in regard to modification attacks.

The emergence of blockchain technology can be attributed to its application in the underlying ledger technology [1] in Bitcoin cryptocurrency system, given by the pseudonym Satoshi Nakamoto. The cryptocurrency system started operating from 2009 onwards. Electronic cash, here, is attached with a digital address and is transmitted from one digital address to another. This is the transaction, and any user of the system, if required, can independently verify it. There existed some electronic cash systems like NetCash, but it never earned widespread use. Although blockchain started as a part of online financial services and also gathered attention in respect of

A. K. Biswas (✉) · M. Dasgupta
Department of Computer Application, National Institute of Technology Raipur, Raipur 492010, India
e-mail: anindya.kr.bws@gmail.com

S. Ray
Department of Computer Science and Engineering, National Institute of Technology Sikkim, Ravangla, Sikkim 737139, India

R. Doriya et al. (eds.), *Machine Learning, Image Processing, Network Security and Data Sciences*, Lecture Notes in Electrical Engineering 946,
https://doi.org/10.1007/978-981-19-5868-7_60

finances, however, there are considerable applications where this technology can give a new yet better direction like Internet of Things (IoT) [2, 3], medicines [4], engineering [5] and education [6, 7]. This has resulted in increased attention from both industry and academics, and huge application prospects are available. One such is the education sector, which has seen renovations in recent years and is still improving.

The candidates who receive the hard copies of various academic certificates from their institutes and recognition certificates from extracurricular activities need to safely store them forever. Being physical quantity, these valuable documents are prone to getting damaged over the course of time, naturally, no matter whatever the precaution taken. An alternative way to achieve peace of mind is to scan them and safely store them. However, when one needs to produce the original certificates somewhere for verification and authentication purposes, those valuable documents (hard copies) need to be taken out and one has to travel the distance to the verification center. Competitors and other mischievous entities might attack and cause permanent and irrecoverable damage to them, resulting in extreme loss to both life and assets. So educational institutes and other organizations can make use of modified blockchain to skillfully tackle this situation, which has the potential to benefit all except adversaries.

This document follows the subsequent organization: Sect. 1 provides introductory framework, Sect. 2 provides the related works in education sectors, Sect. 3 gives the requisite preliminaries, Sect. 4 presents our proposed method, and Sect. 5 finally concludes our research work.

2 Related Works

Applications which are blockchain related can support their division into three phases [8]: (i) blockchain 1.0—the main focus was on financial services like facilitation of simple cash transfer and cryptocurrencies [9], (ii) blockchain 2.0—main focus was on the deployment of smart contracts which enabled fulfillment of automatic criteria and properties and (iii) blockchain 3.0— it opened the door for application development in other sectors like government, education and so on [10]. Blockchain has the potential [11] to be applied in academic domains. However, there are some challenges associated with it [12] in the structure of educational blockchains. Assessment agencies can use services to keep record of learnt data [13] and valuation methods. Despite research in this area, the application deployment is still in rudimentary rungs. Only a handful of institutes have deployed it and that also for sharing students' learning outcomes [14]. Blockchain technology, however, can revolutionize the academics field and probably offer much more. Any educational or allied activities institution can provide with more varied and enhanced learning opportunities instead of just acting as certification agents [15] to students. Getting awarded a certificate is like a digital event in a person's life. This digital event can be made to float throughout the network in a distributed fashion, securely stored by blockchain because of its inherent transparent yet covert nature. Recruitment agencies can utilize its benefit [16] as it makes easier for them and others to access the relevant information [17].

Marks/grades can be stored to provide a convenient access [18]. The core of the system is studied [19], including the backbone and discusses about applications that can be built upon it. Our main application of blockchain is in the education sector.

3 Preliminaries

Over the years, despite various research taking place in development, variations in blockchains were achieved; nonetheless, the core concepts were retained by most. It is a collection of blocks where meta data is stored in block header. Blocks are chained, that is, linked together in a linear fashion resulting in the formation of blockchain. This blockchain is publicly available, that is distributed throughout the entire peer-to-peer network. It consists of evidence, which are assorted chronologically and can access its content if required [20]. However, this chaining of contents in linear manner in its early stages, given by Haber-Stornetta [21]. Here, a part of the first document was linked with the next document. Whenever there was some malicious change in the particular area of first document, the linking from next document onwards would break.

In the bitcoin system, the blockchain is the distributed ledger book, where each block accommodates all the transactions that have taken place during a 10 minute interval. All these transactions, however, are verified before recording it in a block. Despite the fact that everyone can access it, because of the underlying computationally hard problem, none can tamper with it. In the network, there exists devices with very high computation powers. These are known as the miners. The generated transactions are collected together, converted to a $candidate-block$. All the miners compete with each other to now solve the $proof-of-work$. This $proof-of-work$ is used for validation of the $candidate-block.$. Miners, in return, receive payments in BTC (bitcoins, the digital money). As of November, 2012, BTC 50 was the payment for the winning miner. This payment gets reduced to half every four years.

The formation of candidate bock is as follows:

$$candidate-block$$
$$= (\text{Hash}(\text{last block of blockchain})$$
$$(|\text{Merkleroot}(\text{Tx}_{\text{set}})|\text{Timestamp}),$$

where
Tx_{set} is the transactions which have been accumulated during a 10 minute interval,
Merkleroot(Tx_{set}) is the root of the Merkle hash tree, and
Timestamp is the moment when the block was formed.

A transaction $\in Tx_{\text{set}}$ constitutes sender'ss address, the receiver's address and states the amount in BTC, to be transmitted/given. The address of both the sender and the receiver is represented by public keys, which in turn represent the digital wallets.

The content of a single transaction is: $[wallet_{PU_A} sends\ Q\ bitcoins\ to\ wallet_{PU_B}]$, where A is the sender and B is the receiver and PU_A and PU_B are their respective public keys. In order to solve the $proof-of-work$, all the interested miners compete to obtain a value $U = Hash(candidate-block|nonce)$, by changing the value of nonce. This is the BTC hard problem, where different values of U are continuously found out by modifying the parameter nonce. The U should be less than a prespecified value which is followed by some zeros. The hash function employed here is the $SHA-256$ which outputs 64 hexadecimal digits or 256 bits.

Our proposed method demonstrates the way in which blockchain can be made an important part of academic institutions like smart education and smart certificate management system.

4 Proposed Method

Here, we give our proposed method which can enable not only institutes but also recruitment agencies to become smarter, resulting in benefit to candidates. Each institution will create and maintain its own blockchain containing record of all the certificates issued to its candidates, forever. Any concerned entity can access this secure archive of records whenever the need arises. The consensus functions including the $proof-of-work$ will be taken care of by some designated systems ($miners$) deployed by the involved establishments/organizations. However, this necessitates indispensable modifications/implementations on blockchain and is performed by keeping in mind the specific application domain. So, our proposed $genesis$ block, general block and the method/scheme are presented below. Hash function used in our method would be the cryptographic $Hash-256$.

4.1 Our Proposed Genesis Block Structure

Our smart education system, which incorporates smart certificate management, including its issuance, requires a modified $genesis$ block. Each institute/university will have its own $genesis$ block. Each $genesis$ block can link to multiple organization specific blockchains. This block should be able to properly recognize an institute, the courses offered, valid certificates along with the associated public key. All this is done to prevent spread of false information and forgery. Each institute's own $genesis$ block and the demarcation will be based on difference in verifiable yet secure parameter values.

The proposed configuration is as follows:

It contains the following fields:

(i) RC_{Ins}: Registration Certificate of the Institute with Government body depicting the institutes validity and legality to impart education.

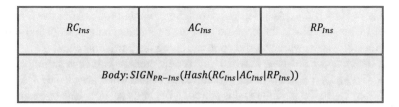

Fig. 1 Proposed genesis block

(ii) AC_{Ins}: The Authentication Certificate of the Institute which helps verify its *private−public* key pairs, including its validity period. This digital certificate is issued from a registered Key Generation Centre (KGC).

(iii) RP_{Ins} : Registered Programs of the Institute provides a list of approved courses, their identification numbers, that the institute can impart to its students. This field also contains the various blockchains (based on courses) linked to this genesis block.

(iv) $SIGN_{PR} - Ins$: It refers to the signature performed using the private key $PR - Ins$ of the concerned institute. A different institute will have different Ins value.

A block, part of a chain, would now be linked to this *genesis* block (Fig. 1).

4.2   *Our Proposed General* **Block** *Structure*

There will exist multiple blockchains depending on separate courses like Bachelor of Technology (B. Tech.), Master of Technology (M. Tech.), Master of Computer Applications (MCA.), Ph. D. and others. Each organization can have its own set of multiple blockchains, depending on registered programs/courses offered by the respective establishments.

Our general block diagram structure is provided in Fig. 2.

The following fields are there in our modified block:

(i) RPI_{id}: The course ID linked with the Registered Program of the Institute.

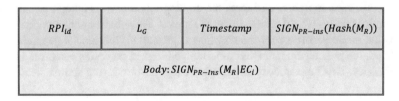

Fig. 2 Our proposed single block structure

(ii) $L_G = \text{Hash}(\text{RC}_{\text{Ins}}|\text{AC}_{\text{Ins}}|\text{RP}_{\text{Ins}})$, from the *genesis* block. After the formation of 1st general block, there would be some parameter changes from 2nd general block onwards, which would continue along the particular chain.

(iii) *Timestamp* : The time at which this (or any general) block is getting created.

(iv) $SIGN_{PR-Ins}$: It refers to the signature performed using private key $PR - Ins$ belonging to the institute and is stored in the body section. The corresponding public key $PU - Ins$ can be obtained from the AC_{Ins} field of the *genesis* block.

(v) M_R: It is the *Merkleroot* of the Merkle hash tree [22], constructed using EC_i, taking two at a time.

(vi) EC_i: It contains all the electronic certificates, for $i = 1, 2, 3, \ldots, n$, that have been issued during one semester, that is, a duration of *six* months. These details are by default encrypted. Decryption needs the corresponding public key. The blockchain would be periodically checked, once every week to ensure integrity is maintained.

The 2nd block, that is, the first block after the *genesis* block is linked using the parameter L_G. The rest of the blocks, that is, from 3rd block onwards (or 2nd block after the *genesis* block, onwards) in the chain would be chronologically linked linearly using modified L_G as $L_P = \text{Hash}(L_{P_j}|\text{Timestamp}|M_R|\text{nonce})$, L_{P_j} is the selected contents of the previous block. For the 1st block, $L_{P_j} = L_G$ derived from the *genesis* block, for the 2nd block, $L_{P_2} = L_{P_1}$ derived from the 1st block and so on. For every 6 months elapsed, a new block would be generated for all the separate streamwise chains (however, integrity check would take place every week). The requirement of *nonce* cannot be underestimated as it helps generate randomized hash values. As the miners are internal to the organization/institute, so, there exists proper coordination and block formation is synchronized. Each generated block is associated with a timestamp (Fig. 2).

In our method, during the process of block formation, we make some modifications in hash formation. Any random *nonce* > 1 will do as we eliminate the requirement to generate any specific hash values. So, it does not matter if any generated hash gets some leading zeros or not. We do this to reduce the computation time and resources. This results in faster and secure block formation. As there are multiple miners (depends on institute) and there exists no need for a specific nonce, so, the opportunity of nonce generation by a particular miner is dependent on the token. The token rotates among the miner nodes in a circular fashion. The node that acquires it generates a random nonce, and then, the cryptographic hash is computed. The rest of the miner nodes would now validate the nonce. There exist archive nodes which stores the entire record of all the certificates generated, the blocks generated and validated, the nonce generated and timestamped logs of activities performed by the miner nodes. This helps rectify any internal irregularities during audits.

4.3   Our Proposed Method and Discussions

The formation of a block, its validation, will proceed as presented in the Sect. 4.2. The certified institutional miners will work together for validation and verification purposes, however, independently for nonce generation. For each blockchain, the 1st field of the header in general block (Fig. 2) will be according to the data stored in RP_{Ins} field of the *genesis* block (Fig. 1). The contents of the first two fields of the header in this block, pre-validates the entire chain structure as well as the issuing organization.

There will be multiple blockchains linked to a single *genesis* block established as per the different streams/courses offered. An interested entity needs adherence to the following:

(i)   If in doubt, the legal existence of any organization can be ascertained. This is because the *genesis* block contains data which can be cross-checked with government records.

(ii)   Find out information about the candidate's present institution or from where qualification/achievement certificates/documents have been obtained.

(iii)   Then access to the institute-specific *genesis* block, see the relevant information like validity, course offered and its id, etc. Based on the obtained information in the 3rd field of the header (Fig. 1), the stream/course ID is obtained. This would provide access to the appropriate streamwise blockchain. This drastically reduces searching time.

(iv)   Now, from the obtained/accessed blockchain, the relevant information can be extracted, like students' information, courses on going and already completed. As record is available in secured, digital and tamperproof format, so it is reliable. Public key would be required for decrypting the relevant information.

If there is a need to access records of multiple streams, then accordingly the relevant information, that is, multiple IDs' based on different streams is to be extracted from the 3rd field in the header of *genesis* block and the process followed, providing access to multiple blockchains instead of just one. This allows interoperability among multi-chains.

The overall structure of the implementation would be as shown in Fig. 3. There is only one genesis block per institute and multiple blockchains linked to it. Each of the chains represents a separate discipline/stream of academic activities containing multiple blocks as $b1, b2, \ldots, so\ on$. An institute can be in possession of k different blockchains if they have k government approved courses and so on.

In our method, although the blockchains are separate, they are linked, like having a common root. Each organization can modify this multi chain structure as per its suitability. The genesis block helps provide interoperability among the various chains of this system. The genesis block stores information in the RP_{Ins} field regarding the number of linked chains. So, one can traverse any of the linked chains.

Although it is not possible, however, hypothetically if an adversary is somehow able to modify some contents of any block, then it would get easily detected as

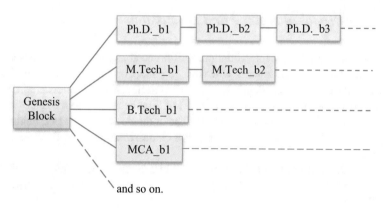

Fig. 3 Our proposed multi-blockchain structure

the chain would cease to hold together, that is, the link would break resulting in easy visibility of malicious activity. In such instances, the concerned institute can reconstruct back the original and error free chain from the data stored in the archive nodes. The contents in the archive nodes are safe as external access to it is not available.

The miners here are not required to be high-end nodes/systems deployed by the institute itself. Therefore, it can be safely assumed that at 100% of the time, all the deployed nodes operated would be non-biased. Also, weekly integrity checks enforce security and eliminate any possibility of forgery taking place. As the entire management is internal, external malicious influences does not make it biased.

5 Conclusion

The advancements and the potentials unlocked by blockchain have resulted in more creative ways of its deployment. Educational sector can surely benefit from it. The traditional academic ideologies are gradually being frowned upon and alternate and smarter ways are being progressively inducted. In this work, we propose efficient and capable methods of blockchain deployment in the academic domain, especially in the field of digital certificate management. Our work provides a smarter yet secured way to keep record of validated and authenticated certificates in a chronological manner and can surely benefit parties belonging to different domains. By our method, verification and on-demand access become a reality. An adversary can never modify the contents illegally, because any modification is always involving very high computation power. Our method also incorporates way to establish any organizations' authority to manage digital certificates.

References

1. Nakamoto S (2008) Bitcoin: A peer-to-peer electronic cash system 2008. https://bitcoin.org/bitcoin.pdf
2. Zhang Y, Wen J (2016) The IOT electric business model: Using blockchain technology for the internet of things. In: Peer-to-Peer networking and applications, pp 1–12
3. Dorri A, Kanhere SS, Jurdak R, Gauravaram P (2017) Blockchain for iot security and privacy: The case study of a smart home. In: IEEE Percom workshop on security privacy and trust in the internet of thing
4. Yue X, Wang H, Jin D, Li M, Jiang W (2016) Healthcare data gateways: Found healthcare intelligence on blockchain with novel privacy risk control. J Med Syst 218
5. Xu X, Pautasso C, Zhu L, Gramoli V, Ponomarev A, Tran AB, Chen S (2016) The blockchain as a software connector. In: The 13th working IEEE/IFIP conference on software architecture
6. Sousa MJ, Machado AdB (2020) Blockchain technology reshaping education: contributions for policy. In: Blockchain technology applications in education. IGI Global, pp. 113–125
7. Al-Barrak A (2020) Workshop 2 Blockchain in education. In: 2020 6th international engineering conference "sustainable technology and development" (IEC). IEEE, pp 242–242
8. Gatteschi V, Lamberti F, Demartini C, Pranteda C, Santamaría V (2018) Blockchain and smart contracts for insurance: Is the technology mature enough? Future Internet 10:20
9. Biswas AK, Dasgupta M (2020) Bitcoin cryptocurrency: its cryptographic weaknesses and remedies. Asia Pac J Inf Syst 30(1):21–30. https://doi.org/10.1109/ICPC2T48082.2020.9071470
10. Biswas AK, Dasgupta M (2021) Blockchain enabled and changeable threshold-based group specific multiple keys' negotiation. In: Sabut SK, Ray AK, Pati B, Acharya UR (eds) Proceedings of international conference on communication, circuits, and systems. Lecture Notes in Electrical Engineering, vol 728. Springer, Singapore. https://doi.org/10.1007/978-981-33-4866-0_18
11. Collins R (2016) Blockchain: a new architecture for digital content. EContent 39:22–23
12. Yang X, Li X, Wu H, Zhao K (2017) Application model and realistic challenge of blockchain technology in education. Mod distance Educ Res 2:34-45
13. Mike S, John D (2016) The blockchain and Kudos: a distributed system for educational record reputation and reward. In: Mike S, Katrien V, Tomazeds K (eds) Proceedings of European conference on technology enhanced learning (EC-TEL 2016)
14. Chen G, Xu B, Lu M, Chen N-S (2018) Exploring blockchain technology and its potential applications for education. Smart Learn Environ 5:1
15. Nespor J (2018) Cyber schooling and the accumulation of school time. Pedag Cult Soc 2:1–17
16. Chen G, Xu B, Lu M, Chen N-S (2018) Exploring blockchain technology and its potential applications for education. Smart Learn Environ 5(1):1
17. Turkanović M, Hölbl M, Košič K, Heričko M, Kamišalić A (2018) EduCTX: a blockchain-based higher education credit platform. IEEE Access 6:5112–5127
18. Rooksby J (2017) Trustless education? A blockchain system for university grades. In: New value transactions: understanding and designing for distributed autonomous organisations, workshop, DIS 2017, June 2017, p 4
19. Garay J, Kiayias A, Leonardos N (2015) The bitcoin backbone protocol: analysis and applications. In: International conferences on the theory and applications of cryptographic techniques, vol. 9057. LNCS, pp 281–310
20. Antonopoulos AM (2014) Mastering bitcoin: Unlocking digital cryptocurrencies, 1st edn. O'Reilly Media, Inc., Sebastopol, CA, USA
21. Haber S, Scott Stornetta W (1991) How to time-stamp a digital document. J Cryptol 3(2):99–111. https://doi.org/10.1007/BF00196791
22. Merkle RC (1979) Secrecy, authentication and public key systems, Ph.D. thesis, Stanford University, Stanford, CA, USA, 1979. Available at: https://www.merkle.com/papers/Thesis1979.pdf

Tracking of Fall Detection Using IMU Sensor: An IoHT Application

Vijay Bhaskar Semwal, Abhishek Kumar, Pankaj Nargesh, and Vaibhav Soni

1 Introduction

1.1 Overview

Generally, human beings have bounded fall recovery capability [1]. This fall recovery depends on various factors like your mental toughness, physical strength, and gender [2]. It gets affected by the energy level of subjects, working environment condition, physical walking condition, and age [3]. These all factors are an important measure to assess human health and their mental status [4]. Fall recovery is a reflexive learning process in which motor neurons are used to learn this behavior with continuous interaction with the environment. [5, 6]. The neurological behavior which is very important to affect the fall recovery used to get affected due to aging, stroke, and some abnormality in the neural system [7, 8]. So, fall recovery and walking analysis are considered important parameters to assist human health [9], to design the assistive technologies [10], various bipedal robotic applications [11], and rehabilitation exercises [12].

Elderly subjects are susceptible to get impacted by external forces. In a human habitual environment, when they are alone at home, they may lose balance performing various activities of daily life such as walking, standing, and jogging [13, 14]. Due to fall, the impact could be very severe which can ultimately lead to an untimely death, loss of memory, multiple injuries or permanent disabilities [15]. To overcome this, fall diagnosis methodology has been developed using an inertial measurement unit (IMU) sensor which can trace them throughout the day with a low-power computing device [16].

V. B. Semwal (✉) · A. Kumar · P. Nargesh · V. Soni
MANIT Bhopal, Bhopal, India
e-mail: vsemwal@manit.ac.in

© The Author(s), under exclusive license to Springer Nature Singapore Pte Ltd. 2023   815
R. Doriya et al. (eds.), *Machine Learning, Image Processing, Network Security and Data Sciences*, Lecture Notes in Electrical Engineering 946,
https://doi.org/10.1007/978-981-19-5868-7_61

Various mobile-based devices are used for data collection in the past [17]. This research has utilized the IMU sensor available with a smartphone to collect the data. Through IMU sensor, the data of linear accelerometer, angular velocity, and orientation are captured for 20 subjects. The androsensor [18] is used as an interface to present and visualize data collected through the sensor.

1.2 Our Contribution

- In this research, we have collected data to identify the human fall recovery behavior in six different categories which are named as follows: normal standing, normal walk, normal run, stand fall, fall during walking, & fall during running.
- With the collected data, we have tried to capture four different postures: before the fall, during the fall, after the fall, and recovery or no recovery from the fall.
- The same experimental setup was utilized to capture human walking trajectories to trace the elderly subjects, trespassers, and their activities.
- The deep learning model is designed to classify the activities into fall or no-fall categories. Four deep learning models, namely convolutional neural network (CNN), LSTM, gated recurrent unit (GRU), CNN + LSTM, are trained on the collected data. The highest accuracy is achieved by LSTM model. For fall detection, the LSTM model has the highest f1-score of 90.48%, and it has recall of 95.00%.
- Apart from these, we have provided 3D plots for fall activities from the data collected through the accelerometer.

2 Literature Review of Related Works

2.1 Related Works

Extensive research has been done in gait analysis and push recovery. Initially, researchers have used a computer vision-based approach, environment-interactive sensor-based approach, and wearable sensor-based approach for data collection [19, 20]. Semwal et al. 2019 have proposed a mobile-based technique to capture the data [21]. However, they have only considered accelerometer data. They have achieved very good performance. Extensive models are created by employing machine learning models [22]. In [17] have collected data of IMU as well as of barometric altimeter located in the lower back. Mekruksavanich et al. have presented work on the gait pattern classification of the wearable sensor using machine learning model [24]. Some recent work of deep learning & machine learning models of wearable sensors reading for gait activity, fall diagnosing & person tracking are listed in these work [25–29].

3 Preliminaries

Deep learning has many good models to be applied on time series data [30, 31]. But, each model has its pros and cons. We have applied many different models, namely CNN [32], LSTM, GRU.

The CNN is good at learning the spatial information in the dataset and computationally cheaper than RNN. The CNN computations can be parallelized as it learns by batch, but RNN computations can not be parallelized as it trains sequentially, and it must wait for the previous computation [33].

The main difference between GRU and LSTM is that GRU uses only two gates to solve the gradient exploding/vanishing problem, while LSTM uses three gates, namely input gate, output gate, & forget gate. That is why GRU is less intricate than LSTM.

4 Proposed Methodology

4.1 Dataset Acquisition

20 persons(13 men + 7 women) volunteered for recording their activities like walking, running, falling during walking, and falling during running. The ethical committee of the institute approved the experiment protocol, and all participants signed the informed consent. We have used the IMU sensor that comes with the smartphone. The IMU sensor was placed on the human center of mass, i.e., navel. Data were collected for each person walking for 500 m. We collected data for fall recovery during another walk for 500 m. Similarly, data were collected for running, standing, and falling. The description of subjects involved in collecting dataset is given in Table 1. The process of collecting data is shown in Fig. 1. In Fig. 1a , the smartphone is placed on the navel of the subject and in Fig. 1b, the subject is falling (Fig. 2).

4.2 Dataset Preprocessing

The information is gathered by IMU sensors. Because collected data can have a wide range of scales and distributions, each variable may have a different scale and

Table 1 Subject health parameters

Sex	Age	Height	Weight
Male	35 ± 10	167 ± 10 cm	69.8–80.0
Female	33 ± 10	161 ± 10 cm	67.7–72.8

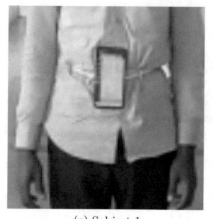
(a) Subject 1

(b) Subject 1 falling

Fig. 1 IMU placed on navel

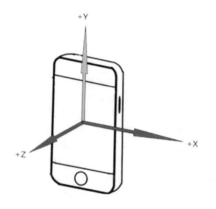
(a) IMU Co-ordinates

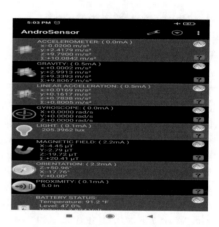
(b) Androsensor layout

Fig. 2 Smart phone-based IMU senor

distribution. Differences in scales in input variables may make the problem more complex to model. The mapping from input variables to output variables is learned by a deep learning model. We should preprocess the data in one of two ways before feeding this to the deep neural network. These are the following methods.

- Data Normalization
- Data Standardization

4.2.1 Data Normalization

Normalization means re-scaling the original range of the data within the range of 0 and 1. For this, we must know or estimate the actual minimum and maximum value in the original data. The equation of normalization is following.

$$ay = (ax - \text{min})/(\text{max} - \text{min}) \tag{1}$$

where max is maximum value, min is minimum value, ax is the data point, and ay is the normalized output value.

4.2.2 Data Standardization

Standardization is the process through which we re-scale the distribution of data such that mean of the observed values becomes 0 and the standard deviation becomes 1. It assumes that the data follow Gaussian distribution, i.e., bell curve. It requires the mean and standard deviation of the observable values. The equation of standardization is given below.

$$ay = (ax - \text{mean})/\text{standard\_deviation} \tag{2}$$

where mean is calculated as

$$\text{mean} = \text{sum}(ax)/\text{count}(ax) \tag{3}$$

where standard deviation is calculated as

$$standard\_deviation = \sqrt{sum((ax - mean)^2)/count(ax))} \tag{4}$$

The data are subtracted from the mean in the numerator is called centering, and dividing by standard deviation is called scaling. Combing both methods, it is called center scaling.

The extracted and preprocessed data are then divided into three sets: training, validation, and testing, on which various classification methods are applied.

4.3 Data Presentation

Figures 3, 4, and 5 shows the accelerometer data for all three category with fall and without fall. A fall event can be characterized by four stages: start, impact, post-impact, and posture, which can be well interpreted from the vertical acceleration pattern generated from smartphones placed on the navel of subjects. We can infer from the figures that the z-axis has the highest variation among all axis in linear

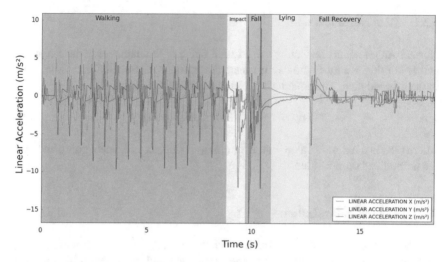

Fig. 3 Accelerometer data for walking with fall

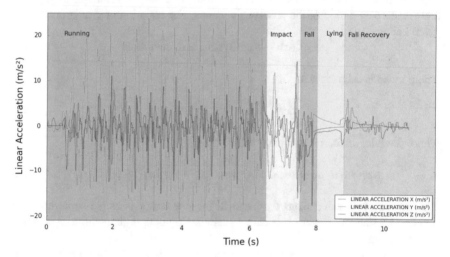

Fig. 4 Accelerometer data for running with fall

acceleration on the impact. We can observe that the acceleration in pre-impact is periodic. But, there is a sudden spike in acceleration value on the impact.

4.4 Proposed Architecture

We have implemented various deep learning architectures in the experiment. Since the workflow of the experiment is almost the same for all deep learning techniques,

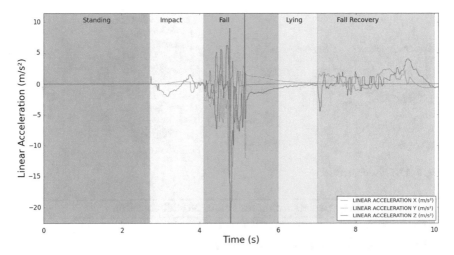

Fig. 5 Accelerometer data for fall during standing

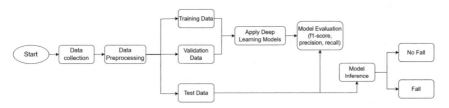

Fig. 6 Workflow of architecture

the workflow is shown in Fig. 6. First, we collect the data; we do data preprocessing as it can increase the quality of data. As real-world data contain noise, missing values, and this may directly affect the efficiency of proposed deep learning models. After this, we do data splitting and apply the models. We evaluate the model on various metrics on test data. Though we have applied 5 models on our data, here, we are presenting the best model architecture that gave the best result. The LSTM and CNN+LSTM gave the best recall value and f1-score for fall detection (see Table 2). The LSTM architecture is given Fig. 7.

4.5 Proposed Algorithm

The details of the proposed work are shown in algorithm 1. Original datasets are used as input in algorithm 1, and the output is measured in terms of precision, f1-score, recall, and classification accuracy. Accelerometer measurements are represented by a_x, a_y, & a_z; gyroscope readings are represented by g_x, g_y, & g_z, and orientation readings are represented by o_x, o_y, & o_z.

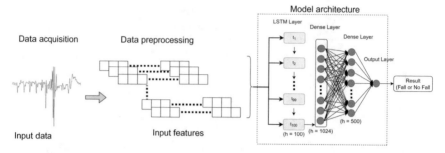

Fig. 7 LSTM architecture

Algorithm 1: Proposed algorithm for Fall or No-fall detection

---

Result: Fall recovery of person using IMU sensor with precision, f1 score, recall and classification accuracy

Input: Raw data collected through 9-degree IMU Sensor;

Output: Classification accuracy, precision, recall & f1 score;

Procedure;

Step 1: Extract the features from raw data using 9-degree IMU sensor.

    1.1 Accelerometer reading are represented using a_x, a_y, & a_z;

    1.2 Gyroscope reading are represented by g_x, g_y, & g_z;

    1.3 Orientation reading are represented by o_x, o_y, & o_z ;

    1.4 Stored the extracted data in to two data-set with respect to fall and no-fall category. ;

Step 2: Apply sliding window and then append the data of each subject corresponding to each features.

    2.1 Prepare samples of the data with sliding window size of sampling frequency i.e., 119 Hz.;

    2.2 Store the labeled records and the corresponding output of last step.;

Step 3: Normalise and standardize the data.

    3.1 Normalisation equation $y = \frac{x - min}{max - min}$

where, y, x, max and min represents output, input data, maximum value and minimum value in data-set.;

    3.2 Standardization Equation $y = \frac{x - mean}{sd}$

where y, x, $mean$, sd represent output, input data, mean of the observable value, standard deviation respectively. ;

Step 4: Shuffle and split the data-set into training set, validation set and testing set.;

Step 5: Apply deep learning algorithm, namely DNN, CNN, LSTM GRU & CNN+LSTM models on the Data-set.;

Step 6: Generate and store obtained classification accuracy, precision, recall & f1 score;

Step 7: Repeat Step 5 and Step 6 by applying other Deep learning algorithms from the list mentioned in Step 5;

---

5 Results and Discussions

5.1 Observation from Data

The result of various models is provided in this section. Precision, recall, f1-score, and accuracy of predicted results of different models are given in Table 2. The 3D plot of dataset is presented in Figs. 8, 9 and 10.

Table 2 Model precision, recall, & f1-score on the test data

Model	Accuracy (in %)	Recall (in %)		Precision (in %)		f1-score (in %)	
		No-fall	Fall	No-fall	Fall	No-fall	Fall
DNN	84.21	85.00	82.35	91.89	70.00	88.31	75.68
LSTM	92.98	97.14	86.36	91.89	95.00	94.44	90.48
CNN	91.22	97.06	82.60	89.18	95.00	92.95	88.37
CNN+LSTM	91.23	94.44	85.71	91.89	90.00	91.15	87.80
GRU	82.46	82.93	81.25	91.89	65.00	87.18	72.22

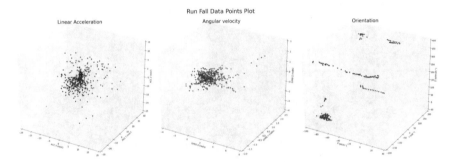

Fig. 8 Run fall in 3D plot

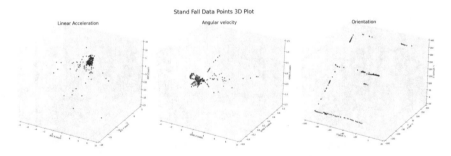

Fig. 9 Stand fall in 3D plot

5.2 Performance Measurement Analysis

The performance of various models has been presented in the last section. This section analyzes the models on the various evaluation metrics listed above. The best metric is the combination of recall and precision, i.e., f1-measure. From the table 2 of models, it can be inferred that LSTM has the highest f1-score for predicting the fall. CNN+LSTM has the highest recall value for no-fall. It is good to have a high recall value for no-fall so that events like the accidental opening of airbags can be avoided. The confusion matrix of the LSTM model is given in Fig. 12 (Fig. 11).

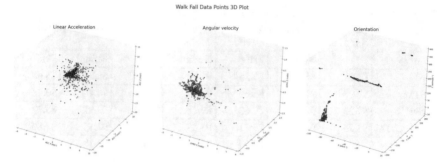

Fig. 10 Walk fall in 3D plot

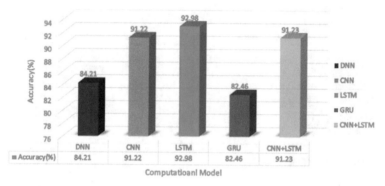

Fig. 11 Accuracy of different models

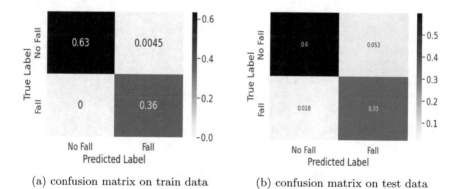

(a) confusion matrix on train data   (b) confusion matrix on test data

Fig. 12 Confusion matrix of LSTM

6 Conclusion, Limitation and Future Research Direction

6.1 Conclusions

The low-cost IoHT system has been designed to detect fall during daily life activities. 20 subjects were considered. 3 different categories walk, stand, and run are being considered for experiment purposes. A clear boundary is drawn between the fall and no-fall categories. The contribution of the vertical component of accelerometer reading is used. The deep learning model has provided quite promising results. The CNN+LSTM and LSTM model has provided the best accuracy of 91.23 and 92.98 %.

6.2 Limitation and Future Research Direction

The future extension of the proposed work can help in the design of a low-cost IoHT device to support edge computing by fusing a compressed deep leaning model. The finding can be utilized to design the bipedal robot with push recovery capability. It can also integrate with brain driven system design.

References

1. Semwal VB et al (2013) Study of humanoid Push recovery based on experiments. In: 2013 international conference on control, automation, robotics and embedded systems (CARE). IEEE
2. Semwal VB et al (2015) Biologically-inspired push recovery capable bipedal locomotion modeling through hybrid automata. Robot Auton Syst 70:181–190
3. Gupta A et al (2020) Multiple task human gait analysis and identification: ensemble learning approach. Emot Inf Process 185–197
4. Semwal VB et al (2015) Toward developing a computational model for bipedal push recovery-a brief. IEEE Sens J 15(4):2021–2022. Semwal VB (2017) Data driven computational model for bipedal walking and push recovery. arXiv preprint arXiv:1710.06548
5. Semwal VB et al (2016) Generation of joint trajectories using hybrid automate-based model: a rocking block-based approach. IEEE Sens J 16(14):5805–5816
6. Bijalwan V, Semwal VB, Singh G, Crespo RG (2022) Heterogeneous computing model for post-injury walking pattern restoration and postural stability rehabilitation exercise recognition. Exp Syst 39(6):e12706
7. Patil P et al (2019) Clinical human gait classification: extreme learning machine approach. In: 1st international conference on advances in science, engineering and robotics technology 2019 (ICASERT 2019)
8. Hsu WC, Sugiarto T, Lin YJ, Yang FC, Lin ZY, Sun CT, Hsu CL, Chou KN (2018) Multiple-wearable-sensor-based gait classification and analysis in patients with neurological disorders. Sens (Basel). 18(10):3397. PMID: 30314269; PMCID: PMC6210399. https://doi.org/10.3390/s18103397
9. Raj M et al (2018) Hybrid model for passive locomotion control of a biped humanoid: the artificial neural network approach. Int J Interact Multimedia Artif Intell 5(1):40–46

10. Nandi GC et al (2016) Modeling bipedal locomotion trajectories using hybrid automata. In: 2016 IEEE region 10 conference (TENCON). IEEE
11. Semwal VB et al (2013) Biped model based on human Gait pattern parameters for sagittal plane movement. In: 2013 international conference on control, automation, robotics and embedded systems (CARE). IEEE
12. Jain R et al (2021) Deep ensemble learning approach for lower extremity activities recognition using wearable sensors. Expert system, Wiley
13. Challa SK, Kumar A, Semwal VB (2021) A multibranch CNN-BiLSTM model for human activity recognition using wearable sensor data. Vis Comput 1–15
14. Dua N, Singh SN, Semwal VB (2021) Multi-input CNN-GRU based human activity recognition using wearable sensors. Computing 1–18
15. Ren L, Peng Y (2019) Research of fall detection and fall prevention technologies: a systematic review, in IEEE Access 7:77702–77722. https://doi.org/10.1109/ACCESS.2019.2922708
16. Bijalwan V, Semwal VB, Mandal TK (2021) Fusion of multi-sensor based biomechanical gait analysis using vision and wearable sensor. IEEE Sens J
17. Semwal VB et al (2017) Robust and accurate feature selection for humanoid push recovery and classification: deep learning approach. Neural Comput Appl 28(3):565–574
18. Fiv Asim (2015) AndroSensor(v1. 9. 6. 3)[Mobile app]. App store http://www.fivasim.comandrosensor.html
19. Gupta JP et al (2014) Analysis of gait pattern to recognize the human activities. Int J Interact Multimedia Artif Intell 2(7):7–16
20. Semwal VB et al (2016) Design of vector field for different subphases of gait and regeneration of gait pattern. IEEE Trans Autom Sci Eng 15(1):104–110
21. Raj M et al (2019) Multiobjective optimized bipedal locomotion. Int J Mach Learn Cybern 10(8):1997–2013
22. Semwal VB et al (2019) Speed, cloth and pose invariant gait recognition-based person identification. Mach Learn Theor Found Pract Appl 39
23. Semwal VB et al (2015) Less computationally intensive fuzzy logic (type-1)-based controller for humanoid push recovery. Robot Auton Syst 63:122–135
24. Mekruksavanich S et al (2019) Classification of gait pattern with wearable sensing data. In: 2019 joint international conference on digital arts, media and technology with ecti northern section conference on electrical, electronics, computer and telecommunications engineering (ECTI DAMT-NCON), Nan, Thailand, pp 137–141
25. Semwal VB et al (2019) Human gait state prediction using cellular automata and classification using ELM. Mach Intell Signal Anal 135–145
26. Semwal VB et al (2021) Pattern identification of different human joints for different human walking styles using inertial measurement unit (IMU) sensor. Artif Intell Rev 1–21
27. Semwal VB et al (2021) An optimized feature selection using bio-geography optimization technique for human walking activities recognition. Computing 1–22
28. Semwal VB, Singha J, Sharma PK, Chauhan A, Behera B (2017) An optimized feature selection technique based on incremental feature analysis for bio-metric gait data classification. Multimedia Tools Appl 76(22): 24457–24475
29. Raj M et al (2018) Bidirectional association of joint angle trajectories for humanoid locomotion: the restricted Boltzmann machine approach. Neural Comput Appl 30(6):1747–1755
30. Bijalwan V, Semwal VB, Gupta V (2021) Wearable sensor-based pattern mining for human activity recognition: deep learning approach. Ind Robot Int J Rob Res Appl
31. Semwal VB, Gupta A, Lalwani P (2021) An optimized hybrid deep learning model using ensemble learning approach for human walking activities recognition. J Supercomput 1–24
32. Zebin T, Scully PJ, Ozanyan KB (2016) Human activity recognition with inertial sensors using a deep learning approach. In: 2016 IEEE Sensors. IEEE
33. Ronao CA, Cho S-B (2016) Human activity recognition with smartphone sensors using deep learning neural networks. Exp Syst Appl 59:235–244

Avenues of Graph Theoretic Approach of Analysing the LIDAR Data for Point-To-Point Floor Exploration by Indoor AGV

Rapti Chaudhuri, Jashaswimalya Acharjee, and Suman Deb

1 Introduction

Indoor robots have been in field for solving a lot of challenging works whether it is support, rescue or exploration. Mostly, indoor robots are the GPS or reference sensor-denied. So, primarily the robot depends on first hand sensor data for analysing proximity or measuring distance from the on-path obstacles. Detecting that obstacle, the robot needs to avoid it and explore free path to reach a specified goal point. Complete coverage path planning (CCPP) algorithms mainly focus on determining optimal path taking obstacles in consideration [1].

Figure 1 exemplifies the working structure of point-to-point robot, where the trajectory of the robot is shown achieved by smoothing operation compared to the actual path through the obstacles. CCPP approaches focuses on navigation coverage in an unknown ambiguous environment. Due to limitations in sensor reading, sometimes difficulties need to be faced in getting the optimal solution with complete workspace coverage. The standard path planning approaches in clude A*, rapidly exploring random trees (RRT), RRT*, artificial potential fields (APF), Voronoi diagram, Dijkstra, Bug Algorithm, cell decomposition approach, etc. Biologically inspired natural selection processes include some of the path planning algorithms like genetic algorithm [2], ant colony and Firefly Algorithm. Table 1 presents theoretical comparison between some commonly used graph theoretic path planning algorithms with space and time complexity. Each algorithm is analysed based on its advantages and disadvantages with respect to path planning strategy and obstacle types detected.

R. Chaudhuri (✉) · J. Acharjee · S. Deb
National Institute of Technology Agartala, Agartala, India
e-mail: chaudhurirapti@gmail.com

© The Author(s), under exclusive license to Springer Nature Singapore Pte Ltd. 2023
R. Doriya et al. (eds.), *Machine Learning, Image Processing, Network Security and Data Sciences*, Lecture Notes in Electrical Engineering 946,
https://doi.org/10.1007/978-981-19-5868-7_62

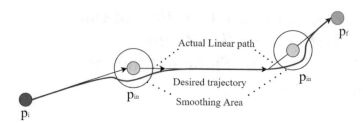

Fig. 1 initial p_i and final goal point p_f with intermediate points p_{in} showing the actual path of the robot movement and desired trajectory covering the smoothing area avoiding intermediate points

Table 1 Theoretical comparison of various path planning algorithms

Method	Advantage	Disadvantage	Path planning	Obstacle type	Space–Time complexity
A* algorithm [2]	Fast, Good Heuristic	Result path tends to stay near obstacles	Smooth, low path cost	Static	$O(b^d)$, $b =$ branching factor, $d =$ depth
RRT algorithm [7]	Fast	No clear guarantee	High path cost, not smooth	Static, dynamic	O(n) & O(nlogn)
Artificial potential field (APF) [15]	Simple, fast convergence	Not-complete, high modelling cost	Not smooth, medium cost	Static, dynamic	$O(MD)$, M = number of nodes, D = Dimension of space
Genetic algorithm (GA) [2]	complete, easy	Complexity increases with dynamicity	Smooth, collision-free, optimized cost	Static, dynamic	O(g(nm + nm + n)), g = number of generations, n = population size, m = size of individual
Voronoi [16]	Guaranteed path clearance	Result path is not smooth	Higher cost	Static	$O((n^2)(\log n))$
Bug [16]	Simple	Slow	Low path cost, not smooth	Static, dynamic	
Vector field histogram (VFH) [16]	Comparatively effective	Less clearance	Smooth, highest cost	Static, dynamic	
Dijkstra's algorithm [2]	Optimal path	Slow and without clearance guarantee	Smooth, low cost	Dynamic	$O(V^2)$ V = vertices in graph

2　Related Work

In the work, [3] presents the new approach of path planning technique in which the virtual size of the obstacle is assumed to be increased approximately $(2n + 1)$ times of the size of the cell. The proposed method reduces chances of collision.

The study [4] proposed genetic algorithm for global path planning by mobile robots. The study [5] proposed A* Algorithm for robotic vehicle navigation system with its optimality and complexity of working. The study [6] proposes robot path planning using turning point algorithm. This proposed algorithm handles two different objectives-path safety and the path length in known environment. The study [7] presents a new approach cell-based bi-directional rapidly exploring random trees (CellBiRRT) for manipulator motion able to handle pose constraints and to operate in difficult environments reducing chances of collision. The study [8] proposed ERRT algorithm for collision free navigation of mobile robots even in dynamic situations. Voronoi diagram is used in [9] for' obtaining shortest optimal path. The study [10] proposes informed RRT* for achieving optimal sampling-based path planning by directly sampling the subset of states present in a path planning by RRT*. The study [11] suggests a new RRT*- inspired online informative path planning algorithm. This method works by continuous expansion of a single tree of candidate trajectories and rewiring of nodes with refinement of intermediate paths. Allowing the algorithm to achieve global coverage and maximizing the utility of a path in a global context by the use of a single objective function. The capability of the proposed algorithm has been experimentally demonstrated in case of autonomous indoor exploration as well as accurate truncated signed distance field (TSDF)-based 3D reconstruction on-board a Micro Aerial Vehicle (MAV). In [12], Neural A* method is proposed which solves a path planning problem by the process of encoding a problem instance to a guidance map followed by performance of the differentiable A* search with the guidance map. Learning to match the search results with preprovided ground truth paths by experts make Neural A* algorithm produce a consistent path in a more accurate and efficient manner.

3　Methodology

First module of the mentioned working architecture includes mobile robot taking input sensor data from RP Lidar. A1M8 360 degree 2D laser scanner model of RPLIDAR is used here. The full 360 degree scanning RPLIDAR–A1M8 (Fig. 2) which can sample 1450 points each round has a scan rate of 2 to 10 Hz, with 12 m detection range, and can determine the general shape of the environment and its content, and can work efficiently in all type of indoor and outdoor areas. It gets accurate estimations on the position of objects within the limit of its triangular measurement system, and has been used as the principal component of obstacle avoidance

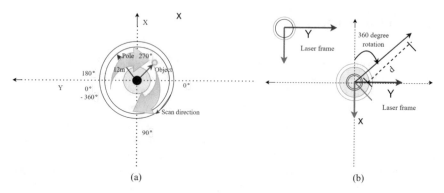

(a)   (b)

Fig. 2 a RPLIDAR rotation and scanning mechanism along polar axis in clock- wise positive direction. **b** RPLIDAR A1M8 series working geometry with reference laser frame

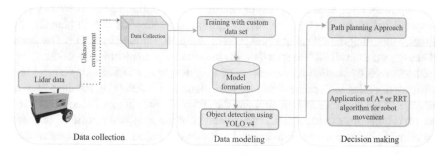

Fig. 3 Proposed working model architecture

system in our mobile robot. It is made to explore various unknown indoor environment several times and the data collected is considered as custom dataset to be trained. The custom dataset is passed through the second moduleand trained forming a model for obstacle detection. Third and last module is path planning achieved by CCPP algorithms mentioned on first section of the paper. Informed and uninformed search constitutes the path exploration process (Fig. 3). All the heuristic algorithms are informed search approaches which uses evaluation function and are more efficient compared to blind search or uninformed search like breadth first search (BFS) and depth first search (DFS) [13].

4 Analysis of Algorithms

Need of obstacle detection is fulfilled by various two-step and one-step object detection methods [14]. Review of many research works introduces many approaches of object identification which includes region-based convolutional neural network (RCNN), Fast-RCNN and Faster RCNN, histogram-based techniques. You only look once (YOLO) is proved to be one of the best real-time object detection machine learning approaches. This process combines classification and detection together. After proper detection of obstacles for optimum path finding many path planning approaches are analysed. Mainly A*, RRT, RRT* and Disjktra's algorithms are analysed with their proper working model and compared the performance of each graphically taking an indoor environment and presentation of performance data are shown in a tabular format.

4.1 YOLOv4 for Object Detection

The backbone is used for feature extraction comprises of three parts: Bag of freebies, bag of specials and CSPDarknet53. The neck is composed of a number of bottom-up and top-down paths, is used for collecting feature maps from different stages. Finally, head performs the final detection. To improve the accuracy of detection during training, the bag of freebies and bag of specials techniques are further used in YOLOv4.

- **Bag of freebies**: YOLOv4 object detector consists of a set of techniques like cost function, data augmentation, class imbalance, semantic distribution bias in datasets, objective function of BBox Regression, etc.
- **Bag of Specials**: It comprises of various post-processing modules and plugins that can act as add-ons for the object detector, involving techniques like non maximum suppression, etc., for improving the accuracy drastically.

After preparing the custom dataset in YOLOv4 format, the data accepted by YOLOv4 is achieved in the format–**object-class, x, y, width and height**. Thus, input information are stored as text file with proper annotations and trained to form model. Based on this formed model, obstacle detection is carried out (Fig. 4).

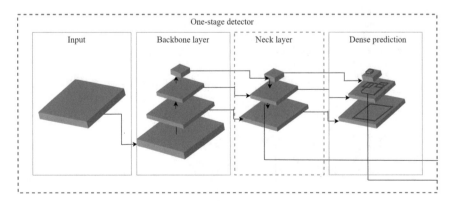

Fig. 4 YOLO V4 architecture for obstacle detection

4.2 *Analysis of Path Planning Techniques*

– *A* Algorithm*

A* algorithm is a heuristic approach of informed search which has been used here in path planning of the mobile robot.

A* firstly calculates $f(n)$, denoting the cost of travelling to neighbouring nodes and that node would be chosen which has comparatively lowest cost. The basic of the algorithm is represented by the equation (as well as in Algorithm 2):

$$f(n) = g(n) + h(n) \tag{1}$$

where $f(n)$ = neighbouring node with lowest cost, $g(n)$ = actual cost from start node to n, $h(n)$ = heuristic approximation of the value of the node and n = neighbouring nodes.

To compute value of h, two methods are proposed: exact and approximation heuristics. In exact heuristics, precomputing the distance and normal euclidean distance are followed to compute the path.

Algorithm 1 YOLOv4 Algorithm

Input: - Input image data
Output: - Custom object detection
1: for Raw input image **do**
2:    Image preprocessing and augmentation
3: **for** Augmented Image data **do**
4:    Feed into CSP-Darknet53 Backbone
5:    Extract the feature maps
6: **for** Feature maps extracted **do**
7:    Feed into PANet for instance segmentation
8:    Preserve spatial information
9: Detection through YOLOv3 Head
10: **for** YOLOv3 Head Detector **do**
11:    Locate bounding boxes
12:    Detect the bounding box coordinates (t_x, t_y, t_w, t_h).
13:    Classify the objects within each bounding box
14:    Calculate confidence score for each class.

$$\lambda_{\text{coord}} \sum_{i=0}^{s^2} \sum_{J=0}^{B} 1_{ij}^{obj} (t_x - \hat{t}_x)^2 + (t_y - \hat{t}_y)^2 + (t_w - \hat{t}_w)^2 + (t_h - \hat{t}_h)^2$$

$$+ \sum_{i=0}^{s^2} \sum_{j=0}^{s^2} 1_{ij}^{obj} (-\log(\sigma(t_o) + \sum_{k=1}^{C} BCE(\hat{y}_k, \sigma(s_k)))$$

$$+ \lambda_{\text{coord}} \sum_{i=0}^{s^2} \sum_{j=0}^{B} 1_{ij}^{noobj} (-\log(1 - \sigma(t_o))$$

15:    Optimization by CIoU loss freebie

Algorithm 2 A* Algorithm

Input: - $node_{leastf}$, *current node, adj node* // list of neighbouring nodes
Output: - *open list* // optimal path to reach the goal
1: *open list* == `null`
2: *closed list* == `null`
3: **while** *open list* $\neq$ `null` **do**
4:     *current node* == $node_{leastf}$
5:     *closed node* == *current node*
6:     **if** *current node* == *goal node* **then**
7:        `return found`
8:     *children.current node* = *adj node*
9:     **for** *children.current node* **do**
10:        **if** *closed list* = *children.current node* **then**
11:           `continue`
12:     *child.g* = *current node.g* + *d child current*
13:     *child.h* = *d child end*
14:     *child.f* = *child.g* + *child.h*
15:     **if** *open list* = *child.position* **then**
16:       **if** *child.g* > *open node.g* **then**
17:          `continue`
18:       *open list*+ = *child node*

In case of approximation heuristics, three approaches are followed:

1. Manhattan Distance: It is calculated by taking the sum of absolute values of differences in the goal's x and y coordinates and that of current cell's x and y coordinates. It is one of the perfect approach of movement of a mobile robot [17]

$$h = absolute\ value(current\ cell.x - goal\ cell.x)$$
$$+ absolute\ value(current\ cell.y - goalcell.y) \qquad (2)$$

   Let X_1 and X_2 be the current position and goal position, respectively, in x coordinate and Y_1 and Y_2 be the current and goal position, respectively, in y coordinate. Then the Manhattan Distance is given by:

$$h = |X_1 - X_2| + |Y_1 - Y_2| \qquad (3)$$

2. Euclidean Distance: This approach is used to move in any direction [18]. It is the normal distance between current cell and goal cell which uses the formula:

$$h = sqrt((current\ cell.x - goal\ cell.x)^2$$
$$+ (current\ cell.y - goal\ cell.y)^2 \qquad (4)$$

   Again, X_1 and X_2 be the current and goal position, respectively, in x coordinate and Y_1 and Y_2 be the current and goal position, respectively, in y coordinate. Euclidean Distance is given by:

$$h = \sqrt{[(X_2 - X_1)2] + [(Y_2 - Y_1)2]} \tag{5}$$

3. Diagonal Distance: It is the maximum of absolute values of differences in the goal's x and y coordinates and that of current cell's x and y coordinates. This approach is used for movement in eight directions.

A dx denotes the absolute value of difference between current and goal state in x coordinate and dy denotes the same in y coordinate.

$$\mathrm{dx} = |X_1 - X_2|$$
$$\mathrm{dy} = |Y_1 - Y_2| \tag{6}$$

h is the required diagonal distance given by:

$$h = D * (\mathrm{dx} + \mathrm{dy}) + (D^2 - 2 * D) * \min(\mathrm{dx}, \mathrm{dy}) \tag{7}$$

$D =$ length of each node, $D^2 =$ diagonal distance between each node.

– *RRT Algorithm*

Sampling-based techniques are computationally less complex. RRT algorithm is a sampling-based algorithm which is very straight forward. Randomly generated points are connected to closest available node. Everytime during vertex creation it is checked that the vertex is outside the obstacle or not, otherwise, the obstacle-free neighbour is chosen, and the tree is formed until the goal region is reached [19]. Based on literature review, RRT algorithm is found to be faster than the basic probabilistic road map approach. RRT always remain connected to the nearest edges as it randomly explores the environment, whereas the probabilistic algorithms face a lot of problem as extra edges are generated during formation of a connected roadmap. Based on the analysis, RRT can be treated as one of the best algorithms to detect collision-free path.

In comparison to A* algorithm, RRT algorithms works better in case of sim ple scenario with infinite time converging to the collision-free desired path. But in case of complex scenarios, A* gives better performance with high speed finding optimum path from start to goal point.

– *RRT* Algorithm*

Optimized version of RRT is RRT*. Basic working principle of RRT* is similar to RRT. Two additional matters of RRT* are it records the distance travelled by each vertex relative to its parent and taken as cost(). After finding the closest node a neighbour vertex in a definite radius from the new node is explored. If its cost() is cheaper, then the proximal node gets replaced by this. The second matter is rewiring of the tree. After connection of the vertex, examination of the cheapest neighbour is done again for ensuring optimal cost. Rewiring of neighbour to the newly added vertex is done to make the path smoother. This approach ensures asymptotic optimality as it is able to find the initial point quickly and goes on optimizing the path with appearance of each sample [20]. Though RRT* successfully reaches to optimal or near-optimal solution, but its convergence rate is comparatively very slow. So, computational time is so high. Below is the RRT* algorithm. To overcome this situation, RRT*-Smart has been came into action destroying the barrier of exploring the optimum path in infinite time. RRT*-Smart results in optimum path in a comparatively finite time.

– *Dijkstra's Algorithm*

It is one of the shortest path planning algorithms [2]. Dijkstra's is extended version of A* algorithm. Working principle of Dijkstra is same as A* algorithm, but A* is its modified version applying intelligent sampling-based technique in exploring the path. Unlike A* Dijkstra's algorithm searches every grid for reaching optimal or near-optimal solution. A* avoids travelling extra grid. In any built environment model, the intersection method of Dijkstra's algorithm to pass and avoid the on-path obstacles by the process of forming a barrier between the specific end points on the graph allows getting multiple graphs consisting of weighted vertex.

This algorithm has been proved to work better in case of maze robot path environment. It makes the mobile robot able to reach the goal node even before searching the entire graph. Complex environment with heavy number of nodes makes the algorithm somewhat difficult and time-consuming. Worst case of its performance is calculated as $O(|V^2|)$, where V is the number of vertices in concerned graph. An auxiliary vector D is introduced first. Length of the shortest path found in current start point from v to each end of v_i is $D[i]$. Initially, $D[i]$ is infinity. So, length is:

$$D[j] = \min_i \ \{D[i] | V_i \in V\} \tag{8}$$

Main logic of the algorithm is:

$$dist[r] = \min(dist[r], dist[q] + \cos t[q][r]) \tag{9}$$

r is the distance vertex adjacent to vertex q will be updated iff (dist[r], dist[q] + cost[q][r]) is less than dist[r] (Fig. 5).

5 Experimental Analysis

The analysis of the results derived out of the experiments are presented below which is obtained by applying each discussed algorithm. The environment has been graphically represented depicting multiple obstacles. The customized robot platform used with two active wheel differential drive design. The wheel circumference measuring 15 cm and runs with maximum 100 rpm that can attain 1 km/hr travel speed. With that constant point to pint robot platform it has been used in full speed and deployed different algorithms to measure travel time as the performance measure that has been presented in Table 2.

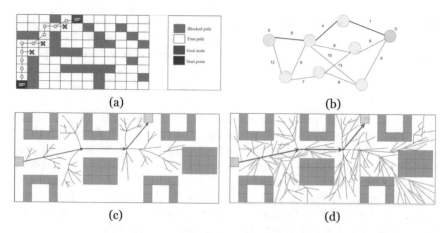

(a)   (b)

(c)   (d)

Fig. 5 **a** Graphical visualization of A* algorithm **b** Dijkstra's **c** RRT **d** RRT* in a proper indoor environment filled up with obstacles having a start point and a desired goal point

Table 2 Experimental comparison between different algorithms

Parameter	A*	Dijkstra	RRT	RRT*
Path (m)	50	50	50	50
Time (s)	180	189.3	3146.42	12892

6 Conclusion

During the analysis of algorithms presented in this work, as precept input 2D RPLIDAR used. The LIDAR data stream is integrated with Robot operating system (ROS) for identification of obstacles in a plane around the sensor. However, other than obstacles in one plane such as hanging obstacles or pits are not captured by RP LIDAR and this may lead to certain instances of collision. For obstacle identification, the applied algorithm YOLO V4 proved to be comparatively more accurate than other versions of YOLO as well as other object detection algorithms like RCNN, Faster RCNN or histogram-based approach. In case of training custom dataset for detecting obstacles that produced more accurate prediction with good probability was the constant environment for path planning performance analysis. Experimental analysis of the proposed graph theoretic approaches for path planning would produce optimal result reducing the possibilities of collision in an unknown amorphous environment. It is found that blending of proper obstacle detection method along with a path planning algorithm results in obtaining accurate point-to-point navigation by an indoor mobile robot to a large extent (Fig. 6).

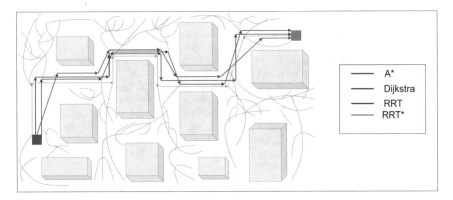

Fig. 6 Graphical experimental analysis of discussed algorithms in a proper in- door environment filled up with obstacles having a start point and a desired goal point

References

1. Cheng KP, Mohan RE, Nhan NHK, Le AV (2019) Graph theory-based approach to accomplish complete coverage path planning tasks for reconfigurable robots. IEEE Access 7:94642–94657
2. Karur K, Sharma N, Dharmatti C, Siegel JE (2021) A survey of path planning algorithms for mobile robots. Vehicles 3(3):448–468
3. Goyal JK, Nagla KS (2014) A new approach of path planning for mobile robots. In: 2014 International Conference on Advances in Computing, Communications and Informatics (ICACCI), pp 863–867
4. Nagib G, Gharieb W (2004) Path planning for a mobile robot using genetic algorithms. IEEE Proc Robot 185189
5. Teleweck PE, Chandrasekaran B (2019) Path planning algorithms and their use in robotic navigation systems. J Phys Conf Ser 1207:012018. IOP Publishing, 2019
6. Hassani I, Maalej I, Rekik C (2018) Robot path planning with avoiding obstacles in known environment using free segments and turning points algorithm. Math Prob Eng 2018
7. Fragkopoulos C, Graeser A (2010) Arrt based path planning algorithm for rehabilitation robots. In: ISR 2010 (41st international symposium on robotics) and ROBOTIK 2010 (6th German conference on robotics), pp 1–8
8. Bruce J, Veloso MM (2002) Real-time randomized path planning for robot navigation. In: Robot soccer world cup. Springer, Berlin, pp 288–295
9. Garrido S, Abderrahim M, Moreno L (2006) Path planning and navigation using voronoi diagram and fast marching. IFAC Proc Volumes 39(15):346–351
10. Gammell JD, Srinivasa SS, Barfoot TD (2014) Informed rrt*: optimal sampling-based path planning focused via direct sampling of an admissible ellipsoidal heuristic. In: 2014 IEEE/RSJ international conference on intelligent robots and systems. IEEE, pp 2997–3004
11. Schmid L, Pantic M, Khanna R, Ott L, Siegwart R, Nieto J (2020) An efficient sampling-based method for online informative path planning in unknown environments. IEEE Rob Autom Lett 5(2):1500–1507
12. Yonetani R, Taniai T, Barekatain M, Nishimura M, Kanezaki A (2021) Path planning using neural a* search. In: International conference on machine learning. PMLR, pp 12029–12039
13. Choset H (2007) Robotic motion planning: A* and d* search. Rob Inst 16–735
14. Bochkovskiy A, Wang C-Y, Liao H-YM (2020) Yolov4: Optimal speed and accuracy of object detection. arXiv preprint arXiv:2004.10934
15. Fan X, Guo Y, Liu H, Wei B, Lyu W (2020) Improved artificial potential field method applied for auv path planning. Math Probl Eng 2020

16. Breitenmoser A, Schwager M, Metzger J-C, Siegwart R, Rus D (2010) Voronoi coverage of non-convex environments with a group of networked robots. In: 2010 IEEE international conference on robotics and automation. IEEE, pp 4982–4989
17. Jing X, Yang X (2018) Application and improvement of heuristic function in a* algorithm. In: 2018 37th Chinese control conference (CCC). IEEE, pp 2191–2194
18. Elizondo-Leal JC, Parra-Gonzalez EF, Ram´ırez-Torres JG (2013) The exact euclidean distance transform: a new algorithm for universal path planning. Int J Adv Robot Syst 10(6):266
19. Karaman S, Walter MR, Perez A, Frazzoli E, Teller S (2011) Anytime motion planning using the rrt. In: 2011 IEEE international conference on robotics and automation. IEEE, pp 1478–1483
20. Islam F, Nasir J, Malik U, Ayaz Y, Hasan O (2012) Rrt* - smart: Rapid convergence implementation of rrt* towards optimal solution. In: 2012 IEEE international conference on mechatronics and automation. IEEE, pp 1651–1656

Combined Cryptography and Text Steganography for Enhanced Security Based on Number System

Bubai Das⬥, Santanu Mondal⬥, and Kunal Kumar Mandal⬥

1 Introduction

Cybercrime is a well-known fact in today's digital world where online data exchange is increasing day by day. One of the biggest problems of today's world is providing Network Security [1]. To protect against unauthorized access, data should be confidential. Cryptography and steganography are the techniques using which we can keep the data confidential. In current days, steganography has attracted more attention to the digital world [2]. Steganography is a technique where data remains hidden in an innocent-looking object called the cover. It conceals the existence of any data.

Steganography differs from cryptography. In cryptography, any intruder if somehow accesses some data, cannot understand the data because here some techniques will be followed using which the data will be changed into another form [3]. Whereas in steganography some techniques will be used to hide the message itself into some other text or audio or video. So here for any intruder, it is very much difficult to understand the existence of the message. Though it is secured still sending any information which is encrypted may draw attention, while invisible information will not. So we can say, cryptography is not the best solution for secure communication, and it is a part of the solution. The meaning of steganography is hidden writing [4]. Here, various methods are used to keep information's hidden from unwanted

B. Das (✉)
J. K. College, Purulia, India
e-mail: bubai.jkc@gmail.com

S. Mondal
Michael Madhusudan Memorial College, Durgapur, India
e-mail: hisan123@gmail.com

K. K. Mandal
Mankar College, Mankar, India
e-mail: kunalkumarmandal@mankarcollege.ac.in

© The Author(s), under exclusive license to Springer Nature Singapore Pte Ltd. 2023
R. Doriya et al. (eds.), *Machine Learning, Image Processing, Network Security and Data Sciences*, Lecture Notes in Electrical Engineering 946,
https://doi.org/10.1007/978-981-19-5868-7_63

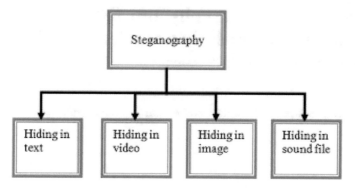

Fig. 1 Type of steganography

persons. In history, there is an example of using steganography which is thought of as the oldest case. In 500 BC Histiaeus who was the ruler of a province, Milteus used a slave to send a message by inking a tattoo on his shaved head. When his hair grew back, he sent him to his son-in-law, Aristagoras. Aristogoras then shaved the slave's head again and got the message [5] (Fig. 1).

2 Previous Work

Image steganography, text steganography, and audio and video steganography are the different types of steganography. It depends on the different cover media. Text steganography can involve different techniques to hide messages [6]. It can be format change of any text, converting word by its synonyms within the text, generating character sequences randomly, etc. [7]. Text steganography is the trickiest because there is no redundant information about the presence of the text in the image file or audio or video file (Fig. 2).

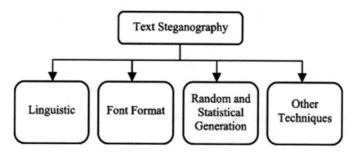

Fig. 2 Type of text steganography

2.1 Hide in a Text

In a normal text file, the rules of steganography can also be applied. Sometimes, the message will be hidden in the blank spaces in between the words. The message will be generated separating the binary lsb from the binary form is separated between the lsb from the binary format throughout the text [8]. Here, the text which will be sent should be proportionately longer than the message which will be hidden in the text. The messages can be hidden in word or PDF documents or any other standards, depending on the user [9].

Compared to image or audio or video file, very less information is kept in the case of a text file. This makes text steganography very much difficult. But it has advantages too [10]. It occupies less memory compared to any other medium. The simple communication method is another advantage of text steganography.

2.2 Based on Format

These methods do not change any word or the meaning of any word or any sentence. It changes the formatting of the text file which will be used to hide any data. use and change the formatting of the cover text to hide data. So, here value or the meaning of any text will not be harmed. Here, to hide any data some extra white spaces will be added to the cover text. Here, a single space will be represented as "0" and double space will be represented as "1." These extra spaces will be added at the end of the words of the text or end of the sentences or the end of the paragraphs of the text file. If we want to hide a large amount of data in this method, then the size of the cover text file needs to be huge [11, 12] (Tables 1 and 2).

The number embedded here is 011011.

Table 1 Normal text

I	T		A	L	W	A	Y	S		S	E	E	M	S		I	M	P
O	S	S	I	B	L	E		U	N	T	I	L		I	T	S		D
O	N	E																

Table 2 White space encoded text

I	T		A	L	W	A	Y	S			S	E	E	M	S			I
M	P	O	S	S	I	B	L	E		U	N	T	I	L			I	T
S			D	O	N	E												

Fig. 3 Word shift coding
example

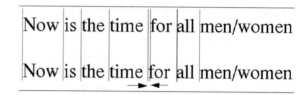

Word-shift coding example

2.3 Word Shift Coding

This technique is used to hide information by shifting slightly the words in the text. Messages will be kept secret by horizontally shifting the words left or right in the text and that will be represented by 0 or 1, respectively [13]. This is less visible to the reader so it is secured but it is necessary to keep the original image of the text or keep the information of the spacing between the words of the plaintext document (Fig. 3).

As the distance between the words in a text is a normal issue, this feature of a document is used to hide any information in this method. Information is hidden here by changing the normal alignments horizontally. It is very hard to understand any existence of a message in this method [14].

2.4 Line Shift Coding

In Line Shift Coding, information is kept hidden by changing the alignment of the lines of the document vertically. Here, encoding can be done by vertically shifting the lines of the text file. It is not very difficult to find out the hidden document here [15]. But it is an easy method where encoding and decoding can be done on the total document file or the bitmap image of the pages of the document. Encoding and decoding can generally be applied either to the format file of a document, or the bitmap of a page image [16] (Fig. 4).

2.5 Random and Statistical Generation Methods

Language has some statistical properties which will be used here to create the cover text file. These methods are based on character and word sequences in the document. Probabilistic context-free grammar generally is used to construct the sentence in the cover text file depending on the secret message need to be hidden. Steganography message will be generated here depending on the grammar used [17, 18].

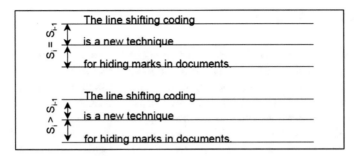

Fig. 4 Line shift coding example

2.6 Linguistics Method

Some Syntactic and semantic methods are known as the linguistics steganography method.

(i) In the Syntactic method to hide any information, some extra punctuation symbols will be inserted in the text. Depending on the grammar used but before that, there must be a clear idea about the proper places or locations in the text where these symbols can be placed [19].

(ii) In the semantic method, information will be kept hidden by replacing some words with their synonyms. Some preselected synonyms of some words in the text will be used to keep information hidden here [20].

2.7 Feature Coding

Here depending on the word some features of the text may or may not be changed. This method can be applied to the text file or bitmap image. Here, character end line is shortened or lengthened randomly and then altered to hide the information in it [21].

2.8 Other Methods

Text steganography by specific characters in words, use of abbreviations or by changing words spelling are some other methods for hiding information in the text besides the above categories [22].

3 Proposed Method

Researchers have discovered a variety of techniques for text steganography. We have used a strategy in this research paper in which a secret message will be sent through a cover-up medium of the number-oriented system on traditional Indian language for the introduced method. In this research paper, we have proposed a proposal where top-secret messages are implanted by applying efficient models of numbering methods. The set is used as a digit of the system, and it is not used to say. We know that in a decimal manner, as Ten digits mean 0 to 9, the same will be done here, but in the method, we will show the display differently. To make the idea clearer, we will now use an example to represent how two numbers are represented in pairs so that a number can be represented. Here, a formula shows how the final value is calculated using two numbers. The concept will become more distinguished after looking at the given example.

Let us assume, 127 is a denary system. So, we can write as $(1*100+2*10+7)$. Same as if this number 127 and represent some other way, suppose base "k," the final value will come out as $(1*k*k + 2*k + 7)$, where k is 10.

It turns out that different number systems have to work in a number system to get the exact value. Only is the calculation different, but proposed methods also work on a number to get the final value. The figure like 127 of decimal is written as (15, 7) in this system. And is calculated by the formula, $((K * (K + 1) / 2) + M)$ for a pairing (K, M). So the couple is (15, 7) specified by $((15 * 16)/2) + 7) = ((15 * 16) + 7) = 120 + 7 = 127$. So, each section like K and M is treated as decimal. Now, the thought is where calculations are prepared in special ways. For example, we all know that long ago they exchanged their goods for other goods. So by value, they cannot represent quantity. The amount is calculated by dividing it into 10 groups according to the rules of the decimal system. Each product is divided into several groups of 10 units, for any two numbers that can be imagined (1,2,3,4,5,6,......10), (11,12,13,14,15,16......20), etc.

The grouping of numbers taken here is no different from a 10-digit number, and the single digits of the number are denoted by the excess of the left number (>10). In this paper, the section is viewed differently. We consider any capabilities of a product, and start as a calculation (Table 3).

That is, from the above table we can infer that the first number carries a single unit, the quantity of elements of group 2 carries 2 units, and the Nth place will have Nth cell numbers. So, the 7th group is numbered by 7 then it has to be represented, (6, 7). So the value of it by the given formula is $(6 * 7/2 + 7) = 21 + 7 = 28$. The italics are given below, and the red color 7 can be verified by calculating the space. This is the 7th number from the left. Thus, the couple (K, M) is prescribed as:

K = Means the number of groups being measured by counting the number is completely done.

M = Leave out the number of additional ingredients.

Table 3 Proposed grouping

GROUP NO	Quantity OF ELEMENTS	Cluster ELEMENT
1	One number	1
2	Two numbers	(2, 3)
3	Three numbers	(4, 5, 6)
4	Four numbers	(7, 8, 9, 10)
5	Five numbers	(11, 12, 13, 14, 15)
6	Six numbers	(16, 17, 18, 19, 20, 21)
7	Seven numbers	(22, 23, 24, 25, 26, 27, 28)
……..	……	……
……..	……	…….
……..	…….	…….
11	……	(56, 57, 58, 59, 60, 61, 62, 63, 64, 65, 66)
12	……	(67, 68, 69, 70, 71, 72, 73, 74, 75, 76, 77, 78)
13	……	(79, 80, 81, 82, 83, 84, 85, 86, 87, 88, 89, 90, 91)
14	……	(92, 93, 94, 95, 96, 97, 98, 99, 100, 101, 102, 103, 104, 105)
15	……	(106, 107, 108, 109, 110, 111, 112, 113, 114, 115, 116, 117, 118, 119, 120)
16	……	(121, 122, 123, 124, 125, 126, 127, 128, 129, 130, 131, 132, 133, 134, 135, 136)
……..	…….	…….
……..	…….	…….
N	N	………….

If we consider the number 6 of the 6th group as an example of the above, then we get that "6" and get 5 complete groups. So next to $K = 5$, we have additional elements left, so $M = 6$. So the coordinator is (5, 6).

4 Technological and Hypothetical Background

The sender and the recipient are aware of the whole process. The sender knows the top-secret message, the way to occult the message and how to send the information and to whom. This is the encoding technique. And the recipient knows the decoding procedure and how to get the secret or original message within the text means also grasps the information about how to extort the top-secret message within the text. This process, unique in nature, can be described entertainingly through a beautiful strategic approach. The cover message is done in such a unique way that the intruder may not understand how the secret message reached the receiver end. We will send the message called "HIJACK" in a very secure way. This time we will understand the

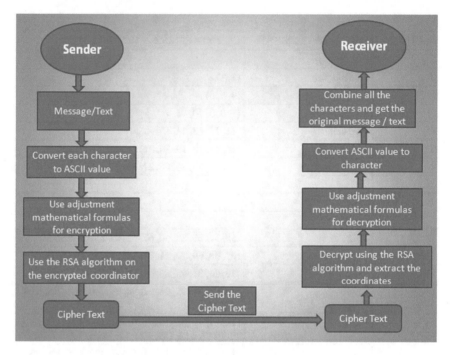

Fig. 5 Encryption-decryption technique

encryption process, encoding algorithm, decryption process, and decoding algorithm very well. The process is described in Fig. 5.

4.1 Encryption Process

We will first extract our secret message from the ASCII table to the ASCII value of each alphabet. We will use our created mathematical formula on each ASCII value. From here, we get some encrypted coordinates. Now, these coordinators together will be called the cover medium. In that cover medium, our secret message is protected. The cover has become so strong that it is very difficult to get the secret message out of here. But we will use RSA Algorithm on this cover medium to make it stronger. This paper used the RSA public key as well as the private key of size 2048 bit with Base64 encoded but anyone can use RSA algorithm with a public key and private key of size either 512 bit or 1024 bit or 2048 bit or 3072 bit and also encoded with 4096 bit and Base64. The cipher text that we receive after using RSA will be sent to the receiver.

Table 4 Character to ASCII conversion

Char	H	I	J	A	C	K
ASCII value	72	73	74	65	67	75
Using our mathematical formula (table)	(11,6)	(11,7)	(11,8)	(10,10)	(11,1)	(11,9)

So, our secret message is "HIJACK," and we will apply our mathematical formula to it and find some coordinates, and this will be our covered medium; in which, the secret message will be protected.

Encoding Algorithm

1. In the secrete message, the first character is = "H" and from the ASCII table, the value is 72, according to our mathematical formula, 72 = (11, 6) [see Table 1] where $K = 11$ and $M = 6$.
2. Second character = "I" and its ASCII value is = 73, according to our mathematical formula 73 = (11, 7) where $K = 11$ and $M = 7$.
3. Third character = "J" and its ASCII value is = 74, according to our mathematical formula 74 = (11, 8) where $K = 11$ and $M = 8$.
4. Fourth character = "A" and its ASCII value is = 65, according to our mathematical formula 65 = (10, 10) where $K = 10$ and $M = 10$.
5. Fifth character = "C" and ASCII value is = 67, according to our formula 67 = (11, 1) where $K = 11$ and $M = 1$.
6. Sixth character = "K" and ASCII value is = 75, according to our formula 75= (11, 9) where $K = 11$ and $M = 9$.

Now it will look like (Table 4),

Each alphabet of the secret message inside all of the above coordinates is very secure. After getting all of the above coordinates, we will apply RSA algorithm techniques to make the cipher text message more secure. Also used RSA algorithm using the public key and private key of size 2048 bit and encoded with Base64. The sender then sends that secure cipher text message to the receiver end.

4.2 Decryption Process

The recipient will apply the RSA decryption technique to the cipher text message received from the sender and get all the coordinators together like (11,6), (11,7), (11,8), (10,10), (11,1), and (11,9). The receiver will apply our mathematical technique to this coordinator and get the alphabets from inside each coordinator, and if put together, will get the original message or secret message.

Decoding Algorithm

1. Receiver examine start all the pairs that is (11,6), (11,7), (11,8), (10,10), (11,1), (11,9) from left to right.
2. A twins like (11, 6) returns $K = 11$ and $M = 6$.
3. Apply K and M values to the mathematical formula $[(K *(K + 1)/2) + M]$ and extract the ASCII value. Like, first couple is (11, 6). So, $K = 11$, $K + 1 = 12$, and $M = 6$. So, $(11 * 12)/2 + 6 = 72$.
4. Collect ASCII values (72) and change characters using ASCII. Thus, in the first pair, the ASCII value is 72 and the corresponding letter is "H".
5. This process will continue (steps 1 through 5) until the original alphabet comes out from all the coordinators.
6. This time the recipient will get the real secret message by combining each alphabet.

5 Conclusion

In this paper, we have been able to send a secret message from the sender to the receiver, using the text message as a cover medium, using the steganography method. Here, the new number system is used to display mathematical formulas and try to make the secret message more secure using RSA algorithms. Attempts have been made to present the idea of steganography differently and as much as possible so that there is no violence to do on the secret message in any way. The basic impetus for raising this technique has been exploited to conceal confidential information with the help of a number system.

6 Future Scope

Finding a powerful cover medium or steganographic algorithm to keep the secret message even more secret. This future study is a big challenge for any researcher. Even if the secret message is a bit big message, it is easy to apply this mathematical formula to it and it is also true that security is a major challenge or concern when it comes to concealing any information, so new security features need to be constantly brought in, other loopholes need to be found and improved over time. If we do not change it in time, we will always face a big challenge.

References

1. Cachin C (1998) An information-theoretic model for steganography. In: Proceeding 2nd information Hiding workshop, vol. 1525, pp 306–318
2. Thangadurai KK, Sudha Devi G (2014) An analysis of LSB based image steganography techniques. In: International conference on computer communication and informatics, pp 1–4
3. Johnson NT, Jajodia S (1998) Steganalysis: the investigation of hiding information. IEEE, pp 113–116
4. Artz D (2001) Digital steganography: Hiding data within data. IEEE Int Comput, pp 75–80
5. Kyriakou G, Kyriakou A, Fotas T (2021) Dermatostiksia (tattooing): an act of stigmatization in ancient Greek culture. History and humanities. Dermatology 112:907–909
6. Wang Z, Zhang X, Qian Z (2020) Practical cover selection for steganography. Signal Proces Lett IEEE 27:71–75
7. Al Hussien SS, Mohamed MS, Hafez EH (2021) Coverless image steganography based on optical mark recognition and machine learning. Access IEEE 9:16522–16531
8. Sun W, Zhou J, Li Y, Cheung M, She J (2021) Robust high-capacity watermarking over online social network shared images. Circ Syst Video Technol IEEE Trans 31(3):1208–1221
9. Satir E, Isik H, Işık H (2012) F A compression-based text steganography method. J Syst Softw 85:2385–2394
10. Osman B, Yasin A, Omar MN (2015) An analysis of alphabet-based techniques in text steganography. J Telecommun Electronic Comput Eng 8(10):109–115
11. Provos N, Honeyman P (2003) "Hide and Seek" an introduction to steganography. IEEE Secur Priv pp 32–44
12. Bennett K (2004) "Linguistic steganography: Survey, analysis, and robustness concerns for hiding information in text". Purdue University, CERIAS Tech. Report 2004-13
13. Moerland T (2003) "Steganography and Steganalysis", 15 May 2003, www.liacs.nl/home/tmo erlan/privtech.pdf
14. Low SH, Maxemchuk NF, Brassil JT, O'Gorman L (1999) "Document marking and identification using both line and word shifting". In: Proceedings of the fourteenth annual joint conference of the IEEE computer and communications societies (INFOCOM'95), vol. 2, pp 853–860
15. Ahvanooey MT, Li Q, Hou J, Mazraeh HD, Zhang J (2018) AITSteg: an innovative text steganography technique for hidden transmission of text message via social media. IEEE Access, pp 65981–65995
16. Yin Z, Ji Y, Luo B (2020) Reversible data hiding in JPEG images with multi-objective optimization. Circ Syst Video Technol IEEE Trans 30(8):2343–2352
17. TAhvanooey MT, Li Q, Shim HJ, Huang Y (2018) A comparative analysis of information hiding techniques for copyright protection of text documents. Secur Commun Netw 2018:22
18. Rafat KF, Sher M (2013) Secure digital steganography for ASCII text documents. Arab J Sci Eng 38:2079–2094
19. Hamdan AM, Hamarsheh A (2016) AH4S: an algorithm of text in text steganography using the structure of omega network. Secur Commun Netw 9:6004–6016
20. Patiburn SAL, Manesh VI, Teh PL (2017) Text steganography using daily emotions monitoring. Int J Educ Manag Eng 1–14
21. Wendzel S, Caviglione L, Mazurczyk W, Lalande J-F (2017) Network information hiding and science 2.0: can it be a match? Int J Electron Telecommun 63:217–222
22. Ramakrishnan BK, Thandra PK, Srinivasula AVSM (2016) Text steganography: a novel character-level embedding algorithm using font attribute. Secur Commun Netw 9:6066–6079

Analysis of Mirai Malware and Its Components

Shubham Kumar and B. R. Chandavarkar

1 Introduction

Mirai malware is one of the most famous malware in the Internet of Things (IoT). It became popular after the famous DDoS attacks around October 2016 on Krebsonsecurity.com, OVH, Dyn, and other Web sites [1]. This attack used a large number of bots, making mitigation of this attack is very challenging [2]. The Web site's incoming request was around 450 K, and out of those requests, the legitimate requests are nearly 20 queries only. Packets were looking like genuine HTTP requests. Earlier, botnet size was around 150–200 K, but Mirai became famous with botnet size started with 600 K and later created 900 K sized botnet [3, 4]. This malware is very less sophisticated and still able to compromise lots of IoT devices. The attacking volume started with 620Gbps and later was able to make attacks in Tbps[1]. Section 3 talks about the Mirai malware in detail. Section 4 talks about the work done on Mirai in this paper. Section 5 talks about the works that need to be done in future.

2 Background

IoT devices are being attacked by malware from the day they came into the industry. Due to its resource constraint, these devices cannot afford a good security level against attacks. Still, in most cases, IoT devices lack some common security issues that can be handled even without additional resource requirements. Hardcoded credentials are one of such major issues. This issue was not targeted for the first time by Mirai malware but was targetted in the past. Malware from the past has used this IoT device's vulnerability to attack and make it a bot for launching DDoS attacks.

S. Kumar (✉) · B. R. Chandavarkar
National Institute of Technology Karnataka, Surathkal, India
e-mail: sshubhamk1@hotmail.com

© The Author(s), under exclusive license to Springer Nature Singapore Pte Ltd. 2023   851
R. Doriya et al. (eds.), *Machine Learning, Image Processing, Network Security and Data Sciences*, Lecture Notes in Electrical Engineering 946,
https://doi.org/10.1007/978-981-19-5868-7_64

However, Mirai malware got much more attention than its predecessor and successor malware. Being so famous is its simplicity, scalability, and portability of code, which made it operate on various architectures. Earlier, IoT malware started with attacking specific architectures, particularly on MIPS architecture. The first multi-architecture supportable malware introduced was Aidra malware, which attacked MIPS, ARM, and PowerPC architectures.

3   Mirai Malware

The first significant Mirai attack was at 8 p.m. ET on Sept. 20, 2016, on krebsonsecurity with approximately 665 gigabits of traffic per second. It was the most powerful DDoS attack done so far on any Web site. Earlier, these kinds of attacks with massive traffic were achieved using DNS reflection attacks [5], but this time it was different. Most of the attacks created a legitimate connection between the attacking host and the target using SYN, GET, or POST flood [6].

A few days later again, Mirai malware launched another DDoS attack, this time with approximately 1Tbps of network traffic on Internet performance management and Web application security company DYN (now oracle) and French hosting firm OVH [7]. These two attacks within a single week made it famous more than any other malware at that moment. Later, the attackers revealed their source code, thinking that availability of source code to everyone might reduce the probability of finding the particular attacker. It also helped researchers to view its actual implementation. Before going through the codes of Mirai malware, let's see the requirements necessary to develop the Mirai malware.

3.1   Mirai Requirements

The software requirement for implementing Mirai malware is following [8]:

- gcc: gcc stands for GNU C compiler. Since the bot program is written in C language, the gcc compiler is used to generate its machine-level code. However, different architectures support different machine codes, and hence, cross-compilers of gcc are used.
- golang: C&C server, scanListen server are implemented in Go language, and hence, Golang is used to compile these programs.
- electric-fence: Bot programs are made memory optimized, and hence, memory leaks and other memory-related errors are needed to be resolved. For this issue to be resolved, electric fence is used.
- mysql-server: User details, attacks details, and Web sited not to be attacked, must be stored in some persistent database to be reused later without any issue. For this purpose, MySQL server is used.

- mysql-client: MySQL client is required to communicate with MySQL server. With its help, data are sent from and to the MySQL server.

3.2 Mirai Implementations

There are various components that all together makes the Mirai malware to be work completely. Those components are following:

- Bot program: The bot program resides inside the IoT device which got infected. It starts with deleting itself after start of execution. Any program on execution first copies the instructions into the memory then starts executing each instruction. Hence, deletion of the program itself won't create any issue. It also helps to remove the evidence of malware so that the researcher won't found any details while doing the malware analysis. Once the program gets deleted, it tries to make change in the watchdog so that the device can't do rebooting by itself. The malware then unlocks the table build within to access various details like the CNC address and other details. It then runs a function ensure_single_instance which makes a connection to the CNC, and if there exist a connection already, it sends a kill signal to it. It then creates child process and starts the attack, killing, and scanning module whose primary task is to perform attack on victim device with provided attack vectors, kill other instances of same application, and to scan other IoT devices in the network to infect it with Mirai malware, respectively. creates a socket for connecting to the CNC server. It uses some of helper modules that are made by the attacker itself, those modules are following:

  - include.h: It includes necessary functions for printing outputs on standard output of the system. All these functions are available in stdio.h file, but the developer made this by himself so that it can be run on any architecture without considering the availability of stdio.h in GCC compilers.
  - table.h: It contains all the necessary details stored in as a separate table entry so that one can modify the program by making changes here only. All the necessary details are kept here with encryption (bit-wise XOR).
  - rand.h: This module is responsible for generating random number,strings. These functions are used mainly for generating random IP address for scanning the Internet for new potential bot devices.
  - attack.h: This module contains different types of DDoS attacks as separate functions.
  - killer.h: This module is responsible for killing all the process in the bot system. So that the bot will be unable to be connected by any other application.
  - scanner.h: This module is for scanning other devices using TELNET protocol. It only works if we are building Mirai malware with TELNET protocol.
  - util.h: It includes functions that are necessary for formatting and copying data from one memory to another.

- resolv.h: This module is for resolving the domain of C&C server and other Web site. Instead of relying on the address written in /etc/hosts file, Mirai malware makes a socket connection to 8.8.8.8 (Google DNS) and resolves the domain from here.

It also defines some of the functions that are following:

- anti_gdb_entry(int): maps to resolv_cnc_addr function when malware is running in debug mode.
- resolv_cnc_addr(void): This function gets the value of CNC domain name, port address.
- establish_connection(void): This function creates a socket connection.
- teardown_connection(void): This function closes the socket connection.
- ensure_single_instance(void): This function ensures that only one connection is made to the CNC server. If any other connection exists, this program will send kill request to that connection.
- unlock_tbl_if_nodebug(char *): This function unlocks table for getting values from it to access CNC and other details using lock mechanism. This mechanism ensures the atomic operation on items of tables.

- C&C Server: This module is responsible for creating the C&C server of Mirai malware. Botmaster maintains control over botnet using this interface. The botnet is provided to any user using this module. All the bots are connected to this server and waiting attack command to be provided.
- debug: This folder contains the output files of the Mirai malware built for debug mode.
- release: This folder contains the output files of the Mirai malware built in release mode. All the binaries are stripped and made optimized, ready to be deployed in the network.
- Tools: This module provides various tools necessary for configuring Mirai malware. It involves various tools for encrypting strings in the malware, tools for removing debugging option, tools for downloading a file from loader through socket connections.
- build.sh: This script is responsible for compiling all the parts of Mirai malware and producing output in debug/release mode.
- prompt.txt: This is a text file that shows some welcome information to the user connected to the C&C server via the telnet protocol. Here, the owner of C&C can write some information and warning related to the C&C server.

3.3 Existing Solutions for Mitigating Mirai

Tanaka et al. [9] gave a unique solution where instead of trying a mitigating mechanism; Hajime (another malware) is spread in the middle of the network to reduce the rate of Mirai spreading in the network. This method reduces the speed of spreading up to 50% and more depending on the network structure.

IoT malware tries to stop other malware. This concept is used here in the solution, which is also a significant motivation for our proposal. While this solution is effective, the major demerit is that it does not mitigate the Mirai malware.

Gopal et al. [10] proposed a method for mitigation of Mirai malware which involves two phases. In the first phase, all the IoT device applications are scanned, and their hashes are stored in the database. This phase is termed a profiling module, where all open applications are whitelisted based on their hashes.

In the second phase, all running processes are monitored. Before executing a process, its hash is computed and compared with hashes stored in the databases. If hash matches, the process is genuine and will be executed. Else, it may be malicious and hence not be permitted for execution and is blocked. Also, the blocked application will be checked later, confirming whether the blocked application is malicious or not. On that basis, it will be allowed/blocked.

This solution is promising. After all, even if a new malware enters the system, it cannot be executed because its hash value will not be stored in the database. Nevertheless, every time calculating hashes of programs before executing, it seems very difficult because calculating the hash of a program requires computation power. IoT devices do not have good computation power [11]; lightweight cryptography will be helpful to an extent in this scenario.

Jaramillo's paper [12] uses free and open source systems for creating a custom anti-virus application with Yara-based rules to detect and prevent Mirai based on their hashes and specific instructions.

An anti-virus application always runs inside a system. Hence, a lot of computation and other resources are continuously used by it. The even bigger system faces this issue, and hence, it is a critical issue while implementing on an IoT device.

Su et al. [13] collected a large number of samples of Mirai and Linux.Gafgyt and used those samples to create a neural network for malware detection. This solution works, but as the obfuscation changes, this method does not detect malware. After the source code of released of Mirai on Github, changing the obfuscation is relatively easy. It hence will be changed with every new variant.

Table 1 shows the advantages and disadvantages of all the available solutions for the mitigation of Mirai.

Tables 2 shows 2 shows the relation between the available solutions and their implementation location. Implementing at the device level consumes more resources, which is unfavorable in IoT devices. Hence, the favorable solution would be implemented at the network level instead of the device level. The two solutions that are implemented at the network level also have issues.[9] is unable to mitigate Mirai malware, and [13] solution does not work on changing obfuscation of the malware. These solutions made us think of another solution that can be implemented at the network level and mitigate Mirai malware even after obfuscation.

This chapter discussed most of the related work of Mirai malware along with the existing mitigation strategy with the issues. The next chapter discusses the proposed methodology for mitigating the Mirai at the network level.

Table 1 Comparisons between the mitigation methods

No.	Paper	Approach	Advantage	Disadvantage
1	Tanaka and Yamaguchi [9]	Another malware	Slow down Mirai by 50%	Unable to mitigate
2	Gopal et al. [10]	Hash based	Full accuracy	Very high computation required
3	Jaramillo [12]	Anti-virus	Free & Open source	Very high computation required
4	Su et al. [13]	Neural network	Lightweight	Doesn't work on changing obfuscation

Table 2 Solution implementation strategy

No.	Reference	Implemented at
1	Tanaka and Yamaguchi [9]	IoT network
2	Gopal et al. [10]	IoT device
3	Jaramillo [12]	IoT device
4	Su et al. [13]	IoT network

4   Related Work

The Mirai malware setup comprises of various components at the time of execution. The whole system is shown in the Fig. 1. All the components are discussed in the upcoming subsections.

4.1   Downloader File

The function of this file is to make a request to the HTTP server and download the Mirai malware to the device on which this file is executing. Downloader files are meant to connect to the HTTP server and download Mirai Malware of their kind. For achieving this purpose, downloader files are also compiled for different architectures.These binaries are kept in the bins folder inside the loader folder. When the loader server starts, it hosts all these downloader files. These downloader files are sent to the bot. On execution of these downloader files, the bot connects to our HTTP server and downloads the Mirai malware itself. The files generated here were following: dlr.arm, dlr.arm7, dlr.m68k. dlr.mips, dlr.mpsl, dlr.ppc, dlr.sh4, dlr.spc.

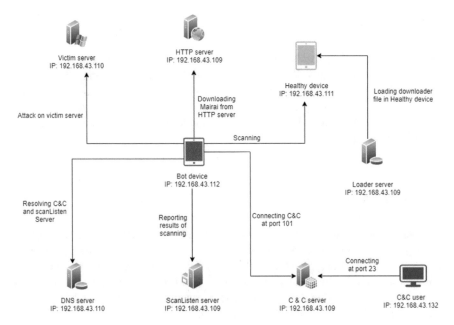

Fig. 1 Implementation of Mirai malware setup

4.2 Mirai File

This is the actual malicious Mirai malware loaded with all the attack vectors and also the program to connect to the C&C server. All files are named as mirai with extension as their supporting architecture types. The files generated here were following: mirai.arm, mirai.arm7, mirai.m68k. mirai.mips, mirai.mpsl, mirai.ppc, mirai.sh4, mirai.spc

4.3 HTTP Server

This server processes a request sent via HTTP protocol by the clients. A predefined Apache server is used for the HTTP server. The public folder in the Apache server is "/var/www," so all copies of Mirai malware should reside in this folder. HTTP server contains the malicious malware compiled for every architecture. For compiling the malware for different architectures, cross-compilers are needed. The ubuntu server running on Raspberry Pi contains these binaries in the "/var/www/html/bins" folder. This location is chosen so that Mirai request on /bins folder will happen.

4.4 DNS Server

DNS server is used to resolve the domain name into its IP address so that a client can access that particular Web site. The bot uses the domain name of the C&C server instead of the IP address. Hence, a DNS server is required to be set up in the environment. DNSmasq application is used in this experiment that is easily available on the apt store for Linux. It helps to resolve the IP address of the C&C server and scanListen server.

4.5 Loader Server

This server is used to load malicious binary to a healthy device while sending the downloader file to the device requires an IP address, port number, username, password, and architecture type. Mirai malware uses hardcoded parameters for the telnet protocol communication. Instead of using the usual method, we are using the SSH protocol to send the downloader file. The architecture type of the device can be checked using the Linux command "uname -m."

4.6 Scanlisten Server

This server is listening for the results from the bots' scanning process. The results include the IP address, port number, credentials, and the architecture of a healthy device. These results come from the bot device whenever it makes a successful attempt of scanning on other devices.

4.7 C&C Server

C&C (Command and Control) controls all the bots infected by malware and sends the command to them. It runs on port 23 so that other users can directly connect to it using Telnet protocol (The default port for TELNET is 23). It uses a MySQL server for storing various types of information. That information is following (Table 3).

C&C server uses MySQL server in the back end to store users' information, attacks, and some safe listed Web sites. The user table stores the details of users that are allowed to connect to the C&C server. The only user with admin privileges is allowed to add another user for the C&C server. The duration field provides the maximum duration for which a user can attack any Web site. The cooldown field represents the minimum time interval between two attacks by the user.

Table 3 MySQL tables

Table name	Description
Users	Stores information about each user of Mirai Malware
History	Stores details of attacks done on victim servers
Whitelist	Stores server address which are not permitted to be attacked

Fig. 2 Interface provided by C&C server at port 23

The login interface is shown in Fig. 2. The first line is taken from the data written in the prompt.txt file, which resides in the same folder. Other than that, the login prompt asks for a username and password to connect to the server. On successful credentials, the user proceeds forward; otherwise, communication finishes at this process.

4.8 Bot Device

The bot device represents the IoT device that is already infected with Mirai malware. One device infected with Mirai malware is required to start the chain reaction. This device starts scanning the network with a random IP address. The random IP address then is checked for its existence. Once the bot makes sure that the IP address is up, it starts connecting with the telnet protocol. Mirai malware comprises of default user-

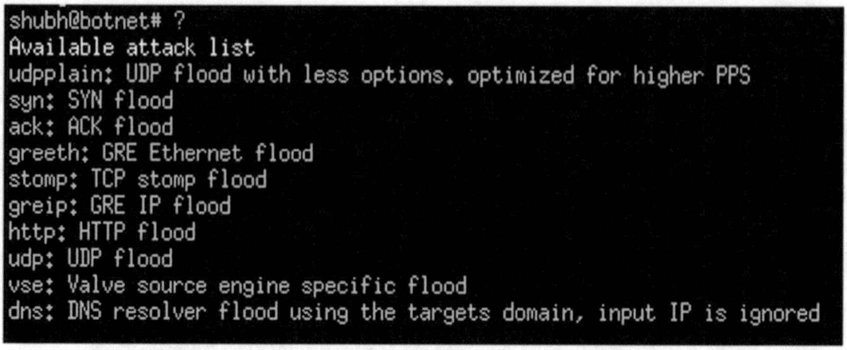

```
shubh@botnet# ?
Available attack list
udpplain: UDP flood with less options, optimized for higher PPS
syn: SYN flood
ack: ACK flood
greeth: GRE Ethernet flood
stomp: TCP stomp flood
greip: GRE IP flood
http: HTTP flood
udp: UDP flood
vse: Valve source engine specific flood
dns: DNS resolver flood using the targets domain, input IP is ignored
```

Fig. 3 Available attacks in Mirai malware

name and password list stored in the table. Those credentials are tried exhaustively until it finds the correct one. A successful guess sends the IoT device's IP address, credentials, and architecture type to the scanListen server. These results are later passed to the loader program to send the downloader file to those IoT devices, and the downloader file would download the Mirai malware and repeat this process again and again. This chain reaction would make the size of the botnet grow very rapidly after some point. Other than scanning, bot also performs attacks on the victim device as commanded by the C&C server. The list of available attacks is showing in Fig. 3.

5 Conclusion and Future Work

Previous sections showed the implementation and working of Mirai malware. It provided various points to defend IoT devices from the Mirai attack. Implementing solutions with multiple checks can be difficult to deploy on IoT devices due to resource constraints. However, small changes in the IoT devices would help to decrease the probability of getting compromised. Knowing the whole procedure of Mirai would help to create the mitigation techniques in future. Researchers should try to defend the attacks strategy mentioned in the Mirai malware and see the possibility of new attacks that the attackers can further add.

References

1. Krebs B (2016) DDoS on Dyn Impacts Twitter, Spotify, Reddit. https://krebsonsecurity.com/2016/09/krebsonsecurity-hit-with-record-ddos
2. Krebs B (2017) How Google Took on Mirai, KrebsOnSecurity—Krebs on Security. https://krebsonsecurity.com/2017/02/how-google-took-on-mirai-krebsonsecurity/

3. Krebs B (2016) New Mirai Worm Knocks 900K Germans Offline—Krebs on Security. https://krebsonsecurity.com/2016/11/new-mirai-worm-knocks-900k-germans-offline/
4. Kolias C, Kambourakis G, Stavrou A, Voas J (2017) DDoS in the IoT: Mirai and other botnets. Computer 50(7):80–84
5. Anagnostopoulos M, Kambourakis G, Kopanos P, Louloudakis G, Gritzalis S (2013) DNS amplification attack revisited. Comput Secur 39:475–485
6. Zebari RR, Zeebaree SRM, Jacksi K (2018) Impact analysis of HTTP and SYN flood DDoS attacks on apache 2 and IIS 10.0 Web servers. In: 2018 international conference on advanced science and engineering (ICOASE). IEEE, pp 156–161
7. Krebs B (2016) DDoS on Dyn Impacts Twitter, Spotify, Reddit. https://krebsonsecurity.com/2016/10/ddos-on-dyn-impacts-twitter-spotify-reddit/
8. Gamblin J (2017) Mirai-Source-Code at master. https://github.com/jgamblin/Mirai-Source-Code
9. Tanaka H, Yamaguchi S (2017) On modeling and simulation of the behavior of IoT malwares Mirai and Hajime. In: 2017 IEEE international symposium on consumer electronics (ISCE). IEEE, pp 56–60
10. Gopal TS, Meerolla M, Jyostna G,Eswari PRl, Magesh E (2018) Mitigating Mirai malware spreading in IoT environment. In: 2018 international conference on advances in computing, communications and informatics (ICACCI). IEEE, pp 2226–2230
11. Kumar S, Lone ZA, Chandavarkar BR (2021) Essential requirements of IoT's cryptographic algorithms: case study. In: ICCCE 2020. Springer, Singapore, pp 163–169
12. Jaramillo LES (2018) Malware detection and mitigation techniques: lessons learned from Mirai DDOS attack. J Inf Syst Eng Manag 3(3):19
13. Su J, Vasconcellos DV, Prasad S, Sgandurra D, Feng Y, Sakurai K (2018) Lightweight classification of IoT malware based on image recognition. In: 2018 IEEE 42Nd annual computer software and applications conference (COMPSAC), vol 2. IEEE, pp 664–669

Realization of 5G NR Primary Synchronization Signal Detector Using Systolic FIR Filter

Aytha Ramesh Kumar, K. Lal Kishore, and Parepalli Sravanthi

1 Introduction

The 5th generation new radio technology is rapidly developing for the latest wireless communications. The 5G specifies the variants of high-speed signal processing, ultra-low latency, massive data conversions, and extensive security with high-end encryption. The mobile cell identification plays a vital role in the accessibility of base station signal at customer end. Also, the inter-channel interference, delay spread, and inter-symbol interference are important criteria which can be overcome by high-performance FIR filters. The aim is to achieve the strong signal at very confined time period, where this can be only obtained with the high-performance components in the DSP units of the wireless devices [1]. The cell identification involves a two-step procedure, such as the primary synchronization signal (PSS) identification and followed by a secondary synchronization signal (SSS) identification. The primary synchronization signal procedure and secondary synchronization signal involve a parallelism of FIR filter units during the filtering of the high data-rate signals and finally capture the relevant cell ID which contributes a high-signal strength [2].

The high-performance FIR filters play a vital role in the wireless data processing algorithms [3]. The work in this paper contributes to a larger extent of designing the high-performance FIR filters using a systolic array architecture, and the MAC units in the FIR filter are incorporated with a high-speed multiplier, i.e., Vedic multiplier and high-speed parallel adder, i.e., carry select adder. The major criteria of designing a high-performance FIR filter are high-speed data processing, ultra-low latency, low-power consumption, and less area utilization [4]. The paper proposes the algorithm

A. R. Kumar (✉) · P. Sravanthi
Department of ECE, VNR VJIET, Hyderabad, India
e-mail: rameshkumar_a@vnrvjiet.in; lncs@springer.com

K. L. Kishore
JNTUA, Anantapur, India

for designing a systolic FIR filter with incorporating the high-performance MAC units. Eventually, the novel matched FIR filters in the primary synchronization signal detector are replaced by the proposed systolic FIR filter. The designed is described using Verilog HDL language in Xilinx VIVADO for design, simulation, synthesis, and implementation. The proposed design is implemented on the ZYNC series-7000 (Zed board).

2 Systolic FIR Filter

The systolic array architecture has become a predominant algorithm for implementation of signal processing video and image processing and latest wireless communication [5]. As the signal processing applications are mainly dependent on the finite impulse response digital filters as they are highly stable and are linear in nature. The vital operations carried over the real-time digital signal processing applications are the additions and multiplications. Thereby the speed of the digital filters mainly depends upon the accurate or overall performance of the Mac units, i.e., the arithmetic functions.

The systolic FIR filter comprises of an array of processing elements that perform computations on every clock cycle. It is fully a pipelined structure which will contribute a high-speed processing and ultra-low latencies [6]. The general definition of the systolic FIR filter is represented as shown below. The coefficients are sequenced as in the following, and the FIR representation is shown in Fig. 1.

$$\{w_1, w_2, ..., w_n\}$$

And the sequences for input

$$\{x_1, x_2, \ldots, x_n\}$$

Finally, the resultant sequence is obtained as

$$\{y_1, y_2, \ldots, y_n\}.$$

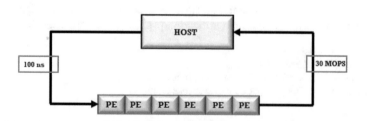

Fig. 1 FIR filter with systolic array algorithm

General expression is given as

$$yi = \sum_{k=0}^{n} h(n)x(k-n) \tag{1}$$

2.1 Proposed Algorithm for Systolic FIR Filter

Step 1: The initial FIR filter is described as a dependence flow graph with resultant, input, and weights. The Figs. 2 and 3 depict the DFG representation of a novel FIR filter. The x, y, and w refer to the initial values of input, result, and the weight, respectively, and the x', y', and w' are their consecutive values where arithmetic operations are performed on the initial vales after passing through the node (i.e., processing element).

Step 2: Select the space time vectors to design the desired systolic FIR filter $d^T = (1\ 0)$, $p^T = (0\ 1)$, and $s^T = (1\ -1)$. The edge is mapped with the scheduling vector and process space vector, the space time representation for the systolic FIR filter is obtained, and the dependence graph with space time representation is shown in Fig. 4; Table 1.

Step 3: The processing element is further designed using this space time representation model. Thereby the processing element is represented with respect to the edge mapping calculations.

Step 4: The processing element represented in Fig. 5 is repeated to build the array of systolic FIR filter. Thereby the N-tap systolic FIR filter, $N = 16$, is represented as shown in Fig. 6.

Fig. 2 Processing element

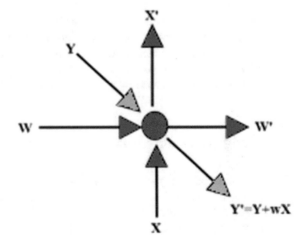

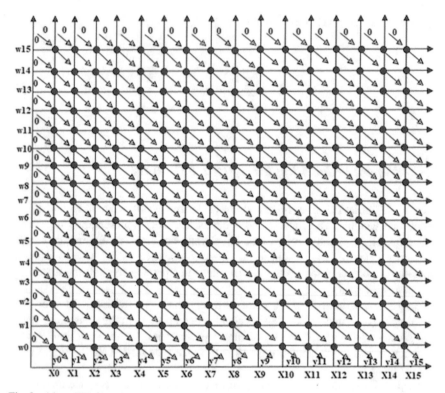

Fig. 3. 16-tap FIR filter dependence graph representation

3 Design of High-Speed MAC Units

The digital filters are made of the basic circuits adders and multipliers to compute the input data signal and perform necessary computations over them and finally determine the final filter output. Several MAC units are required in the partial product generation stage which then affects multipliers, and the accumulated partial products are summated using the adder circuits. Various conventional multipliers and adders with different approaches and low-power techniques are used for designing the digital FIR filters which are proposed by the researchers in the last 20 years.

3.1 Design of 16-Bit Carry Select Adder

The carry select adder algorithm is split into two major phases. Let us consider the higher order bits, i.e., 8-bit, 16-bit, etc. The 1st phase includes the general addition using ripple carry process, and the 2nd phase of addition is carried out by using the maximum possibility of the carry in bits [7]. Thereby the carry in bits will be of two

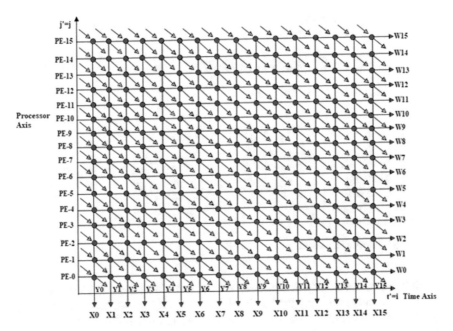

Fig. 4 DFG after applying the space time representation: $j' = j$ (processor axis); $t' = i$ (time axis)

Table 1 Edge mapping of space vectors

Edge (e)	Projection direction ($p^T e$)	Delay ($s^T e$)
Input (0, 1)	-1	1
Weight (1, 0)	0	1
Result (1, -1)	-1	2

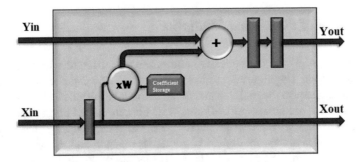

Fig. 5 Processing element using desired space vector set

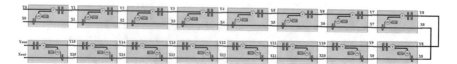

Fig. 6 Proposed 16-bit systolic FIR filter

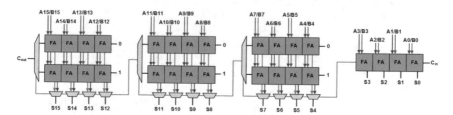

Fig. 7. 16-bit carry select adder

possibilities as such carry in = 0 and carry in = 1. After the 2nd phase performs its respective addition using the possibilities of the carry in bits, then the final carry and final sum bits are determined. The results of the carry select adder depend on the carry out of the 1st phase where in the multiplexor, input is fed from it. Now, considering the select line bit of the multiplexor, the results will be determined or selected for the addition of the two words. Hereby the carry select adder is one of the fastest adders which can perform addition operation in two phase model regardless of the n-bit input. The 16-bit carry select adder is designed using the lower 4-bit carry select adder units as shown in below block representation as Fig. 7.

3.2   Design of 8-bit Vedic Multiplier

The algorithm of Vedic multiplication comprises of a crisscross technique for n-bit multiplication. The algorithm is basically divided into 3 phases of calculation performance, and also the multiplicands used in the multiplication are split into two equal halves and are termed as LSB and MSB bits. In the 1st phase, the LSB bits are multiplied and provided as product; in the 2nd stage, the LSB and MSB bits of both multiplicands are multiplied in crisscross manner, and this partial product is conserved [8]. In the 3rd phase, the MSB bits are multiplied, and the product is obtained. Finally, all the partial products are summed using the respective n-bit adder, and the final product term is generated in a single unit step. Thus, the Vedic algorithm provides a parallel multiplication and thereby is among the high-speed multipliers. The general formula for the Vedic multiplication algorithm is defined as shown below.

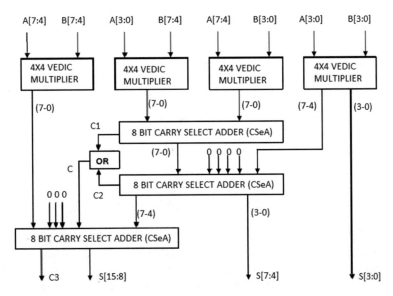

Fig. 8. 8-bit vedic multiplier

$$AM \times BM \dfrac{\begin{array}{cc} AM & AL \\ BM & BL \end{array}}{\begin{array}{c} AM \times BL \\ \downarrow \quad AL \times BM \quad \downarrow \end{array}} AL \times BL$$

The 8-bit Vedic multiplication block is represented in a hierarchical manner by using 4-bit Vedic multiplier units as defined in the Fig. 8.

4 5G NR Cell ID Detection Using Proposed Systolic FIR Filter

The cell ID synchronization and detection play a major role in the cellular system for high-speed wireless communications [9]. The PSS comprises of 127 symbols which are bounded as a wide group of NID2, and this is further communicated as individual group sorting of say 0, 1, and 2. The 5G NR is paired up with the Zadoff-Chu groupings, and these sequences are generated by using an m-sequencer where the computational expressions are defined in Eqs. 2 and 3.

$$x(i + 7) = (x(i + 4) + x(i)) \bmod 2 \tag{2}$$

where the initial input value to the m-sequencer will be

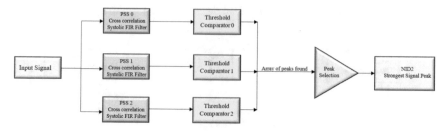

Fig. 9. 5G NR primary synchronization signal detection block representation using proposed systolic FIR filter

$$[x(6)x(5)x(4)x(3)x(2)x(1)x(0)] = [1\ 1\ 1\ 0\ 1\ 1\ 0] \tag{3}$$

The 5G NR PSS block [10] is designed using the proposed systolic FIR filter and is represented as shown in the Fig. 9. The input signal is fed to the proposed systolic FIR filter with different channel coefficients generated by the m-sequencer, and the highest signal peak is populated as the output of the PSS block which is defined as the NID2 signal value.

5 Simulation Results

In the Xilinx Vivado tool, there consists of the design entry, synthesis, and implementation for the desired design that we want to implement. Here, we use the Xilinx tool for designing the proposed systolic FIR filter which comprises of high-performance MAC units in the design and simulations, the final systolic FIR filter is shown in below Fig. 10, and the simulation results are shown in Fig. 11.

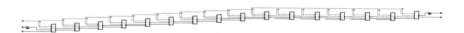

Fig. 10 Schematic block representation of proposed systolic FIR filter

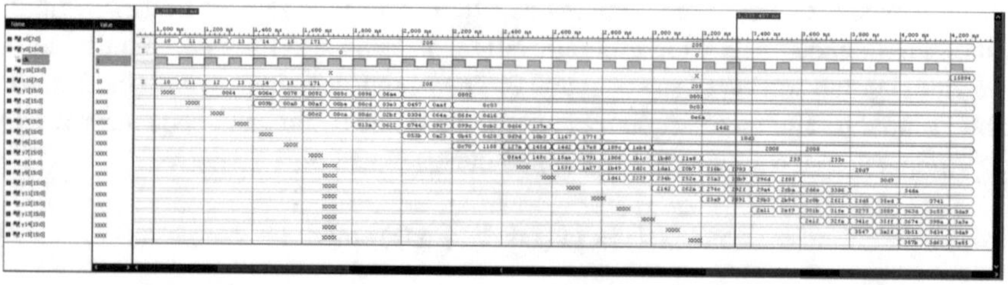

Fig. 11 Simulation waveforms of proposed systolic FIR filter

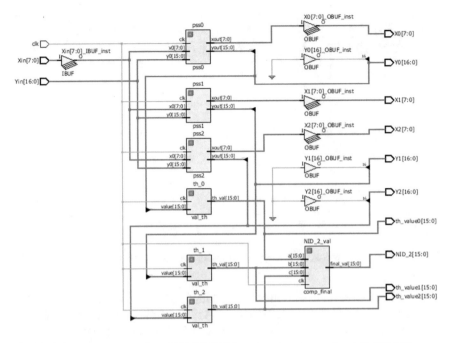

Fig. 12 Schematic representation of 5G NR PSS detector using proposed systolic FIR filter

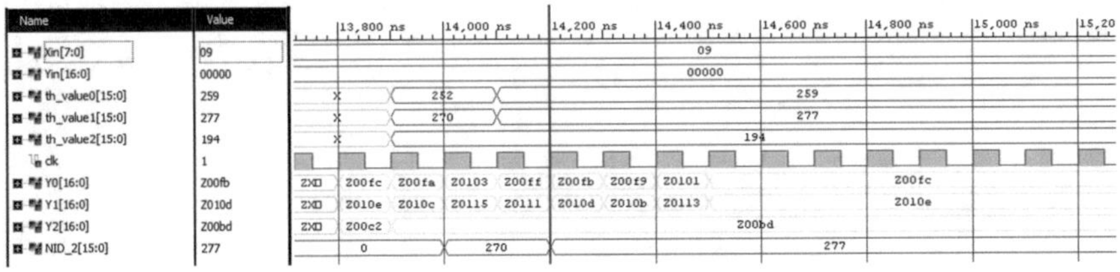

Fig. 13 Simulation waves of directed test verification for 5G NR PSS block

The 5G NR cell ID for detecting PSS [11] is incorporated with the proposed systolic FIR filter algorithm as shown in Fig. 12. The overall performance of the cell ID detection is improved, and the comparisons are done with respect to the existing techniques which are discussed in further session (Figs. 13, 14, 15 and 16).

6 Conclusion

The 5G NR PSS block design incorporated by the proposed systolic FIR filter confirms the high-performance computations when compared to the existing techniques as shown in Table 2 and Fig. 17. The designs are defined in Verilog HDL in

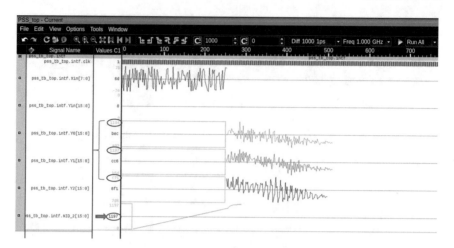

Fig. 14 Simulation waves of constraint test verification for 5G NR PSS block

Xilinx VIVADO 2016.4 and is implemented for ZYNC-7000 series Zed board. The
5G NR PSS block using proposed systolic FIR filter resulted in the reduction in LUT
utilization constituting the total area reduction of 56.2%. The delay parameters were
improved by 78.3% due to the high-speed and low-power MAC units incorporated in
the design. The proposed systolic FIR filter can be extended for the applications of
5G NR SSS, signal processing, 5G image processing, and decision-based algorithms
(Table 3).

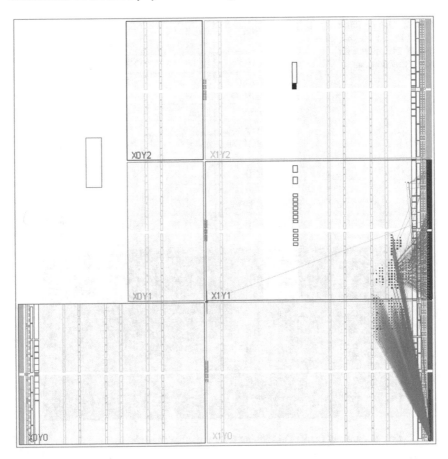

Fig. 15 Implemented design of 5G NR PSS detector incorporated by proposed systolic FIR filter units

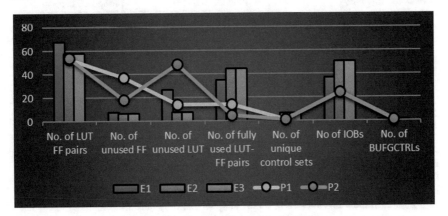

Fig. 16 Device summary for proposed systolic FIR filter w.r.t existing methods

Table 2 Device summary of 5G NR PSS using proposed systolic FIR filter with existing techniques

Utilization summary	Existing method [10]	Existing method [10]	Proposed method
	E1	E2	P1
Numbers of slice registers	594	660	1764
Number of slices LUTs	4556	23075	2169
Number of flip flops	455	10679	848
No of IOBs	70	93	64
No. of BUFGCTRLs	1	1	1
Total delay	41.010 ns	41.554 ns	13.800 ns

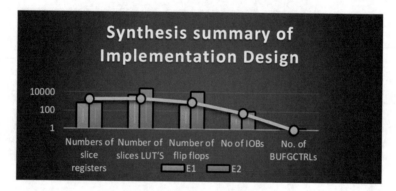

Fig. 17 Device summary for 5G NR PSS block w.r.t existing methods

Table 3 Device summary of proposed systolic FIR filter with existing techniques

Utilization summary	Existing methods [4]			Proposed method	
	E1	E2	E3	P1	P2
No. of LUT-FF pairs	67	57	57	53	54
No. of unused FF	7	6	6	37	18
No. of unused LUT	26	7	7	14	48
No. of fully used LUT-FF pairs	34	44	44	14	5
No. of unique control sets	3	6	6	1	1
No of IOBs	36	50	50	24	24
No. of BUFGCTRLs	1	1	1	1	1

E1- Direct form folded FIR filter using pipelined carry-propagate multiplier
E2- Direct form folded FIR filter using pipelined carry-save multiplier
E3-Direct form transposed FIR filter of pipelined using carry-save multiplier
P1- Proposed systolic FIR filter using Vedic multiplier and carry look ahead adder
P2- Proposed systolic FIR filter using Vedic multiplier and carry select adder

References

1. Razee AM, Dziyauddin RA, Azmi MH, Sadon SK (2018) Comparative performance analysis of IIR and FIR filters for 5G networks. In: Proceedings of 2nd international conference on telematics and future generation networks (TAFGEN), 24–26 July 2018
2. Tsao Y-C, Choi K (2010) Area-efficient parallel FIR digital filter structures for symmetric convolutions based on fast FIR algorithm. In: IEEE transactions very large scale integration (VLSI) system, vol. 20, No. 2, Feb 2010, pp 366–371
3. Ye J, Yanagisawa M, Shi Y (2019) A bit-segmented adder chain based symmetric transpose two-block FIR design for high-speed signal processing. In: Proceedings of IEEE Asia pacific conference on circuits and systems (APCCAS), 11–14 Nov 2019
4. Jayan G, Nair AK (2018) Implementation of folded FIR filter based on pipelined multiplier array. In: Proceedings of the international conference on communication and electronics systems (ICCES 2018), Oct 2018
5. Bougas P, Kalivas P, Tsirikos A, Pekmestzi KZ (2005) Pipelined array-based FIR filter folding. IEEE Trans Circuits Syst Regul Pap 52(1), Jan 2005
6. Jiang H, Liu L, Jonker PP, Elliott DG, Lombardi F, Han J (2019) A high-performance and energy-efficient FIR adaptive filter using approximate distributed arithmetic circuits. IEEE Trans Circuits Syst I Regul Pap 66(1):313–326
7. Dhivya VM, Sridevi A (2014) A high-speed transposed form FIR filter using floating point Dadda multiplier. J Int J Res Eng Sci (IJRES). 2(5):14–20, May 2014
8. Tsao Y-C, Choi K (2012) Area-efficient VLSI implementation for parallel linear-phase FIR digital filters of odd length based on fast FIR algorithm. IEEE Trans Circuits Syst II: Express Briefs 59(6), June 2012
9. Shahbaz MM, Wakeel A (2019) FPGA based implementation of FIR filter for FOFDM waveform. In: Proceedings of 2nd international conference of communication, computing and digital systems, Apr 2019
10. Kumar AR, Kishore KL, Fatima A (2021) Implementation of 5G NR primary and secondary synchronization. Turk J Comput Math Educ 12(8)3153–3161, 20 Apr 2021
11. Krishnamurthy S, Kannan R, Yahya EA, Bingi K (2017) Design of FIR filter using novel pipelined bypass multiplier. In: Proceedings of IEEE 3rd international symposium on robotics and manufacturing automation (ROMA), Dec 2017

Composition of Static and Dynamic Analysis for Algorithmic-Level Code Semantic Optimization

Mehul Thakral, V. C. Skanda, Bhavna Arora, G. R. Dheemanth, and N. S. Kumar

1 Introduction

Code optimization is the process of modifying a piece of code to improve the quality and make it run efficiently. The optimized program may be smaller, i.e., implemented in fewer lines, consume less system memory, execute quickly, or perform fewer I/O operations. The optimized code is expected to have the same output for a given input as its non-optimized version.

This paper suggests a way to perform code optimization at the algorithm level by using the technique of obtaining semantic labels from code semantic detector [1]. A function-level code is taken as an input and suggests the most optimal alternative present in the dataset of known optimized programs with the same semantic label.

The proposed composite metric is calculated using time, space, cyclomatic complexity, and Halstead difficulty metric. The user can tune the weightage for each of those metrics to get the most optimal program depending on what metric is preferred the most.

Time and memory are dynamically calculated metrics. They are calculated by running the program using various input sizes and finding the complexities using

M. Thakral (✉) · V. C. Skanda · B. Arora · G. R. Dheemanth · N. S. Kumar
Department of Computer Science, PES University, Bangalore, India
e-mail: mehul.thakral@gmail.com

V. C. Skanda
e-mail: skandavc18@gmail.com

B. Arora
e-mail: bhavnaaro28@gmail.com

G. R. Dheemanth
e-mail: dheemanthgr@gmail.com

N. S. Kumar
e-mail: kumaradhara@gmail.com

© The Author(s), under exclusive license to Springer Nature Singapore Pte Ltd. 2023   877
R. Doriya et al. (eds.), *Machine Learning, Image Processing, Network Security and Data Sciences*, Lecture Notes in Electrical Engineering 946,
https://doi.org/10.1007/978-981-19-5868-7_66

polynomial regression. Later, integration is done over the domain of inputs to get a value that would further be used to find the composite metric. Cyclomatic complexity and Halstead difficulty metric are calculated statically using the given function snippet.

2   Literature Survey

2.1   Dynamic Versus Static Optimization Techniques for Object-Oriented Languages [2]

This paper introduces the idea of static and dynamic optimization techniques via type inference and type feedback, respectively. Concrete type inference or constraint-based analysis (Static) computes control-flow and data-flow information simultaneously along with static global analysis to compute a type for every expression.

Type feedback (aka profile-guided receiver class prediction) extracts type information from previous executions and feeds it back. Computing control-flow and data-flow information simultaneously using type inference is necessary to analyze dynamically dispatched sends precisely:

- To determine the methods that a send may invoke, the possible classes (i.e., to know type of receiver) and
- To determine the type of send, i.e., to know the method it may invoke.

Although the proposed solution is specific to the SELF-programming language and SELF-like OO languages, the idea of type inference and type feedback play an important role in to analyze the program for optimization capabilities. Type inference helps to reduce the number of dispatches to be completed along with reducing the size of the application through program extraction without relying on runtime information. Type inference does not support extensible programs. Type feedback is suitable for interactive systems that provide high performance consistently by allowing large and extensible systems to scale well. It usually removes fewer dispatches estimated based on the relative frequencies and is dependent on runtime information.

2.2   Predicting Execution Time of Computer Programs Using Sparse Polynomial Regression [3]

This paper highlights the relationship between the execution time of computer programs and the features of the programs. The prediction model is based on program features' data obtained from program execution on sample inputs. The focus is on feature selection and model building to predict the performance metrics (e.g., execution time) on a particular input. The working of the model is given below:

- Feature Instrumentation: obtain values of features of the program (e.g., loop counts, branch counts, variable values)
- Profiling: execute the program with sample input and collect values
- Slicing: a part or subset of a program that contributes to the feature's value. If the whole program is used, the feature is expensive, and if a subset is used, the feature is cheap.
- Modeling: use the feature value and feature costs to build a predictive model on the subset of features

A sparse polynomial regression (SPORE) model can be learned using two algorithms and showed that both algorithms could predict execution time with more than 93% accuracy for the applications they tested.

2.3   Automatic Algorithmic Complexity Determination Using Dynamic Program Analysis [4]

This study introduces a novel approach for determining algorithmic complexity automatically using runtime metrics. A software application's performance is one of the most critical components of any real-world software. However, simulation, profiling, and measurements performed are usually misleading or incomplete. So, an automated tool based on a theoretical model was created to overcome this problem. The main advantage of knowing the complexity of a method is that it gives an insight into the performance of an operation for large input data sizes. The main contribution of this study is to suggest and evaluate a deterministic approach for determining a method's asymptotic algorithmic complexity. The steps in the suggested model are as follows:

- Analyze input code to find out the input and output parameters
- Executes program multiple times to record the time taken
- Use a nonlinear least square data fitting method to find a curve that fits the measured data
- Compute RMSE metric (root mean square error) for choosing the best matching function.

The implemented tool has a higher accuracy of time complexity prediction for both C++ and Java datasets. For the C++ dataset, the accuracy of the benchmarks is comparable to the implemented tool, but for the java dataset, the implemented tool outperforms the benchmark by around 50%.

2.4 Cisco EIGRP Metric [5]

This article provides a way to combine different attribute values based on weights assigned to each to get a single composite value. EIGRP is a Cisco proprietary routing protocol to find the minimum cost path to reach a destination router considering several network parameters like bandwidth, load, delay, and reliability. The minimum cost value was obtained by comparing the composite value (the composition of the above four attributes) for each available path from the source to the destination router.

The weightage provided to each of the above attributes while composing their values is controlled by K-values. The mapping of K-values to the attribute is mentioned below:

– K1 = Bandwidth; K2 = Load; K3 = Delay; K4 and K5 = Reliability

Using these values, they obtain EIGRP composite metric formula. That formula is given in Fig. 1:

The K-values for each attribute can independently vary between 0 and 255, thus deciding the importance of each attribute in the composite value which will be used for comparing across different paths if an attribute needs not to be considered while calculation can be given a value of 0. Since the K-value can go up to 255, we can decide how much consideration can be given to an attribute.

3 System Architecture

The overall system architecture is presented in Fig. 2.

The user gives a function snippet as input. The function is then sent to the code semantic detector and composite metric finder. The function dataset contains functions across multiple semantic labels along with their metrics. The code semantic detector predicts the label, i.e., the main logic behind the function snippet. The composite metric finder measures the function's time, memory, cyclomatic complexity, and Halstead difficulty value and combines them all, which can be used to compare multiple functions with the same semantic label. All programs in the dataset with the same semantic label as the input function are compared based on the composite metric obtained by accounting for the metric preference given in the

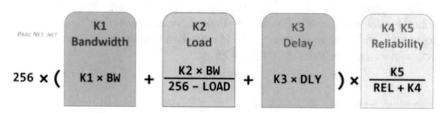

Fig. 1 Cisco metric formula

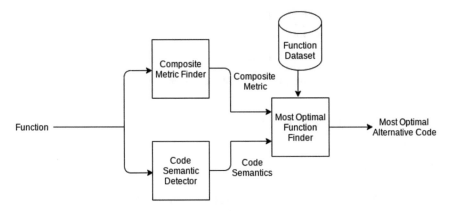

Fig. 2 System architecture

form of weights. The most optimal function finder decides the relevant function to return based on composite value—the lower value of the composite metric, the higher optimized version of the code.

4 Dataset

The dataset is comprised of around 500 Python and 1000 C++ programs scraped from LeetCode belonging to different high-level data structures or algorithmic paradigms. It consists of programs belonging to one of the 25 labels, problems based on arrays, maths, strings, linked lists, trees, graphs, dynamic programming, and backtracking.

The dataset utilized in this study was sourced from code semantic detector [1] that consists of the programs, their vectorized versions, and the respective label. The code semantic optimizer is exposed to a variety of optimized (in terms of the different metrics) and non-optimized versions of the same label to learn, compare, and find the most optimal solution for a label based on the weightage of the metrics.

The programs for each label from the scrapped, preprocessed, and unit tested dataset were passed through a process of calculating all four metrics values and were stored in JSON format, which comes in handy when comparing all the programs with the label same as a test program for the composite metric value based on the weights given by the user.

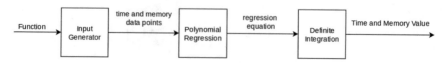

Fig. 3 Flow of operations for dynamically calculated metrics

5 Dynamically Calculated Metrics

5.1 Architecture

The time and memory metrics are calculated dynamically. The given input function is executed on inputs of various sizes. The time taken to execute is recorded along with peak memory used by the function while executing. The upper bound algorithm determines the max input size within which the function can execute for 1 sec. Then, values till upper bound are generated and used for executing the function. Polynomial regression is used to determine the time complexity equation. Later, integration is performed on the obtained equation over the domain of inputs to get the metric values (Fig. 3).

5.2 Input Generator

The input generator uses the upper bound algorithm to find the max input size within which the function can execute in 1 second. The algorithm is explained in Fig. 4. The algorithm is very similar to the binary search algorithm. The time taken and peak memory used is recorded for each run of the function. The polynomial regression algorithm later uses these values.

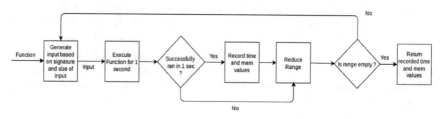

Fig. 4 Input generator

5.3   Polynomial Regression

Polynomial regression is a kind of regression in which the relationship between the independent and dependent variables are modeled as the nth degree of the polynomial of the independent variable.

Using the recorded values from the input generator, the polynomial regression algorithm fits the data to various degrees. The degree varies from 1 to 9. Later, the best polynomial regression model is taken. The R^2 metric is used to select the best model. The algorithm is shown in Fig. 5.

Polynomial regression is used to find the time and space complexities of the given function, which are one of the most crucial measures for evaluating performance. For example, the curve of a $O(n^2)$ algorithm will vary quadratically. This can be found using polynomial regression. So, a polynomial regression model with degree $= 2$ will be the model with the lowest R^2 metric.

5.4   Time and Memory Metric Value Calculation

The equation from polynomial regression cannot be directly used to compare performance. A scalar value is necessary in order to calculate the composite metric. So, the equation obtained is integrated over the domain of inputs in order to get a single scalar value. This is done for both the time and memory equations.

6   Statically Calculated Metrics

Cyclomatic complexity and Halstead difficulty metric are calculated statically from the code. These values are dependent on the control-flow graph and structure of the code. These metrics measure the code's quality and complexity level.

6.1   Cyclomatic Complexity

The order of execution of statements depends on the decision-making statements. The program with more decision statements is expected to be more complex due to more control jumps. The cyclomatic complexity of a code snippet measures the number of linearly independent paths in the code. Cyclomatic Complexity is calculated as $M = E - N + 2P$ where,

- M: cyclomatic complexity
- E: no. of edges in the control-flow graph
- N: no. of nodes in the control-flow graph

Fig. 5 Polynomial regression for finding the time and space complexities

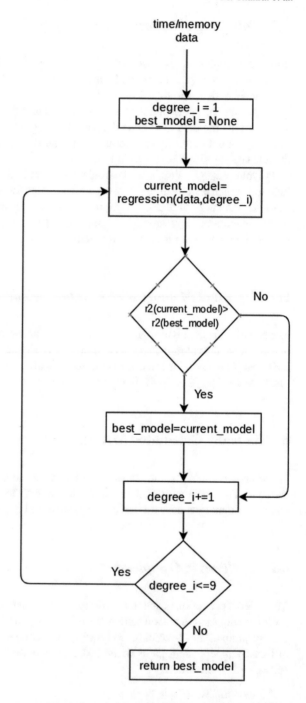

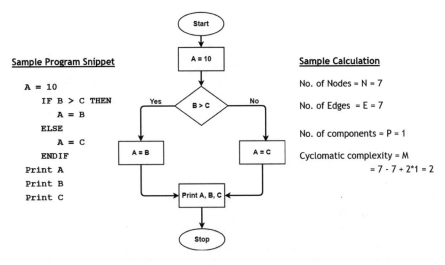

Sample Program Snippet

```
A = 10
    IF B > C THEN
        A = B
    ELSE
        A = C
    ENDIF
Print A
Print B
Print C
```

Sample Calculation

No. of Nodes = N = 7

No. of Edges = E = 7

No. of components = P = 1

Cyclomatic complexity = M
$$= 7 - 7 + 2*1 = 2$$

Fig. 6 Calculation of cyclomatic complexity

– P: no. of connected components.

Refer Fig. 6 for sample program and calculation.

6.2 Halstead Difficulty Metric

The Halstead difficulty metric gives an overview of the redundancy in the code based on the number of operators (n_1) and operands (n_2) with respect to the total number of operators (N1) and operands (N2) in the source code. This is reflected in the actual implementation of the algorithm and is independent of the execution platform. Refer Tables 1 and 2 for Halstead indicators and report generated from these.

Table 1 Indicators to check complexity of a program snippet

Parameter	Meaning
$n1$	Number of unique operators
$n2$	Number of unique operands
$N1$	Number of total occurrence of operators
$N2$	Number of total occurrence of operands

Table 2 Generating Halstead report from indicators

Metric	Meaning	Mathematical representation
n	Vocabulary	n1 + n2
N	Size	N1 + N2
V	Volume	length * log2 (Vocabulary)
D	Difficulty	(n1)/2*(N1)/(n2)
E	Efforts	Difficulty * Volume

6.3 Composition of Metrics

The different static and dynamic metrics are combined similarly as paper [5]. Initially, transformation to the metrics values is applied to ensure all the metrics values have a similar output range to prevent the higher magnitude from dominating the composite value. The transformation chosen is robust scaling. It uses the equations in Eqs. 1 and 2 to get the new values. Since it uses median and interquartile range, hence is robust to outliers and preserves the linear relationship.

$$x_{new} = \frac{x - M}{Q_3 - Q_1} \tag{1}$$

$$x_{new} = \begin{array}{l} < -1, \quad \text{if } x < Q_1 \\ [-1, 1], \text{ if } Q_1 \leq x \leq Q_3 \\ > 1, \quad \text{ if } x > Q_3 \end{array} \tag{2}$$

The values are scaled based on the k values, ranging between 0 and 100. These k values are weights given to each metric by the user to indicate a metric's importance relative to each other. For example, if the given weights for time, memory, cyclomatic, and Halstead difficulty are [2, 1, 0, 0], then it means that the time metric is twice as important as the memory metric, and the other two metrics have no relevance.

These weights and the individual metric values are then combined in the form of a weighted L1 norm (Manhattan distance) to get the final composite metric value as shown in Fig. 7.

7 Results

A test dataset was created to calculate the model's performance which uses an algorithm to obtain an approximate ranking of the programs for each label. The ranking of programs is dependent on the weights of the metrics. This algorithm uses a greedy approach to eliminate the least optimized programs to arrive at a list of the most optimal programs.

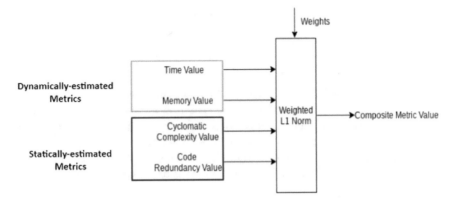

Fig. 7 Composite metric formation

The program suggested by the model should be a part of the list of top optimized programs in the test dataset to be considered accurate. The final accuracies were obtained by executing the model on all the programs with different weight combinations which are presented in Table 3.

Following summarizes the obtained results and experimentation performed:

- Obtained optimization accuracies of both Python and C++ above 85%
- Checked efficacy of different static metrics and memory profilers based on model requirements and ability to implement
- Tried different scaling techniques, namely min–max, standard, but found robust scaling to be robust to outliers

Table 3 Table displaying DS/algorithm-wise accuracy for both python and C++

Data structure/Algorithmic paradigm	Python accuracy (%)	C++ accuracy (%)
Array	85.8	69.1
Math	93.05	86.11
Strings	95.06	73.45
Linked List	88.88	41.97
Trees	78.51	94.96
Graphs	85.18	62.08
Dynamic Programming	91.35	98.76
Backtracking	100	95.06
Overall	88.84	87.33

8 Future Work

Following are some of proposed future works and ideas to enhance the functionality of this paper:

- Extending the development as software for accessing code submission quality in student evaluation systems, online coding platforms, interview settings, and more.
- Using more relevant/impactful metrics, particularly, on statically evaluated part and refining memory profiling on the dynamically evaluated part.
- Setting up a pipeline for automated addition of famous program labels from Leet-Code (or similar coding platforms) and fetching new implementation ways for existing labels.

9 Conclusion

A composite metric approach to finding the most optimal implementation solution for a given program label has been suggested in this paper. The label identification of the unknown program snippet is performed using the code semantic detector. After obtaining the label, the programs with similar labels are compared for their optimality based on the four metrics (i.e., time, space, cyclomatic complexity, and Halstead difficulty) calculated for each program in the dataset. The composite metric is obtained by transforming the individual metric values using robust scaling and getting the weighted L1 norm based on the metric weights given by the user. This composite metric value ranks the programs with similar labels and suggests the most optimal version.

Code semantic detector's labeled C++ and Python languages programs cover the most commonly used programming algorithms. The model developed can suggest the optimal code for a given unknown code snippet with an accuracy above 85% on the test dataset.

References

1. Arora B et al (2021) Code semantic detection. In: 2021 Asian conference on innovation in technology (ASIANCON). https://doi.org/10.1109/ASIANCON51346.2021.9544660, pp 1–6
2. Hölzle U, Agesen O (1995) Dynamic versus static optimization techniques for object-oriented languages. In: Theory and practice of object systems 1(3):167–188
3. Huang L et al (2010) Predicting execution time of computer programs using sparse polynomial regression. Adv Neural Inf Process Syst 23:883–891
4. Czibula IG, Onet-Marian Z, Vida R-F (2019) Automatic algorithmic complexity determination using dynamic program analysis. In: ICSOFT. pp 186–193
5. "EIGRP Metric" (2017) In: Practical networking.net. Available: https://www.practicalnetworking.net/stand-alone/eigrp-metric/ (2017)

A Framework for DDoS Attack Detection in SDN-Based IoT Using Hybrid Classifier

Pinkey Chauhan and Mithilesh Atulkar

1 Introduction

IoT is an emerging paradigm which interconnects different devices in such a manner that the needed information can be given on timely basis without any human interference. It can connect the physical things with virtual world [1]. Smart devices, wearables, cameras, smart lightings along with household appliances like televisions, refrigerators, mobile, wallet, keys, doors, etc., are being connected to the Internet. It gives a rich IoT ecosystem [2]. A typical diagram of IoT is shown in the Fig. 1. The sensors at the left side of the figure are the remote devices that capture the data from different domain. These sensors then transfer the captured data to the Gateway which forwards these data to the servers using wired or wireless media. From the servers, data can be fetched using computer system or mobiles.

Software Defined Network (SDN) is currently an emerging network architecture used in many IT industries and academia to achieve different objectives like Security, Cloud, BigData, Virtualization, etc. Architecture of SDN is shown in Fig. 2. In SDN, there are three layers; infrastructure layer, control layer and application layer. The separation of the control plane from the data plane has given many advantages over traditional network like manageability, programmability, etc. [3, 4]. It gives the controller the capability of global view [4–6] which enables the controller to control all the activities of the network. It is called the brain of the SDN [7, 8]. All the decision making logic resides in the control plane. Due to the growing demand of SDN, many attackers are targeting SDN. DDoS is one among those attacks. In DDoS attacks, a large number of ICMP, TCP or UDP packets are sent to the target and the

P. Chauhan (✉) · M. Atulkar
National Institute of Technology, Raipur, Chhattisgarh, India
e-mail: pchauhan.phd2018.mca@nitrr.ac.in

M. Atulkar
e-mail: matulkar.mca@nitrr.ac.in

© The Author(s), under exclusive license to Springer Nature Singapore Pte Ltd. 2023   889
R. Doriya et al. (eds.), *Machine Learning, Image Processing, Network Security and Data Sciences*, Lecture Notes in Electrical Engineering 946,
https://doi.org/10.1007/978-981-19-5868-7_67

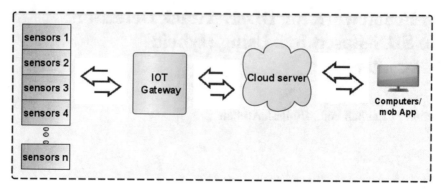

Fig. 1 IoT architecture

response of the target is slowed down. Although, in most of the cases attack is done in the control layer [9] but the data plane is the part from where the devices send the requests to the controller so it is also the equally vulnerable to attack.

SDN-based IoT is that where all the IoT devices send the data to the switch of the dataplane of the SDN through gateway and then next step depends on the decision taken by SDN controller. In this structure advantages is that all the decision is centrally taken by the controller so if any unwanted activity is happening in the network, it can be controlled by the controller. The drawback with this architecture is that the controller which is already loaded with some important decision making works has to participate in the detection of DDoS attack so the performance of the controller degrades. So if the decision making logic is incorporated in the openflow enabled switch of the SDN, the DDoS attack detection can be done in the dataplane

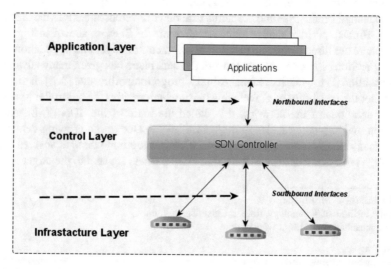

Fig. 2 SDN architecture

itself and hence the performance of Controller can be improved. This is the main contribution of this work. Diagram of SDN-based IoT is shown in the Fig. 3.

For making the communication between the controller and the data plane, openflow protocol is used which is also called south bound interface. The main fields of openflow protocol are shown in the Fig. 4 [10, 11]. When a packet comes to a switch while going to its destination, switch forwards it based on the rules that are available in it is flow table.

The intrusion detection systems (IDS) are categorized into two categories; Sig-nature-based intrusion detection system (SIDS) and Anomaly-based intrusion detection system (AIDS) [12]. SIDS systems work based on pattern matching technique to detect a known attack while in AIDS, a model is trained

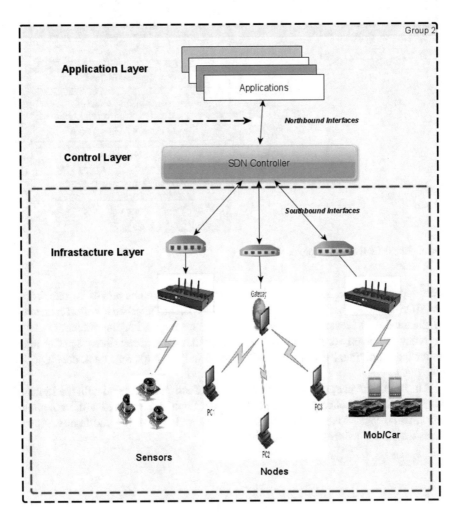

Fig. 3 The SDN-based IoT

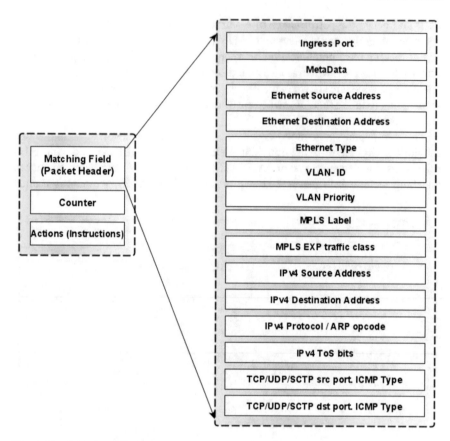

Fig. 4 The field of openflow protocol

then deployed in the network. A deviated traffic is treated as attack. In this work, an AIDS-based stack framework is proposed to detect DDoS attack. Performances of the model is measured on many performance measuring parameters namely, accuracy, precision, recall, F1-value. It is found that stack of classifiers is performing better than individual classifier in SDN-based IoT network for attack detection in data plane.

The rest of the paper is organized as follows. Section 2 is related with the Related Work. Section 3 is concerned with Methodology. Section 4 is related with Implementation while Sect. 5 is related with Experiments and Discussion and finally Sect. 6 deals with Conclusion and Future Work.

2 Related Work

Many works to deal with DDoS attacks for SDN-based IoT have been done. The statistical information entropy-based methods for detection of the DDoS attack is a common method and used in many algorithms. In Kalkan et al. [13], authors have proposed an entropy-based joint scoring system to detect and mitigate it using Ryu controller. They have used Mininet and generated different attacks.

In Giotis et al. [14], authors have used sFlow for sampling of the traffic and entropy based method for the detection and classification of the attack. They have used NOX controller for attack detection and mitigation. In Kumar et al. [15], authors again used entropy method to determine the randomness of the flow data. They have used floodlight controller and Mininet for different scenario.

In Chen et al. [16], authors have used XGBoost classifier for the detection of the attack. They have used Mininet and POX as SDN controller, Hyenae tool to generate the attack and tcpdump to collect the traffic. In Niyaz et al. [17], authors have used deep learning based sparse auto encoder for their malicious defense system. In Haider et al. [18], authors have used a deep CNN to detect the DDoS attack in SDN network and found that this model is performing better than other models under a state of the art dataset.

In Wang et al. [19], authors are deploying multiple controllers in the control plane of SDN. The work of the module in data plane is to detect the anomalous traffic of the network. They have used Mininet emulator and Ryu controller to demonstrate their work.

In Tan et al. [20], authors have experimented trigger based attack detection mech-anism in the data plane of the SDN. Then they used the combined mech-anism on KNN and K-Means in the controller to block the malicious traffic. They are using ONOS as SDN controller and Mininet to create the topology of the network. In Ye et al. [11], authors have performed the work of DDoS attack detection using SVM. They are using Mininet and Floodlight controller.

3 Methodology

In this work, the main objective is to detect the DDoS attack in the data plane of the SDN-based IoT. The DDoS attack is that where multiple nodes in the network start attacking a target using TCP, UDP or ICMP packets in such a manner that target system becomes unable to reply all the sources. In this case the genuine requests are also not replied by the target. There are some solutions proposed for detecting the DDoS attack in the controller of the SDN-based IoT but they are being done in the control plane of the SDN. Using those approaches, the controller has to participate in the detection of DDoS attack and hence the performance of the controller and network degrades.

To enhance the performance of DDoS attack detection in SDN-based IoT, stack of classifiers is proposed to be used in place of a single classifier as AIDS in the switch of SDN-based IoT. For this purpose, SVM and KNN are used as the level 0 classifier and LogisticRegression is used as level 1 classifier. To check the performance of the stack of the classifiers, its performance is checked in terms of Accuracy, Precision, Recall, and $F1$-value using NSL-KDD classifier. The same performance metrics were also calculated for the individual classifiers, i.e., SVM and KNN.

As the NSL-KDD dataset is not in the state to be used directly for training and testing so it was preprocessed first. For this, label encoding, one hot encoding, etc., were performed and then DDoS attack related records were selected. After this, standardization of the data was performed to normalize the data. These records were broken in the ratio of 70 and 30 for the training and testing, respectively.

3.1 Classifiers Used

K-Nearest Neighbor (KNN) is a supervised algorithm which solves classification and regression problems. It is easy to apply but it is said a lazy learner [21, 22]. Reason is, it takes time to calculate the distance between k-nearest points. KNN can handle the noise and provides best accuracy so it works efficiently in case of DDoS attack detection [23]. The KNN classifier uses Minkowski distance by default but the Manhattam distance measuring method is the best method [24, 25] so it has been used in this work. The diagram is shown in Fig. 5.
Support Vector Machine (SVM) is a supervised learning model which can be used as regressor or classifier [3, 26]. It is work depends on hyperplane and vectors. Vectors are points nearest to the hyperplane and hyperplane is a plane in between those vectors whose distance is maximum from the vector points. SVM can be used with different kernels like linear, polynomial, Gaussian, etc., as per the need. Many works [8, 27–29] have been done and suggest that SVM performs better in the case of DDoS attack detection in SDN. The diagram is shown in Fig. 6.
Stack of Classifiers For the better prediction of results, a stack of the classifiers is used where there exists two levels of classifiers namely, level 0 and level 1. In level 0, more than one classifier is used whose predictions are used as the input to the level 1 learner/classifier, i.e., the output of the level 0 classifiers are used as the input to the next level (level 1) classifier. Some research works [30–32] have shown that the prediction by the stack of the classifiers is better than that of individual classifier. The diagram is shown in Fig. 7.

3.2 Dataset Used

The dataset used to measure the performance of the stack of hybrid classifier-based framework to detect DDoS attack in SDN-based IoT is NSL-KDD. Initially the

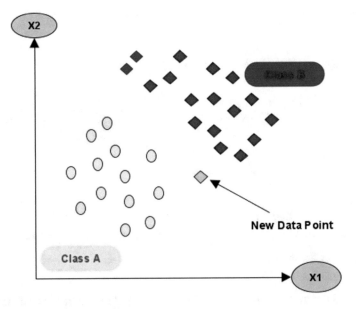

Fig. 5 Diagram of *K*-nearest neighbors

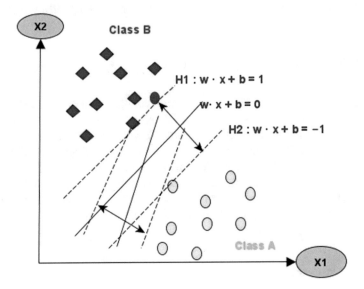

Fig. 6 Diagram of support vector machine

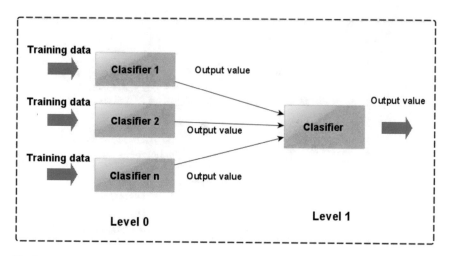

Fig. 7 Stack of classifiers

dataset was not in the form that could be directly used for the training and testing of the model. So, first it was preprocessed and then DDoS attack-based records have been selected. The dataset is split in the ratio of 70:30 for training and testing purpose.

4 Implementation Environment

Operating system used is Ubuntu 16.04 whose configuration is 8 GB RAM, AMD Processor having 1867 MHz speed. Python is used as the base language to implement the work. Sklearn is used as machine learning library. We have used Support Vector Machine classifier, KNN classifier at level 0 and Logistic Regression classifier at level 1 for the stack of hybrid classifier. The dataset used is NSL-KDD to check the performance. For the detection of DDoS attack in the live environment of SDN-based IoT, the trained classifier can be incorporated in any openflow enabled switch of the dataplane where gateway of the IoT devices is connected.

5 Experiments and Discussion

As the NSL-KDD dataset is not in the state to be used directly for training and testing so it was preprocessed first. For this, label encoding, one hot encoding, etc., were performed and then DDoS attack related records were selected. After this, standardization was performed to normalize the data. These records were broken in the ratio of 70 and 30 after shuffling of the record for the training and testing, respectively.

To check the performance of stack of the classifiers, SVM and KNN are used as the level 0 classifier and LogisticRegression is used as level 1 classifier. Preprocessed NSL-KDD dataset is used to check the performance in terms of Accuracy, Precision, Recall, and F1-value using NSL-KDD classifier.

The performance of stack classifier is calculated in terms of Accuracy, Precision, Recall, and F1-value. Formulas to calculate all these values are explained in [33] and are shown in the Eqs. (1–4).

The same metrics are also calculated for individual classifiers, i.e., for SVM and KNN.

$$Accuracy = \frac{TP + TN}{TP + TN + FP + FN} \tag{1}$$

$$Precision = \frac{TP}{TP + FP} \tag{2}$$

$$Recall = \frac{TP}{TP + FN} \tag{3}$$

$$F1\text{ - }Score = \frac{2 * Recall * Precision}{Recall + Precision} \tag{4}$$

The values of Accuracy, Precision, Recall, and F1-value of stack classifier and individual classifiers, i.e., SVM and KNN are shown in Figs. 8a, b, c and d respectively. Also the comparative performance analysis is shown in Fig. 8e

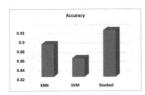

(a) Accuracy Comparison

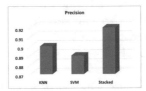

(b) Precision Comparison

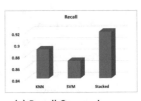

(c) Recall Comparison

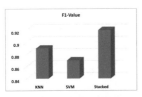

(d) F1-Value Comparison

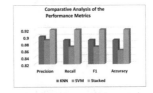

(e) Comparative Analysis of All the Classifiers

Fig. 8 Figures to show different performance measuring metrics. **a** Accuracy comparison, **b** Precision comparison, **c** Recall comparison, **d** F1-value comparison, **e** Comparative analysis of all the classifiers

Table 1 Comparative
analysis of classifiers

Metrics name	KNN	SVM	Hybrid
Accuracy	0.89	0.86	0.91
Precision	0.9	0.89	0.92
Recall	0.89	0.87	0.92
$F1$-value	0.89	0.87	0.91

The accuracy value of KNN, SVM and Stack classifiers are 0.89, 0.86, 0.91, respectively. The precision of these classifiers are 0.9, 0.89, 0.92, respectively. The recall value of KNN, SVM and Stack classifiers are 0.89, 0.87, 0.92, respectively. And the $F1$-Value of KNN, SVM and Stack classifiers are 0.89, 0.87, 0.91 respectively. Looking into all these values, it can be said that the performance of stacked classifier is better than that of individual classifiers in terms of Accuracy, Precision, Recall, and $F1$-value.

6 Conclusion and Future Work

This paper proposes a framework to detect DDoS attack in the SDN-based IoT architecture using stack of hybrid classifier. To accomplish this work, KNN and SVM are used as level 0 classifier and LogisticRegression as level 1 classifier of the stack of hybrid classifier. To check the performance, this stack of hybrid classifier is trained and tested using NSL-KDD dataset and then individual classifier, i.e., SVM and KNN were also trained and tested using the same dataset. There performances were calculated in terms of Accuracy, Precision, Recall and $F1$-value. It is found that performance of stack of hybrid classifier is better than that of individual classifiers.

In future, the same work can be done on other IoT-based datasets. Also, the other well-known classifiers can be used in the level 0 of the hybrid classifier. Moreover, combination of these level 0 classifiers can be used with some other well know classifiers in level 1. As an enhancement of the work the same approach can be done for multi-controller SDN-based IoT.

References

1. Bhunia SS, Gurusamy M (2017) Dynamic attack detection and mitigation in IoT using SDN. In: 27th International telecommunication networks and applications conference, ITNAC 2017, vol 2017-Jan. https://doi.org/10.1109/ATNAC.2017.8215418
2. Gubbi J, Buyya R, Marusic S, Palaniswami M (2013) Internet of Things (IoT):a vision, architectural elements, and future directions. Future Gener Comput Syst 29(7). https://doi.org/10.1016/j.future.2013.01.010

3. Polat H, Polat O, Cetin A (2020) Detecting DDoS attacks in software-defined networks through feature selection methods and machine learning models. Sustainability (Switzerland) 12(3). https://doi.org/10.3390/su12031035
4. Su J, Xu R, Yu SM, Wang BW, Wang J (2020) Redundant rule detection for software-defined networking. KSII Trans Internet Inf Syst 14(6). https://doi.org/10.3837/tiis.2020.06.022
5. Stancu AL, Halunga S, Vulpe A, Suciu G, Fratu O, Popovici EC (2015) A comparison between several software defined networking controllers. In: 12th International conference on telecommunications in modern satellite, cable and broadcasting services, TELSIKS 2015. https://doi.org/10.1109/TELSKS.2015.7357774
6. Mamushiane L, Lysko A, Dlamini S (2018) A comparative evaluation of the perfor-mance of popular SDN controllers. In: IFIP wireless days, vol 2018-April. https://doi.org/10.1109/WD.2018.8361694
7. Mahrach S, Haqiq A (2020) DDoS flooding attack mitigation in software defined networks. Int J Adv Comput Sci Appl 11(1). https://doi.org/10.14569/ijacsa.2020.0110185
8. Meti N, Narayan DG, Baligar VP (2017) Detection of distributed denial of service attacks using machine learning algorithms in software defined networks. In: 2017 International conference on advances in computing, communications and informatics, ICACCI 2017, vol 2017-Jan. https://doi.org/10.1109/ICACCI.2017.8126031
9. Liu Y, Zhao B, Zhao P, Fan P, Liu H (2019). A survey: typical security issues of software-defined networking. https://doi.org/10.23919/j.cc.2019.07.002
10. Ali J, Lee S, Roh BH (2018) Performance analysis of POX and Ryu with different SDN topologies. In: ACM international conference proceeding series. https://doi.org/10.1145/3209914.3209931
11. Ye J, Cheng X, Zhu J, Feng L, Song L (2018) A DDoS attack detection method based on SVM in software defined network. Secur Commun Network. https://doi.org/10.1155/2018/9804061
12. Khraisat A, Gondal I, Vamplew P, Kamruzzaman J (2019) Survey of intrusion detection systems: techniques, datasets and challenges. Cybersecurity 2(1). https://doi.org/10.1186/s42400-019-0038-7
13. Kalkan K, Altay L, Gür G Alagöz F (2018) JESS: joint entropy-based DDoS defense scheme in SDN. IEEE J Sel Areas in Commun 36(10). DOI https://doi.org/10.1109/JSAC.2018.2869997
14. Giotis K, Argyropoulos C, Androulidakis G, Kalogeras D, Maglaris V (2014) Combining openflow and sFlow for an effective and scalable anomaly detection and mitigation mechanism on SDN environments. Comput Network 62. https://doi.org/10.1016/j.bjp.2013.10.014
15. Kumar P, Tripathi M, Nehra A, Conti M, Lal C (2018) SAFETY: early detection and mitigation of TCP SYN flood utilizing entropy in SDN. IEEE Trans Network Serv Manage 15(4). https://doi.org/10.1109/TNSM.2018.2861741
16. Chen Z, Jiang F, Cheng Y, Gu X, Liu W, Peng J (2018) XGBoost classifier for DDoS attack detection and analysis in SDN-based cloud. In: Proceedings IEEE international conference on big data and smart computing, BigComp 2018. https://doi.org/10.1109/BigComp.2018.00044
17. Niyaz Q, Sun W, Javaid AY (2017) A deep learning based DDoS detection system in software-defined networking (SDN). ICST Trans Secur Saf 4(12) (2017). https://doi.org/10.4108/eai.28-12-2017.153515
18. Haider S, Akhunzada A, Mustafa I, Patel TB, Fernandez A, Choo KKR, Iqbal J (2020) A deep CNN ensemble framework for efficient DDoS attack detection in software defined networks. IEEE Access 8. https://doi.org/10.1109/ACCESS.2020.2976908
19. Wang Y, Hu T, Tang G, Xie J, Lu J (2019) SGS: safe-guard scheme for protecting control plane against DDoS attacks in software-defined networking. IEEE Access 7. https://doi.org/10.1109/ACCESS.2019.2895092
20. Tan L, Pan Y, Wu J, Zhou J, Jiang H, Deng Y (2020) A new framework for DDoS attack detection and defense in SDN environment. IEEE Access 8. https://doi.org/10.1109/ACCESS.2020.3021435
21. Dong S, Sarem M (2020) DDoS attack detection method based on improved KNN with the degree of DDoS attack in software-defined networks. IEEE Access 8. https://doi.org/10.1109/ACCESS.2019.2963077

22. Punjabi M, Prajapati GL (2017) Lazy learner and PCA: an evolutionary approach. In: Proceedings of computing conference 2017, vol. 2018-Jan. https://doi.org/10.1109/SAI.2017.825 2120

23. Mishra A, Gupta BB, Perakovic D, Penalvo FJG, Hsu CH (2021) Classification based machine learning for detection of DDoS attack in cloud computing. In: Digest of technical papers—IEEE international conference on consumer electronics, vol 2021-Jan. https://doi.org/10.1109/ICCE50685.2021.9427665

24. Dehkordy DT, Rasoolzadegan A (2020) DroidTKM: detection of trojan families using the KNN classifier based on manhattan distance metric. In: 2020 10h International conference on computer and knowledge engineering, ICCKE 2020. https://doi.org/10.1109/ICCKE50421.2020.9303720

25. Suwanda R, Syahputra Z, Zamzami EM (2020) Analysis of euclidean distance and manhattan distance in the K-Means algorithm for variations number of centroid K. J phys conf ser 1566. https://doi.org/10.1088/1742-6596/1566/1/012058

26. Cortes C, Vapnik V (1995) Support-vector networks. Mach Learn 20(3). https://doi.org/10.1023/A:1022627411411

27. Priyadarsini PI (2021) ABC-BSRF: artificial bee colony and borderline-SMOTE RF algorithm for intrusion detection system on data imbalanced problem. In: Lecture notes on data engineering and communications technologies, vol. 56. https://doi.org/10.1007/978-981-15-8767-2

28. Almomani O (2020) A feature selection model for network intrusion detection system based on PSO, GWO, FFA and GA algorithms. Symmetry 12(6). https://doi.org/10.3390/sym12061046

29. Yang L, Zhao H (2019) DDoS attack identification and defense using SDN based on machine learning method. In: Proceedings—2018 15th international symposium on pervasive systems, algorithms and networks, I-SPAN 2018. https://doi.org/10.1109/I-SPAN.2018.00036

30. Oza NC, Tumer K (2008) Classifier ensembles: select real-world applications. Inf Fusion 9(1). https://doi.org/10.1016/j.inffus.2007.07.002

31. Pavlyshenko B (2018) Using stacking approaches for machine learning models. In: Proceedings of the 2018 IEEE 2nd international conference on data stream mining and processing, DSMP 2018. https://doi.org/10.1109/DSMP.2018.8478522

32. Rajagopal S, Kundapur PP, Hareesha KS (2020) A stacking ensemble for network intrusion detection using heterogeneous datasets. Secur Commun Network. https://doi.org/10.1155/2020/4586875

33. Elhag S, Fern´andez A, Altalhi A, Alshomrani S, Herrera F (2019) A multi-objective evolutionary fuzzy system to obtain a broad and accurate set of solutions in intrusion detection systems. Soft Comput 23(4). https://doi.org/10.1007/s00500-017-2856-4

Modeling Solar Photo-Voltaic Power Generation System with MPPT Controller

Babita Panda, Aman Sharma, Sudip Nandi, Arjyadhara Pradhan, Lipika Nanda, and Sarita Samal

1 Introduction

The limitation of conventional assets such as fossil fuel and nuclear fuel has compelled an exploration of the nonconventional energy sources. Without overexploiting to coal and gas-fueled generations, an advanced approach has to be found to match the generation and demand. Here comes the idea for renewable energy sources. But the power generation from the renewable resources is not that much efficient. Also, a small-scale setup of these generation systems is not capable of fulfilling the needs of the demand. Hence, smart integration of the renewable energy sources will be the better option for shifting from dependence on fossil fuels, while maintaining the balance between the supply and demand.

The solar is the most challenging one, out of all other renewable energy sources. The subject of research is the extraction of power from solar which can replace the conventional energy sources for electricity generation. The solar system can be divided into two types: one is grid connected and another is standalone system. Solar Energy Conversion System (SECS) is the system in which electrical energy is the output from the solar energy. SECS consists of Photo-voltaic Array, MPPT Controller, and Power converter.

In the literary, many MPPT techniques have been found in the category of management [1]. Among all the described MPPT techniques in literature, the perturb and observe (P&O) MPPT technique is most frequently used [2, 3]. It is widely used in commercial PV system because of easy implementation. Still there are many disadvantages out of which the main drawback is the unending oscillation at the MPP

B. Panda (✉) · A. Sharma · S. Nandi · A. Pradhan · L. Nanda · S. Samal
Kalinga Institute of Industrial Technology, deemed to be university (KIIT-DU), Bhubaneshwar, Odisha, India
e-mail: pandababita18@gmail.com

© The Author(s), under exclusive license to Springer Nature Singapore Pte Ltd. 2023   901
R. Doriya et al. (eds.), *Machine Learning, Image Processing, Network Security and Data Sciences*, Lecture Notes in Electrical Engineering 946,
https://doi.org/10.1007/978-981-19-5868-7_68

[3–5]. This drawback is overcome by the INCond. method. During the rapid environmental changes, it can produce more accurate result than the P&O method [6]. The oscillation also reduces in case of INCond. method of MPPT [7]. However, its circuit is more complex and expensive than the others, but its operation will result in the increased efficiency of the system [8–10]. This paper presents an improved fuzzy MPPT method in order to track the maximum power with increased tracking speed.

The primary element of a PV model is the PV cell. The panels or modules can be formed from cells and again large can be formed by grouping the panels. The DC power output from the PV arrays can be used to feed to DC loads. But domestic appliances need power converters to convert the DC power to AC power, as the domestic appliances run on single-phase AC. The power extracted from the PV system will be used to directly feed the load through the inverter connected to the 24 V bus, and simultaneously, it can be used to charge the battery for the backup purpose for the time when there is no sunlight.

2 Modeling of Photo-Voltaic System

Modeling of a fully functional Solar Photo-Voltaic System requires the modeling of the different subsystems involved in the generation of the output.

2.1 Modeling of PV Module

The PV Module can be modeled by using general mathematical equation which can be derived from the equivalent circuit of the PV cell shown in Fig. 1. The system consists of a photo-current source, diode, and two resistors one connected in parallel and another in series [11].

According to Kirchhoff's circuit laws, the equation for photo-voltaic current can be expressed:

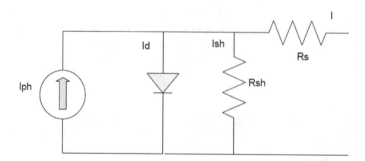

Fig. 1 Equivalent circuit of solar cell

$$I = I_{\text{ph}} - I_0 \left[e^{\frac{q(V+IR_s)}{nKN_sT_c}} - 1 \right] - I_{\text{sh}} \tag{1}$$

where I_{ph} is the light-generated photo-current, I_0 is the saturation current, q is the charge of the electron, n is the cell idealizing factor, K is the Boltzmann constant, T is the cell's absolute temperature, V is the voltage across diode, R_s is the series resistance, and I_{sh} is the shunt current.

The light-generated photo-current (I_{ph}) mainly lean on the solar light and the cell temperature. This is represented by the equation:

$$I_{\text{ph}} = [I_{\text{sc}} + K_i(T - 298)]\frac{G}{1000} \tag{2}$$

where I_{sc} is the short-circuit current, K_i is the short-circuit current of cell measured at 25 °C when an irradiance of 1000 W/m² falls on the panel, T is the cell temperature in Kelvin, and G is the amount of irradiance in W/m².

Saturation current or dark saturation current is a measure of the recombination in a device. It is also the indication of the quality of the cell. Moreover, the cell's saturation current (I_0) changes with the cell temperature expressed as Eq. (3).

$$I_0 = I_{\text{rs}}\left(\frac{T}{T_n}\right)^3 e^{\frac{qE_{g0}\left(\frac{1}{T_n}-\frac{1}{T}\right)}{nK}} \tag{3}$$

I_{rs} is the reverse saturation current of cell and V_{oc} here in the equation for the reverse saturation current Eq. (4) is the cell's open circuit voltage.

$$I_{\text{rs}} = \frac{I_{\text{sc}}}{e^{\left(\frac{qV_{\text{oc}}}{nN_sKT}\right)} - 1} \tag{4}$$

The current through the shunt resistor is given by

$$I_{\text{sh}} = \left(\frac{V + IR_s}{R_{\text{sh}}}\right) \tag{5}$$

Values for the constant(s) taken in the model are listed in Table 1.

The term array is usually employed to describe a group of panels. The PV modules or panels can be connected in series or in parallel or in honeycomb (both series and parallel). Each of the connection types has its own advantages and disadvantages. Here, the parallel connection is being chosen so that even if any of the modules stop working then also it will continue to serve its job. In this work, ten identical modules are parallelly connected to maintain the voltage of the module constant but the output current will be increased to 10 times, hence the power.

Table 1 Parameter values for PV module	K_i (SC current of cell at 25 °C and 1000 W/m^2)	0.0032 A
	q (charge of electron)	1.6e−19 C
	K (Boltzmann constant)	1.38e−23 m^2 kg s^{-2} K^{-1}
	n (ideality factor)	1.3
	E_{go} (Bandgap energy)	1.1 eV
	R_s (Series resistance)	0.221 Ω
	R_{sh} (Parallel resistance)	415.405 Ω
	T_n (Nominal temperature)	298 K
	V_{oc} (OC voltage)	32.9 V
	I_{sc} (SC current)	8.21 A
	N_s (No. of series connected cell)	54

2.2 Modeling of MPPT Controllers

A MPPT is a digital electronic device that maximizes the solar output voltage to such a value at which optimum power of PV module can be extracted. The MPPT tracker considers the output of the system and compares to its previous values and thus generates the triggering pulse for the converter by doing some calculations. So, we can say that the response of the MPPT controller is the duty ratio for the DC–DC converter. Here, three different algorithms are employed for tracking optimum power and comparative analysis is done between the three methods.

2.2.1 P&O Algorithm of MPPT

This is most generally applied Solar MPPT Controllers. Its simple control logic and very few parameter requirements make it one of the most popular architectures for MPP. Basically, if we go through the operation principle, it changes the PV output voltage systematically and then matches the PV power with its previous power value [12].

The working principle of the P&O algorithm is given in Fig. 2. where the $V(t)$, $I(t)$, and $P(t)$ are the present values of voltage, current, and power, and $V(t-1)$, $I(t-1)$, and $P(t-1)$ are their previous values.

Based on the flowchart (Fig. 2), when the power and voltage are increasing in sync, means it is in the left of MPP. Since the duty ratio is related to the output voltage, hence a perturbation step size ΔD will be combined to the duty cycle of previous perturbation cycle. Similarly, when the power is increasing and the voltage is decreasing at the same time means it is in the right of MPP. So, now the step size ΔD is subtracted in the duty cycle.

Again, when the power is decreasing and the voltage is also decreasing it means it is moving toward the left of MPP. So again ΔD is added to the duty ratio. When the

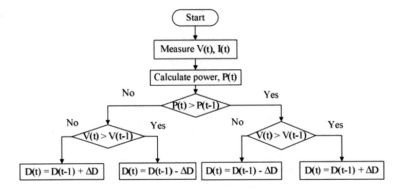

Fig. 2 Flowchart for P&O method

power is decreasing and the voltage is increasing, it means it is now moving toward the right of the MPP. So ΔD is now subtracted from the duty ratio.

2.2.2 Incremental Conductance (INCond.) Method of MPPT

The INCond. method is depending on the most common approach to find the maximum value for a function. The algorithm of the INCond. method of MPP tracking is presented in Fig. 3, where dV, dI, and dP represent the change in voltage, current, and power, respectively.

According to the flowchart, when the PV array voltage is consistent but when the output current increases, duty cycle is increased. Similarly with the decrease of output current, the duty cycle is decreased. The point at which the incremental conductance gets equals to instantaneous conductance, this algorithm searches an appropriate duty. How fast the MPP is achieved is determined by the step size. Increased value for the step size will result in faster tracking but arises the problem of instability. Higher step size will result in the system to oscillate about the MPP. Hence, it is very important to choose the right value of step size in order to get more accurate results.

The main advantage of the INCond. method over previous method is that during sudden environmental changes, it can produce more accurate result. The oscillation also reduces in case of INCond. method of MPPT. However, its circuit is more complex and expensive than the others, but its operation will result in the increased efficiency of the system.

2.2.3 Fuzzy Logic MPPT Design

The FLC controller alters the duty cycle to raise the voltage if the ratio is greater than zero. This process continues until the ratio value is equal to zero. Similarly, the

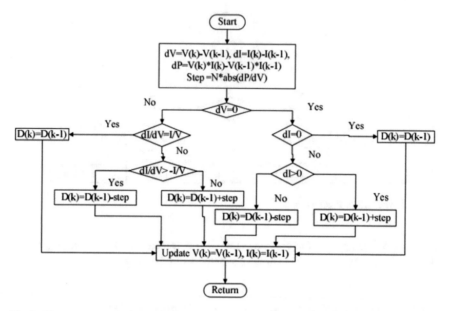

Fig. 3 Flowchart for INCond. method

controller alters the duty cycle to decrease the voltage if this value is less than zero until the ratio value is equal to zero.

FLC has two inputs which are Change in Power (dP) and Change in Voltage (dV) and one output which is the duty cycle of stepdown converter. The input variable is defined as:

$$dP(k) = P(k) - P(k-1)$$
$$= [V(k) \times I(k)] - [V(k-1) \times I(k-1)] \qquad (6)$$

Here, $P(k)$, $V(k)$, and $I(k)$ are the instantaneous power, instantaneous voltage, and instantaneous current from the photo-voltaic system. The primary structure of a fuzzy logic MPPT controller is shown in Fig. 4 and consists of three basic elements: (i) Fuzzification, (ii) Control Rule Base, and (iii) Defuzzification.

(i) Fuzzification:

This process changes input data which are change in Power and change in Voltage into suitable linguistic values.

(ii) Control Rule Base:

In terms of the membership functions, the rules are defined for the required relation between the input and output variables presented in Table 2. *If input* Change in Power (dP) *is* _#Linguistic_Variable#_ *and* Change in Voltage (dV) *is* _#Linguistic_Variable#_, *then the output will be* _#Linguistic_Variable#_.

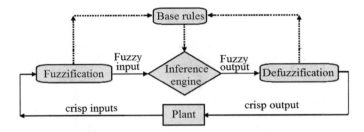

Fig. 4 Basic scheme of the fuzzy logic controller

Table 2 Control rule base for fuzzy controller

dP/dV	NB	NS	ZE	PS	PM
NB	PB	PB	PS	NB	PS
NS	PS	PS	PS	NS	NS
ZE	PS	ZE	ZE	ZE	PB
PS	NS	NS	ZE	PS	PS
PB	NB	NB	ZE	PB	PB

(iii) Defuzzification:

Defuzzification converts linguistic variables to non-fuzzy output which is the duty cycle (D) of power converter:

$$D = \frac{\sum_{j=1}^{n} \mu(\mathrm{d}j) - \mathrm{d}j}{\sum_{j=1}^{n} \mu(\mathrm{d}j)} \tag{7}$$

3 Step Down Converter

A stepdown converter is a class of SMPS typically containing at least a diode D and a transistor Q and a capacitor C, and an inductor L (Fig. 5). To decrease ripple voltage, filters are generally used at the output side and input side of the converter. Considering the buck converter operates in continuous mode, the output voltage can be defined as

$$V_{\text{out}} = D V_{\text{input}} \tag{8}$$

where D is the duty ratio, which is further defined as

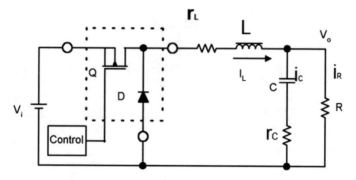

Fig. 5 DC-DC buck converter circuit

$$D = \frac{T_{ON}}{T}$$ (9)

Here T is total time period $= T_{ON} + T_{OFF}$.

4   Simulation Result of the Solar PV System Without MPPT Controller and DC–DC Buck Converter

The VI and PV characteristics of PV system are shown in Figs. 6 and 7, respectively.

To observe the MPPT controller, load is connected to the PV system and the response of the system is observed. A 100 Ω load resistor is connected as load to check the output of the PV system without MPPT controller. Initially, to get the characteristic curve the voltage input to the PV module is given by the ramp function. After that, to observe the actual voltage of the module, the ramp function is replaced with the output voltage of the system as shown in the simulation model. The output

Fig. 6 VI Characteristic of PV array

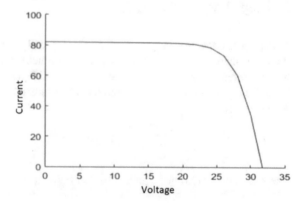

Fig. 7 PV curve of PV array

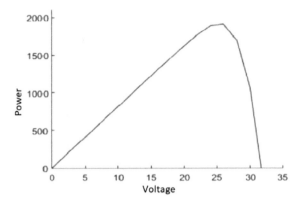

Table 3 PV system output without MPPT

Current (I)	0.3176 A
Voltage (V)	31.76 V
Power (P)	10.09 W

of the system loaded with a 100 Ω resistive load at 25 °C with an irradiance of 1000 W/m^2 is shown in Table 3.

4.1 Simulation Result with MPPT and Buck Converter

The MPPT tracker is fed with the PV system voltage and current. Initially, to get the characteristic curve the voltage input to the PV module is given by the ramp function. After that, to observe the actual voltage of the module, the ramp function is replaced with the output voltage of the system as shown in the simulation model (Fig. 8).

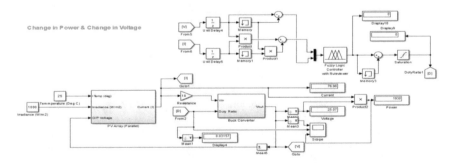

Fig. 8 Simulation model of combined system

Table 4 PV system output with different MPPT controller

PV system output	P&O MPPT	INCond. MPPT	Fuzzy MPPT
Current (I), A	76.21	76.32	76.98
Voltage (V), V	25.15	25.11	25.07
Power (P), W	1916	1916	1930
Duty ratio (D)	0.0330	0.0329	0.0315

The Duty Ratio which is the input of the Converter is given by the MPPT controller. The output of the system loaded with a 100 Ω resistive load at 25 °C with an irradiance of 1000 W/m^2 is shown in Table 4.

All the outputs are verified by the characteristic curves in Figs. 6 and 7. The output of the PV system with all these MPPT controllers in different conditions is shown in Tables 5 and 6.

4.1.1 Temperature is kept constant at 25 °C and irradiance is varied (Table 5, Figs. 9 and 10)

Table 5 Variation of output with irradiation

G	P&O		INCOND		FUZZY	
	V	P	V	P	V	P
1000	25.15	1916	25.11	1916	25.07	1930
800	25.01	1525	25.29	1527	24.97	1531
600	24.96	1132	24.85	1133	24.92	1133
400	24.46	738	24.80	738	24.41	741
200	23.71	349	23.69	349	23.70	354

Table 6 Variation of output with temperature

T	P&O		INCOND		FUZZY	
	V	P	V	P	V	P
20	26.47	2002	26.36	2002	26.46	2006
25	25.15	1916.7	25.11	1916	25.07	1930
30	24.57	1829	24.54	1830	24.55	1833
40	21.94	1661	22.06	1661	22.01	1663
50	20.07	1491	19.55	1487	20.04	1499

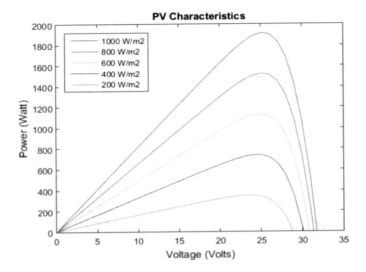

Fig. 9 PV characteristics variation with irradiance

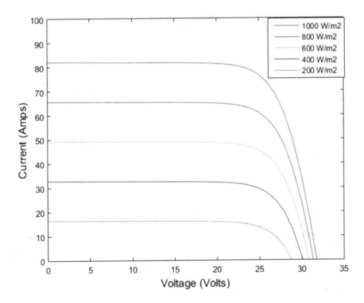

Fig. 10 IV characteristics variation with irradiance

4.1.2 Irradiance is kept constant at 1000 W/m^2 and temperature is varied (Table 6, Figs. 11 and 12)

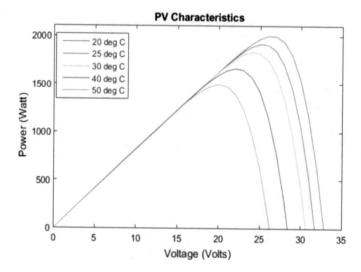

Fig. 11 PV characteristics variation with temperature

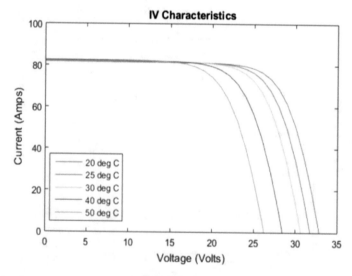

Fig. 12 IV characteristics variation with temperature

5 Conclusion

This paper has analyzed the technique to mathematically model the solar PV system and the MPPT Controllers. The objective of the paper is to control the output voltage of buck converter. Here, P&O algorithm, INCond. algorithm, and Fuzzy logic are employed in the MPPT controllers to compare their outputs and response time and to determine the maximum operating point of the system. The output of the PV system with and without MPPT controller in identical conditions is also compared. From the result, it is observed that all the MPPT are working fine and tracking the MPP for the given conditions. While simulation of P&O MPPT, the outputs are a bit oscillating around the MPP whereas the INCond. MPPT operates with very less oscillations. This is the main advantage of the INCond. method over the P&O method. Also, the required time for INCond. MPPT to reach the MPP is very much less than that of the P&O MPPT. While the Fuzzy MPPT is working much faster than P&O and INCond. Its output has much lower ripples and very closer to the MPP.

References

1. Miyatake M, Veerachary M, Toriumi F, Fujii N, Ko H (2011) Maximum power point tracking of multiple photovoltaic arrays: a PSO approach. IEEE Trans Aerosp Electron Syst 47:367–380
2. Tafticht T, Agbossou K, Doumbia M, Chériti A (2008) An improved maximum power point tracking method for photovoltaic systems. Renew Energy 33:1508–1516
3. Houssamo I, Locment F, Sechilariu M (2010) Maximum power tracking for photovoltaic power system: development and experimental comparison of two algorithms. Renew Energy 35:2381–2387
4. Priyadarshi N, Padmanaban S, Bhaskar MS, Blaabjerg F, Sharma A (2018) Fuzzy SVPWM-based inverter control realisation of grid integrated photovoltaic–wind system with fuzzy particle swarm optimization maximum power point tracking algorithm for a grid-connected PV/windpower generation system: hardware implementation. IET Elect Power Appl 12(7):962–971
5. Jedari M, Fathi SH (2017) A new approach for photovoltaic arraysmodeling and maximum power point estimation in real operating conditions. IEEE Trans Ind Electron 64(12):9334–9343
6. Aamri FE, Maker H, Sera D, Spataru SV, Guerrero JM, Mouhsen A (2018) A direct maximum power point tracking method for single phase grid-connected PV inverters. IEEE Trans Power Electron 33(10):8961–8971
7. Kumar N, Hussain I, Singh B, Panigrahi BK (2018) Framework of maximum power extraction from solar PV panel using self predictive perturb and observe algorithm. IEEE Trans Sustain Energy 9(2):895–903
8. Khan O, Acharya S, Hosani MA, Moursi MSE (2018) Hill climbingpower flow algorithm for hybrid DC/AC microgrids. IEEE Trans Power Electron 33(7):5532–5537
9. Raj A, Gupta M, Panda S (2016) Design simulation and performance assessment of yield and loss forecasting for 100 KWp grid connected solar PV system. In: 2016 2nd International conference on next generation computing technologies (NGCT). IEEE, pp 528–533
10. Pati N, Panda B (2020) Stability analysis of photovoltaic system under grid faults. Int J Power Electron Drive Syst (IJPEDS) 11(2):931–941
11. Sahu JK, Panda B, Sahu S Patra JP (2020) Harmonics estimation of a standalone PV system integrated with a modified SPWM inverter. In: 2020 3rd International conference on smart systems and inventive technology (ICSSIT). Tirunelveli, India, pp 654–656
12. Pradhan A, Panda B, Panda B, Khillo A (2020) An improved MPPT technique for in-creasing efficiency of PV module. In: Advances in electrical control and signal systems, pp 633–644

Printed in the United States
by Baker & Taylor Publisher Services